A CENTURY OF

PSYCHOLOGY
AS SCIENCE

A CENTURY OF

PSYCHOLOGY

AS SCIENCE

EDITED BY

SIGMUND KOCH & DAVID E. LEARY

AMERICAN PSYCHOLOGICAL ASSOCIATION

WASHINGTON, DC

First edition published 1985 by McGraw-Hill. Reissued 1992 by the American Psychological Association with a new Postscript.

Copies may be ordered from
APA Order Department
P.O. Box 2710
Hyattsville, MD 20784

This book was typeset in Electra by Achorn Graphic Services, Inc., Worcester, MA.

Printer: United Book Press, Inc., Baltimore, MD
Cover designer: GrafikCommunications, Ltd., Alexandria, VA
Production editor: Valerie Montenegro

Library of Congress Cataloging-in-Publication Data

A Century of psychology as science / edited by Sigmund Koch. David E. Leary.
    p.   cm.
  Previously published.
  Includes bibliographical references and indexes.
  ISBN 1-55798-171-X (acid-free paper)
  1. Psychology. 2. Psychology—History. I. Koch, Sigmund.
II. Leary, David E.
BF149.C36   1992
    150'.9—dc20   92-20981
                                                              CIP

Printed in the United States of America

Contents

CONTENTS

CONTENTS

IV. PSYCHOLOGY IN RELATION TO SOCIETY, CULTURE, AND SENSIBILITY

Psychology and the Public Good

Psychology as Viewed and Practiced by the Humanist: Four Perspectives

List of Contributors

RICHARD D. ALEXANDER *Museum of Zoology, The University of Michigan, Ann Arbor, Michigan* (CHAPTER 33)

WILLIAM P. ALSTON *Department of Philosophy, Syracuse University, Syracuse, New York* (CHAPTER 27)

RUDOLF ARNHEIM *Professor Emeritus of the Psychology of Art, Harvard University, Cambridge, Massachusetts* (CHAPTER 36)

JACQUES BARZUN *University Professor Emeritus, Columbia University, New York, New York* (CHAPTER 40)

DALBIR BINDRA* *Department of Psychology, McGill University, Montreal, Quebec, Canada* (CHAPTER 14)

ARTHUR L. BLUMENTHAL *Department of Psychology, Sarah Lawrence College, Bronxville, New York* (CHAPTER 34)

DOROTHEA D. BRAGINSKY *Department of Psychology, Fairfield University, Fairfield, Connecticut* (CHAPTER 38)

JOHN B. CARROLL *Kenan Professor of Psychology, The L. L. Thurstone Psychometric Laboratory, Department of Psychology, University of North Carolina at Chapel Hill, Chapel Hill, North Carolina* (CHAPTER 35)

A. CHARLES CATANIA *Psychology Department, University of Maryland, Baltimore County, Catonsville, Maryland* (CHAPTER 13)

STEPHAN L. CHOROVER *Department of Brain and Cognitive Sciences, Massachusetts Institute of Technology, Cambridge, Massachusetts* (CHAPTER 37)

FREDERICK J. CROSSON *Program of Liberal Studies, University of Notre Dame, Notre Dame, Indiana* (CHAPTER 18)

* Deceased

LIST OF CONTRIBUTORS

JOSEPH DE RIVERA *Department of Psychology, Clark University, Worcester, Massachusetts* (CHAPTER 15)

DAVID ELKIND *Eliot-Pearson Department of Child Study, Tufts University, Medford, Massachusetts* (CHAPTER 20)

KENNETH J. GERGEN *Department of Psychology, Swarthmore College, Swarthmore, Pennsylvania* (CHAPTER 23)

JAMES J. GIBSON* *Department of Psychology, Cornell University, Ithaca, New York* (CHAPTER 9)

AMEDEO GIORGI *Department of Psychology, University of Quebec at Montreal, Montreal, Quebec, Canada* (CHAPTER 2)

HENRY GLEITMAN *Department of Psychology, University of Pennsylvania, Philadelphia, Pennsylvania* (CHAPTER 17)

STEPHEN E. GLICKMAN *Department of Psychology, University of California, Berkeley, Berkeley, California* (CHAPTER 32)

RALPH NORMAN HABER *Department of Psychology, University of Illinois at Chicago, Chicago, Illinois* (CHAPTER 11)

MARGARET A. HAGEN *Department of Psychology, Boston University, Boston, Massachusetts* (CHAPTER 10)

RICHARD J. HARRIS *Department of Psychology, University of New Mexico, Albuquerque, New Mexico* (CHAPTER 29)

MARY HENLE *Professor Emerita of Psychology, New School for Social Research, New York, New York* (CHAPTER 5)

WALTER KAUFMANN* *Department of Philosophy, Princeton University, Princeton, New Jersey* (CHAPTER 41)

HOWARD H. KENDLER *Department of Psychology, University of California, Santa Barbara, Santa Barbara, California* (CHAPTER 6)

GREGORY A. KIMBLE *Department of Psychology, Duke University, Durham, North Carolina* (CHAPTER 12)

SIGMUND KOCH *University Professor of Psychology and Philosophy, University Professors Program, Boston University, Boston, Massachusetts* (INTRODUCTION, FOREWORD, CHAPTER 4, AFTERWORD, POSTSCRIPT)

JOHN I. LACEY *Professor Emeritus of Psychiatry, School of Medicine, Wright State University, Yellow Springs, Ohio* (CHAPTER 31)

DAVID E. LEARY *Dean of arts and sciences, University of Richmond, Richmond, Virginia* (INTRODUCTION, CHAPTER 25)

JANE LOEVINGER *Social Science Institute, Washington University, St. Louis, Missouri* (CHAPTER 19)

R. DUNCAN LUCE *Distinguished Professor of Cognitive Sciences, University of California, Irvine, Irvine, California* (CHAPTER 28)

ALASDAIR MACINTYRE *Department of Philosophy, University of Notre Dame, Notre Dame, Indiana* (CHAPTER 39)

WILLIAM J. MCGUIRE *Department of Psychology, Yale University, New Haven, Connecticut* (CHAPTER 24)

GEORGE A. MILLER *Department of Psychology, Princeton University, Princeton, New Jersey* (CHAPTER 1)

* Deceased

WALTER MISCHEL   *Psychology Department, Columbia University, New York, New York* (CHAPTER 22)

ALLEN NEWELL   *University Professor of Computer Science, Department of Computer Science, Carnegie Mellon University, Pittsburgh, Pennsylvania* (CHAPTER 16)

KARL H. PRIBRAM   *Center for Brain Research, Radford University, Radford, Virginia* (CHAPTER 30)

DANIEL N. ROBINSON   *Department of Psychology, Georgetown University, Washington, D.C.* (CHAPTER 3)

SAUL ROSENZWEIG   *Departments of Psychology and Psychiatry, Washington University, St. Louis, Missouri* (CHAPTER 7)

NEVITT SANFORD   *President Emeritus, The Wright Institute, Berkeley, California* (CHAPTER 21)

ROBERT R. SEARS*   *Department of Psychology, Stanford University, Stanford, California* (CHAPTER 8)

ELIZABETH SEWELL   *Formerly Joe Rosenthal Professor of Humanities, University of North Carolina at Greensboro, Greensboro, North Carolina* (CHAPTER 42)

STEPHEN TOULMIN   *Department of Philosophy, Northwestern University, Evanston, Illinois* (CHAPTER 25)

RICHARD M. ZANER   *Ann Geddes Stahlman Professor of Medical Ethics, Department of Medicine, School of Medicine, Vanderbilt University, Nashville, Tennessee* (CHAPTER 26)

* Deceased

Note from the Publisher

The American Psychological Association is proud to reissue this classic historical volume edited by Sigmund Koch and David E. Leary, which, in this printing, includes a new Postscript. The book was originally published in 1985 by McGraw-Hill to celebrate the centenary of Wilhelm Wundt's establishment of the Leipzig laboratory—an event that is generally acknowledged to mark the "birth" of scientific psychology. For a variety of reasons that have to do with the vagaries and complexities of the modern publishing industry, soon after the manuscript was accepted and published, the publisher ceased to promote its social science titles and, in essence, stopped distribution of the book only about a year and a half after its publication. Because of this unfortunate sequence of events, psychology and psychologists were deprived of an ambitious and high-quality compendium of the thoughts and analyses of more than 40 of the preeminent scholars and researchers in the field and in such related fields as biology, philosophy, and the humanities. With this reissuing, APA Books intends to redress the balance.

The *re*-presentation of this widely admired text in conjunction with the centenary of the founding of the American Psychological Association is more than an apt celebratory gesture. It represents the Association's profound conviction that, at this crossroads between a century of the development and evolution of psychology as a science and what appears to be a more highly complex and multifaceted future than ever foreseen by any of the discipline's "founders," it is important to pause and take stock of the opinions, insights, judgments, and prospects offered in this volume. They are as fresh, incisive, and, most important, pertinent today as they were less than a decade ago when they were first presented to the public.

Introduction

SIGMUND KOCH

DAVID E. LEARY

As is well known, the centenary of Wundt's establishment of the Leipzig laboratory was taken by the American Psychological Association (and other groups of psychologists within and outside of the United States) as occasion for the formal celebration of the "hundredth anniversary" of scientific psychology. The American Psychological Association sponsored many activities in recognition of the anniversary, and its 1979 national convention, held in New York City (September 1–5), made the centenary its official theme. The senior editor of this book happened to be president of two divisions of the Association during 1979: the Division of General Psychology (Division 1) and the Division of Philosophical Psychology (24). As one who had given a long career to the analysis of theoretical, methodological, and philosophical problems of psychology, it was natural for him to see the possibility of using the bulk of the convention program time allotted to these two divisions as a vehicle for a serious and comprehensive assessment of the state of the field at the end of its "first" century. The junior editor, whose research efforts have been concentrated on the history of psychology, proved willing to assume the capacity of joint program chairman of the two divisions. Working closely together, we designed a carefully structured program of symposia and invited lectures entitled A *Century of Psychology as Science: Retrospections and Assessments*, and had the great good luck to attract the collaboration of forty-six symposiasts (and twenty chairpersons) whose names read much like an honor roll in the psychological and cognate disciplines.

1

The objective of the symposium series was, of course, to promote a searching backward look at the successes and failures of scientific psychology's first century and a creative effort to discern its prospects as it enters its second. Our distinguished symposiasts were offered total latitude in their choice of role (whether historian, prophet, or somewhere in between), and in the mode of its implementation. Most of them were leaders in some region of the highly specialized tissue of psychological inquiry, and they were asked to focus upon their own fields. Others were distinguished individuals in fields that intersect with psychology, among both the sciences and the humanities; these persons were asked to view aspects of the psychological enterprise from the perspective of their own interests.

No doubt because of the challenge inherent in the ceremonial occasion—and the added circumstance that publication was contemplated from the beginning—participants in the symposium series on which this book is based approached their tasks in high earnest. The result was a program of unusual quality for any scholarly convention. It is to be emphasized, however, that the book is not a "proceedings" but a carefully prepared scholarly work. Virtually all of the papers have been revised in accordance with editorial suggestions made by the senior editor; most include extensive bibliographies and also "supplementary readings" listing landmark publications which register the development of the field under consideration.

After a hundred years of ebullient growth, psychology has achieved a condition at once so fractionated and so ramified as to preclude any two persons agreeing as to its "architecture." Even if an architecture could be reliably discerned, it is doubtful that all of its substructures could be addressed in any single study having a chance of completion before the dawn of psychology's *third* century. To vary the image, current psychology is much like a jumbled "hidden-figure" puzzle that contains no figure. Thus we cannot claim representativeness, still less completeness, for the collection of fields and issues chosen for the originating symposium series and, later, for this book. We did make an effort to include most of the larger, traditionally discriminated subdivisions of fundamental psychology (e.g., perception, learning, motivation, emotion, development, personality, social psychology) and the more prominent intersectional areas (e.g., psychology and mathematics, psychology and philosophy, psychology and neuroscience, psychology and evolutionary biology). Moreover, a number of contributors were asked to confront problems of general systematic import, and another subgroup—including humanists as well as psychologists—inquired into the human impact of psychology. All we can claim is that a sufficient range of historically significant fields and interests were sifted through a sufficient diversity of authoritative sensibilities to provide a telling fix on the state of psychology on the threshold of its second century.

Some major constraints on the representativeness of this book are suggested by considerations that will be addressed in the senior editor's *Foreword*.

1. Evidence will be presented which suggests that the American hegemony in psychology—so patent over a large interval of this century—is decreasing. When, in the early 1950s, the senior editor designed *Psychology: A Study of a Science* (McGraw-Hill, 1959–1963), it was possible for a massive study of the status of psychology to claim adequate representativeness in respect to the discipline, even though the ninety contributing authors (selected on grounds of influence) included only two Europeans and one Canadian. Not a single foreign reviewer of that six-volume enterprise commented on any lack of international representativeness, or even found its overwhelmingly American authorship worthy of comment. One can doubt that the degree of American dominance betokened by such circumstances still prevails. If North America is still the Rome of international psychology in respect to the size of its work force, it is certainly not Athens in respect to its leadership in ideas.

We thus count our failure to include non-American contributors within the present book a distinct limit. All that can be said by way of extenuation is that the time limits—and the fiscal ones—for arranging the originating symposia on which the book is based precluded the invitation of foreign participants. Fortunately, however, the historical reach of many of our contributors extends far past the cozy borders of the United States. Ethnocentrism will not be found a conspicuous trait in the chapters of this book!

2. Evidence will be adduced to document a massive realignment of activity in "fundamental" versus "implemental" (i.e., professional and applied) psychology that has taken place, on a world-wide basis, in recent decades. On that dimension, the representation of fields and topics in this book may be said to be almost perversely skewed. It is. But this selectivity has been a matter of policy!

The raison d'être of the book is the centenary of psychology qua science. Whether the institutionalization of such a discipline be attributed to Wundt or, more generally, to a congeries of late-nineteenth-century developments pointing in a similar direction, the *psychology* at issue was perceived as a "pure," nomothetic, largely laboratory-oriented science which would serve as the foundation discipline of all the human or social sciences. And, on the Wundtian scheme, *Völkerpsychologie*, however nonlaboratory-like or "historical" its methods must be, was also presumed a "pure" discipline. Such a conception of psychology was the lineal progenitor of the vastly altered psychology of the present day. Thus the focus of this book is upon the *fate* of that kind of psychology—psychology qua science—over the past century. If part of its fate has indeed been a diminution of interest in fundamental relative to implemental psychology, *that* is a circumstance worth documenting and pondering. If the activities pursued under the banner of psychology have changed, differentiated, regrouped in ways far outside the range of Wundt's (or the pioneers') anticipations, that, too, is of deep significance. The strategy of choice

3

for the illumination of such matters can only be that of tracing the jagged and extralogical storyline of "scientific psychology" as it branches out from the founding conception.

In this book we have thus concentrated on the representation of fields and issues relating to "fundamental" psychology in some sense of that open-horizon word. One large tradition which developed out of the clinic rather than the scientific psychology of the academy—that of psychoanalytic and dynamic psychologies—will soon merit a centennial volume (or encyclopaedia) of its own. Though the treatment of dynamic psychology in a book such as this must necessarily be a limited one, readers will find its interrelations with fundamental psychology well documented in the chapters of Rosenzweig on experimental psychoanalysis, Sears on psychoanalysis and behavior theory, and of both Sanford and Mischel on personality. The relations of fundamental psychology to human and social affairs are directly represented by the contributions of Chorover and Braginsky, and considerations bearing on the relations between fundamental and implemental psychology are rarely absent in the other chapters of this volume. They are focal in certain of the chapters contributed by our philosophical contingent, such as those of MacIntyre and Zaner.

Broader *direct* representation of the implemental areas would certainly have been desirable, but even an adequate sampling of fundamental psychology is impossible within the limits of any single volume, however ample. We would emphasize, however, that perhaps the most weighty rationale for our concentration upon fundamental psychology is the widespread presumption that what "implemental" psychology implements is, indeed, fundamental psychology. Though a scattering of implemental psychologists have been entertaining doubts about this dependency, the mainstream view of the connection is still very much like the stereotype which presumes engineering to be a wholly derivative and uniquely determined application of "pure" physics. Natural science methodologists already agree that the case for physics and engineering may be far more complicated than the formerly regnant stereotype. It is possible that the case for fundamental-implemental relations in psychology may be even more intricate. Professional and applied psychologists cannot fail to be interested in coming to terms with that issue!

The contents of the book omit but a few of the topics included in the originating symposia, but their sequencing has been rearranged. George Miller's chapter on "The Constitutive Problem of Psychology" was generously written for the book despite the fact that he had been unable to participate in the APA program. Margaret Hagen (also not a symposiast) was equally kind in agreeing to serve as surrogate for James J. Gibson in writing an expository chapter on his important "ecological" theory of perception. The editors had planned to ask Professor Gibson to supplement his laconic but superb critique of "sensation-based" perception theory with a positive statement of his views, but this was precluded by the sad event of his death. Another chapter not based on the original symposium series is Robert Sears's historical overview of "Psychoanalysis and Behavior Theory."

The editorial aim was to secure multiplicity of viewpoint, analytic attack, and style. We hoped for papers that would have a fresh and direct "first person" authenticity rather than be cautious and ritualistic exercises in scholarly apologetics. The results, we think, justify such a hope. The chapters vary widely in the type of task embraced by the author, in style, length, and point of view. The fact that quite a few of the chapters are of moderate length is a boon in several senses—not the least significant of which is that historical assessments cut closer to the bone when not blurred by too much qualifying detail. What the volume projects is the "first century" as filtered through the differing sensibilities and attitudinal frames of intellectually responsible men and women who are very much their own persons and who, for the occasion, are willing to speak with minimal indirection. Moreover, the centennial context did elicit a disposition to inhibit a certain kind of ideational imperialism and truculence that is not unknown in scholarship, and to be uncommonly frank and searching in the delineation of intellectual limits (sometimes limits painful to the writer!) within recent history. We are given, in short, a living registration of psychology *moving* into its second century, rather than an ornate mausoleum in static celebration of its first.

Some insight into the special qualities of this work can be gleaned by comparing it with the large study of the status of psychology at mid-century issuing in the six volumes of *Psychology: A Study of a Science*. The present book can in some ways be seen as a miniature *Psychology: A Study of a Science*, a second probe into the condition of psychology after a quarter-century more of flux. But happily, we think, for the reader, it is a study of far less formal cast. The rather interventionistic editorial methods of the former venture (which sought to ensure uniformity of analytic incidence and something like ultimate detail in the elaboration of arguments) were not deemed appropriate to the present one. Our editorial aim in this project has been to foster heterogeneity, to enhance the timbre of each individual voice, by serving the particular objectives set by each contributor. If a degree of cacophony results, that, too, can teach us much about our curious discipline. Better still, it will enhance and sustain the high interest merited by every page of this book.

The book does not pretend to be a *history* of scientific psychology—far from it! It comprises the variegated efforts of many expert minds to gauge the condition of their special fields at the *end* of the first century. If there is any central emphasis to the questioning, it is *where do we stand at the present time?*—in relation, of course, to the historically constituted objectives of the "new" psychology and the hopes of the founders. Thus the current enterprise—or "study" if you will—is primarily present-centered, and from that center it is as much forward-looking as it is backward-looking. The individual contributors have themselves determined the direction of their glance. Some seek to illumine the present primarily by looking toward the past; others concentrate on what they consider fruitful leads, located either in their own thinking or some more general tendency in their field, which they believe to contain an intimation of the future. Almost all look in *both* directions, but with varying emphases.

This study, then, may be seen as at once an assessment of history and a registration of thought-in-progress which must itself become a part of history, It is as much relevant to the interests of the present student, scholar, or citizen who wishes insight into "modern" psychology in historical perspective as it is to those who in future may wish to understand the psychology of the present period.

A brief "Afterword" by the senior editor (pp. 928–950) identifies certain trends of the book as a whole—some of them so heartening as to encourage anticipations of a second century of increased intellectual dignity. We hope the psychologists (if there be such) of 2079, to whom we dedicate this book, will agree.

We wish to express deep gratitude to Lys Dunlap Koch (the senior editor's wife) for generously placing her long experience as a professional editor at the service of this project. We wish also to thank the senior editor's secretary, Rosalie Carlson, for her impeccable management of the project files and her subtly effective role in serving as a frequent communication link between the editors and contributors. Thomas Quinn, the editor in charge of this book at McGraw-Hill, could not have been more constant in his long-term dedication to the project, or more congenial to work with. Barbara Toniolo, who was the editing supervisor of the book, proved to be brilliant in her technical supervision and a delightful partner.

This is the point for the editors also to thank all contributors for their generous, insightful, and creative efforts. Sadly, it is also a point at which it is appropriate to acknowledge the voices who have been stilled during the interval since initiation of this project: not only James J. Gibson; also Dalbir Bindra, whose brilliant overview of "motivation" is included in the book; Walter Kaufmann, who generously crossed disciplinary lines in serving as one of the few humanist contributors; and Talcott Parsons, who was to have contributed on the relations between psychology and social science.

For the 1992 republication of this book, thanks are due to Julia Frank-McNeil, director of Acquisitions and Development for APA Books, who was the central and constantly nurturant figure in initiating and implementing the project. Thanks are due also to Valerie Montenegro of APA Books for unusually precise and responsive work as production editor of the new book.

We must sorrowfully record the death of an additional participant in the original (1985) publication: Robert R. Sears. Finally, Lys Dunlap Koch, who loaned so much of her editorial wisdom to the original publication, has also died. The senior editor dedicates his own contributions to the book to her memory.

Foreword

WUNDT'S CREATURE AT AGE
ZERO—AND AS CENTENARIAN:
SOME ASPECTS OF THE INSTITUTIONALIZATION
OF THE "NEW PSYCHOLOGY"

SIGMUND KOCH

It is rare that the pursuers of a broad field of inquiry hold an image of their field as having been "founded" at some definite date. One does not encounter multimillennial celebrations of the founding of philosophy (or indeed, physics) by Thales or of history by Herodotus. Painting is not thought to have been initiated in some inaugural atelier, even one provided by a cave. If there be claimants to the invention of literature, they have not carried their case. Virtually all broad areas of inquiring or creative activity now "institutionalized" are seen to meld into history and prehistory. It is as ludicrous to think of them as having commenced on a determinably given date as it is to think of language as having been stipulated into existence by a persuasive primitive linguist. Any definition of what it is to be human must entail that psychological knowledge—both implicit and explicit—has been "owned" and pursued by the race coextensively with its emergence.

Wilhelm Wundt and the "Founding" of Scientific Psychology: As Legend and as Fact

It is significant in a powerful multiplicity of ways when it is said that a man named Wilhelm Wundt *founded* psychology as an independent "science" by inaugurating a "laboratory" for psychological experimentation at Leipzig University in 1879. The *full* significance of that statement could be unpacked only by attempting something very much like an entire intellectual history of the West. This small task we must forego.

What Wundt effectuated by his "founding" was a semantic change: one of very curious character. It was not the beginning of a word, nor even the beginning of a new meaning of a word. It was the stabilization of *a* meaning of a word that had been invited and worked toward over several prior centuries and an arrogation of that "new" meaning to sovereign status relative to all prior usages in the history of thought. Henceforward the core meaning of "psychology" would be dominated by the adjectives *scientific* and *experimental*. And the core imagery suggested by the word would soon commence its well-known evolution from that of bearded savants patiently manipulating Hipp chronoscopes, tachistoscopes, and episcotisters, to clean-shaven laboratory habitués sending forth their obligingly whirring rats upon microjourneys through mazes and obstruction boxes—to the present (and partially retrogressive) imagery of bearded savants algorithmically interrogating their gleaming computers. By comparison with these core connotations of psychology, all prior meanings of the word were rendered contemptible or, at the very least, embarrassing.

The ancient tradition of ardent and disciplined speculation about man's nature and conduct that formed so large a part of the concern of philosophy was now "armchair psychology." Even those philosophers who had argued for, indeed paved the way toward, a scientific conception of psychology—the "early" English empiricists and their associationist and evolutionist successors in the nineteenth century; the French materialists and philosophes of the Enlightenment; the very author of the first treatise on mathematical psychology and one entitled, moreover, *Psychologie als Wissenschaft* (Herbart, 1824–1825)—began to receive but condescending hearing by virtue of their criminally sedentary proclivities. Not a one of them had arisen from his armchair long enough to spin an episcotister! As for the vast reservoirs of psychological knowledge embedded in the history of the humanities, in literature, even within the categories of natural language and the sensibilities of language users, *those* senses of "psychology" were transported beyond the pale.

The massive semantic change precipitated by Wundt was *not* the one he intended to invite. Meanings have a life of their own: an almost perverse capacity to subvert the intent of their author. And, paradoxically, the more prolific an author—and the more differentiated his thought—the less his control over the destiny

8

of his meanings. Psychology was christened a science and installed in a laboratory toward the beginning of an era in which human sensibility would become ever more ahistorical (to the point of bellicosity toward the past) and respect for close scholarship ever more rare. Under these circumstances Wundt, despite his long and remarkably productive career, soon became little more than a perfectly cast character (well-symbolized in those photographs of the mild, neatly bearded, fatherly face) in a legendary inauguration ceremony. A veritable founding father! What historiography there has been concerning the man throughout most of this century has pretty much converged on this legend, supplemented perhaps by a few pages of précis of his 53,735 pages[1] of published writings.

There, of course, *was* no inauguration ceremony, no "founding" in any literal sense. As Boring has said: "Wundt made no special speech, cut no ribbon . . . , dedicated no cornerstone . . . , nor could he have recognized the significance of what was getting under way (1965, pp. 7–8)." Wundt had been assigned a small room at Leipzig University for the storage of demonstration apparatus as early as 1876. During the course of his psychological seminar in the winter of 1879, two of the students—Max Friedrich and Stanley Hall—began to use that space for research: Friedrich as investigator, and Hall as an occasional observer. Wundt also served as observer. The problem, a reaction-time experiment seeking to determine the "duration of simple and complex apperception," formed the basis of Friedrich's 1881 dissertation. (See Bringmann, Bringmann, & Ungerer, 1980, for a detailed archival account of the genesis and later development of the Leipzig laboratory.)

There has, over the years, been a fair amount of squabbling over the date and proprietorship of the first psychological laboratory. For example, should Wundt win, even against himself, by virtue of his having had space for the storage of physiological and psychophysical equipment at Heidelberg as early as 1865? Or should William James get the award for having housed demonstration equipment in a small room at Harvard (Agassiz Hall) as early as 1875? Or was Stanley Hall being as irresponsibly boastful as many have thought him in alleging in 1894 that the first psychological laboratory of appreciable significance was the one he had himself founded at the Hopkins in 1881? There was bad blood between James and Hall over that contention (see Perry, 1935, Vol. II, pp. 6–24).

[1] This is Boring's (1929/1950, p. 345) well-known estimate of the size of Wundt's corpus, based on 491 of the items cited by Eleonore Wundt in her 1927 bibliography of her father's works. The estimate includes all the revised editions of Wundt's works but excludes "mere reprinted editions." Since there has been some quibbling over the accuracy of this estimate, it is only fair to note that Boring embarks upon this computation with the light-hearted proviso that "one must not lose one's sense of humor in so doing." I had long felt Boring's afternoon with his "adding machine," however playful, to be a dismal symbol of the style of historiography practiced during American psychology's long ahistorical interregnum—"why read, if one can count" can seem to be the implicit message. In a more mature and battered frame, I am now inclined to be rather less critical of Boring. Having subsequently made the effort to read a certain amount of Wundt, I consider Boring's decision to count, rather than to read another fifty pages or so, a not excessively vulgar trade-off.

Such nonissues—gleefully resuscitated in recent historical writings—are instructive sequelae of the curious phenomenon, unique in intellectual history, of a "science" legislated into existence by fiat! Whose fiat? Trivia such as "who had the most sophisticated chronoscope stored where, when" have little to do with the true force of the "founding" legend. Wundt qualifies as protagonist in (at least) the following senses:

1. His initially humble but fast-growing laboratory (officially canonized as an *Institut* by Leipzig University in 1882) attracted by far the largest group of students, in the decade or two after 1879, of any center for psychological training in the world. This international cadre of Wundt-trained psychologists became the prime agency for the spawning of new laboratories, during the period at issue, in many European countries and, especially, in the United States.

2. *Philosophische Studien*, the first journal given to experimental psychology, was founded by Wundt in 1882.

3. It was Wundt who more persistently and energetically than anyone generated the rhetoric, the systematic rationale (though a constantly shifting one), and the synoptic early reference sources for the "autonomous" new psychology of experimental cast that had been presaged and invited by so many of his contemporaries and predecessors. This activity was voluminously registered in a stream of publications emanating from his pen throughout most of his Heidelberg period (1857– 1874), especially the *Beiträge zur Theorie der Sinneswahrnehmung* of 1862; the *Vorlesungen über die Menschen- und Thierseele* of 1863; and the influential *Grundzüge der physiologischen Psychologie* of 1874. Moreover, the second edition of the *Grundzüge*—of which there were ultimately to be six—appeared in 1880, only a few months after Friedrich's research had converted Wundt's storage space into a "laboratory." The Leipzig laboratory can thus be seen as a late step in a program which had been evolving for over twenty years; its symbolic and actual significance was not that a space uniquely dedicated to psychological experiment was marked off at some university but that it was *Wundt's* space, a man already world-famous for an authoritative version of a "new" psychology which proclaimed the need for autonomous experimental implementation. It is ironic to contemplate that though Wundt's laboratory achieved rapid world visibility largely because it was Wundt's, Wundt's name remained familiar during most of the twentieth century largely because of his laboratory!

An incipient reassertion of historical interests in psychology over the past few years—some of it precipitated by the very centennial that has occasioned this book—has begun to rectify the schematic image of Wundt that has so long prevailed. It is fortunately now clear to many that Wundt would have perceived as grotesque and unacceptable (and, during his lifetime, did so perceive) many of the aspects of the reconception of psychology set in motion by the symbolism of its "first" laboratory. It is now broadly recognized that his interest in an historico-linguistically oriented cultural psychology, as reflected in the ten volumes of the *Völkerpsychologie* (1900–1920), was not tacked onto his earlier experimental interests as a kind of senile afterthought but, rather, was seen by Wundt, from an early phase, as crucial to any program for a significant psychology. It is clear, also, that the voluminous philosophical writing to which he returned immediately after the founding of the laboratory did not flow from some aberration of multiple personality but reflected his conviction that psychology was propaedeutic to the very serious enterprise of philosophy. It is evident that his philosophical thinking was not, by current standards, antimetaphysical in tenor, but that he was a voluntarist who had been deeply influenced by Leibnitz and other rationalist and idealist philosophers. It is now emphasized that the texture of his psychology had been severely distorted in certain of the secondary accounts thereof (especially in the United States). The "structuralist" version of his approach transmitted to American psychology by his student, E. B. Titchener, is now recognized as a selective derivative in which such central components of Wundt's thinking as his doctrine of apperception, his voluntarism, and actualism have been overlooked or aseptically "positivised." That misreadings so flagrant of any thinker should be in the public domain for the better part of a century has troubling implications relative to the quality of scholarship in our time.

It is well to note, however, that an eighty-year lapse of the historical imagination, and its associated craft, cannot be repaired overnight. The thriving new interest in Wundt (and in history generally) contains potentialities for distortion and selection at least as great as during the era when history was left in the hands of a few devotees (and rarely read at that!). "New" Wundt-images—often rather heroic ones—are proliferating at a rapid rate. It has come as a shock to many that the Wundts now being discovered are at variance with the highly schematic Wundt legends inhabiting psychology's long "ahistorical" interregnum. We are witnessing a massive sense of betrayal over the sudden discovery that Titchener's, or Boring's, or Gardner Murphy's Wundt is not Wundt. This early phase of a laudable wave of antiquarian enthusiasm has resulted in a series of overcorrections—tending more toward *Heldenmusik* than competent scholarship—of the previously regnant Wundt stereotypes. A balanced and critically sober perspective on Wundt's extraordinarily diffuse and inconstant corpus is yet to be achieved.

In the meantime, I would like to report two cautionary impressions.

1. Some of the recent writing on Wundt seems not much less superficial than the sources it seeks to correct—sometimes betraying this circumstance by an imprecise reading of those very sources, brief and simple though they may be. An example is the charge, now fashionable, that Boring and others have overemphasized the significance of Wundt's "elementism" in that they overlook Wundt's frequent metatheoretical assertions to the effect that his elements (e.g., sensations) are "abstractions," and in that they also neglect his correlative emphases upon

process, wholeness, activity, will, and so on. But a reading of almost any of Wundt's writings will show that he is *forced* by his conception of the task of psychology to take these "abstractions" very seriously, for his central concept constitutive of that task (*psychical causality*) requires, via its "law" of "psychical resultants," that the foundational problems of experimental psychology be *posed* and *analyzed* in terms of compositional relations between elements (however abstract) and their "creatively synthesized" resultants or "psychical compounds." Boring is certainly clear enough on this issue, and an historian who cannot perceive that is not the kind of hermeneuticist who can be trusted to digest Wundt's 53,000 pages of convoluted German!

2. Despite Wundt's often meticulous and encyclopaedic reviews of the sensory physiology, experimental psychophysics, and the neurology of his day, and despite his vast erudition in areas as far-flung as natural science, philosophy, and the social, historical, and linguistic studies, his own theorizing is often shockingly arbitrary. Moreover, the frequent emendations in his systematic thinking which some discern as indicative of "development" are often abrupt and but thinly girded by rationale. Not infrequently, one finds—in the midst of some tightly organized and, in the main, well-reasoned analysis—sequences characterized by almost autistic orders of logical elision and ideational inconsonance. These traits must qualify the kind of optimism which views Wundt's systematic thinking as a bypassed treasury of still viable ideas, and perhaps such traits constitute some part of the basis for the rapid passage of his ideas into neglect.[2]

---

[2] The qualities of Wundt's intellectual style that I have sought to convey are brought into vivid focus by the following excerpt from William James's letter to Carl Stumpf, under date of February 6, 1887:

> He says of each possible subject, "Here I must have an opinion. Let's see! What shall it be? How many possible opinions are there? three? four? Yes! Just four! Shall I take one of these? It will seem more original to take a higher position, a sort of *Vermittelungsansicht* between them all. That I will do, etc., etc." So he acquires a complete assortment of opinions of his own . . . (Perry, 1935, Vol. II, p. 69).

Among the many eloquently caustic comments made by James about Wundt, this one (seldom quoted, even though other passages from the same letter have been widely recirculated) seems the least controvertible. It is difficult to read more than a few pages of Wundt and not sense its veracity. If one contemplates also the papal confidence manifested by Wundt in the assertion and defense of his "complete stock of opinions" at any given time (despite their constantly altering character *over* time), one may arrive at a poignant perception of a quality already present in Wundt which became something like a stylistic constant in the subsequent history of psychology: a type of insecurity-induced dogmatism which waxes the more strongly, the more thin or arbitrary the thesis one promulgates. This is perhaps an inevitable symptom among the agents of a "science" that has not yet found its way but that can flourish only under the pretension that it is inexorably moving forward.

One of the truly impressive contributions to the new wave of scholarly interest in Wundt is van Hoorn and Verhave's (1980) analysis of "Wundt's Changing Conceptions of a General and Theoretical Psychology," which documents the instability of Wundt's views on the very definition of psychology over a fifty-year time span. They find, by way of qualifying James's sense of the patchwork quality of Wundt's thinking, but one *"central* idea": that of *"psychische Kausalität"* (psychic causality). This doctrine, and

The "Founding" in Broader Historical Context and in Meaning

The meaning shift triggered by Wilhelm Wundt's laboratory was something for which an eager world had long prepared. Not only had a *science* of psychology been passionately invited and adumbrated by psychologically inclined philosophers for more than two centuries, but the substance of what could be thought an *experimental* psychology had been emerging over an almost comparable interval in physics, in the analysis of the "personal equation" within astronomy, in medicine, in biology, and especially in the work of certain of the great nineteenth-century physiologists and neurologists such as Sir Charles Bell, Marshall Hall, Johannes Müller, E. H. Weber, du Bois-Reymond, Helmholz, Hering, Bernstein, Flourens, Broca, Fritsch, and Hitzig. And, of course, behind Wundt's semantic act of 1879 stood the work of Lotze, Fechner, Stumpf, G. E. Müller, Mach, and others of the free-wheeling German philosophers (some of them, like Fechner and Mach, philosopher-physicists) of the nineteenth century who had already made substantial contributions to experimental psychology. The establishment of the Leipzig "laboratory" can thus be seen—on an obstetrical analogy—as a very late delivery and—on a theological one—an extraordinarily late christening. It was distinctly not an act of conception.

From the vantage of the descriptive historian, the "founding" of psychology as an "independent, experimental science" can hardly seem a matter of surprise in light of its long and laborious gestation. But for those who are driven to make sense of history, it is well to half close one's eyes in hope of admitting the penumbrae of strangeness surrounding facticity. The inception of a laboratory of "experimental psychology" *could have* been a trivial event—noticed, celebrated, and remembered by but a small group of persons isolated from the world by the esotericism of scholarship. Instead, it marked a turning point in world sensibility, culminating in the now accurate cliché that the twentieth is the "psychological century." Why?

Listen to Théodule Armand Ribot conveying *in 1879* to a French audience the achievements of the "new" experimental psychology (in his book, *German Psychology To-day*):

> The spirit of the natural sciences has invaded psychology . . . . One asks whether a collection of ingenious remarks, of fine analyses, of observations clothed in terms of elegant exposition, . . . constitute a body of doctrine, a true science;—whether it

---

five "persistent themes" of metatheoretical and metaphysical cast (e.g., inadequacy of "uncontrolled" introspection, emphasis on process, antimaterialism), emerge as the principal invariants in Wundt's "mature views" (after about 1874). They interpret Wundt's manifold systematic inconsonances and inconstancies rather more generously than did James and others, placing him in the tradition of the typical "German *Gelehrte*" and viewing him as "the last 19th century German metaphysician." Another seminal contribution that can help qualify certain of the excessively heroic images of Wundt now coming into circulation is Solomon Diamond's study of "Wundt before Leipzig" (1980), which explores the characterological basis of Wundt's intellectual and scholarly style.

is not time to resort to a method more rigorous. Thus has arisen the separation, every day more apparent, between the old and the new psychology.

Although it has cut a good figure enough, the old psychology is doomed. . . . Its methods do not suffice for the increasing difficulties of the task, for the growing exigencies of the scientific spirit. It is compelled to live upon its past. . . . Besides, . . . the old psychology rests upon an illegitimate conception, and should perish with the contradictions that are in it. . . . Its essential characteristics remain always the same . . . . In the first place, it is possessed of the metaphysical spirit; it is the "science of the soul"; internal observation, analysis, and reasoning are its favorite processes of investigation: it distrusts biological science . . . . Feeble and old, it makes no progress, and asks only to be let alone, that it may spend its age in peace.

Such a conception is no longer vital. Its metaphysical tendencies exclude the positive spirit, forbid the employ of a scientific method, deprive psychology of the fruits of free research. It does not dare to assert itself as a study of psychic *phenomena* alone, distinct and independent. . . . In proportion as the old habits of mind are effaced, will we see, more and more clearly, that psychology and metaphysics, formerly confounded under the same title, presuppose intellectual aptitudes that are opposite and exclusive. We will perceive that talent in metaphysics bears an inverse ratio to talent in psychology; that henceforth . . . the psychologist should renounce metaphysics and the metaphysician psychology (Ribot, 1879/1886, pp. 1–3).

Do the representatives of the old psychology . . . understand the position they have taken with reference to contemporary science? The physicist and the chemist trust themselves only in their laboratories: the biologist daily adorns his workshop with new machines, arms himself with all his weapons, multiplies his instruments and means of experiment, strives to substitute the passive and mechanical registry of phenomena for their subjective estimation . . .

The new psychology differs from the old in its spirit: it is not metaphysical; in its end: it studies only phenomena; in its procedure: it borrows as much as possible from the biological sciences (p. 5).

. . . we may see the time approaching when psychology will demand the entire power of a man, when he will be psychologist alone, as he is physicist, chemist, physiologist alone. In every science that flourishes and is cultivated with enthusiasm, there is a necessary division of labor. Each important question becomes a field by itself. Will not the profound study of perception alone, for example, be sufficient for the most active mind? Empirical psychology, united to the other natural sciences by a tie of close connection, widens its field; the constant work of analysis enlarges the mass of details. Where the last century had twenty facts to master, we have twenty laws; and next will come laws of laws, that is, the generalization of more and more numerous facts. The human brain has its limits, and is by necessity compelled to concentrate itself upon a single study (pp. 17–18).[3]

---

[3] To these quotations it should be added that Ribot constantly applies such adjectives as "narrow," "childish," "shallow," "verbal," and "scholastic" to the "old" psychology in course of his advocacy of the "new." Such adjectives will have a familiar ring to most psychologists of the present day: they have been echoing for a century in the antimetaphysical and anti-"armchair" rhetoric of scientific psychology.

A passionate set of utterances—and one which could easily be attributed to the Gallic temperament of Monsieur Ribot! But the text as given above was rendered in the words of its American translator, James Mark Baldwin, who, in 1886, undertook the translation "with the feeling that no greater service of the kind could be rendered to the 'new psychology'." Baldwin was, of course, one of the many American students who in the 1880s, along with many other students from other lands, had flocked to the centers of psychological interest in Germany (mainly Leipzig) to study the "new" psychology. Though he had spent there only a year— and only part of that with Wundt in Leipzig—he experienced an "apostolic call to the 'new psychology'" (1930, p. 2). It was in that mood that he discovered Ribot's book and was impelled to translate it into English. It is of interest to note in passing that, after his return, Baldwin established three psychological laboratories on this continent (Princeton, 1893; Toronto, approximately 1900; Johns Hopkins, 1903)— all this despite his ironic confession that: "Already at Princeton the new interest in genetic psychology and general biology had become absorbing, and the meagerness of the results of the psychological laboratories (apart from direct work on sensation and movement) was becoming evident everywhere." He adds: "I began to feel that there was truth in what James was already proclaiming as to the barrenness of the tables and curves coming from many laboratories" (1930, p. 4).

If Baldwin's *initial* enthusiasm for the "new psychology" be perceived as but a sample of the gaucherie of the New World, let us savor the tonality of an influential (and usually restrained) British voice as it invites the new psychology into existence *in 1843*:

> The backward state of the Moral Sciences can only be remedied by applying to them the methods of Physical Science, duly extended and generalized . . . .
>
> If there are some subjects on which the results obtained have finally received the unanimous assent of all who have attended to the proof, and others on which mankind have not yet been equally successful; on which the most sagacious minds have occupied themselves from the earliest date, and have never succeeded in establishing any considerable body of truths, so as to be beyond denial or doubt; it is by generalizing the methods successfully followed in the former inquiries, and adapting them to the latter, that we may hope to remove this blot on the face of science (1843/1862, Vol. II, pp. x, 410–411).

The words, of course, are those of John Stuart Mill, and by the "moral sciences" he meant, in the usage of his day, what we now regard as the social sciences in the sense which includes psychology.

The almost rancorous heat of Mill's invitation and, a third of a century later, the passion of Ribot's remarkably prescient vision of the "new" psychology are but limited and arbitrarily selected symptoms of a broad tendency in Western culture which had been gathering force since the Enlightenment and had become irresistible by the mid-to-late nineteenth century. In simplest human terms, this was the

15

notion that man's earthly destiny is perfectible by rational planning and control and that the content of the rational is coextensive with the methods and findings of natural science. It was this motif which, in social and political relations, found expression in the Utopian and Marxist socialisms, Comte's positivist theocracy, the utilitarianisms, and indeed, the Liberal political and legal reforms of the nineteenth century. In biology and the biologically based theories of man and culture of the post-Darwinian era, its expression took the form of an optimistic evolutionary progressivism. In philosophy, it was expressed as empiricism, naturalism, materialism, and—increasingly—positivism. And a correlative tendency in virtually every field of cultural and practical life was, of course, a growing animosity toward the past: a vertiginous sense that the past was overburdened with exploitative and arbitrary dogma; with a hypersufficiency of inflated intellectual constructions with respect to which there were no rational grounds for choice.

By the third quarter of the nineteenth century, the established natural sciences and their technological offshoots had given such food to humankind's cognitive and material hungers that humanity's appetite had become insatiable. And, by this time, multiple lines of inquiry into the nature and trend of science itself began to focus into an apparently wholesome Victorian vision. It was a vision of a totally orderly universe, totally open to the methods of science, and a totally orderly science, totally open to the stratagems—and wants—of humanity. A point had been reached such that it could actually be believed that knowledge can be beckoned into being by administrative plan. Such a belief—combining as it did with the availability of material resources for its implementation—can be seen as the basis for an unprecedented chapter in cultural history.

A strange chapter: one in which autism and accomplishment can easily interpenetrate; one in which program can seem more palpable than practice; one in which intent and impact, word and meaning, can fall apart.

We need but return to Ribot's statement to illustrate certain of these strange qualities. Ribot gives a prescient registration of the tone, the overarching values, and the ground plan of the psychology of the subsequent hundred years. Yet everything that he says about the "new" psychology can be seen as an autistic misconstrual of the new psychology as it existed when he wrote. In 1879 perhaps not a single representative of the new psychology in the world would have considered himself *exclusively* a psychologist. Most—like Wundt himself—were professors of philosophy and saw their psychological work as intimately related to their philosophic commitments. Few—the outstanding exceptions being Mach (himself primarily a physicist) and Avenarius—would have rejected metaphysics in any sweeping way. Indeed, of the "new" psychologists discussed in extenso in Ribot's book (i.e., Herbart, Lotze, Fechner, Wundt, and Brentano), *all* were metaphysically inclined, while Fechner, primarily a physicist, held some of the most idiosyncratic and (so to say) baroque panpsychic views in the history of thought. It would indeed be some time before any person became "psychologist alone," and it would wait upon the 1890s, or perhaps the beginning of this century, before specialization in psychology began to become as particulate as Ribot anticipated.

It was thus the Ribots who "founded" psychology—in anything like its *currently* institutionalized sense. Wundt started a laboratory which attracted many students, a large subset of whom arrived with (or developed) sensibilities much like Ribot's. It was largely this cadre (numbering perhaps over a hundred by 1900) which soon began founding laboratories throughout Europe and in the New World. Wundt's approximately thirteen American students (until 1900) were especially prolific in this activity. Most of this cadre took to their new locations a dedication to psychology as "independent" and "experimental" (in some sense of those open-horizon terms), but not any marked baggage of Wundt's systematic ideas. Thus the well-known conceptual and programmatic pluralism of modern psychology began its fast-burgeoning course from the very start.

It is in this strangely qualified sense, then, that Wilhelm Wundt's "founding" of his laboratory contributed to the institutionalization of an "independent, experimental psychology." The bounded role which he assigned to experiment became in the hands of many of his students a boundless one. His sense of the "independence" of psychology was that psychology, as the science of "immediate experience" (rather than "mediate experience," the province of physics and natural science), must be construed as an autonomous discipline to be pursued in its own *irreducible* terms. It is doubtful that many of his actual students could have perceived such a position as a declaration of contempt toward *philosophy*, but it did not take long for history to arrive at that reading.

As for "science," yes, Wundt thought psychology a science, but one having characteristics which (as his thinking evolved) increasingly diverged from the standard Anglo-Saxon sense of "natural science." The story of Wundt's changing conceptions of the relations of psychology to the *Naturwissenschaften* on the one hand, and the *Geisteswissenschaften* on the other, is an intricate one (see van Hoorn & Verhave's excellent 1980 treatment). For the purposes of the present glancing discussion, it can be noted that by the early Leipzig years Wundt's particular (and rather Leibnitzian) form of a mind-world parallelism, his voluntarism, his analysis of "psychic causality," and his views concerning *Völkerpsychologie* certainly preclude a positivistic reading of his sense of psychology as science. Indeed, though in the 1873–1874 edition of the *Grundzüge* "Wundt assigns to psychology an *intermediate* position between *Natur- und-Geisteswissenschaften*," by the time of the *Methodenlehre* (1883) "Wundt states unequivocally that psychology must be regarded as the basis . . . of the *Geisteswissenschaften*" (van Hoorn & Verhave, 1980, pp. 90–91). Moreover, at no point in Wundt's thinking concerning the constitutive problem of psychology was it to borrow from natural science anything other than its experimental method—and even this as *transmuted* by application to the controlled observation of "immediate experience" (*Selbst-Beobachtung*). The function of experiment was thus to make rigorous introspection possible by systematic external control and variation of the psychic events to be reported on, but the context of application, unlike the case of physics, was to be the manifold of conscious processes believed to obey sui generis laws of "psychic causality." One can only conclude that psychology, in anything like the mainstream forms that it soon began to assume during its subsequent history, was implemented by the Ribots of this world[4]—of which there were many.

In these cautionary paragraphs, which have sought merely to reduce the vagueness of recently prevailing stereotypes concerning psychology's "founding" as a science, we have necessarily done little justice to the actual tensions, complexities, ironies of the relevant nineteenth-century intellectual history. Though the Ribots of the world, as we have been calling them, flocked to the laboratories, and sought— in increasingly diverse ways—to emulate ever more fetishistically the methods of physical science (as they conceived them to be), there were many countervailing trends. To name but a few: the influential empirical (but *non*experimental) "act psychology" of Brentano; Dilthey's incisively developed conception of psychology and social science as *Geisteswissenschaft* (but in a descriptive and nonexperimental sense quite different from Wundt's conception); the gathering influence toward the end of the century of Husserl's program of phenomenological investigations in psychology and philosophy; the critical skirmishing against the new psychology of residual post-Hegelian idealist philosophers; the French tradition of interest in mental pathology as represented by such thinkers as Charcot and Janet; and, of course, commencing at the turn of the century, the increasingly conspicuous alternative to the scientific psychology of the academy that was to be offered by Freud and his disciples.

The ironies tucked within the interstices of this complex history were legion. I shall develop but one outstanding example: In tandem with the growing ascendancy in psychology of a tight and tidy scientism based on one or another putatively slavish construal of the genius of *Newtonian* physics, there was developing an explosion of doubt *within the physical sciences* concerning the viability of the Newtonian world

---

[4]In a literal age, it is perhaps necessary to state that Ribot's name is used here as a *symbol* for the *attitudes* expressed in the extended quotation (earlier in this *Foreword*) from his 1879 *German Psychology To-day*: attitudes reflecting a strand of late-nineteenth-century sensibility that is continuous with the galloping scientism of twentieth-century psychology. In fact, Ribot himself seceded (up to a point) from our category of "the Ribots of this world." Though—prior to his receipt of the first professorship of experimental psychology in France (College de France, 1888)—he was a radical propagandist for the new experimental psychology and an epiphenomenalist, it was possible for Brett (1921/1965) to conclude that "this excess [the epiphenomenalism] was modified in time and from 1888, the date of his work on *Attention*, Ribot became more truly psychological in his methods and outlook." Brett adds: "The original animosity against metaphysicians, expressed almost violently in the early historical work, ceased to occupy the foreground, though the main principles remain unchanged" (1965, p. 500). It may be added that, subsequent to his appointment as France's first professor of "experimental and comparative psychology," Ribot's actual research, rather than implementing the "new" experimental tradition of Germany, melded with the descriptive and medical strain of French psychology.

view. Stresses upon that view entailed by the Faraday-Maxwell field physics, by empirico-conceptual difficulties with the "ether," and by other anomalies, gave rise to widespread consternation over what was called "the crisis in physics." The very Ernst Mach, himself a significant contributor to the new psychology, whose positivistic views were looked toward well into the present century as *authority* for the essentially Newtonian scientism of experimental psychology, was, qua physicist, centrally and constructively occupied with the "crisis" in physics.[5] Indeed, aspects of Mach's reanalysis of Newtonian physics in *Die Mechanik in ihrer Entwicklung* (1883) were among the influences which played upon Einstein (by his own account) in his work on relativity. It might be added that if psychology at any point after 1905 had sought methodological guidance from the lessons of relativity physics (and, more generally, from what early in this century came to be called the "new physics"), rather than persevering in its simplistic Newtonian mold, it might have developed in a very different direction over most of the present century.

A number of other ironies are implicit in the following considerations.

The persons who actually *forged* psychology in its mid-to-late-nineteenth-century guise (whether loudly "scientific" or merely "empirical")—the pioneers—were persons of substantial complexity and range. They were larger than their specific and technical "psychological" interests. Some were indeed giants. Virtually all saw the character and the prospects of experimental work in qualified terms—sometimes to the point of ambivalence about the sense, significance, nontriviality of what they did qua psychologist. In the person of William James—for whom priority can be claimed as "founder" of American psychology and also as proprietor of a roomful of equipment which preceded Wundt's inaugural laboratory—ambivalence concerning the very conception of an "experimental psychology" assumed agonizing proportions, leaving its mark on virtually every page he penned in the service of psychology.

---

[5] Indeed, in the 1930s psychology was to become massively influenced by the "logical positivism" developed by Mach's successors at the University of Vienna: the "Vienna Circle" of philosophers and scientists (including Carnap, Hahn, Neurath, Frank, Feigl, and others) which had begun to form around Moritz Schlick after the latter had assumed Mach's former chair in the early 1920s. Though their antimetaphysical position and their view of science was strongly influenced by Mach, they soon discarded his phenomenalism in favor of a "physicalism" which resulted in a narrower—and for the psychologist, more inhibiting—conception of science than Mach's. The marriage of the logical positivist reconstruction of science with the orienting attitudes of Watsonian behaviorism was indeed the basis for the "neobehaviorisms" which dominated American psychology from roughly 1930 to 1960. Thus Mach's *indirect* influence on psychology proved far greater than his direct influence—and proved, as most would now agree, more deleterious. The irony is compounded by the fact that Mach's analytical methods did not damp out the profundity of his physical intuition; as Polanyi has pointed out, Mach's critique of Newtonian "absolute space" was essentially correct, despite the fact that Mach's methods caused him to believe such a concept "meaningless." It was Einstein (according to Polanyi, 1958, p. 12) who "showed that the Newtonian conception of space was not *meaningless* but false." It might be added that the ranks of the Vienna Circle included no physicist of comparable genius or penetration to Mach's.

And indeed, many within the initial generation of *students* of the "new" psychology were persons whose intellectual purviews were broader than their specifically psychological interests. They were "converts," young polymathically inclined persons whose initial calling had been to philosophy, to theology, to science, and who attached the idealistic ardor that had brought them to their earlier interests to the heady promise of this new *science* of mind that would ultimately resolve by *experimental* means the ancient backlog of refractory human problems. Such was Carl Stumpf, a student of Brentano and Lotze, who, though he spent most of the working hours of a long career in the empirical and experimental pursuit of his passionate interest in *Tonpsychologie*, felt guilty throughout over his disloyalty to the promptings of his philosophic muse. Such were certain of Wundt's American students (e.g., Stanley Hall, James Mark Baldwin, James McKeen Cattell, Charles H. Judd), who transported the missionary spirit of "experimental psychology" to this country, establishing laboratories, journals, and professional associations, but who, in their own work, soon found themselves drifting away from *experimental* interests. As is well known, Hall turned to genetic psychology, eclectic theoretical and historical writing, and university administration; Baldwin, to genetic psychology and philosophy, and to the broad historical interests represented in his *Dictionary of Philosophy and Psychology* (1901, 1902); Cattell soon became the American pioneer in differential psychology, and later turned his interests to such projects as are represented by *American Men of Science*; and Judd became interested in educational psychology and (what is not so widely known) was perhaps the only American student of Wundt to maintain an abiding interest in the *Völkerpsychologie* and in Wundt's philosophy.

But it is not meet that we engage the terms of literal history—for that will be the province of many of the contributors to this book. However conflicted and uneasy the provenance of scientific psychology may be, the cozy image of a founding father, a distinct location in the distinguished university of a romantic East German city, a definite starting date, and a round century of proliferating effort invites the attempt to align psychology's sprawling present with its past. It is well to ask, after a century of ardent effort, what hath this now vast enterprise wrought? This is more than a *routine* ceremonial question. It is fraught with significance for the human race. It bears on the very definition of what it is to be human.

Psychology at Age One Hundred: An Institutional Profile

The purpose of this book is to record the detailed answers of many expert minds to the large question just raised. It is well, however, to set the stage by examining the disciplinary scope and cultural impact of present-day psychology. What—in the broadest institutional terms—are the current sequelae of psychology's emergence as an "independent science" one hundred years after the event?

The century has seen a vast proliferation of psychological thinking and research modeled, in the main, on the procedures of the natural sciences, a steady differentiation of these efforts into many specialized fields, both "fundamental" and "applied," and an accelerating growth of the psychological work force. At this phase, psychology comprehends one of the largest groupings in contemporary scholarship. In 1981 the American Psychological Association alone had approximately 50,500 members (in 1979, the centennial year, the number had reached 49,047). Since there is evidence that about one-half of the people who qualify, on acceptable definitions, as "psychologist" are not members of the national association, the total number of psychologists in the United States has recently been estimated by one keen student of the matter (Rosenzweig, 1982) as 100,000, and some estimates place the total as high as 120,000. Contrast such figures with the membership of the American Psychological Association in its inaugural year of 1892: a solid total of 42 souls! Consider, further, that in 1879 there was not a single person alive who could have been designated "psychologist alone"!

Joy Stapp (1981, Note 1) has recently reported the astounding finding, based on an analysis of annual National Research Council reports on "Doctorate Recipients from United States Universities," that in 1980 one out of ten doctorates granted in the United States were in psychology. In 1970 psychology doctorates constituted 6.4 percent of all doctoral degrees here; the percentage gradually climbed to 9.9 by 1978, and remained on a plateau through 1980, *despite* the circumstance that the total number of doctorates for *all* scholarly categories began, as early as 1974, to show a mild but fairly consistent decrease (from 33,727 in 1973 to 30,982 in 1980). This suggests that even during a phase in which there has been a downturn in doctoral education, the doctoral-level work force in psychology has continued to grow *relative* to that of scholarship in general. Though, as we shall see, there are indications that the *rate* of growth of psychology as an institution, whether in number of new doctorates per year or on other indices, is decreasing (and may soon become negative), psychology continues to command increasing interest relative to other intellectual and professional pursuits.

Other considerations bearing on the American scene further document the growth and recent status of psychology relative to the culture at large. According to Kiesler (1978), 15 percent of all undergraduate majors in the vast American university system were in 1977 majoring in psychology, and 5 percent of the aggrègate faculties were psychologists. Further data of interest may be gleaned from an authoritative 1978 National Academy of Sciences report on "A Century of Doctorates." Between 1920 and 1974, American universities awarded a total of 32,855 doctoral degrees in psychology; the number of doctorates in physics granted during the same interval was 26,717. If, for the same interval, one aggregates the total number of degrees respectively granted in the two scholarly groupings with which physics and psychology form natural clusters (the so-called "EMP fields" of engineering, mathematics, and physics on the one hand, and the "behavioral sciences" comprising psychology and the social sciences, on the other), the number of

21

"EMP" degrees (146,019) is approximately twice the number of those granted in behavioral science (78,884). That is not a humbling contrast when it is considered that the former disciplines have behind them an institutionalized history several hundred years longer (on some criteria, several thousand years longer) than have the behavioral sciences. The contrast is considerably reduced, however, when it is noted that, during the period at issue, 87,523 doctorate-level degrees were granted in the field of education—an area in which the typical dissertation is wholly or partly addressed to a psychological subject matter. Another instructive comparison is between the aggregate number of doctorates granted in the life sciences (inclusive of all basic medical, biological, and agricultural disciplines) and in the behavioral sciences: the figures (81,316 versus 78,887) are surprisingly close. Perhaps most instructive of all the trends which we have drawn from the National Academy Study is that between 1940 and 1974 psychology (along with engineering and education) was among the three fields in the entire academic spectrum manifesting the highest average annual growth rate in doctorates granted. The rate for psychology was 8.2 percent.

Psychology's American Naturalization

It is not chauvinism that has caused me to concentrate on statistics from the United States to document the explosive growth of psychology over its brief history. In a volume which seeks to assess the first century of psychology, it is profoundly important to note the curious circumstance that over much of the century psychology, despite its European origins, acquired the attributes of an almost uniquely American enterprise. Though I cannot here trace the intricate story of psychology's American naturalization, it must be at least acknowledged. Let it suffice to say that America's founding heritage of Enlightenment values, its almost explicitly "experimentalist" ideology in respect to the translation of such values into social practice, the practical and activist strain of national sensibility induced by the opportunities and challenges of a dynamically expanding and indefinitely expansible frontier—all these were among the broad conditions favoring high receptivity to a "science" that seemed to promise prediction and control of human affairs. From an early point in the twentieth century the United States thus began to achieve a massive hegemony, relative to the rest of the world, in the size of its psychological work force; the number of its psychological laboratories and scholarly periodicals; the number of university and other contexts in which psychology was pursued; and in the amount of public interest, both formal-educational and lay, which the field commanded.

The interaction of American practical and instrumental sensibility with the German, British (and, slightly later, Russian and French) ideas that had fueled the early phase of the new psychology almost immediately began to lend American psychology an indigenous coloration. By the early 1900s, approximately twenty-five laboratories were in operation in this country, but few of them were taking any large part of their marching orders from Leipzig or other German centers. American psychologists were as much looking toward post-Darwinian comparative psychology and British associationism as they were toward any of the German pioneers; they were also looking toward their own philosophers, who were forming such indigenous traditions as pragmatism and, slightly later, neorealism and critical realism, for conceptual guidance. More concretely, New World psychology was putting out pseudopods into *the* world, toward a functional psychology which saw consciousness, in evolutionary perspective, as an instrument of adaptation, and toward an applied psychology of education, of the clinic, and of industry and the marketplace.

At the turn of the century (1898), these influences coalesced in Thorndike's work on "animal intelligence"—heralded as the first actual *experiments* on animal behavior. These studies stand as a perfect symbol—and after that a font—for the indigenous color that American psychology had achieved: the research was biologically oriented and (perforce) "objective" in method; the connectionistic focus of the theorizing was the British "association of ideas" as translated into the Americanese "association of stimulus and reaction"; the overarching explanatory frame of trial-error selection mediated by "success" (later, "satisfiers" and "annoyers") involved a dilute Darwinian model of organism-environment adaptation; the "law of effect" (and supplementary principles) generalizing all of the preceding became the basis of Thorndike's practical and far-reaching work in *educational psychology*; and, finally, that very same generalization, and the types of variables linked by it, became a basis for the later massive American concentration upon S-R learning theory (nowhere more conspicuously than in the enormously influential neobehavioristic "reinforcement" theories of Hull and Skinner, respectively).[6]

[6]It is awesome to contemplate how great a part of the history of fundamental psychology in the United States during the first half of the twentieth century can be seen to relate—either by assimilation, extension, or apposition—to the conclusions that Thorndike based on the informal and crude "experiments" he reported in 1898 (and further elaborated in 1899, 1905, 1911, and many publications thereafter). Thus not only can the "reinforcement" analyses of learning (e.g., Hull) and of performance (e.g., Skinner) which began to dominate fundamental psychology in the 1930s be seen as based on assimilations of the "law of effect" schema, but the central schism among S-R behavior theorists was between those who believed reinforcement a necessary condition of learning and those who stressed some version of associative contiguity (whether S-S or S-R) as alone sufficient. Contiguity theorists (e.g., Guthrie) tended to take Pavlovian CR relationships (so-called "classical conditioning") as paradigmatic of learning, while Hull's maneuver was to seek to derive the Pavlovian conditioning "laws" from the principle of reinforcement. A third class of behavior theorists (e.g., Hilgard and Marquis, Mowrer, Schlossberg) presumed, in one nomenclature or another, that both "types" of learning—Thorndikian and Pavlovian—were fundamental and required recognition as complementary basic "mechanisms" in any full analysis of learning. Skinner can be ambiguously ordered to this class in that, early on, he made joint recognition of "respondent" and "operant" behavior in a manner analogous to the Pavlovian versus the Thorndikian case, but then proceeded to concentrate on operant behavior to the virtual neglect of the respondent type. Amusingly, even Thorndike can be ordered to the "two-factor" class in that, as early as 1905, he included among the laws of learning a principle of "associative shifting" having precisely the same force as Pavlov's "stimulus-substitution" formulation of conditioned response learning.

Moreover, it should be stressed that one of the chief contexts of controversy between Gestalt (or "field") and S-R theorists centered on differential interpretations of the kind of trial-error learning

From Thorndike and from functionalism (which in the hands of Dewey, Angell, and Carr evolved into a formal "school" of psychology at The University of Chicago

phenomena that gave rise to Thorndike's generalizations. The Gestaltists emphasized the primacy in the learning of higher organisms of the type of perceptual-cognitive field reorganization that they associated with "insight," and saw "blind" trial-error learning as a limited case enforced by situations in which the instrumental relationships that could mediate problem solution were hidden or arbitrary. The S-R theorists either derided the very notion of "insight" as extra-scientific, or, like Hull, sought to derive the empirical syndrome definitive of insight-learning (e.g., suddenness, "completeness" on a single trial, and transposability) from "objective" S-R principles.

In the ambience of this vastly ramified impact of Thorndike's 1898 findings, it is instructive to contemplate the following circumstances.

1. The notion of "trial-and-error" had a pre-Thorndikian lineage traceable to Alexander Bain, who had used the phrase descriptively as early as 1855 in his analysis of the "constructive intellect." The term was used by Lloyd Morgan in 1894 in a sense precisely analogous to Thorndike's usage. Morgan had indeed described informal observations of his own dog learning to lift the latch of a gate (a task almost identical to that posed by certain of Thorndike's puzzle boxes) in terms closely presaging Thorndike's characteristic descriptions of his findings, and he had even suggested the desirability of experimentally investigating such processes. The remarkable impact of Thorndike's generalizations upon the ensuing history of research and theory must be attributed to many extrarational factors—not the least of which was his putative priority as the first *experimentalist* in animal psychology.

2. One can find indications in Thorndike's own descriptions (both of the initial studies reported in 1898, in which the subjects were mainly cats, and in later work on Cebus monkeys) of evidence inconsonant with a "blind" law of effect interpretation. Several of his cats, and all three of his Cebus monkeys, did indeed show the kind of sudden drop in time-per-trial that can be associated with insight.

3. The situation-dependent (and cross-cutting this, the individual and species-dependent) character of the gradual trail-and-error "connectionistic" learning that Thorndike believed prototypical across the entire phyletic spectrum, was noted, in one way or another, by many subsequent students of animal behavior. The relevant history is dense and intricate; here it may merely be suggested. By 1901, Hobhouse had designed a number of problems of a sort more open to perceptual survey by the animal, and had found, for a variety of species, evidence of more prompt problem solution than did Thorndike. Köhler's well-known studies (1917/1924) establishing the capacity for (and the *conditions* of) insightful problem solutions in the ape need hardly be cited. Almost never cited, however, is D. K. Adams's important study of 1929, in which Thorndike's 1898 cat experiments are replicated and extended in ways which make possible finer discrimination between circumstances favoring insight-like problem solution and those favoring more gradual solution. Better known are the experiments of Guthrie and Horton (1946), a second semireplication of the Thorndike 1898 study, which—in line with an effort to show the applicability of Guthrie's S-R contiguity theory to puzzle-box learning—employs a box that makes the animal's environment as homogeneous as possible and makes solution contingent upon a highly arbitrary relation between a "chance" contact of the animal with a large vertical lever and the opening of a door permitting escape. This situation elicited precisely what it was designed to effect: marked (though not utter) stereotypy of the successful response. Despite such clear evidence of situation-specific effects on learning as is provided by Thorndike (1898), Adams (1929), and Guthrie and Horton (1946), even in relation to subjects of the same species and problems of the same general type; and despite a massive dispersion of evidence both from the laboratory and the field showing the detailed character of the learning "process" to vary over a wide range of *other* situations and to register also subject variability, occasion variability, and species-specific disposition, American psychology somehow persisted until quite recently in a dominating belief that all learning phenomena were reducible to one basic "mechanism" (in liberal views, two), "objectively" describable in generalizations like the "law of effect."

(See Glickman's superb chapter in this book for extensive discussion of certain of these issues.)

in the early 1900s) it was but a short step to Watsonian behaviorism (about 1912) in that the position can be defined as functionalism sans the methodologically inconvenient baggage of consciousness or mind. The "behaviorist revolution," as it has so often been called, marks the point at which the "new" psychology achieved full American citizenship. It is a paradox that a new selection from the European idea pool soon began to play a role in the behaviorist "revolution": it was Watson who (around 1916) aroused American interest in Pavlovian ideas and methods, and a somewhat garbled version of these soon began to supplement (and, in some contexts, to displace) the Thorndikian generalizations and variables that had been structuring the interest in learning.

Nevertheless, Watson's "revolution" does mark the transition in American psychology between indigenous *color* and indigenous *substance*. If psychology can be said to have been imported from Germany in the 1880s, forty years later it had become an American export commodity which commenced virtually to flood the world market. Incursions from abroad did continue to have an impact on American psychology: one which (after Freud's visit in 1909) ultimately attained a large, if mainly extra-academic, influence was psychoanalysis; in the early 1930s Gestalt psychology found scattered receptivity; in the mid-1950s an extraordinarily belated but enthusiastic discovery of Piaget took place; and also commencing in the mid-1950s, even a few phenomenological viewpoints acquired modest followerships. But these influences were meager in comparison with the extent and depth of the impact of behaviorism on world psychology, especially during the interval (roughly) 1930–1960. During this era of the "neobehaviorisms"[7]—which then held the allegiance of by far the greatest number of theoretico-experimental psychologists in

---

[7] In this era—during which American intellectual influence on world psychology was at something like its zenith—we should again note the paradox of the American work deriving part of its impetus from a European tributary: in this instance, the *philosophic* movement of logical positivism. In a prior footnote, I have already *defined* neobehaviorism as a "marriage" between Watsonian (or "classical") behaviorism and logical positivism. By the early 1930s, the "objective" experimentalism of S-R behavior research had for two decades been generating particulate but unrelated findings—many of little interest. The hope now became that of moving on to rigorous, predictive *theory* which could integrate and guide experimental effort. This initiated what I have called an "Age of Theory" in which psychologists turned to philosophers and methodologists of science for advice concerning what was then called "techniques of theory construction." At that very point in history (the early 1930s), the Vienna Circle was exporting to the scholarly world a newly codified "rational reconstruction" of the nature of theory (based on physical science models) which many were inclined to interpret as a formulary for the construction of theory. This essentially hypothetico-deductive model—combining with cognate procedural directives stemming from such American sources as neopragmatism and operationism—soon stabilized into something like an official epistemology in American psychology. For thirty years (in residual ways, perhaps to the present day) this body of canon law prescribed the conditions of scientific virtue, not only for neobehaviorists but, to some extent, for the contending minority positions. It is worth pondering the fact that the very psychologists who gleefully harnessed themselves to the puppet strings pulled by the philosophers of science were the same who most loudly celebrated the *independence* of psychology from philosophy.

the United States—the disparity between the institutionalization of psychology here and in the rest of the world was perhaps at its greatest. Since that disparity was reflected in the large volume of our periodical and book literature relative to that of other countries, exposure to theorizing and research in the behaviorist frame was inevitable and frequent for any psychologist *anywhere* who wished to remain au courant with fundamental psychology. We are thus confronted with the strange circumstance that Professor Wundt's ornately Germanic creature became transmuted into something like a uniquely American changeling.

Intimations of Waning American Dominance

American dominance in the international psychological community is still very great, but the evidence in the past decade or two seems to indicate a diminution. We are still the font for most current fads and fashions but, amusingly, what we seem to be exporting to international psychology (sometimes, one fears, in garbled and reductively "operationalized" form) are largely ideas that we imported from abroad in the first place. For instance, the widely celebrated "second revolution" in American psychology—the so-called *cognitive revolution* which commenced in the mid-1950s—draws its *substantive* inspiration from the intellectualistic strand within the entire history of philosophy and, more immediately, from Piagetian developmental theory and some of the work on thinking in the Gestalt tradition (see the chapters by A. Newell and M. Henle, included in this volume). What the United States has contributed is the fusion of such ideas with the information theoretic and technological resources of the computer disciplines. It is indicative of the changing dominance relations in international psychology, however, that British, and even Russian, interests in such fusions of psychology and engineering as are marked by fields like "artificial intelligence" and "computer simulation" were asserted not appreciably later than the American interests and, in some contexts, independently of American influence.

Present-Day Psychology in International Perspective

A shrewd analysis of the numbers and distribution of psychologists in the world has been made by Mark Rosenzweig (1982). On the basis of cogent analyses of statistical sources from many countries—together with some clever extrapolations for countries for which data are thin or nonexistent—he estimates the total number of psychologists in the world to be 260,000 (as of spring 1981). The backbone of Rosenzweig's data is provided by the membership totals for each of the national psychological societies which comprise the International Union of Psychological Science (IUPsyS). The Union, formerly called the International Union of Scientific Psychology (IUPS) and founded in 1951, has published membership totals for its component societies in 1970 (when these were thirty-six in number) and 1980 (when the number had grown to forty-four). A comparison of these breakdowns reveals a phenomenal increase in the decade at issue in the number of psychologists represented by IUPsyS: "almost a doubling," in Rosenzweig's words. In 1970 the total was 53,219 members for the thirty-six societies then included; the 1980 aggregate membership of the same thirty-six societies was 101,521; while the aggregate, inclusive of the eight member societies which had subsequently joined the Union, was 102,590.

Rosenzweig's figure of 260,000 for the current world population of psychologists is based on knowledgeable, though perforce uncertain, estimates of ratios of psychologists in each country who meet the criteria for membership in their national societies but who are not members. He also determines rates, per million of population, of the psychologists in each of the forty-four IUPsyS countries in respect both to the national society totals and the inferred "absolute" number of psychologists. These estimates suggest trends—some obvious and some surprising—which cannot be neglected in any portrait of the institutional status of psychology at the end of its first century.

Among the more obvious is the unevenness in the deployment of psychologists around the world: rather predictably, this dispersion is largely correlated with the degree of economic and (by Western standards) educational development of the country or region in question. Nevertheless, some may be surprised by certain details of the distribution. For instance, the figures for "estimated total psychologists" by region show Western Europe with 78,000 psychologists—not far behind the aggregate for the United States and Canada of 106,000. It is also of interest that Latin America has currently the third largest psychologist work force (at least in absolute numbers), with an estimated 45,000 psychologists. This is markedly in excess of the next largest regional work force, that for Eastern Europe (excluding the USSR), which numbers an estimated 11,000. From that point on, there is a sharp break in the regional distribution, the abruptness of which is best indicated by estimates per million of population: taking the rate per million for the United States and Canada as a reference point (424), it progressively drops to 235 for Australia and New Zealand, 222 for Western Europe, 120 for Latin America, and 81 for Eastern Europe; after that point it becomes 7 per million for the USSR, 6 for Asia (exclusive of China), 1 for China. (No estimate is given for Africa, exclusive of South Africa, by virtue of insufficient evidence; the rate for South Africa is 37.)

Though the unevenness in the world distribution of psychologists comes as no surprise, its *extraordinarily* ragged and skewed quality is, perhaps, significant. This enormous variability obviously says something about the dispersion of material and cultural resources in the world, but it may also contain a message about sui generis characteristics of psychology, especially if viewed under the mantle of "science." One can doubt that the variability in the world dispersion of practitioners of the established natural sciences and the life sciences is of a comparable order to that for psychology. Moreover, what psychologists actually *do* by way of research and practice (and also the character and extent of their educational preparation) varies enormously from country to country—and in a degree unmatched by most other disciplines that qualify as "science."

Nevertheless, the most impressive trends that Rosenzweig's analysis lays bare are those which betoken continuing rapid growth in the world psychological work force and, at the same time, a *realignment* of national growth rates in a way which begins to qualify American dominance. However uneven the international distribution of psychologists, the institutionalized pursuit of psychology is indeed becoming *more* international. Rosenzweig's estimates of rates of psychologists per million of population per *country* are especially revealing in this regard. Surveying his relatively hard figures based on actual memberships of the component societies in IUPsyS, one discovers that the density of psychologists in the United States (219 per million of population) is exceeded by five countries: Denmark (365), Finland (275), Israel (437), Norway (246), and Sweden (357); while Australia (188), the Netherlands (192), and Uruguay (172) come within striking distance. Other "high-density" countries are the United Kingdom (137), New Zealand (136), West Germany (89), Ireland (87), and Hungary (83). If we now look at the softer-rate estimates based on the extrapolated *total* number of psychologists per country, the picture changes, but some overtones of the waning American hegemony just documented remain. The United States rate now jumps to 446, but we find that the rate for Spain is 528; while Finland (438) and Israel (437) come out on a par with the United States. Comparisons with the United States rate of some of the other countries which show higher rates on the IUPsyS criterion (e.g., Denmark, Norway, and Sweden) are precluded with respect to the "total psychologists" estimates because these were omitted by virtue of insufficient evidence. It may, of course, be argued that most of the countries which vie with the United States in respect to density of psychologists are small, progressive, welfare-oriented nations; it may be replied that the United States is a large, conservative, welfare-oriented nation—but one with an enormous edge in fiscal resources.

The United States, with approximately 38 percent of the psychologists in the world within its borders, and with recently diminished but still vast institutional and fiscal support of their work, is still the world's greatest engine of psychological activity. But, for the present, there are distinct signs of a slowing of American psychology's rate of growth: membership in the American Psychological Association over the past several years has been at something like a plateau,[8] and the groans of American psychologists over the decreases (commencing in the last decade) in federal research support and academic employment opportunities will surely have

[8] A clarification of the phrase "something like a plateau" may be in order here. *Something like* a plateau is not a literal plateau. Since the end of the 1970s, the membership of the American Psychological Association has increased by approximately 2000 each year. The 1984 membership figure has reached 60,000. The recent fairly constant growth *rate* is consistently less than during earlier decades of this century.

already reached the ears even of transoceanic readers of this book.

Stapp's 1981 analysis of National Research Council annual reports on doctorates granted by American universities (over the interval 1970–1980) shows that the average annual growth in the number of doctoral recipients in psychology declined from 7.9 percent for 1970–1975 to 2.5 percent for 1975–1980. Most of the small increase for the second half-decade took place between 1975 and 1977; the number of degrees granted (slightly over 3,000 per annum) was virtually constant from 1978 through 1980. The dramatic rate of growth of the population of doctoral-level psychologists throughout our "first" century may soon turn negative.

We can conclude that neither intellectually nor institutionally is psychology any longer the overwhelmingly American enterprise that it was over so wide a swath of the twentieth century. At the end of psychology's first century, one can doubt that Professor Wundt's wandering child can ever again establish other than multiple, if not truly international, citizenship.

Some Recent Trends in the Definition, Disciplinary Anatomy, and Human Impact of Psychology

To round out this sketch of the institutional status of psychology at age one hundred, glancing notice must be taken of a number of other matters.

1. The definition of psychology—whether conceptually or professionally—has not achieved stability at any point in the course of its first hundred years. Born in heterodoxy and conflict, it has remained heterodox and conflict-ridden. Perhaps the only period of relative stability was the one marked by the ascendance in the United States (and to some extent, abroad) of the behaviorisms, especially during their "neobehavioristic" phase, which can be roughly placed between 1930 and 1960. But note that it is necessary to pluralize "behaviorism": despite shared epistemological and methodic emphases, there was much internecine conflict, and the period was not devoid of more basic theoretical divisiveness, the most notable contenders being a congeries of Gestalt or "field-theoretical" positions on the one hand, and of psychoanalytic and depth psychologies on the other. Moreover, the fractionation of psychology into diverse specialty areas, both fundamental and applied, was as conspicuous a trend during this interval as it has been throughout all other periods of psychology. The fact that the American Psychological Association currently comprises forty-two specialty-centered divisions barely suggests the incohesiveness of contemporary psychology: each division is in reality a division of divisions, a motley assortment of subgroups the members of which do and believe very different things. At the end of its first century, psychology is marked by so lush a conceptual, methodic, and professional diversity that the label "psychologist" conveys very little information.

29

2. There has over the century been a sweeping realignment of the proportions of psychologists pursuing fundamental (or "pure") and applied objectives. From the very inception of an "independent, experimental psychology," it was, of course, contemplated (by Wundt as by other prophets of the "new" psychology) that the nomothetic principles which would emerge from ardent laboratory effort would cascade into a copious reservoir for the remediation of human problems. And, indeed, a psychology of individual differences, a child psychology, an educational psychology, and a psychology of the clinic (though the last was pursued under the aegis of medicine) were extant before the institutionalization of experimental psychology. Such activities soon became, at least in part, subsumed under the new psychology and were, in turn, augmented by the newly institutionalized discipline from its very early years forward.

It is fair to say, however, that what most excited the bulk of those drawn to the new psychology in the early years was the allure of raising fundamental questions concerning mind, experience, or conduct with the hope, for the first time in history, of gaining determinate answers by rigorous scientific means. Thus, in the main centers of psychological activity—initially Germany, then the United States—the preponderant group within psychology comprised fundamental psychologists working for the most part in university settings. As the discipline grew, that preponderance persisted well into the twentieth century. The pure-applied mix, however, began to change rather dramatically in the immediate aftermath of World War II. In the United States especially, clinical psychology, which before the war had been an area of limited numbers and limited professional responsibilities (by virtue of its subordination to psychiatry in the medical settings which were its chief arena), underwent vast expansion and redefinition of scope under the stimulus of large-scale federally supported Ph.D. programs. Soon the number of clinical Ph.D. candidates in the typical American psychology department began to vie with the number of experimentally oriented students. And other applied fields, ranging from those forms of clinical psychology characterized as "counseling," through areas like educational and "school" psychology, to fields like industrial and management psychology, personnel psychology, survey and "assessment" research, human engineering, and so on, began to burgeon. By the early 1950s, this growing redistribution of the work force became incipiently schismatic within the American Psychological Association, and, by the present date, the redistribution has progressed to a point such that the experimentalist or, more generally, the so-called "academic-research" grouping feels itself to be a thoroughbred dog being wagged by the enormous mongrelized tail of professional and applied psychology. Thus, at the end of our first century, we find the very rationale for psychology's brave declaration of independence as a rigorous experimental science in severe jeopardy.

One can doubt that the ratio of "fundamental" to "implemental" (i.e., professional and applied) psychologists in the American Psychological Association at the present writing is greater than one in five, even when classification of the "fundamental grouping" is sufficiently liberal to include not only experimentally oriented psychologists but *all* who pursue fields known to comprehend a pure-applied mix, such as social psychology, developmental psychology, and personality. Stapp and Fulcher's (1981) weighted-sample estimates of vocational trends (based on actual employment data) among the 44,788 members of APA in 1978 suggest that for all doctoral-level members the ratio of "pure" to implemental psychologists was then one to four. If we use the "hard-nosed" criterion of fundamental psychology prevalent for most of the twentieth century among those American psychologists who consider themselves "basic" scientists (which would translate, in Stapp and Fulcher's specialty categories, into the aggregate number of doctoral-level members of the APA whose specialties were experimental psychology, physiological psychology, comparative psychology, cognitive psychology, and psycholinguistics), the ratio of pure to implemental psychologists (in 1978) becomes less than one to eight.[9] And their rather less certain estimates of the employment status of master's degree-level APA members (again, for 1978) suggests there to be an even more overwhelming preponderance of implemental psychologists over those who pursue fundamental interests (on either of the criteria above defined). If now one seeks to estimate the fundamental-implemental ratio for *all* American psychologists (inclusive of non-members of APA), one is in the context of having to guess rather than manipulate vaguely suggestive numbers. It is a safe inference, however, that the vast majority of those psychologists who are not members of APA work in implemental areas. Thus, of the 100,000 psychologists estimated by Rosenzweig to constitute the total work force in the United States, only a tiny percentage could be construed as pursuing fundamental psychology, whether on our "weak" or our "strong" criterion.

Further insight into the realignment of specialty interests in United States psychology may be derived from Stapp's 1981 analysis of the National Research Council annual doctoral statistics for the years 1970–1980. Her Table I includes figures for the "average annual percent of change" (over 1975–1980) for thirteen subfields of psychology. If one divides these fields on a basis similar to our "weak" criterion for fundamental versus implemental psychology, it will be found that over the half-decade at issue the annual growth rate in the number of Ph.D.s granted in the *implemental* areas was 6.8 percent; the rate for the *fundamental* areas was *negative*, at minus 5.7 percent!

---

[9] Dr. Stapp has called to my attention a point likely to be overlooked by an ancient psychologist like myself who became a certified rat-running member of the Division of Experimental Psychology in 1948: it is, that many of the persons in her sample who report experimental psychology and other hard-core fields, like physiological and comparative psychology, as their vocational specialty actually do *applied* research in a variety of government, business, and other nonuniversity settings. A similar point could, of course, be made in respect to the composition of the corresponding American Psychological Association divisions. Thus my estimated ratios (based on Stapp and Fulcher's data) of fundamental to implemental psychologists *inflate* the fundamental group on both the "weak" and the "strong" criteria that I have used.

Within the implemental grouping, the most populous of the specialization areas is, of course, clinical psychology. From Stapp and Fulcher's data on the specialty distribution of doctoral-level APA members, clinical psychology constitutes 60 percent of the entire implemental work force, and clinical psychology *alone* commands the allegiance of about twice the number of psychologists who, in aggregate, pursue all fields of fundamental psychology (on our "weak" criterion). It is further apparent from a variety of sources that about one-third of all psychologists in the United States are clinical psychologists. To these considerations, it may be added that such clinically related areas as school psychology and counseling psychology have in recent years been burgeoning at a rate far in excess of clinical psychology. For instance, the Stapp 1981 analysis shows that the average annual increase in clinical doctorates over the decade 1970–1980 was 7.4 percent, while that for counseling psychology was 10.8 percent, and for school psychology 16.97 percent!

Reverting to the international scene, it is evident (see Rosenzweig, 1982) that clinical psychology is the largest field of specialization in many countries, preempting 60 percent of the work force in Brazil, 50 percent in Belgium, 50 percent in South Africa, 43 percent in the German Federal Republic, 42 percent in Finland, 40 percent in Colombia, 35 percent in the German Democratic Republic, 32 percent in Hungary, 30 percent in Israel, 30 percent in New Zealand, and 24 percent in Yugoslavia. Rosenzweig notes also that the cognate fields of educational/school psychology and guidance/counseling were often estimated by his IUPsyS informants to be the second largest specialization areas.

It would seem fairly clear that, even though the motley ranges of activities pursued by psychologists vary markedly from country to country, the overwhelming world tendency as psychology expansively enters its second century is a movement out of the laboratory and into the clinic and the consulting room (whether equipped with couch, biofeedback apparatus, or farradic stimulation devices). The nineteenth-century pater familias in Professor Wundt might be a bit uncomprehending if he could confront his unruly child after a century of reeducation by Freud, Carl Rogers, and Joseph Wolpe.

3. The true significance of psychology's trajectory over its first century is not so much to be found in the dramatic growth of the discipline as it is in the vast *impact* of that discipline on world sensibility. The very forces which propelled psychology into existence qua formal "science" rendered the human race voraciously responsive to the authority of its "findings." Given the adulation of science so characteristic of modern sensibility—*and* the volume of human insecurity generated by a century marked by frequent catastrophe of unprecedented scale—how could a *science* of mind, of conduct, seem other than a lifeline if not to salvation at least to transient relief or reassurance? In sum, the ideas, research conclusions, and images of the human condition spawned over a hundred years have not only attracted wide popular interest but have had an intimate influence on the very texture of living, especially in the "advanced" modern societies.

Not a few psychologists, in the first century of their "science," have been willing to serve as self-anointed prophets in relation to virtually any issue that can bear upon the human condition. If that condition be, in any context, problematic (or frustrating, or anxiety-ridden, or even mildly irritating), then surely a *science* attuned to the "lawfulness" of human function will have something to say about the remedy. Perhaps everything to say! Thus, for a century the world has been increasingly rife with scientifically based advice concerning a limitless (if untidy) dispersion of matters such as child rearing, education, marital and familial difficulties, optimal societal organization, technologies of administration or management or work efficiency, blueprints for "self-realization," recommendations and services for the easement of psychic burdens ranging from tics to phobias to stress to depression to genital flaccidity to an assortment of ineptitudes in contexts as diverse as business, warfare, and tennis, to self-hate to self-love to neurasthenia, psychasthenia, or schizophrenia.

Psychotechnologies bearing on such matters as these have been generously offered to society and greedily appropriated by each and every of its institutions: government, education, industry, social service and welfare institutions, the church, and so on. The fact that, at any given time, expert advice is bewilderingly multifarious and that the central tendency or dominant technologies in any given period tend to be fads which are displaced and often reversed, on cycles of a few years, lessens society's enthusiasm not one whit.

Around this core of *qualified* advice and practice (much of it indeed based on disciplined research or training, and some of it effective), it is too easy to discern an enormous industry purveying amateur advice and practice. This is manifested in a vast literature of "how-to" books and periodicals dedicated, via misconstruals of the "latest" scientific findings, to psychic trouble-shooting. It is manifested also by the legions of quacks and quasiquacks offering a motley infinity of psychotherapeutic and potential-releasing services. It is embarrassing to record these well-known circumstances, but one of the hopes animating this book is that it will serve as a time capsule for the psychologists of 2079, and perhaps 2179. These matters must at least be acknowledged as part of the story of our first century.

Perhaps the most pervasive phenomenon definitive of the twentieth as "the psychological century" is the disposition of people everywhere to construe their own reality in categories derivative, however distantly, from lowest common denominator models, metatheories, images of the human condition, conceived (or misconceived) within technical psychology. Often the grateful recipient of such insight is an unwitting eclectic, having acquired his or her categories osmotically from a plethora of sources; sometimes the beneficiary acquires a more monolithic definition of his or her ontology via the psychic building blocks provided by a favored psychotherapist or teacher.

The general consequences of this state of affairs add up to something which is indeed new in human history. There is a tendency for life no longer to be lived but to be "enacted" under the guidance of salubrious scientific rules (whatever their content). A corollary tendency is to become increasingly anesthetic toward, and distrustful of, one's own experience. Should there be conflict between experientially based knowledge (or traditional wisdom) and scientifically sanctioned rule, rule is typically the victor. Many persons no longer *perceive* each other's meanings and intentions; they *infer* them—often on a sophisticated principle which links all "surface" phenomena to ulterior depth "dynamics," or probable reinforcement histories (see the chapter by A. MacIntyre in this book). Many no longer lovingly or hatingly or indifferently or trustingly or suspiciously savor, or communicate with, each other; rather—whether the relation be parent to child, friend to friend, teacher to student, merchant to customer, air hostess to client—they *treat* the other. Minor annoyances or frustrations, which in a less sophisticated day were seen as endemic to the human condition (and often taken as challenges to character), are now seen as pathological disturbances requiring scientific advice or intervention.

Brief discussion of so large and, in some ways, subtle a topic as the present one enforces a mode close to caricature. But it is perhaps precisely the issues that I have here tried to circumscribe which, more than any others, make the *fin-de-siècle* assessment of psychology essayed in this book an essential enterprise.

REFERENCE NOTE

1. Stapp, J. *An overview of the production of doctorates in psychology.* Paper presented at the Symposium on The "Pipeline" in Psychology: Training, Production, and Employment of Psychologists, at the meeting of the American Psychological Association, Los Angeles, August 24, 1981.

REFERENCES

Adams, D. K. Experimental studies of adaptive behavior in cats. *Comparative Psychology Monograph,* 1929 (27).

Bain, A. *The senses and the intellect.* London: Parker, 1855/1864.

Baldwin, J. M. Autobiography. In C. Murchison (Ed.), *A history of psychology in autobiography* (Vol. 1). New York: Russell & Russell, 1961. (Originally published, Worcester, Mass.: Clark University Press, 1930.)

Baldwin, J. M. (Ed.). *Dictionary of philosophy and psychology* (2 vols.). New York: Macmillan, 1901, 1902.

Boring, E. G. *A history of experimental psychology* (2nd ed.). New York: Appleton-Century-Crofts, 1950. (Originally published, The Century Co., 1929.)

Boring, E. G. On the subjectivity of important historical dates: Leipzig 1879. *Journal of the History of the Behavioral Sciences,* 1965, *1,* 5–10.

Brett, G. S. *A history of psychology* (3 vols.). London: Allen & Unwin, 1912–1921; *Brett's history of psychology* (R. S. Peters, Ed.), Cambridge, Mass.: M.I.T. Press, 1965.

Bringmann, W. G., Bringmann, N. J., & Ungerer, G. A. The establishment of Wundt's laboratory: An archival and documentary study. In W. G. Bringmann & R. D. Tweney (Eds.), *Wundt studies: A centennial collection.* Toronto: Hogrefe, 1980.

Diamond, S. Wundt before Leipzig. In R. W. Rieber (Ed.), *Wilhelm Wundt and the making of a scientific psychology.* New York: Plenum, 1980.

Guthrie, E. R., & Horton, G. P. *Cats in a puzzle box.* New York: Rinehart, 1946.

Herbart, J. F. *Psychologie als Wissenschaft, neu gegründet auf Erfahrung, Metaphysik, und Mathematik* (2 vols.). Königsberg: Unzer, 1824–1825.

Hobhouse, L. T. *Mind in evolution.* New York: Macmillan, 1901.

Kiesler, C. A. Contribution to APA Symposium on Psychology and the Future. *American Psychologist,* 1978, *33,* 635–637.

Köhler, W. *The mentality of apes.* London: Kegan Paul, 1924. (German ed., Berlin: Springer, 1917.)

Mach, E. *Die Mechanik in ihrer Entwicklung historisch-kritisch dargestellt.* Prague, 1883. (Translated by T. J. McCormack as *The science of mechanics,* Chicago: 1893.)

Mill, J. S. *A system of logic* (2 vols.). London: Parker, Son, & Bourn, 1862. (Originally published, 1843.)

Morgan, C. Lloyd. *An introduction to comparative psychology.* London: Scott, 1894.

National Academy of Sciences. National Research Council's Board on Human Resource Data and Analyses. *A century of doctorates: Data analyses of growth and change.* Washington, D.C.: 1978.

Perry, R. B. *The thought and character of William James* (2 vols.). Boston: Little, Brown, 1935.

Polanyi, M. *Personal knowledge: Towards a post-critical philosophy.* Chicago: The University of Chicago Press, 1958.

Ribot, T. A. *German psychology to-day.* New York: Scribner's, 1886. (Translation by J. M. Baldwin of *Psychologie allemande contemporaine,* 1879.)

Rosenzweig, M. R. Trends in development and status of psychology: An international perspective. *International Journal of Psychology,* 1982, *17,* 117–140.

Stapp, J., & Fulcher, R., et al. The employment of recent doctorate recipients in psychology: 1975 through 1978. *American Psychologist,* 1981, *36,* 1211–1254.

Thorndike, E. L. Animal intelligence: An experimental study of the associative processes in animals. *Psychological Review Monographs,* 1898, *2*(8).

Thorndike, E. L. The mental life of the monkeys. *Psychological Review Monographs,* 1899, *3*(15).

Thorndike, E. L. *The elements of psychology.* New York: A. G. Seiler, 1905.

Thorndike, E. L. *Animal intelligence: Experimental studies.* New York: Macmillan, 1911.

van Hoorn, W., & Verhave, T. Wundt's changing conceptions of a general and theoretical psychology. In W. G. Bringmann & R. D. Tweney (Eds.), *Wundt studies: A centennial collection.* Toronto: Hogrefe, 1980.

Wundt, W. *Beiträge zur Theorie der Sinneswahrnehmung.* Leipzig & Heidelberg: Winter, 1862.

Wundt, W. *Vorlesungen über die Menschen- und Thierseele* (2 vols.). Leipzig: Voss, 1863.

Wundt, W. *Grundzüge der physiologischen Psychologie* (2 vols.). Leipzig: Engelmann, 1874. (2nd ed., 1880.)

Wundt, W. *Methodenlehre* (Vol. 2 of *Logik*). Stuttgart: Enke, 1883.

Wundt, W. *Völkerpsychologie. Eine Untersuchung der Entwicklungsgesetze von Sprache, Mythos und Sitte* (10 vols.). Leipzig: Engelmann, 1900–1920.

I

THE SYSTEMATIC FRAMEWORK OF PSYCHOLOGY

PSYCHOLOGY AS SCIENCE?
THE DISCIPLINARY STATUS
OF PSYCHOLOGY

1

The Constitutive Problem of Psychology

GEORGE A. MILLER

I grew up in the tradition of experimental psychology that began with Wilhelm Wundt and traced its way down to me through E. B. Titchener, E. G. Boring, and S. S. Stevens. Each of my intellectual fathers put his own interpretation on Wundt's science, but there was a common thread. A bit of all of them lives on in me.

I was educated to believe that psychology is a biological science; that it is concerned with perception, learning, and motivation; that the experimental method provides the key to scientific objectivity; and that pandering to public interest in clinical and social psychology would inevitably weaken and eventually destroy the scientific core that holds the field together as a recognizable and respectable discipline. The odd thing is that part of me still believes all this.

That is to say, I still believe that a discipline of psychology exists for which all those presuppositions are true. In the years since my imprinting, however, I have discovered several other psychologies, all claiming proprietary rights to the label, all competing for disciples, and each contemptuous of the others. In short, I discovered that psychology is an intellectual zoo—a situation that has long prevailed, but from which I was carefully shielded in my youth.

This is not the place and I am not the person to catalogue the zoo. Nor is it the place to argue that psychology either is, or could be, or never will be a science. Parts of psychology are clearly scientific, in the best sense of the term, and other parts are

40

pure moonshine. By picking your examples carefully you can make psychology and psychologists out to be almost anything that pleases your fancy at the moment. But psychology shares at least one attribute with the more mature sciences—it grows and changes. The psychology of 1979 is very different from the psychology of 1879.

As it has grown, psychology has been pulled in two directions (Boring once characterized them as its biotropic and sociotropic poles), one analyzing into smaller elements, the other integrating into larger systems. These opposite approaches create a tension that has persistently frustrated scholars who try to define psychology as a unified discipline. When some biotropic advance occurs, it is seen as either trivial or irrelevant to the sociotropic enterprise; when some sociotropic advance occurs, biotropes can accept it only as description, not as explanation. The conflict has now persisted long enough, and has resisted enough heroic efforts at resolution, that many psychologists are ready, however reluctantly, to accept it as unavoidable.

In his introduction to *Sociobiology: The New Synthesis*, E. O. Wilson (1975) predicted that ethology and its companion enterprise, comparative psychology, are both "destined to be cannibalized by neurophysiology and sensory physiology from one end and sociobiology and behavioral ecology from the other" (p. 6). In Wilson's opinion, behavior will eventually be explained at the molecular level in terms of neural circuits and their sensory transducers. "To pass from this level and reach the next really distinct discipline, we must travel all the way up to the society and the population" (p. 6).

Although Wilson speaks only of comparative psychology and the behavior of animals, the scope of his thesis makes it clear that his prediction can be extended to psychology generally. To a sociobiologist, humankind is merely another primate species; all that is valid in contemporary psychology will eventually be cannibalized either into neurophysiology or into sociobiology.

Such opinions should come as no surprise to psychologists. Did not Wundt, the founding father, limit experimentation to simple sensory processes and warn us that the higher mental processes can be studied only by historical and naturalistic observation? Is this not the same distinction that now threatens to cannibalize Wundt's science?

Well, yes. And then again, no. Yes, because Wundt clearly distinguished between physiological and social psychology. No, because he took the explanation of immediate experience as the subject matter of psychology, and immediate experience is of little concern to either a physiologist or a sociologist. For Wundt, what we feel as a tension between the biotropic and sociotropic poles was merely a matter of methodology, not of substance.

What happened to the unitary substance of Wundt's psychology? An adequate answer would have to recapitulate the history of the field, but it is not too misleading to say that immediate experience took a back seat to other concerns—to behavior, conditioning, the unconscious, mental testing, and a broad range of professional applications in education, industry, and medicine—leading eventually to the intellectual zoo that we inhabit today.

With all of the centrifugal forces presently at work, the real question is not whether psychology is a unified discipline, but why so many psychologists believe it should be. Every large psychology department is today a small college unto itself, with a faculty able to teach a little bit of everything: optics, acoustics, physiology, pharmacology, histology, neuroanatomy, psychiatry, pediatrics, education, statistics, probability theory, computer science, communication theory, linguistics, anthropology, sociology, history, philosophy, logic, and, when time permits, psychology. Does something more than historical accident and administrative convenience hold such an array of talent together?

Obviously, no standard method or technique integrates the field. Nor does there seem to be any fundamental scientific principle comparable to Newton's laws of motion or Darwin's theory of evolution. There is not even any universally accepted criterion of explanation. What is the binding force?

When reason fails, one resorts to faith. But what is the common faith?

Different psychologists articulate their faith differently, usually phrasing it so that the main entrance to the field leads directly into their own work. But I believe the common denominator is a faith that somehow, someday, someone will create a science of immediate experience.

Support for that faith derives from the stubborn fact of consciousness itself. Psychologists who adopt consciousness as the constitutive problem of their field need reject little of what passes for psychology today. They can accept the unconscious, for it defines the boundaries of consciousness. They can accept behavioral analysis, for it provides the evidence for conscious processes. They can accept studies of children and animals, for they reveal the development of consciousness. They can accept computer simulation, for it illustrates the logic of conscious processes. They can accept social attribution, for it shapes our consciousness of others. The central faith is that consciousness is a natural phenomenon and that the discipline—eventually the science—responsible for understanding it should be called psychology.

Unless I have badly misunderstood him, that was the faith that motivated Wundt in the first place. And that is the thread that ties together those who misinterpreted Wundt, and even those who totally rejected him.

But I am less concerned to defend the unity of Wundt's psychology, properly conceived, than to understand why it seems we have made so little progress toward a science of consciousness after one hundred years of effort.

Perhaps we haven't really tried. Perhaps we have been too willing to change the subject, too easily distracted by problems for which we were not yet ready, too uncertain what a science of consciousness would look like. Hilgard (1980) has traced the history of psychological opinion about consciousness; he detects a recent revival of interest after decades of avoidance and neglect. Perhaps we are only now returning to the original commitment.

What would a science of consciousness look like?

Suppose we took as our goal constructing a theory that would explain consciousness to some nonhuman, nonconscious intelligence. To make the goal more specific, imagine that we have been visited by an alien body from outer space, that the thing is apparently both harmless and very intelligent, and that we discern somehow that it wants to understand the human point of view. How would we proceed?

Our first task would be to establish some language, some signaling system in terms of which we could communicate the human point of view. I doubt that any human language could serve; acquiring a human language presupposes too much prior knowledge about the human point of view. I suspect we would have to develop some formal notation with precise and unambiguous definitions of all but a handful of primitive terms, something much like the notations in which scientific theories are expressed.

If we could devise such a notation, coded in a form that the nonhuman intelligence could receive and generate, we could then begin to tell our visitor what we think we know. The first thing we would try to tell it about would be the real world. Just as the real world of an insect is very different from the real world of a mammal, so our real world would be very different from the world of a nonhuman intelligence. What we take to be the real world is constructed by our brains from information received by our senses, so we would have to indicate what kinds of energy we are sensitive to. Fortunately, we already know a good deal about that.

But we could not stop with sensations. Somehow, we would have to communicate our notion of objects—of things that are not merely visual patterns or tactual resistances or sources of noise, but things that integrate all those sensations into coherent percepts. We would have to explain how those objects stand out as units in a three-dimensional space and persist through time and motion. We know a little about that, but probably not enough to make it clear to our visitor.

We would also have to explain how we come to view ourselves as a special class of objects, and how we simplify our perception of events by attributing intentions to the actors in them. We would have to explain our ability to pay attention to some objects and events and ignore others, to seek out some and avoid others. We would have to explain how conformity to social conventions becomes habitual. And we would have to explain how the private processes of thought are communicated to others via the enormously improbable system we call language. Probably the intentional quality of our minds would be the most difficult to explain.

The biotropic and sociotropic poles would still exist, of course. Some parts of our explanation would depend on the neurophysiology of receptors, brain, and effectors; some parts would depend on the social conventions that civilized people must

43

internalize. But an explanation of consciousness could not be cannibalized by either biology or sociology. They might cannibalize explanations of behavior, but behavior is merely the evidence, not the subject matter, of a science of consciousness.

If all this sounds like the contents of an introductory text in general psychology, then you are getting my point. Those contents are precisely the matters we would have to communicate to the nonhuman intelligence for it to appreciate the human point of view. All I have done is to provide an exotic context in which all the familiar aspects of consciousness that we can take for granted by virtue of our human nature would have to be made explicit.

Let me claim, if only to be provocative, that a science of psychology should provide a basis for explaining consciousness to an intelligent being that is not itself conscious. (This is my adaptation of an idea proposed by the philosopher Thomas Nagel, 1979.) Much of what is best in psychology already contributes to such an explanation, but it is obvious how far we still have to go before we will have constructed such a science.

Note, incidentally, that the goal is not to transform the nonhuman intelligence into a human intelligence, but merely to provide the information necessary for understanding the world of human beings. Similarly, comparative psychologists might hope to understand the world of a bee, but they would never expect to experience that world themselves.

It would probably be a great help if we actually had an alien visitor to test our ideas on. When we try to explain consciousness to each other, it is far too easy to take for granted precisely that which most needs explanation—simply because it is perfectly obvious to any conscious person capable of understanding its explanation. Modern computers have helped some psychologists gain this perspective, but they have not yet been able to communicate many qualities of human experience to contemporary machines.

Modern linguistic theory provides an example of the consequences of the perspective I have in mind. Traditional linguists described languages for people who already knew what a language is. Consequently, the most basic concepts did not need explanation—it was assumed (correctly) that they were already known intuitively to anyone capable of understanding an explanation. But not until those native intuitions were themselves subjected to formal analysis could linguistics become a scientific as well as a humanistic study.

Psychologists interested in language have been enormously stimulated by this new approach in linguistics. The reason, in my opinion, is that they have recognized a common concern for the uniqueness of the human point of view, and have been challenged by new ways to characterize and analyze it.

It would delight me to dwell at length on the consequences of shifting the subject matter of linguistics from the description of languages to the explanation of the human capacity for language. But my concern here is with the constitutive problem of psychology, which I take to be the explanation of the capacity for conscious experience. I will only remark in passing that recent advances in linguistic science did not result from better instrumentation, or more accurate measurements, or better experimental design, or new methods of statistical analysis. They resulted from a profound reformulation of our ideas about what it means to be a human being.

I believe that psychologists generally are beginning to understand better what a science of consciousness might be a science of. The revival of work in cognition, spurred by the advent of intelligent machines and a better understanding of the structure of intelligent systems, seems to me a sign of a new awakening. A similar revival in the study of affect, volition, and intention is needed, however, before Wundt's vision can become a reality.

There can be no guarantee of success. Perhaps in the next century we will be able to push the constitutive problem of psychology far enough forward to discover principled limits on our ability to understand ourselves. But think how much more we will have to know about ourselves before anyone can prove that such a science of psychology is impossible.

REFERENCES

Hilgard, E. R. Consciousness in contemporary psychology. *Annual Review of Psychology*, 1980, *31*, 1–26.
Nagel, T. What is it like to be a bat? In *Mortal questions*. New York: Cambridge University Press, 1979.
Wilson, E. O. *Sociobiology: The new synthesis*. Cambridge, Mass.: Harvard University Press, 1975.

2

Toward the Articulation of Psychology as a Coherent Discipline*

AMEDEO GIORGI

Introduction

It is clear to most astute observers of the field that psychology's disciplinary status is ambiguous at best and chaotic at worst. Of course, I do not mean "discipline" in the sociocultural sense, where psychology is as solidly institutionalized and as well organized as most of the other intellectual disciplines, but in the theoretical and scholarly sense, where its precise meaning and its place among the other sciences are still to be determined in a manner acceptable to the majority of psychologists. Throughout its history, psychology has been described as a natural science, a human science, two or more sciences, as intrinsically nonscientific—and other things too numerous to mention. Every decade of its history has been a questioning of psychology's status and a demand that it be conceived as other than it was. One could assemble a series of quotes critical of psychology's foundational status beginning, say, with Franz Brentano in the 1870s and including Carl Rogers in 1973, but I think the ambiguous status of psychology as a discipline can be demonstrated equally convincingly in a briefer way. I shall do this by quoting two evaluations of

*I want to thank Fred Wertz for his critical and helpful comments on this paper.

psychology's status that not only appeared one hundred years apart but exhibited one movement in psychology's self-understanding that goes full circle.

In 1879, the very year of the alleged founding of psychology, G. H. Lewes, a British psychologist-philosopher, wrote:

> In every science we define the object and scope of the search, the motive of the search, and the means whereby the aim may be reached. . . . A glance at the literature of (psychology) discloses the utmost discordance on these cardinal points. The conception of the argument and scope are different and lead to the adoption of antagonistic methods. . . . Of late years, there have arisen writers who have tried to effect a compromise. . . . And yet the constitution of the science still has to be effected. The constitution of a science means first, that *circumscription* of a class of phenomena which, while making its relations to other classes, assigns it a distinctive position in the series of the sciences; and second, that *specification* of the object and method of search which, when aided by fundamental inductions established on experiment, enables all future inquiries to converge towards a self-sustaining and continuous development. In a science thus constituted, the discovery of today enlarges without overturning the conception of yesterday. Each worker brings his labors as a contribution to a common fund, not as an anarchical displacement of the labors of predecessors. Henceforward there is system, but no systems; schools and professors no longer give their names as authorities in place of reasons (1879, pp. 1–5).

In 1979, in an article poignantly enough entitled "Psychology: Science or Non-science," J. R. Kantor wrote: "It is quite apparent that in spite of all the historical efforts to make psychology a science, and the ambitions of psychologists to convert psychology to a science, this discipline cannot fully qualify as a natural science" (p. 159). Kantor continued: "Many persons still regard it as a problem whether psychology is an authentic science or at best only a profession" (p. 155). Elsewhere in the same issue of *The Psychological Record* in which Kantor's article appeared, an anonymous observer wrote:

> But who can ignore the great need for the improvement of psychology as a science? The future of psychology certainly calls for the development of better basic postulates. If psychology is to become a full fledged science, it will be necessary to extrude from it every vestige of transcendental influence. . . . It is a prize necessity to rework the description and theories of all specific psychological events (1979, p. 298).

The fact, I think, that establishes the point I want to make is that one could easily reverse the dates of these two descriptions and find that they are equally applicable. Both make the claim that psychology should be a natural science, and both find it wanting. Moreover, no sense of progress is evident when one compares the two assessments.

47

The following observation provides a second indication of the instability of psychology's disciplinary status. In 1879, in the work I have just quoted, Lewes also wrote: "Until quite recently, universal opinion assigned psychology to the special group of Moral Sciences, both in matter treated and in methods of inquiry" (p. 47). He went on to argue that psychology should actually be included among the natural sciences. Almost one hundred years later, another British psychologist, John Shotter (1975), published a book defending the position, once again, that psychology ought to be a moral science. The one hundred years during which psychology attempted to be a natural science seem not to have settled the issue. A field that can experience such a dramatic reversal after a century of effort certainly cannot consider itself stable.

Indeed, the difficulties surrounding psychology's disciplinary status have been such as to call forth official proclamations of dismemberment from time to time (e.g., Fernberger, 1922; Fearon, 1937). The latest psychologist to champion this view is Sigmund Koch, who writes:

> Psychology . . . *cannot* be a coherent discipline, howsoever "coherence" be defined: whether in terms of subject matter, methodico-strategic commitments, concrete theoretical principles, or some conceivable body of such, conceptual frameworks, or even desirable characteristics of the work force . . . (1976, p. 480).

Koch goes on to state that there are many arguments "in principle" against the view of psychology as a *single* discipline. Certainly, when a psychologist with the experience and stature of Sigmund Koch expresses such strong sentiments, they have to be taken seriously. I agree that his description is accurate so far as the actual state of affairs is concerned. Psychology's crisis is not contemporary but perennial. We did not have an early and adequate coherence that we lost over time; we never were coherent in a mature sense of the term. While from time to time there has been agreement with respect to a label—the study of mind, consciousness, psyche, experience, or behavior—a common in-depth understanding of each of those terms was never achieved. However, I part company with Koch when he elevates this state of factual affairs to the level of principle, although such an impulse is certainly understandable. My reluctance to concede the issue stems from the fact that I remember what Lewes and others said one hundred years ago: that a genuine science can circumscribe a class of phenomena, articulate the object of its study, and specify a method of search based upon the characteristics of the object.

Manifestations of Psychology's Inadequate Scientific Status

A full discussion of the many difficulties encountered in attempting to found a unified scientific psychology would take more space than is available in one chapter. Since the major intent here is to articulate a possible unitary psychology rather than merely to criticize the status quo, and since most of the evidence required to support the points in this section appears in published sources, I shall merely summarize what I think are the major manifestations, cite the appropriate sources, and describe very briefly the major implication(s). The nature of the difficulties encountered sheds some light on how they can be overcome and how the quest for unity can be pursued. As Lewes said, one specifies a method of search based upon the characteristics of the object.

Most of the difficulties cited by psychologists concerning the disciplinary status of psychology can be grouped under three headings: (1) the lack of unity in psychology; (2) the irreconcilable split between the scientific and professional aspirations of the field; and (3) the apparent discrepancy between psychology's commitment to be scientific and its ability to be faithful to either the givens of the human person or the characteristics of concrete phenomena (Giorgi, 1976; 1982).

The lack of unity in psychology (e.g., Hitt, 1969; Brandt, 1975; Lichtenstein, 1967; Royce, 1970) is manifested in various ways, but it can be seen most prominently in terms of two problems: (1) how to find a unified theoretical perspective concerning the whole field rather than more narrowly based unities (e.g., behaviorism, psychoanalysis, Gestalt theory, etc.), and (2) how to establish meaningful relationships between various subfields (e.g., between psychophysics and psychotherapy or between physiological psychology and social psychology). These difficulties point to the lack of a comprehensive central perspective that could clarify the meaning of psychology as such, which in turn would provide the basis for unifying apparently disparate subfields.

The report of the Committee on Scientific and Professional Aims of Psychology (1957) shows how divergent are the perceptions of the meaning of psychology between the "scientist-academic" members of the field and the "professional" members. This debate is often couched in terms like *basic* vs. *applied* or *theory* vs. *practice*, but the difficulty is really deeper, because—whatever the tensions between theory and practice—the relationship between basic psychophysical research and human engineering, or between psychoanalytic theory and practice is not the same as are the differences between "academic-scientific" psychologists and "professional" psychologists. In the latter case, the debate revolves around the very meaning of psychology and its disciplinary status, and the specification of relevant training and professional activities.

The last manifestation of psychology's inadequate scientific status is at the heart of the matter. The very conception of science entertained by psychology is at odds with the subject matter it seeks to comprehend, and thus multiple conceptualizations of both science and psychology abound (e.g., Cole & Arnold, 1976; Koch, 1959). The great division on this issue lies between those who make a commitment to some conception of existing science *first* and then turn to their phenomena of interest armed with the criteria of science as filters, and those who *first* make a

49

commitment to approach human phenomena with fidelity and either ignore the question of scientific approaches or belatedly adopt some procedure of scientific method, which then leads to the same difficulties. Few, however, question whether existing science is appropriate for the study of human psychological phenomena, and many historical reasons exist for raising that question (Giorgi, 1970). Were a theory of science which is compatible with the diversity and complexity of human reality to be attained, the problems of psychology's unity, of the scientist-professional dichotomy, and of the meaning of psychological science could, in principle, be resolved.

The Possibility of Psychology as a Coherent Science

While psychology can make a certain amount of headway with short-term pragmatic solutions, such an approach is not, of course, theoretically satisfying. The history of psychology, it seems to me, has demonstrated two important lessons concerning the establishment of an adequate psychological theory: (1) The unification of psychology is no longer possible merely in terms of an abstract methodology independent of the nature of the phenomena to be studied, and (2) the problems surrounding the genuine subject matter of psychology can no longer be avoided if an adequate science of psychology is to emerge (Giorgi, 1979). Simply calling psychology the science of behavior, or of experience, or of both, will no longer do if one cannot, in turn, say what behavior and experience are. How could a genuine science of psychology be developed without some knowledge of what experience and behavior are like, and how is that possible without some direct contact with these phenomena prior to experimental manipulation? Indeed, after one hundred years of effort, one would think that psychologists would be ready to face squarely the very issue of why we have such a difficult time being scientific with regard to the phenomena of behavior or experience.

Taking a cue from Merleau-Ponty (1942/1963), I would say that the phenomena of behavior and experience have resisted scientific analysis because they have not been conceptualized correctly and therefore we have had difficulty in knowing how to study them. These phenomena are not comprehensible by means of concepts derived from things, where the natural sciences are at home, nor by means of categories derived from pure ideas, where philosophy reigns supreme. Psychology introduces us to a range of phenomena that are different from and prior to natural science and philosophy. This means that nothing short of original description of and reflection on our own phenomena can give us an adequate understanding of psychological science. Moreover, in order to do justice to the originary aspects of psychological phenomena, we should approach them with a minimum number of preconceptions and describe them in an unprejudiced manner so that new conceptualizations have every chance to come forth. In brief, my argument here is that only by means of a theoretical or conceptual achievement, only by grasping correctly the essence of behavior and experience and their variations, can a sound disciplinary basis for psychology be established.

The notion that an originary perspective is essential for psychology has far-reaching implications. It means, for instance, that one cannot pretend to know what science already is and then simply move to subsume psychological phenomena under its categories. Gustav Bergmann (1940), for example, writing from the position of logical positivism, stated that the language of science is "thing language" and then he attempted to show how psychological subject matter could be incorporated into such a perspective. However, if one were apprised that psychological phenomena may be originative with respect to already established languages, then one might try to find new linguistic resources for describing psychological reality rather than using a borrowed language.

Similarly, sensitivity to the possible originality of psychological phenomena might make us more sensitive to the need for reconceptualization. Thus, Skinner (1963) has written that if the mental is really a different sort of thing from the material, then mentalists should be able to come up with a different kind of method to explore it. Skinner tacitly allows the lack of such a method to indicate that the mental is not really different. But perhaps the mental has not as yet been adequately conceived and so an adequate method has not yet emerged. Skinner is right insofar as the mental is not another substance or thing, but it could be a certain complex structure which would require a new form of conceptualization.

Such examples could be multiplied, but I hope that the point is clear. If we can begin our research with the presupposition that those phenomena in which we as psychologists are interested may call forth ways of describing or understanding that are not available in our existing set of concepts, we may become more aware of just what it is we do when we spontaneously recognize psychological phenomena. An obvious problem, of course, is that regardless of how we define the subject matter of psychology—as consciousness, or experience, or behavior—the boundaries of our phenomena are hard to discern. One can separate a clear idea from the stream of thought within which it is embedded, but how do we survey the stream of thought itself? One can hold a body still, but how does one hold behavior still? What are the boundaries of the behavior we wish to study? When does a psychological event end? All perplexing questions, and yet, somehow, we do manage to clarify our thoughts and to explain behavior better after analysis than before. What is it that we are doing right, and how can we come to a better understanding of it? These are the issues to which psychology as a mature science could speak.

I believe that psychology's disciplinary status cannot be solidified until we clarify the meaning of psychology, however difficult that may be. Once we know in depth what we mean by psychology, or precisely how to discern the psychological within the complex world within which we live (which is richer than the psychological perspective we assume with respect to it), then, based upon how the phenomena so

51

selected present themselves to us, we should be able to discover how to approach them systematically and methodically (i.e., scientifically). I do not believe that this is yet a historical, theoretical scientific achievement, even though thousands of practitioners have implicitly and correctly intuited the psychological.

Now, let me return to Koch's statement regarding the impossibility of a coherent psychology. I respect Koch's work, so I take seriously his conclusions with respect to the discipline of psychology. But because I also believe that something in common holds all of us together—however difficult it may be to articulate—I took his statement as a challenge. Could I arrive at a coherent and encompassing picture of the discipline of psychology? Despite the difficulty of the issue and my unreadiness to tackle it, I gave it a try. Mindful of the approaches of the older literature (James, Wundt, Dilthey, Brentano, Titchener, etc.), I will discuss psychology's scope and subject matter in the context of trying to demonstrate the possibility of a comprehensive and coherent science of psychology. Questions of method, untouched here, can only be raised after the subject matter or proper object of a field has been clarified.

Scope

In my view, the psychological has upper and lower boundaries (and I use minimal criteria here to remain as inclusive as possible). At the lower end, the psychological always presupposes life, but more than sheer presence of life is necessary. A sufficient level of sentience, motility, and affectivity apparently has to be present to ensure a minimum of directedness and reflexiveness, that is, the ability of the organism to form presentations (perceptions, memories, etc.) about the environment and its own body, however global and undifferentiated. At the upper level, it seems that pure idealizations escape the psychological as such, although psychological infrastructures would be presupposed. (In other words, just as the psychical presupposes the bodily, but transcends it, so idealizing presupposes the psychological but transcends it.) Higher-level functions and activities include pure logic, mathematics, the contemplation of concepts and pure forms, and so on, which, because of their universality, transparency, and self-reflective character, do not share the qualities of psychological objects. Psychological objects are always more opaque and more physiognomic because they participate in time, worldliness, and embodiment in a more intimate way than ideal objects do. A biologically rooted, world-oriented body is necessary for the presence of the psychological. In other words, the psychological is between the biological and the logical.

This depiction implies that we are dealing with a certain level of functioning of an individual organism. If we take what in naive perception we call a human being, then such a person could be the subject of biological analysis, logical analysis, or psychological analysis. This means that the assumption of a certain perspective is essential to the definition of psychology. It also implies that the psychological is not always "ready-made" for us but that it must be constituted by an observer who assumes a psychological perspective. Of course, the object of observation must fill certain minimum conditions. (One could not constitute the psychological by simply assuming a psychological perspective toward a rock.) It is to this problem that we turn next.

The Proper Object of Psychology

If the term *psyche* were still in good standing, one could say that the psyche was the proper object of psychology. But that term plunged into disuse because of the inability of psychologists to articulate how one is present to the psyche. Is the psychic perceived, and if so, what are its boundaries? Or is it merely an idea that subsumes in a convenient way a vast number of varied behaviors? Such questions were never satisfactorily answered, and thus three main competitive terms for psyche as the subject matter of psychology have arisen: *consciousness, experience,* and *behavior* (or any combination of the three). These terms have both overlapping and unique connotations. How can we sort them out? I suggest that we find a term comprehensive enough to include both their commonality and their differences, and I have settled on the term *expressivity,* or expressiveness. As psychologists we are interested in how organisms or persons *express* themselves in situations.

It seems to me that *expressivity* brings a number of advantages. First of all, it is more comprehensive than the three competing terms we were trying to integrate. Any analysis of expressiveness would have to include what the subject was aware of (i.e., consciousness, if accessible); what other aspects of the situation the subject may have been open to, but perhaps only marginally or even inattentively (i.e., experience); and how the subject performed (i.e., behavior). At the same time expressiveness is more concrete since it automatically includes physiognomic and unique aspects of the subject's relation to the situation. Third, in order for an analysis to do justice to the phenomenon of expressiveness, both internal (subjective) and external (objective) perspectives would have to be considered since what is expressed is divergently but essentially related both to the expressor and to observers of expression. Fourth, expressiveness always requires a vehicle of materiality and so all bodily activities and references are also included by implication. Fifth, because all expressions are situated and take place over time, the situation provides the framework within which more detailed temporal and contextual analyses can take place. Last, expressivity in no way compromises the intentional relation that is essential for any proper understanding of consciousness, behavior, or experience. Indeed it presupposes it. Thus, expressiveness meets the criteria of comprehensiveness, concreteness, the inclusion of internal and external perspectives, bodily reference, context-relatedness, and intentionality.

A possible limit to the term is that expressivity could be understood as a concept polar to *impression* or *impressivity* and thus it would seem to exclude all such phenomena. That is not our intent, however. Whatever the "impressions" taking place in someone, they cannot become accessible for research or any other type of analysis unless they are in some manner expressed—even if only through language, dreams, or thoughts to oneself. Hence, a certain privilege is accorded to the term *expressivity*, but it would include, by implication, whatever "impressions" could be made manifest.

However, if expressiveness is comprehensive enough to synthesize some of the disjunctive features of psychology, it is not sufficient in and of itself to characterize the psychological because it is too broad. One could not differentiate psychology from other human sciences (sociology, history, etc.) that could also claim expressiveness for their subject matter. Consequently, something distinctive would have to be added. I would suggest that psychologists are interested in expressiveness insofar as it reveals the subjectively lived coherent patternings of situations by individuals. This notion will be elaborated in the next section.

Amplification of the Position

Theoretical Elaborations

Psychology as a Certain Level of Analysis   I have mentioned levels already, but I want to say a little more about them. If one turns to the psychological and philosophical literature on consciousness and experience, one soon discovers, among the highly diverse and often contradictory statements, that one way of understanding the relationship between experience and consciousness is to understand consciousness as a higher level of experience. That is, consciousness is experience raised to the level of reflective awareness. Similarly, the relationship between action and behavior is today often viewed in the same way; that is, action is behavior imbued with rationality. The failure to make such distinctions of level is responsible for much confusion in psychology, but it is also true that the state of affairs is indeed complex. If one uses the broader terms (*experience* and *behavior*) one will not be accurate for the higher levels of complexity, but one will be inclusive; whereas if one uses the terms that accurately depict the higher levels of complexity (*consciousness* and *action*), one will be too narrow to include the lower levels. The tension between precision and extensiveness is almost impossible to overcome with these traditional terms. Expressiveness is not laden with the connotations that the other terms have because of their past usage, yet it is broad and flexible enough to allow essential distinctions to emerge. This implies that all psychological research will have to be sensitive to the question of level—both with respect to intrapsychological analyses and for distinguishing between psychological and other types of analyses.

The Psychological as Para-Objective   I have said that psychological phenomena can be described as more than biological and less than logical. Another way of delineating the psychological is to understand it as para-objective, in the full sense of the term. That is, many psychological phenomena are pre-objective (e.g., the monocular images seen prior to stereoscopic perception; the so-called "aura" of the epileptic; the sensorimotor level of cognitive behavior displayed by Piaget's children); others are post-objective (e.g., afterimages; the patterns of fixation of neurotics; functional autonomy); and still others are para-objective in the sense that they are consistently different from the state of affairs known in other ways (e.g., perceptual illusions, hallucinations, delusions). In this discussion, I am using objective as generally synonymous with thematic, reflective knowledge, so that the psychological can then be understood, in Merleau-Ponty's (1942/1963) terms, as the relationship between the lived and the known, or the subjective and the objective. It seems that in psychology we have employed three means of attaining objective or thematic knowledge: (1) through physical description or measurement, which establishes the sense of the psychological in relation to physicality (e.g., afterimages and illusions); (2) through logicality or rationality, which establishes the sense of the psychological in relation to that criterion (e.g., Piaget's sensorimotor level and cognitive dissonance); (3) through intersubjective agreement or intersubjective norms, which establishes the sense of the psychological in relation to a norm (e.g., neurotic patterns and social roles). In each instance, the psychological is seen as a "lived subjective transformation" of what is thematically known by other means. It is as though the "thematically known" could be accessible to the experiencer, but for some reason is not.

This analysis obviously implies that the objective, in the three senses employed here, is necessary but not sufficient to understand the psychological. If the psychological is indeed para-objective, then all efforts to make the psychological objective—in the senses employed here—are misguided. However, one can easily understand the motivation of the search for the objective because without it one would not be able to discern the psychological. But the psychological has to be understood *in relation to* the objective, not as specifications of the objective. This distinction might help avoid some of the confusions of the past.

But matters in psychology are so complicated that even such a broad description is not sufficiently comprehensive. The description above can characterize the psychological in the para-objective sense, but what happens when one is present to the objective rather than to the para-objective? That is, what happens to the psychological when one is being logical or rational, or perceiving in accordance with the physical situation as known in other ways or in harmony with others? Then, I would say, the psychological is not missing but subordinated. It is present, but in a context such that all of the processes are so coordinated that they efface themselves, so to speak, so that the person can be fully and clearly present to the objective features of the situation. The athlete making the great play, the actor who is superb in a role, and all of us living through our daily activities without difficulty exemplify this subordination, this self-effacement of the psychological to the world, to reason, or to harmony with others. Here the coherent subjective patterning is such that it is completely integrated into the total network of relations between the subject and his or her world, and thus in no way stands out. In this latter sense, the psychological as a discrete quasi-autonomous level does not exist. It can, however, be isolated, abstractly constituted, and described.

The Psychological as Relational   Implicit in all of the discussions so far is the idea that the phenomena of psychology have to be understood not as substances but as networks of relationships. The psychological is discovered by means of the subjective in relation to the objective, or one person in relation to another, or an animal in relation to its situation. But more important, even when single labels are used, relations should be understood. Thus, experience can be understood as intentional-presentational-fulfilling relations between a subject and the world (we are in the presence of a world), and behavior as intentional-functional-fulfilling relations (we function in a world). Perception is always perception of an object, emotion a reaction to some situation or event, desiring a desiring for something, and so on. Furthermore there is always the question of the relationship of the present to the past or future, or this part of our experience to other parts or to the totality. Ultimately, one arrives at a network of relationships that first have to be described and then analyzed. In the history of psychology these relationships have not always been understood well: Sometimes a single structure was split into separate elements rather than merely distinguished; at other times structures were understood as simple self-contained substances. Only a relational understanding can do justice to the psychological.

Concrete Elaborations

We have described psychology as dealing with the expressivity of individuals in a situation, and, more specifically, as dealing with the coherent subjective patterning of an objective situation by an individual person or organism. Now, I would like to show, briefly, that this common meaning can be sustained even when cutting across the diverse areas of psychology. In psychophysics, a subject experiences red in relation to what is known as 700 mμ; in a psychological testing situation, a subject performs in such a way that he or she is two standard deviations above the performance of a group of presumably similar individuals; in psychotherapy, a client persists in trying to solve a problem in a particular set way and the therapist tries to bring him or her to a view that logically there are other ways of behaving; a social psychologist tries to understand how a prisoner experiences the world—that is, the social institution known as a prison, cellmates, the particular physical setting in which the prisoner is housed; a hungry rat that initially stumbled through a maze, committing many errors, finally speeds directly to the locus of reward—a location to which the *experimenter* was, of course, privy all along; and so on. In each case, the dimension that makes it possible to bring all of these phenomena under the rubric of psychology is that some sense of "objective situation" is understood in relation to the coherent, lived, subjective patterning of a situation by an individual person or organism.

If we translate these examples of "coherent subjective patterning lived or expressed by individuals or organisms in relation to some sense of objective understanding of the same situation" into more common expressions, we find that we substitute "consciousness," "experience," or "behavior" in the key places. Thus a subject *experiences* red for what is *known* as 700 mμ (physical measurement); a subject *behaves* in a testing situation in reference to *known* standards based on a group of similar individuals (intersubjective standard); a client is *conscious* of only one way of solving a problem but the therapist *knows* (rationality) other possibilities exist; the intention of society in maintaining prisons is presumably retribution (rational value or intersubjective agreement), but a prisoner experiences it as a place in which to become a "better criminal"; an experimenter is interested in observing how long it will take a rat to discover food (behind a white curtain) by living out what the experimenter already *knows* (thematic knowledge). It is also easy to see that some form of the term *expressivity* could have been used in each case.

Conclusion

If all of this withstands criticism, then one could conclude that psychology could be a coherent science because it would deal with the "coherent subjective patternings (presences and functions) of situations by subjects in relation to an objective understanding of the same situation."

Three final comments seem relevant. First, while the above description, if correct, sets limits to the kind of work psychologists should be doing, it also leaves an infinite amount of work to be done. The last word has hardly been said. I mention this because colleagues, by their questions, often seem to imply that if the unity of psychology could be discovered and understood, there would be nothing left to do. Obviously, the truth is just the opposite. Clarity with respect to the meaning of psychology simply sets significant limits for our work and provides a better sense of direction for the work that remains to be accomplished.

Second, I am willing to accept the rejection of any of the substantive statements that I have made about psychology. They could easily be shown to be wrong. But substantive declarations were not my main interest. I attempted to show that psychology could be a coherent science by indicating that the factual absence of such a status is not intrinsic, but, rather, is due to poor theorizing concerning psychological phenomena as well as the meaning of science. Whoever can describe the scope of psychology and specify its proper object can on that basis discover its principle of coherence.

My last comment is a response to a possible criticism. One could easily say that my system might achieve some sense of unity but that it is too general to be of any use. Of course it is general and I certainly do not mean to imply that I am content with it. Quite the contrary. But three points should be kept in mind. First, the differences in psychology across the various subfields are so great that one has to take, at least initially, a great distance in order to see what the similarities might be. Second, due to the lack of unity in psychology, different subfields borrow terms from different universes of discourse. It is hard to overcome this obstacle without using terms of high generality. And last, I tried to show that, in principle, a coherent science of psychology could be possible only if theoretical progress were to be made. Solid, meaningful thinking is necessary for answers to questions such as: What is the meaning of psychological science? What is its scope? What is its proper object? What is its method? What does it mean to assume a psychological perspective toward a phenomenon of the everyday world?

Perhaps it is not entirely out of order to raise these questions again—the questions that our founders raised—as we begin our second century. If we do think about them thematically, work on them, and reemphasize the importance of theory for psychology, then perhaps the community of scholars who call themselves psychologists at the beginning of our third century might have a genuine anniversary to celebrate.

REFERENCES

Bergmann, G. The subject matter of psychology. *Philosophy of Science*, 1940, 7, 415–433.

Brandt, L. W. Scientific psychology: What for? *Canadian Psychological Review*, 1975, 16, 23–34.

Brentano, F. *Psychology from an empirical standpoint* (Linda McAlister, A. Rancurello, D. B. Terrell, trans.). New York: Humanities Press, 1973. (Originally published, 1874.)

Cole, J. F., & Arnold, W. J. (Eds.). *Nebraska Symposium on Motivation, 1975: Conceptual foundations of psychology*. Lincoln: University of Nebraska Press, 1976.

Committee on Scientific and Professional Aims of Psychology. The scientific and professional aims of scientific psychology. *American Psychologist*, 1957, 12, 671–684.

Fearon, A. D. *The two sciences of psychology*. Englewood Cliffs, N.J.: Prentice-Hall, 1937.

Fernberger, S. W. Behaviorism versus introspective psychology. *Psychological Review*, 1922, 29, 409–413.

Giorgi, A. *Psychology as a human science*. New York: Harper & Row, 1970.

Giorgi, A. Phenomenology and the foundations of psychology. In J. F. Cole & W. J. Arnold (Eds.), *Nebraska Symposium on Motivation, 1975: Conceptual foundations of psychology*. Lincoln: University of Nebraska Press, 1976.

Giorgi, A. Phenomenology and psychological theory. In A. Giorgi, R. Knowles & D. Smith (Eds.), *Duquesne Studies in Phenomenological Psychology* (Vol. 3). Pittsburgh: Duquesne University Press, 1979.

Giorgi, A. Issues relating to the meaning of psychology as a science. *Contemporary philosophy: A new survey* (Vol. II). Paris: Institut International de Philosophie, 1982.

Hitt, W. D. Two models of man. *American Psychologist*, 1969, 24, 651–658.

Kantor, J. R. Psychology: Science or nonscience. *The Psychological Record*, 1979, 29, 155–163.

Koch, S. Epilogue: Some trends of Study I. In S. Koch (Ed.), *Psychology: A study of a science* (Vol. 3). New York: McGraw-Hill, 1959.

Koch, S. Language communities, search cells and the psychological studies. In J. F. Cole & W. J. Arnold (Eds.), *Nebraska Symposium on Motivation, 1975: Conceptual foundations of psychology*. Lincoln: University of Nebraska Press, 1976.

Lewes, G. H. *The study of psychology: Its object, scope and method*. London: Trubner and Co., Ludgate Hill, 1879.

Lichtenstein, P. Psychological systems: Their nature and function. *The Psychological Record*, 1967, 17, 321–340.

Merleau-Ponty, M. *The structure of behavior*. Boston: Beacon Press, 1963. (Originally published, 1942; Trans. H. Fisher.)

Observer, Comments and queries. What future for psychology? *The Psychological Record*, 1979, 29, 297–300.

Rogers, C. R. Some new challenges. *American Psychologist*, 1973, 28, 379–387.

Royce, J. (Ed.). *Toward unification in psychology. The first Banff conference on theoretical psychology*. Toronto: University of Toronto Press, 1970.

Shotter, J. *Images of man in psychological research*. London: Methuen, 1975.

Skinner, B. F. Behaviorism at fifty. *Science*, 1963, 140, 951–958.

3

Science, Psychology, and Explanation

SYNONYMS OR ANTONYMS?

DANIEL N. ROBINSON

Only in the present century, and particularly in the past few decades, has there been general acceptance of the view that psychology is a natural science. History, of course, turns up any number of hopeful philosophers who predicted that it would be and argued that it could be, but their optimism culminated only in the incomplete achievement of the Leipzig laboratory. Few of them—writers such as Locke, Hume, Herbart, and John Stuart Mill—would have taken the findings or the program of Wundt and his disciples as actually confirming their predictions or realizing their recommendations. Even where there was close correspondence between a certain principle of philosophy and subsequent research, for example between Hume's associative principles and Ebbinghaus's studies of memory, it is fair to say that the latter were regarded as illustrative of the former but by no means the foundation of a *science* of psychology. Thus, as recently as the early years of the twentieth century, great and grave doubts were expressed regarding the merest possibility of a scientific psychology.

The transition from scepticism to confidence has, therefore, been almost sudden. And it is just this sort of shift in perspective that historians of ideas find summoning since it has not arisen from revolutionary discoveries or original and compelling theories. It cannot, for example, be explained the way one would now account for the adoption of Galileo's physics at the expense of Aristotle's or the abandonment of

Lamarckian theory in the wake of Mendelian genetics. Unlike these historical swings of allegiance, the newly acquired standing of psychology is largely an extrascientific phenomenon inexpressible in the language of discovery.

To comprehend the source of the new confidence, we must recall the grounds of the earlier scepticism. Perhaps it was Kant who spoke most clearly for a veritable army of doubters when he outlined the impossibility of a mind engaging in repeatable and identical acts of self-observation. On yet another basis, J. S. Mill (in 1865) also rejected attempts to found a scientific psychology on introspective grounds:

> We have no means of interrogating consciousness in the only circumstances in which it is possible for it to give a trustworthy answer. Could we try the experiment of the first consciousness in any infant . . . whatever was present in that first consciousness would be the genuine testimony of Consciousness. . . . That a belief or knowledge . . . is in our consciousness now . . . is no reason for concluding that it was there from the beginning (Mill, 1865/1979, p. 140).

Mill's thoroughgoing empirical associationism took for granted that the current mental life of an observer was dominated by notions built up over a course of years and that neither these notions nor the process by which they were installed could be unearthed "introspectively." Thus, even so consistent and devoted a patron of scientific psychology as Mill demanded far more of the discipline than anything likely to be yielded by psychophysical research or studies of learning and memory.

The widespread sentiment, shared by philosophers of otherwise diverging views, was that the determinants of psychological processes and outcomes were simply too varied and numerous to admit of systematic experimental manipulation; that the social, moral, and uniquely personal dimensions of human life were unfit for the sorts of analyses expected of a developed science. Some, like Herbart, argued that a scientific psychology might be *deduced* from a few universal principles of mental function (e.g., the "laws" of association), but even on this supposition there was no way of getting from epistemology to sociology. That is, from the alleged laws of thought it was (is) scarcely likely that one could deduce social or transpersonal phenomena. Wundt himself relegated such phenomena to so special a class and tied them to so special an attribute (human *character*) that his Social Psychology was utterly divorced from his scientific, experimental, and "physiological" psychology. In this, and his own protests to the contrary notwithstanding, he was deeply indebted to the central tenets of that "Romantic Idealism" that dominated German scholarship throughout the nineteenth century. Wundt the *voluntarist*, who thought of the human will as proceeding from the individual *character*, would echo Schelling, Fichte, and Hegel each time he confronted the facts and complexities of social history (Robinson, 1983).

Against this background, how is it that contemporary psychology is so readily accorded scientific status? Have the objections and reservations of Kant, Mill,

61

Wundt, and the rest been answered? Have they been shown to be wrong? Clearly not. Instead, what has happened is that psychologists have jettisoned the very problems and issues that had traditionally excluded psychology from the pantheon of sciences, while at the same time embracing a different class of problems suited to the methods of the developed sciences. The strategy—some might call it a ploy—takes this form. One discovers that the issues bequeathed by history are simply intractable when approached with the tools of experimental science. But, having adopted just these tools, one then proceeds to locate any number of subsidiary problems (or nonproblems) tailored to the now official methods. Then, after years of success solving these, one declares that the original problems were not problems at all, for if they were the official methods would have solved them too!

Several other notions, through uncritical acceptance and vagrant application, have also promoted the discipline at least into the lower ranks of contemporary science. One of these, which we consider later, is Darwinism. Another is "operationism," on whose pithy lexicon more than one fallacy has come to rest. It is important to recall that operationism pertains only to matters of meaning and does not, in and of itself, provide a complete or even a coherent philosophy of science. How one elects to define a term regulates the meaning of those sentences in which the term appears; it does not guarantee that all the sentences taken together will constitute a science or, for that matter, even a valid argument. Long after physics itself learned to live without operationism—because it could not live with it—psychologists are still wed to it in perilous numbers; still convinced that the act of measurement will export meaning to a concept, as if the numbers themselves were meaningful; still wary of "primitive terms" which, as it happens, no science, no system of thought can do without. Nonetheless, having hitched itself to the rapidly falling star of operationism and bedecked itself in the raiment of experimental science, twentieth-century psychology continues to search for a "paradigm." It seems that the old insecurities have been retained by the discipline throughout these recent decades of wide and enthusiastic approval from society and from even the scientific community. As it tells the world it is a science, it tells itself it is not, at least not now—soon, perhaps, but not yet.

A question arising immediately out of this quandary has to do with how one would know that psychology had become a science if, in fact, it were to succeed in its purposes. Would it be content, for example, to remain in the realm of what nineteenth-century German scholars called *Geisteswissenschaft*, forever and in principle cut off from *Naturwissenschaft*? Or is the prevailing urge one that will only be satisfied by full membership in whatever community it is that is now occupied by physics, chemistry, and biology? In either case, what must psychology achieve for it to become a permanent fixture in one of these categories?

Perhaps the most useful way to address questions of this sort is by first eliminating the more common misunderstandings that attach to the idea of science. Alchemy, astrology, and phrenology placed a high premium on controlled observation and measurement, and as high a premium on practicality and prediction. Today, however, it would only be in the purely historical sense that one would refer to "the science of alchemy" or "astrological science" or "phrenological science." That each of these endeavors, once enjoying the loyalty and admiration of many of the best minds, is now recognized as exercises in futility or charlatanism makes up an instructive chapter in the history of thought. It teaches first that quantitative rigor is insufficient to ensure scientific knowledge. It teaches also that even fairly reliable correlations, such as those turned up by Gall and Spurzheim, do not save a discipline from the conceptual assaults of later and clearer reckonings.

There is, of course, no final word on just what makes a body of facts and methods a science. History produces any number of models. Aristotle first attempted to categorize the various modes of human understanding and to establish the nature of scientific understanding within a larger metaphysical context. Fundamental to Aristotle's theory of knowledge is the concept of causation, for on Aristotle's account one may be said to know something only to the extent that one knows its cause.

It will be no digression here to review quickly his four-fold theory of causation since it continues to stand at the center of issues in philosophy of science. Aristotle clearly saw that causation is not a simple process. To inquire into the cause of a particular outcome is to ask questions that may differ radically in their intent. One may account for the Choral movement of Beethoven's Ninth Symphony in terms of (1) the composer's financial needs, (2) Schiller's ode, *An die Freude*, (3) the neuromuscular events necessary for vocalization, (4) the spirit of nationalism and brotherhood in the German states following humiliation at the hands of Napoleon, (5) the black marks on scored paper indicating the sequence of notes to be sung and played by musicians. And this list obviously could be expanded greatly.

As Aristotle examined the various means by which events of one kind produce or make possible those of another, he arrived at his famous set of four causal determinations: the *formal, material, efficient,* and *final* causes of things. Thus, a statue comes into being because certain *materials* (e.g., stone or marble) can be worked (*efficiently*) into certain *forms* that qualify as statuary. The resulting figure depends not only on these three causal antecedents, however, but also on the original design and purpose (*telos*) of the sculptor. It is this design or "end" that constitutes the *final* cause. It is sometimes mistakenly asserted that, for Aristotle, every final cause must have some good as its objective but, as he says in his *Metaphysics,*

> that for the sake of which other things are tends to be the best and the end of the other things; let us take it as making no difference whether we call it good or apparent good (Book V, 1013ᵇ).

In this same work, Aristotle questioned whether a single branch of knowledge, specifically science, might be sufficient to unearth the (four) causes of things.

63

> [I]f there is no substance other than those which are formed by nature, natural
> science will be the first science; but if there is an immovable substance, the science
> of this must be prior and must be the first philosophy, and universal . . . because it
> is first. And it will belong to this to consider being *qua* being—both what it is and
> the attributes which belong to it *qua* being (Book V, 1026ᵃ).

The present context does not admit of a detailed analysis of this important passage. It is enough to underscore the importance of the expression "an immovable substance," for by this Aristotle referred to the rational principle standing behind those phenomena that are not merely "natural." In the *De Anima*, for example, he defines the rational principle (*epistemonikon*) as "that which does not move," and in several other passages in his major essays he establishes *mobility* as the essence of matter. To the extent, however, that entities have real existence—though lacking mass or spatial attributes—natural science cannot be the primary means by which to explain such entities. Thus, all *final causes* are removed from the domain of natural science and become explicable only by metaphysical analysis. In its own sphere of activity, however, science does provide causal explanations, and does so through its universal laws. Its explanations of phenomena are complete to the extent that the phenomena themselves have as constituents nothing "other than those which are formed by nature. . . ." The model of explanation propounded by Aristotle is rationalistic in that it requires universal laws by which specific (singular) instances become deducible. It is also empiricistic in that all such instances amenable to scientific study are drawn from the natural (observable) domain.

Among current philosophies of science, there are striking similarities between the Aristotelian model and that developed by Carl Hempel (1965). Hempel's "covering law" model of science defines the essential character of science according to the logic of explanation. On this account, science consists of explanations of natural phenomena framed by a universal ("covering") law such that, given the law, the phenomena become deductively necessary. The behavior of an apple falling toward the center of the earth is *explained* once it is shown to be a necessary deduction from the universal law of gravitation.

Two characteristics of the "covering law" model are worthy of mention here. One is the requirement that the covering law be *true*, since a false law explains nothing. Note that a false law does not provide a poor explanation but provides no explanation at all. The second is the requirement of *symmetry* between explanation and prediction. This criterion imposes upon bona fide scientific laws the joint burden of predicting the future course of events with the same law invoked to explain past events of the same kind. The gravitation laws, for example, not only explain why apples fall but predict that they will fall under specifiable initial conditions.

It is sometimes argued that the "covering law" model aptly summarizes the salient features of sciences such as astronomy and classical mechanics, but that it is ill-suited both to quantum mechanics and the biological sciences: to the former because quantum mechanical events are inherently statistical and, therefore, violative of any universal law; and to the latter because biological phenomena are best explained by "functional" laws. The first objection misses the mark, for there is nothing in the deductive-nomological model that precludes laws covering inherently statistical events. The formal requirement is that scientific laws be *universal.* Thus, the laws of probability universally cover, for example, the long-run outcomes of tossed coins and the mean and variance of such human phenotypes as height and weight. One does not say that the normal probability distribution "occasionally" or "usually" describes phenotypic frequencies in large and random samples, but that it *always* does. There is an important difference between a law that is valid only "statistically" and a universal law that covers inherently statistical events. In considering several of the so-called "functional laws" of biology, anthropology, and psychology, Hempel has noted that they are often little more than veiled tautologies and that, in any case, they generally if only implicitly make appeals to more fundamental laws (Hempel, 1965, pp. 314–319).

The deductive-nomological model is not the only one available to an aspiring science. One need only recall the *empiriocriticism* of Mach and Avenarius to appreciate the range of possibilities. It was Mach, following in a path first cut by Hume and almost completely cleared by J. S. Mill, who was most steadfast in attempting to rid science once and for all of every trace of "metaphysics." *The Analysis of Sensations* (Mach, 1959), first published in 1886, proved to be a work of such subtlety and power that as unlikely a pair as Freud and Einstein would both claim to find support for their theories in it. Its implicit argument was that the proper business of science is observation, and that the theoretical side of science— to the extent that it has such a side—can be no more than a more formal and systematic redescription of observables. In his Preface to the Fourth Edition (1886) Mach put the case bluntly:

> The opinion which is gradually coming to the front, that science ought to be confined to the compendious representation of the actual, necessarily involves as a consequence the elimination of all superfluous assumptions which cannot be controlled by experience, and above all, of all assumptions that are metaphysical in Kant's sense (Mach, 1886/1959, p. xl).

Recalling that Kant's sense of metaphysics rested on the concept of the pure—that is, *a priori*—categories of the understanding, it is clear what Mach intended to eliminate "above all." And regarding that "monstrous" distinction Kant made between the world of appearance and the world of things-in-themselves, Mach was equally summary in his rejection:

> Since the apparent antithesis between the real world and the world given through the senses lies entirely in our mode of view, and no actual gulf exists between them,

a complicated and variously interconnected content of consciousness is no more
difficult to understand than is the complicated interconnexion of the world (Mach,
1886/1959, p. 28).

In the epistemological patrimony of Hume and Mill, Mach took it as self-evident
that human knowledge was the gift of sensation and that all factual propositions
were, at base, descriptions of actual or possible experience. Descriptions intended to
characterize the external material world were proper to physics; those intended to
characterize directly the intensity and quality of sensations were proper to psychology. But to shift from one to the other involved no more than a change in the
"mode of view." Nature can be examined in either of two aspects: the material,
physical, and external aspect or the sensory, psychological, and experiential aspect.
Both of these proceed from one reality, however, and it is only through the confusions of metaphysics that what is no more than two modes of viewing reality is taken
to prove the existence of two different realities.

On this Machian account, the authority of experience is not simply ultimate, it is
exclusive. Science, which cannot rise above the level of orderly descriptions of
experience, yields laws that cannot go beyond ensembles of perceptual regularities.
It was this ontological purity, this antimetaphysical bias that first captured the
loyalties of the founding members of the Vienna Circle. Note that their first organizational activity proceeded under the label *Verein Ernst Mach* (1928). Taking
Auguste Comte and J. S. Mill as the modern fathers of positivism, it would be
historically proper to call Mach the founder of *neopositivism* and the members
of the Vienna Circle the architects of *logical positivism*. But convention now identifies the Vienna Circle with "neopositivism," a somewhat misleading habit in light
of the several great and irreconcilable disagreements that divided the members
almost from the first. The "circle" began in 1907 as a trio—Otto Neurath, Hans
Hann, and Philipp Frank—later expanding to include Moritz Schlick, Kurt Gödel,
Herbert Feigl, and Rudolf Carnap. The Berlin extension was headed by Hans
Reichenbach and included the young Carl Hempel, although even then (1929) the
match between Vienna's *Verein Ernst Mach* and Berlin's *Society for Empirical
Philosophy* was less than perfect. In the sympathetic periphery of these groups can
be found such influential figures as Wittgenstein and Karl Popper; in America,
Ernest Nagel and Willard Van Orman Quine; in England, A. J. Ayer and Gilbert
Ryle. The founders themselves cited a striking variety of spiritual forebears:
Epicurus, Hume, Mach, Karl Marx, Leibnitz, Helmholtz. This pedigree alone is
enough to convey how uneven and broken a "circle" it was.

What is notable in the history of logical positivism is its early triumphs in
psychology and their continuing hold on psychological thought long after the
defining features of the *ism* were largely rejected by the philosophical and scientific
communities. (Who, after all, besides contemporary psychologists, continues to
believe that "the meaning of a proposition is the method of its verification"?) It is

primarily in the "social" and the "behavioral" sciences that one can still find believers in the possibility of a completely nonmetaphysical body of knowledge; the possibility of an exclusively observational mode of inquiry; the possibility of a *discipline* that never ventures beyond the deceptively safe moorings of "objective description."

Yet, the chief failing of these putative sciences is not simply that they are uncritically anachronous, but that they are untrue even to the defective philosophy of science to which they pay lip service. The positivism defended by Mach and his disciples was one that took the facts of nature as revealed by observation and then legislated the manner in which science was to deal with them. This, however, is quite different from a program or orientation that embraces a particular philosophy of science as a way of avoiding or denying or depreciating any class of facts inaccessible to a chosen method of observation. For Mach especially, any program or orientation that would thus ignore the facts of *mental* life—including thought, feeling, and volition—must be taken as preposterous on its face. His position on such matters was conveyed (in 1886) by a passage in which he attempted to set limits on anthropomorphic explanations:

> We ask whether animals have sensations, when the assumption of sensations helps us better understand their behavior as observed by means of our own senses. The behavior of a crystal is already completely determined for our senses; and thus to ask whether a crystal has sensations, which would provide us with no further explanation of its behavior, is a question without any practical or scientific meaning (Mach, 1886/1959, pp. 243–244).

Nothing is ruled out a priori. Mach's aim is a fuller understanding of that evidence harvested by observations of nature. Given an event, one seeks to understand it and is allowed as many assumptions as may be required for the best understanding.

Contemporary psychology in the Machian tradition is one or another version of behaviorism, especially that defended by B. F. Skinner. But the events examined or admitted for examination by this "school" are generally either of marginal psychological consequence or are *overdetermined* in that more than a description of reinforcing operations is necessary to explain them. In addition to whatever "contingencies" have been set up, prediction of nearly any sample of behavior must take into account the organism's genetic nuances, its age and gender, the time of testing—a veritable sea of variables not embraced by either the concept or the "operation" of reinforcement.

It is true, if somewhat surprising at this late date, that leading behaviorists have now taken to mentioning "genetic endowment" in their attempts to bring the *ism* into line with reality (Skinner, 1974). But there is nothing in this strikingly truant recognition to explain just how the hereditary considerations are to be figured into the behaviorist's program. So much of this writing amounts to no more than adding

67

to behaviorism's original maxim, "As the twig is bent, so grows the tree," another maxim, "You can't make a silk purse out of a sow's ear," that on one construal qualifies it and on another contradicts it. Traditional formulations of behaviorism, at least since the time of Watson, have attracted attention and allegiance primarily through their economical employment of independent variables and their recommendation of essentially dimensionless measures (e.g., rate of responding). It is not clear that such allegiance could survive any serious attempt to refine behaviorism along the lines of modern genetics. The first but by no means the major casualty of such an attempt would be the habit of resting conclusions on the behavior of one organism. Note that, from the modern biogenetic perspective, it is not possible to assign *any* behavior emitted by a single organism either to the category of "learned" or that of "inherited." To adopt the genetic point of view is, ipso facto, to commit oneself to the study of groups of organisms within which estimations of gene frequencies are possible. But beyond this important scientific point is the more important conceptual one by which the very term *genetic behaviorism* becomes something of an oxymoron.

The same is true of all "liberalized S-R models" which, over the past few decades, have increasingly taken recourse to notions of *cognitive mediation* (Tolman, 1948; Kendler, 1964) not to mention still others which leave room for the possibility of "self-determination" through some sort of "reciprocal interaction" between the organism and the environment (Bandura, 1977). A behaviorism that is no more than a set of methodological preferences and habits may rise to the level of engineering but not to that of science or philosophy of science. To propose, for example, that the conduct of organisms is best *explained* by such constructs as cognitive mediation but must be *observed* at the level of molar behavior is to propose the obvious in any setting that is not exclusively introspective. Moreover, it is to acknowledge that the determinants of behavior, at least to this extent, are not entirely external. Of course they are not, but it remains doubtful that behaviorism qua behaviorism can survive the acknowledgment. That it cannot survive the acknowledgment of "self-determination" is beyond doubt, unless "self" is taken to be no more than a homeostatically governed physiological system—that is, the sort of system traditional behaviorism has also been content to ignore.

What these recent trends indicate is a growing awareness within the ranks that a genuine science of psychology would have to outgrow the stage of Baconian descriptivism. However, there is still the stubborn commitment to avoid theory at all cost where *theory* means more than empirical generalization. But behaviorism cannot have it both ways. If, for example, it insists on asserting every now and then some law-like claim of the sort, "For every overt molar response there is in principle a stimulus that will alter its probability," then it must do so at the forfeiture of pure verificationism, since there is no limit to the number of separate verifications required by such claims. Moreover, the expression, "in principle a stimulus" does not refer to any stimulus at all.

What is reflected by the drift toward cognitivism and away from quasi-Machian approaches is not merely an impatience with "pure" description; it is a positive motive to come closer to the nearly universally acknowledged facts of mental life. And it is just this that must urge psychology back to Aristotle and that most fundamental distinction between scientific and metaphysical explanations: the distinction between *causes* and *reasons*.

It is now more than twenty years since William Dray challenged the applicability of the deductive-nomological model to historiography on grounds that are essentially Aristotelian (Dray, 1957). In his essay, Dray argued that the historian's task is often one of determining the rationale, the objectives, and motives of an actor. These do not behave like "efficient causes" or the purely material antecedents in the realm of natural science. Hempel (1965) replied to this criticism by proposing to treat such reasons or motives as nomologically similar to natural causes. Assume, for example, that person A is in a situation of type C and that A is rational. It is now sufficient to show that "in situations of type C, rational beings do X" in order to *explain* A's behavior.

This rejoinder, however, fails on at least three counts. First, the very language of "situations" begs the question raised by Dray, since a "situation" is itself only explicable in rational-historical terms. With all due respect to Kurt Lewin, situations are not akin to magnetic fields and cannot be substituted for those *initial conditions* that serve as minor premises in Hempel's scheme. Second, many significant psychological states do not have public empirical referents. Think, for example, of the *hope* that it will rain on Friday. Finally, the actual and the logical connections between reasons and actions are not the same as those obtaining between causes and effects. The latter are governed by nothing less than logical entailment, since there can be no cause without an effect. But there are *reasons* for action which never lead to action and some that cannot. One may desire to live forever, a wish for which even jogging is not an apt behaviorial correlate. One may also hope that, if there is life on Mars, the laws on Mars be just. Thus, Hempel can only assimilate reasons and rational explanation to the deductive-nomological model by taking the behavioristic ontology for granted, and it is just this that Dray rejects. History, like individual biography, provides ample evidence of reasons that are uncorrelated with actions or whose behavioral correlates are merely incidental and trivial.

Hempel's dictum is not surprising, since one of the requirements of deductive-nomological explanation is that all *explananda* be empirical. The only "public" events routinely taken to be psychological in nature are behavioral (in the wide sense). But examined more closely, such behavior is in fact psychologically neutral for, from any given instance of behavior, any number of psychological inferences may be plausibly drawn. What is genuinely psychological about such events are the cognitive, affective, and volitional antecedents, not the behavior itself. The behavior as such is akin to the results of an opinion poll. One can gauge from these the most common position adopted from a range of options but not the (covert) determinants of the choice itself. Thus, 80 percent of a sample may oppose homicide, but from this fact (this "rate of responding") nothing of explanatory import can be extracted. The opposition might be based on the general desire not to have the tax-base shrink or on fears of the sanitation problems created by unconstrained and mortal assaults. This is just the dilemma facing one who has no more than a given "piece" of behavior before him. It is utterly destitute of psychological significance until theoretical and assumptive colorations are added.

Some might insist that the new "behavioral science" does add such colorations and might point to the recent eagerness of behaviorists to locate their efforts within a neo-Darwinian context. But this context has, after all, been in the background all along, and in making it explicit, the liberated behaviorists have yet to state just how their psychology fits into it. Since they do not know what to do with heredity, since they remain alarmingly aloof to the complex instinctual behavior that flourishes about them, and since their "comparative" psychology is largely exhausted by the pigeon and the rat, what can be made of the assurance that their psychology is somehow a natural science of the Darwinian stripe?

The difficulties do not end, they begin here. Of the many unnecessary and distracting assumptions that have gripped psychology during the past century (Robinson, 1979), perhaps *Darwinism* has had the most untoward effect. It is vital to recognize that the relationship between Darwinism and psychology is that which obtains between a thesis and a body of facts, *not* that obtaining between a scientific law and phenomena allegedly governed by it. In taking Darwin's own daring but purely speculative claims in psychology seriously, modern psychology has remained dangerously loyal to what is often ambiguous, occasionally tautologous, and sometimes ridiculous. In reifying the notions of *function* and *adaptation,* the discipline has been incapable of addressing phenomena that do not lend themselves to functionalistic and survivalistic interpretation. A surprisingly constant picture records modern psychological thought, whether it takes the form of the Freudian tension between the reality and pleasure principles, or the vaunted "law of effect," or that recent narrative that calls itself "sociobiology." On these and similar construals, the organism (or person) is part of a herd, itself driven by the single impulse of the success of the species. Indeed, even the humanistic psychologists have taken to the argot; "self-actualization" is a form of evolution that may be stunted by competitive forces. How much of this, like the theory itself, is but a celebration of the Victorian worldview is a matter historians must settle, but on the plane of conceptual analysis, it can already be judged as inapt and incoherent.

The point here is not to dispute the Darwinian picture of morphological diversity and speciation, the phenomena the theory was designed to explain. Rather, it is to note the obvious—or what should be obvious: the translation of psychological events and processes directly into the language of Darwinism is at best metaphorical, at worst, groundless. Moreover, it has never been a literal or an even faithful translation. Darwinism not only promises, it *legislates* variety. Nothing in the theory requires each species to mimic the rest in its copings and competitions. Human beings may do by art what the baboon does by craft, the spider by instinct. There is, then, nothing especially "Darwinian" about a psychology that denies uniqueness to human intelligence; or the existence of a human moral sense; or the human capacity for abstract thought. Nor is there anything characteristically Darwinian about a psychology that is wed to the laboratory—a setting in which Darwin himself was rarely found and never in connection with his most formidable contributions.

All this aside, there remains the central problem of explanation in psychology, and it is not solved by flashing the theory of evolution each time a sceptic appears. If he is an informed sceptic, he well knows that it is human psychology that stands as the ultimate test of that very theory. Like Alfred Russell Wallace, he will not be persuaded that "selection pressures" are behind non-Euclidean geometries and Bach's *Fugues*; and like Thomas Henry Huxley, he may be inclined finally to treat human ethics less as an expression and more as the adversary of evolutionary forces.

It is in these same regards that the scientific status of a developed psychology cannot be sought in physiological psychology. It must be remembered that the substantial advances of the recent past in the neural sciences—some of them achieved by psychologists—leave remarkably untouched the entire problem of explanation in psychology. To the extent that these advances have proceeded from the developed *sciences* of physiology and biochemistry, they come under those "covering laws" by which genuinely scientific explanations are framed. As such, they allow just those *causal* explanations which, as has been shown, are insufficient for an understanding of psychology. Indeed, it is just the sense in which physiological psychology is *scientific* that it is not *psychology*. One may not doubt that Smith's reason for befriending Jones cannot take place in the absence of a brain, but certainty on this count does not eliminate the need to understand both "reason" and "befriending" according to terms that bear no conceptual relation to neuronal discharges or the synthesis of RNA. What a thoroughgoing *causal* analysis provides is not an explanation of Smith's reasons but a means by which reasons may be ignored. As a gambit or strategy, however, this must fail, if only because Smith's reasons are uniquely *his*, whereas the neural processes are essentially indistinguishable across members of the same (or even diverse) species.

None of this is likely to vex those who have already dismissed philosophy of science as a discipline capable of informing, enriching, and even assessing science itself. In such circles, the connection between the two is generally regarded the way the virtuoso might think of the music critic: as one who cannot perform himself, but who nevertheless presumes to judge the performance of others. This, however, is not an apt analogy. The better one is the relationship between a director and an actor, each taking some responsibility for delivering to the public a creation authored by neither of them. The dictatorial director ultimately produces something

71

closer to an image of himself than to the drama as it is actually conceived. But the stubbornly independent actor, too, presents something no less stereotyped, for all his antics.

It is this actor who seems to characterize much of psychology in recent decades; a psychology that trots out the same data, the same "paradigms," the same slogans in attempting to account for conduct running the gamut from the bar-press to continental invasions. What the audience gets from this is not an explanation of the events under consideration, but a festival of sorts in which the object of the festivity is but a particular school of acting—call it "method acting." At the first few performances, one is tempted to regard the fellow as original, even ingenious. But as he is seen more frequently and in a wider range of settings, one comes to anticipate his formulae and thus see in his actions no more than a device by which he might parade a very limited talent. In the end, his performance is a form of self-parody that elicits the silence of embarrassment rather than that of awe.

As a purely empirical enterprise, modern psychology has added an immense amount to the world's store of factual knowledge, and for this it can expect support and enjoy a measure of pride. Were the discipline to do no more than organize and render more precise even the most commonly and abidingly understood principles of human psychology, its standing would be at least on a par with anatomy. But although it is true that all knowledge begins with classification, it is also true that all explanation goes beyond classification. Furthermore, the only justification for adopting *scientific* modes of classification is the warranted belief that the things thus classified are ultimately to be explained in scientific terms. One surely has no reason to classify orchestras according to the average weight of their members or the speed with which they get from one city to the next *if* the purpose of classification is to establish their musicality or "musicianship." To learn from someone found weighing the members of the horn section that he was doing this because it was the only scale he had would be to prove that the fellow not only had no notion of musicianship but only a childlike understanding of the nature and purpose of measurement. And think of how he might compound his innocence by weighing the *horns* should he have a scale too small to accommodate a person!

The situation within psychology is not unlike that faced by any serious attempt to classify, evaluate, and explain complex phenomena in any sphere of human activity. Some of these phenomena will admit of scientific explanation and others will not. At the stage of classification, therefore, the strategic question pertains to this distinction. Only when this question is settled (provisionally) is it possible to address questions of *tactics*, since one cannot rationally adopt a method of inquiry until he or she has settled on the nature of the thing under examination. Where complex social interactions are involved, or anywhere in which there is unequivocal evidence of human intentions, volitions, and deliberations, it is clear that any coherent explanation will not be of the *causal* variety but will inevitably require the postulation of irreducibly *psychological* dispositions. Recognizing this, the inquirer proceeds to assess the worthiness of those possible methods of investigation which honor the essential character of the phenomena. Depending on the particular event under consideration, the preferred method may be introspective, historical, interrogative, purely conceptual, or experimental. But it is the phenomenon that dictates the method, and not vice versa.

Returning to the title of this essay, is the relationship between psychology and science one of synonymy or antonymy? The answer suggested is that such determinations depend upon the nature of psychological explanation and that this depends upon the nature of the phenomena psychology chooses to address. Those that lend themselves to a purely causal account, requiring no recourse to concepts such as intentionality or rationality, are fit for *scientific* explanation, but the discipline that provides it cannot qualify as psychology. Those that are best or only understood by examining or positing the rational and volitional aspects of the participants must be explained *psychologically*, but the forthcoming explanations will generally lack the nomological features of scientific explanation. There is ample room and considerable need for both a nonscientific psychology and a scientific nonpsychology as human beings go about the important business of understanding themselves. What is not needed are promises that cannot be kept or rhetorical flourishes of the sort Kierkegaard condemned as he criticized an older philosophy:

> What the philosophers say about Reality is often as disappointing as a sign you see in a shop window which reads: Pressing Done Here. If you brought your clothes to be pressed, you would be fooled; for only the sign is for sale (Kierkegaard, 1941).

Readers will no doubt find in the present analysis the sort of distinctions Allport (1937) had in mind when he contrasted *ideographic* and *nomothetic* approaches to psychology. My argument, of course, owes a debt to Allport as it does to Collingwood (1972), Winch (1958), and many other philosophers who have emphasized the need to embrace personal psychological factors in any attempt to explain culturally and socially significant actions. But the present analysis goes beyond Allport's proposals in that it simply discounts the possibility of an ideographic *science*, at least as this noun is understood within the physical and biological disciplines. What is proposed here is not the means by which some new "science" can be brought to bear upon ideographic topics, but the application of tried and true nonscientific methods of analysis to those psychological problems that are nomothetically inexplicable.

Does such a recommendation seek no more than a revival of "armchair" psychology? The answer here depends primarily upon who is in the armchair. But such a question itself betrays the widespread conviction that once psychology moves away from its imitation of science it can aspire to no more than opinion or reckless speculation. On this view, what is in fact a rich trove of insights and possibilities possessed by "folk psychology" is rejected in favor of far less consistent and far more artificial models in some *textbook* psychology (Harré, 1978). Because of this slavish devotion to scientism, modern psychology must be regularly embarrassed by its inability to explain all sorts of occurrences which the lay community has no difficulty explaining at all. Moreover, the counterclaim—that laypeople only *think* they have an explanation but are really deceiving themselves—can only be made by a discipline that has accepted the task of explaining the same phenomenon. In evading the very phenomena that so engage the attention of real people, modern psychology renders itself irrelevant in the most damaging sense of the term and fails in the historic mission facing all serious scholarship—the correction of common errors and the elimination of common prejudice.

REFERENCES

Allport, G. *Personality: A psychological interpretation.* New York: Holt, 1937.

Bandura, A. *Social learning theory.* Englewood Cliffs, N.J.: Prentice-Hall, 1977.

Collingwood, R. G. *The idea of history.* Oxford: Oxford University Press, 1972.

Dray, W. *Laws and explanation in history.* New York: Oxford University Press, 1957.

Harré, H. R. Towards a cognitive psychology of social action: Philosophical issues of a programme. *The Monist,* 1978, *61,* 548–572.

Hempel, C. *Aspects of scientific explanation and other essays in the philosophy of science.* New York: Macmillan, 1965.

Kendler, H. H. The concept of the concept. In A. W. Melton (Ed.), *Categories of human learning.* New York: Academic, 1964.

Kierkegaard, S. *Either/Or* (2 vols.) (D. F. Swenson, L. M. Swenson, & A. Lowrie, trans.). Princeton, N.J.: Princeton University Press, 1941; 1944.

Mach, E. *The analysis of sensations and the relation of the physical to the psychical* (C. M. Williams & S. Waterlow, trans.). New York: Dover, 1959. (Originally published, 1886; trans. from 5th edition, 1906.)

Mill, J. S. *An examination of Sir William Hamilton's philosophy and of the principal philosophical questions discussed in his writings* (Vol. IX). In J. M. Robson (Ed.), *Collected works.* Toronto: University of Toronto Press, 1979. (Originally published, 1865.)

Robinson, D. N. *Systems of modern psychology: A critical sketch.* New York: Columbia University Press, 1979.

Robinson, D. N. *Toward a science of human nature: Essays on the psychologies of Hegel, Mill, Wundt and James.* New York: Columbia University Press, 1983.

Skinner, B. F. *About behaviorism.* New York: Knopf, 1974.

Tolman, E. C. Cognitive maps in rats and men. *Psychological Review,* 1948, *55,* 189–208.

Winch, P. *The idea of a social science and its relation to philosophy.* London: Routledge & Kegan Paul, 1958.

4

The Nature and Limits of Psychological Knowledge
LESSONS OF A CENTURY QUA "SCIENCE"*

SIGMUND KOCH

Throughout the nineteenth century (and indeed, before) an independent scientific psychology was vigorously invited. Toward the end of that century (in 1879, according to prevailing legend), an independent, scientific psychology was bestowed upon the world by the founding of a laboratory and further consolidated some two years later by the inauguration of the first journal for the "new" psychology which, somewhat ironically, was entitled *Philosophische Studien*. And, as we are certainly aware, over the next one hundred years an "independent, scientific psychology" has been enthusiastically enacted by a burgeoning work force that by now constitutes one of the largest groupings within contemporary scholarship. But the frenetic activity of the past hundred years has left the issue in doubt!

If we are "independent"—which, in historical context, is intended to mean aseptically free of philosophy—then why have psychologists been impelled to borrow chapter and verse from one or another presumably authoritative philosophy of science (or indeed, nonscientific philosophy) for every definition of a "proper" subject matter, every procedural or metatheoretical proposal, every substantive

*Presidential address to the Divisions of General Psychology and of Philosophical Psychology at the 1979 meeting of the American Psychological Association. In 1981, the *American Psychologist* published an article based on the address; this chapter is a modified version of that article.

conceptual net put forward *throughout* our century of happy autonomy? If psychology is *a* science, then why have our posits in each of the foregoing categories been so multifarious on each day of that century? And what kind of "science"—independent or otherwise—can we have achieved when it be considered that though our century-long cumulation of a vast technical literature may contain several thousand (perhaps million) law-like statements, not a single such statement can yet be counted a *law*, whether on criteria definitive of lawfulness in the natural sciences that we have been emulating *or* in the simple sense of commanding universal assent.

I am not a historian. But I have lived through a forty-year swath of psychological history from the vantage of a participant-observer whose arrogant construal of his calling has been to explore the prospects and conditions for a significant psychology. At some point near midcareer, I began to feel that my calling had rendered me a human and scholarly cipher in all respects save one: I had developed an uncanny connoisseurship concerning the fine structure and dynamics of pseudo-inquiry, the seamy vicissitudes of the phony scholarship that has characterized so much of the "activity" in my own field, and indeed others, in this century. I became, in fact, the modest founder of a discipline given to the study of misfirings of the scholarly and creative impulse: the field soon to be widely known as the science of "cognitive pathology," the metatheory of which is "epistemopathologistics."

I have tended to be somewhat secretive about this new enterprise. But a few years ago, in the course of an intellectual autobiography I had been asked to present to the APA Divisions of Philosophical Psychology and of the History of Psychology (Note 1), I permitted a brief glimpse of the noble architecture of this discipline. The glimpse apparently piqued curiosity, for after the talk representatives of the same divisions asked whether I would consider giving an "advanced course" in the new discipline on another occasion. That occasion has arrived. What could be a more appropriate one than the centennial of scientific psychology?

Space limits will permit only a précis of the advanced course. But I hope to be able to develop the powerful theoretical structure of this new discipline sufficiently to exhibit certain constraints on the character of the knowledge claims made by the psychology of the past century, as well as some constraints on the character of psychological knowledge in principle. After that, I close with a brief confrontation of the theme of the centennial by asking whether, after the century-long march of psychology under the banner of "independent, experimental science," the field actually is (1) *independent* and (2) a *science*.

The Pathology of Knowledge

Decades of inquiry into the inquiry of others—and into germane processes inside my own head—have induced in me a sense of awe at the plenitude of our gift for the mismanagement of our own minds. It is perhaps the ultimate genius of the race!

If you are a psychologist or social scientist, test any systematic formulation of your choice (whether learning-theoretic, systems-theoretic, information-theoretic, cognitive-genetic, cybernetic or, indeed, phenomenologico-hermeneutic, or, just maybe, behavior-therapeutic) against the following "epistemopathic" peregrinations of the inquiring impulse. (Those who assign passing grades, I shall have to presume either the owners of the formulation under test or first-year graduate students!)

1. Jargon and "word magic."
2. Single-principle imperialism.
3. Substitution of *program* for performance.
4. Tendency to make so restrictive a definition of the field of study as to render the study beside the point or, indeed, finished before begun.
5. Facilitation of progress by making a set of arbitrary and strong simplifying assumptions (e.g., imaginary "boundary conditions," counterfactual assumptions re mathematical properties of the data), proposing an "as if" model observing that set of restrictions, and then gratefully falling prey to total amnesia for those restrictions.
6. Tendency to select—usually on extraneous bases like amenability to "control" or to contemplated modes of mathematical treatment—a "simple case" and then to assume that it will be merely a matter of time and energy until the "complex case" can be handled by application of easy composition rules.
7. Tendency to accept on authority or invent a sacred, inviolable "self-corrective" epistemology that renders all inquiry in the field a matter of application of rules which preguarantee success.
8. Corollary to the preceding, a view of all aspects of the cognitive enterprise as so thoroughly rule-regulated as to make the role of the cognizer superfluous. The rule is father to the thought—and mother, too!
9. Tendency to persist so rigidly, blindly, patiently, in the application of the rules—despite fulsome indications of their disutility—that the behavior would have to be characterized as schizophrenic in any other context.
10. Tendency to accept any "finding" conformable to some treasured methodology in preference to "traditional" wisdom *or* individual experience, no matter how pellucidly and frequently confirmed the nonscientistic knowledge may be.
11. Epistemopathy No. 10, at a certain critical-mass value, results in the *total abrogation* of the criterion that knowledge should *make sense* and in an ultimate distrust of one's own experience. If a finding does make sense, one distrusts *it*.
12. An exceedingly strong reluctance to reinspect one's deeper epistemological and/or substantive commitments. This, in effect, is the theory of truth by individual consistency over time.
13. Ergo—a remarkable and telling disproportion between the attention given to

77

the foundation commitments of one's work and that given to superficial or pedantic details of implemental character. One dwells happily within the "superstructure," however shoddy or wormeaten the "substructure."

14. Tendency to buy into stable or fashionable profession-centered myths with a minimum of prior critical examination, to accept congealed group suppressions concerning bypassed problems or data; or alternative theoretical possibilities; or intrinsic (and sometimes patent) limits on the scope, analytic or predictive specificity, and so on, attainable in the field in question. Ergo, a disposition to become a "central tendency" creature, to hold in check (or happily suffer a reduction of) one's imaginative and critical resources.

The preceding sampling is necessarily a limited exercise in elementary cognitive pathology. My object here is to try to make plausible a large generalization that has come to inundate my mind. It is that there are times and circumstances in which able individuals, committed to inquiry, tend almost obsessively to frustrate the objectives of inquiry. It is as if uncertainty, mootness, ambiguity, cognitive finitude were the most unbearable of the existential anguishes. Under these conditions, able and sincere inquirers become as autistic as little children; they seem more impelled toward the pursuit and maintenance of security fantasies than the winning of whatever significant knowledge may be within reach!

A little reflection will show that such passionately courted cognitive disutilities as these are not exclusive marks of psychological inquiry, but are evident in all contexts of inquiry, both in and out of scholarship. I believe these perversities of cognitive function to be endemic to the human condition, but they have never been manifested more conspicuously (or disastrously) than in our dear century. This darkling hypothesis is not wholly idiosyncratic: It was shared by Bridgman, whose 1959 book, *The Way Things Are*, was animated by a "conviction that there is some fundamental ineptness in the way that all of us handle our minds" (p. 1).

My own epistemopathic observations have not been confined to psychology. Part of my professional commitment has been to philosophy, and I have had a lifelong interest in the arts and humanities. Virtually all fields of cultural life—and too many fields of practical life—are, I think, close to an impasse: an impasse of objective, method, substance, value, and education! Things cannot get much better until we "put our fingers" on the particularities of these blockages. General diagnosis, free-floating existential screams, are not enough.

Localizing the particularities of such blockages against authentic cognition is, of course, an awesome undertaking. Not only are the psychological, historical, and sociological grounds for the ever-accelerating dispersion of epistemopathy vastly ramified and intricately intertwined, but the cognitive pathologist cannot presume to be unafflicted by the disease that he or she seeks to cure. My own feeble efforts have thus far been concentrated on the discrimination of a syndrome that I call "ameaningful thinking" (the prefix has the same force as the *a-* in words like *amoral*) and its detailed contrast to the increasingly rare process of "meaningful thinking" (see Koch, 1965). I have become so obsessed in recent years with the importance of precise and differentiated analysis of the meaning and referential field of the "ameaning" syndrome that it is meet, before going further, to air the suspicion that my own head may be dangerously afflicted with Epistemopathy No. 2 of my sample list, namely, "single-principle imperialism."

In this chapter, I hold myself to the merest sense of the distinction between ameaningful and meaningful thinking. My object here is to develop it only to a point that will enable me to proceed to the consideration of some recent speculations concerning the deeper human context of the ameaning syndrome.

Ameaningful thought or inquiry regards knowledge as the result of "processing" rather than discovering. It presumes that knowledge is an almost automatic result of a gimmickry, an assembly line, a "methodology." It assumes that inquiring action is so rigidly and fully regulated by rule that in its conception of inquiry it often allows the rules totally to displace their human users. Presuming as it does that knowledge is generated by processing, its conception of knowledge is fictionalistic, conventionalistic. So strongly does it see knowledge under such aspects that it sometimes seems to suppose the object of inquiry to be an ungainly and annoying irrelevance. The terms and relations of the object of inquiry or the problem are seen, as it were, through an inverted telescope: detail, structure, quiddity are obliterated. Objects of knowledge become caricatures, if not faceless, and thus they lose reality. The world, or any given part of it, is not felt fully or passionately and is perceived as devoid of objective value. Ameaningful thinking tends to rely on crutches: rules, codes, prescriptions, rigid methods. In extreme forms it becomes obsessive and magical.

The tendency of ameaningful thought to register its object as faceless, undifferentiated, psychically distant—to be, so to say, cognitively anesthetic vis-à-vis its object—I call "a-ontologism" (if the term may be forgiven). Its tendency to subordinate authentic and contextually governed analysis, discovery, or invention to blind application of an extrinsic method, I call "method-fetishism." *A-ontologism* and *method-fetishism* may, in fact, be regarded as the definitive marks of ameaningful thinking.

On the other hand, *meaningful* thinking involves a direct perception of unveiled, vivid relations that seem to spring from the quiddities, the particularities of the objects of thought, the problem situations that form the occasions of thought. There is an organic determination of the form and substance of thought by the properties of the object and the terms of the problem. In meaningful thinking, the mind caresses, flows joyously into, over, around, the relational matrix defined by the problem, the object. There is a merging of person and object or problem. Only the problem or object, its terms and relations, exist. And *these* are real in the fullest, most vivid, electric, undeniable way. It is a fair descriptive generalization to say that meaningful thinking is ontologistic in some primitive, accepting, artless, unselfconscious sense.

Meaningful thinking in its "highest" forms—I do not mean highest relative to a population but relative to an individual ceiling—occurs with extreme rarity at best. As we know from the protocols even of highly creative individuals, its incidence can be maximized only by the most conscientious and delicate husbanding—by arrangements for work that strive to realize a most intricate concatenation of environmental and personal conditions. For *any* individual, the incidence of highly meaningful thought "episodes," though rare, can be modified. If it is valued, meaningful thinking can be "sought" by learning, and causing to be realized, the circumstances that bear some probability relation to its occurrence. Highly meaningful thought episodes can be triggered only under special situational and neural conditions of the organism, some (but not all) of which are accessible to control.

The statistical incidence of highly meaningful thinking in populations—whether these be subparts of a society or culture, entire societies or cultures, or indeed, populations "defined" by historical epochs—varies within limits. Lamentably, the nature of the phenomenon is such that its incidence can probably be made to decrease more easily than to increase. Thus, for any population, the relative incidence of meaningful *or* ameaningful thinking will be determined to a large extent by the values placed by the group upon one or the other. Such values will, of course, be embedded in the ideologies or rationales of knowledge-seeking behavior dominant in the group and will pervade all institutions and agencies that influence intellectual or scholarly style, habit, and sensibility.

The besetting cognitive problems of a culture, a subculture, or an era can thus be very much a reflection of whatever factors lead to the relative valuation of meaningful and ameaningful thinking. One must even face the possibility that cultures can arise which place so limited a value on meaningful thinking that many of its members are deprived absolutely of the possibility of achieving "high" orders of meaningful thought, relative to their capacities, or of discriminating such states— should they occur—as in some sense valuable or even different from ameaningful thinking. I believe that something very much like such a culture has arrived and that the culture in question is the world culture of the twentieth century.

In prior writings, I have sought to delineate the contours of ameaning—and more generally to perform epistemopathic surgery—in a variety of connections. I have, for instance, critically considered *behaviorism* from many angles (e.g., Koch, 1961a, 1964, 1971, 1973, 1976b). Most of these analyses have been trained upon particular formulations and argued in detail. An early artifact of my disenchantment with behaviorism—a study of Hull's systematic work (Koch, 1954)—is probably the most mercilessly sustained analysis of a psychological theory on record.

This body of work on the behaviorisms resists summary, but to convey the flavor of the cognitive-pathological enterprise, I can mention the following surgical efforts. I have tried to show the dependence of behaviorist epistemology on philosophies of science that had begun to crumble even before psychologists borrowed their authority and that are now seen as shallow and defective by all save the borrowers. I have given detailed attention to behaviorism's garbled assumptions concerning the workings of language and the nature of scientific communication; to the undifferentiated, rubbery character, impoverished range, and overblown intension of its major analytical terms ("stimulus," "response," "drive," "reinforcement," and the like); to the inconstant, Pickwickian, and (literally) incoherent discursive practices of its theorists and defenders—practices that render its typical argument forms a species of half-studied and half-unwitting double entendre.

I have in many writings (Koch, 1959, see Epilogue, Vol. 3; 1976a) performed extensive "epistemopathectomies" upon the large segment of twentieth-century psychological history that I have called the "Age of Theory." That happy interval commenced in the early 1930s and may, in modified form, still be with us to this very day. The mark of the Age of Theory, especially in its classic phase (circa 1930–1950), was that all activities were to be subordinated to production of a "commodity" called "theory" *in a quite special sense defined by the Age.* It is as if something called "theory" became an end in itself—a bauble, a trinket—of which it was neither appropriate nor fair, certainly most naive, to inquire into its human relevance. Indeed, most formulations of the era were based on animal data, and some haughtily claimed a restriction of reference to animal (usually rat) behavior. The overarching cosmology of this interval was based on a loose mélange of vaguely apprehended ideas derived from logical positivism, operationism, and neopragmatism—and, it should be added, *not* from these traditions in their full span but merely from a narrow time segment within the early 1930s. These ideas were construed as providing a formulary for the "construction" of theory. Certain epistemological and procedural agreements were absolutely regulative during most of the Age of Theory: in particular, such matters as the regulation of systematic work by the imagery of hypothetico-deduction, the prescriptive lore surrounding operational definition, the lore concerning the intervening variable, the belief in the imminence of precisely quantitative behavioral theory of comprehensive scope, certain broadly shared judgments with respect to strategic foundation data, and the belief in automatic refinement and convergence of theories by the device of "differential test."

Even in an ahistorical era such as the present, most psychologists know something about these agreements, for some of them are still with us. Nevertheless, much of the rationale of the six-volume project, *Psychology: A Study of a Science* (Koch, 1959, 1962, 1963), that I directed at midcentury was to test the official epistemology of the Age of Theory via an apposition of the creative experience of the many distinguished participating theorists with the stipulations of regnant canon law. The results made it possible for me to conclude that the study had subjected that body of law to vast attrition. In continued epistemopathic effort, I have succeeded—at least to my own satisfaction—in demonstrating the dysfunctionality of each statute in the Age of Theory code. But apparently not to the satisfaction of all!

A final context in which I have practiced epistemopathic surgery has been in

81

relation to certain of the scholarly and creative mystiques that have been dominant in both the humanities and the arts in this century (Koch, 1961b, 1969b; Koch, Note 2). I discern in these areas many analogues to the restrictive scientism and rule-saturated ideologies of the psychological and social sciences. I mention this line of interest only to demonstrate that I do not discriminate against psychology.

Despite the extravagant generality into which I am forced by a discussion such as this, I am, by nature and scholarly practice, a particularist. But there is no way of addressing the import of psychology's first century, within a single article, particularistically. My only recourse in the remainder of this article is to move even further away from the surface details of psychological history. I wish to discuss the human wellsprings of the ameaningful epistemopathy that I believe to be so evident in psychology. I propose to do this in artless and nontechnical terms that address humanity's predicament on this planet. I do not project anything so grandiose— indeed, in my belief, insane—as the determination of the *range* of the knowable. Rather, I am groping toward certain constraints inherent in the human situation which would have to condition the form and texture of any knowledge that reflexively bears on human beings as subjects. Perhaps my groping stems more from hesitation or embarrassment than from the difficulty of discerning answers. For I am discussing matters within the ken of every human being which are disquieting to contemplate or address. Indeed, they are matters in respect to which the history of disciplinary inquiry has to some extent been an evasion. It might almost be said that we are increasingly walled off from the matters I have in mind by the overconfident and often spurious knowledge claims disgorged upon the race by certain of the formal disciplines. It is fitting that so arch an introduction point toward a rather odd title. I turn, then, to a consideration of "The Antinomies of Pure Reason and the Antinomies of Impure Living."

The Antinomies of Pure Reason and the Antinomies of Impure Living

Some years ago, while visiting a small liberal arts college, I was asked to have lunch with the resident philosophers. In the formal discussion session that followed the meal, my first questioner was a young faculty member. The tone of his question suggested his expectation of rapid—and final—edification. "Dr. Koch," he said, "what is your solution to the mind-body problem?" I think I mumbled that despite my Hungarian aura of omniscience, my mind was still open on the issue, and that though I considered it an important and meaningful one, I suspected it was undecidable in principle.

Later, it occurred to me that had the question been put to me some thirty years earlier, I would certainly have been able to untuck from my head a confident and final response. I would have said that *because* the question was asked in ontological form (i.e., in what Carnap would then have called "the material mode of speech"), it was undecidable in principle and therefore meaningless. However, if the *intent* of this pseudoquestion could be extricated from its ontological housing and translated into "the formal mode of speech," then it would become the utterly manageable, and therefore meaningful, issue of the relations between the "language systems" of psychology and physiology. Of course, part of me—even then—was surely apprised that both of these languages were woefully asystematic, mixed, and programmatic and, moreover, that each of the languages was not a single language but rather a congeries of languages, each member of which was shared in the typical instance by one person. But that particular part of me did not speak to the rest of me.

Nor did Immanuel Kant speak to me in an especially persuasive way in those days. In the course of his majestic construction of the critical philosophy, he had perceived that humankind is boxed in a curious way. He had discerned that there is a class of questions which human reason must necessarily confront but which are rationally undecidable. These, as every schoolchild knows, are the antinomies of pure reason—issues such that a thesis and its contradictory antithesis can both be proved. The four particular antinomies Kant considers bear, in the usefully brief words of one commentator (Weldon, 1958, p. 81), on "the infinite extent and divisibility of space and time and also the existence of God and the freedom of the will." Post-Kantian sophisticates are fond of noting that the proofs are not formally unassailable, but the impeccability of the specific proofs has nothing to do with Kant's more general insight that there is a class of questions, intensely meaningful to all human beings—questions over which many experience great anguish— which "transcend the competence of human reason." The questions are meaningful but rationally undecidable in principle.

I suggest that the class of such undecidable yet meaningful propositions is far broader than the four antinomies that Kant thought it necessary to develop in pursuit of his systematic objective—which, in the immediate context of the antinomies, was to demonstrate the inadequacy of *dogmatic* metaphysics and theology. Moreover, if metaphorical extension of the notion be permitted, it rapidly becomes evident that a very broad range of human concerns, and even processes, exhibit, as it were, an "antinomal texture." I should like to identify certain consequences of this widespread "antinomality" for human knowledge and also for some characteristics of psychological inquiry in this century. (To emphasize that I am metaphorically building upon the strict logical sense of the term *antinomy*—and also for purposes of euphony—I have substituted these neologisms for the literally correct constructions "antinomial" and "antinomiality.")

First, I shall call upon Bertrand Russell as witness. The quotation from him may seem a bit long, but it will repay attention in better coin than I can mint. In one of his more inspiring moments, he gave the following definition of philosophy:

> Philosophy . . . is something intermediate between theology and science. Like theology, it consists of speculations on matters as to which definite knowledge has, so far, been unascertainable; but like science, it appeals to human reason rather than to authority. . . . *Almost all the questions of most interest to speculative minds are such as science cannot answer,* and the confident answers of theologians no longer seem so convincing as they did in former centuries. Is the world divided into mind and matter, and, if so, what is mind and what is matter? Is mind subject to matter, or is it possessed of independent powers? Has the universe any unity or purpose? Is it evolving towards some goal? Are there really laws of nature, or do we believe in them only because of our innate love of order? Is man what he seems to the astronomer, a tiny lump of impure carbon and water impotently crawling on a small and unimportant planet? Or is he what he appears to Hamlet? Is he perhaps both at once? Is there a way of living that is noble and another that is base, or are all ways of living merely futile? If there is a way of living that is noble, in what does it consist, and how shall we achieve it? Must the good be eternal in order to deserve to be valued, or is it worth seeking even if the universe is inexorably moving towards death? . . . To such questions no answer can be found in the laboratory. . . . The studying of these questions, if not the answering of them, is the business of philosophy.
>
> Why, then, you may ask, waste time on such insoluble problems? To this one may answer as a historian, or *as an individual facing the terror of cosmic loneliness.*

We will skip the historian's answer and continue with Russell's "more personal" answer:

> Science tells us what we can know, but what we can know is little, and if we forget how much we cannot know we become insensitive to many things of very great importance. . . . Uncertainty, in the presence of vivid hopes and fears, is painful, but must be endured if we wish to live without the support of comforting fairy tales. *It is not good either to forget the questions that philosophy asks, or to persuade ourselves that we have found indubitable answers to them. To teach how to live without certainty, and yet without being paralyzed by hesitation, is perhaps the chief thing that philosophy, in our age, can still do for those who study it* (Russell, 1945, pp. xiii–xiv, italics added).

I invite you, in passing, to contrast these attitudes with the following statement by Schlick in the initial paper of the first issue of *Erkenntnis* (1930–1931), the international journal of the Vienna Circle:

> I am convinced that we are in the middle of an altogether final turn in philosophy. I am justified, on good grounds, in regarding the sterile conflict of systems as settled. Our time, so I claim, possesses already the methods by which any conflict of this kind is rendered superfluous; what matters is only to apply these methods resolutely (translated and quoted in Frank, 1950, p. 41).

Schlick's statement is far more characteristic of the dominant tone of philosophy in this century than is Russell's.

It can be seen from Russell's illustrations of "unanswerable" yet, in his view, meaningful and even pressing problems that they include equivalents of Kant's four antinomies but project a considerably broader class. But, if we consider the class of undecidable yet meaningful problems as manifested in the daily preoccupations and concerns of human beings, I think we will all see what we already agonizingly know: that the class is so large as to be nondenumerable in principle. For each of us, of course, there are homely analogues to Kant's four problems and to others cited by Russell; we may not sense them with the finesse of a philosopher, but we certainly feel them in the pit of our stomachs, starting in childhood! And there are others over which we sweat and quake on a day-to-day, or perhaps minute-to-minute, basis.

It does not require an elaborate phenomenological method, but merely honesty, to perceive that very many of the problems—large or small, existential or actional, intellectual or practical—which agitate human beings are indeed meaningful (often intensely so) but undecidable. Moreover, a large fraction of the events, problems, concerns, ruminations, calculations, regrets, evaluations, assessments, projections, and anticipations that populate our existence, whether fleetingly or over a span equivalent to one's biography, are also characterized by something very much like an "antinomal" structure. I do not mean that they pose antinomies in the formal logical sense, of course. What I do mean is that all such moments or units of psychological activity, however configured, involve disjunctive oppositions of meanings, the propositional equivalents of which are not ultimately, or strictly, or even stably decidable. I think I am noting something other than the mere circumstance that decision and action are largely optative or largely determined by "extrarational factors," or that problem solving, and more generally, the movement of cognition, is probabilistic. I *am* comprehending those things in what I say, but I am trying to convey that the residue of mootness, ambiguity, mystery, is appallingly large. Perhaps the only way to convey what I have in mind is through the cumulative impact of varied examples. These I cannot state in orderly echelons, for the "antinomies of impure living" are not deployed by philosophers. Consider, however, the following array.

Let us commence by noting that the child who experiences night-sweats over a dawning sense of the word *eternity* is by way of discovering the Kantian antinomies, but let us leave aside further discussion of those overarching issues concerning origin, destiny, and purpose, which torture us throughout our sentient lives.

Consider now the enormous range of ambiguity inherent in the human condition suggested by, say, the unrecoverability of particular motives and, indeed, the principled impossibility of achieving a full motivational analysis of any action; the ubiquitous problems of self-sincerity, altruism versus egocentrism, guilt versus innocence, sinful versus good deeds, personal responsibility versus shaping or control from without; of whether, in particular instances or in general, one is loved or hated, liked or disliked, or perhaps regarded indifferently; whether one is beautiful

85

or ugly or somewhere in between. Moreover, is one beautiful by virtue of physiognomy or personality or both? When is one lying; when isn't one? When is one being lied to; when not? When is one being treated as an object; when as a person? Is it more desirable to project value, ideal, end state X or Y, or Z or . . . ? Is one (whether in general or in respect to particular endeavors) a success or a failure? If a failure, is it by virtue of having successfully sought failure, or by ineptitude, the fault of others, or just bad luck?

"Do I understand this equation (this line of poetry or prose, this view, theory, subject, person, event)? Really understand, or merely think that I do?" "Do I really like X (any object of taste) or only think that I do because I should? As a matter of fact, should I, really?" "Should I wear X or Y today or are they both inappropriate?" "Am I showing favoritism toward one of my children, or is that child the one who needs special attention?"

"Can I sustain this performance? Am I doing brilliantly or did I lose it somewhere? Does the audience resonate to me or does it loathe me? If the latter, does it loathe my person, my ideas, or merely my words?"

"Sometimes I am convinced that they are about to fire me, but five minutes later the same evidence seems to mean that I am on the verge of being promoted."

The examples thus far have been drawn in a rather bold and structural way. Let me now enter the microstructure of a characteristic human rumination sequence and attempt to give something like the formal pattern of the excogitations that we develop around the small issues which preempt so much of our daily round.

"A said that B said . . . , but B couldn't have said such a thing. Or could he? I don't think A to be a liar, but I could be wrong. Is A trying to get closer to me by upsetting me over B's inconstancy, or is he really being protective? Or (on the other hand) is B trying to send me a message through A which B is afraid to deliver? But B has never been that kind of person. However, C might have said something to B that changed the way he feels, or maybe B has begun to change because of his relationship with D or that nasty pair, E and F. On the other hand, it's more likely that D is exerting a stabilizing influence on B, that is, on the assumption that D has not been subverted by E and F. But why should E and F, however coarse and vulgar, be so strongly set on changing B, or reaching B through D, when it must be clear to them that there is nothing B can do for them? On the other hand, maybe they don't know that B has given up his connection with G, whom B could indeed have influenced in their favor. But I am not even sure that E and F knew that B ever did have a connection with G. Anyway, I'm not sure that E and F know B at all well or have any basis for wishing to influence him. Now, D, on the other hand, could be changing toward B, not because of the influence of E and F but because. . . ."

These examples are, I think, sufficient to make palpable the awesome dispersion of the antinomal, the problematic, the ambiguous, in human experience. It is no great leap to add that the attendant fear, trembling, and uncertainty are comparably awesome in scope and can, for most of us, at times, achieve an intensity that tests the margins of our sanity. It is no part of our talent to live at utter peace with these pressures—though there are graceful philosophies of faith that can be mitigative and that need not be presumed to be any the less warrantable than, say, the ungraceful philosophies of faith associated with the metaphysics of scientism. And there are other mitigative correlates of antinomality, such as the fascination and intrinsic beauty of the experience of awe and mystery in relation to the universe. But there is no denying that the antinomal texture, the uncertainty of our situation, *can* generate a vast skewing effect on cognition, which can create epistemopathy and sustain ameaning. The ultimate "meaning" of ameaning is indeed that it is a fear-driven species of cognitive constriction, a reduction of uncertainty by denial, by a form of phony certainty achieved by the covert annihilation of the problematic, the complex, and the subtle.

Antinomality, in sum, is at the basis of the endemic human need for crawling into cozy conceptual boxes—any box, so long as it gives promise of relieving the pains of cognitive uncertainty or easing problematic tension. This poignant human need, at any cost, for a frame, an abacus, a system, map, or set of rules that can seem to offer a wisp of hope for resolving uncertainty makes all of us vulnerable—in one degree or another—to the claims of simplistic, reductive, hypergeneral, or in other ways ontology-distorting frames, so long as they have the appearance of "systematicity." Moreover, having climbed into our conceptual box, on one adventitious basis or another, we are prepared to defend our happy domicile to the death—meaning, in the typical instance, *your* death. It is not that we don't want you to join us inside (we would be delighted to accommodate the whole human race); it's just that we don't want you tampering with our box or suggesting—by your location in another one—that there are other places in which to live.

The saving grace of the race is the ability of individuals, occasionally, to climb out of such boxes and look around: to see around the edges of our "received" concepts, our technical constructions, our formal belief systems. When the drive toward easy cognitive assurance remains unchecked and unmitigated, it can lead to something very much like mass insanity.

One might think that all I am doing is addressing the facts of human conflict, which are acknowledged in some form by all psychological theories. If I am, I am addressing them in a special sense and from a special incidence: I am talking about the kind of *cognitive* conflict that paralyzes in the sense that I *know* that I *cannot know*, but somehow am compelled desperately to strive to know. It is a mode or aspect of conflict that is not addressed in theories couched in a language of conflicting drives or needs, conflicting systems of personality, or competing responses.

What I mean by "antinomality" is the kind of conflict generated by a proposition that suggests its contradictory (or the domain of its contraries) as strongly as its own affirmation, at the moment of affirmation. Antinomality, in the sense in which I am employing this metaphor, creates a penumbra of uncertainty around the edges of sentience, such that one can rarely be sure who or what one really is, or indeed what (or which of a class of alternates) one is perceiving, cognizing, or doing. Even when the organization of our mental field seems clear and unambiguous, there is still a faint halo of mystery. On a vast gray area of occasions the organization "wants" to shift into its opposite or some range of alternates, or the field is shadowy, indistinct. And finally, there is that black area of interludes in which something like utter "problematicity," chaos, strangeness, terror, and thus depersonalization supervenes. I am, if you will, talking of something like *metaphysical* conflict and saying that we are all born metaphysicians who are destined mainly to fail when we ply our craft. And I am saying that "conflict" of this sort is far more pervasive in our lives than we tend ordinarily to have the courage to admit, either to ourselves or to others.

When dwelling on the pervasiveness of antinomality, determinate and valid knowledge soon begins to seem a miracle—but no more so than our antinomal presence here on Earth is a miracle. Einstein once wrote that "the most incomprehensible thing in the world is that the world is comprehensible."

I think there are contexts of knowing in which the structures, and relations among disparate structures, in our mental field are defined so perspicuously, sharply, compellingly, as to make "verification" seem superfluous. And indeed, as most great discoverers have reported, nature often says "yes" to such visions when meticulously tested and sometimes continues to say yes over an unanticipated range of their consequences. Taking such occurrences as a prototype case of *meaningful* thinking (as I have previously tried to define it), one should note that approximations of this type of occurrence are within the range of all of us, both in daily living and in moments of "formal" or technical ratiocination. I think that much needs to be said about the human being's capacity for discerning islands of order within the antinomal ocean in which we swim and (in the arts) for creating nobly ordered structures that can transcend or illuminate antinomality. Much needs to be said about such matters, but not in an essay of finite length!

This much, however, has been implicit in all I have said: meaningful thinking, as I have sought to define it, is precisely what cannot supervene when we lack the courage to live with our antinomal uncertainties; it cannot be invited by denial of our situation, but only by a kind of fascinated and loving, if ironic, acceptance.

The twentieth century has been far wiser than Kant—and, in dominant tendency, far wiser than the Russell who spoke in the quotation I cited. (There were many Russells over his long career; he, too, was far wiser over long stretches of it!) A conspicuous strand in the philosophy, especially the scientific philosophy, of the twentieth century has been the view that all questions having presumptive cognitive content but which can be shown to be undecidable in principle are meaningless. They are, in other words, pseudoquestions—linguistically illegitimate question forms. Rational hygiene, therefore, dictates that the human race be freed of such illusory preoccupations. This is the view that received its sharpest (and most incantatory) expression in the various forms of the "verifiability theory of meaning" advanced by logical positivism, but it is prominent as well in pragmatism, operationism, and all *consistent* positivistic and empiricist philosophies. Though not a dominant view in earlier centuries, it was clearly adumbrated in Hume and received something close to its canonical formulation (though not application) in Comte.

In the philosophy of *this* century, unqualified forms of the verifiability theory of meaning began to wane along with the waning hegemony of logical positivism, but some would argue that its imprint was visible well into the 1960s in much of analytic philosophy. This smug and restrictive view of meaning is still, however, implicit in the thinking of most natural and social scientists, while in scientific psychology it remains a devout and irrefragable article of faith.

I should like to suggest that such a view of the range of the meaningful has had, and must have, crippling entailments for the character of the psychological enterprise. If empirical decidability (which, incidentally, itself cannot be *decided in advance*) is the criterion for bounding the meaningful, one then has a perfect rationale for selecting for study only domains that seem to give access to the generation of stable research findings. If any domain seems refractory to conquest by the narrow range of methods (usually borrowed from the natural sciences and mutilated in the process) held to be sacred by the work force, then, obviously, *meaningful* questions cannot be asked concerning the domain, and that domain is expendable. If one cannot achieve stable findings when the dependent variable is of "subjective" cast, then eliminate such data and concentrate on behavior! Indeed, why presume that mental events or processes exist? Why study the *subject* at all; why not study something else?

Such a view of the meaningful, then, dooms psychology to be an empty role-playing pursuit which, in the course of enacting a misconstrued imitation of the forms of science, gives free rein to every epistemopathic potentiality of the "inquiring" mind. Buttressed by such a view and by the anemic theory of science in which it is housed, psychology has felt justified in fixing upon totally fictional domains as its objects of study (i.e., on arbitrary and schematic models of the person, or even the organism, rather than on the actual entities—say, a *schematized* rat, or dog, or sophomore; or, perhaps, a telephone exchange, a sewage system, a servomechanism, a computer). A related strategy, of course, has been to select a dependent variable category (whether phrased in terms of "behavior" or in some other way) bearing a trivial relation to human—or even sophomore or dog—reality. Some games—even within scholarship—are relatively innocent; the game at issue poses a severe threat to humankind because it links the authority of science with an imagery of the human condition that can only trivialize and obfuscate its beneficiaries.

Now psychology has presumed, throughout much of the century, that its task is the *prediction* and *control* of behavior (or, less frequently, some other member of a limited class of dependent-variable categories, as, for instance, action, experience, cognitive change, attitude change, etc.). But one can well ask what such an objec-

89

tive might *mean* against the background of the antinomal and ambiguous human events of the sort I have sought to illustrate. Does "prediction" mean that we expect to derive, from some nomological net, the behavioral, experiential, or judgmental *outcome* of such episodes in the quasi-logic of antinomality as I have tried to analyze? Does it mean the capacity to generate a lawful technology that will give human beings the tools to resolve their antinomal "problems" with finality and precision? Does it mean a set of normative rules or maxims that will enable individuals better to resolve their disjunctive quandaries?

Or does prediction mean the erection of a scientistic myth which uses the iconology of science to reassure people that their lives are not that complex, their situations not that ambiguous—and that, therefore, if they are able to understand the profound fact that they really are redundant concretions of dry hardware or wet software (or wet hardware or dry software), all they need do is happily percolate in a way determined by the laws of the particular kind of concretion that the lawgiver prefers?

It is incredible to contemplate that during a century dominated by the tidy imagery of prediction and control of human and social events, the perverse cognitive pathology housed in such imagery has not been rooted out. In fact, such notions have rarely been seen as problematic and still more rarely subjected even to perfunctory modes of analysis.

Coda: The First Century?

And now for some easy questions. We are celebrating the first one hundred years of an independent, scientific psychology! It is appropriate to ask: (1) Have we been and are we now *independent* in the sense intended by those who celebrate the adjective, namely, "independent" of *philosophy*? And (2) Is psychology a science?

Independence

We are of course independent in an institutional sense. We have our own university departments, laboratories, journals, professional organizations, and so forth. Are we *conceptually* independent of philosophy? In a word, *no*. That opinion will come as no surprise by this point in the exposition. Most of our ideas have come from the twenty-six centuries of philosophy preceding the birth of our partition myth and, of course, to some extent, from physics, mathematics, various biological sciences, medicine, the social studies, the nonphilosophical humanities, and, yes, millennia of ordinary human experience.

Robinson (1976) has argued that twentieth-century psychology, even in its experimental reaches, is a "footnote to the nineteenth century" and is apprised, of course, of some large continuities between the nineteenth and not a few earlier centuries. Despite the curious size of the footnote relative to the text, I think him essentially correct. I presume he would agree that a footnote need not be merely ampliative, but can contain refinements here and there and even novelty. For even I believe that some islands of penetrating thinking and research have existed in this century.

Though many of us have generated a vociferous rhetoric of independence in this century (especially those of behaviorist persuasion), one and all have of necessity presupposed strong, if garbled, philosophical commitments in the conduct of their work. Psychology is necessarily the most philosophy-sensitive discipline in the entire gamut of disciplines that claim empirical status. We cannot discriminate a so-called variable, pose a research question, choose or invent a method, project a theory, stipulate a psychotechnology, without making strong presumptions of philosophical cast about the nature of our human subject matter—presumptions that can be ordered to age-old contexts of philosophical discussion. Even our nomenclature for the basic fields of specialized research within psychology (e.g., sensation, perception, cognition, memory, motivation, emotion, etc.) has its origin in philosophy. Let us note, also, that even during the period when the claim to independence was most aggressively asserted (the neobehavioristically dominated Age of Theory that I have already mentioned), we were basing, and explicitly so, our "official" epistemology on logical positivism and cognate formulations within the philosophy of science.

We should also bear in mind that there have been many psychologists in virtually every field throughout the century who have been explicit in their use of philosophical materials and in their awareness of philosophical origins. Within this subset fall virtually all of the nineteenth-century "founders" (most of whom—including the newly rehabilitated version of Wundt's ghost—indeed continued to see philosophy as their *primary* vocation, even after the founding); the personalists; Gestalt and field theorists; phenomenological psychologists; transactionalists; and more recently, contextualists, pursuers of a motley plurality of Eastern philosophies, and so forth. And there have been seminal thinkers, standing either alone or not easily assignable to broad movements, who have been explicit about their philosophical interests and dependencies. William James, John Dewey, Wilhelm Stern, William McDougall, Wolfgang Köhler, E. C. Tolman, Heinz Werner, Henry Murray, and James Gibson are names that rapidly spring to mind in this connection. It might also be worth recalling that this very essay is based on an Address to the Division of Philosophical Psychology, which is a part—though a tenuous one—of the American Psychological Association.

I should add that no clear line can be drawn between the concerns of philosophy and those of psychology, either historically or in the nature of the case. The ameaningful presumption that a clear line *must* be drawn has fostered much of the grotesquerie in modern psychology. I do not, however, wish to suggest that fuller and more explicit knowledge of our philosophical origins, and of the intertwining of

91

philosophical and psychological modes of analysis, will remove *all* of the blockages that have trivialized psychological thought in this century. For it is part of my position qua cognitive pathologist that one can find forms of epistemopathy in philosophy comparable to those I discern in psychology.

Despite the fact that this ancient tradition—which over history has been the font of every special field of scholarship—has produced many of the noblest achievements of the human mind, the philosophic impulse has at times proven extraordinarily vulnerable to the allures of a specious systematicity and comprehensiveness. For philosophy has also produced many of the kinds of conceptual boxes that promise cognitive reassurance too easily and too confidently. Some of these boxes—as in certain of the post-Kantian idealistic systems—are so expansive as to promote a kind of euphoric hyperventilation of the mind, while others—as in the dominant positivistic philosophies of this century—are so constrictive as to promote a form of cognitive anoxia. There is also a quality of *style* in much philosophical writing that in my opinion puts both reader and writer at epistemopathic risk. This is the implicit assumption that the writer's formulation is *final*, even when the writer knows full well that its claims may be quashed (perhaps even by the writer) next week. This quality of "finalism" is certainly to be found among those *psychological* theorists who view their own work as preemptive, but is not quite so pervasive in psychological writing.

Is Psychology a Science?

I have been addressing this question for forty years and, over the past twenty, have been stable in my view that psychology is not a single or coherent discipline but rather a collectivity of studies of varied cast, some few of which may qualify as science, while most do not. I have written widely on this theme (e.g., Koch, 1969a, 1971, and especially 1976a), but must content myself here with a very brief statement of my position, sans the evidence and analysis on which it rests. The reader will be surprised, perhaps, to discover that my proposals are libertarian ones and not devoid of hope.

For some years I have argued that psychology has been misconceived, whether as a science or as any kind of coherent discipline devoted to the empirical study of human beings. That psychology *can* be an integral discipline is the nineteenth-century autism that led to its baptism as an independent science—an autism which can be shown to be exactly that, both by a priori and by empirico-historical considerations.

On an a priori basis, nothing so awesome as the total domain comprised by the functioning of all organisms (not to mention persons) could possibly be the subject matter of a coherent discipline. If *theoretical* integration be the objective, we should consider that such a condition has never been attained by any large subdivision of inquiry—including physics. When the details of psychology's one-hundred-year history are consulted, the patent tendency is toward theoretical and substantive fractionation (and increasing insularity among the "specialties"), not integration. As for the larger quasitheoretical "paradigms" of psychology, history shows that the hard knowledge accrued in one generation typically disenfranchises the regnant analytical frameworks of the last.

My position suggests that the noncohesiveness of psychology finally be acknowledged by replacing it with some such locution as "the psychological studies." The psychological studies, if they are really to address the historically constituted objectives of psychological thought, must range over an immense and disorderly spectrum of human activity and experience. If significant knowledge is the desideratum, problems must be approached with humility, methods must be contextual and flexible, and anticipations of synoptic breakthrough held in check. Moreover, the conceptual ordering devices, technical languages ("paradigms," if you prefer), open to the various psychological studies are—like all human modes of cognitive organization—perspectival, sensibility-dependent relative to the inquirer, and often noncommensurable. Such conceptual incommensurabilities often obtain not only between "contentually" different psychological studies but between perspectivally different orderings of the "same" domain. Characteristically, psychological events—as I have implied throughout the discussion of antinomality—are multiply determined, ambiguous in their human meaning, polymorphous, contextually environed or embedded in complex and vaguely bounded ways, and evanescent and labile in the extreme. This entails some obvious constraints upon the task of the inquirer and limits upon the knowledge that can be unearthed. Different theorists will—relative to their different analytical purposes, predictive or practical aims, perceptual sensitivities, metaphor-forming capacities, and preexisting discrimination repertoires—make asystematically different perceptual cuts upon the same domain. They will identify "variables" of markedly different grain and meaning contour, selected and linked on different principles of grouping. The cuts, variables, concepts will in all likelihood establish different universes of discourse, even if loose ones.

Corollary to such considerations, paradigms, theories, models (or whatever one's label for conceptual ordering devices) can never prove preemptive or preclusive of alternate organizations. This is so for any field of inquiry, and conspicuously so in the psychological and social studies. The presumption on the part of their promulgators that the gappy, sensibility-dependent, and often arbitrary paradigms of psychology *do* encapsulate preemptive truths is no mere cognitive blunder. Nor can it be written off as an innocuous excess of enthusiasm. It raises a grave moral issue reflective of a widespread moral bankruptcy within psychology. In the psychological studies, the attribution to any paradigm of a preemptive finality has the force of telling human beings precisely what they are, of fixing their essence, defining their ultimate worth, potential, meaning; of cauterizing away that quality of ambiguity, mystery, search, that makes progress through a biography an adventure. Freud's tendency to view dissidents and critics in *symptomatic* terms—and to resolve disagreement by excommunication—is no circumscribed failing, but indeed renders problematic the character of his entire effort, not only morally but cognitively. One is tempted to laugh off the ludicrous prescriptionism of self-anointed visionaries like Watson, Skinner, and even certain infinitely confident prophets of the theory of finite automata, but their actual impact on history is no laughing matter.

Because of the immense range of the psychological studies, different areas of study will not only require different (and contextually apposite) methods but will bear affinities to different members of the broad groupings of inquiry as historically conceived. Fields like sensory and biological psychology may certainly be regarded as solidly within the family of the biological and, in some reaches, natural sciences. But psychologists must finally accept the circumstance that extensive and important sectors of psychological study require modes of inquiry rather more like those of the humanities than the sciences. And among these I would include areas traditionally considered "fundamental"—like perception, cognition, motivation, and learning —as well as such more obviously rarefied fields as social psychology, psychopathology, personality, aesthetics, and the analysis of "creativity."

Much of what I have proposed is grounded on an analysis, on which I have been working for over twenty years, of the functioning of lexical units in natural and technical languages (e.g., 1961b, 1964, 1973, 1976a). The work suggests a sensible alternative to the absurdities of the definitional schemata of logical positivism and operationalism, and leads, I think, to fresh insights into problems of inquiry and of knowledge. This analysis shows that definition of abstract, general, or referentially "rich" concepts upon any delimited base of "epistemic simples" (such as a putative class of "physical thing predicates" or of verifying "operations") simply does not work. Such reductive definitional schemata confound symptom and meaning; if taken seriously, they denude the universe of everything worth talking, or indeed thinking, about.

Analysis of the conditions of actual communication will show that effective definition is essentially a matter of perceptual guidance. The definer seeks to guide the addressee toward perception of the intended property, relation, or system thereof. If the referent is a subtle, delicately contoured, or embedded one (which it often is), such guidance may be very difficult indeed. In the ideal case, definition would be a form of ostension via a perceptual display that exhibits the referent in its purest, least masked, most sharply contoured form. Scientific experiment may be interpreted in that light. It is often difficult to approximate the ideal form. Verbal definitions, though limited by their surrogate character, depend for their efficacy on the definer's skill at mobilizing relevant components of the addressee's discrimination repertoire—and whether (or with what precision) the communication actually takes place will depend on the fineness and nicety of the discriminations within the addressee's repertoire. Definition is thus sensibility-dependent and probabilistic:

nothing says that the intended property or relation will be noted—or brought into comparable resolution—by all addressees.

This perceptual theory of definition has many consequences—including certain of the judgments made in earlier paragraphs of this précis of my conception of psychology. But I have yet to underline one obvious set.

The account stresses the continuity between precise, differentiated, and subtle discriminations upon the human universe within the resources of natural language and *technical* knowledge—even of the most abstruse character. It emphasizes the circumstance that the so-called technical languages—whether of science, the psychological and social studies, or the "hard" humanities—develop as differentiations from natural language, and always continue to depend on their embedding context in natural language for their interpretation and use. Particulate and nice *description* is no lowly or easy task: it is the very basis—indeed, the flesh—of all nonspurious knowledge.

In a strong sense psychology was already "established" before it commenced as a science. Once we appreciate the vast resources of psychological knowledge coded in the natural language and internalized in the sensibilities of those who use it well, it should become a paramount matter of intellectual responsibility for those who explore the human condition to ensure that this knowledge not be degraded, distorted, or obliterated in their technical conceptualizations. Such a responsibility cannot be met by experientially impoverished or functionally illiterate persons. Since the task of the psychological studies is not to *supplant* the cognitive achievements stabilized within the natural language but to refine and extend that knowledge, it is incumbent upon its inquirers that they have *extraordinary* capacities for discriminating upon the inner and outer world, and for the precise and supple mapping of language to their discriminations. And *meaningful* pursuit of the widely varied psychological studies will demand of the inquirers in each area rich and specialized sensibilities relevant to the particular phenomenal domain at issue. This means that the psychological studies require a work force of more heterogeneous background and skill than does any other currently institutionalized branch of inquiry.

The psychological studies, when significantly conceived, will be seen as immensely challenging, immensely difficult, and perhaps in some ranges entirely refractory areas of inquiry. As in other serious and dignified fields of scholarship, knowledge exceeding in precision and differentiation what the human race already knows will be won only by the ardent and creative efforts of relevantly equipped and sensitive persons who proceed with a minimum of public relations fanfare. Psychology has been flagrantly and vulgarly oversold. It will find its dignity only to the extent that it retracts the feckless promises, pseudoconceptualizations, and corrupt technologies it has flung out upon the world, and succeeds in reestablishing authentic continuity with the Western scholarly tradition.

95

Conclusion

And so—ponderous scholar and unrelenting epistemopathectomist though I be—I find I have written a sermon. But a moral analysis of the past, by inviting a change of heart, is a surer bridge to a tolerable future than any confident methodological manifesto. I have been inviting a psychology that might show the imprint of a capacity to accept the inevitable ambiguity and mystery of our situation. The false hubris with which we have contained our existential anguish in a terrifying age has led us to prefer easy yet grandiose pseudoknowledge to the hard and spare fruit that is knowledge. To admit intellectual finitude, and to accept with courage our antinomal condition, is to go a long way toward curing our characteristic epistemopathies. To attain such an attitude is to be free.

REFERENCE NOTES

1. Koch, S. Vagrant confessions of an asystematic psychologist: An intellectual autobiography. Address to the Divisions of Philosophical Psychology and of the History of Psychology at the annual meeting of the American Psychological Association, San Francisco, August 28, 1977.
2. Koch, S. Ameaning in the humanities. Presidential address to the Division of Psychology and the Arts at the annual meeting of the American Psychological Association, Washington, D.C., September 1, 1969.

REFERENCES

Bridgman, P. W. *The way things are.* Cambridge, Mass.: Harvard University Press, 1959.

Frank, P. *Modern science and its philosophy.* Cambridge, Mass.: Harvard University Press, 1950.

Koch, S. Clark L. Hull. Section 1 of *Modern learning theory.* New York: Appleton-Century-Crofts, 1954.

Koch, S. (Ed.). *Psychology: A study of a science* (Vols. 1–6). New York: McGraw-Hill, 1959, 1962, 1963.

Koch, S. Behaviourism. In *Encyclopaedia Britannica* (Vol. 3). Chicago: Encyclopaedia Britannica, 1961. (a)

Koch, S. Psychological science versus the science-humanism antinomy: Intimations of a significant science of man. *American Psychologist,* 1961, *16,* 629–639. (b)

Koch, S. Psychology and emerging conceptions of knowledge as unitary. In T. W. Wann (Ed.), *Behaviorism and phenomenology: Contrasting bases for modern psychology.* Chicago: The University of Chicago Press, 1964.

Koch, S. The allures of ameaning in modern psychology: An inquiry into the rift between psychology and the humanities. In R. Farson (Ed.), *Science and human affairs.* Palo Alto, Calif.: Science & Behavior Books, 1965.

Koch, S. Psychology cannot be a coherent science. *Psychology Today*, March 1969, pp. 14; 64; 66–68. (a)

Koch, S. Value properties: Their significance for psychology, axiology, and science. In M. Grene (Ed.), *The anatomy of knowledge*. London: Routledge & Kegan Paul, 1969. (b)

Koch, S. Reflections on the state of psychology. *Social Research*, 1971, 38, 669–709.

Koch, S. Theory and experiment in psychology. *Social Research*, 1973, 40, 691–707.

Koch, S. Language communities, search cells, and the psychological studies. In W. J. Arnold (Ed.), *Nebraska Symposium on Motivation, 1975* (Vol. 23). Lincoln: University of Nebraska Press, 1976. (a)

Koch, S. More verbal behavior from Dr. Skinner (Review of *About behaviorism* by B. F. Skinner). *Contemporary Psychology*, 1976, 21, 453–457. (b)

Robinson, D. N. *An intellectual history of psychology*. New York: Macmillan, 1976.

Russell, B. *A history of Western philosophy*. New York: Simon & Schuster, 1945.

Weldon, T. D. *Kant's Critique of pure reason*. Oxford: Clarendon Press, 1958.

DOMINANT
TWENTIETH-CENTURY
SYSTEMS OF PSYCHOLOGY

5

*Rediscovering Gestalt Psychology**

MARY HENLE

In 1950 E. G. Boring announced that Gestalt psychology "has already passed its peak and is now dying of its success by being absorbed into what is Psychology" (p. 600). Ever since that time we have been invited to funerals of Gestalt psychology. A few years ago, for example, Postman (1972, p. 6) remarked that Gestalt theory "never gained decisive empirical support and gradually lapsed into virtual oblivion." Many other such statements could be cited. Even Mark Twain would have been dismayed by so many exaggerated reports. One cannot escape the thought that a movement that has required so many funerals must have extraordinary vitality. I believe that we still have important things to learn from Gestalt psychology.

It is well known that Gestalt psychology began around 1910, when Max Wertheimer, with an idea that would not wait, got off a train in Frankfurt and began to work with Wolfgang Köhler and Kurt Koffka, then assistants at the Psychological Institute there. The Gestalt movement was officially launched with the publication of Wertheimer's paper on the perception of motion in 1912. The three founders of Gestalt psychology were most productive scientists and, together with their students, worked vigorously in the new direction for the short time until their work was interrupted by World War I. Wertheimer and Koffka—like so many American

*I am grateful to Professor Edna Heidbreder for her penetrating and most helpful comments on an earlier draft of this paper.

psychologists in 1917—were engaged in war work; and Köhler was isolated on the island of Tenerife, where he had gone in 1913 as Director of the Anthropoid Station, intending to stay for a year. He was unable to return to Germany until 1920.

Since Gestalt psychology is now so widely misunderstood,[1] let me indicate briefly some of its central themes and then consider its relation to certain contemporary trends in psychology.

Gestalt psychology arose as a protest against a scientific world that had no room for problems of meaning and value, thus no room for the most urgent problems of human beings. Much more specifically, in psychology the protest was against the atomistic and mechanistic assumptions prevailing in the discipline. In perception, it was simply assumed that a point-for-point correspondence exists between local stimulation and local sensation; it was held, for example, that stimulation of a single retinal point corresponds to a single sensation. This assumption is what the Gestalt psychologists called the "constancy hypothesis" or "mosaic theory." If perception followed it, we could have no contrast, no size or color or brightness constancy,[2] no perception of motion, no geometrical illusions, and other interesting perceptual phenomena would likewise be inexplicable. Since these phenomena were well known, the mosaic theory was bolstered up by various auxiliary assumptions, hypotheses about processes which were supposed to correct or supplement raw sensory data to give us the phenomena of our perceived world. Köhler, in 1913, wrote a critique of these hypotheses (1913/1971), hypotheses so bizarre, as he remarks, that they would never have occurred to anybody if they had not been considered necessary to support the constancy hypothesis.

The constancy hypothesis could not be attacked directly, since it was supported by these auxiliary assumptions. So Köhler directed his criticism against the latter. These are the assumptions he discussed. (1) It was assumed that sensations occur in two forms—noticed and unnoticed. Thus, where it is possible, by assuming the proper (isolating) attitude, to overcome certain illusions, it was concluded that the required sensations were there all the time but remained unnoticed. (2) Sometimes the judgments we make about sensory data deceive us about them, so that we believe we have experienced sensory contents different from those actually present.

[1] See Henle (1977) for a discussion of some of these misunderstandings.

[2] It is unfortunate that the term *constancy* is used both for the *hypothesis* that was the basis of the traditional psychology of perception and for certain *phenomena* which defy that hypothesis. In the former case, the term refers to the assumption that the result of local stimulation is constant, that all local excitations go their own way, regardless of other excitations. In the latter case, the phenomena refer to the facts that, within wide limits, size, color, brightness, and so on remain phenomenally constant despite differences in distance and illumination and corresponding differences in the retinal image.

In 1913, when Köhler wrote his critique of the constancy hypothesis, no such confusion in terminology existed. Size constancy was called "apparent size," color constancy, "memory color," and so forth. Since these expressions imply theories of the constancies—that they are illusory or merely "apparent," that they are the products of past experience—the old terminology had to be discarded.

(3) But if we search our consciousness for such judgments, we are often unable to find them. Then nothing was easier than to apply the first assumption to judgments as well as to sensations: unnoticed judgments are what deceived us about the sensory data. In the extreme case, where only the "error"—that is, the departure from the mosaic theory—is present in awareness, unnoticed judgments might be assumed to be operating on unnoticed sensations to produce the illusion.

Since the assumed judgments were considered to derive from past experience, it is easy to see why the criticisms of Gestalt psychologists came more and more to be directed against certain kinds of empiristic hypotheses.

Koffka considers the following story to illustrate the relation between the constancy hypothesis and its supporting structure of assumptions:

> A man and his small son are viewing with great interest an acrobat walking on the tight rope and balancing himself with a long pole. The boy suddenly turns to his father and asks: "Father, why doesn't that man fall?" The father replies: "Don't you see that he is holding on to the pole?" The boy accepts the authority of his parent, but after a while he bursts out with a new question: "Father, why doesn't the pole fall?" Whereupon the father replies: "But don't you see that the man holds it!"[3]

Köhler's lengthy analysis of the auxiliary assumptions need be treated only briefly here. He notes the absence of independent criteria to decide when these assumptions are to be invoked: the auxiliary hypotheses are called into service only when observation has violated the mosaic theory, and they are allowed to give only the results demanded by that theory. Köhler points to the danger of applying different standards to cases which do not, and those which do, conform to the constancy hypothesis. If our experience is suspect in the one case, it should be equally so in the other. He gives actual instances in which adherence to the traditional theory retarded scientific progress. "The mere term 'error of judgment' thus sometimes carries more weight than the most careful observations—just the phrase alone!" (Köhler, 1913/1971, p. 28). New facts may actually be discovered and then forgotten because they do not conform to the constancy hypothesis.

One would think that the traditional theory would be put to rest by Köhler's analysis in 1913. It was not. It is sufficient here to refer to Koffka's (1915/1938) reply to Benussi and the production theory, which originated with Meinong (see also Heider, 1970); Köhler's criticism (1925/1938) of G. E. Müller's complex theory, which makes perception a function of an unconscious process of collective attention acting to combine elements into wholes; Köhler's (1928/1938) reply to Rignano, for whom wholes are compounded of independent sensory elements by their emotional significance. Similar theories persist to the present day. As a single example, R. L. Gregory adopts a frankly Helmholtzian theory that "perceptions of objects are given by inference, from data given by the senses and stored in memory" (1973, p. 51).

[3] From *Principles of Gestalt Psychology* by K. Koffka, copyright 1935 by Harcourt Brace Jovanovich, Inc.; renewed 1963 by Elizabeth Koffka. Reprinted by permission of the publisher.

These inferences are held to be unconscious. All these theories, while differing in detail, share the assumption that higher mental processes, unnoticed, work over unorganized sensory data to produce perceptual wholes.

As perceptual theories became more simply empiristic, abandoning unnoticed sensations and errors of judgment and resorting simply to previous experience to explain perceptions which do not show a point-to-point correspondence with proximal stimulation, new arguments were brought forth by the Gestalt psychologists. For example, how is a percept possible the *first time*—before there has been any past experience? Again, once the percept is given, it can arouse any amount of past experience, but an organized perception is needed to arouse the traces of previous experience. A constellation may remind us of a dipper, but it must *look like* a dipper before it can do so, that is, before past experience can be brought to bear on the perception. Gestalt psychologists also showed that we find perceived forms which contradict our past experience: a familiar form may be camouflaged in a totally unfamiliar figure (e.g., Gottschaldt, 1926/1938; Kanizsa, 1968; Wertheimer, 1923/1938).

It is an interesting historical fact that empiristic theories have persisted although nobody has refuted the Gestalt arguments.

To reject empiristic theories is not, of course, to deny a role to past experience in perception and other cognitive processes. On this point Gestalt psychology has been much misunderstood. It rejects as unintelligible theories which look to past experience to create organized perceptions out of unorganized sensory data; but once organization exists, previous learning exerts important influences.

Rejection of the empiristic and other auxiliary hypotheses enabled Gestalt psychologists to reject the constancy hypothesis which depended on them; thus they rejected the fundamental atomistic conception on which the traditional psychology rested. Their task was to build a nonatomistic psychology. For this reason, Gestalt theory is sometimes incorrectly called holistic. It is not. Holism, properly speaking, rejects analysis, while Gestalt psychology only rejects analysis into arbitrary and predetermined elements. It proceeds to the analysis of the phenomenal field in terms of the natural units found there. Through the work of Gestalt psychology, the psychology of perception has become the study of phenomenal objects, no longer the analysis into, and study of, presumably elementary sensations. Starting with the phenomenal object, Gestalt psychologists opened the door to a psychology that could deal with meanings and values—the hallmarks of human experience.

Beyond perception, the pitfalls of the traditional approach repeated themselves in connection with other cognitive processes—that is to say, in what was psychology in the first part of this century. Learning, memory, and thinking were dealt with mainly in the terms of associationism, and thus in terms of indifferent connections between unrelated items. This approach was as atomistic and mechanistic as the then traditional psychology of perception. Wertheimer's and Köhler's early work offered new directions for the psychology of thinking.

103

Wertheimer, as early as 1912, became interested in the number concepts of tribal peoples (1912a). He was impressed by the fact that when these people use numerical operations, they respect the natural relations in the material they deal with, whereas any arbitrary division is permitted by our more abstract number system. For them— as often for us in everyday situations—Gestalt qualities or natural groups may serve the same functions that our numbers do. Whole properties, natural parts, and natural groups already point to an approach which transcends the indifferent items of associationism.

Next Wertheimer examined the syllogism (1920/1938) and found that even this simplest of reasoning tasks sometimes yields new discoveries. But more than this, a transformation of one term—a productive process—is sometimes required before a syllogism can be solved; in such cases, a recentering is required.

Turning his attention to problem solving, Wertheimer (1945/1959) again found centering and recentering to be key concepts for the understanding of productive processes; these are whole properties which do not adhere to any item but which belong to the thinking process as a whole. He emphasized outstanding relations in problem solving, "rho-relations," as he called them, relations which are "sensible with regard to the inner structural nature of the given situation" (1959, p. 41). Other whole properties, such as direction, balance, and symmetry figured in his treatment of problem solving, again a wide departure from the connections of unrelated items in terms of which associationists viewed the thinking process.

Köhler's work on problem solving in chimpanzees (1917/1925) is still very well known and is recognized as setting new directions for the study of thinking in human beings as well as for problems in animal psychology. His tests were directed to a simple question: Under favorable conditions, do nonhuman primates behave with insight? Why should we study "the most clumsy form of learning" asks Köhler, rather than help the animal to "master his problem as fast as possible?" (1925, p. 681). This is the whole thrust of his problem-solving tests, as well as the tests of discrimination and of delayed reaction which he also undertook. In all cases, the situation was set up so that all its relevant aspects were surveyable, enabling the chimpanzee to behave in terms of the objectively given possibilities and obstacles in the situation. Given the opportunity to behave intelligently, to show insight, the animals did so.

The term *insight* has been regarded with suspicion, particularly by American psychologists, who thought of it as referring to something mysterious. Actually, the term means no more than the seeing of a relation experienced as depending upon the nature of the related data (e.g., Köhler, 1959, p. 729).

Since some of the work of Gestalt psychologists on memory is discussed below, we shall consider only one instance here. Associations (as well as S-R connections) have commonly been regarded as formed by the connection of items—just any items, regardless of their nature or their relation to each other. Köhler offers the analogy of a string, by which almost any two objects may be connected, and he refers to such connections as "string connections." Gestalt psychologists treated associations as aftereffects of perceptual organization. Thus it was to be expected that, just as perceptual pairs depend on the properties of the items paired, so the nature of the associated items influences ease of association. Köhler (1941) and Asch, in a long series of experiments (e.g., Asch, 1969) showed that associations are more readily formed between some items than others—just the ones that tend to go together in perception are favored in association. Thus even associations were found to resist interpretation in terms of associationism and were brought under the category of Gestalt.

What concepts can be used to develop a nonatomistic, nonmechanistic psychology? Gestalt psychology showed the significance of context in determining the meaning and function, indeed the very identity of an item. Ternus, for example, showed that whether points retain or lose their identity during stroboscopic movement depends upon the whole in which they appear (1926/1938). Many other experiments and demonstrations (for example, the experiments on camouflage by Gottschaldt and by Kanizsa mentioned above) make the same point.

The importance of beginning analysis from above rather than from below follows from this dependence of parts on their wholes. There are situations, it is true, which consist of mutually independent components, and these may be approached from below: the components may be combined, as in the traditional approach, to arrive at a whole. Köhler offers an example: "Three stones, one in Australia, another in Africa, and a third in the United States, might formally be said to constitute a group, but displacement of one has no effect on the others, nor upon their mutual relation" (1920/1938, p. 26).

But in those situations in which parts owe their nature and functions to the whole in which they exist, where they will be changed if removed from their whole, analysis into components is impossible. Here analysis must proceed from above: in Wertheimer's words, "what happens to a part of the whole is, in clear-cut cases, determined by the laws of the inner structure of its whole" (1924/1944, p. 84). Here analysis must begin with the structure of the whole itself. These cases in which determination occurs from above are psychologically the more interesting ones. They include organized perceptions as contrasted with raw sensory data; here belong sensible learning and thinking, as opposed to rote learning which, in limiting cases, may be treated as "and-sums," as summations rather than as wholes.

Gestalt psychology was faced with the problem of explanation of organized perception, of selective groupings in perception and elsewhere, of reorganization in thinking, and the like. The process of organization is not itself present in awareness; only its products are experienced. The process must, therefore, occur in the psychophysical field, the brain field corresponding to the psychological one. Thus it becomes a matter of physical interactions in the brain, a physical system.

Physical interactions do not occur indiscriminately, but depend on the properties of the interacting events; and distance is also a factor in physical interaction.

105

Correspondingly, grouping in perception depends upon such factors as similarity and proximity. A principle of simplicity is likewise characteristic both of physical systems approaching equilibrium and of perceptual processes. Köhler sums up:

> A theory of perception must be a *field theory*. By this we mean that the neural functions and processes with which the perceptual facts are associated in each case are located in a continuous medium; and that the events in one part of this medium influence the events in other regions in a way that depends directly on the properties of both in their relation to each other (1940, p. 55).

Of course, our access to the brain processes corresponding to phenomenal events is at present limited. It is the hypothesis of Gestalt psychology that psychological events are structurally similar to the corresponding brain events. This is the hypothesis of psychophysical isomorphism. If it is correct, it provides an avenue to cortical events from the much more accessible phenomenal ones. The similarities just pointed out between the behavior of physical systems and phenomenal ones make such a hypothesis plausible, and Köhler has worked out much more specific hypotheses of possible cortical correlates of organized perception (1920/1938). His use of this principle as a heuristic led him first to his work on figural aftereffects (Köhler & Wallach, 1944), then to the demonstration of cortical currents which occur during perception and which he believes are the correlates of organized perceptions (e.g., Köhler & Held, 1949; Köhler, Held, & O'Connell, 1952; Köhler, 1959/1971).

Now let us look at the relations between Gestalt psychology and certain contemporary developments. Today we have contextualists and organization theorists in cognitive psychology, interaction theorists in social psychology. If they mention Gestalt psychology at all, it is usually as an antique precursor, often incorrectly described; but in many cases even such reference is lacking. Let us examine some contemporary instances and consider their relations, if any, to Gestalt psychology. It is impossible, of course, to be comprehensive, since a large part of cognitive psychology is involved. We will have to omit social psychology altogether.

In 1974 James Jenkins announced contextualism. Jenkins had previously been a representative of the associationistic tradition in learning, memory, problem solving, and language—a very productive researcher. But he found that this very research led him away from associationism and the mechanistic and empiristic explanations that went with it. This traditional view, Jenkins wrote, was "*so pervasive in American psychology*" as to be "*almost coextensive with being an experimentalist*" (1974b, p. 786). In place of it, he found himself led to contextualism, to the view that "*what memory is depends on context*" (1974b, p. 786).

Jenkins traces contextualism to William James, C. S. Peirce, and John Dewey. It emphasizes the total meaning or quality of the events that make up experience. The quality of an experience, says Jenkins, "is determined by the interaction that he [the experiencer] has with the physical texture presented" (1974b, p. 788).

Except for this last phrase, contextualism begins to sound like Gestalt psychology. (I take exception to the remark just quoted because Gestalt psychologists are more careful to distinguish between the physical and the phenomenal worlds—a problem I shall return to.) To continue with contextualism, textures consist of strands which lie in a context. The only other concept presented in this introductory statement is fusion, considered below.

The statement that "in general, memory is for systems, not for instances" (Jenkins, 1974b, p. 792) is in the spirit of Gestalt psychology. Again reminiscent of Gestalt theory is the caution that "to study memory without studying perception is to invite disaster" (Jenkins, 1974b, p. 794). Gestalt psychologists, it has been pointed out, see associations as aftereffects of perceptual organization; and, more generally, memory, learning, and thinking are viewed in relation to the subject's phenomenal field. In his conclusion, Jenkins writes:

> Unlike the associationist explanation, the contextualist explanation is put together from the top down, rather than from the bottom up; and it is oriented toward the *event* rather than toward the supposed *machinery* (1974b, pp. 794–795).

Now even the terminology reminds us of Wertheimer's and of Köhler's. Wertheimer's distinction between an approach *from below* and one *from above* has already been discussed. I believe that Jenkins's meaning is similar to Wertheimer's, if not in this introductory article, surely by 1978. He reports experiments which, by means of a series of slides, present events such as taking a walk or making a cup of tea. In connection with them, Jenkins and his colleagues comment:

> We see events as natural wholes that are, so to speak, perceived *through* the slides, rather than built up from the slides. The slides are windows through which the specifications of the event are glimpsed; they are not Tinker Toys that are used to construct some kind of event-like edifice (Jenkins, Wald, & Pittenger, 1978, p. 158).

Of course, Jenkins does not go as far as the Gestalt psychologists have in discussing the part-whole relation implied here.

Jenkins's distinction between the event and the machinery suggests Köhler's distinction between dynamics and machine theory, to which I shall return.

My point is not simply that the contextualists have not done their historical homework well enough, although it is unfortunate that they have done it so selectively. I would like to make it altogether clear that I regard contextualism as a welcome development. It might have gone farther in the direction in which it wanted to go if Gestalt psychology had been taken explicitly into account. Contextualism departs from the thinking of associationism. Fine! But there is still a distance to go, both conceptually and empirically.

On the theoretical side, contextualism is very undeveloped. Event, for example, which is regarded as primary, is undefined. "At the outset," say Jenkins and his coworkers, "we shall use the term only in its intuitive sense. We cannot at this time give a satisfactory definition of what an event is" (1978, p. 130). Beyond this, we are told that events are natural wholes (1978, p. 158), and that they are "usually embedded in other events" (1978, p. 130). As the authors are aware, more theoretical work needs to be done. I hope it is not inappropriate to recommend looking at the theoretical work that *has* been done.

We may first consider the concept of fusion. It cannot replace organization, as the term is used in Gestalt psychology, since organization is selective, and its selectivity follows specific rules. Nothing is said about fusion in these respects. Fusion appears to result in global events (Jenkins, 1974b, p. 793); it is "appealed to in explanation of the paucity of analysis available in aesthetic experience or mystical experience" (1974b, p. 790). But such a concept is insufficient for the mundane structure of our phenomenal world. The organized wholes of Gestalt psychology, in contrast to fused events, are articulated and segregated; and they may be analyzed insofar as the analysis respects their natural parts. We need to ask: What fuses with what? Under what conditions do strands *not* "fuse" into an event? "Contextual glue" (Jenkins, 1974b, p. 792) is too global and too vague a metaphor to help with the conceptual problems. I would invite the contextualists to consider the concept of organization as Gestalt psychologists have used it.

Later, the concept of coherence is added to refer to any set of related stimuli (Jenkins et al., 1978, p. 134), but also to recognize stimuli as belonging to the system (1978, pp. 133–134). Fusion now becomes a special case of coherence, in which the details of an event "are almost completely lost or merged in the quality of overall event" (1978, p. 144). What makes the parts of a system cohere? The authors reject the possibility that "it is the raw physical similarity of the slides in the original set" that is responsible (1978, p. 142). But in some situations the raw (phenomenal) similarity of materials does produce what the authors would most likely call fusion. I am referring to *monotonous* similarity as described by Gestalt psychologists. Two similar items in a field of items of a different kind tend to be grouped together in perception. But if the rest of the field is made similar to the original pair, it loses its distinctiveness and no longer stands out in the larger group (see Köhler, 1940, pp. 136–137). That the same considerations hold for recall was shown by von Restorff (see Köhler, 1938, pp. 256–258). As Köhler summarizes, "Members that do not belong to the monotonous part of a series are far better retained and recalled than those which constitute the semi-uniform part of it" (1938, pp. 257–258). He adds that under conditions of monotonous similarity "traces tend to lose their individual characteristics, if thus a standard condition of homogeneity is approximated" (1938, p. 259). Whether *distinctive* similarity is one

108

factor responsible for "coherence" can only be determined when the concept of coherence has been further explicated.

Although they do not formulate it in terms of organization, Jenkins et al. raise the question, "What possible slides could belong to some event?" (1978, p. 161). They are also interested in the conditions under which fusion will be obtained. No answer is attempted, and it is my impression that no general answer can be given to these questions (apart from the role of monotonous similarity just discussed) until they are removed from the specific experimental paradigms employed and related to such concepts as "requiredness," "following from," and the like. A formal analysis of "coherence" or of "fittingness" seems to be essential. The mere reference to relations (as in the authors' description of coherent stimuli as any set of related stimuli, 1978, p. 134) is insufficient, since various relations clearly differ in their functions in a given context. In this connection, Goldmeier's experimental analysis of similarity is relevant: similarity cannot be defined in terms of the sheer numbers of relations two figures have in common without regard for the phenomenal structure of the whole figures (Goldmeier, 1936/1972). More generally, Köhler's analysis of requiredness (1938), Koffka's discussion of belongingness and fittingness (1935), and Wertheimer's treatment of good continuation (1923/1938) would be of value to the contextualists.

Contextualism is also confusing because it is difficult to know when it refers to physical and when to phenomenal facts. Thus textures are described as physical, but they consist of strands which appear to be phenomenal—a contradiction which makes one wonder whether textures, too, are phenomenal. For example, when a listener hears a sentence, if we are concerned with the qualities of the utterance, the texture "consists of the words and grammatical relations between them in that context" (Jenkins, 1974b, p. 787). Words are presumably phenomenal data; although sound waves exist in the world of the physicist, words do not. It is not clear whether grammatical relations are meant as experienced relations, but it is clear that they are not facts known to physics. Strands make up phrases and are thus presumably phenomenal. I suspect that when the author uses the term "physical," he means the phenomenally present environment, its objects and processes. Or possibly he refers to such data as they exist for the experimenter, while events are reserved for the subject. Or again, in our example "physical" may refer to what the linguist or other expert knows. In any case, this whole matter needs to be cleared up if contextualism is to be comprehensible. I believe the contextualists would find Gestalt psychological discussions of this issue helpful (see Köhler, 1966).

While contextualism has done interesting empirical work, it has still not freed itself sufficiently from the traditional experimental paradigms. An illustration taken from Jenkins's introductory article seems to be typical of work still being done (see Bransford, 1979). Jenkins and his associates, starting with free recall of word lists, "decided to see whether *what the subject was doing* when he heard the words had an effect on the recall phenomena" (Jenkins, 1974b, p. 788). This is an admirable

109

procedure, one that Gestalt psychology has consistently employed. In a first example, two groups of subjects were presented the same list of words under conditions of incidental learning. One group was given an orienting task which required comprehension of the words, while the other group was instructed merely to attend to certain formal properties of the words presented. The former subjects showed much better recall than the latter; they also showed associative clustering, which was largely absent in the group who did not attend to the meanings of the words.

This is a good experiment, but it employs a list of mainly *unrelated* words, that is, a list which is not, as such, comprehensible. Of course, it is not only Jenkins who is partial to such material. Word lists and sentence lists are as frequent in cognitive psychology as they are on the blackboard of an elementary school classroom. Unrelated words do not present the most favorable conditions under which to investigate comprehension.

Further support for contextualism is presented in this introductory article (Jenkins, 1974b). Some of it uses more meaningful material than the example cited. Nevertheless, this research still has something arbitrary about it. I need not discuss it further because today there is a strong tendency to use more meaningful materials. As Craik puts it, "It seems that, belatedly, the field [memory research] is working through its natural history phase" (1979, p. 64). This is all to the good; indeed, one might even recommend more boldness in this respect. And more attention needs to be given to what is meant by a meaningful event.

The further investigations of Jenkins and his colleagues illustrate the latter point. These authors presented sequences of slides which together portrayed such events as a woman making a cup of tea, a teenager answering the telephone, a man taking a walk on campus (Jenkins et al., 1978). All these are meaningful events, but they lack the requiredness, the inner relatedness, the necessary connections of more strongly structured events. There is no particular reason why the stroller, for example, should take one course rather than another on his walk, and the details of the other sequences permit considerable variation. By contrast, no such latitude is permitted in the solution of many problems. The conclusion of a syllogism must follow from the premises by necessity; if an ape is to secure an objective placed out of reach, he has no choice but to find a way of overcoming the distance between himself and the prize with the materials at hand. The paradigms of Wertheimer (1945/1959) and of Katona (1940), of Köhler (1917/1925) and of Duncker (1935/ 1945) might still be useful today in the study of truly meaningful learning.

The difference between the two kinds of meaningful learning may be illustrated by comparing one of Jenkins's experiments with one of Katona's. Both investigators presented numbers to their subjects for later tests of retention. Jenkins used thirty even numbers between 0 and 200; no other principle of selection of the numbers was used. Subjects were tested for recognition. To one group, the numbers were exposed in ordinal sequence, to the other, in random order. The two groups gave about equal recognition of the numbers presented; the group receiving the ordered sequence differed from that given the randomized set largely in a considerable percentage of false positive recognitions of even numbers (Jenkins et al., 1978).

Katona (1940) used three groups of subjects. His number series was constructed according to a principle which subjects in one group were able to discover. For this group, given the principle and the starting point, there was no latitude in choice of numbers; each one had to be what it was. In the other groups, subjects were simply asked to memorize the figures, which were grouped in such a way as to prevent discovery of the principle; for them, the same numbers were entirely arbitrary. For one of these groups, the numbers were presented as the amount of federal expenditures during the previous year. The task was thus meaningful in much the same sense as in the contextualists' experiments. But this group still had to memorize the set, and they showed little difference in recall from the group for whom the numbers were simply given as digits to be learned. The first group, the one that had discovered the principle, not only showed much greater retention than did the subjects who memorized; the members learned without repetition, their errors were different in kind, and they were able to correct or to continue a presented series—achievements impossible for the other groups.

When Jenkins's subjects learned "meaningful" material, they still had to memorize it. With Katona's subjects, the process was one of discovery and reconstruction. If contextualism is indeed interested in the total meaning of the events that make up experience, in structures that go beyond chains (Jenkins, 1974b, p. 786), its task would seem to be to go beyond the study of arbitrarily assembled sequences. Jenkins (1974a, p. 18) states that "we are pressing on in the direction of finding more powerful demonstrations of the effects of *comprehension of meaning* on what one remembers and how it is organized." Why not, then, use truly comprehensible material.[4]

---

[4] While this paper was in press, Jenkins published another article (Jenkins, J. J. Can we have a fruitful cognitive psychology? *Nebraska Symposium on Motivation, 1980*. Lincoln, Nebraska: University of Nebraska Press, 1981) which would alter the above discussion in two respects:

1. In 1974, Jenkins rejected mechanism, along with associationism and elementarism (or "simple units," 1974, p. 786). In 1980, he seems to have returned to mechanism. For example, he quotes Walter Reitman, apparently accepting the position that "In all respects except unlimited time, the human being *is* a universal computing device" (p. 215). Again (p. 217): "One question of appreciable importance is, What determines the kind of machine that a person becomes in a particular environmental context?"

There is even the possibility that elementarism is not quite abandoned in the new article: "If it is *relations* among elements that count rather than just the elements alone, then simple research on simple elements *cannot* tell us what we need to know" (p. 223). What Jenkins probably wants to refer to are relations among parts, not relations among elements; I cannot tell whether the problem is semantic or conceptual.

Any return to machine theory or to elementarism, of course, takes Jenkins farther away from the rediscovery of Gestalt psychology.

2. Further evidence that Jenkins may be moving toward an interest in truly meaningful learning (though within a computational framework) is found in his discussion of P. E. Johnson's studies of

111

Now we come to contemporary organization theory. It is, of course, not possible to cover the field. "The view that cognition can be understood as computation is ubiquitous in modern cognitive theorizing," Pylyshyn recently remarked (1980, p. 111). And Estes found it necessary to ask, "Is human memory obsolete?" (1980, p. 62). (He concluded that it is not because it shows differences in certain of its functional properties from those of the digital computer.)

"A modest revolution is afoot today within the field of human learning," wrote Bower in 1970, "and the rebels are marching under the banner of 'cognitive organization' " (1970, p. 18). Three years later, Tulving and Thomson spoke of "the current transition from traditional associationism to information processing and organizational points of view about human memory" (1973, p. 352). The vocabulary of human learning and memory today is that of computers: input, output, encoding, chunking, retrieval, storage—to mention only a few of the terms we have almost forgotten are metaphors, and the debt of this movement to computer technology is clearly recognized.[5] Chomsky and Piaget are also recognized as ancestors. Gestalt psychology is scarcely mentioned in connection with this new development. Postman (1972) does mention Gestalt psychology, setting forth in sequence what he considers to be the major points in its argument and in that of current organization theory. These are hard to tell apart, except that Postman incorrectly attributes to innate dispositions the main work of organization in Gestalt psychology. Nevertheless, Postman states that the conceptual framework and some of the underlying assumptions of the two kinds of theory are clearly different (1972, p. 5). Bower is another organization theorist who does not ignore Gestalt psychology but who makes modest use of its principles of grouping in designing his experiments (e.g., Bower, 1972; Anderson & Bower, 1974). Others mention Gestalt writers in order to refute a version of their theory that Gestalt psychologists themselves would reject.

I find myself in agreement with Postman about the theoretical differences between Gestalt psychology and contemporary organization theory. Since some of the problems and some of the findings of the two kinds of psychology converge, and since some of the concepts, if abstracted from their theoretical framework, look similar, it is important to be clear both about similarities and differences between

---

expertise in pediatric cardiology. It is pointed out that the experts "tend to look at the entire pattern of symptoms" (p. 235). The nature of this pattern is not, however, described; thus the extent to which it is intrinsically meaningful cannot be determined.

It is interesting to note that Katona's name has found its way into Jenkins's bibliography of 1980; and the term *Gestalt* is used (p. 233)—though not in a way in which I would use it.

If this discussion were not relegated to a footnote, other aspects of Jenkins's paper would merit inclusion. Notable among these are the meaning and provenance of the concept *belongingness*.

[5] It is interesting to note that even Jenkins, who has relinquished mechanism, uses such terms as "coded" and "stored," asks "what kind of device scans the stored representations," and believes that "the human being is a marvelous device, shaped by millions of years of evolution and millions of experiences to pick up the qualities of events" (Jenkins et al., 1978, p. 160).

the two approaches. And this, I repeat, is not merely for historical reasons but also because of the possible theoretical gains such an analysis would entail.

Let me now indicate some instances in which Gestalt psychologists have investigated problems or have introduced concepts which are now being newly discovered. I do not know at what date contemporary organization theory begins: perhaps with George Miller's paper of 1956 on "The Magical Number Seven . . . ,"[6] perhaps with Miller, Galanter, and Pribram's *Plans and the Structure of Behavior* of 1960. In any case, it experienced rapid growth after Tulving, in 1962, introduced a measure of subjective organization. Subjective organization is, of course, not new to Gestalt psychology. Köhler and Koffka repeatedly pointed out that where material lacks autochthonous organization, as in the case of lists of unrelated words or syllables, subjects impose organization upon it. "Intentional learning essentially means intentional organizing," Köhler wrote in 1929 (p. 285; see also 1947, p. 263). Both in perception and in recall, organization may be influenced by subjective factors. Under a search attitude, for example, subjects may discover groupings that would not spontaneously appear, or they may recall material that would not spontaneously come to mind (see Köhler, 1940, pp. 138–139; also Koffka, 1935, e.g., on the role of the ego in attention, on the relation of the ego to trace systems, etc.).

Organization theorists do not limit themselves to subjective organization, although Postman, for one, sees highly structured material as of limited value for the study of organizational processes in memory (1972, p. 43). Gestalt psychologists have placed major emphasis, not on subjective, but on autochthonous organization (as it exists, of course, in the individual's phenomenal field).

Tulving and Thomson, in 1973, considered "one of the clearest signs of change" as having "to do with the experimental and theoretical separation between storage and retrieval processes" (1973, p. 352), that is, between retention, on the one hand, and recall and recognition, on the other. Is this distinction so recent? Mandler reminds us that James "informed us about the distinction between retention (storage) and recollection (retrieval) long before anyone dreamed of the computer metaphor" (1979, p. 744). The distinction persisted in classical experimental psychology, and the Gestalt psychologists, too, have relied on it. Discussing forgetting in 1935, Koffka suggests three possible reasons for failure of communication be-

---

[6] Some of these problems and concepts have been anticipated, not only by Gestalt psychology, but by pre-Gestalt experimental psychology. Woodworth (1938, p. 7) notes, for example, that a method for determining immediate memory span has been in use since 1887. As to the span of apprehension, he refers to Sir William Hamilton's crude experiments in 1859 and to the better controlled experiments of W. S. Jevons in 1871; he reports the results of these early experiments and those of later experimental psychologists, which could be summarized as not far from 7 plus or minus 2 (see Woodworth, 1938, pp. 684–692); the idea of grouping as a means of increasing the span is likewise traced to Hamilton.

I do not review this literature here because I am specifically concerned with the relation of current organization theory to Gestalt psychology.

113

tween a present process and a trace or trace system: (1) "disappearance of a trace"; (2) "unavailability of the trace"; and (3) "failure of the process to communicate with an otherwise available trace" (1935, pp. 523–528). The first of these processes concerns a failure of retention; the other two are disturbances of recall or recognition. Ilse Müller, a student of Köhler's, in 1937 began to investigate the question of whether retroactive inhibition affects the products of previous learning—that is, retention—or whether it might also affect the process of recall. Köhler, a few years later, reported an extension of these experiments (1940, pp. 146–149). Thus, if one reads the work of the Gestalt psychologists—as well as much classical experimental psychology—one sees that it is not correct to say that, until recently, the distinction between retention and recall "shaped neither experiment nor theory" (Tulving & Thomson, 1973, p. 352).

Tulving and Thomson, surveying the field in 1973, found no satisfactory theories of retrieval and proposed what they called the encoding specificity principle: "What is stored is determined by what is perceived and how it is encoded, and what is stored determines what retrieval cues are effective in providing access to what is stored" (1973, p. 353). I would translate: The nature of the trace depends on the perceptual-cognitive organization of the given data; and the nature of the trace determines what present process will elicit it. Gestalt psychologists, reviving an argument of Höffding's of 1887, suggest that a present process must establish a functional connection with the corresponding memory trace to produce recall (see Köhler, 1940, pp. 126–130). It is the similarity between process and trace which is responsible for this connection, and thus for the selection of a particular trace among the countless others somehow present in the nervous system of the individual. The Höffding principle sounds a good deal like encoding specificity, although it is more precise.

Another variable to come into prominence recently in the study of recall is distinctiveness. Since I do not want to go into detail, I quote from Craik's recent review: "Many investigators are converging on the view that the detrimental effects on recall caused by prior items (proactive inhibition) are attributable to a loss of distinctiveness or discriminability in the current items" (1979, p. 76). Von Restorff's experiments have already been mentioned. In 1933 she showed that a distinctive item in an otherwise homogeneous series is much better recalled than the other items of the series, and Ilse Müller (1937) found that the inhibitions within such a monotonous series are not to be distinguished from proactive and retroactive inhibition. In 1935 Köhler and von Restorff extended the investigation to spontaneous recall. Here, as Köhler expresses it (1940, p. 137), "It is not so much similarity as such, as it is *distinctive* similarity, which must be the factor that favors 'the step backward' in recognition and in recall"—that is, the factor that favors the Höffding function.

I could continue my list. Redintegration, for example, an old associationistic conception which refers to the revival of a whole by one of its constituents, has been dusted off and found (by an organization theorist) to obey Gestalt principles! (see Craik, 1979, p. 85). As a final example, it has been newly discovered that comprehension increases retention, a major finding of the extended investigation, cited above, by Katona (1940).

I have somewhere read the opinion that it is more efficient to repeat old experiments than to search the literature to make sure that one has not been anticipated. If this is indeed the case, I am not sure that efficiency is the issue. It is very strange that so much good research has been lost and has to be repeated. Forty years is not long in the history even of a science as young as psychology. More important than loss of the research is the loss of its conceptual basis. Still, I will not complain. If many current findings could have been predicted by Gestalt theory or anticipated by Gestalt psychologists, much valuable research is now being done. In this respect, present-day contextualists and organization theorists are supplying the manpower that Gestalt psychology—for historical and other reasons—has always lacked.

I would like to return to matters of theory. Earlier I expressed agreement with Postman about the differences in conceptual framework and basic assumptions between Gestalt theory and current organization theory, despite some apparent similarities. What is the major difference? It is the one that Gestalt psychologists express as the contrast between a dynamic view and a machine theory.

When natural forces are left to themselves, the result is often a remarkably orderly situation. The heavenly bodies, for example, maintain their regular orbits as a result of free dynamics alone, in this case, as a result of gravitational forces. The interactions that are responsible for the outcome depend on the characteristics of the interacting facts in relation to each other. On the other hand, many systems contain fixed arrangements or constraints, which achieve order by limiting the free play of dynamics. As a very simple example, the chair on which one sits serves as a constraint which keeps the body from moving in the direction of the gravitational forces acting on it. In machines, constraints are introduced to eliminate certain directions of action; in the extreme case, only one form of action remains possible. The constraints in the system are not themselves responsible for action, only for eliminating various dynamic components. Here, order depends on the constraints, not on the characteristics of the interacting data in relation to each other. In the one case, to quote Köhler, "the basic forces and processes of nature [are] free to follow their inherent, dynamic, causally determined directions," while in the other case, "the same forces and processes [are] almost or entirely compelled to take courses prescribed by constraints" (1969, p. 81).

In our thinking about the organism and its functioning, both free dynamics and machines have been used as models. There are, of course, many constraints in the human body, but certain orderly outcomes apparently do not depend upon anatomical arrangements. To use one of Köhler's examples, the delivery by the blood of specific substances to various tissues is not accomplished by special conductors for each substance; it depends, rather, on the relation between these substances and the existing state of the tissues (see Köhler, 1929/1947, p. 125). When we come to the nervous system, there are again many constraints—nerve fibers and other structures. But it has been the contention of Gestalt psychologists that within the limits imposed by such constraints, the order of processes in this system is a matter of free dynamics. Many psychological facts, in perception and elsewhere, suggest interactions in the corresponding brain fields, interactions independent of particular pathways which must, therefore, depend on free dynamics.

By contrast, current organization theory, with its computer model and its interest in computer simulation, is necessarily machine theory. Outcomes are determined by the constraints built into the system.

Collins and Quillian, lightheartedly describing the limitations of computers, remark:

> When computers first set out to humble man, they thought it would be good fun to read, and talk, and answer questions. Well, by now they have gotten over their cockiness about reading and the like. . . . Their failure was not for any lack of cleverness though. Their basic mistake probably was in thinking they could skip over evolution, that their adeptness at artificial intelligence would let them fake their way past us in natural intelligence. Now, with humility written all over their inscrutable faces, computers are trying to revive their egos by imitating man (1972, p. 310).

I think these authors are mistaken. Computers do not need evolution. They are amply provided with constraints, which is what evolution contributes to their human friends. Computers require no heredity because they have been given the necessary anatomy by human beings. If they cannot fake their way past us in natural intelligence, I would suggest that it is because these very constraints prevent the free play of dynamics which is so largely responsible for the remarkable achievements of perception and thinking.

For the present, the computer model has enabled cognitive psychologists to a large extent to overcome the atomism of associationism. They tend no longer to think in terms of bits of information, but rather in terms of chunks, propositions, and other larger units. This is a major advance. But now a very interesting development seems to be in process: a change in the relation between current organization theory and associationism.

In 1970 Tulving and Madigan left open the question of this relation (1970, p. 445). This issue has been much discussed in the past decade. Bower, in 1972 (p. 109), suggested that "there is not much substantive conflict between S-R associative versus organizational accounts of free recall." Anderson and Bower, at the same time that they introduce their computer model of human associative memory, see promise in neo-associational models (1974, p. 135). Postman, surveying the field in 1972, finds "no necessary disagreement between exponents of organization and of association about what is learned" (1972, p. 41). He suggests that the difference is largely linguistic, and he offers samples of translation from the one language to the other. A few years later he repeats: "There is no longer a sharp confrontation between the organizational and associationistic points of view" (Postman, 1975, p. 323). Thus Postman makes it a matter of preference whether one speaks of associative chains and networks, on the one hand, or higher-order units and chunks, on the other.[7]

To the outsider, this equation has a certain appropriateness. For associationism, like current organization theory, is machine theory. A particular outcome depends upon the greater strength of one rather than another associative chain or network. Inter-item associations are seen as arbitrary connections between items, not products of interactions which depend on the nature of the interacting partners in relation to each other.

In 1970, Tulving and Madigan, reviewing the fields of memory and verbal learning, deplored the fact that

> At the time when man has walked on the moon, is busily transplanting vital organs from one living body into another, and has acquired the power to blow himself off the face of the earth by the push of a button, he still thinks about his own memory processes in terms readily translatable into ancient Greek (1970, p. 437).

These authors have in mind the dominance of associationism, but the same observation is relevant to machine theory in general. Aristotle, it will be recalled, invoked crystal spheres to keep the stars in their orbits. Not trusting the dynamics of nature, he invented constraints to ensure the order of the heavenly bodies.

But while mechanistic assumptions are common to current organization theory and associationism, the latter theory is inherently atomistic; the former, so far as I can see, is not, or need not be. It seems to me that atomism should be an issue for those who seek a rapprochement between the two kinds of approaches.

I said in the beginning of this paper that today we can still learn from Gestalt psychology. The current trends I have been discussing represent advances over the old associationism. Postman, who seems not to see much difference between current organization theory and associationism, adds that "organization theorists have asked many important and imaginative questions about the conditions of learning and recall that association theorists had not asked" (1972, p. 41). The present emphasis on context, on thinking in terms of higher-order units, the new emphasis on meaning and comprehension—all these are important advances. Such advances should enable us to go one step farther, to discard machine theory, and to look instead to the dynamics of cognitive processes.

[7] If there is indeed a rapprochement between current organization theory and associationism, the oldest theory of them all, one wonders what has become of the modest revolution of 1970.

117

REFERENCES

Anderson, J. R., & Bower, G. H. *Human associative memory*. Washington, D.C.: Hemisphere, 1974.

Asch, S. E. A reformulation of the problem of associations. *American Psychologist*, 1969, 24, 92–102.

Boring, E. G. *A history of experimental psychology* (2nd ed.). New York: Appleton-Century-Crofts, 1950.

Bower, G. H. Organizational factors in memory. *Cognitive Psychology*, 1970, 1, 18–46.

Bower, G. H. A selective review of organizational factors in memory. In E. Tulving & W. Donaldson (Eds.), *Organization of memory*. New York: Academic Press, 1972.

Bransford, J. D. *Human cognition. Learning, understanding and remembering*. Belmont, Calif.: Wadsworth, 1979.

Collins, A. M., & Quillian, M. R. How to make a language user. In E. Tulving & W. Donaldson (Eds.), *Organization of memory*. New York: Academic Press, 1972.

Craik, F. I. M. Human memory. *Annual Review of Psychology*, 1979, 30, 63–102.

Duncker, K. [On problem-solving] (L. S. Lees, Trans.). *Psychological Monographs*, 1945, 58 (5, Whole No. 270). (Originally published, 1935.)

Estes, W. K. Is human memory obsolete? *American Scientist*, 1980, 68, 62–69.

Goldmeier, E. Similarity in visually perceived forms. *Psychological Issues*, 1972, 8, Monograph 29. (Originally published in part, 1936.)

Gottschaldt, K. [Gestalt factors and repetition.] In W. D. Ellis (Ed. and Trans.), *A source book of Gestalt psychology*. London: Routledge & Kegan Paul, 1938. (Reprinted from *Psychologische Forschung*, 1926, 8.)

Gregory, R. L. The confounded eye. In R. L. Gregory & E. H. Gombrich (Eds.), *Illusion in nature and art*. London: Duckworth, 1973.

Heider, F. Gestalt theory: Early history and reminiscences. *Journal of the History of the Behavioral Sciences*, 1970, 6, 131–139.

Henle, M. The influence of Gestalt psychology in America. *Annals of the New York Academy of Sciences*, 1977, 291, 3–12.

Jenkins, J. J. Can we have a theory of meaningful memory? In R. L. Solso (Ed.), *Theories in cognitive psychology: The Loyola symposium*. Potomac, Maryland: Erlbaum, 1974. (a)

Jenkins, J. J. Remember that old theory of memory? Well, forget it! *American Psychologist*, 1974, 29, 785–795. (b)

Jenkins, J. J., Wald, J., & Pittenger, J. B. Apprehending pictorial events: An instance of psychological cohesion. In C. W. Savage (Ed.), Perception and cognition. Issues in the foundations of psychology. *Minnesota Studies in the Philosophy of Science*, 1978, 9, 129–163.

Kanizsa, G. Percezione attuale, esperienza passata e l' "esperimento impossibile." In G. Kanizsa & G. Vicario (Eds.), *Ricerche sperimentali sulla percezione*. Trieste: Università degli Studi di Trieste, 1968.

Katona, G. *Organizing and memorizing*. New York: Columbia University Press, 1940.

Koffka, K. [Reply to V. Benussi.] In W. D. Ellis (Ed. and Trans.), *A source book of Gestalt psychology*. London: Routledge & Kegan Paul, 1938. (Reprinted from *Zeitschrift für Psychologie*, 1915, 73.)

Koffka, K. *Principles of Gestalt psychology*. New York: Harcourt, Brace, 1935.

Köhler, W. [On unnoticed sensations and errors of judgment.] In M. Henle (Ed.), *The selected papers of Wolfgang Köhler*. New York: Liveright, 1971. (Reprinted from *Zeitschrift für Psychologie*, 1913, 66.)

Köhler, W. [*The mentality of apes.*] (E. Winter, Trans.). New York: Harcourt, Brace, 1925. (Originally published, 1917.)

Köhler, W. *Die physischen Gestalten in Ruhe und im stationären Zustand*. Braunschweig: Vieweg, 1920.

Köhler, W. [*Physical Gestalten.*] In W. D. Ellis (Ed. and Trans.), *A source book of Gestalt psychology*.

London: Routledge & Kegan Paul, 1938. (Abridged translation of *Die physischen Gestalten in Ruhe und im stationären Zustand.* Braunschweig: Vieweg, 1920.)

Köhler, W. Intelligence of apes. *Pedagogical Seminary and Journal of Genetic Psychology*, 1925, 32, 674–690.

Köhler, W. [Reply to G. E. Müller.] In W. D. Ellis (Ed. and Trans.), *A source book of Gestalt psychology.* London: Routledge & Kegan Paul, 1938. (Reprinted from *Psychologische Forschung*, 1925, 6.)

Köhler, W. [Reply to Eugenio Rignano.] In W. D. Ellis (Ed. and Trans.), *A source book of Gestalt psychology.* London: Routledge & Kegan Paul, 1938. (Reprinted from *Psychologische Forschung*, 1928, 11.)

Köhler, W. *Gestalt psychology* (rev. ed.). New York: Liveright, 1947. (Originally published, 1929.)

Köhler, W. *The place of value in a world of facts.* New York: Liveright, 1938.

Köhler, W. *Dynamics in psychology.* New York: Liveright, 1940.

Köhler, W. On the nature of associations. *Proceedings of the American Philosophical Society*, 1941, 84, 489–502.

Köhler, W. [Psychology and natural science.] In M. Henle (Ed.), *The selected papers of Wolfgang Köhler.* New York: Liveright, 1971. (Reprinted from *Proceedings of the 15th International Congress of Psychology, Brussels*, 1957 [1959].)

Köhler, W. Gestalt psychology today. *American Psychologist*, 1959, 14, 727–734.

Köhler, W. A task for philosophers. In P. K. Feyerabend & G. Maxwell (Eds.), *Mind, matter, and method: Essays in philosophy and science in honor of Herbert Feigl.* Minneapolis: University of Minnesota Press, 1966.

Köhler, W. *The task of Gestalt psychology.* Princeton, N.J.: Princeton University Press, 1969.

Köhler, W., & Held, R. The cortical correlate of pattern vision. *Science*, 1949, 110, 414–419.

Köhler, W., Held, R., & O'Connell, D. N. An investigation of cortical currents. *Proceedings of the American Philosophical Society*, 1952, 96, 290–330.

Köhler, W., & Wallach, H. Figural after-effects: An investigation of visual processes. *Proceedings of the American Philosophical Society*, 1944, 88, 269–357.

Mandler, G. Retrospective review: *The principles of psychology* by William James. *Contemporary Psychology*, 1979, 24, 742–744.

Miller, G. A. The magical number seven, plus or minus two: Some limits on our capacity for processing information. *Psychological Review*, 1956, 63, 81–96.

Miller, G. A., Galanter, E., & Pribram, K. H. *Plans and the structure of behavior.* New York: Holt, 1960.

Müller, I. Zur Analyse der Retentionstörung durch Häufung. *Psychologische Forschung*, 1937, 22, 180–210.

Postman, L. A pragmatic view of organization theory. In E. Tulving & W. Donaldson (Eds.), *Organization of memory.* New York: Academic Press, 1972.

Postman, L. Verbal learning and memory. *Annual Review of Psychology*, 1975, 26, 291–335.

Pylyshyn, Z. W. Computation and cognition: Issues in the foundation of cognitive science. *The Behavioral and Brain Sciences*, 1980, 3, 111–132.

Ternus, J. [The problem of phenomenal identity.] In W. D. Ellis (Ed. and Trans.), *A source book of Gestalt psychology.* London: Routledge & Kegan Paul, 1938. (Reprinted from *Psychologische Forschung*, 1926, 7.)

Tulving, E. Subjective organization in free recall of "unrelated" words. *Psychological Review*, 1962, 69, 344–354.

Tulving, E., & Madigan, S. A. Memory and verbal learning. *Annual Review of Psychology*, 1970, 21, 437–484.

Tulving, E., & Thomson, D. M. Encoding specificity and retrieval processes in episodic memory. *Psychological Review*, 1973, 80, 352–373.

Wertheimer, M. Über das Denken der Naturvölker: I. Zahlen und Zahlgebilde. *Zeitschrift für*

Psychologie, 1912, *60*, 321–378. (a) [Abridged translation in W. D. Ellis (Ed. and Trans.), *A source book of Gestalt psychology*. London: Routledge & Kegan Paul, 1938.]

Wertheimer, M. Experimentelle Studien über das Sehen von Bewegung. *Zeitschrift für Psychologie*, 1912, *61*, 161–265. (b)

Wertheimer, M. *Über Schlussprozesse im produktiven Denken*. Berlin: De Gruyter, 1920. [Abridged translation in W. D. Ellis (Ed.), *A source book of Gestalt psychology*. London: Routledge & Kegan Paul, 1938.]

Wertheimer, M. [Laws of organization in perceptual forms.] In W. D. Ellis (Ed. and Trans.), *A source book of Gestalt psychology*. London: Routledge & Kegan Paul, 1938. (Reprinted from *Psychologische Forschung*, 1923, *4*.)

Wertheimer, M. [Gestalt theory.] (N. Nairn-Allison, Trans.). *Social Research*, 1944, *11*, 81–99. (An address before the Kantgesellschaft, Berlin, December 17, 1924.)

Wertheimer, M. *Productive thinking* (enl. ed.). New York: Harper, 1959. (Originally published, 1945.)

Woodworth, R. S. *Experimental psychology*. New York: Holt, 1938.

SUPPLEMENTARY READINGS

Arnheim, R. *Art and visual perception* (the new version). Berkeley and Los Angeles: University of California Press, 1974. (Originally published, 1954.)

Asch, S. E. *Social psychology*. New York: Prentice-Hall, 1952.

Duncker, K. [On problem-solving.] (L. S. Lees, Trans.). *Psychological Monographs*, 1945, *58* (5, Whole No. 270). (Originally published, 1935.)

Ellis, W. D. (Ed. and Trans.). *A source book of Gestalt psychology*. London: Routledge & Kegan Paul, 1938.

Flores d'Arcais, G. B. (Ed.). *Studies in perception. Festschrift for Fabio Metelli*. Milan and Florence: Aldo Martello-Giunti, 1975.

Henle, M. (Ed.). *Documents of Gestalt psychology*. Berkeley and Los Angeles: University of California Press, 1961.

Johansson, G. *Configurations in event perception*. Uppsala: Almquist & Wiksell, 1950.

Kanizsa, G., & Vicario, G. (Eds.). *Ricerche sperimentali sulla percezione*. Trieste: Università degli Studi di Trieste, 1968.

Katona, G. *Organizing and memorizing*. New York: Columbia University Press, 1940.

Koffka, K. [*The growth of the mind.*] (2nd ed.) (R. M. Ogden, Trans.). New York: Harcourt, Brace, 1928. (Originally published, 1921.)

Koffka, K. *Principles of Gestalt psychology*. New York: Harcourt, Brace, 1935.

Köhler, W. [*The mentality of apes.*] (E. Winter, Trans.). New York: Harcourt, Brace, 1925. (Originally published, 1917.)

Köhler, W. *Die physischen Gestalten in Ruhe und im stationären Zustand*. Braunschweig: Vieweg, 1920. [Abridged translation in W. D. Ellis (Ed. and Trans.), *A source book of Gestalt psychology*. London: Routledge & Kegan Paul, 1938.]

Köhler, W. *Gestalt psychology* (rev. ed.). New York: Liveright, 1947. (Originally published, 1929.)

Köhler, W. *The place of value in a world of facts*. New York: Liveright, 1938.

Köhler, W. *Dynamics in psychology*. New York: Liveright, 1940.

Köhler, W. *The task of Gestalt psychology*. Princeton, N.J.: Princeton University Press, 1969.

Köhler, W. *Selected papers* (M. Henle, Ed.). New York: Liveright, 1971.

Metzger, W. *Gesetze des Sehens* (3. Aufl.). Frankfurt am Main: Verlag Waldemar Kramer, 1975. (Originally published, 1936.)

Michotte, A. *The perception of causality* (T. R. Miles, Trans.). London: Methuen, 1963. (Originally published, 1946.)

Wertheimer, M. *Drei Abhandlungen zur Gestalttheorie*. Erlangen: Philosophische Akademie, 1925. (Originally published, 1912–1920.)

Wertheimer, M. *Productive thinking* (enl. ed.). New York: Harper, 1959. (Originally published, 1945.)

6

Behaviorism and Psychology
AN UNEASY ALLIANCE

HOWARD H. KENDLER

My aim is to describe behaviorism, not to praise it. Three points of view will prove helpful in accomplishing this task. One, behaviorism must be recognized as a historical movement that has matured over the years. As in any intellectual movement, internal controversy occurred, and so the historian must distinguish between core beliefs adopted by all behaviorists and assumptions accepted only by some behaviorists. In identifying these core beliefs it will not prove helpful to consider as sacrosanct the pronouncements of some self-crowned supreme behaviorist or presumed peerless historian. Two, to evaluate behaviorism as a systematic psychological approach requires a conception of psychology: what it is and what it seeks to accomplish. It is my thesis, a position that most nonbehaviorists will enthusiastically endorse, that more is expected of psychology than behaviorism can offer. The state of affairs may reflect a limitation in behaviorism or unrealistic expectations about psychology. Three, the evaluation of behaviorism's contribution should be assessed on a relativistic basis, not an absolute one. To anticipate the future of psychology, one must judge the successes and failures of behaviorism in comparison to other systematic positions.

What Is Behaviorism?

John B. Watson was the founder of behaviorism partly because he had the necessary qualities for a successful revolutionary: original thinker, articulate spokesman, lucid writer, and energetic polemicist. In psychology, these revolutionary talents are usually associated with a tendency toward oversimplification, a tendency that Watson increasingly exhibited as his career developed and changed directions from a methodologist and theorist to an advertising executive. His polemical zeal frequently corrupted his scholarly efforts. As Skinner (1959) noted, "Polemics led [Watson] into extreme positions from which he never escaped," an observation that Skinner, himself, might have heeded.

It therefore follows that a full understanding of behaviorism cannot be gleaned from the efforts of Watson alone. We must study both important ideas that led to behaviorism and the refinements to that systematic position suggested by Watson's successors. Initially, I would like to discuss three ideas that anticipated Watsonian behaviorism and became core assumptions in behaviorism even though Watson did not fully appreciate their independent status.

Historical Background

The first notion was that the methods of the natural sciences—physics, chemistry, biology—can and should be applied to human events. The behavioristic revolution was encouraged by the promise that if natural science methods would be applied to human and animal behavior, progress in our understanding would be inevitable.

The second important idea was that the dependent variable in psychology should be behavior. The Russian physiologist, Ivan Sechenov, implied this position in 1863:

> A child laughing at the sight of a toy, a young girl trembling at the first thought of love . . . Newton discovering and writing down the laws of the universe—everywhere the final act is muscular movement (Sechenov, 1863/1965).

The third influential notion, perhaps more an attitude than a cohesive position, was that in some very fundamental way phenomenology—the observation and description of mental phenomena—and the scientific method were incompatible. Pavlov (1927) expressed this attitude when he commented that "it is still open to discussion whether psychology," which to Pavlov was the study of the mind "is a natural science, or whether it can be regarded as a science at all." This suspicion of an incompatibility between phenomenology and the methods of natural science was previously expressed by several eighteenth and nineteenth century philosophers (e.g., La Mettrie, Comte) without the benefit of our current knowledge of natural science methodology and systematic efforts to study consciousness.

One might suggest that the application of the scientific method to psychology, the selection of behavior as the dependent variable, and the incompatibility between the study of consciousness and the scientific method are all expressions of the same fundamental notion that psychology should be objective, but historical analysis suggests that these three ideas have independent status.

Structuralism also conceived itself as an extension of the natural science methodology to psychology; Titchener argued that "we must know what the established sciences have in common, and must carry over our conception to the domain of the mind" (Titchener, 1929, p. 27). The fact that structuralists, while perceiving themselves as operating in the traditions of natural sciences, selected consciousness as their subject matter, underlines the point that the decision to employ the scientific method in psychology does not necessarily lead to defining its domain as the study of behavior. Nor does it follow that the selection of behavior as a dependent variable carries with it a methodological rejection of the direct examination of conscious experience. Functionalism sought to investigate behavior and consciousness simultaneously, even in animal psychology, as evidenced by the title of the prebehaviorist John Watson's doctoral thesis, *Animal Education: The Psychical Development of the White Rat*. Finally, many past and current psychologists believe that natural science methodology can combine the study of behavior with the direct examination of mental events without creating any special difficulties.

These three methodological components of behaviorism—natural science methodology, behavior as a dependent variable, and methodological aversion to mental events—require further elucidation, but before doing this, the question of whether other defining characteristics should be added to our conception of behaviorism must be answered. In answering, one must avoid the impression, currently popular, that Watson founded behaviorism and Skinner developed it. Either a gap is assumed to have occurred between the two or the romantic belief is held that Watson actually crowned Skinner as his successor.

An understanding of behaviorism demands an appreciation of the contributions of Edward Tolman's cognitive behaviorism and the neobehaviorism of Clark Hull, Kenneth Spence, and Neal Miller. It is an historical mistake to equate contemporary behaviorism with the methodological position and empirical program of Skinner and his followers. This admonition is not offered to minimize, in any way, the *enormous* contributions of radical behaviorism. Instead, it underlines the important point that Skinner's atheoretical position and views about social engineering are not core assumptions within behaviorism.

Classical Behaviorism

In our attempt to complete an identification of the core beliefs of behaviorism it will prove useful to discuss classical behaviorism during the interval between 1912 and

123

1930. Koch (1964) has suggested that classical behaviorism contains five major orienting attitudes: (1) objectivism, (2) stimulus-response orientation, (3) peripheralism, (4) emphasis on associationistic learning, and (5) environmentalism. If we assume that these five orienting attitudes represent the core of behaviorism at its birth, what remains in its seventh decade of life? Obviously only one: objectivism. Tolman, one of the more sophisticated behaviorists, rejected a stimulus-response model and language, emphasized central processes, and postulated, as did Hull, hereditary factors in his analysis of behavior. Hull, in his analysis of behavior, did not limit himself to associationist processes as his treatment of motivation reveals. Without pursuing this historical analysis further, my conclusion should be clear: behaviorism is not a substantive theory but, rather, a methodological orientation for psychology. The core assumption shared by all behaviorists is a methodological commitment to what early behaviorists described as objective psychology and to what a more sophisticated analysis would reveal to be a set of independent assumptions, some of which have already been mentioned: natural science methodology, behavior as a dependent variable, and the methodological aversion to the direct examination of consciousness.

I do not, however, wish to leave you with the impression that my conclusion that behaviorism is a methodological orientation and not a substantive theory represents an admission that the orienting attitudes of classical behaviorism were either unjustified or inappropriate. Historical forces encouraged them, and their impact on the development of psychology was beneficial in some, if not all, ways.

The stimulus-response orientation has been the source of much controversy, partly because it has been interpreted in a variety of ways (Kendler, 1965). I would suggest that the most appropriate designation is that of a technical language which represents psychological phenomena in terms of three important sets of variables: stimuli, responses, and the association—the hyphen—between them. Probably the greatest impact of S-R language was to force psychologists to think in terms of manipulable environmental variables and measures of objective behavior and thereby to encourage empirical solutions to psychological questions. Two limitations of S-R language should be noted. It was assumed by some and hoped by others that empirical laws between physically defined stimulus variables and behavior could easily and reliably be ascertained. It became apparent that some transformation of the physical stimulus was required for a variety of reasons, not the least of which was the potent influence of the operating characteristics of receptor processes. Second, concepts in addition to stimuli, responses, and associations were required to interpret many forms of behavior. Several theoretically oriented behaviorists recognized this problem, although admittedly they failed to appreciate its complexity.

The peripheralistic bias of early behaviorists resulted from the contamination of theoretical assumptions by methodological principles. In their desire to avoid hiding theoretical processes from public scrutiny, behaviorists committed the error of equating peripheral response measures with central processes. Later on, more sophisticated strategies of theory construction were employed to avoid this error.

The early emphasis on associationist learning represented the merging of associationist traditions in philosophy and early psychology with the theoretical concept of habit and its presumed empirical counterpart, classical conditioning. The questions of whether associationism is an appropriate theoretical representation of learning and memory processes is still with us. The controversy is most often expressed by comparing the concept of association with that of organization. Some are convinced that the principle of organization cannot be reduced to associationist theory, while others argue that the difference between organizational and associative mechanisms is more a matter of semantics than that of substance. Many years ago I suggested (Kendler, 1952) that the kind of theoretical dispute that revolves about the concepts of association and organization, which in those days was the central issue in the latent learning controversy, was irresolvable. I still maintain this position, and will argue later that these irresolvable disputes are an expression by intrinsic limitations in the precision of "black-box" theories, conceptions that do not involve underlying physiological processes.

Although the early behaviorists took a strong environmental position, it was exaggerated by their critics. Watson's widely quoted statement that he could train any child to be any kind of an adult usually omitted his concluding qualification,

> I am going beyond my facts and I admit it, but so have the advocates of the contrary, but they have been doing it for many thousands of years.

He wanted to emphasize the power of educational techniques while encouraging his audience to reject an extreme hereditarian position. He was essentially expressing an American cultural tradition that appropriate educational methods can overcome any psychological limitations. This tradition is still operating today with the confusion between egalitarianism as an ethical precept and as a psychological fact. But Watson did, like his successors, acknowledge, although admittedly he did not fully appreciate its power, the influence of genetic factors: heredity influenced physiological structures which "slanted" an individual's behavior in certain directions.

In sum, the ancillary orienting attitudes of classical behaviorism—stimulus-response, peripheralism, emphasis on associationistic learning, environmentalism—can all be accused of being oversimplifications but not necessarily misdirections, especially when viewed from the perspective of one of the core assumptions of behaviorism that psychology is a natural science. It is to this core belief of behaviorism that I wish now to turn my attention.

Psychology as a Natural Science

The title of the paper, "Behaviorism and Psychology: An Uneasy Alliance," stems from the conclusion, obvious to me, that several segments of the psychological community, consciously or unconsciously, reject the notion that psychology can or should be a natural science. There are several reasons behind such a position, and I will now discuss the more significant ones.

Behaviorists have frequently been accused of succumbing to scientism: the adoration of the methods of the natural sciences, a false god for psychology. The methods of the natural sciences, it is said, may not be appropriate for those of the social, behavioral, or humanistic sciences, and therefore the "scientific method" must be adapted to the special needs of these disciplines.

The essence of such an argument revolves about the meaning of *method*. If one understands *method* to represent specific kinds of research tools and techniques, then quite obviously each scientific discipline must develop its own particular investigatory procedures. Psychology needs standardized tests and operant conditioning apparatuses; physics requires cloud chambers and low temperature laboratories. However, if scientific method is considered a systematic mode for arriving at warranted empirical conclusions, then the *method* transcends the borders of the various scientific disciplines. Regardless of the particular procedures of investigation used, the criteria of empirical truth remains the same. The key question is, how does one know that their psychological interpretations and conclusions are justified? Behaviorists argue that the methods of drawing warranted conclusions about psychological events are the same as those employed by the natural scientists in drawing warranted conclusions about the phenomena with which they deal.

I am fully aware that it is difficult, if not impossible, to draw a precise demarcation line between science and nonscience. There is always a gray area between significant categories, as any hermaphrodite will testify. However, this gray area should not be employed to blur the division between science and nonscience beyond any distinction. We may not know exactly when day becomes night, but the distinction between the two is useful.

Understanding

The one key issue that I have time to deal with in distinguishing between science and nonscience is that of understanding. My thesis is simple. Understanding is a psychological concept, and a sense of understanding can be achieved in a variety of ways. Understanding can be achieved in literature, philosophy, religion, and the arts as well as in science, and one cannot and should not argue that only one kind of understanding represents "true" understanding. However, natural science understanding differs from other forms of understanding.

126

The form of understanding that is usually associated with natural science methodology is deductive. The underlying assumption is that natural events can be interpreted in the form of logical order. Understanding is achieved when an event is deduced from one or more general propositions. The medium for deductive explanations is a "deductive theory," some system of propositions that are logically organized and are coordinated to empirical events in such a manner that legitimate deductions, predictions, or postdictions about the phenomena can be made. The essential characteristics are that a deductive theory possesses an empirical content and is capable of generating deductions that could, in principle, be at odds with the evidence. I am not suggesting that all deductive theories share a fundamental conceptual structure, such as being capable of expression in a formal mathematical model. In fact, from a strategic point of view these tactics at early stages of theorizing may be self-defeating. I am also not implying that deductive theorizing demands an experimental approach. Unfortunately many behaviorists have erred in considering empiricism and experimentation synonymous, an equivalence that Darwin effectively denied.

Some philosophers (e.g., Harré, 1970) would maintain that a deductive theory, in an epistemological sense, is not equivalent to a "realistic" theory which attributes phenomena to the operation of "real" or permanent structures (e.g., the hypothalamus, blood chemistry). Instead of assuming that logical order reflects natural order, the realist maintains that empirical events are explained only when the operation of the permanent structures responsible for the phenomena are described. My own opinion is that realist theories are a form of deductive theories, but for our present purposes we can make the distinction between the two in order to avoid any possible confusion as to what constitutes understanding within the traditions of natural science.

To complete forms of understanding in natural science which are consistent with the behaviorist approach to psychology, it becomes necessary to include the approach to understanding that can be described as knowing through *behavioral control*. One understands an event when one discovers the factors that control its occurrence. Although I myself do not find this criterion of understanding fulfilling, I must recognize that it has played a significant role in operant behaviorism. From animal training to child rearing to educational technology to behavior modification to psychopharmacology, operant methods have contributed important procedures for effective behavior management. And the fundamental reason for its success, in the last analysis, may be that seeking behavioral control is a particularly effective strategy in behavioral psychology. The overwhelming number of causal agents that operate even in the simplest situation makes the problem of deductive theory construction grotesquely difficult. When one is concerned with controlling behavior, one learns very quickly whether one is on the right track. The feedback is rapid, especially when compared to the complicated and lengthy validation procedure associated with deductive theorizing. One can argue, at least at *this stage* of its

127

history, that striving for behavioral control may be the optimal strategy for the complicated science of psychology.

My list of the forms of understanding—deductive and realistic theories and knowing by behavioral control—does not exhaust all possible forms of understanding employed in psychology. Operating within psychology are two strong traditions, one from the so-called human sciences, the other from phenomenology, which provide forms of understanding that are methodologically unacceptable to behaviorists.

The term *science*, unfortunately, has been used in two entirely different contexts, contributing much to the confusion surrounding the question as to whether psychology is a science. Up to this point I have equated science with the method of arriving at warranted conclusions employed in physics, chemistry, and biology. Another conception of science, more common in Europe than in America, is much broader and looser in that it refers to systematic scholarship that offers a coherent interpretation of a set of phenomena. In this looser sense, science, known commonly as "human science," has been applied to a variety of disciplines including history, law, literary criticism, and even religion. An early exponent of this view, Giambattista Vico (1668–1744), a Neapolitan philosopher of history, social theorist, and jurist, denied that the scientific method used to study the physical sciences was the only valid method of scientific inquiry. He insisted that there are different kinds of sciences. For example, history requires a method of study different from that employed in physics. One important feature of this difference is the kind of understanding that can be achieved by historical as contrasted with physical research. Because physicists are external to the inanimate subject matter they study, they cannot achieve the personal understanding that is ultimately available to historians. The historian, a human being studying human events, is capable of empathizing with those who made history and therefore can achieve an intimate acquaintance with the subject matter that is denied the physical scientist.

This notion of human science, with an emphasis on empathic understanding, raises two distinct problems. These problems are the relationship between behaviorism and conscious experience (experiential psychology) and the role of phenomenology in understanding.

Behaviorism and Conscious Experience

John Watson created much confusion in his inconsistent treatment of conscious experience, a confusion that behaviorism has still not fully recovered from. Initially he denied that the analysis of consciousness was the subject matter of psychology because it could not be incorporated within a natural science approach. He did not, however, deny the existence of conscious experience per se:

If you will grant the behaviorist the right to use consciousness in the same way that other natural scientists employ it—that is, without making a special object of observation—you have granted all that my thesis requires. . . . In this sense consciousness may be said to be the instrument or tool with which all scientists work (Watson, 1913, pp. 175–176).

Later on, he shifted his position from methodological behaviorism, with which the above quotation is consistent, to a vaguely expressed metaphysical behaviorism, which denies consciousness per se. "Consciousness has never been seen, touched, smelled, tasted or moved. It is a plain assumption just as unprovable as the old concept of the soul." Bergmann (1956) concludes that, "Watson's particular mistake was that in order to establish that there are no interacting minds, which is true, he thought it necessary to assert that *there are no minds*, which is not only false but silly."

The problem of dealing with conscious experience within a behavioristic framework is to recognize the methodological limitations of directly investigating the mind. A person's behavior cannot be explained by state of mind because private experience is unavailable to the inspection of other observers. This conclusion is clearly supported by the complete lack of success lawyers, psychiatrists, and psychologists have had in distinguishing between mental conditions that are responsible and not responsible for controlling behavior. In a similar vein, the attempts to describe consciousness directly have failed to yield a generally accepted phenomenology but instead have produced different phenomenologies, each dependent, in part, on the modes of self-observation employed.

The exclusion of the direct examination of mental events from behavioristic psychology does not completely rule out "mental processes." If conscious experience is viewed from the methodological perspective, not as direct raw experience but instead as an inferred "state of mind," then its admissibility into a behavioral psychology based upon public observation becomes possible, and, as some would argue, desirable. Adopting the assumption that the subject matter of psychology is publicly observed behavior leaves a wide variety of options in regard to the treatment of phenomenal experience. At one extreme would be an *epiphenomenalistic behaviorism*, which rejects as unnecessary all inferences from mental processes, while at the other extreme would be *subjective behaviorism* which strives to explain behavior in an objective fashion on the basis of a model of the mind. In between would be a variety of forms of *pragmatic behaviorism* that would *infer* phenomenal processes only when the demands for explaining a particular kind of behavior requires it. As an example of behavioristic methodology combined with an inferred view of mental processes would be the information-processing paradigm. In their perceptive analysis of this paradigm, Lachman, Lachman, and Butterfield (1979) list some of its historical influences from behaviorism: "empiricism as its main method of proof," "operationism for describing experiments," and "the rational canons of natural science."

129

Conscious Experience and Understanding

I previously noted that an argument in favor of a human science in contrast to a natural science approach to psychology is that it encourages a personal empathic understanding of human events. The distinction is highlighted by a question I posed to a group of clinical psychologists in an informal discussion: "Would you consider a theory of personality to provide a satisfactory sense of understanding if it could accurately predict your patient's behavior but failed to provide any insight into his inner life?" To a woman they all answered, "No!" Some believed that a deductive theory was incomplete if the proposed theoretical analysis failed to characterize the phenomenological experiences of the patient. Others thought that a deductive theory and a phenomenological theory could be independent, each serving a separate, but essential, need.

This anecdote identifies a crucial problem in contemporary psychology for which there is no simple solution, now or in the future. Behaviorism, with its commitments to a natural science conception of understanding, is incapable of assessing the validity of descriptions of conscious experience. A descriptive phenomenology within the context of natural science *may* be possible when the physiological basis of consciousness is better understood. That is, the suggestion is offered that the direct comparison of inner states is neither logically nor physically impossible but at present is technically impossible. In sum, behaviorists can offer no simple or direct answers to psychologists who yearn to understand the content and quality of human experience. Although to some this would be interpreted as an admission of failure, to the behaviorist it simply recognizes the limits of natural science. Essentially the argument revolves about the criteria employed to evaluate understanding. Whereas humanistic psychologists reject standards of natural science because they cannot yield a veridical account of human experience, behaviorists reject humanistic interpretations because they fail to meet the standards of empirical verification and falsifiability. Although these issues are much too complex to be fully analyzed in a brief time, it may prove enlightening to conclude this discussion with a quotation from Saul Bellow. He describes the desire and effort of his protagonist, Charles Citrine, in his novel *Humboldt's Gift*, to understand the desires of others:

> To do this one had to remove all personal opinions, all interfering judgments: one should be neither for nor against this desire. In this way one might come gradually to feel what another soul was feeling. I made this experiment with my own child Mary. For her last birthday she desired a bicycle, the ten-speed type. I wasn't convinced that she was old enough to have one. When we went to the shop it was by no means certain that I would buy it. Now what was her desire, and what did she experience? I wanted to know this, and tried to desire in the way she desired. This was my kid, whom I loved, and it should have been elementary to find out what a soul in its fresh state craved with such intensity. But I couldn't do this. I tried until I broke into a sweat, humiliated, disgraced by my failure. If I couldn't know this kid's

desire could I know any human being? I tried it on a large number of people. And then, defeated, I asked where was I anyway? And what did I really know of anyone? The only desires I knew were my own and those of nonexistent people like Macbeth or Prospero. These I knew because the insight and language of genius made them clear.[1]

Past Achievements and Future Trends

It should be quite apparent by now that the evaluation of any systematic position in psychology will depend on one's methodological commitments and conception of psychology. Thus the development of sophisticated methods of measuring behavior, both within the behavioristic community of experimental psychologists and the allied group of psychometricians, would be considered a definite plus. If empirical questions are raised about the behavior of individuals or groups, behaviorist achievements and traditions provide the means by which answers can be forthcoming.

The significance of methods to measure behavior objectively has often been overlooked. Only when amateurs attempt this task, and frequently they are members of related disciplines, such as biology and sociology, do we fully appreciate the achievements of psychologists in the technology of measuring behavior. Psychology has developed, and is capable of developing, new measures of behavior that are essential for basic research and for our attempts to cope with significant social phenomena, e.g., drug research, educational practices, and evaluation research of the effects of various social policies.

The merits of a tough-minded approach to the measurement of behavior should not be limited only to its positive contributions. Anyone who abides by the behavioristic traditions tends to avoid getting enmeshed in fuzzy, and sometimes corrupted, issues. I am thinking particularly of the concept of the *image of man*, a concept that behaviorists have been accused of demeaning. One possible interpretation is that behaviorists ignore the fundamental problem of describing the human potential which is sometimes expressed in such terms as self-fulfillment and characterized as becoming "everything that one is capable of becoming" (Maslow, 1954, p. 92). According to contemporary behavioristic conceptions, individuals possess many different potentialities, although certainly not limitless ones. Circumstances of life, representing numerous interactions between nature and nurture, shape individual behavior and determine which potentialities will be achieved and which ones will not. It is not the task of psychologists to tell society which human potentialities are desirable and which are not. Psychologists can assist society in making these decisions by discovering the psychological consequences of adopting different social ideals, but it is inappropriate and dangerous for psychologists to attempt to impose a set of values on society in the guise of scientific evidence. Most religions

[1] From *Humboldt's Gift* by Saul Bellow. Copyright © 1973, 1974, 1975 by Saul Bellow. Reprinted by permission of Viking Penguin Inc.

131

offer an *image of man,* usually justified by a Supreme Being. Psychologists should resist the temptation to believe that their professional competence qualifies them to occupy such a position.

Behaviorism, with its relatively clear-cut empirical approach to psychology, has been instrumental in producing an enormous amount of psychological data. This has proved to be a mixed blessing because much of the evidence is trivial and refractory to any theoretical integration. Certainly if we compare psychology to genetics in the past one hundred years, we would be forced to admit that our progress in achieving understanding has not been close to that of genetics. Why? The major reason is that our efforts to formulate "black-box" behavior theories— those formulations which employ abstract intervening variables to bridge the gap between environmental manipulations and the behavior or organisms—have not been as successful as initially anticipated. Numerous theoretical controversies (e.g., latent learning, cognitive-dissonance, the number of memory stories) in various fields (e.g., learning, memory, social) have proved irresolvable in the sense that the evidence did not clearly favor one side in the controversy as it did in the cases of the Copernican versus the Ptolemaic dispute and the evolutionary versus the creationists positions. A common reaction to these insoluble controversies, which I previously accepted as valid, was that the difficulties stemmed from the ambiguity of the competing formulations. The solution to the theoretical impasse was obvious: behavioral theories must be made more precise. But attempts to do this, in the form of mathematical models, have failed to provide answers to the theoretical questions we sought. At best, the mathematical models offered limited answers to narrow questions.

Another possible explanation of the failure of general environmental-behavioral theories to resolve their controversies is that they suffer both from an empirical openness and a lack of theoretical constraints. The empirical phenomena encompassed by the theory is not a closed system; variables unaccounted for by the theory exert an important influence on behavior. In other words, a lot of noise influences the results. In addition, and probably of greater importance, is that the conceptual network of black-box theories allows for an infinite amount of modifications to accommodate embarrassing data. There appears to be no end to escape clauses for black-box theories. As long as these general conditions remain, there will be a limit to the explanatory capacity of such general theories.

Perhaps the most reasonable strategy to cope with these unresolvable theoretical controversies is to attempt to tighten up the theories, to place some constraints on the system that is to be studied. When possible, the general behavior theorist should shift interest from environmental-behavioral relationships to neurophysiological-behavioral relationships. Neurophysiological hypotheses, when they involve direct interventions into the physiological system, do not have the vast potential for ad hoc theorizing as do black-box conceptions. It is much easier to obtain negative evidence against a hypothesis concerning the operation of some physiological process than it is to discover that a set of abstract theoretical constructs are incapable of

132

explaining a set of behavioral phenomena. This encouragement of a biopsycholog-ical approach should not be interpreted as a rejection of a black-box approach to behavior. Black-box behaviorists have increased our understanding of a wide variety of phenomena in learning, memory, perception, and other fields, as well as in behavior management techniques. But there appears to be a definite ceiling effect in the capacity of these black-box theories to resolve central theoretical issues. Nevertheless these theories, and the data which they generated, can give direction to the biopsychologists in their attempt to achieve a deeper understanding of behav-ior. In addition, it must be noted that black-box behaviorists have provided invalu-able behavioral measurement techniques for biopsychological research.

Quite obviously I could not do full justice to behaviorism, its past and its future, in this brief time. I have been forced to draw strong conclusions in the absence of full and detailed justifications. But I have tried to reflect the basic historical forces that are operating in this multifaceted discipline of psychology (which is very undis-ciplined). History tells us that behaviorism represents a natural-science approach to study of behavior. Although the core methodological framework of natural science is not free of all ambiguities, I reject the notion that it can be conceptualized in any personal subjective manner that one desires. Understanding in natural science is different from understanding in other fields, and behaviorists are committed to explain the phenomena when they deal in a manner consistent with their methodological commitments.

The behaviorist approach to psychology cannot possibly satisfy those who are interested in getting a descriptive phenomenology or in discovering "moral princi-ples . . . which can be scientifically confirmed" (Goble, 1971, p. 91). We must fully recognize the different methodological orientations that pervade psychology and not be misled into believing that they have a common goal anymore than we should think it would be possible to combine the rules of chess and checkers without modifying either game.

Behaviorism has made some progress in understanding a range of phenomena from sensation to social behavior, but the level of our understanding is far short of what was anticipated four decades ago when an easy optimism prevailed about psychology's future successes. This does not deter the behaviorist from persisting in efforts to interpret behavior within a natural-science framework for the simple rea-son that there are no other forms of understanding that meets the needs. The only change that can occur is a change in tactics, and I have suggested that behaviorists returning to the biological orientation from which they sprang will make that change.

REFERENCES

Bellow, S. *Humboldt's gift*. New York: Viking, 1975.
Bergmann, G. The contributions of John B. Watson. *Psychological Review*, 1956, 63, 265–276.
Goble, F. *The third force*. New York: Pocket Books, 1971.

133

I. THE SYSTEMATIC FRAMEWORK OF PSYCHOLOGY

Harré, R. The principles of scientific thinking. Chicago: The University of Chicago Press, 1970.

Kendler, H. H. "What is learned?"—A theoretical blind alley. Psychological Review, 1952, 59, 269– 277.

Kendler, H. H. Motivation and behavior. In D. Levine (Ed.), Nebraska Symposium on Motivation, 1964. Lincoln: University of Nebraska Press, 1965.

Koch, S. Psychology and emerging conceptions of knowledge as unitary. In T. W. Wann (Ed.), Behaviorism and phenomenology. Chicago: The University of Chicago Press, 1964.

Lachman, R., Lachman, J. L., & Butterfield, E. C. Cognitive psychology and information processing: An introduction. Hillsdale, N.J.: Erlbaum, 1979.

Maslow, A. H. Motivation and personality. New York: Harper & Row, 1954.

Pavlov, I. P. Conditioned reflexes (G. V. Anrep, trans.). London: Oxford University Press, 1927.

Sechenov, I. M. Reflexes of the brain. (Reprint of a 1961 translation by S. Belsky, printed in Moscow, of a work published in Russian in 1863.) Cambridge, Mass.: M.I.T. Press, 1965.

Skinner, B. F. John Broadus Watson, behaviorist. Science, 1959, 129, 197–198.

Titchener, E. B. Systematic psychology: Prolegomena. New York: Macmillan, 1929.

Tolman, E. C. Purposive behavior in animals and men. New York: Appleton-Century, 1932.

Watson, J. B. Experimental studies on the growth of the emotions. In C. Murchison (Ed.), Psychologies of 1925. Worcester, Mass.: Clark University Press, 1926.

Watson, J. B. Psychology as the behaviorist views it. Psychological Review, 1913, 20, 158–177.

SUPPLEMENTARY READINGS

Estes, W. K. The statistical approach to learning theory. In S. Koch (Ed.), Psychology: A study of a science. (Vol. 2) General systematic formulations, learning, and special processes. New York: McGraw-Hill, 1959, pp. 380–491.

Guthrie, E. R. The psychology of learning (Rev. ed.). New York: Harper & Row, 1952.

Guthrie, E. R. Association by contiguity. In S. Koch (Ed.), Psychology: A study of a science. (Vol. 2) General systematic formulations, learning, and special processes. New York: McGraw-Hill, 1959, pp. 158–195.

Hull, C. L. The goal gradient hypothesis and maze learning. Psychological Review, 1932, 39, 25–43.

Hull, C. L. Principles of behavior. New York: Appleton-Century, 1943.

Kendler, H. H. Psychology: A science in conflict. New York: Oxford University Press, 1981.

Kendler, H. H., & Spence, J. T. Tenets of neobehaviorism. In H. H. Kendler & J. T. Spence (Eds.), Essays in neobehaviorism. New York: Appleton-Century-Crofts, 1971, pp. 11–40.

Meyer, M. The psychology of the other one. Columbia, Mo., Missouri Book Store. 1921.

Miller, N. E. Liberalization of basic S-R concepts: Extensions to conflict behavior, motivation and social learning. In S. Koch (Ed.), Psychology: A study of a science. (Vol. 2) General systematic formulations, learning, and special processes. New York: McGraw-Hill, 1959, pp. 196–292.

Skinner, B. F. The behavior of organisms. New York: Appleton-Century-Crofts, 1938.

Skinner, B. F. Cumulative record. New York: Appleton-Century-Crofts, 1959.

Spence, K. W. The postulates and methods of "behaviorism." Psychological Review, 1948, 55, 67–78.

Spence, K. W. Cognitive versus stimulus-response theories of learning. Psychological Review, 1950, 57, 159–172.

Tolman, E. C. Purposive behavior in animals and men. New York: The Century Company, 1932.

Tolman, E. C. Operational behaviorism and current trends in psychology. In H. W. Hill (Ed.), Proceedings, 25th American celebration of the inauguration of graduate studies, The University of Southern California. Los Angeles: The University of Southern California Press, 1936, pp. 89–103.

Watson, J. B. Psychology as the behaviorist views it. Psychological Review, 1913, 20, 158–177.

Watson, J. B. Behaviorism (Rev. ed.). New York: Norton, 1930.

Weiss, A. P. A theoretical basis of human behavior. Columbus, Ohio: Adams, 1925.

7

Freud and Experimental Psychology: The Emergence of Idiodynamics*†

SAUL ROSENZWEIG

Preliminaries

The occasion is the centenary of the founding of the first systematic laboratory of experimental psychology by Wilhelm Wundt at the University of Leipzig in 1879 (Rieber, 1980). The fact that Leipzig is presently in East Germany and that the institution is now called Karl Marx University indicates how much has changed, in the political world at least, in the interim. In psychology during that period we have witnessed the life and work not only of Wundt himself but of Pavlov and Freud. It is to the last of that great triumvirate that this contribution will be devoted.

*Copyright © 1985 by Saul Rosenzweig.

† A brief, preliminary version of this treatise was presented in a centenary (1879–1979) symposium at the annual meeting of the American Psychological Association, New York, September 4, 1979. The research for this writing was initially aided by a grant from the National Institutes of Health, MH No. 12673. I am grateful to my colleague Ira J. Hirsh for his critical reading of an early draft of the manuscript and his various helpful suggestions.

EDITORS' NOTE: The exceptional length of this chapter was deemed justifiable in that the large tradition of psychoanalytic and related thought is but thinly represented in the rest of this book.

However, it must at the outset be avowed that, though I shall attempt objectively to present the relationships of experimental psychology to the psychoanalytic orientation of Freud, the account will be what Freud would have called "tendentious." For I have a thesis to expound which gives an evolutionary significance to this centenary. In my view we have witnessed a progression from *experimental psychology*, a physiologically based, nomothetic science, to the *clinical psychodynamics* of Freud, with its stress on experiential, not physiological, constructs and an incipient recognition of the individual as central to psychology; and, finally, in the last quarter of the century, the beginnings of *experimental idiodynamics*—an orientation which firmly focuses the emphasis of research in psychology on the interaction between the specific experimenter and the particular person who complements him or her in the experimental situation.

Another preliminary comment may be helpful. The reading of Freud's writings demands a special orientation that few other psychologists or psychiatrists require. Freud was primarily a writer, not unlike Goethe the scientist; an artist, not unlike Leonardo da Vinci the engineer. His thought as scientist, teacher, philosopher, and even novelist went into literary production as he experienced it at the time. He wrote autobiographically whether he was discussing dreams, or slips of the tongue; whether composing case histories, interpreting famous historical figures, formulating theories of personality, or expounding aspects of social philosophy. All these areas of his experience were given expression and were organically interwoven. Freud made little explicit attempt to integrate them or to reconcile his later with his earlier views. He allowed his life to provide the unity. In other words, he lived his works. It was left for others to understand and try, if they considered it worthwhile, to integrate his experience of his world. To read Freud without this awareness of him as a phenomenon—as a world of unique experience—is to condemn oneself from the start to misunderstanding him. To read Freud as one looks into a phenomenal world with its several levels of expression and its various modes of communication is to treat him idiodynamically—to enter, as it were, into his lifelong self-analysis. To the extent that the following contribution at times departs from this orientation, it will have erred by making certain concessions to the process of abstraction temporarily required by formal research design. But the sensitive reader will, in the end, appreciate that whatever unity lies in this contribution and whatever useful message or messages it delivers are the outcome of the attempt to enter into Freud's life and work idiodynamically.

Freud's Relation to Brücke's Institute of Physiology

Let us begin with Freud's scientific education at the Institute of Ernst Brücke, the Professor of Physiology at the University of Vienna, and his exposure there to the ideas of Helmholtz and, less directly, Fechner—the twin pillars of the arch by which students of psychology entered Wundt's laboratory. Both at some time professors of physics, they were the two indispensable pioneers of experimental psychology as an exact science (Hall, 1912). Helmholtz was the pillar of mechanistic "physicalism"; Fechner, the pillar of panpsychic idealism, a position he developed into psychophysics as a mathematical-experimental solution of the body-mind dichotomy.

Brücke was one of the three friends of Herman Helmholtz who joined him in attempting to give physiology the precision of physics and chemistry by discovering the facts and the nomothetic principles founded upon a physicalist underpinning. In a sense, Helmholtz was even more important than Wundt in giving physiological psychology its scientific basis. He was certainly more inventive and more truly a scientific discoverer of new facts and principles than was Wundt, who cared more for the details of a system than for empirical discoveries. Brücke was the staunch protagonist of the position of Helmholtz, and he was Freud's master for six crucial formative years (1876–1882), a period which left an indelible mark on Freud's later thought (Bernfeld, 1944, 1949; Jones, 1953). During his self-analysis Freud, recalling Brücke's Institute, confessed that there ". . . I spent the happiest hours of my student life, free from all other desires . . ." (Freud, 1899/1953, IV, p. 206). After his first scientific paper on the missing testes of the eel, the product of an assignment under Professor Claus, Freud moved to Brücke's Institute as a "famulus," and on July 18, 1878, he became the proud author of a report on the neural structure of the *Petromyzon* presented by his master at a meeting of the prestigious Vienna Academy of Sciences.

But on the present occasion it is neither possible nor profitable to follow the details of Freud's work in the Physiological Institute. One should, however, note in passing that it was precisely at the zenith of Freud's involvement with Brücke that Wundt in 1879 established the Leipzig laboratory. For the rest, let us explore briefly the evidence of Freud's relation to Brücke (hence to Helmholtz, Fechner, and Wundt) in his development. This evidence is discernible in four fragments of his self-analysis cryptically embedded in his first and most significant book, *The Interpretation of Dreams* (Freud, 1899/1953). In examining this material, one should know that in Brücke's Institute Freud became acquainted with Josef Breuer, Sigmund Exner, Ernst Fleischl, and Joseph Paneth, the first two of whom, along with Brücke, later appeared, for the significance of their contributions to physiological psychology, in the classic *A History of Experimental Psychology* by E. G. Boring (1929). Breuer, for example, who is remembered by most psychologists today for his role in collaborating with Freud on the cathartic theory and therapy of hysteria (Breuer & Freud, 1895/1955), was chiefly known to his scientific contemporaries for his investigations of the sense of equilibrium as mediated by the semicircular canals in the inner ear. It was for this research that William James (1890), for one, referred to Breuer in his *Principles* (Vol. II, p. 89n.), ten years after reviewing it in more detail in a separate article (James, 1880).

137

Although four of Freud's dreams belong here, only one, the last, is examined in detail. As will appear, it is discussed at this point for its accent on Brücke's laboratory in Freud's scientific development, but it recurs later to illustrate the concepts of idiodynamics on the basis of data from Freud's own life.

This *"non vixit"* dream (as it is known to students of the history of psychoanalysis) can be dated almost precisely from Freud's own associations (1899/1953, p. 421f.). He describes it as having occurred "only a few days after" the dedication of the memorial bust of Ernst Fleischl, one of Brücke's assistants and Freud's superior who became a close friend afterwards. Fleischl died in 1891, at the early age of forty-five. The memorial ceremony, which Freud attended, can be dated from public records as held on October 16. As we shall see, "a few days later" probably means October 22.

Freud begins the description of the dream by noting: "I had gone to Brücke's laboratory at night, and, in response to a gentle knock on the door, I opened it to (the late) Professor Fleischl, who came in with a number of strangers and, after exchanging a few words, sat down at his table." Freud then continues by describing a second part of the dream in which his friend Fliess came unobtrusively from Berlin to Vienna in July. Fliess, conversing with Freud's deceased friend P. [Paneth], went with them both to a small table where a conversation ensued concerning the death of a sister of Fliess who had died in youth. Her last hour was described by Fliess who "added some such words as 'that was the threshold'." As the dream continued Freud recognized that P. was not a living person, but only an apparition and, since P. was causing difficulties by his silence, the dreamer gave him a piercing look that caused him to melt away. The dreamer then realized that Fleischl also was only an apparition and that "people of that kind only existed as long as one liked. . . ." In describing P. as an apparition, the dreamer used the (Latin) expression *non vixit* (literally: he did not live), an error for the expression *non vivit* (he is not living).

For us the main point of this dream is Freud's vivid reliving (in his self-analysis) of his experiences at the Brücke laboratory where Joseph Paneth, as well as Fleischl, worked alongside Freud. Paneth, like Fleischl, died prematurely—in 1890, at age thirty-three, just as the sister of Fliess had died prematurely. The dreamer is a survivor over his many rivals, and the piercing look with which he dissolved P. was copied, Freud states in his associations, from a similar gaze with which the great Brücke at one time "annihilated" him for having reported late for work, and not for the first time. So the dreamer identified with the master to assume the ascendant role. Herein lies one wish-fulfillment of the dream, according to Freud's interpretation.

Three further aspects should be noted to bring out the significance of Freud's experience at the Brücke laboratory as a part of his formative education and as preparation for his future work as the founder of psychoanalysis.

1. It will be recalled that the early death of Fliess's sister was described with the unusual expression "that was the threshold." The dreamer is obviously using the word "threshold" in some cryptic way as equivalent to death. In the Brücke context the reason is not difficult to infer if one is familiar with the use of "threshold of consciousness" in the psychophysics of G. T. Fechner, one of the two chief pioneers of experimental psychology. Though Fechner borrowed the term from a predecessor (Herbart, 1816/1977, pp. 12–13), it was he who gave it currency in the laboratories of Brücke and Wundt (Fechner, 1860/1966, Chap. X). Moreover, Fechner developed psychophysics, as we shall see later, to serve as a support for his religious philosophy, and in the latter, the threshold concept was indeed tied to the idea of death and survival. He repeatedly mentions this point in his most popular work, *The Little Book of Life after Death* (Fechner, 1836/1887; 1905). To him, a panpsychist, life was equated with consciousness; it existed both before birth and after death in some form continuous with the consciousness of waking life. The threshold measured not only the reference point for the methods of measurement Fechner employed in his psychophysical experiments; it defined in his philosophy the transitions of birth and death to both of which Fechner denied any lasting significance (Hermann, 1925; Ellenberger, 1970). If one adds to this information the facts, very probably well known in Brücke's laboratory, that October 22 (1850) was the date to which Fechner conspicuously assigned his discovery of the psychophysical law (Fechner, 1860, II, p. 554); and that October 22 was the actual date of Fleischl's death (in 1891), "threshold" becomes a code word for Fechner in re Fleischl. Freud in his brief autobiography (Freud 1925/1959, p. 59) stated: "I was always open to the ideas of G. T. Fechner and have followed that thinker on many important points." The devotion of Freud to the ill-fated Fleischl at the dawn of psychoanalysis is unmistakable as one peruses the biography of Freud by Jones and the various dreams of Freud's self-analysis.[1]

2. Closely linked to the foregoing is the fact that when Joseph Paneth died so prematurely in 1890, Sigmund Exner, the partner of Fleischl as assistants to Brücke, unobtrusively commemorated the sad event by posthumously publishing a brief report of the young scientist's (presumably) last experiment (Paneth, with Exner, 1890). With almost poetic appropriateness the paper dealt with research on the temporal course of memory images. The short account states that Paneth had modeled his research on prior experiments described by Fechner in his *Psychophysik* (Fechner, 1860, II, p. 493). In the next section of that treatise Fechner goes on to discuss apparitions and hallucinations as phenomena of abnormal mental states!

---

[1] From my association with E. G. Boring, head of the Psychology laboratory at Harvard University, I recall (and at one time confirmed by correspondence with him) that in the precincts of the department at Emerson Hall, where psychophysics was given a prominent place, October 22 was regularly celebrated as Fechner Day with an informal party of staff and graduate students. Whether there was a similar practice at Brücke's Institute (or elsewhere), I do not know.

It is inconceivable that Freud did not know about this subtle contemporary tribute paid to Paneth by Exner, particularly when in Freud's free associations to the present dream he mentions, regretfully, that Paneth did not live long enough to earn a memorial bust like Fleischl's.

3. There is a final aspect tending to demonstrate that in the mind of Freud, Paneth was a substitute for his earliest rival, his brother Julius, who died at the age of six months in 1858. Joseph Paneth was born October 1857; Julius Freud, in the same month and year. The significance of the death of Julius, which occurred when Freud was not quite two years old, has been discussed elsewhere (Rosenzweig, 1970a). Here it is of interest that Freud is subtly doing for his deceased brother, still remembered and very much alive in his "unconscious," what Exner had done for Paneth. By having Fliess come to Vienna unobtrusively in *July* (mentioned in the manifest dream but never repeated in the many pages of associations), and by alluding to the ghost of *Julius* Caesar at the end of the first four-page section of these associations, Freud is unquestionably indicating that in his obsessive memories Julius, whose death fulfilled Sigmund's own infantile hostile wishes, had not been forgotten. While Julius died in 1858, the *non vixit* dream occurred in 1898—on the fortieth anniversary of the death.[2]

These testimonials from the self-analysis leave little doubt that the 1876–1882 experience in the Brücke Institute, so closely related to physiological psychology at the very time that Wundt founded the science, made a deep and lasting impression on the budding scholar—an impression that would shape much of his later creative thinking in seemingly unrelated areas.

---

[2] Since the above-mentioned four dreams constitute a series and the earlier three significantly contribute to the relevant evidence, the three earlier ones should be briefly noticed. They all occurred at the zenith of Freud's self-analysis in 1898, one each in the successive months July through October. The first (Freud, 1899/1953, p. 455f.), in July, invoked, in its manifest content, a marine biology station, probably the one at Trieste under the direction of Professor Carl Claus where Freud performed his research on the genital system of the eel. It is striking that to this dream, unlike his numerous others except one (the Irma dream), he assigned a specific date: the night of July 18–19. If one knows, as stated above, that the crowning achievement of the dreamer in his physiological research was the public report by Brücke on July 18, 1878, the date must have entered as a recollection of the twentieth anniversary. But Freud did not trouble to explain why he so explicitly dated this dream, perhaps because this basis for it may have been only one among others. In August occurred the dream of Freud's dissecting his own pelvis (ibid., 1899/1953, p. 452f.). It was "old Brücke" who had set him this strange task. In the course of his associations Freud equated this assignment with his ongoing self-analysis. There followed in September the dream about the Three Fates (ibid., 1899/1953, p. 204f.), who appeared in the manifest content in the guise of three women kneading dumplings (in the kitchen of Freud's childhood). The name of Fleischl occurred in the dream as a play on the German word for "flesh" or "meat." And in the interpretation another play on a proper name occurred, this time a translation of the name Brücke into *bridge*—to create what Freud later called a "verbal bridge" by which the dream-work often accomplishes its unconscious aims. All three dreams thus focus at the manifest level on the Physiological Institute, headed by Ernst Brücke, just as did the *non vixit* dream of October 1898.

By extrapolation the foregoing dream study contributes also to the understanding of one type of creativity. In various instances (e.g., the life and work of Dostoevsky, Hawthorne, Eugene O'Neill), a close encounter with death (of parent or sibling) in childhood or adolescence, under circumstances that instill a sense of guilty complicity in that death, leads to an identification with the dead person (Rosenzweig & Bray, 1943; Rosenzweig, 1943c). An equivalent experience may be a symbolically crippling accident at a critical moment in the life cycle. Personality disorder may be entailed, but in instances where the individual is fittingly endowed, a restitutive process is initiated in which the introjected guilt engenders a creative solution. Idiodynamic research on creativity has included several examples of the process (e.g., that of Henry James; see Rosenzweig, 1943b); but in the present context the most appropriate one is, of course, Sigmund Freud. The *non vixit* dream may thus be viewed not only from the more manifest aspect concerning Brücke's laboratory, just emphasized, but from the more cryptic one concerning the premature death of Freud's brother Julius. In that light, and as already implied, the dream wishfully erected a monument to Julius. Actuated by the undying memory of his dead brother, the survivor, Sigmund Freud, became compulsively dedicated to the process of self- or psycho-analysis, then dedicated himself to the creation of a corresponding discipline.

Freud's "Only Experimental Study"

The period from 1882 to 1893 was a decade of clinical training. Having finally obtained his M.D. degree in 1881, and having met his best beloved, Martha Bernays, in early 1882, Freud left the Brücke Institute to embark upon the clinical experience he needed to prepare for a livelihood by the practice of medicine.

Except for a single experiment devoted to the effects of cocaine on muscular strength, measured by the dynamometer (Freud, 1885), Freud's relations to laboratory research of any kind were from now on negligible. But this unique production deserves special notice. Jones (1953, I, p. 92) comments on it thus: "The paper is of interest as being the only experimental study Freud ever published, and its dilettante presentation shows that this was not his real field." In this light it is more understandable that Freud's friend Josef Herzig, a research chemist, assisted him in the work, as Freud specifically acknowledged. He was apparently aware that he needed help not only from the standpoint of the chemistry of cocaine but in the setting up and analysis of the experimental conditions. This experiment thus affords an opportunity for distinguishing between the type of physiological, specifically histological, observation that Freud performed under Brücke and the type of work, involving independent and dependent variables, which the experimental psychologist is called upon to perform on the model of such established sciences as physics and chemistry. Helmholtz, for example, performed countless such experiments, as did Wundt and his students. So one should recognize that though, as emphasized above, Freud's experience at the Brücke Institute imbued him with the thought patterns of Brücke and Helmholtz, it did not train him in the experimental methods employed by Fechner, Helmholtz, and Wundt. Careful descriptive observation and the special principles associated with Brücke and Helmholtz impressed Freud indelibly, but the methodology of experimental psychology represented a special discipline with which his personal familiarity was very limited. This fact may well have influenced his later limited appreciation of experimental studies of psychoanalytic theory which will be considered below.

Freud now began postgraduate clinical work with hospital patients under such mentors as Meynert, the neurologist, Charcot, the psychopathologist in Paris, and his special patron Josef Breuer. Through Breuer the continuity with the Brücke laboratory was maintained.

In the medical or therapeutic activities of this period of his life, Freud often came into conflict with Breuer because of the latter's conservative stance, not only in things scientific but in therapy as well. Eventually, after the collaborative *Studies on Hysteria* (Breuer & Freud, 1895/1955), the rupture occurred, largely on Breuer's initiative. It is, however, an error to believe that Breuer refused to recognize the importance of sexuality in hysteria; his section on the theory of hysteria in their book completely refutes that allegation.

The Emergence of Clinical Psychodynamics

In the decade 1894–1904, Freud published his basic contributions to the foundation of psychoanalysis as both theory and therapy.[3] There were two landmarks. The first was the unpublished *Project* of 1895, submitted to his friend and correspondent Wilhelm Fliess and preserved by the latter, in which one can observe Freud's painstaking attempts to pass from a neurologically grounded psychology to a psychology of pure experience (Freud, 1895). The concepts of unconscious conflict and ego-defense were thus developed. By the end of the decade came the second and more consequential landmark: the publication of his masterpiece, *The Interpretation of Dreams* (Freud, 1899/1953). In that work he crystallized these concepts by testing them in the crucible of his self-analysis. The most important dreams of that book are his own, and by the method of free association, however discreetly edited for the public view, he presented a theory equally apposite to the neurosis as a dreamlike product and the dream as a codex of neurosis. Both phenomena are rooted in the transformations of libido through conflict and defense, notably repression, and both are amenable to understanding and therapeutic modification by the

---

[3] A careful, critical, and historically based account of the development of Freud's early psychology of the neuroses has been published by Levin (1978).

method of free association in the permissive rapport between the reporter and the observer (patient and therapist). But this experiential system, which in 1896 he dubbed "psychoanalysis" (Freud, 1896/1962a, p. 151), retained the earmarks of the nineteenth-century physicalist school.

An important transitional theory was concerned with the etiology of hysteria to which Freud devoted three papers in a single year (1896/1962a; 1896/1962b; 1896/1962c). In all of them he focused on the seduction of the adult hysterical patient during childhood by a parent, sibling, nurse, or some other close associate. By 1897 he had become disillusioned and wrote to his friend Fliess (Freud, 1954a, p. 215) to this effect: he had been taken in by the patients' fantasies of childhood seduction that had persisted unconsciously and turned up in the analysis as real events. It was, however, not until 1905 that he retracted the seduction theory in his published writings (Freud, 1905/1953, p. 190; 1906/1953, p. 274f.), and then only with reservations to allow for the actuality of some of these memories. But contemporaneously, beginning in 1897, Freud developed his theory of infantile sexuality on the basis of these childhood fantasies. He believed that the child's own libido had created these fantasies in childhood with a vividness that caused them to appear as real events when recalled from the repressed unconscious. It had been the repression of these infantile complexes that, with or without a firm foundation in reality, contributed to the understanding of the adult neurosis. Psychoanalytic therapy consisted, in part, in the resolution of these complexes by the method of free association as aided by the transference neurosis in which the therapist was a surrogate for the parent or other childhood companion. The Oedipal theory was, of course, a derivative of infantile sexuality. By these steps, based on such reconstructions, the psychoanalytic theory of personality (experiential psychodynamics) emerged. In that theory and in the methods employed to implement it in therapy, the psychical rather than the physical (social) reality of the patient's world was emphasized.

It is noteworthy that in today's purview Freud may have been unduly skeptical of the actual facts. One reason for his hesitancy may have been the comment, quoted by him to his friend Wilhelm Fliess, made by Freud's department head, the now famous Richard von Krafft-Ebing, who called Freud's theory a "scientific fairy-tale" (Freud, 1954a, p. 167n.). This evaluation from Europe's leading authority on sex perversions could not but have impressed the young investigator who, no doubt, viewed the remark as referring not only to his theory of the etiology of hysteria but to the implied incidence of child sexual abuse. But in the present-day evaluation, the seductions alleged in Freud's early theory appear less fantastic. In the current phase of the candid "sexual revolution" which Freud largely initiated, a new area of social work and law enforcement has sprung up: child abuse and neglect, more specifically, child sexual abuse which comprises about 15 percent of all such complaints (Kempe et al., 1962; Cantwell, 1981; Williams & Money, 1980). It is striking that it was Robert Fliess, son of Freud's inadvertent analyst (Wilhelm

143

Fliess), who was one of the earliest modern psychiatrists to call in question the devaluation of the seduction theory. He maintained that Freud "went too far in *favoring fantasy at the cost of memory* . . ." (Fliess, 1956, p. xvii), but he attributed such sexual abuse to ambulatory-psychotic adults not found in the usual household visited by the average social worker. In any event, it is instructive that Freud, master of fantasy, was reluctant to credit the social world of the child with the acting out of the endopsychic which his methods brought to light in his patients. Was he perhaps inhibited by a new edition of ego-defense against the facts of his own childhood environment that were emerging in his ongoing self-analysis? Whatever the reason, it was through the seduction theory and its vicissitudes that Freud was led to relinquish his reliance on the facts of the social world, just as he had already given up the attempt to correlate psychological experience with physiology and neurology. In the place of these correlations, he stressed the interrelationships in the patient's endopsychic experience.[4]

[4]The controversy in psychoanalytic circles provoked by Jeffrey Masson's *The assault on truth: Freud's suppression of the seduction theory* (1984), which was summarized earlier in *The New Yorker* by Janet Malcolm (1983; see also Malcolm, 1984), appeared after this paragraph had gone to the typesetter. As will be seen, the paragraph well summarized the current situation regarding the actuality of child sexual abuse, but it also anticipated some of the misunderstanding of Freud which Masson has appeared to foster. Masson has argued that the founder of psychoanalysis deliberately concealed the facts of child sexual abuse after he had maintained emphatically in 1896 that these seductions were at the root of later hysteria, especially in adolescent and adult women. Then, argues Masson, Freud began to fear the effect of these disclosures on his reputation as a professional practitioner so that he retracted fact and substituted fantasy as the important agent in neurosis. On this dubious basis Freud founded his new theory of infantile sexuality. But by this substitution Freud turned his back on external reality.

As stated above, Freud never did completely reject the seduction theory: he admitted only that he had exaggerated the frequency of seduction in childhood because he took his analytic patients too literally. Masson argues that Freud did not take them literally enough and he quotes Freud's retraction by citing 1905 and 1906 (as above). Then comes a surprising ploy. When Masson gets to Freud's most considered statement regarding the seduction theory—the statement in "On the history of the psycho-analytic movement" (1914/1957)—a remarkable ellipsis occurs. Freud there repeats that he had overstated the frequency of seduction in childhood and reiterates his modified position of 1905. He continues with these five crucial lines: "Disposition and experience are here linked up in an indissoluble aetiological unity. For *disposition* exaggerates impressions which would otherwise have been completely commonplace and have had no effect, so that [by exaggeration] they become traumas giving rise to stimulations and fixations; while *experiences* awaken factors in the disposition which, without them, might have long remained dormant and perhaps never have developed" (Freud, 1914/1957, pp. 17–18). Masson (1984, pp. 130–131) has copied out Freud's long statement (pp. 17–18) but in so doing he has omitted the crucial lines in the middle of the passage. Ellipses are substituted [. . .], which clearly indicate that Masson had read the lines. Presumably because they did not accord with his own one-sided thesis, he deliberately suppressed them. What Freud thought and Masson would not even let him state is vital for the present exposition of idiodynamics. Freud, in revising his estimate of actual seductions in childhood, recognized that reality and fantasy are interdependent. He uses the terms *experience* and *disposition* to refer, respectively, to *reality* and *fantasy*, the latter arising from the child's own sexual predisposition. A complementary continuum is postulated (similar to the assumed interaction in discussions of environment and heredity). In the perception of a predisposed child, a pinch of the cheek, a pat on the head, or

Moreover, this psychodynamic system, unlike experimental-physiological psychology, was built on the life experience of the individual as viewed developmentally in relation to his immediate personal environment, especially his family. In its earliest applications, especially in the first edition of *The Interpretation of Dreams*, the free associations of the individual patient were meticulously sought. Freud appeared to eschew the universal symbolism of the popular dream books. But a decade later a change for the worse, not recognized as such by him, took place. In the Preface to the third edition of the book (1911), he acknowledged the influence of Stekel in rearousing his interest in universal dream symbolism, and he reworked much of the discussion in these terms. Similarly, in the second edition of the abbreviated version of his masterpiece (entitled "On Dreams") he added Chapter 12 to take explicit account of this new emphasis, and he cited Stekel's writings in a footnote (Freud, 1901/1911). Stekel's book, *Die Sprache des Traumes*, also appeared that year (1911), but Freud's close association with the author at this period had, of course, acquainted him with its message well before its publication. The deleterious effect of this influence on the future of psychoanalysis as an empirical science can, to this extent, be documented.[5]

While Freud, from 1897 to 1909, was still according due emphasis to the experience of the individual patient, the influence of his exposure to the ideas of Brücke, Fechner, and Helmholtz found implicit expression in the first formulations of his psychoanalytic theory. That subtle influence may have made him more susceptible to the "universal" emphasis in the ideas of Stekel (and Jung). In the present context the striking resemblance between Freud's early formulations and the similar principles of the Helmholtz school are noteworthy.

1. Freud represented the "libido," his equivalent of psychic energy, as a quantity which can neither be increased nor decreased. This energy can only be converted or transformed—an obvious parallel to the principle of the conservation of energy first speculatively formulated by Robert Mayer in 1842 but fully developed in the classi-

---

an affectionate hug may be recalled in later years as a genital seduction, particularly if the incident has undergone the kind of secondary elaboration that Freud's theory of repression implies. On the other hand, actual sexual stimulation may be recalled quite accurately without its necessarily having had dire consequences for later personality development. This statement does not condone sexual seduction in childhood, but neither does it condone exaggeration of the facts. The historian or critic who fails to recognize this principle of interdependence is both psychologically and philosophically naive. To vary an aphorism by Kant regarding percepts and concepts, reality without fantasy is blind and fantasy without reality is empty. A partial portrayal of the truth, presented as "an assault on truth," is a seduction by caricature.

[5]Though Freud himself here credits only Stekel, the influence of C. G. Jung, which reached its zenith in 1910, must surely have contributed to this same shift of emphasis. It was in 1911 that Jung began publishing his landmark volume *Symbols of Transformation* (1911–1912/1956) in which the universal symbolism of the racial archetypes (later called the "collective unconscious") was brought center stage (pp. 177–178).

cal paper by Helmholtz five years later.[6] Fechner applied this principle to psycho-logical sensory phenomena in his *Elemente der Psychophysik* (1860), and Freud carried the principle into the field of motivation, especially sexuality, which he broadly interpreted to allow for its alleged phenomenal transformations.

2. As a corollary of this principle, Freud maintained in his book on dreams that one must understand the *manifest* content of a dream as a transformation of the *latent* content, accomplished by the "dream-work." In so doing, he was using the model of *kinetic* and *potential* energy which, taken together, always represent a constant amount. Work is defined in physics as the transfer of energy from one body or system to another. So Freud was basing his principles on those of Helmholtz, the physicist and physiological psychologist.

3. Freud insisted upon the rule of psychic determinism, especially in his book on slips and accidental events, and this principle clearly corresponds to the physico-chemical determinism of the physicalists. Hence every item of the manifest dream can be seen as a meaningfully determined product of unconscious forces, as much governed by law as are the phenomena of the physical world.

In the theoretical physics of today, where principles derived from nuclear fission and space exploration have taken physical science far beyond Newton, Helmholtz, and even Einstein, these nineteenth-century doctrines are of limited relevance; Freud's analogous ones are regarded by many psychoanalytic theoreticians as simi-larly dated. But the point here is only that, as of the formative period 1894–1904, Freud's scientific model was that of the experimental psychology of his time and place. He was not a speculative mystic, interpreting dreams, slips, and symptoms according to his purely subjective fancy. In his psychodynamic formulations at the turn of the century, he was closer to the formulations of "experimental psychology" than were some less enterprising psychologists who clung to the physiological infra-structure. Thus, for Wundt, whose system opposed the constructs of a dynamic unconscious, Freud had little use. According to Fritz Wittels, Freud's earliest biographer, Freud declared in one of his University lectures (which Wittels at-tended) that Wundt was like the giant in Ariosto's *Orlando Furioso* who, beheaded in the heat of battle, was "too busy to notice it" and went on fighting (Wittels, 1924, p. 130).[7]

[6] At Christmas in 1898 Freud received from his friend Fliess the scientific essays of Helmholtz (1882–1883; see Kris, 1954, p. 10) which included the above-cited classical contribution of 1847 on the conservation of energy. This two-volume edition is extant in the portion of Freud's library housed at his final residence, Maresfield Gardens, London. (See Trosman & Simmons, 1973, p. 666.)

[7] It should not, however, be concluded that Freud completely dismissed Wundt. Though the founder of psychoanalysis had little use for the experimental psychology of conscious processes, he was not unaware that Wundt's scope went far beyond the laboratory and that in these other areas his scholarship demanded respect. Thus in *Totem and Taboo* (Freud, 1955), which first appeared in 1913, he repeatedly

But the advantages of Freud's early adherence to the physicalist school may have prevented his keeping pace with later advances in cultural anthropology and the psychology of the person. His view of the patient (or the normal person) as an "organism" hewed closer to nineteenth-century biology and to traditional medicine. Hence a decade later he began to desert his pristine empirical stance vis-à-vis the patient's own utterances and reverted to the allegedly universal, largely sexual, symbolism of his conceptual predecessors. In this respect he was failing to heed the individual (or idiodynamic) norms that he had at the outset sedulously respected, and he was alienating himself from what will be recognized below as experimental idiodynamics.

In this context, the paradoxical influence of Jung, whom Freud first met in 1907, was twofold. While it impelled him, on the one hand, to look with Jung to experimental supports for his theory of the unconscious (as will presently be described in some detail), it joined with the influence of Stekel, above noted, to foster an interest in archetypal folklore (see Jung, 1911–1912/1956). The paradox lies in the fact that while Freud explicitly repudiated Jung's generalized view of the libido, he did not himself escape the subtler effects of the influence. By the time he explicitly separated from Jung in early 1913 (Freud & Jung, 1974, pp. 538–539), irrevocable damage had been done to his previous, more cautious, empirical stance. (See his *Totem and Taboo*, 1913/1955.)

The Beginnings of Experimental Validation: The Study of Complexes

The year 1904 is notable for a new departure in psychoanalysis—the first attempts systematically to employ an experimental method to study psychoanalytic concepts. The method sought to detect unconscious complexes. The story is, however, less straightforward than has hitherto been thought, and the account here given will selectively stress the less known or unknown aspects. A detailed conventional history and outline of the word-association technique, but lacking these points, may be consulted in the monograph by Kohs (1914).

The method of word association was introduced by Francis Galton (1879, 1879–1880), the British psychologist. He was one of the pioneers of differential psychology in the context of which he used this method, among others. By differential psychology is meant the psychology of individual differences studied systematically by both qualitative and quantitative or statistical means. After publishing several

---

cited the recent volume by Wundt on folk psychology (1912) in which Wundt propounded views on totemism and the related practice of taboo—views which Freud considered important enough to take seriously.

separate papers on word association, mainly with himself as the object of observation, Galton brought together his results on this and cognate topics in his *Inquiries into Human Faculty*, published in 1883. That Freud knew the book early is indicated by his allusion to Galton's composite family portraits at the beginning of *The Interpretation of Dreams* (1899/1953, p. 139). Freud used this photographic device as an analogy for the mechanism of condensation in symbolic dream imagery. But this allusion further points to a probable source of the method of free association as a modification of Galton's word association. Galton had himself pointed out that the results of the method are often so highly autobiographical and intimate that a bolder man than he would be required to reveal the findings. Freud certainly was that bolder man.

From Galton's introduction of the method of word association in 1879 to its adoption in Wundt's Leipzig laboratory, established that same year, was only a matter of weeks. In the summer of 1880, Trautscholdt was using it there in the first known application of it after Galton. Examining Trautscholdt's monograph (1881–1882), one is struck by the fact that among the small number of subjects whose detailed protocols are given Wundt himself served along with G. Stanley Hall, Wundt's first American student. As we shall see more fully later, Hall was, indeed, a pioneer. We see him here in a secondary but significant role in the first use of Galton's method in the first systematic laboratory of psychology.

Other investigations with the method in Wundt's laboratory followed in the ensuing decade. Among the workers was the later famous psychiatrist Emil Kraepelin and the prolific word-association investigator Gustav Aschaffenburg (cf. Kohs, 1914). Toward the end of the decade, Ziehen used the technique with children and he appears to have first disclosed the dynamic significance of delayed responses. But most of the work originating in Leipzig under Wundt or at Jena under Ziehen had little significance for what Freud would soon be calling the unconscious.

An overlooked innovator in this field was Salomon Stricker, the experimental psychophysiologist at the University of Vienna and one of Freud's teachers, who as early as 1883 had published a monograph *Studien über die Association der Vorstellungen* (Studies on the Association of Ideas), in which the term *complex* was repeatedly employed. Stricker defined the source of ideas as words organized into "complexes" (configurations) and he recognized the emotional foundation in which such complexes were often embedded. But neither Gross nor Bleuler, or their respective research students, discussed below, made any mention of Stricker's book.

On the other hand, there is clear evidence that Freud, who used the term *complex* as early as 1895, knew the monograph. In the important and lengthy footnote in the *Studies on Hysteria* (Breuer & Freud, 1895/1955, p. 51) where he discusses what he calls "the compulsion to associate," admitting that he shared this compulsion, Freud related it to a prevailing "complex" or "complex of ideas" with a pervasive feeling tone, usually of anxiety. He avowed that he had discovered this compulsion in himself during a recent period of some weeks when his sleep was disturbed by his having to move to a new and harder bed than he was accustomed to and found, as he repeatedly awoke, that he recalled all the dreams he had had. He wrote down these dreams and traced them back by association to their sources. Here is probably the origin of his method of dream interpretation, fully developed in his subsequent masterpiece. And in the first edition of that book Freud (1899) listed Stricker's above mentioned monograph in the bibliography. The title is, however, tacked on at the end of the reference list, outside the alphabetical order. One infers that it was added at the proof stage and inserted at the end in order to avoid the costly resetting of type for the entire page. Freud would have seen a meaningful parapraxis here: in the context of his book there is evidence that the omission was probably motivated by a "complex." Freud had a grievance against Stricker. Carl Koller, another of Stricker's students, was a rival of Freud's in the demonstration of cocaine as a local anaesthetic. For this achievement Koller became well known and for it Stricker honored him. These circumstances dominate one level of Freud's "dream of the botanical monograph" (1899/1953, p. 169f.).[8]

In 1903–1904, from two independent quarters, the word-association method was applied in the diagnosis of complexes. The first work of C. G. Jung and his associates at the Burghölzli Hospital in Zurich, Switzerland, under the direction of E. Bleuler, appeared in 1904. Various other papers by Jung and his associates (1904–1909/1918, belatedly translated into English) were soon published. It was this research which first brought Jung to the attention of Freud, who at that time saw in the diagnosis of complexes an experimental validation of his conception of unconscious ego-defense. Heralded by these confirmatory studies, Jung visited Freud for the first time in March 1907 to begin a close collaboration that lasted for about five years. During that period, Freud sought almost too assiduously to groom his energetic and enthusiastic younger colleague as his successor in the beleaguered camp of psychoanalysis.

But the method of word association for the discovery of complexes was already being used at the University of Prague under the guidance of Hans Gross, Professor of Criminal Law, who, in the 1890s, founded "criminalistics." The investigators were Max Wertheimer and Julius Klein (1904), two of his students, who applied the technique to diagnose the truth or falsity of legal testimony. The applications to the

---

[8]Another overlooked figure of the 1880s, trained in Vienna as a philosophical psychologist under Franz Brentano, was Richard Wahle (1857–1935). His treatise on the association of ideas (Wahle, 1885) stressed the role of fantasy and wishes in the association process, which he considered as both conscious and unconscious. He coined the term *solicitation* to account for the way in which ideas or images are evoked by other members of a series, often from beyond the threshold of consciousness. This conception was a clear predecessor of what later came to be known as free association. That Freud knew Wahle's work is indicated by the fact that the published dissertation of Wahle (1884) is among the books of Freud's personal collection which found their way from Vienna to the New York Psychiatric Institute in September 1939. However, Wahle in his later writings, which are characterized by a Humean type of skepticism, utterly repudiated psychoanalytic theory as unproved and unprovable (Wahle, 1931, p. 6).

juridical setting were of chief interest to them, just as the psychiatric implications, in reference to the dynamic unconscious, were central for Jung and his associates.

Freud's early awareness of these developments is brought out by a lecture on the topic which he delivered in June 1906 to a university seminar session at the invitation of Alexander Löffler, Professor of Jurisprudence, in Vienna. The paper (Freud 1906/1959) appeared six months later in the *Archiv für Kriminal-Anthropologie und Kriminalistik*, Volume XXVI, edited by the above-mentioned Dr. Gross. In it Freud, for the first time in his writings, alluded to Jung. He also appositely cited the earlier work of Wertheimer and Klein (1904) to whom he attributed the first use of the word-association method to study complexes presumably present in the accused.

Freud's paper is remarkable not only for its timeliness but for other intrinsic reasons. In it he tellingly compared the criminal with the neurotic (Freud, 1906/1959, pp. 108, 111). He posited marked similarities and differences between them even if his treatment of the comparison is exaggerated. He stresses the role of *secrets* in both the criminal defendant and the hysterical patient—secrets which "plague the patient in just the same way as a guilty conscience does." But he distinguished between the two in the crucial respect that the criminal hides his secret from others "whereas in the case of the hysteric it is a secret which . . . is hidden even from himself" (ibid.). This sharp contrast is, of course, open to question. Freud is more circumspect and up to date in his discussion of individuals who, although innocent, react as though they are guilty because of a pervasive neurotic sense of guilt that seizes upon the accusation implied in the examining procedure. Guilty responses from such individuals could mislead the examiner and the magistrate. An extended discussion of the point leads Freud to anticipate the present-day position that limits or excludes lie-detector evidence in courts of law. He did not mention the other extreme of lie-detector fallibility: the fact that habitual liars often come through these tests unscarred.

In any event, Freud was well briefed on one relevant topic when he received Jung as his guest in Vienna in 1907, eight months after the above lecture. They may possibly have discussed, among more important matters, the rivalry between Prague and Zurich which was then brewing. This contest over priority had been provoked by Jung's repeated published assertions that Wertheimer's research had been inspired by his own. Wertheimer (1906) was hence impelled to publish a note of correction in which he demonstrated that, together with Klein, his first publication had antedated Jung's. Though his priority in print was slight, his work with Klein dated back three and one-half years (to 1900) at which time he started by serving as subject in experiments conducted by Klein. Jung (1908) reluctantly acquiesced in a reply in which he stressed that only 12 days separated his own first publication from the earliest one by Wertheimer.[9]

---

[9]It has not previously been noted that Wertheimer, the founder of the Gestalt school of psychology,

Regardless of priority, the so-called complexes were playing the same role for both the legal and the medical examiner. In a legal hearing, where guilt or innocence is in question, evidence of false testimony is meant to cast doubt upon the character of the witness and the acceptability of his or her testimony. Similarly, with neurotic patients, the word-association technique supplemented the method of free association by penetrating the patient's defenses. But in neither instance was there conclusive proof that the complex was truly unconscious. That shortcoming points up the inadequacy of the word-association procedure in fully confirming the alleged basis of Freud's approach—the dynamic unconscious as a scientifically acceptable conception.

Perhaps to compensate for this limitation, the method of word association was soon expanded to include concomitant physiological measures of respiration, heart beat, blood pressure, electrical skin conductance, and muscle tremor. Under the name "polygraph" (or lie detector) this multiple procedure for evaluating the truth of legal testimony today perpetuates the pioneer work of Wertheimer and Klein. But, as above noted, evidence obtained by the polygraph is not legally admissible in most courts of law—a restriction which Freud foresaw with remarkable clarity in 1906. At that time he also relegated the word-association experiments to the status of "dummy exercises" because "you will never be able to reproduce in them the same psychological situation as in the examination of a defendant in a criminal case" (Freud, 1906/1959, p. 114). By these words he was anticipating his later denigrative opinion of the entire experimental approach to psychoanalytic concepts.

Jung's research with the word-association method, which occupied him during 1904–1909, was, as we have seen, of great interest to Freud. Jung had mailed him a copy of the first cumulative monograph on the topic (Jung, 1906) the year before he visited Freud in Vienna, but Freud, acknowledging the gift in his very first letter to Jung, confessed that "in my impatience I had already acquired [it]" (Freud & Jung, 1974, p. 3). Later, Freud's regard for the work diminished. That point is quite evident in his essay on the history of the psychoanalytic movement, published in 1914 (Freud, 1914/1957). He there states (p. 28): "By this means it had become possible to arrive at rapid experimental confirmation of psycho-analytic observations and to demonstrate to students certain connections which an analyst would only have been able to tell them about. The first bridge linking up experimental psychology with psycho-analysis had been built." However, on the next page, having recounted the divergence between himself and Jung, he wrote (p. 29): ". . . I do not value this contribution so highly as others do whose concern with these matters is

---

which arose in opposition to elementary associationism, paradoxically began his research career with publications featuring the method of associated verbal elements. Did he possibly learn from the defects of his initial investigations, or would he perhaps have said that in a sense a "complex" is, indeed, a configuration? Ziehen's equivalent term, as early as 1891, was actually *constellation* (Ziehen, 1891, p. 119; 1895, p. 213).

more remote . . . . It has neither itself produced a psychological theory, nor has it proved capable of easy incorporation into the context of psycho-analytic theory."

The Clark Vigentennial: 1909

In 1908 G. Stanley Hall, the president of Clark University in Worcester, Massachusetts, and one of America's most distinguished psychologists who had essentially founded the American Psychological Association and had started the first professional journal of psychology in this country, began to plan for the twentieth anniversary of the opening of Clark University in 1889, the year of years. He had for his guidance the precedent of the tenth anniversary celebration, at which time he invited world leaders from several sciences, including Forel in psychiatry and related behavioral science and S. Ramón y Cajal, father of the neurone theory. These and other lecturers received honorary degrees. But he had something on a larger scale in mind this time—not just five lecturers in a brief event, but twenty or more participating over a period of at least two weeks. In the field of the behavioral sciences, one of the main areas to be covered, there were to be about ten world leaders in psychology, psychiatry, anthropology, and pedagogy; but there were to be equally distinguished speakers in the physical and in the social sciences. At the ceremonies for conferring honorary degrees, twenty-nine participants were eventually designated. Among them were eight representing the behavioral sciences: Franz Boaz, Leo Burgerstein, Sigmund Freud, H. S. Jennings, C. G. Jung, Adolf Meyer, William Stern, and E. B. Titchener. But for some reason this multidisciplinary, distinguished group were eclipsed for most later psychologists by the legend that the Clark celebration of 1909 was a conference honoring Freud and psychoanalysis. Even so well-informed a historian as E. G. Boring innocently gave currency to the legend in one of his publications (Boring, 1965, p. 9). When I demonstrated the error to him, he accepted the correction but shifted the responsibility for it to his own former mentor, E. B. Titchener, one of the honored participants on that occasion.

As with most legends, a germinal element of fact is discoverable. There can be little doubt that Hall, being himself a psychologist and an educator, was chiefly interested in the behavioral scientists whom he was instrumental in inviting to participate and, even more to the point, he looked forward to the occasion as an opportunity to further his own growing interest in Freud and psychoanalysis. He wanted to effect a reconciliation between that field of psychological knowledge, grudgingly acknowledged in Europe, with the rest of psychology—the experimental science that he knew and had attempted to foster in America. It is this basis of the legend that makes a brief account of the 1909 Clark conference a vital part of the present discussion. Since a more detailed account, including all the correspondence between Hall and Freud before and after the conference, is in preparation for separate publication (Rosenzweig, 1985), the present one stresses only certain high-lights that concern Hall's hope for creating a bridge from Freudian psychoanalysis to experimental psychology or, at any rate, to the broad scientific psychology which he had long fostered.

For further background one must briefly step back to glance at Hall's own early training in psychology. We can then better appreciate what he was attempting at this time: Hall had been a student at European, especially German, universities twice. The first occasion was before he achieved his Ph.D. degree, the second after he had earned it at Harvard under Bowditch (at the Medical School) and William James in the Department of Philosophy. Hall was the first person in America to receive the Ph.D. degree in psychology, and nominally his sponsor was James, although his research was done mainly under Bowditch. After taking his degree in 1878, he traveled in Europe for post-Ph.D. work from 1878 to 1880, at which time he became, as he observed in his letter to Wundt quoted below, Wundt's first American student. But his quest for knowledge was much broader than that affiliation would suggest. The best description of it is found in the following words by E. B. Titchener. It should be noted that Titchener in his remarks is referring to both of Hall's European sojourns.

> Six years in Germany, without the haunting oppression of the doctor's thesis—such was Dr. Hall's opportunity, and he made the most of what was offered. He heard Hegel from the lips of Michelet; he sat with Paulsen in Trendelenburg's seminary; he undertook work of research in Ludwig's laboratory, with von Kries as partner; he experimented with Helmholtz; he was the first American student in Wundt's newly founded laboratory of psychology; he discussed psychophysics with Fechner, the creator of psychophysics; he was present at Heidenhain's early essays in Hypnotism; he attended those lavishly experimental lectures of Czermak, where hecatombs of dogs were sacrificed on the altar of science. . . ; he followed courses in theology, metaphysics, logic, ethics, psychology, the philosophy of religion—in physics, chemistry, biology, physiology, anatomy, neurology, anthropology, psychiatry; he frequented clinic and seminary, laboratory and lecture; and he roamed afield as far as Paris on the west and Vienna on the east (Wilson, 1914, p. 48).

Returning to the 1909 celebration, we may begin by observing that among the very first invitations extended by Hall to prospective participants were two, seemingly of equal importance to him, in letters both dated December 15, 1908: one to Wilhelm Wundt, the creator of the first laboratory of experimental psychology, and the other to Sigmund Freud, the founder of psychoanalysis. Hall's hitherto unpublished letter to Wundt is historically so interesting in all its details that it will be given here in full:[10]

---

[10] I gratefully acknowledge the permission to publish the letters between Hall and Wundt granted me by the Clark University Archives, William Koelsch, Archivist. Translation of Wundt's letter from the German by Saul Rosenzweig.

December 15, 1908

Professor Wilhelm Wundt,
  University of Leipzig
    Leipzig, Germany

My dear Professor Wundt:

The first week in next July marks the twentieth anniversary of the founding of this University, which we wish to celebrate by a congress of American psychologists, at which we are extremely anxious to have you present.

Not only, as you know, have many American professors been your own personal students (and I have always been very proud of having been the first and oldest), but the influence of your thought in this country has been profound and far-reaching.

Moreover, we are now having occasion to greatly refresh our sense of obligation to you, our master, by the efforts being made to cooperate in the approaching celebration of your anniversary at Leipzig, in a way that shall be worthy of you and of us.

Under these circumstances, it has seemed to my advisers and to myself that we may appeal with unusual cogency to you to now visit this country, and allow those psychologists who have, and the far larger number who have not, seen or heard you to have the stimulation of that experience.

As you know, the voyages are now made very easy, quick, and comfortable. We have chosen the best season for temperature and weather here, and hope to be able to give you the best audience the country can afford.

The topics could be either new or old, or anything to suit yourself, and be presented either in German or in English.

We are able to attach an honorarium, to cover all expenses, of $750, or 3000 Marks, together with entertainment as long as you remain in this city.

I am, with great respect,

Sincerely yours,
[G. Stanley Hall]
President

The reply, translated from the German, follows:

Leipzig   5. January, 1909

Dear and Honored Professor Stanley Hall!

Please accept my heartiest thanks for your very friendly invitation to the 20th anniversary celebration of Clark University. I would so gladly come over the ocean to this celebration, especially since I would have the opportunity to see not only you but many other American friends at this single event. But there are two reasons which make it completely impossible for me to accept this enticing invitation. First, I have now reached the stage in life at which such long journeys are not a simple matter, especially when, like me, one is no longer accustomed to such trips. Secondly, our University will be celebrating its 500th Jubilee immediately after your celebration, with a very short period between the two events. Added to this is the fact that I have been requested to give the Jubilee Address on that occasion, a duty which I am afraid could not readily be well discharged if I have just come back from a long journey. My regret in declining is that much greater because I would so much have enjoyed this opportunity to see you again as well as the other American friends who at various times visited the previous Psychological Institute and carried out work there.

Please accept my congratulations on the successful completion of the second decade of Clark University under your direction, and my wishes for its further success, especially in the disciplines of psychology and pedagogy.

With best greetings.

Your,
(signed) W. Wundt

It should be noted that in the invitations Hall extended in December, 1908, the plan was to begin celebrating the twentieth anniversary in early July. This date conflicted with Wundt's already planned participation as primary speaker at the 500th anniversary of Leipzig University, scheduled for the last week of July. (To the latter event Professor Sanford was, in fact, later sent to Leipzig to represent the young sister institution in Worcester.) But Hall made no attempt to prevail over Wundt's various cogent arguments presented in the above-cited letter.

However, when Freud also declined, a second letter of invitation was sent him in February 1909, in which Freud's participation was shifted from July to early September—a more acceptable time for Freud; and two new enticements were included: an increase in the honorarium (to the exact figure which had originally been offered to Wundt, but not to Freud) and a specific mention of the contemplated honorary degree to be conferred during the celebration. This time Freud accepted.

The juxtaposition of Wundt and Freud in these earliest invitations to the conference is emblematic of Hall's personal aim in reconciling by this event two quite disparate branches of psychology, both of which were, in his very broad conception of what psychology should be, essential to an adequate understanding of the totality of human behavior. For this former theological student there was only one area of behavior that he refused to countenance as legitimate for the science of psychology—the area of spiritistic or psychic phenomena. Oddly, this was the very area that Hall's former mentor and colleague William James at Harvard promoted more and more assiduously with the passage of the years. It was one of the bones of contention between these two most prominent American psychologists. In the fuller account of the Clark conference, the rumblings of this contention play an interesting part, and into one aspect of it Freud and Jung were drawn by Hall toward the end of the conference week.

Jung's participation in the conference is, in retrospect, quite consonant with the

155

present theme since two of his three lectures (Jung, 1910) were devoted to the empirical word-association method, a technique in which Hall had been interested, as we already know, from its inception by Francis Galton. Hall had, in fact, used this "Freud-Jung method" (as he called it) earlier in 1909 in some investigations of psychic phenomena, embarked upon in an effort objectively to unmask their insubstantial character. But, contemporaneously, there is some enigma about Jung's invitation to participate, not made any easier by his own incorrect avowal in his autobiography (Jung, 1963, p. 120) that he was invited "simultaneously" with Freud when, in fact, the invitation was surely not extended in 1908 and probably not until May 1909. A probable factor in the delay—or in the first impetus—to extend the invitation may have been the declination by E. Meumann, a Wundtian by training. This surmise is borne out by the circumstance that Meumann was working in learning as applied to pedagogy, and Jung's eventual honorary degree was, unlike Freud's, in pedagogy, not in psychology (as was Freud's). Jung's third and last lecture on the "Psychic Life of the Child" provided only a slim basis for the degree characterized in this way. It is of interest that Jung was only thirty-four years old in 1909, the youngest of the twenty-nine honored with degrees, and young indeed as compared to other behavioral scientists invited as lecturers. (Stern was also exceptionally young—only thirty-seven—but, unlike Jung, he was already the author of several scientific books.) Why and how Jung was invited remains puzzling though in retrospect his later career justified the invitation.

In any event, two of the eight behavioral scientists who lectured during the celebration represented psychoanalysis—a much larger proportion than would have been expected at any similar conference at that time. Moreover, Hall gave special distinction to their presence by having Freud and Jung as his house guests during the week of their participation.

We know from the published letters of William James (James, 1926, II, pp. 327–328) that he attended the Clark conference for one day in order to hear Freud. Afterward he wrote to his friend Théodore Flournoy in Switzerland to share his impressions. With characteristic gentlemanly generosity he told his friend that he hoped Freud and his pupils would carry on their line of work so as to reveal what there was in it, but he confided that Freud impressed him as "a man obsessed with fixed ideas." Freud seems to have been more favorably impressed by James, for in his brief autobiography (Freud, 1925/1959), when commenting on his participation at Clark, he mentions a walk that he took with James during the conference and, with admiration, describes the courage with which his companion excused himself at one point, asked Freud to continue while he remained behind (to recover from what was apparently an angina attack). Freud remarks that he wished he could behave with such fortitude under similar circumstances.

I have been able to reconstruct from newspaper accounts collated against the published lectures the actual order in which Freud treated the topics he presented at Clark. Then using a surviving but unpublished letter from James to Hall, it became clear what topic James heard Freud discuss at the conference. The day was Friday, September 10, the one day James was present, and Freud lectured on his theory of dreams. (On that day the group picture on the steps of the Clark Library must also have been taken, with James prominently in the front row.) It may then not be an unrelated fact that one of the very last papers that James wrote (on December 16–17, 1909, as his diary states) and published in 1910, the year of his death, included several of his own dreams—a unique performance for James. But he gave a quite different kind of interpretation from anything recommended by Freud (James, 1910). To James, these dreams, which he recalled from his sojourn in San Francisco in 1906 during the great earthquake, suggested something bordering on a mystical view of the dissociated dream state. The content of one dream, with affinities to his famous brother Henry's "The Beast in the Jungle," played no part in the interpretation. Could these dreams have entered into the conversation with Freud during the walk in Worcester if, as we may reasonably suppose, that event took place after Freud's lecture (given at 11:00 A.M.)?

More relevant to the present context is the fact that at Christmas, 1909, the annual meeting of the American Psychological Association took place in Cambridge, Massachusetts, and that a session of nearly three hours (on December 29) was devoted to Freud's theories with papers by Ernest Jones, Morton Prince, James J. Putnam, and Boris Sidis (among others). Jones discussed Freud's theory of dreams. Boris Sidis, an outspoken antagonist of Freud's theories and one of James's former Ph.D. students and an active experimentalist in psychopathology, visited his ailing master at his Cambridge home to share the discussion of Freud's ideas at APA (diary of James, Dec. 31, 1909). James condensed that report in the phrase "Jones windfall" but the term *windfall* in 1909 had practically the opposite meaning from its current usage. As Freud's orthodox representative, Jones had apparently been the special object of a vigorous attack by Sidis who, in his own opinion, "blew the man down." Sidis, like Prince and James, was unable to accept Freud's emphasis on sexuality for which Sidis sometimes preferred to substitute the pervasive influence of fear (Sidis, 1916, pp. 43–63).

From the other camp, Hall shared with Freud by letter (December 30, 1909) his very different view of the APA sessions, noting particularly that Sidis "deprecated a Freud cult in this country" and predicted its quick demise; but Putnam put Sidis in his place by noting the indebtedness of Sidis to Freud's work. In response, Freud gratefully wrote to Hall (on January 11, 1910): "I cannot suppress a certain unholy joy that you and Putnam have rejected Boris Sidis who is neither very honest nor very intelligent. I mean he deserved nothing better" (Rosenzweig, 1985). Clearly a prejudiced statement. Sidis (1898) had published a very original book in experimental psychopathology, with an Introduction by James, in anticipation of some of Freud's work and methods. In any event, Sidis and Hall heard the same session with very different selectivity—a presage of the future more widespread debate over psychoanalysis.

157

We may conclude that participation by Freud and Jung in the Clark conference made a strong impression on contemporary American psychologists and psychiatrists, and the event for the first time gave Freud's position a hearing in the scientific forum previously denied it in Europe. But despite this opportunity and the further momentum that this recognition gave to the psychoanalytic movement as such, which had its first formal organization as the International Psychoanalytic Association at a congress in Nuremberg in 1910, Hall did not succeed in gaining wide acceptance for psychoanalysis as a scientific approach. For one thing, the "Boston School" led by Morton Prince, who had founded the *Journal of Abnormal Psychology* in 1906, used the event to begin crystallizing its opposition to psychoanalysis, a confrontation more evident in psychopathology than in general psychology. Freud did, however, gain an important American adherent in the person of James J. Putnam, Professor at the Harvard Medical School, who maintained for many years a friendly debate about Freudian theory with Morton Prince, privately and in print (Hale, 1971).

The Logic of Psychoanalysis as Science

The decade or two following the Clark conference witnessed sporadic efforts to subject aspects of psychoanalytic theory to the test of experimental verification. Beginning around 1930, these forays became more numerous and more systematic until, during the decade of the 1970s, several book-length surveys of such work were published. There were also by this later period various efforts to examine the amenability of psychoanalytic theory to rigorous scientific definition—exercises in the logic of science rather than in laboratory research. Nevertheless, some recognition of these efforts will be a salutary introduction to the review of empirical work.

After this preparation, several typical studies of dreams—Freud's royal road to the unconscious—will be described. This will be followed by a synopsis of the chief published surveys of research on the validation of psychoanalytic concepts. Then a more critical examination will be accorded one selected area of research which began around 1930 and has continued with variations in aim or method ever since: the experimental definition of repression, the keystone of psychoanalytic theory. There flowed from some of the research on repression and related concepts a recognition of the complexities of the human experimental situation. These insights, first formulated systematically in 1933 and revived with special vigor in the 1960s, will be examined as an outgrowth of knowledge about the transference situation in psychoanalysis. It will be maintained that from this nexus arose an experimental idiodynamics of human behavior—an approach in which behavior is experimentally analyzed with the dynamics of the individual considered as a matrix of events.

Though not directly concerned with the experimental or other observational verification of psychoanalytic concepts, the rigorous scrutiny to which psychoanalysis has from time to time been subjected during the last thirty or forty years from the standpoint of the logic of science is an essential aspect of the relation of psychoanalysis to experimental psychology (Horwitz, 1963). Most of these critiques have originated from the position of logical- or neo-positivism. This school grew up in Vienna, incidentally the city of Freud and psychoanalysis. It owes much of its inception to Ernst Mach and his philosophy of science which was closely tied to British empiricism and which influenced some of the later developments in experimental psychology. The early history of this Vienna Circle is ably described in the short book by Kraft (1953).

For present purposes a systematic exposition of the logical critiques of psychoanalysis as science is not possible for a variety of reasons, but the highlights of such critiques can be indicated and some of the chief exponents of these views mentioned. One may begin with a paper by Gustav Bergmann which clearly bears on the present purposes though the main conclusion it reaches reflects a special preference for a certain type of behaviorism.

In "Psychoanalysis and Experimental Psychology," Bergmann (1943), an adherent of logical positivism, points up the necessity for defining the terms employed in psychoanalytic theory. He contrasts the logical stance of psychoanalytic theory with that of learning theory (as presented by Hull and Spence) which, he maintains, can be applied to the empirical content of psychoanalytic theory. The semantic bridge is the *historical* character of many psychoanalytic propositions, on the one hand, and those of learning theory, on the other. These approaches address themselves, macroscopically and microscopically, respectively, to the life history of the individual organism.

But this contribution is not fully typical of the neopositivistic point of view as applied to psychoanalytic theory. More typical are publications by Ayer (1936) which undertake a radical analysis of language as a vehicle of thought and then emphasize the principle of verifiability. Many of the adherents of the Vienna Circle have stressed this important criterion of the meaning of a scientific proposition. On this basis the meaning of a proposition lies in the method of its verification. Thus stated the position approximates to American operationism (Bridgman, 1928).

Several of the contributions in the *Minnesota Studies in the Philosophy of Science* (Feigl & Scriven, 1956) address themselves to the nature of psychoanalytic concepts from the general position of logical positivism where verifiability or testability becomes the basis for accepting a proposition in any science, including psychoanalysis. On this basis, concepts like "libido" are obviously far too vague—too characterized by "surplus meaning"—to serve a scientific purpose. But in this same context behaviorism, especially radical behaviorism, is also rejected by certain critics as unacceptably naive despite its alleged operational basis (Scriven, 1956).

The critique of psychoanalysis from the standpoint of neo-positivism has crested in Popper's principle of falsifiability which he has summarized in the words: ". . .

the criterion of the scientific status of a theory is its falsifiability, or refutability, or testability" (Popper, 1965, p. 37). He continues: "The criterion of falsifiability . . . says that statements or systems of statements, in order to be ranked as scientific, must be capable of conflicting with possible, or conceivable, observations" (p. 39). The bearing of this criterion on many of the investigations reviewed below is obvious. But as will be seen, some of the experiments on repression are relatively sounder than some other investigations in the area of our present concern because they proceed on the basis of hypothetical predictions to be confirmed or disconfirmed by future observation and tested by observations with a control group for whom the conditions are made deliberately different by design.

However, the critique of psychoanalytic theory advanced by Popper (1959; 1965, pp. 34–39) has proved to be very appealing to such prestigious judges as Peter Medawar (1972, pp. 34–36, 62f.). An illuminating rejoinder by Holloway to his argument is generously included by Medawar in his book (1972, pp. 39–50). A more direct response to Popper's own position is to be found in the book by G. S. Jones (1968). That work attempts also to reconcile on psychological grounds the logical postulates of neopositivism and the Freudian mechanisms of irrationality.

In the studies to be discussed below for their bearing on the relationships of experimental psychology to psychoanalysis, the finer logical and philosophical points of interest to the neopositivist have rarely been focal for psychological investigators. These individuals have either lacked the sophistication to recognize the logical pitfalls of their work or they have considered these refinements irrelevant to the commonsense empiricism on which they have been satisfied to proceed with the consent of their peers. In adopting such a stand they have, on the whole, not been too different from empirical researchers in areas other than psychology. Philosophers of science tend not to be practicing scientists and, reciprocally, practicing scientists are not by nature or training philosophically inclined. These remarks are not meant to justify the isolation of the one field of endeavor from the other. It is, however, fair to say that psychologists investigating psychoanalytic concepts are, by and large, no more at fault than are psychologists with other concerns. In the long run, however, it will probably be from the rare psychologist who is able to work empirically and yet think occasionally in more abstract terms that the future breakthroughs so urgently needed to provide coherence to the disparate efforts of the behavioral scientists will emerge.

A final comment may be useful before discussing specific attempts to validate psychoanalytic concepts by experimental methods. It has sometimes been argued that psychoanalytic theory, not being nomothetic, does not call for experimental validation. In other words, cause and effect formulations are not involved in psychoanalysis which is primarily a matter of the individual's life history.[11] The

---

[11] An example of this position is found in an exchange between Havelock Ellis and Freud. In an article Ellis (1917, reprinted in his book *The Philosophy of Conflict*, 1919, Chap. XVIII) called Freud's vocation

obvious answer is that while parts of Freud's overall position are not nomothetic, others are unmistakably so, for example, the pleasure and reality principles (Freud, 1911/1958). In one of the best epitomes of psychoanalysis, Freud (1926/1959a) classified the whole of psychoanalytic theory as consisting of dynamic, economic, and topographical principles, all of which include propositions he considered to be scientific (nomothetic) in intention and scope. The dynamic concept of repression, the cornerstone of psychoanalytic theory according to Freud (1914/1957, p. 16), asserts that experiences which offend the ego are apt to be forgotten while those which gratify it are remembered. Granted that the ego of the particular individual must be taken into account in defining what will or will not be pleasant or unpleasant to the particular ego, the general proposition itself demands verification as do all such propositions. To argue thus is not to say that the individuality of the repressed content can be ignored. It is, however, to deny that such individuality, contrasting with the nomothetic, is to be regarded as idiographic.

In the dichotomy of nomothetic versus idiographic (considered below in more detail), idiographic events are held to be unique and unreplicable. They are facts of history which can occur but once: they can only be described, not predicted or controlled. They are hence not open to verification, as are nomothetic propositions. But in that context the distinction between *idiographic* and *idiodynamic* has to be considered. As will later appear, the idiodynamic refers not to a given unreplicable event but to a *universe* of events which, *unique in configuration through time*, permits prediction (if not always control) and comprehension in its own terms. Knowing some limited portion of the idioverse—the unique universe of events of any given person—it becomes possible to define and to understand the rest of that universe.

It was precisely this idiodynamic orientation that underlay Galton's word-association method and Freud's adaptation of it in his earliest uses of free association, as above described. But when, as will be shown presently, Freud later departed from the strictly idiodynamic interpretations, which free association demands, and embraced instead the universal symbolism employed by Stekel and Jung, he surrendered his own more rigorous orientation. His early opposition to Stekel as a "wild" psychoanalyst and to Jung as "mystical" were quietly abandoned in a regressive

---

"artistic" rather than "scientific." The highly individualized process of free association with its dependence upon the particular life history was offered in evidence. Freud (1920b/1955, p. 263) quickly rejected this characterization: "The aim of this essay [by Ellis] is to show that the writings of the creator of analysis should be judged not as a piece of scientific work but as an artistic production. We cannot but regard this view as a fresh turn taken by resistance and as a repudiation of analysis, even though it is disguised in a friendly, indeed in too flattering a manner. We are inclined to meet it with a most decided contradiction." Five years later Freud devoted an entire paper to "The Resistance to Psycho-analysis" (Freud, 1925/1961) in which the various forms of such resistance and the psychological motives for it were exposed. According to Freud, psychoanalytic theory was to be judged as science comparable to Darwin's theory of evolution and the Copernican theory of the solar system (Freud, 1917/1955).

spirit of competition. The opportunity for psychoanalytic method to become more fully idiodynamic was temporarily lost.

The thrust of the present contribution, as stated at the outset, is toward the validation of psychoanalytic theory to become a harbinger of idiodynamics—a harbinger that awaits fulfillment. That goal can be finally achieved when dynamic psychology advances from an exclusively nomothetic position to embrace the implications of Freud's early clinical interpretations of the individual case (implicitly idiodynamic) and then combines these two positions in *experimental idiodynamics.*

From Early to Recent Attempts to Validate Freud's Theory of Dreams

The first experimental effort in the area of psychoanalysis after the research by Jung and others by word association was the pioneer but short-lived study by Karl Schrötter (1912) which attempted experimentally to produce Freudian dream symbolism as an incidental result by hypnotic intervention. The work was published in one of the first established psychoanalytic journals and was favorably reviewed before publication by Freud himself who mentioned it in his correspondence with Jung (Freud & Jung, 1974, pp. 485–486, 489) as "experimental confirmation of our dream symbolism." He continued, "This marks the beginning of a new branch of experimental psychology." Unfortunately this effort did not pass beyond its preliminary stage because the investigator committed suicide the next year. However, Freud still remembered the research for some favorable mention in a book he published in 1933 (Freud, 1933, p. 36). But he also commented there, somewhat ironically and more generally, on the doubtful necessity for such experimental efforts to validate psychoanalytic theory:

> Only quite recently the physicians at an American university refused to allow that psycho-analysis was a science, on the ground that it admits of no experimental proof. They might have raised the same objection against astronomy; experimentation with the heavenly bodies is after all exceedingly difficult.

One detects a growing ambivalence about this type of research if one compares these comments with Freud's unqualified endorsement twenty years earlier.

A complement to the Schrötter research was a study on daydreams, specifically, the foster-child fantasy, published by an American psychologist. It has somehow escaped most surveys of the verification literature. The work was performed by Edmund S. Conklin (1920) who obtained his Ph.D. under Hall at Clark where he was a student from 1908 to 1911, and he hence very probably heard Freud in 1909. Though the investigation did not involve an induced experimental condition, it appears to have been the first explicit attempt to validate a significant psychoanalytic generalization, an aspect of the "family romance" described by Freud (Rank, 1909) as an extended version of the Oedipus theory. Several psychoanalytic authors asserted with Freud that in the years before puberty children often entertained the idea that their present parents were not their actual ones. Their real ones were of noble birth or otherwise eminent. Psychoanalytic excursions into the nature of folklore and myth in the period from 1909 to 1920 elaborated this generalization, most notably in the work of Otto Rank. Rank's monograph *The Myth of the Birth of the Hero,* translated into English in 1914, first appeared in German in 1909.

Conklin attempted to validate and determine the prevalence of the alleged foster-child fantasy by the administration of a specially prepared questionnaire to about 1,000 subjects ranging in age from fourteen to twenty-five years. Returns from 904 individuals were examined and statistically analyzed under eleven rubrics. A chief finding was that 28 percent of the 904 subjects readily recalled having a foster-child fantasy at one of several stages of development which Conklin described. He concluded that the findings provided "support and amplification of the generalizations from psychoanalysis," especially the assertions made by Rank in his collaboration with Freud.

A cognate but broader investigation was conducted at the end of the decade by G. V. Hamilton (1929), a psychiatrist who worked under Adolf Meyer for a time. Though the focus was on marriage as examined in the light of Freud's theories of sexual development, the work included a section (Chap. XIII) on "Daydreams and Sleeping Dreams." The subjects were 200 married men and women who responded to a detailed, systematic questionnaire, a significant forerunner of the methodology of Alfred C. Kinsey a generation later. Throughout the report Freud's views are cited and subjected to critical scrutiny. Some years earlier the author had published more strictly experimental research concerned with the sexual behavior of monkeys and baboons (Hamilton, 1914). The new empirical investigation of marriage was a pioneer effort that aroused considerable interest not only among psychiatrists but among psychologists and sociologists as well. Hamilton considered his main results to be supportive of Freud's orientation which he epitomized by the "study of the child in the adult" (1914, p. 327).

Of incidental but intriguing interest is the fact that the American playwright Eugene O'Neill and his wife served among the subjects in Hamilton's research. Moreover, in 1926 O'Neill was "analyzed" by Dr. Hamilton for a brief period, the chief complaint being alcoholism (Shaeffer, 1973, pp. 188–190, 233). O'Neill also consulted him about the composition of his most famous play, *Strange Interlude,* and soon after its production, Hamilton published a psychoanalytic review of it in the *Theatre Guild Magazine* (Hamilton, 1928). In his interpretation of the play's protagonist, Nina, as a narcissist, he blended the insights gleaned from his recently completed investigation of marriage with Freud's view of libido economy in women. The relationship between Hamilton and O'Neill strikingly illustrates

163

Freud's growing influence on American culture in the two decades following the conference at Clark University.

These early studies of dreaming (and related Freudian topics) may be profitably compared with their current counterpart which largely resulted from the new knowledge regarding the nature of sleep. This field of research has expanded rapidly during the past twenty-five years, with the combined efforts of physiologists, psychoanalysts, and psychologists, after starting from the accidental discovery of the rapid eye movements (REM) that accompany nightdream imagery. This latter observation was made in 1952 by Aserinsky, a graduate student working with the physiologist Kleitman, and was published the following year (Aserinsky & Kleitman, 1953).[12] Related phenomena, such as a certain type of brain wave, soon came to be recognized as concomitant indicators of dreaming, and a typical sleep cycle which varied with the presence of dreams was soon depicted.

One of the most significant developments was the experimental induction of dream (or REM) deprivation by waking up subjects during REM periods. Such interruption produced a great increase in "dream time" (Dement & Fisher, 1960). "Apparently there is a quantitive dream need . . . ," they state. (This need, a tension reducer, has been the thesis of a book by W. Robert [1886] whom these authors do not mention but whom Freud repeatedly cited in his *Interpretation of Dreams*.) Fisher asserted "that the experiments confirmed Freud's assumptions that dreaming is a necessary psychobiological function," and he speculated that dream deprivation might cause periods of waking mental derangement with hallucinations. However, later research has not always demonstrated such negative effects.

The literature in this rich area is by now so highly specialized that it can only be mentioned in passing. It is included here mainly to indicate the fruitfulness of Freud's theories about the functions of sleep and dreaming, even though the specialists are by no means of one voice in their views regarding the relevance or significance of their results for Freudian theory (Fisher, 1965, 1978; Witkin & Lewis, 1967).

Surveys of Independent Investigations to Validate Psychoanalytic Concepts

The decade of the 1930s was very fruitful in attempts to validate psychoanalytic concepts by experimental and other observational methods. It began with Flugel's

[12] It is historically significant that the first observations of eye movements in dreams were reported by G. Trumbull Ladd sixty years earlier (Ladd, 1892). It is an index of Freud's insightful scholarship that in the very first edition of his book on dreams (1899/1953, pp. 32–33) he cited and discussed at some length this experimental, introspective contribution. Freud fully grasped the precision of this research on visual dreams, the form which, he noted, was commonly taken by the imagery during sleep. He did not, of course, foresee the further experimental possibilities of eye movements.

keynote contribution to *Psychologies of 1930* (Flugel, 1930), which ended with the challenge to "academic" psychologists to apply rigorous experimental and other empirical methods to the verification of the clinically derived seminal but vaguely formulated concepts of psychoanalysis. Flugel concluded:

> . . . it has still to be seen how far the obvious difficulties in applying true experimental methods to psychoanalysis are really insuperable. It may be that a body of psychologists fully trained both in experimental psychology and in psychoanalysis (at present there are scarcely any such) may find means of overcoming many of these difficulties. . . . What eventual success such methods may achieve it is, of course, impossible to say at present. In view of the vast benefits that psychology would be likely to derive, if psychoanalysis could be made amenable to experimental technique, the attempt seems emphatically to be worth the making (1930, p. 394).

Having in the meantime undertaken just such a program of research, with stress on the investigation of repression, I made a somewhat more explicit appeal for this kind of work a few years later (Rosenzweig, 1937a). It began with an epigraph from Claude Bernard (1865/1927) who had done for physiology what needed now to be done for psychology by another form of "experimental medicine." The article passed in review several ongoing programs of research which shared this aim: the behavioristic, largely Pavlovian, orientation; the Gestalt standpoint, represented in particular by Lewin and his students; and the dynamically based, objective approach emanating from the work of Murray, Rosenzweig, and their associates at the Harvard Psychological Clinic. The last of these programs would be partially presented in the book *Explorations in Personality* at that time in preparation and published the following year (Murray et al., 1938). The paper was a rallying call rather than a summary of achieved results.

From the psychology division of the Yale Institute of Human Relations, presided over by Clark Hull with his behavioristic orientation, came the first survey: a review by Sears of accomplished research prepared for the Social Science Research Council (Sears, 1943). In this monograph a variety of studies, experimental and observational, conducted in the interest of defining or redefining psychoanalytic concepts, were summarized and critically appraised. Among the topics covered were: erotic behavior of children, fixation and regression, repression and projection, and the study of dreams. In the concluding chapter stress was laid upon the role of learning, but other systematic reformulations were also considered. Of particular value were the bibliography and synopses which provided the first panoramic outline of "objective" attempts to validate Freudian concepts independently of the psychoanalytic-clinical method.

Of related interest is a handbook compiled and edited by J. McV. Hunt (1944) under the title *Personality and the Behavior Disorders* to which many of the more important workers mentioned by Sears contributed chapters. However, this book was not intended to serve the kind of goal at which Sears had aimed. More strictly relevant is the contribution by Hilgard, "Experimental Approaches to Psychoanalysis" (1952), in which the author evaluates efforts to provide a scientific basis for Freud's concepts but concludes: "Anyone who tries to give an honest appraisal of psychoanalysis as a science must be ready to admit that as it is stated it is mostly very bad science, that the bulk of the articles in its journals cannot be defended as research publications at all" (p. 44). However, Hilgard is more sanguine in his belief that there is much to be learned from these writings and that there is a hopeful future for psychodynamics if the methods of science are critically applied to test psychoanalytic hypotheses.

With a somewhat broader orientation Shakow and Rapaport (1964) evaluated *The Influence of Freud on American Psychology*. The positions of key figures (rather than specific studies of psychoanalytic theory) such as Knight Dunlap, Piaget, Thorndike, McDougall, J. B. Watson, Woodworth, and F. L. Wells are briefly described; but the main goal of the book was to evaluate Freud as a force (comparable to Darwin) in influencing the scientific commitment of American psychology. One chapter is devoted to appraisals, surveys, and reference works by psychologists dealing with psychoanalysis, including "surveys of experiments testing psychoanalytic theory"; and a useful synopsis of leading articles on psychoanalytic themes in the *Psychological Bulletin* during the period 1943–1958 is presented.

The three most inclusive surveys of research directed toward the validation of psychoanalytic theory appeared in the 1970s. The first of these was by Kline (1972), and, despite a certain natural selectivity, it comprehensively devoted four hundred pages, with thirty-four listing references, to the topic in hand. While the author dismissed much of the metapsychology of psychoanalytic theory as unscientific and untestable, he favorably reviewed the evidence accumulated to validate Freudian propositions and concepts such as repression and the Oedipus complex. He found that in most instances the Freudian phenomena could be fitted into some model derived for theories of learning though learning theory as such needed to be enriched and modified by content provided by Freudian observation. The conclusion of the book was that much of Freudian theory had been confirmed by independent research, some had not, and "a huge task of research remains."[13]

---

[13] The second edition (Kline, 1982), which has recently appeared, brings the subject matter up to date. Moreover, critics of the book, such as Eysenck and Wilson, who attempted to refute the author's positive claims on behalf of Freudian concepts, are considered and answered. Kline has also made the most of the cognate volume, published by Fisher and Greenberg in 1977, which is more inclusive but, he states, less critical than his own. He maintains that Fisher and Greenberg "accept results at their face value with almost no consideration of methodological adequacy." But the conclusions he reaches do not differ greatly from those in the first edition. It is noteworthy that in both, the author, in his evaluations, appears to be overly impressed by research methods which depend heavily upon the subject's present perceptions (and memories) which result from the individual past history but are not as such under the control of the experimenter. In that regard Kline is less rigorous than the experimental learning theorists that he emulates and than other investigators of psychoanalytic concepts whom he cites sparingly.

In the following year Eysenck and Wilson (1973) compiled a book of selected, previously published papers reporting research to validate psychoanalytic concepts. Each article was followed by a Comment of critical appraisal by the editors. The sections covered, among other topics, psychosexual development, the Oedipus and castration complexes, repression, humor, symbolism, and theory of psychosis. In a Foreword the writers commended the efforts to subject psychoanalytic propositions to experimental and other empirical testing but in the epilogue a generally negative appraisal, often taking exception to the earlier conclusions of Kline, was made. While some of the critical comments were reasonable and stimulating, the general tenor was influenced by an initial, negative attitude toward psychoanalysis.

The last of the three surveys was by Fisher and Greenberg (1977). It was both more inclusive and more discursive than the two above cited—more inclusive because half the volume was devoted to the evaluation of "Freud's therapy," the other half, to "Freud's theoretical views." The discussions of research on psychoanalytic concepts were much more general and the critiques less incisive than the comparable portions of Kline or of Eysenck and Wilson. But, again, the seventy-five pages of references are a useful compendium even though they suffer from some striking omissions.

The Experimental Study of Repression

Because the construct or constructs of repression represent what Freud himself regarded as the cornerstone of psychoanalytic theory (Freud, 1914/1957, p. 16), a separate discussion of the research on that topic is appropriate. The bibliography includes hundreds of titles, but there is luckily an excellent critical digest of the work during the first thirty years (MacKinnon & Dukes, 1962) which permits the present discussion to concentrate on the contributions made by this writer as a sample of the rest. Since that portion of the total had certain novel characteristics which carry implications not yet fully exploited, the selection appears to be justified.

MacKinnon and Dukes divided their critical survey into three sections that corresponded remarkably well to the three phases of repression depicted by Freud: "primal repression," which, for the reviewers, becomes "denial of entry into consciousness" and was represented by the work on "perceptual defense" that loomed large in the 1950s; "after-expulsion," which translates into the failure to recall earlier unpleasant experiences which have wounded the subject's ego; and "return of the repressed," which appears as a disturbance in the behavior of subjects with known or presumed complexes that are tapped by the word-association method in one or another of its variants. The appraisal of all this work is remarkably thorough and reveals the sometimes very subtle distinctions that have engendered controversy and further research in a complicated progression. The review also presents the

167

reaction of psychoanalysts to these research efforts—rarely favorable. The final overview considers this small but checkered sector of the history of psychology as one of "conquest and expansion" but with no unanimity among psychologists on the significance of what has been achieved. Like good historians the authors outline the options without committing themselves to any of them. It bespeaks their perspicacity that their essay is still required reading if one is to appreciate the later experimental studies of repression, e.g., the very recent research of Erdelyi and Goldberg (1979). That contribution, it should be noted, has an excellent bibliography including research on repression published subsequent to the appraisal by MacKinnon and Dukes in 1962.

Though most of my own research on what I have called "experimental psychoanalysis" was concerned with "after-expulsion," as classified by MacKinnon and Dukes, and involved recall as the dependent variable, some of it fell in the category of "return of the repressed." Subjects were in these latter instances not requested to recall the names of pleasant and unpleasant tasks previously performed but instead were instructed to recognize from a lengthy list with many additional neutral words the names of the tasks (successful and pleasant, unsuccessful and unpleasant) that they had previously performed. There were also experiments to measure (as a "projection" of the repressed) changes in hedonic ratings of the stimuli in word-association lists administered both before and after experiences of success and failure and including the names of the attempted tasks. Differences found in both recognition and rating of the two categories of stimuli tentatively favored the repression hypothesis (Rosenzweig 1938b). Of special import were the results of two interrelated experiments with children. In one of these investigations, preferences in the voluntary repetition of successful or unsuccessful tasks were shown to be correlated with the age of the child; those aged eight years or below preferred to repeat completed (i.e., successful) tasks while those above eight chose the uncompleted (or unsuccessful) (Rosenzweig, 1933b). This was the first experimental corroboration of Freud's "pleasure" and "reality" principles, and was subsequently redefined as increase in frustration tolerance (Rosenzweig, 1945). In the second experiment with the same children, the tendency to *recall* more successful than unsuccessful tasks correlated positively with preferences to repeat the failures (Rosenzweig & Mason, 1934, pp. 254–255). The interpretation was made that when the children were mature enough to be wounded by failure (so that they might try to vindicate themselves by restriving), they were motivated also to forget (repress) the wounding experiences and hence recalled more of the successful or pleasant experiences than of the unsuccessful or unpleasant ones.

To revert briefly to the research on delay of gratification: the findings that demonstrated a consistent increase from age four to nine in the capacity to delay gratification were later independently corroborated by Walter Mischel. From 1958 onward he published a series of studies on the topic, summarized in his textbook on personality (Mischel, 1971, pp. 125–130, 379–390, and 398–400). However,

Mischel did not cite and was apparently unaware of my much earlier experimental work on the topic. The omission is the more remarkable because in 1971 he discussed his findings in terms of "frustration tolerance." Both his work in 1958 and mine in 1933 included a reference to Freud's paper on the pleasure and reality principles (Freud, 1911/1958). But there is also a difference that is worth noting: while my research on preferences in the repetition of successful and unsuccessful activities highlighted ego-involvement, Mischel focused on the capacity to wait for a greater hedonic reward (a *larger* portion of candy) if the child was willing to postpone the pleasure. At this writing the difference also suggests that repetition choice of success over failure at an early age and of failure later on may involve the child's need for mastery in situations which when observed by Freud led him to go *Beyond the Pleasure Principle* (Freud, 1920/1955a) and formulate the repetition compulsion. The need for mastery would not enter into the purely hedonic gratification that Mischel studied. The two techniques, his and mine, applied to the same group of four- to nine-year-old children might, in the light of this theoretical difference, prove illuminating.[14]

The distinctive novelty of all my work on repression was the deliberate induction of pleasant and unpleasant experiences, equated here with success and failure, under lifelike but laboratory-controlled conditions. Moreover, unlike previous retrospective studies of repression, the experiences to be recalled (without the experimentee having been informed in advance) were of a conative nature, that is, they were created *ab initio* and either gratified or offended the concept of the self. Most earlier efforts had involved the differential recall of irrelevant (from the standpoint of Freud's concept of repression) pleasant or unpleasant sensory stimuli, for example, odors; or, again, uncontrolled and broadly defined pleasant and/or unpleasant events which had occurred during a recent vacation period. Though my research employed completed and uncompleted tasks similar to some of those utilized in the work of Lewin's students (Lewin, 1935), the tasks employed were of a uniform, not a heterogeneous, nature, and were intentionally devised for these investigations. Moreover, the aim from the outset was to investigate Freud's formulations regarding the forgetting of the unpleasant.

The two principal papers were published a decade apart though the experiments had been performed in the short interval from 1930 to 1933 (Rosenzweig & Mason, 1934; Rosenzweig, 1943a). In the interim I had published a full summary of this

---

[14]Since this manuscript was completed the foregoing speculations have undergone a preliminary experimental investigation. Approximately 300 school children, age four to thirteen, were administered in one continuous session both repetition choice (success or failure) and, again, a choice between two rewards, the larger of which entailed a delay of gratification. (I am indebted for technical assistance to my students Yvonne Barreto, Matthew Getz, Marie Sutera, and Lori Tenser.) The findings, thus far preliminarily analyzed, demonstrate that each of these aspects of frustration tolerance is (predictively) correlated with age (i.e., development) with about equal validity. The differences between these two aspects of developing frustration tolerance have still to be resolved.

169

and related research in the above-cited volume edited by Murray (Rosenzweig, 1938b).

The overall result of these investigations, which included control groups and other safeguards, was a preliminary confirmation of the proposition that unpleasant experiences (of failure) were less well recalled than were pleasant (successful) ones. Individual differences were observed but could be related to other characteristics of the total situation, for example, teachers' ratings of pupils for the trait of pride, independently assigned; or hypnotizability, for which the experimentees were objectively evaluated. Likewise, the immediate kind of response to experimentally induced success and failure was observed to vary and to affect results. On these grounds a heuristic classification was proposed for types of reaction to frustration (Rosenzweig, 1934). A behavioral test for these types of reaction was devised (1935), and the experimental measurement of these types was explored (1938c). In that same year I introduced the concept of frustration tolerance (1938a, 1938d, pp. 153–154). Its operational superiority to the comparable psychoanalytic concept of "ego strength" is even now insufficiently recognized by many psychologists and psychiatrists.

That concept was developed through a historical review of the discipline of immunology, in particular, the work of Elie Metchnikoff (cf. Metchnikoff, 1921). His theory of phagocytosis (the action of white blood corpuscles in inflammation as a form of defense) emerged in 1883 and was, in fact, given its Greek-derived name during a visit to Professor Claus in Vienna (ibid., p. 119)—the professor who a few years before had supervised Freud's earliest scientific work, his search for the missing testes of the eel. I recognized that Freud's "ego-defenses" (including repression) were extrapolated from the various forms of body defenses well known by 1894 (Rosenzweig, 1938a). Largely in that perspective a comprehensive formulation of three levels of defense—the cytologic, the autonomic, and the cortical—was offered to cover the continuous and interdependent spectrum of reactions to stress (Rosenzweig, 1944a). In recent years this comprehensive approach has been implicitly adopted by many investigators of the so-called immune system (Rogers et al., 1979).

As regards repression itself, another historical perspective generated a triadic hypothesis which combined immediate preferential reaction to frustration, degree of suggestibility, and implicit choice of ego-defense. This hypothesis was experimentally investigated and preliminarily supported (Rosenzweig, 1938b; Rosenzweig & Sarason, 1942). The classification of types of reaction to frustration, after further investigation, was systematically clarified and developed into a psychodiagnostic instrument (Rosenzweig Picture-Frustration [or P-F] Study) which is at present used worldwide (Rosenzweig, 1978a, 1978b).[15] The three types of norms included in

---

[15] The distinction between *types* and *directions* of aggression which emerged from the long series of studies in experimental psychoanalysis and on frustration as related to ego-defense (later termed *etho-*

idiodynamics (see below) are explicitly provided for in the scoring and interpretation of this technique (Rosenzweig, 1978a, p. 13 and passim; 1978b, pp. 7, 13–14).

Reverting to Freud's original conception, we need to observe that, while this experimental research tended to confirm the observable preferences for the recall of pleasant over unpleasant experiences, the work was not primarily concerned with the part played by conscious or unconscious processes in these findings. As is noted below, the orientation of idiodynamics subordinates the conscious-unconscious spectrum to operational levels of communication that are not necessarily either conscious or unconscious. There remains the largely philosophical question as to the function of Freud's concept of the unconscious in assuaging the sense of responsibility and of guilt in the conduct of personal and interpersonal relationships which religion and the legal system have taken as their province in the history of civilized institutions. From that standpoint Freud's role as a moral philosopher rather than as a scientist comes to the fore. But one can no more successfully confine Sigmund Freud to an exclusive social role than one can successfully demarcate the overlapping spheres of science and medicine, religion and law in human existence.

Two Letters from Freud: Resistance to Experimental Verification[16]

What did Freud think of the attempts to validate the concepts of psychoanalysis experimentally? Fortunately, an approximate answer can be given to this question because the investigator, as an aspiring young psychologist, sent Freud reprints of two early papers—one being an investigation touching on the alleged transition from the "pleasure principle" to the "reality principle" (Rosenzweig, 1933b) and the other an experimental study of repression (Rosenzweig & Mason, 1934). Freud responded on February 28, 1934 with a masterpiece of succinctness which, translated from the German (gothic) script (see Figure 7.1), read as follows:

> My dear Sir
> I have examined your experimental studies for the verification of psychoanalytic propositions with interest. I cannot put much value on such confirmation because

defense) became the basis for scoring the Rosenzweig Picture-Frustration (P-F) Study. The work on frustration and its correlates also led to the recognition that aggression, universally present among human beings, can only be understood (and controlled) through multidisciplinary research, ranging in scope from neurology to physiology, psychology and sociology. From this recognition there originated in 1972 the International Society for Research on Aggression, of which the writer was the first president. By its tenth anniversary congress, held in Mexico City in 1982, the membership of this organization included about 300 specialists in all the above disciplines from twenty-six countries. In 1974 *Aggressive Behavior* began publication as the official journal of the Society.

[16] Permission to reproduce these two letters (see Figures 7.1 and 7.2) was kindly granted to me by the late Ernst Freud, the son of Sigmund. Translation from the German is by Saul Rosenzweig.

171

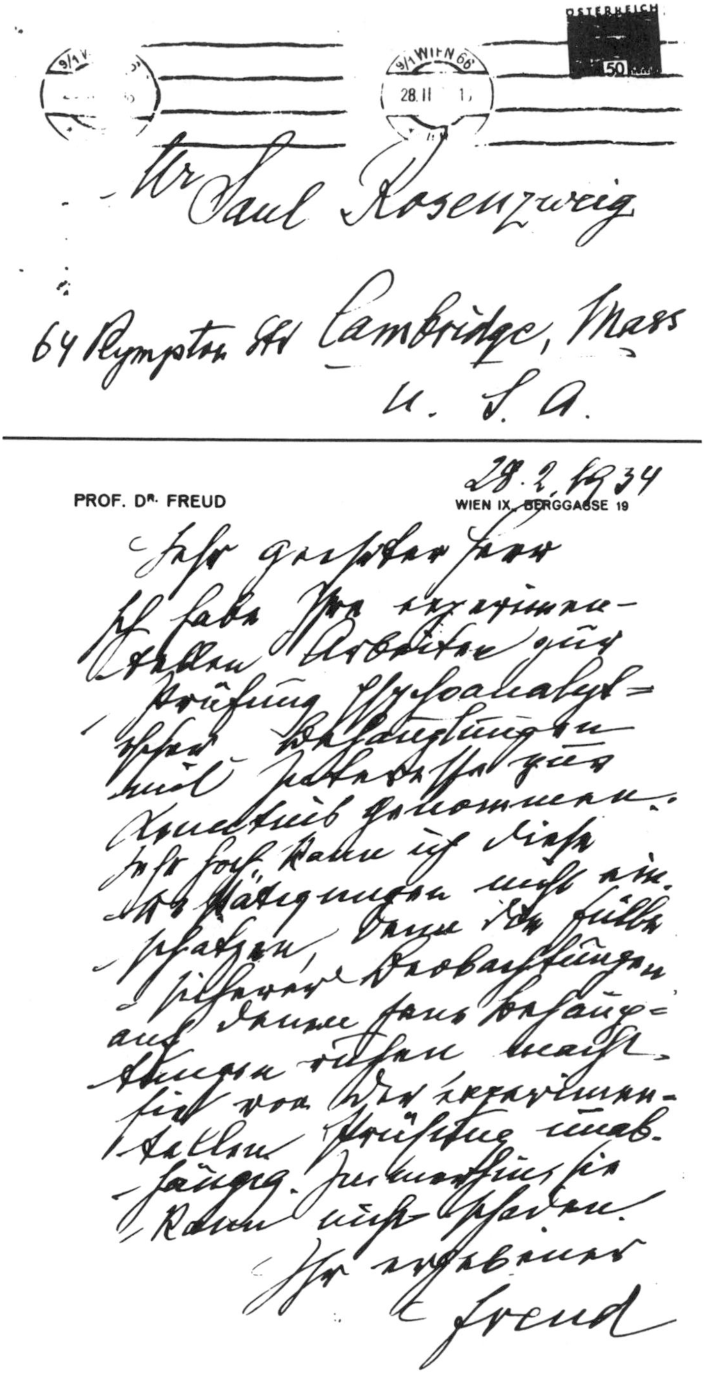

ÖSTERREICH 50

WIEN 66 28.II

Dr Saul Rosenzweig

64 Plympton St Cambridge, Mass

U. S. A.

PROF. Dr. FREUD

WIEN IX, BERGGASSE 19

28.2.1934

Sehr geehrter Herr

Ich habe Ihre experimentellen Arbeiten zur Prüfung psychoanalytischer Behauptungen mit Interesse zur Kenntnis genommen. Sehr hoch kann ich diese Bestätigungen nicht einschätzen, denn die Fülle sicherer Beobachtungen auf denen jene Behauptungen ruhen, macht sie von der experimentellen Prüfung unabhängig. Immerhin, sie kann nicht schaden.

Ihr ergebener
Freud

Figure 7.1. Letter from Freud, 1934.

the abundance of reliable observations on which these propositions rest makes them independent of experimental verification. Still, it can do no harm.

Sincerely yours,
Freud

It is of interest that there was a witness present at the time Freud received these reprints (Grinker, 1940), and he later conveyed Freud's reaction publicly at a professional meeting in St. Louis. He did so during the discussion period of his address (as guest speaker) at a point when he recognized the questioner as the Rosenzweig whom Freud had asked about one morning in 1934 when he, the speaker, had reported for his analytic hour. The speaker was Roy Grinker, who described how Freud, displaying the reprints for his inspection, had inquired what his American analysand knew about their author who was doing research at Harvard. Grinker replied that he knew nothing special about the person except that Harvard had a good reputation in psychology. Thereupon Freud threw the reprints across the table in a gesture of impatient rejection. At a later time the speaker described the same event in roughly similar terms in one of his publications (Grinker, 1958, p. 132).

Various individuals who knew about this letter from Freud have speculated about his negative reaction. On the basis of cognate incidents discussed above, it is possible to achieve a more circumspect interpretation. The reader will recall Freud's harsh judgment in 1909 of Boris Sidis, the experimental psychopathologist trained at Harvard, who was a severe critic of Freud's ideas. Then, after having commended Schrötter's study of hypnotically induced dreams in 1911 as opening up a new field of experimental psychology, Freud added a second mention of it in 1933, with a derisive allusion to "an American University" which repudiated psychoanalysis as a science because "it admits of no experimental proof." (He was referring, in all probability, to the Harvard Medical School, located in Boston, where Hanns Sachs, a member of Freud's most intimate circle, had arrived in September 1932 to take up his duties as a training analyst [Hendrick, 1961, p. 34 and passim]). In 1914 Freud described Jung's work on word association as the "first bridge linking up experimental psychology with psychoanalysis," (Freud, 1914/ 1957, pp. 26–30), but he then dismissed the method as having produced nothing truly useful either in itself or for psychoanalytic theory. As is evident from this account of his relationship with Jung in its entirety, Freud felt that he had naively credited Jung with a devotion to the "cause" which was never very sincere. Freud's final evaluation of Jung's experimental studies in word association (1904–1909), distinctly negative, must be viewed in that context. One may infer that at the time of the rupture Freud had developed a "complex" about Jung and his pioneer attempts to demonstrate the validity of psychoanalytic theory by experimental methods. And it is in the nature of such complexes that they generalize to other similar situations.

173

Freud's letter of 1934, twenty years after the break with Jung, may therefore be viewed as one in a series of reactions which gradually became more negative on a common dynamic basis. He came to regard any experimental approach to the verification of psychoanalytic concepts as harboring an undercurrent of personal "resistance" concealed by respectable scientific intent. He may also have rationalized his own resistance with the opinion that artificial laboratory conditions cannot reproduce the repressions of everyday life.

There is a cross-validation of Freud's negative attitude in the form of a second letter which he wrote me in 1937. The occasion was an invitation that I extended to him under the auspices of the National Research Council. I had been asked to explore the possibility of establishing a new journal for research in experimental psychopathology. By this assignment I sent letters to several potential consulting editors and to five prospective honorary editors. The latter group included Eugen Bleuler, Sigmund Freud, Pierre Janet, William MacDougall, and Adolf Meyer. Of these five, all but Freud endorsed the idea of the proposed journal and accepted the proffered invitation. Freud replied to me at the Worcester State Hospital in Worcester, Massachusetts (home of Clark University), where I was then working as a research associate. He again gave a terse response (see Figure 7.2) which, translated from the roman handwriting[17] that he employed this time, read as follows:

> My dear Colleague
> Within the scope of my orientation, I cannot see that there is a need to create a special journal just for *experimental* research in psychopathology.
>
> Very sincerely yours,
> Freud

There was by now, it thus appears, a consistently negative attitude on Freud's part. In 1937, two years before his death, he expressed it by refusing to encourage the field of experimental psychopathology.[18] Most students of abnormal behavior would not have agreed with Freud's attitude though they might, at the same time, have argued that some of the concepts and claims of psychodynamics are not

---

[17] The difference between gothic script, which Freud employed in his first (1934) letter, and the roman handwriting of his second (1937) letter is notable. One plausible view is that the former usage was more spontaneous, personal, and self-expressive; he wrote in that mode in his dairy and in his letters to his family. The reprints provoked him. When three years later he declined the invitation to lend his name to the Board of Editors of the proposed new journal, he was responding more formally to an individual representing the National Research Council. The view he expressed was more deliberate and was meant to be shared with public figures.

[18] It is noteworthy that Freud had reservations about psychologists only in regard to their scientific (especially experimental) pretensions toward the self-sufficient domain of psychoanalytic theory. As regards the practice of therapy, he was free of the contemporary, medical territoriality. (See Freud, 1926/1959b; Rosenzweig, 1963.)

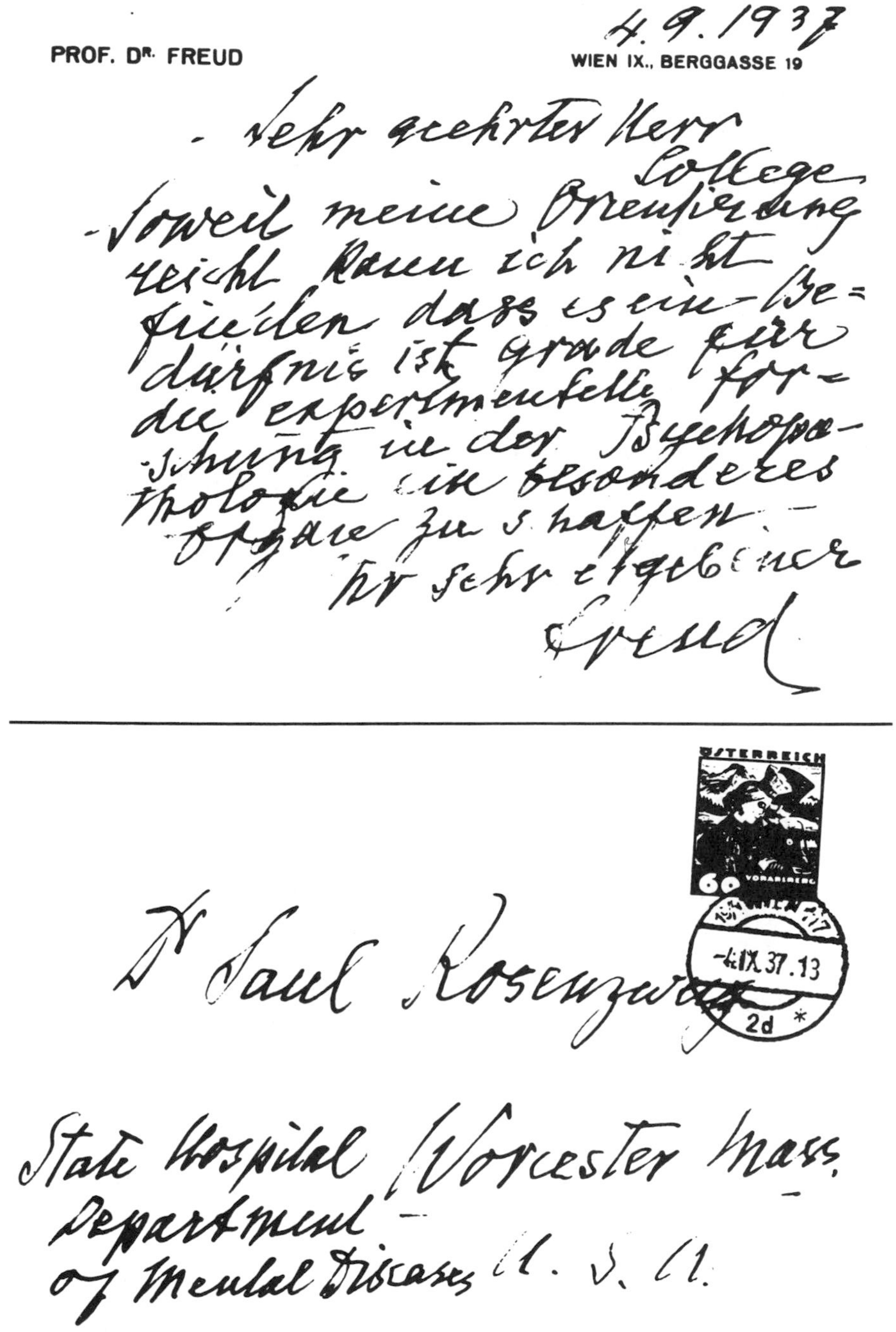

PROF. DR. FREUD

4. 9. 1937

WIEN IX., BERGGASSE 19

- Sehr geehrter Herr
College

- Soweit meine Orientierung
reicht kann ich nicht
finden dass es ein Be-
dürfnis ist grade für
die experimentelle For-
schung in der Psychopa-
thologie ein besonderes
Organ zu schaffen. -
Ihr sehr ergebener
Freud

Dr Saul Rosenzweig

State Hospital Worcester Mass.
Department
of Mental Diseases U. S. A.

Figure 7.2. Letter from Freud, 1937.

175

amenable to experimental or other modes of "objective" verification. As Freud recognized in 1933, there are accepted areas of science that have to wait for nature to supply the (predicted) conditions for testing their constructs (e.g., the well-known case of the solar eclipse that confirmed Einstein's theory of relativity). But Freud's increasing rejection of experimental appraisal must have stemmed from other special personal sources. He fell back in the last analysis on the revelations of his self-analysis, corroborated to his satisfaction by the numerous later analyses of his patients and students in training, which made psychoanalytic theory "independent of further verification."

However, it is noteworthy that wherever experimental confirmation is possible in science, it is the method of choice. A good example is found in the work of Heinrich Hertz (1857–1894), a student of Helmholtz, who encouraged him to perform the experimental research that verified the basic constructs of electromagnetism. Faraday, Maxwell, and Helmholtz himself had already theoretically and mathematically demonstrated that electricity is to be conceived as waves, but Hertz, by his laboratory demonstrations under controlled conditions, established the basis for modern wireless telegraphy, including radio, television, and satellite communication. Marconi and Edison made the essential applications and inventions but, according to historians, these applications might not have occurred or would have been delayed had it not been for the experimental verification by Hertz. (See Buckley, 1927, pp. 124–125.)

Freud the Conquistador

There is another perspective from which Freud's negative response to the experimental approach may be regarded: his self-concept or ego ideal with respect to his role as a scientist. From that standpoint it is relevant that he more than once rejected the evaluation of him by others as a scientific investigator in the strictest sense of the term. In a letter to his friend Fliess (February 1, 1900, unpublished but quoted by Schur, 1972, pp. 201–202), he wrote: "On the whole I have noticed quite often that you habitually overestimate me. The motive for this mistake, however, disarms any reproach. For I am actually not at all a man of science, not an observer, not an experimentalist, not a thinker. I am by temperament nothing but a conquistador, an adventurer, if you want to translate this term—with all the inquisitiveness, daring, and tenacity characteristic of such a man. Such people are customarily valued only if they have been successful, have really discovered something; otherwise they are thrown by the wayside. And this is not altogether unjust." Thirty-seven years later—two years before his death in 1939—Freud repeated the same sentiment to Marie Bonaparte (his former patient and eventual rescuer from the Nazis), who in the context of trying to persuade him not to destroy his letters to Fliess, which she had purchased from a rare book dealer in Berlin, compared Freud to other great men about whom posterity has a right to receive full information: "That is very complimentary, but I can't share your opinion. Not because I am modest, not at all. I have a high opinion of what I have discovered, but not of myself. Great discoverers are not necessarily great men. Who changed the world more than Columbus? What was he? An adventurer" (Jones, 1955, II, p. 415).

Freud had a very modest estimate of his abilities, especially in regard to mathematics, physics, and other hard-science disciplines (Jones, 1955, II, p. 415). He did not aspire to become an experimental scientist, certainly not in the field of psychology. And the self-image of the explorer was with him almost from the beginning of his work as a psychoanalyst. In the landmark paper in which he most fully set forth his theory of the etiological significance of premature sexual experience as a basis for later neurosis, he boldly declared his theory to be "the discovery of *caput Nili* in neuropathology" (Freud, 1896/1962a, p. 203). He was clearly alluding to the much-mooted and contested discovery of the source of the Nile in which Richard Burton and John Speke played conspicuous roles in the years 1856–1864. It was probably not lost upon Freud, who made much of such anniversary dates as these, registered in unconscious memory, that this bitter contest over priority, which included the ambiguously "accidental" death of Speke, occurred in the period of Freud's own early childhood. It was to this period of life that, in his pivotal theory of 1896, he referred the primary etiology of neurosis.

Again, two years later, writing once more to Fliess, he mentioned the publication of the "three volumes of adventures" by the Arctic explorer Fridtjof Nansen (1897–1898) which his whole family was devouring. He stated that he would be able to make good use of the dreams reported by Nansen: they were so similar to his own, "typical of someone who is trying to do something new which makes call on his confidence and [who] probably discovers something new by a false route and finds that it is not as big as he had expected" (Freud, 1954a, p. 260, letter of August 20, 1898).

On the same page Freud refers to Theodor Lipps, Professor of Psychology in Munich, as his chief rival in the exploration of the unconscious. He mentions reading the book by Lipps, *Grundthatsachen des Seelenlebens* (1883), and continues in the same vein the next month (Freud, 1954a, p. 267, letter of September 27, 1898). A copy of this volume by Lipps (a tome of 709 pages) is still extant in the London portion of Freud's surviving library (Trosman & Simmons, 1973) and it has Freud's markings, including those on page 149 which discuss the unconscious (Freud, 1954a, pp. 260–261n.). It is noteworthy that there are seven other volumes by Lipps in this collection of Freud's books—more volumes than those by any other author. At the Third International Congress of Psychology, held in Munich, 1896, Lipps delivered a lengthy paper on the unconscious (Lipps, 1897) with which Freud was familiar. He alludes to it in *The Interpretation of Dreams* (cf. Freud, 1899/1953, p. 701). Jones reports that Freud had intended to attend this Congress but may have changed his mind in the end. But there is no evidence that he did not

177

attend and, in any event, he knew the volume containing the proceedings. From the letters to Fliess, as well as the published book on dreams, it is clear that Freud had been following the work of Lipps since at least 1896. He described Lipps as "the best mind among present-day philosophical writers" (Freud, 1954a, pp. 260–261). In the original edition of his book on dreams he refers to Lipps three times (Freud, 1899, 364–366). The present relevance of this evidence lies in the fact that Lipps, like Freud, regarded the unconscious as being the generic source of mental life out of which consciousness arises under certain special circumstances. To them both this "region" was comparable to a submerged continent.

A third explorer allusion, also involving the North Pole, was not made by Freud himself but occurred by coincidence. He could hardly have failed to be struck by the fact that when he visited the United States in 1909 for the first and only time and lectured at Clark University in early September, the newspapers were ablaze with headlines about the competition between Peary and Cook, each claiming the first actual discovery of the North Pole. This notorious feud and the rival claims of the men are still being sorted out by historians (Wright, 1970).

That the explorer analogy dominated his "unconscious" is shown by a striking dream which he had shortly after the letter about Nansen mentioned above. In this dream he saw himself dissecting his own pelvis—a task assigned him by his former teacher, Ernst Brücke (Freud, 1899/1953, pp. 452–455). He associated to the manifest content by alluding to the novels of Rider Haggard, several of which, notably the famous *She*, featured African exploration. Though Freud mentioned Haggard, he was also probably aware of the earlier African explorations of Dr. David Livingstone, whose *Last Journals* were published in 1874 and were available to Haggard for his later fiction.

The explorer self-image was in Freud's thoughts to the end of his life. The comment he made to Marie Bonaparte in 1937 is relevant here, but a later incident is even more idiodynamically pertinent. Jones, describing Freud's escape from the Nazis in 1938, reports "During the night journey from Paris to London he dreamed that he was landing at Pevensey. When he related this to his son he had to explain that Pevensey was where William the Conqueror had landed in 1066" (Jones, 1957, III, 228). Thus, even in his escape from Vienna a year before his death in exile, Freud saw himself not as a refugee but as a conquistador. But this conclusion raises new questions as to what the conception of the conquistador, as contrasted to the experimental scientist, meant to Freud.

First, and most obvious, is method or mode of performance: the contrast between the patient and painstaking way of the scientific investigator, with or without controlled experimentation, and the impatient adventurer who takes large risks, invests great energy, and even makes costly sacrifices if the stakes are high enough. There is also something ruthless about the conquistador—the adventurer who is impelled by the excitement of a goal the value of which is enhanced by a challenging contest with a rival, or by a dangerous target the attainment of which is worth all hazards.

In the African explorations of the nineteenth century all these features of the conquistador were dramatically present. They were patent in the contest between Burton and Speke to discover the source of the Nile—a goal which, in the end, neither of them attained. In the adventures of Livingstone and his successor Stanley, the same elements were present, and Livingstone, like Speke, died in the pursuit without a successful result; Stanley did not achieve it either. The North Pole offered the same type of challenge to Nansen, who never reached that destination despite his dramatic adventures. Peary and Cook, at the acme in 1909, were even more dramatically vying with each other on almost an hourly basis. If, then, Freud conceived himself as a conquistador, he was not prepared to emulate the slow and painstaking procedures of the scientific investigator who knows that the *experimentum crucis* will occur, if at all, probably by accident. Moreover, to Freud, relishing the contest, the prize would not be conceded readily when, by great personal sacrifice (his self-analysis), he had already produced convincing results.

Also to be considered is the content of the target area. The "unconscious" is too vague an answer. Was there a more specific content for Freud? The answer is at least partly provided by a comment which complements the earlier imagery of the African exploration. Writing in 1926, when he was seventy years old, he confessed to being puzzled still by the essence of womanhood: "The sexual life of adult women is a 'dark continent' for psychology" (1926/1959b, p. 212). (In the original German edition of the book the term *dark continent* was in English.) Plainly he was continuing to employ the metaphor of the African exploration, as he had done in 1896, but now it was the psychology of women, not childhood sexual experience in general, that defined the quest. The phrase rendered in English reveals that he was familiar with the common designation used in the latter part of the nineteenth century for the still unexplored interior of Africa. Did he know the famous book by Henry M. Stanley (the man who found Livingstone in 1871) entitled *Through the Dark Continent* (Stanley, 1878)?[19]

Finally, there is the motivation for the quest which, in a dynamic psychology like that of Freud, must be considered. In addition to the above cited cryptic allusions in the *Interpretation of Dreams* (Freud, 1899/1953, V, p. 619), Freud ascribed to

[19] Freud's first mention of an explorer as "conquistador" occurred in another letter to Fliess (Freud 1954a, p. 253, letter dated April 14, 1898). He was describing an Easter vacation in Italy, where he went with his brother Alexander. He told in detail of a visit to Rudolf's Cave in the Divaca on the Carso. Having enumerated the curious stalactitic formations in the cave, he came to the main point: "Most remarkable of all was our guide, strongly under the influence, but completely sure-footed and humorous and lively. He was the discoverer of the cave, and obviously a genius run to seed. He kept talking about his death, his conflicts with the priests, and his achievements in these subterranean realms. When he said he had already been in thirty-six 'holes' in the Carso I recognized him as a neurotic and his *conquistador* exploits as an erotic equivalent. He confirmed this a minute later, because when Alexander asked him how far one could penetrate into the caves he answered: 'It's like with a virgin; the farther the better.'" Freud joyfully overidentified with this *conquistador*: "I over-tipped the 'biggest blackguard in Divaca,' as he called himself, to help him drink his life away the faster."

children an inordinate curiosity about the genitalia in his paper entitled "On the sexual theories of children" (Freud, 1908/1959). Emphasis was placed on the penis, or, more specifically, the loss of it. Here for the first time he formulated his concept of the girl's "penis envy" and its reciprocal for boys, the "castration complex," which usually develops when the boy first catches sight of the female genital without the penis (pp. 216–218). From his treatment of the topic here, and more fully later, it is evident that Freud was saying more about the boy than about the girl. The mischief begins when the little boy first sees his naked sister or mother. Having described the effect upon the boy, Freud arrived at "penis envy" two pages later. The girl, he stated, has a corresponding lively interest in the boy's penis, with the result that she succumbs to the "sway of envy."

It is significant that in this context Freud advanced the notion (which he later labeled *negation*) according to which neither the little boy nor the little girl is willing to admit the absence of the penis in the female. The little boy says to himself: " 'When she gets bigger it'll grow all right.' The idea of a woman with a penis returns in later life in the dreams of adults; the dreamer, in a state of nocturnal sexual excitation, will throw a woman down, strip her, and prepare for intercourse—and then, in place of the female genitals, he beholds a well-developed penis and breaks off the dream and the excitation" (p. 216).

Here is brought to light a presumably typical male dream. The evidence for the generalization is lacking but, at the very least, Freud was reporting a recurrent dream of his own. Was he also indicating, at least in part, the quest of Freud the conquistador? By his own affirmations, this quest was for the missing penis of the woman—a quest based upon fixation—doomed to failure from the beginning. Its counterpart was the "castration complex" of the male.[20]

[20] In this context belongs Freud's idiosyncratic theory of male fetishism—obsessional reverence for the woman's foot (and shoe)—which he fully *published* for the first time a year after he alluded to the "dark continent" (Freud, 1927/1961). He presented the view that the fetish is a "substitute for the woman's (the mother's) penis that the little boy once believed in and—for reasons familiar to us [castration anxiety]—does not want to give up" (pp. 152–153). He then footnoted his earliest published statement of this interpretation of the fetish—in his study of Leonardo da Vinci (Freud, 1910/1957, p. 96). Drawing upon various case histories, the details of which "must be withheld from publication" for reasons of discretion, Freud then described the male's inextinguishable belief (fixation) in the woman's possession of a penis (cf. his paper on childhood sexual theories, 1908/1959). As is shown by James Strachey in the Editor's Note to this paper (Freud, 1927/1961, pp. 149–151), Freud first discussed male fetishism in detail at a meeting of the Vienna Psychoanalytic Society, February 24, 1909. Strachey states that Freud was at that time "on the point of preparing the 'Rat Man' analysis for publication." (See the allusion to fetishism in that classical case history, Freud, 1909/1955, p. 274n.) But, as Strachey also meticulously shows, Freud was preoccupied with the riddle of fetishism from at least 1905 (Freud, 1905/1953, pp. 153–155) up to the last year or two of his life, at which final time he wrote about ego-splitting (Freud, 1940/1967) and related it to the mechanism of negation and the phenomenon of male fetishism. If, knowing that Freud first discussed fetishism in detail at the Vienna Society, one turns to the volume of the Society minutes (Nunberg & Federn, 1962–1975, especially Volume 2, 1967, p. 163), one discovers that "unfortunately, this record was lost." This loss is, without doubt, a Freudian "accident"—the only instance in these four

It will then come as no surprise to learn that in the aforementioned passage in which Freud described the sexuality of woman as a "dark continent" for psychology, he coupled this characterization with a comment on the female's "envy for the penis" (Freud, 1926/1959b, p. 212). This penis envy, first posited in 1908, was described in context in his first paper wholly devoted to female sexuality (Freud, 1931/1961). He was then seventy-five years old. One year earlier, in 1930, his doting mother had died at the age of ninety-five.

In a complete study of Freud's idioverse, the part played by his bisexuality would unquestionably loom large. The "castration complex" which Freud viewed as a counterpart to female "penis envy" may be viewed without much doubt as in substantial measure a projection of his own sense of inadequacy.[21] But, reciprocally, it is plausible that, had he not been handicapped in this way, he would have been insufficiently motivated to probe those parts of his "unconscious" the exploration of which led to discoveries, no matter how flawed, for which the world will remain indebted to him for a very long time.

Freud, the adventurer-explorer was a tragic hero. He knew from the depths of his painful self-analysis where the "unconscious" was and how it worked. Experimental investigation, especially if undertaken independently of him, was both needless and threatening. The most that he could therefore grant was that such verification "could do no harm." Yet, as he would have been the first to acknowledge in other

volumes in which a meeting is stated to have been held and recorded, with the participants listed, but with the minutes themselves missing. Freud's long essay entitled *Delusion anad Dreams in Jensen's "Gradiva"* (Freud 1907/1959) expressed his first (published) interest in the phenomenon of foot fetishism. The monograph was not, however, a statement of theory but an application of psychoanalytic method to a literary production which had focused on a "delusion" of the protagonist about the female foot and gait. Believing as he did in primal fantasies, Freud read Jensen's tale as a sensitive portrayal of such a fantasy. In this 1907 essay, Freud made no mention of the male's castration complex or its relation to the "missing penis" of the female. But one year later, in his paper on the sexual theories of children, that observation was made; its relation to fetishism was not indicated. On the basis of this sequence, one may safely infer that in the missing presentation made at the Vienna Psychoanalytic Society, February 1909, Freud must have developed the missing-penis theory of fetishism for the first time in detail.

[21] It is worth noting that "castration complex" is, strictly speaking, a misnomer. If, as is repeatedly evident in Freud's writings, he means the arbitrary loss of the penis, the term should be "peotomy complex." (The seldom encountered "peotomy" is the correct surgical term, derived from *peos*, Greek for "penis," and *tomy*, for "cutting.") Castration, as is well known, is accomplished in a very different way, that is, by excision of the testicles. The analyst's response to this "correction" might well be (following Freud) that the little boy observes the absence of the penis in the girl and makes an inference about the potential loss of his own organ. The little boy's knowledge about the role of the testicles is negligible, if present at all. Likewise, the knowledge about the homology between the penis and the clitoris is too recondite for the child of either sex. But any such answer is not truly apposite. If, as Freud states, the boy means loss of the penis (by cutting off), the right term (which was, after all, applied by Freud, the adult) should still have been *peotomy*—unless there was some other unstated reason for the misnomer.

cases, the attitude was irrational—out of proportion to the significance of the experimental work accomplished but threatening in its potentiality.

Despite Freud's negative attitude, experimental research inspired by psychoanalysis has continued and expanded (Eysenck & Wilson, 1973; Fisher & Greenberg, 1977; Kline, 1981). Clinical psychoanalysis developed into experimental psychodynamics by attempting to translate Freud's "unconscious" into operationally defined concepts. Experimental idiodynamics, discussed below, is the next stage of scientific research, and it has just begun.

Freud's Faith in Psychoanalytic Therapy

To round out the picture of Freud's attitude toward the verification of psychoanalytic concepts, it is appropriate to take note of what he had to say about the validation of psychoanalytic therapy. His most pungent comment on this topic occurs at the conclusion of his *Introductory Lectures on Psychoanalysis* (1917/1963, pp. 461–462), twenty years before the second of his letters quoted above. He said:

> Friends of analysis have advised us to meet the threatened publication of our failures with statistics of our successes drawn up by ourselves. I did not agree to this. I pointed out that statistics are worthless if the items assembled in them are too heterogeneous; and the cases of neurotic illness which we had taken into treatment were in fact incomparable in a great variety of respects. Moreover, the period of time that could be covered was too short to make it possible to judge the durability of the cures. And it was altogether impossible to report on many of the cases: they concerned people who had kept both their illness and its treatment secret, and their recovery had equally to be kept secret . . . . There was obviously a prejudice against psycho-analysis . . . . Nothing can be done against prejudices. You can see it again today in the prejudices which each group of nations at war has developed against the other. The most sensible thing to do is to wait, and to leave such prejudices to the eroding effects of time. One day the same people begin to think about the same things in quite a different way from before; why they did not think so earlier remains a dark mystery.

While devout faith on the part of the analysand is ostensibly not an avowed aspect of psychoanalytic therapy, Freud did expect the analyst to have such faith, regardless of independent or outside evidence. The position is not unlike that expressed in his letter of 1934, quoted above.

Freud's special pleading notwithstanding, attempts have been made to validate the results of psychotherapy, including psychoanalysis, and, indeed, he correctly anticipated that prejudice might enter into such evaluations. Perhaps the best known of these attempts was published by Eysenck (1952) who, using reports on the results of psychotherapy, went so far as to maintain that patients treated by psychoanalysis improved at a lower rate than patients who receive no systematic psychotherapy. That clearly flawed appraisal was soon superseded by others which more objectively assessed the results of therapy and took into account the intrinsic difficulties of such evaluations (e.g., Rosenzweig, 1954). The reply I made to Eysenck had grown out of an earlier effort to assay the implicit common factors in diverse methods of psychotherapy (Rosenzweig, 1936). And this latter essay was a corollary of my prior attempts to define the validity of psychoanalytic concepts by experimental or laboratory methods. The well-known "placebo effect" in psychotherapy—the truism that all methods, regardless of rationale, produce in common a very high degree of unexplained positive results—was explained by the recognition of the implicitly shared operative factors of all leading methods. Forty years later, Luborsky et al. (1975) labeled this shared effectiveness the "Dodo verdict." The phrase derived from the epigraph of my 1936 essay, in which I repeated the judgment of the Dodo, the referee in the caucus race of *Alice in Wonderland*: "*Everybody* has won and all must have prizes." But Luborsky and his coworkers drew their conclusions from extensive empirical research involving careful comparative studies of therapeutic methods applied to matched experimental and control groups. By confirming the "Dodo verdict" on such grounds, they, with others, are constructively paving the way for the eventual fitting of selected therapeutic modes to the diagnosed individuality of the patient—the ideal goal of idiodynamic psychotherapy.

This idiodynamic psychotherapy will quite obviously depend heavily on the psychoanalytic orientation. It will, however, derive more from the earlier than the later Freud—the pre-1911 Freud not yet greatly influenced by Stekel and, more particularly, Jung. These disciples tended to corrupt Freud's own implicitly idiodynamic approach. A good epitome of idiodynamic psychotherapy, described in untechnical, common-sense terms, is found in a paper on the psychoneuroses by Henry Head: "Diagnosis of the psycho-neuroses is an individual investigation; they are not diseases but morbid activities of a personality which demand to be understood. The form they assume depends on the mental and physiological life of the patient, his habits, and constitution" (Head, 1920, p. 391). As indicated by this passage, Head, in trying to account for and to treat functional disturbances of behavior, moved progressively toward the replacement of the nomothetic concept of disease by that of idiodynamic personality disorder.

The Experimenter-Experimentee Interaction in Human Laboratory Research

The 1960s and 1970s saw a rapid development of a new field of experimental-social psychology: the social psychology of the psychological experiment. Eventually there were entire books devoted to the area, including two excellent works by Adair (1973) and Silverman (1977). It will here be demonstrated that the provenance of this fruitful area derived in large measure from the experimental approach to psychoanalytic concepts—a fact that has not hitherto been recognized.

Early in the 1930s, against the background of two to three years of intensive experimental research on the validation of psychoanalytic concepts, I published an article under the title "The Experimental Situation as a Psychological Problem" (Rosenzweig, 1933a). It was primarily a methodological analysis of what transpires in the human interaction of the psychological laboratory. A taxonomy of certain types of interaction gave the paper its structure, but there were numerous concrete examples from the writer's current research and from that of previous investigators who had taken the trouble to record artifacts as well as facts. At the time it was not realized how much the interest in and knowledge about psychoanalysis had implicitly influenced the theme of the paper. Today the point seems obvious.

Although published in the prestigious *Psychological Review*, the article attracted scant attention. In the 1950s, when most of the same insights were rediscovered, it was still ignored: the writers were apparently not aware of it. In the 1960s and 1970s the article resurfaced and was appreciatively discussed by several investigators (Lyons, 1964; Silverman & Shulman, 1970; Adair, 1973). Adair (1973, pp. 12–14), in particular, gave a digest of its parts in parallel with the recent rediscoveries.[22]

In the 1933 article, three types of unwitting error or subtle influence in psychological experimentation were defined. These influences, it was argued, made experimentation in psychology more complicated than similar research in the established natural sciences. The first of these influences, called "errors of observational attitude," were peculiar to the introspective work of the Structuralists, with some similarities to Titchener's "stimulus error." The second class included "errors of motivational attitudes," exemplified in both introspective and behavioral experimentation. They stemmed from the unforeseen questions in the mind of the experimentee in the form of opinions about the experiment—about the experimenter's purpose and what the experimentee might reveal about himself or herself in complying with the instructions. Such behavior was called "opinion error." As Adair states, "The opinion error is similar to the concept of demand characteristics" described early in the 1960s (Orne, 1962). In both cases it was recognized that the experimentee was sometimes motivated to protect the experimenter's self-respect.

---

[22] After this chapter was in final form for the publishers, a very recent discussion of the 1933 article came to my attention: Ralph Rosnow's *Paradigms in Transition: The Methodology of Social Inquiry* (1981), pp. 41f. At the other end chronologically is an unpublished paper written by one of my students, Susanne King (1970), that preceded the books by Adair (1973) and Silverman (1977). She surveyed the available literature on the experimental situation as a psychological problem and demonstrated that the various aspects of experimenter-experimentee interaction discovered by Orne (1962), Rosenberg (1965), and Rosenthal (1966) had been anticipated by the 1933 article.

Another basis of the opinion error was pride, which Adair described as "virtually identical to Rosenberg's evaluation apprehension" (Rosenberg, 1965).

The third chief type of artifact was described as "errors of personality influence." These were twofold: (1) those involving the experimenter's personal attributes, such as his race or sex, which could modify the behavior of the experimentee, and (2) "suggestion errors" which, as Adair stated, were "virtually identical to experimenter expectancy effects." These embraced the various "experimenter effects" of Rosenthal (1967).

Adair (1973, p. 14) concluded: "Here in a single paper in 1933 was a concise yet thorough analysis of the experiment as a social situation. Unfortunately, this splendidly critical analysis was ahead of its time; the challenge to reconsider aspects of the research method was not met . . . . Rosenzweig's insights remained buried for 35 years."

As mentioned above, the present aim is to show that such insights as were displayed in the 1933 contribution had their origin in the implicit understanding of the interpersonal situation between analyst and analysand even though, explicitly, the research was intended to verify certain other more circumscribed psychoanalytic concepts. But in the long view the inception of the "social psychology of the psychological experiment" probably represented as important a contribution as any of the more direct validations of psychoanalytic theory. The understanding of the interaction between the experimenter and the experimentee was a new beginning for what has here been described as experimental idiodynamics.

It is of incidental interest, but still significant, that in some degree three of the leading protagonists of the new orientation of the 1960s had some background in psychopathology or psychoanalysis before contributing to the social psychology of experimentation with human subjects. Rosenthal had devoted his dissertation to the experimental induction of the defense mechanism of projection, described in one of his first publications (Rosenthal, 1959). And both Orne and Rosenberg had earlier investigated hypnotic phenomena. But the inference should not be labored. It is mentioned chiefly to point up my own orientation which unquestionably, even if only implicitly, reflected a knowledge of transference and counter-transference (cf. Freud, 1911–1915/1958)—the background for recognizing cognate influence in the interaction between the experimenter and the human subject.

One last aspect concerns a terminological recommendation of the 1933 contribution. On the second page of the article the term *experimentee* was substituted for *subject* and the new term was employed throughout the paper. In a footnote (1933a, p. 338) this usage was justified as follows:

The word "experimentee" is the exact equivalent of the German "Versuchsperson." It is a general designation that may be used to refer to the person, whatever his function (that of observer or that of subject), working in cooperation with, but

185

in a complementary relation to, the experimenter. It is an authorized English word [in Webster] and it is suggested that it be more commonly employed.

In the light of the foregoing discussion, it is obvious that this new designation grew out of the thesis of the paper. Since the *experimental person* (as the Germans expressed it) was not actually *subject* to the experimenter but was largely autonomous, it was reasonable to acknowledge this fact in a change of terminology.

When I subsequently employed the novel term in an article submitted to the *Journal of Experimental Psychology*, an unexpected opposition was encountered, not from the editor of the *Journal* but from the man in charge of the prevailing *Zeitgeist* in my professional niche. Some years later I wrote a commemorative paper about that vibrant individual, with whom I had developed a life-long friendship. In it I devoted a few lines to this encounter, and, because they express as well as I know how what happened at the time and what the implications are for possible future usage, the lines may be repeated. Having mentioned my attempt to introduce the term *experimentee*, I continued:

> I found myself thwarted by a protracted campaign of opposition from him [E. G. Boring], by letter, interview, and memorandum, that eventuated in my diplomatic acceptance of the Department Chairman's judgment. As is now evident, the *Zeitgeist* was then standing in the way of a general insight that a generation later independently inspired a spate of investigations into the experimental situation as a psychological problem. For though Boring's opposition was directed at the novel term experimentee, that term was being employed . . . in the context of a research program that highlighted the social psychology of behavioral research. It was this total context with which my paper was concerned, but the context was lost on him and . . . he prevailed (Rosenzweig, 1970b, p. 68).

Perhaps by this centenary date psychology is better prepared to overcome the inertia of usage and replace the obsolete "subject" with the more appropriate "experimentee."

The evolution from experimental psychology through clinical psychodynamics to experimental idiodynamics is part of a healthy progression toward a science with a more coherent unity. The debatable gains from still continuing attempts to validate specific psychoanalytic concepts must await this eventuality. In the meantime, a significant, if modest, legacy has passed from psychoanalysis to experimental psychology: an appreciation of the experimenter-experimentee interaction.

Experimental Idiodynamics

The upshot of the individual differences in repression, above mentioned, fully appeared only when the conception of idiodynamics was applied to the experimental situation. A twofold groundwork for idiodynamics had already been laid: (1) the recognition of three types of explanatory norms in psychology and (2) the implications of idiodynamics for the projective techniques of psychodiagnosis (Rosenzweig, 1951) and related response-response analysis of behavior.

The three types of norm employed in psychological explanation or interpretation were first designated as universal, group, and individual (Rosenzweig, 1950a, 1958). The function of association, originally offered as an illustration, will bear repetition. The principles of association (similarity, contiguity, etc.), described by the early Greek thinkers and still recognized in present-day theories of learning, employ norms that appear to be *universally* valid. These principles were the basis for the spate of experimental studies carried out in Wundt's first laboratory. But even there it was soon recognized that certain *groups* of individuals, including mental patients of a given diagnosis, produce associations peculiar to or characteristic of these groups. In these terms certain kinds of associations consistently emitted by an individual helped to classify him or her as belonging to a given group (e.g., the clang associations of the manic patient). Finally, in the research on complexes, discussed above, the *individual* or individualized potential of word associations was studied as pointing to a unique organization or constellation of thoughts, images, and feelings in one particular person. This standpoint defined the objective of the investigation and its application to the understanding of the dynamics of one individual.

These three types of norm (or explanation) are now more appropriately designated *nomothetic, demographic,* and *idiodynamic* in order to avoid the quantitative reference misleadingly emphasized by the earlier terminology. The confusion is evident in the writing of Allport (1961, pp. 14–15) where, on the one hand, he commended the formulation I introduced but then erroneously equated each type with the size of the population in question. In other words, he confounded the classification of explanatory norms with the purely actuarial one of Kluckhohn and Murray (1948, p. 35) according to which every human being is in certain respects like all others (i.e., species-specific), like some others (from the same variety of subculture), and like no other (the unique traits that individuals exhibit). This last category pointed to what Allport had earlier espoused as the idiographic approach, but in 1961 Allport made the error of equating the idiographic with the idiodynamic. Since the error arose from the failure to differentiate the actuarial from the explanatory, the more definitive terms *nomothetic, demographic,* and *idiodynamic,* which plainly refer not to population size but to special modes of explanation, are here employed. Under these rubrics the population size is of secondary importance and essentially irrelevant. It is more pertinent to observe that even in the terms of common sense a human being (*Homo sapiens*) is an organism, a citizen, and a person, with one or another of these roles phenomenally dominant at various times. In every instance, however, these three orientations converge in and are definitely modified by the dynamic blending which occurs in the idiodynamic matrix.

To make the distinctions in these new terms clear, examples of each type of norm will be presented. (1) For nomothetic norms: Pavlov's *law of extinction*, according to Woodworth and Schlosberg (1962, p. 543), states that: "If a conditional reflex is elicited without reinforcement by an unconditional reflex, the conditional reflex is weakened or inactivated." Human beings, in common with other mammals, obey this principle of learning. (2) For demographic norms: A *moron*, with IQ in the range of 50–69, as defined by English and English (1958, p. 141), is "a person 'who is capable of earning a living under favorable conditions, but is incapable, from mental defect existing from birth or from an early age, of competing on equal terms with his normal fellows; or of managing himself or his affairs with ordinary prudence.'" This statement (which follows the definition given by an English Royal Commission) is vague and describes "a psychological condition in sociological terms; but it has been very influential." (3) For idiodynamic norms: A recurrent display of self-hatred (intropunitiveness), ostensibly associated with fratricidal guilt during the childhood of a man when his younger brother died under conditions that made the boy feel responsible for the event. He was pursued by this complex throughout his life, as was Orestes by the Furies. He was so obsessed by the memory of the death of this first "rival" that later rivals, especially if they met with death, appeared to him to be copies of the first. The satisfaction of any triumph was mixed ambivalently with a sense of remorse and with a need to make restitution—to make amends by transforming notable successes to the psychological advantage of other persons (social sublimation). Despite achieving fame through many such successes, he apparently did not succeed in fully assuaging his conscience, and in his eighty-fourth year, he died at a time which he chose and which coincided with the Jewish Day of Atonement in 1939.[23,24]

---

[23] The chief reference here is Rosenzweig (1970a). The evidence in that paper highlights the idiodynamic content of Freud's dream of the Three Fates (Freud, 1899/1953, p. 204f.), which occurred during his self-analysis. His associations to it included the thought, "You owe a death to Nature." The dream can be conclusively dated as belonging in the week of the Jewish High Holidays in 1898 which, of course, included the Day of Atonement. This earlier evidence may be supplemented. That Freud elected the day of his demise is shown in the oral history that I obtained about the medical circumstances of Freud's final day from his personal physician (the late Dr. Max Schur), who administered the last injections of morphine. These were repeated, at the patient's request, until their fatal effect was assured. Freud's last words were, "Tell Anna" (Rosenzweig, 1964). (It should be added that during the interview with Dr. Schur there was no mention of Freud's choice of his death day or any reference to the Day of Atonement.) (See also Schur, 1972, p. 529.)

[24] To help round out the interpretation and to illustrate how nomothetic principles are combined with idiodynamic norms, the concept of "nemesism" should be referred to here. Nemesism is a dynamic module which characterizes certain forms of intropunitiveness (self-hatred). The concept was introduced (Rosenzweig, 1935, 1938c) as a parallel to "narcissism." John Flugel (1945, Chapter VII) adopted the concept and supported it with an array of experimental studies. Subsequently nemesism was related to "castration compulsion," to stress the manner in which "the fear of castration" (or demise) is sometimes found neurotically interlocked with the wish for this fate (Rosenzweig, 1956). The wish may be viewed as an expression of femininity in strongly bisexual males. In conjunction with restitution, as employed on page 141 above, bisexuality can sometimes foster the creative process (see Rosenzweig, 1943b).

The single, most remarkable mystery of life, attested to by competent biologists, is the fact that every human individual (indeed every animal organism) constitutes a unique and unreplicated unit. The particular combination of genes and ontogenetic experience is never repeated in nature. Under these circumstances it is incredible that the conception of idiodynamics and the concept of the idioverse have never previously appeared in scientific discourse. One reason for this lack may be the very recent elucidation of the genetic pool. It was, after all, not until 1956— the centenary of Freud's birth—that the correct chromosome number of *Homo sapiens*, 46, was at last determined (Stern, 1973, p. 22). The crucial decade for DNA was also the 1950s.

The eminent geneticist Dobzhansky has repeatedly (1967a, 1967b) stressed the unique organization of genes from which every human being is born. He has strenuously objected to the manner in which types or genotypes have been stressed in classical genetics at the expense of individuality. He has attributed this bias to an implicit Platonic orientation. A typical statement is the following: "It is allegedly not in the province of science, but of insight, empathy, art, and literature to study and understand a person in uniqueness. . . . I wish to challenge this view. Individuality, uniqueness, is not outside the competence of science. It may, in fact, be understood scientifically. In particular, the science of genetics investigates individuality and its causes" (Dobzhansky, 1967a, p. 41). In like manner the uniqueness of the events that constitute the dynamic idioverse is to be understood. When the unique genome develops in its inevitably unique physical and social environments, the idioverse emerges. In a democratic social order equal opportunity not only accepts but encourages such diversity. The problems of reconciling this uniqueness with demographic and nomothetic norms are always present, and these problems can all too readily overshadow the primacy of idiodynamic norms.

Allport's stress on the *idiographic*[25] (as combined with the nomothetic) was intended to underscore personal uniqueness, but his preoccupation with traits, rather than events (dynamic interactions between the organic and the environmental contributions to experience), fell short of what is here meant by idiodynamic. It should now be evident that the *idiodynamic* differs from the *idiographic* by referring not to a statistical N of 1 (with *traits* peculiar to it), but to a universe of *events* (the idioverse). A unique dynamic organization through time distinguishes the person from others by providing an explanation of behavior in terms of a peculiar develop-

---

[25] Allport (1937, p. 22) adopted this term in relation to the psychology of personality from its earlier usage by the philosopher W. Windelband (1904). Windelband divided scientific enterprises into two types: the *nomothetic* or natural sciences, such as physics, chemistry, and biology, which deal in universal, abstract principles; and the *idiographic*, such as history and biography, which focus on the acts and qualities of individual persons or figures. Allport described psychology as belonging to both types of discipline, but formulated the psychology of personality as largely idiographic, a point of view that, he believed, had not been adequately recognized and accepted by the nomothetic, that is, experimental or general, psychologists.

mental history. From the repetitive dynamic events in the idioverse, idiodynamic norms are derived. These norms, in peculiar conjunction with nomothetic principles and the relevant demographic generalizations, afford the necessary keys to a given idioverse.

There have, of course, been various intuitive appreciations of individuality and some tentative formulations concerning it (especially in biological genetics); and there have been biographical studies of individual human beings.[26] But the conception of idiodynamics, recapitulated in the present précis, was not propounded or named until 1950. It should therefore not surprise anyone that it will require decades of detailed research before any notable fruition can occur.

In this perspective, a further word regarding the concept of event is appropriate. While a variable of this kind might have been too vague a generation or more ago, there has now been sufficient advancement in the logic of science and the science of logic to permit the use of such a unit without fear of being charged with intuitive vagueness. As modern physics has continued to demolish the old materialism of the nineteenth century, objects or things have gradually yielded to processes, including dynamic entities such as events. Though this is hardly the place to enter into questions of ontology, mention may be made of some of the recent concerns of symbolic logic with the concept of event and the calculus of the individual (Martin, 1978). A generation earlier there were the pioneering efforts of the theoretical biologist J. E. Woodger (1952, 1956). In neurology the methods and discoveries of Wilder Penfield (e.g., 1958, 1975) point to some of the organic correlates of the registration, retention, and apperceptive recall of individual experiences. Related developments in cognitive psychology are exemplified by the innovative investigations of Crovitz (1970), Crovitz and Schiffman (1974), and Rubin (1982) on memory for autobiographical incidents. Of similar relevance is the important distinction in the field of memory research between "episodic" (or autobiographical) and "semantic" (or generic) memories (Tulving & Donaldson, 1972, Part III). All these contributions demonstrate that the idioverse can be studied as a universe of experienced events—as a population for quantitative as well as qualitative analysis. For present purposes an event is, then, an incident in the chronology of a life that has a demonstrable and significant effect upon a succeeding incident or upon a series of such incidents.

---

[26] One well-known approach is that of H. A. Murray under the heading of "personology." Murray (1938, p. 4) defines it as "The branch of psychology which principally concerns itself with the study of human lives and the factors that influence their course, which investigates individual differences and types of personality . . . ." He continues: "Personology, then, is the science of men taken as gross units. . . ." However, the term *personology* was not coined by Murray. He adopted it from a book by J. C. Smuts (1926, pp. 262, 282–294), who introduced the term there and defined it and discussed it as "the science of personality as a whole." (See Oxford, 1982, III, p. 398.) The book by Smuts greatly impressed Murray in the early 1930s (when I was associated with him at the Harvard Psychological Clinic), but Murray does not cite that author.

190

The implications of idiodynamics in the projective techniques of psychodiagnosis as involving response-response rather than stimulus-response analysis were demonstrated early (1951). With data from an earlier investigation on repression, it was next shown (Rosenzweig, 1952) that that work had inherent in it a grasp of the experimental situation in which individual differences could be analyzed as a predictable result of the response-response conditions. With the data drawn from the cited experiment, it was shown that (a) the actual durations recorded for the separate tasks analyzed demographically failed to reveal differences between the pleasant and unpleasant; but that (b) if the median times spent by individual experimentees were used as an idiodynamic criterion and related to the outcomes of the attempted tasks, significant differences appeared that supported the hypothesis of repression. Idiodynamically defined long successes were recalled better than short successes, and short successes better than short failures; and these last were, in turn, better recalled than long failures. In other words, when the times spent were treated idiodynamically, that is, with the median time on all tasks spent by any given individual as the applicable criterion, the recall results were no longer random. This limited example was then expanded to introduce the paradigm of experimental idiodynamics. In this paradigm the external "stimulus" conditions and the "personality" of the experimentee mutually define the experimental situation, and both must be anticipated and measured. This germinal schema awaits wider adoption and clarification along the lines pursued, for example, by Edelman (1958) in my laboratory.

The hiatus in experimental psychology between nomothetic (universal) principles and demographic (group) generalizations is intended to be filled by idiodynamics. Idiodynamic norms represent the blending of the other two types in the generative matrix of the idioverse. The computer is an excellent tool for nomothetic and demographic data in instances where genetic and cultural generalizations, respectively, are objectively sought. Experimental idiodynamics aims to use these other two types of normative data as regulative criteria against which to assess individual deviations, but these deviations are themselves regarded as normative for the unique universe of events (idioverse). When data are examined idiodynamically, so-called individual differences, ordinarily belittled in both the nomothetic and demographic orientations, point to the very stuff of the idioverse—its peculiar population of events. In this direction lies the mode by which individualized data (in medicine, for example, the clinical) can be translated into valid generalizations that are at the same time consistent with nomothetic and demographic principles.

A preparatory version of what is here called idiodynamics appeared in a paper which interpreted the positions of Allport, Lewin, and Murray as complementary (Rosenzweig, 1944b). That purview prepared the way for the recognition of the three complementary types of norms and, finally, idiodynamics. But more directly relevant and elaborative in the present context is the article (Rosenzweig, 1958) which reexamined the traditional reductive hierarchy of the several sciences and rerepresented them as a horizontal spectrum under the collective name "humanics." (See Figure 7.3.) This collectivity (of the behavioral sciences) viewed as a horizontal rather than a hierarchical structure was seen to extend from physics at one end to sociology at the other and to bring together the "psycho" portions of psychophysics, psychophysiology, psychobiology, psychodynamics, and psychosociology (or social psychology). Each of these disciplines was regarded as retaining a scientific autonomy of its own, even though the place of each in the spectrum had to be recognized in order to provide for the important overlapping functions of the network as a whole. This composite unity had never been explicitly organized as such; implicitly, it was "psychology," but it was now relabeled "humanics." In the center of the humanics gamut resided idiodynamics (or "psychopsychology") which referred the data of direct experience to no other science. The data of idiodynamics thus were to be regarded as autonomous—on a par with those of the other sciences arranged on either side of it in the horizontal spectrum. The peculiarity of idiodynamic data is its consideration of direct psychological experience as completely reducible to no other scientific discipline. It considered such experience to constitute an idioverse of events, as above indicated. It should, however, be observed that in the present exposition idiodynamics is extended to incorporate the *data* of the genetic (primarily nomothetic) and of the cultural (primarily demographic) milieus as these flow into and are transformed by the idiodynamic matrix. "Humanics" is still applicable to the broader perspective in which all three types of norms have their independent *and* interdependent significance.[27]

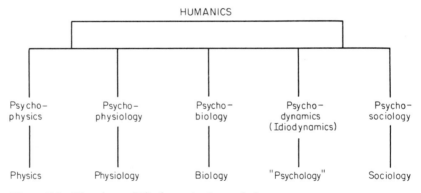

Figure 7.3. The place of idiodynamics in psychology.

[27] Friendly advisers point out that a caveat is needed regarding the intent and scope of idiodynamics lest this approach be perverted into a justification of ruthless individualism. An essential implication of generative idiodynamics, which explicitly posits the organic and cultural milieus as necessary parameters, is that it obliges both the psychologist and the person observed to recognize the interdependence of the individual with other past and present individuals. It has for many years seemed to me self-evident that personality in an untrammeled society proceeds from dependence (childhood), to independence

A Future Paradigm for Dynamic Psychology

There are four isomorphic universes that scientists are just beginning to comprehend. At one extreme is the total interstellar universe. This we may never penetrate except by telecommunication. At the other extreme, in and under our hands, exists the atomic universe that began to be charted at the turn of the century. In between these two is the solar universe. The first manned orbital flight in extraterrestrial space occurred in 1961. Bridging the solar and the atomic universes is the human idioverse which lies before us for aboriginal exploration.

The experimenter-experimentee interaction discussed above implies integration through individuation. There may here be something analogous to the sequence of development first described by the embryologist Coghill (cf. Herrick, 1949), which he extended in later writing to the fields of human motivation and psychopathology (Coghill, 1936). His basic observations showed that the undifferentiated action of the whole animal on first stimulation is followed in the course of growth by differentiated partial patterns and, finally, by an integration of these partial patterns within a total response of the organism. In this course of events the more or less autonomous partial patterns are not added together but combine in an organized fashion whereby the dominant whole supersedes the separate parts to accomplish more complete adaptation. Coghill saw in this sequence a justification for the view that the organism moves toward increased autonomy. He speculated that healthy personality development follows a similar trend. On this model, biological growth at the lowest levels of life already provides a guide to the understanding of the growth of the human individual.[28]

An analogy is suggested macroscopically in considering the development of experimental psychology during the past century. While at the outset experimental psychology under Wundt was a comprehensive but amorphous package (Rieber, 1980), there was soon a splintering of this new discipline into "schools," each of which emphasized a different aspect of the Wundtian broad approach. Under Titchener in America, Structuralism appeared, with a marked emphasis on a highly specialized brand of introspection applied to the study of sense impressions. Behaviorism under John B. Watson and B. F. Skinner went to the other extreme by excluding consciousness altogether and highlighting reflex behavior in conditioning and learning (Skinner, 1956; Rosenzweig, 1972). Psychoanalysis under Freud had also played down consciousness but it focused on behavior determined by unconscious motivation. A similar selective emphasis has been demonstrated for the other

---

(adolescence), to interdependence (maturity). Idiodynamics affords a scientific groundwork for this developmental series. It is surely not a justification for egoism; it assumes instead that mutual regard for the freedom and dignity of the other individual is an essential value of participant democracy.

[28]This orientation has been adopted to comprehend the evolution of human sexual autonomy in terms of ultimate idiodynamics (Rosenzweig, 1973).

dominant schools. Each of these approaches could be interpreted as representing an overarticulation of one segment of the behavioral spectrum which, viewed in perspective, made a complementary total pattern (Rosenzweig, 1937b). The corollary of this developmental conception of the schools, digested through experimental studies of the human experimentee, led to the recognition of the experimental situation as a psychological problem.

Moreover, this recognition prefigured a new integration for the behavioral sciences: experimental idiodynamics emerged. In that conception the individual experimenter and the individual experimentee together constitute a unity in which the concrete experimental situation must be understood as individualized.

It remains to describe the implications of this view of the experimental situation for psychology as a whole and, in particular, for dynamic psychology in which motivation is crucial. The experimentee and the experimenter are seen here as interacting idiodynamically in a new and more mature operational paradigm. In that paradigm the continuously growing individual person holds center stage for the psychological observer.

The ultimate significance of any effort to validate the concepts of psychoanalysis experimentally and to fit them into a scientific psychology can only be appreciated if one takes into account the ideal structure of the discipline in the years ahead. The wider implications of idiodynamics thus become relevant and should, at least, be summarized here. For it is in this perspective that the concepts of both psychoanalysis and of experimental idiodynamics acquire their ultimate significance.

Historically Woodworth's pioneer conception of "dynamic psychology" (1918), revised and updated 40 years later (Woodworth, 1958), is noteworthy.[29] But unlike the position he naturally adopted as a general-experimental psychologist, the focus here is on the individual—on the idioverse.

A future paradigm for dynamic psychology (see Figure 7.4) includes two persisting milieus: from the one side, a genetic (organic) milieu affects the idioverse biogenically; from the other, a cultural milieu contributes sociogenically; and both these relatively permanent transmitters blend in the transitory matrix of the idioverse. In that generative matrix, determinants from the two persisting milieus flow through continuously, are transformed, and provide the idiodynamic signals for a complete understanding of a given human event. While it endures, this

---

[29]The term *dynamic psychology*, introduced in 1918 by R. S. Woodworth, was handily employed by E. G. Boring to name the new division of the Department of Psychology at Harvard University, which was made possible when Morton Prince provided funds in 1928. H. A. Murray joined Prince as his assistant at that time. About ten years later, G. W. Allport adopted from Woodworth's book the conception that mechanisms became drives, which he then rechristened "functional autonomy" (Allport, 1937, p. 191f.). Both these events (at Harvard) lie in the background of my conception of idiodynamics which, despite its marked difference in emphasis from Woodworth, holds with him that dynamic psychology, distinctly not "behavioristic," is a *behavioral* approach. As such it includes both overt and covert (introspective) behavior, but with the overt predominant in empirical research.

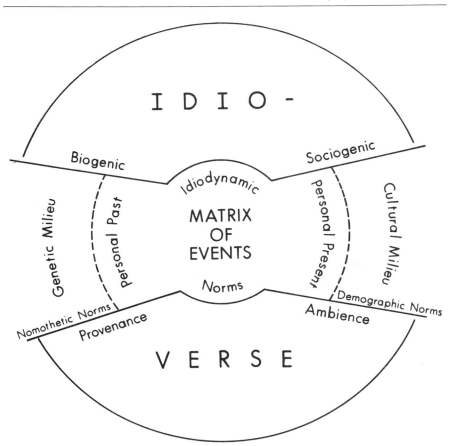

Figure 7.4. Dimensions of the idioverse: a paradigm for dynamic psychology.

vehicle—the matrix of the idioverse—is psychologically paramount, and its norms make intelligible to the prepared observer the person who feels, thinks, and acts.[30]

The temporal aspect of experience is crucial. While in the matrix of the idioverse

[30]A contribution along these lines will be found in the position of the neurobiologist Pierre Karli (1983). In the more directly relevant area of behavioral pathology, the conceptualization regarding schizophrenia as an interactive diathesis-stressor disorder is noteworthy. (See Gottesman & Shields, 1982.) With respect to that formulation (and comparable ones for other personality disorders), an important remaining problem is whether the assumed genetic diathesis is specific to the particular disorder or the result of a generalized vulnerability—a possibly genetic low level of frustration tolerance (discussed above)—or some combination of the two. Further research should take into account not only environmental stressors, but the level of frustration tolerance (conceivably genetic) thus far not sufficiently considered. Nevertheless, in the present context the unusually sophisticated formulations of Gottesman and Shields are instructive.

195

everything is of present tense, the genetic milieu tends to stress derivation from the biological past. These inputs interact with those from the cultural past, and all these inputs converge in the adaptively creative and future-oriented matrix of events. In that matrix the personal present and personal past mingle as do perception and memory.

The above discussed interaction between the experimenter and the experimentee matches recent treatments of the traditional dichotomy of heredity and environment. In most such discussions the interaction is seen not to be additive (H + E) but multiplicative (H × E). In the future, even this sophisticated way of thinking about the relationship between what is inherited and what is externally experienced will be modified by the new knowledge of human genetics which is beginning to include chromosomal microsurgery (see, for example, Berns et al., 1981). Now that it has become possible to rearrange chromosomes and genes in the early stages of embryonic development, heredity is no longer sacrosanct—no longer a given from the past which must be accepted. The genetic code itself can be modified. Intervention in the antenatal milieu is, of course, presently limited, and the future of genetic engineering is fraught with both scientific and ethical problems; but it is inevitable that such modifications of the genome will, for better or for worse, be made in the years ahead. This momentous enlargement of the "environment" will have to be considered in any future conception of the heredity–environment interaction.

The manner in which the three types of explanatory norms previously discussed apply to the parameters of the idioverse represents a problem still not completely solved. It is tempting but only approximately correct to identify the genetic milieu with nomothetic norms and the cultural milieu with the demographic. In truth, each of the three parameters is in some degree open to the three normative types.

The role of communication in and from the idioverse is crucial. In preference to Freud's vaguely denotative conscious, preconscious, and unconscious, the operationally definable immediate, intermediate, and inframediate levels of expression are here proposed. The immediate is the literal story, but in most creative communications it is a blended composite with the other two levels. The intermediate is the allusive level, usually based on some existing model (what Henry James in his *Notebooks*, 1947, called the *donné*), a life situation that suggests a plot. The inframediate is the autobiographical (confessional) component which makes possible the communicator's comprehension of the intermediate and enters intimately into the final combination of all the levels in the peculiar manner that gives the communication its special flavor or appeal.[31]

---

[31] These three levels of communication should not be confused with an earlier distinction among levels of behavior (Rosenzweig, 1950b). This earlier conceptualization was meant to comprehend the methods and results of appraising personality by the most commonly employed devices: the subjective (questionnaire), objective (behavior sampling), and protective techniques (Rorschach inkblots, Thematic

In contradistinction from psychoanalysis, idiodynamics tends to stress conscious over unconscious processes because it can be demonstrated that much of what is explained by followers of Freud as "unconscious" is actually in the fully conscious aspects of the idioverse. The idiodynamic equivalent of Occam's razor is the maxim that the unconscious should not be invoked as an explanation until the conscious has been fully exhausted. In Freudian practice the unconscious is often applied to palliate a person's sense of shame or guilt; the person knows what, in self-defense, he or she denies knowing until self-deception replaces awareness. The strategies employed in these transformations are continuations, but with subtle human refinements, of the disguises and camouflages, well known to biologists, which pervade the entire animal world in the struggle for survival. (See Cott, 1957.) This area of behavior, which might well be designated "cryptergasia," offers potentially rich rewards for the future idiodynamic investigator of both normal and abnormal behavior.

The work of the creative artist resolves itself, in part, in these terms. The artist prides himself on having an expanded awareness which he or she employs to advantage in literary or other productions. Such productions can be fully understood only by empathically informed biographical and historical reconstruction of the levels. The procedure here suggested, and anticipated inchoately in some of Freud's attempts to apply psychoanalysis to the interpretation of literature and art, may be called "psychoarcheology."[32]

Apperception Test). These methods are meant to elicit *opinion*, *overt*, and/or *implicit* levels of response, respectively. There is a rough equivalence between the projective techniques, which seek to yield the implicit level, and the inframediate level of communication. However, the correspondence between the other levels or dimensions is more mixed. This only approximate equivalence is not surprising since the objectives in the two instances are in practice different. In psychodiagnosis one is in direct contact with a living examinee, but in the reconstruction of creative works, it is only the work and the other surviving parts of the worker's idioverse that are available for investigation.

Equivalent levels or layers have been recognized since at least the time of medieval rhetoric, as exemplified in biblical hermeneutics and in classical authors like Dante. Dante discussed the topic in the *Banquet* and in his letter to his friend Can Grande della Scala (Haller, 1973). He distinguished four kinds of meaning: literal or historical, allegorical, tropological or moral, and anagogic. Freud's implicit rediscovery of the levels (through his self-analysis) has not, to my knowledge, been hitherto noted in these terms. The oversight of Freud's use of the standard rhetorical levels may be due to his having assimilated them implicitly in his psychodynamic reformulation. Recognition of this provenance throws new light on the nature of his interpretation of dreams (and the cognate neuroses). The so-called dream work consists largely in a translation of the metaphorical (unconscious) dream content to the manifest (preconscious and conscious) level. The present formulation is more demandingly operational. As such, it has played an important part in much of my still unpublished research on the creative process, exemplified in the works of Freud himself and of such other writers as Hawthorne, Melville, and Henry James.

[32] A pellucid specimen of such psychoarcheology is to be found in "The Ghost of Henry James" (Rosenzweig, 1943b; 1963) viz., in the treatment of "The Story of a Year," if one now adds, for the first time, the intermediate level. That level was afforded to Henry James by the lurid contemporary newspa-

I. THE SYSTEMATIC FRAMEWORK OF PSYCHOLOGY

At some future time a unified system of generative idiodynamics will, one hopes, become fully articulated. That system will supersede the contending factions of dynamic psychology that still gratuitously compete for conceptual dominance. The need for some such comprehensive and viable science of the individual becomes more and more imperative at this stage of global history in which participant–complementary democracy appears to have reached a crossroads.

REFERENCES

Adair, J. G. *The human subject: The social psychology of the psychological experiment*. Boston: Little, Brown, 1973.

Allport, G. W. *Personality: A psychological interpretation*. New York: Holt, 1937.

Allport, G. W. *Pattern and growth in personality*. New York: Holt, Rinehart & Winston, 1961.

---

per accounts in early March 1864 of the death and mutilation of a twenty-one-year-old Union cavalry officer named Ulric Dahlgren. From an earlier military exploit he had suffered the amputation of his right leg, but this deficit in no way deterred him from planning a surprise attack on Richmond, Virginia, in order to free the Northern soldiers confined in the Libby Prison. When the attack failed, he was killed, then mutilated (probably literally castrated), and his body exposed to the gaze of the Confederate citizens. Exactly one year later, James published in the *Atlantic Monthly* his first acknowledged tale, which concerned the curious death of a Northern soldier. Another intermediate strand, not previously stressed, was the participation of Henry James's younger brother, Wilkie, in the assault on Fort Wagner in 1863, from which he returned seriously wounded to recuperate near the family home in Newport (James, 1891). As if to validate the haunting indelibility of all his disastrous experiences during the American Civil War as the context for his first published story we have the testimony of the paper published in March 1916, a few days after his death. In it James conjoins his "fond" and painful memories of that time with his current visits to the European hospitals with their "long wards." There he again ministered to convalescing soldiers, those of World War I (James, 1916). Another piece of evidence, not previously noted in the "Ghost," is the first actual ghost story ("The Romance of Certain Old Clothes"), which he published (James, 1868) three years after "The Story of a Year." It is a tale of mortal sibling rivalry between two sisters—instead of brothers, probably to mask the rivalry of Henry with his elder brother William. One of the sisters marries a man that they both love and when, soon after the birth of a daughter, the wife dies, the rival marries the widower. At his deceased wife's deathbed request, the husband has stored in a locked chest in the attic the clothes that she wanted preserved for her daughter. But the new wife taunts her husband into proving his love for her by asking him to break his vow and give her the key to the chest. The tale ends when the husband at last discovers his second wife kneeling lifeless before the chest in the attic. "Her lips were parted in entreaty, in dismay, in agony; and on her bloodless brow and cheeks there glowed the marks of ten hideous wounds from two vengeful ghostly hands" (James, 1868, p. 220). In this first of his ghostly tales the author has interwoven his indelible sibling rivalry with the theme of the haunting ghost, as if to signify that his feud with William, carefully concealed in their actual intercourse, pursued him in a manner that he could never overcome and which effectually emasculated him—a bachelor, probably bisexual, to the end of his days. (See the attenuated view of this rivalry by Leon Edel [1983, pp. 276–279], who exaggerates the "normal masculinity of William" and takes William's view of Henry too seriously.)

Aserinsky, E., & Kleitman, N. Regularly occurring periods of eye motility, and concomitant phenomena, during sleep. *Science*, 1953, *118*, 273–274.

Ayer, A. J. *Language, truth and logic*. London: Gollancz, 1936.

Bergmann, G. Psychoanalysis and experimental psychology: A review from the standpoint of scientific empiricism. *Mind*, 1943, *52* (n.s.), 122–140.

Bernard, C. *An introduction to the study of experimental medicine* (L. J. Henderson trans.). Introduction by L. J. Henderson. New York: Macmillan, 1927. (Originally published, 1865.)

Bernfeld, S. Freud's earliest theories and the school of Helmholtz. *Psychoanalytic Quarterly*, 1944, *13*, 341–362.

Bernfeld, S. Freud's scientific beginnings. *American Imago*, 1949, *6*, 163–196.

Berns, M. W., Aist, J., & Edward, K., et al. Laser microsurgery in cell and development biology. *Science*, 1981, *213*, 505–513.

Boring, E. G. *A history of experimental psychology*. New York: The Century Company, 1929.

Boring, E. G. On the subjectivity of important historical dates: Leipzig 1879. *History of the Behavioral Sciences*, 1965, *1*, 5–9.

Breuer, J., & Freud, S. *Studies on hysteria. Standard edition of the complete psychological works of Sigmund Freud* (Vol. II). London: Hogarth, 1955. (Originally published, 1895.)

Bridgman, P. W. *The logic of modern physics*. New York: Macmillan, 1928.

Buckley, H. *A short history of physics*. London: Methuen, 1927.

Cantwell, H. B. Sexual abuse of children in Denver, 1979: Reviewed with implications for pediatric intervention and possible prevention. *Child Abuse & Neglect*, 1981, *5*, 75–85.

Coghill, G. E. Integration and motivation of behavior as problems of growth. *Journal of Genetic Psychology*, 1936, *48*, 3–19.

Conklin, E. S. The foster-child fantasy. *American Journal of Psychology*, 1920, *31*, 59–76.

Cott, H. B. *Adaptive coloration in animals*. London: Methuen, 1957.

Crovitz, H. F. *Galton's walk: Methods for the analysis of thinking, intelligence, and creativity*. New York: Harper & Row, 1970.

Crovitz, H. F., & Schiffman, H. Frequency of episodic memories as a function of their age. *Bulletin of the Psychonomic Society*, 1974, *4*, 517–518.

Dement, W. C., & Fisher, C. Studies in dream deprivation and satiation. *Psychoanalytic Quarterly*, 1960, *29*, 607–608. (Abstract.)

Dobzhansky, T. Of flies and men. *American Psychologist*, 1967, *22*, 41–48. (a)

Dobzhansky, T. On type, genotype, and the genetic diversity in populations. In J. N. Spuhler (Ed.), *Genetic diversity and human behavior*. New York: Wenner-Gren Foundation for Anthropological Research, 1967. (b)

Edel, L. *The stuff of sleep and dreams*. New York: Harper & Row, 1983.

Edelman, J. An idiodynamic approach to ego-defensive behavior. Doctoral dissertation. St. Louis: Washington University, 1958. *Dissertation Abstracts*, 1958–1959, *19*, 3021.

Ellenberger, H. F. *The discovery of the unconscious*. New York: Basic Books, 1970.

Ellis, H. Psycho-analysis in relation to sex. *Journal of Mental Science*, 1917, *63*, 537–555. (Reprinted in his book *The philosophy of conflict*. Boston: Houghton Mifflin, 1919.)

Ellis, H. *The philosophy of conflict*. Boston: Houghton Mifflin, 1919.

English, H. B., & English, A. C. *A comprehensive dictionary of psychological and psychoanalytical terms*. New York: Longmans, Green, 1958.

Erdelyi, M. H., & Goldberg, B. Let's not sweep repression under the rug. Toward a cognitive psychology of repression. In J. F. Kihlstrom & F. J. Evans (Eds.), *Functional disorders of memory*. Hillsdale, N.J.: Erlbaum, 1979.

Eysenck, H. J. The effects of psychotherapy: An evaluation. *Journal of Consulting Psychology*, 1952, *16*, 319–324.

199

I. THE SYSTEMATIC FRAMEWORK OF PSYCHOLOGY

Eysenck, H. J., & Wilson, G. D. (Eds.). *The experimental study of Freudian theories*. London: Methuen, 1973.

Fechner, G. T. *The little book of life after death*. With an Introduction by William James. Boston: Little, Brown, 1905. (Originally published, 1836; 3rd ed. 1887.)

Fechner, G. T. *Elemente der Psychophysik* (2 vols.). Leipzig: Breitkopf & Hartel, 1860. (H. E. Adler trans. Vol. I only. New York: Holt, Rinehart & Winston, 1966.)

Feigl, H., & Scriven, M. (Eds.). *The foundation of science and the concepts of psychology and psychoanalysis. Minnesota Studies in the Philosophy of Science* (Vol. I). Minneapolis: University of Minnesota Press, 1956.

Fisher, C. Psychoanalytic implications of recent research on sleep and dreaming. *Journal of the American Psychoanalytic Association*, 1965, *13*, 197–303.

Fisher, C. Psychological significance of the dream-sleep cycle. In H. A. Witkin & H. B. Lewis (Eds.), *Experimental studies of dreaming*. New York: Random House, 1967.

Fisher, C. Experimental and clinical approaches to the mind-body problem through recent research in sleep and dreaming. In N. Rosenzweig & H. Griscom (Eds.), *Psychopharmacology and psychotherapy*. New York: Human Sciences Press, 1978.

Fisher, S., & Greenberg, R. P. *The scientific credibility of Freud's theories and therapy*. New York: Basic Books, 1977.

Fliess, R. *Erogeneity and libido*. New York: International Universities Press, 1956.

Flugel, J. C. Psychoanalysis: Its status and promise. Chap. 20 in C. Murchison (Ed.), *Psychologies of 1930*. Worcester, Mass.: Clark University Press, 1930.

Flugel, J. C. *Man, morals and society: A psycho-analytical study*. New York: International Universities Press, 1945.

Freud, S. Beitrag zur Kenntniss der Cocawirkung. *Wiener medizinische Wochenschrift*, 1885, *35*, 129–133.

Freud, S. *The origins of psycho-analysis. Letters to Wilhelm Fliess, drafts and notes: 1887–1902.* London: Imago, 1954. (a)

Freud, S. Project for a scientific psychology. Unpublished, 1895. In S. Freud, *The origins of psychoanalysis. Letters to Wilhelm Fliess, drafts and notes: 1887–1902.* London: Imago, 1954. (b)

Freud, S. Heredity and the aetiology of the neuroses. *Standard edition of the complete psychological works of Sigmund Freud* (Vol. III, 143–156). London: Hogarth, 1962. (Originally published, 1896.) (a)

Freud, S. Further remarks on the neuro-psychoses of defense. *Standard edition of the complete psychological works of Sigmund Freud* (Vol. III, 162–185). London: Hogarth, 1962. (Originally published, 1896.).(b)

Freud, S. The aetiology of hysteria. *Standard edition of the complete psychological works of Sigmund Freud* (Vol. III, 191–221). London: Hogarth, 1962. (Originally published, 1896.) (c)

Freud, S. *Traumdeutung*. Vienna: Deuticke, 1899.

Freud, S. The interpretation of dreams. *Standard edition of the complete psychological works of Sigmund Freud* (Vols. IV–V). London: Hogarth, 1953. (Originally published, 1899; 3rd ed. 1911.)

Freud, S. *Ueber den Traum*. Wiesbaden: Bergmann, 1901. (2nd ed. 1911.)

Freud, S. Three essays on the theory of sexuality. *Standard edition of the complete psychological works of Sigmund Freud* (Vol. VII, 135–243). London: Hogarth, 1953. (Originally published, 1905.)

Freud, S. My views on the part played by sexuality in the aetiology of the neuroses. *Standard edition of the complete psychological works of Sigmund Freud* (Vol. VII, 271–279). London: Hogarth, 1953. (Originally published, 1906.)

Freud, S. Psycho-analysis and the establishment of the facts in legal proceedings. *Standard edition of the complete psychological works of Sigmund Freud* (Vol. IX, 103–114). London: Hogarth, 1959. (Originally published, 1906.)

Freud, S. Delusions and dreams in Jenson's *Gradiva*. *Standard edition of the complete psychological works of Sigmund Freud* (Vol. IX, 7–95). London: Hogarth, 1959. (Originally published, 1907.)

Freud, S. On the sexual theories of children. *Standard edition of the complete psychological works of Sigmund Freud* (Vol. IX, 209–226). London: Hogarth, 1959. (Originally published, 1908.)

Freud, S. Notes upon a case of obsessional neurosis. *Standard edition of the complete psychological works of Sigmund Freud* (Vol. X, 155–318). London: Hogarth, 1955. (Originally published, 1909.)

Freud, S. The origin and development of psychoanalysis. *American Journal of Psychology*, 1910, 21, 181–218.

Freud, S. Leonardo da Vinci and a memory of his childhood. *Standard edition of the complete psychological works of Sigmund Freud* (Vol. XI, 63–137). London: Hogarth, 1957. (Originally published 1910.)

Freud, S. Formulations on the two principles of mental functioning. *Standard edition of the complete psychological works of Sigmund Freud* (Vol. XII, 218–226). London: Hogarth, 1958. (Originally published, 1911.)

Freud, S. Papers on technique. *Standard edition of the complete psychological works of Sigmund Freud* (Vol. XII, 91–171). London: Hogarth, 1958. (Originally published, 1911–1915.)

Freud, S. Totem and taboo. *Standard edition of the complete psychological works of Sigmund Freud* (Vol. XIII, 1–161). London: Hogarth, 1955. (Originally published, 1913.)

Freud, S. On the history of the psycho-analytic movement. *Standard edition of the complete psychological works of Sigmund Freud* (Vol. XIV, 7–66). London: Hogarth, 1957. (Originally published, 1914.)

Freud, S. A difficulty in the path of psycho-analysis. *Standard edition of the complete psychological works of Sigmund Freud* (Vol. XVII, 137–144). London: Hogarth, 1955. (Originally published, 1917.)

Freud, S. Introductory lectures on psycho-analysis. *Standard edition of the complete psychological works of Sigmund Freud* (Vols. XV–XVI). London: Hogarth, 1963. (Originally published, 1917.)

Freud, S. Beyond the pleasure principle. *Standard edition of the complete psychological works of Sigmund Freud* (Vol. XVIII, 7–64). London: Hogarth, 1955. (Originally published, 1920.) (a)

Freud, S. A note on the prehistory of the technique of analysis. *Standard edition of the complete psychological works of Sigmund Freud* (Vol. XVIII, 263–265). London: Hogarth, 1955. (First published anonymously over the signature 'F', *Internationale Zeitschrift für Psychoanalyse*, 1920, 6, 79.) (b)

Freud, S. An autobiographical study. *Standard edition of the complete psychological works of Sigmund Freud* (Vol. XX, 7–74). London: Hogarth, 1959. (Originally published, 1925.)

Freud, S. The resistances to psycho-analysis. *Standard edition of the complete psychological works of Sigmund Freud* (Vol. XIX, 213–224). London: Hogarth, 1961. (Originally published, 1925.)

Freud, S. Psycho-analysis. *Standard edition of the complete psychological works of Sigmund Freud* (Vol. XX, 263–270). London: Hogarth, 1959. (Originally published, 1926.) (a)

Freud, S. The question of lay analysis. *Standard edition of the complete psychological works of Sigmund Freud* (Vol. XX, 183–258). London: Hogarth, 1959. (Originally published, 1926.) (b)

Freud, S. *Die Frage der Laienanalyse*. Leipzig, Vienna, and Zurich: Internationaler Psychoanalytischer Verlag, 1926.

Freud, S. Fetishism. *Standard edition of the complete psychological works of Sigmund Freud* (Vol. XXI, 149–157). London: Hogarth, 1961. (Originally published, 1927.)

Freud, S. Female sexuality. *Standard edition of the complete psychological works of Sigmund Freud* (Vol. XXI, 225–243). London: Hogarth, 1961. (Originally published, 1931.)

Freud, S. *New introductory lectures on psychoanalysis*. New York: Norton, 1933.

Freud, S. Splitting of the ego in the process of defence. *Standard edition of the complete psychological works of Sigmund Freud* (Vol. XXIII, 1967, 275–278, unfinished). (First published posthumously, 1940.)

Freud, S., & Jung, C. G. *The Freud/Jung letters*. W. McGuire (Ed.). Princeton, N.J.: Princeton University Press, 1974.

Galton, F. Psychometric facts. *Nineteenth Century*, 1879, 5, 425–433.

Galton, F. Psychometric experiments. *Brain*, 1879–1880, 2, 149–162.

Galton, F. *Inquiries into human faculty and its development*. London: MacMillan, 1883.

I. THE SYSTEMATIC FRAMEWORK OF PSYCHOLOGY

Gottesman, I. I., & Shields, J. *Schizophrenia: The epigenetic puzzle.* London and New York: Cambridge University Press, 1982.

Grinker, R. R. Reminiscences of a personal contact with Freud. *American Journal of Orthopsychiatry,* 1940, *10,* 850–854.

Grinker, R. R. A philosophical appraisal of psychoanalysis. Pp. 126–142 in J. H. Masserman (Ed.), *Science and psychoanalysis* (Vol. I). New York: Grune & Stratton, 1958.

Hale, N. G., Jr. *James Jackson Putnam and psychoanalysis.* Cambridge, Mass.: Harvard University Press, 1971.

Hall, G. S. *Founders of modern psychology.* New York: Appleton, 1912.

Haller, R. S. *Literary criticism of Dante Alighieri.* Lincoln: University of Nebraska Press, 1973.

Hamilton, G. V. A study of sexual tendencies in monkeys and baboons. *Journal of Animal Behavior,* 1914, *4,* 295–318.

Hamilton, G. V. Nina: An interpretation. *Theatre Guild Magazine,* 1928 (Dec.), 19–22.

Hamilton, G. V. *A research in marriage.* New York: A & C Boni, 1929.

Head, H. Observations on the elements of the psycho-neuroses. *British Medical Journal,* 1920, *1,* 389–392.

Helmholtz, H. *Wissenschaftliche Abhandlungen* (2 vols.). Leipzig: Barth, 1882.

Hendrick, I. (Ed.), *The birth of an institute.* Freeport, Maine: Bond Wheelwright, 1961.

Herbart, J. F. *Lehrbuch zur Psychologie.* Königsberg: Unzer, 1816. (2nd ed. 1834.) (English translation [1891] reprinted: *Textbook in psychology.* Washington, D.C.: University Publications of America, 1977.)

Hermann, I. Gustav Theodor Fechner: eine psychoanalytische Studie. *Imago,* 1925, *11,* 371–420.

Herrick, C. J. *George Ellette Coghill, naturalist and philosopher.* Chicago: University of Chicago Press, 1949.

Hilgard, E. R. Experimental approaches to psychoanalysis. In E. Pumpian-Mindlin (Ed.), *Psychoanalysis as science.* Stanford: Stanford University Press, 1952.

Horwitz, L. Theory construction and validation in psychoanalysis. Chap. 27 in M. Marx (Ed.), *Theories in contemporary psychology.* New York: Macmillan, 1963.

Hunt, J. McV. (Ed.), *Personality and the behavior disorders* (2 vols.). New York: Ronald Press, 1944.

James, G. W. The assault on Fort Wagner. In *Military order of the loyal legion of the United States. Wisconsin Commandery. War papers read before the Commandery of the state of Wisconsin.* Milwaukee, Wisconsin, 1891.

James, H. The romance of certain old clothes. *Atlantic Monthly,* 1868, *21,* 209–220.

James, H. The long wards. In E. Wharton (Ed.), *The book of the homeless.* New York: Scribner's, 1916.

James, H. Notebooks. F. O. Matthiessen & K. B. Murdock (Eds.). New York: Oxford University Press, 1947.

James, W. Review on experimental and critical contribution to the physiology of the semicircular canals. *American Journal of Otology,* 1880, *2,* 341–343.

James, W. *The principles of psychology* (Vol. II). New York: Henry Holt, 1890.

James, W. Diary for 1909. Unpublished MS. Harvard University, Houghton Library. Cambridge, Massachusetts.

James, W. A suggestion about mysticism. *Journal of Philosophy, Psychology, & Scientific Methods,* 1910, *7,* 85–92.

James, W. *The letters of William James* (2nd ed. 2 vols. in one). Edited by his son Henry James. Boston: Little, Brown, 1926.

Jones, E. *The life and work of Sigmund Freud* (Vol. I). New York: Basic Books, 1953.

Jones, E. *The life and work of Sigmund Freud* (Vol. II). New York: Basic Books, 1955.

Jones, E. *The life and work of Sigmund Freud* (Vol. III). New York: Basic Books, 1957.

Jones, G. S. *Treatment or torture: The philosophy, techniques, and future of psychodynamics.* London: Tavistock Publications, 1968.

Jones, V. C. *Eight hours before Richmond*. New York: Henry Holt, 1957.

Jung, C. G. (Ed.). Diagnostische Assoziationsstudien: Beiträge zur experimentellen Psychopathologie (Vol. I). Leipzig: Barth, 1906.

Jung, C. G. *Studies in word-association*. London: Heinemann, 1918. (Originally published, 1904–1909.)

Jung, C. G. Zur Tatbestandsdiagnostik. *Zeitschrift für angewandte Psychologie und psychologische Sammelforschung*, 1908, *1*, 163.

Jung, C. G. The association method. Three lectures at Clark University, September 1909. *American Journal of Psychology*, 1910, *21*, 219–269.

Jung, C. G. *Symbols of transformation*. London: Routledge & Kegan Paul, 1956. (Originally published, 1911–1912.)

Jung, C. G. *Memories, dreams, reflections*. Recorded and edited by Aniela Jaffé. New York: Pantheon Books, 1963.

Jung, C. G. Experimental researches. *Collected Works* (Vol. 2). Princeton, N.J.: Princeton University Press, 1973.

Karli, P. Human aggression and animal aggression: A unifying view of the brain-behavior relationship involved. *Aggressive Behavior*, 1983, *9*, 94–102.

Kempe, C. H., Silverman, F. N., Steele, B. F., Droegemueller, W., & Silver, H. K. The battered child syndrome. *Journal of the American Medical Association*, 1962, *181*, 17–24.

King, S. The experimental situation as a psychological problem. Unpublished article. St. Louis: Washington University, 1970.

Kline, P. *Fact and fantasy in Freudian theory*. London: Methuen, 1972 (2nd. ed. 1981).

Kluckhohn, C., & Murray, H. A. *Personality in nature, society, and culture*. New York: Knopf, 1948.

Kohs, S. C. The association method in its relation to the complex and complex indicators. *American Journal of Psychology*, 1914, *25*, 544–591.

Kraft, V. *The Vienna circle: The origins of neo-positivism*. New York: Philosophical Library, 1953.

Kris, E. Introduction. In S. Freud, *The origins of psycho-analysis*. London: Imago, 1954.

Ladd, G. T. Contribution to the psychology of visual dreams. *Mind*, 1892, *1* (n.s.), 299–304.

Levin, K. *Freud's early psychology of the neuroses: A historical perspective*. Pittsburgh: University of Pittsburgh Press, 1978.

Lewin, K. *A dynamic theory of personality*. New York: McGraw-Hill, 1935.

Lipps, T. *Grundthatsachen des Seelenlebens*. Bonn: Cohen, 1883.

Lipps, T. Der Begriff des Unbewussten in der Psychologie, *Dritter Internationaler Congress für Psychologie in München, 1896*. Munich: Lehmann, 1897.

Livingstone, D. *The last journals of David Livingstone in Central Africa* (2 vols.). H. Waller (Ed.). London: John Murray, 1874.

Luborsky, L., Singer, B., & Luborsky, L. Comparative studies of psychotherapies. *Archives of General Psychiatry*, 1975, *32*, 995–1008.

Lyons, J. On the psychology of the psychological experiment. Pp. 89–109 in C. Scheerer (Ed.), *Cognition: Theory, research, promise*. New York: Harper & Row, 1964.

MacKinnon, D. W., & Dukes, W. F. Repression. In L. Postman (Ed.), *Psychology in the making*. New York: Knopf, 1962.

Malcolm, J. Annals of scholarship: Trouble in the archives. *The New Yorker*, 1983, December 5, 59–152; December 12, 60–119.

Malcolm, J. *In the Freud archives*. New York: Knopf, 1984.

Martin, R. M. *Events, reference, and logical form*. Washington, D.C.: The Catholic University of America Press, 1978.

Masson, J. M. *The assault on truth: Freud's suppression of the seduction theory*. New York: Farrar, Straus & Giroux, 1984.

Medawar, P. B. *The hope of progress*. London: Methuen, 1972.

I. THE SYSTEMATIC FRAMEWORK OF PSYCHOLOGY

Metchnikoff, O. *Life of Elie Metchnikoff: 1845–1916*. Boston: Houghton Mifflin, 1921.

Mischel, W. *Introduction to personality*. New York: Holt, Rinehart & Winston, 1971.

Murray, H. A., et al. *Explorations in personality*. New York: Oxford University Press, 1938.

Nansen, F. *In Nacht und Eis* (3 vols.). Leipzig: Brockhaus, 1897–1898.

Nansen, F. *Farthest north: Being the record of a voyage of exploration of the ship "Fram" 1893–96 and of a fifteen months' sleigh journey by Dr. Nansen and Lieut. Johansen* (2 vols.). New York: Harpers, 1897.

Nunberg, H., & Federn, E. *Minutes of the Vienna Psychoanalytic Society* (4 vols.). New York: International Universities Press, 1962–1975.

Orne, M. T. On the social psychology of the psychological experiment: With particular reference to demand characteristics and their implications. *American Psychologist*, 1962, *17*, 776–783.

Oxford English dictionary, a supplement to. R. W. Burchfield (Ed.). (Vol. III). Oxford: Clarendon Press, 1982.

Paneth, J. Versuche über den zeitlichen Verlauf des Gedächtnissbildes. *Centralblatt für Physiologie*, 1890, *4*, 81–83. (Reported after the author's death by Sigmund Exner.)

Penfield, W. *The excitable cortex in conscious man*. Springfield, Ill.: Thomas, 1958.

Penfield, W. *The mystery of the mind*. Princeton, N.J.: Princeton University Press, 1975.

Popper, K. R. *The logic of scientific discovery*. New York: Basic Books, 1959.

Popper, K. R. *Conjectures and refutations: The growth of scientific knowledge* (2nd ed.). New York: Basic Books, 1965.

Rank, O. *Der Mythus von der Geburt des Helden*. Leipzig and Vienna: Deuticke, 1909. (With a section, pp. 64–68, by S. Freud, on the "family romance.") (English translation: *Myth of the birth of the hero* by O. Rank. New York: Nervous and Mental Disease Publishing Co., 1914. Pp. 63–68 by S. Freud.)

Rieber, R. W. (Ed.), *Wilhelm Wundt and the making of a scientific psychology*. New York & London: Plenum, 1980.

Robert, W. *Der Traum als Naturnothwendigkeit erklärt*. Hamburg: Herman Seippel, 1886.

Rogers, M. P., Dubey, D., & Reich, P. The influence of the psyche and the brain on immunity and disease susceptibility: A critical review. *Psychosomatic Medicine*, 1979, *41*, 147–164.

Rosenberg, M. J. When dissonance fails: On eliminating evaluation apprehension from attitude measurement. *Journal of Personality & Social Psychology*, 1965, *1*, 28–42.

Rosenthal, R. The experimental induction of the defense mechanism of projection. *Journal of Projective Techniques*, 1959, *23*, 357–364.

Rosenthal, R. *Experimenter effects in behavioral research*. New York: Appleton-Century-Crofts, 1966.

Rosenthal, R. Covert communication and tacit understanding in the psychological experiment. *Psychological Bulletin*, 1967, *67*, 356–367.

Rosenzweig, S. The experimental situation as a psychological problem. *Psychological Review*, 1933, *40*, 337–354. (a)

Rosenzweig, S. Preferences in the repetition of successful and unsuccessful activities as a function of age and personality. *Journal of Genetic Psychology*, 1933, *42*, 423–441. (b)

Rosenzweig, S. Types of reaction to frustration: A heuristic classification. *Journal of Abnormal & Social Psychology*, 1934, *29*, 298–300.

Rosenzweig, S. A test for types of reaction to frustration. *American Journal of Orthopsychiatry*, 1935, *4*, 395–403.

Rosenzweig, S. Some implicit common factors in diverse methods of psychotherapy. *American Journal of Orthopsychiatry*, 1936, *6*, 412–415.

Rosenzweig, S. The experimental study of psychoanalytic concepts. *Character & Personality*, 1937, *6*, 61–71. (a)

Rosenzweig, S. Schools of psychology: a complementary pattern. *Philosophy of Science*, 1937, *4*, 96–106. (b)

Rosenzweig, S. A dynamic interpretation of psychotherapy oriented towards research. *Psychiatry*, 1938, *1*, 521–526. (a)

Rosenzweig, S. The experimental study of repression. In H. A. Murray (Ed.), *Explorations in personality*. New York: Oxford University Press, 1938. (b)

Rosenzweig, S. The experimental measurement of types of reaction to frustration. In H. A. Murray (Ed.), *Explorations in personality*. New York: Oxford University Press, 1938. (c)

Rosenzweig, S. Frustration as an experimental problem. *Character & Personality*, 1938, *7*, 126–160. (d)

Rosenzweig, S. An experimental study of 'repression' with special reference to need-persistive and ego-defensive reactions to frustration. *Journal of Experimental Psychology*, 1943, *32*, 64–74. (a)

Rosenzweig, S. The ghost of Henry James. *Character & Personality*, 1943, *12*, 79–100. (b) (Reprinted with a postscript in *Modern criticism*, edited by W. Sutton & R. Foster. New York: Odyssey Press, 1963, 401–416.)

Rosenzweig, S. Sibling death as a psychological experience with special reference to schizophrenia. *Psychoanalytic Review*, 1943, *30*, 177–186. (c)

Rosenzweig, S. An outline of frustration theory. In J. McV. Hunt (Ed.), *Personality and the behavior disorders* (Vol. I). New York: Ronald Press, 1944. (a)

Rosenzweig, S. Converging approaches to personality: Murray, Allport, Lewin. *Psychological Review*, 1944, *51*, 248–256. (b)

Rosenzweig, S. Further comparative data on repetition-choice after success and failure as related to frustration tolerance. *Journal of Genetic Psychology*, 1945, *66*, 75–81.

Rosenzweig, S. Norms and the individual in the psychologist's perspective. In M. L. Reymert (Ed.), *Feelings and emotions: The Mooseheart symposium*. New York: McGraw-Hill, 1950. (a)

Rosenzweig, S. Levels of behavior in psychodiagnosis with special reference to the Picture-Frustration Study. *American Journal of Orthopsychiatry*, 1950, *20*, 63–72. (b)

Rosenzweig, S. Idiodynamics in personality theory with special reference to projective methods. *Psychological Review*, 1951, *58*, 213–223.

Rosenzweig, S. The investigation of repression as an instance of experimental idiodynamics. *Psychological Review*, 1952, *59*, 339–345.

Rosenzweig, S. A transvaluation of psychotherapy: A reply to Hans Eysenck. *Journal of Abnormal & Social Psychology*, 1954, *49*, 298–304.

Rosenzweig, S. Unconscious self-defense in an uxoricide. *Journal of Criminal Law, Criminology and Police Science*, 1956, *46*, 791–795.

Rosenzweig, S. The place of the individual and of idiodynamics in psychology: A dialogue. *Journal of Individual Psychology*, 1958, *14*, 3–20.

Rosenzweig, S. Hubbub at the hub. Special review of *The birth of an institute*, edited by Ives Hendrik. *Contemporary Psychology*, 1963, *8*, 225–228.

Rosenzweig, S. Interview with Dr. Max Schur regarding the final illness and death of Sigmund Freud. Unpublished, January 30, 1964.

Rosenzweig, S. The day of Freud's death: A thirtieth anniversary note. *Journal of Psychology*, 1970, *74*, 101–103. (a)

Rosenzweig, S. E. G. Boring and the *Zeitgeist: Eruditione Gesta Beavit*. *Journal of Psychology*, 1970, *75*, 59–71. (b)

Rosenzweig, S. The impact of B. F. Skinner on psychiatry. *Medical World News*, 1972, *13*, Supplement "Psychiatry," 54–55, 59–60.

Rosenzweig, S. Human sexual autonomy as an evolutionary attainment, anticipating proceptive sex choice and idiodynamic bisexuality. In J. Zubin & J. Money (Eds.), *Contemporary sexual behavior: Critical issues in the 1970s*. Baltimore: Johns Hopkins University Press, 1973.

Rosenzweig, S. *The Rosenzweig Picture-Frustration (P-F) Study: Basic manual*. St. Louis: Rana House, 1978. (a)

205

Rosenzweig, S. *Aggressive behavior and the Rosenzweig Picture-Frustration Study*. New York: Praeger, 1978. (b)

Rosenzweig, S. *Freud, Jung and the kingmaker: The visit to America, with the letters of Sigmund Freud and G. Stanley Hall, 1908–1923, and Freud's five lectures at Clark University 1909*. St. Louis: Rana House, 1985 (in press).

Rosenzweig, S., & Bray, D. Sibling deaths in the anamneses of schizophrenic patients. *Archives of Neurology & Psychiatry*, 1943, 49, 71–92.

Rosenzweig, S., & Mason, G. An experimental study of memory in relation to the theory of repression. *British Journal of Psychology* (General Section), 1934, 24, 247–265.

Rosenzweig, S., & Sarason, S. An experimental study of the triadic hypothesis: Reaction to frustration, ego-defense, and hypnotizability. *Character & Personality*, 1942, 11, 1–19, 150–165.

Rosnow, R. L. *Paradigms in transition: The method of social inquiry*. New York: Oxford University Press, 1981.

Rubin, D. C. On the retention function for autobiographical memory. *Journal of Verbal Learning & Verbal Behavior*, 1982, 21, 21–38.

Schrötter, K. Experimentelle Träume. *Zentralblatt für Psychoanalyse*, 1912, 2, 638–646.

Schur, M. *Freud: Living and dying*. New York: International Universities Press, 1972.

Scriven, M. A study of radical behaviorism. Pp. 86–130 in H. Feigl & M. Scriven (Eds.), *The foundations of science and the concepts of psychology and psychoanalysis. Minnesota Studies in the Philosophy of Science* (Vol. I). Minneapolis: University of Minnesota Press, 1956.

Sears, R. R. *Survey of objective studies of psychoanalytic concepts*. New York: Social Science Research Council, Bulletin No. 51, 1943.

Shaeffer, L. *O'Neill: Son and artist*. Boston: Little, Brown, 1973.

Shakow, D., & Rapaport, D. *The influence of Freud on American psychology. Psychological Issues*, Vol. IV, No. 1, Monograph 13. New York: International Universities Press, 1964.

Sidis, B. *The psychology of suggestion: A research into the subconscious nature of man and society*. With an introduction by William James. New York: Appleton, 1898.

Sidis, B. *The causation and treatment of psychopathic diseases*. Boston: Richard G. Badger, 1916.

Silverman, I. *The human subject in the psychological laboratory*. New York: Pergamon, 1977.

Silverman, I., & Shulman, A. D. A conceptual model of artifact in attitude change studies. *Sociometry*, 1970, 33, 97–107.

Skinner, B. F. Critique of psychoanalytic concepts and theories. Pp. 77–87 in H. Feigl & M. Scriven (Eds.), *The foundations of science and the concepts of psychology and psychoanalysis. Minnesota Studies in the Philosophy of Science* (Vol. I). Minneapolis: University of Minnesota Press, 1956.

Smuts, J. C. *Holism and evolution*. New York: Macmillan, 1926.

Stanley, H. M. *Through the dark continent* (2 vols.). London: Low, Marston, Searle & Rivington, 1878.

Stekel, W. *Die Sprache des Traumes*. Wiesbaden: Bergmann, 1911.

Stern, C. *Principles of human genetics* (3rd ed.). San Francisco: Freeman, 1973.

Stricker, S. *Studien über die Association der Vorstellungen*. Vienna: Wilhelm Braumüller, 1883.

Trautscholdt, M. Experimentelle Untersuchungen über die Association der Vorstellungen. *Philosophische Studien*, 1881–1882, I, 213–250.

Trosman, H., & Simmons, R. D. The Freud library. *Journal of the American Psychoanalytic Association*, 1973, 21, 646–687.

Tulving, E., & Donaldson, W. *Organization of memory*. New York: Academic Press, 1972.

Wahle, R. *Gehirn und Bewusstsein: Physiologisch-psychologische Studie*. Vienna: Alfred Hölder, 1884.

Wahle, R. Bemerkungen zur Beschreibung und Eintheilung der Ideenassociationen. *Vierteljahrschrift für wissenschaftliche Philosophie*, 1885, 9, 404–432.

Wahle, R. *Grundlagen einer neuen Psychiatrie*. Vienna: Steyermühl-Verlag, 1931.

Wertheimer, M. Zur Tatbestandsdiagnostik: Eine Feststellung. *Archiv für die Gesamte Psychologie*, 1906, 7, 139–140.

Wertheimer, M., & Klein, J. Psychologische Tatbestandsdiagnostik. *Archiv für Kriminal-Anthropologie und Kriminalistik*, 1904, *15*, 72–113.

Williams, G. J., & Money, J. (Eds.), *Traumatic abuse and neglect of children at home*. Baltimore: Johns Hopkins University Press, 1980.

Wilson, L. N. G. *Stanley Hall: a sketch*. New York: G. E. Stechert, 1914.

Windelband, W. *Geschichte und Naturwissenschaft*, 3rd ed. Strassburg: Heitz, 1904.

Witkin, H. A., & Lewis, H. B. (Eds.), *Experimental studies of dreaming*. New York: Random House, 1967.

Wittels, F. *Sigmund Freud: His personality, his teaching, and his school*. Translated from the German. London: Allen & Unwin, 1924.

Woodger, J. H. *Biology and language. An introduction to the methodology of the biological sciences including medicine*. Cambridge (England): Cambridge University Press, 1952.

Woodger, J. H. *Physics, psychology and medicine: A methodological essay*. Cambridge (England): Cambridge University Press, 1956.

Woodworth, R. S. *Dynamic psychology*. New York: Columbia University Press, 1918.

Woodworth, R. S. *Dynamics of behavior*. New York: Holt, 1958.

Woodworth, R. S., & Schlosberg, H. *Experimental psychology* (rev. ed.). New York: Holt, Rinehart & Winston, 1962.

Wright, T. *The big nail: The story of the Cook-Peary feud*. New York: John Day, 1970.

Wundt, W. *Elemente der Völkpsychologie*. Leipzig: Alfred Kröner, 1912. (English translation, 1916.)

Ziehen, T. *Leitfaden der physiologischen Psychologie*. Jena: G. Fischer, 1891.

Ziehen, T. *Introduction to physiological psychology*. London: Swan Sonnenchein, 1895. (English translation of the German 2nd ed., 1893.)

207

8

Psychoanalysis and Behavior Theory: 1907–1965

ROBERT R. SEARS

The relationship between psychoanalysis and the rest of psychology was a bit stormy from the beginning. The structural psychology of consciousness that dominated the last part of the nineteenth century was not prepared for the unconscious or for a motivational theory of the thought processes. When Freud added the subject matter of sexual development to the cognitive dynamics of dream theory, there seemed no possible bridge between the two kinds of psychology. There was not, and structuralism simply disappeared.

The credit goes more to behaviorism than to psychoanalysis, of course. Academic psychology was already becoming more functional, and the birth of behavior theory provided a new potential partner for psychoanalysis. The difficulties were as great as they had been with structuralism, however. The methods, the data obtained, and the philosophical underpinnings of the two theories were incompatible. Nevertheless, over the years to come, quite a few behavior theorists and several psychoanalysts made valiant efforts to integrate their separate bodies of knowledge into a single system. It was a difficult task, and it had not been accomplished at the end of the first half century. But while psychoanalysis remains as rigidly limited in method, data, and type of theory as it was seventy years ago, behavior theory has been a considerable gainer from the effort. My aim is to record the main elements of the who, what, when, and where of this long encounter.

Psychoanalysis and behavior theory both took shape in the last decade of the nineteenth century. Psychoanalysis was a little the forerunner, with the publication in 1895 of Breuer and Freud's *Studies on Hysteria*. The beginning of behavior theory came soon after, with Thorndike's *Animal Intelligence*, published in 1898. There was little to connect the two, but over the next half century two major successive waves of effort bent toward creating a linkage. The first, lasting into the 1930s, stemmed from the biologically oriented theory then developing around the research of Thorndike, Yerkes, and Watson. The chief architect was G. V. Hamilton, a young psychiatrist who had studied with Yerkes at Harvard while serving as a resident with Shepherd Ivory Franz at the nearby MacLean Hospital. This first effort to link psychoanalysis and behavior theory stemmed from the need for more effective ways to understand the causes and to treat psychological disorders. The second effort to join the two theories was made by a group at Yale who were influenced by the newer behavior theory of Clark Hull. These were psychologists and anthropologists whose primary aim was to construct a unified social science. Though successive, these two waves were not altogether independent. Hamilton's work led to some important generalizations about reactions to frustration, and much later, the second wave contributed significantly to the therapeutic task via Dollard and Miller's *Personality and Psychotherapy* (1950). But initially little interaction took place between the earlier therapists and the later social scientists.

Our first protagonist is the young Gilbert Van Tassell Hamilton.[1] He was born in 1877 in a small Ohio town, received his undergraduate degree at Ohio Wesleyan University, and completed his medical training at Jefferson Medical College in 1901. He served an internship year in Philadelphia and three more years as a hospital psychiatrist. This experience disillusioned him, and he saw the serious need for research on mental disorders. In 1905 he secured the residency at MacLean Hospital, where he remained until 1908, and began to serve as a part-time postdoctoral collaborator in Yerkes's animal laboratory. It was from that hospice, in 1907, that he published his first paper, an experimental examination of a dog's reactions to an insoluble problem (Hamilton, 1907).

Only in retrospect is it clear that this minor research not only began the interaction of behavior theory with psychoanalysis, but opened an entirely new domain for behavior theory itself. Thorndike, Yerkes, and Watson had concerned themselves with the learning process, that is, how and under what conditions animals used cues to improve their performance in a problem situation. As a psychiatrist, Hamilton saw his patients as being more influenced by the insoluble problems of life than the soluble ones. His genius as a scientist was in reversing the older convention that

[1] I am much indebted to Dr. H. W. Magoun and Mrs. Roberta Yerkes Blanshard for help in reporting on Hamilton's life. This is a difficult task, for his personal papers have disappeared, as has the manuscript of his autobiography, which he was revising for publication by Harpers at the time of his sudden death by coronary occlusion in 1943.

sought the conditions for success in order to study the outcome of imposed failure and frustration.

Hamilton's experiment was simple. He placed his dog in a four-exit multiple choice apparatus and gave it an incentive to escape. There were ten trials a day for many days. Only a single exit was open on any trial, and the only consistency was that the same exit was never open on successive trials. Initially, Hamilton's dependent variables were cognitive, namely, the dog's ways of choosing its exit—the extent to which it made rational choices—but later he turned to affective variables as well. This method was the prototype for several more intensive investigations Hamilton made in the next few years to study more formally, and in much greater detail, the various types of cognitive and affective reactions of many different species of animals to baffling disadvantage. His subjects ranged from gophers to human children (Hamilton, 1911a, 1914, 1916).

The year 1907 was noteworthy in two other respects. Adolf Meyer recommended Hamilton to a wealthy family who were maintaining a home for a schizophrenic son in Santa Barbara. Hamilton accepted the position with the agreement that he could build and maintain a primate colony as a research laboratory. His enthusiasm for this venture was aroused by the other event of 1907, his reading of Freud's *Three Essays on the Theory of Sexuality* (1905). He was struck instantly by its breadth and realistic quality. But while he was attracted to the factual material, he was offended by what he called the "psychomorphic" character of the theory in which the observations were embedded. To him, sex was one of the major cravings of mammalian organisms, a drive that activated great domains of both individual and social behavior. Freud (1905/1953) viewed sex as experience, an internal event that was related to the external world only by ideational representation. Hamilton was a psychobiologist, oriented toward the observation of behavior in other species as well as human beings, and he preferred a theoretical formulation that did not rest upon the language habits of a single species.

During the next nine years, Hamilton's research had two themes. One was the study of mammalian reactions to baffling disadvantage, i.e., to insoluble problems. This was, in fact, the first sophisticated empirical study of reactions to frustration. The other theme was sex behavior among monkeys and baboons, both in confinement and in the free-ranging state permitted by a large ranch (Hamilton 1914). Both sets of studies were relevant to the psychological problems that were at the heart of psychoanalytic theory. The multiple-choice apparatus permitted a detailed comparison of species, and of individuals within species, with respect to their modes of responding to frustrations. Hamilton distinguished five types of reaction, ranging from the most rational possible—Type A—to an extremely persistent nonadjustive reaction—Type E. The relative frequency of the more adjustive responses increased up the phylogenetic scale and with age among monkeys and human children. (Years later Patrick [1934] used a similar method with college students as subjects and found that relatively low drive stimulation also induced a more rational response.)

The observations of sexual behavior in monkeys and baboons confirmed the polymorphous perverse quality of sexual behavior. They revealed the effects of required monogamous mating, and the liberating effect of release from captivity. With reduction of external interference, there was a reduction in aggression connected with sexual activity.

These various research reports deserve careful study in their own right, but their findings are brought together most forcefully in the context of patient diagnosis and treatment. Earlier, Hamilton (1911b) had published a brief article on neurasthenia. In it he described several patients' symptoms as persistent, nonadjustive reactions to baffling disadvantage. Some of these difficulties were sexual, or at least marital; others were more related to achievement and work. The baffling disadvantages sometimes arose from external circumstances and sometimes from self-defeating habits of response. The primary presenting complaints of neurasthenia were physical, however, and not easily conceptualizable as habitual. These organic symptoms offered a separate problem. At that time, clinical and research findings on the autonomic nervous system were much in the forefront of psychiatric thinking. Speculating beyond either psychoanalysis or behavior theory, Hamilton interpreted flatus, palpitation, fatigue, headaches, and other imprecisely definable disabilities as the products of autonomic nervous system exacerbation. Now, with substantial research findings on both sex and frustration, and with the growing body of neurological knowledge, Hamilton felt that it was time to try out his interpretive theory with a larger number of patients. So with his entry into military service in World War I, he discontinued both his primate research and his psychiatric service to his single patient.

After the war, Hamilton spent a year as a practicing psychiatrist in his old home town in Ohio, accepting referrals from the other local physicians. He chose this setting deliberately because he knew that a knowledge of the values, beliefs, customs, and the social milieu in which his patients lived was essential to an understanding of the problems they faced. His own theory was essentially a theory of individual behavior, and he had to rely on his nontheoretical knowledge of the social system and the substantive contents of his patients' thoughts and feelings to set his theory to work.

Hamilton reported the results of his year's practice in a 1925 volume entitled *An Introduction to Objective Psychopathology*. In it he presented more than a hundred cases with detailed diagnoses in terms of reaction to the baffling disadvantages the patients suffered in their efforts to satisfy major cravings. These vignettes, together with a lengthy explanation of the behavior theory itself, constituted a landmark in the attempt to draw psychoanalysis and behavior theory into a workable partnership. So far as American psychiatry was concerned, however, it was ahead of its time; it received a vilifying review in the *Journal of Nervous and Mental Diseases* (1927).

This was the end of Hamilton's formal effort to construct an objective behavior theory. His final published research was the famous *Research in Marriage* (1929), conducted in New York. It was essentially a continuation, with human subjects, of his earlier studies of sexual behavior in monkeys and baboons. It was not observational, of course, but made use of a standardized interview. He had finally accepted the need to deal specifically with language when dealing with the human animal.

Hamilton returned to private practice in Santa Barbara after completing the manuscript of his marriage study. In a letter to Yerkes in 1941 he said that he had become purely a psychoanalyst, but he spoke wistfully of his earlier dreams of creating a more objective psychopathology, and he expressed his interest in the new work on frustration that was coming out of Yale.

Hamilton was only the first of the practitioners who made an effort to *integrate* psychoanalysis and behavior theory. Indeed, with one exception, the first wave of the interaction was led entirely by therapists, and integration was their aim. The exception was the philosopher E. B. Holt, whose *The Freudian Wish* (1915) was a sophisticated attempt to translate psychoanalytic motivation theory into behavioristic terms. But in the main, the integrators were therapists. In 1920 E. J. Kempf of St. Elizabeth's Hospital published his mammoth *Psychopathology* in which he illustrated with many cases an integration of psychoanalysis, conditioned reflexes, and a somewhat speculative neurophysiology of the autonomic nervous system. English Bagby published his *Psychology of Personality* in 1928; this was based on a systematic behavior theory that incorporated a considerable amount of psychoanalytic conceptualization, particularly that of the defense mechanisms. In the early 1930s, two psychoanalysts developed integrative theories. One was Thomas M. French of the Chicago Institute, whose paper on conditioned reflexes (1933) was in part a plea for cross-theoretical research, a suggestion he repeated a decade later (French, 1944). The other was David M. Levy, whose theory underlying his experiments on sucking behavior in puppies (1934), his observations on human maternal reactions toward infants (1937), and his studies of overdependent children (1943) came directly from psychoanalysis. This first wave of attempted integration was essentially an effort on the part of clinicians to broaden the theoretical basis for their diagnosis and therapy. Only Hamilton and Levy carried the task into the empirical research arena.

In the meantime—and now I can supplement my role as historian with that of a participant-observer—several young psychologists had begun a new approach to psychoanalytic theory. The group included Helen Koch at Chicago, Saul Rosenzweig and Henry A. Murray, Jr., at Harvard, Ross Stagner at Wisconsin, and me at Illinois. These people were attempting to *verify* psychoanalytic observations and theoretical constructs by so-called "objective" methods. (For reviews of this work and citations to the many relevant publications, see Sears, 1943, 1944, and Hilgard, 1952.) Analysts insisted that from one patient to another there was appropriate replication of findings on such matters as sexual development, dream interpretive principles, and both observations and conceptualizations of defense mechanisms (see French, 1944). The psychologists, without direct experience of the clinical method, were skeptical. They wanted more precise measures than clinical judgments of similarity, and they tried to devise test procedures that would capture the effects of such mechanisms as repression, projection, and displacement, or to construct experiments which created the necessary conditions for producing them. These researches did not involve any systematic behavior theory, and hence would be of only tangential interest to the present discussion except for two things. One was intellectual and the other personal. On the intellectual side, these verification studies were preparatory for the next step, because the very process of designing nonpsychoanalytic behavioral research methods required an interpretation of psychoanalytic theory into behavioral terms. For that, a well-integrated behavior theory was obviously the most efficient medium. Translation, therefore, succeeded verification.

On the personal side, my first verification study of projection, which I reported at the 1934 APA meetings, aroused Hull's interest in a possible integration of the two theories, and his personal enthusiasm was the crucial element in the next stage of development.

As I have indicated, the first wave developed within the context of that loose turn-of-the-century behavior theory surrounding conditioned reflexes and the law of effect. The translations by French and by Holt belonged to that era. The second wave took advantage of Clark Hull's more systematic learning theory of the early 1930s. Quite by accident I provided the first example of translation within that context. I was an instructor at Illinois, two years beyond my degree at Yale. My interest in psychoanalysis stemmed from my teaching responsibilities, and I had started a series of verification studies on projection and repression. John McGeoch, the editor of *The Psychological Bulletin*, knew of this, so when he commissioned Arthur Melton to do a literature review on experimental studies of normal memory, he also invited me to do one on functional abnormalities of memory. As I waded through the literature on amnesias and repression, I thought that Freud's concepts of cathexis and anticathexis were another way of talking about Hull's fractional anticipatory goal responses. By midsummer of 1935 I was able to send Hull a rough draft of my translation. The article was in two parts, one a summary of the psychoanalytic theory of repression, the other the translation proper. Hull replied on August 28 with great praise for the former ("I have read it several times and have by no means digested it all. You have done an excellent job of condensation"). As to the second part, he said, "I have scribbled numerous comments on the margins. In general, I should say that it is a fine beginning. I hope you publish it." In a postscript he added, "I think I may wish to borrow copies of your manuscript for my seminar around October?" I think I did not send him the final draft because

McGeoch promised publication in early 1936. Hull bought some reprints of the paper (Sears, 1936), but by that time the famous "Hull's Seminar" of 1935–1936 was nearly over, and the minutes contain no reference to it.

Now as to that seminar. The first three months were simply a continuation of Hull's usual seminar on learning. But suddenly, on January 22, something very different occurred. The usual seminar announcement began: "This is the first of a proposed series of seminars which will be devoted to an attempt to integrate the major concepts and principles of the conditioned reaction with those of psychoanalysis" ("Notice of Informal Seminar," initialed C.L.H., dated January 20, 1936). Subsequent meetings were devoted to an exhaustive examination of libido, cathexis, fixation, regression, and repression. Earl Zinn, John Dollard, and, on one occasion, Erik Erikson served as the informants on psychoanalysis. Ruth Washburn, H. M. Halvorsen, Burton Castner, and Frances Ilg provided clinical and experimental information about infant behavior. Hull contributed a steely demand for logic and rigor, while his students presented relevant research reports from animal studies. The seminar met most Wednesday evenings through the rest of that academic year, with Hull as chairman and O. H. Mowrer as a superlatively skillful scribe. Neither Neal Miller nor I was there that year—he was in Vienna having an analysis with Heinz Hartmann, and I was still at Illinois—and the minutes reflect the presence mainly of Dollard, Zinn, and Mowrer among those who would become prominent members of the "Yale Group" in the Institute of Human Relations during the next few years (Hull & Mowrer, 1935–1936). The outcome of this integrative effort was disappointing. The analysts could not operationalize analytic concepts in the style that Hull desired, nor could he himself reach a solid conclusion that conditioned reflex principles were fully encompassing the complexities of the neuroses or the intangible qualities of the basic analytic concepts. A new approach was needed.

The time was propitious. Mark May had taken over the directorship of the floundering Institute, and in the fall of 1936 he had brought together a group of mostly young research psychologists, anthropologists, and psychoanalysts. Their mission was to construct a unified social science. May was the entrepreneur and Hull was the intellectual leader and provocateur. The troops included psychologists Leonard Doob, Neal Miller, Hobart Mowrer, Carl Hovland, Richard Sollenberger, Donald Marquis, and me; the anthropologists were G. P. Murdock, Clellan S. Ford, and John Whiting; the psychoanalysts were John Dollard and Earl Zinn. The Wednesday Night seminar began again, and after a couple of months of joint fumbling for a new approach, Dollard and Miller came forth with a quite startling formulation. This was the rudiment of the notion that later came to fruition in the book *Frustration and Aggression* (1939). The substantive leadership drifted away from Hull to the younger people, because Hull, primarily interested in his learning theory, saw psychoanalysis as but a new channel for its expansion. This shift was a matter of substance only. There was no shift in logic. Hull's famous imitation of the deductive logic of Newtonian physics permeated all our work. My ancient files from that year are loaded with enough definitions, assumptions, postulates, and theorems (all followed by the ritualistic Q.E.D.) to create a dozen unified social sciences.

The integration Hull had sought required the application of that logic to the subject matter of psychoanalysis. This simply did not work. As an alternative, Dollard and Miller proposed that a single proposition be abstracted from psychoanalysis, that it be converted to behavioral concepts, and that it be embedded in the current behavior theory. Frustration thus became the stimulus and aggression the response. After that theoretical leap, all that remained was to derive the consequences by the customary hypothetico-deductive logic, Q.E.D. Ultimately this is just what happened; the earlier approaches via integration, translation, and verification gave way to absorption. Behavior theory absorbed the subject matter, concepts, and principles from psychoanalysis but ignored the analytic method, theoretical structure, and operations that served to define the concepts.

But that is looking too far ahead. The actual events of the 1936–1937 year in the Institute were far removed from the cool directedness of this intellectualized description. Nearly everyone caught fire with the frustration-aggression idea, and a new seminar was started for its discussion. This was the beginning of the Monday Night meetings that continued as the core of the Institute's activity until Pearl Harbor put an end to that part of history. These meetings provided the forum for discussion of the new theory and for reporting the rapidly accumulating empirical data. Hull's health was precarious and he was intensely anxious to get on with work on his learning theory. The action theory of the frustration-aggression hypothesis was not to his taste. In his "idea book" he wrote on January 4, 1937, "Let the Monday Night group carry on the work I have started" (Hull, 1962). Nevertheless, on the same page, he made notes for some possible seminars to have; these were still in the mold of the broader conceptualizing that had governed his seminar the preceding year. He remained faithful enough to the Institute program, through the following years (see IHR 1938–1939), but he never did in fact publish anything that bore on the problem of the relation between psychoanalysis and behavior theory. *Frustration and Aggression* was the link accomplished between the two.

The theory underlying it was mainly about action, rather than learning. Behavior change was inherent in the treatment, but it was explicit only with respect to the effects of anticipated punishment for aggression, discussed in Chapter 3 of the book, and in the discussion centering on socialization of aggression in Chapter 4. The former chapter was drafted by Neal Miller and the latter by John Dollard. With the completion of the book, each of us moved on to his or her own interests. Miller and Dollard chose learning theory. In 1941 they published *Social Learning and Imitation*, which provided the theoretical basis for the next major development in the psychoanalysis-behavior theory theme. In terms of psychoanalytic metapsychological parameters, *Frustration and Aggression* had dealt mostly with the economic and dynamic. Now it was time to attack the developmental. In the Yale

215

Institute Zeitgeist, this meant the application of learning principles to the socialization process, especially to child rearing.

The first move was John Whiting's study of the Kwoma (1941), an anthropological investigation of the child-rearing procedures and their outcomes in a primitive society. Whiting did his field work during the late 1930s. While others of us were working on aggression, he was discovering the origins of dependency in the oral frustrations of early childhood. In some respects the necessary use of a single culture was as troublesome as the psychoanalysts' use of single cases. To overcome this handicap, Murdock and Ford began construction of the Cross-Cultural Area files to provide comparable data on many cultures.

Then came Pearl Harbor and four years of war. The Institute was decimated. Miller went into the Army, Hovland and Doob went to Washington, the anthropologists went into the Navy, and in the summer of 1942 I became Director of the Iowa Child Welfare Research Station and, by fiat, a child psychologist. This of course provided a perfect setting and opportunity to take the next developmental steps. The first was fortuitous, an opportunity to study some infants who had been cup-fed from birth, and thereby to test a translated theory of oral drive development. We found that infants who were breast-fed and had to suck hard to get their milk developed stronger oral habits than infants who were cup-fed with soft nipples on bottles (Davis et al., 1948; Sears & Wise, 1950). This was in opposition to Levy's interpretation of psychoanalytic theory, and in support of a behavior theory deriving from Miller and Dollard's drive-reduction model.

The next step was more intentional. In anticipation of the time when we could mount a full-scale study of the effects of child rearing on personality development, I spent what time I could filch from war research working with students on the development of measuring techniques for relevant personality variables. These included doll-play methods, with George Bach (1945) and Leon Yarrow (1948), and time-sample observations with Barbara Merrill (1946). When the war ended, I was able to induce Vincent Nowlis and John Whiting to join me at Iowa. Whiting had already begun work with Irvin Child on a cross-cultural study of the effects of child rearing on cultural beliefs about the origins of disease. Their data came partly from the new Area Files, while the propositions they were testing stemmed directly from psychoanalytic theories of development (Whiting & Child 1953). These provided several useful behavior concepts that could be transported directly into the child-training arena (Sears, 1948). With this background, in 1947 Whiting, Nowlis, Pauline Sears, and I undertook a correlational study of the effects of child rearing (punishment, reward, nurturance, permissiveness) on two personality variables (aggression and dependency). It was completed by 1949 but not published until 1953. One finding suggested the importance of the process of identification in determining the amount and direction of the expression of aggression. Other findings, such as those relating the severity of punishment to aggressiveness and nonnurturance to dependency, were far more robust, but in some respects these

216

were less exciting because they followed easily from behavior theory without benefit of psychoanalytic theory. It gives a measure of the strength of our continuing allegiance to the latter, therefore, that when the Whitings and Sears moved to Harvard in 1949, our first thought was to pursue the child-rearing antecedents of identification rather than the other more promising leads.

With new collaborators—Eleanor Maccoby, Harry Levin, and Edgar Lowell —we designed another correlational study in which child-rearing practices and attitudes were again measured by structured interviews; the consequent variable of identification was measured by doll play. The interviews gave us a substantial amount of information about the conditions of learning for several dimensions of personality, especially sex, aggression, dependency, and conscience; they also provided a lot of comparative data for interpreting the secondary effects of the child's gender, ordinal position, and social class. We published a full-length report of these findings in 1957 as *Patterns of Child Rearing*. However, the theory testing of the identification process was handicapped by the too-limited character of the doll-play measures of the dependent variable. Having moved to Stanford, I now found two new colleagues—Lucy Rau Ferguson and Richard Alpert—who joined me in a much more intensive study that utilized many real-life assessment situations and behavior observations to measure the hypothesized effects of identification. This enterprise proved far more successful for hypothesis testing than the Harvard study. The translated theory of primary anaclitic identification was reasonably well supported for girls; and for boys, the secondary defensive process gained at least modest affirmation. Partly for extraneous reasons and partly because of the massive intercorrelational character of the data, the published report, *Identification and Child Rearing*, did not appear until 1965. But the research was planned and executed just at the end of the half century that began with Hamilton's little study of the dog's reaction to an insoluble problem, and it belongs to that period.

What did psychology gain from these long and sometimes contentious efforts to integrate, verify, translate, and absorb? The net effect for psychoanalysis was minimal, I think. Its leadership withdrew behind a wall impervious to those who did not subscribe solely to that method and that theory. But the outcome for behavior theory was quite the opposite. Over the half century, psychoanalysis had opened a whole new world to behavioral research. If you look at the developmental area as an example, it is instructive to note the chapter headings of the two books I have mentioned; they include feeding, toilet training, dependency, aggression, sex, adult role, and conscience. These come from the central core of psychoanalytic theory—totally redefined and totally behaviorized, to be sure, but a clear measure of the extent to which the absorption stage had influenced the content of behavior theory by the end of the 1950s.

So much for history. The events of the most recent quarter century are too close at hand to be viewed in perspective. As psychologists have moved professionally into psychoanalysis, their training has introduced a new element in the field. Social

217

psychology and linguistics appear promising as possible contributors to a revivified psychoanalytic theory. On the other hand, the cognitive revolution in both psychology and anthropology seems to have wiped out some of behavior theory's gains from the earlier encounter. Until the pendulum swings back—as it always does—behavior theory will no doubt continue to suppress the problems of passion and unreason that so engrossed it in the earlier time. Nowadays feeding and toilet training have been cleansed of orality and anality and returned to the pediatricians; dependency has been devitalized into infantile attachment; sex has gone by default to the pornographers; and conscience has disappeared altogether. Aggression remains as a healthy substantive residue, of course, and I do not fear but that the other subjects will return eventually.

One thing is certain: the main source of conflict between psychoanalytic and behavior theory has gradually been destroyed. At the turn of the century, psychology and medicine—indeed all of Western science—were contaminated by the medieval assumption of the duality of mind and body. These were defined as incommensurable. In psychological science, battle lines were drawn between those who wanted a mentalistic theory and those who wanted a physicalistic one. Psychoanalysis was mentalistic in the sense that it dealt with the structure and dynamics of consciousness and the unconscious. Behavior theory was physicalistic in the sense that it dealt with objectively measurable environmental events, physicochemical changes in the body, and overt behavior of the organism. The assumption of incommensurability created what we now know to have been an entirely artificial barrier to integration of the two theories. Hamilton's protest at the "psychomorphic" character of psychoanalytic theory was but a sample of the effort by late nineteenth-century objective biologists and early twentieth-century behaviorists to reject the mental and adopt the physical as the proper scope for a science of human beings. Freud, on his side, was insistent on converting the language data from the analytic couch into a theory composed of mentalistic constructs. Both sides seemed to miss the fact that the content of language in the human species is one of the two essential elements in the data bank from which the science of human being's social and emotional life must be constructed. I am pretty sure, therefore, that the linguists will eventually give us a third kind of theory. If so, it will be created in conjunction with the second essential element, the massive matrix of facts and theories developed by biological, medical, and psychological science concerning the interaction between internal physicochemical events, the language reports of feelings, and other forms of overt behavior. Curiously enough, Hamilton, Cannon, Kempf, Hoskins, Adolf Meyer, and many others who struggled with the beginnings of what we now call by such labels as hormonal regulation and biofeedback foresaw the ultimate destruction of the assumption of incommensurability between the mental and physical spheres, though they were too close to the nineteenth-century Zeitgeist to know how to rid themselves of it. Modern psychology and medicine get along very well indeed without that medieval homunculus.

218

Philosophy was at the root of the trouble, but there were other sources of difficulty, too—some personal, some social, some even reasonably intellectual. Looking back on those first fifty years, one is tempted to ask the "what if" questions: What if Freud had been more open to the heterodoxy of Jung, Adler, Rank, and Ferenczi? What if Watson and Lashley had been responsive to the substantive variables of psychoanalysis instead of being hostile to its necessary concern with consciousness and the unconscious? What if psychoanalysts had begun by eagerly teaching nonanalysts to understand the theory rather than by hiding it away behind the ritual of a personal analysis? And most telling of all—what if G. V. Hamilton, instead of the Kraepelinian Eugen Kahn, had been appointed professor of psychiatry at Yale in 1929, the year Hull went there in the Institute of Human Relations?

It is too bad that the history of science cannot be an experimental science. I would so much like to vary some of these "what if" variables and try the whole enterprise over again.

REFERENCES[2]

Bach, G. R. Young children's play fantasies. *Psychological Monographs*, 1945, 59 (No. 272).

Bagby, E. *Psychology of personality*. New York: Holt, 1928.

Bandura, A., & Walters, R. H. *Adolescent aggression*. New York: Ronald Press, 1959.

Breuer, J., & Freud, S. *Studies on hysteria*. New York: Basic Books, 1957. (Originally published, 1895.)

Davis, H. V., Sears, R. R., Miller, H. C., & Brodbeck, A. J. Effects of cup, bottle and breast feeding on oral activities of newborn infants. *Pediatrics*, 1948, 2, 549–558.

Dollard, J., Doob, L. W., Miller, N. E., Mowrer, O. H., & Sears, R. R. (in collaboration with C. S. Ford, C. I. Hovland, & R. T. Sollenberger). *Frustration and aggression*. New Haven: Yale University Press, 1939.

Dollard, J., & Miller, N. E. *Personality and psychotherapy*. New York: McGraw-Hill, 1950.

French, T. M. The interrelations between psychoanalysis and the experimental work of Pavlov. *American Journal of Psychiatry*, 1933, 12, 1165–1195.

French, T. M. Clinical approach to the dynamics of behavior. In J. McV. Hunt (Ed.), *Personality and the behavior disorders* (Vol. I). New York: Ronald Press, 1944.

Freud, S. *Three essays on the theory of sexuality. Standard edition of the complete psychological works of Sigmund Freud* (Vol. VII). London: Hogarth, 1953. (Originally published, 1905.)

Hamilton, G. V. An experimental study of an unusual type of reaction in a dog. *Journal of Comparative Neurology and Psychology*, 1907, 17, 329–341.

Hamilton, G. V. A study of trial and error reactions in mammals. *Journal of Animal Behavior*, 1911, 1, 33–66. (a)

Hamilton, G. V. The etiological significance of persistent affective states in neurasthenia. *California State Journal of Medicine*, 1911, 9(1), 37–41. (b)

Hamilton, G. V. A study of sexual tendencies in monkeys and baboons. *Journal of Animal Behavior*, 1914, 4, 295–318.

Hamilton, G. V. A study of perseverance reactions in primates and rodents. *Behavior Monographs*, 1916, 3(13), 1–65.

Hamilton, G. V. *An introduction to objective psychopathology*. St. Louis: Mosby, 1925.

Hamilton, G. V. *A research in marriage*. New York: Albert & Charles Boni, 1929.

[2]Asterisks indicate publications of special historical importance.

219

I. THE SYSTEMATIC FRAMEWORK OF PSYCHOLOGY

*Hilgard, E. R. Experimental approaches to psychoanalysis. In E. Pumpian-Mindlin (Ed.), *Psychoanalysis as science*. Stanford: Stanford University Press, 1952.

Holt, E. B. *The Freudian wish and its place in ethics*. New York: Henry Holt, 1915.

Hull, C. L. Mind, mechanism, and adaptive behavior. *Psychological Review*, 1937, *44*, 1–32.

Hull, C. L. Psychology of the scientist: Passages from the "idea" books of Clark L. Hull. (Ruth Hays, Ed.) *Perceptual and Motor Skills*, 1962, *15* (Monograph Supplement 9).

Hull, C. L., & Mowrer, O. H. (No title. Announcements and minutes of Hull's Informal Seminars) Mimeographed. Institute of Human Relations, Yale University, 1935–1936.

Institute of Human Relations. Abstracts of S-R Sessions of Monday Night Group. Mimeographed. Yale University, 1938–1939.

Kempf, E. J. *Psychopathology*. St. Louis: Mosby, 1920.

Levy, D. M. Experiments on the sucking reflex and social behavior in dogs. *American Journal of Orthopsychiatry*, 1934, *4*, 203–224.

Levy, D. M. Primary affect hunger. *American Journal of Psychiatry*, 1937, *94*, 643–652.

Levy, D. M. *Maternal overprotection*. New York: Columbia University Press, 1943.

Merrill, B. A. Measurement of mother-child interaction. *Journal of Abnormal and Social Psychology*, 1946, *41*, 37–49.

Miller, N. E. Theory and experiment relating psychoanalytic displacement to stimulus-response generalization. *Journal of Abnormal and Social Psychology*, 1948, *43*, 155–178.

Miller, N. E., & Dollard, J. *Social learning and imitation*. New Haven: Yale University Press, 1941.

Mowrer, O. H. A stimulus-response analysis of anxiety and its role as a reinforcing agent. *Psychological Review*, 1939, *46*, 553–565.

Mowrer, O. H., & Kluckhohn, C. Dynamic theory of personality. In J. McV. Hunt (Ed.), *Personality and the behavior disorders* (Vol. I). New York: Ronald Press, 1944.

Patrick, J. R. Studies in rational behavior and emotional excitement. II. The effect of emotional excitement on rational behavior in human subjects. *Journal of Comparative Psychology*, 1934, *18*, 153–193.

Review of Hamilton's Objective psychopathology. *Journal of Nervous and Mental Diseases*, 1927, *64*, 214–216.

Sears, R. R. Functional abnormalities of memory with special reference to amnesia. *Psychological Bulletin*, 1936, *33*, 229–274.

*Sears, R. R. *Survey of objective studies of psychoanalytic concepts*. New York: Social Science Research Council, Bulletin 51, 1943.

*Sears, R. R. Experimental analysis of psychoanalytic phenomena. In J. McV. Hunt (Ed.), *Personality and the behavior disorders* (Vol. I). New York: Ronald Press, 1944.

Sears, R. R. Personality development in contemporary culture. *Proceedings of the American Philosophical Society*, 1948, *92*, 363–370.

Sears, R. R., Maccoby, E. E., & Levin, H. *Patterns of child rearing*. Stanford: Stanford University Press, 1957.

Sears, R. R., Rau, L., & Alpert, R. *Identification and child rearing*. Stanford: Stanford University Press, 1965.

Sears, R. R., & Wise, G. W. Relation of cup-feeding in infancy to thumbsucking and the oral drive. *American Journal of Orthopsychiatry*, 1950, *20*, 123–138.

*Shakow, D., & Rapaport, D. *The influence of Freud on American psychology*. New York: International Universities Press, 1964.

Thorndike, E. L. Animal intelligence: An experimental study of the associative processes in animals. *Psychological Review Monographs*, 1898, *2* (Whole No. 8).

Whiting, J. W. M. *Becoming a Kwoma*. New Haven: Yale University Press, 1941.

Whiting, J. W. M., & Child, I. L. *Child training and personality: A cross-cultural study*. New Haven: Yale University Press, 1953.

Whiting, J. W. M., & Mowrer, O. H. Habit progression and regression. *Journal of Comparative Psychology*, 1943, *36*, 229–253.

Yarrow, L. The effect of antecedent frustration on projective day. *Psychlogical Monographs*, 1948, *62* (No. 293).

II

THE SPECIAL FIELDS
OF PSYCHOLOGY

SENSORY PROCESSES AND PERCEPTION

9

Conclusions from a Century of Research on Sense Perception

JAMES J. GIBSON

A hundred years ago the new experimental psychology accepted as valid two tasks. The first was to make a sort of *inventory* of the basic sensations. The second was to discover the process by which they were converted into perceptions, that is, to formulate the theory of perception and to verify it by experiment.

The inventory was to be taken by classifying the elementary sense impressions of the normal human adult. They had to be catalogued since they were the *data* for perception. The inventory could be tested by finding the receptors of the body to which the sense impressions were specific, and the correspondence could be checked by stimulating them experimentally to see if they did in fact yield the sense impressions. The program was perfectly straightforward: introspection provided the inventory, anatomy and physiology provided the list of receptors, and controlled applications of physical energy to these receptors provided the check. You could even apply stimuli to your *own* receptors and observe the resulting sensations.

The process of perception was to be discovered by formulating testable theories and determining the best. A good theory had to answer several questions and explain certain phenomena. First, how do the relevant sensations get *selected out* of the bombardment of nervous impulses from the receptors; how are they *attended to*? Second, how do perceptions come to have *meaning* if they are based on meaningless sensations? Third, how are the *depth* and distance of objects perceived if the sensations coming from the retina and the skin are flat? Fourth, how can the

224

constant form and size of objects be seen despite the changing form and size of their sensations? Fifth, how is the *persistence* or *permanence* of objects perceived despite the fact that their sensations are interrupted? Sixth, how are *motions* perceived or, more exactly, *events*? Seventh, how is the concurrent awareness of the self to be explained along with the perceptual awareness of the external world? Some of these questions go back more than a century. Some can be phrased in various terms, but they have been recognized as puzzles for psychology more and more clearly as time goes on (Boring, 1942).

Taking Inventory of the Sense Impressions

Consider the first task, and whether or not it has been accomplished. Sense impressions were assumed to be the irreducible data for perception, which is to say, what was given to the mind. They were the "bare" impressions, or the "raw" material. They were taken to be *discrete*. Perhaps they were the original impressions experienced at birth by the infant, but this assumption of an innate repertory was debatable, as I shall show.

They were supposed to be triggered by stimuli at receptors. Receptors on the surface of the body were to be found in banks like the retina and the skin. A given sensation came from either a single receptor with a punctate stimulus or perhaps a group of receptors with a pattern of stimuli. This was also debatable.

Different modes of sensation occurred in different areas of the cerebral cortex called projection areas. Each was (more or less) "projected" to the brain by a bundle of nerve fibers from the sensory mosaic, each fiber conducting impulses independently.

The sensations were specific to the receptors only, not to the applications of stimulus energy that could excite them, and certainly not to the external objects that were the sources of stimuli. This was the doctrine of Johannes Müller (Boring, 1942, pp. 68–78). The modern theory that a sensation comes from a group of receptors, a receptive unit triggered by a stimulus pattern, is a partial departure from this doctrine, but only partial.

Receptors could be classified by the kinds of stimulus energy to which they were especially sensitive, as mechanoreceptors, chemoreceptors, and photoreceptors. But they could also be triggered by inappropriate stimuli, even if partly protected against this by the anatomy of the sense organs.

Receptors could also be classified by their location in the body, as interoceptors in the internal organs; proprioceptors in the muscles, joints, and the vestibular organ; and exteroceptors in the skin, the retina, and the cochlea. This classification was due to Sherrington (Boring, 1942, Chap. 14). Note that on the skin and the retina (but not the cochlea) punctate sensations were supposed to have "local signs" (Chap. 1).

225

Sensations were also supposed to fall into "modalities," depending on the sense organs in which the receptors were located. But the ancient assumption of five senses became doubtful, and the number of distinct modalities has not been agreed upon.

Has the inventory been accomplished? In a whole century of research, I suggest, nothing like a catalogue of sense impressions has been achieved. It *could* not be achieved. I think the task was misconceived at the outset.

For one reason, there are kinds of general awareness for which no sense impressions can be discovered. An example is the continuous neural inflow from the utricle, saccule, and semicircular canals during posture and movement. Another is the kind of awareness that Michotte called *amodal* such as occurs in the perception of a surface that is progressively occluded at an edge (Michotte, Thines, & Crabbé, 1964).

For another reason there are kinds of awareness like the so-called "obstacle sense" of the blind where the sensations reported are cutaneous impressions localized on the face but the information utilized is auditory, consisting of the echo-latency of footsteps. The sensations are not the basis of the perception.

For another reason, the assumption of an innate repertory of sensory inputs makes the gradual development of discrimination and the learning of perception very hard to conceive (Gibson & Gibson, 1955). If all infants could do was to enrich their sensations with memories or mix them with innate ideas, the little creatures would not be able to do what they do. A repertory of basic sensations at birth, like a repertory of innate reflexes on which to build, is a myth.

Another reason, even more compelling, is simply that sensory impressions are not discrete and, if so, they cannot be inventoried. Titchener believed at one time that there were 32,820 colors and 11,600 tones. But later he retracted and concluded that sensations were actually only their attributes. The dimensions of variation were what was important. A sensation was only an expression of the ability to distinguish an instance of stimulation from other instances of stimulation. Even from the beginning of psychophysics some had suspected that sensitivity to *differences* was prior to sensitivity to *stimuli*.

This theory of a growing capacity to discriminate seems to have supplanted in some quarters the search for an inventory of sensory inputs. Perhaps it is a step in the right direction, but it is far short of the theory of a growing capacity to extract invariants. Note what it entails. A discrimination is not an input. If you accept discrimination, you cannot accept the straightforward doctrine of sensory inputs. You have to abandon the old assumption that inputs from different receptors are simply different. You have to assume that sensations first have to be *separated* from one another before they can be associated or organized or "processed."

Dimensionalism is a persuasive formula, but it flies in the face of sensory physiology as now understood—the theory of afferent *impulses*, of sensory nerve *conduc-*

tion, of ingoing *signals*. Moreover it does away with the difference between sensation and perception; it sweeps the problem under the rug instead of cleaning it up.

Note that modern theories of so-called "information processing" *accept* the doctrine of afferent neural inputs inasmuch as what their adherents call incoming *information* is a pattern or sequence of inputs. In my opinion, they cheat by simply *calling* inputs information. They try to substitute Claude Shannon for Johannes Müller! They attempt to slip around the old perplexities. They neglect the history of sense perception; they do not seem to know sense physiology. Signal detection indeed!

Has anything been accomplished? In a hundred years psychologists have found out a great deal about input thresholds, about the impressions that correlate with intensity of stimulation, about methods for applying stimuli to an observer so as to elicit judgments; and physiologists have found out how to do microelectrode recording. But these curiosities seem to me irrelevant and incidental to the practical business of perception.

The Explanation of Sense Perception

We now come to the second undertaking of experimental psychology, the establishing of a theory of perception. What were the processes in the brain that converted the sensory inputs into perceptions of the outer world? Or, in other terms, what were the operations of the mind on the deliverances of the senses? A good theory, I suggested, had to provide answers to several questions concerning selective attention, meaning, depth and distance of objects in space, constancy of objects, the phenomenal permanence of objects, the awareness of motions, and the concurrent awareness of the self.

Consider some of the processes that have been postulated in the attempt to answer these questions. Here is a list.

1. The *filtering* of sensory inputs, perhaps by neural inhibition and facilitation.
2. The *laying down of traces* considered as copies of sensations.
3. The *storing* of traces, that is, engrams, images, representations or memories. Each new trace must be stored together with the class of earlier traces to which it belongs.
4. The *accrual* of associated memories to the present core of sense impressions.
5. The *organization* of sense impressions and memories, in accordance with the laws of organization.
6. The *assimilation* of sensations to existing concepts, either learned concepts or innate ones.

227

7. A process of *compensating* for the changing perspective transformations of the retinal images of objects as the observer moves.
8. A process of *unconscious inference* as to the external objects, or some process analogous to the *interpreting of signals*, the *decoding of messages*, or the *understanding of signs* (Gibson, 1979, pp. 251ff.).

Are these hypothetical processes good enough? Do they, singly or in combination, provide a theory that will answer the questions about attention, meaning, depth, constancy, and so on? No. We do not have a theory, only arguments among theorists. After a century, it seems to me, we should begin to suspect that they are the wrong questions. Answers to the wrong questions cannot be right. Explanations of phenomena that take for granted sensation-based perception cannot be found if it is not based on sensations. The processes that I have just listed, without exception, presuppose the doctrine of passive channels of sense. The alternative notion of active perceptual systems, with continuous adjustments of the "sense organs" so as to extract information from the available stimulation, is not recognized.

Has anything been achieved? What most experimenters have been trying to do is to impoverish the stimulation so as to allow the processes of perception to manifest themselves in purer form. The internal contribution to perceiving, they assume, can be separated from the external contribution and the former is to be studied. The sensory share in beholding is not crucial; the beholder's share is what counts. Hence the tachistoscope is used to reduce the flow of stimulation to a snapshot. Or a point stimulus is applied so as to reduce the stimulation even further. Is the tachistoscope an achievement? It seems to me to be a calamity. Far from reducing visual experience to its simplest form, it prevents the visual system from operating normally.

What about psychophysics as prescribed by Fechner? The law relating the psychic realm to the physical realm has not been agreed upon. The very notion of two realms of reality, two environments, two worlds that *need* to be correlated, has come under suspicion. As for the ambition to show the physicists that we too can measure and quantify as they do and are therefore scientists as they are, it is a futile enterprise.

What, Then, Are Sense Impressions?

If sensations, sense data, or sensory inputs are not the foundation of sense perception, what on earth can they be? Note that the verb *to sense* ordinarily does not mean *to have a sensation*. When one says "I sensed that I was being followed," one had a perception without sensation; and when one says "I had a sensation of ringing in the ears," one had a sensation without perception. The word is slippery, and the various meanings confuse us. I am not at all sure how to use the term, but here are some tentative suggestions.

There are abnormal sensations and normal sensations. Abnormal sensations are the product of overstraining the capacity of a perceptual system to pick up information, as when one has an aftersensation or afterimage, or as when the finger in warm water feels cool after holding it in hot water. Normal sensations are the kind that can accompany ordinary perception when the perceiver pays attention to the stimulation as such, instead of the information in stimulation. They are an *awareness of being stimulated*. Sometimes they are *obtrusive*. They become more obvious when discrete stimuli are imposed, as in the laboratory, but not obvious when a stimulus flux is obtained, as in life. They are incidental symptoms of normal perception. They are products of an introspective attitude. An example of such normal sensations is the illusory "double-imagery" of single objects in the binocular field of view. The binocular *disparity* is the information that the perceptual system picks up; the apparent "doubleness" of objects nearer or farther than the one on which the eyes converge is purely incidental. It can only be noticed if you hold both eyes fixed on the same point. It is a curiosity, like the so-called "blind spot" in monocular vision. It points to facts about the anatomy of the eyes and the retina. But not to facts about the perception of objects.

I am suggesting that most people never notice the subjective sensations that may accompany objective perception. If you feel the edge of the table, what you feel is the edge. You can also feel the impression the edge makes on your skin if you introspect, but who wants to do that except introspectionists?

Another meaning of the term *sensation*, then, is *an experience that refers to the body of the observer*. These are sensations that may (or may not) go along with looking, listening, and feeling. But there are also sensations that refer *only* to the body of the observer, like aches and pains, and fatigue or hunger. No one ever suggested that they were the basis of perceiving the world. They constitute one kind of what has been called *somaesthesis*, that is, awareness of the body. But there is more than one kind of awareness of the body. One can see one's body, hear one's body speaking, and feel one's body in contact with the surface of support. Are these visual, auditory, and haptic experiences to be called sensations? I am uncertain. When it comes to these, the term has lost all meaning.

In short, so-called "sense impressions" do not make a single class of experiences. Receptor awareness is one thing, the color patchwork of the monocular visual field is another, somaesthesis is still another, and they do not go together. Most of what we have learned about them is not applicable to the problems of psychology.

Conclusions

The conclusions that can be reached from a century of research on perception are insignificant. The knowledge gained from a century of research on sensation is incoherent. We have no adequate theory of perception, and what we have found in the search for sensations is a mixed batch of illusions, physiological curiosities, and bodily feelings. The implications are discouraging. A fresh start has to be made on the problem of perception. And we should abandon the study of so-called "sensations" to the input physiologists. Some day, they will learn how to study *systems*, and when they do, we can begin to listen to them again.

Our experiments have been misconceived. We have supposed that the study of illusions would somehow reveal the process of perception, as if the defects in a system described the system. We have tried to manipulate "cues" considered as signs of reality with imperfect probabilities of being valid (Brunswik, 1956), instead of trying to discover invariants. We have assumed that the controlling of the physical variables of stimuli at the sense organs of a perceiver would relate the physical to the psychical, as if what he needed to perceive was physics. The experiments we need to design in future should control the display of stimulus information, not the physical variables of stimuli. Or, for that matter, perfectly good experiments can be done outdoors under the sky without having to construct an artificial display.

REFERENCES

Boring, E. G. *Sensation and perception in the history of experimental psychology*. New York: Appleton-Century-Crofts, 1942.

Brunswik, E. *Perception and the representative design of psychological experiments*. Berkeley: University of California Press, 1956.

Gibson, J. J. *The ecological approach to visual perception*. Boston: Houghton Mifflin, 1979.

Gibson, J. J., & Gibson, E. J. Perceptual learning: Differentiation or enrichment? *Psychological Review*, 1955, 62, 32–41.

Michotte, A., Thines, G., & Crabbé, G. Les complements amodaux des structures perceptives. In *Studia Psychologica*. Louvain: Publications Université de Louvain, 1964.

10

James J. Gibson's Ecological Approach to Visual Perception

MARGARET A. HAGEN

Gibson's Conclusions from a Century of Research on Sense Perceptions

In his retrospective critique of one hundred years of theory and research in the field usually called perception, James Gibson wrote:

> The conclusions that can be reached from a century of research on perception are insignificant. The knowledge gained from a century of research on sensation is incoherent. We have no adequate theory of perception, and what we have found in the search for sensations is a mixed batch of illusions, physiological curiosities, and bodily feelings. The implications are discouraging (pp. 229–230 of this volume).

In support of his abandonment of traditional theories of perception, Gibson (1979) explained that "the perennial doctrine that two-dimensional images are restored to three-dimensional reality by a process called depth perception will not do." And neither will the related idea that flat images become transformed by slant and distance cues so as to give the impression of size and shape constancy in object perception. "The simple assumption that perceptions of the world are caused by stimuli from the world will not do." And neither will the notion that stimuli cause sensations that then combine with memory traces of old sensations to yield perceptions of the world. He wrote that "the established theory that exteroception and proprioception arise when exteroceptors and proprioceptors are stimulated will not do" in part because the assumptions of special channels of sensation corresponding to specific nerve bundles has been abandoned

Along with sensationism, Gibson rejected the belief of empiricists that the perceived values and meanings of things come from the past experience of the observer. "But even worse is the belief of nativists that meanings and values are supplied from the past experience of the race by way of innate ideas." He argued lastly that not even the modern translation of sensationism into cognitive information processing will do because it is based, as was its predecessor, on hypothetical operations of the mind upon the impoverished deliverances of the senses in service of the creation of meaningful percepts.

> Information processing in cognitive theory is really information generation, but the information generated is all too often illusions, physiological curiosities, and bodily feelings bearing little or no relation to the properties of the world perceived (1979, p. 238).

Traditional Issues, Traditional Approach

In his listing of the traditional issues of concern to sense perceptionists, Gibson cited the problems of selecting out and attending to specific sensations; of adding depth, distance, and meaning to sensations depthless and meaningless; of achieving constancy, persistence, or permanence in the face of constant change; of perceiving motions or events; and the problem of perceiving the self along with awareness of the world. Some of these questions go back over one hundred years.

In his initial approach to these problems of perception, Gibson retained the classic Helmholtzian processing model and attempted to compensate for its weaknesses. In step with the Gestaltists, Gibson noted that a major area of weakness lay in the impoverished character of the Helmholtzian stimulus and the consequent constructive processes required to enrich the pitiful input. Accordingly, Gibson devoted much of his early work to a stimulus analysis embracing variables of much greater complexity and informative richness than were ever proposed before. It seemed to a good many people that an adequate perceptual theory could be obtained by a rather simple wedding of Gibson's stimulus analysis to Helmholtz's processing analysis.

This notion provided the basis for what Gibson tried to do in his *The Perception of the Visual World* (1950). However, this apparently good idea does not work—for all the reasons Gibson has taken pains to adduce in his chapter in the present volume. Over the last thirty years of Gibson's work, he came to realize more and more that the old model simply would not do, that the assumptions on which it was based

232

were wrong, and the questions it generated inappropriate and uninformative about perception. Gibson is many things to many people, but generally he is understood in terms of whichever of his three books was in vogue during one's graduate-school years. For some people, Gibson is *The Perception of the Visual World* (1950); for others, he is *The Senses Considered as Perceptual Systems* (1966); for students today, he is *The Ecological Approach to Visual Perception* (1979). It is not possible to understand Gibson's ecological theory of perception without a thorough study of the last book, and one's understanding of the last book is much enhanced by a reading of the two versions of the developing theory that came before. That there will be no additional books is an incalculable loss.

The very long way Gibson came from any possible rapprochement with a Helmholtzian model of perception is best appreciated by reading Gibson, but a brief presentation of some aspects of the Gibsonian approach to perception can whet the appetite. Insight into the character of Gibson's thinking perhaps can best be facilitated by concentrating on his mature views concerning the traditional issues of the sense perceptionists. In his own elegantly concise chapter in this book, Gibson confines himself to the effort to show the artificiality of many of the traditional questions, and the untenability of the "sensation-based" perception theorists' answers. By adopting a strategy of summarizing Gibson's positive reformulations of the traditional issues, and the alternate analyses he makes by way of "answer," one can hope to make both the special force and something of the contour of his theorizing manifest.

Gibson's Approach to Traditional Sense Perception Issues

Perception of the Character of Objects and Their Arrangements in Space

The traditional questions about the perception of the character and arrangements of objects center around how we perceive the properties and layout of visual space—the color, form, location, orientation, distance, and motion of objects and surfaces around us, each independent of our momentary viewing position and distance from the scene. Gibson's answer? We don't. It is trivial but necessary to note that space has no perceptible intrinsic properties and that such traditional word uses lead to terrific muddles. Gibson (1979) wrote that what we perceive mainly are objects, places, and, more basically, surfaces and substances, together with events which are changes in the surface layout. To perceive these things is to perceive what they afford, what they offer, for good or ill. Also, the continuous act of perceiving necessarily involves the coperceiving of the self, a notion intimately linked to the idea of the direct perception of "affordances."

"Color, form, location, space, time, and motion—these are chapter headings

233

that have been handed down through the centuries, but they are not what is perceived" (1979, p. 240). We perceive both persistence and change—the persistence of places, objects, and substances along with whatever changes they undergo. "Everything in the world persists in some respects and changes in some respects. So also does the observer himself. And some things persist for long intervals, others for short" (pp. 246–247). Gibson wrote that the perceiving of persistence and change can be stated in terms of the observer separating the change from the nonchange, noticing what stays the same and what does not, or seeing the continuing identity of things along with the events in which they participate.

> The question, of course, is how he does so. What is the information for persistence and change? The answer must be of this sort: The perceiver extracts the invariants of structure from the flux of stimulation while still noticing the flux. For the visual system in particular, he tunes in on the invariant structure of the ambient optic array that underlies the changing perspective structure caused by his movement (p. 247).

Structured Light   The ambient optic array is the light to a possible point of observation structured by the differential reflectance properties of surfaces as a function of their textures or substances, pigmentation, structural relations or arrangements with respect to other surfaces, and participation in events. Gibson suggested that the terms *persistence* and *change* be used to refer to the environment and preservation and disturbance of structure be used to refer to the optic array. Preservations and disturbances of structure are both classes of invariants, aspects of optical structure univocally related to the environmental object or event determining by its own reflectance character the structure of the light. Optical information is specific to its environmental source, not ambiguous, random, or equivocal. It affords direct perception of the environment without mentalistic enrichment or interpretation of an insufficient stimulus.

This is the kernel of Gibson's theory: that there exists a cluttered world with sky overhead; that overhead and upright, down there and horizontal are ecologically determined, not invented; that the ground plane is the basic reference surface, and most other surfaces rest on it or rest on surfaces resting on it; that the ground surface and most other surfaces are more or less regularly textured in that they have a more or less homogeneous substance or composition; that every difference in surface texture causes a border in, a change in quality of, the light reflected from it, that every change in slant will also cause a change in the structure of the light reflected from a surface; that such structures in the light are specific to their sources, and, as such, are therefore directly informative about these sources.

Much of the Gibsonian enterprise, in terms of work performed by Gibson himself as well as the work of disciples, has been directed toward the description and demonstration of optical structures as specific information for various aspects of the environment, like the size, shape, slant, and distance of various objects. Most of the early work from the 1940s and 1950s was concerned with the specification of such information. Examples of this work are the determinations of the minimal texture information needed for the perception of a surface; descriptions of the families of perspectivities specific to different classes of objects under transformations like rotation; and formulations of the various static monocular gradients as sources of information for slant, shape, and distance. It is this kind of work that comprised the core of Gibson's earliest answer to questions of how we perceive "space." It seemed at the time like a rather good answer, at least a rather good route to an answer, so why did Gibson largely leave this path?

Development of the Concept of Information   Gibson's disaffection arose for several related reasons implicit in the traditional wording of the question. Countless workers have asked how it is that we perceive different aspects of the environment independently of our own actions, despite variations in momentary position and distance from objects or scenes viewed? Over years of research, Gibson came to believe profoundly that we do not. We perceive the world as *independent* of our own actions, but we do not perceive it *independently* from our own actions in it. This realization was born in the motion picture testing and research work that dealt largely with the specification of patterns of flow of optical textures, very fancy but mathematically specifiable forms of structural change in the light to the eye, that take place when a perceiver moves around the environment (see Gibson, Olum, & Rosenblatt, 1955).

Every pattern of optical flow is specific *both* to the layout of the surfaces reflecting the light to the observer *and* to the observer's position and actions relative to those surfaces, be it landing a plane on one of them or walking directly into another. Out of many years of such work came the understanding that environmental "stimuli" are not in any strict sense external to the observer or independent of momentary position or action. It was for this reason that Gibson rejected the traditional notion of "stimulus" altogether as an intrinsically passive idea implying the inevitable imposition of a stimulus "out there" onto the hapless and helpless (frequently one-eyed and completely paralyzed) observer. In its place is the concept of *invariant information*, an idea that has increased in complexity as it has increased in specificity over the years.

The monocular gradients, like that of the ever-increasing compression of optical texture with increasing distance, were quite easy to describe mathematically, and this gave many people easy access to the concept of invariants. It was quite clear that for any more-or-less regularly textured surface, the elements of texture projected in the light to the eye will get smaller and smaller with ever-increasing distance in a gradient function, the first derivative of the curve describing the changing projected sizes. As the observer walks along such a surface, the gradient remains invariant in a nice commonsensical way, as long as the slant of the surface does not change. It

235

also happens that this gradient derives from an invariant of projective geometry, the invariant cross-ratio of points and lines which relates to flat surfaces (planes) and straight edges (lines). So optical gradients are invariant in both a pragmatic and a geometrical sense.

It is this dual use of the word *invariant* that causes so much confusion. For those of us who went to graduate school between Gibson's second and third books, the mathematical description of an invariant, following a practical demonstration of the situation for which it is informative, was considered to be the top of the line in perceptual research. We clung to the belief that even the very difficult-to-describe optical flow patterns accompanying different types of locomotion would eventually lend themselves to an economical mathematical analysis. We no longer believed in the efficacy of static monocular gradients for much of anything but picture perception—after all, how often does an observer sit perfectly still scanning his perfectly still environment?—but we certainly believed in the informative quality of the patterns and gradients of optical flow and expansion. And we knew that with sufficient effort they would yield to mathematical exposition and control. Gibson knew that too.

However, it was around the time of his second book—the mid- to late-1960s—that Gibson began to argue also for the importance of invariant patterns of persistence and change *not* readily amenable to a simple analysis in terms of the invariants of projective geometry. Why does a bird flying usually look like a bird flying? What makes a waterfall perceptible as such? Worst of all for the future of geometric analysis of information, Gibson became interested in the phenomenon of optical occlusion, the simultaneous deletion and accretion of optical texture of a surface at the leading and trailing edges of another surface "optically passing" in front of the first. Gibson had been well aware in the mid-1960s of the changes in vistas as an observer walks around the environment, of what was usually called "motion perspective." Motion perspective referred to all the changes in the projected sizes and shapes of surfaces with changes in distance and angle of view attendant on locomotion. The kinds of invariants preserved are projective and definable under reversible transformations.

This idea is simply a more complex example of the families of perspective views of single objects undergoing single transformations which were found, some time ago, to be informative for the perception of rigidity and elasticity, as well as for the nature of the transformation itself. Motion perspective, then, is not a particularly daunting concept as a source of invariant information for the layout of surfaces; it simply requires simultaneous considering of many nested surfaces in addition to a reference surface. Put these together with the gradients and patterns of optical expansion and flow and one has information for the nature and the path of locomotion as well as for the layout and composition of surfaces. The observer-environment relation generates a wealth of information about both environment and observer all amenable, within constraints, to description in terms of the trans-

236

formations and invariants of projective geometry (and its subordinate geometries, of course).

Problem of Occlusion   Such descriptions yielded a wealth of information indeed, but they did not cover by any means *all* of the available information. They did not even touch on the occlusion information, much less describe or explain it. As I look down at the typewriter I notice (because I am writing this particular paper) that certain parts of the desk supporting it are hidden from view. As I move to the right or the left, a previously hidden area of desk on one side of the typewriter comes into view while an area on the other side goes out of view. This is the accretion and deletion of optical texture of a farther surface by a nearer one, with rate a function both of distance from observer and distance between surfaces. The rate component of occlusion is little removed from old familiar motion parallax—the differential rate and extent of translation of optical texture across the retinae as a function of distance. As such, it lends itself to a gradient analysis, to an analysis in terms of projective invariants.

The aspect of occlusion that involves the appearance and disappearance of optical texture, the coming into view and going out of view, does *not* as easily lend itself to geometrical description. Gibson pointed out that projective transformations (with a couple of exceptions) are one-to-one mappings of planes onto planes, of surfaces onto surfaces. Occlusion, involving as it does the accretion and deletion of visibles, is not a one-to-one mapping of what is visible now with what is visible later. I cannot map my present view of the desk supporting my typewriter with my view after (or during) movement unless I am allowed to map the whole desk, hidden areas as well as visible ones. This holistic surface approach was appealing to Gibson because he believed that the accretion and deletion of texture at an edge is direct information for the continuity of the farther surface. If a surface was discontinuous at the edge of visibility, observer motion would reveal no accretion and deletion of texture but rather the discontinuity of texture. This holistic approach restores the possibility of employing a projective analysis for the exposition of occlusion, but only in a rather abstract sense. Likewise, the fact that ordinary occlusion involves a reversible transformation with accretion becoming deletion and vice versa, while true appearances and disappearances, if there are such things outside magic shows, are not reversible, at least not by any action of the perceiver, also strongly suggests the continued utility of the geometrical approach to optical information.

However, it really cannot be argued that Gibson in his last book believed that all invariant visual information would yield to geometrical description. He wrote rather:

> It would simplify matters if all of these kinds of change in the optic array (change of illumination, change of point of observation, change in samples, and local distur- bances of structures) could be understood as transformations in the sense of map-

pings, borrowing the term from projective geometry and topology. The invariants under transformation have been worked out. Moreover it is easy to visualize a form being transposed, inverted, reversed, enlarged, reduced, or foreshortened by slant, and we can imagine it being deformed in various ways. But, unhappily, some of these changes cannot be understood as one-to-one mappings, either projective or topological (1979, p. 310, parenthetical phrases added).

Instead, Gibson divided visual information into four classes of invariants, some of which he thought were geometric and some not.

Four Classes of Visual Invariants

1. *Invariants of optical structure under changing illumination.* Gibson (1979) wrote that sunlight, moonlight, and artificial light can change in amount of intensity, in direction and in color, thus changing the quality of light reflected from surfaces. Since we still perceive those surfaces, their layout, relative brightnesses, and colors, there must be invariants underlying the changes that permit us to do so. According to Gibson, these invariants almost certainly involve ratios of intensity and color. Thus they are (or will be) mathematically specifiable, but it is not at all clear that they are geometrically describable. Ratios in length are geometrical, but are ratios of intensity?

2. *Invariants of optical structure under change of the point of observation.* Change of the point of observation is what happens whenever we move.

Some of the changes in the optic array are transformations of its nested forms, but the major changes are gain and loss of form, that is, increments and decrements of structure, as surfaces undergo occlusion. Proportions and cross-ratios underlie the transformations, however, and extrapolations, interpolations, gradients, and horizon-ratios underlie the increments and decrements (1979, p. 310).

As noted above, Gibson saw the first kind of change as geometrical but not the second. However, it should not be forgotten that the gradients derived from projective invariants and the horizon-ratio (see Sedgwick, 1980) can be understood as a similarity transformation. Increments and decrements of structure are probably not as removed from the realm of geometrical description as Gibson thought.

3. *Invariants across the sampling of the ambient optic array.* Gibson described "looking around" as the reversible sweeping of the field of view over the whole optic array with continuous successive overlaps of views. Gibson argued that across the sliding sample of views there was some common structure and that it was reasonable to call such common structure "invariant." Again, adjacencies share a limited point-to-point correspondence, but sections of the optic array considerably removed need not. Yet there is a degree of persistence of the changing structure across the whole that warrants common description. It isn't clear whether the concept of

geometrical transformation can do the job—although neither is it clear that it cannot, particularly in light of the advances in ecological geometry made by Gibson in *The Ecological Approach to Visual Perception*.

4. *Local invariants of the ambient array under local disturbances of its structure.* Global transformations of the optic array happen when the observer moves around; local disturbances happen when other things move around as well, or otherwise change. Local events include everything from the blooming of a rose, to the aging of the human face, to the flying of birds, the falling of water, the bouncing of balls, the fluttering of leaves, the stretching of cats, the approach of a car or another person. Across all these local disturbances is invariant information for the nature of the change itself, as well as invariant information for the object undergoing change. Some of the changes are not difficult to describe as geometrical transformations, either projective, or topological, or a combination of the two, and some of the invariants are familiar from geometry. Whether all the changes and all the instances of nonchange in the face of change that serve as information for their sources will be adequately described by geometry is not yet known. In his last book, Gibson very much doubted that they would. In view of the fact that there are intermodally specified invariants (e.g., optical-acoustical), there have to be other forms of description—for space, consider echolocation and location visually.

Gibson's Approach to the Perception of "Space"   Gibson's answer, then, to how we perceive the intrinsic properties of visual space independent of our momentary viewing position and distance from the scene is not quite as abrupt as "we don't." His answer was fifty years in the making, and the making was not finished when he died. His answer involved the continual and increasing reformulation of the question, along with an ever growing rejection of the philosophical baggage—the assumptions, values, and goals—of the traditional constructivist position in perception.

It is certainly true that Gibson much increased our understanding of the richness and complexity of the optical stimulus, but it must not be forgotten that he also completely revamped the conceptualization of what a stimulus actually is. He obliterated the clean distinction between organism and environment, pointing out that each is defined, pragmatically and not just formally, in terms of the other. A stimulus is not applied, but information about the environment and about the activity of the self in the environment is obtained in the multiplicity of events that make up the organism-environment whole. In context of this principle of mutuality, then, Gibson would say that we perceive the persistence of places, objects, and substances, along with whatever changes they undergo, in conjunction with a coperception of the activities of the self by extracting the invariant structures of the ambient optic array that specify those objects, places, substances, activities, and events.

239

Role of "Processing"   This answer by no means precludes the legitimate investigations of the physiologists, although it is certainly an attempt to redefine both what gets processed and the relationship between processed and processor. As Gibson put it:

> The theory of information pickup requires perceptual systems, not senses. Some years ago I tried to prove that a perceptual system was radically different from a sense (Gibson, 1966), the one being active and the other passive. People said, "Well, what I mean by a sense is an *active* sense." But it turned out that they still meant the passive inputs of a sensory nerve, the activity being what occurs in the brain when the inputs get there. That was not what I meant by a perceptual system. I meant the activities of looking, listening, touching, tasting, or sniffing. People then said, "Well, but those are responses to sights, sounds, touches, tastes, or smells, that is, motor acts resulting from sensory inputs. What you call a perceptual system is nothing but a case of feedback." I was discouraged. People did not understand (1979, p. 244).

In his last book, Gibson attempted one more time to describe the necessary outlines of the pickup systems, distinguishing them from senses. He wrote that a sense is defined by a bank of receptors or receptive units that are connected with a presumed projection center in the brain. Local stimulation at the sensory surface causes local firing of neurons in the appropriate projection center. Adjustments of the organ, for example, an eye, containing the receptive units, are not included in the usual definition of the sense. In contrast, a perceptual system "is defined by an organ and its adjustments at a given level of functioning, subordinate or superordinate. At any level, the incoming and outgoing nerve fibers are considered together so as to make a continuous loop" (1979, p. 245).

He used the eye as an example to explain how the different levels of functioning of a perceptual system all serve the pickup of information. He argued that the first level, the lens, pupil, chamber, and retina together comprise an organ whose appropriate adjustments include accommodation, intensity modulation, and dark adaptation. At the second level, the eye with its muscles in the orbit make up an organ with the attendant movements of compensation, fixation, and scanning. The third-level organ is comprised of the two eyes in the head with level-specific adjustments of convergence/divergence and disparity pickup. At the fourth level, the eyes in a mobile head that can turn constitute an organ for the pickup of ambient information through all the possible various movements of the head. Even more extensive movements of the body accompany the fifth-level organ, "the eyes in a head on a body comprise a superordinate organ for information pickup over paths of locomotion" (p. 245). Such an analysis certainly presupposes a number of

240

interrelated, nested, physiological structures, but it takes a radical approach both to the size of the systems and to the nature of the receptors.

Gibson stressed repeatedly that a critical difference between sense and perceptual system is the assumption that senses are passive receivers of stimuli, whereas in a perceptual system, the input-output loop obtains information actively. "Even when the theory of the special senses is liberalized by the modern hypothesis of receptive units, the latter are supposed to be triggered by complex stimuli or modulated in some passive fashion" (p. 245). The possibility of learning also distinguishes a perceptual system from a sense. A sense is sensitive to a certain fixed number of sensations innately given, or perhaps, stretching it, subject to a certain limited degree of expansion through physiological maturation. With practice, a perceptual system picks up information that is ever more subtle, elaborate, and precise. The palate can be improved as long as life goes on. A sense allows us to experience only the receptor sense itself and not the world that presumably occasioned the sensations; perceptual systems pick up information specific to the qualities of things in the world, especially, according to Gibson, their affordances.

This point requires the breakdown of the organism-environment dichotomy and runs counter to centuries of Western philosophy. Gibson notes that in traditional theory strenuous efforts must be made to avoid the shocking conclusion that we cannot know the "outer world." Helmholtz invented unconscious inferences to get us from our sensations to the world, but he did so realizing that an assumption of veridicality as the normal case was critical if the inferences obtained were to be reliable guides to behavior. Nearly all perceptual theorists have realized that they somehow must deal with the fact that many organisms avoid death in a dangerous world long enough to breed and rear their young, a remarkable feat which requires the assumption of a modicum of veridicality in perception, or at least a most fortuitous correspondence between inner and outer states. Helmholtz argued that correspondence was sufficient to the theory, but he himself assumed veridicality— more by assertion than by argument. "Modern" perceptual psychologists who are not Gibsonians rely on perceptual clues or cues to the state of the world, with the sources of the resemblances, however minor, between cue/clue and world being both mysterious in origin and again fortuitous.

Gibson has pointed out repeatedly that "it seems to be that all such arguments come down to this: we can perceive the world only if we already know what there is to be perceived. And that, of course, is circular" (p. 246). The alternative is to assume that the information generated by organism/environment mutuality is sufficient to specify the qualities of the world in relation to the observer and that the perceptual systems pick up the information directly. A theory of direct perception is only possible because there is information in the ambient array that *specifies* events, objects, and so forth in the world (the word *direct* here does not refer particularly to a processing theory). It is only in this limited sense that the Gibsonian analysis of available information can be seen to substitute for a "processing analysis"; in the Gibsonian approach, there is a great deal more to be "processed" and the process of "processing" is considerably different. Gibson's approach increases the complexity of the physiology to be studied and understood, it does not claim to replace it.

Objects and Space: Related Issues   Because Gibson's proposed answers to other aspects of the traditional "objects and space" questions are implicit in the rather extended answer to the general question above, a considerably briefer treatment should suffice. After all, this chapter is intended only to whet one's appetite for Gibson.

A major traditional question is, how do we perceive the three-dimensionality of space and the "proper" shapes and locations of objects? Gibson's answer? How could we not? To begin to understand the Gibsonian approach to this question, it would be helpful to assume for a moment that we do *not* perceive the three-dimensionality of space, that we do *not* perceive the three-dimensional shapes and locations of objects. What then do we, can we, perceive? No one ever assumes that we see in four- or five-dimensional space because the assumption means nothing to the nonmathematician. It certainly means nothing to most perceptionists. What we usually overlook is that the assumption they *do* make means nothing either. Many traditional perceptionists assume that people, and, presumably, frogs and cats, see, at least in early youth, in two dimensions. They assume that we see not the world, but pictures of the world, and that these pictures are two-dimensional until we learn to add depth to them.

Now, this makes no sense at all. Where are the pictures? Somewhere out in front of the body? At the bridge of the nose? On the retinae? Does this mean that we perceive the pictures to be painted on the retinas, or that we experience the world as a plane slicing through our bodies? The pictorial assumption makes perception very difficult; the two-dimensional assumption makes it impossible. If visual perception is to be considered truly two-dimensional, then the observer must experience the self, the ego, as a point on some two-dimensional plane. This makes reaching rather difficult since it restricts the range of adaptive movements to that plane. If the plane is somewhere in front of the body—perhaps in the plane of clear focus, eight to twelve inches from the body at birth, on the average—then three-dimensional space is defined by the introduction of an ego point not on the plane. Assuming that such picture-gallery vision is what is meant by the assertion that we see in two dimensions, then the problem for the traditional perceptionist has been the addition of depth cues or clues to the picture to make its several parts recede variously in space. The proposed solution is that we learn the depth cues by moving around in space and observing the correlations between the picture cues and the consequences of our movements for relative distance.

This unlikely scenario seems to have arisen from the discovery that the light reflected from world surfaces to the eye is projective in character and from the observation that the eye has certain properties in common with manufactured image-forming devices. An additional assumption was critical to the traditional formulation of the problem of three-dimensional perception: it was that the visual system works essentially like a camera, shooting and storing still pictures that serve as stimuli for the visual process. Under this set of assumptions, depth perception certainly is a problem. Gibson approached the problem by rejecting the last assumption that still pictures provide the stimuli for perception. He argued that the information for both persistence and change is given by the invariant structures in the ambient array that occur over time. The visual system picks up invariants precisely through the detection of nonchange across change, not through tortuous interpretations of single still shots.

Gibson also denied the existence of the retinal image, the core of the picture theory of natural vision. He did not deny that it is possible to remove a vertebrate eyeball and under careful conditions use it to construct images; he denied that such a procedure was involved in normal vision. He stressed the continual movements of the eye, head, and body that make it so difficult to argue that vision is based on the pickup of still pictures and pointed out the irrelevance of images to vision in organisms with compound eyes. Invariants in the light are available to all sighted organisms, and little pictures in the eyes are not necessary to their pickup (see Schiff, 1965).

Because traditional perceptionists have accepted the snap-shot theory of vision, they are confronted as well with the problem of integration of snapshots across both eye and body movements. Again, the problem does not arise unless we assume pictorial units stored and compared to be the basis of vision. This assumption is so strong that so-called "evidence" can be found at will to support it. The modern researcher can easily set up an experiment to show the existence of what information processors like to call the "icon." Present the observer with a clear, bright stimulus, usually a picture of something, for a short time, usually a few hundred milliseconds, then show a blank field, and what do you discover? The "icon"! You discover that after the stimulus has been removed, chemical transformation of retinal pigments continues for some time, neuronal impulses continue to travel for some time, and cortical neurons continue to fire for some time—not a great while, mind you, but for varying numbers of milliseconds. A far more interesting discovery would be that all neurophysiological activity ceased instantaneously—a logical and biological impossibility. Nevertheless, the fact that bodily activity and attendant awareness persist in real time is considered evidence for the existence of the "icon" and for the importance of its role in visual perception, despite the absence of a logical or empirical basis for the connection.

The gulf between this model and Gibson's argument that perception is based not on stored still pictures but on the pickup of invariants that persist *across* both time and space cannot be bridged by any known brand of constructivism, however modern its terminology. The information processors' "icon" assumption simply

243

revamps the centuries-old question of how we perceive form in modern, quasiphysiological dress.

The Problem of Form: Traditional and Gibsonian Approaches

Gibson's answer to the traditional question of how we perceive form is the same as his answer to the "space" question—that is, we don't. We do not perceive form as a component of the perception of the ordinary environment if by form is meant the flat projection of three-dimensional solids on a picture plane. However, if form means the patterns on the surfaces of objects, then we perceive form when we read, pick out wallpaper, stroll through the Museum of Modern Art, or design fabric. We are certainly capable of perceiving two-dimensional design on surfaces, and we do so in exactly the same manner as we perceive the boundaries of the surfaces themselves. No special explanation for the perception of form in this sense of the word is required.

However, if form is used in the traditional sense to refer to the shape of projected solids on the retina, then there is no reason to believe that it figures in perception at all. A fixed retinal image is a fiction outside the laboratory, and there is little reason to believe that observers are even aware of the momentary stable appearance of things. It is possible to train yourself to notice what the shapes of things, the distances and the angles, would be if those solid things were centrally projected, surface by surface, onto a sheet of glass mounted vertically in front of the face. Western post-Renaissance artists used to train themselves to notice these forms and to reproduce them. However, the artists were concerned specifically with the activity of projecting solids sitting on a horizontal surface into plane figures on a vertical surface, establishing an approximate projective equivalence between the two. Under certain highly restricted conditions of observation, the scene and the projectively equivalent picture should look more or less alike in certain important respects.

What has this to do with ordinary visual perception? Nothing. There is no vertical canvas in the eye, and no one to look at it if there were. No evidence whatsoever suggests that people can match the projected shapes of solids that would be present on the curved retinas if such images really existed. The few studies on such matching, like Thouless's classic work (1931) on phenomenal regression to the real object, investigated shape matches with stimuli that fell between the veridical, e.g., 90° angle between two sides of a cube, and the pictorial, e.g., the projection of the 90° angle onto a flat vertical surface. There were *no* curved "retinal" stimuli available. It's no wonder that Thouless found that people unfamiliar with Western projective art persisted in showing considerable phenomenal regression to the veridical shapes.

Form perception is interesting as it pertains to picture perception, particularly to the perception of pictures that are not Western. Form perception is important to our

244

understanding of the reading of verbal language and of music and of much of design. But special explanations of form perception are not required. Two-dimensional forms are on surfaces and those surfaces move or we move in relation to them. The printed page undergoes numerous translations and rotations across which the invariant features of the letters printed thereon remain invariant, just as the shape of the page itself does under the same transformations. The problem, the information, and the process of pickup are the same. We can even learn, as Leonardo did with reading and writing (for heaven knows what reason), to pick up form invariants under unfamiliar transformations like reflection. That it is so simple to do so is most instructive about form perception, an ordinary event much in need of a new name. It's too bad that "pattern perception" is already in such regrettable use, because the perception of surface design patterns is all that is really meant by the term *form perception* under any reasonable definition of *form*.

The Traditional Issue of Color Perception: Gibson's Approach

Gibson approached the problem of color perception, as he approached every other problem of perception, from an ecological point of view. He argued that for human beings and some animals the perception of colors of *surfaces* was more important than the perception of the colors of such events as rainbows and sunsets because surface color is informative for aspects of the environment critical for living, like the colors of ripened and unripened fruit. He believed that surface color was insepar-ably connected to surface texture, that every surface has a characteristic color just as it has a characteristic texture. Characteristic color is the characteristic distribution of the reflectance ratios of the different wavelengths of the light striking the surface.
Gibson wrote:

> How the differential colors of surfaces are specified in the optic array separately from the differential illumination of surfaces is, of course, a great puzzle. The difference between black and white is never confused with the difference between lighted and shadowed, at least not in a natural environment as distinguished from a controlled laboratory display. There are many theories of this so-called constancy of colors in perception, but none of them is convincing (1979, p. 91).

Gibson's ecological approach considers the problem in context of the "fact" that the sun moves constantly across the sky from morning to night, that in the natural environment the pattern of illumination is always changing. "I suggest that the true relative colors of (the) adjacent surfaces emerge as the lighting changes, just as the true relative shapes of the adjacent surfaces emerge as the perspective changes" (1979, p. 89). What is the information in the light that specifies the true relative colors of surfaces? To understand the source of the invariant information for color, it is necessary to realize that the natural environment outside the laboratory is

245

cluttered with surfaces arranged both in series of adjacencies and in a nested hierarchy of sizes. Thus the color of any surface is not an absolute color, rather it is relative to the colors of adjacent surfaces, up, down, and sideways; the reflectance ratio of a particular surface is specified only in relation to the reflectance ratios of other surfaces in the same layout. (Try matching paint and wallpaper without placing samples of each side by side.)

In a normal optic array, a whole range of black, white, and gray surfaces and a range of chromatically colored surfaces are projected in an arrangement of solid angles.

> The colors are not seen separately, as stimuli, but together, as an arrangement. And this range of colors provides an invariant structure that underlies *both* the changing shadow structure with a moving sun and the changing perspective structure with a moving observer. The edges and corners, the convexities and concavities, are thus specified as multicolored surfaces, not as mere slopes; as speckled or grained or piebald or whatever, not as ghostly gray shapes (1979, p. 91).

Relative to other aspects of perception, Gibson spent little time on the problem of color perception itself. Gibson saw color perception much as he saw texture perception in the 1950s. Gradients of texture can provide information for slant and distance; discontinuities of texture provide information for changes of surface. There are no known informative gradients of surface color, but discontinuities of color, changes in ratios of spectral reflectance, generally, though not always, provide information also for changes in surface. Color and texture changes generally go together, providing redundant information for surface change, as long as one defines color broadly enough to include chromatically variegated surfaces like bricks and linoleum.

Thus it was the discontinuities of texture and color rather than the homogeneities that occupied most of Gibson's attention. Gibson did not doubt that we can discriminate one grade of sandpaper from another or one color of pinpoint cotton from a second, but other than pointing out that ratios, proportions, and relations of other kinds were the proper units of analysis for the specification of invariant information, he spent little time on the problem. In contrast, during the last years of his life he devoted most of his time to the problem of meaning.

The Perception of Meaning and the Meaning of Perception

The traditional approach to the problem of meaning argues that the objects of perception are meaningless and that meaning is somehow added to these strange unknowns through "cognition" and/or "memory." This position was admirably expressed by Berkeley in his "Essay Towards a New Theory of Vision" in which he explained that the objects of vision are given meaning only through association with the tangible ideas of things touched in the past. Helmholtz, Titchener, and all of the structuralists, introspectionists, and later constructivists believed in some version of this position as a fundamental article of faith. They believed that the objects of vision, the stimuli, cues, clues, or information for vision are meaningless, or at the very least inadequately meaningful (a truly wonderful concept with no logical integrity at all), and that the meaning must be added by the perceiver either through higher mental processes like unconscious inference or through associated memories of past experiences. It is clear to traditionalists that stimuli are physical and meaning is mental.

The modern sensationists, the information processors, have added nothing to this point of view; the relabeling of traditional constructs with terms from computer language has advanced the field not one step. Traditional perceptual theory has never dealt adequately with the question of how the meaningless stimulus fortuitously triggers the appropriate associated meaningful memories—how do meaninglessness and meaning ever manage to get together?

Gibson's approach to the problem of meaning is the first radically different approach since (at least) Berkeley's. He gave us the theory of "affordances." Gibson (1979) explained that the environment can be described both in terms of the surfaces that separate substances from the medium in which animals live, and in terms of what it *affords* animals for contact and behavior, i.e., terrain, shelter, food, water, fire, other animals, objects, and so on. He then asked, "How can we go from surfaces to affordances?" If there is information in the light for surfaces, does it necessarily follow that there is information in the light for affordances as well? The answer is yes.

Gibson argued that in a very fundamental sense the layout and composition of surfaces constitute what they afford, so to perceive layout and composition is to perceive affordances. It is in this very important sense that values and meanings of objects and events can be considered external to the perceiver. He wrote:

> The *affordances* of the environment are what it *offers* the animal, what it *provides* or *furnishes*, either for good or ill. The verb *to afford* is found in the dictionary, but the noun *affordance* is not. I have made it up. I mean by it something that refers to both the environment and the animal in a way that no existing term does. It implies the complementarity of the animal and the environment (1979, p. 127).

As an example of an affordance, Gibson used a terrestrial surface nearly horizontal, nearly flat, sufficiently extended relative to the size of the animal, and sufficiently rigid relative to the weight of the animal—such a surface affords support to the animal and is perceived as doing so. Gibson noted that the four properties—horizontal, flat, extended, and rigid—must be measured relative to the animal because the scale is different for elephants and spiders. This species specificity is true for all types of affordances—what Gibson called the climb-on-able, the fall-off-able, the get-underneath-able, the graspable, and so on. "Different layouts afford different behaviors for different animals, and different mechanical encounters" (p. 128). This is true even within species, for as Gibson pointed out, knee-high is not the same for a child as for an adult, so what affords sitting for an adult need not afford sitting for a child.

In relation to a species, however, Gibson argued that the concept of ecological niche, the lifestyle of a species, is best understood as a set of affordances. Again, such a concept can be understood only in a context of understanding the reciprocity between organism and environment.

> An important fact about the affordances of the environment is that they are in a sense objective, real, and physical, unlike values and meanings, which are often supposed to be subjective, phenomenal, and mental. But, actually, an affordance is neither an objective property nor a subjective property; or it is both if you like. An affordance cuts across the dichotomy of subjective-objective and helps us to understand its inadequacy. It is equally a fact of the environment and a fact of behavior. It is both physical and psychical, yet neither. An affordance points both ways, to the environment and to the observer (p. 129).

Gibson's position, then, on *where* meaning lies is clear, but it is clearer still when considered in terms of invariant information. Visual information for affordances, like the information for composition and layout, is in the light. Indeed, the information for affordances is the information for composition and layout—but for many aspects of composition and layout at the same time. Horizontality, flatness, rigidity, and extension are all specified in the light; when they are all specified together, then there is information available for a surface of support. Thus, the information for affordances is an invariant cluster of individual invariants.

> Nevertheless, a unique combination of invariants, a compound invariant, is just another invariant. It is a unit, and the components do not *have* to be combined or associated. Only if percepts were combinations of sensations would they have to be associated. Even in the classical terminology, it could be argued that when a number of stimuli are completely covariant, when they *always* go together, they constitute a single "stimulus." If the visual system is capable of extracting invariants from a changing optic arrary, there is no reason why it should not extract invariants that seem to us highly complex (1979, p. 141).

Gibson's position on the problem of meaning is undoubtedly radical—the aspect of his ecological approach to visual perception most difficult to accept for those of us who went to graduate school before 1979. Gibson's position on affordances, however, is all of a piece with his approach to the nature of optical information and his redefinition of the organism-environment relation in terms of mutuality.

248

Affordances are a logical extension of the work begun over forty years ago, and to be understood they must be seen as such.

Gibson's Proposal for the Next Century of Research

Before his last book was published, Gibson experienced a considerable degree of pressure, primarily from students, to entitle it *The Theory of Ecological Optics*. He refused. He called it instead *The Ecological Approach to Visual Perception*, with careful consideration of each word selected. Gibson's conclusions to his last book dealt primarily with the problems confronting those who would take this approach to perceptual research, particularly problems in the design and display of information. Gibson wrote that the approach needs to be tested experimentally, it needs to be clarified further, and its implications need to be followed up, and he praised the efforts of many researchers in these respects. His last words on the subject were

> These terms and concepts are subject to revision as the ecological approach to perception becomes clear. May they never shackle thought as the old terms and concepts have! (James J. Gibson, 1979, p. 311).

REFERENCES

Berkeley, G. Essay towards a new theory of vision. In A. A. Luce & T. E. Jessop (Eds.), *The works of George Berkeley Bishop of Cloyne*. London: Thomas Nelson, 1948. (Originally published, 1709.)

Gibson, J. J. *The perception of the visual world*. Boston: Houghton Mifflin, 1950.

Gibson, J. J. *The senses considered as perceptual systems*. Boston: Houghton Mifflin, 1966.

Gibson, J. J. *The ecological approach to visual perception*. Boston: Houghton Mifflin, 1979.

Gibson, J. J., Olum, P., & Rosenblatt, F. Parallax and perspective during aircraft landings. *American Journal of Psychology*, 1955, 68, 372–385.

Schiff, W. Perception of impending collision. *Psychological Monographs*, 1965, 79 (No. 604).

Sedgwick, H. A. The geometry of spatial layout in pictorial representation. In M. A. Hagen (Ed.), *The perception of pictures* (Vol. I). New York: Academic Press, 1980.

Thouless, R. H. Phenomenal regression to the real object. *British Journal of Psychology*, 1931, 21, 338–359.

Thouless, R. H. A racial difference in perception. *Journal of Social Psychology*, 1933, 4, 330–339.

11

Perception

A ONE-HUNDRED-YEAR PERSPECTIVE

RALPH NORMAN HABER

I am a rather ahistorical person, preferring to leave history to the historians. This is particularly easy when talking about visual perception, since the big questions one hundred or even two hundred years ago are the same ones which occupy our attention now. In fact, Wundt in 1879 was a latecomer to this area of psychology, as there already had been over fifty years of solid empirical and theoretical work on perception predating the founding of his laboratory. So rather than trace the rise and fall of individuals or ideas, I shall first single out what I consider to be the current formulation of these big questions, and then provide some evaluative or speculative comments about the future of each.

First Big Question: How Do We Perceive the Layout of Space?

This is the granddaddy of big perceptual questions—ancient and modern. In its modern form, it has many components. How do we perceive the three-dimensionality of space so that objects are seen in their proper shapes and locations with respect to one another as well as to us? How do we perceive the intrinsic properties of visual space: the color, shape, texture, orientation, and distance of objects and surfaces around us, each independent of our momentary viewing position and distance from the scene? How do we integrate the continually changing visual results of our own movements as we locomote in space? How do we integrate the successive glances that arise as a result of our eye movements into a single panoramic view of the visual space around us?

That we do perceive the intrinsic properties of visual space, in vivid three dimension, has not been in question. But how do we do it? The answer has never seemed very simple (and it is not simple) because the question has usually been posed in the context of how can we see the world in three dimensions when our retinas are two dimensional and we have no "distance receptor" to register directly how far away a surface is when it reflects light to the eye. Without such a distance receptor, most theorists have argued that the third dimension of space has to be derived from other sources of information, and the theoretical battles have concerned those other sources. As is often the case, the ultimate battle is over how the initial question is framed.

We have had nearly a century of two polarized theories that account for how we perceive the layout of space. One of these polar positions received its clearest exposition in the work of Helmholtz, in Volume II of his three-volume *Treatise on Physiological Optics*, published in 1866. He treated information about space as separate and distinct cues, including those of retinal size, retinal shape, aerial perspective, interposition, and binocular disparity, as well as nonsensory knowledge and assumptions about the arrangements of the scene being viewed. The perception of space was, then, the result of an unconscious inference or processing of these various cues, in which the information value of the cues is combined so as to arrive at the proper view of the scene. Helmholtz applied his concept of unconscious inference to the various aspects of space perception with great power and productivity, and his approach blended well with the subsequent American commitment to empiricism and acquired experience.

The other pole did not receive adequate voice until Gibson began his research nearly fifty years ago. His work has remained the single most sustained and towering challenge to Helmholtz. They differ on every point of issue. Most important, Gibson demands that we understand the richness of the stimulation reaching us from visual space before inventing nonvisual mediators to account for space perception. Further, he argues that this richness is not to be ascribed to separate, addable cues. The information in the entire pattern of light reaching the eye is already combined, and therefore already informative of the layout of space; no further information or processing is required.

As is often the case with such explicitly opposed approaches, the two have never really confronted each other, but have continued to coexist as independent conceptions of how we perceive. Let me illustrate what I mean.

Helmholtz and his often feuding descendents, such as Ittelson (1960), Rock (1977), Epstein (1973), and Hochberg (1979), each focus on processing: how we take the information that falls on the retina and transform it into a perception of space. This approach creates a processing analysis of space, and fits naturally with

251

information-processing theories and models of all cognitive processing (see the fourth question below). Processing models of space concentrate on isolated features on the retina and ask how these are processed, that is, altered, constructed, or reconstructed, so we can infer from them the intrinsic properties of the stimulus in space. For example, since the size of the retinal image of an object is a function of the object's distance from the perceiver, and there is no "distance receptor," how does the perceiver process or adjust retinal size in order to perceive intrinsic size? The answer, according to Rock (e.g., 1977) or Epstein (e.g., 1973), is to take distance into account: we infer the true intrinsic size by calculating distance, as given by the size-distance invariance hypothesis. This calculation requires a separate source of information about distance, and then a calculation or inference process, what Epstein (1973) describes as solving an algorithm to arrive at each intrinsic property of space.

This model of space perception demands careful laboratory studies, using controlled variables under very simple conditions of stimulation. It has been a very powerful model of space perception and has led to a large body of research on different and presumably independent sources of information about the layout of space perception. Each aspect of space, such as the size of an object, is treated in isolation, and for each, the cues provide independent sources of information. Each of these aspects enter into separate computations, so that we perceive the size of an object by one algorithm, its shape by another, its relative position by yet another, and so forth.

One example of the kind of approach used by the Helmholtzians concerns the integration of information sources to perceive motion. The proper cue to motion, dating back to Helmholtz (1866/1924), is the successive stimulation of adjacent retinal loci. It took nearly a century before we knew the neural mechanism by which this is encoded, but Barlow (1953) and especially Hubel and Wiesel (1962) showed the presence of simple neural units in the cortex that respond to successive stimulation of adjacent retinal loci, selectively as a function of speed, direction, shape of moving pattern, and locus.

Given Helmholtz's specific definition of the cue to motion, the question arises as to how perceivers tell whether the motion across the retina is due to some object moving in space, or merely to an eye or head movement of the perceiver. I say merely because if the latter is the cause, no motion should be perceived, as indeed none is. Helmholtz (1866/1924) reasoned that that information must be available either as afferent feedback from the muscles of the eye or as an efferent correlary signal that produced the eye movement in the first place. If the magnitude of the eye position shift, measured either afferently or efferently, just matches the amount of shift of stimulation on the retina, then the two cancel and no motion is perceived. Any mismatch implies that an eye movement cannot account for the retinal image displacement, and so motion in space is perceived. This processing model is a very simple and elegant one, capturing the spirit of the unconscious inference approach.

Helmholtz (1866/1924) reported an experiment to test this model, an experiment since replicated by von Holst (1954) and Stevens, Emerson, Gerstein, Kallos, Neufeld, Nichols, and Rosenquist (1976) among others. Each provides evidence of at least the efferent correlary signal as the source of information to be added to the retinal information of motion (see Gyr, 1972; Gyr, Willey, & Henry, 1979, for reviews). In the von Holst version, the eye muscles of a perceiver are paralyzed so that the eye cannot move in a given direction, and then the perceiver is instructed to move his eye in that direction, say, to the right. This instruction, which presumably produces an efferent command but no resulting displacement on the retina (the eye cannot execute the command), results in the perception of the visual world moving to the right. In a second condition, von Holst moved the paralyzed eye mechanically to the right instead of instructing the perceiver to move it. In this case, there should be no efferent command, but now there is retinal displacement. Here also, the perceiver reports seeing movement of the visual world, but now he sees it moving to the left, as would be expected. In a third condition, von Holst instructs the perceiver to move his paralyzed eye, and at the same time von Holst moves the eye mechanically in the same direction. In this case there is both an efferent command and a retinal displacement, so the effects found in the first and in the second conditions should just cancel. As expected, the perceiver reports that the visual world is stationary. These three conditions provide evidence that the perception of motion, at least under these circumstances, includes a comparison or correlation between the efferent commands to muscles with the resulting visual afferent consequences.

The difficulty with this Helmholtzian approach is not its processing emphasis, but its failure adequately to describe the information that has to be processed. This failure has a number of causes. First, because the Helmholtzian approach focuses on single, isolated variables, it ignores the richness of stimuli in the real world. Thus, this approach does not attempt to describe completely the patterns normally on the retina when the retina is exposed to a real scene in space. Second, also because of the focus on isolated variables, visual space is often simulated with extremely simple and even impoverished stimuli. Third, the Helmholtzian approach is rarely applied to successive glances at a scene, so that no integration processes are included. Finally, it gives little attention to differences between central and peripheral processing on the retina, or to eye movements, or to the interactions of these variables.

There are, of course, differences among the various Helmholtzian disciples, with Hochberg the most difficult to categorize. Hochberg (e.g., 1974) focuses on the mental structure of expectancies created by the perceiver about the scene being viewed. Since these expectancies include anticipations about what will be seen in each successive eye movement, he emphasizes the integration of successive glances, considering the perception of the entire scene as a unity, rather than each aspect of each object separately. His work represents virtually the sole exception in the Helmholtz tradition of ignoring stimulus properties within processing models of space perception. Even so, Hochberg fits into the Helmholtzian tradition because his major focus is on how information is processed.

The Helmholtzian tradition has had over one hundred twenty-five years of impetus in the laboratory behind it. The alternative view, represented best by the nearly fifty years of work by James Gibson, is dramatically different in nearly all respects—philosophical persuasion, theoretical modeling, and experimental method. But I think the differences between the Gibsonians and the Helmholtzians reduce down to only one factor, a focus on stimulus versus a focus on process.

Gibson (1950, 1966, 1979) objects to the assumptions underlying the whole line of processing work, because, he rightly argues, the information in the stimulus itself is sufficiently rich to provide the layout of space for the perceiver. Locked into their studies of single variables, the Helmholtzians have ignored the informativeness of the interaction of real stimuli in the real world.

Gibson begins his stimulus approach by examining the transformations that occur between the pattern of light reflected from surfaces in the visual scene and the optical projection of that pattern on the retina. He details these transformation rules, especially the different varieties of perspective transformations.

When we look at a scene, the pattern of light on each retina can be described in terms of three different but equivalent perspective transformations, all involving distance. Thus, when viewing any scene which has a continuous surface, such as the ground stretching away from the viewer, the relatively uniform surface texture of that ground produces a continuous gradient or perspective of texture density in the light projected across the two retinal surfaces. Since this perspective change begins at the feet and stretches away in all directions, the pattern of light on the retinas provides a continuous scale of visual space, a scale on which all objects in the scene are anchored.

A second though entirely equivalent scale of space arises from the pattern of binocular disparities between the two retinas, a pattern of differences which varies directly with the distance between the perceiver and each part of the scene. For every momentary fixation into space, the direction and magnitude of the disparity in the optical pattern between the two eyes provides a continuous scale for all surface qualities nearer and farther away than that point of fixation.

The third scale arises when the viewer moves around in the visual scene. The changes in the pattern of light reflected to each retina has a perspective over time so that light reflected from nearby surfaces is displaced farther across the retinas than light from far surfaces. This motion perspective also is perfectly correlated with the other two scales, but it is available obviously only when the position of the perceiver's head changes with respect to the scene being viewed. Gibson's recent theoriz-

254

ing, especially 1979, places greatest weight on the information provided by motion perspective resulting from the perceiver's own movements in space.

Gibson has provided here a geometrical analysis of the ways in which the pattern of reflected light is transformed when projected on surfaces such as retinas, as a function of distance, movement, and separation of the two retinas. It is a stimulus analysis exclusively, relying on no principles of psychology, perception, or cognition. It is the proper starting analysis, because it tells us what kinds of patterns of light to expect to find on the retinas when real observers, who have peripheral retinas as well as foveas, and who move their eyes, heads, and bodies, view real scenes. Gibson has shown, when viewing the normally rich visual world, how the entire surface of each retina has patterned light projected over it; and how the various visual properties of the world are represented in variation in those patterns. Once we know this, and only then, can we begin to ask questions about how the process of space perception occurs. The failure of the Helmholtzians has been their insistence on using impoverished, line-drawn stimuli, all too often stimuli that indeed do not convey much information to the eye about the layout of space, and certainly nothing about the redundancies in the three scales of space detailed above. It is not surprising that if the perceiver is denied most of the information he typically uses, then he is forced to resort to nonvisually based assumptions, or to make up visual data to describe what he is looking at.

How does Gibson use his stimulus analysis to describe what the viewer perceives about the layout of space? Consider size constancy and motion perception again. From his point of view, no Helmholtzian (processing) mechanism, such as computation or inference, is necessary in either case, and certainly no prior knowledge or nonvisual information, such as that about eye or head position, as long as the scene is complete. For size, Gibson argues that we have to attend to the information over the entire retinal surface, not just the retinal size of the object in question. The full retinal scales of space contain all that is necessary and more, in order to determine all of the sizes (and locations, orientation, colors, and the like) of each object, as long as there is a full complete scene reflecting light to the eye. Nearby objects intersect the ground where the surface scale of the ground is coarse, whereas far objects intersect the ground scale where it is fine. The gradient of change of the scale is proportional to distance. If the ground extends up to the observer, as it usually does, then every object is located on the scale with respect to its distance from the observer and from other objects. The disparity between the two eyes generates a second completely redundant scale, and the same information is provided by the motion perspective scale if the observer moves. Further, each object occludes part of the ground scale, proportional to its size (and orientation). For a fixed intrinsic size, regardless of the distance of an object from the viewer, the amount of the ground texture occluded is constant. Hence, the same object at different distances appears to be the same (intrinsic) size because its relation to the ground remains constant.

255

The story about motion is similar. Gibson argues that when looking at a full scene, there can never be any ambiguity in the information provided by the light reflected from the scene as to whether some one object in the scene moved, the eye(s) of the perceiver moved, or any combination of these. Ambiguity arises only when the scene is a single object that is not attached to a ground stretching away from the perceiver. Consider what happens on the retina when looking at a landscape with a bird flying to and fro. If the perceiver holds his head and eyes still, the only change in the light pattern is that reflected from the bird. All of the retinal image is stationary except that one part. Geometrically, the only occurrence that can cause this is the description given above. There are no other arrangements and changes in space that can produce that pattern. Hence the optical changes above are sufficient to specify the physical changes. Take another case: the observer looks at this scene with the moving bird and makes saccadic eye movements from tree to tree, as if searching for a wood nymph. With the head still, each saccade displaces the retinal image across the retina by the amount of the movement, but without any other change in the image except covering and uncovering at the edges. There is no stretching, compression, or expansion. The only physical circumstance that produces an exact translation of an unchanging retinal image across the retina is an eye movement directed at a stationary scene. Again the optical information at the eye is sufficient to specify the physical circumstances, and no efferent signal concerning eye position is necessary.

The other combinations of viewing can all be worked out in like fashion. If the scene is natural and visually rich, as nature nearly always makes scenes before our eyes, then there is no ambiguity in the information available to the eyes about who moved. Ambiguity only exists at the level of a single motion detector. There is none when the entire retina is considered.

I have tried to couch this analysis entirely in terms of the information available to the retina. That is all a stimulus analysis can do. It specifies what information is theoretically available, but it says nothing about how that information is used. It is at this point that Gibson fails.

Gibson tries to substitute his superb stimulus analysis for a legitimate processing analysis as well. The existence of transformation rules does not tell us how they are used, how they are acquired, how they are developed or modified, or how individual differences occur or what they are. Nor do they tell us anything about the order in which rules are applied or how assumptions or expectations may affect their use. Gibson has simply assumed that because these transformation rules are describable, the stimulus information on the retina from the scene is the same thing as the perception of that scene. It is in this sense that Gibson has a theory of the direct perception of space. However, it is not a theory of space perception, but only a stimulus analysis about information arising from space. For example, the evidence that perceivers use efferent eye position information when they perceive space (e.g., von Holst, 1954) is not sufficient to disapprove or support Gibson. Since most of that evidence is obtained with flat displays, Gibson's analysis makes it clear that these contain ambiguity which could only be resolved with further (presumably eye efferents) information. But maybe perceivers use efferent information even when they have sufficient visual information. After all, the eye efferents and the various visual scales of space share the same redundancies. Which conditions determine which sources of information are used is an empirical question. But that kind of question rarely is addressed.

Hence, for the last fifty years we have had two parallel paths of work: a processing analysis based on a totally unrealistic stimulus description, and a stimulus analysis with no processing specification at all.

We have to have both a stimulus analysis and a process analysis to understand space perception. Neither one alone is adequate, no matter how good a job it does on its own half of the problem. The Helmholtzians (e.g., Gyr, Willey, & Henry, 1979; Ullman, 1980) have to stop attacking "direct perceptions" and latch on to Gibson's real contribution, while the Gibsonians (e.g., Turvey, 1977) need to recognize that having information available and using available information are not the same thing.

I feel that as soon as we create a truly *Gibholtzian* theory of space perception, this merger will produce a breakthrough in our understanding of space.

The stimulus analysis of space, as developed by Gibson, represents an explicit description of the full stimulus context for space perception. But when Gibson goes on to argue that no further information is needed, nothing from assumptions, prior knowledge, past experience, or processing strategies, he is also explicitly rejecting all other contexts. In current parlance, he believes space perception to be entirely data-driven (Bobrow & Norman, 1977). The modern Helmholtzians, on the other hand, wish to enlarge the process of space perception so that it includes a healthy slice of either assumption or prior perception. For them space perception is a combination of data-driven and resources-driven processing, and what we perceive is determined in part by what we expect to see or by what we have seen before. The expectancy modelling of Hochberg (e.g., 1979), the computational approach of Pylyshyn (e.g., 1980) or Ullman (e.g., 1979), the algorithmic approach of Rock (e.g., 1981), and the current work on computer vision with artificial intelligence (e.g., Winston, 1975) represent some of the more promising lines of work that stress the combined contributions of data and resources. But the final answers about space perception are not in yet, in large part because the proper experiments have yet to be done. I will be very surprised if those answers support an entirely data-driven description of space perception. In the two examples to follow, I have selected what I consider to be very promising lines of work that best exemplify attention to both stimulus and process. The first is more data-driven than the second.

Regan (e.g., Regan, Beverley, & Cynader, 1979) has done a careful stimulus analysis of the optical changes associated with radial motion, as when an object is thrown toward the perceiver, or the perceiver is walking through a scene toward a

257

target in the distance. From that analysis he has then looked specifically for a neural apparatus that might be specialized to respond to that optical information.

If a ball is thrown directly toward one eye, the retinal image of the ball expands, from moment to moment, with its rate of expansion proportional to its velocity. When the path is directly toward the eye, then the successively larger optical patterns are concentric, whereas if the path of the ball misses the eye, then the expansion patterns do not share the same center but drift across the retina as the ball gets closer. Hence, expansion itself is a source of information about an approaching object, and the concentricity of the expansion is information about its path. But what happens in the other eye? If the ball heads toward one eye, it will miss the other. Hence there is no drift of the expanding pattern in the eye to be hit, whereas in the other the pattern drifts outward. If the ball is aimed toward the nose, each expansion pattern drifts outward across each retina, with the rate of drift exactly equal and opposite. Finally, consider what happens if the path misses the head altogether: now there is a drift across both retinas, but they always are in the same direction, and if their drift rates are exactly equal, the ball is on a path perpendicular to the line of sight.

Up to this point, this is a stimulus analysis. From it, Regan argues that as perceivers, we care most about objects that might collide with us, so we should be most sensitive to patterns that drift oppositely across the two retinas, as compared to those where both patterns drift in the same direction. This concern specifies only a few degrees of radial motion, but these degrees are the only ones we cannot afford to misinterpret.

Therefore, Regan argues, because we are so good and so fast at detecting and responding to collision motion, we must have specialized detectors just for those stimulus features—in this case the relative drift in opposite directions of the retinal images across the two retinas. This is exactly what he has found. First, using a variation of a stereoscopic display, he projected an image on each eye which he could then move across the retina under his control. When he varied the patterns as the stimulus analysis described, his subjects reported perception of the appropriate movement. Second, he measured the subject's sensitivity to the detection of oscillatory motion on different collision, near collision, and miss paths. Then he had the subject watch a simulated object move back and forth along one pathway for twenty minutes. Following this adaptation, the subject's sensitivity was tested again. Regan found that there was a specific loss in sensitivity for radial motion along the pathway adapted. Finally, Regan repeated the experiment in cats, measuring the electrical activity of certain cells in the visual cortex thought to be responsive to motion. He had no trouble finding cells that were responsive only to particular combinations of drift across the two retinas. These cells were not responsive to drift over only one retina, so they were responding only to the specific stimulus information about collision. Regan found most sensitivity for motion that would either hit the head or just narrowly miss the head, but relatively little sensitivity for all other directions.

This is an example of an excellent stimulus analysis that guided the search for specific kinds of processing—in this particular case, processing at a relatively peripheral site in the visual nervous system. It seems likely to me that most aspects of the motion perspective scale of space are processed in similar ways, if only we look for them. And at least in this one example, Gibson's claim that optical information is sufficient appears to hold up to experimental scrutiny.

The second example concerns how we integrate the information from successive views from each of our two eyes as we scan a scene into a single panoramic representation of that scene. Hochberg (1968, 1974; Hochberg & Brooks, 1978) has best recognized the complexity of the processing problem, and most of his work has focused on the processing side. But the complexity arises because of what a proper stimulus analysis reveals.

One of the most striking (and virtually ignored) aspects of perception is the stability and fixity of the visual scene in spite of the myriad pattern of eye movements made while viewing it. This has to imply that we perceive the scene in its own frame or coordinates, independent of the particular locations of stimulation on our retinas at any one moment. Yet when we fixate our eyes first on one part and then on another, each of those fixations produces an image of a particular view of the scene. And when the successive views result from a change in accommodation, as when shifting our gaze from near to far space, or from our movements in the scene when we walk through it, there is no way for a simple alignment of views to be possible. The successive retinal images stretch or contract unevenly, and the areas of maximum sharpness, clarity, and contrast continually change. Finally, we have two retinas, not one, and the image on one never exactly matches that on the other.

Yet not only do we know it is the same scene being viewed by each eye in each glance, but even more important, we perceive only one scene, fixed out there in the world, unmoved by our movements and undoubled by our two eyes.

The undoubling part is well on the way to being understood. The perspective geometry of the disparity between the two images was fully described by Helmholtz (1866/1924), though its description even predated him, and almost a century and a half ago Wheatstone (1838) built a device to simulate stereoscopic perception from separate images in much the same way that Regan did for radial motion. So we have known that the pattern of disparity between the two eyes is always proportional to the distances of all objects from that point in the scene at which we are momentarily fixated. As such, the disparity provides a source of information about distance, and it is a single value, reflecting differences between the two retinas at each point, rather than separate values for each retina.

It has been much more recently that we have had the evidence that the visual nervous system is wired so as to encode the disparities directly. For example, Hubel and Wiesel (1968) found single cells in the visual cortex whose response is proportional to the disparity in stimulation between the two retinas; yet these cells are not responsive to stimulation of either retina alone. Since disparity is proportional to

259

distance, this is evidence for the existence of cells that process distance based on binocular disparity. Since there are cells that are responsive to disparity between every paired location across the two retinas, the pattern of activity in these cells constitutes the initial processing of the binocular scale of space. Other experiments (see Julesz, 1971; Richards, 1975) have convincingly shown that nonvisual variables are irrelevant to this processing: for example, we do not need to add eye position or movement information in order to process disparity.

But what about the succession of images over time? How do we perceive the intrinsic scene and not the succession of retinal images? Here we have less to go on, mainly because much less has been done. Most researchers in the Helmholtzian tradition have ignored the problem, mainly because they find it easier to control the stimulus by limiting the presentation to only one glance. So they have rarely had to worry about integration built up across several glances. When they do try, they get stuck with their pictorial assumption that it is each retinal image that has to be combined or aligned, in much the same way one might try to make a composite photograph by arranging and superimposing a set of photographic negatives, each taken from a different position or direction. This works if only one eye moves in a stationary head, and there are no changes in accommodation (distance into the scene being fixated). Since such restrictions can never be realistic, and because they can be applied in the laboratory and never in the natural perception of the world, the solution cannot be based on alignment of images.

Hochberg (1968; Hochberg & Brooks, 1978) argues that no stimulus analysis contains sufficient optical information to create integration and perception of the stable intrinsic scene. The solution to the problem therefore depends, according to him, on the perceiver's creating and using a schema to construct a single panoramic representation out of the information that comes in successively. Hochberg has reported experiments that vary the degree of overlap of successive views (a visual source of information) and the orderliness of predictability of the sequence (a nonvisual source). Both factors are found to be important, so that an observer can only perceive the entire scene flowing across before him if the simulated eye movements are not too large, and if he has some idea of what is being displayed. If either does not hold, intrinsic perception fails.

Much more work is needed on integration. A more detailed stimulus analysis is required than Hochberg offered. And since Hochberg's displays are pictorial and not actual scenes, it is possible that real scenes do contain sufficient information to make the expectancies unnecessary. Nevertheless, his approach, like Regan's studies of radial motion, exemplifies what I see as the proper direction of future research in the perception of space: the combined theoretical account and analysis of stimulus and process.

Before leaving the topic of space perception, I want to comment briefly on two developments in other disciplines that have had a profound impact on this field.

The first is based on discoveries from sensory neurophysiology; the second, on discoveries made by perceptual development research.

We are now in the midst of a revolution in sensory neurophysiology. With only a few exceptions, until twenty-five years ago both the predominant view and the evidence supported an isomorphic mapping of connections from the retina to the cortex, in such a way that patterns on the retina were reproduced in the cortex. (See Polyak, 1957, for the best evidence of neural interconnections known at that time.) This meant that the retina was merely a relay station, as in a switchboard. The simultaneous and independent publications by Barlow and by Kuffler in 1953, in parallel with the pioneering work by Bekesy (1960) and by Hartline and Ratliff (1957), provided the first organized view of the retina as a neural coding device based upon a receptive field structure. This exploded the isomorphism of the previous one hundred years and fundamentally changed every concept that we have on how information from light is coded and propagated throughout the visual system.

Unfortunately, the fruits of this revolution have not permeated very far into perceptual theory. First, the neurophysiologists tend to avoid visual displays for which their subjects might have prior experience or interest or reasonable response strategies; they also maintain a traditional aversion to viewing displays under normal conditions of eye and head motion. Knowing how a cortical cell responds to a moving bar provides convincing evidence about how processing works only when that bar is an object in a scene, and the eye and head are able to move. Only then can we tell how motion perception occurs, and only then will we have a proper analysis of the role that motion detector cells in the cortex play in that process. As yet, nothing from the neurophysiology of motion corresponds to any reasonable stimulus analysis of motion perception.

Second, perception researchers, especially those concerned with space, objects, or forms, continue to ignore even the most rudimentary neurophysiological knowledge. How many perception models include or recognize any of the following: the nonuniformity of sensitivity across the retinal surfaces, with the markedly different properties of the central as compared to the peripheral areas; the almost continuous motion of the eyes and the head; receptive-field coding processes rather than a simple one-to-one projection from retina to cortex; or the dramatic changes that occur in retinal organization with shifts in adaptation. And so forth and so on. Failure to recognize any of these tends to lead to silly notions and very limited theories. Tachistoscopic studies of single-glance presentations to an immobilized eye can only tell us something about how we read during a lightning storm. Don't we want to know more than that?

I see neurophysiology and perception to be mutually compatible, but only if each uses the knowledge of the other. It is certainly acceptable for a high-level theory to start at a high level and not to include details of its component parts. But such a

261

presentation cannot assume components that are fundamentally different from those we know actually exist.

The other set of discoveries with dramatic implications for the study of space perception concern perception in newborns, who lack prior experience or knowledge. While philosophers and psychologists have recognized for over two millennia that to understand perceptual development one has to start with newborns, only in the past two decades have we successfully done so, beginning with the pioneering work by Fantz (1961) and by Kessen (e.g. Kessen, Haith, & Salapatek, 1971) and the students he has trained in his laboratory at Yale. This work, in only twenty years, has spectacularly changed our thinking about perception itself.

We now know, for example, that a human newborn has a functioning visual system at birth. What he sees is not the "blooming buzzing confusion" described by James (1890), but the beginning of an orderly world of edges, colors, and shapes (Cohen & Salapatek, 1975), and he has available some evidence that objects are located in space (Bower, 1974). Within just the first few months, familiar objects are sorted out from novel ones (Haith, Bergman, & Moore, 1977), spatial arrangements become fully articulated (Bower, 1974), and complex processing of information begins under the control of selective attention, memory, and expectations (see Haith, 1981). None of these results were even dreamed of just thirty years ago, when our beliefs about perceptual development were still firmly anchored in a tabula rasa tradition of John Locke (1690/1959). In these few decades, we have come to appreciate how much of visual processing occurs without benefit of extensive practice or even specific visual experience.

The evidence on the latter point has come mainly from research with young animals tested after various conditions of deprivation of vision (Mitchell, 1978). The findings suggest that a critical period of normal exposure to patterned light is required for perceptual functions to develop properly. But the exposure is not for the purpose of learning about the specific characteristics of the visual world, but rather to allow the neural coding processes governing relatively low-level features of the visual scene (e.g., edge, motion, and binocular disparity detectors) to mature. These results have certainly moved us a long distance from Bishop Berkeley's (1709/1910) description of perceptual learning as a slow buildup of associations between the way the visual scene appears and the motion responses we have to make to interact with that scene. Depth perception no longer appears to be learned as a consequence of an infant's reaching behavior.

Newborn research has changed the field of perception because it has provided hard evidence to counter the traditional American empirical viewpoint that the fundamental aspects of perception are learned. It has spelled out techniques first for sorting and then for determining the interplay of initial perceptual abilities and subsequent perceptual experience, and it has shown that this interplay is essential for normal development. It no longer allows the glib answer to the nature-nurture question (it's both nature and nurture), since we now can explore exactly how the two interact.

Second Big Question: How Do We Perceive Form?

It is possible to ask about the name of a figure's shape (for example, a square or a triangle), or the name of a visual pattern (for example, a letter A), or even the identity of a complex pattern (for example, a pine cone from a pinion pine tree). These constitute some of the questions addressed under the topic of form. As such, these all seem to be quite different from the topics considered in space perception. But the difference is deceptive, and keeping the two topics apart has played havoc with what we have learned about forms and perceptions of forms.

There have been two quite independent approaches to form. The Gestalt tradition has provided the greatest theoretical legacy through its demand to know the factors that account for why we perceive stimulation in one way rather than in another: why are some elements (now called features) seen as belonging together and others as separate? The most basic division or separation was spelled out by Rubin (1921), who detailed the stimulus features and the resulting perceptual organizations that differentiate figure from ground. Then, to describe figures, the Gestalt psychologists asked what determines that some elements are seen as part of the figure and others as different—either another figure, or the background. This led to a number of descriptions of organizational principles of forms, such as the laws of similarity, closure, Pragnanz, and so forth. Thus, elements that are similar are seen as belonging together, as are elements that are near each other in two-dimensional space (hence, near each other in the retinal image). These so-called Gestalt laws are statements of perceived organization. It is this focus on organization that has provided the greatest contribution of Gestalt psychology to visual perception (see Hochberg, 1973 for the best critical evaluation and review). What defines perceived forms is a transcendant organization that is independent of the particular features that comprise it. Thus, we can see a form as square irrespective of how the sides are constructed, be they black lines on white, white on black, or even a discontinuous series of little dots, triangles, or splotches. All that is required is a certain relationship among the features that is invariant over all of these transformations.

Such a description has been most useful in talking about what constitutes a form, considered as perceived structure, so that Gestalt laws are mainly rules that define the different forms in terms of what happens when they are perceived. Recent enlargements on this approach have described forms by their information content (e.g., Attneave, 1954), or minimal number of possible structures (Hochberg & McAlister, 1953). Thus, the structure that is perceived from the stimulation reaching the eye is determined by the redundancy or predictability among the elements.

In contrast, the other major theoretical approach to form has concentrated entirely on recognition and identification processes, and paid little attention to what defines a form in the first place. It has evolved independently of Gestalt theory, almost entirely within the context of computer and information processing. Three rather different models of the pattern-recognition process have been described (see Neisser, 1967, or Sutherland, 1974, for good descriptions of the models and their problems).

The most literal machine model refers to the matching of the pattern on the retina against a set of stored templates, with "recognition" occurring when a good match is found. This template model has been useful in tasks which permit no variation in pattern or viewing conditions (e.g., machine visual number processing on the bottoms of bank checks). But this model, in any reasonable form, can be shown to be unwieldy or simply inadequate when trying to handle even simple patterns that can vary in composition (such as handwriting or typeface styles), or in location, size, or orientation on the retina, as would occur in free viewing.

To overcome the variation in both the pattern itself and in its registration on the retina, a feature model suggests that the pattern to be recognized is decomposed into a set of distinctive visual features, and it is those features which are compared to stored feature lists of all possible patterns. Since the features are invariant or irrelevant to retinal position, size, or orientation, and even the features of each of the letters of the alphabet are pretty much the same regardless of typeface, a feature model solves the problems that confound templates. E. J. Gibson (e.g., 1969) has developed a detailed feature model for letter recognition (see Haber & Haber, 1981a for a detailed review), but the Pandemonium feature model developed by Selfridge (1959), and described in more detail by Lindsay and Norman (1978), is treated as the more general form of a feature model.

Feature models have their failures, too. Some patterns with vastly different meanings differ by only small details, such as a capital O and Q. How does the model discount large-scale noise and attend to small-scale critical differences? Further, the feature model provides no way to describe the arrangement of features. While a capital letter H has two vertical lines and one horizontal line, there are many ways to arrange those three features, only one of which "looks like" an H. It has been difficult to include the relation aspect into a feature-list description without the list becoming as long as to be silly, or the result being the same as a template.

To repair these problems, a third constructive model (see Haber & Hershenson, 1980, for details) has appealed to the perceiver's expectancies about which features or elements might go together or appear at all, based upon what he knows already about the possible patterns that could be present. In this view, the perceiver forms an abstract representation of the stimulus pattern, guided by the organizational properties of the stimulus. The perceiver then makes hypotheses based on expectancies about what the stimulus might be. The hypotheses take into account the

264

current stimulation in terms of visual features as well as the rules of similarity, redundancy, and probability that the perceiver has formed in past experience with the visual world. In the construction process, one particular pattern of segmentation might be tried and rejected when it results in an inconsistent, incomplete, or improbable representation. Then other hypotheses or constructions would be tried until one is found that matches most of the incoming information. The one that works best is the abstract construction that is then stored as a representation of the stimulus. The act of forming hypotheses and constructions is the act of perceiving and recognizing patterns.

There have been few experiments that have compared either the different models, or how recognition would proceed under any one of the models. Much more has been said in proposing or criticizing the models than in testing them. Certainly, for some tasks, each of the models seems reasonable. And Lindsay and Norman (1978) have been able to integrate a vast amount of cognitive psychology into an expanded version of the Pandemonium model, incorporating aspects of both features and expectancies.

However, despite the obvious productiveness of both directions of thinking about form, I think that form, either as perceived organization or as feature, has very little relevance to general theories of perception. The research on form has become almost entirely anchored in tasks of recognizing particular forms. Models have been generated to explain how we perceive alphabetic characters, abstract designs, geometric shapes, aircraft silhouettes, or faces. These models often work for the tasks for which they were designed, but they are not integrated into a more inclusive theory, either for other forms, or for space perception, or for cognitive theory in general. The models are ad hoc. They are designed to fit the demands of the particular application. Because of their great power, they represent one of the brightest stars of perceptual research in this past century. They also represent one of its greatest failures, for there has been no generalization.

The reasons for the failure to integrate models of form perception into general perceptual theory are easy to discover. Form perception has from the beginning been considered a separate and prior process from that of space perception. Gestalt psychology has lots of laws of organization, but all of them are basically for two-dimensional forms of line elements or their equivalent. Little of the content of these laws recognizes that a central property of organization is three dimensionality. Space is not treated as a property or dimension of form. In addition, most theorists assume that the form of objects is perceived first and only then is the three-dimensional layout of space perceived. This assumption justifies research on form without any need to integrate it into theories about space perception in general.

True, some forms do not have spatial layout in three dimensions—letters of the alphabet, for example—so that the specialized models of form perception can be applied. Theories to account for such forms cover very special cases and lead to dead ends when we attempt to generalize beyond them. Flat forms have even

265

seduced us into thinking that because there is no depth, there is no other larger context either. Thus, I similarly object to feature models of letter recognition (see L. R. Haber & R. N. Haber, 1981; R. N. Haber & L. R. Haber, 1981a, 1981b). Fluent readers cannot start from a feature analysis of letters alone. Readers may begin with some features, but only in the context of what the whole passage is about. We have to work in both directions at once, just as we must for objects in space. The form of an object does not exist independent of the object, nor does the object exist independent of its location in visual scene. To isolate just those features that define the form alone, independent of all of the richness of the scene to which it belongs, is to extend the errors that underlie much of Helmholtzian space perception research into that form and pattern as well.

I believe that the organization of perceived space occurs before form and object recognition. They never occur in fixed processing order of first form, then space. To understand what features are perceived together, or how particular arrangements of features are perceived together, or how a particular arrangement of features is recognized, we have to refer to theories about space.

It is only when there is no space, as in patterns known to be flat, such as letters, that specialized pattern recognition models work. But it seems likely that perceivers treat most flat patterns or forms drawn on a flat picture plane as if they are objects in a scene. This undoubtedly accounts for many of the visual illusions produced by two-dimensional geometric designs (see Coren & Girgus, 1977), in which the perceiver acts as if the information reaching the eye comes from a scene in depth, and uses the information accordingly. It is in this sense that the processing of objects in depth comes first and then the isolated form of each can be ascertained if needed. But a form drawn on a picture surface is equivalent to a momentary retinal image. The visual nervous system is designed to perceive the intrinsic object which produced that momentary view. To do so, all of her available information is used as well. If there is no other information, or the other information is ambiguous, it is not surprising that perceivers often misperceive. Thus, nature produces virtually no visual illusions because it always displays scenes that are meant to be perceived as three-dimensional. (Note that the moon illusion, a natural event that seduces nearly all of us, violates the main demand of a stimulus-controlled perception—there has to be a ground that stretches away from the perceiver on which most of the objects in the scene are anchored. This is true for neither the horizon moon nor for the zenith moon. Typically perceivers have no information other than retinal size and luminance as to the distance of any moon except one about to set or one having just risen.)

Similar observations about the primacy of space perception can be made regarding how we perceive depth in pictures. The older assumption had been that because pictures have one less dimension than does space and a closer resemblance to the retinal image, pictures are easier to perceive than the scenes they represent (see Hagen, 1980b, 1981, for the best historical and current perspectives on pictures perception). But the current view is just the opposite now (Haber, 1980a, b)—it is more complex to process the depth in a picture than from a scene. In fact, children make many mistakes in working out the layout of objects in pictures. Apparently, they treat pictorial displays as if they were actually windows opening into the scene they represent. This poses no problems as long as the children view the picture from the proper station-point (Pirenne, 1970), but from any other place, the surface perspective information from the picture is not consistent with what it would have been from the scene itself, hence the error. With practice or experience, adults are able to use the information that the picture surface is flat in order to compensate for any incorrect viewing position. If the flatness information of the picture surface is removed, adults misperceive the depth and object arrangement in pictures, too (see Hagen, 1974, 1976, for evidence on these conclusions).

As a final and perhaps most important example of space-before-form, consider the problem of contrast and lightness constancy. One of the intrinsic properties of an object is its surface reflectance, which determines both its lightness and its color. A piece of coal reflects relatively little of the light that falls on it and hence is perceived as black, whereas the paper in this book reflects most of the light, making it appear white. These differences in appearance hold regardless of the overall illuminative level falling on the coal or paper. This means that to perceive the intrinsic surface property—lightness constancy—we must be able to perceive the reflectance of the surface, independent of illumination. But the light reaching our eye from a surface is the product of illumination times reflectance (a proportion from 1.00 to .00). How can we tell the difference between a low reflecting surface under high incident light and a high reflecting surface in dim light, when both end up sending the same amount of light (luminance) to the eye?

While Helmholtz had the general principle, it was not until Wallach (1948) worked out the details of contrast that we had a reasonable answer. Wallach showed that lightness is perceived on the basis of the luminance of the object to the luminance of the background when both are illuminated by the same light source. Since the ratio is of two luminances, each being illumination times reflectance, and since the two illumination terms in the ratio are the same, they cancel, leaving a ratio of the two reflectances themselves. Thus, with a single light source, Wallach showed that information regarding the lightness of an object (its reflectance) is available independent of the momentary light level. The ratio is the same in high or in low light—it is constant.

There are two important properties to Wallach's ratio rule. First while we can perceive lightness independently of illumination, we still have a ratio of reflectances to contend with. This means that a given surface appears lighter if the background against which it is viewed is made darker (a lower reflectance). This is the well-known effect of lightness contrast. A tree seen against snow appears to have a darker bark than one of the same species seen against the earth—a failure to achieve an intrinsic perception of the lightness of the bark. If there are lots of trees of different

267

barks all standing in the snow, all are affected by contrast. But given the common background of snow for all, a ratio of ratios of luminances cancels out the reflectance of the snow and yields a reflectance value for each tree. And if some of the trees are on snow and some on low-reflectance earth, then the ratio of luminance at the snow-earth boundary still provides a reflectance value for all trees separately. The critical part of this analysis is that neither a display of a single object by itself nor even a single object on a visible background is sufficient to permit perception of its reflectance. What is needed is a scene full of objects seen against their various backgrounds. Saying this another way, we need to perceive space before we can perceive the properties of single surfaces.

The second property of Wallach's ratio principle is one of limitation. The taking of a ratio of luminances is only useful if the edge between the two luminance areas is caused by a difference in reflectance and not by a difference in illumination. Katz (1935) showed clearly that lightness constancy fails if the perceiver cannot tell what kind of edge is present, especially when the edge arises from different illuminations falling on the same surface. Gilchrist (1977, 1979) verified these findings with quite different procedures. This means that the perceiver must first determine what kind of edges separate the surfaces, and only then take the ratios. If an edge on the retina arises because of two different surfaces abutting together, then the ratio taking is appropriate as a way to perceive the reflectance of the surfaces. But if the edge is due to a shadow lying across a single surface, which produces an illumination edge, then taking a ratio is a mistake, since it attributes two different reflectances rather than two different illuminations to the surface. This suggests that before the lightness of a surface can be perceived, the object arrangements of the scene have to be worked out—again, space before form.

Cornsweet (1970) provides a powerful description of how lateral inhibitory mechanisms in the retina account for the perception of contrast, and he uses his powerful explanation to cover lightness constancy (and color constancy) as well. The thrust of his work is to place the neural coding of contrast and constancy very peripherally in the visual nervous system. While his model can be questioned on its own terms [e.g., inhibiting processes would have to work across large distances, much larger than have ever been demonstrated on the retina (see DeValois & DeValois, 1975)], its more serious failure arises in the present context. How can the retinal inhibiting mechanisms occur prior to the classification of edges? Rather, edge classification has to come first, and only then can a decision be made about whether contrast is taken across the edge or not. Clearly a peripheral mechanism cannot be the end of the story.

All of these arguments suggest that most of the current and past research on form perception is misguided. Form perception, as currently understood, can only be useful in explaining how some explicitly defined flat pattern might be perceived or recognized. We need theories of form that treat form as a property of objects in space, not as a precursor of space.

Third Big Question: How Do We Perceive Color?

Not everyone would include this as a Big Question, even though color is uniquely visual and has no counterparts in other senses, either in its stimulus properties or in how it is processed. I treat it as a big question for six different reasons. First, it is the single most studied topic in vision, and perhaps in all of perception. Second, the best work in vision has been done on color vision. Third, we are probably closer to a complete understanding of the retinal mechanisms by which color is processed than we are for any other single topic. Fourth, research and theory on color includes the best integration between psychophysical, neurophysiological, and phenomenological approaches to perception—integration that I see as the necessary and vital component of future work in perception. Fifth, the resulting models of color vision are quite different from the perception of other attributes of visual stimuli, such as intensity, movement, or form. And finally, theories about color as perception are virtually nonexistent. Boynton's (1979) book on color vision provides a superb account and justification for the first five of these reasons. Since he mentions nothing about the sixth, he justifies that reason as well.

The resolution of the great nineteenth-century debate between Helmholtz (taking a position formulated earlier by Young in 1801) and Hering on the nature of the neural coding of color has produced most of the excitement in color vision research. In simple terms, Young argued that since we can create any hue by the appropriate additive combination of only three light sources, each of a different wavelength, the neural coding system need only contain three different receptor types, each sensitive to a different region of the wavelength spectrum. The outputs of these three receptor types are added together to achieve perception of the stimulus color. Hering (1888) argued that an additive system could not work since certain so-called "complementary" colors cancel each other. Therefore, he proposed that the coding had to be by opposites and that it could not be additive at all. Helmholtz and Hering each spent the latter part of the nineteenth century marshalling evidence to support their opposing positions, drawing on evidence from color blindness, color matching, color appearance, color adaptation, and the like. It has taken the sophisticated technology of the past thirty years to show them both right and to reveal how the neural codes work, or at least how the beginning steps work.

We now know that there are three cone types, just as Young had speculated. This evidence comes from a vast variety of techniques and is uncontestable. (DeValois & DeValois, 1975, have a good review.) However, just as Hering had suggested, the outputs of the cones are not added together but rather contrasted or treated in opposition. Thus, the output from a cone most sensitive to the long wavelength end of the spectrum and a cone from the middle wavelength part mutually inhibit each other in an antagonistic receptive field structure, thereby accounting for why mixing equal parts of red and green light produce achromatic gray.

Thus, while light to the retina stimulates the three cone types differently, depending upon their absorption properties, the outputs of the three cones are contrasted, so that by the level of the ganglion cells, the code is in terms of the differences in output of the three types of cones, not their sum. This is revealed by recordings of neural activity at the ganglion level.

This is a story of the great success of remarkable experiments guided by remarkable models of neural coding. But like the story for form, I see it as very limited, for it tells us only how variation in wavelength is encoded by the peripheral visual nervous system. It does not tell us how we perceive color. Hence, I want to comment only on the sixth reason above—we know little about how perception of color occurs.

In the laboratory, most research on color vision uses two-dimensional displays to illuminate adjacent areas of the retina with light of differing spectral compositions. This makes the psychophysical task very easy, since the subject can easily locate the colors and assign them to the proper display surface.

But how is color attached to objects or surfaces when the surfaces also have to be perceived? Our theories today simply assume that color, like form, is another attribute of stimulation, an attribute that is independently processed and then used to fill in the surfaces of objects. In their boldest form, our theories argue that the color we perceive in a particular place in space is entirely explained by the excitation of those receptors that correspond to that particular place at that moment in time, and by the unvarying chain of neural events that is inevitably set in motion by the activation of those receptors. But we know that this has to be naive. It holds true only for trivial two-dimensional displays such as those typically used. For the same reason that form cannot precede space, neither can color. The perceived color of the surface depends on how we perceive the surface itself in space, especially its orientation and distance, as well as the arrangements of lighting (see Hochberg, 1971; Beck, 1972). Color is no more an absolute or primitive property of perception than are shape, form, and so on. Hence, a full understanding of color perception also requires that color theory be integrated into general models of space perception. Unfortunately, even such a superb scholar as Boynton (1979) never even mentions the perception of the color of real objects, or any of the contributions to color perception made by properties of space. Hopefully, we will not need another century before this is done.

Fourth Big Question: How Do We Perceive Meaning?

The history of perception research and theory over the past century reveals an inconsistent attitude toward meaning. Sometimes, the proper study of perception involved isolating it from all variables that might be called the meaningfulness of the stimulus, as if they could contaminate the purity of perception. This is quite similar to what Ebbinghaus (1885/1913) believed: that we can study memory independent of meaning. To prove it, he invented the nonsense syllable, and we struggled for a half century before we realized that memory implied meaning and the whole enterprise of nonsensical memory was nonsense. But we have been repeating the same mistake in studying perception and meaning. With the indiscriminate use of devices such as tachistoscopes, we act as if their use can prove that we need no more of a perceptual context than a one hundred millisecond slice of perceiver's life.

Research on meaning over the past century has not always been based on this approach. At times the pendulum would swing, allowing researchers at least to ask whether perception was affected by meaningfulness, or past experience, or anticipation. One such swing began about thirty-five years ago, but then took a dramatic swerve. Instead of asking whether meaning affects perception, the question is now whether the meaningfulness of the task and/or display determines not only what is perceived but the very process of perception itself. And since meaning implies some residue from prior contact with the display or prior knowledge about such displays in general, the distinction between perception and memory and perception and thought collapsed. All are now conjoined into cognition, or, more narrowly, the information-processing approach to perception. I have written two brief histories of this swerve (Haber, 1969, 1974); a more general history of cognition, by Posner and Shulman, was published in 1979.

The greatest productivity of the information-processing approach has been within the more traditional domains of verbal learning and memory, language processing of listening and reading, as well as in search, decision-processing, and reasoning. Historically these are all topics distinct from perception, topics that presumably would have to be eliminated or controlled if perception itself can be analyzed and investigated in a pure state. But in the late 1940s we began to grapple experimentally with larger contexts, trying to show that perception was influenced and often determined by motivation, expectation, and meaning. Bruner's theoretical model (1957) and the research that led up to it provided this first focus in what was called the "new look" in perception (see Erdelyi, 1974, for a more modern translation). The seminal papers by Miller and by Garner, Hake, and Eriksen, both in 1956, provided a fresh impetus by suggesting new conceptual tools and methodological operations. Their concern in each case was to show that what is perceived at any one instant cannot be treated separately from what had been previously seen—that is, from the knowledge possessed by the perceiver. Perception occurs in a context; it cannot be distinct from memory.

Context is the principle of overriding concern of the information-processing approach in this current swing. All cognitive activities, including perception, occur in a context—a context of current stimulation, of assumptions about that stimulation, or prior knowledge about such displays and tasks, and of procedures for processing and retaining the current stimulation.

271

The dramatic swerve of the current pendulum swing has enlarged the focus and blurred the boundaries of once clearly isolated topics. Now we are asking for details about the initial perceptual stages of each of these broader topics. To take just one example, that of reading, we have a resurgence of interest in eye movements in reading (e.g., Monty & Senders, 1976; Rayner, 1978); in the direction of scan (Pollatsek et al., 1981); in visual feature processing of letters (E. J. Gibson, 1969; Bouma, 1971; see R. N. Haber & L. R. Haber, 1981a for a review); in the visual processing of the shapes of words (e.g., R. N. Haber & L. R. Haber, 1981b); and in the general role of peripheral vision and the size of the visual field during reading (Rayner, 1975; McConkie, 1976). These can all be considered perceptual components of reading.

The blurred boundaries allowed other changes in focus as well. Continuing the same example, are these perceptual components altered by subsequent nonperceptual ones? Does it take less time to perceive a grouping of letters if those letters spell a familiar word? Cattell (1885) answered yes a hundred years ago, but his evidence was dismissed as a result of mere guessing (decision making) and not as a result of knowledge affecting the perception itself. Now the issue is joined again, since we have the same evidence even with guessing biases controlled (e.g., Reicher, 1969; Johnston, 1978; see Krueger, 1975, for a review).

If it is true that the meaningfulness of a word affects its perceptability directly, how do we account for this? Do we enlarge the stimulus analysis to include the meaning of the stimulus as part of the stimulus itself, or do we enlarge the processing variables to include the subject's knowledge of that meaning? Consider what appears to be a simpler case than that of reading. Using any one of a variety of tasks, it is easier, faster, or more accurate to respond to a nonsense sequence of letters that are pronounceable as compared to a sequence that cannot be pronounced. The rules of English that specify the allowable co-occurrences of phonemes in a single morpheme are highly regular and greatly restricted, and fully described by Whorf (1956). The mapping of letters to sounds, while not as regular, is sufficiently precise so that most reader-speakers of English agree on most pronunciations (see Venezky, 1970). These rule systems together represent a description of the stimulus letter sequence—is it pronounceable or not, and if not, what is the nature of the violations of pronunciation? This is a description of the stimulus, based upon an analysis of the regularities found in English. It can be carried out by examining words without recourse to any subject. Yet these rules also are known to each adult native English speaker, and to lesser degrees by younger subjects, non-native speakers, nonreaders, or those with various kinds of developmental disabilities. So the pronunciation differences among different sequences can be described as an aspect of the letter sequences themselves, and as part of a knowledge system of the subject. We need each description: a full description of the stimulus (rules restricting letter sequences), readers' knowledge of such rules, and the way in which that knowledge is then used to respond to any particular sequence of letters. For completeness, we also need to know the process by which this knowledge of the rule systems was acquired, since only then can we properly account for the performance differences between normal native adults and native children, non-native adults or children, and developmentally disabled children and adults.

This example from word recognition illustrates the same theoretical analysis as should properly be applied to every other task in perception. We need to know the stimulus, the aspects of the stimulus known by the perceiver (especially the rules which govern its organization), and how those rules are typically used by that same perceiver. If we as theorists and experimenters attend to only some of those, the analysis can be incorrect and our understanding of the phenomenon inadequate.

Contextual analyses have not sprung forth full-blown. In fact, in spite of their commitment to context, information-processing theories have been remarkably slow to pursue the full implications of this commitment. Consider the subcomponent skills and processes that are part of the context of reading. Probably the single most studied topic in cognitive psychology is that of word recognition. A variety of research designs are used to assess the variables that affect the identification, recognition, or comparison of sequences of letters that may or may not spell a real word. Virtually all of these designs involve the presentation of the stimulus in isolation. The important variables affecting a nonword include the pronounceability of the letter sequence and the regularity of its spelling patterns (intrinsically confounded with pronounceability, at least in English). The major variables affecting a real word are the frequency with which the word has appeared in print and the expectancy that a particular word might be presented.

However, since we rarely encounter nonwords, and almost as rarely encounter real words in isolation from a context of a full sentence set in a larger context of a passage of sentences, can the results from word perception research in isolation explain how we perceive words in context? I think not. With respect to regularity of pronunciations and spelling of nonwords, these findings are as yet irrelevant to the perception of real words, since all real words are by definition pronounceable and properly spelled. If these variables are to be made useful at all (a dubious enterprise), we need to have a metric for the degree of regularity of spelling and pronunciation among real words. Are some real words easier to see because their spelling patterns are more regular than some other words? While it may be possible to construct such a metric, no one has ever tried to apply one to perception of words.

Despite this limited utility, variables of pronounceability and spelling have been used in testing theories of the reading process. For example, the still on-going debate about whether normal skilled reading has a necessary subvocal translation component from print to speech has been fueled by findings that the pronounceability of nonword letter sequences affect their identification, recognition, or comparison. While there is other evidence relevant to both sides of this debate (see Levy, 1978, for a review), unless the pronounceability among real words varies and effects their perception, such evidence regarding nonwords ought to be irrelevant to the question of speech recoding in reading.

The real word variables of frequency and expectancy are equally uninformative. Frequency of occurrence in print, which presumably reflects the number of encounters a reader has had with a printed word before, does not, by itself, tell us why a more frequent word is easier to see. We need to run further experiments to isolate the different effects frequency of prior occurrence might have. Does a more frequent word have specific properties that differentiate it from a less frequent one? Several possibilities exist. Frequency and length are correlated in English (the shorter the word, the more frequent it is likely to be), as is frequency and part of speech (function words being much more frequent than nouns or verbs, for example). Further, it is possible that the more often a word is perceived, the more likely its letter units are to combine into a larger single unit (Healy, 1980) so that the letters do not have to be processed one by one. Each of these are possible consequences of frequency and need to be studied in their own right.

The expectancy variable is the most interesting one, for it shows that it is easier to perceive a particular word when that word is expected to occur than when it is not. One obvious aspect of context is to provide information that changes expectancies about any particular item appearing. Thus, showing that the manipulation of expectancies can change perception provides evidence that context is capable of exerting an influence on perception. The next task is to describe the context fully so that the various sources of information that affect expectancies are explicated and tested, something that is not done by merely showing that expectancy affects perception. Thus, we need for printed text a complete stimulus analysis comparable to what J. J. Gibson accomplished for space.

For all of these reasons, then, the proper way to study word recognition is to study reading in full context. Only within a passage can we determine the variables that affect whether we will perceive a particular word or not—in isolation, the perception of that word may be determined by an entirely different set of combinations of variables, combinations that do not generalize to the context case at all. This is the same argument advanced earlier. If most of the richness of information about the layout of space or text is withheld from the perceiver, it is not surprising if he utilizes novel or different processes, or calls upon normally unused sources of information.

Without an adequate stimulus description in reading, that is, a full linguistic description of how meaning is represented in text, we continue to repeat in reading research the Helmholtzian mistakes made in research on space. We select one narrow, local, visible aspect of the stimulus—a letter or a word—and ask how that element is processed into meaning, or into comprehension, in just the same way that we singled out retinal size, or luminance, or an edge, and asked how that is processed into an object or scene. Independent combinations of single letters or words can no more be mapped into the meaning of a story or a conversation or a poem than a concatenation of independent edges can be mapped onto a scene out the window.

Since so much of our research has been based on looking at single elements, it is not surprising that many theories of reading treat these single elements as the basic units of meaning. Thus, the current bottom-up models of reading (e.g., Gough, 1972) argue that the perceiver begins with the lowest level of visual features of the letters, uses those to build whole letters, then goes from letters to words, and so forth, without any reference to prior knowledge of spelling rules, syntax, or expectations about what the topic of the passage might be.

If there is one result of Gibson's work, it has been to show us the richness of the information available to the eyes, richness in the sense that this information can describe the entire structure of visual space. A comparable analysis is needed for language stimuli. Chomsky's work (1957, 1965) made the best start we have, for he has tried to provide a structural analysis of language in which meaning is described by linguistic structure. Such an analysis of structure can be carried out in an armchair, without recourse to experimental data, in the same way that a geometrical analysis of the mapping of space onto a projection surface such as the retina is possible in the absence of a real perceiver. Only when we know how meaning is represented in text can we begin to ask questions about how perceivers acquire that meaning.

The reliance on procedures which present isolated elements, seen in a single glance, without a context, is declining. With the decline, our research is being replaced with fuller and more accurate descriptions of the organization of the stimulus, such as the full text in reading research. That description then permits us to determine the interaction of processing strategies with that text and to have some hope of learning about the perceptual components of the reading process. I have singled out reading as an example, but the questions of the perception of meaning occur in issues of language processing more generally, familiarity in scenes and pictures, decision making, and all of the topics of cognitive psychology. If we can keep the focus on the role of context, we can expect an explosive century on this big question.

The discussion in this section on meaning has focused primarily on the pitfalls of trying to study meaning without knowing what it is. Two other kinds of errors have beset current information-processing work. The first of these concerns the relationship of theories of information processing of meaning to theories of information processing of space.

The perceiver of color, or form, or meaning, is the same perceiver who perceives space. Any theory that isolates these perceivers and treats their abilities as unrelated should be considered most suspiciously. As only one example, consider the invention of the concept of iconic memory (see Haber, 1983, for a more detailed description of this sad story).

Sperling (1960) demonstrated that for a short time following the termination of a brief tachistoscopic flash, the perceiver had available all of the information that had been in the stimulus presentation itself. He called this a visual information store, and likened it to a persisting visual image. Neisser (1967) renamed this persistence an icon. Subsequent evidence supported Sperling's findings, specifically that the icon possessed very high capacity and decayed rapidly. Other studies showed that visual persistence following a brief flash could be measured directly, which further supported these properties (e.g., Haber & Standing, 1970). From these results, the icon has been treated as the initial storehouse of information, and while it lasts only a quarter second or so, that time has been considered the base from which all subsequent processing and extraction of information occurs.

What has been overlooked is that this type of sensory memory occurs only following brief tachistoscopic flashes that themselves last less than about a quarter-second. Such presentations have no natural counterpart in nature, unless you are trying to read during a lightning storm. There are no natural occasions in which the retina is statically stimulated for less than about a quarter of a second, preceded and followed by blankness. Rather, with stimulation controlled by saccadic eye movements, the stimulus itself is always available for a minimum of a quarter of a second, and often much longer. There is no need for a persistence mechanism to extend brief stimulation up to a quarter of a second: the stimulus itself does it for us. Any icon would not only be superfluous, it would never be noticed because the stimulus itself would provide much better stimulation, stimulation that did not decay.

So icons are silly to have during saccadic control of perception, as in visual exploration, search, or reading. But they are worse than silly when we are moving through visual space, as we are doing almost all of the time. Most of the information we receive about the layout of space, the location and shapes of objects, and of our position in space comes through the continuous motion perspective changes that occur in stimulation reaching the retina as a result of our bodily movements. Under such circumstances there never is a fixed snapshot-like retinal image, frozen in time, but rather a continuously changing one. Again, any persistence, even if one were generated, would be superfluous and probably detrimental to accurate perceiving.

These observations are not new (see Hochberg, 1968; Neisser, 1976; Turvey, 1977; Haber, 1983), but they are not taken seriously because our models are kept isolated from everyday perception. The icon was born in the laboratory, and it has life only there and nowhere else. Out in the real world we have no need to invent a sensory memory device. Where we do need one, the stimulus itself provides it. The rest of the time, the concept of an icon, or of sensory memory, makes no sense at all.

I have singled out the icon as an example where laboratory analysis of memory is isolated from general perception, but there are others as well. Information-processing research has to keep in mind that not much of perception occurs only for two-dimensional static displays such as print. And when that is the stimulus, the perceptual process has demands placed on it that are rather atypical. Information-processing researchers have to consider all the circumstances in which we process information, in order to be sure they do not invent silly concepts. It is critical that a theory constructed to account for how we process meaning in print also be applicable to how we process the identification of the three-dimensional objects we normally view.

A second error in information-processing research concerns the specificity of our operations and the narrow range of tasks and data to which they apply. We have been incredibly ingenious in the design of perception experiments, especially in the application of converging operations to information processing. The use of concepts developed by signal-detection theory has virtually removed criterion-bias problems from psychophysical research. Our ability to specify levels of processes and to isolate component parts is now very much better than even a decade ago.

But all this experimental sophistication brings serious problems with it due to the absence of corresponding growth in our knowledge of how to create theories. Our methods are now far better than our theories. Any experiment now can provide enough evidence to reject any version of a general theory applied to it. We have so much power in our methods that we have been forced to reduce the breadth of our theories. They have a narrow base, limited range, little integration with other theories, and no generality. Each has its own minor theory. Whether we are going to back off the power on the one hand or devise some ways of making more general theories on the other is not yet clear, but something has to give soon.

This brings me to the end of my brief review of four big questions of the perception of space, form, color, and meaning. I cannot defend these questions as the only ones of importance in the past century, but they do illustrate most of the richness of the century, and many of its failures as well.

I have described the failures and increasing success of our recent work within a matrix of two main frameworks: our growing integration of stimulus analyses and analyses of processing, and the recent focus on larger contexts on which to base this integration.

In conclusion, I have not tried to provide a historical perspective, but rather an appraisal of the current scene. This has been a great century for perception, probably better for perception than for any other area in psychology. A hundred years ago we were farther along than the rest of psychology, and I think we have more than kept pace. The next century should be even better, especially if we can keep in mind that we evolved our visual system in order to be able to perceive visual space around us. Only by studying perception in that context can we come fully to appreciate how it functions. I think we are now able to do this, so I am very optimistic about the future.

277

II. THE SPECIAL FIELDS OF PSYCHOLOGY

REFERENCES

Attneave, F. Some informational aspects of visual perception. *Psychological Review*, 1954, *61*, 183–193.

Barlow, H. B. Summation and inhibition in the frog's retina. *Journal of Physiology*, 1953, *119*, 69–88.

Beck, J. *Surface color perception*. Ithaca, N.Y.: Cornell University Press, 1972.

Bekesy, G. Von. Neural inhibitory units of the eye and skin: Quantitative description of contrast phenomena. *Journal of the Optical Society of America*, 1960, *50*, 1060–1070.

Berkeley, G. An essay towards a new theory of vision. In A. C. Fraser (Ed.), *Selections from Berkeley*. Oxford: Clarendon, 1910. (Originally published, 1709.)

Bobrow, D. G., & Norman, D. A. Some principles of memory schemata. In D. G. Bobrow & A. M. Collins (Eds.), *Representation and understanding*. New York: Academic Press, 1977.

Bouma, H. Visual recognition of isolated lower case letters. *Vision Research*, 1971, *11*, 459–474.

Bower, T. G. R. *Development in infancy*. San Francisco: Freeman, 1974.

Boynton, R. M. *Human color perception*. New York: Holt, 1979.

Bruner, J. S. On perceptual readiness. *Psychological Review*, 1957, *64*, 123–152.

Cattell, J. McK. Ueber die Zeit der Erkennung und Benennung von Schriftzeichen Bildern und Farben. *Philosophische Studien*, 1885, *2*, 635–650.

Chomsky, N. *Syntactic structures*. The Hauge: Mouton, 1957.

Chomsky, N. *Aspects of a theory of syntax*. Cambridge, Mass.: M.I.T. Press, 1965.

Cohen, L. B., & Salapatek, P. (Eds.). *Infant perception: From sensation to cognition*. (2 Vols.) New York: Academic Press, 1975.

Coren, S., & Girgus, J. S. Illusions and constancies. In W. Epstein (Ed.), *Stability and constancy in visual perception*. New York: Wiley, 1977.

Cornsweet, T. N. *Visual perception*. New York: Academic Press, 1970.

DeValois, R. L., & DeValois, K. K. Neural coding of color. In E. C. Carterette & M. P. Friedman (Eds.), *Handbook of perception* (Vol. 5). New York: Academic Press, 1975.

Ebbinghaus, H. *Über das Gedächtnis*. Leipzig: Duncker, 1885. (H. Ruyer & C. E. Bussenius, trans. [*Memory*].) New York: Teachers College, Columbia University Press, 1913.

Epstein, W. The process of "taking-into-account" in visual perception. *Perception*, 1973, *2*, 267–285.

Erdelyi, M. A new look at the new look: Perceptual defense and vigilance. *Psychological Review*, 1974, *81*, 1–25.

Fantz, R. L. The origin of form perception. *Scientific American*, 1961, *204*, 66–72.

Garner, W. R., Hake, H. W., & Eriksen, C. W. Operationism and the concept of perception. *Psychological Review*, 1956, *63*, 317–329.

Gibson, E. J. *Principles of perceptual learning and development*. Englewood Cliffs, N.J.: Prentice-Hall, 1969.

Gibson, J. J. *The perception of the visual world*. Boston: Houghton Mifflin, 1950.

Gibson, J. J. *The senses considered as perceptual systems*. Boston: Houghton Mifflin, 1966.

Gibson, J. J. *The ecological approach to visual perception*. Boston: Houghton Mifflin, 1979.

Gilchrist, A. L. Perceived lightness depends on perceived spacial arrangement. *Science*, 1977, *195*, 185–187.

Gilchrist, A. L. The perception of surface blacks and whites. *Scientific American*, 1979, *240*, 112–124.

Gough, P. B. One second of reading. In J. P. Kavanagh & I. G. Mattingly (Eds.), *Language by ear and by eye*. Cambridge, Mass.: M.I.T. Press, 1972.

Gyr, J. W. Is a theory of direct visual perception adequate? *Psychological Bulletin*, 1972, *77*, 246–261.

Gyr, J., Willey, R., & Henry, A. Motor-sensory feedback and geometry of visual space: An attempted replication. *Behavioral and Brain Sciences*, 1979, *2*, 59–94.

Haber, L. R., & Haber, R. N. Visual processes in reading. In F. J. Pirozzolo & M. C. Wittrock (Eds.),

Neuropsychological and cognitive processes in reading. New York: Academic Press, 1981, pp. 167–200.

Haber, R. N. Introduction to information processing. In R. N. Haber (Ed.), *Information processing approaches to visual perception.* New York: Holt, 1969, pp. 1–15.

Haber, R. N. Information processing. In E. C. Carterette & M. P. Friedman (Eds.), *Handbook of perception* (Vol. 1). New York: Academic Press, 1974, pp. 313–333.

Haber, R. N. How we perceive depth from flat pictures. *American Scientist,* 1980, *68,* 37–380. (a)

Haber, R. N. Perceiving space from pictures: A theoretical analysis. In M. A. Hagan (Ed.), *The psychology of representational art* (Vol. 1). New York: Academic Press, 1980, pp. 3–31. (b)

Haber, R. N. The impending demise of the icon, and good riddance. *Behavioral and Brain Sciences,* 1983, *6,* 1–55.

Haber, R. N., & Haber, L. R. Visual components of the reading process. *Visual Language,* 1981, *15,* 147–182. (a)

Haber, R. N., & Haber, L. R. The shape of a word can specify its meaning. *Reading Research Quarterly,* 1981, *13,* 334–345. (b)

Haber, R. N., & Hershenson, M. *The psychology of visual perception* (2nd ed.). New York: Holt, 1980.

Haber, R. N., & Standing, L. Direct estimates of apparent duration of a flash followed by visual noise. *Canadian Journal of Psychology,* 1970, *24,* 216–229.

Hagen, M. A. Picture perception: Toward a theoretical model. *Psychological Bulletin,* 1974, *81,* 471–497.

Hagen, M. A. The development of sensitivity to cast and attached shadows in pictures as information for the direction of the source of illumination. *Perception and Psychophysics,* 1976, *20,* 25–28.

Hagen, M. A. (Ed.). *The perception of pictures I: Alberti's window. The projective model of pictorial information.* New York: Academic Press, 1980. (a)

Hagen, M. A. (Ed.). *The perception of pictures II: Dürer's devices. Beyond the projective model of pictures.* New York: Academic Press, 1980. (b)

Haith, M. M. *Rules that newborns look by.* Hillsdale, N.J.: Erlbaum, 1981.

Haith, M. M., Bergman, T., & Moore, M. J. Eye contact and face scanning in early infancy. *Science,* 1977, *198,* 853–855.

Hartline, H. K., & Ratliff, F. Inhibitory interaction of receptor units in the eye of Limulus. *Journal of General Physiology,* 1957, *40,* 357–376.

Healy, A. F. Proofreading errors on the word "the": New evidence on reading units. *Journal of Experimental Psychology: Human Perception and Performance,* 1980, *6,* 45–57.

Helmholtz, H. von. *Treatise on physiological optics* (Vol. II) (J. P. Southall, Ed. and trans., from the 3rd German ed.). Rochester, N.Y.: Optical Society of America, 1924. (Originally published, 1866.)

Hering, E. Über die Theorie des simultanen Kontrastes von Helmholtz, Vierte Mitteilung. *Pflüger's Archiv,* 1888, *43,* 1–21.

Hochberg, J. In the mind's eye. In R. N. Haber (Ed.), *Contemporary theory and research in visual perception.* New York: Holt, 1968.

Hochberg, J. Perception: I. Color and shape. In J. Kling & L. A. Riggs (Eds.), *Handbook of experimental psychology.* New York: Holt, 1971.

Hochberg, J. Organization and the Gestalt tradition. In E. C. Carterette & M. Friedman (Eds.), *Handbook of perception* (Vol. 1). New York: Academic Press, 1973.

Hochberg, J. Higher order stimuli and interresponse coupling in perception of the visual world. In R. B. Macleod and H. L. Pick, Jr. (Eds.), *Perception: Essays in honor of James J. Gibson.* Ithaca, N.Y.: Cornell University Press, 1974.

Hochberg, J. *Perception* (2nd ed.). Englewood Cliffs, N.J.: Prentice-Hall, 1979.

Hochberg, J., & McAlister, E. A quantitative approach to figural "goodness." *Journal of Experimental Psychology,* 1953, *46,* 361–364.

279

Hochberg, J., & Brooks, V. The perception of motion pictures. In E. C. Carterette & M. P. Friedman (Eds.), *Handbook of perception* (Vol. 10). New York: Academic Press, 1978.

Holst, E. von. Relations between the central nervous system and the peripheral organs. *British Journal of Animal Behavior*, 1954, 2, 89–94.

Hubel, D. H., & Wiesel, T. N. Receptive fields, binocular interaction and functional architecture in the cat's visual cortex. *Journal of Physiology*, 1962, 160, 106–154.

Hubel, D. H., & Wiesel, T. N. Receptive fields and functional architecture of monkey striate cortex. *Journal of Physiology*, 1968, 195, 215–243.

Ittelson, W. H. *Visual space perception*. New York: Springer, 1960.

James, W. *The principles of psychology*. New York: Holt, 1890.

Johnston, J. C. A test of the sophisticated guessing theory of word perception. *Cognitive Psychology*, 1978, 10, 123–153.

Julesz, B. *Foundations of cyclopean perception*. Chicago: The University of Chicago Press, 1971.

Katz, D. *The world of color* (R. B. MacLeod & C. W. Fox, trans.). London: Kegan Paul, 1935.

Kessen, W., Haith, M. M., & Salapatek, P. H. Infancy. In P. H. Mussen (Ed.), *Carmichael's manual of child psychology* (3rd ed.). New York: Wiley, 1971.

Krueger, L. E. Familiarity effects in visual information processing. *Psychological Bulletin*, 1975, 82, 949–974.

Kuffler, W. S. Discharge patterns and functional organization of mammalian retinas. *Journal of Neurophysiology*, 1953, 16, 37–68.

Levy, B. A. Speech processes during reading. In A. M. Lesgold, J. W. Pellegrino, S. D. Fokkema, & R. Glaser (Eds.), *Cognitive psychology and instruction*. New York: Plenum, 1978.

Lindsay, P. H., & Norman, D. A. *Human information processing* (2nd ed.). New York: Academic Press, 1978.

Locke, J. *An essay concerning human understanding* (A. C. Fraser, Ed.). New York: Dover Publications, 1959. (Originally published, 1690.)

McConkie, G. W. The use of eye-movement data in determining the perceptual span in reading. In R. A. Monty & J. W. Senders (Eds.), *Eye movements and psychological processes*. Hillsdale, N.J.: Erlbaum, 1976.

Miller, G. A. The magical number seven, plus or minus two. *Psychological Review*, 1956, 63, 81–97.

Mitchell, Donald E. Effect of early visual experience on the development of certain perceptual abilities in animals and man. In R. D. Walk & H. L. Pick, Jr. (Eds.), *Perception and experience*. New York: Plenum, 1978.

Monty, R. A., & Senders, J. W. (Eds.). *Eye movements and psychological processes*. Hillsdale, N.J.: Erlbaum, 1976.

Neisser, U. *Cognitive psychology*. Englewood Cliffs, N.J.: Prentice-Hall, 1967.

Neisser, U. *Cognition and reality*. San Francisco: Freeman, 1976.

Pirenne, M. *Optics, painting, and photography*. Cambridge: Cambridge University Press, 1970.

Pollatsek, A., Bolozky, S., Well, A. D., & Rayner, K. Asymmetrics in the perceptual span for Israeli readers. *Brain and Language*, 1981, 14, 174–180.

Polyak, S. L. *The vertebrate visual system*. Chicago: The University of Chicago Press, 1957.

Posner, M. I., & Shulman, G. L. Cognitive science. In E. Hearst (Ed.), *The first century of experimental psychology*. Hillsdale, N.J.: Erlbaum, 1979.

Pylyshyn, Z. W. Computation and cognition: Issues in the foundations of cognitive science. *Behavioral and Brain Sciences*, 1980, 3, 111–169.

Rayner, K. The perceptual span and peripheral cues in reading. *Cognitive psychology*, 1975, 7, 65–81.

Rayner, K. Eye movements in reading. *Psychological Bulletin*, 1978, 85, 1–50.

Regan, D. M., Beverley, K., & Cynader, M. The visual perception of motion in depth. *Scientific American*, 1979, 241, 136–151.

Reicher, G. M. Perceptual recognition as a function of meaningfulness of stimulus material. *Journal of Experimental Psychology*, 1969, *81*, 275–280.

Richards, W. Visual space perception. In E. C. Carterette & M. P. Friedman (Eds.), *Handbook of perception* (Vol. 5). New York: Academic Press, 1975.

Rock, I. In defense of unconscious inference. In W. Epstein (Ed.), *Stability and constancy of visual perception*. New York: Wiley, 1977.

Rock, I. Anorthoscopic perception. *Scientific American*, 1981, *244(3)*, 145–153.

Rubin, E. *Visuell wahrgenomenne Figuren*. Copenhagen: Gyldendalske, 1921.

Selfridge, O. G. Pandemonium: A paradigm for learning. In *The mechanization of thought processes*. London: H. M. Stationery Office, 1959.

Sperling, G. The information available in brief visual presentation. *Psychological Monographs*, 1960, 74(11, Whole No. 498).

Stevens, J. K., Emerson, R. C., Gerstein, G. L., Kallos, T., Neufeld, G. R., Nichols, C. W., & Rosenquist, A. C. Paralysis of the awake human: Visual perceptions. *Vision Research*, 1976, *16*, 93–98.

Sutherland, N. S. Object recognition. In E. C. Carterette & M. P. Friedman (Eds.), *Handbook of perception* (Vol. 3). New York: Academic Press, 1974.

Turvey, M. T. Contrasting orientations to the theory of visual information processing. *Psychological Review*, 1977, 84, 67–88.

Ullman, S. *The interpretation of visual motion*. Cambridge, Mass.: M.I.T. Press, 1979.

Ullman, S. Against direct perception. *Behavioral and Brain Sciences*, 1980, 3, 373–416.

Venezky, R. L. *The structure of English orthography*. The Hague: Mouton, 1970.

Wallach, H. Brightness constancy and the nature of achromatic colors. *Journal of Experimental Psychology*, 1948, 38, 310–324.

Wheatstone, C. Contributions to the physiology of vision, I. On some remarkable and hitherto unobserved phenomena of binocular vision. *Philosophical Transactions of the Royal Society*, 1838, *128*, 371–394.

Whorf, B. L. Linguistics as an exact science. In J. B. Carroll (Ed.), *Language, thought and reality*. New York: Wiley, 1956.

Winston, P. H. *The psychology of computer vision*. New York: McGraw-Hill, 1975.

Young, T. On the theory of light and colours. In *Lectures in natural philosophy* (Vol. 2). London: Printed for Joseph Johnson, St. Paul's Church Yard, by William Savage, 1807.

LEARNING

12

*Conditioning and Learning**

GREGORY A. KIMBLE

The scientific study of the psychology of learning originated in the late nineteenth century in three very different parts of the world. In Russia the great physiologist Ivan Petrovich Pavlov turned from work on digestion to the investigation of classically conditioned reflexes. In America Edward Lee Thorndike did his early studies of animal intelligence that were somewhat complex versions of what later came to be called "instrumental" or "operant conditioning." In Germany Hermann Ebbinghaus invented the nonsense syllable and began his self-inflicted studies of human verbal learning and memory. In this paper we review the history that grew out of the first two of these contributions.

Setting the Methodological Stage

To appreciate the history of conditioning and learning one must understand the scholarly climate in which this study emerged. By the end of the nineteenth century, dominant decisions had been made about human nature and how to know it. The most influential scholars in those days had taken a stand in favor of certain

* A somewhat expanded version of this chapter appears in G. A. Kimble and K. Schlesinger, *Topics in the History of Psychology* (New York: Wiley, 1984).

methodological "isms" that specified the framework within which the psychology of learning developed: empiricism, elementism, associationism, and materialism.

Empiricism

The most important ideas determining the nature of the emerging scientific study of learning were put forth by the British empiricists over a period of some three hundred years, from about 1600 to about 1900. All of the methodological principles just mentioned appeared in their writings. Possibly the most basic of these was the proposal that knowledge comes from experience with the world. This idea has two closely related consequences. The first is that it carries a directive as to the nature of scientific procedures: they must be based upon observation rather than opinion, intuition, or authority.

The second is more closely related to the psychology of learning. John Locke (1632–1704) put the position in its most quotable form. The mind of the child, he said, is a blank slate (tabula rasa) upon which experience writes. Adult mental life is merely the record of the previous history of the person. Although today we recognize such statements as too radically empiristic, they legitimized the study of a person's history of experience, one way of considering the process of learning.

Elementism

The major goal of the British empiricists was to understand the mind or consciousness. In their striving toward such understanding, they relied upon the method of analysis which had achieved such success in physical science, especially chemistry. Consciousness, they held, consisted of mental elements. These were ideas, and because each corresponded to a unit of experience, it was sensory or perceptual in nature. This conception led to efforts to determine the number of mental elements in existence—to discover a psychological "periodic table." The question of how these elements combined to recreate consciousness as we know it was answered in terms of associationism, which, in the words of John Stuart Mill (1806–1873), was the essential process of the new "mental chemistry."

Associationism

The assignment of this basic role to association and the attempted descriptions of the process led to the formulation of several sets of proposed laws of association. The law proposed most often was a *law of contiguity* which states that associations are most easily formed between experiences that occur closely together in time and space. Other suggested laws of association were those of *similarity, contrast, vividness, frequency,* and *recency.* Although they are seldom, if ever, called laws, these conceptions have survived and appear in discussions of learning and memory today.

285

Materialism

Although some of the British empiricists interpreted the sensory elements in terms of physicalistic "vibrations" in the brain, the most significant materialistic themes were developed in the field of biology. René Descartes (1596–1650), sometimes called the father of physiology, made modest beginnings. He developed the view that the material human body is controlled by an immaterial soul. Descartes believed that the site of this interaction was the pineal gland which, under the direction of the soul, controlled the flow of animal spirits through nervous tubules to determine bodily actions. Among Descartes's contributions was a clear statement of the concept of reflex. Later on in the history of our topic, reflexes were to become an alternative to sensations as the fundamental elements out of which psychological processes are built.

In the course of this history two developments had a particular significance for the study of learning. The first was the independent discovery by Sir Charles Bell (1774–1842) in England and by François Magendie (1783–1855) in France that a segregation of function occurs in the nervous system at the level of the spinal cord. Sensory nerves enter by way of the dorsal roots and motor fibers exit by way of the ventral roots. The importance of this discovery is related to the concepts of elementism and associationism. Now a new stimulus-response form of associationism became possible. A century later the question of whether associative learning involves stimuli and responses or sensations (the *ideas* of the British empiricists) had become the focus of bitter dispute.

In the meantime Charles Darwin (1809–1882) had published his theory of evolution and had added a new perspective to the developing materialistic view of behavior, the concept that it is adaptive. This was the second development in biology of significance for the psychology of learning. Later on, the functionalists were to make the concept of the adaptive value of mental processes central to their theory.

Russian Reflexology

The founding father of Russian reflexology was Ivan Michailovich Sechenov (1829–1905). The details of his writings show that, at least in those days, the dominant intellectual themes in Russia were the same as in the West. On empiricism, Sechenov maintained that ". . . 999/1000 of the contents of the mind depends upon education in the broadest sense, and only 1/1000 depends on individuality" (1863/1935, p. 335). The features of elementism and materialism were closely related to each other. Sechenov nominated the reflex as elementary unit of behavior and this was a materialistic proposal. Sechenov was quite specific on the point that all behavior was built up of reflexes piece by piece. In addition he accepted Darwin's proposal that reflexes are adaptive, calling attention to the way in which the reflexes of blinking, sneezing, and coughing expelled injurious foreign objects from the body. Finally, Sechenov supported associationism as the mechanism by which the creation of complex behavior is accomplished and described the process of association as one in which the proprioceptive stimulus produced by a first reflex is connected to the stimulus that elicits a second reflex. Thus Sechenov's associationism was stimulus-stimulus (S-S) association. All of these ideas were to become a part of Pavlovian theory.

Ivan Petrovich Pavlov and Classical Conditioning

The basic idea behind the study of conditioning seems to have suggested itself during Pavlov's earlier work on digestion for which he received the Nobel Prize in 1904. In much of this work Pavlov used dogs with esophageal and stomach fistulae, as shown in Figure 12.1. In the condition illustrated, these animals "ate" the food provided for them but it never reached the stomach. In spite of this the stomach secreted gastric juice much as it would have had the food been eaten normally. This could only mean that the taste of food and/or the acts of chewing and swallowing were stimulating gastric secretion, presumably by connections through the brain.

Conditioning Experiments

With this simple but brilliant insight Pavlov turned to his studies of salivation which was much easier to measure than gastric activity. All that was necessary was to make a minor incision in a dog's cheek and to bring the parotid gland outside the cheek to allow the measurement of the amount of salivation secreted. As is well known, Pavlov did his conditioning experiments on dogs prepared in this way. In these experiments, Pavlov (1927) discovered most of the basic phenomena of condition-

Figure 12.1 Dog with esophageal fistula and gastric fistula (Asratyan, 1949).

ing, which there is room here only to list (see Kimble, 1961, pp. 44–108, for a more complete description): acquisition, extinction, spontaneous recovery, higher-order conditioning, the generalization of excitation and inhibition, differential conditioning, summation, external inhibition, conditioned inhibition, and inhibition of delay.

The general character of these phenomena has suggested to many psychologists that Pavlovian conditioning is of significance only for simple behavior in simple organisms. Pavlov, himself, did not see it that way. He believed that the mechanisms of conditioning could explain the most elaborate features of human behavior.

Assessment

Pavlov's Huxley Lecture, delivered at the Charing Cross Hospital in London in 1906, on the scientific investigation of the psychical faculties in animals appeared in *Science* and became available to Western psychology. Details of Pavlov's experiments were summarized three years later in a review by Yerkes and Morgulis (1909). This information did not, however, lead to any immediate replications of Pavlov's work in America. There are probably several reasons for this. A minor problem was that American investigators had difficulty with the Pavlovian techniques of collecting saliva. A more important point was that other methods had developed, and, without recognizing that there might be an important difference, American investigators had turned to a variety of instrumental, or operant, conditioning procedures.

What, then, was Pavlov's contribution to the psychology of learning? From a later perspective, there appear to have been two contributions. The first was a factual one. Most of the conditioning phenomena discovered by Pavlov turned out to be general ones that appeared in other forms of learning. Thus Pavlov contributed knowledge out of which psychology hoped to create a scientific account of human and animal behavior. The second contribution was that Pavlov's method provided an alternative to the introspectionistic psychology that was dominant in those days, but seemed inappropriate to psychology as it was developing.

American Functionalism

In early twentieth-century America, the leader of experimental psychology was Edward Bradford Titchener (1867–1927), whose thinking was in the tradition of the British empiricists. He identified the subject matter of psychology as the mind or consciousness, and its most important method as introspection. The purpose of this method was to analyze the content of consciousness into its elements. The general idea was that these elements were the basic building blocks of the mind, the units of its structure. Hence the position was called *structuralism*.

As early as 1884, in an article in *Mind* entitled "On Some Omissions of Intro-spective Psychology," William James was writing in a vein that was very critical of structural psychology. The difference between James's position and that of the structuralists was basic. Whereas the structuralists presented a picture of mind as composed of static content, James spoke of a "stream of consciousness," made up of substantive terms that are "stopped over" for an instant, only to give way to transitive "moments of flight." One difficulty with introspective psychology is that it cannot handle these moments of flight. For to introspect upon them is to stop them, to make them substantive, and to lose the very object of introspection. Directing the light of introspection against the stream of thought is like turning up the gas lamp to see how the darkness looks.

A related criticism made by James in the same article, and by many others elsewhere, was that an awareness of our subjective states modifies them. We have all had the experience of examining a mood of joy or anger only to find ourselves a little less joyous or a bit less angry. Particularly the emotions, but to a degree all mental states, present this problem for the introspective method.

A third criticism that James had for the structuralists involved their obsession with analysis: "What God has joined together, they resolutely and wantonly put asunder." This James considered to be the root of all introspective evil. Typically, as James saw it, introspection analyzed the unanalyzable and then indulged itself in the meaningless exercise of trying to synthesize the original object of analysis. James gave this procedure short shrift in the observation that two pinks (the products of analysis) do not make one scarlet (the mental state with which the analysis began).

There were also other dissatisfactions with the structuralist position, particularly with the introspective method. Psychology was developing an interest in child development, mental disorder, and animal behavior. Introspection was peculiarly unsuited to the study of any of these areas. In the face of such pressures, a new psychology began to take form in which the ideas of Darwin played a central role. This new psychology stressed the adaptive value of mental processes and asked about their functions, hence its name, *functionalism*.

The Basic Tenets of Functionalism

James Rowland Angell (1869–1949) put the functionalist position before psychol-ogy in a paper entitled "The Province of Functional Psychology" (1907). He pre-sented functionalism as a return to established themes in psychology from which structuralism had briefly strayed. In the writings of Angell and the other important functionalists, Harvey Carr (1863–1954), John Dewey (1859–1952), and Robert Woodworth (1869–1962), functionalism developed as more of an attitude or gen-eral orientation than a well-defined school. Some of the features of their orientation were the following:

Mental processes have two aspects, a structural one and a functional one. It is

289

important to develop a psychology of both. Upon analysis it turns out that some psychological phenomena (e.g., idea, image) are more structural in nature; others (e.g., attention, thinking) are more functional. The basic error of structuralism lay precisely in the fact that it limited its interest to just one of these aspects. Since functionalism concerned itself with both of them, it was broader than the structural psychology with which it competed.

Functionalism was also broader in another way. The basic functionalist question is that of the adaptive value of the mental processes, the question of what they are for. This concern for the functions of mental processes led easily to a tolerance for applied psychology and an interest in mental tests, educational psychology, child development, and psychopathology. It also laid the foundation for a new view of psychology which took *behavior* rather than the mind to be the basic subject matter of the field.

Taking the cue from Darwin, seeing mental activity as involved in the struggle for .survival and as showing an adaptive function, led easily to an interest in learning. Well-ingrained habits and reflexes were seen as automatic ways of adapting to the routine requirements of existence. Functioning automatically, they allowed the mind to free itself for higher activities, coming down to these everyday matters only after moments of conflict or decision. In the language of maze learning, which came on the scene at about the same time as functionalism did, "consciousness arises at a choice-point."

Instrumental (Operant) Conditioning and Selective Learning

The study of animal learning developed in the functionalist context, and Edward Lee Thorndike (1874–1949) was the scholar in this tradition whose contribution now seems greatest. For the purpose of this record, Thorndike's most important work was his doctoral investigation of selective learning in a variety of species, including cats, dogs, chicks, fish, and monkeys. His most famous experiments were carried out with cats learning to escape from a "puzzle box" to obtain release and a bit of food as a reward. In the apparatus in the illustration (Figure 12.2), the response required of the cat was to press a treadle. In other versions, the cat learned to turn a latch, to pull a string, or to perform one or more other responses. The major data in Thorndike's experiment were from 13 cats and 3 dogs. It is probably safe to say that never in the history of psychology has so much controversy arisen from such a modest basis in fact. The controversy was, of course, not about the facts, but about three points of interpretation (Thorndike, 1911).

Stimulus-Response Connectionism

Two of these three controversial items were stated as formal laws. The third was not. This last was the concept that learning consisted of stimulus-response (S-R) connec-

Figure 12.2 Thorndike's "puzzle box" apparatus.

tions rather than the association of ideas, as the British empiricists had suggested, or stimulus-stimulus (S-S) connections as Pavlov believed. The S-R position was so essential to the statement of Thorndike's two major laws, however, that there never was any doubt as to where Thorndike stood on the issue.

The Law of Effect

Thorndike believed that reward and punishment played a critical role in learning and stated (1911) that belief as follows.

> The Law of Effect is that: Of several responses made to the same situation, those which are accompanied or closely followed by satisfaction to the animal will, other things being equal, be more firmly connected with the situation, so that, when it recurs, they will be more likely to recur; those which are accompanied or closely followed by discomfort to the animal will, other things being equal, have their connections with that situation weakened, so that, when it recurs, they will be less likely to occur. The greater the satisfaction or discomfort, the greater the strengthening or weakening of the bond (p. 244).

The law of effect came under immediate attack on two main fronts. Some claimed that the law could not be universally true. How, these critics asked, do reward and punishment play any part when we happen to remember (and therefore must have learned) that there is a mail box along the route we normally take when we walk to work? Others objected on methodological grounds, claiming first that the term "satisfier" was unscientifically subjective and that the law of effect was circular. The charge of circularity went this way: The law of effect proposes that S-R connections are strengthened because a response is followed by a satisfier; but how does one know that an event is a satisfier? By its ability to strengthen S-R connections.

This objection should never have been raised. On the page following the statement of the Law of Effect, Thorndike (1911, p. 245) made the concept of satisfier what we would now call an intervening variable and also broke the circle by giving an independent definition of a satisfier: "By a satisfying state of affairs is meant one which the animal does nothing to avoid, often doing such things as attain and preserve it." Eventually most psychologists who accepted a version of the law of effect also accepted this way of stating the logical situation.

The Law of Exercise

Thorndike's third controversial proposal was the law of exercise stated as follows.

> The Law of Exercise is that: Any response to a situation will, other things being equal, be more strongly connected with the situation in proportion to the number of times it has been connected with that situation and to the average vigor and duration of the connection (1911, p. 24).

What made the law of exercise controversial was the explicit statement that learning is gradual rather than sudden or insightful.

Later Developments

By the early 1930s Thorndike had modified his position considerably. The law of exercise was repealed (1932) largely on the basis of the observation that repetition appeared to produce no increase in the strength of strong connections. The law of effect was modified (e.g., 1932) but also strengthened. The modification was one that enhanced the importance of reward and minimized the importance of punishment in learning. This was because a variety of experimental demonstrations seemed to indicate that an annoying aftereffect did not weaken the tendency that produced it. The strengthening of the law of effect took the form of a statement that *any* S-R connection could be strengthened by a satisfying aftereffect.

The statement that *any* connection could be strengthened by reward carried an important proviso, however. Thorndike had noted that the responses an animal learned often seemed "natural" to the situation and "relevant" to the animal's wants. They somehow "belonged" to the learning situation. According to Thorndike such responses were easier for animals to acquire than others and specifically could be learned with a greater delay of satisfaction than unnatural or irrelevant responses. Thirty years later (see p. 315) this law of belongingness received full confirmation in studies of learned aversions to tastes.

Behaviorism

Behaviorism may be said to have been launched with the publication of Watson's paper, "Psychology as the Behaviorist Views It" (1913). As usual, however, many of the important concepts had been developed by others, and possibly earlier. In this case, one of the most significant early figures was a Russian contemporary of Pavlov.

Bekhterev

Vladimir M. Bekhterev (1857–1927) began his systematic investigation of "association-reflexes" during the winter of 1906–1907. In his experimental work, he used human subjects as well as dogs to study the conditioning of withdrawal and respiratory responses evoked by electric shock. Bekhterev's *Objective Psychology*, describing this work, appeared serially from 1907 to 1912, published, of course, in Russian. By 1913, however, Bekhterev's work had been translated into French and German, languages with which the psychologists of the West were familiar (a knowledge of these two languages then being required in all American doctoral programs). The translations of Bekhterev's work were widely read by American investigators, and most of them adopted his motor methods rather than the salivary method of Pavlov.

Even more important than Bekhterev's experimental contribution was his more basic methodological contribution. This took the form of a strong case for the exclusive use of objective observation, a case Bekhterev made with the aid of the now familiar "man from Mars" metaphor. Suppose, he argued, that you are a creature from another planet, that you arrive somehow on earth, and that you get interested in the activities of the species called "man." After a period of informal observation, you decide that you will try to develop a science of these activities. What methods would you have at your disposal? Being from another world, you could not possibly rely upon your intuitions, for they depend too much upon your own experience. This rules out the major method which psychology tends to use. You could not interview these beings, because you do not know how to communicate with them. That eliminates another common method. Finally, you realize there are available to you only two kinds of materials: the things these people do (responses) and the situations in which these responses occur (stimuli). If you could find dependable relationships between the responses and the stimuli in whose presence they occur, that would be a science of "man's" behavior. It was such a program that Bekhterev and, almost simultaneously, Watson urged as the appropriate method for psychology.

Watson

John Broadus Watson (1878–1958) was born near Greenville, South Carolina. He received Bachelor and Master degrees from Furman University. After that, he went to the University of Chicago to study philosophy. There the great functionalist psychologist, James Rowland Angell, soon turned his interest to psychology.

Two programs of research associated with Watson's name were most important. The first was on the "sensory control of the maze." Its basic question was: What contributions do each of the sensory departments make to the rat's mastery of the maze habit? The issue was studied by systematically depriving the rat of sight, hearing, smell, and tactile sensitivity provided by the vibrissae and then measuring maze performance. The results of decades of such work can be described briefly. Loss of any sensory department interferes with maze learning; the more senses that are lacking, the greater the impairment, but the loss of all of these senses still leaves the rat capable of learning the maze, albeit slowly. The second important program was on human fear conditioning. The best known of these studies was that carried out with Rosalie Rayner in which the boy Albert was conditioned to fear a white rat (Watson & Rayner, 1920).

It was not Watson's experimental work that was so significant, however. It was his theoretical work which came to be known as behaviorism. The important systematic point in this theorizing was an extreme environmentalism. Watson's most quoted statement sums up this aspect of his position very well:

> Give me a dozen healthy infants, well-formed, and my own specified world to bring them up in and I'll guarantee to take any one of them at random and train him to become any type of specialist I might select—doctor, lawyer, merchant-chief and, yes, even beggarman and thief, regardless of his talents, penchants, tendencies, abilities, vocations and race of his ancestors (1925, p. 104).

In his presidential address to the American Psychological Association in 1915, Watson put forth the conditioned reflex as the agent for such training. Watson rejected all psychological concepts that seemed to him "subjective." He did not care much for the concept of reinforcement employed by Pavlov, let alone for Thorndike's theory of satisfiers. He substituted for the law of effect a principle of recency, according to which connections are formed on the basis of temporal contiguity. He reduced pleasure to a matter of stimuli originating in peripheral erogenous zones and thought to implicit subvocal speech. Such treatments were what led Tolman to criticize Watson for creating a "muscle-twitch psychology."

Watson's behavioristic proclamation now appears to have had its greatest impact as a negative statement. It told psychology what it must not do: it must not deal with anything mentalistic. The cost of attempting to comply with Watson's program was enormous. Psychology lost its mind, its will, and its consciousness. It received a cold Watsonian stare of disapproval if it thought, made a judgment, experienced an emotion, had an attitude, or even paid attention. Watson created this unpsychological psychology by reducing the basic subject matter to stimuli and responses defined in a very narrow way. Stimuli were such things as rays of light of different wave lengths, sound waves of different amplitude, length, phase, and combinations, and gaseous particles of such small diameters that they affect the membrane of the nose. Responses were such things as muscle contractions and glandular secretions.

The most effective critic of this position was Edward Chace Tolman (1886–1959). In a paper entitled "A New Formula for Behaviorism," published in 1922, Tolman proposed a liberalization of the concepts of stimulus and response. Presenting himself as still a behaviorist, he substituted the concepts of *stimulating agency* for stimulus and *behavior act* for response:

> The stimulating agency may be defined in any standardized terms, those of physics, of physiology, or of common sense, and it constitutes the independent, initiating cause of the whole behavior phenomena. . . .
> . . . The behavior act is simply the name given the final bits of behavior as such. The behavior act together with the stimulating agency constitutes the fundamentals upon which the rest of the system is based . . . they alone . . . tell us all that we know of . . . an organism's mentality (even when that organism is another human being who can introspect).

Later on, Tolman and others would refer to this type of psychology, in which the concepts of situation or stimulating agency and behavior were the basic terms, as a *molar behaviorism*. Such a system was adopted by almost all behavioristic psychologists as more attractive and more realistic than Watson's *molecular* ("muscle-twitch") *behaviorism*. This is a point that deserves clearer understanding than it has received. The critics of behaviorism, almost without exception, resurrect the dead horse of Watsonian behaviorism and beat it in their destructions of behaviorist psychology.

Operationism

In several papers published in the next half dozen years, Tolman sought to show how such mentalistic concepts as instinct, emotion, sensory quality, ideas, insight, consciousness, and purpose (all discarded by Watson) could be retained in a behavioristic psychology. A few key sentences, not in sequence, from Tolman's (1925) treatment of purpose will serve to illustrate the procedure.

> When one observes an animal performing, one knows nothing concerning possible "contents" of the latter's "mind" and to assume such contents seems to us to add nothing to one's description. One does, however, see certain aspects of the behavior itself which are important and for which the term "purpose" seems a good name.

> When an animal is learning a maze, or escaping from a puzzle box, or merely going about its daily business of eating, nest building, sleeping and the like, it will be noted that in all such performances a certain *persistence until* character is to be found. Now it is just this *persistence until* character which we will define as purpose.

> . . . we, being behaviorists, *identify* purpose with such aspects . . . and there is no additional explanatory value, we should contend, in making the further assumption that such responses are accompanied by a mentalistic something, also to be known as "purpose."

In this statement, Tolman was saying that this aspect of persistence until a goal was reached in the behavior of an animal could provide an objective definition of the purpose of the animal to achieve that goal. This is the essential idea of the movement called *operationism* which psychology was to discover in the writings of the Harvard physicist Percy Bridgman (1927). Unobservables, mentalistic concepts, for example, are acceptable in science if they can be given *operational definitions* that relate them to observables. In physical science these operations are usually operations of measurement. In psychology they more frequently are statements of the objective bases used to introduce an unobservable into our scientific vocabulary. The impact of operationism on the psychology of learning was enormous. For the next two decades, the most deadly sin a psychologist could commit was to fail to define his terms operationally.

Hypothetico-Deductive Method

Operationism deals with the factual aspects of science. An important development was also occurring on the theoretical front. This was an application of the deductive methods of physics in psychology. The first important spokesman for this position was Clark L. Hull. Modeling himself on Newton, Hull undertook the ambitious task of developing a deductive theory of the phenomena of learning. As Newton had done in his *Principia*, Hull's plan was to assemble a set of basic laws that would serve as postulates or basic *hypotheses* in a *deductive* system. The theorems deduced from these postulates would constitute the essential proof or disproof of the system.

This strategy was widely accepted and came to be known as the *hypothetico-deductive* method.

Taxonomies of Learning

By the late 1920s (see Konorski & Miller, 1937) a number of psychologists had recognized an important operationally defined difference between the Pavlovian and Thorndikean experiments. In the Thorndikean case, there is a contingent relationship between responses and reinforcement. The cat receives food if, but only if, it pulls the string or makes some other specified response. In the Pavlovian case, no such contingency exists. The dog receives food at a specified time after the presentation of the CS whether or not it salivates. Although the expressions "Pavlovian conditioning" and "Thorndikean learning" were sometimes used to refer to these different procedures, it became more conventional to refer to the former as "classical" or "respondent conditioning" and to the latter as "instrumental" or "operant." Hilgard and Marquis (1940) popularized the classical-instrumental terminology. B. F. Skinner (1938) suggested the respondent-operant distinction.

It is important to note that these different procedures provide *operational definitions* of two different methods of conditioning. They say nothing about differences in underlying processes. The important question, of course, involves this latter point: do classical and instrumental operations produce different forms of learning? A good many psychologists claimed that they did. The important proposed distinctions are summarized in Table 12.1.

TABLE 12.1 Proposed Differences between Pavlovian and Thorndikean Learning

	Pavlovian procedure	*Thorndikean procedure*
Procedural distinction	No contingency between response and consequence	Response-consequence contingency
Type of response	Elicited by US, reflexive involuntary	Emitted without discoverable stimulation, voluntary
Neural mechanisms	Autonomic nervous system	Skeletal nervous system
Essential law of learning	Contiguity	Reinforcement (effect)
What is learned	S-S connections, expectancies, preparatory responses	S-R connections, habits

These differences have now been the object of experimental work for half a century. The two specific key questions have been these: (1) Is it possible to obtain instrumental conditioning of elicited, reflexive responses of the autonomic nervous system? For example, can the galvanic skin response of a human subject be conditioned by making reward contingent upon the appearance of such a response? (2) Can emitted "voluntary" skeletal responses be conditioned classically? For example, can the key-pecking response of a pigeon be conditioned by the mere pairing of a light and the presentation of food? Although the returns are not all in, the tentative answer to both of these questions seems to be "yes." Kimmel (e.g., 1973) has provided a number of demonstrations of instrumental conditioning of the GSR. The phenomenon of *autoshaping*, to be considered later, is often presented as a case of classical conditioning of an emitted response. Such results mean, in short, that the classical-instrumental distinction may be a purely definitional one.

Varieties of Instrumental Learning

In their influential book, *Conditioning and Learning*, Hilgard and Marquis (1940) first made the distinction between classical and instrumental conditioning and then went on to distinguish among four different types of the latter form of learning: (1) *reward training* (Skinner-box experiments where a rat receives food for pressing a bar); (2) *escape training* (a rat learns to run off an electrified grid when the shock comes on); (3) *avoidance training* (given a signal that shock is about to come on, the rat leaves the grid before the shock appears); and (4) *secondary reward training*. Early experiments on secondary reward training were those of Wolfe (1936) and Cowles (1937). In these experiments chimpanzees first learned to deposit tokens about the size of poker chips into a vending machine ("chimp-o-mat") to obtain a bit of fruit. Later on, the subjects would perform a series of other tasks for which the reward was a token. The token was a *secondary reward* because its value as a reward was learned. Food itself was a *primary reward*.

Hilgard and Marquis arrived at their classification by thinking in terms of the effects of primary rewards and punishments in situations where they were either present or absent. Thus, reward training was produced in situations where the primary reward was present but the secondary reward training occurred when it was absent. Escape training occurred where the primary punisher (shock) was present. Avoidance training occurred where it was absent.

In his revision of Hilgard and Marquis's *Conditioning and Learning*, Kimble (1961) also proposed a four-fold classification of types of instrumental conditioning, but on a partially different basis. He defined the types in terms of reward and punishment again, but his second defining variable was whether the specified response led to the presence or absence of a reward or punishment. This classification resulted in these types of instrumental conditioning: (1) *reward training* (if the response occurs, reward occurs); (2) *omission training* (if the response occurs, reward is withheld); (3) *punishment training* (if the response occurs, punishment occurs); and (4) *avoidance training* (if the response occurs, punishment is withheld). More recent taxonomies of learning have built on this last one, adding another dimension, whether or not a signal indicates the beginning of a trial. This added variable creates eight types of instrumental learning produced by all combinations of whether or not a signal is used, whether reward or punishment is used as a reinforcer, and whether the response produces the reinforcer or eliminates it.

Assessment

While this work was going on, the psychology of learning was developing delusions of grandeur. Although Hull had put the point most strongly, the whole field (except for Skinner) had accepted the view that the road to progress lay in the development of deductive treatments of learning. This meant that the right scientific strategy was to discover the elementary laws of learning which then could be put together to account for complex behavior. On this ground, research on complex learning gave way to simpler studies involving single-unit T-mazes, straight alleys, the Skinner box, and eyelid conditioning. The theories of learning, to which we turn now, were grounded in research of that type.

Hull and Spence

Pavlov died in 1936. By the same date Thorndike had left the field of his early work and had moved into educational psychology where he was the most significant individual on the scene. The vacuum left by the departure of these giants was destined to be filled by Clark L. Hull (1884–1952) and Kenneth W. Spence (1907–1967). Although these men disagreed on many specific points of interpretation, their goals were so much the same that the position they represented came to be called the Hull-Spence theory.

Early Work

Hull's most important early work in learning represented an attempt to analyze complex behavior in terms of the principles of conditioning. The analysis of certain aspects of maze learning with the aid of the *habit-family hierarchy* and the *goal-gradient hypothesis* concepts was typical. The idea essential to the habit-family hierarchy was that in most situations where there is a goal to be attained, the organism has at its disposal several different responses (a habit-family) to use to attain that goal. At the same time, however, these habits vary in strength (form a hierarchy). The strength of the habit determines the probability that it will be used.

One of the most straightforward applications of this concept was to the explanation of trial-and-error learning. Hull saw the process as a matter of reordering the strengths of the various habits in the hierarchy. Since the situation is a learning

299

situation, the strongest habit cannot be the correct one. For such learning to occur, this strongest incorrect habit must be weakened and a habit that is initially weaker must be strengthened. The mechanisms put forth to accomplish these effects were reinforcement and extinction. In an early paper on the habit-family hierarchy, Hull (1934) used these ideas to explain the occurrence of errors in a multi-unit maze. For example, one of the strongest habits in the animal's hierarchy is that of approaching goals once their location is recognized. This leads to errors made by entering goal-pointing blind alleys and difficulty in elimination of these errors.

Even earlier, Hull (1932) had presented the *goal-gradient hypothesis* this way, ". . . the goal reaction gets conditioned the most strongly to the stimuli preceding it, and other reactions get conditioned to their stimuli progressively weaker as they are more remote (in time or space) from the goal." In this statement Hull conceived of any behavioral situation as capable of being analyzed into a series of S-R links. He then proposed that the strength of the connections was a function of the distance of the particular link in time or distance from the goal. Hull used the goal-gradient hypothesis to explain a dozen different features of maze learning. The most important of these involved speed of running and the order in which blind alleys are eliminated in maze learning.

Principles of Behavior

The most influential Hullian theory was developed in his *Principles of Behavior* (1943). Here Hull presented what he believed to be the fundamental laws of all behavior and an organization of these principles into a formal deductive system. Although the theory was expressed mathematically and also had a neurophysiological component, its enduring contribution can be presented as a chain of hypothetical processes that connected stimuli on the one hand with responses on the other. As this statement suggests, Hull was clearly in the camp of the S-R theorists.

Habit Formation   The central concept in Hull's theory was that of *habit*, which he defined in Thorndikean terms. Habits were (1) stimulus-response connections which (2) developed gradually (3) as a result of reinforcement. This last assumption was Hull's version of the law of effect. Hull proposed that reinforcement consisted in a process of *drive reduction*: food is reinforcing for a hungry organism because it reduces the drive of hunger.

For Hull, stimulus generalization was also a part of the process of habit formation. Hull recognized that stimulus situations would vary slightly trial by trial and that an organism could never learn anything unless habits generalized to these different stimuli.

Performance   An important aspect of Hull's theory was an acceptance of the learning-performance distinction. *Learning* he conceived as a permanent product of previously reinforced pairings of stimuli and responses. *Performance* was the manifestation of these products in behavior. The concept of *drive* allowed Hull to take a first step toward an explanation of an organism's ability to make use of what it has learned.

The most interesting aspect of Hull's treatment of drive was that he made it exclusively a performance variable which gave habits the energy required to produce performance but which played no role in learning. Given a level of drive sufficient to produce responding and to make a reinforcer, such as food reinforcing, learning should be the same at all drive levels. This prediction received support in a number of drive-shift experiments (see Figure 12.3). In these experiments, different groups of subjects began training under two or more different levels of drive. This produced differences in performance; the stronger the drive, the better the performance. In a second stage of the experiments, a portion of the animals in each group were switched to higher or lower levels of drive. The result favoring Hull's theory was that under the new drive level the subjects behaved as if they had been trained at that drive level from the beginning. Differential drive levels, in other words, had no differential effect on learning.

Inhibition   Following the lead of Pavlov, Hull included an inhibitory concept in his theory to account for extinction, spontaneous recovery, discrimination learning, and the like. Hull proposed that two inhibitory mechanisms were required to account for various inhibitory phenomena. The first of these, *reactive inhibition*, developed with the occurrence of every response, whether reinforced or not, and

		Drive level during later training	
		High	Low
Drive level during original training	High	High – High	High – Low
	Low	Low – High	Low – Low

Figure 12.3 Design of a typical experiment intended to determine whether motivation affects learning. Animals are first trained on two different drive levels (rows in the figure). Then each of these two groups is divided (represented by the columns in the figure). Half of the subjects continue under the original condition of drive; the other half are switched to the alternative condition. The performance of interest is that occurring following the switch. If performance differs for the two groups *trained* under different drives, then motivation affects learning.

dissipated with rest or nonresponding. Hull considered reactive inhibition to be a fatigue-like state with motivational properties. This latter assumption meant that the dissipation of inhibition would be reinforcing because it was drive-reducing. With reinforcement thus provided, Hull argued that nonresponding could be conditioned to the stimuli in any situation. In this way Hull deduced the existence of a second form of inhibition, *conditioned inhibition*, which added to the effects of reactive inhibition. Both forms of inhibition reduced the level of performance.

These ideas bought a great deal for Hull in the way of interpretation of experimental data. The theory predicted that performance under distributed practice would be superior to performance under massed practice, that extinction would occur with the development of inhibition, and that spontaneous recovery would occur with rest as a result of the dissipation of inhibition. Since part of the inhibitory process was a habit, the theory also predicted that spontaneous recovery would not restore performance to its complete preextinction level. Conditioned inhibition would continue to suppress it. Results of experiments supported all of these predictions.

Response Evocation   Hull developed two final concepts that were required in order to account for certain details of performance. The first of these was a concept of *oscillation*. On the basis of several lines of evidence, Hull assumed that response tendencies varied randomly from moment to moment. Second, Hull introduced a concept of *threshold* which these tendencies had to exceed if a learned response were to occur. Hull used these ideas to explain the facts that sometimes many reinforcements had to occur before the appearance of the first learned response and that frequently learning curves showed an initial period of positive acceleration.

Summary of Hull-Spence Theory

It is useful to think of the Hull-Spence theory as a chain of concepts connecting a set of independent variables with a set of dependent variables. Figure 12.4 displays the links in this chain. An important thing to notice is just the general structure of the theory as a serial chain of concepts describing the mechanisms thought to take place between the independent variables on the left and the dependent (response) variables on the right. Some important questions to ask about the theory concern its obvious complexity. Can a theory so elaborate be manageable? Is it realistic? Answering the second question first: unfortunately it begins to appear that behavior is at least that complexly determined. But manageable is something else. The increasing cumbersomeness of Hull's theory, as it was revised in later versions, was one of the important factors leading to its downfall.

302

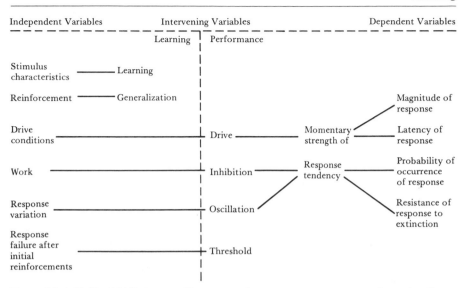

Figure 12.4 Hull's (1943) theory of learning. The important points to get from this figure concern the structure of the theory, because the competing theories had very similar structures as will emerge in Figures 12.5, 12.7, and 12.8. Note that Hull's theory is of the intervening variable variety and that it incorporates a distinction between learning and performance.

Tolman

In the 1940s the theory which stood as the main alternative to Hull's was that of Tolman. Tolman's most important theoretical statement of that period was contained in his paper, "The Determiners of Behavior at a Choice Point" (1938). In this paper Tolman presented the outline of a theory designed to answer the simple question, what accounts for the probability that a rat will turn to the left at an intersection in a T-maze? The answer, he claimed, would be in terms of the effects of a set of independent variables. In quasiformal terms $P_{BL} = f_1(x_1, x_2, \ldots, x_n)$; that is, the probability of left-turning behavior will be a function (f_1) of the values of the independent variables x_1, x_2 to however many there are (x_n).

Tolman identified ten variables as probably among the most important. Six of these were environmental variables: maintenance schedule or drive (M), the appropriateness of the goal object (G), types of stimuli provided (S), types of responses required (R), nature and number of trials [we use the symbol N, although Tolman called it Σ (OBO)], and pattern of maze units (P). The other four were individual difference variables: heredity (H), age (A), previous training (T), and special endo-

303

crine, drug, or vitamin conditions (E). Thus, Tolman's f_1 function would be:

$$P_{BL} = f_1(M, G, S, R, N, P, H, A, T, E)$$

Although this statement may seem complex enough already, Tolman introduced further complexities, claiming that even the more elaborate expression was surely an oversimplification. To illustrate just one of the complicating aspects, Tolman maintained that the individual difference variables interacted with each of the environmental variables and would influence the effect of each. Anticipating a more explicit later statement by Feigl (1945), Tolman saw that he could simplify things by breaking the f_1 function down into two subfunctions with the aid of *intervening variables*. His specific proposal was to introduce these intervening variables as functions (f_2) of the independent variables and then to relate them to behavior by a third set of functions (f_3). Tolman did not attempt to state these functions quantitatively but, instead, presented them in the diagram presented in Figure 12.5. This figure is similar to Figure 12.4 and makes the very important point that the theories of Tolman and Hull were not dissimilar in structure. The main points of conceptual disagreement are reflected in the positions Tolman and Hull took on certain experimental questions.

Expectancy versus Habit   Although Tolman called himself a behaviorist, and in 1938 set his goal as that of explaining a simple item of behavior, he did not think of learning in terms of stimulus-response connections or habits. He spoke instead of the development of knowledge, expectations, cognitions, or stimulus-stimulus associations. What a rat running a maze actually learns, he sometimes said, is a knowledge of what leads to what in this situation. More specifically (to show why the theory was a stimulus-stimulus theory), Tolman proposed that the rat learns that given such-and-such a first stimulus, it will arrive at such-and-such a second stimulus if it performs a particular response. This contrasts sharply with the theories of Hull and Thorndike, who proposed that learning involves the formation of stimulus-response associations.

Reward versus Incentive   A second Thorndikean point upon which Tolman and Hull disagreed had to do with the role played by reward in learning. As we have seen, Hull made reinforcement the essential condition of *learning*. Tolman, on the other hand, believed that cognitions could develop without reward just on the basis of experience with successions of stimuli in the environment. For him, reward was a *performance* variable. It functions as an *incentive* and simply provides the learner with a good reason for producing responses that it has learned. The *latent-learning* experiment was designed to provide evidence for such an interpretation.

The reference latent-learning experiment is that of Tolman and Honzik (1930) in which rats ran a maze for ten days with (control group) or without (one experimen-

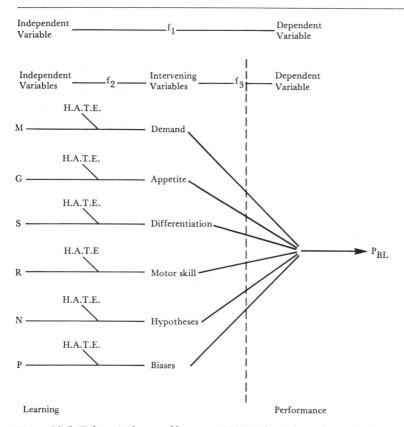

Figure 12.5 Tolman's theory of learning (1938). The independent variables are listed at the top of the figure. The theory itself has the same major features as Hull's theory depicted in Figure 12.4.

tal and one control group) reward. On the eleventh day, reward was introduced for the experimental group previously run without reward. The results of this experiment showed that the introduction of reward on the eleventh day led to an immediate decrease in number of errors in the group treated this way. This last observation is the most direct kind of evidence for the existence of latent learning. It was as if the rats in this group had *learned* considerably more about the maze than their previous *performance* indicated, and all that was required to make them show it was an adequate reason (incentive). The crux of such an interpretation is in the assumption that reinforcement has its effects on performance rather than on learning.

305

S-S versus S-R Associations

One line of experimentation in favor of Tolman's stimulus-stimulus position was the phenomenon of *sensory preconditioning*. These studies proceeded in three stages: (1) two neutral stimuli were presented together for many trials; (2) one of the stimuli then became the conditioned stimulus paired with an unconditioned stimulus; (3) finally, there was a test with the second stimulus. If this stimulus now elicited a response, the interpretation was that the paired presentations in stage 1 had produced a stimulus-stimulus association between the two neutral stimuli. Obviously there would not be much point in describing such experiments if they had not come out positively.

The case for pure stimulus-stimulus associations was not so strong as this may suggest, however. The diagram in Figure 12.6 gives a stimulus-response interpretation of the process by showing what might theoretically happen at each stage of the experiment where the neutral stimuli are a tone and a light, and the unconditioned stimulus is a shock which produces flexion as the unconditioned response.

The important point to note is that CS_2 actually does produce a response that is conditioned to the tone in stage 1 of the experiment. The lowercase r is a common notation to represent a covert response, in this case perhaps a partial blink or pupillary constriction. Note that this fractional response has a consequence in the form of proprioceptive stimulation (s), perhaps kinesthetic feedback.

In stage 2, according to this theory, both CS_2 and s serve as stimuli to which flexion gets conditioned. This means that in stage 3 the tone elicits r—s, and s elicits the conditioned response. This mechanism, incidentally, is perhaps the best

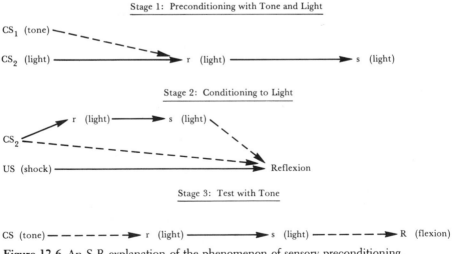

Figure 12.6 An S-R explanation of the phenomenon of sensory preconditioning.

example available of a process of *mediation* which S-R psychologists frequently used to explain mentalistic phenomena.

Continuity versus Noncontinuity

A final point of disagreement between Tolman and certain other theorists was that Tolman believed that learning sometimes occurs suddenly (insightfully), whereas Hull, in particular, had argued that learning is a gradual process. In this difference of opinion, Hull took the continuity position; Tolman, the noncontinuity position. One set of experiments designed to evaluate these two positions was the *discrimination reversal* experiments.

In these studies rats were run in a simple, single-choice apparatus, perhaps a T-maze where they had to learn to go to a black alley rather than a white one. Trial by trial the black and white alleys were shifted randomly from the right side of the apparatus to the left. For the rat, the mastery of such a discrimination is not easy. It performs at a chance level for a long *presolution period* before it begins to respond to the positive stimulus. The continuity and noncontinuity theories had different accounts of what went on during the presolution period. The noncontinuity position was that the animal entertained a series of *hypotheses* during this period, for example, "go left," "go right," "first go left then go right," "choose black." All of these except for the last two would lead to reinforcement 50 percent of the time, whenever black and the choice based on the hypothesis happened to coincide. An important element of the noncontinuity position was that testing a wrong hypothesis had no effect upon the strength of a tendency to choose the black side of the maze. The continuity theorists made the opposite assumption, namely, that chance reinforcements following a response to the correct stimulus add an increment to the strength of the tendency to respond to this stimulus again.

The test of these alternatives involved the discrimination reversal experiment. If positive and negative stimuli were switched during the presolution period, this manipulation, according to the noncontinuity theorists, should have no effect. According to the continuity theorists, the reversal should slow up mastery of the discrimination, because it would be necessary for the animal to unlearn the developing habit to go to the now incorrect stimulus. Many experiments of the type just described were carried out between 1930 and 1950. The preponderance of results favored continuity theory—that is, reversing the contingency of reinforcement slowed up mastery of the discrimination (Krechevsky, 1932; Spence, 1940, 1945).

Guthrie

Edwin R. Guthrie (1886–1959) was an S-R theorist who reduced the learning process to the simplest possible formula. As Guthrie saw it, what happens in any

307

learning situation is like this: the organism makes a variety of responses. If one of these responses produces a significant change in the situation or removes the animal from it, that response is the one that will occur upon a later occurrence of the same situation. Rewards and punishments have nothing to do with the process except that they are ways of producing dramatic changes in the situation (Guthrie, 1935).

Act versus Actone

Guthrie was the only important learning theorist of the period under discussion to retain the Watsonian molecular form of behaviorism. Whereas other theorists concentrated on behavior *acts* defined in terms of such environmental consequences as reaching the end of a maze or pressing a bar, Guthrie emphasized the detailed movements (*actones*) which occurred as an organism performed the response being learned.

Guthrie did very few experiments. His most important one, done in collaboration with G. P. Horton, made the argument for this approach fairly convincingly. In this experiment, cats learned to escape from a puzzle box by tilting a pole in the center of the apparatus. The response also operated a camera which took a picture of the behavior as it occurred. The "data" of the experiment were sequences of pictures of the animals making the escape response on successive trials in the experiment. Tracings of these pictures obtained on such a series revealed that the details of the cats' movements do, in fact, remain quite constant trial by trial.[1]

Although this part of Guthrie's theory received support from this investigation, such results were not enough to lead to general acceptance of the position. This is because the act-vs.-actone aspect was not one of the issues central to the theoretical dispute. We turn now to the issues deemed more important.

Contiguity versus Reward

Guthrie rejected Thorndike's law of effect and offered in its place a law of contiguity. All that is necessary for learning to take place is for a response to occur in the presence of a stimulus. Under those circumstances, the association is automatic.

This aspect of Guthrie's theory did not fare well when subjected to experimental tests. Several experimenters showed that animals failed to learn a response if they were removed from the apparatus immediately after making it or if the response changed the situation, for example, by turning the room lights on or off. Although these procedures produce important changes in the situation, learning was either slow or nonexistent, or else it was easy to detect the existence of a reward.

[1] Later research was to show that this consistency comes about because the cats were performing unlearned "greeting" responses for the experimenters who were present in the laboratory (Moore & Stuttard, 1979). This demonstration obviously came long after the Guthrie and Horton study had had an effect on the history of the psychology of learning.

Continuity versus Noncontinuity

The second major assumption in Guthrie's theory was that the S-R association was complete after just one pairing. Guthrie, like Tolman, was a noncontinuity theorist. Guthrie approached the issue from a different angle, however. Faced with the fact that learning as it actually happens is usually gradual and not sudden, Guthrie proposed that this is because learning situations do not repeat themselves exactly trial by trial. The learner must attach the response to all of these variations of the situation before learning is complete. In this way, he argued, what seems to be gradual learning is really many one-trial learnings to make a response to what are actually somewhat different situations.

Later (1950) Estes was to make such an interpretation central to a *statistical theory of learning*. In this theory, Estes treated the stimulus side of learning as a large, but finite, collection of stimulus elements, comprising a stimulus population. On any given trial, only a sample of the stimuli in the population is assumed to be present. Those which are present are conditioned to the response on that trial. After the first trial, the stimulus sample on later trials will consist of some stimuli which have been previously conditioned to the response and some which have not. With continued practice, the number of stimulus elements not conditioned to the response will diminish, and the number which have been conditioned will increase, until the entire population of stimuli has been conditioned to the response. Assuming that the proportion of previously conditioned stimuli present in the sample on any trial represents the probability that a conditioned response will occur on that trial leads to the prediction of a gradual increase in response probability with practice. The exact form of the function will depend upon the trial-to-trial variability in the stimulus situation. If the situation is perfectly controlled so that the sample of stimuli is exactly the same from trial to trial, one-trial learning should occur. In a general way, this prediction is that learning will be more rapid in a very constant situation than it will be in a highly variable one. There is considerable reason to accept this idea as a valid one. We know from Pavlov's work, for example, that extraneous stimuli disturb the course of acquisition through external inhibition. In order to guard against the effects of uncontrolled disturbances of this sort, Pavlov eventually had to build a laboratory carefully shielded from outside stimulation.

Figure 12.7 is a diagram of Guthrie's theory as developed by Estes. Comparison reveals that it has much in common with the theories of Hull and Tolman.

Skinner

A final important psychologist who presented the first detailed statement of his position in this period was B. F. Skinner. In his book, *Behavior of Organisms*, Skinner (1938) described the results of a series of experimental studies, begun in

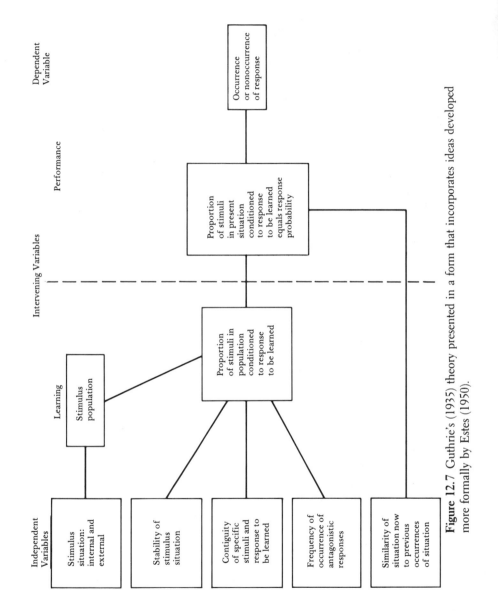

Figure 12.7 Guthrie's (1935) theory presented in a form that incorporates ideas developed more formally by Estes (1950).

1930, of the bar-pressing behavior of rats. Skinner offered an approach to the study of learning and to learning theory that differed sharply from that of the other theorists. (1) He rejected the hypothetico-deductive method, proposing instead to determine the quantitative properties of behavior and, through induction, to establish the laws of behavior. (2) He came out against physiological hypotheses, claiming that the gains from such approaches were far outweighed by "all the misdirected experimentation and bootless theorizing that have arisen from the same source." (3) He studied behavior in a free-responding situation, whereas all of his opponents were attempting to understand how learning proceeded trial by trial. (4) He concentrated on the behavior of individual organisms, whereas other psychologists studied groups of individuals, the larger the group the better. (5) He presented his data in the unorthodox form of cumulative records produced on a kymograph as the rats pressed the lever in the Skinner box. For all these reasons, the immediate reception of Skinnerian psychology was not enthusiastic.

The irony of it all is that by 1975 or so Skinner had come to be recognized as the most important psychologist of his era because of his consistent adherence to a concept with which his earlier contemporaries agreed. This was the concept that behavior is *determined*, a position that was expressed most forcefully in Skinner's controversial publication, *Beyond Freedom and Dignity* (1971). There he took the position that everything we do and everything we are is controlled by our history of rewards and punishments. Even what we say we do "on purpose" or "through an act of personal will" is actually an expression of what we have been rewarded or punished for doing or not doing in the past.

Skinnerian "Theory"

Skinner sometimes (e.g., 1950) argued that theories of learning are unnecessary and claimed not to have one. In fact, he used very few intervening variables—drive and emotion were the main ones—and he limited his treatment to an analysis of two measures of behavior, the number of responses emitted in extinction and the rate of responding under a variety of circumstances.

As a shorthand for the first of the aspects of behavior, Skinner spoke of a *reflex reserve*, the store of unreinforced responses that the organism had available to emit in extinction. The size of the reflex reserve depends upon the number of reinforcements the organism has received, the quality and quantity of such reinforcements and, most important, the schedule on which the reinforcements were delivered.

Schedules of Reinforcement　The pattern of trials or responses on which a learner receives or does not receive reinforcement is called a *schedule of reinforcement*. At the extremes are continuous reinforcement, where reinforcement occurs after every response, and extinction, where it never does. In between, it is possible to identify numerous schedules of partial or intermittent reinforcement. One of Skinner's important contributions was a systematic investigation of many of them (Ferster & Skinner, 1957).

The most basic schedules of partial reinforcement are defined either in terms of numbers of responses or in terms of their timing. The first of these are *ratio schedules*, where reinforcement occurs after some number of responses. The second are *interval schedules*, where reinforcement occurs for the first response after a specified period of time.

The number of responses or the amount of time involved in a schedule may be either *variable* or *fixed*. Combining these bases for defining schedules yields four varieties: *variable-interval, variable-ratio, fixed-interval,* and *fixed-ratio*. In the variable schedules, reinforcement occurs after some average number of responses or minutes, but the exact number changes from reinforcement to reinforcement. In the fixed schedules, the number of responses or minutes is always the same.

Ratio schedules lead to rapid rates of responding in which as many as several hundred unreinforced responses may occur prior to the reinforced one. In fixed-ratio schedules, there is often a long pause after the reinforced response before responding resumes. Variable ratios produce a steadier rate of responding.

Fixed-interval schedules produce a pattern of responding often called a *fixed-interval scallop*. Early in the interval, responding is slow, but as time passes, rate of responding picks up and is greatest at the moment when the reinforced response occurs. Variable-interval schedules produce low but very stable rates of responding and are often used in studies to determine the effects of other variables, such as the administration of a drug.

Other schedules of reinforcement put rate requirements on performance. For example, reinforcement may occur only if the organism performs at a slow rate or a fast one. Organisms learn to respond slowly or rapidly under such contingencies. Still other, more complex, schedules can be produced by combining the basic schedules in various ways. A discussion of such schedules can be found in Ferster and Skinner (1957).

By comparison with continuous reinforcement, extinction following partial reinforcement is very slow. This partial-reinforcement effect (PRE) has been the object of a considerable amount of theoretical conjecture. It now appears to be explainable in terms of a theory that relies on two assumptions. (1) Traces of nonreinforcement are a part of the stimulus complex that comes to control responding. Nonreinforcement in extinction creates these same stimuli, thus supporting the response. And (2) the discrimination between acquisition and extinction is easier following continuous reinforcement than following partial reinforcement. The omission or reinforcement in extinction following continuous reinforcement creates a different situation, and the learned response loses strength through generalization decrement. To return to Skinner's theory, however, it will be sufficient to note that the effect of partial schedule is to enlarge the reflex reserve, the number of responses available in extinction.

Drive and Punishment   An important form of support for the concept of reflex reserve came from the results of studies of levels of motivation during acquisition and mild punishment early in extinction. These results can be summarized very quickly: neither variable had an effect upon the total number of responses obtained in extinction; that is, the size of the reflex reserve remained the same. However, there frequently was an impressive effect upon the *rate* at which this fixed total of responses was emitted. To take the most famous case, an apparatus that delivered a slight slap to the paw of the rat whenever it pressed the bar, during the first ten minutes of extinction, slowed up responding considerably. The number of responses produced by the rat before extinction was completed was the same as for an unpunished animal, however. Punishment had affected rate of responding but not the size of the reflex reserve (Estes, 1944).

Subsidiary Reserve   Other observations, of which the phenomenon of spontaneous recovery is a good example, forced Skinner to develop a concept that was a bit more theoretical than anything mentioned so far in this account. In the bar-pressing situation, spontaneous recovery appears as a small flurry of rapid responses that occurs when extinction begins again after a rest. After that, performance settles down to something more like the prerest rate until all of the responses in the reserve have been exhausted. The brief period of rapid responses suggested to Skinner that there might be a "secondary," "momentary," or "subsidiary" reserve where responses are stored for a while just prior to their emission. These responses can be emitted faster than they can be replaced by additional responses from the basic reserve. The various aspects of Skinner's concept can be summarized in a diagram of the type that appears (with apologies to Skinner) in Figure 12.8. It is important to mention that, except for the hypothetical plumbing, this representation leaves Skinner's theory with a certain resemblance to those of Hull, Tolman, and Guthrie.

Decline and Fall

The period we have just looked at has sometimes been called the "Age of Grand Theory" in the psychology of learning. Although the classical theories were formulated and tested in terms of simple learning, behind the scenes there was always the presumption that these theories could be applied to all behavior—that is, they were grand in scope. The theories were also grand in their estimation of where the psychology of learning stood in its history, the presumption being that most of the basic laws of learning had already been discovered and all that remained was the minor problem of resolving the few systematic issues that separated the major theorists. Disillusionment came more quickly than the classical theorists could possibly have anticipated. By the middle of the century it had become clear that the classical theories of learning were limited in scope and that the state of our scientific

313

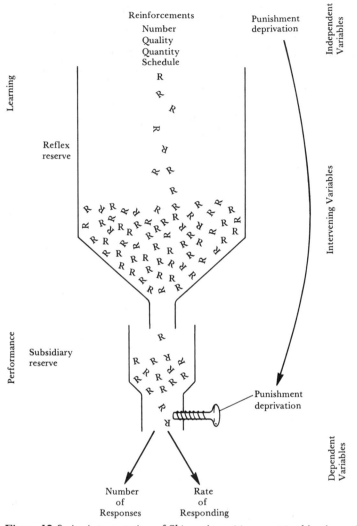

Figure 12.8 An interpretation of Skinner's position contrived by the author of this chapter.

knowledge was pre-Galilean rather than post-Newtonian, as Hull and others had thought. This reevaluation laid the ground for major changes in the field.

The "Cognitization" of Learning Theory

The most fundamental mistake of the Grand Theories had been to underestimate the extent to which the characteristics of the organism affect the progress of learn-

314

ing. Both individual and species differences were involved, and the tradition out of which the classical theories came had not prepared them to cope with such factors.

Equipotentiality versus Preparedness   An extreme example of this position assumed the complete generality of the conditioning process. For example, Kimble (1956), commenting on research related to this point, held that

> a great deal of such research may be summarized by saying that it indicated that just about any activity of which the organism is capable can be conditioned, and these responses can be conditioned to any stimulus that the organism can perceive (p. 195).

Kimble should have known better. As early as 1930, C. W. Valentine had reported being unable to repeat Watson's demonstration of fear conditioning in children, using a pair of opera glasses instead of a white rat as the conditioned stimulus. It was well-known laboratory lore that training a rat to press a bar or a pigeon to peck a key to turn off shock was next to impossible. More formal evidence along these lines was soon to accumulate to prove that the assumption of *equipotentiality* is wrong: animals are *prepared* to form certain associations and counterprepared to form others (Seligman & Hager, 1972).

For example, rats are prepared to form associations between novel tastes and a subsequent experience of sickness. In one experiment, rats were made sick by X-radiation after they had sampled saccharin-flavored water from a drinking bottle. In subsequent tests they avoided the sweet solution. Comparable procedures designed to establish an association between a visual-auditory stimulus and nausea were unsuccessful. On the other hand, the visual-auditory stimulus was easy to condition to an avoidance response based on shock. This is to say that the rat is prepared to form an association between sickness and taste or between pain and visual-auditory stimuli. It is *counterprepared* to form associations between sickness and visual-auditory stimulation or pain and taste (Garcia & Koelling, 1966).

The phenomenon of autoshaping provides a particularly impressive demonstration of the importance of preparedness. If a hungry pigeon is shown a lighted key for a few seconds before grain is delivered by a food magazine, the pigeon comes to peck the key without any special training. Pigeons are so thoroughly prepared to peck for food that they teach (shape) this response to themselves (auto) (Brown & Jenkins, 1968).

The significance of the rejection of the assumption of equipotentiality is far-reaching. On the one hand, it means that the universal laws of learning put forth by the grand theorists are not universal. They are pretty flimsy material out of which to construct a general theory. At the same time, the concept of preparedness opens anew the possibility that there may be capabilities which the human organism is uniquely prepared to develop. Language is the clearest example. Although inves-

315

tigators have had impressive success in teaching chimpanzees to perform language-like behavior, even more impressive is the difficulty of such training. The human two-year-old picks up language effortlessly and without any special program of training. For the chimpanzee it takes intensive tutelage. It is as if the human being is prepared to develop linguistic skill in a way that the chimpanzee is not.

A Force for Change

As the psychology of learning gradually assimilated these lessons, it took on an appearance that sounds more like Tolman's S-S expectancy position than Hull's S-R habit position. The transition just discussed has sometimes been presented as if this is a good way to describe it. There is a sense in which this is true, but it would be wrong to say that the psychology of learning has given up Hull and accepted Tolman—if only because the theories of Tolman and Hull were so similar in structure. What has happened is more basic, and it relates to the issue of objectivism which has come up before here.

Looking back, it now appears that strict operationism represented a necessary stage in the development of our field. Prior to the acceptance of this position, psychology had been far too subjective to become an experimental science. Watson had led a movement away from such subjectivism, but he went too far. Too many topics of interest were banished from the field.

Even in Watson's day there were those, most notably Tolman, who attempted to bring mentalistic-sounding concepts back into psychology by means of what amounted to operational definitions. In a general way, the operational point of view did nothing more than insist that terms designating unobservables be defined in ways that relate them to observables. From there it proceeded to a further insistence that concepts defined in this way must have a relationship to behavior. In this way these concepts became *intervening variables,* ones that stand between observable antecedent conditions on the one hand and behavior on the other. The diagram below serves to summarize this point:

Antecedent Conditions—Mentalistic Concepts—Behavior
Independent Variables —Intervening Variables—Dependent Variables

Obviously there is nothing in this formula to exclude mentalistic concepts. In fact, the whole point of it is to admit unobservables. But the damage had been done. In mid-century American psychology, it would have cost a career to publish on mind, consciousness, volition, or even imagery. Established opinion seemed to maintain that such terms were somehow irretrievably subjective in a way that "habit," "drive," or even "expectation" were not. In addition to its illogicality, this stance led to a period of pretty dreary science because most of the interesting topics seemed to be beyond the pale.

By the early 1960s these unattractive features of the traditional psychology of learning had led to considerable unrest in the field, and many investigators turned to the study of topics that would have been forbidden a decade or two earlier: stimuli as carriers of information (Egger & Miller, 1962); the relativity of reinforcement (Premack, 1965); and biological constraints on learning (Seligman & Hager, 1972). The psychology of learning was entering a new phase that is still too young to evaluate as history.

Conclusion

Although the concept of association was familiar to Aristotle, the experimental study of conditioning and simple learning did not begin until the late 1800s. Initial progress was very rapid, however. By the turn of the century, Pavlov had discovered many of the phenomena of "classical" conditioning and Thorndike had done his early studies of instrumental learning. Thorndike had also put forward an S-R, continuity, reinforcement account of the learning process that was to set the stage for controversy for the next half century.

The explanations of learning advanced by Pavlov and Thorndike both fit the general methodological scheme that had evolved from British empiristic philosophy and European physiology. Both were empirical in that they used the experimental method and presented objective, even quantitative, data. Both were elementistic in that they analyzed their subject matter into simple units—reflexes to be conditioned, stimuli and responses to be connected. They were associationistic in that each built a psychology of learning in which connections among elements was a basic process. They were both physiologically oriented and, therefore, materialistic in outlook.

In spite of this nearly perfect match to the methodological spirit of the times, the psychology of learning remained at the periphery of scientific psychology for the first quarter of the century, for a number of reasons. For one thing, in America where the psychology of learning later found a comfortable home, experimental psychology was dominated by the tradition of Titchener. The most important research was in the areas of the sensory processes and perception. J. B. Watson, who might have led the psychology of learning to a position of prominence, left academic work for a career in business. Moreover even Watson's behavioristic psychology lacked one feature that had to be incorporated before the psychology of learning would come fully into its own.

Hull's landmark publication, "A Functional Interpretation of the Conditioned Reflex" (1929), made him the most important psychologist of learning in the world.

The key to his instant eminence was the word "functional" in the title of his paper. Even before Watson, a new school of psychology had been gaining adherents. This school, called Functionalism, took a theme from Darwin and concerned itself with the purposes or the functions of mental processes. Functionalism appealed to the practical American mind. It was Hull's combination of this view with the objective approach of Pavlov that caught the fancy of so many psychologists in the field of learning.

To say that Hull was the leading figure in the psychology of learning is not to say that he had no competitors. He had many, as well as one most powerful supporter, in the person of Kenneth W. Spence. The three most important individuals in the opposition were Tolman, Guthrie, and Skinner. Each of these men—even Skinner—developed theories that seemed quite different from Hull's theory at that time. All of them used different concepts and advocated different laws of learning, and Skinner had more basic differences at the level of methodology. In retrospect, all of these positions look very similar in structure. All of them took the intervening variable approach; all of them made a learning-performance distinction; all of them dealt with similar variables and phenomena.

The intervening variable approach to psychology was the result of the most important methodological development of the twentieth century—the nearly universal acceptance of logical positivism and the cognate emphases of operationism as the appropriate philosophy of science for psychology. The impact of the operational movement was enormous. It affected the types of research being done, standards of editorial review, what appeared in the textbooks, and what was taught in the classroom. So powerful was this influence that by 1940 psychology had invented an eighth deadly sin. In addition to greed, lust, the misuse of chi-square, and the rest, there now was added the failure to define one's variables operationally.

The domination of psychology by operationism from about 1940 to about 1960 was both good news and bad news for the field. The good news was that it fostered an objectivism that was badly needed in the psychology of learning; the bad news was that operationism, applied in the tradition of Watson, led to an exclusion from the field of too much that was interesting and important. By 1980 or so, one of psychology's major accomplishments had been a liberalization of operationism so that such topics as consciousness, imagery, and even volition had become acceptable subjects for study. With this relaxation of the operational regulations, and the roughly simultaneous demise of the grand theories, the psychology of learning is now entering the second century of its official existence. It does so in high spirit and the expectation of great accomplishment in the next phase of its history.

REFERENCES

Angell, J. R. The province of functional psychology. *Psychological Review*, 1907, *14*, 61–91.
Asratyan, E. A. *I. P. Pavlov, his life and work*. Moscow: Foreign Languages Publishing House, 1949.

318

Bekhterev, V. M. *La psychologie objective*. Paris: Alcan, 1913.

Bridgman, P. W. *The logic of modern physics*. New York: Macmillan, 1927.

Brown, P. L., & Jenkins, H. M. Auto-shaping of the pigeon's key-peck. *Journal of the Experimental Analysis of Behavior*, 1968, *11*, 1–8.

Cowles, J. T. Food-tokens as incentives for learning by chimpanzees. *Comparative Psychology Monographs*, 1973, *14*(No. 71).

Egger, M. D., & Miller, N. E. Secondary reinforcement in rats as a function of information value and reliability of the stimulus. *Journal of Experimental Psychology*, 1962, *64*, 97–104.

Estes, W. K. An experimental study of punishment. *Psychological Monographs*, 1944, *47*(No. 263).

Estes, W. K. Toward a statistical theory of learning. *Psychological Review*, 1950, *57*, 94–107.

Feigl, H. Operationism and scientific method. *Psychological Review*, 1945, *52*, 250–259.

Ferster, C. B., & Skinner, B. F. *Schedules of reinforcement*. New York: Appleton-Century-Crofts, 1957.

Garcia, J., & Koelling, R. Relation of cue to consequence in avoidance learning. *Psychonomic Science*, 1966, *4*, 123–124.

Guthrie, E. R. *The psychology of learning*. New York: Harper, 1935.

Guthrie, E. R., & Horton, G. P. *Cats in a puzzle box*. New York: Rinehart, 1946.

Hilgard, E. R., & Marquis, D. G. *Conditioning and learning*. New York: Appleton-Century-Crofts, 1940.

Hull, C. L. A functional interpretation of the conditioned reflex. *Psychological Review*, 1929, *36*, 498–511.

Hull, C. L. The goal gradient hypothesis and maze learning. *Psychological Review*, 1932, *39*, 25–43.

Hull, C. L. The concept of habit-family hierarchy and maze learning. *Psychological Review*, 1934, *41*, Part I, 33–52; Part II, 134–152.

Hull, C. L. *Principles of behavior*. New York: Appleton-Century-Crofts, 1943.

Hull, C. L. *A behavior system*. New Haven: Yale University Press, 1952.

James, W. On some omissions of introspective psychology. *Mind*, 1884, *9*, 1–26.

Kimble, G. A. *Principles of general psychology*. New York: Ronald, 1956.

Kimble, G. A. *Hilgard and Marquis' conditioning and learning*. New York: Appleton-Century-Crofts, 1961.

Kimmel, H. D. Instrumental conditioning. In *Electrodermal activity in psychological research*. New York: Academic Press, 1973.

Konorski, J., & Miller, S. On two types of conditioned reflex. *Journal of General Psychology*, 1937, *16*, 264–272.

Krechevsky, I. "Hypotheses" versus "Chance" in the pre-solution period in sensory discrimination-learning. *University of California Publications in Psychology*, 1932, *6*, 27–44.

Moore, B. R., & Stuttard, S. Dr. Guthrie and *Felis Domesticus* or: Tripping over the cat. *Science*, 1979, *205*, 1031–1033.

Pavlov, I. P. The scientific investigation of the psychical faculties or processes in the higher animals. *Science*, 1906, *24*, 613–619.

Pavlov, I. P. *Conditioned reflexes* (G. V. Anrep, trans.). London: Oxford University Press, 1927.

Premack, D. Reinforcement theory. In M. R. Jones (Ed.), *Nebraska Symposium on Motivation, 1965*. Lincoln: University of Nebraska Press, 1965.

Sechenov, I. M. *Selected works*. Moscow: State Publishing House, 1935. (Originally published, 1863.)

Seligman, M. E. P., & Hager, J. L. (Eds.). *Biological boundaries of learning*. New York: Appleton-Century-Crofts, 1972.

Skinner, B. F. *The behavior of organisms*. New York: Appleton-Century-Crofts, 1938.

Skinner, B. F. Are theories of learning necessary? *Psychological Review*, 1950, *57*, 193–216.

Skinner, B. F. *Beyond freedom and dignity*. New York: Knopf, 1971.

Spence, K. W. Continuous versus non-continuous interpretations of discrimination learning. *Psychological Review*, 1940, *47*, 271–288.

Spence, K. W. An experimental test of the continuity and non-continuity theories of discrimination learning. *Journal of Experimental Psychology*, 1945, 35, 253–266.

Thorndike, E. L. *Animal intelligence*. New York: Macmillan, 1911.

Thorndike, E. L. *The fundamentals of learning*. New York: Teacher's College, 1932.

Tolman, E. C. A new formula for behaviorism. *Psychological Review*, 1922, 29, 44–53.

Tolman, E. C. Behaviorism and purpose. *The Journal of Philosophy*, 1925, 22, 36–41.

Tolman, E. C. The determiners of behavior at a choice-point. *Psychological Review*, 1938, 45, 1–41.

Tolman, E. C., & Honzik, C. H. Introduction and removal of reward, and maze learning in rats. *University of California Publications in Psychology*, 1930, 4, 257–275.

Valentine, C. W. The innate basis of fear. *Journal of Genetic Psychology*, 1930, 37, 394–419.

Watson, J. B. Psychology as the behaviorist views it. *Psychological Review*, 1913, 20, 158–177.

Watson, J. B. *Behaviorism*. New York: Norton, 1925.

Watson, J. B., & Rayner, R. Conditioned emotional reactions. *Journal of Experimental Psychology*, 1920, 3, 1–14.

Wolfe, J. B. Effectiveness of token rewards for chimpanzees. *Comparative Psychology Monographs*, 1936, 12(No. 60).

Yerkes, R. M., & Morgulis, S. The method of Pavlov in animal psychology. *Psychological Bulletin*, 1909, 6, 257–273.

SUPPLEMENTARY READINGS

The preceding reference list includes most of the major systematic statements of the theorists covered in this chapter: Guthrie (1935), Hull (1943), Pavlov (1927), Skinner (1938), Thorndike (1911), Tolman (1938), and Watson (1925).

The most significant publications of this type not included in the reference list are the following:

Koch, S. (Ed.). *Psychology: A study of a science (Vol. 2). General systematic formulations, learning, and special processes*. New York: McGraw-Hill, 1959.

Written by these theorists or their very close associates, this volume contains treatments of the theories of Guthrie, Hull/Spence, Skinner, and Tolman. There is an important statement by Neal E. Miller aimed at liberalizing the S-R point of view and a chapter by Harry Harlow, whose error-factor theory would be covered in a more complete history of the topic of conditioning and learning.

Pavlov, I. P. *Lectures on conditioned reflexes (Vol. 1). Twenty-five years of objective study of the higher nervous activity (behavior) of animals*. London: Lawrence & Wishart, 1928.

Pavlov, I. P. *Lectures on conditioned reflexes (Vol. 2). Conditioned reflexes and psychiatry*. London: Lawrence & Wishart, 1941.

This two-volume set, translated by W. H. Gantt, was also published separately by International Publishers of New York in 1928 and 1941.

Pavlov, I. P. *Selected works*. Moscow: Foreign Languages Publishing House, 1955.

Pavlov, I. P. *Experimental psychology and other essays*. New York: Philosophical Library, 1957.

Among them, these four books and the 1927 volume contain something like 90 percent of Pavlov's published work, all translated into English.

An interesting fact about the theorists of learning is that all of them, sometimes through disciples, made strong efforts to demonstrate the relevance of their work to practical problems. Among the most significant of these attempts are the following:

Guthrie, E. R. *The psychology of human conflict*. New York: Harper & Row, 1938.

Dollard, J., & Miller, N. E. *Personality and psychotherapy*. New York: McGraw-Hill, 1950.

Miller, N. E., & Dollard, J. *Social learning and imitation*. New Haven: Yale University Press, 1941.

The last two books listed are extensions of Hullian theory to the areas suggested.

Skinner, B. F. *Walden two*. New York: Macmillan, 1948 (a utopian novel).

Skinner, B. F. *The technology of teaching*. Englewood Cliffs, N.J.: Prentice-Hall, 1968.

Tolman, E. C. *Drives toward war*. New York: Appleton-Century-Crofts, 1942.

Students interested in commentary on the psychology of learning as well as critical evaluation might consult one of the following:

Bower, G. H., & Hilgard, E. R. *Theories of learning* (5th ed.). Englewood Cliffs, N.J.: Prentice-Hall, 1981.

Kimble, G. A. *Foundations of conditioning and learning*. New York: Appleton-Century-Crofts, 1967.

MacCorquodale, K., & Meehl, P. H. In *Modern learning theory*. (Chap. 2, on "Edward C. Tolman.") New York: Appleton-Century-Crofts, 1954.

The Bower and Hilgard volume is a well-balanced coverage which brings the classical theories up to date. Kimble's book presents several major theories briefly, but in more detail than this chapter does. *Modern Learning Theory* contains critical reactions to these theories and was published at a time when the theories flourished.

13

The Two Psychologies
of Learning
BLIND ALLEYS AND NONSENSE SYLLABLES

A. CHARLES CATANIA

The history of the psychology of learning is a tale of confusions and controversies. It has more often been told in terms of theorists and their systems than in terms of the phenomena of learning. Although learning has typically been regarded as a fundamental part of experimental psychology, it was overshadowed in the psychological laboratories of the late nineteenth century by other issues, issues such as sensation and reaction time and attention. We may acknowledge the founding of Wundt's laboratory in 1879, but we must recognize that the main accomplishment was to give experimental psychology a home within the universities. Two decades had passed since the publication of Darwin's *Origin of Species* (1859), and that work had already stimulated research on animal behavior by Lubbock and others (e.g., Lubbock, 1882; Romanes, 1892). By that date also, Ebbinghaus had begun the experiments on human memory that he was to publish in 1885. Both of these historical lines were to become well-established within university laboratories by the turn of the century, in such work as that by Loeb and Jennings on the one hand and by Calkins and Müller on the other (e.g., Calkins, 1894, 1896; Jennings, 1906; Loeb, 1900; Müller & Pilzecker, 1900). At various universities in succession, the lines of research diversely housed in physiology and philosophy began to acquire shared residence within the single discipline of psychology. From then on, their proximity was forced; nevertheless, these two branches of the psychology of learning remained separate.

In animal learning, attention shifted from invertebrates to vertebrates. With Thorndike's puzzle boxes and the mazes of Yerkes and Small (Small, 1899–1900; Thorndike, 1911; Yerkes, 1907), experimental psychology gained the topic of instrumental learning. Thorndike soon set an example by moving from animal studies to analyses of human verbal learning (e.g., Thorndike, 1921), but in so doing he was exceptional. Later students of animal learning were more likely to make the extension through theoretical elaboration than through experiments. For example, following his demonstrations of respondent conditioning, Pavlov manifested an interest in human language in his theory of the second signal system (Pavlov, 1957, p. 285), but his impact on American psychology was based on his canine research (Pavlov, 1927). With instrumental and respondent conditioning established as phenomena in the early decades of the twentieth century, the stage was set for the elaboration of discrimination learning—experimentally in the progression from Lashley's jumping stand to Skinner's rat chambers and pigeon boxes, and theoretically in the evolution from Skinner's pseudo-reflex to his three-term contingency (e.g., Lashley, 1930; Skinner, 1930, 1938). The phenomena of reinforcement schedules were to follow later (Ferster & Skinner, 1957).

With the advent of Watsonian behaviorism (1919), which was strengthened by the parallel development of logical positivism in philosophy and operationism in physics (Ayer, 1959; Bridgman, 1927), the stage was set for the era of grand theories that emerged in the 1930s and 1940s. Give or take a name or two, Hull and Skinner and Tolman and Guthrie and one or more Gestalt psychologists are still likely to appear in chapter headings of texts on learning theories. Consistent with their professed generality, the theories, mostly based on animal data, retained a concern with human behavior and language. For example, Hull included rote learning, concept formation, and hypnosis among his research concerns (e.g., Hull et al., 1940). Of the several theorists, Skinner eventually provided the most substantial extension to human language in his *Verbal Behavior* (1957), one of the few treatments in psychology that placed more weight on the functions of language than on the structural features of syntax and semantics. Other attempts to integrate the processes of animal learning with the properties of language, as in the subsequent work of Mowrer (1960), lost influence in parallel with the declining fortunes of stimulus-response connectionism and other variations on classical associationism.

In the field of human learning and memory, it is more difficult to catalog the events of the same period in terms of individual researchers or theorists. Ebbinghaus (1885) had outlined major issues, and his precedence dominated subsequent detailed studies of serial-position effects, massed vs. spaced practice, meaningfulness, backward associations, interference, and so on. The shape of the learning curve was at issue, and the plateaus in Morse Code learning that were demonstrated by Bryan and Harter (1899) at the turn of the century remained as part of psychological lore until well into the 1950s, when Keller (1958) put the phantom phenomenon to rest. Thorndike and Woodworth (1901) began to investigate transfer of training, probably

323

inspired in part by questions about the educational value of such classical disciplines as Latin and Greek. These and other findings made the potential practical relevance of studies of human learning seem obvious. The effects on verbal learning of such variables as sleep, distraction, and motivation became the basis for advice on study habits. An important result of these researches was that the differentiation among such topics as acquisition and retention and transfer was sharpened. Despite the different content, however, the theoretical underpinnings of these areas were the same as those of animal learning. Contiguity, association, generalization, and the law of effect were the links that gave a superficial appearance of unity to the two disparate experimental lines.

By the 1940s, the pattern was firmly entrenched and is most clearly illustrated by two textbooks of the time. The first, in 1940, was Hilgard and Marquis's *Conditioning and Learning*, devoted primarily to research on animal behavior. The second, in 1942, was McGeoch's *Psychology of Human Learning*, concerned mainly with human learning and remembering. Both were best sellers by scholarly standards, and each reappeared in subsequent editions, the former in Kimble's 1961 revision and the latter with Irion's 1952 collaboration. Although they had relatively short histories to cover, both missed some classic work. For example, Stratton's name appears in McGeoch but neither book refers to his work with inverting prisms (Stratton, 1897). That research is usually regarded as relevant primarily to perception, but among other things Stratton had shown how the consequences of eye movement can be learned: if when we look down we see the ceiling rather than the floor, we learn to look up when we drop something. How differently might the concept of reinforcement have evolved had it been tied to such elementary consequences of behavior. Esper's name is missing from both bibliographies. His work on novel verbal responses generated by the intersection of independently learned response classes (Esper, 1918, 1933), with its implications for syntax and for metaphor, did not fit comfortably into the associationist mold of the period. What might psycholinguistics have become if it had developed primarily within psychology instead of being catalyzed from without by progress in linguistics.

Every psychology department in this country presumably gives some attention to learning in its introductory course and offers advanced courses devoted exclusively to the topic, though the role of the latter as requirements for or as electives toward the psychology major undoubtedly varies. The name for such a course is typically "the psychology of learning" because some university faculties will not allow the word *learning* to stand alone in a course title. Learning is, of course, the business of the entire university and cannot be preempted in its entirety by a psychology department or, worse yet, by an individual faculty member. Nevertheless, this offering is often colloquially "the learning course." In the singular, however, that title is a misnomer, because in different universities or even in different semesters within the same university two offerings of learning may have as little overlap as did the Hilgard and Marquis and the McGeoch books of the 1940s. Corresponding to these courses we still have texts that exclusively treat one or the other area, such as Rachlin's *Behavior and Learning* (1976) and Crowder's *Principles of Learning and Memory* (1976). This is not to fault such texts; they often treat the material within their province exceedingly well. The point is that in the face of such differences it is difficult to speak of a single entity called "the psychology of learning."

Some texts do treat both the literature of animal learning and conditioning and that of human verbal learning and memory, with varying degrees of emphasis on one or the other area (e.g., Donahoe & Wessells, 1980; Hulse, Deese, & Egeth, 1975). In such texts, the transition between the two areas is often abrupt and lacking a rationale; sometimes too they end suddenly, with a final chapter on some specific topic such as concept formation or long-term memory but with no overview or summary statement. On occasion, the courses correlated with these texts cover all the topics, either within a single semester or in two successive semesters, and in some departments separate courses in the two areas of learning are explicitly arranged. But it is also not unusual for an instructor to stop at the transition, having covered only the sections on animal learning and conditioning in the available time. Of course innumerable variations are defensible in organizing the psychology of learning, and a single learning course will at least be more effective in introducing students to the phenomena of learning than a little learning treated in passing in a course on developmental or cognitive psychology or presented only indirectly in a course on theories of learning. But if we judge the integrity of the psychology of learning from the consistency of psychology curricula, we may wonder what justifies celebrating the role of learning in the centennial of experimental psychology. Two psychologies of learning are one too many.

Certainly we understand more about learning now than we did one hundred years ago. The title of my earliest draft of this chapter, "Learning: Increments, Cumulations, and Insights," alluded to our progress. Some readers will also know that I attempted to address some of the preceding issues in my own 1979 text, *Learning*. The main purpose of that book was to demonstrate the feasibility of a coherent psychology of learning encompassing both literatures. Whether that effort was a failure or a partial success is not for me to say, and it is impossible here to detail the arguments implicit there. But I do assert that those who wish to speak for the priority of one or another component of the psychology of learning must be well-informed about the alternatives. To say that the literature has grown too large or that our competencies have become too specialized is an inadequate excuse for ignorance.

The reader who here detects a certain petulance must understand that one source of it is the recurrent and erroneous judgment from some cognitive theorists who should know better that all varieties of behavior analysis entail associationist principles that lead inevitably to stimulus-response or mediational accounts of sequential behavior. We may leave aside the defenses of mediational accounts that might have been offered by admitting the possibility of simultaneous and interacting behavior chains; that avenue merely illustrates our prejudices with regard to whether organisms can do only one thing at a time. Whether mediational accounts can be salvaged, however, is not at issue. The point instead is that some behavioral accounts parted company with associationism decades ago, and some of our colleagues seem not to know that yet.

For example, Skinner was familiar with Lashley's (1951) treatment of the problem of serial order in behavior, and in the work of Dews (1962) sequential behavior not interpretable in terms of chaining has been demonstrated even with pigeons. The very fact that among Skinner's categories of verbal responses he included intraverbals as the response classes generated by chaining should have made it obvious that processes besides chaining were involved in other classes and therefore were recognized in his analysis of verbal behavior. But Chomsky (1959) missed the point, and the consequences of that misunderstanding are still with us more than two decades after his critical review of Skinner's *Verbal Behavior* (1957). What followed in theories of language acquisition was closer to creationism than any other part of contemporary psychological research.

To argue that one kind of process can occur in behavior is not to imply that all other kinds of processes must be rejected. The issue can be converted from a theoretical to an empirical one. Unlike the grand theories that sought to account for all learning in terms of a limited number of principles, we can admit the existence, on the one hand, of behavior sequences that are temporally extended units in their own right and, on the other, of sequences in which early responses produce stimuli that occasion later responses that in turn produce new stimuli, and so on. The difference between the two kinds of sequences is that the latter can be fractionated in ways that the former cannot. The true accomplishment of contemporary behavioral analysis is not that it has been able to explain varied behavior in terms of a minimal set of assumptions, but rather that it has developed criteria for distinguishing among different sorts of behavior. It is important to be able to differentiate between this behavior as reinforced and that as species-specific, or between this behavior as elicited and that as occasioned by a discriminative stimulus, because an adequate taxonomy of behavioral processes is a prerequisite for any effective theory of learning. It may even be appropriate to argue that such a taxonomy is itself a kind of theory, though of a considerably different sort from those that have previously been dominant. Thus, the demonstration, by Sidman and his colleagues, that the equivalence classes established through matching procedures with humans are not necessarily reducible to simpler discriminations (e.g., Lazar, 1977; Sidman, Cresson, & Willson-Morris, 1974) did not initiate a theoretical crisis but simply added a new process to those that had already been recognized.

Imagine what biology would be like if osmosis was a theoretical issue. Judging whether fluids moved through a membrane in various preparations would be a test of the generality of the theory. Consider then how the phenomenon of active transport might be received, and what theoretical controversy would be engendered.

Yet the point is not to choose between osmosis and active transport; rather the significance of active transport can only be appreciated in the context of an understanding of osmotic phenomena and the ways in which active transport operates in an environment of osmotic gradients. When we observe complex behavior, we must similarly examine the ways in which the component processes combine and interact. We need not choose among the components as if they were mutually exclusive alternatives.

Even the concept of reinforcement has been treated as if we had to choose between reinforcement as a cause of all behavior or no reinforcement at all. But only a few die-hard behaviorists would claim that all behavior can be attributed to reinforcement, and it is therefore ironic to see Skinner arguing that behavior has both phylogenic and ontogenic sources while being taken to task on that point by a former student on the grounds that even phylogenically determined behavior can involve reinforcement (Herrnstein, 1977a, 1977b; Skinner, 1977). The phenomenon of reinforcement remains controversial not because there is any question that some events will increase responding when they are made consequences of responding. Rather, the issues are those of what determines when events can function as reinforcers, and those issues are more empirical than theoretical (e.g., Morse & Kelleher, 1977; Premack, 1965).

The dichotomies within the contemporary psychology of learning, however, cannot simply be laid at the feet of antibehavioral critics. The divisions that originated in the earliest days of experimental psychology nurtured a latter-day parochialism in animal learning that perhaps even provoked the eventual clash between cognitive and behavioral psychologies. Sometimes the differences between animal nonverbal and human verbal research interests were only latent, as when the conflicts between behavior analysis and more traditional approaches dominated animal learning. The separation between animal and human learning was not the only division within psychology, nor was it the same as that between structuralism and functionalism or other dominant schools (see Catania, 1973, 1978). Inevitably a brief account oversimplifies complex issues. It is clear, however, that intellectual chauvinism is often reciprocated, and our concern should not be whether students of animal behavior endeared themselves to their colleagues or to each other. Rather, for our present purposes we should be interested in what they knew of each other's work. There were times when they seemed unwilling to acknowledge that their colleagues were studying phenomena different from theirs in ways appropriate to those issues and not their own phenomena in different and debatably effective ways.

The logic of experimental analysis, which was concerned not with explanations of behavior but rather with the rationale for defining behavior classes, might have been brought to bear on those complex activities called "remembering" and "attending" and "thinking." This is not to say that better experiments would have been conducted; given the research available on classes of remembering and visual imagery and the psychological reality of syntactic structure such an assertion would be presumptuous indeed. But perhaps the separate research lines might have been drawn together if there had existed research issues of genuinely mutual concern. When two topographically different responses that have similar consequences vary together, we say that the responses are members of the same operant class. When responses do not change together, we speak of them as belonging to different classes. As described by Skinner (1935, p. 40), behavior breaks along these natural lines of fracture. In other words, reinforcement and other operant procedures are the basis for discovering behavior classes. They are not phenomena to be explained by those classes.

But now consider remembering. Remembering is behavior, even if it is not a response. Much research effort has been devoted to attempts to explain remembering, usually in terms of metaphorical accounts of storage and retrieval. But another approach is to see how behavior classes can be defined by what is remembered. Some work on memory has emphasized the properties of what is differentially remembered (e.g., Bousfield, 1953; Conrad, 1964; Paivio, 1971; Sachs, 1967; Tulving, 1972; Wickens, 1970). When some things are more likely to be remembered together than others, we speak of the organization of memory. When we note that the content of sentences is better remembered than their grammatical structure, we define semantic and syntactic properties of language. When we identify correspondences between verbal and nonverbal items remembered, we justify the distinction between imagery and verbal ideation. When we classify the kinds of errors that occur in remembering in terms of the vocabulary of encoding, we describe the kinds of behavior that are occasioned when items are to be remembered. None of these approaches explains remembering. All are concerned in one way or another with the definition of behavioral classes, and they are among the most successful lines of research on human memory. In the face of these similar features of the research strategies within the two areas of research, debates over the priority of behavioral and cognitive vocabularies seem mere digressions. Yet few researchers seem to regard the fields of animal learning and conditioning and of human verbal learning and memory as having any important relation to one another.

What a strange subject matter is learning. For some time during its history it was not even clear whether particular phenomena came within its purview until after those phenomena had been studied. For example, research on the behavior of unicellular organisms declined with the successive discoveries of artifactual sources of the changes in behavior that had once been taken as instances of learning. Experiments with paramecia, amoebae, and stentors illustrated in microcosm the range of phenomena with which studies of animal learning were concerned. Habituation was demonstrated early, and then one by one procedures established with mammals were adapted for their microscopic counterparts. The literature for paramecia alone includes studies of maze learning, escape from enclosed spaces, respondent conditioning, discrimination learning, and operant responding, but in none of these cases did the results stand as examples of learning (e.g., Best, 1954; Jensen, 1957). For that reason, their historical impact was slight, but we are justified in noting them because they were so clearly designed not to explain a phenomenon or to support a theory but simply to determine whether certain phenomena occurred and, if so, what properties they had. It is true that the results were negative, but in their concern with the nature and range of learning phenomena such studies provide the very foundations of our subject matter.

The point of coming back from human learning and remembering not even to vertebrate responding but to the behavior of protozoa is that it is time to address the question of whether there is any point to treating these disparate subject matters together. Now that we have examined the history, we may wish to conclude that animal learning and conditioning and human learning and remembering are so little relevant to each other that they should go their separate ways, the former to provide us with substrates for studies in psychopharmacology and psychophysiology and maybe even with techniques for training pets and other domesticated animals, and the latter to provide findings not only of interest in their own right but also presumably relevant to the practical problems of education. I will maintain here, however, that such a course would be a serious mistake. There are obviously the simple arguments that the learning phenomena studied with animals also occur in human behavior, and that the nature of complex human learning is clarified by an understanding of more elementary processes. But I believe that a more important reason is that human behavior is characterized by an interplay between the verbal and the nonverbal, and we have yet to understand the origins and priorities of each.

In *The Origin of Consciousness in the Breakdown of the Bicameral Mind*, Jaynes (1977) describes some ways in which the progress of his own research duplicated the history we have just considered:

> After failures to find learning in the lower phyla, I moved on to species with synaptic nervous systems, flatworms, earthworms, fish, and reptiles, which could indeed learn, all on the naive assumption that I was chronicling the grand evolution of consciousness. Ridiculous! (p. 7).

His account points to assumptions about the evolution of human behavior that were implicit throughout the history of the psychology of learning. If pressed to hypothesize about the evolution of learning, we might proceed as follows. Over the epochs of evolution, some organisms became responsive to their environments, developing reflexes and then simple varieties of conditioning that adapted them to survive and reproduce in a complex world. Their behavior also became sensitive to its own consequences, in the operant relations of reinforcement and punishment, and then sensitive to different consequences in different settings, in discrimination learning or stimulus control. But still their behavior was subject to the vagaries of accidental correlations among events and changing natural contingencies. Then came verbal behavior, and subsequent human history is a chronicle of how language—and ultimately the science and logic made possible by language—brought reason into the world. Human beings could now overcome the behavioral constraints by which other organisms were bound. With language, rule-governed behavior replaced contingency-shaped behavior, and because such higher-order capacities as deliberation, consciousness, and self-control had become possible, humans no longer had to remain victims of the ways in which the immediate consequences of action could outweigh important but more remote consequences.

Is this a plausible account? We recognize all too well that language need not be an instrument of reason, and yet even those who have warned of the traps that can be created by verbal behavior, such as Korzybski (1941) on general semantics and Chase in his *Tyranny of Words* (1938), have typically spoken of such problems of language as if they were temporary aberrations of recent origin. What if the preceding scenario has things backward? From the work on bait-shyness by Garcia and Revusky and their colleagues (e.g., Revusky & Garcia, 1970), for example, we know that nonverbal organisms need not be lured by immediate contingencies to become victims of remote contingencies: rats who have recovered from poisoning subsequently avoid the poisoned food even if the symptoms of poisoning follow only a considerable time after ingestion. And in the research of Rachlin and others, we have begun to be able to specify nonverbal processes that must enter into self-control and free-choice preference (e.g., Catania & Sagvolden, 1980; Rachlin & Green, 1972). Perhaps the problems of human history are not in the slowness with which language has transcended nonverbal behavior but in our assumptions about the role of language in the evolution of human behavior.

Jaynes has given us a glimpse of an alternate possibility. Suppose that language evolved primarily through the elaboration of its instructional functions. The calls of the leader may once have controlled the behavior of members of the group as reliably as any other releaser elicits a fixed-action pattern. With the differentiation of more varied vocal calls corresponding to a more extensive repertory of instructed classes of behavior, and with the singling out of instructional control over individual members by distinctive calls that would eventually become names, and with repetition by others of the leader's utterances not only initiating the relevant vocal behavior in the leader's successors but also creating the precursors of verbal memory by establishing conditions under which instructions might be followed in the leader's absence, a cohesive social group would have been developed, the coordinated behavior of which would give each of its members a survival advantage relative to those in competing groups, even though the instructed behavior would inevitably be relatively insensitive to modification by its natural consequences.

If such instructional functions were involved in the origins of language, recent human history might be regarded as a chronicle of the emergence of other functions of language and their substitution for instructional control. But the phenomena of religious fanaticism and political dogmatism suggest that some strongly determined instructional components of language have remained with us instead of becoming vestigial. Perhaps the contingency–sensitive part of the evolution of language has only just begun. From this perspective, contemporary human achievements are not merely those of developing and refining language but, perhaps more fundamentally, those of freeing language from its origins in social control. Galileo's problem is simply stated: some of his verbal behavior was under the control of what he saw through his telescope and not of what he had been told by others, and some of those others would not even look. In the evolving functions of language, the promise of science is that it may bring human behavior back into contact with natural contingencies again, and perhaps in new and more effective ways.

This is admittedly a speculative account, but it is offered in the service of our progress in the psychology of learning, and at least it illustrates how extensive are our areas of ignorance. We must discover not only which properties of behavior are unique to humans but also which we hold in common with other organisms. The task is one of behavior synthesis as well as behavior analysis. For example, attempts to establish language in chimpanzees (e.g., Gardner & Gardner, 1969; Premack, 1970; Rumbaugh & Gill, 1976) demonstrate how some properties of verbal behavior can emerge when simpler behavioral processes are combined. Given the varied properties of language, we must assume that both the elementary phenomena of animal learning and conditioning and the complexities of human learning and remembering will enter into any effective account (see Catania, 1980). For this reason, we cannot allow the subject matter to remain divided. One psychology of learning is enough. The psychologists of future centennials may then be able to say of the later decades of the twentieth century that these were the times when experimental psychology recognized that the psychology of learning had too long been presented as two to many.

REFERENCES

Ayer, A. J. (Ed.). *Logical positivism.* New York: The Free Press, 1959.

Best, J. B. The photosensitization of paramecia aurelia by temperature shock. *Journal of Experimental Zoology,* 1954, 126, 87–99.

Bousfield, W. A. The occurrence of clustering in the recall of randomly arranged associates. *Journal of General Psychology,* 1953, 49, 229–240.

Bridgman, P. W. *The logic of modern physics.* New York: Macmillan, 1927.

Bryan, W. L., & Harter, N. Studies on the telegraphic language. The acquisition of a hierarchy of habits. *Psychological Review,* 1899, 6, 345–375.

Calkins, M. W. Association. *Psychological Review,* 1894, 1, 476–483.

Calkins, M. W. Association. II. *Psychological Review,* 1896, 3, 32–49.

Catania, A. C. The psychologies of structure, function, and development. *American Psychologist,* 1973, 28, 434–443.

II. THE SPECIAL FIELDS OF PSYCHOLOGY

Catania, A. C. The psychology of learning: Some lessons from the Darwinian revolution. *Annals of the New York Academy of Sciences*, 1978, *309*, 18–28.

Catania, A. C. *Learning*. Englewood Cliffs, N.J.: Prentice-Hall, 1979.

Catania, A. C. Autoclitic processes and the structure of behavior. *Behaviorism*, 1980, *8*, 175–186.

Catania, A. C., & Sagvolden, T. Preference for free choice over forced choice in pigeons. *Journal of the Experimental Analysis of Behavior*, 1980, *34*, 77–86.

Chase, S. *The tyranny of words*. New York: Harcourt, Brace, 1938.

Chomsky, N. Review of B. F. Skinner's *Verbal behavior*. *Language*, 1959, *35*, 26–58.

Conrad, R. Acoustic confusions in immediate memory. *British Journal of Psychology*, 1964, *55*, 75–84.

Crowder, R. G. *Principles of learning and memory*. Hillsdale, N.J.: Erlbaum, 1976.

Darwin, C. *On the origin of species*. London: John Murray, 1859.

Dews, P. B. The effect of multiple S^Δ periods on responding on a fixed-interval schedule. *Journal of the Experimental Analysis of Behavior*, 1962, *5*, 369–374.

Donahoe, J. W., & Wessells, M. G. *Learning, language, and memory*. New York: Harper & Row, 1980.

Ebbinghaus, H. *Über das Gedächtnis*. Leipzig: Duncker und Humbolt, 1885.

Esper, E. A. A contribution to the experimental study of analogy. *Psychological Review*, 1918, *25*, 468–487.

Esper, E. A. Studies in linguistic behavior organization. *Journal of General Psychology*, 1933, *8*, 346–381.

Ferster, C. B., & Skinner, B. F. *Schedules of reinforcement*. New York: Appleton-Century-Crofts, 1957.

Gardner, R. A., & Gardner, B. T. Teaching sign language to a chimpanzee. *Science*, 1969, *165*, 664–672.

Herrnstein, R. J. The evolution of behaviorism. *American Psychologist*, 1977, *32*, 593–603. (a)

Herrnstein, R. J. Doing what comes naturally: A reply to Professor Skinner. *American Psychologist*, 1977, *32*, 1013–1016. (b)

Hilgard, E. R., & Marquis, D. G. *Conditioning and learning*. New York: Appleton-Century-Crofts, 1940.

Hull, C. L., Hovland, C. I., Ross, R. T., Hall, M., Perkins, D. T., & Fitch, F. B. *Mathematico-deductive theory of rote learning*. New Haven: Yale University Press, 1940.

Hulse, S. H., Deese, J., & Egeth, H. *The psychology of learning* (4th ed.). New York: McGraw-Hill, 1975.

Jaynes, J. *The origin of consciousness in the breakdown of the bicameral mind*. Boston: Houghton Mifflin, 1977.

Jennings, H. S. *Behavior of the lower organisms*. New York: Macmillan, 1906.

Jensen, D. D. Experiments on learning in paramecia. *Science*, 1957, *125*, 191–192.

Keller, F. S. The phantom plateau. *Journal of the Experimental Analysis of Behavior*, 1958, *1*, 1–13.

Kimble, G. A. *Hilgard and Marquis' Conditioning and learning*. New York: Appleton-Century-Crofts, 1961.

Korzybski, A. *Science and sanity: An introduction to non-Aristotelian systems and general semantics* (2nd ed.). Lancaster, Pa.: Science Press, 1941.

Lashley, K. S. The mechanism of vision. I. A method for rapid analysis of pattern vision in the rat. *Journal of Genetic Psychology*, 1930, *37*, 453–460.

Lashley, K. S. The problem of serial order in behavior. In L. A. Jeffress (Ed.), *Cerebral mechanisms in behavior*. New York: Wiley, 1951.

Lazar, R. Extending sequence-class membership with matching to sample. *Journal of the Experimental Analysis of Behavior*, 1977, *27*, 381–392.

Loeb, J. *Comparative physiology of the brain and comparative psychology*. New York: Putnam, 1900.

Lubbock, J. *Ants, bees, and wasps*. New York: D. Appleton, 1882.

McGeoch, J. A. *The psychology of human learning*. New York: Longmans, Green, 1942.

McGeoch, J. A., & Irion, A. L. *The psychology of human learning* (2nd ed.). New York: Longmans, Green, 1952.

Morse, W. H., & Kelleher, R. T. Determinants of reinforcement and punishment. In W. K. Honig & J. E. R. Staddon (Eds.), *Handbook of operant behavior.* Englewood Cliffs, N.J.: Prentice-Hall, 1977.

Mowrer, O. H. *Learning theory and the symbolic processes.* New York: Wiley, 1960.

Müller, G. E., & Pilzecker, A. Experimentelle Beiträge zur Lehre vom Gedächtnis. *Zeitschrift für Psychologie*, 1900, Ergänzungsband 1.

Paivio, A. *Imagery and verbal processes.* New York: Holt, 1971.

Pavlov, I. P. *Conditioned reflexes* (G. V. Anrep, trans.). London: Oxford University Press, 1927.

Pavlov, I. P. *Experimental psychology and other essays.* New York: Philosophical Library, 1957.

Premack, D. Reinforcement theory. In D. Levine (Ed.), *Nebraska Symposium on Motivation, 1965.* Lincoln: University of Nebraska Press, 1965.

Premack, D. A functional analysis of language. *Journal of the Experimental Analysis of Behavior*, 1970, *14*, 107–125.

Rachlin, H. *Behavior and learning.* San Francisco: Freeman, 1976.

Rachlin, H., & Green, L. Commitment, choice and self-control. *Journal of the Experimental Analysis of Behavior*, 1972, *17*, 15–22.

Revusky, S., & Garcia, J. Learned associations over long delays. In G. H. Bower (Ed.), *The psychology of learning and motivation* (Vol. 4). New York: Academic Press, 1970.

Romanes, G. J. *Animal intelligence.* New York: D. Appleton, 1892.

Rumbaugh, D. M., & Gill, T. V. The mastery of language-type skills by the chimpanzee (*Pan*). *Annals of the New York Academy of Sciences*, 1976, *280*, 562–578.

Sachs, J. S. Recognition memory for syntactic and semantic aspects of connected discourse. *Perception and Psychophysics*, 1967, *2*, 437–442.

Sidman, M., Cresson, O., Jr., & Willson-Morris, M. Acquisition of matching to sample via mediated transfer. *Journal of the Experimental Analysis of Behavior*, 1974, *22*, 261–273.

Skinner, B. F. On the conditions of elicitation of certain eating reflexes. *Proceedings of the National Academy of Sciences*, 1930, *16*, 433–438.

Skinner, B. F. The generic nature of the concepts of stimulus and response. *Journal of General Psychology*, 1935, *12*, 40–65.

Skinner, B. F. *The behavior of organisms.* New York: Appleton-Century-Crofts, 1938.

Skinner, B. F. *Verbal behavior.* New York: Appleton-Century-Crofts, 1957.

Skinner, B. F. Herrnstein and the evolution of behaviorism. *American Psychologist*, 1977, *32*, 1006–1012.

Small, W. S. Experimental studies of the mental processes of the rat. *American Journal of Psychology*, 1899–1900, *11*, 1–89.

Stratton, G. M. Vision without inversion of the retinal image. *Psychological Review*, 1897, *4*, 341–360; 463–481.

Thorndike, E. L. *Animal intelligence.* New York: Macmillan, 1911.

Thorndike, E. L. *Educational psychology. Volume II. The psychology of learning.* New York: Teachers College, 1921.

Thorndike, E. L., & Woodworth, R. S. The influence of improvement in one mental function upon the efficiency of other functions. *Psychological Review*, 1901, *8*, 247–261.

Tulving, E. Episodic and semantic memory. In E. Tulving & W. Donaldson (Eds.), *Organization of memory.* New York: Academic Press, 1972.

Watson, J. B. *Psychology from the standpoint of a behaviorist.* Philadelphia: Lippincott, 1919.

Wickens, D. D. Encoding categories of words: An empirical approach to meaning. *Psychological Review*, 1970, *77*, 1–15.

Yerkes, R. M. *The dancing mouse.* New York: Macmillan, 1907.

SUPPLEMENTARY READINGS

Baddeley, A. D. *The psychology of memory.* New York: Basic Books, 1976.

Baer, D. M., Peterson, R. F., & Sherman, J. A. The development of imitation by reinforcing behavioral similarity to a model. *Journal of the Experimental Analysis of Behavior*, 1967, *10*, 405–416.

Bechterev, V. M. *General principles of human reflexology* (E. Murphy and W. Murphy, trans. from the fourth Russian edition, 1928). London: Jarrolds, 1933.

Bolles, R. C. Species-specific defense reactions and avoidance learning. *Psychological Review*, 1970, *77*, 32–48.

Boren, J. J., & Devine, D. D. The repeated acquisition of behavioral chains. *Journal of the Experimental Analysis of Behavior*, 1968, *11*, 651–660.

Catania, A. C. Chomsky's formal analysis of natural languages: A behavioral translation. *Behaviorism*, 1972, *1*, 1–15.

Catania, A. C. Operant theory: Skinner. In G. M. Gazda & R. J. Corsini (Eds.), *Theories of learning*. Itasca, Ill.: F. E. Peacock, 1980.

Dawkins, R. *The selfish gene.* New York: Oxford, 1976.

Day, W. F. On certain similarities between the philosophical investigations of Ludwig Wittgenstein and the operationism of B. F. Skinner. *Journal of the Experimental Analysis of Behavior*, 1969, *12*, 489–506.

Estes, W. K., Koch, S., MacCorquodale, K., Meehl, P. E., Mueller, C. G., Jr., Schoenfeld, W. N., & Verplanck, W. S. *Modern learning theory.* New York: Appleton-Century-Crofts, 1954.

Gallistel, C. R. *The organization of action: A new synthesis.* Hillsdale, N.J.: Erlbaum, 1980.

Garcia, J., & Koelling, R. A. Relation of cue to consequence in avoidance learning. *Psychonomic Science*, 1966, *4*, 123–124.

Glucksberg, S., & Danks, J. H. *Experimental psycholinguistics.* Hillsdale, N.J.: Erlbaum, 1975.

Guthrie, E. R. *The psychology of learning.* New York: Harper, 1935.

Guthrie, E. R., & Horton, G. P. *Cats in a puzzle box.* New York: Rinehart, 1946.

Harris, M. *Cannibals and kings.* New York: Random House, 1977.

Hull, C. L. *Principles of behavior.* New York: Appleton-Century-Crofts, 1943.

Johnston, J. M., & Pennypacker, H. S. *Strategies and tactics of human behavioral research.* Hillsdale, N.J.: Erlbaum, 1980.

Kelleher, R. T., & Morse, W. H. Schedules using noxious stimuli. III. Responding maintained with response-produced electric shocks. *Journal of the Experimental Analysis of Behavior*, 1968, *11*, 819–838.

Köhler, W. *The mentality of apes* (2nd rev. ed., E. Winter, trans.). London: Routledge & Kegan Paul, 1927.

Köhler, W. *Gestalt psychology.* New York: Liveright, 1929.

MacCorquodale, K. On Chomsky's review of Skinner's *Verbal behavior*. *Journal of the Experimental Analysis of Behavior*, 1970, *13*, 83–99.

Mackenzie, B. D. *Behaviourism and the limits of scientific method.* Atlantic Highlands, N.J.: Humanities Press, 1977.

Malcolm, N. The myth of cognitive processes and structures. In T. Mischel (Ed.), *Cognitive development and epistemology*. New York: Academic Press, 1971.

Matthews, B. A., Shimoff, E., Catania, A. C., & Sagvolden, T. Uninstructed human responding: Sensitivity to ratio and interval contingencies. *Journal of the Experimental Analysis of Behavior*, 1977, *27*, 453–467.

Paivio, A. Neomentalism. *Canadian Journal of Psychology*, 1975, *29*, 263–291.

Premack, D. Catching up with common sense or two sides of a generalization: Reinforcement and punishment. In R. Glaser (Ed.), *The nature of reinforcement*. New York: Academic Press, 1971.

Rozin, P., & Kalat, J. W. Specific hungers and poison avoidance as adaptive specializations of learning. *Psychological Review*, 1971, 78, 459–486.

Ryle, G. *The concept of mind.* New York: Barnes & Noble, 1949.

Schoenfeld, W. N. Some old work for modern conditioning theory. *Conditional Reflex*, 1966, *1*, 219–223.

Sechenov, I. M. *Reflexes of the brain* (S. Belsky, trans.). Cambridge, Mass.: M.I.T. Press, 1965. (Originally published, 1863.)

Sherrington, C. *The integrative action of the nervous system.* New York: Scribner's, 1906.

Sidman, M. *Tactics of scientific research.* New York: Basic Books, 1960.

Skinner, B. F. The operational analysis of psychological terms. *Psychological Review*, 1945, *52*, 270–277.

Skinner, B. F. *Contingencies of reinforcement.* New York: Appleton-Century-Crofts, 1969.

Thorndike, E. L. Animal intelligence: An experimental study of the associative processes in animals. *Psychological Review Monograph Supplements*, 1898, 2 (No. 4).

Tolman, E. C. Cognitive maps in rats and men. *Psychological Review*, 1948, *55*, 189–208.

335

MOTIVATION, EMOTION, AND VALUE

14

Motivation, the Brain, and Psychological Theory

DALBIR BINDRA

Hippocrates (circa 400 B.C., cited by Allport, 1937) talked of the four humors that make people sanguine, melancholic, choleric, or phlegmatic. St. Thomas Aquinas (thirteenth century, cited by Beach, 1955) talked of instincts that do for animals what reason does for man, and Freud (1915/1925) of the Id and the Superego. Descartes (1650) talked of passions of the soul that arise from bodily agitation and heat, and Darwin (1872) of emotions that link the human to the animal species. Spencer (1872–1873) talked of pleasure and pain, Papez (1937) of limbic circuits of the brain, and Hebb (1955) of arousal. Spranger (1928) talked of aesthetic, economic, and other values that define types of persons, McDougall (1908) of sentiments, and Allport (1937) of personality traits. And the current talk is of psychoactive drugs (see Seiden & Dykstra, 1977), self-systems (Bandura, 1978), and neuromodulators (see Wise, 1979). All these terms, spanning two millennia, contain the common idea that thought and action are governed, at least in part, by certain changing but more or less enduring dispositions, moods, interests, temperaments, or what in modern psychology has come to be called "the motivational state."

Three observations point to the need for some dispositional concept, such as motivation, in completing a psychological account of behavior. One is that over the period of a year, or a week, or a day, an individual distributes its time among several different actions, now it eats or drinks, now it grooms or sleeps, now it copulates or fights, now it sleeps or nurses the young, now it explores or marks its territory. The second observation is that these changes in the direction or goals of actions are not wholly tied to any specific situational stimuli, as when a woman may on occasion be edgy and self-deprecatory in situations in which she has normally been calm and self-confident. The third observation is that any particular goal-directed action does not always involve the same movements, as when a young chimpanzee may obtain a banana from a dominant adult by stealing, begging, or trickery, each method involving different patterns of movements, utilizing widely different musculature.

These three observations—that the goals of our actions change from time to time, that these changes in goals are not wholly determined by any specific situational alterations, and that an invariant goal may be reached by several alternative sets of movements—compel the conclusion that such variations in goals of actions are not explainable in terms of specific stimulus input or specific motor outflow. Rather, they suggest the existence of certain dispositions of broader scope that give direction to actions and save them from becoming either haphazard scrambles of purposeless movements or rigidly stereotyped reactions to prevailing stimuli. Some of the dispositions are short-lived and are usually called "impulses," "drives," and "emotions"; others are more lasting and are called "interests," "attitudes," and "sentiments"; and still others are even more stable and are called "temperament," "personality traits," and "values."

In this paper I want to retrace the path of ideas along which we have come in the past hundred years or so, and to relate that lineage to the newer ideas about the nature of the motivational factor. In a word, my conclusion is that our understanding of both the behavioral and neural aspects of the motivational factor has progressed a good deal since the founding of psychology, and this now makes it possible to deal with the diverse phenomena subsumed under the heading of motivation, emotion, and personality within a unified theoretical framework.

An Historical Glimpse

Any serious account of motivation must deal with two problems. One, what is the nature of the motivational factor: What is a motive? What is the origin of motives? How do they become active or change from time to time? Two, how does a prevailing motive influence actions—response output? Does a motive influence behavior through perception or by direct motor instigation? By what process is this influence effected? Numerous ideas on these questions have been proposed during the past century. For convenience I shall group these ideas under eight headings: motive as instinct; motive as drive; drive as need; drive as strong stimulation (afferent discharge); drive as excitation of specific brain sites; drive as an ad hoc instigational factor; incentive motivation; and the process of response production.

Motive as Instinct

The use of the term motive in its modern, psychological sense is traceable to Schopenhauer (1836, cited by M. J. Morgan, 1979). He proposed that a motive is a mental cause in the same way as a force is a physical cause, and that energy and direction of both types of causes have fixed—determined and automatic—outcomes or goals. The related broader notion that inherent purposive strivings lie behind all that is observed in nature was promoted by the writings of Nietzsche (1883/1932) and von Hartmann (1893) and became very influential in the intellectual circles of Europe in the latter half of the nineteenth century. It influenced psychology through the writings of McDougall (1908, 1923) and Freud (1915/1925), who gave distinct purposive dimension to the old concept of instinct by endowing each instinct with a specific energy and a specific direction aimed at a certain goal. McDougall called instincts the "essential springs or motive powers" that make all animal and human behavior possible, and regarded each instinct as an innate propensity or energy source that, once excited, determines the immediate goal of mental activity and thereby promotes specific thoughts and actions. The characterization of instinct given by ethologists (Lorenz, 1937; Tinbergen, 1951) followed McDougall's ideas closely (see Hinde, 1960).

The essential feature of the instinct doctrine was that it assumed the existence of several innate, goal-specific or action-specific energy reservoirs or instincts, each postulated to explain a particular type of behavior. Motive a, action-specific energy for foraging, instigates directed behavior in relation to goal A, food; motive b, aggression, instigates directed behavior in relation to goal B, victim; motive c, gregariousness, instigates directed behavior in relation to goal C, friends, and so on. The complete circularity (and, therefore, theoretical emptiness) of this model was partly dispelled because its proponents tried to specify the process by which an instinct, once excited, influences the behavioral outcome. McDougall was quite clear on this point. According to him, an excited instinct creates a perceptual disposition to attend to certain classes of environmental objects, an affective disposition to experience a certain kind of emotional excitement in relation to the perceived objects, and finally a disposition to act in a goal-directed way in relation to that object. For example, an excitation of the instinct of fear results in selective perception of dangerous objects, an impulse or emotion of trepidation, and a tendency to run away. McDougall looked upon the effective impulse or emotion as the process that integrates the cognitive and conative aspects of mental life and accounts for the directedness of actions.

The essential weakness of this model was that it failed to specify the conditions that produce changes in the goals of actions from time to time, that is, conditions that make for the excitation of now one and now another instinct. Further it did not adequately deal with the fundamental question of the nature or source of various instinctive energies, except to say that they were universal and innately determined.

340

Criticisms of the instinct doctrine on these grounds have been continually made since around 1920 (see Bindra, 1959, Chap. 1). The most recent important additions to these criticisms are those of Hinde (1960) and Lehrman (1953), which deal mainly with the instinct theories developed by ethologists (Lorenz, 1950; Tinbergen, 1951).

Spirited discussions of the concept of instinct since the 1920s have continued to prompt useful investigations of the exact bases of actions that were presumed to be produced by specific instincts. Kuo (1928) showed that individual experience plays a significant part in the development of predatory behavior in the cat, and Wiesner and Sheard (1933) revealed some of the hormonal and experiential factors that control maternal behavior of the rat. These pioneer studies were followed by investigations of hoarding (Bindra, 1948; C. T. Morgan, 1947), sexual behavior (Beach, 1942, 1965; Lehrman, 1965), bird songs (Marler, 1970; Thorpe, 1961), imprinting (Bateson, 1973), and various other what are now called "species-typical actions." These investigations have shown in general that such actions are neither uniform nor unified (all-or-none), but that each component of such actions depends on the sequential and interactive operation of several different types of organismic, situational, and experiential factors. The factors that combine to produce such an "instinctive action" are too varied and numerous to be subsumable within the connotations of the concept of instinct. As knowledge of the role of such specific factors has increased, the use of the concept of instinct has declined (Beach, 1955). In the past, psychologists tended to be concerned primarily with the specifications of organismic and experiential factors, while ethologists concentrated on the analysis of situational "releasing stimuli," but happily the two emphases have merged in the more recent investigations (Bateson, 1973; Hinde, 1966; Marler, 1970; Mayer & Rosenblatt, 1979). One interesting recent development is that of "human ethology," which is concerned with the analysis of stimuli that tend to elicit various aspects of human emotional and social behavior (see Eibl-Eibesfeldt, 1979; also see von Cranach et al., 1979).

Motive as Drive

In his *Dynamic Psychology*, Woodworth (1918) pointed out that nerve and muscle cells have intrinsic energy which can be released by appropriate stimulation. Therefore, there was no reason to postulate a separate source of instinctive energy for each type of goal-directed action; the energy required for an action is *not* distributed from a special instinctive reservoir, but rather is provided by the energizing or excitation of successive components of the response mechanisms involved. For example, in the case of a reflex such as an eye-blink, the external stimulus (puff of air) is the triggering event that excites the sensory neurons, the excited sensory neurons then excite the sensory-motor links, and so on until the muscle is excited. Woodworth further suggested that the brain mechanisms for consummatory reactions (eating, drinking, etc.) once excited, have the property of serving as strong and persisting excitors or stimulators for several other mechanisms. Such a strong and persisting stimulation he called a *drive*. According to him, drive has no intrinsic goal-directional capability but instigates goal-directed actions by selective excitation of response mechanisms related to particular goals (consummatory actions).

This idea of a stimulation that drives or propels response mechanisms was proposed just as the instinct concept was beginning to appear untenable, so that *drive* quickly replaced instinct as the name for the motivational factor in behavior. But in the rapid acceptance of the concept of drive, Woodworth's idea that mechanisms, when excited, become drives for subsequent mechanisms was distorted into the simpler notion that drive is a particular type of triggering event that directly activates a specific type of goal-directed action. Thus action-specific instinctive energies got replaced by action-specific drive triggers. This prompted a search for the stimulations that serve as appropriate triggering events or "drives" for various types of goal-directed actions.

Drive as Bodily Need

Common observation suggests that bodily needs, such as hunger and thirst, promote goal-directed actions, such as eating and drinking. Cannon's (1915/1929) elucidation of homeostatic control of the internal bodily environment made it plausible to think of a bodily need as a deviation (increase or decrease) of bodily processes from a certain normal, balanced state. The idea that bodily needs, defined as deviations from homeostasis, may directly trigger action received some support from Richter's (1922, 1927) work on the general activity of the rat. He showed that food deprivation, water deprivation, and estrus produce marked increases in the level of general activity of the rat. Following Woodworth (1918), Richter (1927) called the bodily states correlated with increase in general activity *internal drives*. But the correlations Richter established were between such biological or homeostatic drives and the level of *general activity*; these correlations did not prove that specific goal-directed actions of eating, drinking, or copulation are instigated by the corresponding needs. However, gradually the investigations became more specific both in regard to the definition of bodily needs and the measurement of particular types of goal-directed actions.

At present, the investigation of the relation between needs and behavior continues as a search for the sensory and chemical consequences of bodily needs that may serve "to regulate" particular types of goal-directed actions. Studies of the regulation of eating (see Hoebel, 1971; Teitelbaum, 1961) and drinking (see Wayner, 1964; Blass, 1975) have revealed several internal organismic variables that can promote or suppress these actions. These organismic variables include sensory inputs reflecting stomach distension or dryness of the mouth, nutritional variables, such as sugar, salt, fat, and water levels of the blood, and hormonal variations, such as those of insulin and angiotensin. In general, such "set-point" models of motivation assert that appropriate action is taken when an actual physiological variable departs from a set point (Grossman, 1967; Oatley, 1967). A critical review of such models appears in a paper by Toates (1981).

As an illustration of the difficulties with such a model, consider Epstein's account of thirst. According to Epstein (1973, p. 315), bodily depletion of water results in several sensory and chemical changes in the body, and these changes result in characteristic neural changes or signs of bodily need, and together these neural changes comprise the real "neural thirst." This neural thirst is the drive that instigates specific goal-directed actions of water-seeking and drinking. There are two difficulties with this kind of model of motivation. First, it is contradicted by the evidence (Scott, Scott, & Luckhardt, 1938; Fitzsimmons, 1971; Le Magnen, 1971) that normally eating or drinking does not wait for the buildup of bodily needs for food or water and may occur in the absence of any marked sensory or chemical signs of depletion. Thus many of the bodily factors that have been demonstrated to influence eating and drinking under conditions of experimental depletion and other manipulations may have little to do with their regulation under normal conditions. Second, the need model fails to deal with the problem of how the neural thirst, once generated, results in appropriate water-directed actions. It is noteworthy that while instinct theorists have concentrated on how an activated instinct leads to appropriate behavior and neglected to specify the origins of the instinct energy, the need theorists have tended to concentrate on specifying the origins of the need—neural need signals—and have failed to address the essential question of how such a neural need gets translated into an appropriately directed action. This failure to deal with one-half of the problem of motivation is a common shortcoming of most physiological accounts of motivation; many physiological accounts seem to assume that the problem of motivation will be solved if one could specify the neural basis of needs because each need would "naturally" lead to appropriate action.

Drive as Strong Stimulation

Incorporating the idea of biological needs within a stimulus-response view of behavior, Hull (1943) suggested that the drives or action-instigating factors were internal, need-related sensory stimuli. The strong sensory discharges arising from such stimuli related to needs of hunger, thirst, sex, and pain he regarded as the primary drives or motivations. He also suggested that several secondary or acquired drives could be generated by external (conditioned) stimuli that might become associated with primary drives. His view was that adaptive actions were directed at reducing need-related stimulation, comprising primary or secondary drives, through commerce with particular types of environmental objects, called *reinforcers* (food, water, etc.).

Hull's view of motivation was subjected to two main criticisms. First, that several

343

actions of animals are clearly not directed at reducing either primary or secondary hunger, thirst, sex, or pain drives. Nissen (1953) pointed out that mutual grooming in chimpanzees is not a drive-reducing action and yet they engage in it for long periods of time. Hebb (1946) demonstrated that chimpanzees show spontaneous fear of strange objects (cast of a snake, skull of a monkey) which the chimpanzees have never encountered before and which certainly have not been previously associated with pain. Further, Harlow (1953) and Berlyne (1950, 1954) pointed to exploratory behavior and made the point that distal environmental stimuli rather than only internal stimuli can serve as drives; this also implied that animal actions may at times be directed not at decreasing but at increasing sensory stimulation (Butler, 1953; Hebb, 1955). Finally, contrary to Hull's drive-reduction view of behavior, animals seek out and ingest pleasant-tasting substances, such as a sucrose or saccharin solution, even when they are neither hungry nor thirsty (Young & Shuford, 1955; Sheffield & Roby, 1950).

The second difficulty with Hull's view arises from his emphasis on current *peripheral* stimulation as the basis of drive. In fact, there is little evidence to show that continuous stimulation arising from need-related organs is necessary for the maintenance of goal-directed actions. As Lashley (1938) noted, "The rat in the maze does not stop running between hunger pangs." Rats whose stomachs have been denervated continue to eat and perform food-related actions fairly normally (Bash, 1939). Sexual responses can also occur in the absence of sensory stimulation from the genitals (Ball, 1934; Bard, 1935). Finally, the elimination by blocking of autonomically controlled visceral changes accompanying electric shock fails to eliminate shock-avoidance behavior (Wynne & Solomon, 1955). All these findings indicate that drives, or any other motivational factors capable of producing persisting goal-directed actions, may be largely independent of phasic peripheral sensory stimulation but are likely to have a continuous central existence.

Drive as Excitation of Specific Brain Sites

As early as the 1930s Hess (1957) showed in his Zurich laboratory that electrical stimulation of various particular sites of a bird's brain produced some typical bird actions. This line of investigation gradually expanded and revealed that several different goal-directed actions, such as eating, drinking, copulating, attacking, and so forth, can be produced by appropriate electrical—and to some extent chemical—stimulation of particular brain sites. Some of the most effective sites were found to be in the hypothalamic region, and soon various hypothalamic sites were identified as drive sites for eating, drinking, sex, attack, and so on (Glickman & Schiff, 1967). Such sites have also been located in human neurological patients who, for medical reasons, have had several electrodes implanted in particular sites of their limbic structures. When appropriate electrical pulses are passed through an electrode, a remarkable and sudden change frequently occurs in the patient's mood as judged by the nature of the patient's verbal remarks and the direction in which he or she pursues a conversation. For example, Heath describes the case of a patient on the verge of tears as he was describing his father's near-fatal illness, but when the septal region was stimulated, he immediately terminated this conversation and within fifteen seconds exhibited a broad grin as he discussed plans to date and seduce a girl friend. When asked why he had changed the conversation so abruptly, he replied that the plans concerning the girl suddenly came to him.

There are three features about these studies that make them particularly important for the theory of motivation. One is that the stimulation of a site produces the corresponding behavior even if the animal would not normally display that behavior at that time; thus sated animals will eat and animals that have copulated to exhaustion will copulate again at the mere flick of an electrical switch. The second feature is that the stimulation-induced responses cannot be specified in terms of movements but can be specified in terms of goals; thus, stimulation of the eating site will result in the performance of whatever arbitrary instrumental response is required to gain access to food in the given situation (Miller, 1957, 1961) and the stimulation of an attack site will make a cat traverse a runway to gain access to an attackable object (Roberts & Kiess, 1964). The third feature is that a given behavior produced by stimulation is subject to the same influences as when that behavior is produced normally; thus, when electrical stimulation of the eating site produces eating, the likelihood and vigor of eating can be influenced by such normally effective factors as the palatability of food, size of food pellets, any trained food aversions, familiarity of the test situation, and so on (Wise, 1974).

A related discovery is equally important. In the 1950s it was found that electrical stimulation of certain brain sites could produce reinforcing—rewarding or punishing—effects (Olds & Milner, 1954; Delgado, Roberts, & Miller, 1954) and thus could be used to train different types of instrumental responses. The most effective of the positive reinforcing sites were found also to lie largely in the hypothalamic-limbic regions (Olds, 1958) and to overlap with the drive sites (Glickman & Schiff, 1967). These findings suggested that the so-called drive and reinforcement sites may have a common neural substrate.

The above features of the electrical stimulation studies leave little doubt that the stimulation of each site under the conditions of these experiments produces a drive—that is, a motivational state—rather than a specific set of movements. On this point there is now no disagreement. Further there now seems to be some consensus that the stimulation of any one drive site probably produces some of the same neural consequences as are produced when that drive is produced normally (Glickman & Schiff, 1967; Miller, 1961; Wise, 1974); in other words, the electrical stimulation of drive sites produces genuine drives under the given experimental conditions. In this context, the finding that the stimulation of each different hypothalamic-limbic site (under given experimental conditions) promotes a certain goal-directed action has been widely interpreted as showing that a drive or motivation is wholly a matter of the excitation of such sites. This is challengeable.

The difficulty is that the motivation generated by electrical stimulation—as indicated by a particular type of goal-directed action—does not bear an exclusive relation to any particular site of stimulation. Valenstein, Cox, and Kakolewski (1968) and Roberts (1969) have shown that the actions emerging from stimulation at a certain hypothalamic site can vary a good deal, depending on the experience of the animal and the nature of incentive objects present in the test situation. Suppose we stimulate a lateral hypothalamic site that normally produces eating in the test situation, but instead of presenting food to the animal we present some other incentive object, such as a piece of wood, a few nursing pups, water, or nesting material. Now the stimulation at the same site may well produce goal-directed actions that are appropriate for one or more of the incentive objects present at the time of stimulation. This means that the locus of stimulation does not by itself determine what motivational state will be generated, but that motivational state or states generated are also determined by the nature of the incentive objects present in the situation. In the absence of appropriate incentive objects, the electrical stimulation produces no effect that is interpretable as motivational.

There is another reason for concluding that the electrical stimulation of such hypothalamic sites does not by itself generate a motivational state. It is that the actions of the animal, though goal-directed, remain highly stimulation bound. Thus if a satiated rat is made to eat a pellet of food by electrical stimulation of the lateral hypothalamus, and then the stimulation is suddenly turned off, the rat drops the pellet immediately; there is no lingering interest in eating after the termination of stimulation. The corresponding observations have been made in the case of electrically induced predatory attack and copulation. The type of lingering mood that may be observed in the course of normal eating, attack, or copulation is not observed when these actions are induced by electrical hypothalamic stimulation. Thus hypothalamic sites are not the loci of motivation per se. It is likely that they are the loci of integration of the regulatory reflexes that control various aspects of the organismic state of the animal. It is therefore reasonable to suppose that electrical stimulation of each particular site leads to the transmission of information about the levels of certain visceral and humoral organismic variables to some other sites, which are the true motivational sites. Normally this transmission depends on actual organismic-state changes, but hypothalamic stimulation may transmit the same organismic information in the absence of actual organismic changes.

Drive as an Ad Hoc Instigational Factor

Despite the untenability of all the different interpretations of the drive view of motivation, the concept of drive has continued to be widely used as the main motivational construct all across the wide spectrum of psychological studies—from physiological to social. In the absence of the specific characterizations of drive as neural representations of bodily needs or as need-related stimulation, the concept of drive has become increasingly vague. It now serves as a general rubric for an internal impulse, craving, or urge arising from a "homeostatic" discrepancy (Stagner, 1977) of an unspecified nature that somehow acts as an instigator of the type of behavior under consideration. So we have aggressive drive (Feshbach, 1964), a conditioned craving for morphine or morphine drive (Solomon & Corbit, 1974), a drive to reduce cognitive dissonance (Festinger, 1957), an achievement drive (McClelland, 1955), and the drive of self-actualization (Maslow, 1962). McDougall's (1908) list of instincts pales into insignificance in comparison to the list of drives that can be drawn from even a casual reading of today's psychological literature. The point to note is that in each case the postulated drive is considered to be an internal state, though it may be internally or externally activated, inherent or acquired, individual or universal, but no exact specification is given of its nature or how it produces the type of action it is invoked to explain. The implicit assumption seems to be that such an "appropriate" instigational drive would "naturally" facilitate the type of behavior in question. Action-specific triggers again!

What none of the drive views of motivation make clear is how an internal state, whether its causes lie in internal metabolic processes or in external stimulation, could possibly produce goal-directed actions. Merely asserting, for example, that neural hunger naturally leads to eating and that drive achievement leads to hard work is equivalent to saying that hunger is the eliciting stimulus for eating and that drive achievement is the eliciting stimulus for hard work. But this is absurd. The critical eliciting stimulus for eating is food, not hunger; and the critical stimulus for drinking is not thirst but water, for copulation it is certainly an appropriate sexual partner, for escape a region of safety, and for hard work it is a situation where hard work leads to success and rewards. In a recent paper, Wise (personal communication, 1979) has made this point eloquently. I quote,

> The flaw in the view that hunger is a stimulus to eat or to explore is that the response is not defined by "eat" or "explore." Eat what? Explore where? Eat and explore . . . must be qualified by the terms of external space. Hunger cannot tell us to go left or right, the response of turning left must be a response to a stimulus that tells us what is to be found to the left. . . .

The point is that all goal-directed actions are addressed, and must be addressed, to environmental stimuli—so that the basis for goal-direction must be provided by the environmental stimuli, not by internal needs or drive stimuli. How can an internal, spatially nonspecific instigational factor direct behavior in relation to specific external goals? The primary role in goal-directed actions must necessarily be that of environmental goal stimuli or of their central representations; the internal factors can have only a secondary, even though at times necessary, role.

347

Motivation as Incentive Stimulation

From a psychological perspective, objects and events in the world may be divided into two broad categories: those that are hedonically (affectively) potent, and those that are hedonically relatively uninteresting or neutral. As compared to neutral stimuli, hedonically potent stimuli have the property of reliably producing appetitive or aversive reactions and being affectively pleasing or discomforting. Such stimuli include sights, sounds, tastes, odors, temperatures, and cutaneous textures that are provided by such biologically important objects, events, and situations as food, water, a sexual partner, a nest, the call of a distressed offspring, the shape of a predator, and injurious levels of heat or cold. Such hedonic stimuli include what are variously called "emotional stimuli," "reinforcing stimuli," "appetitive stimuli," "aversive stimuli," "releasing stimuli," and "incentive stimuli." I shall use the term *incentive stimuli* to denote such reliably potent environmental stimuli.

The behavioral importance of incentive stimuli has long been recognized; they are known to have reinforcing—rewarding or punishing—effects on behavior, as well as motivational—goading or tempting—effects on behavior. For example, one morning if you receive a flattering message in a letter, you may repeatedly go to your desk, unfold the letter, and read the message again and again. These might be called reinforcing effects of the letter, the stimulus that has served as an appetitive incentive. But the letter may also induce an expansive mood that makes you stride through the center of the hall rather than shuffle along its sides, look others in the eye rather than avert your eyes, be unusually affable and talkative at the coffee break, and so on. These are the motivational effects of the same incentive. Such motivational effects were not clearly separated from the reinforcing effects until recently. Indeed, men like Machiavelli, Hobbes, Bentham, and Freud, who wrote about the control of human actions by incentive stimuli, were unclear on this point and failed to separate the two effects.

In psychology, the reinforcing—rewarding or punishing—effects of incentive stimuli were emphasized in the writings of Spencer (1872–1873) and Bain (1868), and this tradition was followed by Thorndike (1911), Hull (1943), and Skinner (1953), to the utter neglect of the motivational role of such stimuli. Indeed, so great was the supremacy of the response-reinforcement view, that those who, like Craig (1918), Troland (1932), Young (1948), and Schneirla (1959), emphasized the motivational or response-promoting role of incentive stimuli were hardly mentioned in discussions of behavior theory. When Hull (1952) was forced to accept the motivational role of incentive stimuli, he proposed the concept of *incentive motivation*. Hull thought of incentive motivation as less important than and subsidiary to his main motivational factor, drive, and he also thought of incentive motivation as a learned, secondary factor acquired by environmental stimuli that are associated with drive reduction. Amsel (1962) and Spence (1960), who elaborated this concept, continued to argue that incentive motivation is a subsidiary and secondary motivational factor and that it enhances performance through feedback stimuli from anticipatory goal responses.

The realization that certain incentive stimuli may have important and primary motivational properties that are independent of their reinforcing or drive-reducing properties emerged slowly. First came a general attack on the hypothesis that incentive stimuli reinforce because they reduce drives. Several psychological experiments showed, for example, that rats will work for an opportunity to copulate even if ejaculation is prevented (Sheffield, Wulff, & Backer, 1951), that monkeys will work for interesting sights and sounds (Butler, 1953, 1957), and that chimpanzees will be scared and panic-stricken on seeing strange objects that had never been associated with pain (Hebb, 1946). Then came studies (Harlow, 1953; Pfaffmann, 1960; Schneirla, 1959; Young, 1948) showing that many sights, sounds, textures, odors, and tastes have inherent properties that attract or repel members of certain species; in other words, the motivational properties of incentive stimuli need not be acquired or secondary but may be primary. Finally, the work of ethologists (Lehrman, 1965; Tinbergen, 1951) led to the specification of certain particular features of environmental objects that give those objects response-eliciting or motivational properties. By 1960 it was evident that any psychological account of motivation must attribute a central role to environmental incentive stimuli, and that the motivational properties of environmental stimuli may be inherent and species-typical, as in the case of unconditioned or primary incentive stimuli, or they may be acquired and variable, as in the case of initially neutral stimuli that have acquired conditioned or secondary incentive properties through individual experience.

Motivation and Response Production

Turn now to the second main question about motivation: how does the motivational factor, once generated, actually influence behavior? How does it promote the production of appropriate responses at a given time? The two major theories of adaptive behavior that dominated the psychological scene around the middle of this century, those of Hull (1943) and Tolman (1932), approached this question in essentially the same way. Both Hull and Tolman made a sharp distinction between a motivational process and a response-selection process. For Hull the motivational process was drive (D) and the response-selection process, habit ($_SH_R$); for Tolman the motivational process was incentive "demand" and the response-selection process, expectancy or means-end-readiness. Both these views held that a repertoire of habits (Hull) or means-end-readiness (Tolman) is developed through learning and exists in the animal's head. An action gets performed when an appropriate habit or means-end-readiness is first selected on the basis of stimulus-response associations or of situational knowledge, and then the selected entity is energized by the motivational factor, leading to the observed performance. Note that in the accounts of both Hull and Tolman, the motivational factor in itself has no directional influence but only an instigational influence on responses that have already been picked out by some sort of a selection process; direction in behavior is provided only by the response-selection process.

The general idea that a directional, response-selection process combines with a motivational, instigational process to produce goal-directed actions was widely held in the 1950s. It may have influenced the interpretation placed on the discovery of the ascending reticular activating system of the brain stem (Moruzzi & Magoun, 1949). This discovery pointed to the existence of two anatomically distinct sensory systems: one, the traditionally known topographically precise sensory system, consisting of tracts of parallel fibers, provides detailed stimulus information and is the basis of sensory-motor coordinations; and two, the newly discovered reticular activating system that is topographically diffuse, consisting of fibers that diverge or fan out to various parts of the brain and activate the neurons at the sites at which they end. In interpreting the significance of this finding for psychological theory, Hebb (1955) suggested that the classical, topographically precise sensory system serves a steering or directional function, that the new reticular activating system serves an arousal or instigational function, and that the two combine to produce adaptive behavior. According to Hebb, then, the central arousal system, rather than peripheral stimulation, was the source of drive.

The common fault of all these views is that the motivational factor is identified wholly with the instigational process—drive, demand, or arousal—and is made completely separate from the directional or steering function. If motivation and response-selection processes are in fact so separate, then how are they coordinated to produce a specific motivationally relevant response? Why, for example, does a hungry animal seek food but not water or nesting materials, or a thirsty animal seek water but not food or its offspring? None of the traditional accounts of behavior, Hull's (1943, 1952), Tolman's (1932, 1949) or Skinner's (1938, 1953), gives an adequate explanation of the remarkable coordination between the motivation-inducing operations, such as food deprivation, and the particular types of goal-directed actions displayed, such as eating. Instead of addressing this problem which is central to the understanding of how motivation works, most theorists have tended to assume that somehow the prevailing motivation and the selected response get matched. "It's natural."

Nor have the traditional theorists tried to explain how, if responses exist ready-made in a central response store and are instigated by internal motivational factors, does the response adjust to the details of the situation (changing patterns of light and shadows on the ground, unexpected obstacles, and so forth) in which the response is performed. In other words, the critical problem of flexibility of behavior has not been adequately addressed. Insofar as the Hullian and Skinnerian response-reinforcement frameworks are concerned, the two basic assumptions—the idea of stimulus-response association and the response-reinforcement principle—have been contradicted by the facts of motor equivalence and flexibility (or "intelli-

350

gence") in behavior, as well as by the fact of the emergence of new forms of actions in the absence of both reinforcement and prior performance (see Bindra, 1978; Bolles, 1972; Kimble, 1961). Insofar as the Tolmanian, cognitive framework is concerned, it does not even deal with the problem of response production, saying simply that when an animal has the necessary knowledge or expectancy, the appropriate response somehow gets produced. It has therefore been clear for some time that any new view of motivation requires a new revised view of how adaptive behavior is produced.

Summary and Conclusion

By way of concluding this sketchy historical review, it may be said that by the end of the 1960s it was clear that the formulation of any new ideas about motivation must be guided by the following five considerations.

1. The motivational factor is neither an energy reservoir nor a set of neural structures specialized for generating and distributing action-specific energy; rather, the energy required for goal-directed actions is generated by the excitation of the receptors, neurons, and muscle fibers involved in those actions.

2. The motivational factor cannot be equated with drive, whether a drive is regarded as a bodily need, a collection of strong stimuli or receptor discharges, excitation of certain hypothalamic sites, or any other type of internal state; an internal, spatially undifferentiated instigational factor as such can have no directional influence on behavior.

3. The motivational factor, inasmuch as it both prompts action and gives direction to it, is likely to be closely linked to environmental incentive stimuli, unconditioned or conditioned; it is these environmental stimuli in relation to which spatially and temporally organized goal-directed actions are performed.

4. Any complete account of motivation must indicate how the motivational factor enters into the mechanisms of response production so as to match the motivation with the response. Since the traditional theories of adaptive behavior are inadequate in this regard, the formulation of any new view of motivation must go hand-in-hand with the formulation of a new framework for explaining adaptive behavior in general.

5. Motives or motivational states exist in the central nervous system and some of the neural substrates of different types of central motivational states have been elucidated. For those interested in a theoretical account of motivation, it would seem self-defeating to ignore these neurobehavioral findings.

The Current Scene

The ideas about motivation that have emerged in recent years may be briefly summarized as follows.

The Nature of Motivational States

The ideas of Woodworth (1918), Lashley (1938), and Hebb (1955) are reflected in the current assumption that the basis of a specific central motive state (cms), as defined by behavioral direction toward a certain type of goal, lies in the excitation of a particular set of central neural circuits. A strong central motive state reflects a state of high excitation of certain circuits and a weak central motive state reflects a state of low excitation of those circuits.

Variations in the level of excitation of such motivational circuits are determined jointly by internal organismic variables and external incentive stimulation (Bindra, 1968, 1974; Milner, 1977; Mogenson & Huang, 1973; Pfaff & Pfaffmann, 1969; Soltysik, 1975). Several formal accounts have recently been proposed regarding how the organismic and the incentive factors may combine to generate a motivational state (e.g., Booth, 1980; McFarland, 1976; Sibly, 1975; Toates, 1981). The common requirement of these accounts is that the organismic information and incentive information reach some common motivational circuit. One view of such confluence may be sketched as follows.

There are neural events that reflect the current organismic condition of the animal, including circadian metabolic fluctuations and the levels of various nutritional and hormonal factors often subsumed under the concepts of need or drive. Information about these organismic variables is distributed widely or "broadcast," neurally or humorally, over different areas of the brain and determines the *excitability* of various motivational circuits. Further, there are neural events that reflect certain affective or hedonic stimulus aspects (such as odor, taste, color, pattern, and intensity) of environmental incentive objects and events. This incentive information follows specific sensory channels, is topographically represented, and determines *which* motivational circuits will be excited. The actual level of excitation of any given motivational circuit, say one concerned with food, depends (1) on the excitability of that circuit, as determined by the neural consequences of the relevant organismic variables (e.g., food depletion, muscular weakness, plasma insulin level, etc.) and (2) on the neural consequences of the affective characteristics (e.g., odor quality and odor intensity) of food objects in the environment. The organismic information influences the excitability level, serving as a gate that determines the effectiveness of incentive input in enhancing the probability of excitation of the circuit.[1]

[1] In this connection it is interesting to note that in current discussions of the neurochemical mechanisms, a distinction is beginning to be drawn between the action of neurotransmitters and that of neuromodulators (Krivoy, 1961, cited by Wise, 1979). While a neurotransmitter (e.g., acetylcholine) is a substance released at a synapse that effects transmission across the synapse to a certain target cell, a neuromodulator (e.g., dopamine) is thought to be a substance that does not by itself effect transmission but facilitates the firing of a target cell when some other (neurotransmitter) input arrives at the same synapse. Wise (1979) has suggested that motivation may represent the action of neuromodulators, while the activity of actual sensory motor transmission pathways may depend on neurotransmitters.

Note that it is the incentive characteristics that determine the nature of the motivational state, for it is incentive information that is directed to a certain specific motivational circuit. If the same circuit also happens to receive relevant (i.e., effective) organismic information, then the level of excitation of that circuit will be further enhanced, but organismic information by itself, in the absence of incentive stimulation, will be incapable of generating any particular central motive state (enhancing excitation level) regardless of how strong the relevant organismic conditions may be. It follows that the strength of a central motive state may be influenced merely by varying the stimulus characteristics of the incentive object. For example, for any specified level of food deprivation, the amount eaten depends on the stimulus features that define the palatability of food (Young, 1948); without any deprivation, sweetened chocolate may be eaten, pastry nibbled on, and ordinary food rejected. Ethologists (Lorenz, 1950) too have emphasized the reciprocal relations between the appropriateness of an incentive (or releasing) stimulus and the stringency of the organismic conditions required for particular types of goal-directed actions.

Some Implications

Some of the implications of this interactional model have been elaborated. Consider a few of these.

Multiple Interactions   According to the above formulation, a given organismic variable may be relevant to more than one motivational state, and that depending on what incentive stimuli are present in the environment, several different central motive states may exist simultaneously, that is, several motivational circuits may be at a substantial level of excitation at any given time. This feature of the model points up two misleading assumptions of the traditional views of motivation. One is that each organismic variable is relevant to the generation of only one motivational state; for example, that blood-glucose level or stomach distension is relevant only to a food-oriented motivational state, that the level of circulating angiotensin II or blood dehydration is relevant only to the water-oriented motivational state, and that the testosterone level of the male is relevant only to sexual motivation. But this is obviously false. Blood-sugar level may be relevant to irritability or aggression as well as to eating, dehydration may be relevant to motivation for nursing the young as well as to motivation for water, and testosterone may contribute to the generation of aggression as well as to sexual motivation.

The second traditional assumption that has been misleading is that an animal's action in relation to a goal, such as food, sexual partner, or offspring, is the outcome of a single motivational state. It is obvious that the actual action that an animal displays in a given situation and at a given time must depend on more than one motivational state; eating depends not only on food-related motivation but also

353

on how familiar the animal is with the situation, what other opportunities or dangers lie in the situation, what effort is required to obtain the food, and so on. It is well known that a hungry rat introduced into a novel environment which contains food may spend considerable time "freezing," exploring, and sitting, and may take an hour or more before it starts to eat. Similarly, the actions of a nursing she-wolf, when an intruder arrives at the lair, must arise from a mixture of attachment for the infants and hostility toward the intruder. The connections between organismic variables and motivational states, and between motivational states and actions are not one-to-one; rather they are one-to-many and many-to-one. This consideration suggests that caution should be exercised in drawing inferences from particular actions observed to the underlying motivational states and organismic variables even in the case of simple actions. The model being proposed here assumes multiple interactions.

Motivation and Emotion   This model implies no fundamental distinction between the phenomena of motivation and those of emotion. The basis of both these sets of affective phenomena lies in the generation of central motive states by joint actions of internal organismic conditions and environmental incentive stimuli. Organismic conditions appear to be somewhat more important in what are usually called motivational phenomena, such as the phenomena of eating and drinking, and environmental incentive stimuli appear to be somewhat more important in what are usually called emotional phenomena, such as fear, anger, and love or attachment. But organismic conditions constrain emotional episodes as much as they do motivational episodes. The discipline of psychopharmacology is based on the importance of organismic variables in the control of anxiety, depression, aggression, and so on.

Whatever the apparent differences in terms of which distinctions between motivation and emotion are usually drawn, the fundamental organismic-incentive interactions and neural substrates of the two sets of phenomena are the same; neurally the central motive states of motivation and emotion are identical. Because there can be innumerable combinations of organismic conditions and incentive stimuli, many distinguishable motivational-emotional states can be generated, each determined by a unique combination of varying levels of excitation of different motivational circuits. Further, because actions of an animal in a given situation depend on the excited motivational circuits and on the current situational layout of important stimuli, the number of distinguishable types of affective episodes must be countless. What emotion is experienced depends on the nature of the total effective episode. Common-sense motivational and emotional terms (e.g., maternal love, frustration, anxiety) represent a rough classification of such episodes on the basis of their social, communicative relevance (Bindra, 1969).

Acquired Motivation   An important implication of the emerging interactional model concerns the mechanism of acquired or secondary motivation. In the enthusiasm generated by the publication of Hull's (1943) *Principles of Behavior*, it was widely held that the vast amount of behavior not directly related to primary, biological, or species-typical drives would be explainable by adding the concepts of acquired or conditioned drives and of secondary or conditioned reinforcers. For example, Miller and Dollard (1941) and Dollard and Miller (1950), among others, elaborated on how secondary drives and reinforcers could account for many phenomena of neurosis and of social behavior. The general idea was that by being associated with primary drives (i.e., strong need stimuli), initially neutral stimuli become capable of generating "secondary drives" in the absence of actual drive stimuli. Similarly, by being associated with primary reinforcers, initial neutral stimuli will acquire "secondary reinforcing" properties, so that they serve as reinforcers in the absence of actual (primary) reinforcers or incentive stimuli. In terms of the interactional model, the question to be posed is this: do the observed acquired motivational effects arise from conditioned organismic conditions or conditioned incentive stimuli, or both?

One answer that has been proposed is this. Because the organismic conditions (e.g., hunger) do not excite motivational circuits but determine only their excitability, and because the nature of a central motive state (the particular circuits excited) is dependent on incentive stimulation, the only basis of acquired or conditioned motivation lies in the conditioning of the neural effects of environmental incentive stimuli (Bindra, 1976, Chap. 9). In other words, an initially neutral conditioned stimulus (CS) can acquire incentive properties, and as such can generate a motivational state, but only when an appropriate organismic condition is actually present. That is, in generating a conditioned, secondary, motivational state, an incentive stimulus can be represented by a conditioned stimulus but the appropriate organismic condition cannot be represented by a conditioned stimulus. The particular values of organismic variables required must be produced by usual metabolic processes. Thus, whatever acquired motivational effects are observed in a study, they must be attributed wholly to conditioned or acquired incentive properties. In traditional terms, then, there is no such thing as an acquired drive but there is such a thing as an acquired reinforcer. This conclusion is supported by the empirical corroboration of the concept of conditioned reinforcers or incentives (see Wike, 1966) and the lack of such corroboration for the concept of conditioned drive (Cofer & Appley, 1964; Cravens & Renner, 1970; D'Amato, 1974). Essentially, the evidence shows that when appropriate experimental safeguards for adventitious reinforcing effects are present, conditioned stimuli paired with the presence of a primary drive (organismic condition) do not acquire any motivational properties.

A slightly different view of secondary motivation attributes an important role to "drive stimuli" (arising from organismic conditions). Thus Deutsch (1960), Gallistel (1973), and Milner (1977) have suggested, essentially, that drive stimuli become conditioned to the representations of incentive stimuli (reinforcers) and thereby excite the motivational circuits that would normally require unconditioned or conditioned incentive stimuli. Drive stimuli thus become not only representations of organismic conditions but also excitors of specific incentive circuits. It seems difficult to reconcile this idea with the fact that the same organismic factors (i.e., drive stimuli) may enhance the effectiveness of several different incentive stimuli. Do, then, the same drive stimuli generate two or more different motivational states?

Response Production   Another implication of the interactional view of motivation is that the environmental stimulus that generates a motivational state is also the momentary goal stimulus to which the animal may direct its actions. When a food substance or some other food-related stimulus has generated a motivational state, the goal object (food) to which the behavior must be directed is already present in the environment. Thus the problem of matching the motivation to the object of the animal's directed actions is solved by the mere fact that the environmental stimulus whose perception generates a motivation is also the stimulus that serves as the goal of action. Specifically, it has been suggested (Bindra, 1976, 1978) that motivational states influence response production by priming the central perceptual representations (gnostic-assemblies) of certain environmental stimuli, and that the form of the response is then determined by those stimuli. Since the motivational states are determined by certain unconditioned or conditioned incentive stimuli, the stimuli whose central representations are primed turn out to be the very unconditioned or conditioned stimuli which have generated the current motivational states. In other words, a motivational state generated or enhanced by a certain (incentive) stimulus configuration in turn primes the perceptual representation of the same stimulus configuration and thereby renders it a more effective response elicitor. No representation or "response concept" as such (e.g., James, 1890; Konorski, 1967; Milner 1977) is required to produce a motivationally appropriate response. This provides an uncomplicated mechanism for the coordination of motivation and action and solves a problem that was largely ignored by the traditional theories of behavior. According to this view, what are called discriminative stimuli, secondary reinforcers, and conditioned incentive stimuli all have acquired incentive properties; the differences in their influence on behavior arise from their spatiotemporal position in relation to the primary incentives in the course of training. More detailed views of the motivational influence on response production have recently been proposed by Asratyan (1976), Gallistel (1980), and Mogenson, Jones, and Yim (1980).

Some Prospects for the Future

Concerning possible future developments, three trends may be worth watching, and, in my view, worth promoting.

1. The sway that the need, drive, and related internal instigational views of motivation have held on psychological theory is finally coming to an end. The basic

theoretical difficulty with the internal-instigational views of motivation is their failure to say how spatially nonspecific organismic variables can guide environmentally addressed goal-directed actions. The gradual downfall of this view of motivation will be accompanied, I think, by a gradual acceptance of a view of motivation that ascribes a primary role to environmental incentive stimuli as the generators of motivational states and elicitors of action.

This trend is already evident. For example, the traditional drive interpretations of aggression (Dollard et al., 1939; Feshbach, 1964) are being replaced by ones in which the role of environmental stimuli receives more emphasis. I refer here to Flynn's (1967) stress on the stimulus features of the prey in eliciting the cat's predatory attack, to Moyer's (1968) neuropsychological model of aggression in animals and man, to demonstrations that certain characteristics of children invite battering by their parents (e.g., Friedrich & Boriskin, 1976), and to evidence provided by ethologists (Eibl-Eibesfeldt, 1967; Lorenz, 1966) that certain behavior on the part of potential victims is likely to promote or suppress attack. Similarly, environmental incentive stimuli—odors, tastes, textures, sounds, and visual features—have been shown to be important in developing an infant's attachment to its mother (Harlow & Harlow, 1965; Rosenblatt, 1976). Further, incentive interpretations of "sex drive" (Hardy, 1964) have recently been offered, and situational analysis is playing an increasing role in personality research (Bem & Funder, 1978). Finally, the phenomenon of rewarding effects of intracranial brain stimulation, which used to be interpreted as representing drive or reinforcement manipulations (Deutsch, 1964; Gallistel, 1973; Mendelson, 1970; Olds & Milner, 1954) are increasingly being interpreted in terms of the acquired incentive motivational properties of environmental stimuli associated with intracranial stimulation (Trowill, Panksepp, & Gandelman, 1969). In general, then, the trend toward replacing interpretations in terms of drive and reinforcement concepts by incentive-motivational interpretations seems to be gathering momentum, and there is little doubt that it will soon become the generally accepted—conservative—view of the nature of motivation.

2. The second trend concerns practical applications of motivational theory. The importance of organismic variables in the generation of motivation continues to be useful in encouraging the investigation of various internal, organismic variables—sensory, nutritional, hormonal, neural—that can influence the occurrence of particular types of goal-directed actions. Further advances in this knowledge may provide a basis for some chemical and surgical methods of controlling and alleviating behavioral aspects of disorders such as anorexia, hyperphagia, polydipsia, sexual frigidity and impotence, maternal neglect, drug addiction, and aggression. However, because motivational states are determined only partly by organismic variables, such methods can be only partially effective as treatments.

Recent research on the factors that control drug self-administration point to an important role for unconditioned and conditioned (incentive) stimuli in producing

357

drug-seeking behavior and subjective reports of craving (Gerber & Stretch, 1975; Meyer & Mirin, 1979). An analysis of the basis of such incentive-induced self-administration suggests that drug-seeking behavior can be "primed" by the drug or by conditioned stimuli associated with drug infusion (de Wit & Stewart, 1981). These developments suggest that attempts to develop fully effective methods for treating such behavioral disorders will increasingly include manipulation of environmental incentives and training in relation to those incentives.

3. A third trend that may gain acceptance in the next decade is that of integration of motivational ideas into the fields of perception and thinking. Such a motivation-cognition connection has been long overdue but has failed to materialize. However, the emerging ideas point to a possible way in which motivation and cognition may be integrated. Since motivational arousal depends on the perception of incentive objects and since perceptions are determined partly by current thinking sets, the cognitive factor must influence motivation. And because motivational priming influences perception and perception influences thinking, motivation must also influence cognition. It is the continual influences of cognition on motivation through perception and of motivation on cognition also through perception that may comprise the fabric of our mental life.

REFERENCES

Allport, G. W. *Personality: A psychological interpretation.* New York: Holt, 1937.

Amsel, A. Frustrative nonreward in partial reinforcement and discrimination learning. *Psychological Review,* 1962, *69,* 306–328.

Asratyan, E. A. Some aspects of the problem of motivation in the light of Pavlovian teaching. *Acta Physiologicia Academiae Scientiarum Hungaricae,* 1976, *48,* 323–334.

Bain, A. *The senses and the intellect* (3rd ed.). London: Longmans, Green, 1868.

Ball, J. Sex behavior of the rat after removal of the uterus and vagina. *Journal of Comparative Psychology,* 1934, *18,* 419–422.

Bandura, A. The self system in reciprocal determinism. *American Psychologist,* 1978, *33,* 344–358.

Bard, P. The effects of denervation of the genitalia on the oestrual behavior of cats. *American Journal of Physiology,* 1935, *113,* 5.

Bash, K. W. An investigation into a possible organic basis for the hunger drive. *Journal of Comparative Psychology,* 1939, *28,* 109–134.

Bateson, P. P. G. Internal influences on early learning in birds. In R. A. Hinde & J. Stevenson-Hinde (Eds.), *Constraints on learning.* New York: Academic Press, 1973.

Beach, F. A. Analysis of the stimuli adequate to elicit mating behavior in the sexually inexperienced male rat. *Journal of Comparative Psychology,* 1942, *33,* 163–207.

Beach, F. A. The descent of instinct. *Psychological Review,* 1955, *62,* 401–410.

Beach, F. A. (Ed.). *Sex and behavior.* New York: Wiley, 1965.

Bem, D. J., & Funder, D. C. Predicting more of the people more of the time: Assessing the personality of situations. *Psychological Review,* 1978, *85,* 485–501.

Berlyne, D. E. Novelty and curiosity as determinants of exploratory behaviour. *British Journal of Psychology,* 1950, *41,* 68–80.

Berlyne, D. E. A theory of human curiosity. *British Journal of Psychology*, 1954, *45*, 180–191.

Bindra, D. What makes rats hoard? *Journal of Comparative and Physiological Psychology*, 1948, *41*, 397–402.

Bindra, D. *Motivation, a systematic reinterpretation.* New York: Ronald, 1959.

Bindra, D. Neuropsychological interpretation of the effects of drive and incentive-motivation on general activity and instrumental behavior. *Psychological Review*, 1968, *75*, 1–22.

Bindra, D. A unified interpretation of emotion and motivation. *Annals of the New York Academy of Sciences*, 1969, *159*, 1071–1083.

Bindra, D. A motivational view of learning, performance, and behavior modification. *Psychological Review*, 1974, *81*, 199–213.

Bindra, D. *A theory of intelligent behavior.* New York: Wiley, 1976.

Bindra, D. How adaptive behavior is produced: A perceptual-motivational alternative to response-reinforcement. *The Behavioral and Brain Sciences*, 1978, *1*, 41–52.

Blass, E. M. The physiological, neurological, and behavioral bases of thirst. In J. K. Cole & T. B. Sonderegger (Eds.), *Nebraska Symposium on Motivation, 1974.* Lincoln: University of Nebraska Press, 1975.

Bolles, R. C. Reinforcement, expectancy, and learning. *Psychological Review*, 1972, *79*, 394–409.

Booth, D. A. Conditioned reactions in motivation. In F. A. Toates & T. R. Halliday (Eds.), *Analysis of motivational processes.* London: Academic Press, 1980.

Butler, R. A. Discrimination learning by rhesus monkeys to visual-exploration motivation. *Journal of Comparative and Physiological Psychology*, 1953, *46*, 95–98.

Butler, R. A. The effect of deprivation of visual incentives on visual exploration motivation in monkeys. *Journal of Comparative and Physiological Psychology*, 1957, *50*, 177–179.

Cannon, W. B. *Bodily changes in pain, hunger, fear and rage.* New York: Appleton, 1929. (Originally published, 1915.)

Cofer, C. N., & Appley, H. M. *Motivation: Theory and research.* New York: Wiley, 1964.

Cravens, R., & Renner, K. E. Conditioned appetitive drive states: Empirical evidence and theoretical status. *Psychological Bulletin*, 1970, *73*, 212–220.

Craig, W. Appetites and aversions as constituents of instincts. *Biological Bulletin*, Woods Hole, No. 2, 1918, 91–107.

D'Amato, M. R. Derived motives. *Annual Review of Psychology*, 1974, *25*, 83–106.

Darwin, C. *The expression of emotions in man and animals.* London: Murray, 1872.

Delgado, J. M. R., Roberts, W. W., & Miller, N. E. Learning motivated by electrical stimulation of the brain. *American Journal of Physiology*, 1954, *179*, 587–593.

Descartes, R. In J. W. Reeves (Ed.), *Body and mind in Western thought.* Harmondsworth, Middlesex: Penguin Books, 1958.

Deutsch, J. A. *The structural basis of behavior.* Chicago: The University of Chicago Press, 1960.

Deutsch, J. A. Behavioral measurement of the neural refractory period and its application to intracranial self-stimulation. *Journal of Comparative and Physiological Psychology*, 1964, *58*, 1–9.

de Wit, H., & Stewart, J. Reinstatement of cocaine-reinforced responding in the rat. *Psychopharmacology*, 1981, *75*, 134–143.

Dollard, J., & Miller, N. E. *Personality and psychotherapy.* New York: McGraw-Hill, 1950.

Dollard, J., Miller, N. E., Doob, L. W., Mowrer, O. H., & Sears, R. R. *Frustration and aggression.* New Haven: Yale University Press, 1939.

Eibl-Eibesfeldt, I. Ontogenetic and maturational studies of aggressive behavior. In C. D. Clemente & D. B. Lindsley (Eds.), *Aggression and defense.* Berkeley: University of California Press, 1967.

Eibl-Eibesfeldt, I. Human ethology: Concepts and implications for the sciences of man. *The Behavioral and Brain Sciences*, 1979, *2*, 1–57.

Epstein, A. N. Epilogue: Retrospect and prognosis. In A. N. Epstein, H. R. Killileff, & E. Stellar (Eds.), *The neuropsychology of thirst.* New York: Winston, 1973.

359

Feshbach, S. The function of aggression and the regulation of aggressive drive. *Psychological Review.* 1964, *71*, 257–272.

Festinger, L. *A theory of cognitive dissonance.* Stanford: Stanford University Press, 1957.

Fitzsimmons, J. T. The physiology of thirst: A review of the extraneural aspects of the mechanisms of drinking. In E. Stellar & J. M. Sprague (Eds.), *Progress in physiological psychology* (Vol. 4). New York: Academic Press, 1971.

Flynn, J. P. The neural basis of aggression in cats. In D. C. Glass (Ed.), *Neurophysiology and emotion.* New York: The Rockefeller University Press, 1967.

Freud, S. Instincts and their vicissitudes. In *Collected papers* (Vol. IV). London: Hogarth, 1925. (Originally published, 1915.)

Friedrich. W. N., & Boriskin, J. A., The role of the child in abuse: A review of the literature. *American Journal of Orthopsychiatry,* 1976, *46,* 580–590.

Gallistel, C. R. Self-stimulation: The neurophysiology of reward and motivation. In J. A. Deutsch (Ed.), *Basis of memory.* New York: Academic Press, 1973.

Gallistel, C. R. *The organization of action: A new synthesis.* Hillsdale, N.J.: Erlbaum, 1980.

Gerber, G. J., & Stretch, R. Drug-induced reinstatement of extinguished self-administration behavior in monkeys. *Pharmacology, Biochemistry, and Behavior,* 1975, *3,* 1055–1061.

Glickman, S. E., & Schiff, B. B. A biological theory of reinforcement. *Psychological Review,* 1967, *74,* 81–109.

Grossman, S. P. *A textbook of physiological psychology.* New York: Wiley, 1967.

Hardy, K. R. An appetitional theory of sexual motivation. *Psychological Review,* 1964, *71,* 1–18.

Harlow, H. F. Motivation as a factor in the acquisition of new responses. In J. S. Brown et al., *Current theory and research in motivation: A symposium.* Lincoln: University of Nebraska Press, 1953.

Harlow, H. F., & Harlow, M. K. The affectional systems. In A. M. Schrier, H. F. Harlow, & F. Stollnitz (Eds.), *Behavior of nonhuman primates* (Vol. 2). New York: Academic Press, 1965.

Hebb, D. O. On the nature of fear. *Psychological Review,* 1946, *53,* 259–276.

Hebb, D. O. Drives and the C.N.S. (Conceptual Nervous System). *Psychological Review,* 1955, *62,* 243–254.

Hess, W. R. *The functional organization of the diencephalon.* New York: Grune & Stratton, 1957. (*Das Zwischenhirn,* published in 1949.)

Hinde, R. A. Energy models of motivation. *Symposium of the Society for Experimental Biology,* 1960, *14,* 199–213.

Hinde, R. A. *Animal behaviour.* New York: McGraw-Hill, 1966.

Hoebel, B. G. Feeding: Neural control of intake. *Annual Review of Physiology,* 1971, *33,* 533–568.

Hull, C. L. *Principles of behavior.* New York: Appleton-Century, 1943.

Hull, C. L. *A behavior system.* New Haven: Yale University Press, 1952.

James, W. *The principles of psychology.* (2 vols.) New York: Holt, 1890.

Kimble, G. A. *Hilgard and Marquis' conditioning and learning* (2nd ed.). New York: Appleton-Century-Crofts, 1961.

Konorski, J. *Integrative activity of the brain.* Chicago: The University of Chicago Press, 1967.

Krivoy, W. A comparison of the action of substance P and other naturally occurring polypeptides on spinal cord. *Proceedings of the Scientific Society of Bosnia and Herzegovina-Yugoslavia,* 1961, *1,* 131–137.

Kuo, Z. Y. The fundamental error of the concept of purpose and the trial and error fallacy. *Psychological Review,* 1928, *35,* 414–433.

Lashley, K. S. Experimental analysis of instinctive behavior. *Psychological Review,* 1938, *45,* 445–471.

Lehrman, D. S. A critique of Lorenz's theory of instinctive behavior. *Quarterly Review of Biology,* 1953, *28,* 337–363.

Lehrman, D. S. Interaction between internal and external environments in the regulation of the reproductive cycle of the ring dove. In F. A. Beach (Ed.), *Sex and behavior.* New York: Wiley, 1965.

Le Magnen, J. Advances in studies on the physiological control and regulation of food intake. In E. Stellar & J. M. Sprague (Eds.), *Progress in physiological psychology* (Vol. 4). New York: Academic Press, 1971.

Lorenz, K. Ueber den Begriff der Instinkthandlung. *Folia biotheoretica*, 1937, 2, 17–50.

Lorenz, K. The comparative method in studying innate behavior patterns. *Symposia of the Society of Experimental Biology*, 1950, 4, 221–268.

Lorenz, K. *On aggression*. London: Methuen, 1966.

Marler, P. A comparative approach to vocal learning: Song development in white-crowned sparrows. *Journal of Comparative and Physiological Psychology Monograph*, 1970, 71 (Whole No. 2, Part 2).

Maslow, A. *Toward a psychology of being*. Princeton, N.J.: Van Nostrand, 1962.

Mayer, A. D., & Rosenblatt, J. S. Hormonal influences during the ontogeny of maternal behavior in female rats. *Journal of Comparative and Physiological Psychology*, 1979, 93, 879–898.

McClelland, D. C. Some social consequences of achievement motivation. In M. R. Jones (Ed.), *Nebraska Symposium on Motivation, 1955*. Lincoln: University of Nebraska Press, 1955.

McDougall, W. *An introduction to social psychology*. London: Methuen, 1908.

McDougall, W. *An outline of psychology*. London: Methuen, 1923.

McFarland, D. J. Form and function in the temporal organization of behaviour. In P. P. G. Bateson & R. A. Hinde (Eds.), *Growing points in ethology*. Cambridge: Cambridge University Press, 1976.

Mendelson, J. Self-induced drinking in rats: The qualitative identity of drive and reward systems in the lateral hypothalamus. *Physiology and Behavior*, 1970, 5, 925–930.

Meyer, R. E., & Mirin, S. M. *The heroin stimulus: Implications for a theory of addiction*. New York: Plenum, 1979.

Miller, N. E. Experiments on motivation. *Science*, 1957, 126, 1271–1278.

Miller, N. E. Learning and performance motivated by direct stimulation of the brain. In D. E. Sheer (Ed.), *Electrical stimulation of the brain*. Austin, Texas: University of Texas Press, 1961.

Miller, N. E., & Dollard, J. *Social learning and imitation*. New Haven: Yale University Press, 1941.

Milner, P. M. Theories of reinforcement, drive, and motivation. In L. L. Iverson, S. D. Iverson, & S. H. Solomon (Eds.), *Psychopharmacology* (Vol. 7). New York: Plenum, 1977.

Mogenson, G. J., & Huang, Y. H. The neurobiology of motivated behavior. In G. A. Kerkut and J. W. Phillis (Eds.), *Progress in neurobiology*. New York: Pergamon Press, 1973.

Mogenson, G. J., Jones, D. L., & Yim, C. Y. From motivation to action: Functional interface between the limbic system and the motor system. *Progress in Neurobiology*, 1980, 14, 69–97.

Morgan, C. T. The hoarding instinct. *Psychological Review*, 1947, 54, 335–341.

Morgan, M. J. Motivational processes. In A. Dickinson & R. A. Boakes (Eds.), *Mechanisms of learning and motivation*. Hillsdale, N.J.: Erlbaum, 1979.

Moruzzi, G., & Magoun, H. W. Brain stem reticular formation and activation of the EEG. *Electroencephalography and Clinical Neurophysiology*, 1949, 1, 455–473.

Moyer, K. E. Kinds of aggression and their physiological basis. *Communications in Behavioral Biology*, 1968, 2, 65–87.

Nietzsche, F. W. *Thus spake Zarathustra*. (T. Common, trans.) London: Macmillan, 1932. (Originally published, 1883.)

Nissen, H. W. Instinct as seen by a psychologist. In W. C. Allee, H. W. Nissen, & M. F. Nimkoff, A re-examination of the concept of instinct. *Psychological Review*, 1953, 60, 287–297.

Oatley, K. A control model of the physiological basis of thirst. *Medical and Biological Engineering*, 1967, 5, 226–237.

Olds, J. Self-stimulation experiments and differentiated reward systems. In H. H. Jasper, L. D. Proctor, R. S. Knighton, W. C. Noshay, & R. T. Costello (Eds.), *Reticular formation of the brain*. Boston: Little, Brown, 1958.

Olds, J., & Milner, P. Positive reinforcement produced by electrical stimulation of septal area and other regions of rat brain. *Journal of Comparative and Physiological Psychology*, 1954, 47, 419–427.

361

Papez, J. W. A proposed mechanism of emotion. *Archives of Neurology and Psychiatry*, 1937, 38, 725–743.

Pfaff, D., & Pfaffmann, C. Behavioral and electrophysiological responses of male rats to female rat urine odors. In C. Pfaffmann (Ed.), *Olfaction and taste*. New York: Rockefeller University Press, 1969.

Pfaffmann, C. The pleasures of sensation. *Psychological Review*, 1960, 67, 253–268.

Richter, C. P. A behavioristic study of the activity of the rat. *Comparative Psychology Monographs*, 1922, 1 (2).

Richter, C. P. Animal behavior and internal drives. *Quarterly Review of Biology*, 1927, 2, 307–343.

Roberts, W. W. Are hypothalamic motivational mechanisms functionally and anatomically specific? *Brain, Behavior and Evolution*, 1969, 2, 317–342.

Roberts, W. W., & Kiess, H. O. Motivational properties of hypothalamic aggression in cats. *Journal of Comparative and Physiological Psychology*, 1964, 58, 187–193.

Rosenblatt, J. S. Stages in the early behavioral development of altricial young of selected species of nonprimate mammals. In P. P. G. Bateson & R. A. Hinde (Eds.), *Growing points in ethology*. Cambridge: Cambridge University Press, 1976.

Schneirla, T. C. An evolutionary and developmental theory of biphasis processes underlying approach and withdrawal. In M. R. Jones (Ed.), *Nebraska Symposium on Motivation, 1959*. Lincoln: University of Nebraska Press, 1959.

Scott, W. W., Scott, C. C., & Luckhardt, A. B. Observations on the blood-sugar level before, during, and after hunger periods in humans. *American Journal of Physiology*, 1938, 123, 243–247.

Seiden, L. S., & Dykstra, L. A. *Psychopharmacology, a biochemical and behavioral approach*. New York: Van Nostrand Reinhold, 1977.

Sheffield, F. D., & Roby, T. B. Reward value of a nonnutritive sweet taste. *Journal of Comparative and Physiological Psychology*, 1950, 43, 471–481.

Sheffield, F. D., Wulff, J. J., & Backer, R. Reward value of copulation without sex drive reduction. *Journal of Comparative and Physiological Psychology*, 1951, 44, 3–8.

Sibly, R. How incentive and deficit determine feeding tendency. *Animal Behaviour*, 1975, 23, 437–446.

Skinner, B. F. *The behavior of organisms: An experimental analysis*. New York: Appleton-Century, 1938.

Skinner, B. F. *Science and human behavior*. New York: Macmillan, 1953.

Solomon, R. L., & Corbit, J. D. An opponent-process theory of motivation: Temporal dynamics of affect. *Psychological Review*, 1974, 81, 119–145.

Soltysik, S. Post-consummatory arousal of drive as a mechanism of incentive motivation. *Acta Neurobiologiae Experimentalis*, 1975, 35, 447–474.

Spence, K. W. *Behavior theory and learning. Selected papers*. Englewood Cliffs, N.J.: Prentice-Hall, 1960.

Spencer, H. *The principles of psychology* (2 vols.). New York: D. Appleton, 1872–1873.

Spranger, E. *Types of men*. Halle: Niemeyer, 1928.

Stagner, R. Homeostasis, discrepancy, dissonance: A theory of motives and motivation. *Motivation and Emotion*, 1977, 1, 103–138.

Teitelbaum, P. Disturbances in feeding and drinking behavior after hypothalamic lesions. In M. R. Jones (Ed.), *Nebraska Symposium on Motivation, 1961*. Lincoln: University of Nebraska Press, 1961.

Thorndike, E. L. *Animal intelligence*. New York: Macmillan, 1911.

Thorpe, W. H. *Bird song*. Cambridge: Cambridge University Press, 1961.

Tinbergen, N. *The study of instinct*. Oxford: Clarendon Press, 1951.

Toates, F. M. The control of ingestive behaviour by internal and external stimuli: A theoretical review. *Appetite*, 1981, 2, 35–50.

Tolman, E. C. *Purposive behavior in animals and men*. New York: Century, 1932.

Tolman, E. C. There is more than one kind of learning. *Psychological Review*, 1949, *50*, 144–155.

Troland, L. T. *The principles of psychophysiology* (Vol. 3). New York: Van Nostrand, 1932.

Trowill, J. A., Panksepp, J., & Gandelman, R. An incentive model of rewarding brain stimulation. *Psychological Review*, 1969, *76*, 264–281.

Valenstein, E. S., Cox, V. C., & Kakolewski, J. W. K. Modification of motivated behavior elicited by electrical stimulation of the hypothalamus. *Science*, 1968, *158*, 1119–1121.

von Cranach, M., Foppa, K., Lepenies, W., & Ploog, D. (Eds.). *Human ethology*. Cambridge: Cambridge University Press, 1979.

von Hartmann, E. *Philosophy of the unconscious*. London: Kegan Paul, Trench, Trubner, 1893.

Wayner, M. J. (Ed.). *Thirst*. First international symposium on thirst in the regulation of body water. Oxford: Pergamon Press, 1964. (Distributed by The Macmillan Company, New York.)

Wiesner, B. P., & Sheard, N. M. *Maternal behaviour in the rat*. Edinburgh: Oliver & Boyd, 1933.

Wike, E. L. *Secondary reinforcement: Selected experiments*. New York: Harper & Row, 1966.

Wise, R. A. Lateral hypothalamic stimulation: Does it make animals hungry? *Brain Research*, 1974, *67*, 187–209.

Wise, R. A. Drives and the CNS: An update of the conceptual nervous system in relation to motivation. Personal communication, 1979.

Woodworth, R. S. *Dynamic psychology*. New York: Columbia University Press, 1918.

Wynne, L. C., & Solomon, R. L. Traumatic avoidance learning: Acquisition and extinction in dogs deprived of normal peripheral autonomic function. *Genetic Psychology Monographs*, 1955, *52*, 241–284.

Young, P. T. Appetite, palatability and feeding habit: A critical review. *Psychological Bulletin*, 1948, *45*, 289–320.

Young, P. T., & Shuford, E. H., Jr. Quantitative control of motivation through sucrose solutions of different concentrations. *Journal of Comparative and Physiological Psychology*, 1955, *48*, 114–118.

15

Biological Necessity, Emotional Transformation, and Personal Value

JOSEPH DE RIVERA

Anyone who honestly surveys the past hundred years of work on the emotions must surely experience both humility and impatience. The sheer volume of the literature is overwhelming. Shibles's (1974) general bibliography lists about five hundred studies while Hillman (1961), who concentrates on the theoretical literature, refers to over five hundred studies which are largely *different* from those listed by Shibles. When we turn to the various specialties within the field, the literature becomes a quagmire. Izard's (1971) bibliography of work relevant to the facial expression of emotion, Arnold's (1960a, b) account of the relevant physiological literature, Bandura's (1973) account of the work relevant to aggression, each lists over five hundred different references; and one can only speculate as to the number of completely different references to love, to fear, or to emotion within the psychoanalytic literature. Furthermore, while much of this work has merit, many investigators seem either to ignore or misunderstand the work that preceded their own, and many theories seem quite unrelated to either the facts or to other theories. Hence, we have a situation such that Hillman's careful delineation of theories requires the presentation of eighteen different *types* of theories of emotion. (There are over a hundred distinguishable theories and definitions of what an emotion is.) In order to see what we have learned about emotion, we must select, and this very selection may blind us to other visions. In defense of my own portrait of this complex field, I can only plead my dedication to its subject matter and my commitment to an inclusive rather than a narrow vision.

An Historical Approach

If we ask what has been learned about emotion from a detached historical perspective, we may note at least four major theoretical traditions which have evolved. The important facts about emotion may usually be related to one of these theoretical viewpoints. Since any attempt at synthesis must necessarily abandon historical detachment, let us begin by reviewing these four approaches.

Emotions as Functional Patterns of Behavior

The first tradition focuses on emotion as functional behavior that enables the organism to adapt to its environment. For example, Darwin's (1872/1904) classic work treats emotional expression as related to adaptive behavior. He suggests that the facial expression of sorrow, which involves the contraction of muscles around the eyes, may function to prevent hemorrhage during severe crying. Likewise, although concerned with physiological rather than expressive processes, Cannon (1915, 1927, 1939) takes the same general stance when he conceives of emotions as thalamic processes which involve the body in maneuvers that are adaptive for fight or flight. Today, evidence requires us to add the hypothalamus and limbic system, and to see portions of the neocortex as playing an excitatory rather than inhibiting function. However, the basic idea remains the same—emotions are seen as patterns of adaptive behavior which are controlled by the central nervous system. (The fundamental developments within this area have been well reviewed by Arnold [1960b]; see also Delgado [1966].) In a similar manner, when dealing with purposive behavior, McDougall's (1908/1923) focal idea is of a central emotional mechanism whose adaptive character has been determined by natural selection. McDougall had a conception of these "instincts" as central mechanisms linked to the environment by flexible afferent and motor components which were open to learning and imprinting. In fact, it may be shown (see de Rivera, 1977, pp. 130–134) that McDougall's "instinct" is a hypothetical construct with complete formal similarity to Cannon's thalamic activations and Marston's (1928) "central motor responses," as well as to intervening variables in learning theory such as the "fear" proposed by Miller (1951) and the various emotions proposed by Mowrer (1960).

In contemporary theorizing, there are some important variations within this general functionalist tradition. For example, in Tomkins's (1962) theory, emotions amplify rather than produce drive stimuli, providing positive or negative signals which we work to obtain or avoid. Thus, his central emotional states do not

365

motivate particular behavioral response patterns (with the exception of facial expressions); rather, they regulate behavior indirectly by their reinforcing effect. Nevertheless, the major features of the functional-mechanistic approach are maintained—that is, the theorist proposes a relatively small list of basic emotional mechanisms that function in an adaptive way. Plutchik (1980) has attempted to use this approach to synthesize different work on emotions, abstracting eight prototypical patterns of adaptive behavior that may be applied to all animals and related to specific "primary" emotions.

This tradition's concern with recognizable patterns of response has been the basis for a series of empirical investigations on facial expressions (see Ekman, 1971; Izard, 1971; Eibl-Eibesfeldt, 1973). These studies have established that there are at least a few expressive patterns (e.g., the smile of happiness) that are recognized in widely diverse cultures. The approach has also served as a way of comprehending a number of observations of emotional phenomena that have occurred in connection with investigations into the central nervous system. For example, behavioral patterns such as the attack or flight patterns elicited in cats by stimulation of the hippocampus (Kaada et al., 1953) and hypothalamus (Gloor, 1954), or the impulsive aggressive behavior exhibited by humans with tumors in the midbrain or temporal lobe (see Poeck, 1969) or subjected to subcortical stimulation (see Delgado, 1969). Work within this tradition reminds us that there are recognizable patterns of emotional behavior, that these response patterns have an impulsive deterministic quality, and that many of these seem of a basically functional nature.

Since theories within this tradition relate emotions to recognizable patterns of behavior, they focus on the deterministic, impulsive aspect of emotional reaction as it involves the organism with its environment. Thus, Zajonc (1980) emphasizes the independence and immediacy of affective preference. This energetic quality is sometimes contrasted with the structural quality of cognition, as Piaget (1954) does when he attempts to relate affectivity to intelligence. However, we find a second theoretical tradition which asserts that emotions are best regarded as a form of knowing.

Emotion as the Appraisal of Value

Theorists in this tradition argue that while emotions may sometimes involve organized behavior patterns, the different emotions are basically ways of assessing whether an object in the environment (or our own action) is good or bad for us. Rather than viewing the organism as adapting to the environment by means of a reactive set of central emotional mechanisms, they assert that the organism, or at least a person, adapts emotionally by means of an overall appraisal of the situation. It is this appraisal (and its consequent reaction) that is experienced as emotion and, hence, the appraisal of value is an essential aspect of emotion. Further, since this appraisal is an *act* (rather than a stereotypical response), emotion is seen as having

366

an active component rather than being simply a reactive mechanism. The history of this viewpoint, from the thinking of Aristotle to the experiments of Michotte (1950), has been summarized by Arnold (1960a), who suggests that it is the intuitive appraisal of our situation which initiates the action tendencies experienced as emotions.

Of course, there are variations on this theme. Angyal (1941), for example, asserts that our experience of an emotion is actually a *symbol* for our welfare within a given situation, and Solomon (1977) stresses that emotions involve judgments which actually *constitute* what is valuable. And there are expansions of the theme, as when Chein (1972) proposes that some emotions are assessments about whether one's own activity is or is not successful; when Bowlby (1969) points out that emotions as appraisals also help the self monitor its own behavior and communicate the welfare of the self to others; and when Lazarus (1970) suggests that the appraisal of one's situation includes an evaluation of what actions might be taken. Nevertheless, all of these theorists seem to be in essential agreement.

An important advantage of this approach is that it relates affect to perception in a way that prevents an oversimplistic separation of affect and cognition and encourages research into emotions and feelings as ways of knowing. On the one hand, we may speak of "correct" and "incorrect" emotions in much the same way as we distinguish between true and false ideas (that is, according to whether or not they correspond to objective reality). Thus, Macmurray (1935) points out that a feeling of love is correct to the extent that it reflects a person's genuine concern for the other and is mistaken to the extent that the person is really concerned for the self. On the other hand, to the extent that emotions do enable us to assess situations, we would expect emotions to be useful in what are ordinarily regarded as "cognitive" tasks. Several recent studies support this idea. For example, Sommers (1978) shows that those subjects who use more emotion terms (when telling a story) give more adept performances on a cognitive role-taking task. And Hoffspiegel (1980), using an impression formation task, shows that when persons respond affectively, they are less likely to be fixated on primacy effects. (Subjects who were asked to report their feelings in addition to their cognitions were able to adapt more rapidly to changing information about the target of their perception.)

Emotion as Self-Perception

A third, quite different, theoretical tradition has focused on emotion as involving the perception of bodily cues. James (1890/1950) and Lange (1885/1912) advanced the position that an emotion is simply our perception of the bodily changes aroused by our reactions to situations. While both James and Lange postulated that the feedback came from the skeletal musculature and the viscera *after* the body reacted, Bull (1951) has suggested that felt emotion must also include feedback from the person's postural attitude, from the *readiness* to act. Evoking different emotions

367

under hypnosis, she demonstrated that definitive postural patterns were produced. Recent experimentation has taken the direction of producing different bodily patterns and then demonstrating emotional affects. Brown (1977) has shown that when subjects are asked to hold their heads in different positions, they report different emotional reactions, Laird (1974) has shown that facial expression can affect what emotion is experienced, and Lowen and Lowen (1977) have developed a number of different expressive exercises that may be used therapeutically to evoke different emotional reactions.

While it has been possible to specify a half dozen different bodily response patterns, the number of these patterns is nowhere near the number of emotional experiences which the average person can distinguish (we have about four hundred emotion names in English). Consequently, Schacter and Singer (1962) have suggested that in addition to bodily cues, persons may use situational cues in labeling their emotional state. Subsequently, rather than believing that felt emotion is simply sensory feedback from the body, self-attribution theorists (e.g., Laird and Crosby, 1974) have taken the position that emotional experience is inferred or constructed from an array of both bodily and situational cues. While the work stemming from the first two theoretical approaches suggests that there is much more involved in emotional experience than bodily and situational cues, work in this third tradition has clearly established that emotion is always *embodied* and may often be influenced by altering body position, facial expression, and autonomic functioning.

Emotion as an Alternative to Action

A fourth theoretical tradition has been primarily concerned with *when* emotions occur and with their relationship to action. Since behavior, appraisal, and bodily changes are going on all the time and yet we do not continuously experience emotion, emotions must not simply be behavior patterns, or appraisals, or bodily and situational cues. The theorists in this tradition argue that emotions must involve some disturbance of normal action. However, this disturbance may be conceived in quite different ways. Paulhan (1884/1930) suggested that emotion occurred whenever the quantity of psychological energy was too great to be used in systematic behavior, and the early psychoanalytic tradition tended to adopt an analogous view. Rapaport (1942) postulated that when unconscious instinctual energies were not free to discharge in voluntary action (e.g., when instinctual demands conflicted with one another or the demands of reality) their energy would be discharged as emotion. As a person developed emotional control, affective discharges would not be as overwhelming and could be used as signals of impending distress or of one's general condition. Such a model accounts for some of the aspects of emotionality that are observed clinically, such as emotional abreactions and

368

floodings (see Volkan, 1976). However, there are a number of serious objections to such an energy model (see Bowlby, 1969, pp. 18–21).

A related model that may be easier to defend was proposed by Dewey (1895). He argued that whenever a situation automatically elicited a single behavior pattern, no emotion would be aroused. However, if a situation elicited a number of different possible responses, a conflict would ensue. If, for example, the situation suggested a desirable end which might be reached by some alternative behaviors, then action would have to be inhibited until the most adaptive action was selected, and there would be a tension between the various possible actions and the ideal, imagined end. For Dewey, it was this tension or adjustment that was experienced as emotion; and thus emotion, though born of conflict, was what freed the organism from simple automatic responses. This basic idea—that conflicting alternatives and imagination lies at the heart of emotion—has been advanced by a number of thoughtful investigators (e.g., Angier, 1927; Bartlett, 1925; Nahm, 1939) and keeps reappearing. However, for some (nonobvious) reason this line of theory has not led to much research. An exception is Luria's (1932/1960) little known experimental work on affect as a form of behavioral disorganization.

Yet a third variety of theory within the "blocked-action" tradition has been articulated by Sartre (1948), who suggests that consciousness becomes emotional when a person finds it impossible to act within the world. At such an impasse, consciousness returns to a more primitive attitude and envisages a magical, nondeterministic world in which the person is no longer so separated from objects. (For example, a person who suddenly sees a strange face pressed against the window may experience a surge of horror which completely ignores the fact that the window is between him and the face.) It is interesting to note that a more recent model that is couched in neurological terms (see Pribram & Melges, 1969) is formally similar. Emotion is postulated to occur when organized behavior is disrupted by the failure of the person's plans within the perceived situation. This failure disequilibrates the neural system (the "plan" of action). Just as Sartre's emotion magically changes one's world to reduce tension, Pribram's emotions equilibrate by regulating the *stimulus* input to the system (that is, how the world is perceived). (For a more detailed discussion of these theories and their similarities, see de Rivera, 1977.) Note that in these theories the emotion does not function by leading to a patterned response but by transforming perception. In a somewhat different vein, Mandler (1975) suggests that the interruption of organized behavior arouses the autonomic nervous system, stimulating a reevaluation of the situation. As in the Schacter and Singer (1962) model, the emotion which is experienced is the result of both the autonomic arousal and the cognitive interpretation.

Theories in this tradition keep raising disquieting questions as to the exact condition under which emotions occur, how emotion is precisely related to action, and how emotion systematically functions in a person's life. While there are not many

369

systematic empirical studies which are based on these theories, numerous clinical and introspective observations may be related to them. To some extent, they are also supported by the evidence that links emotion to imaginative activity (see Hillman, 1961), or that relates emotion to primary-process thinking. For example, if the TAT stories of persons waked from deep sleep are compared with the stories of persons waked in the midst of a dream, the former are sparsely pragmatic while the latter are laden with affect. Thus, the imaginative, primary-process mode may exist in the waking state and influence the perception of situations (see Fiss, Klein, & Bokert, 1966). In this vein, consider the fact that prefrontal lobotomy diminishes both imagination and affect, or Hebb's (1954) important observation that emotionality appears to increase with cortical development.

At this point we could continue with our objective survey and become involved in some interesting historical questions. For example, how did Cannon's vigorous (and largely successful) experimental attack on the James-Lange theory result in keeping the theory alive while Dewey's untested (and possibly more viable) theory passed into history for lack of interest? Or what demands of method, theory, and scientific acceptability have led so much recent research on facial expressions to focus on the use of only six highly selected expressions, in spite of the fact that Duchenne (1862) gave detailed descriptions of how the electrical stimulation of isolated groups of facial muscles created the appearance of over twenty different emotional expressions? However, since I am a theorist rather than an historian, I distrust my ability to be historically objective and prefer to attempt a synthesis of the four theoretical traditions I have just outlined.

Since it would be impossible to achieve a true synthesis of such disparate traditions from a position of historical objectivity, I shall have to abandon a detached perspective in order to assert a new theoretical position. However, I shall take care to show the historical roots of this new position and, once it is developed, attempt to show how it may be used to subsume the theories and data we examined earlier.

Emotions as Transformations

Back in the early 1920s, Stumpf asked Kurt Lewin to bring will and emotion into the laboratory, to try to submit these phenomena to experimental investigations. And although Lewin's later work had an immense influence on psychology, this earlier work has been rather ignored. To reduce a brilliant series of experiments and hundreds of pages of data to a paragraph, Lewin (see de Rivera, 1976) demonstrated that when a person *wills* something—that is, when he intends to perform some action—his will operates in much the same way as a need operates, if by "need" one means something very similar to one of Dr. Bindra's central motive states (see his chapter in this volume, pages 338–363). That is, the intention system does not passively lie in wait for some stimulus to trigger it, nor does it directly motivate

370

consummatory action; rather it either searches for the necessary stimulus conditions or influences the perception of objects in the environment so that objects acquire a "valence" or "demand character" that controls the person's activity. Thus, if we intend to mail a letter, a mailbox will catch our attention and exert a field force in its direction. Intentions, like needs, transform our environment so that consummatory activity may occur. Conceptually, Lewin represented both an intention and need by the same construct—a tensed region within the person.

Of course, there are times when the environment appears to have a will of its own—the chair entices us to sit down, the cookie to eat it, the nice day to take a walk. For Lewin, such valences were, in fact, related to the person's own needs—his or her fatigue, hunger, restlessness—or, in the case of "induced" valences, to the will of some authority figure. In all cases, he believed there was an intimate link between environmental valence, need, and activity. Indeed, as the experimental work progressed, Lewin became convinced that the basic unit of psychology, the actor who behaves, was not really the person or organism which we ordinarily conceive but, rather, a "life-space"—a Gestalt unit of action that included both the person and the person's environment. Behavior was a function of the overall state of the life-space and might consist of either a "locomotion" of the person within the life-space or a restructuring of the life-space.

Continuing this analogy between intended activity and need, Karsten (1976), one of Lewin's students, showed that intended activities *satiate* in much the same way needs do. That is, if a subject is asked to repeat an activity, he or she gradually begins to change it—to introduce variations—and if these variations are prevented, the activity disintegrates, the subject stops the activity and literally cannot go on. In addition to working with complex activities such as reading poetry, Karsten used simple repetitive tasks, such as making repeated short strokes with a pencil. She shows that pleasant tasks actually satiate more rapidly than neutral tasks; the more the person is involved with the activity, the more rapidly satiation progresses.

While Lewin never proposes a theory of emotion that may be compared with his theory of will, one of his students, Tamara Dembo (1931/1976) succeeded in synthesizing an emotion in the laboratory—the emotion of anger. It should be noted that most experiments on emotions do not really *synthesize* an emotion, they merely *instigate* an emotion by, for example, insulting or threatening a subject. Such a procedure tells us very little about the nature of emotion. Dembo, however, consciously constructs a field of forces which leads to the development of anger. First, she involves the subject in a task: she seats each subject on a chair within a rectangle and asks him or her to obtain a flower from a nearby vase which is just out of reach. (The instructions make it clear that both feet must remain within the rectangle.) After an initial success (the subject discovers that the flower can be reached by leaning upon the chair) the subject is asked to discover a second solution and runs into a barrier—for there *is* no second solution and, hence, the goal cannot

371

be reached and the person is frustrated. Contrary to the frustration-aggressive hypothesis, there are no signs of aggressive activity at this point, rather the subject simply turns away from the activity and attempts to assert that there is no solution and that he or she is ready to leave.

Dembo prevents these attempts to leave by creating an "outer barrier" that imprisons the subject in the situation: she insists that there *is* a second solution and she is sure it can be discovered by the subject. The only possible escape route requires the subject to return to attempts to reach the blocked goal. Now, the subject begins to experience increased frustration, and the situation becomes oppressive and filled with tension. Dembo details how the person then attempts to escape the field of force by moving up to a level of fantasy where barriers do not exist and wishes can come true. Ultimately, however, the person must return to the level of reality, where tension continues to accumulate. This tension begins to obliterate the various boundaries within the field: the boundaries that distinguish between the real goal and an easy substitute (a nearby flower that is easily reached but is not the real goal and will not provide a real escape), between the level of reality and the level of fantasy, between what is private and what is public. Consequently, subjects begin to engage in minor irrationalities—finding themselves holding the nearby flower, thinking that perhaps they really *can* do an impossible feat (such as hypnotizing the flower), telling the experimenter something that is really too personal to share, and so forth. Subjects struggle against this process, but the tension continues to mount until the field becomes homogenized and the boundary between the self and the environment can no longer be maintained. At this point in the experiment, some trivial event (a smile, a cough) will suddenly be perceived as a provocation and the subject explodes with anger.

It should be noted that Dembo describes the development of an emotion by describing a transformation in the subject's overall life-space rather than simply a change within the person. Thus, rather than a region of tension within the person transforming the situation (as in the case with will or need), we have the situation itself becoming filled with tension and transforming the person. And rather than locomotion within the life-space, we have a restructuring of the field. In fact, Dembo suggests that the intensity of an emotion is best conceived in terms of the emotion's ability to transform the person's life-space.

When Koffka (1935) reviews Dembo's work, he fully accepts the idea that emotions should be conceived as dynamic organizations but (I believe mistakenly) suggests that they are related to states of tension *within* the ego. However, when he discusses physiognomic character—"the horrible, the majestic, the enchanting"— he proposes that these qualities occur when a state of tension exists *between* the object and the ego, and that the type of tension determines the response, "attack, flight, approval, succourance." In fact (I believe correctly) he contrasts this physiognomic character with the demand character described by Lewin (where the valence depends on tensions *within* the person part of the life-space—viz., will or need). I would like to propose that Koffka's description of the physiognomic field is actually a good description of emotion. That is, emotion involves a physiognomic transformation of the life-space, and each different kind of emotion involves a particular type of dynamic tension between the object and the person, a dynamic which produces the particular transformation. As we continue, I hope to show that the particular details of these different transformations may be specified with a considerable degree of precision. Such transformations coincide with a dissolution of the boundary which separates the ego from other aspects of the life-space so that, as Koffka implies, the field is unified in a way that reduces the overall tension in the field.[1]

Dembo's study portrays emotion as occurring when the field is unified by increasing tension and the destruction of boundaries. That this is not necessarily the case is shown by Reichenberg (1939), who was inspired to try a positive version of Dembo's experiment. She gave her subjects, who were school children, one of the activities with which Karsten had demonstrated satiation effect. She asked them to make repeated strokes with a pencil and, of course, after a couple of pages the children wanted to stop. She then gave the children an emotional experience which she labels "joy." She led the children to a treasure chest where they became involved in the challenge of opening the lock. After a protracted struggle, but before any discouragement occurred (she could manipulate the device so that the child was always successful), the child succeeded in opening the chest. There, inside, were candy and toys—which the child could keep—and all the children exhibited positive emotional behavior. After about ten minutes, the experimenter again asked the children to do the activity on which they were previously satiated. In thirty-four of thirty-five cases, the children produced more strokes than they did before—and better quality strokes. They produced page after page of carefully done marking. Particularly convincing is the photographic reproduction of the work of one child who had a behavior disturbance and could only make scrawls before the emotional experience. After the experience, his marks are distinct marks—the emotional experience has clearly transformed the field in a way which unifies and organizes behavior.[2]

Our account of emotional transformation is not restricted to persons. Rather, I believe that we must recognize the existence of patterns of emotional transformations in animals as well as human beings. I do not mean the sort of mechanistic phenomena the ethologists study (releaser stimuli and the like); I mean full transformational patterns of behavior. (This is not to say, of course, that animals are

---

[1] Such a view is compatible with Werner's (1948) view of physiognomic perception, with Angyal's (1941) organismic theory (where emotion involves a reunification of the ego with portions of the self from which it has been separated) and with Hillman's (1961) Jungian theory (where emotion occurs when the object of the emotion is a symbol that unites conscious and unconscious processes).

[2] I do not know of a single citation to this study. How can the results be explained by any of the traditional theories, and what happens to results which we cannot explain?

conscious of these patterns as we human beings are.) Of dozens of naturalistic accounts that could be given, consider the following account by John Muir (1916), certainly a careful observer.

Muir was on an Alaskan expedition, and one of his companions brought along a dog named Strickeen, who had a rather aloof character structure—a loner who went his own way and exhibited little attachment behavior and no emotionality. Muir states, "He sometimes reminded me of a small, squat, unshakable desert cactus." One day a storm developed, and Muir and the dog became trapped on a sort of glacial island that was isolated by deep crevices. The only way off the island was by a narrow ice bridge, which Muir managed to straddle over but could not get the dog to cross. The dog *might* make it across safely. Now Muir encourages him to try, but for the first time the dog shows fear—highly justifiable fear—howls despondently, and refuses to try. Muir pretends to leave—but, of course, the dog does not budge. Finally, Muir *has* to leave, and once the dog *knows* that Muir is really going, he makes the attempt. He creeps across the bridge, leaning into the wind, and finally arrives at the toughest point, the upward slope to the top of the crevice. While Muir is wondering how he can possibly help, the dog observes every detail of the ascent and, suddenly, scrambles up to the bank in one burst of perfectly coordinated energy. He has succeeded! He is alive!

Muir writes, "Never before or since have I seen anything like so passionate a revulsion from the depths of despair to exultant, triumphant, uncontrollable joy. He flashed and darted hither and thither as if fairly demented, screaming and shouting, swirling round and round in giddy loops and circles like a leaf in a whirlwind, lying down, and rolling over and over, sidewise and heels over head, and pouring forth a tumultuous flood of hysterical cries and sobs and gasping mutterings. When I ran up to him to shake him, fearing he might die of joy, he flashed off two or three hundred yards, his feet in a mist of motion; then, turning suddenly, came back in a wild rush and launched himself at my face, almost knocking me down, all the time screeching and screaming, and shouting as if saying, 'Saved! Saving! Saved!' Then away again, dropping suddenly at times with his feet in the air, trembling and faintly sobbing."

Later, Muir observes, "Thereafter Strickeen was a changed dog. During the rest of the trip, instead of holding aloof, he always lay by my side, tried to keep me constantly in sight, and would hardly accept a morsel of food, however tempting, from any hand but mine. . . ."

Note that again we see emotion as a complex transformation of the entire life-space with subsequent effects on the organism's behavior. A search of the experimental animal literature does not reveal many investigators using emotion names—except as cautious labels for intervening variables. However, Crespi's (1942, 1944) studies are a notable exception. Crespi unexpectedly increased (or decreased) the amount of the reward his rats were used to finding at the end of a straight alley maze. He showed that there was an immediate impact on their running speed and refers to their degree of "eagerness," to their "elation," their "frustration" and their "depression." Crespi specifies the behaviors involved and I would like to encourage the description of such transformational patterns of behavior with careful attention to exactly what labels are used.

Specifying Transformational Structures

I believe that emotion names are just as useful as, say, tree names. There is a difference between a maple and a spruce. The leaves differ, the bark differs, they grow in different conditions, the former's wood is harder to cut and burns longer. Our names for these trees refer to these very real differences. In the studies conducted by me and my students at Clark and at New York University (see de Rivera, 1977), we took advantage of the English language in order to specify the exact nature of the transformations involved in different emotions. We postulated that there is a different transformational structure for each emotion, and, thus far, we have been able to specify these structural wholes in terms of four interrelated parts. Each emotion involves: (1) a specific situation with which the person must deal (the perception of this situation is actually a part of the emotion, a transaction between the person and the environment which gives physiognomic meaning to the situation and, hence, is part of the transformation the emotion affects); (2) a particular transformation of the person's body and the manner in which the self relates to the environment (this is a direct emotional response to the new situation); (3) a specific "instruction" as to how the person should behave or transform this new situation (this instruction is experienced as the impulse or motivation of the emotion); and (4) a unique way in which these transformations advance the person's values.

As an example, let us consider the four parts of the structure of the emotion of anger. (1) The situation is transformed into one in which the person experiences a *challenge* to what the person believes *ought* to exist. This challenge is experienced as stemming from the will of an other who is held responsible for the challenge. (2) The transformation of the body involves a stiffening of the person's own will. (3) The emotion's instruction is to remove the challenge. (4) These transformations serve to protect the person's values (what ought to exist) and to preserve the integrity of the relationship with the other.

For every emotion we have studied to date, we have had remarkable success in specifying such structures in a way that differentiates the particular emotion from others and makes clear its particular set of transformations. Let me give just one example, a study by Lindsay-Hartz (1975) which examined the differences between elation, gladness, and joy.

One might think that persons use such words unreliably—that they all just mean "good." But, in fact, relatively educated persons—that is to say, college students—use such words quite precisely. They know exactly when to say "glad" although, of course, they cannot themselves specify how they are able to use the term. When we ask a person to give an example of a time when he or she felt elated, we find that the experience is structured quite differently than it is in times of gladness or joy. What are these structures like?

Elation occurs when our mundane world is jarred by the unexpected fulfillment of a *wish*. Wishes operate on a fantasy level—the level of unreality we discussed earlier in the Dembo experiment. When a wish comes true, it appears that the person has to go up to the level of unreality in order to realize that the wish has come true—otherwise the wished for news is too good to be true. Hence, one of the transformations of elation involves the experience of being lifted (as might be suspected from the etymology of the word). Nor is this description loosely metaphorical. While, of course, the person's body does not literally go off the ground, the person's behavior is literally transformed. Thus, if a student who has just received a high mark is asked to establish the height of a horizon line that is directly opposite to the eyes, he or she will set the line higher than will the nonelated person (Wapner, 1957). And elated persons go out of contact with the mundane reality in which the rest of us remain. If you have ever tried to talk with a person who is "high," you will recognize the phenomenon—there is often a grin on the face and the person cannot seem to hear what you are trying to communicate. In fact, the person is too busy telling you about the wonderful thing that has happened—for the wish or impulse of elation is to announce the person's new position. And this announcement is in the service of elation's function—to help the person realize his or her transformed situation.

In gladness, on the other hand, we find that a *hope* has been fulfilled. Now unlike wishes, hopes are grounded in reality. But hopes are dependent on circumstances beyond our control. We must wait for what we hope for, and we cannot be sure it will occur. Hence, there is a sort of cloud on the horizon when we hope. When a hope is fulfilled, we do not go up; rather the cloud lifts and the horizon becomes transformed—things look brighter. Rather than a grin, we see brighter eyes. And rather than wishing to announce his or her new position, the person wishes to *welcome* the hoped-for event. Gladness functions to enable the person to continue to depend on whatever ally helped fulfill the hope.

Joy differs in yet other ways. Most persons are rarely in direct contact with reality; it is as though there is a veil between us and a perfectly clear perception of the world. But there are times when this veil lifts—when a person experiences the full presence of another person, or a work of art, or a part of nature. This "meeting" is the occasion for joy, and persons report a transformation that involves an increased sense of closeness and harmony with the world and an increased sense of grounding in their bodies. The impulse of joy is to *celebrate* the certainty of meaningfulness that the person experiences, and joy functions to affirm the existence of meaning.

How can we be sure that such descriptions are valid? We can check them in a number of ways. The method used by Lindsay-Hartz involved asking a sample of persons to give an example experience for each of the three emotions. Then each of these persons was provided with the four different parts of each of the three structural descriptions, without any identifying cues as to the emotion they were supposed to portray. The subjects were then asked to match the abstract structural descriptions with their concrete descriptions of the different emotions. Most were able to do this, and the statistics suggest that it is highly unlikely that such matching could occur by chance.

The descriptions of emotional experience which may be obtained by structural analysis provides discriminations that are important both in theory construction and in clinical work (see, for example, Goodman's [1975] differentiation between the experience of anxiety and the experiences of panic, fear, and terror).

However, structural analysis would merely be an interesting approach to the description of individual emotions were it not for two significant aspects of the structures: (1) their form suggests a synthesis of the major theoretical traditions with which we began our discussion; (2) the structures of the individual emotions appear to be related to one another to form an emotional system that regulates object relations and may be related to biological necessity and personal value.

Emotional Structure as an Integration of Prior Traditions

Let us see how the structural form suggests a theoretical synthesis. We have noted the four parts of an emotion's structure: the way in which the emotion transforms the person's situation, the way in which it transforms the body and the relationship to the environment, the specific instruction as to how to transform the situation, and the way the emotion functions to maintain the person's values. I believe that each of the theoretical traditions may be related to a different one of these parts.

The way in which the emotion transforms the person's situation, by its interpretation of events, may be related to the second tradition which stresses that emotions involve a form of knowing, a way of assessing whether objects or situations are good or bad, or going well or poorly for us. This view of emotion corresponds to the part of the emotion's structure which we have termed the emotion's "situation." Since we usually think of an emotion as occurring as a response to a situation, it may seem strange to think of the situation as part of an emotion, but certainly each emotion does structure or interpret the situation in a particular way. If a stranger shakes a fist at a person, the person may interpret the gesture as a challenge (anger), a dangerous threat (fear), a bit of incongruity (amusement), and so on. The emotion is an assessment of the situation, and these assessments are not simple mechanical reactions but true *transactions* between the person and the environment, giving the situation its meaning. Thus, part of the structure of an emotion reflects an unconscious "choice" about how to perceive one's situation. If emotions were only fixed behavior patterns, they would be as inflexible as reflexes; but since they operate by

377

assessing a situation, by participating in the creation of its meaning, they provide a more flexible means of adapting to the environment.

The particular way in which an emotion transforms the body and its relationship with the environment may be related to the third tradition, which stresses the participation of the body in emotion and its influence on what emotion is experienced.

I believe these embodied patterns are much more specific than has yet been demonstrated. As I have said, it seems that the body expresses itself, and is perceived, quite differently in emotions as closely related as elation, gladness, and joy. Rather than working with isolated facial or postural expressions, it may be more fruitful to develop and utilize phenomenological descriptions of bodily responses such as Straus's (1966) description of sighing, Funk's (1974) description of laughing, and Laban's (1960) elaborate descriptive system of patterns of movement.

While the body is crucial to emotion, it does not seem likely that emotional experience is only based on sensory feedback or that it is only a cognition based on bodily and situational cues. Rather, it seems to be a reflection of all the transformations that constitute the emotions. How then may we explain the fact that bodily manipulations may affect emotional experience? I believe that when experimenters manipulate the body, they are not simply providing cues which are then interpreted as an emotion. Rather, they have created the bodily (or situational) component of a particular emotion's structure, and this part has evolved the whole structure and, hence, the emotion. That is, as Koffka (1935) asserted, it seems probable that the evocation of a part of a whole will evoke the entire gestalt. In this view, the manipulation of bodily responses and situational cognitions may *evoke* an emotion rather than simply affect the interpretation of cues.

The specific instruction as to how to transform the situation, and the way in which an emotion functions to maintain a person's values, may relate to the first and fourth traditions. There is an obvious conflict between the first theoretical tradition we considered, with its view of emotions as motives for action or functional patterns of behavior, and the fourth tradition, which sees emotion as an alternative to action. In fact, it should be noted that the relationship between emotion and action is far from obvious. When we examine the stream of behavior in everyday life (see Barker, 1963) it is often easy to observe an emotional tone to the activity, or to observe emotional incidents, but the functional relationship between expressive and instrumental action is quite unclear.

Consider, for example, the relationship between anger and aggressive behavior. Observation clearly shows that an angry person may have an impulse to attack, and it has been shown experimentally that an angered person is more likely than an unangered person to use an opportunity to hurt another person (Hartmann, 1969) and that the sight of another's pain is more likely to be a positive reinforcer to an angry person (Feshback, Stiles, & Bitter, 1967). However, observation also shows that anger does not necessarily lead to aggressive behavior. In fact, even when an attack would be completely safe, when a person's anger leads to direct assertive action there may be a complete absence of aggressive impulses. Likewise, it is clear that attacking behavior can be learned in the absence of anger (see Bandura, 1973). In fact, Hartmann's (1969) experiment shows that simply watching a violent film is more effective in producing attack behavior than is the arousal of anger. This is not to say that no emotions occur in attack behavior. The sheer enjoyment of being active and of mastering an attack may be involved when a child models an attack. And, as Bandura shows, the behavior is much more apt to be modeled when it is successful. Also, when a child is feeling bad (e.g., has lost a competition), he or she is more apt to adopt a model's aggressive behavior. But our point is that the emotion of *anger* is not necessarily connected with the attacking behavior which we associate with it.

Now in my view, the first tradition is correct in viewing emotions as functional, as specific, and as involving "impulses" or "energy." Thus, each emotion invokes specific "instructions" which function to impel the person to transform the situation in particular ways. However, these instructions are not mechanistic. In the first place, they are relative to the perceived situation (as interpreted by the emotional structure). If the situation acquires a different meaning, the emotion and its instructions will immediately change. In the second place, while the instructions are specific (such as anger's "remove the challenge" or joy's "celebrate"), they do not specify the particular behavior pattern to be used. That is, the angry person does not necessarily have an impulse to hit or scratch, or swear, or even attack. The instruction is simply the imperative "remove the challenge." In fact—and here is where I believe the fourth tradition is correct—the emotion only occurs when "direct" instrumental behavior is insufficient and, ideally, the emotion suffices to transform the situation independently of direct instrumental behavior. Thus, in the case of anger, the mere assertion of what ought to be, often psychologically removes a challenge (just as, to take an animal example, the mere growl of a dog may remove a challenge without any attack). When immediate instrumental behavior is involved, as when a child learns to hit or kick, the behavior is congruent with the instruction of removing the challenge; it may be influenced by the particular dynamics of the structure, but it is not a mechanistically determined part of the emotion.

The fourth tradition asserts that emotion occurs in situations where instinctive, habitual, or planned action cannot occur; hence, emotion is seen as an alternative to action. In like manner, the structural theory asserts that emotions are transformations of the person's way of relating to the emotional object rather than direct sources of instrumental action. The instruction of the emotion is, ideally, accomplished by the transformational power of expressive behavior. As Sartre (1948) remarks, the instrumental behavior which may occur is the result of a failure of the emotion's power to restructure the situation. However, while Sartre, like many of the theorists within this tradition, tends to view emotion as a rather functionless and

379

magical substitute for action, our structural theory asserts that emotional transformations are basically functional, particularly within the interpersonal field where emotional expression can often effect changes that instrumental action cannot accomplish (as in convincing another person of one's sincerity).

Such interpersonal consequences of the emotion are related to the fourth aspect of our structural analysis—the way the emotion functions to transform how the person relates to others. Again, we postulate that each particular emotion functions to preserve or advance the person's values in a particular way. For example, while anger removes a challenge, it often functions not only to preserve the person's values but to preserve a kind of closeness with the person at whom one is angry. This is true because anger presumes that the other is responsible and that there *is* a common set of values (otherwise the person could not challenge what ought to exist). Hence, an alternative to anger is always to create distance between the self and the other by seeing the other as not really responsible (insane, a child, a psychopath) or by realizing that one does not have shared values.

It may be objected that emotions are often mistakes, that they may disorganize us and get us into trouble. But the same may be said of ideas. My point is not that emotions are always functional but that emotions are basically designed to be functional, though they may be misused. Imagine a new drug or operation that could eliminate specific emotions; in a given clinical case, one might want to eliminate guilt, anxiety, euphoria, anger, but would one want to eliminate any emotion from the human repertoire? Perhaps even hate and envy have their place and function in a human life.

If the four aspects of an emotion were only a list of unrelated items, we could hardly claim a synthesis of the various theories, but, in fact, the aspects are interrelated parts of a whole and form a true structure. One cannot really separate the emotion's instruction (e.g., remove the challenge) from the emotion's situation (the perception of a challenge, which *is* something to be removed). Nor can one implement this instruction without the body being transformed (a stiffening of the person's will). Nor could all of this organization exist were it not motivated by the way the emotion functions interpersonally (that is, the perception of a challenge, which can be removed, functioning to maintain a shared unity of values and, hence, avoiding the creation of distance). To summarize: every emotion may be conceptualized as a dynamic structure which transforms the person's situation by affecting how the objective situation is perceived, how this perceived situation is altered, how the body behaves, and how the person relates to his or her values and to significant others.

The many different ways in which emotion can be expressed and communicated may be related to the various components of emotional structure. While most research has focused on studies of facial expression (an aspect of how the body is transformed), Benson (1967) has shown how emotion is often conveyed in literature by a description of the object of the emotion or how the world is perceived when one has the emotion (an aspect of the situational transformation). And the Gestalt psychologists have emphasized how the expression and perception of emotion often involve the quality of expressive movement—slow and draggy, jerky, soft and flowing—(an aspect of the instructional transformation). These various aspects of emotional transformation probably have isomorphic resemblances and are ordinarily perceived physiognomically. Clearly, the dynamics of the various emotional structures play an important role in artistic communication. Arnheim (1974) has analyzed the dynamics of expressive structures in art and architecture, Langer (1953) has shown how the artist uses these imagined forms to create the semblance of time and emotion in music, the semblance of power and force in dance, and so on, and Dewey (1934) convincingly argues that the unity of a work of art is dependent upon the integrity of the emotional form that holds the work together.

Emotions as the Transformation of Personal Relations

We have seen that it is possible to describe structures which discriminate between different emotions and that the general form of these structures provides a way to synthesize the various approaches to the nature of emotion, but emotions themselves are but an aspect of those more inclusive affective organizations which McDougall (1908/1923) termed "sentiments" or which psychoanalysts term "object relations," or which we may call "love relationships."[3] As Macmurray has pointed out, each person is born into a love relationship. Because of this, the fundamental unit of psychology must be greater than the individual and even than the life-space of the person-in-environment. "The fundamental unit of the personal is two persons in community with one another and in relationship with a common Other" (Macmurray, 1957).

What do the various emotions, each with their particular structure, have to do with love relationships? We have already noted that one part of an emotion's structure has to do with the functioning of the emotion as it relates to the person's values and relationships with others. When we examine a number of different structures, we begin to become aware that the various structures are related to each other, that they are parts of a more inclusive affective organization, and that each of them appears to have to do with the enhancement and preservation of what is "good" and the avoidance of what is "bad" within the context of the love relationship. In fact, personal values might be said to stand behind emotional transformations in much the same way that motives stand behind actions.

---

[3]While we cannot discuss the literature on object-relations here, the interested reader may want to consider the affective relationship between mother and child as portrayed by Mahler, Pine, and Bergman (1975), the changing viewpoint within psychoanalysis (Green, 1977; Blanch & Blanch, 1973), and the interesting speculations of D.H. Lawrence (1960).

381

One whole class of emotional structures may be called "it"-emotions because they appear to have an object—anger, love, admiration, horror, for example. These deal with the value of the other's actions as perceived by the self. In anger, for example, the other never simply frustrates the person. At the moment of anger, the other is experienced as "bad" or "wrong" in the sense that the person *ought* not to be acting in the way he or she does (as we have noted, an alternative to anger is always to "distance" the other, to make the other not responsible for his or her action). Another class of structures, the "me"-emotions—depression, shame, pride, joy, for example—deal with the self as valued in the eyes of the other. Now the very idea of the self as seen by the other is at the core of symbolic interactionism (see Mead, 1934) and is fundamental for the development of language and culture. Yet here we see it embodied in emotional structures. What is fascinating is that each of these me-emotions appears to be paired with a corresponding it-emotion with a mirror-image structure. For example, if the person experiences *himself* rather than the other as bad, we have a depression rather than an anger structure. Just as anger occurs when a challenge is posed by another, depression occurs when a person acts against his or her own value and thus becomes a self-challenger (see Kane, 1976). Clinicians have always recognized a close link between anger and depression. Now we have a theoretical understanding of the relationship. And the relationship is not only between anger and depression: all emotions are paired. If we are correct, love and serenity, admiration and pride, horror and guilt are all structurally similar, differing only insofar as the other or the self is the object of the valuing process. In fact, the whole affective structure appears to be concerned with *dyadic* relationships such as merger and separation, recognition and dismissal as a group member, and the acceptance and rejection of meaning.

The fact that the other is as intrinsic a part of the emotional system as is the self—that the system is fundamentally dyadic—leads me back to the idea of biological necessity. While the more precise ethologists are much more sensitive to species differences than the average psychologist and are careful not to generalize their findings, the very use of terms such as *attachment* and *territory* suggests a kind of generality, and we find that these same terms are useful in describing different emotional transformations. Thus, in spite of the fact that our own species has its unique behavioral propensities, and in spite of the fact that our specific behavior is largely shaped by cultural factors, I believe that there are fundamental structural similarities across cultures and between our species and many other species. These similarities are none other than the emotional transformations which I have been describing, and these must reflect the biological necessities involved in attaching ourselves to others, dealing with the challenges posed by others to our position, defending ourselves against the dangers posed by others, caring for others who are valued.

Yet in our four-aspect analysis, only one aspect of an emotion is impulsive (the "instruction") and only one aspect of an emotion pertains to its embodiment. Since the emotion structures its own situation, there is an enormous freedom and flexibility possible in how we respond to situations, in the meaning we give them. And since emotions are in the service of what is valued, cultures are as free to use our inherent emotional structures to promote cooperation, creativity, and synergy (see Maslow, 1972) as to establish competition and destruction.

This is not the place to develop these thoughts to the extent that is obviously required, and I have been proceeding at so abstract a level that I want to conclude with a concrete example. In 1869, Wallace wrote the following description of the behavior of a young orangutan:

> For the first few days it clung desperately with all four hands to whatever it could lay hold of . . . hair more tenaciously than anything else. . . . When restless, it would struggle about with its hands up in the air trying to find something to take hold of, and when it had got a bit of stick or rag in two or three of its hands, seemed quite happy. For want of something else, it would often seize its own feet, and after a time it would constantly cross its arms and grasp with each hand the long hair that grew just below the opposite shoulder. . . . Finding it so fond of hair, I endeavored to make an artificial mother, by wrapping up a piece of buffalo skin into a bundle, and suspending it about a foot from the floor. At first this seemed to suit admirably, as it could spread its legs about and always find some hair, which it grasped with the greatest tenacity. I was now in hopes that I had made the little orphan quite happy; and so it seemed for some time, till it began to . . . try to suck. It would pull itself up close to the skin, and try about everywhere for a likely place; but, as it only succeeded in getting mouthfuls of hair and wool, it would be greatly disgusted, and scream violently, and after two or three attempts, let go altogether (cited in de Vore, 1965, p. 520).

Note that quite apart from the specific behavioral mechanisms that are mentioned—the grasping for hair, the motivated search for a stimulus to release sucking behavior—Wallace mentions a number of emotional transformations: the clinging has a "desperate" quality, the orangutan is "restless," when it achieves contact it is "happy" and later it is "disgusted" (in the angry sense of the word). And by now the reader will realize that I do not think that Wallace is being anthropomorphic but, rather, is referring to different emotional structures that are just as present as the grasping. What I am suggesting is that such emotional transformations are related to a valuing process that is bound up with our relations to others (in this case, to the infant orangutan's relationship to the mother), and that it is this valuing process that is just as crucial a part of our biological inheritance as are any specific releaser stimuli. Without such a valuing process, the organism would only exhibit inflexible instinctual mechanisms. For example, the young orangutan would mechanistically continue its search for a nipple rather than emotionally realizing that it was dealing with a bad mother.

We do not restrict our account to the orangutan's behavior. Notice *Wallace's* behavior—his obvious concern for the infant—hoping that he had made it happy. Is there any doubt that a success would result in the transformation of gladness? And note our *own* reaction to Wallace, in his hut in Malaysia, attempting to manufacture an artificial mother for the "little orphan," "finding it so fond of hair," as he did. If the reader values nurturance, as I personally do, *we* may feel a bit of fondness for Wallace, thus experiencing a small emotional transformation of our own—supporting our values as we symbolically join another member of our species who manifests caring.

Appendix

Concerning the "Energetics" of Emotions and Their Expression

While it is not possible to maintain a simple energy model of the emotions, there are many phenomena which require us to recognize the "energetics" of emotional organization and the relative autonomy of these dynamics.

1. When an emotional structure occurs, it shapes a person's experience, assimilating objects and events into its organization of reality. As Dewey (1934) observes,

> In the development of an expressive act, the emotion operates like a magnet drawing to itself appropriate materials: appropriate because it has an experienced emotional affinity for the state of mind already moving. Selection and organization of material are at once a function and a test of the quality of the emotion experienced (p. 69).

2. There are instances where an emotional structure seems to impose its situation on the objective situation in a way which distorts its reality. For example, a person in a situation which is experienced as frustrating may, at first, "contain" or suppress any anger. Later, however (often in a situation where it is safer to express anger), the person becomes angry at a relatively trivial instance (see Dollard et al., 1939). Or a person experiencing loneliness finds himself pretending that an obviously unsuitable other is a potential lover. Or a soldier who experiences "shell-shock" keeps living in a world that is completely dominated by the terror of being trapped in a burning tank or the horror of being splattered by his friend's body. The emotion's influence persists until it (or some other intense emotion) is relived (see Sargent, 1975).

3. In other cases, the absence of an emotional structure that seems to be called for by the objective situation prevents a transformation of the situation, which then persists in a distorted form. For example, persons who suffer the loss of a loved one

but are not able to grieve, often continue to behave as though the dead person is still really present (see Volkan et al., 1977). Or a person who never experiences anger feels no anger upon being abandoned by his or her spouse but develops an ulcer. (Note that in this view the ulcer is not an unconscious expression of anger so much as a failure of anger to occur.)

From our perspective, all of these "energetic properties" may be related to the structural dynamics of each particular emotion and how its structure relates the person to the situation he or she is in. We do not need to speak of quantities of aggressive drive or postulate four hundred different types of emotional energy. There is only one type of "emotional energy," but it is transformed by the different forms the emotional structures can take. Thus, the "energy" of depression may be transformed into the energy of hate—and even into the energy of love—according to the structure the person uses.

Rorty (1978) has written an interesting essay on the different ways in which we may explain the persistence of tenacious or inappropriate emotions. One of these ways has to do with the effects of past experience on our perception of the current situation. There are two ways to conceptualize this effect. Leeper (1970), one of the theorists who has recognized a close tie between emotion and perception, has demonstrated that earlier perceptual experience establishes a "set," so that a person will not be aware of the ambiguity of the present stimulus situation (the different ways in which it may be interpreted) but will simply see it as it was perceived in the past. Differences in past experience account for one reason why the same objective situation will evoke different emotional structures in different persons, and why a given person will tend to persist in his or her emotional structuring of the situation. A somewhat different dynamic has been articulated by Mucchielli (1970), who shows how past emotional structures may persist as unfinished tasks which affect the person's present construal of emotional situations. In a sense, this is a rather straightforward interpretation and extension of the phenomena which Freud elaborated—for example, the persistence of an unresolved Oedipal situation.

There are many other aspects of personality that affect how emotion is experienced. As persons develop, they specialize in different ways of controlling strong emotional reactions (see Lazarus, 1968) and cultivate different "tastes" for emotions, some specializing in wonder and a quest for stimulation, others developing an appetite for anger or the thrills of fear (see Dahl, 1979). And as Schafer (1964) suggests, different personalities treat their emotions quite differently, some making a display of their emotions, others conceiving them as dangerous but precious, to be hoarded or given as presents.

Just as individuals tend to specialize in certain emotions and ignore others, cultures appear to build their institutions on the elaboration and repression of different emotional structures. Briggs (1970), who provides an account of the emotion terms used by the Utku Eskimoes, describes how the Utku feel that anger is

385

only appropriate in small children and white foreigners. Adults cultivate an accept-ing attitude, and do not make assertions about the way things ought to be, and do not feel challenged and angry. (Still, one notes some evidence of the deleterious consequences of having an emotion be unacceptable. For example, Briggs describes Utku men going out of the igloo to beat their dogs—without experiencing any anger or being able to offer an explanation for this action.) On the other hand, a culture may provide opportunities for ritualized expression of emotions. Among the Gahuku in New Guinea, the violent expression of anger is sanctioned in one ceremony which allows the oppressed women to vent hostility against the domineering males (Read, 1965).

Within our own culture, the Japanese psychiatrist Doi (1973) has pointed out the relative absence of an emotion which is quite prevalent in Japan. The Japanese term *amae* refers to an emotional structure for which we have no term in English, but which we might call "passive dependency love." The emotion reflects the need to be taken care of, and the person expressing the emotion assumes that the other will take care of him or her. Of course, we may observe this emotion in children, and it plays a prominent role in Balint's (1965) theory of object-relations. However, while the Japanese build upon the emotion and make it the cornerstone of the reciprocal dependency relations which hold their families and industries together, we ordinar-ily look down upon the expression of *amae*, discouraging it as antithetical to our own valuing of independence and our ideology of self-sufficiency.

On a more abstract level, a number of psychologists have worked with the emotional dynamics that hold a group or a culture together. While Freud's (1913/1950) theory and Slater's (1966) observations stress the theme of a common identification with a primal leader, Redl (1942) has specified a number of other emotional relationships which may bind a group together. In a related vein, Den-nison (1928) has used historical examples to show how different patterns of love relationships may be used to hold a cultural group together, and Ricoeur (1972) has described different ways in which peoples have structured their sense of evil.

REFERENCES

Angier, R. The conflict theory of emotion. *American Journal of Psychology*, 1927, *39*, 390–401.

Angyal, A. *Foundations for a science of personality*. Cambridge, Mass.: Harvard University Press, 1941.

Arnheim, R. *Art and visual perception*. Berkeley: University of California Press, 1974.

Arnold, M. *Emotion and personality* (Vol. 1). New York: Columbia University Press, 1960. (a)

Arnold, M. *Emotion and personality* (Vol. 2). New York: Columbia University Press, 1960. (b)

Balint, M. *Primary love and psychoanalytic technique*. New York: Liveright, 1965.

Bandura, A. *Aggression: A social learning analysis*. Englewood Cliffs, N.J.: Prentice-Hall, 1973.

Barker, R. G. *The stream of behavior: Explorations of its structure and content*. New York: Appleton-Century-Crofts, 1963.

Bartlett, B. Feeling, imaging and thinking. *British Journal of Psychology*, 1925, *16*, 16–29.

Benson, J. Emotion and expression. *Philosophical Review*, 1967, 76, 335–357.

Blanch, R., & Blanch, G. The transference object and the real object. *International Journal of Psychological Analysis*, 1973, 58, 33–44.

Bowlby, J. *Attachment and loss* (Vol. 1). New York: Basic Books, 1969.

Briggs, J. L. *Never in anger*. Cambridge, Mass.: Harvard University Press, 1970.

Brown, R. A. *Kinesthetic and cognitive determinants of emotional state: An investigation of the Alexander Technique*. Unpublished doctoral dissertation, Tufts University, 1977.

Bull, N. The attitude theory of emotion. *Nervous and Mental Disease Monograph*, 1951 (No. 81).

Cannon, W. B. *Bodily changes in pain, hunger, fear and rage*. New York: Appleton, 1915.

Cannon, W. B. James-Lange theory of emotions: A critical examination and an alternative theory. *American Journal of Psychology*, 1927, 39, 106–124.

Cannon, W. B. *The wisdom of the body*. New York: Norton, 1939.

Chein, I. *The science of behavior and the image of man*. New York: Basic Books, 1972.

Crespi, L. P. Quantitative variation of incentive and performance in the white rat. *American Journal of Psychology*, 1942, 55, 467–517.

Crespi, L. P. Amount of reinforcement and level of performance. *Psychological Review*, 1944, 51, 341–357.

Dahl, H. The appetite hypothesis of emotions: A new psychoanalytic model of motivation. In C. E. Izard (Ed.), *Emotions in personality and psychotherapy*. New York: Plenum, 1979.

Darwin, C. *The expression of the emotions in man and animals*. London: Murray, 1904. (Originally published, 1872.)

Delgado, J. M. R. *Emotions*. Dubuque: W. C. Brown, 1966.

Delgado, J. M. R. *Physical control of the mind*. New York: Harper & Row, 1969.

Dembo, T. The dynamics of anger. In J. de Rivera (Ed.), *Field theory as human-science*. New York: Gardner Press, 1976. (Originally published, 1931.)

Dennison, J. H. *Emotion as the basis of civilization*. New York: Scribner, 1928.

de Rivera, J. *Field theory as human-science*. New York: Gardner Press, 1976.

de Rivera, J. A structural theory of the emotions. *Psychological Issues*, Monograph 40. New York: International Universities Press, 1977.

de Vore, I. *Primate behavior*. New York: Holt, 1965.

Dewey, J. The theory of emotion II. *Psychological Review*, 1895, 2, 13–32.

Dewey, J. *Art as experience*. New York: Minton, Balch & Co., 1934.

Doi, T. *The anatomy of dependence*. Tokyo: Kodansha, 1973.

Dollard, J., Doob, L. W., Miller, N. E., Mowrer, O. H., & Sears, R. R. *Frustration and aggression*. New Haven: Yale University Press, 1939.

Duchenne, B. *Mechanisme de la physionomie humaine ou analyse electro-physiologique de l'expression des passions*. Paris: Bailliere, 1862.

Eibl-Eibesfeldt, I. The expressive behavior of the deaf-and-blind-born. In M. von Cranach & I. Vine (Eds.), *Social communication and movement*. New York: Academic Press, 1973.

Ekman, P. Universals and cultural differences in facial expressions of emotions. *Nebraska Symposium on Motivation. 1971*. Lincoln: University of Nebraska Press, 1971.

Feshback, S., Stiles, W. B., & Bitter, E. The reinforcing effect of witnessing aggression. *Journal of Experimental Research in Personality*, 1967, 2, 133–139.

Fiss, H., Klein, G. S., & Bokert, E. Waking fantasies following interruption of two types of sleep. *Archives of General Psychiatry*, 1966, 14, 543–551.

Freud, S. *Totem and taboo*. London: Kegan Paul, 1950. (Originally published, 1913.)

Funk, J. *A phenomenological investigation of laughter*. Unpublished master's thesis, Clark University, 1974.

Gloor, P. Autonomic functions of the diencephalon: A summary of the experimental work of Professor W. R. Hess. AMA *Archives of Neurological Psychiatry*, 1954, 71, 773–790.

387

Goodman, S. E. A clinically-oriented phenomenological investigation of the experiential referent of the word "anxiety" as distinguished first from the experiential referent of the word "panic" and then from the experiential referent of the words "apprehension," "fear," and "terror." Unpublished doctoral dissertation, New York University, 1975.

Green, A. Conceptions of affect. International Journal of Psycho-analysis, 1977, 58, 129–156.

Hartmann, D. P. Influence of symbolically modeled instrumental aggression and pain cues on aggressive behavior. Journal of Personality and Social Psychology, 1969, 11, 280–288.

Hebb, D. O. The social significance of animal studies. In G. Lindzey (Ed.), Handbook of social psychology. Cambridge, Mass.: Addison-Wesley, 1954.

Hillman, J. Emotion, a comprehensive phenomenology of theories and their meanings for therapy. Evanston, Ill.: Northwestern University Press, 1961.

Hoffspiegel, J. The role of affect and cognitive organization during impression formation. Unpublished doctoral dissertation, Rutgers University, 1980.

Izard, C. E. The face of emotion. New York: Appleton-Century-Crofts, 1971.

James, W. The principles of psychology. New York: Dover, 1950. (Originally published, 1890.)

Kaada, B. R., Jansen, J., & Anderson, P. Stimulation of the hippocampus and medial cortical areas in unanesthetized cats. Neurology, 1953, 3, 844–857.

Kane, R. Two studies on the experience of depression. Unpublished master's thesis, Clark University, 1976.

Karsten, A. Mental satiation. In J. de Rivera (Ed.), Field theory as human-science. New York: Gardner Press, 1976.

Koffka, K. Principles of Gestalt psychology. New York: Harcourt, Brace, 1935.

Laban, R. The mastery of movement. London: Macdonald, 1960.

Laird, J. D. Self-attribution of emotion: The effects of expressive behavior on the quality of emotional experience. Journal of Personality and Social Psychology, 1974, 29, 475–486.

Laird, J. D., & Crosby, M. Individual differences in self-attribution of emotion. In H. London & R. Nisbett (Eds.), Thinking & feeling: The cognitive alteration of feeling states. Chicago: Aldine-Atherton, 1974.

Lange, C. The emotions. Translated in B. Rand (Ed.), The classical psychologists. Boston: Houghton Mifflin, 1912. (Originally published, 1885.)

Langer, S. K. Feeling and form. New York: Scribner, 1953.

Lawrence, D. H. Psychoanalysis and the unconscious. New York: Viking, 1960.

Lazarus, R. S. Emotions and adaptation: Conceptual and empirical relations. Nebraska Symposium on Motivation, 1968. Lincoln: University of Nebraska Press, 1968.

Lazarus, R. S., Averill, J. R., & Opton, Em M., Jr. Towards a cognitive theory of emotion. In M. B. Arnold (Ed.), Feelings and emotions. New York: Academic Press, 1970.

Leeper, R. W. The motivational and perceptual properties of emotions as indicating their functional character and role. In M. B. Arnold (Ed.), Feelings and emotions. New York: Academic Press, 1970.

Lindsay-Hartz, J. A phenomenological investigation of elation, gladness, and joy. Unpublished master's thesis, Clark University, 1975.

Lowen, A., & Lowen, L. The way to vibrant health. New York: Harper & Row, 1977.

Luria, A. R. The nature of human conflicts (W. H. Gantt, trans.). New York: Grove, 1960. (Originally published, 1932.)

McDougall, W. An introduction to social psychology. London, Methuen, 1923. (Originally published, 1908.)

Macmurray, J. Reason and emotion. London: Faber, 1935.

Macmurray, J. Persons in relation. New York: Harper, 1957.

Mahler, M. S., Pine, F., & Bergman, A. The psychological birth of the human infant. New York: Basic Books, 1975.

Mandler, G. Mind and emotion. New York: Wiley, 1975.

Marston, W. M. *Emotions of normal people.* New York: Harcourt, Brace, 1928.

Maslow, A. H. *The farther reaches of human nature.* New York: Viking, 1972.

Mead, G. H. *Mind, self and society.* Chicago: The University of Chicago Press, 1934.

Michotte, A. E. The emotions regarded as functional connections. In M. L. Reymert (Ed.), *Feelings and emotions.* New York: McGraw-Hill, 1950.

Miller, N. E. Learnable drives and rewards. In S. S. Stevens (Ed.), *Handbook of experimental psychology.* New York: Wiley, 1951.

Mowrer, O. H. *Learning theory and behavior.* New York: Wiley, 1960.

Mucchielli, R. *Introduction to structural psychology.* New York: Funk & Wagnalls, 1970.

Muir, J. Strickeen. Republished in E. M. Toppan (Ed.), *Stories of nature.* Boston: Houghton Mifflin, 1916.

Nahm, M. The philosophical implications of some theories of emotion. *Philosophy of Science,* 1939, *6,* 458–486.

Paulhan, F. *The laws of feeling.* New York: Harcourt, Brace, 1930. (Originally published, 1884.)

Piaget, J. Intelligence and affectivity (T. A. Brown & C. E. Koegi, trans.). Separate monograph of the *Annual Review of Psychology,* 1954.

Plutchik, R. *Emotion: a psychoevolutionary synthesis.* New York: Harper & Row, 1980.

Poeck, K. Pathophysiology of emotional disorders associated with brain damage. In P. V. Vinken & B. W. Bruyn (Eds.), *Handbook of clinical neurology* (Vol. 3). New York: Wiley, 1969.

Pribram, K. H., & Melges, F. T. Psychophysiological basis of emotion. In P. J. Vinken & G. W. Bruyn (Eds.), *Handbook of clinical neurology.* Amsterdam; North-Holland, 1969.

Rapaport, D. *Emotions and memory.* Baltimore: Williams & Wilkins, 1942.

Read, K. E. *The high valley.* New York: Scribner, 1965.

Redl, F. Group emotion and leadership. *Psychiatry,* 1942, *5,* 573–596.

Reichenberg, W. An experimental investigation on the effect of gratification. *American Journal of Orthopsychiatry,* 1939, *9,* 186–202.

Ricoeur, P. *The symbolism of evil* (E. Buchanan, trans.). Boston: Beacon, 1972.

Rorty, A. O. Explaining emotions. *Journal of Philosophy,* 1978, *75,* 139–161.

Sargent, W. *The mind possessed.* New York: Penguin, 1975.

Sartre, J. P. *The emotions: Outline of a theory.* New York: Philosophical Library, 1948.

Schacter, S., & Singer, J. E. Cognitive, social, and physiological determinants of emotional states. *Psychological Review,* 1962, *69,* 379–399.

Schafer, R. The clinical analysis of affects. *Journal of American Psychological Association,* 1964, *12,* 275–299.

Shibles, W. *Emotion: The method of philosophical therapy.* Whitewater, Wisconsin: Language Press, 1974.

Slater, P. E. *Microcosm.* New York: Wiley, 1966.

Solomon, R. C. *The passions.* Garden City, N.Y.: Doubleday, 1977.

Sommers, S. *The undivided mind: The relationship between affect and social cognition.* Unpublished doctoral dissertation, Boston University, 1978.

Straus, E. W. *Phenomenological psychology.* New York: Basic Books, 1966.

Tomkins, S. S. *Affect, imagery, consciousness.* (Vol. 1) *The Positive Affects.* New York: Springer, 1962.

Volkan, V. D. *Primitive internalized object relations.* New York: International Universities Press, 1976.

Volkan, V. D., Cilluffo, A., & Sarvay, T. Re-grief therapy and the function of the linking object as a key to stimulate emotionality. In P. Olson (Ed.), *Emotional flooding.* New York: Penguin Books, 1977.

Wapner, S., Werner, H., & Krus, D. M. The effect of success and failure on space localization. *Journal of Personality,* 1957, *25,* 752–756.

Werner, H. *Comparative psychology of mental development.* New York: International Universities Press, 1948.

Zajonc, R. B. Feeling and thinking. *American Psychologist,* 1980, *35,* 151–175.

389

COGNITION

16

Duncker on Thinking
AN INQUIRY INTO PROGRESS IN COGNITION*

ALLEN NEWELL

Introduction

How to cast light on what we have learned about cognition in the last one hundred years? It seems a pleasant enough task, as part of the American Psychological Association's centenary celebration of the establishment of Wundt's Laboratory in Leipzig. Yet, though initially pleasant to accept and contemplate, and also pleasant in the final delivery, difficulties arise in bridging the gap between the acceptance and the delivery—a gap noticeable in this as in every other genuine cognitive problem.

Cognition is only a part of psychology, and for much of the century, a minor part. This derives from a larger history—of how associationism and then behaviorism gave a particular cast to the study of the mind, of how that cast emphasized learning, of how the reactions to that, especially Gestalt psychology, found their main ground in perception. The last quarter of this century has witnessed the return of the oppressed to a position of prominence. There is a story to tell about this

* This research was sponsored by the Defense Advanced Research Projects Agency (DOD), ARPA Order No. 3597, monitored by the Air Force Avionics Laboratory under Contract F33615-78-C-1551.

   The views and conclusions contained in this document are those of the author and should not be interpreted as representing the official policies, either expressed or implied, of the Defense Advanced Research Projects Agency or the U.S. Government.

revolution, though it too is generally familiar in its major outlines. But science celebrates its history, not by recounting it, but by critical appraisal.

What have we learned? My solution is to consider a particular scientist, Karl Duncker, and indeed a particular work, *Zur Psychologie des produktiven Denkens*, originally published in 1935 and translated as *On Problem Solving* in 1945 as a *Psychological Monograph*. Duncker studied how human adults solved various mathematical and practical problems. The most well known is the X-ray problem: how can a beam that destroys all tissue, healthy and diseased alike, be used to destroy only a tumor, sparing the healthy tissue? Duncker used *thinking-aloud* protocols as a source of data, analyzing in detail the processes that his subjects went through and how the solutions they found (or failed to find) reflected the structure of the task. The concept of *functional fixity*, familiar to all psychology students (at least to a decade ago), originated in this study. What have we learned since Duncker? What did he know and what were his scientific tasks? What do we know now about cognition, and where do we stand on Duncker's tasks? How did I ever think of this solution to the problem of dealing with the whole history of cognitive psychology? In fact, the thought came a long time ago. I do not recall exactly when I first read Duncker, but it was during the late 1950s.[1] Having had no formal training in psychology, I was exploring what was already known as my interests deepened in problem-solving and cognition. Duncker made a strong impression on me. Now, the opportunity for an appreciation and critique has arisen. Having seized that opportunity, my first obligation is to put Duncker into his historical place.

The Historical Context

A Hundred Years of Cognition

Table 16.1 lays out the hundred-year time line. Duncker (1935) occurs at about the halfway mark in the century, bracketed by its direct predecessor (Duncker, 1926), his master's thesis at Clark, and by the translation to English (Duncker, 1945). Duncker was a student of Max Wertheimer and Wolfgang Köhler, and he dedicates his work to them jointly. This monograph reports essentially the only research Duncker did on problem-solving, his other work being mostly in perception. This may have been because he died early, in 1940 when he was only 37 (he was then at Swarthmore with Köhler). In any event, our inquiry can be neatly focused on this one work.

The great cluster of events that occurs in the second half of the 1950s, below the

[1] After the work on the Logic Theorist program (Newell, Shaw, & Simon, 1958), while working on the General Problem Solver, GPS (Newell, Shaw, & Simon, 1957, 1960).

TABLE 16.1   Key Events in One Hundred Years of the Study of Cognition

1890s	James. *Principles of Psychology*. 1890. Thorndike. Animal intelligence. 1898.
1910s	Dewey. *How We Think*. 1910. Selz. *Zur Psychologie des produktiven Denkens und des Irrtums*. 1922 (1913).
1920s	Köhler. *The Mentality of Apes*. 1925 (1917). . Duncker. A qualitative study of productive thinking. 1926.
1930s	Maier. Reasoning in humans. 1930, 1931. Tolman. *Purposive Behavior in Animals and Men*. 1932. Duncker. *Zur Psychologie des produktiven Denkens*. 1935.
1940s	Katona. *Organizing and Memorizing*. 1940. Luchins. Mechanization in problem solving. 1942. Duncker. On problem solving, 1945 (translation of Duncker, 1935). Wertheimer. *Productive Thinking*. 1945.
1950s	Humphreys. *Thinking*. 1951. Vinacke. *The Psychology of Thinking*. 1952. Johnson. *The Psychology of Thought and Judgment*. 1955.

Start of shift to information-processing viewpoint
  Tanner & Swets. Signal detection theory. 1954.
  Bruner, Goodnow, & Austin. *A Study of Thinking*. 1956.
  Miller. The magical number seven, plus or minus two. 1956.
  Chomsky. *Syntactic Structures*. 1957.
  Broadbent. *Perception and Communication*. 1958.
  Newell, Shaw, & Simon. Elements of a theory of human problem solving. 1958.

1960s	Newell & Simon. GPS: A program that simulates human thought. 1961. Neisser. *Cognitive Psychology*. 1967.
1970s	Estes (Ed.). *Handbook of Learning and Cognition* (6 vols.). 1975–1978. Johnson-Laird & Wason (Eds.). *Thinking*. 1977.

line, signifies the start of the shift to an information-processing viewpoint—the start of the revolution in cognition. It can be seen in the variety of different strands—Broadbent, Miller, Bruner-Goodnow-Austin, Chomsky, Tanner-Swets, and so on. All were generated out of a rapidly shifting conceptual base growing out of the development of communications and computer technology, plus the mathematics of systems, as in game theory and operations research. The confluence of these strands, each distinct in many ways—their *unity in diversity*, to use a well worn phrase—produced a conceptual explosion. We have documented our assessment of this critical period (Newell & Simon, 1972); recently a short note by George Miller agrees (Miller, 1979).

"What have we learned in cognition?" must have as a primary sense, "What has this shift to the information-processing paradigm wrought in comparison to what we knew before?"

Three textbooks on thinking (Humphrey, 1951; Vinacke, 1952; Johnson, 1955), written just before the '58 *tsunami*, provide a neat fix on what had been learned to that point.[2] They show that the work of Duncker was indeed an important and accepted component of the then current view of thinking. The "then current view" was not exactly coherent. With due regard to their authors, these books make dull reading, providing a congeries of assorted experimental facts, tenuously related theoretical ideas, and historical notes on different schools. Duncker's work appears as one thread among many, as the following historical breakdown will show.

Duncker

Duncker was a Gestalt psychologist. Though the principle focus of the Gestalt work was in perception, both his mentors had worked on thinking: Köhler (1925) with the apes at Tenerife in 1914–1917; Wertheimer (1945) with children in the classroom. Both efforts emphasized the understanding of relationships and the suddenness of insight. Both were justly famous. Köhler and Wertheimer were also two-thirds of the Gestalt triumvirate. It follows, then, that Duncker is a minor character on the stage of scientific history. Boring (1950) allots him just two sentences, followed immediately by the plaint that the mere listing of names is the bane of scientific histories. But that did not keep Duncker's work from being extremely well known and giving impetus to much subsequent research.

Duncker is therefore part of what the textbooks called "the Gestalt theory of thinking." Gestalt psychology was a reaction to associationism and its behavioristic follow-on, and it never gave up its rhetoric of protest, even when, as Boring (1950) believed, it was "dying of success," its main points assimilated. However, in the study of higher mental processes it had the field somewhat to itself. The behaviorists made only occasional forays into the area, engaging in their own reductionist rhetoric to the effect that thinking and problem-solving are nothing but learning. Duncker's work bears strong kinship with others (Katona, 1940; Luchins, 1942; Maier, 1930, 1931), and this group in total occupied a prominent position in a nonprominent province of psychology. Duncker himself exhibits little of the Gestalt family's need to score on the behaviorists. He finds good things in everybody, even Thorndike (1898) with his studies on cats in puzzle boxes, taken by most to be the

---

[2]These authors have each written a book on thinking well after the shift to an information-processing viewpoint (Humphrey & Coxon, 1963; Johnson, 1972; Vinacke, 1974). They provide interesting data on the extent to which new paradigms are universally perceived and taken up. It is barely apparent in these later works that anything specifically of an information-processing nature has happened, though both Johnson and Vinacke speak in terms of the explosion of work on thinking and problem-solving.

395

hard rock on which the behaviorists cast out insightful problem-solving and replaced it with trial-and-error.

Duncker jumps in at midcentury. We have neglected earlier work on thinking, though a few antecedents appear in the table, because our need is for the cumulated knowledge about cognition as it existed just before the advent of information-processing psychology, and Duncker suffices for this. How psychology arrived at Duncker is not our problem.[3]

The Cognitive Revolution

The post-1950s development is called both the information-processing approach and the new cognitive psychology. It is perhaps soon to be called *cognitive science*, if the nascent movement to provide an umbrella name for linguistics, artificial intelligence, and cognitive psychology takes firm root. Substantively, its underlying proposition is that theories of human voluntary behavior are to be sought in the realm of *information-processing systems*. This is to be understood in the same sense that theories of macrophysics are to be sought in the realm of *differential equation systems*. There is a type of system—called an "information-processing system"— that consists of *memories* and *processors* (also *transducers, switches, controls, data operations,* and *links,* to be complete). The system works on an internal medium of *data structures,* which represent things and situations. It performs operations on these representations to compute new representations and thereby generally manage its affairs in the world. This is an immense class of systems, all with a family resemblance—active, autonomous, rule-governed, limited structural and resource capacities, discrete, and so on. The central agreement is that a human is this kind of a system, it being open and the object of empirical investigation to find out the particulars. Other major attempts to understand human nature can also be described in terms of the underlying system posited: the *stimulus-response* systems of behaviorism; the *fields* of Gestalt psychology; the *hydraulic* systems of Freudian psychology; the *Markov* systems of mathematical psychology.

The information-processing revolution has in common this fundamental system view. It is otherwise importantly diverse, as the cluster of work in 1958 in Table 16.1 indicates. Broadbent (1958) represents the line from control and communication engineering; it has focused on working out the structure of the basic perceptual

---

[3]The earlier period has been treated neatly by the Mandlers (Mandler & Mandler, 1964) in *Thinking: From Association to Gestalt,* which starts with Aristotle and ends with Duncker. In particular, they treat Otto Selz (1913, 1922) (1881–1943), the repeatedly rediscovered skeleton in cognitive psychology's closet (Humphrey, 1951; DeGroot, 1965), who understood essential elements of a processing explanation of thinking, and who could also have served for a centennial comparison.

and processing mechanisms. Miller's paper on chunking and the limits of short-term memory can be taken as part of that, as can the introduction of signal detection theory by Tanner and Swets (1954). Our own work (Newell, Shaw, & Simon, 1958) can be taken to represent the line from programming and artificial intelligence (also to some extent from rational economics and decision theory). This is the *symbolic* level of information processing and is to be distinguished from the *register-transfer* level considered by Broadbent and company exactly as software from hardware. These would be considered two entirely distinct system views except that the study of computer systems has unified them (Bell & Newell, 1971). The symbolic level, represented also by Bruner, Goodnow, and Austin (1956), provides the notions of *plans, programs, procedures,* and *strategies.* Later, it provides the organization of knowledge in long-term memory (Anderson & Bower, 1973; Quillian, 1968). Chomsky (1957) represents the line from linguistics, with the view—new to linguistics as well—of rule-governed generative systems. This oversimplified picture does most violence here, since Chomskian linguistics contains strong elements of the structuralist tradition, which is distinct from the engineering and mathematical tradition I am taking as the central source for this cognitive revolution.[4]

As this diversity implies, the study of thinking and problem-solving is only one component of cognitive psychology. It is not even the dominant component. Neisser's 1967 book, entitled *Cognitive Psychology,* crystallized for many the revolution and became its defining document. Yet this book deals only with perception and basic processing and ignores higher mental functions—no problem-solving, no concept formation, no planning. Duncker is not mentioned in it except for a perceptual experiment. This view is carried through Blumenthal's (1977) recent review of cognitive psychology, and onto an even more recent treatment that claims explicitly to lay out the cognitive paradigm (Lachman, Lachman, & Butterfield, 1979). Analyzing Duncker for what we have learned in cognition taps only one particular aspect of the total field.

This is enough historical context to consider what Duncker knew and how it compares with what we now know—or think we know. The next three parts of this chapter correspond to the three parts of Duncker's monograph: (1) the structure and dynamics of the problem-solving process; (2) insight, learning, and simple finding; and (3) fixedness of thought-material. Each part leads to a separate aspect of our general question.

---

[4]This perspective places the source extraordinarily external to psychology. It conceals that the revolution was largely shaped by the psychologists themselves and merged with their internal traditions of experimentation and hypothesis-testing.

The Structure and Dynamics of the Problem-Solving Process

Duncker was clear about what he wanted to know: "How does the solution arise from the problem situation?" (p. 1).[5] The question was not innocuous, however it may seem now. The dominant theory of thinking to that point, as defined by James, Dewey, Thorndike, Watson, and others, was, roughly speaking, that the solution did not arise from the problem situation, but from trial-and-error or, at best, the experience of the problem-solver.

The heart of the Gestalt position was that genuine problem-solving behavior arises from the *demands* of the situation. Duncker in 1935 is rather nonpolemical, but in 1926 (at age 23) he was more feisty:

> As the point of departure for the present study I have chosen James' Chapter on "Reasoning". . . . The gap which yawns in the great majority of theoretical or experimental studies upon thinking has nowhere else, as far as I know, been brought to such an extent of yawning as just there. . . . James is right [that reasoning proper is marked off from "mere revery or associative sequence" by the extraction of the essential aspect out of a given fact], but now the fatal question arises: What makes the reasoner pick out just that fitting aspect . . . ? But we might as well let James himself raise the questions: "To reason, then, we must be able to extract characters, not any characters, but the right characters. Here, then, is the difficulty. . . ." . . . Thus we get the following list [after reviewing the answers of James, Dewey, Mach and Whewhell]: Interest in the interrelations of the facts, attentive scanning of the terrain, abstraction, imaginative activity, and—opportune moment. The same yawning gap, carefully filled up with some general and formal attitudes (Duncker, 1926, pp. 642–647).

What Duncker Knew

Duncker had a well-developed view of the main mechanisms by which problem-solving occurs, much of it already in place in the 1926 paper. He used the first part of the 1935 monograph to lay out these mechanisms, working from thinking-aloud protocols of adults on a handful of different problems. The protocols have the flavor of *demonstrations that make evident*, rather than *experiments that discriminate*, much in the style of Wertheimer's book on productive thinking.

Let me sketch this model of the processing in my own terms, supported by quotations from Duncker.

1. The subject has a *goal*; the goal becomes a *problem* if it cannot be reached immediately by obvious actions.

---

[5] Throughout the paper, unless otherwise indicated, all quotations are from Duncker's monograph, "On Problem Solving" (1945), and all italics in the quotations occur in the original. Insertions in brackets are by the author of this chapter.

A problem arises when a living creature has a goal but does not know how this goal is to be reached. Whenever one cannot go from the given situation to the desired situation simply by action, then there has to be recourse to thinking. (By action we here understand the performance of obvious operations) (p. 1).

2. Problem-solving consists of a sequence of *phases*; each phase is a *reformulation* of the problem.

. . . the solution of a new problem typically takes place in successive phases which (with the exception of the first phase) have, in retrospect, the character of a solution and (with the exception of the last phase), in prospect, that of a problem (p. 18).

3. The intermediate phases (tentative solutions) embody the *functional* value of the ultimate solution.

The functional value of a solution is indispensable for the understanding of its being a solution. It is exactly what is called the sense, the principle or the point of the solution (p. 4).

4. The sequence of phases constitutes a sequence of *further specifications* of the functional character of the solution.

The final form of an individual solution is, in general, not reached by a single step from the original setting of the problem; on the contrary, the principle, the functional value of the solution, typically arises first and the final form of the solution in question develops only as this principle becomes successively more and more concrete (p. 8).

5. There is search, which occurs in the space of functional specifications.

It will be realized that, in the transition to phases in another line, the thought-process may range more or less widely. Every such transition involves a return to an earlier phase of the problem; an earlier task is set anew; a new branching off from an old point in the family tree occurs. Sometimes a S returns to the original setting of the problem, sometimes just to the immediately preceding phase (p. 13).

6. The phases are under the control of *general heuristic methods*.

We can therefore say that *"insistent" analyses of the situation, especially the endeavor to vary appropriate elements meaningfully sub specie of the goal, must belong to the essential nature of a solution through thinking.* We may call such relatively general procedures, *"heuristic methods of thinking"* (p. 21).

In a general thinking process, certain heuristic methods play a decisive role in mediating the genesis of successive solution-phases (p. 24).

399

7. The solution depends on details fully specified to the problem situation.

Thus every solution takes place, so to speak, on the concrete, specific substratum of its problem situation (p. 20).

The key concept in this model is *function*. Its nature is clear enough in particular cases from the protocols of Duncker's subjects. For the X-ray problem there is the functional value: *no contact between rays and healthy tissue*; this is realized in the protocol statements "direct the rays by a natural approach," "expose by an operation," "protective wall," and so on. A different functional value is: *less intensity on the way, great intensity in the tumor*; this shows in the protocol statement "concentration of diffuse rays in the tumor." Duncker gives trees of functions for two problems, aggregated from the data of many subjects, with increasingly specific functions as the tree branches down. These trees constitute the space in which subjects search for a solution.

Functions play a double role for Duncker. They are the crucial mediating construct in his theory, the central realization that comes to the subject when engaging in thinking. But functions are also crucial in the Gestalt protest against associationistic psychology. They represent the demands of the problem situation, being just what association theory of problem-solving did not have (see quote on page 399). Though essentially nonpolemical, the monograph retains a strong flavor of forward search as meaningless nonunderstanding behavior, whereas working with functions is meaningful, understanding behavior.

I should like to name the first way the "organic" one. Here from the "function" . . . arises the embodying material, the instrumental means. The second and opposite way is the "mechanical" one (p. 44).

He who merely searches his memory for a "solution of that such-and-such problem" may remain just as blind to the inner nature of the problem-situation before him as a person who, instead of thinking himself, refers the problem to an intelligent acquaintance or to an encyclopedia. Truly, these methods are not to be despised; for they have a certain heuristic value, and one can arrive at solutions in that fashion. But such problem-solving has little to do with thinking (p. 20).

The first quote lays down the famous distinction between working backward as organic and working forward as mechanical. The second quote continues the same attitude, but significantly treats problem-solving on its own terms. This open attitude of Duncker's leads (in my estimation) to his full-bodied model of problem-solving. Here, for example, is his characterization of *Generate and Test*:

This suggestion of the functional value from below is even the rule in problems where a number of objects are offered to begin with, with the instruction to choose from among them an appropriate tool for such and such a purpose. Especially when only a few objects are concerned, thinking will tend to proceed by looking things over, i.e., it will test the given objects one after the other as to their applicability and no attempt will be made to conceive the appropriate functional value first (p. 12).

This last quote leads to another key feature of Duncker's model, which is rather easy to overlook—the plethora of general heuristic methods. In fact, the first section appears to ramble, because Duncker, after introducing the basic notions of functions and successive reformulation phases, works through a large number of methods:

1. *Suggestion from below:* The materials of the problem suggest what needs to be done.
2. *Learning from mistakes:* Incorporation of the avoidance of the evil as an additional demand in finding a new line of approach.
3. *Finding solutions through resonance:* Finding a solution by a memory search with cues taken from the problem: "The problem is: *?Rb; aRb* exists in the thinker's experience; by reason of the partial correspondence with *?Rb, aRb* and therefore *a* are aroused" (p. 19).
4. *Analysis of the situation as conflict:* Asking ". . . *Just why doesn't it work?* or, *What is the ground of the trouble (the conflict)?*" (p. 21) as a means of finding what element of the situation to vary.
5. *Analysis of the situation material:* "*What can I use?*" (p. 21) as a deliberate question to analyze the situation. A special case is *Explication of the premises* in mathematical propositions.
6. *Analysis of the goal:* "*What do I really want?*" "*What can I dispense with?*" "*What does one do, in general, when one . . . ?*" (p. 23) as questions to free the subject from fixations.
7. *Par-force solutions:* "In solving problems, one may very often be guided by natural reactions to forcible demands in the direction of the problem's goal . . . ." (p. 29).
8. *That reminds me of. . . . :* There are problems whose solution depends on the problem situation reminding the subject of some obscure fact or experience. But special cases are more directed, e.g., "*What theorems are there about such a thing . . . ?*" (p. 37).

Duncker investigates each of these, usually with some data. Not all of these are well worked out total methods; many are more like the heuristic suggestions in Polya (1945). Yet he makes clear these are methods; e.g., after a subject's explicit asking about theorems (above) he remarks "(An important heuristic method!)" (p. 37). Not all of these methods and heuristics are original with Duncker. He deals rather carefully with existing work. For instance, he understands Selz thoroughly and the method of *solution through resonance* is identified with Selz's *method of determined means-abstraction*. Or consider:

> Intelligent heuristic methods can be observed in the most primitive animal experiment. Thorndike, in his famous experiments on cats . . . , could in this way establish that the "tendency to pay attention to what it is doing" (instead of blind struggling) increased in the course of the experiment (p. 24).

In sum, Duncker had a rather complete process model. At the center was the concept of function, but it had a diverse apparatus of methods. Comparison with others of the same era (Luchins, 1942; Katona, 1940; Wertheimer, 1945) reveals great agreement on the notion of function as meaningful problem-solving and the response to the demands of the situation—namely, on the tenets of the Gestalt position. However, Duncker's total process model appears to be by far the most explicit of his contemporaries. It seems far from their major concerns.

There were limitations to the structure Duncker presented. He never attempted to characterize what a function is—to describe the space of all functions. The common-sense notion sufficed, illustrated by some demonstrated effects of problem structure and hints. The entire edifice is informal—the quotes above being as precise as the monograph gets. Thus, whether the scheme is actually sufficient to account for any specific problem-solving cannot be determined. In this respect, Duncker's use of protocols was coarse grained (about one statement every several minutes), capturing only the subject's major hypotheses about how to solve the problem (invariably a statement of function).

What We Now Know

The modern state need not be set out beyond the earlier introduction. After all, we are—for today, at least—the moderns and it is our work. Instead, we can focus narrowly on particular features of modern work that illuminate advances beyond Duncker in areas directly related to his work.

We start with the model of means-ends problem-solving provided by GPS (Newell & Simon, 1961; Newell & Simon, 1972), which can be epitomized by a trace of its typical behavior:

$$S1 = \text{Given situation}$$
$$S0 = \text{Desired situation}$$

G1: Transform S1 into S0
    Match S1 to S0 to get difference $\Rightarrow$ D1
    G2: Reduce D1 between S1 and S0
        Select operator relevant to D1 $\Rightarrow$ Q1
        G3: Apply Q1 to S0
            Produce new situation $\Rightarrow$ S2

G4: Transform S2 into S0
  Match S2 to S0 to get difference $\Rightarrow$ D2
G5: Reduce D2 between S2 and S0
  Select operator relevant to D2 $\Rightarrow$ Q2
G6: Apply Q2 to S2
  Produce new situation $\Rightarrow$ S3
G7: Transform S3 into S0

Comparing this with Duncker's scheme reveals some obviously familiar elements: goals (the Gs); the repeated phases (at G1, G4, G7); and the general heuristic method that is used to generate the steps in the phases. In terms of general outline, GPS is just an instance of Duncker's scheme.

One thing not found in Duncker is indicated by the literals, the Gs, Ss, Ds, and Qs. These are specific symbolic structures in a well-defined symbol system, such as the programming language Lisp. Though the means-ends analysis scheme of GPS is often discussed in general terms, its usefulness derives from GPS having been demonstrated to be a *sufficient* scheme for the tasks to which it has been seriously applied. This is the gold-backing for the theory of means-ends analysis represented in GPS. It supports, for instance, comparison between GPS and behavior at a much finer level of detail (5–10 seconds) than Duncker used.

This may be summarized in two claimed advances over Duncker:

Advance: Theories of problem-solving have been shown to be sufficient for problem-solving.

Advance: An underlying symbol system has been posited in which cognition takes place.

Consider now the role of the *differences* in the GPS scheme. Taking an early example from logic:

S1: $(R \supset \neg P) \wedge (\neg R \supset Q)$
S0: $\neg(\neg Q \wedge P)$

D1a: Delete R
D1b: Decrease the number of terms
D1c: Change the sign of the main connective

These difference terms—*delete term, decrease the number of terms, change connectives*—are clearly Duncker's functional values. They operate exactly as they should in Duncker's theory. They represent an analysis of the situation by the subject, characterizing what must be done and directing the search for something to accomplish that function, that is, an operator. They can be seen in the perceptual structure of the situation, exactly as required by Duncker's theory. What they

403

provide that Duncker's treatment of functions does not is an actual explication of what the functional values are, how they arise, and how they have their effects. This produces a third claim:

Advance: We now have an instance of a precise theory of functional value.

However, the theory of means-ends analysis embodied in GPS is not all gain. It is only an *instance* of a precise theory. Having the functions in the little logic task is far from having a general theory of functions. A trade-off invariably occurs when attaining added precision in theoretical formulation. We can project from this what a general theory of functions might actually be like, but GPS hardly provides this, nor does other modern work.

The GPS-related theory also falls shy of Duncker's scheme in being only a single method. As Duncker showed, there are many different general methods. Here the the difficulty is merely with GPS, and not modern work generally, which has led to a ramified investigation of general problem-solving methods and executive organizations. These are relatively content free, hence widely applicable. They organize activity, but do not provide strong direction; that must come from the concrete details of the task which they are capable of absorbing. Here are some of them, though their details need not detain us:

Generate and test: Generate in any way possible (e.g., systematically or haphazardly) a sequence of candidate states, testing each for whether it is the desired state.

Heuristic search: Apply heuristics to reject possible operators from the current state and to reject newly produced states; remember the states with untried operators in some systematic way (different schemes yield search strategies, such as *depth first, breadth first, best first, progressive deepening*).

Hill-climbing: Generate and apply operators from the current state; select one that produces a state with an improved evaluation and move to it.

Means-ends analysis: Compare the current state with the desired state to detect any difference; use that difference to select an operator that reduces or eliminates it; otherwise proceed as in heuristic search.

Operator subgoaling: If an operator cannot be applied to a current state, set up a subgoal to find a state in which the operator can be applied; otherwise proceed as in heuristic search or means-ends analysis.

Planning: Abstract from the present state (by processing only selected information throughout) and proceed to solve the simplified problem; use what is remembered of the path as a guide to solving the unabstracted problem.

The striking difference from Duncker's list is the emphasis on *search*. At the center of the modern theory of intelligence is the notion that all intelligent activity is carried on within the matrix of search, with devices for controlling or warding off incipient combinatorial explosion by bringing knowledge to bear. This runs directly

404

counter to the basic Gestalt position in which search in all its various forms was the indicator of blind meaningless activity. That working forward (heuristic search, hill-climbing, and generate and test) and working backward (means-ends analysis) would be symmetrically considered, as opposed to being contrasted as *mechanical* or *organic*, runs against the Gestalt grain. This should be recorded as yet one more claim of what we have learned:

Advance: All intelligent activity is based in search.

We must be careful in this claim. First, Duncker genuinely makes room for search in his theory, separating himself thereby from the other Gestaltists. Second, though abating, controversy still exists in artificial intelligence over the role of *general methods* (often called *uniform procedures*) vs. *expert knowledge.*

Finally, GPS appears to operate in a different space, namely the space of objects or situations. Sitting at a present situation, it characterizes its difference from the desired goal situation functionally, then uses that functional value to do something. On the contrary, in Duncker's theory the functional idea, once created, undergoes a series of refinements. Again, however, GPS-style means-ends analysis is simply one mechanism of many. Much recent work has occurred on schemata and frames, structures that are more direct realizations of successive refinement and instantiation (Schank & Abelson, 1977; Bobrow & Winograd, 1977). These share the precision and concreteness of GPS.

Insight, Learning, and Simple Finding

Part Two of Duncker's monograph has three chapters: On Total Insight or Evidence; On Learning and Partial Insight; and On Solutions Through Resonance. It appears as a curious and obscure interlude between two readily comprehensible parts, the first on the general dynamics of problem-solving (as we have seen) and the third on the special problem of functional fixity. Most commentators skip over these middle chapters, remarking on Duncker's grappling with philosophical problems:

> Duncker's work is not easy. . . . He hated any compromise with vague terms which give an appearance of knowledge while they actually hide problems. He simply would not let go until he knew the very anatomy of a concept. Thus in some chapters we find the author far within philosophy because the ramifications of insight would not become clear without that transgression (Köhler, Introduction, p. iv).

> The philosopher will find especially interesting the account of the psychology of "synthetic" insight in the Kantian sense, which is derived from Husserl's premises as contrasted with those of Kant (Humphrey, 1951, p. 170).

405

Let us see how Duncker posed the problems for these chapters:

> As happens particularly with mathematical problems, the method of solution may consist, for example, in making appropriate deductions from the proposition or from the premises. But then the psychologist must still discover the psychological meaning of "making deductions from," must discover how, from one fact, thinking actually brings about the intelligent transition to another, new fact. . . . How does thinking succeed in reading off the cause from an effect, or the effect from a cause? (p. 47).

Evidently, Duncker has left the realm of problem-solving. That he has entered that of philosophy can be inferred from the following:

> DEFINITIONS: A *connection of two data* a *and* b *may be called "totally intelligible," if it can be directly understood from* a *that, if* a *is valid, then* b *and precisely* b *is valid. (A connection is therefore "unintelligible" to the extent to which it is to be "accepted as mere fact.") A connection may be called "partially intelligible."* . . . The definition given above of intelligibility has reference to a fundamental statement from Hume's "Inquiry Concerning Human Understanding" (Sec. 7, Part 2): "When any natural object or event is presented, it is impossible for us, by any sagacity or penetration, to discover, or even to conjecture, without experience, what event will result from it . . ." (p. 47).

Although the commentators exude fair-mindedness, the inference seems inescapable that this part is of little central interest to psychology. Furthermore, *insight* was a notorious Gestalt concept. Any residual content of this second part is easily dismissed as flowing from general Gestalt attitudes and polemics:

> As prototype of entirely unintelligible connections we may cite one of those if-then relations which Thorndike imposed on his cats. If the cat licks itself, then the cage door opens, or if it presses on a certain knob, then the same happens. From the circumstance—to be understood quite literally—that a cat licks itself or presses on a certain known, it appears in no way intelligible that the cage door should open (p. 48).

An Alternative View

An alternative view of these three chapters is possible, which bears on what we have learned since Duncker. This view requires some preparation. Let me state it as an hypothesis, then state and explain the advance that I think has happened before I come back to examine Duncker's work.

Hypothesis: Duncker is trying to discover the machine within which problem-solving occurs.

The term *machine* is deliberate to make explicit the connection to the claimed advance:

Advance: Modern cognitive psychology has the concept of *architecture*, which is the physical machinery that realizes a symbolic system.

This concept of architecture needs expansion.

Computer simulation of problem-solving has been important in modern cognitive psychology, but exactly what is going on has been less than clear to those involved.[6] Some see it as a discipline to enforce operationalism. Some see it providing a language of processes. Some see the computer and its program as the computational means for producing the step-by-step consequences of a theory stated mathematically, as in computer simulation generally. Some see the program itself as a theory.

The confusion has been compounded, because simulations are written in programming languages. Clearly not psychological theories in general, some programming languages, especially the list-processing languages, appear to have psychological import. However, no matter what language is used, much of any complex simulation program is detailed housekeeping required just to make the program complete enough to run. Moreover, whether intrinsically or because of this extra detail, simulation programs are big, complex, hard to understand, and hard to communicate (Reitman, 1965).

Clarity seems to be emerging (Newell, 1973; Pylyshyn, 1980). As noted earlier, modern cognition asserts that humans have *symbol systems* (Lachman, Lachman, & Butterfield, 1979; Newell, 1980), i.e., a collection of mental entities called symbols, whose tokens occur in symbolic expressions or structures. These are the carriers of information, stored in memory and the objects of processing. This symbolic level corresponds to the programming level in computers.

Symbol systems must, of course, be realized by some physical system. It has become customary in computer science to refer to this physical structure as the *architecture*, i.e., an architecture supports a symbol system. Different architectures yield different flavors of symbol systems. Though these may differ radically in many ways, they will all have the properties we associate with programming languages— i.e., what is common to Fortran, Lisp, Snobol, Algol 68, Pascal, myriad assembly languages, and so on. To draw the obvious conclusion: if the human has a symbol system, the human has an architecture that supports that symbol system. Within that architecture, programs (i.e., symbolic expressions that designate the human's own mental processes) correspond to psychologically meaningful actions and thoughts.

---

[6] Newell (1970) has an extended discussion of the variety of these views with appropriate references and quotations.

If a simulation were programmed on a computer that had the same architecture as the human, *all* its properties would be of psychological interest and *all* the details of the programs would be psychologically relevant. The role of simulation would become transparent. The architecture plus the program is a theory of the human cognitive system. Such a situation would be essentially different from using a computer (i.e., an architecture plus a programming language) to simulate (say) a business inventory system. This latter is both possible and useful, but the aspects relevant to the inventory system must be declared (by describing the model of the inventory system in independent terms and thinking of the program as simply implementing the computations dictated by the model).

We can now turn back to Duncker. He had seen, as reflected earlier, a variety of high-level cognitive activity. He sought the grounds on which this occurred. He certainly did not have the notion of a symbolic processor (this was the early 1930s). Rather, he had the Gestalt notions of organization, insight, and field (the physical substrate). Yet in these chapters he takes up a series of issues which seem quite close to trying to specify the nature of the architecture—of the underlying processing system. There is space to deal only with a single example, but it is a fascinating one.

A Computational Model of Insight

The example concerns the nature of *insight*. Duncker took insight as occurring when a functional value was seen as following from the givens of the problem situation. For example, a subject sees that *no contact between rays and healthy tissue* is demanded by the X-ray problem.

The example Duncker worked out in most detail was:

From $a > b$ and $b > c$ to understand that $a > c$.

The ingredients of his solution are laid out in Figure 16.1. There is a data structure, which is a *model* in the formal (model-theoretic) sense of the term in modern logic (Addison, Henkin, & Tarski, 1972). The givens are interpreted in the model by means of constructions (*write* operations). The conclusion is extracted from the model by a *read* operation, i.e., by seeing what is now true in the model. The *mind's eye* watches over everything as the executive control. Let the model be an internal line; then $a > b > c$ is layed off internally as three points and the eye can see (read-off) that $a > c$, because it is now true in the model.

This technique of computing is not familiar, but it does occur and can be quite effective. For instance, IBM cards can be decoded by writing them out to memory as 12 rows of 80 bits (as they come in from the card reader) and then reading them back in as 80 columns of 12 bits, which can be interpreted as numbers. Our immediate concern is not the scheme per se, but how Duncker saw it.

Here is how Duncker describes the operation of insight:

> How about the example: "From $a > b > c$ it follows that $a > c$?" I can demonstrate the meaning of "greater" on all kinds of pairs of objects. With the help of the concept so obtained, a clear "paradigmatic" situation: "*a* greater than *b* and *b* greater than *c*," can be constructed. From the situation so constructed, the fact: "*a* greater than *c*" may now be *read off. Yet—and this is the important point—this fact was not needed in the construction of the situation, the "foundation" from which it is now being read off* (p. 49).

Duncker makes clear he knows the standard way of applying the transitive law as a rule—and that he intends something different:

> For the modern mathematician, the straight line is that entity—originally undefined—which receives definition from the axioms about it, nothing more. And the relation: "greater than" acquires its transitiveness in mathematics merely by logical deduction from certain postulates, from the axioms about the relations: "between" and "congruent" (p. 50).

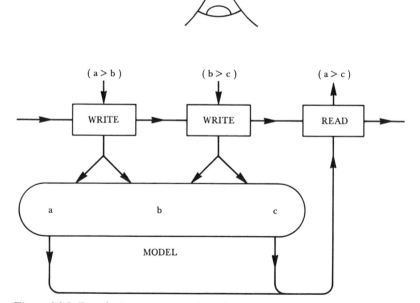

Figure 16.1 Duncker's computational model of insight.

There is no objection to this procedure. The mathematician and logician may proceed thus. As a matter of fact, mathematics and logic would "function" even if all principles were nothing but postulates. In short, "postulation" and "evident following from" are equivalent in respect to their logical achievements. . . . However, even though certain if-then relations *may* be treated as mere postulates, they can also be seen in a different light. Perhaps this other conception is irrelevant to the *purely logical* structure of mathematics. It nevertheless corresponds to actual facts in thinking (p. 51).

Construction and reading-off is not simply a way of stating that some process takes inputs and delivers outputs:

Now, one might be tempted to generalize from this [the example] and to say: "Synthetic evidence [i.e., this particular subspecies of insight] obviously consists in the fact that the new characteristics resulting from a new structuring of given elements are read off from these elements." But with this one would have lost again the specific meaning of evidence and of "insight." For if one properly combines pure hydrogen and pure oxygen . . . and if one reads off the results: the explosion and the formation of water, then to be sure, something very important is read off, but certainly no synthetic evidence. . . .

In short, synthetic insight cannot consist simply in the fact that the result of a new organization is read off. In order to be comprehensible as an instance of synthetic evidence, the example . . . must therefore be otherwise interpreted. . . . *But this means that it remains identical in the respect in which it serves as "foundation" for the two successive functions* (p. 54).

If this condition of identity be given sufficient attention, there will be no danger that the subject regard something as intelligible just because, in the moment of inspection, it happens to be apparent. Suppose, in the moment of reading off from: $a > b$ and $b > c$, the a were suddenly and maliciously to shrink (or turn red). Surely, under these circumstances the subject would not be doomed unsuspectingly to regard as evident from the premises that a must be less than c (or redder than c).

Synthetic evidence is possible through the fact that from a situation given in a certain structuring and characterized by certain functions (aspects), without any change in essential foundations new functions (aspects) may be read off by virtue of new organizations (p. 54).

Thus, the model must remain under computational inspection so the subject can know that the result being read out of the model is due only to what was read into the model. This is the essential—and computationally novel—function of the *mind's eye*.

410

Duncker understands that just having a model for an inference does not establish its validity:

> How is the generality of a given insight possible, although each time such evidence results from only *one* paradigm [model]? . . . Obviously no more is necessary than that, in employing a concept—e.g., the concept "greater than"—I am able to distinguish the essential from the non-essential characteristics of an object. Thus I must distinguish the characteristic: "greater than" from the characteristic: "about 2.5 meters greater than," more particularly from the entirely non-essential green-ness of the tree which is greater than the bush. I can in fact do this, as truly as I can conceive and employ concepts at all. Consequently, I can also recognize, during inspection, what characteristics of the foundation enter into the given evidence present and what others do not (p. 55).

> We shall call a situation "paradigmatic" if it is constructed for the mind's eye by the exclusive use of the concepts expressly contained in the premises (p. 49).

This computational scheme does not produce *necessarily valid* inferences, but Duncker is not claiming such (though he makes no explicit disavowal). He is laying out the computational steps that lead *the subject* to see new information as following necessarily from given premises. But the subject can be fooled; i.e., understanding can be mistaken.

This is as far as we can take this example. The evidence seems compelling that Duncker was taking an essentially computational view. Insight for Duncker was a particular set of cognitive operations that cooperated to establish conditions under which understanding would accrue. The set of conditions is genuinely ingenious. Though the matter cannot be pursued here, their investigation would be an excellent research bet.

Other Mechanisms

There is no space for other examples in sufficient detail to be convincing. Duncker's Chapter 6 contains an extensive characterization of the process of memory search, which is clearly aimed at understanding another primitive operation of the architecture. Duncker seeks to establish that a search model is set up by understanding the task instructions, so a stage of search formulation occurs prior to the search itself. Then the search proceeds by a series of perusals of the search field, these perusals being according to the nature of the field, e.g., geographically (in the mind's eye) if looking for cities, and so forth. The approach is similar to Shiffrin's (1970) model of long-term memory search (probably the best modern treatment), though without any of the mathematical apparatus, precision, or data. This chapter adds a good second data point to the claim that Duncker was attempting to formulate the architecture.

Chapter 5 is less rewarding. Duncker focuses on the nature of the world rather than the human processor. What structure must it have to suggest clues about causal relations. He assumes the human is built to be a *coincidence detector*, but doesn't pursue the matter on the architecture side.

Limitations

To summarize the point: Duncker was attempting to pose the question of what elementary information processes need to exist for the problem-solver to reason. He was not saying that some special and unanalyzable process called insight occurred. On the contrary, insight was for him a special computational device where, having encoded the knowledge, the computation could be made by recognition (accessing) under special conditions, which themselves could be enforced by recognition. He did not concern himself exclusively with insight, though we did not establish this so clearly. He recognized the appropriate role of associations as well as the operation of searches of long-term memory.

Such questions are now more easily put. The proposal to explore the architecture of the human mind is a coherent research proposal. We do not know how clear Duncker was about his own project; we certainly know that he did not communicate this to the world, neither to the mainstream world of behavioristic psychology, from which he was distant, nor to the Gestalt world, of which he was a part, nor even to the information-processing world of 1958, if my own reading then is an indicator.

There are limits to anticipation. Though Duncker was led to take mental operations seriously, he was not led to deal with the control structure, i.e., with the overall operating structure of the mind. There was still a subject whose *inner eye* watched the computation occurring in inner space, to become convinced and attain understanding if it had witnessed all the conditions satisfied.

The lack of concern for control structure and for reduction to mechanism can also be clearly seen in Duncker's treatment of general heuristic methods. They are formulated in natural language (e.g., "analyze the goal"), and it is simply assumed that we understand how a human could behave in such a way. Though he came to ask reductionistic questions—i.e., what mechanisms underlie the human's ability to solve problems meaningfully—he did not seem to be aware of the need at this level.

In sum, there was still the *homunculus*. In this respect we are much better off:

Advance: The homunculus can (on occasion) be banished.

With computer simulation has come a research style in which the homunculus can finally be exorcised. GPS has no homunculus, nor do many other simulation

412

programs. However, the advance remains limited, for even a casual perusal of the modern literature of cognitive processes shows the homunculus well in evidence in many areas.

Duncker was also not sensitive to computational issues of representation. What sort of data-structures his functions could be was not something that he could easily have addressed. However, he does not quite completely ignore it. In discussing the nature of experience in Chapter 5, he addresses directly what is learned, and makes the following remark, which is clearly pertinent to recent discussions on representation:

> "Experiences" are not in general crystallized in statements, but in attributes of objects. . . . Ground-consequence experiences or end-means experiences are embodied in "functional characters" of the objects themselves. The hammer is something for driving nails, the bench is something for resting on (p. 73).

Fixedness of Thought Material

The last part of Duncker's monograph concerns finding materials that satisfy the functions required by a problem. It flows directly from Duncker's theory of problem-solving, which puts the functional characterization of a problem as the decisive cognitive step. The focus is on a particular phenomenon, *functional fixity*, which causes subjects to fail, even though actively looking. Here is the situation:

The subject is looking for an object to perform a new function, F_{new}.

An object exists in the situation that could provide F_{new}.

This object is already characterized as providing a different function, F_{old}.

This decreases the chance of finding the object for F_{new}.

In Duncker's language: F_{old} becomes *fixed* to the object, so that the subject does not see it as available for F_{new}. Such fixation is a priori surprising, because functions are not *objective* properties of an object, but constructs of the subject.

This is the smallest part of the monograph—twenty-six pages vs. forty-five and thirty-four, respectively, for the first two parts. Yet it had by far the largest impact. Functional fixity generated one of the major streams of research in problem-solving until the shift in the mid-1950s to information processing. Part I of the monograph was included in the descriptions in textbooks and reviews of the nature of problem-solving and thought. Part II was dismissed, either as another exposition of the Gestalt position on *insight* or as a philosophical excursion. But Part III generated research. In a theory-less experimental science, the ability to capture the experimenter-hours of your colleagues ultimately defines influence. Thus, we need to understand what Duncker discovered in this third part, why the psychology of midcentury took it up so vigorously, and how our own modern position on this phenomena compares.

What Duncker Knew

Duncker's style of investigation in each of the three parts was quite distinct. In this last part, having focused on the phenomena of fixedness, he performed many small experiments to reveal many factors that affect the amount of fixedness that a subject shows. An abbreviated (somewhat cryptic) list gives the flavor. Implicit in each factor is a comparison of two experimental situations.

1. The object is characterized by a different function (F_{old} not the same as F_{new}). (Restating the basic phenomenon) [**More**]
2. The object is considered as being used only for the different function (i.e., for F_{old}). [**More**]
3. The new function (F_{new}) is considered to be uniquely satisfied by a different kind of object. [**More**]
4. The new function is less obvious perceptually (*pregnant*) in the object. [**More**]
5. The functions (F_{new} and F_{old}) are quite dissimilar types (heterogeneous). [**More**]
6. The functions (F_{new} and F_{old}) are quite similar types (homogeneous). [**Less**]
7. The object is called to attention somehow (i.e., in ways not related to its function). [**Less**]
8. The object is central to the task (and F_{old} may be strong). [**Less**]

Duncker had no theory of functional fixity, beyond that implicit in the metaphor of *fixing* plus some notion that F_{old} *interferes* with F_{new}. This leads him to be surprised about items 5 and 6 (the closer two items, the more they should interfere) and 8 (the more central the object, the stronger it should bind its function).

Why Psychology Took Up Functional Fixity

Functional fixity did not stand by itself as an isolated experimental phenomena. It became included in the topic of *set*, the general factor in the organism that prepares it to respond or perceive the environment in a given way, enhancing or inhibiting responsiveness as the situation agrees or not with the preparation. Set was a general psychological phenomena, but within problem-solving, the work of three people dominated its investigation: Duncker on *functional fixity*; N. R. F. Maier (1930,

1931) on *direction* in problem-solving (recall the two-string task); and Luchins (1942) on the *Einstellung effect* (recall the water-jug task). As one indication of its importance, the 1955 *Annual Review of Psychology* discussion on thinking and problem-solving (Taylor & McNemar, 1955) devotes a third of its pages to set, with major subsections on Einstellung and functional fixity.

No point is served by reciting what was learned by others about set in general or functional fixity in particular. There followed an enumeration of independent variables that affected the formation of set of one kind or another, with experimental demonstrations of which way the effects went. I have not done a literature count; my estimate is that the whole tradition produced a few hundred experimental variations. It is not an exciting and integrated literature. The results seem, at this remove, just like so many facts: anxiety increases set; pressure increases set; time dissipates set; individuals differ.

Little increase occurred in understanding theoretically what processes caused set. This simply reflects the general distance of the 1940s and 1950s from an adequate and accepted model of processing, the area being no wise special vis-à-vis the larger Zeitgeist of experimental psychology. This provides a direct explanation of why psychology chose this third part of Duncker, leaving all the rest either unattended or simply grist for overviews and reviews. Duncker's own approach in this third part meshed exactly with the experimental attitudes and capabilities of the times, and his findings were provocative enough to provide issues to pursue.

The story cannot end quite here, as if just fitting into the paradigm style were enough. As the concordance of the issues by Maier, Luchins, and Duncker indicates, something in the issue of set was especially exciting and provocative to the times. Perhaps it was the notion of a *hidden* factor, not accessible to consciousness or introspection, that made tasks difficult or gave them direction. Certainly many of the issues that fascinated psychology in this period have a similar flavor—latent learning, the *new look* in perception, unawareness in concept formation. However, tracking this down would take us not only beyond Duncker, but beyond the spirit of the monograph, which, despite the third part, is strongly focused on process.

The Position of Modern Cognition

Hardly any studies of functional fixity (or other phenomena of set) have occurred since the early 1960s, which is to say, since the cognitive revolution. The research did not stop because nothing more could be learned about functional fixity, Einstellung, and the rest (in the modern view, not much had been learned). The research simply ceased, because modern cognitive psychology shifted its concerns to internal memory structure and problem-solving processes.

Duncker did not develop a process model of functional fixity. It is easy enough to do, given our current knowledge. Here is a simple model from which all Duncker's phenomena follow.

To find an object to perform a (new) function, the subject must engage in a two step process:
1. A recognitional scan to identify candidates.
2. An evaluation of the resulting candidates for appropriateness.

The subject has no way to *enumerate* the items in a task environment and evaluate them all. The environment is always so rich that the first stage must be recognitional. There is a large dependency in this first stage on both the *surface* aspects of the task and on aspects that can be selected a priori, i.e., without knowledge of the objects to be found. The subject will miss objects that cannot be acquired in this fashion. Once acquired, for whatever reason, the evaluation of whether an object can perform a function goes relatively easily.

The ability to generate reasonable theoretically based explanations can be taken as one more advance.

It is tempting to invoke the Kuhnian model (Kuhn, 1962) to explain the failure of modern cognition to pursue functional fixity—the paradigm shift, scientific elites talking past one another, and so on. In part the story fits, especially the shift to new questions and derivations from different models. However, in one important way it will not do. The underlying role of functions—how they affect the course of reasoning and the difficulty of problems—is as important for the modern theory of cognition as for Duncker. Duncker made a good case for the contribution of functional fixity to the difficulty of problems. Though we may be·cavalier about a processing theory of functional fixity as just one more phenomenon to be modeled, we are every bit as concerned with why problems are difficult and what can be done about it. The modern theory of problem-solving has not made great strides in predicting why problems are difficult. Functional fixity remains an item on our agenda, though there seems no way to predict when it will capture our attention again.

Conclusion

Our exploration of Duncker on problem-solving is completed. Where do we stand in sum? Duncker's 1935 monograph itself stood almost exactly halfway between Wundt and the present celebration, though it was not until the 1950s—almost four-fifths of the way—that the field moved substantially beyond it. However, we must separate what Duncker himself knew from what the field as a whole knew.

Duncker interpreted everything through Gestalt spectacles, in terms of task demands, functions, blind solving, understanding, insight. Yet, as an acute observer of the actual problem-solving behavior of his subjects, in his understanding of process he moved beyond anything to be found in the other Gestaltists. He understood much that we now see in modern information-processing terms: the structure of general heuristic methods, means-ends analysis, search. He was even reaching for how to characterize the underlying processing structure—the architecture.

Turning to the field at large in Duncker's era, concern with processing structure and underlying architecture is all but nonexistent. In its stead is experimental variation of independent variables, the modus vivendi of experimental psychology. It is no surprise that the field took from Duncker what was amenable to experimental variational thinking. Facts about functional fixity could be accumulated indefinitely without making substantial progress on the mechanisms that generate it or its role in the larger scheme of cognitive life.

Contrasting our own state in problem-solving with that of Duncker himself, the advances we have claimed seem primarily of the form "we now have more precise models." That might seem a modest claim. I do not think so. Casting the problem of cognition within a world of mechanism generated the conceptual storm of the 1950s and the waves that swept all before them.

It is not enough just to have a notion of mechanism. The Gestaltists had such a notion—the physical field. So too did Freudian psychology—the psychic energy in a hydraulic-like system. From our present vantage point, these notions are simply not the right mechanism. The human being is a processor of *information:* he or she is not like a physical field; he or she is not like a libido-conservative energy system. Ground can be gained (and was gained) by working under the aegis of these other metaphors. However, they eventually come to hinder more than they help.

Some feel the notion of information processing to be simply another metaphor, like that of field or psychic energy. Only the future can tell. Though it does not seem so to me, spelling out the grounds of that belief is not the business of this paper (Newell, 1980). In all events, the notion of symbolic information processing has provided us with new and striking high-water marks for the detailed understanding of human cognition. Succeeding reformulations will have to move up to still higher ground. That can only be to the great advantage of us all.

Reviewing this excursion into Karl Duncker, recorded twenty years late, I find myself pleased and also confirmed in my assessment (both rational and emotional) about the course of modern cognitive psychology and the advances it has made. More important, I have found things in Duncker I did not find or understand twenty years ago. These seem central to his own research—therefore not of my own construction—and also consistent with what modern cognitive psychology is trying to do and understand. Could anything more be asked from a modest historical exercise? Yes, perhaps one more thing: that we not forget how far Duncker had come in his understanding.

REFERENCES

Addison, J. W., Henkin, L., & Tarski, A. (Eds.). *The theory of models.* Amsterdam: North Holland, 1972.

Anderson, J. R., & Bower, G. *Human associative memory.* Hillsdale, N.J.: Erlbaum, 1973.

Bell, C. G., & Newell, A. *Computer structures: Readings and examples.* New York: McGraw-Hill, 1971.

Blumenthal, A. L. *The processes of cognition.* Englewood Cliffs, N.J.: Prentice-Hall, 1977.

Bobrow, D. G., & Winograd, T. An overview of KRL, a knowledge representation language. *Cognitive Science,* 1977, *1,* 3–46.

Boring, E. G. *A history of experimental psychology* (2d ed.). New York: Appleton-Century-Crofts, 1950.

Broadbent, D. M. *Perception and communication.* London: Pergamon, 1958.

Bruner, J. S., Goodnow, J. J., & Austin, G. A. *A study of thinking.* New York: Wiley, 1956.

Chomsky, N. *Syntactic structures.* The Hague: Mouton, 1957.

DeGroot, A. D. *Thought and choice in chess.* The Hague: Mouton, 1965.

Dewey, J. *How we think.* Boston: Heath, 1910.

Duncker, K. A qualitative (experimental and theoretical) study of productive thinking (solving of comprehensible problems). *Pedagogical Seminary,* 1926, *33,* 642–708.

Duncker, K. *Zur Psychologie des produktiven Denkens.* Berlin: Springer, 1935.

Duncker, K. On problem solving. *Psychological Monographs,* 1945, *58,* 1–113 (Whole No. 270).

Estes, W. (Ed.). *Handbook of learning and cognition* (6 vols.). Hillsdale, N.J.: Erlbaum, 1975 (1975–1978).

Humphrey, G. *Thinking.* Oxford: Oxford University Press, 1951.

Humphrey, G., & Coxon, R. V. *The chemistry of thinking.* London: Pergamon, 1963.

James, W. *The principles of psychology* (2 vols.). New York: Holt, 1890.

Johnson-Laird, P. N., & Wason, P. C. (Eds.). *Thinking.* London: Cambridge University Press, 1977.

Johnson, D. M. *The psychology of thought and judgment.* New York: Harper, 1955.

Johnson, D. M. *A systematic introduction to the psychology of thinking.* New York: Harper & Row, 1972.

Katona, G. *Organizing and memorizing.* New York: Columbia University Press, 1940.

Köhler, W. *The mentality of apes.* London: Routledge & Kegan Paul, 1925.

Kuhn, T. S. *The structure of scientific revolutions.* Chicago: The University of Chicago Press, 1962.

Lachman, R., Lachman, J. L., & Butterfield, E. C. *Cognitive psychology and information processing: An introduction.* Hillsdale, N.J.: Erlbaum, 1979.

Luchins, A. S. Mechanization in problem solving: The effect of *Einstellung. Psychological Monographs,* 1942, *54,* 1–95 (Whole No. 248).

Maier, N. R. F. Reasoning in humans. I: On direction. *Journal of Comparative Psychology,* 1930, *10,* 115–143.

Maier, N. R. F. Reasoning in humans. II: The solution of a problem and its appearance in consciousness. *Journal of Comparative Psychology,* 1931, *12,* 181–194.

Mandler, J., & Mandler, G. *Thinking: From association to Gestalt.* New York: Wiley, 1964.

Miller, G. A. The magic number seven, plus or minus two: Some limits on our capacity for processing information. *Psychological Review,* 1956, *63,* 81–97.

Miller, G. A. A very personal history. Talk to Cognitive Science Workshop, M.I.T., June 1, 1979.

Neisser, U. *Cognitive psychology.* New York: Appleton-Century-Crofts, 1967.

Newell, A. Remarks on the relationship between artificial intelligence and cognitive psychology. In R. Banerji & J. D. Mesarovic (Eds.), *Theoretical approaches to non-numerical problem solving.* New York: Springer-Verlag, 1970.

Newell, A. Production systems: Models of control structures. In W. C. Chase (Ed.), *Visual information processing.* New York: Academic Press, 1973.

Newell, A. Physical symbol systems. *Cognitive Science*, 1980, *4*, 135–183.

Newell, A., Shaw, J. C., & Simon, H. A. *Preliminary description of general problem solving program-1 (GPS-1)*. Technical Report, Carnegie Institute of Technology, December 1957.

Newell, A., Shaw, J. C., & Simon, H. A. Elements of a theory of human problem solving. *Psychological Review*, 1958, *65*, 151–166.

Newell, A., Shaw, J. C., & Simon, H. A. Report on a general problem-solving program for a computer. In *Information processing: Proceedings of the International Conference on Information Processing*. Paris: UNESCO, 1960.

Newell, A., & Simon, H. A. GPS: A program that simulates human thought. In H. Billing (Ed.), *Lernende Automaten*. Munich: Oldenbourg, 1961. (Reprinted in E. Feigenbaum & J. Feldman (Eds.), *Computers and thought*. New York: McGraw-Hill, 1963.)

Newell, A., & Simon, H. A. *Human problem solving*. Englewood Cliffs, N.J.: Prentice-Hall, 1972.

Polya, G. *How to solve it*. Princeton, N.J.: Princeton University Press, 1945.

Pylyshyn, Z. W. Computation and cognition: Issues in the foundations of cognitive science. *The Behavior and Brain Sciences*, 1980, *3*, 111–169.

Quillian, M. R. Semantic memory. In M. Minsky (Ed.), *Semantic information processing*. Cambridge, Mass.: M.I.T. Press, 1968.

Reitman, W. *Cognition and thought*. New York: Wiley, 1965.

Schank, R. & Abelson, R. *Scripts, plans, goals and understanding*. Hillsdale, N.J.: Erlbaum, 1977.

Selz, O. *Uber die Gesetze des geordneten Denkverlaufs*. Stuttgart: Spemann, 1913.

Selz, O. *Zur Psychologie des produktiven Denkens und des Irrtums*. Bonn: F. Cohen, 1922.

Shiffrin, R. M. Memory search. In D. A. Norman (Ed.), *Models of human memory*. New York: Academic Press, 1970.

Tanner, J. P., Jr., & Swets, J. A. A decision-making theory of visual detection. *Psychological Review*, 1954, *61*, 401–409.

Taylor, D. W., & McNemar, O. W. Problem solving and thinking. *Annual Review of Psychology*, 1955, *6*, 455–482.

Thorndike, E. L. Animal intelligence. *Psychological Monograph*, 1898, *2*.

Tolman, E. C. *Purposive behavior in animals and men*. New York: Appleton-Century-Crofts, 1932.

Vinacke, W. E. *The psychology of thinking*. New York: McGraw-Hill, 1952.

Vinacke, W. E. *Psychology of thinking* (2d ed.). New York: McGraw-Hill, 1974.

Wertheimer, M. *Productive thinking*. New York: Harper, 1945.

17

*Some Trends in the Study of Cognition**

HENRY GLEITMAN

When I agreed to write a chapter on what we have learned about cognition since Wilhelm Wundt, I thought my only problem would be one of selection. For after all, how could we *not* have gone beyond Wilhelm Wundt, whom I—like so many of us—had been taught to regard as someone posterity can safely patronize: an indefatigable, erudite, but slightly pedantic champion of an outmoded elementarism, a man whom Stanley Hall called a "wonderful compiler and digester" (Hall, 1921); of whom William James said that "he wasn't a genius but a professor . . . an example of how much mere education can do for a man" (H. James, 1920, p. 263); whom Edna Heidbreder likened to "a careful housewife, industriously picking up after a growing science that . . . has not yet learned . . . to be neat. . . ." (Heidbreder, 1933, p. 96).

I soon discovered (greatly helped by several recent authors, e.g., Blumenthal, 1970, 1975) that this picture of our official founding father is simply false. It is a painting that is reminiscent of those purchased by Gilbert and Sullivan's Major

* Many of the ideas here presented come from a longtime collaborator who helped me with this paper, as with so many others, to the extent of being a de facto co-author—Lila R. Gleitman. I am also very grateful to several friends and colleagues who have been extremely generous in discussing this paper with me at various stages in its preparation: John Flavell, Julian Hochberg, John Jonides, Ulric Neisser, Elissa Newport, and Elizabeth Spelke.

General Stanley, who bought an ancestral home and then acquired a gallery of ancestor portraits to go along with it. Psychology is like General Stanley. It manufactures its ancestors to justify what it is doing now, creating a past that flatters its present.

Poor Wundt is a victim of this Stanley effect. For one thing, he never held the passive conception of mental life he is so often charged with. On the contrary, he might well be regarded as a forerunner of various constructive approaches to perception and memory. As he saw it, conscious experiences generally include elements of forward-looking anticipation which bind the future to the present.

Nor was Wundt the elementarist that later critics, such as the Gestalt psychologists, held him to be. (In this regard, they probably confused him with his American St. Paul, E. B. Titchener.) Consider some of his comments on language, which sound almost like a Wagnerian prelude to a work authored at M.I.T. Here is how he put it in the *Völkerpsychologie*:

> . . . A sentence does not consist of separate mental structures that emerge in consciousness, one by one, each existing as an individual word or an individual sound while all before and after sinks into oblivion. It rather remains in consciousness as a totality while it is being uttered. . . . As a result, all relevant components of a sentence are already mentally given in the brief moment when one first begins to utter it. . ." (Wundt, 1900, p. 235).

There is evidently more to Wundt than met the textbook writers' eyes. How much more I cannot say, for I do not have the stamina to go through the thousands of printed pages (according to some estimates, sixty thousand) that he bequeathed to posterity.

Under the circumstances, I had to change my approach to the question "What have we learned since Wilhelm Wundt?" I cannot very well assess how far we have come (especially given that I do not really know where we started from), for that would be too presumptuous. I do not want to chronicle the historical details of our intellectual pilgrimage, for that would be too tedious. Nor do I wish to relate our long wanderings through the behaviorist wilderness (during which cognition finally became respectable when it was found in rats), for that would be too depressing.

I will instead trace a few themes in the way several areas of cognition have been conceived. My focus will be on the *what* of cognition rather than on its *how*, on structure rather than on process: the way it is organized as we perceive objects, comprehend meanings, and make out another person's intentions, and the way these structures enter not just into what we know but also into what we know we know.

It is probably no coincidence that some of these themes have been foreshadowed by nineteenth-century psychologists, especially by Wilhelm Wundt.

421

A Parallel

A common theme runs through three different domains of cognitive life: visual perception, language, and the interpretation of behavior. Its basis is the distinction between two levels of psychological structure, one more peripheral and the other more central—the difference between what in language is called "surface" and "underlying structure."

In Language

In language, this distinction is by now a commonplace. There is a first-level organization of linguistic input that more or less corresponds to the sentences we actually hear—the surface form. This is somehow organized into a structure that is a closer approximation to the underlying sentence meaning—the underlying structure.

To recapitulate an oft-told tale, these two levels—surface and underlying structure—are very different. One demonstration is the fact that two or more different surface forms can go back to the same underlying structure. Thus:

The princess kissed the frog.

and its passive form,

The frog was kissed by the princess.

both refer to a common proposition and are to this extent paraphrases.

Another demonstration of the surface–underlying structure distinction comes from certain kinds of *ambiguities*. These show that one and the same surface form may go back to two or more different underlying structures. Examples include sentences such as

Kissing frogs can be amusing . . .

and

Smoking volcanoes can be dangerous . . .

In Visual Perception

As several psycholinguists have noted, the surface–underlying structure distinction drawn by linguists has an analogue in visual perception (e.g., Bever, 1970; Fodor, Bever, & Garrett, 1974). Here, surface structure corresponds to something close to the proximal stimulus on the retina, perhaps something which E. B. Titchener would have called the visual sensation (Titchener, 1896). The underlying structure, on the other hand, corresponds to the perception of the distal stimulus—the rock or the tree out there in the world rather than its projection on the retina. It is worth noting that the self-conscious demonstration of this distinction dates back to the Gestalt psychologists and their unceasing war against what they called the *constancy hypothesis*—the assumption that what we perceive corresponds directly to the proximal stimulus on our retina (Koffka, 1935). Their weapons in this war were analogous to those the linguists used to document the surface–underlying structure distinction: ambiguity and paraphrase. Thus they continually emphasized that the same proximal pattern can be perceived in two or more ways, as shown by an unending parade of ambiguous figures of which the Necker cube and the young woman/old woman picture are among the most familiar. The complementary side of their argument came from demonstrations that different proximal stimuli may all be perceived as equivalent in some important regard. Doors seen from different slants cast different trapezoidal images on the retina, but they are all perceived as rectangular; trees at different distances cast images of different size, but they are all perceived as having the same size. These various constancies— here, of shape and size—are the perceptual analogues of language paraphrase. Our perceptual system is somehow able to operate on all of the various trapezoidal images that the doorframe gives rise to and interpret them as a rectangle.

In Behavior

Something akin to the surface–underlying structure distinction may apply to yet another domain: our apprehension of behavior. As Tolman and other theorists taught us, we can look at behavior in both a *molecular* and a *molar* sense (Tolman, 1932). The molecular level corresponds to a surface organization: it is described as a series of particular movements. The molar level is closer to the center and thus more like the underlying structure: it is usually described as the goal or intention.

There is no doubt that any particular molar pattern can be expressed in a number of different molecular forms. This holds for rats who may traverse a path to the same goal in any number of ways—running, swimming, hobbling, or short-cutting, depending upon how Tolman and Lashley had rearranged their maze or brain (e.g., Woodworth, 1938, pp. 133–134). Much the same holds for people who may try to reach a goal by many different molecular means: thus slapping, jabbing, and punching may all be different behavior-surface forms that refer to a common underlying intentional structure. In effect, they are behavioral paraphrases. Their opposite is also found: two acts that are more or less alike on the surface but have two different underlying goal directions, thus representing the behavioral analogue of ambiguity. An example is violently shoving someone standing in the road. Is this a surface manifestation of intense dislike or an attempt to push the victim out of the path of a runaway truck? Another example was used in an episode of the late-lamented television series "Mary Hartman, Mary Hartman": mouth-to-mouth contact between man and woman, which may be kissing or artificial respiration.

Hierarchies of Levels

We should add a qualification. In both goal-directed behavior and in language (and perhaps in visual perception too), there are hierarchies of structure. As a result, the terms *surface* and *underlying form*—at least in an extended sense—are relative. In language, the levels of primary interest have been those that involve the sentence. But one can go below and consider morphological and phonological structures. Or one can go above and look at discourse. What serves as paraphrase or ambiguity will then depend upon the level under consideration. Given an appropriate discourse level, a sentence such as

> *The witch's curse was foiled*

might then be an acceptable paraphrase for our initial sentence about the frog-kissing princess.

A similar multileveled hierarchical structure characterizes goal-directed behavior. There are not only goals but subgoals and subsubgoals and so on down the hierarchy until we finally reach the ultimate surface level of the muscle twitch. Which particular levels of the hierarchy shall we choose as the behavioral analogues of surface and underlying structure? In a way, the problem is quite analogous to that encountered in the analysis of language structures, but there is an important difference. The linguists have some agreed-upon conceptions about the various levels of the linguistic hierarchy. There is a phonological basement, a phonemic first story, and so on, all the way up to the levels of sentence meaning, with some interesting plans for the construction of several discourse penthouses. As far as I know, behavioral analysis has not yet reached this happy consensus (though there have been some attempts in this direction, e.g., Schank & Abelson, 1977). Suppose a smiling man lifts a baby to his head and plants his lips to the infant's. What is the appropriate description of the intention, the underlying behavioral structure? Is he kissing the baby? Pleasing its mother? Running for president? Thus far, there is no agreement. So, in the realm of behavioral description, one man's molecule is another's mole.

How Genuine Is the Analogy?

One may argue that the analogy sketched here is rather superficial. For there is little doubt that the mechanisms by which one moves from surface to underlying structures are quite different in the three domains. Perhaps so. But my point is not directed at the processes that underlie the traffic from cognitive periphery to center.

424

It merely notes that such a traffic occurs and that it is in some ways similar in the three cognitive realms. In all three, the would-be knower confronts a similar problem: how to apprehend an underlying sameness in a welter of changing surface forms. How this task is accomplished—by extraction of stimulus invariants, by various forms of inference, by the gradual development of internal rule systems whose forms may be in some sense pregiven—is another matter entirely.

A further argument for my cavalier disregard of mechanisms is provided by the perceptual constancies: of lightness, size, and shape. All three are phenomena within the same cognitive realm of visual perception. But we already know that the processes that underlie them are very different. Lightness constancy is ours largely by courtesy of evolution and lateral inhibition. Size and shape constancy may very well turn out to be based on early learning, at least in part. But this does not change the fact that all three belong to the same conceptual family and are so viewed by most perception psychologists. For in each case, the perceiver is posed with a similar problem and solves it successfully. Since this is so, all three are traditionally subsumed under the same general rubric. If this can be done within a given cognitive domain, why not across different ones?

I am arguing for an analogy based on structure rather than on process, but it is worth noting that there may be some similarities of process too. Consider the perception of size which clearly requires so-called "cues" for distance. By utilizing these cues (however this is done), the observer can see that he is dealing with an object of a given size and at a given distance. Psycholinguists point out that something like cues exist in language, whose role may be quite equivalent to those played by various cues to distance, orientation, and the like in visual perception. Thus passive forms such as

Noun verb -*ed by* Noun

provide cues in the form of -*ed by* which indicate that the conversational focus is on the object of the underlying sentence proposition rather than the subject. This allows us to extract the underlying proposition, a procedure that works even for nonsense words. Given the pseudosentence

The dax was riffed by the zup.

we immediately suppose that the *zup* was the *riffer*, the *dax* the *riffee*.

By and large this supposition will be correct, but sometimes it won't. If *dax* stands for *pig*, *rif* for *slaughter*, and *zup* for *gate*, the sentence becomes

The pig was slaughtered by the gate.

In this case the *zup* does not function as the *riffer*. Here, the -*ed by* provides a misleading cue to focus. But then the same sometimes happens in visual perception, where distance cues may also turn out to provide false information.

425

Collapsing Time

Suppose we grant that there is something valid about the notion of surface–underlying structure distinction that runs across a number of cognitive domains. What accounts for this dual structure? I believe that its essence has to do with the compression of time.

Consider the underlying structures which—crudely speaking—correspond to our mental representations of purpose, object, and meaning. These mental entities are themselves timeless, but I believe that they all refer to events that necessarily occur over time. They are reminiscent of T. S. Eliot's lines in "Burnt Norton":

> *Time present and time past*
> *Are both perhaps present in time future,*
> *And time future contained in time past.*

It seems to me that this describes a crucial facet of our mental structures. Purpose, object, and meaning are mental packagings of temporal unfoldings, but they themselves are outside of time. In this regard they are quite unlike the surface forms which do occur over time—almost by definition.

Collapsing Surface Behaviors—Purpose

Let us start with purpose. There is no one way in which we can divine another creature's purpose except by observing its behavior over time: its start, its progression, and its finish. Nor is one sequence of outward behavior patterns enough. As Tolman told us, one of the defining characteristics of purposive behavior is its docility: if one means does not attain the end, the organism will choose another (Tolman, 1932). At least in principle, our knowledge of another's purpose is similarly based on the observation of several different surface behaviors. We must know what happens when the starting point is altered, when obstacles are erected, and so on. Needless to say, we generally reach our cognitive decision on the basis of much less information, deciding that, say, Joe wants Mary without actually observing that he takes the appropriate detours when his normal path to Mary is blocked. But the point is that this cognitive decision about Joe's goal boils down to a prediction of his outward behavior on an infinite set of tests (all designed with appropriate qualifications about performance limitations). Will he climb over hurdles to reach his beloved (assuming that he can climb)? Will he swim across moats (assuming he can swim)? And so on and so on. The underlying mental structure we call *purpose* is a kind of mental shorthand which collapses all of these surface behavior forms which do take place in time, encapsulating them in a timeless mental structure in which temporal events exist only as a potentiality.

Collapsing Surface Perceptions—Object

One can argue that an analogous process of time packaging underlies the perception of objects. Consider a table. In the real world—of Newton, or of God—it doubtless exists as a genuine entity whose every parts (legs, tabletop) are simultaneously present in space. But psychologically speaking, our perception of the table is necessarily drawn out in time. Theorists of perception disagree about how this perception is achieved, but, however different their proposals, a reference to temporally extended events is a crucial component of virtually all (Gestalt psychology may be an exception). Thus John Stuart Mill regarded objects as "the permanent possibility of a sensation" (Mill, 1865). Helmholtz described the perception of a table as a compact mental expression of what would reach the eyes if the observer walked around it (Helmholtz, 1866/1962). Gibson emphasized stimulus invariants that necessarily extend over time, such as gradients of motion parallax (Gibson, 1950, 1966), while modern perceptual constructionists such as Hochberg and Neisser regard perceptual figures as a set of anticipations about the visual consequences of eye movements or other explorations (Hochberg, 1970, 1978; Neisser, 1976). In all these accounts, the underlying mental structure—the perception of the object—is a timeless expression of a potentially infinite set of sensory surface forms.

Surface and Deep Structure in Language

The analogy can probably be pursued into language as well. Language utterances are obviously sequential while their mental representation is not. Here again, we are faced with the phenomenon of temporal collapsing and the various issues it poses. As in the perception of objects and purpose, the mental representation of sentence meaning is—among other things—a timeless potentiality for a large number (in principle, an infinite number) of temporally extended utterances.

But in the case of language, several new problems crop up. For language is after all a device for communicating meaning between two sentient persons. To this extent, the transmission of meaning is necessarily different from, say, the perception of objects. Rocks and trees have no particular interest in letting us know of their existence; if we want to perceive them, we must willy-nilly rely on the kind intermediation of temporally extended proximal stimulus events. But why did evolution force us to use an analogous procedure when we try to communicate our meanings to other hearers? Why do we have to go through a cumbersome sequential apparatus in which our meaning is first stretched out in time (as we speak) and is then collapsed again (as our hearers understand)? The answer may be that there was no alternative. Given the limitations of our motor, sensory, and cerebral equipment, and the fact that human languages must convey an infinite set of possible messages with a finite set of means, the only way was to string the message units out in time. A further question arises when we consider the two syntactic organizations of a

427

sentence: surface and underlying structure. Both represent hierarchical organizations that are superimposed upon a sequential arrangement. But why do we need two? Why can the speaker not simply articulate what is, so to speak, at the bottom level of the underlying structure, going from left to right? Would that not save an extra step for both speaker and listener?

There are many answers, some of which depend upon the particular version of modern grammatical theory one subscribes to. For our present purposes, I will adapt an approach (loosely patterned after Chomsky, 1971) which emphasizes the communicative function of the message, a function that is best served by having *both* a surface and an underlying structure. The underlying structure is a marvelously transparent rendering of the propositions that a sentence contains. Take our old standbys

The princess kissed the frog.

The frog was kissed by the princess.

What the princess did was to kiss the frog . . .

These and other amphibian tales all contain the same proposition about princess, kissing, and frog. But the surface structures tell us something else. Among other things, they specify which part of the proposition is in focus. This in turn is related to various presuppositions the speaker entertains about the listener's prior knowledge. If the hearer is already aware that the princess did something but does not know just what, one is likely to say

The princess kissed the frog . . .

If one presupposes that the hearer already knows that something happened to a frog, one is likely to inform him that

The frog was kissed by the princess . . .

To the extent that this is true, the active and passive forms (and many others) are not complete paraphrases. They contain the same underlying proposition, but they also include something else: the conversational focus, which typically indicates the speaker's beliefs about the listener's prior knowledge and conversational interests. Without these, we would prattle on endlessly and be even greater bores than we normally are. To avoid this, we must tell our conversational partners what we presuppose they already know, and this is one of the contributions of the surface form.

This function of language surface structure is again analogous to some phenomena of object perception. For there too, paraphrase is not complete. The size of a given object is perceived to be the same, whether it is far off or nearby. But this does not mean that we see no difference. Of course we do; the object looks further away in one case, and closer by in the other. The partial perceptual paraphrase that occurs (that is, size constancy) has obvious survival value. Our primitive ancestors would have been in considerable trouble if they mistook a saber-tooth tiger in the distance for a pussy-cat close at hand. But size constancy alone is clearly not enough. We have to know the properties of the object itself, but we must know more. We have to know our own relation to it: our distance from it, our orientation, and so on. And this is partially given by the perceptual equivalent of the surface structure—the particular pattern of sensory stimulation in the here-and-now. This too is relevant to survival. It pays to know just how far the saber-tooth tiger actually is so we can take the proper steps in preparation: run away if he is far away and pray if he is nearby.

Metacognition

These comments have been about ways in which we come to know. But we do not just know; we often also know that we know (and even more often, that we do not). This point predates official, scientific psychology by millennia. It is probably implicit in Aristotle's differentiation between memory and recollection; it appears in St. Augustine's contrast between memories that rush forth unbidden and others that have to be dragged out of hiding; it is found in John Locke's description of the two ways of gaining knowledge, empiricial experience and reflection. Our more immediate founding fathers, Wundt and James, were also sensitive to this distinction. Wundt contrasts the influence of past experiences of which one is not aware with those which are recognized as such, where there is an explicit awareness that one is dealing with memory (Wundt, 1918, p. 293). To James, the very term *memory* (or more precisely, secondary memory) is reserved for just those experiences that have this self-conscious, reflective property. As he put it: "[Memory proper] . . . *is the knowledge of an event or fact, of which meantime we have not been thinking, with the additional consciousness that we have thought or experienced before . . ."* (James, 1890, I, p. 648). To these fathers and great-great-grandfathers of our discipline, it was evidently clear that there is a psychology of knowing about knowing as well as a psychology of knowing.

That such subtle distinctions were ignored during much of the twentieth century, especially in America, is not surprising. A behaviorist-dominated era that had little patience with the study of knowledge was going to have none at all for the study of knowledge of knowledge. But by now this state of affairs exists no longer. A fair number of investigators have finally chosen to look where Aristotle and James looked before them, asking what people know about their own cognitive operations, what they know about the way they remember, solve problems, deal with language, and so on—a topic that generally goes under the somewhat portentous name of *metacognition*.

Method of Investigation

An explicit definition of metacognition is hard to come by, for it is not always clear where cognition ends and metacognition begins. But for the time being, I sidestep such boundary problems and deal with relatively clear cases. One such is meta-memory, as recently studied by a number of investigators whose primary focus is on developmental issues, Anne Brown, for example, and John Flavell (e.g., Brown, 1978; Flavell, 1978; Flavell & Wellman, 1977). One question concerns the extent to which the subjects know about their own memory. Do they know that a given item is in their memory store even though they cannot recall it at present? Can they assess how likely they are to recover it later on, or how much they would be helped by various prompts? Another question concerns the subject's knowledge (and command) of various strategies for memorizing and retrieving, such as rehearsing, organizing, and the like. To the extent that the subject does use a deliberate strategy (say, appropriate categorizing), we can be sure that there is metamemory as well as memory. The subject evidently anticipates that the present will soon become the past, and makes appropriate provisions to recover it in some future. By doing so, he shows that he knows something about his own mental operations.

A different topic of inquiry concerns metalinguistic abilities. Such abilities have provided the bulk of the data on which modern accounts of grammar rest. Chomsky's transformational accounts, and the variety of revisions and expansions that have followed, were ultimately based on the capacity of adult human speakers to reflect upon their language and give reports on whether sentences are well-formed, to judge and create paraphrases, and to note ambiguities. More recently, these metalinguistic abilities have been studied in their own right, often in a developmental context (e.g., H. Gleitman & L.R. Gleitman, 1979; L. R. Gleitman & H. Gleitman, 1970; L. R. Gleitman, H. Gleitman, & Shipley, 1972).

Some General Findings

What have such investigations taught us? To begin with, they have shown that cognitive and metacognitive achievements are, to some extent at least, separable. A number of examples come from language. Suppose a five- or six-year-old is presented with various sentences and asked "if they are good or if they are silly." Given the sentence

John and Bill is a brother.

one child responded:

Sure, they could be brothers. I know them. They are brothers.

The child's verbal *production* is fine. There is verbal concord in his own answer. But his metalinguistic judgment did not correspond to his linguistic act. His verbal production apparatus evidently knew about subject-verb agreement, but *he* did not (L. R. Gleitman, H. Gleitman, & Shipley, 1972).

Another finding is that metacognitive abilities increase with age and seem to show greater variability in the population than the cognitive capacities which underlie them. This point has been thoroughly documented in metamemory and in what might be called metaproblem-solving. Thus younger children are less able than older ones to predict their own memory span, do a poorer job at memory monitoring, use fewer and less sophisticated memorial strategies if they use any at all, are less competent in formulating problem-solving plans, and so on (e.g., Brown, 1978; Flavell & Wellman, 1977; Markman, 1977). Similar differences have been found in comparisons of normal with retarded populations.

The same general trend holds for metalinguistic skills. Differences between adults and between adults and, say, five-year-old children are relatively small and subtle with respect to their syntactic usage and their phonology. The pattern is very different when we turn to metalinguistic judgments where both populational variability and developmental differences are considerable.

Metacognition Is Easier for Underlying than for Surface Structures

Another finding brings us back to the surface–underlying form distinction with which we began. By and large, metacognition seems to be harder for surface than for underlying forms.

Let us begin with language. A number of investigators have shown that the lower the level of language feature, the harder it is to access metalinguistically. Consider meaning. When asked whether various sentences are "good" or "silly," kindergartners have much less trouble in commenting on matters of meaning and plausibility than in responding to syntactic issues. Take the sentence

The color green frightened George.

One five-year-old rejected this on the grounds that "Green can't stand up and go 'Boo.' " This contrasts with the seven-year-old who said, "Doesn't frighten me but it sounds OK" (L. R. Gleitman, H. Gleitman, & Shipley, 1972).

A similar pattern holds when we consider surface and underlying structure and the *detection of ambiguity*. To get at this relation, we studied children's explanations of jokes that are based on various kinds of language ambiguity. Children from six to twelve were read a number of jokes and were asked to rate each joke's "funniness" and also to explain just what it was that made it funny (Hirsh-Pasek, L. R. Gleitman, & H. Gleitman, 1978). Some jokes—such as they were—turned on ambiguities of surface structure, such as

Where would you go to see a man eating fish?

A sea-food restaurant.

431

Others hinged on underlying structure ambiguity. An example is

We're going to have my grandmother for Thanksgiving dinner.

You are? Well, we're going to have turkey.

The results showed that the underlying-structure jokes were easier to get and to explain than were those that depended on surface ambiguity.

The greater difficulty of metalinguistic access to surface as opposed to underlying forms is brought out most clearly when we turn to the most surfacey of all surface aspects of language: its sound pattern. Paul Rozin and Lila Gleitman have argued that metalinguistic awareness of this facet of language is enormously difficult to achieve; in their view, this is one of the important obstacles in learning to read an alphabetic script. While five-year-olds can be taught to distinguish between the concepts of sentence and word fairly easily, they find it much harder to distinguish between word, syllable, and sound. They have considerable trouble in segmenting words into syllables, and the greatest difficulty of all in segmenting words or syllables into phonemes (Rozin & Gleitman, 1977).

Related facts concern the difficulty of different reading systems. Logographies, which render meaningful words abstractly are easier to learn than the alphabetic system—a system that, not coincidentally, has been invented only once in human history (Gleitman & Rozin, 1977).

To sum up, there seems to be an orderly progression. The lower—the more surfacey—the level of linguistic representation, the harder it is to cope with metalinguistically.

This is not to say that these lower levels are not processed by the child as he hears or speaks. Of course they are. There is a well-known test of reading-readiness which evidently correlates well with later reading performance. Some children cannot correctly say "same" or "different" when confronted with pairs of words that differ in one phonological segment, such as *bat* versus *cat*. But there is evidence that the children who fail this test respond quite appropriately to sentences such as "Point to the bat" and "Point to the cat." They can hear and they can understand. What they *cannot* do is to make a metalinguistic judgment about a linguistic surface feature (Blank, 1968).

What about cognitive domains other than language? The immediate temptation is to see an analogue to memory, given the general run of the depth of process findings (e.g., Craik & Lockhart, 1972), better recall for underlying syntactic structure than for surface forms (e.g., Sachs, 1967), and similar effects. Even so, I am a bit worried. Do the memory results reflect a metamemory effect (in which case the analogy fits), an effect of memory proper (in which case it does not), or some interaction of the two? It is hard to say.

More directly relevant are metacognitive effects in the two realms which provided

432

the initial parallel to the surface–underlying structure distinction—that is, visual perception and goal-directed behavior. There have been relatively few modern studies on metacognition in these areas (though some exciting beginnings are now being made by Flavell and his associates, e.g., Flavell, Shipstead, & Croft, 1978). But I believe that we have a great deal of informal evidence that here too metacognitive awareness is easier for underlying than for surface forms. This is clearly so for visual perception. Most of us are conscious only of its end-product and content ourselves with reports of seeing the various objects of the visual world. Unless of course we are painters, especially Renaissance painters. In that case, we may well be masters of visual surface structure and be able to report—by brush, if not by mouth—on all manners of delicate, proximal-stimulus-related detail. Similarly for the perception of behavior. On watching a Monday-night football game, most of us are only aware that, say, the middle linebacker plunked himself on top of the opposing quarterback. We see the intention and its fulfillment, the behavioral underlying structure. The coaches—not to speak of Howard Cosell—can do more. They are exquisitely aware of many specific details of the linebacker's actual movements. They (and the player himself) note the surface as well as the underlying structure.

Further support for this general contention comes from the work of the men who provide the occasion for this centennial. For Wundt and his students may well be regarded as the first official students of metacognition. Consider Titchener. He and his students found that it was murderously difficult to focus on mental surface forms. It was too easy to fall into what Titchener called the *stimulus-error*. In studies of perception, this so-called "error" was to describe the stimulus (that is, the *object*) that produced the sensation rather than the sensation itself. In studies of thinking, it was to describe the *meaning* of the thought rather than such surface contents as images and feelings (Titchener, 1909).

An example is a Cornell study on touch blends in which subjects had to analyze the feeling of "clammy." They were blindfolded, required to touch a bunch of live oysters, and asked to describe their mental experience. After much urging and reinstructing, they finally came up with an acceptable catalogue of surface mental contents, such as "cold," "wet," "soft," "yielding to pressure," and "unpleasant imagery" (Zigler, 1923). It would have been much easier to give in to the stimulus error and describe the object as "a bunch of oysters," and one's own intention, "I'd like to get out of here."

Whether Titchener and Wundt were successful in their attempts to describe certain aspects of mental surface structures is debatable. But what is not debatable, and what they themselves would certainly have conceded, is that such surface metacognition (assuming it exists) is very much more difficult to describe than the metacognition of underlying structure forms.

What accounts for this pattern of relationships? What I have to say is probably just a restatement. Cognitive processes are generally directed toward some ends. If

433

asked to reflect on one's cognitions, it is easier to describe these end-states (the perceived object or meaning or goal) than to describe the steps by which these ends are reached. This may be because we can only access our own mental operations through the time-collapsed mental packagings which these end-states represent. Or perhaps metacognition is a by-product of a set of internal monitoring systems (of a kind envisaged by, among others, Marshall & Morton, 1978) which somehow check on whether goals are reached, whether sentences make sense, and whether perceptual anticipations are met.

Given how little we know about cognition, it is hardly surprising that we know even less about metacognition. But at least we know that there is a distinction between the two. This distinction may very well help us to resolve some past debates, including some about consciousness. What Titchener called consciousness is a kind of metacognition of mental surface structures, which is hard if not impossible to attain. What Gestalt psychologists called consciousness might be regarded as metacognition of underlying structures. Perhaps we can take an even wilder step and suggest that what Freud called unconsciousness might be most usefully reinterpreted as a form of meta-noncognition, in which the patient ends up *not* knowing that he knows.

I have tried to sketch a few themes that characterize cognition as we have thought about it during the one hundred years since Wundt. I do not know whether we have progressed that much beyond him. Our techniques are more sophisticated, and there are many more of us, so we can inundate each other in a mass of facts. But much of what we now do and think was already implicit in Wundt, and in other nineteenth century figures. We could do worse than to go back for an occasional glance at our intellectual origins, if only to have a sense of what posterity will do for us one hundred years from now at Wundt's *bi*centennial, when some future Major General Stanley acquires *our* portraits.

REFERENCES

Bever, T. G. The cognitive basis for linguistic structures. In J. R. Hayes (Ed.), *Cognition and the development of language*. New York: Wiley, 1970.

Blank, M. Cognitive processes in auditory discrimination in normal and retarded readers. *Child Development*, 1968, 39, 1091–1101.

Blumenthal, A. L. *Language and psychology: Historical aspects of psycholinguistics.* New York: Wiley, 1970.

Blumenthal, A. L. A reappraisal of Wilhelm Wundt. *American Psychologist*, 1975, 30, 1081–1088.

Brown, A. L. Knowing when, where and how to remember: A problem of meta-cognition. In R. Glaser (Ed.), *Advances in instructional psychology*. New York: Halstead Press, 1978.

Chomsky, N. Deep structure, surface structure, and semantic interpretation. In D. Steinberg & L. A. Jabobovits (Eds.), *Semantics*. London: Cambridge University Press, 1971.

Craik, F. I. M., & Lockhart, R. S. Levels of processing: A framework for memory research. *Journal of Verbal Learning and Verbal Behavior*, 1972, *11*, 671–684.

Flavell, J. H. Meta-cognitive development. In J. M. Scandura & C. J. Brainerd (Eds.), *Structural/ process theories of complex human behavior*. Alphen a.d. Rijn, The Netherlands: Sijthoff and Nordhoff, 1978.

Flavell, J. H., Shipstead, S. G., & Croft, K. Young children's knowledge about visual perception: Hiding objects from others. *Child Development*, 1978, *49*, 1208–1211.

Flavell, J. H., & Wellman, H. M. Meta-memory. In R. V. Kail & J. W. Hagen (Eds.), *Perspectives on the development of memory and cognition*. Hillsdale, N.J.: Erlbaum, 1977.

Fodor, J. A., Bever, T. G., & Garrett, M. F. *The psychology of language*. New York: McGraw-Hill, 1974.

Gibson, J. J. *The perception of the visual world*. New York: Houghton Mifflin, 1950.

Gibson, J. J. *The senses considered as perceptual systems*. New York: Houghton Mifflin, 1966.

Gleitman, H., & Gleitman, L. R. Language use and language judgement. In C. J. Fillmore, D. Kempler, & W. S-Y. Wang (Eds.), *Individual differences in language ability and language behavior*. New York: Academic Press, 1979.

Gleitman, L. R., & Gleitman, H. *Phrase and paraphrase*. New York: Norton, 1970.

Gleitman, L. R., Gleitman, H., & Shipley, E. The emergence of the child as a grammarian. *Cognition*, 1972, *1*, 137–164.

Gleitman, L. R., & Rozin, P. The structure and acquisition of reading I: Relations between orthographies and the structure of language. In A. S. Reber & D. Scarborough (Eds.), *Toward a psychology of reading*. Hillsdale, N.J.: Erlbaum, 1977.

Hall, G. S. In memory of Wilhelm Wundt: By his American students. *Psychological Review*, 1921, *28*, 154–155.

Heidbreder, E. *Seven psychologies*. New York: Appleton-Century-Crofts, 1933.

Helmholtz, H. von. *Treatise on physiological optics* (Vol. 2) (J. P. C. Southall, Ed. and trans. from 3d ed., 1909). New York: Dover Press, 1962. (Originally published, 1866.)

Hirsh-Pasek, K., Gleitman, L. R., & Gleitman, H. What did the brain say to the mind? In A. Sinclair, R. Jarvella, & W. J. M. Levelt (Eds.), *The child's conception of language*. New York: Springer-Verlag, 1978.

Hochberg, J. E. Attention, organization and consciousness. In D. I. Mostofsky (Ed.), *Attention: Contemporary theory and analysis*. New York: Appleton-Century-Crofts, 1970.

Hochberg, J. E. *Perception* (2d ed.). Englewood Cliffs, N.J.: Prentice-Hall, 1978.

James, H. (Ed.). *The letters of William James* (2 vols.). Boston: Atlantic Monthly Press, 1920.

James, W. *The principles of psychology* (2 vols.). New York: Holt, 1890.

Koffka, K. *Gestalt psychology*. New York: Harcourt, Brace, 1935.

Markman, E. M. Realizing that you don't understand: A preliminary investigation. *Child Development*, 1977, *48*, 986–992.

Marshall, J. C., & Morton, J. On the mechanics of Emma. In A. Sinclair, R. J. Jarvella, & W. J. M. Levelt (Eds.), *The child's conception of language*. New York: Springer-Verlag, 1978.

Mill, J. S. *An examination of Sir William Hamilton's philosophy*. London: Longman, Green, Longman, Roberts and Green, 1865.

Neisser, U. *Cognition and reality*. San Francisco: Freeman, 1976.

Rozin, P., & Gleitman, L. R. The structure and acquisition of reading II: The reading process and the acquisition of the alphabetic principle. In A. S. Reber & D. Scarborough (Eds.), *Toward a psychology of reading*. Hillsdale, N.J.: Erlbaum, 1977.

Sachs, J. S. Recognition memory for syntactic and semantic aspects of connected discourse. *Perception and Psychophysics*, 1967, *2*, 437–442.

Schank, R., & Abelson, R. *Scripts, plans, goals and understanding*. Hillsdale, N.J.: Erlbaum, 1977.

Titchener, E. B. *An outline of psychology*. New York: Macmillan, 1896.

435

Titchener, E. B. *Lectures on the experimental psychology of the thought processes.* New York: Macmillan, 1909.

Tolman, E. C. *Purposive behavior in animals and men.* New York: Century, 1932.

Woodworth, R. S. *Experimental psychology.* New York: Holt, 1938.

Wundt, W. *Völkerpsychologie* (Vol. 1). Leipzig: Verlag von Wilhelm Engelmann, 1900.

Wundt, W. *Grundriss der Psychologie* (13th ed.). Leipzig: Alfred Kröner Verlag, 1918.

Zigler, M. J. An experimental study of the perception of clamminess. *American Journal of Psychology,* 1923, 34, 550–561.

18

Psyche and the Computer
INTEGRATING THE SHADOW

FREDERICK J. CROSSON

Some of the most seminal work in recent years in the sciences of mankind has been directed toward discerning the structures which constrain fields of human activity previously seen as more reflective of the creative or free productions of the human spirit. I think, for example, of the project of sociobiology, of the work of Propp in the analysis of the formal structure of folktales, of the theory of myth of Lévi-Strauss, which views myth as the mediation of binary functions, expressed in images of opposition and dilemma. Lévi-Strauss is quite explicit that latent structures are not conscious to the individual and that they are rooted ultimately in the nervous system as their organic base. Propp's formalist analysis of folktales is expressed in a symbolism which can be flow-charted, and an Israeli group has already computerized some of these functions in a "generative poetics" to analyze and construct stories on the computer. The uniformities which Propp discovered are not culture-specific, which suggests deeper, psychological origins for the regularities. In these cases and others, we are led to the inference of *internal* formal constraints on social organization, on myth-making, on story-telling. And there are "computational" transformations involved in each process, some of which can be formally represented and derived.

Many of these constraints—formal conditions of our doing and making—are most saliently rendered in the digital computer, that universal machine (for which we may perhaps borrow a term from the new kitchen armament and call it simply "La Machine"). The computer is, many of us have come to believe, made in the image and likeness of man, at least of man's mind. But just as theologians differ over what the *imago dei* means, so psychologists differ over how one is to understand the computer's information processing as *like* human information processing. Is it the generic identity of species of information-processing systems, or are we dealing only with an analogy or metaphor? Note that *either* of these disjuncts may be illuminating for psychological investigation. Even if people and machines are *not*, in the same generic sense, information-processing systems, even if the machine's states and operations are only analogous to those of man, the analogy may be far-reaching and provide us with a fruitful way of thinking about ourselves.

With respect to scientific psychology, the two most important developments in the last thirty years have been the work of Chomsky on transformational linguistics and the work on artificial intelligence, that is, the programming of computers to simulate human achievements. As these two areas have progressed, they have had the effect of nudging aside the behaviorist proscription on psychological theories about internal structures, in particular, innate or genetically programmed structures. The notion that there is a set of innate grammatical rules and of preprogrammed ("wired-in") cognitive structures has opened up or reopened a new dimension for psychological inquiry. In particular, the work in artificial intelligence showed that we could find an information-processing system capable of cognitive tasks which was certainly quite independent of neurology and whose achievements were based on design rather than wholly due to learned procedures.

Although these two developments are by no means obviously complementary, since one of them deals with a theory of structure and competence while the other deals with performance, the combined effect of their success has been to recover the field of internal formal structures for psychological theory. Moreover, they concur in not appealing to consciousness or to introspection for the evidence of their claims, and it is this which has helped to lend them the credibility of scientific theories.

It is of course to the computer model that I shall speak, and I want to touch briefly on the history of its present status, to make some remarks about the idea of a model, and finally to discuss some problematic areas of "cognitive psychology," which I shall take as a general name for that movement of psychological theorizing which accepts the computer as a model for its inquiries about internal structures. Skinner has said that the computer is a bad model, and it is far from clear that there are not serious deficiencies in it as a model. But there is no doubt that it is a major alternative to radical behaviorism at the present time if psychology is to be scientific in some traditional sense of that term.

From Performance to Theory

Computers were developed of course as *instruments*, that is, they were developed in the "performance mode," to take over certain human tasks (solving differential equations) which were too complicated and/or time-consuming for people to do. No attempt is made, of course, in the performance mode of utilizing computers to simulate the psychological manner in which a human thinker fulfills the same task. It is indeed still common to begin the performance of such a task by adverting to the manner in which a human being approaches the task, collecting protocols as the person consciously expresses how he or she goes about addressing the task. But then the project is to find a way to achieve that same end by whatever means are efficient, however distant this may be from the manner in which the person consciously proceeds. Thus, recent chess-playing programs trace the possible moves to be considered as much as thirty-some moves ahead, while even the most expert human player never explicitly envisages more than four or five moves ahead within the context of a general strategy.

McCulloch and Pitts had already noted in the early 1940s that there was a structural similarity between the binary character of logical inferences and the neural networks of the brain. But the workers in the computer field, at that time, were oriented toward performance, and although the similarities were interesting, they did not provoke a concern with the *psychological* dimension.

It was indeed the paper of A. M. Turing, "Computing Machinery and Intelligence," published in the *philosophical* journal *Mind* in 1950, which boldly proposed a test for deciding the question of whether machines could be said to think, and which argued that computers could eventually be programmed to exhibit the information and intelligence necessary to have that psychological predicate ascribed to them. Within five years, the first papers on pattern recognition (by Selfridge, 1955, and Dineen, 1955), claiming artificial intelligence for computers, were published. The later 1950s and 1960s saw a veritable explosion of work in artificial intelligence, most of which did not take the form of psychological inquiry but, rather, simulated human cognitive performances. But some psychologists had already been asking questions about psychological processes in a way which made them open and receptive to these developments in artificial intelligence.

Hebb had published his *Organization of Behavior* in 1949, and later he described his approach in these terms:

> The significance of the theory is principally in trying to get these central processes out of the bushes where we can look at them. Everyone knows that set and expectancy and the stimulus trace exist. How are we to learn more about these ideational or mediating processes, and the limits on their role in behavior, except by forming hypotheses (as explicit as we can reasonably make them) and then seeing what implications they have for behavior, and whether these implications are borne out in experiment. By all means, if you will, call these central events mediating processes instead of ideas or cell assemblies, but let us get busy and investigate them (Hebb, 1959, pp. 629–630).

By 1960, the work of Miller, Galanter, and Pribram, *Plans and the Structure of Behavior*, was assimilating the work that had been done by computer scientists in such a way as to make it relevant to the situation of psychological research.

Influential in these developments was the work of Newell, Shaw, and Simon on the Logic Theorist (1957) and, of course, the GPS, or General Problem Solver (1963). Simon compared the importance of the computer for psychology to that of the microscope for biology. It provided a way to set up experiments in such a manner as to test constructs which had been formulated for psychological processes in a sharp and unequivocal manner. (If only that were *less* an analogy, and we were able to *see directly* with the computer!) The computer has gone through several generations in the last thirty years, and the field of artificial intelligence has expanded similarly: from pattern recognition and checker playing in the early 1950s, through theorem proving in logic and mathematics, chess, natural language interpretation, IQ tests, music composition, and the construction of robots equipped with sensory inputs and effectors. Psychological theory which takes the computer as a model has not developed at anything like that mushrooming speed, but that is in large part a reflection of the fact that artificial intelligence has worked largely in the performance mode, and as we have seen, this is sometimes without any immediate illumination for the related psychological processes.

In any case, computers are the best model we have now as an alternative to the model which behaviorism began from: namely, less complex animals. Like those animals, it appears to lend itself to objectivity in research because it does not involve us with the problem of subjective interpretation. We have designed the computer to perform *some* human functions, but no one has seriously suggested that we have to worry about computers deceiving us—yet. And the analytic rigor which programming forces on us demands that the operations be univocally defined, leaving no room for the kind of interpretation which, say, psychoanalysis requires.

The computer presents itself as a model because, it is argued, when it succeeds in simulating a human cognitive function, the program constitutes *a* theory of how the function is computed from (presumably) the same type of input data; and the programmed computer is therefore a model of the way in which the human agent computes the same function. (I shall postpone for the moment more detailed comment on the model notion.)

Note that it is not the mere external simulation that grounds the likeness: a tape recorder can replicate my speaking, but it offers no ground to be described as a psychological model for my speaking. There must also be in the model the simulation of my linguistic *capacities*: vocabulary, ability to generate phrase structures and grammatically valid sentences, response to questions, and so forth. And finally there must be—most crucial and problematic—simulation of the psychological *processes* by which I exercise those capacities. It is not, of course, physiological or neurological sameness of processes which is in question here but, rather, the computing of the function in the same way.

440

Some caveats have been raised about the cognitive starkness of the computer model, e.g., the absence of any affective dimension or any sense of "style." (Samuel, 1959, has noted that checker champions who played against his very successful program commented on the absence of any sense of overall strategy or style of play in the game.) But one must begin somewhere, and it is at least arguable that the cognitive functions are logically distinct, if not normally separated in fact, from noncognitive factors in human beings.

What distinguishes the computer as a model is the internal complexity of its possible interconnections and the sequencing of subroutines in the execution of any effective procedure, that is, any function which we can divide exhaustively into univocally specifiable parts. It disposes of a complex logical space by means of internal representations of the possible relevant subfunctions which constitute the effective procedure required.

Now it is precisely this flexibility, this capacity to employ now this path, now that, depending on the task to be performed, that leads—that has led—to the ascription of intentional predicates to the programmed computer-based system. We speak of the system as responding on the basis of the *way in which it represents* the task to be executed, on the basis of the way it "understands" the input, of the way it "believes" the input is to be taken. It is just this characteristic which leads to speaking of agency, of acting rather than simply reacting, and which therefore takes us out of a pure S-R or radical behaviorist framework. Just as human persons act not simply in response to an environmental stimulus but on the basis of the way they *construe* that stimulus, *represent* that stimulus—the *proximal* stimulus, as the Gestaltists said, as distinguished from the *distal* stimulus—so the computer responds on the basis of the way it construes or represents the input.

No one has argued for this model more intelligently, ambitiously, or effectively, to my mind, than Jerry Fodor in his book, *The Language of Thought* (1975). He takes every psychological event to be a physical event, but shows that this is not reductionist—psychology cannot be replaced by neurology or physics—because the psychological events are not identical with the natural unities, the natural *kinds* of entities that physics (or neurology) studies, any more than the notion of a monetary exchange in economics can be given a *physical* description which would be a proper predicate for a law of physics.

The machine language of the computer he holds to be one whose semantic properties "correspond directly to computationally relevant physical states and operations of the machine." It is in this "innate" language that the representations of the inputs are couched for every available level on which the inputs can be meaningfully analyzed, and it is this language into which the compiler translates the programming language. As a psychological model, the programming language corresponds to our natural, learned language, which we acquire by constructing, so to speak, a compiler which matches the truth conditions of the predicates in the natural language with those of the genetically innate ("machine") language of

441

thought. We learn what a predicate means by representing in that innate language a hypothesis about its extension, that is, about the rules for its attribution. And, Fodor asserts, we have "no notion at all" of how a first language might be learned except by such a process of hypothesis formation and confirmation.

There is, of course, no claim that we are *conscious* of all of these representations and computations: what is offered is a *theory* about what conditions seem to be necessary in order to explain perception, motivation, learning, and so on. The ground of the theory is, on the one hand, reflection about what shape a psychological theory of such cognitive processes seems to require, and, on the other hand, a certain amount of experimental evidence which seems to confirm the postulated states and operations.

I am tempted to characterize Fodor's theory (it is more, as he says, the *schema* of a theory) as hylomorphic, because (1) it holds that every psychological event is a physical event—that is, has both a physical and a psychological (intentional or semantic) description; (2) it rejects a reductionist identity theory; (3) it is not a psychophysical parallelism theory; (4) it does not appeal to consciousness as the defining characteristic of the psychological.

Be that as it may, I have brought it in here because I believe it to be a most cogent defense of the computer as a model for psychology, and one which faces candidly some of the basic problems with that model. I return to its problematic aspects in the following sections.

One final observation about a related field. Information theory, which has been closely related to some work in computer science, has not had the same influence on psychological research as the computer has. Some effort was made in the 1950s and 1960s to utilize information theory in the analysis of perception—I think particularly of the work of Fred Attneave (e.g., 1959)—but it seems to have had no widespread continuing issue. I believe this is because, although the experimental work that was done was intriguing, it involved the artificial gridding of the perceptual input in order to identify or designate the bits which served as units of information-theoretic analysis. But defining the elementary *psychological* units of perception is a problematic affair: even on the neurological level, the interconnection of sensory cells and related inhibition of firing and the feedback from central assemblies to peripheral transducers limit the extent to which a one-to-one analysis of *perceptual* bit and cell response is feasible.

To put this in another way, the information-theoretic analysis of perception would seem to be necessarily extensional, and, as we have seen, what marks the computer model is the tendency to attribute intentional states to the cognitive process, states not reducible to equivalent extensional description.

But it may be that a way will be found to make this approach more fruitful once again. (My colleague Ken Sayre has pursued this direction in several challenging works.) In neurological study of the brain, at any rate, where information units are more naturally discriminated and quantified, information theory is likely to be more productive. Conversely, the computer model for neurobiologists seems unhelpful. Francis H. C. Crick (1979) has expressed a forthright refusal of the computer as a model for brain research on the grounds (among others) that the brain exhibits nonbinary coding, multiplex parallel processing, and redundancy.

Metaphor, Model, Theory

I want now to look more closely at the notion of a model, because we are considering here the programmed computer as a model for psychological inquiry.

Let us begin with the notion of a metaphor. A metaphor is the ascription of a predicate from one domain, where it has a literal sense, to a subject which does not belong to that domain, and hence where the ascription is not literal but nevertheless is somehow revealing, meaningful. Some metaphors are poetic—their power lies in their immediate juxtaposition, they are not meant to be unpacked, to draw causal consequences from. But some metaphors are explanatory: they suggest ways to think about the subject to which they are applied, they function heuristically.

A model is a metaphor of a particular kind. (It will become apparent that I am going to be using the term *model* as it is used in scientific *inquiry*, e.g., water waves as a model for explaining sound and light.) A metaphor moves toward becoming a model not only when we know it better in some respect than we know the subject to which it is applied—this characterizes any explanatory metaphor—but when we have or develop a logical or mathematical *theory*, however rudimentary, for the metaphorical predicate and we try to extend that theory to the subject, the explanandum.

Consider the following model for a memory trace, taken from René Descartes in the seventeenth century:

> . . . these traces are nothing but the fact that those pores of the brain through which the [animal] spirits have formerly passed . . . have in that way acquired a greater facility than the other [pores] for being once more opened by the animal spirits. . . .[1] (*The Passions of the Soul*, 1649, Article 62).

The model suggests a hydraulic theory of the brain. It draws on phenomena which are more familiar and accessible than the postulated brain traces in order to try to understand some properties of long-term memory. (Descartes is of course following in the footsteps of Harvey, who a little earlier had successfully applied a hydraulic model to the cardiovascular system; he spoke of the "locks" and "canals" of the system.)

---

[1] For "animal spirits" read "neural impulse" and for "pores" read "synapse."

We can say that the theory is *instantiated* by the model. But we are inquiring whether, on the basis of the similarity expressed by the metaphor, we can *extend* the theory to the *explanandum*. If the extension succeeds, then the model becomes unnecessary, it ceases to serve any heuristic purpose because we can apply the theory *directly* to the phenomena of the explanandum.

Newell, Shaw, and Simon wrote some years ago (1962) that a successful artificial intelligence program is a model or theory of the human thinking which it simulates. This statement mixes two senses of "model" whose distinction we need to be aware of.

One sense is this: Weizenbaum (1976) rightly says that a program can be characterized as a theory, but it is not a model: the model is the programmed computer which executes the program. In this sense, he goes on to say, "the connection between a model and a theory is that a model *satisfies* a theory." In fact, of course, the computer is *built* to satisfy a theory of computability. But often in the history of science, a theory is worked out to account for what is *already* perceived as a model or analogy. And this is the *other* sense of model, the one based on metaphor. It is in *this* sense that we speak of water waves as a model for light.

The second sense might be described as the heuristic model, or the inquirer's model. It differs from the first sense of model by including a heuristic or indeterminate element. More adequately we can say that the inquirer's model has *some* properties *similar* to those of the explanandum, some properties *different* from the explanandum, and *some whose status is unclear*, just so long as it functions as a heuristic model. And it is just the latter properties which lead to new predictions about the explanandum. So the model, in its indeterminate aspects, has an essential role in guiding inquiry.

In contrast, the sense of model as that which satisfies the theory has no indeterminate elements: this is to say it simply and clearly satisfies the theory.

For example, when the properties of light were being explored by Huyghens on the model of waves, he did not know how many of the mathematically related properties of waves would turn out to have correlates with the phenomena of light: reflection, diffraction, frequency, amplitude, medium of propagation?

So to say that the theory of the model *is* the theory of the explanandum is to run together these two senses of "model." That is why I think Weizenbaum is right to insist that it is not the theory/program that is the model, the programmed computer is. And it is relevant here to advert again to the fact that Fodor finds analogies for psychology in the internal mechanisms of the computer, e.g., the compiler.

This is also why I should want to consider the claims that man and computer are two species of the genus "information-processing system" as a hypothesis. Perhaps that is the case, as water and sound waves are two different embodiments of the same formal theory. But the fact that a model computes the same function— simulates the performance—does not necessarily imply that the theory of the model *is* the theory of the explanandum.

444

As Flavell (1963) has written in making a similar point about Piaget's theory of cognitive structures, "logically possible cognitive structures" are not the same as "empirically discovered logical structures." The evidence for the claim that the same, that is, isomorphic structures and processes are in the explanandum cannot come from the fact that they are derivable in the theory and instantiated by the model which simulates the performance in question. Whether the same process of derivation is followed by the organism is an empirical question, and to address it we need to design experiments which confirm the hypothesis without begging the question.

As Skinner (1974) and others have insisted, there is, for example, *no behavioral or introspective* evidence of a search and retrieval process for many of the performances which we term *remembering*. But unless we define psychology by those two dimensions, there is no obstacle in principle to confirming the hypothesis of non-conscious psychological events. Mendel was ingenious enough to devise experiments which confirmed microstructures inaccessible by any other means at the time (and for long afterward).

So, I should say, the computer model (in the heuristic sense) still seems promising: one must simply be wary of the temptation to which behaviorism succumbed and which is a temptation for any elaborated theory, namely the procrustean bed of ignoring the phenomena that don't fit, of *defining* psychological processes to fit the theory.

God knows, there are enough dissimilarities to give one pause, phenomena which we understand too poorly simply to set aside: hemispheric differentiation; sleep; the unconscious; the emotions. Maybe these are all separable dissimilarities which do not ingress upon cognitive processes. Maybe not.

All one can do in the present situation, before we have a computer analogue for these—and at present it is unclear what it would be like to represent, say, the unconscious in a computer—or have evidence of the separability of cognitive processes from such phenomena, all we can do is assume that they *are* sufficiently separable until contrary evidence emerges.

Ordinary Language, Introspection, and Tacit Knowing

I want now to touch on three problems, of different degrees of seriousness, concerned with the formulation of cognitive theories and their confirmation. I shall mention the form in which the issues occur in Fodor's book, but I believe they are quite general problems.

First is the problem of the language in which we describe the phenomena to be accounted for.

When we are guided by a model or explanatory metaphor, it is perfectly natural and legitimate to attempt to describe the psychological events to be explained in

445

some, at least, of the language appropriate to the model. (Compare the extension of the notion of a medium of propagation for light waves, though this subsequently turned out to be an element of dissimilarity, that is, proper only to the model.) At the same time, some of the ordinary language terms which have been used to designate or describe the psychological phenomena will have to shift their meaning in order to conform to the requirements of the model.

Consider two such ordinary-language terms: internal *representations* are *assigned* to environmental stimuli, to behavioral options, to hypotheses about the truth-conditions of predicates being learned, and so on. Both of these terms, *representations* and *assign*, have ordinary language connotations which must be pruned to fit the description, guided by the model.

"Representation" is the name for a triadic relation: x represents y for (or to) z, the conscious organism. But to be consistent with the model that is guiding us, we need a sense in which x represents y without any reference to such a z. Is that a consistent sense? Possibly so. Compare the analogy of the genetic "code" which conveys instructions without any reference to a reader of the code.

"Assigns" is harder. We can understand a first sense in which we assign interpretations or representations to ambiguous figures—we can often do that consciously at will (the proximal stimulus). The phenomenon is quite general: every sentence is, after all, an "ambiguous figure" at many levels of analysis—phonetic, syntactic, semantic. Every sentence can receive an indefinite variety of representations at each level. Sometimes we are *conscious* of a variety of representations; always we can voluntarily assign a variety of interpretations.

Here again, to fit the model, we need a sense of "assign" which does not necessarily connote conscious and voluntary assigning. This is crucial to sustain the claim that "causal relations between stimulus and response are *typically* mediated by the organism's internal representations of each." Representations, Fodor argues, are not *elicited* (then we would be back with associational stimulus-response chains) but assigned, and "*which* representation is assigned is determined by calculations which rationally subserve the utilities of the organism."

Once again: is there a consistent sense in which we can say a representation *is* assigned without implying necessarily an agent or quasi-agent who does the assigning? Perhaps. But even if there is, we have to be wary that we do not surreptitiously carry over the ordinary language sense and implicitly appeal to *that* sense of the term in our argument. (The same caveat applies to the, again quite normal, retroactive extension of terms from the sphere of the explanandum to that of the model.)

Another problematic area of cognitive theory where the danger of surreptitious baggage occurs is in the regular appeal, in getting arguments off the ground, to introspection. Professor Skinner prudently avoided appeals to conscious experience, as the jogger avoids the swamp. (Personally, I don't think we can completely avoid the swamp, though the sooner we get out, the better. If we can. Maybe the whole field is swampy.) In any case, beginning with the protocols of problem-solvers, chess players, and so on has been standard practice for AI in order to get the analysis of a task under way. Fodor constantly appeals to our experience and introspection of understanding sentences, imagining, learning, and so forth.

The case never rests there, to be sure. Experimental evidence is often cited, though often, too, we are limited to the conjecturing of intelligent hypotheses about nonconscious psychological processes, cast in the language of representations and their computational transformation.

The problem is whether introspective descriptions can be reliably adequate to the phenomena they attempt to capture. Francis Crick (1979) asserts flatly that "we are deceived at every level by our introspection." *His* reason is the neurological one that "what we can report is only a minute fraction of what goes on in our head." But Michael Polanyi (1964, 1966) made the same point without any neurological reference in asserting that we know more than we can tell. The danger is always that in giving or accepting a focal, specific description of any phenomenon, we may be dealing with a caricature because we cannot render explicit all of the clues which enter into our discerning of the phenomenon. Behind every cognitive performance, Polanyi argued, however simple in appearance, lies a skill which relies on a multitude of unspecifiable (at least, not exhaustively specifiable) clues.

To say they are unspecifiable is, of course, to say they are nonconscious, and indeed it is just the effort of cognitive psychology to formulate hypotheses (and confirm them) about what the nonconscious factors responsible for our states and operations are. The question I am raising is whether the digital computer, for which every element of a representation and computation must be simply present or absent, in which everything must be spelled out, is an *adequate* model for the *exercise* of such tacit knowing? How is the *tacit* knowledge of a grammatical rule to be represented in a computer where representations are, like the symbols on a Turing machine tape, either present or absent? It is not enough for the rule to be "wired-in" but not known, for then the utterances would merely *satisfy* or conform to the rule.

This issue can be expressed in a different way in the terms of Fodor's theory (1975). He speaks generally of a representation as a psychological entity, a sort of atomic substate of the organism. To assign a representation is, for example, to give a physical stimulus-event a meaning (for some level of analysis). But what makes a representation present one or another significance is the field or context to which it is assimilated. This is why the inference from input to percept is nondemonstrative. (Think how you could give the phrase "his grip is worse" different semantic representations *by thinking of different situations* in which it might be spoken.)

In discussing perception, for example, Fodor speaks of the perceptual analysis of an event being determined by the integration of sensory information and "*background* knowledge" brought to the task ("two kinds of information"). The perceptual representation *does not stand alone*, it bears its meaning only in the context of that (indefinitely large and unspecifiable) background knowledge. What characterizes

447

our awareness of meaning in any modality, it seems to me, is just that it is constituted by the copresence of the explicit and the tacit, the occurrence of an event inside our body (a neural event) and our making sense of it by assimilating it to a context.

Conclusion

Let me conclude. This is by no means a counsel of despair. I believe it is certainly possible to identify nonconscious psychological entities, both in theory and experimentally. To say that they are psychological is to say that they have a *sense* for the organism, but not an explicit consciousness. (Actually, phenomenology after Husserl has moved in the same direction of extending the notion of sense or significance to the explanation of the behavior of organisms: Merleau-Ponty, Ricoeur.) I suspect that some of the experimental work done under a behaviorist aegis could be reread under this perspective and provide indications for further work.

The great advantage of the computer is that it provides us with a model of ratiocination where all data must be explicit, and it therefore forces us to specify the elements which enter only tacitly (nonconsciously) into our cognitive performances. This is, to my mind, what provides the intellectual challenge and fascination of work in simulation. But I do not see that there is any a priori reason, neurological or psychological, to suppose that the computer will prove to be an *adequate* model for these performances. It may only reveal to us how deeply our cognitive processes are embedded in inarticulate skills.

If that is right, we will learn something about ourselves by pursuing that model just as the programs for machine translation of natural languages taught us so much about the relations of syntax and semantics in natural languages. And artificial intelligence in the performance mode will, I believe, outstrip us in all those areas where ratiocination is of the essence. But the shadow which psychology may have to integrate is more likely to be the tacit dimension than the computer.

REFERENCES

Attneave, F. *Application of information theory to psychology: A summary of basic concepts, methods, and results.* New York: Holt, Rinehart & Winston, 1959.

Crick, F. H. C. Thinking about the brain. *Scientific American*, 1979, 241, 219–232.

Dineen, G. P. Programming pattern recognition. *Proceedings of the Western Joint Computer Conference* (Institute of Radio Engineers), 1955, 94–100.

Flavell, J. H. *The developmental psychology of Jean Piaget.* New York: Van Nostrand, 1963.

Fodor, J. A. *The language of thought.* New York: Crowell, 1975.

Hebb, D. O. *The organization of behavior: A neuropsychological theory.* New York: Wiley, 1949.

Hebb, D. O. A neuropsychological theory. In S. Koch (Ed.), *Psychology: A study of a science* (Vol. 1). New York: McGraw-Hill, 1959.

McCulloch, W. S., & Pitts, W. H. A logical calculus of the ideas immanent in nervous activity. *Bulletin of Mathematical Biophysics*, 1943, *5*, 115–133.

Miller, G. A., Galanter, E., & Pribram, K. H. *Plans and the structure of behavior*. New York: Holt, Rinehart & Winston, 1960.

Newell, A., Shaw, J. C., & Simon, H. A. Empirical explorations with the logic theory machine. *Proceedings of the Western Joint Computer Conference* (Institute of Radio Engineers), 1957, 230–240.

Newell, A., Shaw, J. C., & Simon, H. A. The processes of creative thinking. In H. E. Gruber, G. Terrell, & M. Wertheimer (Eds.), *Contemporary approaches to creative thinking*. New York: Atherton, 1962.

Newell, A., & Simon, H. A. GPS, a program that simulates human thought. In E. A. Feigenbaum & J. Feldman (Eds.), *Computers and thought*. New York: McGraw-Hill, 1963.

Polanyi, M. *Personal knowledge: Towards a post-critical philosophy*. New York: Harper & Row, 1964.

Polanyi, M. The logic of tacit inference. *Philosophy*, 1966, *41*, 1–18.

Samuel, A. L. Some studies in machine learning using the game of checkers. *IBM Journal of Research and Development*, 1959, *3*, 210–229.

Sayre, K. M. *Consciousness: A philosophic study of minds and machines*. New York: Random House, 1969.

Sayre, K. M. *Cybernetics and the philosophy of mind*. Atlantic Highlands, N.J.: Humanities Press, 1976.

Selfridge, O. G. Pattern recognition and modern computers. *Proceedings of the Western Joint Computer Conference* (Institute of Radio Engineers), 1955, 91–93.

Skinner, B. F. *About behaviorism*. New York: Knopf, 1974.

Turing, A. M. Computing machinery and intelligence, *Mind*, 1950, *59*, 433–460.

Weizenbaum, J. *Computer power and human reason: From judgment to calculation*. San Francisco: Freeman, 1976.

SUPPLEMENTARY READINGS[2]

The following works provide useful introductions to the field covered in this chapter. Many of the classic articles in this field have been reprinted in the collective volumes indicated under their editors in this selective bibliography.

Abelson, R. P., & Carroll, J. D. Computer simulation of individual belief systems. *American Behavioral Scientist*, 1965, *8*, 24–30.

[2] A great deal of the current work is in the form of technical reports, especially from the artificial intelligence labs at Stanford and the Massachusetts Institute of Technology. These have been omitted because of their restricted circulation. In addition to the specific titles listed, the following annuals and journals may be consulted for ongoing research and further reference:

Proceedings of the First International Joint Conference on Artificial Intelligence. Washington, D.C.: 1969. Second, 1971; Third, 1973; Fourth, 1975.

Journal of the Association for Computing Machinery.

Machine Intelligence 1. Edinburgh: Edinburgh University Press, 1967. 2, 1968; 3, 1968; 4, 1969; 5, 1970; 6, 1971; 7, 1972. (Originally published by Oliver & Boyd.)

Cognitive Psychology.

Abelson, R. P., & Rosenberg, M. J. Symbolic psycho-logic: A model of attitudinal cognition. *Behavioral Science*, 1958, 3, 1–13.

Arbib, M. A. *The metaphorical brain: An introduction to cybernetics as artificial intelligence and brain theory*. New York: Wiley, 1972.

Boden, M. A. *Purposive explanation in psychology*. Cambridge, Mass.: Harvard University Press, 1972.

Chase, W. G. (Ed.). *Visual information processing*. New York: Academic Press, 1973.

Chase, W. G., & Simon, H. A. Perception in chess. *Cognitive Psychology*, 1973, 4, 55–81.

Clippinger, J. H. *Meaning and discourse: A computer model of psychoanalytic discourse and cognition*. Baltimore: Johns Hopkins University Press, 1977.

Colby, K. M. *Artificial paranoia*. New York: Pergamon, 1975.

Crosson, F. J. (Ed.). *Human and artificial intelligence*. New York: Appleton-Century-Crofts, 1970.

Dennett, D. C. *Content and consciousness*. London: Routledge & Kegan Paul, 1969.

Dreyfus, H. L. *What computers can't do: A critique of artificial reason*. New York: Harper & Row, 1972.

Ernst, G. W., & Newell, A. *GPS: A case study in generality and problem solving*. New York: Academic Press, 1969.

Feigenbaum, E. A., & Feldman, J. (Eds.). *Computers and thought*. New York: McGraw-Hill, 1963.

Fodor, J. A. *Psychological explanation: An introduction to the philosophy of psychology*. New York: Random House, 1968.

Goffman, E. *Frame analysis: An essay on the organization of experience*. New York: Harper & Row 1974.

Lettvin, J. Y., Maturana, H. R., Pitts, W., & McCulloch, W. S. What the frog's eye tells the frog's brain. *Proceedings of the Institute of Radio Engineers*, 1959, 47, 1940–1959.

Lindsay, P. H., & Norman, D. A. *Human information processing: An introduction to psychology*. New York: Academic Press, 1972.

Loehlin, J. C. *Computer models of personality*. New York: Random House, 1968.

McCulloch, W. S. A heterarchy of values determined by the topology of nervous nets. *Bulletin of Mathematical Biophysics*, 1949, 11, 89–93.

Mackay, D. M. A mind's eye view of the brain. In N. Wiener & J. P. Schadé (Eds.), *Progress in brain research, 17: Cybernetics of the nervous system*. Amsterdam: Elsevier, 1965.

Meehan, J. Using planning structures to generate stories. *American Journal of Computational Linguistics*, 1975, Microfiche 33, 77–93.

Michie, D. *On machine intelligence*. Edinburgh: Edinburgh University Press, 1974.

Miller, G. A., & Johnson-Laird, P. N. *Language and perception*. Cambridge, Mass.: Harvard University Press, 1976.

Minsky, M. L. (Ed.). *Semantic information processing*. Cambridge, Mass.: M.I.T. Press, 1968.

Minsky, M. L., & Papert, S. *Artificial intelligence*. Eugene, Oreg.: Condon Lecture Publications, 1973.

Moser, Ulrich, von Zeppelin, I., and Schneider, W. Computer simulation of a model of neurotic defense processes. *Behavioral Science*, 1970, 15, 194–202.

Neisser, U. *Cognitive psychology*. New York: Appleton-Century-Crofts, 1967.

Newell, A., & Simon, H. A. *Human problem solving*. Englewood Cliffs, N.J.: Prentice-Hall, 1972.

Pylyshyn, Z. W. What the mind's eye tells the mind's brain: A critique of mental imagery. *Psychological Bulletin*, 1973, 80, 1–24.

Pylyshyn, Z. W. Minds, machines, and phenomenology: Some reflections on Dreyfus' "What computers can't do." *Cognition*, 1974, 2, 20–42.

Raphael, B. *The thinking computer: Mind inside matter*. San Francisco: Freeman, 1976.

Reitman, W. R. *Cognition and thought: An information-processing approach*. New York: Wiley, 1965.

Schank, R. C. Conceptual dependence: A theory of natural language understanding. *Cognitive Psychology*, 1972, 3, 552–631.

Schank, R. C. (Ed.). *Conceptual information processing*. New York: American Elsevier, 1975.

450

Schank, R. C., & Colby, K. M. (Eds.). *Computer models of thought and language.* San Francisco: Freeman, 1973.

Simon, H. A. *The sciences of the artificial.* Cambridge, Mass.: M.I.T. Press, 1969.

Sloman, A. *The computer revolution in philosophy: Philosophy, science, and models of mind.* Hassocks, Sussex: Harvester Press; N.J.: Humanities Press, 1978.

Wiener, N. *Cybernetics, or control and communication in the animal and the machine.* New York: Wiley, 1948.

Wilks, Y. A. *Grammar, meaning, and the machine analysis of natural language.* London: Routledge & Kegan Paul, 1972.

Wilks, Y. A. Dreyfus' disproofs. *British Journal of Philosophical Science,* 1976, 27, 177–185.

Winograd, T. *Understanding natural language.* New York: Academic Press, 1972. (Revised version of *Procedures as a representation for data in a computer program for understanding natural language.* AI-TR-17. Cambridge, Mass.: M.I.T. AI Lab., 1971.)

Winston, P. H. (Ed.). *The psychology of computer vision.* New York: McGraw-Hill, 1975.

Yovits, M. C., Jacobi, G. T., & Goldstein, G. D. (Eds.). *Self-organizing systems 1962.* Washington, D.C.: Spartan, 1962.

DEVELOPMENT

19

A Century of Character Development*

JANE LOEVINGER

Interest in the development of character is at least as old as written history; there-fore, to speak of a century of studying character development is arbitrary. It serves, however, to limit our purview, which would otherwise be boundless. Let us, then, look at some of the main trends in its study during the hundred years that have seen the rise of modern experimental-statistical psychology.

There was a period in recent history when study of character development was neglected, an embarrassing if not actually taboo topic. This was probably because of the problem which Köhler (1938) called "the place of value in a world of facts." Psychologists, shaky about their standing as scientists, tried to avoid any topics that were possibly tainted with values. In contrast, during the nineteenth century, character development was considered a central problem of pedagogy and the very reason that pedagogy needed to be grounded in psychology (Leary, 1979). In prescientific psychology, character development was a central preoccupation. Of course it has always been of immense importance to some educators. Wundt himself, who wrote a book on ethics (1886/1897–1901), would certainly not have scorned the topic.

The last decade of the nineteenth century saw important books by James Mark

*Preparation of this essay was supported by Research Scientist Award MH-00657 from the National Institute of Mental Health, U.S. Public Health Service, and by a grant from the Spencer Foundation.

Baldwin (1897/1902) and Sigmund Freud (Breuer & Freud, 1895/1955; Freud, 1900/1953), which initiated the seminal contributions of those two gigantic figures. Their lines of thought are still reverberating in some of the most recent work in the field. One of Baldwin's central contributions he called the "dialectic of personal growth." The infant first learns to distinguish persons from other objects in the environment; then he learns to see himself as a person among persons, but having feelings he cannot observe in others; then he learns to think of others as having feelings he has discerned in himself. This dialectical process, the child seeing self in the light of what he or she observes in others and inferring in others what he or she feels within self, is repeated over and over, each time at a higher level of complexity. As a result, the content of ego and alter ego are much the same; one thinks of self and others in the same terms.

The young child, according to Baldwin, imitates those more powerful, and toward them he or she is altruistic; but he or she practices on those less powerful, and toward them is apt to be aggressive and selfish. Gradually the child learns to see both sides of himself or herself, both the aggressive egoist and the accommodating pupil, and then he or she learns to see both possibilities in others. Another element is added when he or she constructs an ideal self, a "copy for imitation," at first modeled after parents, but gradually generalized so that even his or her models are required to adhere to it. But as I learn to conform to it, said Baldwin, "I forever find new patterns set for me; and so my ethical insight must always find its profoundest expression in that yearning which anticipates but does not overtake the ideal" (Baldwin, 1897/1902, p. 42).

In emphasizing that these ideas are to be found in Baldwin's 1897 book, I do not mean to imply that he had no predecessors, simply that later authors have been given credit for originating these same ideas. The moving principle in development was, for Baldwin, a kind of instinct of imitation, and that sounds foreign to our ears. But *instinct* for him never meant something hereditary or an innate releasing mechanism. Strike the obsolete word *instinct*, go back to his text, and Baldwin was talking about what the social learning theorists call *modeling*. What Baldwin called the *ideal self* is just about exactly what Freud later, in the essay on narcissism (1914/1957), called the *ego ideal*. Those two terms, *ideal self* and *ego ideal*, may sound slightly different, but Freud was not writing English, and translated into German, Baldwin's term could as well have been the same as Freud's. That personal growth is a dialectical process has an ultramodern sound, and finally, most sophisticated of all, Baldwin clearly expressed the idea that the ideal self becomes an internalized *pacer* for development. The concept of pacer has a firm foundation in laboratory studies of cognitive growth (Dember, 1965), and at least one psychoanalyst (Loewald, 1960) has characterized the superego as an internalized pacer for ego development.

Freud, who, by the way, was familiar with some of Baldwin's writings, began by setting his drive psychology over against ego psychology. So *character development* in psychoanalytic literature was taken to mean fixation at one or several psychosexual stages together with the resultant personality sequelae. The relative importance to be given to the ego and the drives was always an issue; in fact, it was the issue over which Freud and Adler parted company in 1911.

So far as academic psychology was concerned, Watsonian behaviorism became the new broom that swept out the ego psychology descended from Baldwin. Psychoanalysis and all its variants still had little toehold in psychology, despite G. Stanley Hall's courageous invitation of Freud and C. G. Jung to the Clark University celebration in 1909. The advent of behaviorism did not improve the prospects of psychoanalysis.

Whereas Baldwin and those influenced by him, such as William McDougall, G. H. Mead, and John Dewey, were interested in the origins of morality in the individual, anthropology in the early years of this century saw the publication of important books on the origins of morality in society, particularly Hobhouse's *Morals in Evolution* (1906) and Westermarck's *The Origin and Development of the Moral Ideas* (1906–1908). No anthropologist today could write such books. Anthropology, like psychology, has turned to more rigorous methodologies. That methodological fastidiousness cannot be undone, but something has been lost, something of the broad view those early twentieth-century authors had. The *Ethics* of John Dewey and James Tufts (1908) is a readable source of much of the materials reported by Hobhouse and Westermarck. Heinz Werner's *Comparative Psychology of Mental Development* (1926/1940) was an influential book, especially in Europe (where the original German edition appeared in 1926), in the grand tradition of Hobhouse and Westermarck, although it reviewed much experimental work as well as field studies. Werner's biogenetic law, that development proceeds by increasingly complex differentiation, integration, and hierarchization, holds especially strongly in the field of character development, at least for one school of contemporary thought.

Turning now to the early behavioristic psychology, the definitive behavioristic study of character development was of course that of Hartshorne and May and their collaborators, J. B. Maller and F. K. Shuttleworth (1928, 1929, 1930). Mark May, whose life span, 1891 to 1977, corresponds to the period I am reviewing, was a remarkable psychologist. The Reverend Hugh Hartshorne was a religious educator from Union Theological Seminary. May had been a student there also, but finding that "there were more sinners in Union than there were on the streets of New York," had switched to psychology at Columbia (May, 1978). After World War I, when E. L. Thorndike was given a large grant to study character education, he brought Hartshorne and May together for the now-famous studies. Everyone knows some of their main results: disappointingly low correlations between cheating in one situation, such as grading one's own test, and another situation, such as party games. There have been many attempts to explain away these results. For one thing, psychologists today are accustomed to correlations that are disappointingly

456

low. As Guilford (1948) put it, "We must face the fact, unpleasant though it may be, that in human behavior, complex as it is, low intercorrelations of utilizable variables is the general rule and not the exception. Highly valid predictions must ordinarily be based on multiple indicators" (p. 5). Another consideration is that the tasks that Hartshorne and May presented were not necessarily sufficiently ego-involving to engage the character structure of the children (Allport, 1943). Backing up that point, Piaget (1932/1965) and Norman Bull (1969) have pointed out that cheating is not usually considered a very heinous offense by children, however it may be looked on by their elders.

The main thrust of the Hartshorne and May studies is often forgotten. Their purpose was to investigate the effectiveness of deliberate attempts to inculcate adult norms of right conduct into children. On the whole, those attempts were ineffective. Children did not become much less likely to cheat with age. Children who belonged to supposedly character-building organizations—we are not told whether it was the Boy Scouts or something else of the sort—were not less likely to cheat, nor were children who went to Sunday school. If that research purpose sounds naive, it is only because we now know their results. My own experience is that advanced, progressive schools whose teachers are eager to introduce the most modern methods of character development into the curriculum still have the same agenda: how can we cut down on stealing, fighting, and cheating? Would that psychologists knew the answer.

Few people get as far into Hartshorne and May as their third volume, the studies that are concerned specifically with the organization of character. To measure deceit, they gave each test twice, with an opportunity for surreptitious cheating the first but not the second time. The score difference they took as a measure of cheating. Scores were standardized and normalized for the various tests and situations. Thus each child had a distribution of honesty scores, and the standard deviation of the distribution was considered a measure of integration. Their estimate of the correlation between honesty and integration, corrected for attenuation, was .78. They concluded that while dishonesty is specific to the situation, honesty may be an integrated character trait. It is remarkable that this fine set of studies is almost always cited as supporting specificity rather than organization of character. But whatever else one may say about the Hartshorne and May studies, they initiated empirical research on character development. For psychologists there was no going back to the wise essay.

Two years after their third volume, Jean Piaget published another watershed study, *The Moral Judgment of the Child* (1932/1965), though it was some years before respectable academic psychologists paid attention to the book. In stunning contrast to the methods of Hartshorne and May, Piaget's prototypic situation was the game of marbles, precisely because grown-ups do not consider that a moral situation. Piaget wished to study the evolution of the child's moral reasoning. He saw that situations such as Hartshorne and May were studying would elicit simply

457

how willingly the child conformed to adult norms, quite another thing from moral reasoning. Thus his approach to the study of character development was as revolutionary as his approach to the study of intelligence. Adaptations of his *methode clinique* are the preferred approach in the largest group of contemporary studies of character development.

If we skip to World War II, we find not much going on in reference to character development in academic psychology, but psychoanalysis was flourishing, both in its orthodox version, now turning to ego psychology, and in its many variants and offshoots, usually called neo-Freudian but more properly called neo-Adlerian (Ansbacher & Ansbacher, 1956). An interest in character development was important to authors in both groups.

The high point of the tradition beginning with Baldwin and Adler and running through G. H. Mead was Sullivan's interpersonal theory of psychiatry (1953). Sullivan was admittedly influenced by Freud, but he was also strongly impelled to differentiate his system of ideas from those of Freud, which he considered philosophically faulty. Whether as cause or effect of that push away from Freud, he clarified aspects of ego psychology and character development that had been only meagerly treated in the Freudian literature.

The central conception of Sullivan's interpersonal psychiatry was the *self-system*, his term for approximately what others call "ego" or "character structure." His very terminology emphasizes the social origin of the self (*interpersonal*) and its structural nature (self-*system*). Although he did not state matters exactly this way, what later psychologists have gleaned from his account of the development of the self-system is that the *stages* of character development generate the diversity of character *types* of adult life. This idea is one of the distinctive marks of the current cognitive-developmental school and related theories. The difference between Sullivan's idea and the somewhat similar theory of psychosexual stages and types in Freud is that there is no necessary connection between the outcome of one psychosexual stage and that of the next one, whereas, with the self-system, being arrested at one stage virtually precludes advancing to the problems of the next one.

Another contribution of Sullivan's is his description of the importance of the chumship of the preadolescent period. It is with the chum, prior to the rise of imperative sexual needs, that one learns to value another as one values oneself, Sullivan maintained. Surely that ability is a crucial aspect of the most mature character development.

Among orthodox Freudians, there are many who have not gone beyond Freud's contributions in their own thinking. Indeed, it is questionable whether some analysts have caught up yet with the ideas of Freud's final burst of creativity. In 1914 in the essay on narcissism, Freud proposed a theory of how the ego ideal is itself derived from fundamental sexual drives. This is an extraordinary idea, and in the long run it weakened the drive paradigm. To put the issue crudely, a drive that can be satisfied by forming an ideal is a long way from being a biological or tissue need, as Freud characterized drives elsewhere (Freud, 1915/1957). Another aspect of the theory of the ego ideal, whose formation is of course a major step in character development, is that progression can be predicated on or can require a prior regression. In the essay on narcissism (Freud, 1914/1957) that is stated in terms of the ego ideal involving a regression to narcissism, but in other psychoanalytic writings the principle is used in other contexts. This principle is a truly original theoretical contribution by Freud. The conception of the ego ideal, however, with which his admirers often credit him, was taken from the common domain, being found in Baldwin, James, and others.

Freud's ideas on character development are often encapsulated, not to say caricatured, in the sentence, "The superego is heir to the Oedipus complex." That idea is part of a complicated sequence whose keystone is something much less hackneyed, namely, that the child masters the frustration of his aggressive impulses by identifying himself with the parent who imposes control (Freud, 1923, 1930). This identification results in a more complex ego or character development, since the child is now, so to speak, internally divided, functioning at once in the impulsive and controlling roles. The concept of identification, at least in this sense, seems to have originated with Freud.

In 1945 a British psychologist and psychoanalyst, J. C. Flugel, published a wise book called *Man, Morals, and Society.* Although it had no startlingly original ideas, it was a learned book and still makes good reading. Flugel took many insights from the writings of McDougall and Baldwin and united them with insights from Freud to make a comprehensive picture of the origins of conscience and moral character. Shortly before its publication, a book appeared by the French psychoanalyst, C. Odier (1943), which seems not to have been translated into English but whose title is descriptive of their joint message: *Les Deux Sources, Consciente et Inconsciente, de la Vie Morale.* Flugel discerned four sources for a mature conscience: first, the ideal self or ego ideal; second, incorporation of moral attitudes or precepts of others, particularly parents; third, aggression turned against the self; fourth, sadomasochism or the need for mastery. The first two sources together he called the *ego ideal,* the last two the *superego.* The first two were known to psychologists before Freud, particularly Baldwin and McDougall; the last two were distinctive contributions of psychoanalysis. The parts of conscience that Flugel called the superego are the earliest to arise developmentally. Even in a very young infant, one can observe anger arising from nonfulfillment or postponement of wishes; Flugel observed that one target for baby's aggression that is always present and within reach is himself. Control of impulse, even control motivated by narrow self-interest, comes later than structuring of impulse as such. So long as expression of impulse is more compelling than any calculation of self-interest requiring control, turning aggression against the self is a likely outcome. The most important transmutation of this aggression against the self is simply impulse control per se, a process to which psychoanalysts sometimes apply the hideous word *countercathexis.*

459

The drive for *mastery*, a term I prefer to Flugel's emphasis on sadomasochism, cannot be structured in a child until there is some capacity to distinguish impulse and control. Whether the drive for mastery is allied to or derived from an aggressive drive, or whether it originates separately from the aggressive drive, with each capable of being turned against the self, I need not decide. The specifically psychoanalytic version of the drive for mastery is that one must do what one has suffered, that experience is mastered by actively repeating frustrating experiences one has passively undergone. This principle is invoked at various points in psychoanalytic theory, to account for children's play, for altruism and identification with the aggressor (A. Freud, 1936/1946), and, as I have just explained, for the resolution of the Oedipus complex. The law of the talion is an early version of this principle. The part that the law of the talion plays as a primitive precursor of conscience and a sense of justice is often neglected, but it has been emphasized by John Stuart Mill (1859/1975), by Westermarck, by Hobhouse, and among psychoanalysts, by Odier. The developmental psychologist should always remember that the early stages of a mature faculty may seem to be its opposite, as different as talion revenge is from a compassionate sense of justice.

The third source, the formation of the ego ideal or ideal self, and the fourth, the incorporation or acceptance as one's own of parental standards, prohibitions, and ideals, need no further explanation. To these four sources of conscience one can add a fifth, drawn from Sullivan: valuing another person equally with oneself, or, as others have put it, valuing persons as ends rather than as means, which includes seeing from the other person's point of view. Only with achieving that capacity can one become truly disinterested and achieve what lawyers called the "judicial temperament," a manifestation of the highest estate of conscience and character.

To Erik Erikson (1950a, b), beginning with his contributions to the discussion of the "healthy personality" at the Midcentury White House conference, we owe an increased appreciation of the importance of adolescence as a developmental period. That has come as a useful antidote to the idea attributed to Freud and psychoanalysis, perhaps unjustly, that the important aspects of character are fixed by the age of four or six or seven. That may be true for character considered as a manifestation of psychosexual constitution (a topic outside my purview), but it is surely not true of the aspects of character being discussed here. Character in our sense is probably the last major aspect of the person to reach its apogee, after physical and intellectual growth have essentially stopped.

Another milestone publication in 1950 was *The Authoritarian Personality*, the Berkeley studies of Adorno, Frenkel-Brunswik, Levinson, and Sanford. The authors had set out to study character structure in psychoanalytic terms in the shadow of fascism and the Holocaust. Like Hannah Arendt (1964), what they found was more banal than what they expected. Their results forced their attention away from psychosexual development and toward a continuum that I now call ego development. Using in-depth interviews, Else Frenkel-Brunswik contrasted groups of people high in ethnocentrism or prejudice with those low on those traits. The greatest differences were in their cognitive structure and their attitudes toward their current self. The highly prejudiced were conformist, given to use of cliches, intolerant of ambiguities, and given to moralistic condemnation of unconventional people. Their relations with people tended to be exploitive and manipulative and concerned more with things than with feelings. They tended to be conventional, particularly about sex roles, and to think of their work in terms of competition, power, and status. The present self and parents were described in idealized terms, but there were few spontaneous references to childhood. Those low on prejudice were often unconventional and were tolerant of individual differences. Their relations with others were dominated by a search for companionship and affection. They dwelt on their own faults and conflicts, including conflicts over sex roles and conflicts with parents. They described other people, including their parents, vividly and realistically, as having good and bad traits. They tended to think in terms of achievement or social values and ideals. They spontaneously explained their present self in terms of development from childhood. Thus in that book one can see an instance of the evolution of the psychoanalytic conception of character from psychosexual to ego development as it happened. Because of the distinguished authors, this was that rarity, a psychological study to which psychoanalysts as well as psychologists paid attention.

The major factor which directed the attention of psychoanalysts, or at least some of them, away from complete preoccupation with drives and toward greater interest in ego development was disappointment in results of some analyses. That, in turn, was at least partly the consequence of results so encouraging in other cases that they were led to extend the method to previously excluded cases, particularly those of the psychoses and delinquencies. Generally disappointing results with psychoses, delinquencies, and so-called borderline conditions led to a renewed interest in theory of ego development. Because their interest came from this direction, psychoanalysts' interest in ego development was inevitably colored by problems of pathology and particularly preoccupation with the earliest stages of ego development. Moral development, however, is to a large extent an adolescent phenomenon; hence much of what psychoanalysts study under the heading of ego development has minimal pertinence to character development in the sense in which I am using the term.

At the same time, the theory of ego development implicit in the writings of Freud, beginning about 1920, contains the most profound insights into the dynamics of the sequence that we have even today (Loevinger, 1976, 1979). The first of Freud's theoretical principles states that experience is mastered by actively repeating what we have passively suffered. This principle was first stated in a famous passage in *Beyond the Pleasure Principle* (Freud, 1920/1955), one to which Freud and Anna Freud referred repeatedly in later writings on ego functioning and ego development. The second principle, in part a consequence of the first, is that intrapersonal schemes are shaped by interpersonal ones, that is, intrapersonal differentiation is

461

both modeled on and spurred by interpersonal interactions. This principle made its first appearance in a somewhat implausible context in "Mourning and Melancholia" (Freud, 1917/1957), but later came into its own in relation to the resolution of the Oedipus complex and formation of the superego (Freud, 1923/1961) and in relation to the development of conscience, character, and even civilization (Freud, 1930/1961). The third principle, that progression is, sometimes at least, based on regression, made its first appearance in the essay on narcissism (Freud, 1914/1957). The psychoanalysts Erikson (1950a, 1956) and Loewald (1951, 1960, 1971) and the philosopher Ricoeur (1970) have made these principles central to their own reconstruction of the psychoanalytic paradigm, but one cannot claim that the mainstream of psychoanalytic theory today similarly recognizes the import of these principles. (Undoubtedly the intertwining of the first principle with the generally unacceptable idea of the death instinct has had much to do with their neglect.)

Psychoanalysis is often criticized or even ridiculed for its personification of inner forces or agencies. Certainly at its worst psychoanalytic theorizing can give the ridiculous impression of people within people, making choices, in contention with each other, and so on. And yet the foregoing principles and the observations on which they are based show that there is some justification for seeing psychic agencies—call them conscience, superego, ego ideal—as originally embodiments of the voices of others, particularly parents. Freud was not naive. "The hypothesis of the super-ego really describes a structural relation and is not merely a personification of some such abstraction as that of conscience," he wrote (Freud, 1933/1964, p. 64) in the same passage in which he described the superego as the outcome of the Oedipus complex. Mead's (1934) theory of the origin and growth of the self depends on a similar process. Mead saw the child as first taking the role of others in play, advancing finally to take the role of the "generalized other."

Although grand theorizing is a lapsed tradition, there is one recent exception, *The Origin of Consciousness in the Breakdown of the Bicameral Mind*, by Julian Jaynes (1977). The personification of psychic agencies is a central topic of this book also. His argument does not, like that of Freud and Mead, depend on observations or reconstructions of children's development, however. His argument rests on a variety of other sources, including examination of classical texts such as the Iliad and the Old Testament, archaeological records, and studies of split-brain patients. In Jaynes's reconstruction, modern "consciousness," and, by extension, modern character and conscience, had as precursors in primitive peoples auditory hallucinations of the voices and particularly of the commands of absent or dead fathers, chiefs, and kings. Today we also can hear the voices of dead friends and relatives, but since most of us do not believe that ghosts can make themselves heard, we class the voices as memories rather than as presences. In the transition several millennia ago when the belief in the real presence of the hallucinated voices largely broke down, obedience to them also broke down. The historical period that followed was marked by unrestrained opportunism and cruelty. Modern consciousness and conscience gradually developed to fill the void left by the decline in belief of the reality of ancestral voices. Though this summary is too brief to represent Jaynes's thesis fairly, it does show that Freud was not the only psychologist to struggle with the problem of a quasipersonified agency of self-regulation.

Another line of research, prominent among child psychologists in the 1950s and 1960s and continuing today, is concerned with identifying parental behaviors that are antecedent to and presumably responsible for favorable outcomes of childrearing. Various aspects of character and conscience come under the heading of favorable outcomes, as, for example, in the study of Sears, Maccoby, and Levin (1957), based on interviews with 379 mothers. This line of research must assume an answer to the question which is of greatest current interest, namely, that of the essential nature and general course of character development. For how one answers that question determines what one should look for by way of parental and other environmental influences. Peck and Havighurst (1960) studied character development in terms of parental practices. Their approach was more inferential and less behavioristic than that of Sears, Maccoby, and Levin, and in some ways it anticipated the contemporary structural approach.

Among current researchers in the field of character—they are far too numerous to be mentioned individually—there are three general types of answers to the question of the nature of character development: the specifist-situationist models, characteristically using an experimental approach; the trait models, often using objective tests; and the structural models, often using projective tests or clinical interviews. The best known current advocates of these approaches are probably Albert Bandura and Walter Mischel, the situationists (who call themselves "social-learning theorists"), Robert Hogan, the trait theorist, and Lawrence Kohlberg, the structuralist. Obviously today I can give only skeletal accounts of these theories to bring out their contrasts.

According to Bandura (1978) and Mischel (Mischel & Mischel, 1976), moral development may superficially look like stage models depict it, but in fact that development is an artifact of the child's growing cognitive abilities and changing demands made on the child by parents and others. If two people respond differently to a given situation, that is because they have different life histories, different experiences, and they have experienced different patterns of rewards, punishments, and modeling. Seemingly earlier stages can in fact be made to follow seemingly later ones by suitable patterns of reinforcement. But it is the immediate situation that Mischel sees as the major factor in a child's reaction to a situation that could be called "moral," or "protomoral," as his favorite research paradigm must be. This model involves studying the conditions under which a child will elect to wait longer for a better, larger, or more preferred reward, rather than take a smaller reward sooner. The use of experiments as his investigative tool naturally brings out situational factors with special clarity. As Mischel has often documented, the literature offers ample evidence of short-term effects of reward, punishment, and modeling,

463

but to what extent those factors can be held accountable for long-term effects, that is, for character structure, which is our present topic, seems more hypothetical than firmly proved. Pushed to its logical extreme, their position would seem to be that there is no such thing as character structure. Morality is learned as other behaviors are learned, and each of us is totally the creation of the situation, usually the immediate one, and if not that, then past ones. To some extent that formula is a blank check, for any surplus effects can be laid to unknown past history. Probably every system of thought has to have such a blank check somewhere, but that should not be confused with what can be proved. Gewirtz (1969) seems to take the extreme position, but Mischel (1973) no longer seems to, acknowledging instead cognitive factors in general and self-conception in particular as stable sources of personality and conduct.

Hogan (1973; Hogan, Johnson, & Emler, 1978) differentiates role structure from character structure. Roles, self-images, and life-styles are typically conscious, sensitive to demands of specific situations, and directly reflected in overt behavior. Together they make up role structure. Character structure, by contrast, is stable and enduring, unconscious, and manifested only indirectly through attitudes and attitude statements. The most important of the attitudes is that toward rules.

Character structure, Hogan hypothesizes, has three dimensions, conceptually independent and operationally discriminable. They are socialization, empathy, and autonomy. The first dimension, socialization or rule attunement, represents the extent of internalization of social rules. Hogan believes it can be measured quite effectively by the socialization scale of the California Psychological Inventory (CPI). The second dimension, empathy or social sensitivity, is the ability and disposition to accommodate one's actions to the expectations of others. Whereas socialization is believed to develop in response to parental demands, empathy may develop more in response to peer demands. It can be assessed by the empathy scale of the CPI. The third dimension, autonomy, is the ability to make moral decisions independently of peers and authorities; it is based on self-awareness. An autonomous person complies with social rules to maintain self-respect or refuses to comply for the welfare of the group, not his personal welfare. It is measured by the autonomy scale of the CPI. A person high on empathy, socialization, and autonomy is the rare morally mature person. Normally, these traits develop in that order, but any status on any of the three is possible with any status on the other two; there are no logically necessary "stages." Evidently, with his heavy reliance on CPI scales, Hogan is not breaking any new ground methodologically. Rather, he is defending classical or usual personality tests in application to the field of character structure.

You might think that Mischel, with his criticism of "state-trait theorists" and of depth psychology, and Hogan, with his allegiance to tests of traits and to depth psychology, would be squaring off at each other, but I have not noticed them doing so. Instead, each seems to reserve his most extensive criticism for Kohlberg (1976). Since you can hardly pick up a popular magazine without reading about his six stages, I will not repeat them, except to remind you that they are divided into three main levels, the premoral level, the level of conventional role conformity, and the level of self-accepted moral principles. There are two stages within each level. The stages are articulated in a Piagetian manner, as involving a structure or inner logic that governs the equilibration at each stage and the progress to the next one.

Kohlberg's test of moral maturity is a modified extension of the *methode clinique* of Piaget in the *Moral Judgment of the Child* (1932/1965). The conception of stages, however, is drawn from Piaget's work on cognitive development, since Piaget demurred at finding stages of moral development. Kohlberg's cognitive-developmental view of moral development is opposed to a purely or predominantly maturational view, which some versions of psychosexual development may approximate, and it is opposed to a predominantly environmental view, which learning and social-learning theories uphold. The moral thinking of the parents or the society is not "stamped in," whatever the pattern of punishment, reasoning, or modeling. Rather, the child constructs his own structure of moral reasoning, with the stages always following in fixed order. The premoral stages always precede those of conventional role conformity, which always precede (but are not always followed by) morality of self-accepted principles. That fixed order is not, however, determined genetically but rather by the internal logic of the successive stages, a point some of his critics overlook.

Social experience can retard or accelerate progress, but it cannot fundamentally change the sequence, according to Kohlberg. The social experiences most useful in this respect are opportunities for role-taking. Each stage evolves from the preceding one on the basis of the interaction of the child with his environment, not the unfolding of a preformed plan and not the impression on the child of an environmental pattern. Optimal conditions for growth require an environment just slightly ahead of where the child is, or at least an environment that constantly presents a pattern just ahead of the child's current level. This represents a level of disequilibrium too great to be assimilated to the current stage, but not so discrepant as to be unintelligible. Thus the child can eventually accommodate to it and move ahead.

There are many other major figures within each of these traditions. Bandura (1978), the major theorist in the social-learning group, has been formulating a theory of self within that paradigm. I think Kohlberg's earlier criticism still holds. Bandura can with some effort talk about character development within that framework, but it is a translation of findings made within other frameworks, not a means for making new discoveries. Justin Aronfreed (1976) has an extensive program using a resistance-to-temptation paradigm. In one way, Aronfreed has compounded the flaw in the resistance-to-cheating model, for the temptation to which he typically exposes children, playing with an attractive toy, is not bad by any criterion other than that of an artificial adult prohibition, and it is surely not regarded as bad by children.

Among Kohlberg's followers and colleagues there are now many who are making

465

their own original contributions. Damon (1977) has studied the child's social development, particularly the development of the child's sense of justice; Selman (1976) is studying the development of the ability to take the role of another, particularly with respect to the child's conception of friendship and of personality; Turiel (1975) has turned to the development of the child's ideas of customs and conventions; Broughton (1978) to the development of sense of self, and so on.

There are two of us who can be considered F-1 hybrids: James Rest (1979) has contrived an ingenious objective test of moral maturity based on a version of Kohlberg's stages. My group has been working with a conception of ego development, derived originally from the conception of interpersonal integration of Sullivan, Grant, and Grant (1957), but closely allied to the Kohlberg conception and, like it, covered by the term *character*. Our chief instrument, however, has not been the clinical interview but a sentence completion test, semiprotective in format but semiobjective in scoring, thanks to an extensive scoring manual (Loevinger & Wessler, 1970; Loevinger, Wessler, & Redmore, 1970).

Incidentally, I am often criticized for not defining my terms, in this case, *character*. In Wundt's day I suspect that would not have been considered necessary. Further, if you look at how research workers define their fields of study, you will frequently find that they build their conclusions into their definition, or, at least, they define their field so that their own research is its inevitable core and centerpiece. I could define the field to make my work, Kohlberg's, and that of our likeminded colleagues the only research that matters. But in fact Hogan and Mischel do consider their approaches as alternative ones, and they do cover a partly overlapping though not identical territory. I am trying to acknowledge that community of interest, at the expense of using *character* in inconsistent ways.

In addition to the foregoing and related lines of research, several important research programs within social psychology are germane to this field; the vast literature on socialization and conformity and on altruism are examples, though much of the work is oriented specifically to behavior rather than to character per se. The research on empathy is another controversial example; Hogan considers it directly relevant to or part of character, whereas some of the rest of us consider it peripheral or irrelevant.

Psychoanalysis continues of course as a school—or group of schools—in its own right, though not exactly a school of academic psychology. Within psychoanalysis one must distinguish, at a minimum, two schools of ego psychology. For the Hartmann-Rapaport school, ego psychology is an addition to drive psychology, and cathexis or psychic energy remains its central concept (Hartmann, 1939/1958; Hartmann, Kris, & Loewenstein, 1945–1962/1964; Rapaport, 1959). For Erikson and for most academic psychologists who are actively identified with psychoanalysis, the relation between drives and ego has been reconceptualized, with emphasis on concepts such as mastery and identification, deleting the obscure concept of cathexis (Holzman & Gill, 1976).

466

There is even a small but growing group of psychoanalysts who are working out cognitive-dynamic paradigms. Bruch (1973), for example, stresses cognitive errors as the fundamental factor in some cases of anorexia nervosa. Wishnie (1977) has a method of cognitive diagnosis and treatment of adult impulsive personalities, such as delinquents and addicts. An interesting feature of his method is that the therapist and the patient work out the cognitive diagrams together. Horowitz (1977, 1979) has a similar method of diagramming changes in cognitive states; he is applying his technique in situations calling for short-term therapy of stress-response syndromes. Bruch, Wishnie, and Horowitz are clinicians and their contributions are clinical. Although many psychological researchers in the field of character development would acknowledge some influence of psychoanalysis on their thinking, no systematic experimental or research paradigm has emerged based on the ego psychology of Freud's final period or that of the post-Freudians. So the principles of psychoanalytic ego psychology are not yet integrated with empirical research approaches to character development.

The trait theorists clearly are direct descendants of the psychometric tradition in psychology. The Berkeley study of the authoritarian personality united that tradition with the classical psychoanalytic one.

Behaviorism was the background of Thorndike and hence of Hartshorne and May; social-learning theory comes out of that tradition. Modeling, however, also draws from Baldwin, who was no behaviorist. Sears was a product of the Yale tradition, uniting behavioristic learning theory with psychoanalytic drive theory, a movement that flourished with the encouragement of that remarkable psychologist, Mark May.

The immediate ancestors of the cognitive-developmental or structural school are Piaget, Sullivan, and Erikson. From Erikson they draw the emphasis on adolescence as a significant developmental period (which shows that an idea can be psychoanalytic without being Freudian). From Sullivan, they draw the idea of adult character as the trace of an invariant sequence of developmental stages, an idea that sounds as if it comes from Freud, but in Sullivan's version came close to Werner's conception of hierarchization and Piaget's of equilibration. From Piaget they draw both his clinical interview method and the idea of structure, that is, of hierarchical stages and equilibration. Freud was a major influence on Erikson, of course, and on Sullivan; Baldwin influenced Piaget and Sullivan, the latter via Charles Horton Cooley and Mead.

All of this activity bespeaks a healthy state of affairs, not to say a booming business. But despite the large amount of empirical work and significant additions to knowledge, I have an uneasy feeling. In regard to the larger issues to which our work ought to be and often is intended to be relevant, I am not sure that the certified scientists at present are much closer to answers than were our "unscientific" predecessors. Our data, at their best, are more certain than Baldwin's or Sullivan's unstandardized observations, but often less relevant. The leap from meticulously

467

watching children eat little pretzels rather than waiting for a large dish of ice cream to any real knowledge of character is a long one.

Sometimes it seems as if we do not take our theories seriously enough; that is, we pretend that discoveries that actually were made under the star of quite a different theory are the property of our own. For example, did Bandura and Mischel "discover" the importance of the sense of self by following the logic of social-learning theory, or by forgetting social-learning theory and following common sense? Similarly, did Hartmann "discover" autonomous ego functions by following psychoanalytic method and logic? Or did he discover ego autonomy by setting aside his psychoanalytic scruples long enough to follow common sense? The point is reinforced by the fact that Allport (1937) was stressing a similar conception of "functional autonomy of motives," similar to Hartmann's "secondary autonomy of ego functions," at the same time, obviously on the basis of wholly different assumptions.

On other occasions, we take our theories too seriously; those are the cases in which theories become blinders, preventing us from seeing the other fellow's discoveries, rather than what theories should be, ways to see better, to help us discover and formulate new knowledge.

Thus character development, which sounds at first like a narrowly specialized topic, turns out to be a broad field, encompassing a range of schools and points of view and active controversies today. In that field one can still see the footprints of giants: Baldwin, Freud, Adler, Sullivan, Werner, Piaget.

REFERENCES

Adorno, T. W., Frenkel-Brunswik, E., Levinson, D. J., & Sanford, R. N. *The authoritarian personality*. New York: Harper & Row, 1950.

Allport, G. W. *Personality: A psychological interpretation*. New York: Holt, 1937.

Allport, G. W. The ego in contemporary psychology. *Psychological Review*, 1943, 50, 451–478.

Ansbacher, H. L., & Ansbacher, R. R. (Eds.). *The individual psychology of Alfred Adler*. New York: Basic Books, 1956.

Arendt, H. *Eichmann in Jerusalem: A report on the banality of evil*. New York: Viking, 1964.

Aronfreed, J. Moral development from the standpoint of a general psychological theory. In T. Lickona (Ed.), *Moral development and behavior: Theory, research, and social issues*. New York: Holt, 1976.

Baldwin, J. M. *Social and ethical interpretations in mental development*. New York: Macmillan, 1902. (Originally published, 1897.)

Bandura, A. The self system in reciprocal determinism. *American Psychologist*, 1978, 33, 344–358.

Breuer, J., & Freud, S. *Studies on hysteria. Standard edition* (Vol. 2). London: Hogarth Press, 1955. (Originally published, 1895.)

Broughton, J. M. The development of concepts of self, mind, reality and knowledge. In W. Damon (Ed.), *New directions for child development* (Vol. 1). San Francisco: Jossey-Bass, 1978.

Bruch, H. *Eating disorders: Obesity, anorexia nervosa and the person within*. New York: Basic Books, 1973.

Bull, N. J. *Moral judgment from childhood to adolescence.* Beverly Hills, Calif.: Sage Publications, 1969.

Damon, W. *The social world of the child.* San Francisco: Jossey-Bass, 1977.

Dember, W. N. The new look in motivation. *American Scientist,* 1965, *53,* 409–427.

Dewey, J., & Tufts, J. H. *Ethics.* New York: Holt, 1908.

Erikson, E. H. *Childhood and society.* New York: Norton, 1950. (a)

Erikson, E. H. Growth and crises of the "healthy personality." In M. J. E. Senn (Ed.), *Symposium on the healthy personality. Supplement II. Problems of infancy and childhood.* New York: Josiah Macy Jr. Foundation, 1950. (b)

Erikson, E. H. The problem of ego identity. *Journal of the American Psychoanalytic Association,* 1956, *4,* 56–121.

Flugel, J. C. *Man, morals and society.* New York: International Universities Press, 1945.

Freud, A. *The ego and the mechanisms of defense.* New York: International Universities Press, 1946. (Originally published, 1936.)

Freud, S. *The interpretation of dreams. Standard edition* (Vols. 4 & 5). London: Hogarth Press, 1953. (Originally published, 1900.)

Freud, S. *On narcissism: An introduction. Standard edition* (Vol. 14). London: Hogarth Press, 1957. (Originally published, 1914.)

Freud, S. *Instincts and their vicissitudes. Standard edition* (Vol. 14). London: Hogarth Press, 1957. (Originally published, 1915.)

Freud, S. *Mourning and melancholia. Standard edition* (Vol. 14). London: Hogarth Press, 1957. (Originally published, 1917.)

Freud, S. *Beyond the pleasure principle. Standard edition* (Vol. 18). London: Hogarth Press, 1955. (Originally published, 1920.)

Freud, S. *The ego and the id. Standard edition* (Vol. 19). London: Hogarth Press, 1961. (Originally published, 1923.)

Freud, S. *Civilization and its discontents. Standard edition* (Vol. 21). London: Hogarth Press, 1961. (Originally published, 1930.)

Freud, S. *New introductory lectures on psychoanalysis. Standard edition* (Vol. 22). London: Hogarth Press, 1964. (Originally published, 1933.)

Gewirtz, J. L. Mechanisms of social learning: Some roles of stimulation and behavior in early human development. In D. A. Goslin (Ed.), *Handbook of socialization theory and research.* Chicago: Rand McNally, 1969.

Guilford, J. P. Some lessons from aviation psychology. *American Psychologist,* 1948, *3,* 3–11.

Hartmann, H. *Ego psychology and the problem of adaptation.* New York: International Universities Press, 1958. (Originally published, 1939.)

Hartmann, H., Kris, E., & Loewenstein, R. M. Papers on psychoanalytic psychology. *Psychological Issues,* 1964, *4* (2, Whole No. 14). (Originally published, 1945–1962.)

Hartshorne, H., & May, M. A. *Studies in the nature of character.* Vol. 1. *Studies in deceit.* New York: Macmillan, 1928.

Hartshorne, H., May, M. A., & Maller, J. B. *Studies in the nature of character.* Vol. 2. *Studies in service and self-control.* New York: Macmillan, 1929.

Hartshorne, H., May, M. A., & Shuttleworth, F. K. *Studies in the nature of character.* Vol. 3. *Studies in the organization of character.* New York: Macmillan, 1930.

Hobhouse, L. T. *Morals in evolution.* New York: Holt, 1906.

Hogan, R. Moral conduct and moral character: A psychological perspective. *Psychological Bulletin,* 1973, *79,* 217–232.

Hogan, R., Johnson, J. A., & Emler, N. P. A socioanalytic theory of moral development. In W. Damon (Ed.), *New directions for child development* (Vol. 2). San Francisco: Jossey-Bass, 1978.

Holzman, P., & Gill, M. (Eds.). *Psychology versus metapsychology: Psychoanalytic essays in memory of George S. Klein. Psychological Issues,* 1976, *9* (4, Whole No. 36).

469

Horowitz, M. J. Structure and the process of change. In M. J. Horowitz (Ed.), *Hysterical personality*. New York: Aronson, 1977.

Horowitz, M. J. *States of mind: Analysis of change in psychotherapy*. New York: Plenum, 1979.

Jaynes, J. *The origin of consciousness in the breakdown of the bicameral mind*. Boston: Houghton Mifflin, 1977.

Kohlberg, L. Moral stages and moralization. In T. Lickona (Ed.), *Moral development and behavior: Theory, research, and social issues*. New York: Holt, 1976.

Köhler, W. *The place of value in a world of facts*. New York: Liveright, 1938.

Leary, D. A century of social concern. *APA Monitor*, June 1979, p. 3.

Loevinger, J. *Ego development: Conceptions and theories*. San Francisco: Jossey-Bass, 1976.

Loevinger, J. Psychoanalysis as a quasi-scientific paradigm. In J. Loevinger, *Scientific ways in the study of ego development*. Worcester, Mass.: Clark University Press, 1979.

Loevinger, J., & Wessler, R. *Measuring ego development 1. Construction and use of a sentence completion test*. San Francisco: Jossey-Bass, 1970.

Loevinger, J., Wessler, R., & Redmore, C. *Measuring ego development 2. Scoring manual for women and girls*. San Francisco: Jossey-Bass, 1970.

Loewald, H. W. Ego and reality. *International Journal of Psycho-Analysis*, 1951, 32, 10–18.

Loewald, H. W. On the therapeutic action of psychoanalysis. *International Journal of Psycho-Analysis*, 1960, 41, 16–33.

Loewald, H. W. Some considerations on repetition and repetition compulsion. *International Journal of Psycho-Analysis*, 1971, 52, 59–66.

May, W. W. A psychologist of many hats: A tribute to Mark Arthur May. *American Psychologist*, 1978, 33, 653–663.

Mead, G. H. *Mind, self and society*. Chicago: The University of Chicago Press, 1934.

Mill, J. S. *On liberty*. New York: Norton, 1975. (Originally published, 1859.)

Mischel, W. Toward a cognitive social learning reconceptualization of personality. *Psychological Review*, 1973, 80, 252–283.

Mischel, W., & Mischel, H. A cognitive social learning approach to morality and self-regulation. In T. Lickona (Ed.), *Morality: Theory, research, and social issues*. New York: Holt, 1976.

Odier, C. *Les deux sources, consciente et inconsciente, de la vie morale*. Neuchâtel, Switzerland: De la Baconnière, 1943.

Peck, R. F., & Havighurst, R. J. *The psychology of character development*. New York: Wiley, 1960.

Piaget, J. *The moral judgment of the child*. (M. Gabain, trans.) New York: Free Press, 1965. (Originally published, 1932.)

Rapaport, D. The structure of psychoanalytic theory: A systematizing attempt. In S. Koch (Ed.), *Psychology: A study of a science*. Vol. 3. *Formulations of the person and the social context*. New York: McGraw-Hill, 1959.

Rest, J. *Development in judging moral issues*. Minneapolis: University of Minnesota Press, 1979.

Ricoeur, P. *Freud and philosophy: An essay on interpretation*. New Haven: Yale University Press, 1970.

Sears, R. R., Maccoby, E. E., & Levin, H. *Patterns of child rearing*. Evanston, Ill.: Row, Peterson, 1957.

Selman, R. Social-cognitive understanding: A guide to educational and clinical practice. In T. Lickona (Ed.), *Moral development and behavior: Theory, research, and social issues*. New York: Holt, 1976.

Sullivan, C., Grant, M. Q., & Grant, J. D. The development of interpersonal maturity: Applications to delinquency. *Psychiatry*, 1957, 20, 373–385.

Sullivan, H. S. *The interpersonal theory of psychiatry*. New York: Norton, 1953.

Turiel, E. The development of social concepts: Mores, customs, and conventions. In D. J. DePalma & J. S. Foley (Eds.), *Moral development: Current theory and research*. Hillsdale, N.J.: Erlbaum, 1975.

Werner, H. *Comparative psychology of mental development.* New York: Harper, 1940. (Originally published, 1926.)

Westermarck, E. *The origin and development of the moral ideas* (2 vols.). London: Macmillan, 1906–1908.

Wishnie, H. *The impulsive personality.* New York: Plenum, 1977.

Wundt, W. M. *Ethics: An investigation of the facts and laws of the moral life* (Trans. from 2d German ed. by E. B. Tichener, J. H. Gulliver, & M. F. Washburn). New York: Macmillan, 1897–1901. (Originally published, 1886.)

20

Child Development Research

DAVID ELKIND

History can be written in many ways and from many different perspectives. This chapter takes two different approaches. The first is a brief chronological record of the evolution of child development research and theory over the past century and its reception by society at large. The second section considers some of the major ideas of the discipline contributed by individual investigators, viewing their achievements in the light of their personal histories.

A Brief History of Child Development Research in America

According to the social historian Philippe Ariès (1962), the concept of childhood as a distinct period of life, although accepted in ancient times, was lost during the middle ages—only to be rediscovered in the seventeenth century. Child portraiture, toys unique to children, and clothing, games, and literature designed for them began to appear at that time. Although childhood was not understood in the sense that it is today, the notion that childhood was different from adulthood, that children were not just small adults, was planted during the late Renaissance.

The conception of childhood as a distinct period of life is a necessary prerequisite for its scientific study. But such study took its major impetus only after the publication of Charles Darwin's work on evolution in general and his work on the evolution of emotions in animals and man (1872) in particular. Darwin's work suggested that human behavior could be observed and studied in much the same way that physical phenomena could be explored.

The first systematic accounts of child development and behavior began with the infant biographies of workers such as Bronson Alcott (1830) and Milicent Shinn (1900). In these documents, careful records of children's motor behavior, their language, play, and intellectual achievements were reported in great detail. Such biographies have retained an important place in child development research. Jean Piaget's classic studies of his own three infants (1936/1952, 1937/1954, 1945/1962) are mature examples of this genre. And studies of language such as Roger Brown's *A First Language* (1973) also make use of careful records of the individual histories of a few children.

The official "foundation" of child study as a discipline in this country was the work of G. Stanley Hall. Toward the end of the last century, at the bequest of Jonas Clark, Hall established Clark University in Worcester, Massachusetts, and built a strong psychology department with an emphasis on child study. Hall himself was an evolutionist who subscribed to the now-discredited "recapitulation" theory which postulated that in its development the child went through the same stages as had mankind in its progression from the Stone Age to the present. Hall's attempt to support this theory in his two-volume work *Adolescence* (1904) was impressive in the range and breadth of documentation he brought to bear on the topic. But recapitulation turned out to be a romantic metaphor rather than a testable scientific hypothesis.

Hall was particularly interested in the relation between child development and education. He saw clearly that a true scientific pedagogy had to be built upon the systematic study of children. This point, also made by Piaget in his book *The Science of Education and the Psychology of the Child* (1969/1970), is still not broadly accepted today. In order to pursue this scientific pedagogy, Hall started the "Child Study Movement" by having teachers and parents collect data (through questionnaires) on a wide range of topics, from religion to sex. Although certain of the data were interesting (Hall published some of it in the journal that he founded, *Pedagogical Seminary*, which later became the *Journal of Genetic Psychology*), the movement soon came under attack from investigators in the fledgling science of educational psychology.

Educational psychology took its roots from the work of English psychologists Galton (e.g., 1883) and Pearson (1900) who were concerned with mental measurement. And it took its model from Alfred Binet (e.g., 1905) who, together with Simon, gave the world its first reliable measure of intelligence. The Binet-Simon scales provided a model for test building that was quickly taken up in America. Tests of all kinds soon proliferated, and the theory and rationale of mental testing grew apace. It was from the relatively sophisticated standpoint of the mental test

473

movement that the "home-made" questionnaires used by Hall and his followers came under attack. Reliability and validity were the hallmarks of a good test, but Hall ignored these criteria in the construction of his questionnaires. Consequently much of the data that had been collected were discarded, and the questionnaire method itself fell into disrepute.

G. Stanley Hall also had an indirect impact upon the history of child study. In 1909 he brought Sigmund Freud to the United States for his first and only trip to this country. Freud delivered several lectures at Clark University that increased the interest in his work—an interest that had been growing. In particular, Freud's conception of infantile sexuality, and his postulation of the origin of neurosis in childhood, furthered an interest in the emotional disturbances of children. Freud's visit helped promote the growth of child clinical psychology and the child-guidance movement in this country.

Before World War I, therefore, some of the major themes of child study had been articulated and were being pursued. The study of infants (which is so prominent in child study today) was anticipated in the infant biographies; the study of children's ideas (later stimulated by Piaget's work) was initiated by Hall's questionnaires; mental measurement was given impetus by Binet's test; and child clinical psychology, and the study of personality and social interaction that it abetted, were promoted by Freud's visit to America.

After World War I, the field of child study split along philosophical and methodological lines, a schism that continues to characterize it today. One of these lines was that initiated by G. Stanley Hall: it was decidedly developmental in orientation. Researchers of this persuasion such as Arnold Gesell (e.g., 1940), a student of Hall's, Heinz Werner (1926/1940), and Piaget were concerned with the systematic changes that occur in children's behavior, thinking, language, and social interactions as they mature. The aim of most of this research and theory was normative—to describe with as much detail and precision as possible the course of growth and development followed by the *average* child.

Research along these lines was accelerated by some major foundation grants (The Laura Spellman Foundation, The Rockefeller Foundation) to various universities for longitudinal investigations. At Stanford, for example, Terman (e.g., 1925) was able to undertake his longitudinal study of children with high IQs. At Berkeley, a comprehensive investigation of the physical, intellectual, social, and emotional development was undertaken under the direction of Nancy Bayley (e.g., 1949). Data from that investigation are still being mined, and publications based on those data are still appearing in the literature.

The developmental approach was also reinforced by the emigration to the U.S. of a number of distinguished psychologists from Europe before World War II. Heinz Werner was one of these emigrants, and eventually he arrived at Clark University where he continued in the tradition of Hall's broad-based developmental approach. Kurt Lewin, at Iowa and at M.I.T., introduced mathematical models and a field approach to the study of social behavior (e.g., 1946). The Gestalt psychologists, Köhler (e.g., 1917/1925), Koffka (e.g., 1921/1924), and Wertheimer (e.g., 1945) brought new concepts and new ways of looking at the development of children's perception, reasoning, and creative thought. The Europeans gave a decidedly mentalistic cast to research and theory in developmental psychology.

Much of the work of the developmental group was published in the *Journal of Genetic Psychology* and then in *Child Development*—the journal of the Society for Research in Child Development. This society, founded in 1930 as a multidisciplinary research group, now includes thousands of members, and its biennial meetings are attended by investigators from all over the world. In addition to *Child Development*, the Society publishes a monograph series and an annotated *Abstracts* and *Bibliography*.

Though developmental psychology was not broadly pursued in the U.S. in the interval between (roughly) 1930 and the mid-1950s (largely because of the dominant preoccupation with large-scale behavior theories of nomothetic cast), from the late 1950s onward interest grew dramatically by virtue of a variety of new circumstances. One of these was the growing Civil Rights movement and its emphasis upon the disadvantaged. Government programs in the 1960s, such as Head-Start, required child psychologists for evaluation and instrumentation, including curriculum writing. Also, the appearance of Sputnik, in 1957, brought about a reevaluation of educational practice and of school curricula. Investigators from many disciplines were recruited to write new curricula, and the testing and implementation of these required psychologists. Even some psychologists who had not previously concentrated on child study, such as Jerome Bruner (e.g., 1960), were recruited into the developmental fold. Finally, the rediscovery of Piaget (his work received but a brief nod of interest in the 1930s) brought about a burgeoning of fresh interest in infancy, in cognitive functioning, and moral development.

Many of these emphases continue today, as developmental psychology, like social science generally, prepares for a period of retrenchment. The training of developmental psychologists, greatly expanded in the 1960s and 1970s, is already being cut back. As the government withdraws research support, developmentalists, like other social scientists, will have to rely upon their own ingenuity and other sources of support to continue their research.

A quite different strand of child study, emerging in the 1920s, was the behavioristic approach exemplified by the work of John Watson. While the developmental strand of child study was founded on the metaphor of the child as a growing plant, the behaviorist metaphor was that of raw material capable of being shaped entirely by environment. As Watson said: "Give me a dozen healthy infants . . . and I'll guarantee to take any one at random and train him to become . . . a doctor, lawyer, artist, merchant-chief and, yes, even . . . beggarman and thief" (1926, p. 10).

The emphasis of behaviorism was learning theory, and it was presumed that the

475

principles of learning were universal across species and, by extension, across age levels. The early studies of children undertaken from this perspective were modeled after investigations first conducted with animals. Such studies are still being pursued. Discrimination learning studies are of this variety. The emphasis of these investigations is on experimental rigor and methodological and technical sophistication. Children in these investigations are regarded as young, inexperienced organisms, rather than as developing ones.

The experimental approach to child study has yielded important information about children's learning and memory, but it was not until the work of B. F. Skinner (e.g., 1953) that the experimental approach was applied to practical issues. Skinner, who introduced his own conception of learning (operant conditioning), has been concerned with "behavioral engineering"—the use of behavioral principles to accomplish socially accepted or desired goals. Under the label "behavior modification," the principles of operant conditioning are now being widely applied in schools and clinics.

Like the developmentalists, the experimentalists have their own journal and organizations. The *Journal of Experimental Child Psychology* reports only experimental studies, and the Psychonomic Society, while not reserved for people in child study, provides a more congenial organization for experimental students of child behavior than does the Society for Research in Child Development.

The distinction between the developmental and experimental approaches to child study is a useful device for describing the history of the discipline. In fact, of course, the lines are not clearly drawn. Many workers in the field publish in both *Experimental Child Psychology* and *Child Development*, and the majority of workers—regardless of persuasion—belong to the Society for Research in Child Development. Most investigators use both experimental and developmental methodologies in their research so that even this division is not absolute.

It should also be noted that *normative* developmental psychology has stimulated a number of practical applications: Piaget's work has been translated into educational practice; Lawrence Kohlberg's work on moral development (e.g., 1967) has been translated into training programs in schools and prisons. Just as experimental child study found an applied dimension in Skinner's work, the developmentalists have found one in the work of Piaget and Kohlberg, among others. Some of the new directions in child study, such as social cognition and family studies, combine the research and applied perspectives of both developmental and experimental approaches.

Indeed, it appears that some of the past ideological struggles between the learning theorists and the developmentalists have lessened, and that a re-approachment is under way. When behaviorism, particularly of the Skinnerian variety, was new, it tended to be stated as a set of preemptive truths. The same can be said for the developmentalist position as represented by Piaget. Now that both positions are established, extreme stances are no longer necessary, and accommodation is possible and underway. Child study today builds upon the strength of both its experimental and its developmental heritage.

"Child Sense" and Child Development Research

In this section I take a psychohistorical approach to the evolution of child psychology as a discipline. That is to say, I shall try to show how an investigator's "child sense" (unique conception of childhood) relates to his or her personal history on the one hand and research endeavors on the other.

Before proceeding, some definitional matters are in order. First of all, the phrase "child sense" as it is used here does not refer to a general understanding of children, an ability to get along with them, talk comfortably with them, and so on. That is child "know-how," or child competence. Many teachers and a goodly number of parents have child competence without having child sense. *Child sense*, as it is used here, refers to a special insight into children and childhood that has roots in the investigator's personal history and which is expressed in a particular line of research and mode of theoretical construction.

Perhaps more detail about this concept of "child sense" is in order. The contention here is that each person's childhood has a kind of focus, a unique setting, theme, character, or mood which informs the whole of that person's childhood. This central motif, because it is experienced from the standpoint of a child and because it is experienced broadly, gives the person a special insight into child life. Although most people have a child sense of this sort, relatively few people use it. On the other hand, writers like Maurice Sendak, who wrote *In the Night Kitchen* (1970) and *Where the Wild Things Are* (1963), capitalize upon their child sense and can speak meaningfully to children. In the same fashion, developmental psychologists who tap into their child sense are likely to make original contributions to the field.

Second, the term *research* is used here in the broad sense of systematic study ranging from anecdotal observation to controlled experimentation. I stress the multifaceted nature of research because so much emphasis in our training of young people is placed upon experimentation. My impression is that the child sense of many young investigators is blunted and aborted by an overemphasis on experimental rigor. I firmly believe that if we permitted and encouraged more natural history in child-development research, we would have much less trivia and much more basic data about children. Experimental knowledge is a goal worth aiming for; it is not the bedrock upon which a discipline is based.

I hope that I will be excused, therefore, if I choose for my examples some well-known figures who are better known for their fruitful insights into child life than they are for the sophistication of their research. I hope, too, that everyone will appreciate, as I do, the extraordinary complexity of the relationships to be described

477

here. In relating an investigator's achievements to his or her child sense and personal history, I in no way want to reduce those achievements to these factors. Creative achievements in science, like those in the arts, are unique constructions that derive from the individual's talent, motivation, life circumstance, personal history, and much more. In this regard, child sense can be regarded as a mediating structure that relates a person's life history to his or her work. It does not explain that work or the history; it merely forms a connection between the two. Let me give a few examples of what I have in mind.

G. Stanley Hall

It seems fitting to begin with G. Stanley Hall (Ross, 1972), who has a legitimate claim to being the founder of developmental psychology in America. He not only founded the *Journal of Genetic Psychology*, he also initiated the turn-of-the-century "child-study movement." Hall was also a true developmentalist in that he wrote about all stages of the life cycle, including senescence. Although he was more of a conceptualizer and synthesizer than a researcher, some of the early work from the child-study movement on "the contents of children's minds" (1883) has stood the test of time. He was also a great supporter of research, and many of his students—such as Arnold Gesell—have contributed richly to our field.

Hall's unique child sense probably grew out of the confluence of his particular life circumstances, his particular talents, and the Zeitgeist. As to his life circumstances, he came from a relatively poor New England farming family that both admired and distrusted his scholarly leanings. Although directed toward the ministry, he soon turned to more secular pursuits and became increasingly estranged from his pietist Yankee background. Trips to Europe to study German philosophy and psychology made the estrangement even stronger.

If Hall was an outsider to his family, he was also one to the academic community. Although he was asked to deliver lectures at Harvard (the then president having ridden up on horseback to invite him), he never received a permanent appointment there. And his funny mix of applied, theoretical, and research interests made it difficult to pigeonhole him into a neat academic department. Even at Johns Hopkins, where he eventually received a professorship, he was something of a maverick. Perhaps that is why he took up Jonas Clark's offer to found a new university at Worcester, Massachusetts.

My contention is that Hall's position as a kind of outsider—to his family, the church, and the academic community—contributed to his unique child sense. What Hall accepted, and what seems so difficult for many psychologists (even today) to accept, is that children's minds and thinking are qualitatively different from those of the adult. But how was this difference to be conceptualized? Hall borrowed from the biology of his time, namely, the doctrine of recapitulation, and argued that in its evolution the child's mind followed the sequence of development to be found in cultural history. This grandiose concept was an apt vehicle for Hall's all-encompassing intelligence and allowed him to bring together his extraordinary erudition in science, history, philosophy, and religion.

A few comments are in order here. The postulation of a particular child sense as a mediator between an individual's life history and his or her achievements might seem to be rather arbitrary and entirely post hoc. There is, however, a kind of negative test—in Piagetian terms a *contre-epreuve*—that one can apply in support of the hypothesis. The test might show that a given person's child sense, his or her special insight into child life, helps to account for *failures* as well as successes. If this can be demonstrated, if the negative as well as the positive outcomes of a particular child sense can be shown, then the case for a particular child sense is thereby made stronger.

In this connection we can look at G. Stanley Hall's contribution. His particular child sense was his sense of being an outsider, and this gave him an appreciation of the difference between children and adults. But he carried the sense of difference too far. In advocating a recapitulation theory, Hall missed the inherent continuity of biological development. He attributed characteristics of a particular age group to a particular stage of social-historical development and thus missed the psychological continuity of stages, how they build upon one another and deal with the same problems at increasingly higher levels. In a very real way, therefore, Hall's child sense, his sense that children are different from adults, was carried too far, and he missed or underemphasized the essential continuity of development. In Hall's case, his child sense helps explain his failures as well as his successes.

Maria Montessori

Perhaps it will not be taken amiss if an educator, namely Maria Montessori, is the next person introduced here. Her contributions to our knowledge about children are many (e.g., 1912/1964), if unheralded. Montessori was, perhaps, the first environmental psychologist, stressing the role of the "prepared environment" in children's learning and behavior. In addition, her method of breaking down complex tasks into smaller behavioral components, manageable by young children, surely anticipates the task analyses and programming of contemporary behavior modification procedures. And her emphasis upon the motoric aspects of learning preceding the symbolic is clearly echoed in the research and theory of Piaget. Many other insights about children offered by Montessori could be listed but these should suffice.

Whence this child sense? One could, it seems, trace it to some facets of her childhood. Growing up as an only child in an aristocratic family in Italy, she was required to do something daily for the poor. Her efforts to befriend a poor hunchbacked girl, however, backfired because of the contrast in their appearances and positions. Early experiences such as this helped Maria Montessori to understand

479

that there are different ways of helping those who are less fortunate and that what seems like help may in fact be a hindrance. Later she was to place great emphasis upon arranging materials so as to enable children to do for themselves what others used to do for them.

Early in her adolescence Montessori's parents moved to Rome and encouraged her to become a school teacher. But her fierce independence, shown since early childhood, came to the fore. She proposed becoming an engineer because of her exceptional mathematical abilities. It was, of course, unheard of for women at that time to enter engineering. But Montessori persevered until she tired of the subject and decided that medicine was a better outlet for her talents and interests. Although initially opposed, her parents eventually supported her determination to become a physician.

Montessori was the first woman in Italy to enter medical school and her admission did not go unresisted. Once in medical school Montessori was the subject of jokes and ridicule. In addition, she had to suffer special privations. For example, she had to dissect her cadavers at night because it was not seemly for her to be with her male counterparts in the presence of nude bodies. Despite the special difficulties she encountered, Montessori graduated at the head of her class and was chosen to give the commencement address.

One might argue that Montessori's struggle for independence gave her a special insight into children's need for independence. She wanted them to do as much for themselves as they were capable of doing just as she wanted that for herself. In the upper classes of Italian society, as in other European countries, women and children were coddled; she wanted none of that for herself nor for her charges. Many of the materials she developed were self-didactic: errors were immediately obvious and children could correct themselves. (Again, in this she anticipated contemporary learning materials.) She understood that children are willing and eager to do things for themselves if the task is at their level—the problem of the match, as J. McV. Hunt (1961) has called it.

Where Montessori's child sense deserted her was in the domain of play. She seemed to distrust play and fantasy as somehow trivial. Perhaps because she herself was such a hard and dedicated worker, she generalized this to children and saw this as their nature too. One of the dangers of child sense, and the one I want to highlight here, is that it can deceive even those who possess it. Montessori believed she had the same insight into children's play that she had into their learning. Unfortunately she did not.

At the time she wrote, play was thought to be the natural activity of children; it was the way in which they learned about the world and prepared for adult life. But Karl Groos (1899/1901), whose well-known books on play in human beings and animals were a basis for Montessori's thinking, recognized two facets of play. There was a personal, expressive, aesthetic side to play which developed into the arts. And there was a social adaptive part to play which was the forerunner of socially prescribed behaviors and work. It is important to note that in this context play is defined in relation to its orientation—personal or social adaptation—and not in terms of affect. Play can be pleasant or unpleasant, and the same is true for work.

Montessori, while she recognized the personal, expressive side of play, accorded it little value. She wrote:

> Imagination has always been given a predominant place in the psychology of childhood and all over the world people tell their children fairy stories that are enjoyed immensely, as if children wanted to exercise this gift which imagination undoubtedly is. Yet if we are all agreed that a child loves to imagine, why do we give him only fairy tales and toys on which to practice this gift? If a child can imagine a fairy and fairyland, it will not be too difficult for him to imagine America. Instead of hearing it vaguely in conversation, he can help clarify his own ideas of it by looking at the globe on which it is shown (1949/1967, p. 177).

For Montessori, play was the child's work and had to be taken in all seriousness. And to this day, in traditional (but by no means all) Montessori schools expressive play is really not permitted except upon the playground.

In short, as the case of Maria Montessori demonstrates, an investigator's personal value system and life experience can give rise to a child sense that provides creative insights into some domains of child behavior but which can also block insights into others.

John B. Watson

Montessori is an example of an investigator's personality and life circumstance giving rise to a child sense that stressed children's activity and independence. A radically different child sense and correspondingly different child psychology was arrived at by John Watson (1928). In his autobiography (1930) Watson describes an unhappy childhood in a small Southern town. He was an indifferent student and athlete and seems to have taken most pleasure in bullying blacks—a common and accepted practice at the time. One gets the feeling from Watson that he did not like the relative powerlessness of childhood and that his aggressive acting out was a reaction to the inherent physical and societal inferiority of the childhood estate.

As he matured, Watson's intellectual brightness brought him to the university. But he seems always to have distrusted books and "hand-me-down" knowledge. He was often able to get good grades by dint of prodigious memorizing but retained little after the examinations were over. On the other hand, he was good at building and making things. He could build experimental apparatus and he liked designing and running experiments. But when he moved to psychology from biology, he discovered that human "Os" were more recalcitrant than most laboratory animals. Consequently, following Thorndike, Watson began using animals to get at basic principles of human behavior.

481

The psychology that evolved from his research and from the work of others, such as Pavlov and Thorndike, was "Behaviorism" (e.g., 1924). Although Watson's behaviorism, particularly as it applied to child psychology, seems naive today, it contains a certain truth. Watson's child sense, his own childhood sense of powerlessness and passivity, of anti-intellectualism, and an excessive pride in craftsmanlike skills informed his view of children. Children are in some respects passive, anti-intellectual, and "activity" oriented. Watson did see clearly into one facet of child life.

The problem was, of course, that he mistook the part for the whole. As we have observed with other workers, the very child sense that provides insight blocks it at the same time. Watson could only see the passivity of childhood, not its active constructing, creating side. Children were completely malleable and he could make anyone into butcher, baker, "beggarman and thief" (1926, p. 10). As an adult, in control and active, Watson had to see children as passive and lacking in control. It is not surprising that when he left psychology he went into advertising. The advertiser, too, sees himself as active and his audience as a passive response system manipulable by the exercise of a few basic advertising principles.

The behaviorism of today is, of course, far different from the behaviorism of Watson. But it still retains some of the characteristics of his child sense: a kind of anti-intellectualism (e.g., Skinner's *Beyond Freedom and Dignity*, 1971); an emphasis upon apparatus; and a need to see the world as passive and manipulable. It would be wrong to dismiss this insight into child life because we find it dismal. Rather, it is important to recognize that Watson's child sense, like that of the other investigators described here, was limited. A child-sense approach to child development history thus allows us to appreciate an investigator's positive contributions as well as his or her negative impact.

Harry Stack Sullivan

Another sort of child sense is exemplified by our most creative American psychiatrist, Harry Stack Sullivan. Perhaps more than anything else, Sullivan is known for the interpersonal focus he placed upon all emotional difficulties (1953). He believed that emotional illness was social, not individual, and emerged in the process of interacting with others. Mental illness, in Sullivan's view, was never encapsulated in a patient's head but always existed in that person's interactions with others.

Sullivan placed great emphasis upon human development. He stressed the importance of interpersonal processes for the child's developing sense of self. Indeed, some of his concepts—such as "trust" and "intimacy"—anticipated similar concepts in Erik Erikson's (1950) conception of the life cycle. Of particular importance to Sullivan was what he called the "chumship"—a relationship between like-sexed peers in early adolescence that paved the way for true intimacy in all future interpersonal relationships.

What lay behind Sullivan's unique insight into the interpersonal dimension of childhood? His own childhood in upstate New York provides a clue. Sullivan grew up as an only child in a farm community in which there were no other Catholic children. He was generally ostracized and never experienced the close companionship of peers that he was to highlight as so significant for healthy development.

Perhaps because of this lonely childhood, Sullivan developed his special sense of the need for social interaction, his unique child sense. It was this insight into the child's continuing social needs that informed all of Sullivan's original contributions to psychiatry. His concerns went beyond children, patients, and families. After World War II he literally gave his life in pursuit of world peace.

Sullivan's emphasis upon the social and interpersonal inevitably produced its own blind spot. He did not see how critical the sense of personal identity, of uniqueness, is to adolescence. It took Erik Erikson (1950), with a very different social history, to focus upon personal identity, rather than social self, as a fundament of child life.

Jean Piaget

When we turn to Jean Piaget it is hardly necessary to chronicle his enormous contributions to developmental psychology. Perhaps Piaget's most distinctive emphasis is on the continuity between biology and the higher mental processes, his demonstration that human intelligence is an extension of biological adaptation processes. In addition, Piaget's work is particularly noteworthy for the insights it provides into the child's view of the world. At each stage of development, the child creates and recreates reality out of his or her experiences with the world. The child thus has a progressive series of realities, each of which is broader and more intricate than its predecessor.

What was Piaget's child sense and what sort of early childhood experiences contributed to it? Perhaps the first thing to be said is that Piaget was a true genius. Like most men of genius, Piaget demonstrated his talents early. He published his first paper at the age of ten. By the age of sixteen his bibliography was comparable to that of a productive senior professor.

Piaget's early involvement in matters intellectual was probably spurred by a somewhat conflict-ridden home situation. The religious piety of his mother was in sharp contrast with the academic liberalism of his university professor father. By pursuing his intellectual interests, Piaget was perhaps able to block out this family discord and also identify himself more closely with his father and uncle, both of whom were men of broad intellectual interests. One might speculate that because of his unique intellectual talents and the quality of his home life, Piaget was deprived

483

of a true childhood, which could help account for his very special child sense. He has a deep and abiding empathy with children. This comes through particularly in his early writings (e.g., 1923/1950, 1924/1928, 1932/1965) but marks all of his work. This special empathy, this unique insight into the child's view of the world, could stem from his own aborted childhood. In Jungian (1943/1966) terms, the child dimension of his personality was never realized. But in discovering how children come to construct reality, he is able, however vicariously, to realize the child in himself.

But Piaget's type of child sense, like Montessori's, has its limits and can be deceptive. Perhaps because Piaget is so identified with the child, he was never able to give much weight to the adult's role in development. Children do not really grasp the role of the adult in their intellectual formation. Adults are seen as providing the materials and the problems, but children feel that they are doing all the work. Piaget's view of child development is of this sort. It is the *child* who constructs and reconstructs reality out of his or her experiences with the environment. And, in education Piaget (1969/1970) argues that children should not be given knowledge but rather should invent or reinvent it. In Piaget's scheme, the adult plays only a secondary role in the child's construction of reality.

The secondary role of the adult may hold true for the acquisition of the basic mental operations described in Piaget's stage theory. But in the acquisition of cultural knowledge, adults do play a role. There is increasing evidence, from different lines of research, for what might be called "mediating structures" that intervene between the Piagetian operations and knowledge or skills per se. Whether these are called "strategies" or "styles" or "plans" or "learning to learn" or "metacognitions" is less significant than the fact that they in some ways intervene in the learning process and are acquired through interaction with adults.

There have been, and continue to be, many criticisms of Piaget, but a number of these seem to me ill-founded, since they blame him for not solving problems that he never proposed to tackle. I feel that he is to be most faulted in having left adults out of the child's developing intelligence (except for his inclusion of the vague "social experience"). In his own terms, Piaget views intelligence as an extension of biological adaptation. But what he fails to recognize is the adult's critical role in that adaptation at both the biological and psychological levels. While this failure does not in any way vitiate the value and significance of Piaget's work, it leaves us with the enormous task of somehow writing the adult into the developmental equation.

Erik Erikson

Perhaps the clearest example (because he has elaborated it himself) of the relationship between child sense and child development research is to be found in the work of Erik Erikson (1950). As he himself has documented, Erikson was the outsider *par excellence*. As a boy he grew up in a Jewish home and community that was discrepant with his Nordic appearance. As a young man he became a wandering artist, a direction much at variance with the professional orientation of his background. As an adult he became a psychoanalyst without formal academic training. In America he taught at major universities such as Harvard, Yale, and Berkeley without a B.A., much less an M.A. or Ph.D. It is probably fair to say that Erikson's sense of difference was present from an early age.

Erikson's unique child sense, therefore, was his insight into the child's need continually to integrate the disparate parts of himself or herself. Using his clinical and anthropological field experiences, Erikson was able to show how this need for a sense of personal identity could be a force for healthy mental growth and how its interference could lead to mental illness. To be sure, Erikson's child sense, had it not been combined with many clinical and artistic gifts, could not have been realized in the form of developmental theory. But it is hard to believe that Erikson would have arrived at the centrality of the child's need for a sense of personal identity unless spurred by his own extraordinary life experience.

If Erikson's unique child sense, his insight into the child's need to experience himself or herself as an integrated whole, gave us a new understanding of the adolescent, it also gave us a distorted view of the young child. This shows another limitation to child sense. An insight appropriate to a given age level may not be appropriate for all age levels. The limitation of Erikson's child sense can best be seen in his description of play in early childhood.

In his chapter on "Toys and Reasons" in *Childhood and Society* (1950), Erikson makes an important addition to the Freudian conception of play. He maintains that play is not merely a catharsis for emotional conflicts but can also be an outlet for the healthy problems of growing up. He gives a telling example from *Tom Sawyer* in which Tom's friend, Ben Rogers, imitates a steamboat with his whole body. Erikson argues that such play is healthy and provides a symbolic mode by which a young man who is in the midst of a growth spurt can master the disparate parts of himself.

While one can applaud this broadened conception of play as a means to promote healthy growth in addition to its role in dealing with emotional conflicts, it is less easy to applaud Erikson's Montessorian identification of work with play in early childhood. In contrast to Piaget (1945/1962) and Freud (1900–1914/1938), both of whom clearly distinguish between work and play (accommodation and assimilation for Piaget, and secondary and primary process for Freud), Erikson insists upon integrating the two. He gives an anthropological example of a little girl learning to close a heavy door and insists that this is play as well as work. In so doing he loses the important distinction, maintained by both Piaget and Freud, between personal and social adaptations. In early childhood it is necessary that personal adaptation and social adaptation be two separate strands of development, if eventual solid integration is to occur (Elkind, 1981). In Erikson, then, as in the other innovators presented earlier, the very child sense that brings insight into one domain of child life may block it in another. In science, as in life, there are no unmixed blessings.

485

Many other illustrations of the role of child sense in child-development research could, of course, be given. One thinks, for example, of John Bowlby (1977), who has lived almost all his life in a particular section of London. This must surely relate to his special child sense into the meaning and importance of attachment in child life. One thinks also of Vygotsky (1930–1934/1978) and of his ill health as a child and adult. This may have limited his childhood experiences and given him an empathy of the Piagetian sort for children. Indeed, some of the parallels between the two men may derive from a commonality of their child sense. It might be fruitful to isolate groupings of investigators who share a common child sense in future explorations of the history of our discipline.

Concluding Comments

In writing this paper I have taken a number of risks. I have oversimplified interactions that are, as we all know, enormously complex. Perhaps a greater risk, relative to a psychological readership, was to use a method of historical analysis that is to some extent subjective and speculative. But speculations of the present sort help make a point that perhaps cannot be made in any other way. Child sense is critical to valid insights into child life. Understanding children is extraordinarily difficult in that layer upon layer of experiential, conceptual, and operational sediment lie in the way. Child sense allows us to bore through these layers and to make contact with the workings of children's minds. Though child sense is not an unalloyed good and has its dangers, perhaps one must pay some price for its benefits.

I am much impressed by the quality of work that I see in our field and by the many new talents that are emerging. At the same time, I am dismayed by the large amount of methodologically sophisticated but conceptually sterile research generated by bright and competent young people. Our training philosophy may be to blame for this—together with the publish-or-perish mentality of the university structure. Too often the young become wedded to conceptualizations and methodologies that are ill-matched to their child sense. In our training programs we must devise ways to help students discover and explore their own special child sense so that they may find the research domain in which they can work most fruitfully. If this discussion, with all its limitations, encourages some young researchers to activate their child sense, it will have served a second purpose—the primary one having been historical.

REFERENCES

Alcott, A. B. *Observations on the principles and methods of infant instruction.* Boston: Carter & Hendee, 1830.

Ariès, P. *Centuries of childhood* (R. Baldick, trans.). London: Jonathan Cape, 1962.

Bayley, N. Consistency and variability in the growth of intelligence from birth to eighteen years. *Journal of Genetic Psychology*, 1949, *45*, 1–21.

Binet, A., & Simon, T. Méthodes nouvelles pour le diagnostic du niveau intellectuel des animaux. *Année Psychologique*, 1905, *11*, 191–244.

Bowlby, J. John Bowlby. APA *Monitor*, 1977, *8*, 6–7.

Brown, R. *A first language: The early stages.* Cambridge, Mass.: Harvard University Press, 1973.

Bruner, J. S. *The process of education.* Cambridge, Mass.: Harvard University Press, 1960.

Darwin, C. *The expression of emotions in man and animals.* London: Murray, 1872.

Elkind, D. *Children and adolescents* (3d ed.). New York: Oxford, 1981.

Erikson, E. *Childhood and society.* New York: Norton, 1950.

Erikson, E. *Young man Luther.* New York: Norton, 1968.

Freud, S. *The basic writings of Sigmund Freud* (A. A. Brill, trans.). New York: Modern Library, 1938. (Originally published, 1900–1914.)

Galton, F. *Inquiries into human faculty and its development.* London: Macmillan, 1883.

Gesell, A. *The first five years of life.* New York: Harper, 1940.

Groos, K. *The play of man* (E. L. Baldwin, trans.). New York: Appleton, 1901. (Originally published, 1899.)

Hall, G. S. The contents of children's minds. *Princeton Review*, 1883, *11*, 170–182.

Hall, G. S. *Adolescence* (2 vols.). New York: Appleton, 1904.

Hunt, J. McV. *Intelligence and experience.* New York: Ronald, 1961.

Jung, C. G. *Two essays on analytical psychology* (R. F. C. Hull, trans.). Princeton, N.J.: Princeton University Press, 1966. (Originally published, 1943.)

Koffka, K. *The growth of the mind* (R. M. Ogden, trans.). New York: Harcourt, Brace, 1924. (Originally published, 1921.)

Kohlberg, L. Moral and religious education and the public schools: A developmental view. In T. R. Sizer (Ed.), *Religion and public education.* Boston: Houghton Mifflin, 1967.

Köhler, W. *The mentality of apes* (E. Winter, trans.). New York: Harcourt, Brace, 1925. (Originally published, 1917.)

Lewin, K. Behavior and development as a function of the total situation. In L. Carmichael (Ed.), *Manual of child psychology.* New York: Wiley, 1946.

Montessori, M. *The Montessori method* (A. E. George, trans.). New York: Schocken, 1964. (Originally published, 1912.)

Montessori, M. *The absorbent mind* (C. A. Claremont, trans.). New York: Holt, Rinehart, & Winston, 1967. (Originally published, 1949.)

Pearson, K. *The grammar of science* (2d rev. ed.). London: Black, 1900.

Piaget, J. *Judgment and reasoning in the child* (M. Gabain, trans.). New York: Harcourt, Brace, 1928. (Originally published, 1924.)

Piaget, J. *The language and thought of the child* (M. Gabain, trans.). London: Routledge & Kegan Paul, 1950. (Originally published, 1923.)

Piaget, J. *The psychology of intelligence* (M. Piercy & D. E. Berlyne, trans.). London: Routledge & Kegan Paul, 1950. (Originally published, 1947.)

Piaget, J. *The origins of intelligence in children* (M. Cook, trans.). New York: International Universities Press, 1952. (Originally published, 1936.)

Piaget, J. *The construction of reality in the child* (M. Cook, trans.). New York: Basic Books, 1954. (Originally published, 1937.)

Piaget, J. *Play, dreams, and imitation in childhood* (C. Gattegno, & F. M. Hodgson, trans.). New York: Norton, 1962. (Originally published, 1945.)

Piaget, J. *The moral judgment of the child* (M. Gabain, trans.). New York: Free Press, 1965. (Originally published, 1932.)

Piaget, J. *The science of education and the psychology of the child* (D. Coltman, trans.). New York: Orion Press, 1970. (Originally published, 1969.)

Ross, D. G. *Stanley Hall*. Chicago: The University of Chicago Press, 1972.

Sendak, M. *Where the wild things are*. New York: Harper & Row, 1963.

Sendak, M. *In the night kitchen*. New York: Harper & Row, 1970.

Shinn, M. W. *Biography of a baby*. Boston: Houghton Mifflin, 1900.

Skinner, B. F. *Science and human behavior*. New York: Macmillan, 1953.

Skinner, B. F. *Beyond freedom and dignity*. New York: Knopf, 1971.

Sullivan, H. S. *The interpersonal theory of psychiatry*. New York: Norton, 1953.

Terman, L. M., et al. *Genetic studies of genius. Vol. I: Mental and physical traits of a thousand gifted children*. Stanford, Calif.: Stanford University Press, 1925.

Vygotsky, L. S. *Mind in society* (M. Cole et al., Eds.). Cambridge, Mass.: Harvard University Press, 1978. (Originally written, 1930–1934.)

Watson, J. B. *Behaviorism*. New York: Norton, 1924.

Watson, J. B. What the nursery has to say about instincts. In C. Murchison (Ed.), *Psychologies of 1925*. Worcester, Mass.: Clark University Press, 1926.

Watson, J. B. *Psychological care of the infant and child*. New York: Norton, 1928.

Watson, J. B. John Broadus Watson. In C. Murchison (Ed.), *History of psychology in autobiography* (Vol. 3). Worcester, Mass.: Clark University Press, 1930; New York: Russell & Russell, 1961.

Werner, H. *Comparative psychology of mental development* (E. B. Garside, trans.). New York: Harper, 1940. (Originally published, 1926.)

Wertheimer, M. *Productive thinking*. New York: Harper, 1945.

PERSONALITY

21

What Have We Learned about Personality?

NEVITT SANFORD

The editors of this book evidently thought that if I could write a piece about personality for *Psychology: A Study of Science* (Sanford, 1963) and then expand and update that piece to make my book *Issues in Personality Theory* (Sanford, 1970b), I could easily tell what we have learned about personality since the year 1.

Part of my problem is the delusion that people have read, and remembered, what I have written about personality. Actually, I have no hard evidence that anybody has read *Issues in Personality Theory*, except Salvatore Maddi, who reviewed it for *Contemporary Psychology* (Maddi, 1971), Ross Stagner, who is an old colleague, and maybe a few graduate students at the Wright Institute.

I do want to undertake what the editors suggested: to discuss some things we have (and have not) learned about personality over the past one hundred years—and, I would add, some things that we have forgotten—to speak of some major developments, make some assessments, and offer some suggestions for the future. My remarks are arranged not in chronological order, but according to a number of themes which I keep following and circling, something in the manner of a scout.

I must ask first, "Who is *we?*" in the question "What have we learned?" Perhaps the word refers to psychologists in general, or to those who think of psychology as their discipline. "We," however, might as well refer to the whole scientific and scholarly community, at least to everybody who studies personality. When Gordon

Allport entitled his great 1937 book *Personality: A Psychological Interpretation* (Allport, 1937), he made clear that there were other interpretations. He proceeded briefly to consider various theological, philosophical, juristic, sociological, and biosocial as well as psychological meanings of "personality" before setting forth his own famous definition.

Unfair, Perhaps, but Propaedeutic

I take this multiplicity of approaches seriously, and would say at the outset that personality is rapidly becoming (or is already) a subject for interdisciplinary study. I am sorry that the organizers of the centennial symposium on which this book is based did not list "Psychology and Politics" in their section on "Psychology and Its Intersecting Disciplines." Wundt himself, as Allport reminds us, argued for a characterology that would be propaedeutic to politics and history, the way Francis Bacon had demanded. I have some feelings about this, because at a time when *The Authoritarian Personality* (Adorno et al., 1950) was being widely ignored by psychologists it was kept alive (and improved upon) largely by political scientists (e.g., Greenstein, 1968; Knutson, 1973; Di Renzo, 1977).

When I taught a course in personality at Stanford in the early 1960s, I gave two lectures on authoritarianism in personality quite early in the quarter, referring mainly to a case study from our book. I hoped to give students an idea of the breadth and complexity of our subject. After one of these lectures a student said to my teaching assistant, "It isn't fair. I thought this was a course in psychology but it's not. It's a course in political science."

It would make sense to speak of what we personality psychologists, or personologists, have learned, but even here generalizations would be difficult. I know that more than a few influential personologists believe that interest in their field has slackened, that it is harder than ever to get money for good projects, that the Society for Personality and Social Psychology is dominated by the experimental social psychologists. But all this is relative. If we go back to 1950, say, or to a time when there were only fifteen divisions in APA, the prominence of personality as a field was certainly much greater than today. But if there is a sense among personality psychologists of having taken a back seat, this is mainly due, it seems to me, to a fantastic expansion in other fields of psychology rather than to any shrinkage of their own field. When, in the 1970s, Ross Stagner came to prepare the fourth edition of his 1937 textbook, having published the third in 1961, he found himself faced with "a truly overwhelming mass of material" that called for evaluation and summarization. He was able to mention in his book less than 50 percent of the publications he had examined.

491

An Imaginary Bandwagon

Perhaps the safest course for me is to explain what I think I have learned about personality, hoping to find out later how many colleagues agree. Here I must warn you of an old trick used by psychologists, ministers, politicians, and other propagandists. They say that what they want to happen *is* happening, hoping thereby to discourage their enemies and lead others to get on an imaginary bandwagon. If I were to say that cognitive variables and phenomenological perspectives had gained their proper place in the study of personality, opening the way to the study of adult development and to the effective countering of psychoanalytic reductionism; that this had been accomplished without any really crippling damage to the traditional psychodynamic point of view; that recent years had brought fresh understanding of the interactions between personality and the social environment, helping us to see how deep structures of personality are sustained by social structures and how the adult personality may be changed through changes in behavior and through self-insight; that great strides had been made toward understanding the role of culture in personality and of personality in culture; that psychoanalysis, which suffered a decline in influence in the 1950s and 1960s was staging something of a comeback; that greater appreciation of the wholeness of personality and of the embeddedness of this whole in the social environment had given rise to dissatisfaction with those one-shot experiments in which two or three variables are removed by abstraction from their living contexts and to a longing for "scientific revolutions" and to a new interest in and respect for general systems theory, field theory, phenomenology, grounded theory, and qualitative methods; if I were to say these things you would assume, reasonably enough, that I had spoken of what I want to see happen.

To get to what has actually been learned: one thing that everybody has learned (something that official psychology, social scientists, and the man in the street seem quite certain about) is that there *is* such an entity as personality.

Courses in personality are taught in most psychology departments today, it has a place—often a prominent place—in elementary textbooks, and it was listed among the special fields of psychology by the organizers of the centennial symposia, right alongside sensory processes, perception, learning, and so forth.

Quite Suddenly in the 1930s

When were these things not so? I have long had the impression, derived in large part, as I thought, from being on the scene at the time, that personality quite suddenly became a field in the middle 1930s. I have confirmed this impression by referring to Gardner Murphy's *Historical Introduction* (1949). Stagner's systematic text, based mainly on social-cultural dynamics, and Allport's great integrating treatise were both published in 1937, while Murray's *Explorations in Personality* came

492

in 1938. *Frustration and Aggression* (Dollard, Doob, et al., 1939), a product of Yale's baptism in psychodynamic theory, appeared the next year.

It is interesting to note that Lewin's *Dynamic Theory of Personality* was published earlier than any of these, in 1935. Gordon Allport called the title a misnomer, since the book contained mainly reports of general psychological experiments based on Gestalt theory. But it also included the long paper on feeblemindedness, with its representation of the person. Students in my course in the history of psychology who by the time we get to Lewin have read some of Titchener, James, Freud, Jung, and McDougall, find it quite stunning to see that Lewin so neatly conceptualized the whole personality and that changes in that whole (such as thickening of all the boundaries separating regions) go with changed conditions in the environment, and therefore can be induced experimentally. Of course, Freud and Jung also had conceptions of the whole person, but this often does not come through at a first reading, which is likely to focus upon particular concepts.

Why was the establishment of personality as a field so long delayed? There was a lot of psychology around by 1935 (I started to say an awful lot). Studies of individual differences and case histories of patients in clinics had been accumulating in this country since 1896. When I was at Columbia in 1929, the curriculum was almost as broad as it is today, though less differentiated or specialized. The knowledge, speculations, and methods that Stagner and Allport were to bring together were available in quantity. Drawing upon this legacy, Allport was able to deal with an enormous range of personality characteristics—traits, attitudes, values, competencies—and to list (and discuss briefly) fifty-two methods for measuring variables and assessing aspects of personality.

Psychoanalysis Comes to America

Psychoanalysis, in the decade of the 1930s, was Jungian (Jung, 1954) and Adlerian (Adler, 1929) as well as Freudian (Freud, 1917/1943). After the famous symposium at Clark University in 1909, where both Freud and Jung held forth, some of the psychological journals began to accept papers about psychoanalysis, and by 1920 influential university professors were willing to say a good word about the subject— for example, Terman at Stanford, Tolman at Berkeley, Dollard at Yale, Willoughby at Clark, Wells at Harvard.

Before the middle 1930s, however, psychoanalysis was taken seriously, worked at, and used in practice almost exclusively in clinics and mental hospitals. In these settings the word "personality" was in fairly common use and formal definitions had been offered, even before 1920. Clinicians were willing to use anything that promised help in dealing with their cases, and they were not much troubled by the differences between psychoanalysis and behaviorism.

To be established as a field, personality had to make its way into the university. It had to connect itself with, and acknowledge its indebtedness to, general psychology. In the case of psychodynamically oriented personality theory and research, this turned out to be exceedingly difficult. Part of the difficulty is shown by Allport's skimpy treatment of psychoanalysis in his 1937 text. He explained in a footnote that psychoanalysis dealt with the abnormal, and besides it had been fully treated elsewhere (he didn't say that about any other subject). In other words it belonged in the clinic. Allport's personality psychology, I am afraid, was to remain a psychology of the parlor or living room; it hardly concerned itself with what went on in the bedroom, bathroom, or kitchen (the kitchen is where the murders take place).

The trouble that personology encountered in the university was not primarily the kind of resistance that psychoanalysts talk about or even the behaviorists' dislike of dealing with anything they couldn't, so to speak, get their hands on. The greatest trouble, I think, was the fear on the part of academic psychologists that the empirical science they had been building up for nearly fifty years would be damaged or threatened by adopting problem areas that did not lend themselves well to attack by experimental or rigorously quantitative methods. There would be a lowering of standards or, perhaps, a change in the prevailing conception of science itself. Their fears were not groundless. The psychoanalysts and other clinicians did not show great interest in empirical demonstrations of their theories, or if they did, they found such demonstrations extraordinarily difficult. They argued, of course, that method ought to be suited to the problem rather than the other way around.

Morton Prince and Henry Murray, in setting up the Psychological Clinic at Harvard in 1927, agreed with this argument, but they made clear to colleagues that they intended to stay within the bounds of empirical science. Nevertheless, in reviewing Murray's *Explorations in Personality* (1938) Richard M. Elliott, despite his admiration for the boldness and imaginativeness of the enterprise, expressed considerable dismay at what he considered a tendency of the researchers to find what they were looking for. And he predicted, rightly, that the *Explorations* would run a gauntlet of criticism (Elliott, 1939).

With Joy and Excitement

And so the battle was joined. Indeed it had been joined five or six years before the *Explorations* was published. Allport as well as Murray believed that personality entered into the determination of all behavior. Those who ignored this basic truth would never enter the Kingdom of Heaven. Extraordinarily able polemicists, these two men gave as good as they got in the controversy that raged throughout the 1930s.

But apart from their common accent on wholeness, these two men were not very close in their views. Allport was the great integrator, but Murray was the one who knew where to find the skeletons. He not only saw personality as an organic whole but proceeded to conceptualize this whole, and to conceive and carry out a grand design for studying it. And his was a dynamic personology which gave plenty of room for unconscious processes. It was the inside structuring of personality that had to be uncovered, and those of us who were lucky enough to be Murray's students in the 1930s delved into it with joy and excitement—which could be fully explained only by reference to a breakthrough of infantile curiosity.

I have been parochial in referring so much to Harvard. Actually there was readiness for a dynamic psychology of personality all around the country, and work along this line was being done at centers whose reputation for scientific rigor was much higher than at the Harvard Psychological Clinic. For example, Robert Sears, a Yale man, first published on his experimental studies of projection in 1935, and his Survey of Objective Studies of Psychoanalytic Concepts (Sears, 1943) included many studies carried out in the decade of the 1930s in diverse psychology departments.

The struggle to implant dynamic psychology of personality firmly in the university was dramatic. Fierce loyalties and persistent enmities were generated; there were, as followers of Gregory Bateson would say, "schizmogenetic confrontations." I imagine myself writing a history of this struggle and have already thought of some original titles for its various phases: "The Gathering Storm," "Blood, Sweat, and Tears," "Their Finest Hour," and now "The Grand Alliance."

In Response to Hitler

As early as 1933 there began to arrive in this country refugees from Hitler's Germany, many of whom were to join forces with our native psychodynamic personologists. There were not only psychoanalysts, representing various degrees of orthodoxy (e.g., Fenichel, 1945; Alexander, 1937) and revisionism (e.g., Fromm, 1941; Horney, 1937; Reich, 1946), but field theorists (e.g., Lewin, 1935; Werner, 1948), general system theorists (e.g., Bertalanffy, 1943), organismic personologists (e.g., Goldstein, 1939; Angyal, 1941), psychodynamically oriented psychologists from the universities which were already involved in the studies of life-cycle development (e.g., Bühler, 1935; Frenkel-Brunswik, 1942), and social philosophers with advanced ideas about the embeddedness of personality in the social system (e.g., Adorno, 1946; Horkheimer, 1949). The alliance of these scientists and scholars with the American students of personality gave the field a major forward thrust.

World War II further boosted the fortunes of personality psychology. Psychodynamic psychologists did not immediately embrace the conceptual scheme and the general method of Murray's *Explorations*, but they seized upon the projective techniques described there, particularly the Thematic Apperception Test. This was particularly true of clinical psychologists, who, as we know, will use anything that

495

promises to help them with their problems. Use of this test involved concepts referring to unconscious processes.

It is commonly said that World War II did for clinical psychology what World War I had done for intelligence testing. Almost immediately after the war the Veterans Administration and the U.S. Public Health Service began pouring money for clinical training into the universities. Everybody who was on the scene at the time will recall the influx of able and eager veterans who wanted a psychology that was useful. At Berkeley in the late 1940s a question often heard from graduate students was "Where can I get an inexpensive analysis?"

In September of 1947 the APA accepted the report of its Committee on Training in Clinical Psychology. As its chairman, David Shakow, has written (Shakow, 1977), this report meshed with the Zeitgeist. While general psychology and standard research methods were required in the curriculum (the clinician was to be a psychologist first), all the good things that the personologists could ask for were also included—psychodynamics of behavior, diagnostic methods, including of course the projective techniques, psychotherapy, and lots more. The activities of the Veterans Administration and the U.S. Public Health Service meant that money, in large amounts, was behind these new programs.

Station S and the Practice of Assessment

These trends were strengthened by the establishment of the OSS assessment centers during the war and the setting up of such centers at universities after the war. Henry Murray again. The method at Station S, which Murray headed, was to have numerous observers see subjects in various situations—ranging from depth interviews to situational tests. This was the way not only to select people for important jobs but also to study personality (OSS Assessment Staff, 1948). More than a few psychologists left Station S after the war determined to set up similar centers at their own universities, and some succeeded. Various other psychologists who worked in war-related jobs returned home with the expectation of doing psychological work that was useful in practice.

Now we come to "Triumph and Tragedy." In the personality psychology of the late 1940s psychodynamic or psychoanalytic psychology was riding high. One of the most respectable kinds of experiments one could do featured some cognitive or learning process as the dependent variable and some psychodynamic process as the independent one. In 1949 Klein and Schlesinger asked, "Where is the perceiver in perceptual theory?" And the answer was, right there at the center of the whole thing. Instead of relating behavior to an external stimulus while holding personality processes constant, the style was to relate behavior to personality variables, and personality variables one to another while giving due attention to the environment.

Personality psychologists thought this style was firmly established. They were to learn to their sorrow that it was not. In the early 1950s a reaction set in. To me it seemed sudden, though it probably had been building for some time. By 1955, surely, the reaction was plain. True enough, the outpouring of personality research continued, and courses were still taught. The editions of Hall and Lindzey's textbook (1957, 1965, 1972) helped to insure that thousands of students learned something about personality. But much of the life had been drained from the great movement of the 1930s and 1940s. Most (if not all) of the theorists discussed by these authors had done their great work in the decades before.

Without Looking at It

By the 1950s, according to Robert White, there were hundreds of research projects supposedly about personality which showed "no trace of organismic thinking, of field theory, or of awareness of complexity" (White, 1980). He described this type of research as "studying personality without looking at it." I think it is safe to say that much of this work is no improvement over the studies of individual differences carried out in the 1920s.

What happened? Clinical psychology had overextended itself. There were far too few well-trained clinical psychologists to staff the programs established in the 1940s, far too few who could do the clinical training and at the same time maintain the research productivity demanded by the universities. Also, the clinical psychologists of that time were not sufficiently social in their orientation; they failed to take sufficiently into account the political and social structural processes of the psychology departments, the universities, and the funding agencies. Nonclinical personality psychologists, including some who had become associated with centers modeled after the OSS assessment program, suffered a failure of nerve. Unwilling or unable to make common cause with the failing clinicians, they fell back upon the tried and true, or the fashionable, where methodology was concerned. Important new leads in personality research were turned into methodological problems.

Personologists in the Murray tradition, seeing they could do little to influence the course of events, began to take stock. Here I believe some real learning took place. These psychologists began to see what others had pointed out, that they had overstated their case and had perhaps even overstressed the inner at the expense of the outer. Murray's *Explorations in Personality* (1938), of course, had much to say about the importance of the contemporary environment. His concept of "press"—especially of Alpha and Beta press—was one of his happiest. And the "vast and intricate architecture" of personality included just about everything anyone could think of—mature and proactive processes as well as infantile fixations and their derivatives. But there is no denying that Murray and his circle gave special attention

497

to the "unity thema" of a personality central to which were unconscious processes set going early in life.[1]

A Love of Early Determinants

Things were much the same when it came to *The Authoritarian Personality* (Adorno, Frenkel-Brunswik, Levinson, & Sanford, 1950). We were willing to allow all sorts of contemporary environmental determinants of prejudice; and we were careful to say that we were talking about the *potential* for fascism in the personality. We said enough about society and its processes so that a famous sociologist called our book a Leninist tract. Yet there is no denying that *The Authoritarian Personality* is a book about personality, considered mainly within a psychoanalytic frame of reference. A colleague told me recently that the reason he and a lot of other people didn't read the book was because it did not suggest what to do about fascism now. He certainly didn't want to wait until the next generation had been reared.

It is a little embarrassing to admit, but as late as 1950–1951 some of us were on the same old track. At the Institute of Personality Assessment and Research in Berkeley, under the direction of Donald MacKinnon, we carried out a three-day assessment of graduate students from various departments of the University using the OSS model (OSS Assessment Staff, 1948). We set out to explain, on the basis of life histories and psychodynamic theory, variations in creativity, personal soundness, and potential for success. It never occurred to us, as far as I know, to ask what, if any, were the impacts upon these students of being in graduate school.

What now seems clear is that childhood determinants are readily found in adult personalities by anyone who has the data. Erik Erikson has unpublished case histories to show that themes found in the play constructions of twelve-year-olds were still ramifying throughout their personalities when they were forty-five. Every year, it seems to me, someone produces a dissertation, based on data available at the Institute of Human Development in Berkeley, confirming some psychodynamic hypothesis concerning the relations between present personality characteristics and childhood experience.

Open Systems to the Rescue

Let us agree, however, that there are in everyone, normal and abnormal, processes that are not dominated by unconscious processes but governed instead by well-established principles of learning. Young adults may take new directions in their

---

[1]Robert White's "The Case of Ernst" in *Explorations* (1938) remains the best model of a search for a unity thema.

development through responding to challenges put in their way (White, 1952, 1963; Sanford, 1962a,b, 1980). The personalities of young adults, and other people, are best conceived as open systems—which means that they have some freedom from entropy. Education, and much psychotherapy, can be considered as the expansion of those parts of the personality that are not dominated by unconscious processes. Such expansion can change the relationship between the conscious and the unconscious parts of the personality and, quite conceivably, lead to some shrinkage of the latter.

If all this leads to the threat of the warm embrace of the more extreme wing of the humanistic psychologists, one can always come up with a few Freudian interpretations.

This open-systems view clearly enhances the role of cognitive processes in personality functioning and development. The authors of *The Authoritarian Personality* included rigidity, intolerance of ambiguity, and other cognitive variables within the authoritarian syndrome, but they consistently saw psychodynamic factors as determining. I now happily admit that in a syndrome which embraces both psychodynamic and cognitive processes, a change in cognitive functioning can bring a change in the whole thing.

My favorite story about this concerns a professor in a Southern institution who broke up an authoritarian structure in one of her students by teaching her some statistics. After class one day the professor found this young woman in the rest room, crying bitterly. "You are ruining my life," she said. "You are knocking down everything I have believed in." What had happened, it seemed, was that the study of probability, distribution curves, and so forth had made it impossible for her to maintain the stereotypes and rigid categories with which she had structured her world. A change in cognitive behavior brought change in the personality as a whole. But, not to leave the psychodynamic entirely out of account, it seems to me likely that this student would not have caught the lessons in statistics had she not liked and admired her teacher.

Self-Insight and Behavior

As this story suggests, change in personality requires a change in behavior. For a long time behaviorists who insisted on this position and paid no attention to self-insight have argued with psychodynamically oriented psychologists who saw self-insight as the royal road to personality change. Today most of the energy seems to have gone out of this debate. I think most personality psychologists could not object to the formulation that a developmental change in personality, in the case of an adult or a college student, requires both behavior change *and* self-insight in order to endure (Sanford, 1980). The change in behavior must be integrated with the personality, and this requires the kind of self-reflection that leads to insight. If the

499

young woman in the story really did largely overcome her authoritarian tendencies, this was due in large part to her reaching a place where she could recall with amusement the episode in the rest room and differentiate easily between her present and her former selves.

Conceiving of personality as an open system draws attention not only to the role of cognitive processes but to the interaction of the person and the social environment. Twenty years ago (it seems only yesterday), I stated that personality was more "social" than it used to be (Sanford, 1963).

> With the development of anthropology and sociology, evidence has gradually accumulated and has become rather overwhelming that virtually all distinguishable features of personality are correlated with features of the cultural or social environment of the individual now or in his past.

Accent on the social environment of the past as a determinant of present dispositions in the person has, as I have indicated, long been the stock in trade of the traditional personality psychologists of the psychodynamic persuasion. This stemmed largely from Freud's emphasis on the events of early childhood. But it also stemmed from his explicit insistence upon the role of other people in the development of personality. Although well-known as a biological determinist, and the propounder of instinct theory, by 1922 Freud became a self-styled social psychologist. In *Group Psychology and the Analysis of the Ego*, he wrote:

> It is true that Individual Psychology is concerned with the individual man and explores the paths by which he finds satisfaction for his instincts; but only rarely and under certain exceptional conditions is Individual Psychology in a position to disregard the relation of this individual to others.
>
> In the individual's mental life someone else is invariably involved, as a model, as an object, as a helper, as an opponent, and so from the very first Individual Psychology is at the same time Social Psychology as well—in this extended but entirely justified sense of the words (Freud, 1921/1960, pp. 1–2).

The issue which Freud was here trying to resolve was the ancient one concerning biological versus social-environmental determination of human behavior and mental life. Since the turn of the century, or before, sociologists and behavioristic psychologists had been trying to refute or correct the instinct theories of Freud (1917/1943) and McDougall (1908). Well before 1922 it was clear that the environmental determinists were winning the day. In America, Charles Cooley (1902) and E. A. Ross (1908) were arguing that human personality was determined not by instincts but by the "social order." These writers were enormously influential. It may be doubted that they influenced Freud. But the ideas they espoused were

500

certainly in the air in Europe, put there by such figures as Hegel, Marx, and Comte—and by Freud's contemporary Gabriel Tarde (1890/1903).

How Do We Feel a Social Force?

In the perspective of today it is possible to see that the "social forces" posited by the early sociologists were not very well differentiated, and the conception of personality was too simple. Even more disabling, the processes by which the social forces were said to become established within the latter—processes such as imitation and conformity—were not adequate to the complexity of the interaction between personality and the social environment. The early behavioristic psychologists were quite precise about ways in which the environment wrought some of its effects on the person, but they had only limited conceptions of personality or of the broader social environment.

It remained for the anthropologists (and a few early social and personality psychologists) to grasp the significance of Freud's complex conception of personality, and his theories about the ways in which the predispositions which the infant brings into the world are shaped by early events in the setting of family life. Margaret Mead was, as far as I know, the first anthropologist to test psychoanalytic theory through field studies in remote cultures (Mead, 1928/1949, 1930/1953). She and other leading anthropologists such as Ruth Benedict (1934) and Ralph Linton (1936) brought together masses of material to show that what McDougall called "instincts" were not universal in the species but were, instead, patterns of behavior that depended on the social environment—as shown by the fact that they varied from one culture to another. When anthropologist Edward Sapir was chosen to write the piece on personality for the 1934 *Encyclopedia of the Social Sciences* (Sapir, 1934), he devoted the most space to Freud, Jung, and Adler and stated his preference for the "psychiatric definition" of personality: a structure of reactivity essentially fixed by the age of two or three. All these anthropologists were greatly influenced by Freud and thus put heavy emphasis upon early childhood as the time when basic erotic and aggressive impulses were shaped in accord with the demands of social life.

A Comparative Study of Structures

It is sometimes forgotten that in the "culture–personality movement" of the 1930s the relations between culture and personality were seen as a two-way street. Culture shaped personality, but culture evolved in part out of the needs, conflicts, and anxieties of individuals. Malinowski was willing to take Freud's *Totem and Taboo* (Freud, 1913/1961) seriously. In that work Freud wrote as if the Oedipus complex

501

were universal, as if the patterns of love and hate and the mechanisms of defense found in children and neurotic adults in Vienna were revealed in such cultural institutions as exogamy, taboo, and totemism. Malinowski, in his *Sex and Repression in Savage Society* (1937), observed that basic childhood patterns of love and hate in the matrilineal society of the Trobriand Islanders were not the same as in the Viennese society of Freud's day. Thus Malinowski could argue that Frued's Oedipus complex was not universal, but he did not doubt that the repression of sexual and aggressive impulses and the transformations that followed were important sources of culture.

Abram Kardiner, an avowed Freudian, proposed in 1939 that each culture has a "basic personality structure," a pattern of deeply based attitudes and beliefs compatible with a given system of social institutions and traditions (Kardiner, 1939). It was in terms of such structure that one could describe the basic personality differences between a Trobriand Islander and one of those middle-class patients of Freud. Similar to Kardiner's idea was Erich Fromm's concept of "social character," a socially shaped structure embodying deeply based emotional needs and common to most members of the group in question (Fromm, 1941).

David Riesman, who was a close student of Fromm, wrote in *The Lonely Crowd* (1950) of a new "social character" emerging in the bureaucratic salaried classes of this country, and W. H. Whyte in his *The Organization Man* (1956) described the same kind of thing. Michael Maccoby (1977), who collaborated with Fromm in their *Social Character in a Mexican Village* (1970), is still making good use of the concept.

Where Is the Pattern to Be Found?

One way to grasp what is involved here is to ask about a structure such as authoritarianism whether it is "in" the culture, or "in" the personality, or "in" both? The authors of *The Authoritarian Personality* (1950) found, among other things, that ethnic prejudice goes with idealization of parents, which goes with punitiveness toward nonconformists, which goes with rigid conception of sex roles, which goes with intolerance of ambiguity, and so on; and they saw in this covariance a deeply based structure of personality. Others, for example, Selznick and Steinberg (1969), while accepting these findings, have held that authoritarianism should be regarded as an aspect of the "common" as opposed to the "enlightened" culture of the United States. If it makes sense to speak of an authoritarian culture or social character, as I believe it does, the common culture of the United States is not a very good example of it; but the crucial question here is what makes the elements named above go together to form a pattern.

This question is the same whether we are talking about a personality pattern or a culture pattern. And, in my view, the only way to gain an adequate understanding of the dynamic interrelationships of the elements in a culture pattern is through the intensive study of individuals. Here it is important to note that a culture pattern, or some variety of social character, can exist not only in exotic tribes or in nation states but in reference groups such as professional psychologists or a manufacturers' association and in face-to-face groups within colleges and corporations. I first encountered this use of the concept in Elliott Jacques's book *The Changing Culture of a Factory* (1951), and not long after that my colleague John Bushnell (1962) was writing about student culture at Vassar College.

In the 1950s I stressed the point that personality psychology was becoming more social with respect not only to variables but also to the locus of organizing principles. Citing Bettelheim's (1943) observations of life in a German concentration camp and my own observations of the loyalty oath controversy at the University of California (Sanford, 1953), I wrote as follows:

> Increasingly we realize that we do not detract from such favorite concepts as the superego, ego identity, or self-concept by supposing that—despite their relative stability and autonomy—they are to some degree sustained as well as formed by forces in the social environment and may be altered radically by extreme social change (Sanford, 1970b, p. 62).

Furthermore, self-concept or other aspects of personality might be altered by social factors in the present or very recent past of an adult as well as in childhood or youth. Personality psychologists paid increasing attention to what an adult had recently learned through exposure to the environment, using such concepts as role dispositions, interpersonal reaction systems, and social values. I would say now that this inclination to see individuals in their social context is becoming more and more firmly established.

The Importance of Studying Adults

An important case in point is Daniel Levinson's (1978) concept of "the individual life structure—the underlying pattern or design of a person's life at a given time." It embodies "all the relationships with individuals, groups and institutions that have significance for" a person. This concept is at least as social or sociological as it is personal. Levinson is out to develop what he would call a truly social psychology.

It is no accident that Levinson arrived at his conception of the individual life structure through his study of adult development. If we believe that adults can develop and should, we naturally examine their contemporary environment with a view to identifying components that favor development. We do well, too, to take a fresh look at personality, asking ourselves which of its components or aspects can develop and by what processes.

503

Here we owe much to Erik Erikson (1950). His concept of "ego identity" signaled, for many of us, a major advance in psychoanalytic thinking. Conceived as a central structure of personality, ego identity was clearly still being formed, as Erikson saw it, in young adulthood. And, as I think he would say today, issues of identity are never settled once and for all in the course of a lifetime.

Robert White has also been a major contributor to the field of adult development. In *Lives in Progress* (1952) he reported intensive and comprehensive case studies of people who had been seen once when they were in college and again five to ten years later. He then went on to describe some major changes in personality that had occurred in the interval between the two sets of interviews, and then, using both psychodynamic and social learning concepts, he presented a theory concerning the conditions and processes of change.

My colleagues and I leaned heavily on the work of Erikson and White when we carried out our studies of personality development in college students (Sanford, 1956). This line of inquiry has been followed up by numerous investigators whose work has been summarized by Feldman and Newcomb (1969) and by Chickering (1969). I would say today that almost any tendency in the person can be profoundly changed by education, broadly conceived. What holds for college students holds for graduate students as well (Katz & Hartnett, 1976) and, as we are beginning to learn, for faculty members (Freedman et al., 1980). Less research has thus far been done on the development of people other than students or teachers, but theory suggests that investigation into their potential will also be rewarding.

In arriving at this conception of adult potentialities, I and more than a few colleagues of the old school have come quite a long way. We have given significant ground to the cognitive theorists, to the social theorists, even to the situationists. This raises the question—to paraphrase Professor Higgins in *My Fair Lady*—why can't *they* be like us—so friendly and tolerant, so broadminded and flexible, so eager to learn?

The Scandal of the Dynamic Unconscious

Much of the trouble, surely, lies in the continuing unwillingness or the inability of many psychologists to come to terms with the dynamic unconscious. Many are saying, in effect, "Anything you can explain by reference to unconscious processes, I can explain better in terms of social-learning theory." Thus for thirty years refutations have been raining on *The Authoritarian Personality*, whose major findings have long since found a place in the culture of social science. It is, of course, the duty of scientists to be critical of works that appear to be significant—but to keep reinventing the same critiques for thirty years? It seems too much. Some psychologists just can't seem to let the matter drop.

Recently I read a research proposal by a man who was out to demolish the original work on authoritarianism by redefining the concept. In order to get results which promised to support a social-learning theory, he limited his definition to authoritarian submission, authoritarian aggression, and conventionalism—patterns which subjects might conceivably have learned from their parents. He simply set aside patterns such as anti-intraception, overaccent on power and toughness, and projectivity, all of whose intercorrelation and correlation with the above patterns really call for psychodynamic theory. Stubbornly to neglect it is to face the problems of the world with one hand tied behind one's back (to use Henry Murray's imagery).

Such sins of omission may be due merely to preference for one theory over another, or to loyalty to mentors or schools of thought, but sometimes we have to deal with old-fashioned Freudian "resistance." Some of my students and I came up against this recently. I teach a year-long course the first half of which is devoted to the history of psychology, the second half to my *Self and Society* (1966a). We got along fine until we came to the chapters entitled "Masculinity and Femininity in the Structure of Personality" and "Changing Sex Roles, Socialization, and Education." We found ourselves unable to have a rational discussion of these topics. Before we knew what was happening the air was filled with anger, anxiety, and embarrassment, with too many people talking at once.

Having used our two hours without getting anywhere, we decided to try again the following week. Our efforts were still confused and very unsatisfactory. One trouble, I thought, was that some of the more aggressively feminist women were sure there was something sexist in the material but could not put their fingers on it. At the same time, there was unspoken opposition to assigning psychodynamic interpretations to what these women saw as a political problem. We agreed, however, that we had allowed our unconscious processes to interfere with our reasoning.

Fragmented into Triviality

Changing sex roles are precisely the stuff that psychoanalysts should be interested in, since it is their duty to be countercyclical, to talk about what people do not want to talk about. I am not aware, however, that they have taken a leading role in the public discussion of women's liberation, changing sex roles, or homosexuality, although there can be no doubt that these issues must arise daily in their practices. One might suppose, too, that psychologists interested in personality dynamics would want to examine the ways in which people today manage their conscious and unconscious dispositions toward femaleness and maleness. Some psychologists are interested, but I would not bet a nickel on their chances of getting funding, except, of course, for "studies of personality without looking at it," studies of variables instead of people, studies limited to objective tests.

The commitments of academic psychologists to the experimental or quantitative study of functional relationships among a few variables seem as firm as ever (Epstein, 1979). Many of these psychologists seem to define science as the proper use of these methods. For the foreseeable future we can expect little change: this outlook finds support in the general academic culture, the structure of the university, and well-established practice in the government funding agencies.

At the same time, counterforces which have been present all along are increasing in strength. For example, there has been a revival of interest in the study of lives. The determined efforts of the Committee on Personality of the Society for Personality and Social Psychology are beginning to bear fruit. The several celebrations of the fortieth anniversary of the publication of Murray's *Explorations in Personality* produced some major statements favoring the grand tradition in personality research (Block, 1980; Epstein, 1979; Levinson, 1980; White, 1980; Sanford, 1980), and wide interest was aroused. And the establishment of the Murray Center for the Study of Lives at Radcliffe provides a new source of data on sex roles, women's lives, and related topics. I hope the new Center will help to put psychohistory on a firmer footing. Psychohistorians have contributed a lot to the study of personality, but sometimes their embrace of classical psychoanalysis has been too passionate, to the neglect of what Erikson calls the "historical moment."

Paths to Revitalized Research

Political scientists also have made and are making major contributions to the study of personality, and the founding of the International Society of Political Psychology, a broadly interdisciplinary group, has been a major stimulus to people interested in the study of the person in society.

There are stirrings in anthropology also. A couple of years ago, as an observer, I attended a national conference of anthropologists. To my delight, the group was made up of "oldsters"—people trained by the founders of American anthropology—and "youngsters." The people who are currently running Anthropology—whom I took to be the "hardnosed" set—were referred to as "the excluded middle." Never was better advantage taken of the fact that grandparents and grandchildren communicate better than do parents and children. Personality and culture and psychoanalysis were discussed freely and creatively, and much satisfaction was taken in the fact that anthropology is still one of the humanities. The youngsters wanted action—action anthropology—while the oldsters very tactfully let it be known that they had been involved in action anthropology from the beginning.

Coming back closer to home and to the need for new paradigms, I believe it is fair to say that qualitative research, exploratory research, and phenomenological methods have won for themselves a new legitimacy. Daniel Levinson and as-

506

sociates, in producing their very interesting book *The Seasons of a Man's Life*, might have sat down with the data from their forty-five subjects and correlated everything with everything. Instead, Levinson familiarized himself with all the cases, immersed himself in the data, took time for a lot of thought, and then proceeded to write what is by common consent a major contribution to the socio-psychological study of life-cycle development. One psychologist said on reading the book that he hated it when he found that all of his principles concerning method were either violated or neglected *and* that his own formula had been spelled out.

It is not possible, of course, to get any grant money for research on new paradigms, but graduate students, happily, have to do research whether they are paid or not. Many seize the opportunity to work at some problem or phenomenon with which they have had some experience, in which they are deeply interested, and which needs to be approached through the intensive study of cases—necessarily a limited number.

Thus in the interdisciplinary program at the Wright Institute, for example, we have approved dissertations based on the study of five white families who had adopted black children at least fifteen years before, on nine cases of divorced women who had found the going much tougher than they expected, on twelve cases of young female social scientists, on six cases of professional women in the People's Republic of China. Such dissertations always include a section on "method" in which students argue for suiting the method to the problem at hand, citing such authorities as Churchman (1979) on general systems theory; Bateson (1972) on context and reality; Polanyi (1958) on subjectivity and objectivity in science; Ziman (1968) on the inadequacy of physical science's "two-valued logic" when it comes to the study of social problems; Gendlin (1965–1966), Diesing (1971) and Schachtel (1959) on phenomenology; Glaser and Strauss (1967) on grounded theory; Becker (1963) on participant observation; Gouldner (1970) and Reinharz (1979) on the rehumanization of sociology; Devereux (1967) and Briggs (1970) on the encounter between anthropologists and their informants; and Allport (1937), White (1938), and Sanford (1943, 1953) on the case study. These dissertations have been read by various visiting committees from our accrediting association and from NIMH and, although a few of these studies arched some eyebrows, we passed muster.

What It Means to Know People

In personality research the pattern is the thing—a pattern of interrelated dynamic and cognitive processes which makes sense when considered in the light of a theory. Recently a student interviewed people who had come to the Wright Institute in response to an ad asking the help of people who had recently quit smoking. He started with a comprehensive interview schedule being used around the Institute in

507

other studies. He found, however, that his schedule got in the way of what the visitors really wanted to say, that if he relaxed and let them talk, one thing suggested another until their own pattern emerged—and this he found more interesting.

Had he stayed with the interview schedule he could have obtained measures on, say, eighty-seven variables which, when manipulated by appropriate statistical procedures, would have yielded some patterns, some of which would resemble those that emerged directly when his interviewees were allowed to tell their stories. In that case, however, none of his statistically derived patterns would have fit any particular interviewee precisely, or well enough so that intervention could be confidently planned.

Patterns discovered through close-in work with individuals can be demonstrated by means of our traditional quantitative methods. We simply shift from a multitude of variables observed in a small number of cases to a few variables in many subjects. But when it comes to action affecting individuals or groups, far more than these isolated patterns needs to be taken into account. There is no way to avoid making use of the best of all computers, the mind of the action researcher. The functioning of this computer can always be improved through further training and experience, but I have often been impressed by what third-year graduate students can do, especially if they know their subjects or clients or client-subjects well, compare or group them on the basis of the patterns discovered in accord with theory, and ask which actions have what effects with which subjects.

I had a student who recently carried out a study in the manner of the original *The Authoritarian Personality* (Adorno et al., 1950), using various objective and projective tests, life-history interviews, and case studies. He had great difficulty in writing up one of his cases, in arriving at what might be called the "dynamic formulation" of the case. He said he had finally gotten things into place by looking at himself and asking what he would have done in the circumstances that faced his subject. This subject had majored in psychology, earned an M.A. in the subject, and read almost everything worth reading about personality theory before he arrived at the Wright Institute. Later, when he was about to hand in his thesis, he said, "I am beginning to feel like a psychologist." This young man will always be a psychologist, whether he gets a job in this field or not.

It is a fine thing to know another person well. It increases our humanity and our love of humankind. A student in my personality course at Stanford, required to do a case study of an acquaintance, studied his mother. He was amazed and delighted when she turned out to be a real person, interesting beyond anything he had imagined. It changed their whole relationship.

The biographical interview should be taught in high school and college, alongside of how to write a composition. If all graduate students in psychology were required to begin their work by doing such interviews and writing a case history, the whole face of psychology would be changed.

508

Research as Action, Action as Research

What researchers bent on the discovery of personality patterns do to gather their data, to get to know their subjects well, is already an action that affects the researcher as well as the subject. Wise Allen (1976), who did the study of white families who had adopted black children, inevitably became their counselor and friend, and while helping them he acquired some general knowledge and enriched his own life. Myra Wise (1977) drew her nine cases of divorced women from her practice of counseling and psychotherapy. While she was helping them, they helped her by supplying special data that she needed for her dissertation. Emily Serkin's (1980) interviews with the young female social scientists undoubtedly enhanced their sense of themselves and assisted their decision-making even as she—a young female social scientist herself—increased her control of her own life. Diana Wu (1980), who lived the first eighteen years of her life in mainland China, knew in advance of her visit there that her subjects would have no conception of social science as we know it, and that in China, as elsewhere in Asia, you establish a relationship before you get down to business. Thus her interviews were essentially conversations in which interviewer and interviewee took turns telling about their work, their children, their husbands, and so on. Naturally, Wu and her subjects became friends. After two years they still correspond, Wu joining the others in affirming that the research encounter was one of the most significant experiences of their lives.

The conception of action research with which I have sought to familiarize students at the Wright Institute and other people (Sanford, 1965, 1966b, 1969, 1970a) owes more to Freud than to Lewin (1947). Freud is supposed to have said that a psychoanalyst needed at least three patients, one who could pay, one who could be cured, and one from whom something could be learned. Regardless of the resources or promise of his patients, however, psychoanalysis in Freud's hands was a cooperative undertaking in which both analyst and patient learned in order to act, and acted in order to learn. In the interaction, both became emotionally involved, both learned.

It is unfortunate that Freud's method has been thought to belong only to the consulting room. The fact is that the well-motivated investigator does not need to be paid or to cure anybody in order to carry on activity that is enlightening and otherwise beneficial to both researcher and researched. The main thing to bear in mind is that in the research encounter, each of the actors is a whole person, a thinking, feeling, valuing individual, possessed of unconscious as well as conscious dispositions.

I have elsewhere tried to describe and explain, on the basis of experience with college students and faculty members, the benefits to an adult of being interviewed (1970a, 1971–1972, 1980). Suffice it to say here that interviewees have a chance to say things for which there had not previously been an appropriate audience; they can put into words ideas and thoughts that had been only vaguely formulated, and when they are met with attention and interest, self-esteem is raised. People who are interviewed have a chance to reflect upon their lives, take stock, think out loud about alternatives. They often gain some self-insight. Professors who are interviewed usually become more open to themselves and, hence, to their students; accordingly, interviews with professors have become regular features of faculty development programs.

It is interesting to recall in this connection that in the experiments that got started in Wundt's laboratory the person whom today we are likely to call a "subject" was called an "observer." These observers were real, live, whole persons, key figures in the interaction, who could be counted upon to take responsibility for their actions, to tell the truth, to keep their promises.

Years ago, when I was a graduate student I think, I heard Gardner Murphy say concerning Wilhelm Wundt, whom he credited with being the founder of modern psychology, that none of his findings were to be fully supported by later research. It would be ironic if his methods, which were designed to bring psychology into line with the natural science of his day, went the way of his findings. It would be ironic but not tragic. What would be tragic would be a failure of psychologists to accord their subjects the humanity that Wundt accorded his.

REFERENCES

Adler, A. *The practice and theory of individual psychology.* New York: Harcourt, Brace, 1929.

Adorno, T. W. Anti-Semitism and fascist propaganda. In E. Simmel (Ed.), *Anti-Semitism: A social disease.* New York: International Universities Press, 1946.

Adorno, T. W., Frenkel-Brunswik, E., Levinson, D. J., & Sanford, N. *The authoritarian personality.* New York: Harper & Row, 1950.

Alexander, F. *The medical value of psychoanalysis.* New York: Norton, 1937.

Allen, W. *The formation of racial identity in Black children adopted by White parents.* Unpublished doctoral dissertation, The Wright Institute, 1976.

Allport, G. W., *Personality: A psychological interpretation.* New York: Holt, 1937.

Angyal, A. *Foundations for a science of personality.* Cambridge, Mass.: Harvard University Press, 1941.

Bateson, G. *Steps toward an ecology of mind.* New York: Ballantine, 1972.

Becker, H. *Outsiders: Studies in the sociology of deviance.* New York: Free Press, 1963.

Benedict, R. *Patterns of culture.* Boston: Houghton Mifflin, 1934.

Bertalanffy, L. Von. An outline of general systems theory. *British Journal of Philosophical Science,* 1943, 134–165.

Bettelheim, B. Individual and mass behavior in extreme situations. *Journal of Abnormal and Social Psychology,* 1943, 38, 417–425.

Block, Jack. Some enduring and consequential structures in personality. In A. Rabin (Ed.), *Future explorations in personality.* New York: Wiley, 1980.

Briggs, J. Kapluna daughter. In P. Golde (Ed.), *Women in the field: Anthropological experiences.* Chicago: AVC, 1970.

Bugental, J. F. T. *The search for authenticity.* New York: Holt, 1966.

Bühler, C. The curve of life as studies in biographies. *Journal of Applied Psychology*, 1935, *19*, 405–409.

Bushnell, J. Student culture at Vassar. In N. Sanford (Ed.), *The American college.* New York: Wiley, 1962.

Chickering, A. *Education and identity.* San Francisco: Jossey-Bass, 1969.

Chickering, A. (Ed.). *The modern American college.* San Francisco: Jossey-Bass, 1981.

Churchman, C. W. *The systems approach and its enemies.* New York: Basic Books, 1979.

Cooley, C. *Human nature and the social order.* New York: Scribners, 1902.

Devereux, G. *From anxiety to method in the behavioral sciences.* New York: Mouton-Hawthorne, 1967.

Diesing, P. *Patterns of discovery in the social sciences.* Chicago: AVC, 1971.

DiRenzo, G. *We the people: American character and social change.* Westport, Conn.: Greenwood Press, 1977.

Dollard, J., Doob, L., Miller, N., Mowrer, H., & Sears, R. *Frustration and aggression.* New Haven: Yale University Press, 1939.

Elliott, R. M. The Harvard explorations in personality. Review of *Explorations in personality* (H. A. Murray, Ed.), *American Journal of Psychology*, 1939, *52*, 453–462.

Epstein, S. Explorations in personality today and tomorrow: A tribute to Henry A. Murray. *American Psychologist*, 1979, *34*, 649–653.

Erikson, E. *Childhood and society.* New York: Norton, 1950.

Feldman, K., & Newcomb, T. *The impact of college on students.* San Francisco: Jossey-Bass, 1969.

Fenichel, O. *The psychoanalytic theory of neuroses.* New York: Norton, 1945.

Freedman, M., et al. *Academic culture and faculty development.* Orinda, Calif.: Montaigne, 1980.

Frenkel-Brunswik, E. Motivation and behavior. *Genetic Psychology Monographs*, 1942, *26*, 121–265.

Freud, S. *A general introduction to psychoanalysis.* Garden City, N.Y.: Doubleday, 1943. (Originally published, 1917.)

Freud, S. *Group psychology and the analysis of the ego.* New York: Bantam Books, 1960. (Originally published in German, 1921).

Freud, S. *Totem and taboo.* In J. Strachey (Ed.), *The standard edition of the complete works of Sigmund Freud.* London: Hogarth Press, 1961. (Originally published, 1913.)

Fromm, E. *Escape from freedom.* New York: Farrar and Rinehart, 1941.

Fromm, E., & Maccoby, M. *Social character in a Mexican village.* Englewood Cliffs, N.J.: Prentice-Hall, 1970.

Gendlin, E. T. Experiential explication and truth. *Journal of Existentialism*, 1965–1966, *22*, 1–33.

Glaser, B., & Strauss, A. L. *The discovery of grounded theory: Strategies for qualitative research.* Chicago: AVC, 1967.

Goldstein, K. *The organism.* New York: American Book, 1939.

Gouldner, A. *The coming crisis of Western society.* New York: Basic Books, 1970.

Greenstein, F. *Personality and politics.* Chicago: Markham, 1968.

Hall, C., & Lindzey, G. *Theories of personality.* New York: Wiley, 1957, 1965, 1972.

Horkheimer, M. Authoritarianism and the family today. In R. H. Ashen (Ed.), *The family: Its functions and destiny.* New York: Harper & Row, 1949.

Horney, K. *The neurotic personality of our time.* New York: Norton, 1937.

Jacques, E. *The changing culture of a factory.* London: Tavistock, 1951.

Jung, C. G. *The collected works of C. G. Jung* (H. Read, M. Fordham, G. Adler, & W. McGuire [Eds.]. R. F. C. Hull, trans.). Princeton, N.J. Princeton University Press, 1954.

Kardiner, A. *The individual and his society: The psychodynamics of primitive social organization.* New York: Columbia University Press, 1939.

Katz, J., et al. *No time for youth: Growth and constraint in college students.* San Francisco: Jossey-Bass, 1968.

II. THE SPECIAL FIELDS OF PSYCHOLOGY

Katz, J., & Hartnett, R. *Scholars in the making: The development of graduate and professional students.* Cambridge, Mass.: Ballinger, 1976.

Klein, G., & Schlesinger, H. J. Where is the perceiver in perceptual theory? *Journal of Personality,* 1949, *18,* 32–47.

Knutson, J. (Ed.). *Handbook of political psychology.* San Francisco: Jossey-Bass, 1973.

Korchin, S. *Modern clinical psychology.* New York: Basic Books, 1976.

Levinson, D., et al. *The seasons of a man's life.* New York: Knopf, 1978.

Levinson, D. Explorations in biography. In A. Rabin (Ed.), *Further explorations in personality.* New York: Wiley, 1980.

Lewin, K. *Dynamic theory of personality.* New York: McGraw-Hill, 1935.

Lewin, K. Frontiers in group dynamics. I. *Human Relations,* 1947, *1,* 5–41.

Linton, R. *The study of man: The cultural background of personality.* New York: Appleton-Century-Crofts, 1936.

Maccoby, M. *The gamesman.* New York: Simon & Schuster, 1977.

Maddi, S. Review of *Issues in personality theory* by N. Sanford. *Contemporary Psychology,* 1971, *16,* 199–201.

Malinowski, B. *Sex and repression in savage society.* New York: Harcourt, Brace, 1937.

McDougall, W. *An introduction to social psychology.* Boston: J. W. Luce, 1908.

Mead, M. *Coming of age in Samoa.* New York: Mentor, 1949. (Originally published, 1928.)

Mead, M. *Growing up in New Guinea.* New York: Mentor, 1953. (Originally published, 1930.)

Murphy, G. *Historical introduction to modern psychology* (2d rev. ed.). New York: Harcourt, Brace, 1949.

Murray, H. A. (Ed.). *Explorations in personality.* New York: Oxford University Press, 1938.

OSS Assessment Staff. *Assessment of men.* New York: Holt, 1948.

Polanyi, M. *Personal knowledge: Towards a postcritical philosophy.* Chicago: The University of Chicago Press, 1958.

Reich, W. *The mass psychology of fascism* (3d rev. ed.). New York: Orgone Press, 1946.

Reinharz, S. *On becoming a social scientist.* San Francisco: Jossey-Bass, 1979.

Riesman, D., et al., *The lonely crowd.* New Haven: Yale University Press, 1950.

Ross, E. A. *Social psychology.* New York: Macmillan, 1908.

Sanford, N. Individual and social change in a community under pressure: The oath controversy. *Journal of Social Issues,* 1953, *9,* 25–42.

Sanford, N. Personality development during the college years. *Personnel and Guidance Journal,* 1956, *35,* 74–80.

Sanford, N. Developmental status of the entering freshman. In N. Sanford (Ed.), *The American college.* New York: Wiley, 1962. (a)

Sanford, N. (Ed.). *The American college: A psychological and social interpretation of the higher learning.* New York: Wiley, 1962. (b)

Sanford, N. Personality: Its place in psychology. In S. Koch (Ed.), *Psychology: A study of science* (Vol. 5). New York: McGraw-Hill, 1963.

Sanford, N. Social science and social reform. *Journal of Social Issues,* 1965, *21,* 54–70.

Sanford, N. *Self and society.* New York: Atherton Press, 1966. (a)

Sanford, N. The study of human problems as an approach to greater knowledge about man. In J. Fishman (Ed.), *Expanding horizons of knowledge about man.* New York: Ferkauf Graduate School of Humanities and Social Sciences, Yeshiva University, 1966. (b)

Sanford, N. Research with students as action and education. *American Psychologist,* 1969, *24,* 544–546.

Sanford, N. Whatever happened to action research? *Journal of Social Issues,* 1970, *26,* 3–23. (a)

Sanford, N. *Issues in personality theory.* San Francisco: Jossey-Bass, 1970. (b)

Sanford, N. Academic culture and the teacher's development. *Soundings*, Winter, 1971–1972, 357–371.

Sanford, N. *Learning after college*. Orinda, Calif.: Montaigne, 1980.

Sanford, N., Adkins, M., Miller, R. B., & Cobb, E. Physique, personality and scholarship. *Monographs of the Society for Research in Child Development*, 1943, 8 (No. 1).

Sapir, E. Personality. In *Encyclopedia of the social sciences*, 12, 85–88. New York: Macmillan, 1934.

Schachtel, E. G. *Metamorphosis: On the development of affect perception, attention and memory*. New York: Basic Books, 1959.

Sears, R. *Survey of objective studies of psychoanalytic concepts*. Social Science Research Council Bulletin, No. 51. New York: Social Science Research Council, 1943.

Selznick, G., & Steinberg, S. *The tenacity of prejudice: Anti-Semitism in contemporary America*. New York: Harper & Row, 1969.

Serkin, E. *The development of personality in the first two decades of adult life among a selected group of professional women*. Unpublished dissertation, The Wright Institute, 1980.

Shakow, D. Clinical psychology: Two aspects. A paper presented at the annual convention of the *American Psychological Association*, San Francisco, August 29, 1977.

Stagner, R. *Psychology of personality*. New York: McGraw-Hill, 1937.

Tarde, G. *The laws of imitation* (E. C. Parsons, trans., from 2d French ed.). New York: Holt, 1903. (Originally published, 1890.)

Werner, H. *Comparative psychology of mental development*. Chicago: Follett, 1948.

White, R. W. The case of Ernst. In H. A. Murray (Ed.), *Explorations in personality*. New York: Oxford University Press, 1938.

White, R. W. *Lives in progress*. New York: Holt, 1961. (Originally published, 1952.)

White, R. W. (Ed.). *The study of lives*. New York: Atherton Press, 1963.

White, R. W. Exploring personality the long way: The study of lives. In A. Rabin (Ed.), *Further explorations in personality*. New York: Wiley, 1980.

Whyte, W. H. *The organization man*. New York: Simon & Schuster, 1956.

Wise, Myra. *The aftermath of divorce: A study of women and latency age children*. Unpublished doctoral dissertation, The Wright Institute, 1977.

Wu, Diana. *Beyond the bamboo door: A psychosocial study of women and organizations in metropolitan China*, 1978–1979. Unpublished doctoral dissertation, The Wright Institute, 1980.

Ziman, J. *Public knowledge*. Cambridge, England: Cambridge University Press, 1968.

SUPPLEMENTARY READINGS

Hampden-Turner, C. *Maps of the mind: Charts and concepts of the mind and its labyrinths*. New York: Macmillan, 1981.

A comprehensive attempt to collect, describe, and diagram the most important concepts of the mind put forth not only by the world's greatest psychologists but by the greatest philosophers, writers, and painters. An extraordinary scholarly achievement.

Peters, R. S. (Ed.). *Brett's history of psychology* (abr. ed.). Cambridge, Mass.: The M.I.T. Press, 1953.

The most scholarly and complete of all the histories of psychology. Peters's summary of twentieth-century theories is masterful. In preparing this paper I benefited a great deal from his judgments of issues and trends.

Sanford, N. *Learning after college*. San Francisco: Jossey-Bass, 1980.

> Chapters 6 and 9 give a partial picture of what it was like to be in graduate school in the 1930s when so much history was being made. Graduate students might well find something useful in Chapter 12, "Advice to a Recent Ph.D."

Shneiderman, E. S. (Ed.). *Endeavors in psychology: Selections from the personology of Henry A. Murray*. New York: Harper & Row, 1981.

> Murray is one of the most influential figures in American psychology—a fact that is becoming increasingly well recognized. This book collects in one volume the writings which together constitute the essentials of Murray's psychological and philosophical thought.

22

*Looking for Personality**

WALTER MISCHEL

Let me begin with a rapid survey of what I see as some of the highlights of the field of personality. Historically the field has been influenced by a few main positions of which one of the oldest and most enduringly influential is trait psychology. Beginning at about the turn of the century, and inspired primarily by the success of the intelligence-testing movement and especially by the work of Alfred Binet, psychologists became interested in seeing whether the success achieved with mental measurement might be repeated if one tried to quantify social characteristics.

The Psychometric Trait Approach

The trait theories of the 1920s and 1930s became primarily a psychology of common sense in which the layperson's theory of what people are like became the scientific theory of what people are like on "dimensions" like friendliness or honesty or conscientiousness or aggressiveness. The scientific innovation—and it was a most important one—was the attempt to provide a method to dimensionalize these qualities systematically and to quantify them rigorously and carefully. The re-

*This chapter is adapted from Mischel (1979) and Mischel (1981), which present similar material.

515

sponses of the subject were primarily self-reports, mostly check marks on multiple choice or true-false inventories and questionnaires. Recall, for example, the Bell Adjustment Inventory, or the Woodworth Personal Data Sheet of the World War I period (e.g., "I am a good mixer"; "I am at ease with people"). These were quite reasonably intended as short cuts for the *actual* sampling of behavior (for instance, as short cuts for the psychiatric interview).

But I think a giant step was taken at that time. This was the jump from sampling people's specific *performances* by assessing what they could do (which was the heart of intelligence testing) to asking people to report about what they are like in general, in a relatively situation-free fashion: that is, to capture the gist of themselves, their "average" or "typical" behavioral dispositions, on such broad dimensions as friendliness, conscientiousness, or introversion. These responses were used not as *samples* of the respondents' relevant behavior, but as *signs* or indicators of their generalized dispositions. The implications of this jump have been emerging over the past ten or twenty years with the growing recognition of the conceptual and methodological problems that one gets into if one does not carefully distinguish people's judgments and subjective categorizations about themselves (and about others) from the objective sampling of what they actually do, i.e., their performance under specific circumstances. We see what people do, for example, when we ask them to count the beads or arrange the blocks or say the digits backward, or when we directly observe their behavior as it unfolds. Such specific behaviors are very different from how people characterize and abstract themselves in their global descriptions, and the differences have serious measurement implications (see Mischel, 1968).

Early trait psychology was a psychology guided mostly by the dictionary, as in Allport and Ogden's search for trait names, yielding the 1,800 or so terms that they finally culled from a much larger number of adjectives. Other trait psychologists attempted to find ways to hone down this list, using a variety of often ingenious techniques, most notably factor analysis. The struggle became one of finding a finite and, it was hoped, relatively small taxonomy of the basic characteristics, "the dimensions," of personality and social behavior. And that remains one of the main objectives of the field—with a distinctive methodology and with distinctive uses, contributions, and limitations.

The lone voice speaking out critically against this dimensionalization of personality with numbers was Gordon Allport, who, beginning in the 1930s, eloquently defended an "idiographic" approach stressing each person's uniqueness and individuality. Most who heard him were excited by his arguments for such an approach. But curiously his own inventory-value-survey work inspired still more attempts to categorize people on the slots or dimensions that were the preferred yardsticks of the psychologist (rather than the equivalence classes of the person being assessed). More forcefully than others before him, Allport (1937, p. 3) articulated the essence of the trait position, claiming that the individual is an "amazingly stable and self-contained system" that contains enduring, generalized dispositions. Our task, in his view, was to search for those stable, broad dispositions as manifested by their behavioral "signs" or "indicators." And that has been the major mission of trait psychology for many decades.

How fruitful has this search been? In trying to answer this question it is important to discriminate clearly between demonstrations of impressive temporal stability and cross-situational generality. More than a decade ago the available research, in my view, provided evidence for significant temporal stability but also (and far more surprising at the time) for discriminativeness or "specificity" and ideographic organization in how behavior is generalized and patterned across situations. I concluded: "Although behavior patterns often may be stable, they usually are not highly generalized across situations" (Mischel, 1968, p. 282).

No one can seriously question that lives have continuity and that we perceive ourselves and others as individuals who have substantial identity and relative stability over time, even when our specific actions change across situations (Mischel, 1968, 1973, 1977). But while temporal stability in the patterning of individual lives, in self-perceptions, and in how others view us seems evident, there is room for serious disagreement about the nature, degree, and meaning of the cross-situational breadth of behaviors assessed by objective measures of the behaviors as they unfold.

Are the "erratic and uneven" relationships typically found when cross-situational consistency is studied with objective measures of behavior reflections of measurement problems (see Block, 1977; Epstein, 1979) or are they indicative of the actual discriminativeness of social behavior across psychologically (subjectively) nonequivalent situations? Better measures would surely provide better support for the existence of meaningfully organized behavior patterns. (Discriminative behavior and idiographic organization imply neither chaos nor unpredictability.) But, in my view, better measures and more fine-grained analyses would also make it even more apparent that individuals organize and pattern their behavioral consistencies and discriminations in terms of their subjectively perceived equivalences and their personal meanings, not those of the trait psychologist who categorizes them. While sometimes the subject's equivalences will coincide with the nomothetic trait categories of the assessor, often they will not (Mischel & Peake, 1982). Whether or not the degree of correspondence is judged adequate and useful depends on many considerations, and especially on one's purpose (Mischel, 1979, 1984).

From my own cognitive social-learning perspective, temporal stability would be expected to the degree that such qualities as the person's competencies, encodings, expectancies, values, and goal-plans endure (Mischel, 1973). While the pursuit of durable values and goals with stable skills and expectations would surely involve coherent and meaningful patternings among the individual's efforts and enterprises, the degree of "cross-situational consistency" might be high, low, or intermediate, depending on a multitude of considerations—including the type of data one examines, the structure of the perceived cross-situational contingencies, and the subjective equivalences among the diverse situations sampled.[1]

Trait psychology has had a significant, enduring, but nevertheless limited impact on our field. This is so not merely because human consistencies and psychological equivalences are more complex than nomothetic trait theory suggests but also because its focus is not dynamic, not addressed to the flow of behavior, not in any way linked to the interactions that take place while people are actually living their lives. It has to do instead with efforts to cut up human qualities and the stream of action into neat dimensions, to provide some kind of taxonomy which puts people in their places—but on the psychologist's theoretically preferred, favorite dimensions, not on the person's. The result is a focus on between-person differences, between-person variance, rather than on *within*-person variance as it relates to environmental changes. These efforts have consumed much energy and yielded many interesting, useful classificatory schemes. In addition to advances in ability testing, especially notable was the development of criterion-analysis and of sophisticated actuarial methods by Meehl (1956), Gough (1957), and others so that self-reports could be used to generate a variety of predictions and descriptions of group differences for many practical purposes. Unfortunately, the processes underlying personality are not addressed; the tendency is to classify subgroups of people rather than to capture and explain the ongoing flow of their behavior.

The Psychodynamic Challenge

It is, I think, because of the static, descriptive, nonanalytic quality of trait psychology that many of us were so excited when we first came across the psychodynamic approach. Freud (and those who have extended and revised his views) seemed to offer a way of getting beyond labeling people, and ordering them into groups, by providing a mode of access into the individual's unique psyche. The appeal of the psychodynamic approach when I first encountered it as a graduate student was that

---

[1] While the typical "personality coefficient" may average something like a statistically significant but modest .30, higher coefficients have been, and will continue to be, obtained in personality research. For example, consider the phenomenon of selective attention to the self-relevant information. Over five years ago, my associates and I assessed the correlations between scores on a self-report trait measure (the R-S Scale based on the MMPI; see Byrne, 1964) and attention to one's personal assets and liabilities as measured (Mischel, Ebbesen, & Zeiss, 1973). We found that people who presented themselves in a positive rather than self-critical ("sensitizing") fashion on this 127-item scale also tended to spend more time attending to positive (.51) and less time to negative (−.61) information about themselves on the behavioral measure of selective attention. Likewise, substantial cross-situational consistency can be demonstrated at least for some behaviors (e.g., aggression) for subjects who are extreme on those behavioral dimensions (Mischel, 1984). But to me the discovery of the discriminative conditions under which correlations like these do *not* hold is at least as theoretically interesting as the demonstration that sometimes consistencies can be found.

at last there seemed to be a way of studying equivalences, of finding consistencies as they exist for the individual in ways that are not obvious at the level of surface behavior. These equivalences are not found by the kind of counting of specific behavioral similarities that characterized the work of Hartshorne and May (who in the 1920s attempted to show that the child who is honest in not cheating on an arithmetic test is also honest in not cheating when it comes to a spelling test). Instead, psychodynamic theorists realized that the relationships between the indicators which putatively sample an individual's dispositions may not be direct, cumulative, and additive (as the trait approach assumes). The relationship between sign and disposition may be subtle, indirect, and contradictory, and may involve all kinds of transformations.

Indeed, much of the excitement of the psychoanalytic approach was that it provided the notion of transformation: the notion that the same motive, the same wish or impulse, could manifest itself in all sorts of nonobvious ways, displaying a wide range of vicissitudes. Thus Veronica, who repeatedly says she is very aggressive on questionnaires, may *not* be more aggressive than Charles, who claims to be unaggressive and endorses mostly timid adjectives; indeed, the more Veronica insists on her aggressiveness, the *less* aggressive and the more passive-dependent she might really prove to be, while Charles, the ostensibly passive one, may indirectly reveal himself to be a cauldron of stifled aggressive impulses. The hope was that recognition of "genotypic" underlying equivalences might enable one to see the similarities beneath all kinds of phenotypic surface variations and seeming contradictions in behavior. The excitement here was that at last there was attention to causal dynamics, with a recognition that what people do is selective, that it is motivated and conflictful, and that it has to be unscrambled in terms of what it really means rather than how it merely seems.

Unfortunately, the initial exuberance, the high promise of the psychodynamic approach, was soon followed by a sobering and generally dismal flood of empirical studies that deeply questioned the nature, importance, and even the very existence of such basic psychodynamic processes as repression (see Mischel, 1976). But because the studies themselves could readily be accused (often justifiably) of flaws and limitations in scope and method, the psychodynamic approach itself tended to withstand the empirical assaults on its key constructs. The most serious disillusionment with psychodynamic approaches began to arise, in my view, not so much from the failure to validate crucial constructs experimentally as from the clinical experiences of the 1950s and early 1960s with clients seeking help. It was in that context, not in the laboratory, that clinicians became increasingly dubious about the value of the psychodynamic "portraits" to which they were devoting so much of their time (e.g., Mischel, 1968; Peterson, 1968; Vernon, 1964).

Guided by the view that test responses are merely "indirect signs" of underlying psychodynamics, assessors had for years elicited signs such as picture drawings, or associations to inkblots, or stories told to ambiguous pictures, whose relations to the

519

individual's important life behaviors tended to be tenuous and remote. Skepticism about the utility of such assessments arose from a growing worry that the resulting psychodynamic "personality diagnostics"—too often formulated with little regard for the client's own construction of his or her life and specific behaviors—might be exercises in stereotyping (like those of trait psychology) that miss the uniqueness of the individual and pin people instead to a continuum of theory-supplied labels. But a focus on the immediate behavioral troubles of the client was for many years widely regarded as naive and hazardous because these problems (e.g., phobias, sexual dysfunctions, fetishes) were construed merely as "symptoms" or even as manifestations of "resistances." Traditionally, the clinician's task was to go beyond behavioral complaints to underlying psychodynamics, and the fear of "symptom substitution" led many to eschew direct behavior intervention. However, the fear of symptom substitution turned out to be largely unjustified (e.g., Grossberg, 1964). Clients whose maladaptive behaviors were directly alleviated, rather than becoming victimized by substituted symptoms, appeared more likely to show generalized gains from overcoming their original handicaps (e.g., Bandura, 1969).

Empirical Dilemmas of Psychodynamic Approaches

In the 1950s and 1960s many empirical studies investigated carefully the utility of clinicians' efforts to infer broad dispositions indirectly from specific symptomatic signs and to unravel disguises in order to uncover the hypothetical dispositions that might be their roots. The results indicated that the disillusionment beginning to be expressed by skeptical clinicians was, in general, justified. The findings tended to call into question the utility of clinical judgments even when the judges are well-trained, expert psychodynamicists, working with clients in clinical contexts and using their own preferred techniques. Research surveys indicated, on the whole, that clinicians guided by concepts about underlying genotypic dispositions have not been able to predict behavior better than have the person's own direct self-report, simple indices of directly relevant past behavior, demographic variables, or, in some cases, their secretaries (e.g., Mischel, 1968, 1972; Peterson, 1968). Moreover, dispositional labels and the psychodynamic portraits formulated might reflect at least to some degree illusory correlations perpetuated by shared semantic organizations and belief systems (e.g., D'Andrade, 1970; Chapman & Chapman, 1969; Shweder, 1975). Increasingly it appeared that the hypothesized psychic structures and dynamics that clinicians elaborated at case conferences may have added more to the weight of the clients' diagnostic folders than to the design of treatments tailored to their specific needs and circumstances. And, as distressing as the failure to demonstrate convincingly the utility of the inferences and predictions of psychodynamically oriented clinicians was the evidence on the limitations of psychodynamic treatments. While at times psychodynamic psychotherapy seemed to do better than no-treatment controls, the approach lacked efficacy when compared to more parsimonious alternatives (e.g., Bandura, 1969; Kazdin & Wilson, 1978). Moreover, skeptics noted perceptively that some psychodynamic "cures" may be better characterized as an ideological conversion to the belief system of the therapist.

In sum, the problem for me—and I suspect for many of us—in trying to apply the psychodynamic approach, both clinically and in research, was that we discovered the fallibility of the clinician, the fallibility of the judge (see Mischel, 1968; 1973). The focus in psychodynamically oriented measurement had turned away from assessing the reliability and validity of tests to the measurement of the clinician, in the hope that one could calibrate the judge and establish his or her validity, reliability, and utility. And that effort has had (at least in my eyes) a disappointing history.

Consequently we have had to limit greatly our conclusions about the nature of psychodynamics and the predictive skills of the clinician. But we have learned much about the ways in which the hypotheses of the judge (the constructions, expectancies, scripts in his or her head) interact with, structure, and inform whatever data there might be "out there" in the world of the perceived. And that is, after all, one of the fundamental, enduring messages that seems to be coming from the fields of both personality and cognitive psychology. Indeed since the 1940s and the now old "new look in perception" (e.g., Bruner, 1957), we have come to recognize that there are cognitive heuristics (distortions, simplifications, and biases that channelize what we expect and how we act) through which we go rapidly beyond the given information.

Discovering Our Fallibility

Especially in the last decade, research in cognitive and social psychology (most notably investigations of how people categorize, simplify, and process information when making social judgments) has illuminated the cognitive bases for many of the paradoxes and dilemmas of the clinicians (e.g., Nisbett & Ross, 1980; Tversky & Kahneman, 1974, 1978). For example, such studies have shown elegantly how certain everyday heuristics of inference may bias the judge (whether layperson or clinician) to ignore base rates (unless they are causally relevant) and the reliability of evidence. The "representativeness" heuristic, for instance, leads one to predict incorrectly extreme values and low probability events when they happen to resemble what one is trying to predict. The same heuristic also helps to account for other common judgmental embarrassments found in the literature on clinical inference (e.g., Mischel, 1968, Chap. 5). Indeed the "illusion of validity" (Kahneman & Tversky, 1972, p. 249) arises and persists because the very factors that enhance the judge's subjective confidence—such factors as the consistency and extremity of the data—often are in fact correlated negatively with the accuracy of predictions, creating the paradox of confident predictors who persist in practices that are objectively unjustifiable. Moreover, the layperson, like the clinician, eagerly seeks *causal* explanations of events (Tversky & Kahneman, 1978), and in these explanations tends most readily and naturally to attribute causality to the enduring dispositions of actors rather than to the particular circumstances in which they act. The growing insights into our cognitive processes and fallibility as intuitive psychologists are an important part of the general recognition of what might be called "cognitive economics": the recognition that people (including Ph.D.s in personality) are flooded by information which somehow must be reduced and simplified to allow efficient processing and to avoid an otherwise overwhelming overload.

Phenomenology and the Self

Coming from a quite different direction (beginning in the 1940s and 1950s) was the phenomenological and self-theory, of which perhaps the most influential modern spokesman was Carl Rogers. He was adamant in asserting that our *perceptions* of events, more than their objective reality, guide how we act. And he was one of the first in psychology to recognize that the self provides a most important organizing unit. If I sense correctly what is happening in the field now, there is a new concern with cognition generally and with the self particularly as an organizing structure that provides coherence and unity in the face of behavioral diversity (e.g., Cantor & Kihlstrom, 1980). It is to be hoped that the current approaches will not create the tautologies that undermined the usefulness and credibility of the concept of self in earlier formulations.

George Kelly was another exciting historical force in the same vein, although his full influence is just beginning to be felt. Kelly (1955) noted in his personal construct theory that we perpetuate a curious dichotomy in how we practice psychology. Traditionally, when we talk about people they are "subjects" whose behavior is governed by laws and depends on motives, contingencies, and reinforcement conditions. But when we talk about ourselves, when we focus on our activity as psychologists, we use an entirely different idiom. We see ourselves as cognitive beings, rational scientists forming and testing hypotheses in efforts to validate our constructions and ideas. Kelly suggested (long before others) that the same orientation and principles ought to be used in talking about our "subjects" and about ourselves as scientists. He thus foreshadowed much in contemporary psychology and his wisdom has not yet been fully recognized (Mischel, 1980). His notion that a person is always capable of constructive alternativism, of creating alternative worlds, is especially appealing today. He insisted that while cognition may not be able to change an event at all (constructs do not undo a broken arm), one is free to reconstrue the meaning of the event and control its impact. And I think that is an extremely important idea, introducing the possibility of freedom through reconstruing, through recategorizing, through cognitive transformations that allow us to build alternative ways of seeing and being.

One reason that Kelly's approach has not had the impact it deserves is that it was hard to apply in research. To the degree that there was a method—the REP test—it was used mostly like a tool of trait psychology, with researchers counting to see whether people had many constructs or few constructs and whether the constructs were permeable or not permeable, thus turning constructions into trait-like dispositions. Moreover, many critics saw Kelly's constructs as free-floating and not properly linked either to historical antecedents or to subsequent behavior (e.g., Mischel, 1976). And while the exploration of personal constructs was surely an important part of psychotherapy, most clinicians were puzzled about how to produce construct changes that might really alleviate their client's anxieties, inhibitions, and dysfunctional, disadvantageous behaviors.

Cognitive Social-Learning Approaches

With the nomothetic trait orientation as one prevailing force and the psychodynamic approach as the other, the advent of the behavioral (social-learning)[2] approach to clinical problems in the 1960s seemed especially refreshing for many personologists and clinicians who were increasingly frustrated both by their research-based correlation coefficients and by their treatment experiences. For me, the original excitement of the behavioral approach (e.g., Bandura, 1969; Bandura & Walters, 1963; Mischel, 1968; Rotter, 1954; Skinner, 1953) lay in its promise to focus on the client-defined problematic behavior in its context rather than on the clinician's inferences about the symptomatic meaning of that behavior as a sign of generalized dispositions or psychodynamics. At last a client who complained, for example, of sexual performance problems, or of fears of going outdoors, might achieve help with the behaviors of concern rather than be given insights of uncertain validity into their hypothetical origins or symptomatic significance. Here, it seemed, was an approach that would (in the form of functional analyses of peoples' real-life problems) pay more than lip service to each individual's uniqueness and deal with behavior at the level at which the person categorized and lived it.

The behavior-theory contribution of special interest for personality psychology is the view that discontinuities—real ones, not merely superficial or trivial surface changes—are part of the genuine phenomena of personality (Mischel, 1968, 1973). This perspective suggests that an adequate conceptualization of personality has to

---

[2] I refer here to the behavioral-learning approaches that began with an explicit break from the earlier Miller-Dollard translations of psychodynamic theory into the language of learning and that have become increasingly cognitive and social in orientation (see Mischel, 1976).

recognize that people change as the conditions of their lives change and these changes are genuine, not merely phenotypic. In that view, an adequate account of personality must have as much room for human discrimination as for generalization, as much place for personality change as for stability, and as much concern for man's self-regulation as for his victimization by enduring intrapsychic forces or momentary environmental constraints.

Some early versions of the behavioral approach tended to focus on the role of external variables in the regulation of behavior (and hence emphasized contingencies and the objective "controlling" environment). The rapid growth in recent years of the behavioral approach was soon accompanied by an increasing focus on the social and psychological environments in which people live. (The sharp rise of interest in the environment as it related to the person is seen in the fact that from 1968 to 1972 more books appeared on the topic of man-environment relations from an ecological perspective than had been published in the prior three decades [Jordan, 1972].) As is true in most new fields, a first concern in the study of environments has been to try to classify them and provide taxonomies. Depending on one's purpose, many different classifications are possible and useful (e.g., Magnusson & Ekehammar, 1973; Moos, 1973, 1974). But I believe it would be as futile to seek any single "basic" taxonomy of situations as it is to search for a final or ultimate taxonomy of traits: we can label situations in at least as many different ways as we can label people. We should not settle for a trait psychology of situations in which events and settings rather than people are merely given different labels. The naming of situations is no substitute for analyzing the process of *how* conditions and environments interact with the people in them. We must go beyond descriptions of the environment (of the climate, buildings, social settings, etc., in which we live) to the psychological processes through which environmental conditions and people influence each other reciprocally (Mischel, 1984).

There has been a rapid movement beyond the objective external environment and increasing interest in cognitive-symbolic processes in the human actor and perceiver as being not only vital for social learning (e.g., Bandura, 1969) but also key components of individuality (e.g., Mischel, 1973). Going beyond the habit-learning and drive formulations of earlier learning models, a focus on the role of subjective expectancies, values, and goals (e.g., Rotter, 1954) and of self-instructions, plans, and self-regulatory systems (Bandura, 1977; Meichenbaum, 1977; Mischel, 1973, 1979) has increasingly characterized applications of the behavioral approach to the study of persons.

Contemporary versions of behavior theory thus recognize and emphasize the role of self-systems in the regulation of behavior. They take pains to note that what one does and experiences depends on self-evaluative processes, self-standards, and self-estimates and not merely on environmental and external circumstances (e.g., Bandura, 1977; Kanfer, 1975). They continue to cognitivize traditional behavior theory and thus begin to approach the self (and to converge with phenomenological viewpoints) in emphasizing that *how* events are interpreted may be more crucial than the events themselves. Moreover, they view the individual's awareness of the contingencies in the situation (his or her understanding of what behavior leads to what outcome) as a crucial determinant of the resulting actions and choices. And they stress that any objective stimulus condition may have a variety of effects, depending on how the individual construes and transforms it (e.g., Mischel, 1974). The result is a much less mechanical, much less simple view of the individual and of the determinants of behavior. And while we can claim some real progress in the last hundred years, the search for more useful and illuminating theoretical insights into the human being continues so vigorously as to ensure that today's cherished personological insights will be superceded by the wisdom of the future.

REFERENCES

Allport, G. W. *Personality: A psychological interpretation.* New York: Holt, 1937.

Bandura, A. *Principles of behavior modification.* New York: Holt, 1969.

Bandura, A. *Social learning theory.* Morristown, N.J.: General Learning Press, 1971.

Bandura, A. *Social learning theory.* Englewood Cliffs, N.J.: Prentice-Hall, 1977.

Bandura, A., & Walters, R. *Social learning and personality development.* New York: Holt, 1963.

Block, J. Advancing the psychology of personality: Paradigmatic shift or improving the quality of research. In D. Magnusson & N. S. Endler (Eds.), *Personality at the crossroads: Current issues in interactional psychology.* Hillsdale, N.J.: Erlbaum, 1977.

Bruner, J. S. On perceptual readiness. *Psychological Review,* 1957, *64,* 123–152.

Byrne, D. Repression-sensitization as a dimension of personality. In B. A. Maher (Ed.), *Progress in experimental personality research* (Vol. 1). New York: Academic Press, 1964.

Cantor, N., & Kihlstrom, J. (Eds.). *Personality, cognition, and social interaction.* Hillsdale, N.J.: Erlbaum, 1980.

Chapman, L. J., & Chapman, J. P. Illusory correlations as an obstacle to the use of valid psychodiagnostic signs. *Journal of Abnormal Psychology,* 1969, *74,* 271–280.

D'Andrade, R. *Cognitive structures and judgments.* Paper presented for T.O.B.R.E. research workshop on cognitive organization and psychological processes. Huntington Beach, Calif., August, 1970.

Epstein, S. The stability of behavior: I. On predicting most of the people much of the time. *Journal of Personality and Social Psychology,* 1979, *37,* 1097–1126.

Gough, H. G. *Manual for the California Psychological Inventory.* Palo Alto, Calif.: Consulting Psychologists Press, 1957.

Grossberg, J. M. Behavior therapy: A review. *Psychological Bulletin,* 1964, *62,* 73–88.

Jordan, P. A real predicament. *Science,* 1972, *175,* 977–978.

Kahneman, D., & Tversky, A. Subjective probability: A judgment of representativeness. *Cognitive Psychology,* 1972, *3,* 430–454.

Kanfer, F. H. Self-management methods. In F. H. Kanfer & A. P. Goldstein (Eds.), *Helping people change.* New York: Pergamon, 1975.

Kazdin, A. E., & Wilson, G. T. *Evaluation of behavior therapy: Issues, evidence, and research strategies.* Cambridge, Mass.: Ballinger, 1978.

Kelly, G. A. *The psychology of personal constructs* (2 vols.). New York: Norton, 1955.

Magnusson, D., & Ekehammar, B. An analysis of situational dimensions: A replication. *Multivariate Behavioral Research*, 1973, *8*, 331–339.

Meehl, P. E. Wanted—A good cookbook. *American Psychologist*, 1956, *11*, 263–272.

Meichenbaum, D. *Cognitive-behavior modification*. New York: Plenum, 1977.

Mischel, W. *Personality and assessment*. New York: Wiley, 1968.

Mischel, W. Direct versus indirect personality assessment: Evidence and implications. *Journal of Consulting and Clinical Psychology*, 1972, *38*, 319–324.

Mischel, W. Toward a cognitive social learning reconceptualization of personality. *Psychological Review*, 1973, *80*, 252–283.

Mischel, W. Processes in delay of gratification. In L. Berkowitz (Ed.), *Advances in experimental social psychology* (Vol. 7). New York: Academic Press, 1974.

Mischel, W. The self as the person: A cognitive social learning view. In A. Wandersman, P. Poppen, & D. Ricks (Eds.), *Humanism and behaviorism: Dialogue and growth*. New York: Pergamon, 1976.

Mischel, W. The interaction of person and situation. In D. Magnusson & N. S. Endler (Eds.), *Personality at the crossroads: Current issues in interactional psychology*. Hillsdale, N.J.: Erlbaum, 1977.

Mischel, W. On the interface of cognition and personality: Beyond the person-situation debate. *American Psychologist*, 1979, *34*, 740–754.

Mischel, W. George Kelly's anticipation of psychology: A personal tribute. In M. J. Mahoney (Ed.), *Psychotherapy process: Current issues and future directions*. New York: Plenum, 1980.

Mischel, W. Personality and cognition: Something borrowed, something new? In N. Cantor & J. F. Kihlstrom (Eds.), *Personality, cognition, and social interaction*. Hillsdale, N.J.: Erlbaum, 1981.

Mischel, W. Convergences and challenges in the search for consistency. *American Psychologist*, 1984, *39*, 351–364.

Mischel, W., Ebbesen, E., & Zeiss, A. R. Selective attention to the self: Situational and dispositional determinants. *Journal of Personality and Social Psychology*, 1973, *27*, 129–142.

Mischel, W., & Peake, P. K. Beyond deja vu in the search for cross-situational consistency. *Psychological Review*, 1982, *89*, 730–755.

Moos, R. H. Conceptualizations of human environments. *American Psychologist*, 1973, *28*, 652–665.

Moos, R. H. Systems for the assessment and classification of human environments. In R. H. Moos & P. M. Insel (Eds.), *Issues in social ecology*. Palo Alto, Calif.: National Press Books, 1974.

Nisbett, R. E., & Ross, L. D. *Human inference: Strategies and shortcomings of informal judgment*. Century Series in Psychology. Englewood Cliffs, N.J.: Prentice-Hall, 1980.

Peterson, D. R. *The clinical study of social behavior*. New York: Appleton-Century-Crofts, 1968.

Rotter, J. B. *Social learning and clinical psychology*. Englewood Cliffs, N.J.: Prentice-Hall, 1954.

Shweder, R. A. How relevant is an individual difference theory of personality? *Journal of Personality*, 1975, *43*, 455–485.

Skinner, B. F. *Science and human behavior*. New York: Macmillan, 1953.

Tversky, A., & Kahneman, D. Judgment under uncertainty: Heuristics and biases. *Science*, 1974, *185*, 1124–1131.

Tversky, A., & Kahneman, D. Causal schemas in judgments under uncertainty. In M. Fishbein (Ed.), *Progress in social psychology*. Hillsdale, N.J.: Erlbaum, 1978.

Vernon, P. E. *Personality assessment: A critical survey*. New York: Wiley, 1964.

SOCIAL PSYCHOLOGY

23

*Social Psychology and the Phoenix of Unreality**

KENNETH J. GERGEN

And every natural effect has a spiritual cause, and not a natural: for a natural cause
only seems, it is a delusion.

> William Blake
> *Milton.* Plate 26:46.

If one surveys the vast corpus of Wilhelm Wundt's contributions to psychology, one
is struck by what appears to be a significant evolution in orientation. In his early
work, such as the *Principles of Physiological Psychology* (1874/1904) and *Lectures on
Human and Animal Psychology* (1863–1864/1894), Wundt helped to chart the
terrain that was later to become the private reserve of American experimental
psychology. It is to this work that Boring's (1929) classic history devotes such
singular attention. Yet, during the culminating years of his career, Wundt turned
from the task of isolating biologically based mechanisms of psychological function-

*The preparation of this paper was facilitated by a grant from the National Science Foundation
(#7809393). For their critical appraisal at various stages of preparation, grateful acknowledgment is
extended to Erika Apfelbaum, Michael Basseches, Mary Gergen, Horst Gundlach, Marianne Jaeger,
Hugh Lacey, Ian Lubek, Alexandre Métraux, Jill Morawski, Barry Schwartz, and Wolfgang Stroebe.
Although relieved of responsibility for its failings, Sigmund Koch must be credited for furnishing both
the initial inspiration and final clarification of the paper.

ing to the problems raised by social pattern. The bases of such patterns do not lie primarily within the nervous system, argued Wundt, but are essentially human creations. Patterns of religious activity and governance, for example, along with such culturally significant concepts as honor or truth, are products of people at particular points in history. As such, they demand forms of exploration that differ from those of the experimentalist (Blumenthal, 1975, 1979; Mischel, 1975). *Völkerpsychologie* (1900–1920), the ten-volume work that was to occupy Wundt for the last twenty years of his career, represents his exploration into this alternative form of inquiry. As is apparent from the history of American social psychology, it is Wundt the experimentalist, and not the author of *Völkerpsychologie*, to which the discipline turned for a model of investigation.

Wundt's concept of social psychology is an interesting one and much deserving of contemporary scrutiny. For Wundt the guiding metaphor for social psychology was not that of natural science but, rather, that of historical analysis (*Geschichte*). Rather than searching for general laws of psychological functioning, the task of the social psychologist was to render an account of contemporary behavior patterns as gleaned from the culture's history. Toward this end the laboratory experiment could contribute very little. The method for social psychology developed from the documentation and explanation of historical patterns as they emerged over time. The function of social psychology was not that of making predictions. Consistent with Popper's (1957) views of behavioral science, Wundt did not believe in the inevitability of social patterning. Rather than prediction, the goal of the social psychologist was to render the world of human affairs intelligible. This task was to be carried out by examining the etymology of contemporary patterns.

Yet, in spite of the enticing implications of this line of thought, it is Wundt's conflict between fundamental conceptions of science that furnishes us with a base for examining social psychology's history and its critical standing today. For Wundt's conflict may be viewed as but a localized instance of an antinomy of longstanding and profound consequence both within the intellectual sphere and without. Like many of his contemporaries, Wundt was grappling with competing metatheoretical assumptions concerning human knowledge and its relationship to the natural world.[1] Although these competing assumptions may be characterized in many ways, it will prove useful to center our attention on the critical conflict between environmental versus person-centered theories of knowledge. On the one hand, human knowledge in ideal form may be viewed as a reflection of the real world or a map of nature's contours. From this standpoint, empirical entities are granted preeminent status in the generation of human knowledge; the human mind

---

[1] For further analysis of Wundt's paradigmatic conflict see Blumenthal (1975) and Danziger (1980). Wundt's attempt to distinguish two forms of psychological science, the one concerned with natural process and the other with human artifacts, was paralleled by many others, including Dilthey, Rickert, Troeltsch, and Windelband.

529

best serves the interests of knowledge when it operates as a pawn to nature. In contrast, the human mind can be viewed as the origin of knowledge, a font of conceptual construction, or a source of thought-forms that frame both the questions that may be put to nature and the answers derived therefrom. It is the former view that spurred Wundt's concern with the physiological mechanisms driven by or reliably dependent on variations in the natural environment; it is the latter view which sustained Wundt's inquiry into the historically relative patterning of ideas. Elements of this antagonism now insinuate themselves into all aspects of psychological inquiry, including the development of theory, choice of methods, and mode of application.

It is an account of this conflict as it has developed over the past century and its repercussions in contemporary social psychology that I wish to examine. I choose this task for purposes of enlightened self-consciousness and also because I believe not only that we have witnessed a profound shift in the balance of power between these antagonistic views but that we are currently on the threshold of moving beyond them. The redistribution of power is one to which social psychologists have indeed contributed, and it is also one that now promises to thrust the discipline into a pivotal position vis-à-vis the broad intellectual community. My first task, then, is to sketch out an account of the role played by this conflict over epistemic assumptions during the past century, both in psychology more generally and social psychology in particular. This historical résumé will function as a necessary prolegomenon to the central concern of this paper, namely the critical shift taking place in contemporary psychology.

To appreciate properly the historical context of the antagonism, a brief précis is required concerning the protagonists. Let us first employ the term *exogenic* to refer to theories of knowledge granting priority to the external world in the generation of human knowledge, and *endogenic* to denote those theories holding the processes of mind as preeminent.[2] Although one can scarcely locate a pure exemplar of either variety, many philosophic writings may be singled out for the inspiration they have furnished to those of one or the other persuasion. Surely John Locke's arguments against innate ideas, along with his analysis of the means by which elementary sensations give rise to the development of complex ideas, has played a major role in the history of exogenic thought. Similarly, Hume's tracing of compound ideas to the association of simple impressions and Mill's view of the mind as an accumulation of sensations driven automatically by physical inputs have contributed substantially to the exogenic polarity. Although one may draw a meaningful parallel between traditional empiricist philosophy and what is here termed exogenic

---

[2]The distinction between the exogenic and endogenic views may be usefully compared with such analytic distinctions including mechanistic versus organismic views (Reese & Overton, 1970); plastic versus autonomous (Hollis, 1977); structuralist versus functionalist (Rychlak, 1977); and mechanistic versus person-centered (Joynson, 1980).

thought, the relationship between endogenic thinking and either rationalist or idealist philosophy is more clouded. However, certain rationalist arguments, including Spinoza's attempt to derive knowledge not from experience but deductively from propositions and Kant's theory of a priori constructs of time, space, causality, and so on, must surely be viewed as seminal contributions to endogenic thought. However, lodged against these rationalist arguments and sustaining the endogenic line are Schopenhauer's later tracing of knowledge to the wellsprings of will and Nietzsche's arguments for knowledge not as a reflection of fact but as an outgrowth of motives for power.

Lest this metatheoretical antagonism seem pallid, let us glimpse a number of localized conflicts of more pungent familiarity. As an ideal typification, it may be said that:

1. Those who favor an exogenic world view are likely to argue that because the external environment drives the senses in predictable ways, objectively grounded knowledge about this environment is possible. In contrast, those who take an endogenic perspective are likely to argue against the possibility of objective knowledge. Because knowledge is primarily a product of the processing agent, traditional criteria of objectivity are rendered suspect.

2. The exogenic thinker tends to believe that because there are objectively correct and incorrect answers about the world, people of sound mind should reach common agreement. Science should thus ideally strive for consensus among practitioners. For the endogenic thinker, however, multiple interpretations of experience are usually held to be both legitimate and desirable. Thus, if total accord exists within a group, it may be a signal either of oppressed minority views or shallow conformity. The process of generating knowledge, from this standpoint, holds conflict to be superior to consensus.

3. The exogenic thinker, arguing that reality is independent of the observer, may frequently argue for scientific neutrality. If the scientist allows his or her values to guide the course of observation, the result may be a faulty recording of the state of nature. For the endogenic thinker, however, recordings of reality are not so much correct or incorrect as they may be held to be creations of the observer. If scientific statements are not data driven but psychologically generated, then in what sense can one be neutral or independent of what is known? The possibility for scientific neutrality is thus obscured.

4. For the exogenic thinker, it is often argued that the empirical world impinges on the senses and may thus be considered the determinant of psychological states. Such environmental determinism may be direct, in terms of immediate sensory input, or indirect, as in the case of the continuing effects of previous learning experiences. The causal locus for human action is thus placed in the environment: human behavior is dependent on or determined by antecedent environmental events. In contrast, for the endogenic thinker, the individual may be viewed as free

531

to construct or interpret sense data furnished either from the environment or from memory. The causal locus of human action thus tends to be placed within the individual: for the endogenic thinker, environmental determinism is often replaced by voluntarism.

5. Because of the emphasis on environmental determinism and the related belief in a separation of fact and value, the exogenic theorist is likely to view questions of moral value as beyond the scope of the discipline. From the endogenic perspective, with its emphasis on personal constructions of reality and the inseparability of fact and value, moral issues often seem inescapable. To declare them irrelevant may itself be morally culpable.

6. The exogenic thinker is likely to place strong emphasis on methods of measurement and control because it is through such methods that one may obtain unbiased assessments of the facts. For many endogenic thinkers, however, "correct assessments" are suspect. Thus, empirical methods may be seen as means of sustaining theoretical positions already embraced. Given a particular theoretical standpoint, methods may be anticipated that will yield support. Methods thus furnish rhetorical rather than ontological support for the scientist.

With the lines of battle thus drawn, let us follow the example set by Wundt and attempt an understanding of the present complexion of the discipline by examining its historical development.

Exogenic-Endogenic Détente: The Reality of the Internal

It is no intellectual accident that psychology as a science was given birth at the close of the nineteenth century. One might indeed ask if it was not a sign of lassitude that it was so late beginning.[3] The foundations had long been laid. The concept of an empirical science had been well developed since the time of Newton, and the function of laboratory experimentation had been impressively demonstrated by Lavoisier, Berzelius, the Curies, and Rutherford. Coupled with this self-conscious attempt to unlock nature's secrets through systematic empirical study was a long-standing belief in mind as an empirical entity. Thinkers from Plato to Descartes had granted the mind ontological status, and by the late nineteenth century, philosophers such as John Locke, David Hume, David Hartley, and J. S. Mill had supplied rather detailed theories of mental processes. For almost a century, German thinkers

---

[3] Kirsch (1976) has argued that the emergence of psychology as an empirical science can largely be attributed to developments in German physiology, where attention was being directed to the physiological basis of experience. Mackenzie (1976) maintains that the development of Darwinism was the essential catalyst for the emergence of an empirically oriented psychology. Ben-David and Collins (1966) trace the impetus to the shifting structure of German academic institutions of the time.

had also given careful thought to the relationship between mental elements and the physiological system. In effect, there existed in the 1900s an auspicious conjunction between the exogenic and endogenic perspectives: mind was an empirical entity that could be studied with no less rigor and precision than the surrounding environment. There remained only the task of welding the belief in the palpability of mental entities with the experimental orientation of the natural sciences to give birth to the science of psychology. This was fully accomplished in late-nineteenth-century Germany.[4]

Yet, while the late 1800s were optimal years for the growth of psychology as a science, they were simultaneously unfavorable to the development of a social psychology. If the mind was the focus of empirical study, if mental operations and their biological coordinates furnished the essential questions, there was little obvious role for a uniquely social psychology. Social stimuli had no distinctive properties; they were essentially patterns of light, sound, and so on to be processed like any other stimuli. Neither was it necessary to develop a special category for social as opposed to nonsocial behavior. An understanding of all behavior patterns should ultimately be derived from thorough knowledge of basic psychological process.[5]

As a result, to develop his *Völkerpsychologie* Wundt had to begin an entirely separate enterprise. Virtually none of his experimental work, nor the contributions of Fechner, Helmholtz, Weber, and the like, made their way into his historical account of social institutions. And when the first two American texts on social psychology appeared in 1908 (one by William McDougall; the other by E. A. Ross), neither drew significantly from the empirical study of mind. McDougall's book relied heavily on an evolutionary perspective, while Ross's work drew sustenance from earlier sociological thinking. For neither of them was it possible to

---

[4]The concept of a détente between the exogenic and endogenic views falls far short of representing the full range of opinion during this period. Indeed, the concept of an empirical science of mind was hotly debated in many circles. Dilthey, Windelband, Rickert, Hensel, and others all carried out strong attacks against the empiricist position. In the same way, pockets of strong endogenic thought continued to exist during the hegemony of American behaviorism. In the latter case, for example, Havelock Ellis's 1923 volume, *The Dance of Life*, presents science as an aesthetic creation no more objectively valid than religion, dance, or literature. As Morawski (1979) points out, Ellis here followed Vaihinger's doctrine of fictions. "Matter is a fiction, just as the fundamental ideas with which the sciences generally operate are mostly fictions, and the scientific materialization of the world has proved a necessary and useful fiction, only harmful when we regard it as a hypothesis and therefore possibly true" (Ellis, 1923, pp. 91–92).

[5]The exogenic-endogenic détente is also evident in Comte's analysis of the social sciences. As Samelson (1974) points out, in *la morale* ("the sacred science") the subject and the object coincide. In this composite is reached "the definitive stage of human reason . . . the establishment of a subjective synthesis" (Comte, 1854; quoted by Samelson, 1974, p. 203). And, consistent with the endogenic position, Comte saw a close relation between value and science. Science was to be used in the service of reforming society. In the United States, Hugo Münsterberg was also attempting to synthesize the laws of nature with social idealism (Hale, 1980). As Münsterberg wrote in his diary of 1900, his aim was "the harmonization of a positivistic study of human life with an ethical idealism in the direction of Kant's and Fichte's philosophy" (Hale, 1980, p. 71).

discern useful connection between social activity and the laboratory study of mental process.[6]

It was primarily William James who carved out a niche for social psychology within the domain of psychology proper.[7] As he reasoned, there might be certain psychological processes that were distinctly social in their implications. His discussion of the basic senses of self, along with his formula for determining the individual's self-esteem (by dividing success by pretension), informed later generations of social psychologists that if they wished a place in psychology, they must identify mental processes that are uniquely social in implication. From this standpoint, the very most social psychologists could anticipate was a small piece of the mental pie. As we shall soon begin to see, however, there is good reason to believe that social psychology may serve a far more pivotal role in understanding human action. Indeed, the mental pie may be viewed primarily as a social creation.

The Exogenic Succession: Toward Public Reality

The conjunction between the exogenic and endogenic perspectives that served to give birth to early psychology was not to last. Within the robust realism of the American climate assumptions concerning the character of "the mind" soon became targets of attack. American culture, faced with the zesty promises of an expansive environment, was yielding up a philosophy of its own, namely pragmatism. For the pragmatist, nothing was considered real unless it made a difference in practice. With such major thinkers as John Dewey, William James, and Charles Pierce contributing both to the philosophy of pragmatism and to theoretical psychology, American psychology could hardly remain unaffected. There were also seemingly insoluble theoretical squabbles emerging in German circles regarding the nature of mind, and the introspective method allowed no hope of solution. Simultaneously there were the impressive experiments of Pavlov that demonstrated systematic behavioral changes without reliance on experiential analysis. Finally, the

[6]Texts are, of course, only one marker for an emerging discipline. However, even in the 1860s journal *Zeitschrift für Völkerpsychologie und Sprachenwissenschaft* and in the French "protosocial psychologies" of the mid-nineteenth century (along with the later works of the Tardes), virtually no mention was made of developments in experimental psychology (Apfelbaum, 1979; Lubek, 1979).

[7]It would be a mistake either to view James as a full proponent of the exogenic-endogenic détente or to assume that the détente was enthusiastically endorsed in all circles. For James, along with Josiah Royce, Henri Bergson, and others the central intellectual problem of the age was to identify "a transcendental source of values and purpose in a world where science had transformed nature into the blind interaction of atoms and where history had relativized all cultural standards of beauty, morality and truth" (Hale, 1980, p. 70). For James this search ultimately led to his severing of his connections with psychology and to the publication of *The Varieties of Religious Experience* (1902/1961).

mentalistic concerns so strongly represented in German psychology must surely be counted among the casualties of World War I.[8]

It was thus in 1924 that J. B. Watson could boldly contrast the "old psychology" which viewed "consciousness" as its subject matter with the "new" psychology of behaviorism which

> holds that the subject matter of human psychology is the behavior or activities of the human being. Behaviorism claims that "consciousness" is neither a definable nor a usable concept; that it is merely another word for the "soul" of more ancient times. The old psychology is thus dominated by a kind of subtle religious philosophy (p. 6).

This shift toward an exogenic psychology was further stimulated by the rise of logical positivist philosophy. Based on the writings of Schlick, Neurath, Ayer, Frank, and others, behaviorist psychologists could draw sustenance from the early positivist argument that assertions closed to empirical verification are without positive function in a mature science. Thus, concepts of psychological process, whether driven by environmental stimuli or autonomously operative, were all subject to disapprobation. Further, the psychologist could draw comfort from the logical positivist arguments for the unity of science. If all theoretical statements in psychology could be linked to an observation language, and all observation language could ultimately be translated into the language of physics, then psychology could anticipate ultimate assimilation into the family of natural sciences.

Social psychologists of the time had much to gain by joining the exogenic succession. Social activity was, after all, publicly observable and could therefore be placed at the center of scientific concern rather than serving as a peripheral derivative of mental process. Social psychology had also been criticized as "hopeless, speculative and verbose,"[9] and a shift of emphasis to observable entities held out promise for greater scientific respectability.[10] Floyd Allport wrote in the preface to his important text, *Social Psychology* (1924): "There are two main lines of scientific achievement which I have tried to bring within the scope of this volume. These are the *behavior viewpoint* and the experimental method" (p. 12). It was largely through

[8] For amplification see Blumenthal (1977) and Rieber (1980).

[9] See E. B. Holt's 1935 essay on the "whimsical condition" of social psychology.

[10] In his 1930 review of "recent social psychology," Sprowls argues that the establishment of prediction and control of human behavior as chief aims of social psychology was largely in response to the demands of American politics, philanthropy, industry, and other social institutions. He also agrees with the dominant view of the time that "behavior patterns" should take "first place" among the concerns of the profession. See also Murchison (1929) for a reiteration of the behavioral viewpoint in social psychology.

535

his efforts that the scattered social experimentation of Triplett and others became amalgamated into a "scientific discipline."[11]

Exogenic Liberalization: Personal Reality as Hypothetical Construction

The hegemony of radical empiricism proved short-lived within psychology. As logical positivist philosophy flourished and became extended in the 1930s and 1940s, it became increasingly clear that the demand for science without reference to unobservables was far too stringent. In physics, concepts such as "energy," "wave," and "field" were usefully employed, none of which could be directly represented by empirical operations. There appeared no good reason for excluding such terms in psychology. Terms that did not refer to immediate observables thus came to be viewed as "hypothetical constructs" (MacCorquodale & Meehl, 1948). They were to be admitted into the science provided that one could ultimately tie them, through a series of linking definitions, to public observables. Under these conditions it was possible to readmit internal or psychological states into proper study as hypothetical constructs. Personal experience once again had scientific credentials—only on a hypothetical level.[12]

This loosening of the criteria for mature science was enthusiastically received in many quarters of psychology. Many influential thinkers, including Woodworth, Tolman, Cattell, and Gordon Allport had never been moved by radical behaviorism and had continued to place a major emphasis on psychological process.[13] The 1940 publication of *Mathematico-Deductive Theory of Rote Learning*, reflecting the efforts of Clark Hull and his colleagues in both psychology and philosophy, also demonstrated the seeming precision with which such hypothetical terms could be used. And finally, the 1930s exodus from Germany of Gestalt thinkers Köhler, Wertheimer, and Koffka sparked an innervating romance with endogenic thought. To the extent that autochthonous psychological processes enabled the organism to create figure, ground, form, groupings, and movement from a stimulus array that did not itself contain such properties, then a concept of self-directing, internal process seemed inescapable. The liberalization of the positivist-behaviorist orientation was in full force.[14]

---

[11] In their challenging analysis of the Triplett study, Haines and Vaughan (1979) argue that contrary to common belief, the research does not occupy a unique place in the history of social psychology, and that the claim for Triplett's being the first experiment functions only as an "origin myth."

[12] Koch's 1959 analysis of this liberalization is perhaps definitive.

[13] Critical reactions to the inception of the behaviorist movement have been nicely documented by Samelson (1981).

[14] For an analysis of the Gestalt movement as a revolt against positivist science, see Leichtman (1979).

Had the empiricist liberalization not occurred, Kurt Lewin might today be an obscure and lonely figure. Arriving in the United States in 1933, Lewin was indeed in treacherous waters. With philosophers Husserl and Cassirer as his intellectual forebears, his endogenic commitment was not easily reconciled with the dominant empiricist temper of the times.[15] For Lewin, the chief subject of attention was the mental world of the individual, not the world of surrounding nature. Empirical reality of the positivist variety indeed occupied a nebulous position in Lewinian theory—never quite absorbed but not entirely rejected. This ambivalence was also reflected in Lewin's use of the term "external reality." At times the concept referred to public observables, but at others to the internal or psychological construction of the world (Deutsch, 1958). This ambiguity in the status of empirical reality is nicely illustrated in Lewin's 1935 essay on environmental forces. At times he argues for an independent reality capable of altering the psychological field. As he points out,

> The mere knowledge of something (e.g., of the geography of a foreign country . . .) does not necessarily change the child's life-space more than superficially. On the other hand, psychologically critical facts of the environment, such as the friend-liness of a certain adult, may have fundamental significance for the child's life-space . . . (p. 74).

But are these "critical facts" to be viewed as existing entities? Lewin's explication is fully equivocal: "The environment is for all its properties (directions, distances, etc.) to be defined . . . according to its quasi-physical, quasi-social, and quasi-mental structure" (p. 79). Further comment proves equally ambiguous: "Environment is understood psychologically sometimes to mean *momentary situation* of the child, at other times to mean the *milieu*, in the sense of the chief characteristics of the permanent situation" (p. 71). To further complicate the argument, Lewin then speaks as if the psychological world is the empirical world. "These imperative environmental facts—we shall call them valences—determine the direction of the behavior" (p. 77). As the present analysis makes apparent, Lewin's classic equation, $B = f(P,E)$—behavior is a function of the personal construction *and* the environment—represents his attempt to conjoin two fundamental epistemologies. In tracing behavior to psychological process, he reflects his longstanding immersion in endogenic thought; in tracing behavior to environmental determinants, he caters to exogenic interests.[16]

It was left to Lewin's students, Back, Cartwright, Deutsch, Festinger, Kelley, Pepitone, Schachter, Thibaut, and others to reconcile fully Lewin's endogenic

---

[15] As Koch has pointed out (personal communication), Lewin finally capitulated to the dominant empiricist metatheory in his (1940) article, "Formalization and Progress in Psychology," where he attempts to elucidate hypotheses for experimental evaluation.

[16] For further discussion, see Miriam Lewin's 1977 paper.

leanings with mainstream empiricist psychology. This was accomplished first by the adoption of the hypothetico-deductive form of exposition so impressively represented by Hull and his colleagues. Within this mode, the task of the scientist is that of developing and testing hypotheses about the world of observable fact.[17] Festinger's (1954) widely heralded theory of social comparison furnished an impressive model for social psychology. Here Festinger layed out a series of formal assumptions, each accompanied by supportive research findings. The reconciliation with empirical psychology was further achieved through the virtually exclusive adoption of the experimental method.[18] Importantly, this modus operandus also resembled that developed by the major competition—the Hullian satellites. Thus the theories and experiments of the Lewinians, along with such publications as *Frustration and Aggression* (Dollard et al., 1939) and *Communication and Persuasion* (Hovland, Janis, & Kelley, 1953) furnished a univocal model for scientific conduct. It was in this mold that social psychological inquiry was contentedly, if not enthusiastically, cast until the present era. In effect, by the late 1960s social psychology had witnessed the apotheosis of neobehaviorism.

But let us observe more carefully the fate of the endogenic perspective during this period. Clearly the scientists themselves were following empiricist doctrine with respect to their own conduct. From the guild standpoint, they were attempting to map reality as accurately and systematically as possible and to test such maps against reality in dispassionate fashion. However, the endogenic perspective so strongly represented in Lewin's orientation remained. Where? Essentially it became embodied in the theories under empirical study. People other than scientists were said to be dominated by cognitive construction, motives, needs, and so on. *They* lived in a world of mental process. It is this ironic duality—the scientist employing an exogenic theory to guide his or her own conduct, while assuming an endogenic basis for others' actions—that now returns to haunt us.

[17] Social psychology was hardly independent in the development of its central paradigms. In fact, its form may be viewed as an emulation of mainstream experimental psychology, which by 1938 was characterized as *empirical, mechanistic, quantitative, nomothetic,* and *operational* (Bills, 1938). In their 1940 review of the preceding fifty years of social psychology, Bruner and Allport largely agree that such a designation had also come to be applicable to the social domain as well. The only important deviation appeared to be in the concomitant concern of social psychologists with research on social problems.

[18] The Yale group, with its close attachment to the exogenic roots of learning psychology, tended to place a strong emphasis on the manipulation and measurement of observables with a secondary emphasis on mental processes, while the endogenically oriented Lewinians tended to emphasize mental process and place secondary emphasis on accounting for a multiplicity of stimulus or behavioral variables. This difference in epistemological orientations explains McGuire's description of convergent versus divergent forms of research (Chapter 24, this volume). However, the differential emphases were not sufficiently radical to prevent relatively easy transition from one camp to the other. Lewin's student, Harold Kelley, could thus become an important contributor to the Hovland program in attitude change (see Hovland, Janis, & Kelley, 1953) and to later accounts of internal process (see Kelley, 1967). Festinger (1954) incorporated both exogenic and endogenic bases into his theory of social comparison by distinguishing between two realities, the one physical and the other social.

Exogenic Deterioration and the Cognitive Revolution: The Return of Subjectivity

In order to appreciate recent developments in social psychology, it is again necessary to take account of the intellectual ethos. As we have seen, an important interplay has taken place between psychological thought and contributions to exogenic and endogenic thinking more generally. The recent past seems no exception. In particular, one cannot but be impressed with what appears to be a broad-scale disenchantment with exogenic assumptions in philosophy. This disenchantment appears to be highly correlated with both the cognitive revolution in psychology and with what has been termed "the crisis" in social psychology. Let us deal first with the deterioration of the exogenic position in philosophy and the growth of cognitive psychology. We may then turn more directly to the position of social psychology today.

The contemporary deterioration in exogenic epistemology may be traced to three major lines of thought. The first is the *broad reassessment of empiricist philosophy of science*. At the outset, those philosophers most closely identified with the founding of logical positivism themselves retreated over time from the bold and invigorating promise of certainty in science. By 1932 Neurath was prepared to argue that verification is a relation between propositions and not between propositions and experiences; Carnap ultimately gave up his early argument that meaning in the sciences was to be identified as translatability into experience; and Ayer finally argued that sense data cannot be conclusively used to prove assertions about the physical world.

In the meantime, Karl Popper (1957) argued persuasively against the classic view that scientific knowledge can be built up from pure observations and against the positivist view that empirical confirmation of a theory constitutes a proper means of accumulating knowledge. (In effect, Popper's arguments militate against the common practice in psychology of verifying hypotheses.) It is usually possible to find some evidence in favor of a given theory, argued Popper; the critical question is whether the theory can withstand evidence brought against it. Yet, even the falsification thesis has not resisted deterioration. As Quine (1953) demonstrated, along with Duhem (1906/1954) long before, falsification is a problematic process. For one, the defender of a given theory can typically locate auxiliary theoretical assumptions to discredit or absorb the disconfirming evidence. Further, because what counts as data relevant to a theory's falsification cannot easily be specified outside the language of the theory itself, the range of potential threats to a theory may be severely truncated. In effect, what counts as a fact cannot be separated easily from theoretical premises.

The break with empiricist philosophy of science became fully apparent with Kuhn's (1962/1970) account of scientific progress. As Kuhn argued, shifts from one major theoretical paradigm to another in the sciences do not generally depend on either confirmation or falsification. Rather, what appears to be "progress" in science represents a shift in perspectives based on a confluence of social factors, along with the generation of anomalies that are simply irrelevant to previously favored theories. The new theories are not improvements over the old in terms of predictive power: primarily they represent differing frameworks of understanding. More polemically, Feyerabend (1975) has argued that rules for induction and deduction, along with methods of hypothesis testing are basically irrelevant to scientific progress. Necessary for a flourishing science is procedural anarchy, argued Feyerabend, where hypotheses contradicting well-confirmed theories should be championed, and social and ideological persuasion should be given equal footing with evidence. To be sure, brisk argument continues in virtually all these sectors. The major point is that the weight of the argument has shifted substantially over the past forty years, so that the chorus of lusty voices that once sang hosannas to empiricist rules of science has now been replaced by a cacophony of dissidents.

A second major contribution to the erosion of the exogenic commitment has been made by *ordinary language philosophy*. Stimulated largely by the work of Moore, Russell, and Wittgenstein, concern shifted away from the problem of relating experience to knowledge, to the way in which claims about knowledge and experience functioned within the language. As it was argued, problems within both philosophy and everyday life are often created by the language, and their solution may thus require an analysis and possibly purification of that language. Of particular concern for the behavioral sciences, increasing attention was given by philosophers such as Ryle, Anscombe, Hamlyn, and Austin to the language of person description.

And, as such concepts as mind, motivation, intention, and behavior were scrutinized, increasing attention was paid to the forms of discourse used in the behavioral sciences. From such analyses a fundamental critique of the empiricist-behaviorist orientation emerged. In particular, it is argued (Hamlyn, 1953; Hampshire, 1959; Peters, 1958; Taylor, 1964; Winch, 1958) that human action cannot be rendered intelligible in strictly physical terms—that is, by referring to the physical properties of the stimulus, physiological process, or resulting behavioral events. To take account of the temperature, the wind velocity, the pitch and magnitude of vocal tones, and so on to which John Jones is exposed on a given occasion, and to relate these systematically and precisely to subsequent movements of his arms, legs, mouth, and so on is not to "make sense" of his behavior. Such an account would indeed leave one mystified. However, this form of empirically based discourse, often termed *causal*, may be contrasted with another which enables immediate comprehension. If we simply point out in this case that John Jones is "greeting his neighbor," we have informatively explained his actions. This level of discourse, often termed *reasoned*, typically requires that reference be made to reasons, motives, purposes, or intentions. When we know what the person is trying or intending

540

to do, his or her actions are typically made intelligible.[19] Thus it could be concluded that endogenic concepts of reason, intention, motive, and so on are fundamentally indispensable to a behavioral science. Concomitantly, the role of environmental stimulus and response became increasingly unclear. If intention is built into our language of understanding, then environmental stimuli cannot easily be viewed as the cause of action. And, if action can only be identified by knowing its intentional basis, then behavioral observation plays an ancillary role to symbolic interpretation (Gergen, 1980).

Coupled with these two important philosophic movements has been a third force antagonistic to the traditional exogenic commitment in behavioral science, that is, the flourishing of "the critical stance" within the social sciences. In part because of hostility toward the U.S. military deployment in Vietnam, a wide variety of potentially culpable institutions, such as government, industry, and education, have undergone critical scrutiny within the past decade.[20] Among the institutions under fire was the scientific establishment. Of particular importance, questions have been raised concerning the ideological implications of what appeared, on the surface, to be value-free description. It is argued, for example, that in exploring the various personal characteristics of participants in race riots the investigator implies that the rioters are responsible for their actions. It is to assume that their character must be changed if rioting is to be reduced. Such a position removes responsibility from institutions practicing racial discrimination, and such institutions are thus protected by what the investigator may assume is nothing but an attempt to study existing correlations. One of the most powerful arguments of this sort was contained in Alvin Gouldner's *The Coming Crisis in Western Sociology* (1970). Gouldner demonstrates how structural-functional theory in sociology, although impeccably neutral in its scientific credentials, lends strong implicit support to the status quo and is inimical to social change. Other accounts have demonstrated the ideological underpinnings of historical accounting (Zinn, 1970) along with behavioral theory in political science (see Surkin & Wolfe, 1970). Such queries also rekindled interest in the earlier writings of Habermas, Adorno, and other members of the Marxist-oriented Frankfurt School (Jay, 1973). As the critical mode became increasingly well-developed, it also became apparent that the empiricist assumption of a value-neutral social science was deceptively misleading (see Unger, 1975). Social science knowledge is not an impartial reflection of "the way things are," as the empiricists would have it, but reflects the vested interests, ideological commitments, and value preferences of the scientists themselves.

[19]To clarify, one could not "make sense" of language through an exhaustive study of its phonetics. It is only when such sounds are transformed into morphemes that we understand the language.

[20]Leo Marx (1978) has argued that indeed the current era is witnessing a "neo-romantic" revolution against the cold formalism of "science" more generally.

It is difficult to ascertain precisely how and where these shifts in philosophic perspective influenced the course of psychological thought, or even whether such influence was unidirectional in its effects. However, it does seem clear that the three major developments just outlined are quite compatible with what is now viewed in psychology as the "cognitive revolution." Several reasons may be offered for this compatibility. Among them, the philosophy of science ceased to offer encouragement and guidance to those who wished to purify the language of psychology of mentalist terms. The door was open for what now may be seen as a wholesale reification of mental process. Terms such as "concept," "memory," and "decoding" have come to acquire an ontic status similar to that granted to the "facts of consciousness" by the nineteenth-century German mentalists. A second fillip to cognitive study was furnished by the philosophic shift toward linguistic analysis. Such work furnished a basis for useful interchange between philosophers and psychologists. The boundaries between the disciplines were often obscured. In some of the work of Noam Chomsky (1968), for example, one finds the reincarnation of the nineteenth-century philosopher-psychologist. And as the present analysis makes clear, the debate between Chomsky (1959, 1964) and Skinner (1957) was not only a scientific disagreement over which theory best fits the data (see also Dixon & Horton, 1968), it was also a recapitulation of the fundamental conflict between exogenic and endogenic worldviews.

This same shift from the exogenic to the endogenic perspective is evident throughout the cognitive domain. Ittelson (1973) has nicely traced the subtle but significant change in the concept of stimulus in the history of perceptual study. As he shows, the traditional view is one that views the stimulus as "physical energy outside the organism which, when it impinges on the organism, initiates processes, the end product of which is a response wholly determined, and predictable from the nature of the stimulus" (p. 8). Exogenic thought could have no clearer exemplar. However, this line of argument has gradually been eroded. For example, Gibson (1950) stated that "the term 'stimulus' will always refer to the light change on the retina" (p. 63) but, by 1966, he had reconsidered this position, stating that his early definition "fails to distinguish between stimulus *energy* and stimulus *information* and this difference is crucial" (p. 29). In effect, information is a concept that recognizes the autonomous processing capacities of the organism; it assumes an organism that is in search of and uses stimulation to fulfill its goals. The quandary over exogenic and endogenic views has now become a focal point of discussion. In his popular text on cognition, we find Neisser (1976) agonizing, "No choice is ever free of the information on which it is based. Nevertheless, that information is selected by the chooser himself. On the other hand, no choice is ever determined by the environment directly. Still, that environment supplies the information that the chooser will use" (p. 182). Finally, we must consider the work of Piaget (1952, 1974). From the present perspective we find Piaget undertaking the titanic challenge of integrating both the exogenic and endogenic worldviews in a single theory.

542

He wished simultaneously to accept a real world about which true knowledge could be obtained, along with an active organism that formulates and interprets. Thus, Piaget's concept of accommodation yields to exogenic assumptions, while the concept of assimilation emphasizes his commitment to endogenic thought. Development becomes an epistemological see-saw.

To be sure, social psychological thinking has been much influenced by the shift toward cognitive formulations in the field more generally. However, social psychologists were amply prepared. As we have seen, early formulations of the Lewin group planted important seeds for endogenic thought within the discipline. The more general deterioration of the behaviorist-empiricist orientation furnished a context in which such thought could reach fruition. Thus, with Schachter's two-factor theory of emotional labeling (Schachter, 1964; Schachter & Singer, 1962), cognitive processes replaced biological determinism as the basis of behavioral explanation. Festinger's (1957) theory of cognitive dissonance, which began with the supposition that people's actions are driven by inherent cognitive tendencies, came to serve as the battle cry for virtually a small army of social psychologists (see Brehm & Cohen, 1962; Wicklund & Brehm, 1976). Yet, few investigators bothered themselves with the earlier empiricist demand for an independent behavioral anchoring of hypothetical constructs. Balance formulations (Abelson et al., 1968; Heider, 1946; Newcomb, 1961) also came to demand equally wide attention. Again, such formulations assumed the existence of autonomous tendencies toward cognitive equilibrium, tendencies that were not clearly products of previous environmental influences.[21] This variety of formulation continues to the present day. Reactance (Brehm, 1966; Wicklund & Brehm, 1976), equity (Adams, 1965; Walster, Walster, & Berscheid, 1978), self-awareness (Duval & Wicklund, 1972), uniqueness striving (Snyder & Fromkin, 1980), and many similar concepts have all been added to the arsenal of cognitive tendencies.

Heider's (1958) theory of causal attribution also demonstrated its origins in German endogenic thought. For Heider the experience of causality was not given in the movement of relationships among environmental entities: it was rather a phenomenological necessity inherent in mental functioning. Although an overwhelming number of studies were inspired by Heider's formulation, much of this work has attempted a reconciliation with the empiricist roots of experimental social psychology. That is, the inherent mental tendencies so fundamental to the endogenic basis of the theory gave way to traditional exogenic thinking. In the Jones and Davis (1965) and Kelley (1972) formulations, both pivotal to attribution inquiry,

---

[21] It is of historical interest to note the shift from exogenic to endogenic assumptions in the Yale volumes on attitude change. Although early volumes were largely concerned with isolating external determinants of attitude change, with the 1960 publication of *Attitude Organization and Change* the endogenic metamorphosis was virtually complete: concern had shifted almost entirely from external determinants to internal process.

internally driven cognitive tendencies are largely eschewed. Instead the perceiver becomes a rational being weighing the evidence supplied by the senses. Indeed the Kelley formulation uses as its basis John Stuart Mill's canons of logical inference, long a mainstay in empiricist philosophy.

In adopting a cognitive basis of explanation, social psychologists have also been successful in linking their interests with adjacent domains. Beginning with the attempt of dissonance researchers to account for biological motives (see Brehm & Cohen, 1962), of research relating psychological states of helplessness and control to health related actions and symptoms (see Seligman, 1975; Rodin & Langer, 1977), and of more recent work on stress and coping strategies (see Glass, 1977; Glass & Singer, 1972), social psychologists have helped form the basis for what has become behavioral medicine. And, with the more recent work on cognitive processes underlying social decision-making (see Nisbett & Ross, 1980) and on person memory (Hastie et al., 1980), social psychology has allied itself once again with traditional experimental psychology. So enthusiastically have such enterprises been pursued that many social psychologists have come to fear that concern with fundamental social process may be relegated to a secondary position. Social psychology may become an ancillary discipline whose concerns will be dictated by either applied or experimental psychology.

The Struggle Toward a New Psychology: Mind as a Social Creation

That which we call the world, the objective world, is a social tradition.

Miguel de Unamuno
The Tragic Sense of Life

Thus far we have seen that the breakdown of empiricist metatheory has been a congenial context for the flourishing of cognitive theory. However, of greater importance, this breakdown has also been accompanied by widespread reconsideration of the nature of behavioral inquiry. Within the fields of sociology and political science, philosopher Richard Bernstein (1978) has spoken of an "emerging new sensibility" in respect to the aims and functions of such disciplines, one that holds promise for fundamental transformation. It is apparent that this new sensibility, so widely evident in our adjoining disciplines, is abundantly manifest within the central ranks of psychology. For example, Meehl's 1978 critique of traditional hypothesis testing along with the Popperian view of science, Cronbach's (1975) lament over the cumulativeness of experimental findings, Sarbin's (1977) argument for a contextualist orientation to understanding human action, Neisser's (1976) misgivings about the predictive capability of cognitive research, Bronfenbrenner's (1977) concern over the ecological irrelevance of much developmental research, Argyris's (1975) elucidation of the manipulative implications of much social theory, Riegel's (1972) attack on traditional developmental psychology for its historical and ideological insensitivity, Fiske's (1978) dismay with the meager progress of personality research, along with recent portrayals of research on learning and memory as both ideologically and historically bound (Schwartz, Lacey, & Schuldenfrei, 1978; Meacham, 1977; Kvale, 1977) are all indicative of a major evolution in thinking.[22] Such generalized ferment has not taken place in psychology since the advent of radical behaviorism in the 1920s.

It is also apparent that what has been termed "the crisis" (Elms, 1975; Lewin, 1977; Sherif, 1977; Graumann, 1979; Silverman, 1971; Mertens & Fuchs, 1978) in recent social psychology is not a matter of localized dyspepsia. Within the manifest discontent with the experimental method (see McGuire, 1973; Gergen, 1978; Gadlin & Ingle, 1975), misgivings concerning the capacity of present research to solve pressing social problems (Helmreich, 1975), arguments against the generation of transhistorical predictions (Gergen, 1973; Hendrick, 1976), arguments for breaking the link between understanding and prediction (Thorngate, 1976), the exploration of the human image implied by social theory (Shotter, 1975), doubts about the cumulativeness of programmatic research (Smith, 1972; Cartwright, 1973), and concern with the ethical foundations underlying psychological research (Kelman, 1972; Mixon, 1972; Schuler, 1980; Smith, 1974), social psychologists are critically confronting the empiricist tradition. Further, in the questioning of the value bases implicit within descriptive theories (Archibald, 1978; Apfelbaum & Lubek, 1976; Sampson, 1977, 1978, Hampden-Turner, 1970), in our growing concern with the effects of social context on social psychological knowledge (Buss, 1979), in our probing the extent to which scientific theory creates social phenomena (Gergen, 1979), in our exploration of the rule following basis of social action (Harré & Secord, 1972; Harré, 1979; Ginsburg, 1979), in the probing of dialectic theory (Buss, 1979; Cvetkovich, 1977) and the interpretive bases of social life (Gauld & Shotter, 1977), in the exploration of the extent to which people may voluntarily escape the predictive efforts of the science (Scheibe, 1978), in the search for biases underlying the discipline's history (see Morawski, 1979; Samelson, 1974; Baumgardner, 1977), and in the various conferences and colloquia devoted to the nature

---

[22] Such citations are only representative of a much broader array of critical self-appraisals within recent psychology. Sigmund Koch's (1959) work may be viewed as prophetic in this regard. However, many others must be added to the list, including Allport, 1975; Bakan, 1969; Campbell, 1969; Chein, 1972; Deese, 1972; Hermann, 1976; Holzkamp, 1976; Hudson, 1972; Israel & Tajfel, 1972; Lorenz, 1967; Mahoney, 1976; McKeachie, 1974; Mishler, 1979; Morawski, 1979; Petrinovich, 1979; Rychlak, 1975; Sampson, 1978; and Shotter, 1975.

of the discipline and its potential (see Armistead, 1974; Strickland, Aboud, & Gergen, 1976; Israel & Tajfel, 1972), we are breaking clear of a tradition that, for all its solidifying capacities, had become strangulating in its singularity. Such metatheoretic analysis may be viewed, then, as a salutory sign that the field is healthily linked to the broader intellectual community and is making a serious attempt to reach solutions in its own terms.

In this attempt at solutions can one anticipate the emergence of a "new psychology"? This is indeed a momentous question, and its answer will ultimately depend on a confluence of many factors, including intellectual, political, and economic ones. Although criticisms of the empirical tradition seem virtually lethal, assumptions on which such criticisms are based have not been sufficiently tested against the crucible of counterattack. Such assumptions require more complete elaboration and examination. Further, the critics have been unable in most cases to offer compelling alternatives for everyday activity in the science. One often encounters the comment that although traditional practices seem problematic, they are comfortably programmatic and have reward value within the profession. Regarding professional politics, those committed to the empiricist traditions currently occupy most positions of authority and control within the discipline. If the continuation of critical probing succeeds in alienating rather than inviting dialogue, movement toward alternative forms of inquiry may be vitally impeded. And, with respect to economics, as the availability of academic positions continues to recede, many institutions may prefer to select a traditional candidate over one searching, but uncertain. Those who wish to fly on new wings may continue to dream of fairer weather.

Should these and other complex problems be solved, what form of psychology might one anticipate? As an initial answer one might conjecture that no single form will emerge; rather, a variety of competing alternatives will be developed, each of which will vie for centrality. In effect we may see a fragmentation of paradigms. To support this view one might point to the steadily increasing number of social psychologists pursuing the ethogenic orientation, dialectic theory, philosophical psychology, interpretive (hermeneutic) analysis, the critical orientation, historical-social psychology, metatheoretical and historical analysis of social psychology, and ethnomethodology. Scholars in each of these areas have criticized the traditional hypothesis-testing orientation in social psychology and are now searching for viable alternatives for research. Yet it is my belief that there are certain metatheoretical assumptions that would elicit substantial agreement among scholars in each of these seemingly disparate enterprises. That is, when carefully examined, one may find sufficient accord among these orientations that one could, on an abstract level, envision a unified alternative. It will prove useful to elucidate several of these key assumptions about which agreement might be secured. The reader who wishes to trace the assumption back to specific works may consult an earlier paper (Gergen & Morawski, 1980).

Knowledge as Socially Constituted

From the traditional empiricist standpoint, the investigator ideally serves as a passive recording device, sensitive to the patterns of nature. Theoretical description properly serves to map the existing pattern. As we have seen, this view of the scientist has come under brisk attack, both within the philosophy of science and within the behavioral sciences themselves. At the same time, within both circles attention is being increasingly directed toward the relationship between what is taken for knowledge at any point and processes of social interchange. As the reasoning goes, knowledge systems are fundamentally linguistic systems, sounds or markings that are used by people in relationships. In this respect, knowledge would appear vitally dependent on the vicissitudes of social negotiation. Its constraints would not essentially be experiential but social. From this standpoint, the existence of aggression, altruism, attitude change, conformity, reciprocity, socioeconomic class, and the like are not matters of ontological significance; statements about them are not fundamentally subject to empirical test. Rather, statements employing such terms may or may not be supported by observation depending on how one chooses to relate such terms to observation. Typically such relationships depend importantly on the usage of the terms within social interchange. However, it may be ventured that because such usage depends on coordinated actions among people, or "joint action" in Shotter's (1980) terms, knowledge in its linguistic sense can be viewed as fundamentally a social product.

While sensitive to the many persuasive arguments for the "social construction of reality" this view does not simultaneously commit the scientist to the endogenic extreme: reality as subjective. That is, one may accept the empiricist assumption of a real world, or reliable sensory experiences, as one might have it. However, one may simultaneously separate the construction of knowledge systems, or the way one communicates about experience, from the experience itself. One may experience without communication about an entity and communicate without benefit of experience. Knowledge about social life is not to be viewed as a "reflection" of what there is, but as a "transformation" of experience into a linguistic ontology. To reiterate, from this perspective the constraints on knowledge as a language are not furnished by reality but by social process.

This line of argument would apply no less strongly to statements about psychological states or processes (see Coulter, 1979). That is, one may argue that what we take to be psychological knowledge is not fundamentally dependent upon self-experience but is a system of talking governed by continuously evolving rules. In the case of talk about psychological states, however, we may anticipate a particularly elastic set of rules with a high degree of terminological negotiation. This is because the process of pointing, or saying, *"That's* what I mean by X" cannot be easily accompanied by shared experience. In saying "he possesses a *concept* of writing," for example, one cannot conveniently point to what we take to be an object as a way

547

of furnishing an experiential anchor for the term "concept." One can usually do so when saying, *"That* is a book."

As this discussion suggests, under favorable circumstances the social psychologist could come to play a critical role in the intellectual community. To the extent that the generation of knowledge is a social process and the social psychologist is committed to an understanding of such processes, then social psychological inquiry does not parallel that of the physicist, chemist, historian, or economist, for example; rather, the social psychologist could become indispensable in elucidating the grounds upon which physical, chemical, historical, or economic knowledge is based. In no way is the discipline prepared for such an undertaking at the present time. However the seeds for such an enterprise are sown both within the discipline and its adjoining domains.

Order as Socially Constituted

Exogenic thought has often placed a strong emphasis on the determined order of events in nature, and such thought sustains the scientist's concern with tracing relationships between antecedents and consequents. Social psychologists have fallen heir to this legacy, and the tradition has thus been committed to generating "basic principles" or "laws" of human interaction. Much of the critical literature cited above has found this view problematic. Rather, on both ontological and humanistic grounds it has been argued that the vast share of human activity is not fruitfully assumed to possess an order favored by nature. The range and variations of human activity seem enormous. Although biology may set limits on human potential, within these limits lies a virtual infinity of possible patterning. And at any point virtually any action within the available repertoire may be used as a "response" to any "antecedent stimulus." On this account there is little necessary connection between a given antecedent, in terms of an environmental event, and any subsequent action. To the extent that this line of thinking can be sustained, it becomes useful to view the ordered activity of human beings not as governed by natural law but as conforming in various degrees to localized and historically situated rules. Rules may be developed within the culture to reduce the threat of chaos and to secure needed ends. However, people remain fundamentally free to obey the rules, break them, or to attempt their alteration. In this respect, the new psychology might replace the mechanistic with a voluntaristic base of human activity.[23]

Within this argument one may also discern the germ of what could become a

---

[23] Even in the domain of cognitive psychology the search for fundamental principles of cognition seems to be ebbing. Such concepts as "cognitive heuristics," "scripts," and "plans" suggest that the range of cognitive orientations could be virtually infinite. Thus, the existing configuration or distribution of cognitive dispositions within the culture must be viewed primarily as a matter of historical concern. Contemporary cognitive research may tell us what people can do; it tells us little about what they must do.

liberation of theoretical explanation in social psychology. When order is assumed to be under human control, the causal power previously granted to the environment (stimulus or reinforcement) within the traditional exogenic framework is thereby diminished. The environment ceases to be "responsible" for human activity, and one cannot thus continue to "scan the landscape of observables" to answer the question of "why" a given pattern occurs. In this context the theorist is granted broad liberties with respect to explanation—where causal power is placed and how it is to be understood. Many of the theoretical departures within the cognitive movement may be viewed as precursors of what could become a far-reaching enrichment of the explanatory vocabulary. Of particular promise is the form of explanation suggested in Wundt's *Völkerpsychologie*, that is, historical or diachronic explanation. Contemporary social psychology is based almost entirely on a logic of efficient cause; it searches for the immediate antecedents, both necessary and sufficient, for a given action. Yet the same action may also be understood in terms of its place in an historical process, both with respect to the individual and the culture. How and why have such patterns been developed in the life of the individual or within the society more generally? What transformations have such patterns undergone over time, and what functions have these transformations served? Such questions open an exciting range of new theoretical possibilities.

Theory as Agency

As we have seen, the empirical tradition has typically considered theoretical description and explanation as mapping devices. From this standpoint, social theory serves society by furnishing reliable predictions in the world as given. However, we have also seen that this characterization of theory appears critically flawed. It may be more fruitful to view theories as linguistic signals with a negotiable relationship to experience. If we further accept the argument for a socially constituted order and grant a functional link between the linguistic practices of the culture and its other patterns of conduct, then alterations in linguistic practices have implications for the social order. In this way social psychological theory acquires an "agentive" role in social life. It can serve as a linguistic tool to be employed by the theorist or others to strengthen, sustain, or obliterate various forms of human activity. As such terms as *equity, reciprocity, conformity, reactance*, and so on enter the scientific vocabulary, they also enter the ontological system in its linguistic aspect. When such terms are then used to "describe" various actions, one's dispositions toward such actions may be vitally altered. For example, to say that one pattern of action is equitable and another inequitable, one is conforming and another autonomous, and so on is to have implications for the continuation of such actions.

This line of argument places the social psychologist in a position at once enviable and precarious. To the extent that society furnishes the means by which the psychologist gains special proficiency within language and communication, it also

549

grants him or her enhanced power to alter or sustain patterns of social life. The public thus entrusts to the psychologist skills that may affect its well-being. Further, when the psychologist is looked to for authoritative descriptions and explanations of human activity, he or she is being granted license to employ that skill. The theorist may thus acquire what could in some cases become enormous powers of influence in society. The theorist's hope "to be useful" in the culture need not await the practitioner's attempt to derive predictions in applied settings; the chief lever of social change may lie in the theoretical interpretation of social life.

At the same time, this position confronts social psychologists with a range of formidable problems—in fact, those which many exogenic thinkers had misleadingly argued were irrelevant to behavioral inquiry. These are problems of value—what forms of social life are to be favored, which are to be discouraged? If the language of theoretical description and explanation inevitably carries with it implications for action, as widely and persuasively argued, then the scientist can no longer take refuge in the Shangri-La of "pure description." To describe is inherently to prescribe. The social psychologist is thus invited, if not compelled, to return to the moral concerns so central to Auguste Comte's view of the science. Moral debate may thus come to play an increasingly important role in the new psychology.

Research as Vivification

If these various arguments are sustained and amplified over time, we may also anticipate fundamental alterations in the place of research. Since the 1930s the discipline has primarily been devoted to the empirical testing of hypotheses. The hope has been that with the accumulation of enough reliable facts, one might build inductively toward a fully general and empirically grounded theory. Yet, as critics of this orientation have argued, induction in the sciences is misconceived, the facts of social life are seldom stable, and factual data are negotiable. In effect, the place of empirical work in the sciences must be reassessed.

At the outset, it is clear from these suppositions that within the scholarly setting empirical study may be viewed as ancillary to theory construction. It is the theoretical interpretation of experience that has the capacity to transform social life and not the empirical evidence itself. The data themselves are mute. Further, it can be argued, it is the theory that gives rise to the empirical study and not the other way around. Within this setting the empirical study gives up its former, ill-claimed role as crucible for theoretical accuracy. Rather, research may be viewed as a means of enhancing the efficacy of theoretical communication. In a certain sense the researcher may be considered an artist who fashions the world in such a way that a theory is made palpable, dramatic, or life-like. And, as implied by the earlier arguments, researchers may wish to concern themselves not only with the ethics of observation, but with the ethics of communication about observation. The experiment, once interpreted, enters the common consciousness—to favor and threaten various forms of activity. In effect, the empirical study becomes an instrument for altering or sustaining social patterns—an instrument for good or ill according to moral or ideological criteria.

What does this mean for the researcher in the applied setting—one who wishes to assess the probability of suicide, auto accidents, needs for therapy, or the success of a public policy? In many cases such a researcher may not wish to escape conventional definitions. That is, the applied researcher may agree to common definitions of such terms along with their associated value investments and to furnish data within this framework. However, as the present arguments indicate, the researcher should be aware of the extent to which he or she is acceding to convention. The applied researcher does not at all escape the moral repercussions of "mere description," but joins the scholar as an artisan of symbols.

Should social-psychological study shift in the direction adumbrated by these assumptions, it may find enthusiastic support within other academic domains: vital movements within philosophy (see Taylor, 1971; Gadamer, 1975; Ricoeur, 1970), sociology (Bauman, 1978; Berger & Luckmann, 1966; Giddens, 1976; McHugh, 1970), anthropology (Geertz, 1973; Douglas, 1975), political science (Hirschman, 1970), and literary analysis (Fish, 1979; Hirsch, 1976; Burke, 1966). Ethnomethodological inquiry (see Garfinkel, 1967; Cicourel, 1968; Kessler & McKenna, 1978) must be singled out as well for its pivotal focus on the negotiation process through which verbal constructions become objectified. In effect, should a relatively unified reconstruction in social psychology occur along the lines suggested above, a rich exchange might be anticipated within the broader intellectual milieu.[24]

To conclude, during the past century social psychology has participated in one of humankind's greatest intellectual adventures. It has, in J. L. Austin's (1962) terms, joined in the "pursuit of the incorrigible," or certain knowledge, a pursuit that has challenged thinkers from Heraclitus to the present. Early in this century it appeared that the means had been discovered for gaining certainty in the behavioral sciences. Yet, subsequent examination has found such means sadly wanting. The search for certainty is a child's romance, and as in most romances, one holds fast to even the most fragile shard attesting to continued life. The question that must now be confronted is how to pass successfully into the maturity of a second century. A new romance may be required to extinguish the old, and possibly the signals of its inception are at hand.

REFERENCES

Abelson, R. P., Aronson, E., McGuire, W. J., Newcomb, T. M., Rosenberg, M. J., & Tannenbaum, P. H. (Eds.). *Theories of cognitive consistency: A sourcebook.* Skokie, Ill.: Rand McNally, 1968.

[24]For a more extended analysis of the development of a transformed psychology see Gergen, 1982.

551

II. THE SPECIAL FIELDS OF PSYCHOLOGY

Adams, J. S. Inequity in social exchange. In L. Berkowitz (Ed.), *Advances in experimental social psychology* (Vol. 2). New York: Academic Press, 1965.

Allport, D. A. The state of cognitive psychology. *Quarterly Journal of Experimental Psychology*, 1975, 27, 141–152.

Allport, F. H. *Social psychology*. Boston: Houghton Mifflin, 1924.

Apfelbaum, E. Some overlooked early European social psychologies. Paper presented at the 1979 meeting of the American Psychological Association, New York.

Apfelbaum, E., & Lubek, I. Resolution vs. revolution? The theory of conflicts in question. In L. Strickland, F. E. Aboud, & K. J. Gergen (Eds.), *Social psychology in transition*. New York: Plenum, 1976.

Archibald, W. P. *Social psychology as political economy*. New York: McGraw-Hill, 1978.

Argyris, C. Dangers in applying results from experimental social psychology. *American Psychologist*, 1975, 30, 469–485.

Armistead, N. (Ed.). *Reconstructing social psychology*. Harmondsworth: Penguin, 1974.

Austin, J. L. *Sense and sensibilia*. London: Oxford University Press, 1962.

Bakan, D. *On method*. San Francisco: Jossey-Bass, 1969.

Bauman, Z. *Hermeneutics and social science*. New York: Columbia University Press, 1978.

Baumgardner, S. R. Critical studies in the history of social psychology. *Personality and Social Psychology Bulletin*, 1977, 3, 681–687.

Ben-David, J., & Collins, R. Social factors in the origins of a new science: The case of psychology. *American Sociological Review*, 1966, 31, 451–465.

Berger, P., & Luckmann, T. *The social construction of reality*. Garden City, N.Y.: Doubleday, 1966.

Bernstein, R. J. *The restructuring of social and political theory*. Philadelphia: University of Pennsylvania Press, 1978.

Bills, A. G. Changing views of psychology as a science. *Psychological Review*, 1938, 45, 377–394.

Blumenthal, A. L. A reappraisal of Wilhelm Wundt. *American Psychologist*, 1975, 30, 1081–1086.

Blumenthal, A. L. Wilhelm Wundt and early American psychology: A clash of two cultures. *Annals of the New York Academy of Sciences*, 1977, 291, 13–20.

Blumenthal, A. L. The founding father we never knew. *Contemporary Psychology*, 1979, 24, 547–550.

Boring, E. G. *A history of experimental psychology*. New York: Century, 1929.

Brehm, J. W. *A theory of psychological reactance*. New York: Academic Press, 1966.

Brehm, J. W., & Cohen, A. R. *Explorations in cognitive dissonance*. New York: Wiley, 1962.

Bronfenbrenner, U. Toward an experimental ecology of human development. *American Psychologist*, 1977, 32, 513–531.

Bruner, J. S., & Allport, G. W. Fifty years of change in American psychology. *Psychological Bulletin*, 1940, 37, 757–776.

Burke, K. *Language as symbolic action: Essays on life, literature and method*. Berkeley, Calif.: University of California Press, 1966.

Buss, A. R. (Ed.). *Psychology in social context*. New York: Irvington, 1979.

Campbell, D. T. A phenomenology of the other one: Corrigible, hypothetical and critical. In T. Mischel (Ed.), *Human action: Conceptual and empirical issues*. New York: Academic Press, 1969.

Cartwright, D. Determinants of scientific progress: The case of research on the risky shift. *American Psychologist*, 1973, 28, 222–231.

Chein, I. *The science of behavior and the image of man*. New York: Basic Books, 1972.

Chomsky, N. A review of B. F. Skinner's *Verbal Behavior*, *Language*, 1959, 35, 26–58.

Chomsky, N. Current issues in linguistic theory. In J. A. Fodor & J. J. Katz (Eds.), *The structure of language*. Englewood Cliffs, N.J.: Prentice-Hall, 1964.

Chomsky, N. *Language and mind*. New York: Harcourt, Brace, 1968.

Cicourel, A. V. *The social organization of juvenile justice*. New York: Wiley, 1968.

Coulter, J. *The social construction of the mind*. London: Macmillan, 1979.

Cronbach, L. J. Beyond the two disciplines of scientific psychology. *American Psychologist*, 1975, 30, 116–127.

Cvetkovich, G. Dialectical perspectives on empirical research. *Personality and Social Psychology Bulletin*, 1977, 3, 688–698.

Danziger, K. Wundt and the two traditions of psychology. In R. W. Rieber (Ed.), *Wilhelm Wundt and the making of scientific psychology*. New York: Plenum, 1980.

Deese, J. *Psychology as science and art*. New York: Harcourt, Brace, 1972.

Deutsch, M. Field theory in social psychology. In G. Lindzey (Ed.), *Handbook of social psychology*. Reading, Mass.: Addison-Wesley, 1958.

Dixon, T. R., & Horton, D. L. (Eds.), *Verbal behavior and general behavior theory*. Englewood Cliffs, N.J.: Prentice-Hall, 1968.

Dollard, J., Doob, L., Miller, N. E., Mowrer, O. H., & Sears, R. R. *Frustration and aggression*. New Haven: Yale University Press, 1939.

Douglas, M. *Implicit meanings*. London: Routledge & Kegan Paul, 1975.

Duhem, P. *The aim and structure of physical theory* (P. Wiener, trans.). Princeton, N.J.: Princeton University Press, 1954. (Originally published, 1906.)

Duval, S., & Wicklund, R. A. *A theory of objective self-awareness*. New York: Academic Press, 1972.

Ellis, H. *The dance of life*. Boston: Riverside, 1923.

Elms, A. C. The crisis in confidence in social psychology. *American Psychologist*, 1975, 30, 967–976.

Festinger, L. A theory of social comparison process. *Human Relations*, 1954, 7, 117–140.

Festinger, L. *A theory of cognitive dissonance*. Evanston, Ill.: Row, Peterson, 1957.

Feyerabend, P. K. *Against method*. London: Humanities Press, 1975.

Fish, S. Normal circumstances, literal language, direct speech acts, the ordinary, the everyday, the obvious, what goes without saying, and other special cases. In P. Rabinow & W. Sullivan (Eds.), *Interpretive social science: A reader*. Berkeley, Calif.: University of California Press, 1979.

Fiske, D. W. *Strategies for personality research*. San Francisco: Jossey-Bass, 1978.

Gadamer, H.-G. *Truth and method* (G. Barden and J. Cumming, Eds.). New York: Seabury, 1975.

Gadlin, H., & Ingle, G. Through the one-way mirror: The limits of experimental self-reflection. *American Psychologist*, 1975, 30, 1003–1009.

Garfinkel, H. *Studies in ethnomethodology*. Englewood Cliffs, N.J.: Prentice-Hall, 1967.

Gauld, A., & Shotter, J. *Human action and its psychological investigation*. London: Routledge & Kegan Paul, 1977.

Geertz, C. *Interpretation of cultures*. New York: Basic Books, 1973.

Gergen, K. J. Social psychology as history. *Journal of Personality and Social Psychology*, 1973, 26, 309–320.

Gergen, K. J. Experimentation in social psychology: A reappraisal. *European Journal of Social Psychology*, 1978, 8, 507–527.

Gergen, K. J. The positivist image in social psychological theory. In A. R. Buss (Ed.), *Psychology in social context*. New York: Irvington, 1979.

Gergen, K. J. Toward intellectual audacity in social psychology. In R. Gilmour & S. Duck (Eds.), *The development of social psychology*. London: Academic Press, 1980.

Gergen, K. J. *Toward transformation in social knowledge*. New York: Springer-Verlag, 1982.

Gergen, K. J., & Morawski, J. An alternative metatheory for social psychology. In L. Wheeler (Ed.), *Review of personality and social psychology*. Beverly Hills, Calif.: Sage, 1980.

Gibson, J. J. *The perception of the visual world*. Boston: Houghton Mifflin, 1950.

Gibson, J. J. *The senses considered as perceptual system*. Boston: Houghton Mifflin, 1966.

Giddens, A. *New rules of sociological method*. New York: Basic Books, 1976.

Ginsburg, G. P. (Ed.). *Emerging strategies in social psychological research*. New York: Wiley, 1979.

Glass, D. C. *Behavior patterns, stress and coronary disease*. Hillsdale, N.J.: Erlbaum, 1977.

Glass, D. C., & Singer, J. E. *Urban stress.* New York: Academic Press, 1972.

Gouldner, A. *The coming crisis in Western sociology.* New York: Basic Books, 1970.

Graumann, C. F. Die Scheu des Psychologen vor der Interaktion. Ein Schisma und seine Geschichte. *Zeitschrift für Sozialpsychologie,* 1979, *10,* 284–304.

Haines, H., & Vaughan, G. M. Was 1898 a "great date" in the history of social psychology? *Journal of the History of the Behavioral Sciences,* 1979, *15,* 323–332.

Hale, M., Jr. *Human science and social order: Hugo Münsterberg and the origins of applied psychology.* Philadelphia: Temple University Press, 1980.

Hamlyn, D. W. Behaviour. *Philosophy,* 1953, 28 (No. 105).

Hampden-Turner, C. *Radical man: The process of psycho-social development.* Cambridge, Mass.: Schenkman, 1970.

Hampshire, S. *Thought and action.* London: Chatto & Windus, 1959.

Harré, R. *Social being.* Oxford: Blackwell, 1979.

Harré, R., & Secord, P. F. *The explanation of social behaviour.* Oxford: Basil Blackwell & Mott, 1972.

Hastie, R., Ostrom, T., Ebbesen, E. B., Wyer, R. S., Hamilton, D., & Carlston, D. E. (Eds.). *Person memory: The cognitive basis of social perception.* Hillsdale, N.J.: Erlbaum, 1980.

Heider, F. Attitudes and cognitive organization. *Journal of Personality,* 1946, *21,* 107–112.

Heider, F. *The psychology of interpersonal relations.* New York: Wiley, 1958.

Helmreich, R. Applied social psychology: The unfulfilled promise. *Personality and Social Psychology Bulletin,* 1975, *1,* 548–560.

Hendrick, C. Social psychology as history and as traditional science: An appraisal. *Personality and Social Psychology Bulletin,* 1976, *2,* 392–403.

Hermann, T. *Die Psychologie und ihre Forschungsprogramme.* Göttingen: Hogrefe, 1976.

Hirsch, E. D., Jr. *The aims of interpretation.* Chicago: The University of Chicago Press, 1976.

Hirschman, A. *Exit, voice and loyalty: Responses to decline in firms, organization and states.* Cambridge, Mass.: Harvard University Press, 1970.

Hollis, M. *Models of man: Philosophical thoughts on social action.* Cambridge, England: Cambridge University Press, 1977.

Holt, E. B. The whimsical condition of social psychology, and of mankind. In H. M. Kallen & S. Hook (Eds.), *American philosophy today and tomorrow.* New York: Furman, 1935.

Holzkamp, K. *Kritische Psychologie.* Hamburg: Fischer Taschenbach Verlag, 1976.

Hovland, C. I., Janis, I. L., & Kelley, H. H. *Communication and persuasion.* New Haven: Yale University Press, 1953.

Hudson, L. *The cult of the fact.* New York: Harper Torchbook, 1972.

Israel, J., & Tajfel, H. (Eds.). *The context of social psychology: A critical assessment.* New York: Academic Press, 1972.

Ittelson, W. H. (Ed.). *Environment and cognition.* New York: Seminar Press, 1973.

James, W. *The varieties of religious experience.* New York: Collier, 1961. (Originally published, 1902.)

Jay, M. *The dialectical imagination.* London: Heinemann, 1973.

Jones, E. E., & Davis, K. E. From acts to dispositions. In L. Berkowitz (Ed.), *Advances in social psychology* (Vol. 2). New York: Academic Press, 1965.

Joynson, R. B. Models of man: 1879–1979. In A. J. Chapman and D. M. Jones (Eds.), *Models of man.* London: British Psychological Society, 1980.

Kelley, H. H. Attribution theory in social psychology. In D. Levine (Ed.), *Nebraska symposium on motivation,* 1967. Lincoln: University of Nebraska Press, 1967.

Kelley, H. H. *Causal schemata and the attribution process.* Morristown, N.J.: General Learning Press, 1972.

Kelman, H. C. The rights of the subject in social research: An analysis in terms of relative power and legitimacy. *American Psychologist,* 1972, *27,* 989–1016.

Kessler, S. J., & McKenna, W. *Gender: An ethnomethodological approach.* New York: Wiley, 1978.

Kirsch, I. The impetus to scientific psychology: A recurrent pattern. *Journal of the History of the Behavioral Sciences*, 1976, *12*, 120–129.

Koch, S. Epilogue. In S. Koch (Ed.), *Psychology: A study of a science* (Vol. III). New York: McGraw-Hill, 1959.

Koch, S. Psychology as science. In S. C. Brown (Ed.), *Philosophy of psychology*. London: Macmillan, 1974.

Koch, S. Language communities, search cells, and the psychological studies. In W. J. Arnold (Ed.), *Nebraska Symposium on Motivation, 1975*. Lincoln: University of Nebraska Press, 1976.

Kuhn, T. S. *The structure of scientific revolutions* (2d ed.). Chicago: The University of Chicago Press, 1970. (Originally published, 1962.)

Kvale, S. Dialectics and research on remembering. In N. Datan & H. W. Reese (Eds.), *Life-span developmental psychology*. New York: Academic Press, 1977.

Leary, D. The philosophical development of the conception of psychology in Germany. *Journal of the History of the Behavioral Sciences*, 1978, *14*, 113–121.

Leichtman, M. Gestalt theory and the revolt against positivism. In A. R. Buss (Ed.), *Psychology in social context*. New York: Irvington, 1979.

Lewin, K. *A dynamic theory of personality*. New York: McGraw-Hill, 1935.

Lewin, K. Formalization and progress in psychology. *Studies in Topological and Vector Psychology*, 1940, *1*, 9–42.

Lewin, M. Kurt Lewin's view of social psychology: The crisis of 1977 and the crisis of 1927. *Personality and Social Psychology Bulletin*, 1977, *3*, 159–172.

Lorenz, K. *On aggression*. New York: Bantam, 1967.

Lubek, I. The relatively unknown social psychologies of Gabriel Tarde and sons. Paper presented at the 1979 meeting of the American Psychological Association, New York.

MacCorquodale, K., & Meehl, P. E. On a distinction between hypothetical constructs and intervening variables. *Psychological Review*, 1948, *55*, 95–107.

Mackenzie, B. Darwinism and positivism as methodological influences on the development of psychology. *Journal of the History of the Behavioral Sciences*, 1976, *12*, 330–337.

Mahoney, M. J. *Scientist as subject*. Cambridge, Mass.: Ballinger, 1976.

Marx, L. Reflections on the neo-romantic critique of science. *Daedalus*, 1978, 61–74.

McGuire, W. J. The yin and yang of progress in social psychology: Seven koans. *Journal of Personality and Social Psychology*, 1973, *26*, 446–456.

McHugh, P. On the failure of positivism. In J. D. Douglas (Ed.), *Understanding everyday life*. Chicago: Aldine Press, 1970.

McKeachie, W. J. The decline and fall of the laws of learning. *Educational Researcher*, 1974, *3*, 7–11.

Meacham, J. A. A transactional model of remembering. In N. Datan & H. W. Reese (Eds.), *Life-span developmental psychology*. New York: Academic Press, 1977.

Meehl, P. E. Theoretical risks and tabular asterisks: Sir Karl, Sir Ronald, and the slow progress of soft psychology. *Journal of Consulting and Clinical Psychology*, 1978, *26*, 806–834.

Mertens, W., & Fuchs, H. *Krise der Sozialpsychologie?* Munich: Franz Ehrenwirth Publishers, 1978.

Mishler, E. G. Meaning in context: Is there any other kind? *Harvard Educational Review*, 1979, *49*, 1–19.

Mischel, T. Psychological explanations and their vicissitudes. In W. J. Arnold (Ed.), *Nebraska Symposium on Motivation, 1975*. Lincoln: University of Nebraska Press, 1976.

Mixon, D. Instead of deception. *Journal of the Theory of Social Behaviour*, 1972, *2*, 145–177.

Morawski, J. *Human interest and psychological utopias*. Unpublished doctoral dissertation, Carleton University, 1979.

Mueller, C. G. Some origins of psychology as science. *Annual Review of Psychology*, 1979, *30*, 9–29.

Murchison, C. *Social psychology*. Worcester, Mass: Clark University Press, 1929.

Neisser, U. *Cognition and reality*. San Francisco: Freeman, 1976.

Newcomb, T. M. *The acquaintance process*. New York: Holt, 1961.

II. THE SPECIAL FIELDS OF PSYCHOLOGY

Nisbett, R. E., & Ross, L. *Human inference: Strategies and shortcomings of social judgment.* Englewood Cliffs, N.J.: Prentice-Hall, 1980.

Peters, R. S. *The concept of motivation.* London: Routledge & Kegan Paul, 1958.

Petrinovich, L. Probablistic functionalism. *American Psychologist,* 1979, *34,* 373–390.

Piaget, J. *The origins of intelligence in children.* New York: Norton, 1952.

Piaget, J. *Understanding causality* (D. Miles & M. Miles, trans.). New York: Norton, 1974.

Popper, K. R. *Logik des Forschung.* Vienna: Springer, 1935. (Trans. as *The logic of discovery.* London: Hutchinson, 1959.)

Popper, K. R. *The poverty of historicism.* London: Routledge & Kegan Paul, 1957.

Quine, W. V. O. *From a logical point of view.* Cambridge, Mass.: Harvard University Press, 1953.

Reese, H., & Overton, W. Models of development and theories of development. In L. R. Goulet & P. B. Baltes (Eds.), *Life-span developmental psychology: Research and theory.* New York: Academic Press, 1970.

Ricoeur, P. *Freud and philosophy: An essay on interpretation.* New Haven: Yale University Press, 1970.

Rieber, R. W. Wundt and the Americans. In R. W. Rieber (Ed.), *Wilhelm Wundt and the making of scientific psychology.* New York: Plenum, 1980.

Riegel, K. F. The influence of economic and political ideologies upon the development of developmental psychology. *Psychological Bulletin,* 1972, *78,* 129–141.

Rodin, J., & Langer, E. J. Long-term effects of a control-relevant intervention with the institutionalized aged. *Journal of Personality and Social Psychology,* 1977, *35,* 897–902.

Rychlak, J. F. Psychological science as a humanist views it. In W. J. Arnold (Ed.), *Nebraska Symposium on Motivation, 1975.* Lincoln: University of Nebraska Press, 1976.

Rychlak, J. F. *The psychology of rigorous humanism.* New York: Wiley, 1977.

Samelson, F. History, origin, myth, and ideology: "Discovery" of social psychology. *Journal for the Theory of Social Behavior,* 1974, *4,* 217–231.

Samelson, F. Struggle for scientific authority: The reception of Watson's behaviorism, 1913–1920. *Journal of the History of the Behavioral Sciences,* 1981, *17,* 399–425.

Sampson, E. E. Psychology and the American ideal. *Journal of Personality and Social Psychology,* 1977, *35,* 767–782.

Sampson, E. E. Scientific paradigms and social values: Wanted—a scientific revolution. *Journal of Personality and Social Psychology,* 1978, *36,* 1332–1343.

Sarbin, T. R. Contextualism: A world view for modern psychology. In A. W. Landfield (Ed.), *Nebraska Symposium on Motivation: Personal Construct Psychology, 1976.* Lincoln: University of Nebraska Press, 1977.

Schachter, S. The interaction of cognitive and psychological determinants of emotional states. In L. Berkowitz (Ed.), *Advances in Experimental Social Psychology* (Vol. 1). New York: Academic Press, 1964.

Schachter, S., & Singer, J. Cognitive, social and psychological determinants of emotion. *Psychological Review,* 1962, *69,* 379–399.

Scheibe, K. E. The psychologist's advantage and its nullification: Limits of human predictability. *American Psychologist,* 1978, *33,* 869–881.

Schuler, H. *Ethische Probleme der psychologischer Forschung.* Toronto: Hogrefe, 1980.

Schwartz, B., Lacey, H., & Schuldenfrei, R. Operant psychology as factory psychology. *Behaviorism,* 1978, *6,* 229–254.

Seligman, M. E. P. *Helplessness: On depression, development, and death.* San Francisco: Freeman, 1975.

Sherif, M. Crisis in social psychology: Some remarks towards breaking through the crisis. *Personality and Social Psychology Bulletin,* 1977, *3,* 368–382.

Shotter, J. *Images of man in psychological research.* London: Methuen, 1975.

Shotter, J. Action, joint action and intentionality. In M. Breuner (Ed.), *The structure of action.* Oxford: Blackwell, 1980.

Silverman, I. The experimenter: A (still) neglected stimulus object. *Canadian Journal of Psychology*, 1971, *15*, 258–270.

Skinner, B. F. *Verbal behavior*. New York: Appleton-Century-Crofts, 1957.

Smith, M. B. Is experimental social psychology advancing? *Journal of Experimental and Social Psychology*, 1972, *8*, 86–96.

Smith, M. B. *Humanizing social psychology*. San Francisco: Jossey-Bass, 1974.

Snyder, C. R., & Fromkin, H. L. *Uniqueness: The human pursuit of difference*. New York: Plenum, 1980.

Sprowls, J. W. Recent social psychology. *Psychological Bulletin*, 1930, *27*, 380–393.

Strickland, L. H., Aboud, F. E., & Gergen, K. J. (Eds.). *Social psychology in transition*. New York: Plenum, 1976.

Surkin, M., & Wolfe, A. (Eds.). *An end to political science*. New York: Basic Books, 1970.

Taylor, C. *The explanation of behaviour*. London: Routledge & Kegan Paul, 1964.

Taylor, C. Interpretation and the science of man. *The Review of Metaphysics*, 1971, *25* (No. 1).

Thorngate, W. Possible limits on a science of social behavior. In L. Strickland, F. E. Aboud, & K. J. Gergen (Eds.), *Social psychology in transition*. New York: Plenum, 1976.

Unger, R. M. *Knowledge and politics*. New York: Free Press, 1975.

Walster, E., Walster, G. W., & Berscheid, E. *Equity, theory and research*. Boston: Allyn & Bacon, 1978.

Watson, J. B. *Behaviorism*. Chicago: The University of Chicago Press, 1924.

Wicklund, R. A., & Brehm, J. W. *Perspectives on cognitive dissonance*. Hillsdale, N.J.: Erlbaum, 1976.

Winch, P. *The idea of a social science and its relation to philosophy*. London: Routledge & Kegan Paul, 1958.

Wundt, W. *Lectures on human and animal psychology* (Trans. of 2d ed. by J. E. Creighton & E. B. Titchener). New York: Macmillan, 1894. (Originally published, 1863–1864.)

Wundt, W. *Principles of physiological psychology* (Partial trans. of 5th ed. by E. B. Titchener). New York: Macmillan, 1904. (Originally published, 1874.)

Wundt, W. *Völkerpsychologie* (Vols. 1–10). Leipzig: Engelmann, 1900–1920.

Zinn, H. *The politics of history*. Boston: Beacon Press, 1970.

24

Toward Social Psychology's Second Century

WILLIAM J. McGUIRE

A description of where social psychology has been and where it will or ought to be going should start with a definition of the field, but the very ambiguity which requires a definition makes it difficult to formulate. The vicissitudes of social psychology's evolution, like those of other disciplines, have produced a conglomeration of topics whose definition must violate either history or logic. One strategy is to define social psychology by its independent variables as "the branch of psychology that studies human thoughts, feelings, and actions insofar as they are affected by other people." However, this criterion leaves out some archetypal topics which get included if we define the field in terms of dependent as well as independent variables as "the study of human thoughts, feelings, and actions insofar as they affect or are affected by other people." In general, as our definition becomes more inclusive to do justice to heterogeneous accumulations of topics, it tends to lose the conceptual tidiness that is a major purpose of definition.

Granting that social psychology is a field of knowledge, we can conclude (even without defining adequately just which field of knowledge it is) that it, like other fields of knowing, is both a process and a product. Professionals within the field, being preoccupied with its methods of inquiry and discovery, tend to stress its process aspect, while the outside laity (if interested at all) is interested in social psychology as a product, a body of established knowledge. The ambiguity often produces tension and misunderstanding when insider and outsider discuss the topic in the classroom, the conference room, or the dining room. The social psychologist is inclined to talk about method and how she or he proceeds, pointing out that findings can be misleading when presented outside the context of their mode of discovery. The nonprofessional, as a consumer rather than producer of social psychology, wants to know about its product and what new verified knowledge it has discovered and complains that the social psychologist is forever talking about methods, the process of discovery, without ever revealing what of interest has been discovered. This tension between process and product on the part of the producers and consumers of social psychology provokes a useful dialectic: as process, social psychology's theories guide its empirical inquiries; as product, empirical findings guide its theory formation.

To describe adequately social psychology's past and prescribe its future, we shall consider here both its process and product aspects. Our first section describes the four basic aspects of social psychology as process, namely, how topics are selected for inquiry, how one's research progresses programmatically from study to study, how one creatively generates hypotheses to describe the phenomena selected for study, and how the issues are developed in confrontation with empirical observation. Our second major section describes social psychology as product, not by presenting a detailed propositional inventory of specific social-psychological findings, but on a more abstract level in terms of the broader theoretical views of the person that have emerged from social-psychological research, including both its systems theories and its guiding-idea theories.

Social Psychology as Process

Even the most doctrinaire rationalist, while insistent that the formal product of thought be systematically organized, will probably admit that the course of human thought as it produces knowledge tends to be untidy and disorganized. In describing here the discovery process in social psychology as four successive steps (problem selection, programmatic progression, hypothesis generation, and empirical confrontation), we do not mean to imply that the social psychologist typically goes consciously and systematically through these separate phases. In actuality, one or more of the phases is likely to be left implicit in any one thought session, and a great deal of backtracking is likely to occur. But each of the four phases is important in the overall discovery process in social psychology and so deserves to be described here.

Topic Selection in Social Psychology

The first step in the social psychology discovery process is picking a topic for study. Over the years the research attention paid to various topics has fluctuated a great deal. Such hardy perennials as intergroup conflict (Deutsch, 1973; Billig, 1976; Tajfel, 1978), cultural influence on cognition (Cole & Scribner, 1974; Triandis & Lambert, 1979), socialization (Percheron, 1974; Jennings & Niemi, 1974), intragroup processes (Back, 1972; Triandis, 1977), aggression (Zillman, 1979), interpersonal attraction (Berscheid & Walster, 1978; Kelley, 1979), helping behavior (Staub, 1979), and so forth always receive some research attention, but a given topic tends to fluctuate from center stage to relative neglect from one period to the next. In the 1920s and early 1930s the most exciting topic was attitudes, particularly attitude measurement (Thurstone & Chave, 1929; Likert, 1932; Bogardus, 1933; LaPiere, 1934, etc.). By the 1940s and 1950s the fashion had shifted to group dynamics (e.g., Newcomb, 1943; Sherif, 1936; Lewin, 1947/1966; Festinger et al., 1950). By the late 1950s and 1960s, interest had moved back to attitudes, particularly attitude change (persuasive communications, dissonance theory, etc.: Hovland et al., 1953; Festinger, 1957), which in turn has given way to the 1970s preoccupation with social perception as in attribution (Kelley & Michela, 1980) and person perception (Schneider, 1979; Hastie et al., 1980). Underlying these fluctuations in what topics become fashionable in social psychological research are three factors: individuals' predilections for research topics, consensus in the judgment of where the action is at any period, and historical forces that suggest it is time for a change.

Individual's Topic Choices   Biography is destiny as far as the individual's selection of research problems is concerned (Wechsler, 1978; Coan, 1979). Some students in graduate school acquire from their mentors a topic interest which dominates their work for years. There is even negative teacher influence, as with a faculty member in my own graduate-school days who was so obnoxious that an appreciable portion of my fellow graduate students adopted their earliest theoretical stance and topic interest mainly to refute his theory. One's job is often the determinant, most obviously when one is in an applied setting where one's research may be prescribed by the organization, but even in a more permissive academic setting, a research topic often emerges from one's teaching assignments or search for a niche not already occupied by colleagues. Colleagues and students may influence the direction of our research, as may a striking journal article or even events in our nonscientific life (Reinharz, 1979).

Group Designation of Fashionable Topics   With so many social psychologists affected by such a diversity of influences, it is likely that at any period some research attention is being paid to each topic in the spectrum of social psychology. Which of these will take off and become the "in" topic among fashionable researchers is affected not only by internal factors but also by social forces extraneous to the field. For example, the preoccupation with attitude measurement during the 1920s and early 1930s was probably affected by public concern over the changing morality and behavior patterns, especially among the youth, during the 1920s. The subject matter used by these attitude researchers reflects such a concern in that their measuring instruments usually focused on then-controversial moral issues such as religiosity, birth control, political and economic conservatism, racial relations, and the effect of motion pictures.

If becoming fashionable required only an intrinsically interesting topic with the example of some interesting individual research, the study of groups, rather than attitude research, might have been the rage of the 1920s and early 1930s. Good research on "cold" groups was already being published in the early 1920s by Moede (1920) in Leipzig (his work perhaps being transmitted to the New World when Münsterberg moved to Harvard), followed by F. Allport (1924) and Dashiell (1935) in this country. And Bechterev (1932) in the Soviet Union and Watson (1928) in the United States were already studying "hot" groups (for example, the effects of face-to-face discussion on problem-solving) in the 1920s. But it was not until the worsening economic, political, and military disturbances of the 1930s, along with the resulting revolution, destitution, and migration which weakened accustomed cultural, political, religious, and familial guidelines and modes of social control that research on groups, focusing on compensatory themes of group cohesiveness, peer influence, cooperation and competition, and leadership styles, became popular in the 1940s and 1950s.

More recently, heightened sensitivity to violence during the late 1950s and early 1960s, associated with rising crime rates, political assassinations, extralegal modes of agitating for one's desires, and so forth influenced the recent preoccupation in social-psychological research with topics such as aggression (Feshbach & Fraczek, 1979), prosocial behavior (Staub, 1979), effects of television (Comstock et al., 1978), social modeling (Bandura, 1976), and so on. Also during the 1960s, affluence in the Atlantic countries allowed the emergence of a youth culture whose aspirations could shift from material success to meaningful interpersonal relationships; it is no accident that contemporaneous social psychological research showed a growth in popularity of topics such as interpersonal attraction (Berscheid & Walster, 1978), affect states, apathy, and alienation. In such an atmosphere, an isolated incident like the Kitty Genovese tragedy evoked the flurry of social-psychological research on "good Samaritan" helping behavior phenomena (Latané & Darley, 1970; Staub, 1979).

Historical Change in Topic Popularity   So far in this discussion of problem selection in social psychology we have concentrated on the influence of the idiosyncratic personal experiences of the researcher and social forces from outside the field. Shifts are also affected by forces intrinsic to the research development itself. Most generically, a healthy yin and yang of interest on any given topic is part of the research progression. When an innovative researcher makes some striking discoveries about a neglected topic, this tends to recruit to the topic other adventurous researchers whose early investigations of the underworked field produce a high yield of interesting findings for the first few years. But gradually entropic tendencies dampen the creative dividend: the easy, interesting questions tend to be answered early, leaving difficult and complex problems to be investigated. The original clean oversimplifications give way to baroque conceptual distinctions and arcane elaborations of the initial partial views, leaving them still interesting enough to the initiates but without the appeal to attract new and creative recruits. In time, even the initiates tend to drift to other topics. That momentary fads arise is a healthy tendency, since many researchers operate more effectively in a communal atmosphere that involves mutual stimulation and competition. And it is probably equally healthy that the fad wanes when the original creative insights have become blunted through use, leaving the field to lie fallow for a time until it is revived through the introduction of new and different insights. Werskey (1978) reviews the sociology of these "high science" fluctuations.

The microprocesses involved in the demise of fashionable research topics become clearer if we look more closely at examples, such as the waning of the attitude measurement enthusiasm in the mid-1930s or of the group dynamics research in the mid-1950s. One stifling outgrowth of success is that the fashionable topic tends to become suffocated by an extravagant overgrowth of conceptual elaboration. The review of the attitudes field by G. Allport (1935) shows how a decade of fashionability resulted in the accumulation of endless definitions and distinctions, etc.; likewise, by the end of the 1950s, exciting and superficially simple independent variables that had earlier attracted research to group dynamics had become encumbered with elaborate partial definitions of reference groups, cohesiveness, leadership styles, etc. A second natural but stifling development accompanying social psychology fashionability is a tendency toward quantification. By the 1930s, attitude scaling had resulted in a measurement precision which made attitudes disdainful of keeping company with the more primitive, qualitatively scaled independent variables. A third embarrassment of success is a tendency toward practical application, such as the applied attitude research on religiosity, race relations, etc. from the 1930s and the application of group research in the form of sensitivity training, for example, from the 1950s (Back, 1972). There seems to be a mandarin aesthetic in many basic researchers that causes the practical application of a topic to drive them off.

In fingering conceptual precision, quantification, and social application as stifling concomitants of research fashionability which eventually dampen interest in the topic, we are not implying that these are undesirable developments. On the contrary, while bad for the health of the field in which they grow, they are good in themselves and desirable in the total scheme of things. Even for the field itself their stifling effect is a Good Thing, like 1066 and all that, in that they promote the healthy yin and yang of interest in the field, at first advancing the field and then resulting in entropic accumulations that cause its being left to lie fallow for some years, after which a new generation will find it more rich and fertile due to the embellishments added by these three tendencies, together with the freshness provided by the years of benign neglect in which they eventuated.

Styles of Programmatic Research in Social Psychology

Our discussion of problem selection has concerned content and the tactical level of research. Now, in turning to the second step in the research process, we deal with the more stylistic, strategic aspects having to do with how we approach the topic and proceed from study to study of it. There are two rather contrasting styles of pursuing topics in social psychology, the divergent and the convergent. While both styles tend to be represented among the active researchers in any period, one or the other tends to carry the Establishment imprimatur at any given time. For the third quarter of this century, the divergent style was in the ascendance but later the consensus shifted toward the convergent. To put the contrast most succinctly, the convergent stylist is phenomenon-preoccupied while the divergent stylist is theory-preoccupied. The convergent researcher's point of departure is an effect (e.g., interpersonal liking, group productivity, persistence of induced attitude change); the divergent stylist's point of departure is a theoretical notion (e.g., reinforcement, dissonance, attribution).

An exemplar of a convergent-style researcher is Carl Hovland, who was typically preoccupied with a phenomenon such as delayed action effects in persuasion or the primacy versus recency phenomenon (Hovland et al., 1949, 1953). He proceeded eclectically, utilizing independent variables from a diversity of theories, bringing the insights from each convergently to bear on the phenomenon of interest, using any one theory only partially but by the whole set of theories accounting as fully as possible for the observed variance in the delayed-action, primacy/recency, or whatever, phenomenon. Leon Festinger (1957, 1964) can serve as an exemplar of the divergent stylist, typically preoccupied with a theoretical notion such as social comparison or dissonance, and making maximum use of its insights by applying it diversely to a wide variety of phenomena, accounting for only a small amount of variance in any one phenomenon but for some of the variance in each of a large set of phenomena.

The contrasting orientations and aims of the two styles result in their giving rise to distinctive patterns of inquiry, as summarized in Table 24.1. For example, the convergent, phenomenon-centered stylist, attached only loosely to any one theory, tends to be somewhat cavalier about independent-variable manipulations, typically settling for an operationally defined gross manipulation in a group testing situation. But as regards dependent-variable measurement, the convergent stylist tends to be quite demanding, often using a multi-item instrument, or even multiple instruments, careful scaling, reliability checks, and so forth. The divergent theorist, on the other hand, tends to be rather off-hand about the dependent-variable measure,

TABLE 24.1 Convergent versus Divergent Research Styles as Regards
Pursuit of Issues from Study to Study

RESEARCH ASPECT	STYLE	
	Convergent	*Divergent*
Focus	A phenomenon	A theory
Aim	To account fully for the phenomenon, using such theories as necessary	To utilize the theory fully, applying it to as many phenomena as possible
Yield	Explaining a great deal of the variance in the single phenomenon	Explaining a small amount of the variance in many phenomena
Example	Hovland's studies of delayed action effects, of primacy/recency	Festinger's utilization of social comparison theory, of dissonance theory
Independent-variable manipulation	Gross operational manipulation in a group setting	Precise and intricately staged manipulation in a one-on-one situation
Dependent-variable measure	Elegantly scaled, multi-item	Gross, dichotomous single measures
Test situation	Group testing	Individual testing
Number of cases	Large N	Small N
Design	Multiple independent variables	Single independent variable
Extraneous variables	Introduced as additional, orthogonal variables in the design	Eliminated or held constant by elaborate situational devices
Inferential statistics	Elaborate regression analysis (ANOVA, CANOVA, trend analysis)	Less parametric statistics (chi-square, t-test)
Interaction effects	An encouraging indication of contact with complex reality	A discouraging indication of crude independent-variable manipulation

often settling for a single dichotomous measure, such as whether the participant asks for supportive or for attacking material or does or does not sign a petition; but as regards independent-variable manipulation, divergent theorists tend to be careful and elaborate, often using intricately staged situations to establish the different levels, applying them in one-on-one testing situations and eliminating participants who internal checks suggest have not been manipulated to the intended independent-variable level.

Consequences of the two styles extend to experimental design and statistical analysis. The convergent researcher tends to use rather elaborate designs, often handling worrisome extraneous variables by introducing them as additional independent variables in an orthogonal design. Relatively large Ns are used, with elaborate statistics such as higher-order analysis of variance and even analysis of covariance to adjust for intervening processes, and trend analyses to detect divergences from an underlying relationship. The divergent researchers, on the other hand, tend to use simple one-variable designs, concentrate on first-order effects, and attempt by elaborate situational staging to eliminate or hold constant the extraneous variables. These divergent stylists are restricted to a relatively small number of cases with their one-on-one testing, in contrast to the large number used by the convergent researchers in their less sensitive group administrations. The divergent theorists, in consequence, tend to use relatively simple, less parametric statistics, such as the sign-test or chi-square.

The difference between the two styles in both their productive and critical thinking is epitomized in their contrasting attitudes toward interaction effects. The convergent researcher is rather enamored of higher-order interaction, his or her phenomenon-focused thinking leading naturally to perceiving causation as flowing from a variety of interacting independent variables. Hence, the finding of higher-order interactions tends to be thought-stimulating to the convergent researcher and reassuring that one is closer to depicting reality as it is. Divergent researchers, on the other hand, taking rather abstract theories as their point of departure and attempting to assay their limited role in affecting each of a whole series of dependent variables tend to find more creative stimulation and reassurance in main effects and are annoyed by interaction effects as perhaps indicative of a fuzzy manipulation of the theory's independent variable.

While researchers are seldom articulate about these divergent/convergent stylistic proclivities, they tend to sense communalities and differences based on them. During the Establishment ascendance of the theory-oriented divergent style in the third quarter of the twentieth century, peripheral convergent stylists were perceived as stumbling, deficient in direction, and lacking in imagination and theoretical coherence. Reciprocally, as systems stylists move progressively into the ascendance in the final quarter of the century (McGuire, 1983), they perceive divergent researchers as lacking in relevance and seriousness, engaging in hit-and-run fun and games as they flit from one topic to another. Some researchers are stimulated by such hostilities and competitiveness, whether on matters of content or style, so let us leave them working away, happily unhappy about their unstylistic colleagues. The more ecumenical among us will recognize that each style provides a dynamic tension and internal coherence capable of instigating and guiding inquiry. Each researcher should march to the drummer with whose cadences he or she best resonates. The field might progress more rapidly and quietly if each researcher, while working in his or her own authentic stylistic idiom, would concentrate on moving ahead rather than firing at alternative stylists on their flank.

Modes of Generating Hypotheses

Here we turn to the third aspect of the research process: how the researcher, having decided what topic to study, proceeds creatively to generate hypotheses about it. For the convergent researcher, who begins with a phenomenon to be explained, this hypothesis generating involves the creative identification of powerful and interesting independent variables; for the divergent thinker, initially focused on a theory-derived independent variable, hypothesis formation involves identifying a dependent variable on which this factor will have an interesting effect.

Some researchers would question the usefulness of discussing creative modes of hypothesis generating, feeling that the creativity level of the researcher is a given, and that creative techniques cannot be taught or even described. A number of the factors which affect the researcher's level of creativity are not susceptible to easy change by classroom teaching: for example, the sociocultural conditions of one's time and place in history as described by Popper (1972), Merton (1968, 1980), and other sociologists of science; by one's more immediate working environment, as described by industrial psychologists like Pelz and Andrews (1976) and Andrews (1979) who have investigated productivity in different types of research laboratories; and by one's idiosyncratic life experiences, as described by Stein (1975). Besides these situational factors, there are a number of fairly persistent personal factors that affect research creativity, including both dynamic factors like motivation, cognitive style, and personality, and ability factors like intellectual aptitude and breadth of knowledge, all of which tend to be "givens," not susceptible to appreciable manipulation in a year or two of research training (Arieti, 1976).

But beside these more structural determinants, research creativity is also affected by the use of tactical-level creative heuristics that can be described and perhaps taught. This writer has criticized graduate programs in psychology for the fact that they invariably have methodology courses—often the only required courses in the program—but, although it is generally recognized that the research process includes both creatively generating as well as critically evaluating hypotheses, these methodology courses deal almost exclusively with the latter, critical, aspects of science. Methodology courses have traditionally dealt almost exclusively with the specifics and generalities of how one tests hypotheses (measurement, experimental design, statistics, etc.), ignoring completely how one goes about formulating the hypothesis to be tested. Our graduate programs in psychology have forgotten the first law of cooking, that to make Welsh rabbit, one must first catch a rabbit.

In a previous article (McGuire, 1973) we mentioned that we had observed a dozen creative heuristics used by various social-psychological researchers and we described a series of these. A few months after the article appeared, one careful reader wrote me saying that I had referred to a dozen techniques but had described only nine, and he wondered if I might let him know what the other three were. At first I regarded this letter as coming from an unusually pedantic and concrete

566

mind but when, within the next several weeks, I received two more inquiries asking, "And where are the other three heuristics?" I began to worry that the FTC might cite me for false labeling. Hence, in a frenzy of anxiety I proceeded to dig up at least three more creative heuristics, but the fear-propelled momentum carried me through a list of forty-five, shown in Table 24.2.

There is not space enough to describe each of these forty-five creative techniques and illustrate its use by one or more social psychologists during the past hundred years. We shall have to settle simply for little more than listing them and hoping that their names will be self-explanatory. The reader, for an exercise, can think of examples of each from the past productive research in social psychology. The heuristics are shown grouped into five classes going from more unstructured, a priori heuristics, progressively toward more formal, analytical heuristics. For illustrative purposes, we describe and give an example of one heuristic from each of the five classes. Additional examples can be found in McGuire (1980).

The first class of creative heuristics all involve some kind of observation and analysis of naturally occurring phenomena. Illustrative is heuristic 2, the analysis of paradoxical occurrences. Many researchers have fixated on such paradoxical incidents and, instead of ignoring them as aberrations, used them to produce new insights into the workings of the person or society, insights that could be further developed in confrontation with empirical data. For example, rather than taking for granted that people are entertained by tragedies, tear-jerkers, and scary stories, Aristotle fixated on the pervasiveness and the paradoxical quality of this aesthetic reality to develop his catharsis theory of entertainment. Similarly, Freud (1900/ 1953), noted how paradoxical it is that dreams, which would seem to be an opportunity for creating a wish-fulfilling fantasy life to escape a harsh world, are so often nightmares, to explain which Freud was led to creative ideas about the human personality. Bettelheim's (1943, 1960) observations of peculiarities of behavior in the concentration camps (a case of the peculiar within the bizarre) led to interesting extensions of the "identification with the aggressor" phenomenon. Festinger (1957), in analyzing the nature of rumors, was led by the peculiar occurrence of rumors of impending disasters following a past disaster to develop the basic insight of dissonance theory.

Our second class of approaches groups together a dozen modes of thinking which involve simple direct conceptual analysis. As an illustration of this class we will discuss heuristic 13, taking a commonsense hypothesis, reversing the direction of the relationship between two variables, and thinking up circumstances under which the counterintuitive direction of relationship might obtain, a conjecture that can be subjected to an empirical confrontation. For example, while it is generally agreed that a persuasive communication will be more convincing if the receivers are not aware of its persuasive intent, we have in several places (McGuire & Millman, 1965; McGuire, 1969a) hypothesized specific conditions that will reverse this relationship, so that people will be more persuaded when they are aware in advance of

TABLE 24.2   Creative Heuristics Used in Social Psychological Research

A. ANALYSIS OF NATURALLY OCCURRING PHENOMENA
   1. Intensive case study
   2. Analyze paradoxical occurrences
   3. Collect practitioner's rules of thumb
   4. Integrate and interpret folk wisdom on the topic
   5. Search for similar problems already solved
   6. Search for opposite problem
   7. Introspect on own experiences in comparable situation
   8. Role-play (self or another) in the situation
   9. Participant observation

B. DIRECT, SIMPLE CONCEPTUAL ANALYSIS
   10. Push a reasonable hypothesis to point where its implications become implausible
   11. Mentally reduce factor to zero in a given situation
   12. Explore the limits
   13. Reverse a commonsense hypothesis as regards the direction of the relationship
   14. Reverse a commonsense hypothesis as regards the direction of causality
   15. Functional (adaptivity) analysis
   16. Linguistic analysis
   17. Remove focus from dependent variable (or IV) to independent variable (or DV)
   18. Utilize imagery (e.g., physiognomic perception, right-hemisphere thinking)
   19. Disrupt ordinary state of consciousness
   20. Focus on essentials and diverge; refocus
   21. Analyze into (sequential) subcomponents

C. MEDIATED, COMPLEX INFERENTIAL ANALYSIS
   22. Posit multiple mediators (and/or limits) of a known relationship
   23. Induce a broader generalization and then deduce further implications
   24. Hypothetico-deductive method
   25. (Computer) simulation
   26. Generate a list and organize it
   27. Construct a heuristically provocative generating structure (e.g., matrix)
   28. Analogy; transfer a conceptual scheme from one area to another
   29. Transfer a relationship, reverse the known and unknown

D. ANALYSIS OF PREVIOUS RESEARCH
   30. Reconcile conflicting outcomes (or, at least, failures to replicate)
   31. Deviant case analysis
   32. Interpreting serendipitous interaction effects
   33. Analyzing nonmonotonic relationships into simpler underlying processes
   34. Positing factors that account for irregularities in obtained relationships
   35. Write a review article (e.g., via PASAR)
   36. Bringing together two striking past experiments

E. COLLECTION OF NEW DATA
   37. Pitting two factors against one another
   38. Direct measuring and subtracting out a given mediating process
   39. Mathematical modeling

TABLE 24.2 *Continued*

40. Multivariate fishing expedition
41. Adding exploratory independent variables for serendipitous interactions
42. Allow open-ended response and do content analysis
43. Active participation in research routine (data collection, etc.)
44. Explore a new technique
45. Statistical discovery methods

persuasive intent. Indeed, we predicted that in these circumstances there would be an anticipatory belief change in the forewarned direction, even before the persuasive message is communicated. Or again, it is commonly hypothesized that people like best those who are most like themselves demographically, ideologically, and in lifestyle, but it is an easily met creative challenge to reverse this hypothesis and generate circumstances under which people will dislike others to the extent they are like themselves (McGuire, 1985).

Our third category of creative approaches includes eight heuristics involving mediated conceptual analysis of somewhat greater complexity than the dozen in the second class. We can illustrate this class by heuristic 22, positing multiple mediators for a known relationship. All too often researchers stop when they generate a first underlying process to explain a relationship and ignore or even adopt an antagonistic relationship to other explanations. This anxiety about multiple explanatory processes is understandable since testing such processes is so tedious that one can do empirical justice only to very few. But the creative researcher should continue beyond the first, generating a half dozen or more underlying processes, even when she or he plans to investigate only one empirically. For example, when Hovland et al. (1949) observed a delayed action effect of persuasive communications, they hypothesized and described half-a-dozen underlying processes that could account for it, even though they pursued experimentally only the "discounting cue" explanation.

The seven heuristics that are included in the fourth class, all involving analysis of previous research results, can be illustrated by heuristic 30, reconciling conflicting outcomes of previous research. For example, in the 1960s there was a tremendous flurry of attitudes research on the "forced compliance" phenomenon provoked by a variety of attempts to reconcile the finding by some researchers that counterattitudinal advocacy produced internalized opinion change in direct proportion to the reinforcement while other researchers found an inverse relationship (Collins & Hoyt, 1972). Good work was also stimulated by attempts to reconcile the findings that a pair of opposed arguments presented successively sometimes showed a primacy and sometimes a recency effect (Wilson & Miller, 1968). Work by the writer and his students (e.g., McGuire, 1968) on personality and persuasibility was designed to test an elaborate theory constructed to explain why some researchers find a positive and others a negative relationship between personality variables like intelligence, self-esteem, anxiety with susceptibility to social influence.

The fifth and most formal category, under which we list nine heuristics, includes techniques that use data collection, not simply to test whether a priori hypotheses are or are not correct, but to provide new insights into the phenomenon of interest, a procedure that is discussed further in the next section as constituting the contextualist approach. These techniques involve collecting more suggestive types of data and analyzing the data in ways that suggest new insights. Illustrative is heuristic 42, using probes that elicit open-ended responses whose content can be analyzed to provide new insights into the content and form of thought. We have used this heuristic in our own work on the spontaneous self-concept (McGuire, McGuire, & Winton, 1979; McGuire, 1984), eliciting unexpected information on what dimensions people use in thinking about themselves. The "cognitive response" approach to persuasion (Petty et al., 1980) also illustrates heuristic 42. Another example of this fifth category is heuristic 45, the use of statistical analyses as a discovery method rather than simply as a testing procedure to determine whether one was right in the first place. Illustrative here are Mosteller's (1977) techniques in exploratory data analysis and Tukey's (1977) resistant statistical measures.

Each of the forty-five heuristics listed in Table 24.2, as well as the dozens more which readers can add, deserves extensive discussion and illustration from past social psychological research. Such extensive treatment could form the basis of a methodology course that would correct the current overemphasis on the critical, "hypothesis-testing" aspect of the research process by focusing more on the creative aspect, that is, how we generate our hypotheses and theories.

Empirical Confrontation

Once one generates a hypothesis describing or explaining an aspect of the world, one typically proceeds to some further action on the basis of it. In our daily life, an interpretation of events having been generated, it may lead us, e.g., to make a decision, or to become indignant, or to stop worrying. If we develop the insight as an artist, we then try to depict its working out within the constraints of our artistic medium. If we have formed the hypothesis as a humanistic scholar, we may seek to show how it relates to comparable notions and to illustrate within the material of our discipline how it manifests itself. The social psychologist, being an empirical scientist, acts after generating a hypothesis by subjecting it to an empirical confrontation. The description and prescription of this empirical confrontation comprise the fourth and final step that we shall discuss in this review of social psychology as process.

For over a dozen years I have been publishing (McGuire, 1967, 1969b, 1972, 1973) my notions that the social psychology Establishment has been erroneously depicting this empirical confrontation as a test of the hypothesis and that this misperception has distorted and delayed social-psychological research during the past quarter century. I have been arguing that the logical empiricism paradigm when first introduced was a useful corrective to the preceding, more positivistic conception of the nature of the empirical confrontation, and so represented a step forward during the middle third of the twentieth century. However, it has now outlived its usefulness in that its corrective insights have been adequately absorbed by the field and its shortcomings are warping research. It should now be replaced by a new approach, which we call "contextualism." Our revisionist analysis will be better understood if we first describe three paradigms which preceded logical empiricism and then describe how logical empiricism marked an advance on these, before pointing out its own shortcomings and the new contextualist approach that we think will and ought to guide our thinking about the empirical confrontation stage of the social-psychological research process during the next quarter-century.

Three Earlier Positions: Dogmatism, Rationalism, and Positivism It has always been the dominant Establishment view within Western thought that our conceptualizations and hypotheses can be seriously entertained only insofar as they have external validity ascertained through some kind of empirical confrontation (albeit with perennial resurfacing among *intelligentsia* and *narod* minorities of the view that truth comes also from divine infusion, LSD, flying saucers, etc.). Where the Establishment consensus has varied considerably over Western history, however, is in regard to the nature of this empirical confrontation, with five successive paradigms discernible over the last two millennia, as shown in Table 24.3. For the first thousand years of the Common Era the shared paradigm might be called "dogmatism," though perhaps we should define the time span as the half-millennium between the Roman and the Carolingian empires to avoid confusing the separate strands of the Classical and the Judeo-Christian tradition. During this dogmatic half-millennium, the kind of external validation insisted upon by intellectual leaders such as Athanasius, Augustine, Gregory, Bede, Rashi, and John Damascene was that one's hypotheses measure up to the external standards of truth provided by the evidence epitomized in the Judeo-Christian scriptures and the teachings of the Church. While dogmatism has not for the past millennium been the dominant position in the Western intelligentsia, it still survives in many respectable ecclesiastical circles and within highly productive schools of thought such as dialectical materialism and Freudianism (Popper, 1962). It should be understood that dogma-

TABLE 24.3 Five Successive Dominant Views within Western Thought Regarding How the Production of Knowledge Involves Empirical Confrontation

1. Dogmatism (e.g., Athanasius, Augustine, Gregory, Bede, Rashi)
2. Rationalism (e.g., Anselm, Abelard, Averroës, Maimonides, Aquinas, Duns Scotus, Nicholas)
3. Positivism (e.g., F. Bacon, Locke, Hume, Condillac, Comte, Spencer)
4. Logical empiricism (e.g., Schlick, Carnap, Hempel, Feigl, Bergmann)
5. Contextualism (e.g., Russell, McGuire)

tism does not ignore empirical observation as a criterion of truth but rather asserts that a specified compendium of doctrines is the best representation of observed reality.

By the onset of the second millennium of the Common Era, this dogmatic paradigm had already begun to give way to rationalism as the Establishment position. The rationalists' epistemology begins with self-evident axioms (such as the principle of sufficient reason) and firmly established inductive postulates (such as the principle that all life comes from life) and generates and evaluates specific theorems in terms of their deducibility from the general principles. By 1077 Anselm had already written *Monologium* in response to his monks' requests for a treatise that would establish everything about God by reason without making use of Scripture; and by 1117, Abelard, in his *Sic et Non*, assembling quotes from Scripture and the other authorities on both sides of most issues, raised questions as to whether Scripture was not only dispensable but perhaps even inadequate for arriving at the truth. By the thirteenth century there were gothic intellectual cathedrals to match those in stone which, like Thomas's *Summae*, used the rationalist approach to construct and evaluate contemporary representations of the material and spiritual worlds.

The flamboyant intellectual monuments of the thirteenth century, embellished by subtle thinkers like Duns Scotus, grew into progressively more rococo rationalist systems that provoked critics like William Occam to wield their razors against unnecessary multiplication of being. But it was not until three centuries ago that the opening of the European mind produced by geographic and speculative voyages of discovery firmly established the dramatically different positivistic paradigm. Then Francis Bacon not only whittled down Duns Scotus but stood him on his head, replacing the rationalists' deductive with the positivists' inductive paradigm. By the nineteenth century a series of British and French empiricists such as Locke, Hume, Condillac, Comte, and Spencer had firmly established the positivistic position that theory should be developed inductively from observation, the knower starting with an open mind, observing phenomena to perceive regularities, and then inducing a general principle to describe these regularities, with broader theories ultimately constructed to integrate these inductively derived principles.

Logical Empiricism   A half-century ago the intellectual Establishment shifted to the new logical empiricist paradigm that has dominated scientific notions of the relationship between theory and observation until the present. In the golden twilight and afterglow of the early twentieth-century Hapsburg Vienna, the unlikely site of so many intellectually revolutionary systems associated with Freud, Herzl, Mahler, and Wittgenstein, was also the meeting place of the circle of physical scientists, mathematicians, and philosophers who developed the new logical empiricism paradigm. After they were scattered in the 1930s by the return of Vienna's failed artist, their views spread to become, by midcentury, psychology's Establishment epistemology. Logical empiricism constitutes a particularly elegant leap forward. Its own predecessor, positivism, had been related to its rationalist antecedent simply by an antagonistic thesis/antithesis relationship, the extreme positivist inductivism being a contrary reaction to rationalism's extreme deductivism. Logical empiricism's advance was a more productive synthesis of the thesis/antithesis relationship constituted by its two predecessors, making creative use of the richness of each. Logical empiricism accepts the rationalist notion that the theory and its derived hypotheses should precede and guide observations; but it also accepts the positivist tenet that the ultimate criterion of the truth (and even meaning) of the theory is putting the question to nature to determine whether derived hypotheses survive an observational test. The genius of the logical empiricist was to give the first word to deductive theory and the last word to empirical observation. The logical empiricist epistemology has become so dominant within social psychology that for the past quarter-century, at least, teacher and student take for granted that our field progresses by our having a theory from which we derive testable hypotheses which are then put in jeopardy by an empirical test, and the hypothesis and theory from which it is derived are accepted or rejected depending on the outcome of this test.

The Contextualist Approach For a dozen years or more we have been urging that social psychology move beyond logical empiricism to a new epistemological paradigm. The considerable intellectual stimulation and clarification inherent in logical empiricism have been largely absorbed, while its shortcomings are with increasing uniformity distorting the way we think about and describe our work. The new position that we have been urging as a successor to logical empiricism incorporates some of its tenets and rejects others. We call our new position "contextualism" because it recognizes the role of empirical observation, not to test theories as in logical empiricism, but as an aid for discovering contexts in which a given theory leads to useful insights and contexts in which it is misleading. Contextualism incorporates two basic premises of logical empiricism, that a theory-embedded hypothesis should precede and guide our formal observational undertaking, and that the interpersonal meaningfulness of the theory derives from its being subjected to an empirical confrontation and illustration. Where contextualism departs radically from logical empiricism is in its position on the nature of this empirical confrontation. In logical empiricism, the purpose of the empirical work is to test the theory; in contextualism, the purpose of the empirical work is to construct the theory by clarifying its meanings and implications, its hidden assumptions and limitations, and revealing contexts in which it does and does not hold. In contrast to logical empiricism's contention that some theories are right and some wrong and that the function of the empirical work is to test which of several opposed theories is right, contextualism asserts that each of the several different theories is right and that the empirical work is conducted in order to reveal the contexts in which each of the complementary theories obtain.

We can illustrate the difference between logical empiricism and contextualism by using some half-roasted chestnuts from social psychology's recent past where different theories made opposite predictions about a relationship. For example, consider the forced compliance controversy regarding the relationship of incentive size on the effect of counterattitudinal advocacy on subsequent internalized belief change; here, learning theorists predicted a positive and dissonance theorists a negative relationship (McGuire, 1966b). Alternatively, consider the Good Samaritan controversy, whether the likelihood of coming to the aid of a person in distress is increased or decreased by the presence of other observers; here again different theoretical orientations have led to opposite predictions (Latané & Darley, 1970). The logical empiricism paradigm would have social psychologists think of their research as putting their derived hypothesis to an empirical test: Perhaps using an elaborate laboratory or field manipulation experiment, they see themselves as exposing a series of participants to a situation in which a victim appears to be in need of help, the situation being standardized except that the number of onlookers (besides the experimental participant) is randomly varied. The extent to which the experimental participant comes to the aid of the victim is then measured and correlated with the number of people present; if the correlation is positive, the hypothesis predicting a negative relationship and its embedded theory is rejected as untrue; if the obtained correlation is negative, then the theory yielding the hypothesis of a positive relationship is rejected. The researcher thinks of the work and describes it in the published version as if this were the actual mode of procedure.

The actual procedure is rather different, with the researcher, even if a logical empiricist of the strict observance, probably all too aware and solicitous of the ambiguity, tenuosity, and vulnerability of his or her theory. Rather than deriving the hypothesis, setting up and conducting a test, and accepting or rejecting the hypothesis and its theory on the basis of the outcome, the researcher proceeds in a more circuitous manner. Aware of the differing predictions derivable from various theories, probably one does some thought experiments to generate insights into the circumstances assumed by one's own theory; sometimes one actually conducts prestudies to perfect the material, measures, procedures, etc., that increase the sensitivity of the design, that is, set the conditions to increase the likelihood that the experiment will come out "right." If the polished experiment as ultimately devised does support the theory, the researcher publishes a sanitized description of the ultimate experiment, avoiding space wastage (the editor assisting toward this end) by eliminating the armchair thinking and the prestudies which probably reveal a more complex, "iffy" set of outcomes than does the final polished study. If the study does not come out right, one looks for flaws in, e.g., the procedures, corrects them, and tries again. In actuality one is testing not the theory but the "test."

The contextualist position which we urge, far from criticizing these meandering preliminaries, asserts that they are the heart of the scientific method and contain more information than does the ultimate polished experiment, information which is largely lost within the logical empiricist fictions that guide our thinking about and published descriptions of our work. The contextualist position is that the empirical confrontation is a discovery process which, rather than testing the hypothesis, serves by making its meaning (and that of the theory from which it is derived) clearer to ourselves and others. This clarification involves making explicit the hidden assumptions of the formulation and describing the contexts when it will obtain as compared with those in which the different predictions derivable from alternative theories will obtain.

This difference between logical empiricism and contextualism regarding the nature of the empirical confrontation, the one saying that it is a test and the other that it is a discovery procedure regarding the hypothesis, derives from a more fundamental difference between the two paradigms as regards the distribution of truth values over theories. Underlying logical empiricism is the notion that some theories are empirically valid and others are not, and that when two theories yield contradictory predictions, at least one must be wrong. Contextualism asserts outrageously that all theories are true, or in Blake's words, "Everything possible to be believ'd is an image of truth." That is to say, if a reasonable person (or even a rather unreasonable one) makes some assertion such as "The greater the reward for counterattitudinal advocacy, the less internalized attitude change that will result," or "The more bystanders that are present when one sees a victim needing help, the less likely it is that one will come to the aid of the victim," then these assertions are almost certainly true. That is, under the conditions that the speaker has in mind when asserting the hypothesis, or at least under some conditions that could be devised by a creative proponent of the hypothesis, the relationship probably does hold. But likewise, when another researcher coming from another theoretical orientation makes the opposite assertion (that the more bystanders, the more likely one will come to the victim's aid, or whatever), then this contrary hypothesis is also true, again assuming a certain set of circumstances such as the second theorist has in mind, no doubt quite different from those in terms of which the first theorist is thinking. The contextualist position that all hypotheses are true simply calls our attention to the likelihood that almost any conceivable hypothesized relationship probably does obtain in some circumstances that exist in the real world and/or could be created in the laboratory (though the ecological validity or range of circumstances under which alternative hypotheses obtain can vary considerably).

In asserting that all conceivable hypotheses are true, even the members of contradictory pairs of hypotheses, the contextualist position does not deny the principle of contradiction. The contextualist, in a less provocative or less sanguine moment, might equally say that all theories are false. The basic point is that any hypothesis is derivable from a theory only with the aid of additional implicit or explicit assumptions about limited sets of circumstances under which the predicted relationship will be confirmed. Given a theory's assumed circumstances, the predicted relationship will probably obtain; given the circumstances assumed by an alternative theory making the opposite prediction, the opposite relationship will obtain. The empirical confrontation procedure prescribed by the contextualist pushes the researcher to consider alternative theories bearing on the relationship between the dependent and independent variables of interest, making a deliberate effort to include theories making opposite predictions, as in the method of strong inference (Platt, 1964). But then, rather than proceeding to devise an experiment to test which of the contending theories is valid, the researcher should do thought experiments and other conceptual clarifications to make explicit the hidden assumptions of the various theories and derive predictions about the differing circumstances in which each of the theories makes a valid prediction, perhaps refining the thought experiments by prestudies. Then the formal study to be published should be designed to include, besides the independent and dependent variables of initial interest, also a variety of other interacting independent variables and mediating dependent variables which bear on the different assumptions made by the alternative theories regarding the circumstances under which the predicted relationships will obtain. With this more ecumenical stance, the researcher then publishes the study, not to show whether his or her theory is true, but rather to clarify the meaning of the several theories and the circumstances under which each is more informative.

We believe that this contextualist position which we have been urging during the past dozen years is indeed struggling toward Bethlehem to be born and that we are entering a contextualist quarter-century in which we shall be exploiting more fully the information inherent in the empirical confrontation by considering it not as a test but as a voyage of discovery to specify the contexts in which each of the alternative partial views of the person and society is most informative in guiding our depictions of reality.

Social Psychology as Product

We have described the four aspects of social psychology as a process and now shall describe social psychology as product, depicting its past and projecting its future as a body of knowledge yielded us by the processes just described. Were there world enough and time, one could describe the social-psychological product on a very concrete level, in the form of a detailed propositional inventory of what is known about human thoughts, feelings, and actions insofar as they affect or are affected by other people. We choose rather to summarize the social-psychological content on a more abstract level, in terms of the theories of the person and society that have developed within social psychology during the past century and which will be the foundation on which the next century's edifice will be constructed. Choice of this abstract theoretical level is ordained not so much by lack of the time and space needed for a more concrete propositional inventory as by recognition that knowledge is an abstraction and an oversimplification of the reality it is depicting. The limitations of the human intellectual apparatus require our oversimplifying the complexities of reality, depicting it by abstract theories. These abstract depictions of the person and society furnish more usable tools for our labor of understanding than do the more concrete specifics (though these latter may be more serviceable for a prescribed application). We shall describe two types of theories: systems theories and guiding-idea theories.

Systems Theories in Social Psychology

Social-psychological theories are conveniently divisible into two types, systems theories and guiding-idea theories. A social-psychological systems theory consists of a set of independent postulates typically numbering a dozen or so, each a broad generalization about the person or society, from which can be derived a hierarchy of hypotheses about how human thoughts, feelings, or actions will affect or be affected by various aspects of other people's thoughts, feelings, and actions. The prototypic example of a systems theory is the geometry of Euclid, consisting of a set of axioms that allow the derivation of an endless set of theorems, corollaries, and scholia about spatial relationships. In the empirical sciences, system theories tend to be developed by the hypothetico-deductive method, beginning with observations of regularities from which are abstracted the general postulates, which, in turn, serve as principles from which are deduced hypotheses for further empirical confrontation on the basis of which the initial set of principles is augmented or adjusted. Examples of systems theories used in social psychology include general behavioristic (or "learning") theories and psychoanalytic theories insofar as they have been used to derive hypotheses about person-societal relationships. While these general theories may be called social-psychological in the sense that they have been widely used within this field, they actually derive from other subdisciplines: behavioral theory from general experimental psychology and psychoanalytic theory from clinical psychology or psychiatric practice.

For systems theories that are more thoroughly social-psychological in that they have their origin as well as use in this field, we must confine ourselves to miniature systems constructed to describe the relationships among variables in circumscribed personal-societal domains. The writer's own work provides several examples of these miniature systems theories. For example, in McGuire (1968) we use a systems theory of six postulates to describe how individual differences affect susceptibility to social influence under a wide range of conditions. Also, our probabilogical theory (McGuire, 1960, 1981) uses a larger set of postulates to describe cognitive organization as it affects the ramifications of persuasive communication through the belief system.

The second quarter of psychology's twentieth century was an "age of systems" when the broad theoretical formulations provided creative impetus and feeling of community to most researchers. During the third, just-ended quarter of the century, the broad systems theories became progressively less fashionable. Instead, cliques have formed mainly around the "guiding-idea" theories that will be considered in the next section. During the final quarter of the twentieth century we expect that computer-inspired information-processing notions will provide an increasingly popular systems theory within social psychology. However, various guiding-idea theories (among the ones considered in the next section) will continue to become successively popular rallying points for subgroups of social psychologists. Since the guiding-idea theories are more primitive formulations than systems theories, we expect or at least hope that during the next few decades miniature systems theories will become more popular relative to the guiding-idea theories.

Guiding-Idea Theories in Social Psychology

Most of the theories that currently guide research in social psychology consist of partial views of the person, focusing on some one human aspect to predict how several independent variables will affect the person's action in or reaction to a specifiable set of conditions. They may depict the person as an ego-defender, a consistency-maximizer, a stimulation-seeker, etc., and on the basis of this one partial view predict how the person will behave under given circumstances, ignoring other human aspects. Indeed, a person is to some extent a consistency-maximizer, but she or he is also other things; hence, any guiding-idea theory will be found valid under some circumstances but inadequate or misleading under others. One does not have to be a contextualist to grant this, though it helps.

Since guiding-idea theories have been the point of departure for so much social psychological research in the past and promise to continue in this role in the future, a review of these partial views of human nature provides a useful summary of social psychology as product, of the field's body of knowledge, on an intermediate level of abstraction.

To assemble an economical set of the partial views of human nature that underlie and grow out of social psychological research we used creative heuristics 26 and 27 (Table 24.2). We first assembled a list of the more obvious partial views of human nature that underlie social psychological research (the person as reward-maximizer, stimulation-seeker, ego-defender, etc.). We then analyzed the guiding-idea theories on this initial list in order to abstract the underlying dimensions that distinguish them, for example, being versus becoming theories (i.e., those that depict the person as Apollonian, homeostatic, and organized to maintain or restore the current equilibrium versus those stressing the Dionysian, growth aspects of the person, the striving to attain a new level of complexity). After abstracting and dichotomizing several such conceptually orthogonal dimensions that differentiate social psychology's guiding-idea theories, one can construct a matrix whose cells are defined by the dimensions. The theories in one's initial list can be assigned to the various cells of such a matrix, while the characteristics of the empty cells suggest new guiding-idea theories actually or potentially usable in social psychology.

Ultimately, we ended up with a conceptual space defined by four dichotomous orthogonal dimensions as shown in Table 24.4. Besides the stability versus growth dimension mentioned above, the theories differ in that some view the person as actively initiating behavior while others depict the person as responding reactively to outside forces; some depict the person as tending toward a specifiable cognitive state while others posit an affective end state; and finally the state whose attainment terminates action is seen by some as involving internal adjustment among aspects of the personality and by others as involving external adjustment of the self with the environment. Each of the sixteen cells in the resulting 2^4 structure produced by these four dichotomous dimensions includes a family of guiding-idea theories as shown in Table 24.4. Space limitation requires selectivity in discussing these guiding-idea theories: we shall discuss briefly only one guiding-idea theory from each of the four quadrants of the Table 24.4 matrix, starting with the upper left cell of the four cognitive stability theories in the upper left-hand quadrant of the matrix and, continuing clockwise, one cell from each of the other blocks of four. A fuller description of all sixteen families of guiding-idea theories can be found in McGuire (1985).

Cognitive-Stability Guiding-Idea Theories   The four types of theories shown in the upper left quadrant of Table 24.4 all agree in depicting the person as striving to preserve the current stability rather than to grow to new levels of complexity; they agree also in depicting the person as tending toward a cognitive rather than an affective end state. To illustrate the four families of guiding-idea theories shown in this cognitive-stability quadrant, we shall discuss only consistency or balance theories, shown in the upper left cell 1.

This upper left cell, like each of the other fifteen cells of the matrix, includes a whole family of theories. These cell 1 consistency theories agree in depicting the person's beliefs, feelings, and actions as interconnected and the person as tending toward maintaining coherence among these interconnected parts. When one's beliefs get out of line with one's feelings or actions, or when one behaves at variance with one's feelings, this incongruity causes a strain toward adjusting the mismatched aspects of the self in a way that will restore internal harmony. The optimal-consistency criterion varies from theory to theory, but many imply a least-squares-deviation solution that minimizes the extent to which any one aspect of the self is left with a large discrepancy from the other aspects.

Consistency formulations were the dominant guiding-idea theories of social psychology during the 1950s and 1960s and include many variants. Heider's (1958) balance notion and the Osgood-Tannenbaum (1955) congruity model were early examples, and Festinger's (1957) dissonance theory is the best known. Other important consistency theories include Newcomb's (1953) symmetry notions, Abelson and Rosenberg's (1958) psycho-logic model, Cartwright and Harary's (1956) graph theoretical approach, McGuire's (1960) probabilogical theory, Adam's equity

579

TABLE 24.4   Guiding-Idea Theories: Partial Views of Human Nature That Lie Behind Social Psychological Research in the Twentieth Century

ACTION INITIATION

ACTION TERMINATION	Need for Stability		Need for Growth	
	Active Instigation	*Reactive Instigation*	*Active Instigation*	*Reactive Instigation*
COGNITIVE STATE — Internal Relationship	1. Consistency (balance) Heider; Festinger; Osgood/Tannenbaum; Newcomb; McGuire	2. Categorization (perceptual) Külpe; Bartlett; Sherif; Asch; Lévi-Strauss; Piaget	5. Stimulation (exploratory) Harlow; Hebb; Berlyne; Kendler; Dember; Fowler	6. Problem-solving (utilitarian) Lewin; Tolman; M. B. Smith; Bauer; M. Rosenberg; Fishbein
External Relationship	4. Hermeneutic (attribution) Helmholtz; Michotte; H. Kelley; E. E. Jones; Rotter/Phares	3. Induction (self-observational) W. James; G. H. Meade; Cooley; Soc. Comparison; Bem; Duval/Wicklund	8. Autonomy (control) G. Allport, Murray; Maslow, Erikson; Brehm; Steiner	7. Teleological (template, script, cybernetics) N. Weiner; Ashby; Miller/G/P; Powers
AFFECTIVE STATE — Internal Relationship	13. Tension—(drive-)reduction Buddha; Freud; Hull; Spence; Miller/Dollard	14. Ego-defensive (functional) Adorno/Frenkel-Brunswick; M. B. Smith; D. Katz; I. Sarnoff; M. Jahoda	9. Attraction (empathy) Ribot; Kropotkin; Sorokin; Giddings; Byrne; Staub	10. Identification (role-playing) Linton; Sarbin; Newcomb; Goffman; Garfinkle; Blumer
External Relationship	16. Expressive (acting out) Huizinga; Leont'ev; Bühler; Peak; Arnold; Stephenson	15. Repetition (habituation behavioristic, S-R) Pavlov; Thorndike; Janis; Staats; R. F. Weiss; R. M. Baron	12. Assertion (achievement) Hobbes; Nietzsche; A. Adler; McClelland; Lorenz; Morris	11. Contagion (modeling, social learning) LeBon; Charcot; Doob et al.; Berkowitz; Bandura; Gambrill

theory (1963), and so on. A succinct analysis of these consistency theories can be found in McGuire (1966) and an extensive exposition of them in Abelson et al. (1968).

The Cognitive-Growth Theories   The four partial views of human nature found in the upper right quadrant of Table 24.4 all agree with the previous tetrad in depicting the person as tending toward a cognitive rather than affective end state, but differ from them in depicting the person as tending toward growth rather than a homeostatic maintenance of stability. Cognitive growth theories tend to be espoused by those with humanistic inclinations, often inspired by notions derived from Freud or Marx though typically purged of their reductionist and materialistic aspects.

For brevity, we shall let the lower left cell 8 of this cognitive growth quadrant illustrate the tetrad. This family of cell 8 "autonomy" theories share an emphasis on the person as striving for freedom and autonomy and at least the illusion of control over his or her own destiny and over the external environment. According to this notion, people strive to maximize the options available to them and their freedom to choose among the options. When conditions are imposed upon people, they tend to become uncomfortable even if they would have selected these conditions had they been free to choose; conversely, people tend to be satisfied with even an aversive condition if they are allowed some degree of choice among the negative alternatives.

This partial view of human nature as striving toward autonomy was quite popular in the personality theories underlying social-psychological research at midcentury, deriving from G. Allport (1937), H. Murray (1938), Maslow (1954/1970), and Erikson's (1950) theory of psychosocial development. It received less attention in the 1960s when consistency theories were more dominant, but has seen a strong revival in the 1970s with formulations such as Brehm's reactance theory (Wicklund, 1974) and Steiner's (1970) illusion of freedom research. In applied social-psychological research, particularly the active fields of behavioral medicine and environmental psychology, much has been made of the need for autonomy and control in recent years by researchers (Rodin & Langer, 1977; Lazarus & Monat, 1977) who demonstrated that frustration of the person's need for control causes physiological as well as psychological suffering.

The Affective-Growth Theories   The tetrad of theories shown in the lower right quadrant of Table 24.4 agree with the four just discussed in stressing the growth rather than the homeostatic aspects of the person; but the theories in the two quadrants differ in that this tetrad in the lower right depicts the person as tending toward affective rather than cognitive growth.

The assertion (dominance, power, achievement) guiding-idea theories shown in cell 12 illustrate the affective-growth theories. These assertion theories stress the

581

aspect of the person involving self-aggrandizement and include concepts such as egotism, power, and mastery. In this partial view, the person is depicted as achievement-oriented, seeking success, mastery over the environment, and superiority over other people. Rather than passing through life in an Apollonian harmony with nature, the person is viewed as trying to give meaning to his or her life by making a difference and leaving a mark on the world. Some of the theories in this family stress interpersonal aspects, such as the person's striving to attain recognition by others or competing to outdo others and dominate over them.

This assertion or achievement aspect of the person has been stressed by a number of students of human nature including social philosophers like Hobbes and Nietzsche. Alfred Adler, the most socially oriented member of the Vienna psychoanalytic school, placed the power need at the center of human personality, and it underlies a number of his concepts having to do with inferiority, overcompensation, sibling order, and so on. McClelland (1975) has stressed the person as achievement- and power-oriented. More recently the "fear of success" notion (Horner, 1970) has introduced an interesting reversal of the classic "fear of failure" theme of these theorists. This predatory view of the person has also influenced the thinking of social Darwinists such as Spencer and has been revived more recently in the emphasis on human aggressiveness by ethologists such as Lorenz (1966) and the "naked ape" school of popular writers such as Morris (1967), Ardrey (1961), and Tiger and Fox (1971).

The Affective-Stability Theories The final four theories constituting the lower left quadrant of Table 24.4 agree with the tetrad just considered in stressing affective rather than cognitive needs of the person, but differ in that they stress the person's tending toward homeostatic stability rather than growth and as tending toward an effective rather than a cognitive end-state. Affective theories tend to be more staid and traditional than cognitive theories, and the stability-affective theories particularly so; however, they are no less respectable because of their age, and a number of them have been perennial goads to social-psychological research.

This tetrad is illustrated in terms of the family of theories in its upper left cell, namely, the cell 13 partial views of human beings as operating on a tension-reducing economy. This notion has proved attractive to theorists across the spectrum, from materialism to pantheism. It underlies Freud's (1920/1955) notion, derived from the second law of thermodynamics, that pleasure consists of release from tension; likewise, it is the basis of the drive-reduction theory of reinforcement that lies at the core of the Hullian (Hull, 1952; Spence, 1956; N. Miller, 1963) school of behaviorism. At the other extreme, the same notion inspires the pantheistic Buddhist concept of happiness as involving the attainment of nirvana, a state of zero arousal characterized by the abolition of self-consciousness and desire.

Social psychologists have made wide use of the orthodox psychoanalytic notion that any erotic or thanatotic arousal is painful and its reduction pleasurable so that the person develops a wide range of defense mechanisms to prevent tension accumulation and of adjustment dynamisms to provide tension release. The sophisticated behaviorists in the Hullian tradition have united to these Freudian ideas the conditioning concepts of Pavlov and Thorndike to explain or suggest the wide range of social-psychological phenomena having to do with imitation, personality devel opment, psychotherapy, and so forth.

It is important to keep explicit that any one of the sixteen families of guiding-idea theories shown in Table 24.4 stresses just one aspect of the person. In keeping with the contextualist epistemology, it should be recognized that each of the guiding-idea theories is true in that it correctly guides our thinking about the behavior of the person to some slight extent in many situations and to a considerable extent in a few situations; but each is also false in that the other aspects of human nature (stressed in other guiding-idea theories) will also be affecting behavior, so that the outcome in any one situation may well be the opposite to that predicted by a given theory. Each of these partial views provides creative impetus by concentrating our attention on certain important tendencies in the person that are likely to prove determining in the situations which initially suggest the theory. However, as the guiding-idea theory is extended further and further from its original source of inspiration, the elected ignorances and systematic distortions contained within it tend to make it increasingly misleading.

Within the contextualist epistemology, it is best to derive hypotheses from several guiding-idea theories and to design research confrontations to include interacting independent variables and direct measures of hypothetical mediating variables, so that the outcome of the research will clarify the interactions and the underlying processes which define the domain of applicability of each theory. Unfortunately, proponents of a given guiding-idea theory often regard theories within the other cells (and sometimes even variants within the same cell) as antagonistic rather than complementary.

A Great Proposal for a Modest Leap Forward

We started this chapter by pointing out that social psychology is a branch of knowledge and, after a half-hearted attempt to define which branch, described social psychology in terms of its process of knowing and the knowledge it has produced. Throughout the discussion of process and product of knowing, our claims for the validity of knowledge were modest: in discussing the research process, our contextualist position emphasized that all imaginable theories are occasionally or potentially correct but usually wrong; in discussing the theoretical product of the social-psychology inquiry, we emphasized that our theories overemphasize and distort a few aspects of reality while ignoring the others. In order to clarify what can be expected of social psychology, we shall close by discussing more fully the limitations of knowledge.

We humans seem to have evolved with a need to know, a need to represent reality to ourselves insofar as our cognitive apparatus allows. This representational or knowing process appears to be a crucial aspect of our mode of coping with the environment. It is the tragedy of knowledge that this process, which we cannot do without, we cannot do well: it inevitably misrepresents the environment both by oversimplifying and by distorting it. Oversimplification occurs because our cognitive limitations require such reductions as slicing the seamless web of reality rather arbitrarily into thought-sized chunks; abstracting a few features of reality while electing ignorance of the others; focusing on the relationships between a few "variables" while illogically assuming that everything else is constant, and so on. More serious than these oversimplifications are the distortions inherent in knowing, such as assimilating observations to such ill-fitting mental categories as we may have available; lumping diverse entities in a common concept by ignoring their essential peculiarities; and warping our perceptions and inferences to conform to our values, desires, and expectations. These limitations are not peculiar to social-psychological knowledge (though some optimists have argued that they arise only in fields like ours because of some special contradictions and/or special interests in social science topics or methods). It can be shown that the tragedy of knowledge—that our necessary representing of reality necessarily misrepresents it—pertains equally to the natural sciences, to humanistic and artistic modes of knowing, to informal musings, and to ecstatic epiphanies.

We more senior social psychologists need reminding of the limitations of knowledge because we grew up in a peculiarly rationalistic moment, with the optimistic view that knowledge was a promising path, not only to truth, but also to beauty and goodness. Such an apotheosis of intellect occurs rarely in the time space of history, being represented in Western culture by the brilliant Hellenic century two-and-a-half millennia back, by the thirteenth century of the Common Era, by the Enlightenment, and the first half of the twentieth century. Even in these intellectualistic moments there has been a core of epistemological anxiety. In the Hellenic period it was not atypical that Parmenides found it necessary to write two tomes, one on the world as it is and the other on the world as it is not, the latter being the world as known. And while Socrates struggled unendingly against the Sophists whose leader, Gorgias, maintained cynically that nothing exists, or if it did it could not be known, or that if it were known it could not be communicated, Socrates himself held the melancholy position that such claim as he had to wisdom was in knowing how inadequate was his knowledge, a position equally espoused by other rationalist thinkers, such as Nicholas of Cusa during the height of medieval intellectualism. And during our own dimming Enlightenment, rationalists and positivists have stressed that we see through a glass, darkly. Kant pointed out that our knowledge reflects the nature of our own thought apparatus as much as it does the thing known;

Dilthey (see Hodges, 1952) struggled to span the paradox of the hermeneutic circle that we can know the parts of our world only insofar as we know the context in which they appear but that we can perceive the total context only insofar as we perceive its parts; and the arcane Heidegger, who after twenty-two volumes has managed to keep his secret still intact, has made at least one thing perfectly clear in *Sein und Zeit* (Heidegger, 1927/1962), that our knowing is necessarily distorted by *Vorverständnis* and the human necessity of analyzing the essential complexity of reality into intelligible bits. Even the more sanguine British empiricists acknowledged their failure to solve "Hume's problem" regarding the impossibility of inductively establishing the validity of induction, Russell pointing out that while empiricism is a practical necessity, it is necessarily arbitrary.

Our cautionary tale, that we have only modest expectations for scientific inquiry, is directed at the older generation, wholly and holily wedded to rationalism and empiricism. The reminder is less necessary for the baby-boom cohort come of age; in the last quarter-century the bond uniting the elite to intellectual thought modes has, like so many other marriages, been dissolving. Increasingly during recent decades, charismatic, mystical, irrational modes of thought have been moving from the Eleusinian caves and provincial forests to center stage, to the paperback book, even to the classroom (or at least the dormitory room) of the university. If the more senior social psychologists have to be urged to expect less from scientific inquiry, the coming generation may need encouragement to use scientific inquiry with more confidence and courage, lest these teeny-boppers wait for enlightenment to come instead on a flying saucer with the Reverend Moon in the nose cone and the Reverend Jones at the tail gun (Bromley & Shupe, 1979; Nugent, 1979).

In stressing the limitations of knowledge in social psychology (or in any other domain) my purpose is not to ride the wave of an irrational future or to deride the social psychology we have constructed so far by scientific inquiry. Granted, I have pointed out that our social psychological knowledge is a delusional system which represents reality only poorly, the representation being oversimplified by our limited intellectual apparatus and distorted by our cognitive systems and our wishes, values, and expectations. But while knowledge is not so deep as a well nor so wide as a church door, 'twill do, 'twill serve. It had better serve, since it is the least flawed tool we have. The only thing more outrageous than using our faulty intellectual processes, including scientific inquiry, to arrive at a representation of reality is not to use them. When we notice the slightness of the advancement of knowledge deriving from all this social psychological research, we can draw some solace from remembering that this area too had once been one of the dark places of earth. That scientific inquiry or any other knowledge process is bound to be limited by our cognitive categories and distorted by our values does not mean that we should abandon intellect but that we should try harder, recognizing the limitations of knowledge and working to minimize the havoc of oversimplification and distortion.

It is further cause for discouragement to recognize that even if we social psychologists ourselves keep the faith in scientific inquiry, our progress may be slowed by external forces. One threat, depressing though not likely to prove decisive, is the growing strength of irrationalism, manifested in a subgeneration that veers from primal scream through vacant meditation to chemical vision, taking social form in the growing membership in pseudoscience and antiscience cults and in the increasing popularity of the occult and the macabre in entertainment. Turning our attention from the asses to the masses, we notice additional signs of public hostility to (social) science. A recent court decision (Kiesler, 1980) may have left the golden fleece in need of a hair implant, but more significant than its momentary legal status (or the malice or inequity with which the fleece may have been perpetrated) is the glee with which the cheap shot has been received by the public, or at least by the non-social-science segments of the Establishment. There seems to be increasing awareness that in the past money has been given and received under false pretenses and that much of the support for social scientific research has been wasted on busywork, fun and games, and hobby-horse riding. As it becomes necessary to lighten the load, it is always possible that society will leave behind Philoctetes as well as the ballast. I doubt it will come to this, but even if it does, we, like that abandoned malcontent, must limp along on our island, working away despite our incurable wound until the time comes when the anti-intellectual armies which contend in the night return for our help, recognizing that our flawed tool is the best hope.

Whether we social psychologists continue to live off the fat of the land or on the gleanings of a desert island, what should we be doing? In my remarks about the process and product of social psychology there are a number of prescriptions. As regards the choice of topics, I am hesitant to be prescriptive or even descriptive of what problems we ought to study; if there is anything not in short supply, it is problems worthy of inquiry. My own suspicion is that the 1980s will see the growth of a third wave of attitude research, following the first wave on attitude measurement and the second wave on attitude change. This third coming will, I think, focus on attitude systems as they function in the broader directive and dynamic structures. As regards theoretical guidance, I expect a resurgence of systems theories, probably a systems theory based on the broader information-processing conceptualizations that have evolved from the computer analogy, but augmented by a fuller appreciation of motivational aspects and of memory limitations and costs.

As regards empirical confrontation, I anticipate a more explicit utilization of the contextualist approach that would enrich both the creative and the critical side of our methods. Our methods courses will probably give fuller attention to the construction of theory and hypotheses, correcting their present exclusive emphasis on hypothesis "testing." A more ecumenical attitude toward theories will lead us to appreciate more fully the complexities of the phenomena we are studying, so that we shall generate multiple theories and hypotheses. We shall recognize that the purpose of the empirical work is not to test which of several formulations is right but to explore the circumstances under which each is right. Hence, our research designs will include more independent variables whose interactions with the main independent variable will be the basis for our exploring their limits as well as more direct measurement of intervening variables that will allow us to check the operation of the hypothesized mediating processes. I also anticipate that the analytic processes to which we subject the collected data will be less inspired by the Student and Fisher model of statistics-as-testing and more by the Mosteller (1977) and Tukey (1977) model of statistics-as-discovery. Evolution in these directions requires recognizing that knowledge is tragedy, but a great tragedy.

REFERENCES

Abelson, R. P., Aronson, E., McGuire, W. J., Newcomb, T. M., Rosenberg, M. J., & Tannenbaum, P. H. (Eds.). *Theories of cognitive consistency.* Chicago: Rand McNally, 1968.

Abelson, R. P., & Rosenberg, M. J. Symbolic psycho-logic: A model of attitude cognition. *Behavioral Science,* 1958, 3, 1–13.

Adams, J. S. Toward an understanding of inequity. *Journal of Abnormal and Social Psychology,* 1963, 67, 422–436.

Allport, F. H. *Social psychology.* Boston: Houghton Mifflin, 1924.

Allport, G. W. Attitudes. In C. Murchison (Ed.), *A handbook of social psychology.* Worcester, Mass.: Clark University Press, 1935.

Allport, G. W. *Personality: A psychological interpretation.* New York: Holt, 1937.

Andrews, F. (Ed.). *Scientific productivity: The effectiveness of research groups in six countries.* New York: Cambridge University Press, 1979.

Ardrey, R. *African genesis.* New York: Atheneum, 1961.

Arieti, S. *Creativity: The magic synthesis.* New York: Basic Books, 1976.

Back, K. W. *Beyond words.* New York: Russell Sage, 1972.

Bandura, A. *A social learning theory.* Englewood Cliffs, N.J.: Prentice-Hall, 1976.

Bechterev, V. M. *General principles of human reflexology.* New York: International, 1932.

Berscheid, E., & Walster, E. H. *Interpersonal attraction* (2nd ed.). Reading, Mass.: Addison-Wesley, 1978.

Bettelheim, B. Individual and mass behavior in extreme situations. *Journal of Abnormal and Social Psychology,* 1943, 38, 417–452.

Bettelheim, B. *The informed heart.* Glencoe, Ill.: Free Press, 1960.

Billig, M. *Social psychology and intergroup relations.* New York: Academic Press, 1976.

Bogardus, E. S. Social distance and its practical implications. *Sociology and Social Research,* 1933, 17, 265–271.

Bromley, D., & Shupe, A. D., Jr. *"Moonies" in America: Cult, church and crusade.* Beverly Hills, Calif.: Sage, 1979.

Cartwright, D., & Harary, F. Structural balance. *Psychological Review,* 1956, 63, 277–293.

Coan, R. W. *Psychologists: Personal and theoretical pathways.* New York: Halstead, 1979.

Cole, M., & Scribner, S. *Culture and thought.* New York: Wiley, 1974.

Collins, B. E., & Hoyt, M. F. Personal responsibility-for-consequences: An integration and extension of the forced compliance literature. *Journal of Experimental Social Psychology,* 1972, 8, 558–593.

Comstock, G., Chaffee, S., Katzman, N., McCombs, M., & Roberts, D. *Television and human behavior.* New York: Columbia University Press, 1978.

587

Dashiell, J. F. Experimental studies of the influence of social situations on the behavior of individual human adults. In C. Murchison (Ed.), *Handbook of social psychology*. Worcester, Mass.: Clark University Press, 1935.

Deutsch, M. *The resolution of conflict*. New Haven: Yale University Press, 1973.

Erikson, E. H. *Childhood and society*. New York: Norton, 1950. (2nd ed., 1963.)

Feshbach, S., & Fraczek, A. (Eds.). *Aggression and behavior change*. New York: Praeger, 1979.

Festinger, L. *A theory of cognitive dissonance*. Stanford, Calif.: Stanford University Press, 1957.

Festinger, L. (Ed.). *Conflict, decision and dissonance*. Stanford, Calif.: Stanford University Press, 1964.

Festinger, L., Schachter, S., & Back, K. *Social pressures in informal groups*. New York: Harper & Row, 1950.

Freud, S. *The interpretation of dreams*. London: Hogarth, 1953. (Originally published, 1900.)

Freud, S. *Beyond the pleasure principle*. London: Hogarth, 1955. (Originally published, 1920.)

Harvey, J. H., & Smith, W. P. *Social psychology: An attribution approach*. St. Louis: Mosby, 1977.

Hastie, R., Ostrom, T. M., Ebbesen, E. B., Wyer, R. S., Jr., Hamilton, D. L., & Carlston, D. E. (Eds.). *Person memory: The cognitive basis of social perception*. Hillsdale, N.J.: Erlbaum, 1980.

Heidegger, M. *Being and time*. New York: Harper & Row, 1962. (Originally published, 1927.)

Heider, F. *The psychology of interpersonal relations*. New York: Wiley, 1958.

Hodges, H. A. *The philosophy of Wilhelm Dilthey*. London: Routledge & Kegan Paul, 1952.

Horner, M. S. Femininity and success achievement: Basic inconsistency. In J. M. Bardwick, E. Douvan, M. S. Horner, & D. Guttman (Eds.), *Feminine personality and conflict*. Belmont, Calif.: Brooks/Cole, 1970.

Hovland, C. I., Janis, I. L., & Kelley, H. H. *Communication and persuasion*. New Haven: Yale University Press, 1953.

Hovland, C. I., Lumsdaine, A. A., & Sheffield, F. *Experiments on mass communication*. Princeton, N.J.: Princeton University Press, 1949.

Hull, C. L. *A behavior system*. New Haven: Yale University Press, 1952.

Jennings, M. K., & Niemi, R. G. *The political character of adolescence*. Princeton, N.J.: Princeton University Press, 1974.

Kelley, H. H. *Personal relationships: Their structures and purposes*. New York: Halstead, 1979.

Kelley, H. H., & Michela, J. L. Attribution theory and research. In M. R. Rosenzweig & L. W. Porter (Eds.), *Annual review of psychology*, 1980, *31*, 457–501.

Kiesler, C. A. Hutchinson versus Proxmire. *American Psychologist*, 1980, *35*, 689–690.

LaPiere, R. T. Attitudes *vs* action. *Social Forces*, 1934, *13*, 230–237.

Latané, B., & Darley, J. M. *The unresponsive bystander: Why doesn't he help?* New York: Appleton-Century-Crofts, 1970.

Lazarus, R. S., & Monat, A. (Eds.). *Stress and coping*. New York: Columbia University Press, 1977.

Lewin, K. Group decision and social change. In H. Proshansky & B. Seidenberg (Eds.), *Basic studies in social psychology*. New York: Holt, 1966. (Originally published, 1947.)

Likert, R. A technique for the measurement of attitudes. *Archives of Psychology*, 1932, *22* (No. 140).

Lorenz, K. *On aggression*. New York: Harcourt, Brace, 1966.

Maslow, A. H. *Motivation and personality*. New York: Harper & Row, 1954. (2nd ed., 1970.)

McClelland, D. C. *Power: The inner experience*. New York: Halstead, 1975.

McGuire, W. J. A syllogistic analysis of cognitive relationships. In C. I. Hovland & M. J. Rosenberg (Eds.), *Attitude organization and change*. New Haven: Yale University Press, 1960.

McGuire, W. J. The current status of cognitive consistency theories. In S. Feldman (Ed.), *Cognitive consistency*. New York: Academic Press, 1966. (a)

McGuire, W. J. Attitudes and opinions. In P. R. Farnsworth, O. McNemar, & Q. McNemar (Eds.), *Annual review of psychology*, 1966, *17*, 475–514. (b)

McGuire, W. J. Some impending reorientations in social psychology. *Journal of Experimental Social Psychology*, 1967, *3*, 124–139.

McGuire, W. J. Personality and social influence. In E. F. Borgatta & W. W. Lambert (Eds.), *Handbook of personality theory and research*. Chicago: Rand McNally, 1968.

McGuire, W. J. Suspiciousness of experimenter's intent. In R. Rosenthal & R. Rosnow (Eds.), *Artifact in behavioral research*. New York: Academic Press, 1969. (a)

McGuire, W. J. Theory-oriented research in natural settings. In M. Sherif & C. W. Sherif (Eds.), *Interdisciplinary relationships in the social sciences*. Chicago: Aldine, 1969. (b)

McGuire, W. J. Social psychology. In P. C. Dodwell (Ed.), *New horizons in psychology-2*. Middlesex, England: Penguin, 1972. (2nd ed., 1980.)

McGuire, W. J. The yin and yang of progress in social psychology: Seven koan. *Journal of Personality and Social Psychology*, 1973, *26*, 446–456.

McGuire, W. J. The development of theory in social psychology. In R. Gilmour & S. Duck (Eds.), *The development of social psychology*. London: Academic Press, 1980.

McGuire, W. J. The probabilogical model of cognitive structure and attitude change. In R. E. Petty, T. M. Ostrom, & T. C. Brock (Eds.), *Cognitive responses in persuasion*. Hillsdale, N.J.: Erlbaum, 1981.

McGuire, W. J. A contextualist theory of knowledge: Its implications for innovations and reform in psychology research. In L. Berkowitz (Ed.), *Advances in experimental social psychology. Vol. 16*. New York: Academic Press, 1983.

McGuire, W. J. Search for the self: Going beyond self-esteem and the reactive self. In R. A. Zucker, J. Aronoff, & A. I. Rabin (Eds.), *Personality and the prediction of behavior*. New York: Academic Press, 1984.

McGuire, W. J. Attitudes and attitude change. In G. Lindzey & E. Aronson (Eds.), *Handbook of social psychology* (3rd ed.). Reading, Mass.: Addison-Wesley, 1985.

McGuire, W. J., McGuire, C. V., & Winton, W. Effects of household sex composition on the salience of one's gender in the spontaneous self-concept. *Journal of Experimental Social Psychology*, 1979, *15*, 77–90.

McGuire, W. J., & Millman, S. Anticipatory belief lowering following forewarning of a persuasive attack. *Journal of Personality and Social Psychology*, 1965, *2*, 471–479.

Merton, R. K. *Social theory and social structure*. Glencoe, Ill.: Free Press, 1957. (Rev. ed., 1968.)

Merton, R. K., & Riley, M. W. (Eds.). *Sociological traditions from generation to generation*. Norwood, N.J.: Albex, 1980.

Miller, N. E. Some reflections on the law of effect produce a new alternative to drive reduction. In M. R. Jones (Ed.), *Nebraska Symposium on Motivation, 1963*. Lincoln: University of Nebraska Press, 1963.

Moede, W. *Experimentelle Massenpsychologie*. Leipzig: Hirzel, 1920.

Morris, D. *The naked ape*. New York: McGraw-Hill, 1967.

Mosteller, F., & Tukey, J. W. *Data analysis and regression*. Reading, Mass.: Addison-Wesley, 1977.

Murray, H. A. (Ed.) *Explorations in personality*. New York: Oxford University Press, 1938.

Newcomb, T. M. *Personality and social change*. New York: Dryden, 1943.

Newcomb, T. M. An approach to the study of communicative acts. *Psychological Review*, 1953, *60*, 393–404.

Nugent, J. P. *White night*. New York: Rawson, Wade, 1979.

Osgood, C. E., & Tannenbaum, P. H. The principle of congruity in the prediction of attitude change. *Psychological Review*, 1955, *62*, 42–55.

Pelz, D. C., & Andrews, F. M. *Scientists in organizations: Productive climates for research and development*. Ann Arbor, Mich.: Institute for Social Research, University of Michigan, 1976.

Percheron, A. *L'univers politique des enfants*. Paris: Colin, 1974.

Petty, R. E., Ostrom, T. M., & Brock, T. C. (Eds.). *Cognitive responses in persuasion*. Hillsdale, N.J.: Erlbaum, 1980.

Platt, J. R. Strong inference. *Science*, 1964, *146*, 347–353.

II. THE SPECIAL FIELDS OF PSYCHOLOGY

Popper, K. *Conjectures and refutations: The growth of scientific knowledge.* New York: Basic Books, 1962.

Reinharz, S. *On becoming a social scientist.* San Francisco: Jossey-Bass, 1979.

Rodin, J., & Langer, E. Long-term effects of a control-relevant intervention with the institutionalized aged. *Journal of Personality and Social Psychology,* 1977, 35, 897–902.

Schneider, D. J., Hastorf, A. H., & Ellsworth, P. C. *Person perception* (2nd ed.). Reading, Mass.: Addison-Wesley, 1979.

Sherif, M. *The psychology of social norms.* New York: Harper & Row, 1936.

Spence, K. W. *Behavior theory and conditioning.* New Haven: Yale University Press, 1956.

Staub, E. *Positive social behavior and morality* (2 vols). New York: Academic Press, 1978, 1979.

Stein, M. I. *Stimulating creativity. Vol. 1. Individual procedures. Vol. 2. Group procedures.* New York: Academic Press, 1974–1975.

Steiner, I. D. Perceived freedom. In L. Berkowitz (Ed.), *Advances in experimental social psychology* (Vol. 5). New York: Academic Press, 1970. Pp. 187–248.

Tajfel, H. (Ed.). *Differentiating between social groups: Studies in the social psychology of intergroup relations.* London: Academic Press, 1978.

Thurstone, L. L., & Chave, E. J. *The measurement of attitude.* Chicago: The University of Chicago Press, 1929.

Tiger, L., & Fox, R. *Imperial animal.* New York: Holt, 1971.

Tillich, P. *The courage to be.* New Haven: Yale University Press, 1952.

Triandis, H. C. *Interpersonal behavior.* Monterey, Calif.: Brooks/Cole, 1977.

Triandis, H. C., & Lambert, W. W. (Eds). *Handbook of cross-cultural psychology.* (6 vols.). Boston: Allyn and Bacon, 1979.

Tukey, J. W. *Exploratory data analysis.* Reading, Mass.: Addison-Wesley, 1977.

Watson, G. B. Do groups think more efficiently than individuals? *Journal of Abnormal and Social Psychology,* 1928, 23, 328–336.

Wechsler, J. (Ed.). *On aesthetics in science.* Cambridge: M.I.T. Press, 1978.

Werskey, G. *The visible college.* London: Lane/Penguin, 1978.

Wicklund, R. A. *Freedom and reactance.* New York: Wiley, 1974.

Wilson, W., & Miller, H. Repetition, order of presentation and timing of arguments and measures as determinants of opinion change. *Journal of Personality and Social Psychology,* 1968, 9, 184–188.

Zillman, D. *Hostility and aggression.* Hillsdale, N.J.: Erlbaum, 1979.

III

PSYCHOLOGY AND ITS INTERSECTING DISCIPLINES

PSYCHOLOGY AND
PHILOSOPHY

25

The Cult of Empiricism in Psychology, and Beyond*

STEPHEN TOULMIN

DAVID E. LEARY

At some stage in its development, any field of intellectual discussion or scientific speculation may reach a point at which it begins to generate large numbers of "empirical" questions, that is, questions whose answers must refer to carefully documented observations, or even to controlled experiments. In physics, this happened most strikingly in the course of the seventeenth century; in biology, the comparable stage was not reached until around 1770, rising to its peak in the course of the nineteenth century (Toulmin, 1972; Toulmin & Goodfield, 1962); whereas in psychology, it has become customary—though a trifle arbitrary—to argue that this happened just one hundred years ago, with the establishment of Wilhelm Wundt's pioneer psychological laboratory in Leipzig in 1879.

There need be no serious objection to saying this, on one condition. If we speak of Wundt and 1879 as defining the moment at which scientific psychology became a genuinely "empirical" science, we must take care to talk about Wilhelm Wundt himself, as he existed historically in late nineteenth-century Germany, and not

* Revisions of this paper were written while the senior author was a Fellow at The Hastings Center, Institute of Society, Ethics, and the Life Sciences, Hastings-on-Hudson, N.Y. and the collaborating author was a Fellow at the Center for Advanced Study in the Behavioral Sciences, Stanford, Calif. Acknowledgment is made to the National Endowment for the Humanities (Grant No. FC 20029-82) and to the National Science Foundation (Grants No. SES 80-08051 and BNS 82-06304).

about the Wundtian heritage that has developed during the subsequent hundred years, particularly in the United States. For, in some significant respects, the intellectual constraints that American psychologists have tended to place upon themselves since Wundt—in the name of "empiricism"—have been far more rigorous and exacting than any which Wundt himself intended, and also far more rigorous and exacting than was ever the case in other fledging sciences. Neither in physics nor in biology did the introduction of experimental procedures lead scientists to cut their diplomatic relations with the larger philosophical debates out of which their newly defined "empirical" questions had emerged and from which those questions had acquired their original meaning. On the contrary: in both sciences, an elaborate analytical and theoretical debate continued for most of a century after the onset of this new "empirical" phase of investigation. These debates were concerned with two groups of theoretical issues carried over from the preceding period. On the one hand, there were conceptual discussions about the fundamental nature of matter and force (or life and adaptation), discussions that had already been under way before the beginnings of the new empirical physics and biology; and on the other hand, there were discussions about the intellectual relevance of the new empirical investigations to the larger theoretical issues from which they had developed. These latter discussions were aimed, in particular, at clarifying the question, "What *is* an empirical science of physics or biology, and what should it become?"

Wundt's Dual Program for Psychology and Its Bifurcation

If we look at Wundt's own case, we find just the same sort of thing happening once again in psychology. The establishment of Wundt's new laboratory was not intended to inaugurate a separate, autonomous field of experimental psychology, independent of all other subjects (Leary, 1979; Métraux, 1980). Rather, Wundt saw it as contributing toward *one* legitimate research program, among others. In Wundt's own hands, psychological issues initially retained their earlier connections with the logic and epistemology of Immanuel Kant, the physiology of Hermann von Helmholtz, and the psychophysics of Gustav Theodor Fechner (Wundt, 1862, 1863; Richards, 1980; Woodward, 1982); and even after he had defined his narrower research program for the experimental study of "the manifold of consciousness" (Wundt, 1874), he never suggested that this should constitute the entirety of psychology, still less that the results obtained from this new program could be used to build a psychological science free of all more general intellectual connections, either with philosophical arguments or with contemporary theoretical issues in neighboring fields of science. Indeed, Wundt (1880–1883, 1886) went to considerable effort to develop his own systems of logic (including epistemology) and ethics—not to mention his own system of philosophy (1889)—each of which he saw as

595

intimately related to, and dependent upon, psychology. Conversely, psychology itself, in his scheme, was *and should be* susceptible to philosophical analysis. The depth of Wundt's belief in this two-way interdependence between psychology and philosophy was perhaps best illustrated in his (1913) vehement opposition to the proposed separation of psychology and philosophy in German universities (see Ash, 1980). According to Wundt, neither empirical observation (or experiment) nor rational analysis alone could constitute true, complete science. Neither psychology nor philosophy could fulfill its task without the other. In taking this stand, Wundt showed that he was clearly aware of the historical dependence of psychology—even the new experimental psychology—upon the discipline of philosophy. (On the indebtedness of the so-called "new psychology" to philosophy, see Leary, 1978, 1979, 1980a, 1980b, 1982.)

To put the point in a word, Wundt was not a "positivist," though he did share with Ernst Mach (and many others) a view of experience as the primary "given" from which the different natural sciences arrive at their respective subject matters by various distinctive modes of abstraction. Although he was cautious in his metaphysical speculation, he did not shrink from the discussion of the nature of his subject matter, which he construed as consciousness, or the mind. Besides formulating a rather dynamic view of the mind as "actuality," he also pointed out the practical (as well as intellectual) necessity for a philosophical doctrine about the relation between mind and body: methodological decisions—i.e., day-to-day empirical procedures—are dependent upon such a doctrine. For himself, he preferred and argued for a psychophysical parallelism, at least on a pragmatic level; ultimately, this parallelism reflected Wundt's double-aspect monism (Blumenthal, 1980; Richards, 1980). Still, the point is that Wundt, the "physiological psychologist," argued on essentially philosophical grounds for an autonomous psychology, i.e., a nonreductionistic psychology; and he saw no other way to argue the point, pro or con.

In addition to his belief in the integral relationship between psychology and philosophy—and in addition to his belief that psychologists should continue to address the epistemological, ethical, and ontological issues that had given rise to psychological science in the first place—Wundt held yet another supposition that helped to define his research program. We are referring to the distinction he made between different aspects of mental life, i.e., between those that do and those that do not lend themselves to investigation by experimental methods. His view was that purely experimental methods were appropriate only to a restricted range of mental activities and phenomena. In particular, he excluded from their scope just about all those aspects of mental life that are nowadays classified under the heading of "higher mental functions." These other aspects of mental life could be brought within the grasp of a scientific psychology, but only if they were handled in quite different ways. So Wundt conceived a kind of historico-anthropological method for investigating the "higher" modes of mental functioning (see van Hoorn & Verhave, 1980; Leary, 1979). This is best exemplified in Wundt's own later volumes on

596

Völkerpsychologie (1900–1920), a title that is perhaps best translated as "cultural psychology."

In Wundt's conception, the subject matter of this nonexperimental cultural psychology included such phenomena as language, myth, custom, social structure, law, culture itself, and history, all of which reflect the higher-level working of the human mind (in contrast to basic sensation and perception, for example). Wundt believed, in brief, that the rigorous demands of experimental control, and the equally compelling demand for phenomenal authenticity, could not be simultaneously met in the study of these higher-level phenomena. To take a single example: in the study of language, one must either forfeit control of experimental subjects' prior experience (and hence, idiosyncratic associations) with natural language or set up a strictly controlled study of previously nonexperienced nonsense language, which is, of course, no real language at all. The same sort of dilemma can be posed for the study of social-group processes, and so on. In each case, Wundt felt, experimentation is doomed to failure. What he proposed in its stead was a careful, historical, and cross-cultural investigation of the various products of higher mental functioning. In addition to mere data-gathering, he argued for the extensive use of rational and comparative analysis as the optimal method for this kind of psychology. (In many ways his analytic method was analogous to reductive analysis of the Kantian sort. Wundt asked, in essence, what must be the nature of the human mind for it to produce these kinds of phenomena.) Although the actual execution of some parts of his program for cultural psychology have been subjected to criticism, it is noteworthy that Wundt's study of language has recently been acknowledged as a significant forerunner of contemporary psycholinguistics (Blumenthal, 1970).

All in all, then, the real Wundt had a more complex and richly stocked mind than one might guess from reading various histories of psychology (e.g., Boring, 1950) or the polemics of Wundt's critics at Würzburg and elsewhere. (For recent revisions of Boring's account of Wundt, see Blumenthal, 1975, 1979; Danziger, 1979, 1980a, 1980b, 1980c; Leary, 1979; Mischel, 1970; Woodward, 1982.) This fact needs to be borne in mind when we consider the influence Wundt had on psychology in various countries, particularly as regards the two branches of his dual program for psychology. In Germany, the United States, Russia, Britain, and even xenophobic France, the work of Wundt was of real importance, but the existing intellectual traditions in each of these countries led psychologists to select out rather different things from the Wundtian corpus for use in their own locales. For the most part, they selected out his experimental psychology (and then, only a strange facsimile of it), leaving his cultural psychology to have an impact, as it did, only on other disciplines, such as linguistics, sociology, anthropology, and even psychoanalysis. (An interesting exception evolved in Russia, where the work of Lev Vygotsky and Alexander Luria has represented both sides of the Wundtian heritage: the experimental and the cultural. See Toulmin, 1978.)

In the United States, which will be the locus of our concern, this bifurcation of Wundt's psychological program was carried yet another step further. Virtually de facto, in its transatlantic migration the new experimental psychology was divorced from the philosophical context that had originally nurtured its existence. At the same time, it was transplanted into a pragmatic soil that, with each tilling, abided overt philosophical nurturance less and less. Although some Americans, such as William James, agreed with Wundt in espousing a fundamental relation between psychology and philosophy, as a matter of fact their philosophy was such that it tended to discourage (or disguise) the free exercise of the philosophic imagination. And many others simply denied the need for any philosophy—or even any preliminary *thinking*—at all. Edward B. Titchener was not of this persuasion, but his positivistic rendering of Wundt's psychology did much to instigate the movement toward a reductionistic (albeit introspective) empiricism in American psychology (see Danziger, 1979; Leahey, 1981; Tweney & Yachanin, 1980). It was, however, Titchener's friend (and systematic opponent), John B. Watson, who best symbolized the trend toward reductionistic empiricism in the United States, especially as it became aligned with the development of so-called "objective" psychology. As this trend enveloped more and more American psychologists, empiricism ceased to be the legitimate source of creative innovations that it had been in physics two hundred years before and in biology one hundred years before. Instead it became what we shall call a cult.

The Temporary Divorce of Psychology from Philosophy in the United States

Interestingly, Watson's famous behaviorist manifesto (1913) appeared in the same year as Wundt's equally impassioned defense of the alliance between the "new psychology" and philosophy. To be sure, Watson's proclamation was not simply a reaction against Wundt, or even against the derivatives of Wundt's psychology in America. In fact, from an historical point of view, Watson's manifesto was actually only one of a much larger set of factors that contributed to the movement of American psychology toward a simplistic form of empiricism. Many of these were operative well before and after 1913. Although we cannot review them all, we can at least discuss them briefly under several general headings.

First of all, as we said, the national setting itself made a difference in the assimilation and shaping of the new psychological science. Broadly speaking, the practical character of the American temperament, blending at that point in history with the progressivist movement toward political and social reform (Goldman, 1955; Wiebe, 1967), provided a context within which American psychologists were called upon, and willingly offered, to apply their new-found methods to the solution of real-life problems. Even formerly intransigent "pure" psychologists such as the immigrant Hugo Münsterberg (1908, 1909a, 1909b, 1913, 1914) were converted to, and developed, the various fields of applied psychology. This trend toward the practical drew American psychologists away from the former intellectual concerns of their field, so much so by the 1920s that it has been argued (O'Donnell, 1979a) that the first (1929) edition of E. G. Boring's classic history text was written as a defensive reaction against the threat of total encroachment (even within academia) by "professional" psychology. At any rate, it is clear that Watson's promise of an "objective" science of psychology that would lead (in short order) to the prediction and control of behavior was precisely what the reformers, politicians, and businessmen-trustees wanted to hear (Burnham, 1968; O'Donnell, 1979b). The fit between perceived social needs and the goals of applied, and particularly behavioristic, psychology was fortunate, to say the least.

Within this context, it is not surprising that the apparently successful applications of psychology accelerated the trend away from a conceptually rich interdisciplinary psychology (see Crennan & Kingsbury, 1923). Indeed, even some of the less valid applications, as in the army intelligence testing program during World War I (Samelson, 1979), passed for major achievements which buttressed the legitimacy of the new profession. In order to understand the emergence of the cult of empiricism, it is necessary to acknowledge the imagined as well as the real accomplishments of the first generation of applied psychologists.

Meanwhile, at the same time that psychology was moving away from philosophy under its own momentum, American philosophy itself reinforced psychology's trajectory. Although this is rarely appreciated, it was *not* generally the case (Harvard being a notable exception) that psychologists had to fight their way out of philosophy departments, and thus away from their past associations with philosophy. As often as not, philosophers were in the vanguard of the movement calling for an autonomous psychology. Sometimes crying "psychologism," they argued that the alliance between psychology and philosophy had to be broken, for the sake of philosophy as much as psychology. There were clearly economic motives involved in this campaign, but there were also intellectual reasons (Leary, 1979). Increasingly, around the turn of the century, philosophers became aware that their goals, methods, and interests were not always coextensive with those of psychologists. As a result, in 1901 they founded the American Philosophical Association as a splinter group from the American Psychological Association, which had served as a professional organization for both psychologists and philosophers since its inception in 1892. Even after 1901, the psychologists and philosophers continued for a time to meet together. (In many cases, of course, the psychologist and philosopher was one and the same person.) But over the next decade the connections dwindled. Still, the point is that the numerous debates that were held in the early 1900s regarding the proper affiliation of psychology—whether it should maintain its traditional relation to philosophy or become one of the natural sciences—helped to set the scene for

Watson's later proclamation (see Smith, 1981). Watson was no more the first to call for psychology's independence from philosophy than he was the first to call for objective methods and the extirpation of subjectivist terminology from psychology.

In fact, a select group of philosophers foreshadowed and influenced subsequent developments in this latter respect. Building upon the earlier pragmatism of C. S. Peirce and William James, neorealists such as Edwin B. Holt and Ralph Barton Perry called for an objectivistic interpretation of sensation, perception, consciousness, cognition, behavior, purpose, and so on (see Holt et al., 1910, 1912). Their philosophical orientation had a very profound influence, for example, upon the thinking of Edward C. Tolman (see Smith, 1982). Although their stance was not entirely antimetaphysical, their works (and those of other neorealist philosophers) contained antispeculative undertones. Contemporaneously, another philosopher, E. A. Singer (1911), anticipated the main emphases of Watsonian behaviorism, directly influencing the career choice of Edwin Guthrie (Smith, 1981, pp. 34–35). It is probable that acquaintance with the works of such philosophers predisposed some of the more philosophically inclined psychologists toward objective modes of analysis. Together with the later development of critical realism and neopragmatism, their views would have reinforced the movement toward an empiricistic psychology.

Of course, some American psychologists simply had no taste for philosophical discourse. Among these were certainly Watson and Edward L. Thorndike, whose unhappy experiences with John Dewey and Josiah Royce, respectively, had left unpleasant associations (Smith, 1981). Following in the footsteps of Charles Darwin, George J. Romanes, and C. Lloyd Morgan—and together with Robert M. Yerkes, among others—they turned away from traditional introspective, human psychology and did pioneer research in the area of animal psychology. This research clearly influenced their later approach to human psychology, serving as a natural prologue to their articulation of a behavioral point of view. In addition, Watson was influenced by the objectivistic biology of Jacques Loeb, the zoological research of H. S. Jennings, and (after 1913) the reflexology of Ivan Pavlov and Vladimir Bekhterev (Watson, 1936), much as B. F. Skinner was later influenced by William J. Crozier's approach to the study of physiological "conduct" (Skinner, 1979, pp. 44–46). This shift of allegiance from philosophy to the biological sciences did not mean, of course, that they—or any other "objective" psychologists— avoided taking philosophical stances in their work: it was (and is) impossible to avoid such stances. But in their attempts to get out of the orbit of philosophical discourse, these psychologists produced an antiphilosophical rhetoric that came to typify behavioral psychology in the United States. Although many other psychologists were less drastically disaffiliated from philosophy than they, this rhetoric, wedded to the slowly evolving modern psychology-journal style, operated as something of a self-fulfilling prophecy. When psychologists and philosophers began to find themselves in separate departments, speaking different languages and publishing in different journals, the long-time public marriage of their disciplines was temporarily over. Psychologists had heard the "empiricist message," and they proceeded to emphasize empirical work at the expense of psychological theory (see Bruner & Allport, 1940).

Watson's Empiricistic Program for Psychology and Its Constrictive Influence

Although his so-called "classical" behaviorism did not take over American psychology as instantaneously and completely as sometimes thought (Samelson, 1981), Watson's psychology strongly contributed to the development of the cult of empiricism in American psychology. If the inspiration of his creed came from animal psychology and objectivistic biology, Watson's ultimate model was derived from physics. His resolution was to make psychology as close to experimental physics as he knew how, banishing all subjective appeals to introspectable data and focusing exclusively on public, observable reactions to arbitrary stimuli. Despite his insistence on objective techniques of observation, it is interesting to note that his consequent use of basic terms such as "stimulus" and "response" was anything but precise and consistent, as he himself admitted (Watson, 1919, pp. 9–15). In fact, Watson's continual reliance on mechanical analogies in his published works served as a sort of verbal camouflage for the fact that the empiricism he espoused was more of an idealized prescription than a real description of his own work. This is partly what we mean when we speak of empiricism becoming the object of a cult: it was more praised in omission than honored by commission. This point would be driven further home if we could take the time to analyze Watson's basically ad hoc, metaphorical, extrapolative use of the notion of the reflex and Pavlovian conditioning. Under present constraints, however, we shall simply invite the reader to consider Watson's views (1924, Chap. 12) on the reduction of personality to reflexology, and try to find an adequate evidential basis for his claims.

The postulation of objective technique and the focus (however fuzzy) on stimulus-response relations led naturally enough to the other major characteristics of Watsonian behaviorism—its peripheralism, its emphasis on learning, and its environmentalism (Koch, 1961; 1964, pp. 7–9). Even at the "periphery" of the organism, however, basic activity is not always so easily observed. As a consequence, Watson's assertion that certain "inner" responses (such as thinking) are effectively "represented" by various muscular movements (such as those of the larynx) was far less influential than his attempts to correlate external "stimuli" with subsequent overt physical "responses" (Watson, 1919, Chap. 9; 1924, Chap. 10). Thus, in practice, the classical behaviorist program led toward a radical shrinking of the range of topics for psychological investigation *and theorizing*, despite Watson's avowed intention to account for a broad spectrum of psychological phenomena, including thinking.

This constriction of the subject matter of psychology was furthered by the behaviorist emphasis on learning and on the influence of the environment. Coming from a background in animal psychology, Watson wanted to focus on the adaptation of the organism to its environment; and because he held certain utopian ideals about the improvement of the social order, he was also interested in the possibility of the prosocial, behavioral adaptation of the organism to an environment manipulated according to human design (see Morawski, 1982). It is not surprising, then, that Watson's psychology became almost entirely a psychology of acquired adaptive responding. But as behaviorism exerted more and more influence on the psychological scene, this emphasis on learning, and on the impact of the environment, became rather too preemptive, and psychologists began to overlook even the basic processes underlying their vaunted empiricism: for several decades, sensation and perception were methodologically taken for granted but theoretically and empirically ignored by the majority of American psychologists. Perhaps nothing illustrates so well the development of a naive, cult-like empiricism as this basically know-nothing attitude toward the fundamental processes underlying the acquisition of empirical knowledge.

New Links between Psychology and Philosophy

For some time now, we have been pointing our fingers at Watson's psychology. But, of course, classical behaviorism is something of the past, even if its legacy is not. Not all the evils of subsequent times can be laid directly at its door. The orthodoxy that controlled American psychology from the 1930s until (approximately) the mid-1950s was not Watsonian but "neobehaviorist"; and there were not one, but several forms of this orthodoxy (see Koch, 1959, 1964, 1976). It was under the aegis of these revisionist versions of behaviorism that the cult of empiricism achieved its most complete formulation and its practical dominion over American psychology. What is particularly remarkable, in view of the putative banishment of philosophy from psychology, is the way in which this formulation and domination was effected with the complicity of a certain kind of philosophy. By the 1930s, psychologists had apparently gained enough confidence in their new experimental discipline that they began to listen to philosophers once again, and they liked what they heard: for they listened to a group of philosophers—by and large, the Viennese logical positivists—who were speaking a dialect closely related to their own objectivistic language. That they were attracted to the neopositivist philosophers was natural enough. Given their common empiricist heritage, the behaviorists and logical positivists had a good deal in common. In fact, through the earlier influence of Watson on Bertrand Russell, and Russell's impact on the logical positivists, there was an actual historical link between behaviorism and logical positivism (Smith, 1981). It is not surprising, then, that logical positivism provided support for the major orientations of the newly developing versions of behaviorism.

Indeed, it is only a slight caricature to represent neobehaviorism as the product of the remarriage of psychology, in the guise of behaviorism, and philosophy, in the guise of logical positivism (Koch, 1961; 1964, p. 12). Although there were internal trends within behaviorism itself, as well as philosophical and methodological trends indigenous to the United States, that led toward the redefinition of the behaviorist program, the confluence of behaviorism and logical positivism constituted the major factor in the development of the orthodoxy that ruled American psychology for at least twenty years, and still remains a tangible, if somewhat less reputable, directive force. For a marriage of limited fertility, and a marriage in which one of the partners (logical positivism) retreated from its vows almost from the beginning, this is truly amazing. In fact, it is difficult to explain the abiding hold of the neopositivist philosophy of science without reference to the cult-like belief that the marriage inspired.

The first step toward understanding this resilient belief in the complex of assumptions propagated by the behaviorist-positivist alliance can be taken by examining the context within which the belief was generated in the first place. By the late 1920s and early 1930s, it had become apparent that the promise of classical behaviorism remained unfulfilled. Rather than solving all the intellectual problems of the discipline and curing the various practical problems of the world, behaviorism had failed even to silence the cacophony of voices within psychology. Although the general objectivistic orientation of behaviorism had gained a wide range of adherents, other "schools of psychology" had continued to develop throughout the 1920s (see Heidbreder, 1933; Murchison, 1926, 1930; Woodworth, 1931). Objectivism in data collection was one thing; agreement about specific modes of objectivism, and about the theoretical implications of "objective" data, was something else. What was needed was some sort of "decision procedure" (see Koch, 1959, p. 371ff.; 1964, p. 9ff.), by which psychologists could reach agreement not only about the specifics of methodological procedure, but also about the appropriateness and definition of theoretical terms and the proper conduct of theoretical discourse. In the midst of apparent conceptual anarchy, even those who had banished speculative, metaphysical theory from psychology decided that psychologists had to adopt some sort of technique for reaching consensus about the meaning of their empirical results.

Within this context, logical positivism satisfied the needs of the moment. First of all, it passed inspection by being as virulently antimetaphysical as the most dogmatic form of behaviorism. At the foundation of the logical positivist program was the belief that all statements are either analytic (and thus tautological), empirical (and thus verified by observation), or meaningless (Carnap, 1932/1959a). As a result, according to the original logical positivist creed, theoretical statements were either logical tautologies, propositions reducible to empirical content, or nonsense. Any theories exceeding (even if not contradicting) the restrictive domain of verified observation were consigned to the latter category. This included carefully conjectural considerations of fundamental issues as well as out-and-out metaphysical speculations about the nature of the mind, organism, behavior, and so on—the kind of speculations that typified early (as well as later) theoretical discourse in the natural and biological sciences. Thus, the "new philosophy," which had modeled itself on a particular conception of science, legitimized (we might have said "sanctified") the empiricism of "objective" psychology. Psychologists were only too eager to pledge allegiance to this new code since it seemed to provide a program by which they could finally achieve scientific—not to mention philosophical—respectability. It had become only too embarrassing for them to contemplate the empirical state of affairs in their less than unified and progressive discipline.

In corroborating the behaviorists' emphasis on objectivism, logical positivism offered a specific criterion by which the meaning of terms could be empirically defined. "Physicalism," as the logical positivists defined it, entailed the formulation of a data-base language in which all terms could be defined by reference to intersubjectively observable, physical objects and events. This criterion formalized the behaviorists' own objectivistic leaning and made it prescriptive for all the sciences. As a result, it brought psychology (at least potentially) within the fold of so-called "unified science." One of the major logical positivists, Rudolf Carnap (1932/ 1959b), applied the physicalist criterion directly to psychology, admitting that the successful adoption of such a criterion would depend upon the open-mindedness of psychologists who might well have an "emotional resistance" to the prospect of a physicalistic psychology.

The neobehaviorists, of course, had no such emotional reaction. The message of physicalism seemed to corroborate not only their own unsophisticated objectivism, but also the recent proclamation of operationalism by the Harvard physicist Percy W. Bridgman (1927). This operationalism had a substantial impact on American psychologists. Early on, it was reflected in the methodological orientation of E. G. Boring (1933); later, it was given influential formulation by S. S. Stevens (1935a, 1935b, 1939); and under the joint inspiration of neorealist philosophy, it led to the tradition of "intervening variables" begun by E. C. Tolman (1935, 1936) and relied upon by Clark Hull (1943a). Strengthened and justified by its fusion with the meaning-criterion of early logical positivist philosophy of science, the influence of the operationalist approach to the definition of theoretical terms can be seen in American psychology to this very day, despite the criticism and recantations of the former promoters of orthodox logical positivism (Koch, 1964, 1976).

Indeed, by the mid-1930s, Carnap (1936–1937) and other neopositivist philosophers of science (e.g., Hempel, 1935/1949) had begun to realize that their early interpretation of the criterion of meaning, especially as applied to psychology, was unrealistic, and they continued to liberalize the logical positivist position—almost beyond recognition—over the subsequent decades (see Hempel, 1950; Toulmin,

1969, 1977). But as Sigmund Koch (1964, pp. 21–25) has noted, this liberalization was hardly noticed, much less imitated, by the neobehaviorists and their successors, who held (and continue to hold) on to earlier operationalistic conceptions in a manner that can only be described as wish-fulfilling (or fetishistic). As Smith (1981) has pointed out, several of the leading logical positivists have admitted that "progress in psychology has been impeded by the influence of the earlier strict versions of the meaning criterion" (p. 36; see Carnap, 1956, p. 70; Feigl, 1951, pp. 201, 204–205).

The logical positivist creed also offered the neobehaviorists a view of scientific laws that helped psychologists resolve their uncertainty about the structure of theoretical discourse. The logical positivist prescription for a theory appeared in different variations (see Suppe, 1977), but all these variations required that a theory be capable of being "rationally reconstructed" into a deductive form. Working from the top down, scientific theories (in this general conception) must provide a set of statements from which the pertinent empirical phenomena can be deduced. In practical terms, scientific theories should be composed of fundamental laws or hypotheses that are asserted as postulates. From these, lower-level theorems should be deducible by the strict application of the rules of logic and/or mathematics. These theorems should then be testable by experiment (in the course of which scientists should use physicalist [translate: operational] modes of definition). In summary, proper scientific theory should constitute a hypothetico-deductive system.

As is well known, Clark Hull (1943b, 1951, 1952) became the major advocate of this form of theorizing in psychology. Indeed, he made it the supreme goal of psychological science. Without a hypothetico-deductive system of theory, he was convinced, psychology would be no science at all. He believed this, we should point out, despite the evidence of history which attests to an almost unending panoply of "scientific" forms. If Hull used Newtonian science as the prototype of a hypothetico-deductive system, he might just as well have used it, in another of its aspects, as the prototype of an empirico-inductive discipline (see Guerlac, 1965; Schofield, 1970, esp. Chap. 1). His acceptance of the logical positivist prescription of hypothetico-deductive systematization must be seen, on the historical evidence, as the acceptance of a corroboration of a personal viewpoint, not some timeless or necessary truth. Hull's own bias for logical, hierarchical explanations preceded his contact with logical positivism; indeed—unlike many of the psychologists who inherited his hypothetico-deductive zeal—he did not in his writings appeal to logical positivism for authority, nor is it clear that he was a keen student of the position (Smith, in press).

Through his station as a major teacher and leader at the Yale Institute of Human Relations, as well as through his influential publications, the hypothetico-deductive model achieved near hegemony in the heyday of neobehaviorism. Only when his own drastic revisions (Hull, 1951, 1952) of his own hypothetico-deductive system (Hull, 1943b) were published did his espousal of a radically logical, hierarchically structured, unified theory of psychology come to be seen as vastly premature at best (Koch, 1954). But in many ways Hull's philosophy of science endures, in somewhat attenuated form, to the present time—in the many minisystem models that have taken the place of his grand theory, in the prescribed format style for dissertations and journal articles, in the introductory chapters of psychology textbooks, and thus in the general lore of the field. And again, these conceptual straitjackets persist despite all the reactions, and all the developments, in the philosophy of science over the past decades.

There were, of course, some neobehaviorists who escaped the influence of the logical positivists. B. F. Skinner, for instance, took his inspiration from the older positivism of Ernst Mach (see Skinner, 1979, pp. 66–67). But this only means that his is an even sparer form of empiricism. Trying to banish not only metaphysics but also theory from his psychology, Skinner has relied on the most naive form of empiricism imaginable, assuming that the "facts" will speak for themselves. This is perhaps the ultimate expression of the cult of empiricism—of faith in the data. Ironically, such naive empiricism, precisely *because* it disavows its dependence upon the theoretical realm, is all the more likely to be a vehicle of unexamined metaphysical assumptions about the nature of the data, the organism, and the world.

In concluding this discussion of neobehaviorism, it is only proper to acknowledge that not all psychologists in America between the 1930s and 1950s were neobehaviorists. Yet it seems entirely safe to say that the neobehaviorists, particularly Hull, set the dominant tone for this period. Additionally, the general characteristics we have outlined—the antimetaphysical temper, the operationalist approach, and the hypothetico-deductive ideal—governed the activity of the majority of psychologists throughout this period, whether they were behaviorists or not. Clearly, there were exceptions. Egon Brunswik (1943, 1947), for example, rejected the hypothetico-deductive ideal, even though he accepted the other basic tenets of neobehaviorism. But the exceptions proved the rule. Although Brunswik was highly respected, his critique was neither understood nor accepted. Even nonbehaviorists, such as Kurt Lewin (1943), rejected Brunswik's criticism of the dominant prescription. Yet from an historical perspective we can see once again that the dominant prescription was just that: a prescription. Since the publication of the multivolumed *Psychology: A Study of a Science* (Koch, 1959–1963), it has been clear that much of the theorizing that had been going on in psychology had not conformed to the requirements of hypothetico-deductive systematization (see Koch, 1959). Nor for that matter had psychologists really avoided all metaphysical commitments; nor had they always utilized—or even believed—in the lore about operationalism! But this acknowledgment was rather tardy. During the "age of theory" (Koch, 1959), psychologists had not so readily confessed their sins against the god of Empiricism.

The Cult of Empiricism and Its Results

With all the foregoing as historical background, we can now (finally) explore several features of what we are here calling the "cult" of empiricism among American psychologists. Although we have already suggested a number of reasons for referring to a cult of empiricism, we should once and for all justify our deliberate choice of a prejudicial word. To recapitulate and expand our argument: among experimental psychologists in the United States from roughly the 1920s on, a commitment to "empiricism" rapidly became something which (like the doctrine of the Trinity) it was more important to accept than to understand. These experimental psychologists came to regard theoretical questions that were not tied directly to the analysis of "controlled experiments" as self-discrediting: self-discrediting as arguments, since their nonempirical origins were sufficient to demonstrate their emptiness; and self-discrediting even as speech acts, since any psychologist who spent time on such irrelevant matters would be talking evident nonsense and so be professionally unsound. And this was something that had never happened, either in physics after 1650, or in biology after 1780. Newton and Leibniz, Bichat and Müller, Helmholtz and Bernard had all had broad and highly philosophical interests.

Stepping back from our earlier historical survey, we want now to present a conceptual overview and analysis of this cult of empiricism. We shall argue that this cult rested on three distinguishable but connected strands of argument. These had to do (1) with the nature and purpose of "scientific" observations and, more specifically, with the purpose of "controlling" those observations; (2) with the need to limit theoretical hypotheses and constructions to those arising out of, and securely supported by, the results of "controlled observations"; and (3) with the prize that could seemingly be won only by confining oneself to this particular empirical model, viz., universality (which would be expressed, for most of the neobehaviorists, as some sort of law in the upper reaches of a hypothetico-deductive system). Only those who stuck to narrowly controlled experimental procedures (it was believed) could hope to formulate theories guaranteed to apply to all human beings (not to mention animals), regardless of all the diversities associated with cultural variations and historical changes.

Once these three claims are set out separately in this way, it becomes clear why one must speak of this as a cult of "empiricism" rather than of "experimental method." Since the time of Francis Bacon—long before the advent of logical positivism—items 2 and 3, in particular, have been essential elements within the tradition of *philosophical* empiricism. Empiricist philosophers have repeatedly claimed that controlled observations alone, as prescribed under item 2, provide the indispensable means to achieve universalizable results, as specified in item 3. The empiricist formula for establishing universal generalizations has been, precisely, to confine theoretical speculation to the results of controlled observation. Furthermore, while we can distinguish these three elements in the program of American

607

experimental psychology in retrospect, they were originally conceived as three aspects of a single program, and in actual practice they worked together. According to this program, as we have seen, it was assumed that psychology could make progress as a science only by taking three closely related steps. First, psychologists had to cut themselves loose from all the verbiage of earlier philosophical speculation; next, they had to create for themselves a theoretical tabula rasa—an empty field or flat conceptual space, awaiting the erection of some vast and disinfected scientific emporium; and, finally, they had to throw up new "logical constructions" de novo, as building material became available from controlled experiments.

In the last fifty years, the discussion among psychologists about "theory construction" (to use a phrase that is unknown in physics and biology) has gone through two successive phases, both of which have been influenced by arguments within neopositivist philosophy of science and inductive logic. In the first place, as we have seen, American experimental psychologists followed the recipes for theory construction put forward by such philosophers as Rudolf Carnap and C. G. Hempel in their debates, e.g., about the legitimacy of using "intervening variables" in psychological explanations and theories. What was called "theory construction" had thus, in actual fact, nothing to do with the older traditions of scientific theorizing as developed by physicists and biologists. Instead, it represented a kind of "logical construction" of more complex propositions out of simpler ones, according to models set out by Gottlob Frege, Bertrand Russell, and their successors in the program of twentieth-century symbolic logic (Toulmin, 1969).

For the time being, it escaped the notice of working psychologists that the positivist account of natural science was a formal logicians' fiction and had only a very limited application to real-life science. It could not be applied to contemporary physics: Carnap himself (1950), for instance, refused to address questions about quantum mechanics, on the ground that the quantum theory had never been "formulated according to the rigorous standards of modern logic" (p. 243). And it gave an impoverished account of biology: Carl Hempel (1965), for instance, dismissed Darwin's theory of evolution as not really being "scientific" at all, at least by the formal standards of logical empiricism (p. 370). Since they allied themselves with a particularly narrow and dogmatic school of philosophers, then, it is not surprising if the psychologists' own results were themselves narrowly dogmatic. In the extreme case, only those theoretical statements that could be "logically constructed" out of observational measurements alone were regarded as "well-founded" in experience; and it became the ambition of some, following Hull's example, to leap directly to a theory of psychological phenomena as fully axiomatic as Newton's theory of dynamics in the *Principia*.

Subsequently, from the mid-1950s on, many psychologists became disappointed at the scanty results achieved as a consequence of all this "theory construction" and "axiomatization." They also wanted to escape from the dominance of the neobehaviorists and began to espouse pluralism in the methods and concepts of psychology. This was, in its own way, a promising enough move. If their pluralism had been grounded in a proper understanding of the relations between the methodologies of the different branches of psychology—like the understanding that validates, for example, the division of authority in biology between cell biology, general physiology, developmental biology, and evolution theory—all might yet have been well. But that would have meant confronting the problems of psychology head on, and analyzing them in their own terms—i.e., generating a truly *theoretical* account of those problems. Most psychologists were not yet ready to do so. Instead, they were content to go on as before, taking as their guide and authority the outdated words of logicians and philosophers of science, rather than the digested fruit of their own experience. Then, under the influence of T. S. Kuhn's *Structure of Scientific Revolutions* (1962), the move toward pluralism quickly lapsed into a shallow relativism—"You choose your paradigm, and leave me to choose mine." This second phase is, of course, still with us.

Meanwhile, the other two elements in the empiricist program have also generated lasting difficulties of their own. These requirements were (to recall) the necessity to perform only "controlled" experiments and the desirability of achieving "universality" in the resulting generalizations. On the one hand, the recipe for "controlling" psychological experiments was commonly interpreted as requiring the elimination of all external, situational cues by which experimental subjects might be led to attribute "meaning" to the stimuli that were the subject matter of experiments. On the other hand, the goal of "universality" was typically construed as requiring psychologists to begin by abstracting from all possible historical epochs and cultures, with the intention of eliminating all the local or temporary (and so presumably *non*universalizable) influences that are the subject matter of "cultural psychology," or *Völkerpsychologie*.

The first of these demands explains the widespread emphasis, found in much American experimental psychology since the 1920s, on the need for experimental arrays of stimuli or attributes to be purely *arbitrary*—i.e., thought up ad hoc by the experimenter. Only such arbitrary experimental material was supposedly controllable enough to yield "objective" results. Only in this way, it seemed, could experiments be insulated from the extraneous influence of current preexisting "meanings" and associations. Unfortunately, this demand for "culture-free" observations had the effect of destroying the entire "sense" of the material under investigation. In particular, it prevented experimental psychologists from considering how any given body of experimental material related to the larger-scale human enterprises from which it drew its significance in actual practice. A classic illustration is provided by Clark Hull's (1920) study of concept formation, which utilized arbitrary Chinese characters as experimental stimuli. More recent is the account given by W. C. Holz and N. H. Azrin (1966) in their survey article, "Conditioning Human Verbal Behavior." This article attempted to provide an exhaustive account of recent research on the subject, and the authors set out to achieve true "objectivity" by dint of

609

rejecting all observations that had not been totally shielded from all extraneous contextual cues. The result of insisting on this demand for absolute objectivity was striking and drastic: Holz and Azrin found themselves with nothing to report aside from experiments on meaningless vocalizations—e.g., the learning of nonsense syllables, the utterances of lunatics, and techniques for improving subjects' capacity to articulate sibilants!

As for the second demand (that experimental psychology should guarantee its own universality by abstracting in advance from all possible cultural differences), this requirement has tended, in practice, to blind experimental psychologists to *actual* "cultural universals," and these are now proving to be of considerable significance. In this respect, indeed, the novel methods of investigation of actual constancies in human nature developed by the crosscultural psychologists—e.g., Brent Berlin and Paul Kay (1969) and Eleanor Rosch (1973, 1977, 1978) in their studies on color perception and categorization (see Mervis & Rosch, 1981, for a review)—represent a major break with the assumptions underlying much American experimental psychology since the 1920s. If many of the people involved in this novel crosscultural work have come to experimental psychology from cultural anthropology or animal-behavior studies, that is no accident. For the new field of "crosscultural psychology" successfully straddles Wundt's dividing line between "experimental psychology" and "cultural psychology." And this gives us a way of moving not only beyond the narrower limits set by Wundt's American successors but also outside the more generous limits set by Wilhelm Wundt himself.

Beyond Wundt and Beyond the Cult of Empiricism: Toward a More Unified and Expansive Conception of Psychology

Wilhelm Wundt (as we have seen) understood cultural psychology, on the one hand, and experimental psychology, on the other, to be concerned with phenomena that could be distinguished and separated *in advance*. Some human mental activities and functions lent themselves, in Wundt's eyes, to experimental study, while others lent themselves rather to historico-cultural investigation; and, once this division had been clearly made, there was no way of going back on it. By contrast, the crosscultural psychologists of the 1970s and 1980s see experimental psychology itself as having something to learn from the results of anthropological studies. Instead of *abstracting* from all possible cultures and so losing the significance of all "meanings," the crosscultural psychologists seek to *generalize* from all actual cultures and so to discover what "meanings" are in fact universal, and so, generalizable. Eleanor Rosch's (1973) work on "salient colors," following Berlin and Kay's (1969) pioneer work in the linguistics of color, is an excellent example. What it illustrates is that by making a preliminary digression into *Völkerpsychologie*, we are not banishing ourselves from experimental psychology in perpetuity. On the contrary, we may subsequently be able to come back out of *Völkerpsychologie* into experimental psychology and enrich it with new discoveries of kinds that were precluded both by Wundt's dichotomization of psychology and by the traditional methodology of experimental psychology in America.

To spell this point out more clearly: the experimental psychology that has lent itself to an honest marriage with cultural anthropology, and so helped to create the crosscultural psychology of the present day, is not the dogmatic, positivistic psychology of the 1920s to 1950s. It is not, in other words, the psychology that had condemned itself to incoherence and meaninglessness as a result of its own chosen methods and assumptions. Rather, it is the more modest experimentalism that had originated in the psychophysics of Weber and Fechner and in the sensory psychology (the so-called "physiological optics") of Hermann von Helmholtz, before being taken up and developed by Wundt and his contemporaries. For in psychology, as in physics and biology earlier, a sufficiently unpretentious experimentalism allied to clearheaded analytical arguments (philosophical, conceptual, or theoretical, call them what you will) was quite capable of keeping out of trouble. And the experimental procedures of (say) a Helmholtz can usefully be taken into the field and employed for the purpose of crosscultural inquiries, in New Guinea or Nigeria as well as in New Hampshire or Nebraska.

In this respect at least, we have at last reached a point at which Wundt's two separate research programs for psychology are beginning to come together. It is reasonable to hope that, from now on, those who are concerned with the study of the cultural aspects of higher mental functioning will, increasingly, take with them into the field methods of inquiry developed by the experimental psychologists. Conversely, we can hope and expect that the outcomes of their cultural investigations will, increasingly, feed back illuminating concepts and generalizations suitable for study within the experimental laboratory. If this occurs, the dividing line between the two classes of mental functions and activities that lend themselves to investigation by experimental and historico-cultural methods, respectively, will be seen to be a good deal more fuzzy and blurred than Wundt originally assumed.

Even more subversive, from the standpoint of hardline experimental methodology, is another conclusion to which the new crosscultural psychology has recently been leading. To quote an observation by Eleanor Rosch (1978):

> When a context is not specified in an experiment, people [i.e., experimental subjects] must contribute their own context. Presumably . . . in the absence of specified context, subjects assume what they consider the normal context or situation for the occurrence of that object [i.e., the situation or stimulus under experimental investigation] (pp. 42–43).

If these observations are correct, then all the precautions that hardheaded American experimental psychologists have relied on since the 1920s in order to ensure the "objectivity" of experimental material by insulating it against extraneous associa-

611

tions have been in vain. For the only effect of these precautions has been to drive experimental subjects back to their unanalyzed assumptions about "the normal contexts" and the actual patterns of events in daily life that lead us to impute "meanings" to objects. In short, the emergence of crosscultural psychology makes it not merely *possible* to bring back into experimental psychology material from which it has been cut off for quite some time: it makes it *compulsory* to do so.

At the same time, with reference to the residual dogmatic empiricism that is the legacy of the neobehaviorist era, we can hope and expect that an increased freedom of thought will typify future psychology. We are not thinking here of a lazy, undisciplined, relativistic approach to psychological theory. Empiricism has its own legitimate role, as does the quest for universality. The search for empirically grounded theories of broad scope has characterized science in all its many forms. But there needs to be room for the creative play of the scientific imagination. History abounds with instances of important empirical observations that were made only after—and on account of—the formulation of significant theoretical insights. To cite one example alone: John Hughlings Jackson's important discoveries regarding the neurophysiological correlates of aphasia were dependent upon Jackson's belief in Herbert Spencer's theory of evolutionary associationism (Young, 1970, Chap. 6). In addition, there needs to be room for serious thinking about the fundamental (including metaphysical) issues that underlie the field of psychology. Even Ernst Mach (1896), the arch-positivist, insisted that great scientific investigations could be "carried out only by a [person] who is inspired by a great and philosophically most profound view of the world" (p. 240). In recent years, in some of the "harder" areas of psychology (e.g., Eccles, 1953; Pribram, 1971; Sperry, 1969), serious reflection of the sort we are suggesting has begun to take place. This is a trend that deserves to continue.

One last comment: it is not only *thinking* that suffered because of American psychology's cult of empiricism. As we have tried to indicate, empiricism itself suffered because of the rigid, experimental fetters that were placed upon it. Surely there should be room too for a retreat, at least by some, from *experimental* empiricism. All science, and probably all speculation, originates at a more basic level of empiricism: the level of experience. In a discipline that is often confused about its subject matter, it is not a bad idea to return to basic experience from time to time. The natural taxonomy that arises therefrom is much more likely to provide a useful framework for experimental work than the artificial taxonomies that structure so much of the field today.

REFERENCES

Ash, M. G. Wilhelm Wundt and Oswald Külpe on the institutional status of psychology: An academic controversy in historical context. In W. G. Bringmann & R. D. Tweney (Eds.), *Wundt studies*. Toronto: Hogrefe, 1980.

612

Berlin, B., & Kay, P. *Basic color terms: Their universality and evolution.* Berkeley, Calif.: University of California Press, 1969.

Blumenthal, A. L. *Language and psychology: Historical aspects of psycholinguistics.* New York: Wiley, 1970.

Blumenthal, A. L. A reappraisal of Wilhelm Wundt. *American Psychologist,* 1975, *30,* 1081–1088.

Blumenthal, A. L. The founding father we never knew. *Contemporary Psychology,* 1979, *24,* 547–550.

Blumenthal, A. L. Wilhelm Wundt—problems of interpretation. In W. G. Bringmann & R. D. Tweney (Eds.), *Wundt studies.* Toronto: Hogrefe, 1980.

Boring, E. G. *A history of experimental psychology.* New York: Century, 1929.

Boring, E. G. *The physical dimensions of consciousness.* New York: Century, 1933.

Boring, E. G. *A history of experimental psychology* (2nd rev. ed.). New York: Appleton-Century-Crofts, 1950.

Bridgman, P. W. *The logic of modern physics.* New York: Macmillan, 1927.

Bruner, J. S., & Allport, G. W. Fifty years of change in American psychology. *Psychological Bulletin,* 1940, *37,* 757–776.

Brunswik, E. Organismic achievement and environmental probability. *Psychological Review,* 1943, *50,* 255–272.

Brunswik, E. *Systematic and representative design of psychological experiments: With results in physical and social perception.* Berkeley, Calif.: University of California Press, 1947.

Burnham, J. C. On the origins of behaviorism. *Journal of the History of the Behavioral Sciences,* 1968, *4,* 143–151.

Carnap, R. The elimination of metaphysics through logical analysis of language. In A. J. Ayer (Ed.), *Logical positivism.* New York: Free Press, 1959. (Trans. by A. Pap from *Erkenntnis,* 1932, 2.) (a)

Carnap, R. Psychology in physical language. In A. J. Ayer (Ed.), *Logical positivism.* New York: Free Press, 1959. (Trans. by M. Black from *Erkenntnis,* 1932, 3.) (b)

Carnap, R. Testability and meaning. *Philosophy of Science,* 1936, *3,* 420–468; 1937, *4,* 1–40.

Carnap, R. *Logical foundations of probability.* Chicago: The University of Chicago Press, 1950.

Carnap, R. The methodological character of theoretical concepts. In H. Feigl & M. Scriven (Eds.), *The foundations of science and the concepts of psychology and psychoanalysis* (Minnesota Studies in the Philosophy of Science, Vol. 1). Minneapolis: University of Minnesota Press, 1956.

Crennan, C. H., & Kingsbury, F. A. Psychology in business. *Annals of the American Academy of Political and Social Science,* 1923, *110,* 1–232.

Danziger, K. The positivist repudiation of Wundt. *Journal of the History of the Behavioral Sciences,* 1979, *15,* 205–230.

Danziger, K. The history of introspection revisited. *Journal of the History of the Behavioral Sciences,* 1980, *16,* 241–262. (a)

Danziger, K. Wundt and the two traditions of psychology. In R. W. Rieber (Ed.), *Wilhelm Wundt and the making of a scientific psychology.* New York: Plenum, 1980. (b)

Danziger, K. Wundt's theory of behavior and volition. In R. W. Rieber (Ed.), *Wilhelm Wundt and the making of a scientific psychology.* New York: Plenum, 1980. (c)

Eccles, J. C. *The neurophysiological basis of mind.* Oxford: Clarendon, 1953.

Feigl, H. Principles and problems of theory construction in psychology. In W. Dennis, R. Leeper, H. F. Harlow, J. J. Gibson, D. Krech, D. McK. Rioch, W. S. McCulloch, & H. Feigl, *Current trends in psychological theory.* Pittsburgh: University of Pittsburgh Press, 1951.

Goldman, E. F. *Rendezvous with destiny: A history of modern American reform* (2nd rev. ed.). New York: Vintage, 1955.

Guerlac, H. Where the statue stood: Divergent loyalties to Newton in the eighteenth century. In E. R. Wasserman (Ed.), *Aspects of the eighteenth century.* Baltimore: Johns Hopkins Press, 1965.

Heidbreder, E. *Seven psychologies.* New York: Century, 1933.

Hempel, C. G. The logical analysis of psychology. In H. Feigl & W. Sellars (Eds.), *Readings in*

613

philosophical analysis. New York: Appleton-Century-Crofts, 1949. (Trans. by W. Sellars from *Revue de Synthese,* 1935, *10.*)

Hempel, C. G. Problems and changes in the empiricist criterion of meaning. *Revue Internationale de Philosophie,* 1950, *4,* 41–63.

Hempel, C. G. *Aspects of scientific explanation.* New York: Free Press, 1965.

Holt, E. B., Marvin, W. T., Montague. W. P., Perry, R. B., Pitkin, W. B., & Spaulding, E. G. The program and first platform of six realists. *Journal of Philosophy,* 1910, *7,* 393–401.

Holt, E. B., Marvin, W. T., Montague, W. P., Perry, R. B., Pitkin, W. B., & Spaulding, E. G. *The new realism.* New York: Macmillan, 1912.

Holz, W. C., & Azrin, N. H. Conditioning human verbal behavior. In W. K. Honig (Ed.), *Operant behavior: Areas of research and application.* New York: Appleton-Century-Crofts, 1966.

Hoorn, W. van, & Verhave, T. Wundt's changing conceptions of a general and theoretical psychology. In W. G. Bringmann & R. D. Tweney (Eds.), *Wundt studies.* Toronto: Hogrefe, 1980.

Hull, C. L. Quantitative aspects of the evolution of concepts. *Psychological Monographs,* 1920, *28* (No. 123).

Hull, C. L. The problem of intervening variables in molar behavior theory. *Psychological Review,* 1943, *50,* 273–291. (a)

Hull, C. L. *Principles of behavior.* New York: Appleton-Century-Crofts, 1943. (b)

Hull, C. L. *Essentials of behavior.* New Haven: Yale University Press, 1951.

Hull, C. L. *A behavior system.* New Haven: Yale University Press, 1952.

Koch, S. Clark L. Hull. In W. K. Estes, S. Koch, K. MacCorquodale, P. E. Meehl, C. G. Mueller, Jr., W. N. Schoenfeld, & W. S. Verplanck, *Modern learning theory.* New York: Appleton-Century-Crofts, 1954.

Koch, S. (Ed.). *Psychology: A study of a science* (6 vols.). New York: McGraw-Hill, 1959–1963.

Koch, S. Epilogue. In S. Koch (Ed.), *Psychology: A study of a science* (Vol. 3). New York: McGraw-Hill, 1959.

Koch, S. Behaviourism. *Encyclopaedia Britannica,* 1961, *3,* 326–329.

Koch, S. Psychology and emerging conceptions of knowledge as unitary. In T. W. Wann (Ed.), *Behaviorism and phenomenology.* Chicago: The University of Chicago Press, 1964.

Koch, S. Language communities, search cells, and the psychological studies. In W. J. Arnold & J. K. Cole (Eds.), *Nebraska Symposium on Motivation, 1975.* Lincoln: University of Nebraska Press, 1976.

Kuhn, T. S. *The structure of scientific revolutions.* Chicago: The University of Chicago Press, 1962.

Leahey, T. H. The mistaken error: On Wundt's and Titchener's psychologies. *Journal of the History of the Behavioral Sciences,* 1981, *17,* 273–282.

Leary, D. E. The philosophical development of the conception of psychology in Germany, 1780–1850. *Journal of the History of the Behavioral Sciences,* 1978, *14,* 113–121.

Leary, D. E. Wundt and after: Psychology's shifting relations with the natural sciences, social sciences, and philosophy. *Journal of the History of the Behavioral Sciences,* 1979, *15,* 231–241.

Leary, D. E. The historical foundation of Herbart's mathematization of psychology. *Journal of the History of the Behavioral Sciences,* 1980, *16,* 150–163. (a)

Leary, D. E. German idealism and the development of psychology in the nineteenth century. *Journal of the History of Philosophy,* 1980, *18,* 299–317.(b)

Leary, D. E. Immanuel Kant and the development of modern psychology. In W. R. Woodward & M. G. Ash (Eds.), *The problematic science: Psychology in nineteenth-century thought.* New York: Praeger, 1982.

Lewin, K. Defining the "field at a given time." *Psychological Review,* 1943, *50,* 292–310.

Mach, E. *Die Principien der Wärmlehre.* Leipzig: Barth, 1896.

Mervis, C. B., & Rosch, E. Categorization of natural objects. In M. R. Rosenzweig & L. W. Porter (Eds.), *Annual Review of Psychology* (Vol. 32). Palo Alto, Calif.: Annual Reviews, Inc., 1981.

Métraux, A. Wilhelm Wundt und die Institutionalisierung der Psychology. *Psychologische Rundschau,* 1980, *21,* 84–98.

Mischel, T. Wundt and the conceptual foundations of psychology. *Philosophy and Phenomenological Research,* 1970, *31,* 1–26.

Morawski, J. G. Assessing psychology's moral heritage through our neglected utopias. *American Psychologist,* 1982, 37, 1082–1095.

Münsterberg, H. *On the witness stand: Essays on psychology and crime.* New York: McClure, 1908.

Münsterberg, H. *Psychology and the teacher.* New York: Appleton, 1909. (a)

Münsterberg, H. *Psychotherapy.* New York: Moffat, Yard, & Co., 1909. (b)

Münsterberg, H. *Psychology and industrial efficiency.* Boston: Houghton Mifflin, 1913.

Münsterberg, H. *Psychology and social sanity.* New York: Doubleday, Page, & Co., 1914.

Murchison, C. (Ed.). *Psychologies of 1925.* Worcester, Mass.: Clark University Press, 1926.

Murchison, C. (Ed.). *Psychologies of 1930.* Worcester, Mass.: Clark University Press, 1930.

O'Donnell, J. M. The crisis of experimentalism in the 1920s: E. G. Boring and his use of history. *American Psychologist,* 1979, 34, 289–295. (a)

O'Donnell, J. M. *The origins of behaviorism: American psychology, 1870–1920* (Doctoral dissertation, University of Pennsylvania, 1979). *Dissertation Abstracts International,* 1979, 40, 3493A. (University Microfilm No. 79-28159.) (b)

Pribram, K. H. *Languages of the brain.* Englewood Cliffs, N.J.: Prentice-Hall, 1971.

Richards, R. J. Wundt's early theories of unconscious inference and cognitive evolution in their relation to Darwinian biopsychology. In W. G. Bringmann & R. D. Tweney (Eds.), *Wundt studies.* Toronto: Hogrefe, 1980.

Rosch, E. On the internal structure of perceptual and semantic categories. In T. E. Moore (Ed.), *Cognitive development and the acquisition of language.* New York: Academic Press, 1973.

Rosch, E. Human categorization. In N. Warren (Ed.), *Studies in cross-cultural psychology* (Vol. 1). London: Academic Press, 1977.

Rosch, E. Principles of categorization. In E. Rosch & B. B. Lloyd (Eds.), *Cognition and categorization.* Hillsdale, N.J.: Erlbaum, 1978.

Samelson, F. Putting psychology on the map: Ideology and intelligence testing. In A. R. Buss (Ed.), *Psychology in social context.* New York: Irvington, 1979.

Samelson, F. Struggle for scientific authority: The reception of Watson's behaviorism, 1913–1920. *Journal of the History of the Behavioral Sciences,* 1981, *17,* 399–425.

Schofield, R. *Mechanism and materialism.* Princeton, N.J.: Princeton University Press, 1970.

Singer, E. A., Jr. Mind as an observable object. *Journal of Philosophy, Psychology, and Scientific Methods,* 1911, *8,* 180–186.

Skinner, B. F. *The shaping of a behaviorist.* New York: Knopf, 1979.

Smith, L. D. Psychology and philosophy: Toward a realignment, 1905–1935. *Journal of the History of the Behavioral Sciences,* 1981, *17,* 28–37.

Smith, L. D. Purpose and cognition: The limits of neorealist influence on Tolman's psychology. *Behaviorism,* 1982, *10,* 151–163.

Smith, L. D. *Behaviorism and logical positivism: A revised account of the alliance.* Stanford, Calif.: Stanford University Press, in press.

Sperry, R. W. A modified concept of consciousness. *Psychological Review,* 1969, 76, 532–536.

Stevens, S. S. The operational basis of psychology. *American Journal of Psychology,* 1935, 47, 323–330. (a)

Stevens, S. S. The operational definition of psychological concepts. *Psychological Review,* 1935, 42, 517–527. (b)

Stevens, S. S. Psychology and the science of science. *Psychological Bulletin,* 1939, 36, 221–263.

Suppe, F. (Ed.). *The structure of scientific theories* (2nd rev. ed.). Urbana, Ill.: University of Illinois Press, 1977.

III. PSYCHOLOGY AND ITS INTERSECTING DISCIPLINES

Tolman, E. C. Psychology versus immediate experience. *Philosophy of Science*, 1935, 2, 356–380.

Tolman, E. C. Operational behaviorism and current trends in psychology. In *Proceedings of the twenty-fifth anniversary celebration of the inauguration of graduate studies at the University of Southern California*. Los Angeles: University of Southern California Press, 1936.

Toulmin, S. From logical analysis to conceptual history. In P. Achinstein & S. F. Barker (Eds.), *The legacy of logical positivism*. Baltimore: Johns Hopkins Press, 1969.

Toulmin, S. *Human understanding* (Vol. 1). Princeton, N.J.: Princeton University Press, 1972.

Toulmin, S. The structure of scientific theories. In F. Suppe (Ed.), *The structure of scientific theories* (2nd rev. ed.). Urbana, Ill.: University of Illinois Press, 1977.

Toulmin, S. The Mozart of psychology. *New York Review of Books*, September 28, 1978, pp. 51–57.

Toulmin, S., & Goodfield, J. *The architecture of matter*. New York: Harper & Row, 1962.

Tweney, R. D., & Yachanin, S. A. Titchener's Wundt. In W. G. Bringmann & R. D. Tweney (Eds.), *Wundt studies*. Toronto: Hogrefe, 1980.

Watson, J. B. Psychology as the behaviorist views it. *Psychological Review*, 1913, 20, 158–177.

Watson, J. B. *Psychology from the standpoint of a behaviorist*. Philadelphia: Lippincott, 1919.

Watson, J. B. *Behaviorism*. New York: Norton, 1924.

Watson, J. B. Autobiography. In C. Murchison (Ed.), *A history of psychology in autobiography* (Vol. 3). Worcester, Mass.: Clark University Press, 1936.

Wiebe, R. H. *The search for order, 1887–1920*. New York: Hill & Wang, 1967.

Woodward, W. R. Wundt's program for the new psychology: Vicissitudes of experiment, theory, and system. In W. R. Woodward & M. G. Ash (Eds.). *The problematic science: Psychology in nineteenth-century thought*. New York: Praeger, 1982.

Woodworth, R. S. *Contemporary schools of psychology*. New York: Ronald, 1931.

Wundt, W. *Beiträge zur Theorie der Sinneswahrnehmung*. Leipzig: Winter, 1862.

Wundt, W. *Vorlesungen über die Menschen- und Thierseele* (2 vols.). Leipzig: Voss, 1863.

Wundt, W. *Grundzüge der physiologischen Psychologie*. Leipzig: Engelmann, 1874.

Wundt, W. *Logik* (2 vols.). Stuttgart: Enke, 1880–1883.

Wundt, W. *Ethik*. Stuttgart: Enke, 1886.

Wundt, W. *System der Philosophie*. Leipzig: Engelmann, 1889.

Wundt, W. *Völkerpsychologie* (10 vols.). Leipzig: Engelmann, 1900–1920.

Wundt, W. *Die Psychologie im Kamp ums Dasein*. Leipzig: Kröner, 1913.

Young, R. M. *Mind, brain and adaptation in the nineteenth century*. Oxford: Clarendon, 1970.

SUPPLEMENTARY READINGS

Achinstein, P., & Barker, S. F. (Eds.). *The legacy of logical positivism*. Baltimore: Johns Hopkins Press, 1969.

Ayer, A. J. (Ed.). *Logical positivism*. New York: Free Press, 1959.

Bergmann, G. The contribution of John B. Watson. *Psychological Review*, 1956, 63, 265–276.

Borger, R., & Cioffi, F. (Eds.). *Explanation in the behavioural sciences*. Cambridge, England: Cambridge University Press, 1970.

Boring, E. G., Bridgman, P. W., Feigl, H., Israel, H. E., Pratt, C. C., & Skinner, B. F. Symposium on operationism. *Psychological Review*, 1945, 52, 241–294.

Bringmann, W. G., Bringmann, N. J., & Ungerer, G. A. The establishment of Wundt's laboratory: An archival and documentary study. In W. G. Bringmann & R. D. Tweney (Eds.), *Wundt studies*. Toronto: Hogrefe, 1980.

Brown, S. C. (Ed.). *Philosophy of psychology.* New York: Barnes & Noble, 1974.

Feigl, H. The Wiener Kreis in America. In D. Fleming & B. Bailyn (Eds.), *The intellectual migration: Europe and America, 1930–1960.* Cambridge, Mass.: Harvard University Press, 1969.

Feigl, H., & Blumberg, A. E. Logical positivism. *Journal of Philosophy,* 1931, 28, 281–296.

Feigl, H., & Brodbeck, M. (Eds.). *Readings in the philosophy of science.* New York: Appleton-Century-Crofts, 1953.

Feigl, H., & Scriven, M. (Eds.). *The foundations of science and the concepts of psychology and psychoanalysis* (Minnesota Studies in the Philosophy of Science, Vol. 1). Minneapolis: University of Minnesota Press, 1956.

26

The Logos of Psyche
PHENOMENOLOGICAL VARIATIONS ON A THEME

RICHARD M. ZANER

Introduction: Phenomenology as a Philosophical Tradition

Phenomenological philosophy and psychology have had a long and mutually deepening relationship over the past century. Not only Edmund Husserl, founder and still central figure of the phenomenological movement (see Spiegelberg, 1960), but many of the other major phenomenological thinkers (Gurwitsch, 1964, 1966; Goldstein, 1948; Straus, 1966; Merleau-Ponty, 1962; Sartre, 1956; Ricoeur, 1966, 1970) have had an abiding concern for the discipline of psychology. Indeed, there has been an impressively substantive influence of phenomenological writings on many of the social sciences since the mid-1960s in this country (Natanson, 1973a; Schutz, 1973). Despite all this, psychologists in the American milieu have for the most part known very little about phenomenology, whether intrinsically or actually, in terms of its relevance for psychological inquiry.

It thus seems appropriate to preface this essay with some consideration of phenomenology's specifically philosophical character. But there is, in fairness, another reason for such a preface. When reading phenomenological literature, the impression one often gets is that the method of "reduction and epoché," of which so much has been written, is not only impossibly difficult and complex, but that it is a frank embarrassment, an effrontery to cognition. Phenomenologists who write about this

618

method can seem, if not utterly obscurantist, then at least self-indulgent. The situation seems little better when it comes to such central concepts as "intentionality," "constitution," and still others. Space prohibits detailed discussion of such matters here (see Ricoeur, 1967; Zaner, 1970; Natanson, 1973b); nevertheless, it might be helpful to give some hints at least about the sense and aims of phenomenological philosophy.

The problem of method has loomed large in its literature, and it centers on the concepts of "epoché" and "reduction." Unlike what has come to be known as "reductivism" (e.g., in philosophy of science), the phenomenological "reduction" has nothing whatever to do with any effort to simplify or to economize, much less to explain one region of objects by trying to show that it is reducible to another (e.g., psychological processes to physiological ones). Rather, its meaning is to be found in the literal, etymological sense: a leading back to origins, to beginnings which have become obscure, hidden, or taken for granted. The fundamental idea is to throw light on a rudimentary and unquestioned "natural" commitment within each conscious subject to there being "the world" with all its multiple and varied objects, human and nonhuman, animate and inanimate. Not unlike what Santayana called "animal faith" (1923/1955), or Hume "belief" (1888), Husserl wrote of the "natural attitude" and its "general thesis" as fundamental to human consciousness. This "thesis" and its underlying "attitude" are not so much explicit judgments as they are expressive of a rudimentary stance toward "what is"—namely, *that* there is a "world" taken to be independent of human experience, and *that it is* over and above whatever may be "cancelled out" of it under the name of hallucination, illusion, deception, or error.

This fundamental attitude (*Einstellung*) at the root of our every experience of things (as things *within the world*) is an "attitude," i.e., an orientation toward things, a way of regarding which at every point implicitly *informs* our experience and awareness of them (that these "things" exist in the world around us, and more crucially that the world itself "is"). It is, moreover, "natural," i.e., it is expressive of the fundamental tendency of our consciousness to "posit" or "take a stance toward" whatever it may be that is encountered or experienced, and in whichever way it may be so encountered (perceptually, memorially, in anticipation, emotively, valuatively, judgmentally, reflectively, and so on). The phenomenological epoché and reduction is the systematic effort to bring that natural attitude itself into focus, to enable its deliberate and rigorous study as completely as possible.

To the extent that it is the inherent tendency of consciousness or mental life to "posit" or "take a stance toward" whatever it may be, any particular process or act of awareness is a specific "orientation" with respect to such "objects," and thus the latter always have a specific and determinable "sense" or "meaning" strictly correlated to the specific type of orientation at hand in any particular case. For instance, if one reaches for a vase when an intruder sneaks in, the vase has the sense "weapon." Or, while driving my injured son to the hospital and coming upon a red traffic light, I find that the light has the sense not only of "stop" (thanks to the context of traffic rules), but also of "critical interruption," possibly "disastrous," precisely as a correlative function of "what I am trying to do now" (get my son to medical help). That is to say, my "stance" toward such objects of awareness, in these specific circumstances, "constitutes" them as having a specific "sense" for me, but one wholly understandable by other persons (e.g., police officers). It is the same, the phenomenologist contends, for every actual and even every possible mode of awareness and its correlated object(s).

Thus, the phenomenologist insists (1) that every awareness (even the simplest) is not merely an awareness *of* something, but involves necessarily some modality of "positing" (*Positionalität*)—usually including not only a "belief" of some kind (e.g., that "there *is* the traffic light"), but also emotive ("it is disastrous"), valuative ("would it were not there!") and volitional ("I must press through it to the hospital") aspects. With careful focusing, these can and must be explicated *precisely as they present themselves* to our reflective regard, if we are to understand the full complexus of mental life and its remarkable variety of objects. But, (2) the phenomenologist also contends that every *awareness-of-something*, and *that-of-which* there is the awareness, are essentially *correlated*. Hence, to analyze any objectivity whatever commits one as well to the analysis of its correlated mode of awareness, through which that objectivity is at all presented or otherwise encountered, and in whichever way it may be. But also, to analyze any awareness (perception, memory, anticipation, judgment, symbolization, etc.) necessarily commits one to the analysis of its correlated objectivity. This awareness side (the *noesis*) has its objective correlate (the *noema*), and neither can be understood without the other. Nor is this all: for since every such experience is that of an embodied human being, the analysis must as well, at some point, delineate the specific modes of bodily awareness present in each case (see Zaner, 1981). This essential correlativity, or contextuality as it may be called, is what is expressed by the central phenomenological concept of intentionality (*Intentionalität*).

To be sure, most of the time we are not explicitly aware of things as they are presented through specific acts of consciousness, any more than we are explicitly aware of our own acts of awareness as consciousnesses of specific objective correlates and embodied in determinable ways in and by bodily attitudes, stances, movements, and the like. That is, our focal attention is for the most part captured by and directed simply to objects, and only rarely to *objects-as-meant* or *intended*. The methodical step expressed by "reduction" is designed expressly to enable the reflecting inquirer to bring that correlational a priori to explicit attention, so that it may be rigorously studied—for its own sake, and also in relation to other contexts of embodied awareness.

In different terms, the reduction is a *strictly methodical* step to enable the investigator *to make explicit* what is all along implicit and taken for granted by each of us. Thus, the philosopher's reflective attention must, as Henri Bergson once put it, "do violence" to our otherwise "natural" ways of thinking (see 1949, pp. 50–51): we must explicate (make explicit) what is taken for granted, hidden, habitual, in every dimension of human engagement. In these terms, phenomenology is at bottom an exercise in systematic *criticism*; it is a discipline of thought which, as should be clear, lies at the heart of every effort to know anything (see Zaner, 1970).

There is nothing magical or recondite about this cognitive effort. What is required to grasp and then explicate this "natural attitude" is to *shift one's focal attention* to it, specifically to the strictly correlational context of awareness/object-of-awareness/mode of embodiment—to probe and examine it with the resolve to stop at nothing or to "go to the things themselves," in Husserl's well-known phrase. This deliberate, explicitly adopted philosophical shift of cognitive attention is precisely what is to be understood as the "phenomenological epoché"; the resultant "orientation" or "attitude"—that self-consciously maintained resolve to reflect radically on whatever then presents itself, and just as it presents itself—is what is meant by the "reduction." With this, it becomes clear that there are a number of other possible shifts of attention, with their consequent reflective orientations (I may, e.g., focus solely on what is *actually* the case, or on what is essentially *possible*, or on what is *normatively* the case, etc.). The epoché and reduction thus signify only that one's focal attention has been shifted in order to view whatever complex of affairs it may be, to view it or them for their own sakes, and to explicate whatever is then found.

To the extent that a psychologist will focus only on a particular range of affairs (say, designing a personality test), it is perfectly clear that that inquiry is intrinsically *incomplete* as such, that it takes certain key things for granted. Thus, to design such a test presupposes a well-conceived idea of what constitutes "personality," what formal meaning is to be given to "test," and even whether "personality" is the sort of affair which can be "tested." Beyond that, it presupposes as clear as possible a range of application, that is, which human beings are specifically testable (children, retardates, those from other cultures, etc.). Clearly, the sort of inquiry which delineates the meaning of "personality" is at a *different level* than that which works out the test itself. As I suggest shortly, the work of conceptual clarification is philosophical, whether a philosopher or someone else actually attempts it. Thus, psychological inquiry relates directly to philosophical inquiry. Beyond this, of course, it is also presupposed that those who are "personalities" to be "tested" are human beings, and thus that there is conceptual clarity about that difficult topic. The point here is that the initial inquiry necessarily involves a crucial albeit usually unnoticed *decision to restrict* the field of objects (and, of course, the range of focal attentiveness) to just certain ones and not others—in this case, to *actual* human beings of specifiable sorts. Thus restricted, such a de facto inquiry is similarly restricted to only those sorts of evidences which are determinably appropriate to just those sorts of actual entities (see Zaner, 1972, 1973).

Noticing this decision to restrict the field of inquiry, however, makes it clear that

621

there are other *levels* of inquiry, levels whose epistemological sense is that they go to *complete* the inquiry. Thus, since every actuality is in one key sense a possibility which has been actualized, and since epistemic completeness ("knowledge") demands at some point that each level of inquiry be justified and made accountable, it is clear that the very sense of de facto restrictions demands completion at these other, more fundamental levels of inquiry. Every actual human being is also a possible human being; that is, the actual exemplifies the possible, and phenomenological philosophy seeks specifically to delineate the region of the purely possible—or of what Husserl called "essences" in the most unrestricted sense (see Zaner, 1978).

Epistemic completeness demands inquiry at other levels, and that level suggested above forms what phenomenologists term the "transcendental" level. It is, one hopes, clear that, however ethereal it might appear, any such study of the purely possible has a quite direct bearing on the study of the actual: if any possible human being must show certain features in order for it to be human, then so must actual human beings show these. Here, of course, complex and passionate issues arise: is an autistic child also a "person"? Is it a "self"? Is a fetus a "person," or only a "potential" person? And, if potential, what sense must we give to that: is it potential in the way a sleeping adult is potentially awake? Is a retarded person nevertheless a person and thus to be accorded all the moral and legal stature of "normal" persons? Do they have "personalities" and thus can they be "tested?"

But the reverse relation is also manifestly true: psychological inquiry has a direct bearing on philosophical inquiry. Since judgments about the purely possible, as also about justifiable concepts, concern every possible case, including actual ones, anything discovered in empirical inquiry can and does serve to illuminate philosophical inquiry. The point here is basic, and it is at the heart of the relationship of phenomenology to psychology: there is a profound *reciprocity* among all levels of inquiry, just as there is a profound reciprocity between actual and possible examples and that of which these examples are examples. More simply, philosophical and de facto levels of inquiry are epistemically bound in a continuum defined by increasing completeness inherent to the very idea of knowledge, but it is a continuum with inherent levels.

A final comment seems desirable. Phenomenologists often characterize their inquiries as transcendental, and some of them, following Husserl, go on to term them transcendental "idealism"—a claim which has led some to reject some of Husserl's ideas. At the same time, Husserl just as often spoke of phenomenology as a genuine "empiricism," and this has given other commentators a comparable case of the philosophic willies. Surely such labels can too easily become mere catchwords, stirring up much dust and conveying little of substance. For me, as I have tried to make clear (but with perhaps unpardonable brevity), phenomenology is quite properly conceived not only as transcendental idealism but also as a new empiricism—but such terms are admissible only if they carry the sense which Husserl gave to them.

It is transcendental because it is foundational inquiry: it seeks to uncover and explicate analytically the necessary presuppositions of every actual and possible object and mode of awareness—in this sense it seeks epistemic completeness, that demanded by our every effort to know anything at all in the first place. Ultimately, phenomenology seeks to explicate the grounds for philosophical reflection itself. It is therefore also "idealism" because, as criticism, it is obliged to turn to consciousness itself as a complex of acts and processes by and through which alone are objects of any and all types whatever presented, experienced, or otherwise made known to us. This, obviously, *in no way* entails the claim that objects are either "mental" or "reduced to consciousness"; to the contrary, objects are quite obviously for the most part transcendent (i.e., outside) consciousness, and a great many of them are quite clearly nonmental and are experienced precisely as such.

The "empiricist" feature consists in this: that this philosophy insists that positing anything beyond all possible experience of any kind is sheer nonsense, and that it is to the things themselves of experience, and precisely as experienced (in whatever way), that one must ultimately appeal for all evidence and knowledge. But it is a "new" empiricism, because "experience" is in no way restricted merely to sensory data, or even to sensory perception (as in traditional empiricism). Rather it becomes disclosed as manifestly richer and enormously more stratified and differentiated than any traditional empiricism could see: all modes of encounter are legitimately and necessarily included in "experience," whether they be visual, auditory, and the like, or emotive (to dislike something is to experience it in determinable ways), valuational, or volitional, or for that matter judgmental, memorial, imaginal, and so on. Human experience is plainly, richly complex and varied; to "go to the things themselves" thus requires that our understanding of the "things" of human experience be equally complex and varied. Phenomenology is thus ultimately the rigorous effort to reclaim the full reach and context of human life.

Phenomenology and Psychology

It is a point of no small significance for the understanding of phenomenological philosophy's relations with psychology to recognize that Edmund Husserl, the founder and still the central figure of phenomenology, came to his crucial decision to change his focal concern from mathematics to philosophy during his period of study with the psychologist Franz Brentano (see Brentano, 1955). While Husserl shortly became quite critical of Brentano's work, especially of his version of the intentionality of mental processes, it seems clear that it was Brentano who convinced him of the possibility and indeed the necessity of systematic inquiry into mental life for its own sake. Although Husserl's earliest concerns were to account for the foundations of mathematical operations and their specific, correlated objectivities, and then those of logic, his inquiries very quickly expanded to the point where he was able to claim that he had come upon a veritably new and densely populated territory, whose many promontories had occasionally been noted by other explorers, but whose manifold depths and interwoven connections had hardly been suspected.

In a clear sense, the key to his and subsequent phenomenologists' explorations is found in psychology's basic theme and task: to inquire rigorously and systematically, that is, *scientifically*, into the regions of *mental life*—to develop a *logos of psyche*, so far as possible strictly for its own sake (see Husserl, 1965). Only after having accomplished at least the essential lines of that project would it then be possible to take up the systematic study of the multiple and complex relations between mental life and other regions—corporeal phenomena, natural things, social configurations, and so on. It was Husserl's conviction that the kinds of inquiry needed to unravel the complex of material nature had pretty much been laid out, and that many lasting insights had already been achieved. He thus stood in profound admiration of the sciences of nature, of their hard-won explanatory insights and especially of their self-corrective and rigorous methods of inquiring into material, natural affairs. But he came to be convinced that a too-naive and unselfcritical acceptance of natural science on the part of too many psychologists and others had led them to an over-hasty belief that every other phenomenon could and must be approached with the same methods and conceptual framework as those belonging to material nature. That position was seen as a plain bias, uncritical and unjustifiable, for it presumes and does not demonstrate that the range of specifically mental phenomena are the same as, or are for purposes of knowledge precisely like, specifically material phenomena. And the work of Brentano, Stumpf, von Ehrenfels, Meinong, William James, and others, as well as his own early studies, convinced Husserl that that "naturalization of consciousness," that bias, was simply and deeply wrong. This set up, however, the critical issue: is it possible, and if it is, how is it possible, to gain access to mental life as it is in and for itself? For, as Wilhelm Dilthey had insisted in his classic, if nonetheless only, programmatic essay on descriptive and explanatory psychology, in 1894, only if there is such a demonstrable and defensible way of getting at "the mind" itself is psychology even conceivable, much less conceivable as "science" (see Dilthey, 1977). Researchers in the natural sciences had for a long time conducted their inquiries into physical, chemical, and biological affairs by systematically ignoring or disregarding all actual and possible relations between these and mental processes; it is now necessary, said Husserl, along with psychologists such as Brentano and Stumpf, to study the mind in a similar way—i.e., for its own sake and, so far as possible, independently of its actual and possible relations to the somatic and the physical.

However, while such a scientific project seemed secure as regards physical and biological nature, it appeared to those in the mainstream of philosophy and espe-, cially psychology to be a wholly improbable if not impossible and incoherent proposal as regards mental phenomena, despite the growing sense in the late nineteenth and early twentieth centuries that there were profoundly troublesome enigmas and paradoxes in the mainstream view of the matter.

It is worth noting, if only in passing, the historical irony in all this. It was the signal work of Descartes, in his bifurcation of reality into mind and matter, which at once secured the legitimacy of the Galilean mathematization of nature (see Husserl, 1962/1970), and, in a way, gave theoretical license to the subsequent developments leading clearly to the naturalization of consciousness—whether in subsequent dualisms or the varieties of idealisms and materialisms, all of which, as Hans Jonas has brilliantly shown (1966), are essentially children of the Cartesian parent. While it was the shadow if not the actual presence of that dualism which gave, and still gives, seeming force to the summary dismissal of the proposal to study mind—i.e., subjectivity—in and for itself, neither Descartes nor his empiricist critic, John Locke, had the least difficulty with that proposal (see Zaner, 1981). Nor, it is interesting to note, did others in the empiricist tradition. Thus Descartes not only was convinced that consciousness can be directly inspected, but he believed it was actually easier to do so than to study nature. Locke, too, claimed that it is the "understanding that sets man above the rest of sensible beings," and it must therefore be man's first and primary object of inquiry. Indeed, for him as, later, for Hume, to claim to know anything else is to presuppose that one knows that which knows that something else, and thus the sciences of the mind are seen by Hume as the central, indeed the paradigmatic ones. Locke especially appreciated that knowing one's own faculty of knowledge is difficult:

> The understanding, like the eye, whilst it makes us see and perceive all other things takes no notice of itself; and it requires art and pains to set it at a distance, and make it its own object. But whatever be the difficulties that lie in the way of this inquiry, whatever it be that keeps us so much in the dark to ourselves, sure I am that all the light we can let in upon our own minds, all the acquaintance we make with our own understandings, will not only be very pleasant, but bring us great advantage in directing our thoughts in the search of other things (Locke, 1959, pp. 25–26).

Still, by the time psychology began to see itself as a "science," notably in the nineteenth-century German physiological laboratories and then in this country, it is clear that this proposal was already anathema to mainstream thinkers and researchers. The mathematization of nature was now to be matched by an imitative mathematization of mind. Subsequent to the Galilean-Cartesian stripping away of nature to the bare-bones category of extension (i.e., quantity), and the resultant shunting of the rich, observably opulent other qualities of the experienced world into the dark dungeon of "mere subjectivity" (for not only was beauty thought to be "in the eye of the beholder," but practically everything else as well) (see Koyré, 1958), there followed the effort in psychology to naturalize consciousness: the "subjective" is knowable, if at all, only by reducing, translating, or otherwise forcibly rendering it amenable to the much-admired methods and concepts of the successful natural sciences. And thereby, Dilthey caustically remarked in 1894, psychology became a "theory" (*logos*) of the "soul" without a "soul" (*psyche*) (1977, p. 42).

******

Not so very long ago, Sigmund Koch echoed Husserl's and Dilthey's judgment, stressing with some melancholy perhaps but also with trenchancy that the discipline to which he has devoted so many years of study and work has in effect pursued a pipe dream:

> The test of the Millian hypothesis has not been a sleazy one. In my estimation, the hypothesis has been fulsomely disconfirmed. I think it by this time utterly and finally clear that *psychology cannot be a coherent science*, or indeed a coherent field of scholarship, in any specifiable sense of coherence that can bear upon a field of inquiry. It can certainly not expect to become *theoretically* coherent; in fact, it is now clear that no large subdivision of inquiry, including physics, can be (Koch 1973, p. 86).

Nor is Koch's judgment a sleazy one; his indictment of "scientific psychology" is neither unfounded nor uninformed, whatever one may think about the inquiries of physics. I think that both his criticisms of psychology and his own positive suggestions about its central tasks are not only sufficiently important to deserve critical attention, they will also help considerably in elucidating phenomenology's relation with psychology.

In the "Epilogue to Study I" of his classic, *Psychology: A Study of a Science* (1959, pp. 729–788), Koch contends that psychology's "age of theory" has been productive mainly of a "kind of pseudo-mathematized jargon" (p. 770), and it has been "permeated with an 'imagery' of hypothetico-deduction—the use or presence of which often seemed interpreted as equivalent to hypothetico-deductive practice" (p. 777). Through these and other "idols of the laboratory," as Suzanne Langer calls them in her splendid work on mind and feeling (1967, I, pp. 33–57), psychologists have seemed more concerned to imitate what was thought to be "real" laboratory science than they were to initiate careful studies conforming to their own specific objects of inquiry. As mentioned, such criticisms echo the earlier ones by Husserl and Dilthey. With Koch, however, there is a twist. Arguing that we now stand "at a grave impasse in the history of scholarship—indeed the history of intelligence," he makes a plea for rethinking the basic tasks of psychological studies along with those of the *humanities*, and especially their relationships. The latter, he argues:

626

. . . *should* be more like an identity than any other type of connection. The central psychological task is to disembed subtle relational unities within the flux of experience. That, too, is the central task of the humanist. Let each humanist construct his own psychology. Let each psychologist reconstruct his own humanity (1973, pp. 90, 91).

This must seem an alarming fate: to find oneself classed along with these loosely organized, conceptually cluttered, and pitiably funded "humanities," those (as James acidly remarked) "soft-headed" fields in which not only does science seem remote but even conceptual rigor, if anything, striking by its sheer absence! Part of the uneasiness any would-be scientist senses when faced with such a suggestion, of course, has to do with the peculiar status of the "humanities": few persons within or without seem to be able to present a convincing case for conceiving these as more than a sort of clustering for administrative and fiscal convenience, or sometimes by appeal to outmoded intellectual history. Here, but also for the reforming of psychology, Langer stresses:

The basic need is for powerful and freely negotiable concepts in terms of which to handle the central subject matter, which is human mentality—properly, and not foolishly, called "mind." But such concepts are still missing, or at least unrecognized; and as long as they are missing there will always be some primitive, scientifically useless entity—soul, entelechy, metaphysical Subject or vital essence—ready to slide into the vacant place to work havoc with the incipient science (1967, p. 51).

But there is a critical need as well, I believe, for gaining legitimate *access* to that subject matter, for without that there can be no hope for acquiring those "powerful and freely negotiable concepts," no way either to secure insights expressed through such concepts or even to make coherent sense. So far and so long as "mind"—that is, subjectivity—is regarded as either inaccessible to rational inquiry or accessible solely by means of reduction to and translation into terms other than its own, there follows the exclusion, or at a minimum the grievous distortion of the bulk of distinctively human life: feeling, symbols, concepts, fantasy, religion, speculation, personhood, morality, indeed science itself precisely inasmuch as it likewise is a specifically human activity involving all those characteristics and more—theorizing, judging, calculating, concluding, inferring, observing, thinking, talking, and so on. As Langer remarks, to exclude or distort such as these, "for the sake of sure and safe laboratory methods is to stifle human psychology in embryo" (1967, I, p. 38).

Thus, just as Husserl and other phenomenologists, Koch and Langer call for a thorough rethinking of the very sense and tasks of psychology. To accomplish that, however, phenomenologists have insisted, and Langer agrees, to use her words, ". . . means going back to the beginnings of thought and mental phenomena and

627

starting with different ideas, different expectations, without concern for experiments or statistics or formalized language . . ." (ibid.).

It may well be that after a "turbulent intellectual gestation period," as Langer put it (p. 52), psychology will not only be able to achieve a genuinely scientific stature, it may merge with others of the sciences as mature disciplines. It is, however, equally possible that that labor will demonstrate that mental and sociocultural phenomena will turn out to be more akin to those of history, jurisprudence, politics, or art theory—all highly developed disciplines, but as Dilthey came to believe and as is now advocated by Paul Ricoeur (1970), more interpretative and *hermeneutical* than "natural scientific." In that event, the "commitment to 'scientific methods,' " especially as currently found in such sciences as physics or chemistry, "could be seriously inimical to any advance of knowledge in such important but essentially humanistic pursuits" (Langer, 1967, p. 53). It would seem, for all its curiosity value and even though it has surely exposed him to all manner of lampooning, that this is precisely what Koch means by the "identity" of the tasks of psychology and the humanities.

Whether psychology turns out to be "scientific" or "hermeneutical"; whether it eventually embodies strands of both; or, indeed, whether some psychological inquiries are in the main scientific and others predominantly hermeneutical—none of these possibilities can be decided in advance of the initial labor of acquiring these "powerful and freely negotiable concepts" without which psychology cannot be a coherent set of studies in any sense. But, once again, the fundamental problem centers in that "initial labor"—and although it must be stressed that phenomenological philosophy and psychology have already learned a great deal from one another and have developed many of these concepts since the early decades of this century, the key to their historical and systematic relationship is to be found in the initial task of gaining access to and subsequently explicating mental phenomena themselves. Thus, as Langer points out, the formulation of those crucial concepts "is often the work of empirical investigators, but it is philosophical, nonetheless, because it is concerned with meanings rather than facts, and the systematic construction of meanings [i.e., concepts] is philosophy" (1967, p. 52). Thereby, as Husserl insisted in his famous 1910 article, "Philosophy as Rigorous Science," "for essential reasons psychology must be more closely related to philosophy (i.e., through the medium of phenomenology), and must in its destiny remain most intimately bound up with philosophy" (1965, p. 92).

Dilthey also clearly understood the point and went on to stress that the systematic study of mental life is essential for the whole spectrum of the "human studies" (*Geisteswissenschaften*). In his words, "the first condition of [history as a discipline] lies in the consciousness that I am myself a historical creature, that the one who examines history also makes history" (1927/1958, p. 278). To ground knowledge of historical affairs—i.e., diaries, letters, documents, poems, laws, inventions, and so forth—*as* historical expressions of individuals and peoples, we must first of all understand in principle how it happens that "mind," the mental activities and expressions of such historical persons, makes itself objectively manifested in and through such products. And this requires sound knowledge of the mind itself. But anyone who studies such mental phenomena is himself a mind, and only thereby is it even possible for the mind itself to be studied. I can thus readily rephrase Dilthey's point: "the first condition for the possibility of a psychology lies in the consciousness that I am myself a consciousness, that the one who examines consciousness also by the fact exhibits consciousness."

To "go back to the beginnings of thought about mental phenomena" (Langer), or to "disembed subtle relational unities within the flux of experience" (Koch), therefore, is to find straightaway that that "thinking about mental phenomena" or that "disembedding" within experience is itself the fundamental "mental phenomenon." In a word, the study of mental life is essential to the very possibility of the study of history as of social and cultural configurations, art, or religious life; indeed, it is necessary for the understanding of science itself, whatever kind it may be.

Clearly, as Koch emphasizes, that domain—whether conceived as the totality of the functioning of all organisms, or, as I have said, the total domain of all mental activities, from the cognitive to the emotive, volitional, and valuational—is surely awesome. And while, as he insists, it seems impossible to view it as subject matter of a single coherent discipline on the model of the Millian hypothesis, phenomenologists, such as Husserl, Gurwitsch (1964), and Merleau-Ponty (1962), and psychologists, such as Goldstein (1948), Straus (1966), Minkowski (1970), Bosch (1970), and Giorgi (1970), have gone to some pains to point out that the possibility of rigorous, objective study of the mind is not at all dependent on the acceptance of that conception of science. For one thing, since, to paraphrase Locke, it is our own understanding, our own consciousness, which makes us acquainted with everything else, the rigorous study of this is presupposed by the study of anything else. Thus, even the negative judgment that the subjective, the mind, cannot be known in and for itself presupposes that we have sound evidence to back up the claim, and this presupposes that we do indeed have access to our own understanding, however difficult it may be to distance ourselves from it.

For another thing, however, Koch's point is in a sense quite well taken: only if all mental activities were of the same sort and functioned at the same level with the same structure and objects would it all make sense to conceive the study of mental life in the monolithic way he has found to be such a failure. Clearly, even if, as phenomenologists are wont to insist, there are certain determinably essential characteristics of mental phenomena, this by no means indicates either that there is nothing else to be said or that there is only one way to study them. Rumors about phenomenology to the contrary notwithstanding, it is precisely because mental activities go on at quite different levels and in quite different directions that phenomenology has consistently advocated the necessity for a whole *battery* of methods for studying mental life. Rather than being monistic, even as regards the specifically

629

philosophical tasks, phenomenology has been pluralistic, for the very good reason that every study must take its clues for methods from the region of things studied and not bring them in ad hoc.

******

Recognizing the pathos of any time-bound enterprise—that not everything can be said and many essential things must be left unsaid—I want now to bring all this to some semblance of closure. How does it stand with the science of the psyche from the perspective of phenomenology?

1. In the first place, psychology of any sort and in respect of any of its subregions—clinical, social, experimental, educational, and so on—purports to be one of the many studies focusing on human life. Those studies which focus on animal life—apes, or monkeys, or what have you—are thus of interest here solely to the extent that they purport to be relevant for understanding human life (and *whether* they are relevant or not can be left open for my purposes, even though there is surely much that is problematic about such a claim). As such, psychology, like every other human study (sociology, economics, history), epistemically focuses on some particular region of actual human life. It makes claims about that region and thus implicitly appeals to some modes of experience or apprehension of that region of actual affairs which then function as evidences for or against those claims. In this fashion any regional inquiry *presupposes some mode of access* (experience, apprehension, mode of givenness) with respect to its "objects" of study. Hence, every psychologist in a strict sense is of necessity in the *embrace of a circle*: he or she must already be in possession of the very thing ("psychic life") that he or she, on the other hand, supposedly sets out to study (see Zaner, 1978). To inquire into psychic life, I must already be able to recognize it when I come across it, for otherwise I might well find myself interviewing the sky or clinically treating street curbs.

2. The circle cannot be ignored. With us, at least since Plato put Meno through its apparent dilemma, it forms *the very condition of the human studies*. As psychologists, we seek to understand, say, human behavior, and we are often instructed to do so "objectively." This, in turn, is often thought to require us, among other things, to refrain from allowing our perspectives, beliefs, values, and so on to interfere with the behavior we study. Yet, it is perfectly obvious (and to many, a source of much dismay) that *these behaving creatures*, which we seek to take into account, ineluctably *take us into account*. Human beings interpret the world around them, behave in myriad ways toward it and its various objects, and among the latter are other human beings (which include us psychologists). My talking to you is essentially an act presupposing your listening to me, and my "talk" necessarily takes that into account, as does your "hearing" me take my talk into account. My observing you embraces of necessity my being observed (or observable) by you. *This distinctive mutuality of human life*—which holds as well, though with important differences,

for human-to-animal and animal-to-animal, behaviors—such that our behaviors "reckon with" one another, is precisely what must be studied in the human studies, psychology included. And yet, since the "studiers" are themselves not only scientists but human agents as well, within the world of human life more generally, it is precisely this essential characteristic which seems to mitigate against the very possibility of a "science." The "data" are irascible: they are not and cannot be simply "data," for these "data" *take us scientists as "data" too!* Or, what we seek to interpret interprets us, interprets other human beings, and interprets the world around us—including interpretations of what we psychologists "do," i.e., our very "science" is interpreted by our "data"!

3. The situation of psychology is complicated even more than others of the human studies, however. On the one hand, seeking to be a rigorous study requires gaining access to the best possible instances of its objects: psychic life. Yet it has frequently been taken as self-evident that my sources are drastically limited. I seem to have the best access only *to my own psychic life*, whereas the lives of others are at best only indirectly, if at all, given to me. How can I say anything at all about these others, much less scientifically? Am I not constrained to being merely my own autobiographer if "psychic life" is what I am supposed to study? Each psychologist, his own humanist; each humanist, his own psychologist!

On the other hand, even if one says that after all I do have access to other persons—they talk to me and to one another, they act in various ways, they write letters and articles, books, and diaries—how could such as these provide the kind of evidentiary base needed to warrant genuinely scientific claims? Either rhapsodies, or nothing at all—such seems the choice.

Nor is this all. For if, as Dilthey maintained, history and all the other human studies *presuppose* psychology as a science of psychic life, and if the very thing psychology is all about is so intractable—indeed, a veritable "catch-22" of enigmas—where does this leave us?

David Hume, it might fruitfully be recalled, landed in just this situation. Positing the "moral sciences" as the ground of all the others, the course of his inquiry and assumptions inevitably took him to the position of recognizing that everything has a merely subjective source. Every causal connection "lies merely in ourselves, and is nothing but that determination of the mind, which is acquired by custom . . ." (Hume, 1888, p. 266). Given this, that the very basis of all science is merely subjective, he announces that "we have, therefore, no choice left but betwixt a false reason or none at all" (p. 268). The only thing which saved him from the complete skepticism this implies, as he knew well, is that it matters not in the least for us in our daily lives. "Carelessness and in-attention alone can afford us any remedy," for if we believe, for instance, "that fire warms, or water refreshes, 'tis only because it costs us too much pain to think otherwise" (pp. 218, 230).

Without pursuing the matter too much further here (see Zaner, 1975, pp. 14–30), suffice it to point out that psychology thereby seems to be in a most precarious

631

position, and it has been that position which has concerned phenomenologists ever since the early work of Husserl. For when one considers the matter, it is striking indeed how potent and even happy is that "inadvertence" of daily life. It is impressively potent, for, after all, as Hume himself insisted, it is precisely the character of daily life that it alone is capable of overcoming the subjectivism and inevitable relativism of Hume's professed skepticism. It is also a strikingly happy inadvertence for, in Husserl's terms, it is again daily life which effectively resolves the riddle which otherwise infects Hume's (and others') works—the riddle, namely, "of a world whose being is a *being produced from subjectivity* . . ." (Husserl, 1962/1970, pp. 96–97).

While Hume was, Husserl earlier remarked, the "first to *treat seriously the Cartesian focusing purely on what lies inside*" (Husserl, 1929/1969, p. 256), he nevertheless did not systematically explicate the remarkable character of those entrenched beliefs and customs one quickly finds when "what lies inside" (in the mind) is treated seriously. For we do indeed believe that fire warms and water refreshes, and we have a myriad of beliefs as well about objects, other people, institutions, and values—whether past, future, present, or even imaginary. And while it may well "cost us too much pain to think otherwise," the truth is that we do not think otherwise. Each of us believes in, has feelings and desires about, values and conducts himself or herself with respect to, argues and comes to agreement about an incredible variety of affairs: mathematical, physical, social, and biological matters, not to mention those involving music, painting, and literature, for example, along with norms, reasons, causes, motivations, and so on. And, beyond that, we are aware of (in ourselves and in others) and we practice, make claims, and argue about mental activities of all sorts: learning, remembering, expecting, fearing, inferring, touching, wishing, and on and on.

Indeed, to "focus on what lies purely inside" is to find oneself promptly directed to that myriad of objective affairs. Far from finding any sort of insulated, encapsulated, and essentially recondite sphere of utter privacy, careful reflection on "the mind" discloses that it is necessarily and essentially *intersubjective;* that a "sphere of privacy" is in truth not a given but a positive accomplishment within our common social milieu (see Zaner, 1981). Such complex beliefs, in short, turn out to be not only *susceptible* of rigorous inquiry, but quite necessary to study if we would understand anything else—and just this, phenomenology has insisted, is the task of both psychology and philosophy. If any common imperative is suggested by the experience of the two disciplines in the almost hundred-year history of phenomenology's movement, it is this: that reflection or even introspection is precisely what systematically opens up that world of common experience for rigorous study.

4. In slightly different terms, it is just here that the basic theme of a phenomenological psychology was, and is, found. The conditions for the possibility of the human sciences in general include (a) that such scientists are themselves human beings in the common social world who have already been engaged in what they

later seek to do with greater care and deliberateness, and (b) that the products of their various sciences are the products of specific, determinable mental activities. Long before such persons became scientists, they were already doing very much the sorts of things they now do: each has already interpreted human actions (his own included), "asked" questions, "taken examples," "inquired," "inferred," "observed," "talked" with others to elicit information, "tried to explain," and so on and on. *Such activities, and especially our multiple modes of "talking" and "listening," are ways by which we not only "know" one another, but in general give order or structure to and account for ourselves, for others, and for the world of human life,* as well as that of nature. In these terms, learning to become a psychologist is fundamentally and necessarily an act of learning to become reflexively aware of what one has been engaged in all along in the world of daily life, and doing so now with the express and deliberate effort to understand systematically what has hitherto gone unnoticed, taken for granted, or inattentively believed.

5. In view of this, it seems obvious enough that however important is a science of behavior, for instance, it necessarily must *presuppose* a pure internal psychology having the specifically human mental life as its object of rigorous study. The reason is also obvious: no "behavior" could present itself to anyone, behaviorist or not, as specifically "human behavior" (hence as relevant for study) unless one already comprehended or understood it as the objective manifestation of human mental activities—volitions, emotions, valuations, and cognitions, and so on. Thus, as Jonas once put it:

> The evidence we find in ourselves is an integral part of the evidence concerning life which experience puts at our disposal. That it must be used critically to avoid the pitfalls of anthropomorphism goes without saying. But used it must be—and as a matter of fact, most of the time it is, however much biologists and behaviorists may assure us and themselves of the contrary. Else they would altogether miss the existence of life around them and thus have no object for inquiry . . . to begin with (1966, p. 91).

For a pure internal psychology, neither beliefs, nor values, nor overtly manifested behavior (much less behaviors not overtly manifested, such as decisions not to sell stocks) can be regarded as dependent variables observable from without in the manner of rocks or atoms. To the contrary, beliefs, values, and the like—as expressed in the myriad ways we know them to be—as also overt behaviors themselves, are expressions of the meaning of the subject's history and intentional life (the subject, namely, whose beliefs, values, or behaviors are in question in the first place). As Paul Ricoeur expressed a similar point, arguing against a Skinnerian reductivism of psychoanalytic theory, behavioral facts

> do not function as observables, but as signifiers for the history of the desires. The signification is precisely what Skinner casts into the outer darkness, into the general

633

catch-all of theories about mental life and of prescientific metaphors. However . . . strictly speaking, there are no "facts" in psychoanalysis, for the analyst does not observe, he interprets (Ricoeur, 1970, pp. 364–365).

To my point, then. It is because of the *reflexiveness* and *mutuality* of human life that a psychology which takes these, in their many worldly expressions, as its specific subject matter is not only possible but necessary. What Ricoeur says of psychoanalysis is true of "scientific psychology" in its core discipline—the one which has as its principal theme the foundations of psychology, i.e., phenomenology.

6. Finally, it is not as if those enigmas mentioned before have suddenly disappeared. Rather, what can now be seen is that they are disclosures of the textures of human life; in different terms, *they are enigmas solely to the extent that one fails to distinguish between different levels of epistemic inquiry.* What is puzzling about Descartes's "cogito, ergo sum," for instance, is that he fails to see that the "cogito" he discloses is taken by him to be merely a piece of the world, ontically on a par with everything else: his ontology is unileveled despite the fact that it is consciousness (turned onto itself) which alone discloses anything else. As if a mere part of a whole could serve to account forthwith for the very whole of which it is a part!

What is enigmatic about Hume's conclusion, satyric or not, is that he fails to see the sense of his own claims about the subjective source of knowledge: such claims, even to make sense, could not possibly be "merely subjective" in the way that what he claims to be talking about is said to be! In brief: Descartes did not notice that *his own cognitive apprehension of the "cogito" must of necessity lie at a different level from that of the cogito itself*; Hume, on the other hand, fails to note that *the grounds for saying that one has no choice except between a false reason or none at all are neither the one nor the other, and that the claim is itself perfectly "reasonable"* (however mistaken it might be).

Similarly, everything said in this paper about psychology was in no sense said from within the science itself; rather, my claims issued from that other level of inquiry, i.e., phenomenological philosophy.

If psychology has a pivotal place among the human studies (which the phenomenological tradition firmly contends), this is because its focal point of concern is the "mental"—that, thanks to which there is any awareness, experience, apprehension, or even argument as regards anything whatever, including itself. But psychology's particular orientation toward psychic life is that of a de facto, empirical science, not that of philosophy. The point and conclusion here can thus be readily expressed. Insofar as mental life manifests itself outwardly in various "acts," "works," "products," and "languages," and even more complex social, political, artistic, and religious products, empirical psychology is as Koch says identical with a properly reconceived humanities; that is, they are *hermeneutic disciplines*, interpretations of de facto, actual objective manifestations and the modalities by which these actual products become thus objectivated—precisely what Dilthey had with great insight set out.

That I believe there to be a profound *reciprocity* and *mutuality* between phenomenological philosophy and the range of the human studies (and especially psychology) is by this juncture certainly evident. It may need emphasis, however, that this mutuality of levels of inquiry is to be taken most seriously. Just as the study of autism as a mode of human life would be empty-headed speculation in the absence of actual, concrete instances (and variations of these), and just as the clinical treatment of autistic children would be blind, unguided probings and soundings in the absence of some clear cognition of the sense of autism itself—just so are philosophy and psychology (and the other human sciences) closely tied to one another (see Bosch, 1970). It is not only the case that the philosophical examination of human life and its empirical study are conjoint conditions to epistemic completeness. It is also true that philosophy, indeed even transcendental phenomenology, must continuously be checked (if not held in check) by psychology and the human studies. Philosophical and empirical inquiries are thus bound together in a continuum defined by increasing epistemic completeness inherent to the very idea of knowledge, but it is a continuum with internal levels and corresponding orientations. It is this which ultimately gives the lie to the false and divisive territorialities—and to the bureaucratization—of knowledge so prevalent today. It is the deployment of ardent effort along such a continuum which can ultimately recover the sense of human subjectivity, countering the deeply seated relativisms and crises of our time.

REFERENCES

Bergson, H. *An introduction to metaphysics*. New York: Bobbs-Merrill, 1949.

Bosch, G. *Infantile autism: A clinical and phenomenological/anthropological investigation taking language as the guide* (D. I. Jordan, trans.). Foreword by Bruno Bettelheim, Berlin/New York: Springer-Verlag, 1970.

Brentano, F. *Psychologie vom empirischen Standpunkt* (Vol. I). Hamburg: Felix Meiner, 1955.

Dilthey, W. *Gesammelte Schriften* (Vol. VII, 2nd ed.). Stuttgart: B. G. Teubner, 1958. (Originally published, 1927.)

Dilthey, W. Ideas concerning a descriptive and analytic psychology (1894). In W. Dilthey, *Descriptive psychology and historical understanding* (R. M. Zaner & K. L. Heiges, trans.). Introduction by R. A. Makkreel. The Hague: Martinus Nijhoff, 1977.

Giorgi, A. *Psychology as a human science: A phenomenologically based approach*. New York: Harper & Row, 1970.

Goldstein, K. *Language and language disturbances*. New York: Grune & Stratton, 1948.

Gurwitsch, A. *The field of consciousness*. Pittsburgh: Duquesne University Press, 1964.

Gurwitsch, A. *Studies in phenomenology and psychology*. Evanston, Ill.: Northwestern University Press, 1966.

Hume, D. *A treatise of human nature* (L. A. Selby-Bigge edition). Oxford: Clarendon, 1888.

III. PSYCHOLOGY AND ITS INTERSECTING DISCIPLINES

Husserl, E. Philosophy as rigorous science. In E. Husserl, *Phenomenology and the crisis of philosophy.* (Notes and introduction by Q. Lauer, trans.) New York: Harper Torchbooks, 1965.

Husserl, E. *Formal and transcendental logic* (D. Cairns, trans.). The Hague: Martinus Nijhoff, 1969. (Originally published, 1929.)

Husserl, E. *The crisis of European sciences and transcendental phenomenology.* (Introduction by D. Carr, trans.) Evanston, Ill.: Northwestern University Press, 1970. (Originally published, 1962.)

Jonas, H. *The phenomenon of life: Toward a philosophical biology.* New York: Delta Books, Dell, 1966.

Koch, S. Epilogue to Study I. In S. Koch (Ed.), *Psychology: A study of a science* (Vol. III). New York: McGraw-Hill, 1959.

Koch, S. Psychology cannot be a coherent science. In F. W. Matson (Ed.), *Without/within: Behaviorism and humanism.* Monterey, Calif.: Brooks/Cole, 1973.

Koyré, A. *From the closed world to the infinite universe.* New York: Harper Torchbooks, 1958.

Langer, S. K. *Mind: An essay on human feeling* (Vol. I). Baltimore: Johns Hopkins, 1967.

Locke, J. *An essay concerning human understanding* (Vol. I). (A. C. Fraser edition). New York: Dover, 1959. London/New York: Routledge, n.d.

Merleau-Ponty, M. *The phenomenology of perception* (C. Smith, trans.). London: Routledge & Kegan Paul, 1962.

Minkowski, E. *Lived time: Phenomenological and psychopathological studies.* Introduction by N. Metzel, trans.). Evanston, Ill.: Northwestern University Press, 1970.

Natanson, M. (Ed.), *Phenomenology and the social sciences* (2 vols.). Evanston, Ill.: Northwestern University Press, 1973. (a)

Natanson, M. *Edmund Husserl: Philosopher of infinite tasks.* Evanston, Ill.: Northwestern University Press, 1973. (b)

Ricoeur, P. *Freedom and nature: The voluntary and the involuntary.* (Introduction by E. Kohak, trans.) Evanston, Ill.: Northwestern University Press, 1966.

Ricoeur, P. *Husserl: An analysis of his phenomenology.* (E. G. Ballard & L. E. Embree, trans.) Evanston, Ill.: Northwestern University Press, 1967.

Ricoeur, P. *Freud and philosophy: An essay on interpretation* (D. Savage, trans.). New Haven: Yale University Press, 1970.

Santayana, G. *Scepticism and animal faith.* New York: Dover, 1955. (Originally published, 1923.)

Sartre, J.-P. *Being and nothingness: An essay on phenomenological ontology* (H. Barnes, trans.). New York: Philosophical Library, 1956.

Schutz, A., & Luckmann, T. *The structure of the life-world* (R. M. Zaner & H. T. Engelhardt, Jr., trans.). Evanston, Ill.: Northwestern University Press, 1973.

Spiegelberg, H. *The phenomenological movement: A historical introduction* (2 vols.). The Hague: Martinus Nijhoff, 1960.

Straus, E. W. *Phenomenological psychology: Selected essays* (E. Eng, trans.). New York: Basic Books, 1966.

Zaner, R. M. *The way of phenomenology: Criticism as a philosophical discipline.* New York: Pegasus, Bobbs-Merrill, 1970.

Zaner, R. M. Reflections on evidence and criticism in the theory of consciousness. In L. E. Embree (Ed.)., *Life-world and consciousness: Essays for Aron Gurwitsch.* Evanston, Ill.: Northwestern University Press, 1972.

Zaner, R. M. Examples and possibles: A criticism of Husserl's method of free-phantasy variation. *Research in Phenomenology,* 1973, 3, 29–43.

Zaner, R. M. Hume and the discipline of phenomenology: An historical perspective. In *Phenomenological perspectives: Historical and systematic essays in honor of Herbert Spiegelberg.* The Hague: Martinus Nijhoff, 1975.

Zaner, R. M. Eidos and science. In J. J. Bien (Ed.)., *Phenomenology and social science.* The Hague: Martinus Nijhoff, 1978.

Zaner, R. M. *The context of self: A phenomenological inquiry using medicine as a clue.* Athens, Ohio: Ohio University Press, 1981.

SUPPLEMENTARY READINGS

Casey, E. S. *Imagining: A phenomenological study.* Bloomington and London: Indiana University Press, 1976.

Engelhardt, H. T., Jr. *Mind-body: A categorical relation.* The Hague: Martinus Nijhoff, 1973.

Farber, M. *The foundation of phenomenology.* Albany, N.Y.: The State University of New York Press, 1943.

Gadamer, H. G. *Truth and method.* New York: The Seabury Press, 1975.

Grene, M. *The knower and the known.* New York: Basic Books, 1966.

Gurwitsch, A. *Human encounters in the social world.* (F. Kersten trans.) A. Metraux (Ed.). Pittsburgh: Duquesne University Press, 1979.

Kockelmans, J. J., *Edmund Husserl's phenomenological psychology.* Pittsburgh: Duquesne University Press, 1967.

Kockelmans, J. J., & Kisiel, T. J. (Eds.). *Phenomenology and the natural sciences.* Evanston, Ill.: Northwestern University Press, 1970.

Natanson, M. *Phenomenology, role, and reason.* Springfield, Ill.: Charles C Thomas, 1974.

Scheler, M. *The nature of sympathy* (P. Heath, trans.). Introduction by W. Stark. New Haven: Yale University Press, 1954.

Sokolowski, R. *Husserlian meditations: How words present things.* Evanston, Ill.: Northwestern University Press, 1974.

Spiegelberg, H. *Phenomenology in psychology and psychiatry.* Evanston, Ill.: Northwestern University Press, 1972.

Straus, E. W. Natanson, M., & Ey, H. *Psychiatry and philosophy.* M. Natanson (Ed.). New York: Springer-Verlag, 1969.

Wieder, D. L. *Language and social reality.* The Hague: Mouton, 1974.

27

Conceptual Analysis and Psychological Theory

WILLIAM P. ALSTON

For my contribution to this volume, I shall deal with the interaction of philosophical analysis and psychology, both as it has been and as it might conceivably be.

To begin at the most fundamental level, the analysis of concepts is an essential part of every intellectual enterprise. If one is engaged, as psychologists are, in formulating and testing general hypotheses, explaining phenomena, and building theories, one is well-advised to become as explicit as possible about the shapes of the concepts one is using. For depending on the character of those concepts, one will get one or another answer to such questions as: "What are the implications of this hypothesis?" "What is the explanatory force of this theory vis-à-vis those data?" "Of what sorts of tests is this hypothesis susceptible?".

When a philosopher seeks to analyze concepts, we simply have (usually) a more elaborate and (ideally) a more expert example of the same activity. Whereas psychologists are trained in statistics, experimental design, and sampling techniques, philosophers, at least those in the amorphous and ill-defined group known as "analytic philosophers," learn to flush out crucial features of the meaning of key words and phrases, to uncover crucial ambiguities, and to discern patterns of implication. One could, in principle, do one's own plumbing, but it is often advisable to call in an expert.

The picture just drawn is one of happy and fruitful cooperation. But, alas, 'tis not always thus. There are barriers from both sides. Psychologists seldom feel a need to call the plumber; and if one appears, unsummoned, at the door, he is likely to be sent packing. From the other side, when analytical philosophers have directed their attention to psychology it has been, more often than not, with hostile intent. I shall now cast a critical eye on some examples of these less-than-friendly ventures, as a prelude to illustrating how I think it should go.

Ordinary-Language Philosophy

After World War II, the English-speaking philosophical world was afflicted with an aberration known as "ordinary-language philosophy." Based on the later work of Ludwig Wittgenstein in Cambridge and the work of Gilbert Ryle and J. L. Austin in Oxford, it came to dominate especially the latter of these institutions (and hence is often called "Oxford philosophy," thereby causing many Oxford greats of bygone areas to execute the well-known necrophilic motions). From thence it spread to the United States and other former British colonies. Though, of course, different philosophers within the movement disagreed on various points, the overall character of the movement might be summed up in the following convictions.

1. Many traditional philosophical problems are pseudoproblems that arise from misuses of ordinary language (without putting anything intelligible in its place).
2. If we will attend carefully to the ordinary use of the crucial expressions, we can diagnose the pseudoproblems and allay philosophical puzzlement.
3. More positively, a careful delineation of the ordinary use of key terms like *know, can, cause, true,* and *reason* can illuminate our thinking in many areas.

Thus Wittgenstein, J. O. Urmson, and P. F. Strawson have suggested that Hume and others have been baffled over how to justify induction only because they have failed to realize that, as the term *reason* is actually used, when one has strong inductive evidence for a belief this is a paradigm case of having adequate *reasons* for the belief. Or consider the following puzzle about time. "Only the present exists, for the past is gone and the future is not yet real. But at any moment, only an extensionless instant is *present*, for what is before that instant is past and what comes after it is future. Thus nothing that requires a temporal duration for its existence, such as a movement, ever exists at any time." This puzzle is said to be resolved by noting that terms like *now* and *present* are designed to pick out a temporal slice with some extension, not an unextended instant.

When ordinary-language philosophers turn their attention to psychology, they often make the same moves. That is, they often try to show that certain psychological inquiries or theories are vitiated through insufficient attention to the character of

639

the terms involved. I will illustrate this with two examples—Gilbert Ryle on perception and R. S. Peters on motivation.

Before coming to Ryle's more serious point about the psychology of perception, I will just mention a point that figures prominently in his very influential book, *The Concept of Mind*, since it typifies an approach that is all too common in these writings. In the chapter entitled "Sensation and Observation" Ryle decries the tendency to explain perception by postulating "paramechanical" goings-on within the perceiver's mind or nervous system. After saying

> The questions, that is, are not questions of the para-mechanical form "How do we see robins?", but questions of the form "How do we use such descriptions as 'he saw a robin'?".

Ryle goes on to say:

> We do not, that is, want tidings or hypotheses about any other things which the listener may have privily done or undergone. Even if there had taken place three, or seventeen, such *entr'actes*, news about them would not explain how detecting a mosquito differs from having a shrill singing in the ears. What we want to know is how the logical behaviour of "he detected a mosquito" differs from that of "there was a singing in the ears . . ." (Ryle, 1949, p. 225).

Taken literally, this last passage is of only sociological interest. The fact that well-brought-up denizens of Oxford senior common rooms are interested in the one question rather than the other does not, in itself, tell us anything about the viability of the psychology of perception. If such pronouncements are to have any bearing on the point at issue, they must reflect a conviction that psychologists really set out to explain *what it means to say* that a person heard a mosquito, and that it is only because they are confused about their own enterprise that they try to discover what was going on in the person's mind and/or nervous system that is responsible for the fact that he did recognize what he heard as a mosquito. But surely it is obvious to anyone at all conversant with the psychology of perception that the initial aim was the latter rather than the former.

The more serious point is found in the chapter on perception in Ryle's book *Dilemmas*. Here he tries to show that "there is something which is drastically wrong with the whole programme of trying to schedule my seeing a tree either as a physiological or as a psychological end-stage of processes" (Ryle, 1954, p. 101). The point is that "seeing a tree is not an effect—but this is not because it is an eccentric sort of state or process which happens to be exempt from causal explanations but because it is not a state or process at all" (Ryle, 1954, p. 102). To put it briefly, Ryle's claim is that perceptual verbs like *see* and *hear* are "success words"; they mark cognitive successes. Just as winning a race, unlike running the race, is not something that takes time, that has a beginning, middle, and end, so with hearing a mosquito or seeing a robin, as contrasted with looking for a robin or straining to hear a mosquito. This is shown by noting, for example, that I can say "I've seen a robin" as soon as I can say "I see a robin," and by noting that the present continuous tense "I'm seeing a robin" is ill-formed, except for very special purposes. The claim is that the questions that launch the psychology of perception are based on a failure to appreciate the "logic" of perceptual terms.

But this is a feeble dart, and it is not difficult to see how the psychologist may evade it. Grant all Ryle's contentions about perceptual verbs. Psychologists may habitually talk as if seeing a robin is a process or a state, but they need not. Having recognized that to see a robin is to score a cognitive success rather than to undergo a certain process, they can still ask: "By virtue of what internal neurophysiological or psychological processes does one score this cognitive success? What internal processes make the difference between the winner and loser, when both are bombarded with identical peripheral stimulation?" And the psychology of perception can go on as before.

Ryle does not bother to cite any actual psychological literature; and, indeed, one often gets the impression that his real target in psychology is the largely armchair variety practiced in Oxford around the turn of the century. Let's consider a case in which an ordinary-language philosopher tries to come to grips with what psychologists do. For this purpose I choose R. S. Peters's book, *The Concept of Motivation*, which was published in 1958 in a series called *Studies in Philosophical Psychology*.

The central theme in Peters's book is an attack on the idea that "there can be an all-inclusive theory of human behaviour from whose basic postulates answers to all forms of the question 'Why does Jones do X?' will eventually be deduced" (Peters, 1958, p. 148), the sort of theory classically exemplified by Hull. Peters's attack is a many-pronged one. For one thing, he alleges with some justice that these all-embracing theories confuse different kinds of explanation. Here I want to concentrate on his contention that the imperialist pretensions of motivation theories stem from insensitivity to the restricted range of terms like *motive, need,* and *satisfaction.* First *motive.*

> It has been argued that the term "motive" is used predominantly in contexts where there is a breakdown in conventional expectations, when a man acts "out of character", and that it points to the goal towards which his behaviour is actually directed. . . . to explain *everything* a man does in terms of "motives" is logically inappropriate because it lumps together acting purposefully according to rules, acting with a goal but according to no established rules, and cases where something happens to a man and it is odd to say that he *acts* at all. Psychologists, therefore, who say that all behaviour is motivated are using the concept too widely if by this they mean that we have a motive for everything we do (Peters, 1958, p. 152).

Peters feels that the term *need* is similarly misused in theories of motivation.

> . . . at a common-sense level, the term "need" is mainly normative. It prescribes one of a set of standard goals. It usually functions as a diagnostic term with remedial implication. It implies that something is wrong with a person if certain conditions are absent. . . . In other words the notion of "need" in ordinary language is seldom *explanatory*. It is used to point out what a person ought to be doing rather than to explain what he is doing (Peters, 1958, pp. 17–18).

> Need-reduction explanations are a particular instance of a very common sort of explanation which will be termed "explanations in terms of end-states" . . . . It will probably be found that all such explanations share the logical features revealed in the specific case of need-reduction. These are (i) the generalization of a type of explanation that applies properly only to a very limited class of phenomena and (ii) the use of a term with highly general normative implications which obscure its emptiness as a highly general *explanation* (Peters, 1958, p. 20).

Peters then goes on to make analogous remarks about another sort of "end-state" explanation, that in terms of "satisfaction" or "pleasure" (pp. 22–25).
   Peters acknowledges that:

> It might well be objected that psychologists use terms like . . . "need" and "motive" in a technical sense and that, provided that they give their own rules for using the term, it does not matter much what term they choose (Peters, 1958, p. 154).

To this he might have replied that psychologists have not done an adequate job of supplying new "rules" for the uses of these terms or of explaining in any other way what technical senses they are designed to carry, and that they are in fact depending on our acquaintance with the ordinary uses of these terms, without acknowledging, or even realizing, that they are doing so. Instead he responds as follows.

> In my view it would be a profound mistake for psychologists to take such a cavalier attitude towards ordinary speech. For the different terms employed by ordinary educated people incorporate distinctions which may be unwarrantably ignored by theorists. Drive theorists, for instance, use the term "drive" in such a way that a man can have a hunger drive, a drive to play poker rather than tennis, a drive to repeat acts in a compulsive manner, and even a drive to know. Now surely this leads to confusion. For apart from the fact that it is logically absurd to say that one could be driven to know anything, the use of the same term for all these very different types of action, is a case of unwarrantable assimilation in the interest of an over-all theory. Ordinary language would only use the term "drive" in the case of compulsive repetition and, perhaps, in cases of extreme hunger, as when a man eats his hat. This is no accident; it is not a matter merely of terminology. For there are very important distinctions between the types of behaviour in question. In cases like this, ordinary language, by being specific in its employment of a concept,

singles out differences in behaviour which are theoretically as well as practically important. Would it not be better, therefore, for psychologists to confine a concept like that of "drive" to cases where in ordinary language, a man could properly be said to be "driven" to act? The difficulty about developing a science of psychology is that, in a sense, we already know too much about human behaviour, albeit in a rather uncoordinated manner. Common-sense, which is incorporated in the concepts of ordinary language, has creamed off most of the vital distinctions. Psychology has the task of systematizing what is already known and adding, albeit in rather a piecemeal manner, bits of special theory to supplement common-sense.

This does let the cat out of the bag. It is not that one could not make different uses of the terms of ordinary discourse. It is rather that everyday psychological terms acquire their use within the context of what is, in the main, the correct psychological theory, or better, correct theoretical standpoint. Hence, if psychologists seek to develop theories based on other conceptual frameworks, they are doomed to failure, the inevitable fate of those who set themselves against the wisdom of the ages.

Well, Peters is entitled to his opinion, but to me it seems a rash leap of faith to be so confident that "common-sense has creamed off most of the vital distinctions," so confident as to close ones mind against novel possibilities. Admittedly, no radically new conceptual scheme has yet taken over the field. Admittedly, psychology's most notable successes have been of the piecemeal variety. Nevertheless, the history of science indicates that one cannot predict radical conceptual shifts. (If one could, one would be making them.) Would it not be more reasonable to keep an open mind, to let a thousand flowers bloom, to take seriously the possibility that conceptual innovations may prove fruitful in psychological theory. From this point of view, it is not enough to point out that Hull or Tolman deviates from the ordinary use of "need," or joins together what ordinary language has put asunder. We must consider whether the concepts thus spawned have any determinate shape, whether they are being wielded clearly and consistently, whether they are playing the role for which they were intended, and, last but not least, whether the theoretical matrix in which they are embedded is a successful one.

A Different Use for Conceptual Analysis

An application of conceptual analysis to psychology that is in the spirit of these last remarks would be a very different kettle of fish from the sort exemplified by Ryle and Peters. Let me elaborate on this in the context of a general assessment of "ordinary-language philosophy" and the prospects for its transmogrification.

Even though the characterization of traditional philosophical problems as pseudoproblems was absurdly overdrawn, Wittgenstein et al. were following a sound insight in supposing that philosophy needs a careful delineation of the ordinary use of key terms. The potential payoff is high in this case just because

643

philosophers are, or should be, using key terms in their ordinary senses, though this is often concealed, even from themselves. We are interested in whether we can know anything about the external world in some ordinary sense of "know," not in some special technical sense of the term. Similarly, when we want to know whether human beings can act freely, it is in the sense of "free" in which it figures in, for example, questions about moral responsibility as they come up in everyday thought. When we ask whether we are ever obliged to go against our own self-interest, we are using the term *obliged* in a common moral sense. Hence when we are interested in such questions, it behooves us to become as clear and explicit as possible about the character of those ordinary senses, for that determines just what question we are asking, and, hence, just what constraints there are on an answer.

I do believe, though I cannot pause to argue the point, that psychologists also typically place a heavy, and often unacknowledged, reliance on the ordinary senses of their crucial terms. This is most marked in social psychology and personality theory, but it is far from absent in perception and other cognitive fields, in motivation, and in learning. To the extent that this is so, ordinary-language analysis will have the same kind of bearing on psychology that it has on philosophy; whatever the field, the good worker should know his or her tools and keep them in good working order. But as suggested above, the philosopher should not just assume that t'will be ever thus. He or she should be alive to conceptual innovations.[1] However, and this is the crucial point, the conceptual analyst has at least as important a job to perform with respect to *novel technical* concepts. There, no less than with borrowings from common sense, it is imperative that the inquirer be alive to the nature and powers of conceptual tools.

In the light of all this, here is my suggested program for an analytical philosophy of psychology. Philosophers will approach a branch of psychology with a concern for uncovering the structure and function of its key concepts. Alive both to carry-overs from nontechnical thought and to conceptual innovations, they must eschew any prior assumption that either of these possibilities covers the whole field. Furthermore, they will in the first instance see themselves as, in Locke's phrase, "underlaborers," clearing away brambles and weeds, preparing the ground for those who are actually cultivating the field. In more prosaic terms, they will concentrate on problems that have some discernible bearing on the primary work of psychology, rather than exploring a stretch of conceptual territory for its own sake. That is, they will seek to bring out those features of the relevant concepts that have implications for such matters as explanatory force, theory construction, and empirical testing; and they will be especially on the lookout for ambiguities or indeterminacies that affect such matters. Finally, they may well seek to take a step or two beyond the humble role of tool sharpener—in two respects. First, they may go beyond the

[1] Again this point holds across fields. Even if reliance on ordinary language seems more ineluctable in philosophy, still the analytical philosopher should not confront what seem to be technical uses of terms in philosophy with a rigid "Thou shalt not pass!"

concepts they actually find psychologists employing and suggest some alternative conceptual schemes, drawn from commonsense thought or elsewhere. In fact, since any conceptual analysis involves some tidying up of the raw material, there is no sharp line between simply analyzing what is already there and suggesting new alternatives. Second (and this is where the line between philosopher and psychologist becomes quite blurred), once the analytical philosopher abandons a dogmatic commitment to commonsense psychology or to any other particular conceptual framework, he or she will have to recognize that the acceptability of any set of concepts for psychology, or any other discipline, ultimately depends on how adequate a job can be done with their use in the pursuit of the distinctive goals of the discipline.

The ultimate test of a conceptual scheme for psychology is the adequacy of the theories that make use of it. An analytical philosopher of psychology may think, and may even rightly think, that he or she is in as good a position to make these assessments as the psychologist. Of course the psychologist is closer to the subject matter; but then the philosopher has the compensating advantage of being able to take a wider view of the situation, and, in addition, training renders him or her more sensitive to issues involved in the comparative evaluation of theories and of conceptual schemes. Thus the analytical philosopher of psychology may well feel inclined to join forces with the practicing psychologist at this culminating point of the endeavor and speak his or her piece on the comparative evaluation of conceptual schemes *in the light* of the empirical results of psychological research. Here conceptual analysis merges into psychological theorizing, thereby reflecting the intimate connection of concept formation and theory construction in science generally.

An Application to Personality Theory

Against this background I would like to present briefly a conceptual investigation of my own, as a fragmentary example of how conceptual analysis might be useful to psychology and so as to have a real-life "good guy" to contrast with the "bad guys" I have already presented. The investigation in question concerns concepts of personality characteristics (hereinafter Cs), an area not frequented by philosophers. More specifically, I have identified what I take to be a crucial conceptual distinction within this field, a distinction that carries important implications for the use of C-concepts in personality assessment and in personality theory.[2] This presentation stops far short of the empyrean heights envisaged at the end of the last paragraph, but it will at least serve to illustrate the more modest underlaborer role that philosophical analysts may usefully play. One side of the distinction is embodied in a

---

[2] For more detailed expositions, see Alston (1970, 1975).

model many personologists regard as applicable to all Cs. This is often presented as a definition of the term *trait*, as it is by Cronbach:

> A trait is a tendency to react in a defined way in response to a defined class of stimuli (Cronbach, 1960, p. 499).

Since the term *stimuli* is unrealistically physicalistic, let's change it to the more inclusive *situation*, and perhaps you will allow me to change *tendency* to *disposition*, since I will make a different use of the former term. With these alterations, we may say that a concept that conforms to this model is a concept of a disposition to emit responses of a certain category (R) when in a situation that belongs to a certain category (S). I shall call such dispositions "Ts" (for *traits*), and I shall confine the term "T" to those S-R dispositions in which the S- and R-categories range over empirically accessible states of affairs. Some familiar T-concepts, each with its distinctive S- and R-categories, are the following.

Domineeringness:	(R) takes advantage of (S) opportunities to control the behavior of others.
Persistence:	(R) continues an activity (S) in the face of difficulties.
Cooperativeness:	(R) complies with (S) request.

Needless to say, these dispositions are not conceived to be invariable but rather to vary in strength as a function of the frequency of Rs in a wide spread of Ss, as well as other factors, such as the average magnitude of the Rs. As a more explicit (though still highly schematic) model for the analysis of T-concepts, I offer the following.

> P is T to the degree $n =_{df}$. P is so constituted that if P is in an S on a large number of occasions, then P will emit R in m proportion of those occasions, the Rs having average magnitude o.

Construed in this way, Ts are what we may call "S-R frequency dispositions."

Although many concepts employed in personality description conform to the T-model, many do not. The latter group include such familiar items as desires, needs, motives, interests, attitudes, abilities, self-esteem, and the self-concept. Call the members of this group PC concepts, for reasons to be made explicit shortly.

The most obvious deviation of PCs from the T-model is this. T-strength, as we have seen, is a function of the frequency with which the person emits Rs of the appropriate category in a wide spread of Ss of the appropriate category. It could not be correct to call a person *very* domineering unless, given a large number of opportunities, he or she actually made many attempts to control the activities of others. But a like principle does not hold for PCs. No doubt, for any PC there are types of correlated Rs that we might call "manifestations" of that PC. Thus if a

646

person has a strong need, or desire, to dominate others, we would expect him or her to:

1. Seek to control the behavior of others
2. Feel elated when he or she succeeds in doing so
3. Frequently think of dominance-related matters

Nevertheless, PC strength does not necessarily vary with the frequency of such Rs. One can have a strong desire to dominate others without frequently emitting such Rs. One's inclinations to seek to control others may be inhibited by a fear of rejection or by strong scruples. Thoughts of dominance may be excluded from consciousness if it would be too painful to entertain them. And delight in achieving dominance may be smothered by contrary affects, such as guilt or fear of retaliation. Similar points hold for other PCs. A person may have abilities that he or she rarely exercises; one may have negative attitudes without "doing anything about it." Since it is possible to have a PC, even to a high degree, without emitting a relatively large number of Rs in a wide spread of Ss, a PC cannot be construed as an S-R frequency disposition.

But then how are desires, needs, interests, and the like to be conceived? It is my view that they spring from a familiar model of motivation, what we may call the "purposive-cognitive (PC) model." According to this way of thinking, one which in its gross outlines is familiar to all of us from early childhood, intentional action is undertaken in order to reach certain goals, the particular means employed being a function of the agent's beliefs as to what, in the current situation, is most likely to attain that goal. Sam is starting his car because the dominant goal for him at present is to arrive at his office at 9:00 A.M., and because he believes that the best way of ensuring this is to drive his car to a certain parking lot and that in order to do that he has to start the car. In stark outline this model features three basic types of inner psychological determinants: *desires*, which, so to speak, mark out certain states as "to be striven for"; *beliefs*, which provide bases for selecting certain lines of action as the most promising ways of reaching those goals; and *abilities*, which delineate the response repertoire from which the desire-belief combinations make their selections.

Typically more than one desire (including aversions under that heading) is activated at a given moment; and for any given goal, typically more than one means is envisaged. This means that usually there is conflict as to which of several alternative lines of action is most promising vis-à-vis a given goal, and there is conflict as to which goal is to be actively pursued. These facts force us to complicate the model by inserting a "field" of "tendencies" between the activated desires and beliefs on the one end and the actual responses on the other. An appropriate desire-belief pair would, in the absence of contemporaneous competition, give rise to the actual deployment of the means in question, assuming they are within the subject's power.

647

Where there is competition, we may think of *each* desire-belief pair as giving rise to a *tendency* to a certain response, where to say that P has a "tendency" to R at time *k* is to say that in the absence of interference, and assuming that R is within his power, P emits R at *k*. Thus we get a field of such tendencies, and out of the interaction within that field, some particular R emerges. The PC model, though deeply rooted in commonsense thinking, has been given a more technical elaboration by such psychologists as Lewin and Tolman, and more recently by Atkinson and Birch (1970).

To return to our conceptual problems, a desire or belief, I would suggest, is conceived as what occupies a certain position in motivational processes as depicted by the PC model. A desire for a goal, G, is that psychological state which, together with a belief that doing A is likely to contribute to the realization of G, will give rise to a tendency to A; that state which, together with a belief that G has been attained, gives rise to a tendency to feel elated, and so on. A complementary statement can be given as to what a belief is. I shall use the term *PC-concept* for the concepts that are spawned by PC theory.

We can now see *why* it is conceptually possible to have a strong desire without frequent manifestations. Whether the tendencies to which a desire is a disposition are actually carried out depends not just on *their* character, but also on the competition they encounter in the current psychological field. A strong desire will (given suitable beliefs) necessarily give rise to one or more strong *tendencies*, and its strength *is* a function of the strength of those tendencies. But whether those tendencies will frequently, or even ever be carried out is not a function of their strength alone. Thus even a strong desire may fail to be frequently manifested if frequently confronted by even stronger contrary desires.

Now for a brief look at the importance of this distinction for the psychology of personality. First consider the validation of measures. A distinction is often made between validation against a "criterion" and "construct validation." Their interrelation is a matter of controversy. But one thing that is practically never suggested in these discussions is that the way we conceptualize the C to be measured influences the kind of validation appropriate. This seems to be a grievous lack, for our distinction has a crucial bearing on the matter. To put the point shortly, criterion validation is possible for Ts in a way in which it is not for PCs. A T, as we have seen, is conceived in terms of a certain S-R frequency. This means that it follows from the very conception of a T that there is, in principle, a uniquely direct and decisive way of measuring the degree of T-possession. Observe the subject in a wide spread of Ss and determine the proportion of Rs (along with their magnitude and whatever other dimensions are relevant). The decisiveness of this particular test is rooted in the very concept of a T. We can't mean what we do by "cooperativeness" and still doubt that a person who has acceded frequently over a wide spread of requests is a very cooperative person. This "time-sampling" procedure has a special status as a *criterion* against which other proposed measures can be validated.

With PCs, on the contrary, no such uniquely privileged criterion is determined by the constitution of the concept. We have seen that a desire, for example, cannot be construed as a disposition to empirically accessible Rs. It is, rather, a disposition to develop tendencies to Rs, and the frequency of actual overt Rs is not a function just of the strength of the tendencies to R that are aroused on the relevant occasions but also of the strength of the competing tendencies roused on those occasions. Hence the concept of, for example, a desire to cooperate does *not* mark out frequency of cooperations as a decisive test of strength. With PCs, construct validation is the only available alternative.

As a second illustration, consider the search for nomological relationships, in other words, the use of C-concepts in general hypotheses. More specifically, let's consider hypotheses concerning the influence of Cs on Rs. The basic point is simply this. Each T, by its conceptual structure, is fitted to be used in isolation for the prediction of restricted types of Rs, while a given PC, by its conceptual structure, is fitted rather to enter with other variables into an indefinitely large number of combinations that can be used to predict and explain an indefinitely large range of Rs.

First an elaboration of the T side of the contrast. In attributing a high degree of a given T—aggressiveness, for example—to a person P, what we are *saying* is that that P is so constituted as to emit a large proportion of Rs of a given category in a wide spread of Ss of a given category. Therefore that attribution, just by virtue of its content, puts us in a position to predict such Rs, or some subclass thereof; and, on the level of general hypotheses, the concept warrants us in embracing any hypothesis that attributes to high-T persons a high frequency of any Rs that fall under the appropriate category. Just by virtue of what is meant by "aggressiveness," we are justified in supposing that a very aggressive person will be likely to take vigorous steps to defend himself if charged with a criminal violation, that such a person will protest vigorously if someone tries to get ahead of him in a queue, that he will retort to slurs rather than ignoring them, and so on.

PC-concepts, on the contrary, carry no such predictive power in isolation. A given PC-concept is not tied to any particular S-R frequency. If all we know about a person is that he has a very strong desire for recognition, that will not, by itself, give us a strong basis for predicting that he will frequently seek recognition. To have a strong basis for such predictions we would have to consider also what other strong needs, aversions, or fears he has—a strong fear of failure, for example—and whether the need for recognition might be overborne by some of these. By way of compensation, however, a PC-concept, by its very constitution, is fitted to enter with other factors into an indefinite variety of explanations of an indefinitely wide variety of Rs. We conceptualize a desire, for instance, as the kind of psychological state that combines with beliefs in a certain way to produce certain kinds of action tendencies, combines with beliefs in another way to produce certain kinds of affective reaction tendencies, and so on. The tendencies formed at a given moment

649

interact with each other in some kind of "force-field" to produce actual responses. Since a PC, by its very conception, is embedded in this kind of systematic matrix, it contains, so to say, plugs and sockets for making connections with other factors for the complex determination of an indefinitely wide range of responses. Thus if all we know about P is that he has a strong need for recognition, that gives us innumerable leads as to how pieces of further information can combine with this to provide explanations of an indefinitely wide range of Rs. When this need is activated and combined with the belief that the most likely way of securing recognition is to publish carefully worked out papers in his field, he will have a strong tendency to do so; combined with another belief, for example, that his most likely route to recognition is through making himself agreeable to powerful individuals, the same need will give rise to a strong tendency to that. Whether such tendencies will actually be carried out (and in what proportion of the cases) will further depend on their competition, and so the model directs us to look for possible competitors—a fear of having the papers rejected, for example—and to make an estimate of their strength. There is virtually no kind of R that might not be explained by this desire in combination with various other factors. The very thing that prevents a PC from being unilaterally related to Rs, viz., its embeddedness in a complex model of motivation, is the source of its unlimited potential for entering into systematic explanations.

Ts, by contrast, are not inherently fitted to enter into such systematic combinations: T-concepts contain no plugs and sockets. With Ts, the only bearing on Rs suggested by the concept is the S-R frequency explicitly contained therein. Just because a T-concept does not emerge out of a theoretical background, it is *conceptually* isolated.

I hope that even this fragmentary example may go some way toward illustrating how the analytical philosopher may use his special skills in a way that will be helpful to the psychologist.

REFERENCES

Alston, W. P. Toward a logical geography of personality: Traits and deeper lying personality characteristics. In *Mind, science, and history: Contemporary philosophic thought.* The International Philosophy Year Conferences at Brockport (Vol. 2). Albany, N.Y.: State University of New York Press, 1970.

Alston, W. P. Traits, consistency and conceptual alternatives for personality theory. *Journal for the Theory of Social Behavior,* 1975, 5, 17–48.

Atkinson, J. W., & Birch, D. *The dynamics of action.* New York: Wiley, 1970.

Cronbach, L. J. *Essentials of psychological testing.* New York: Harper & Row, 1960.

Peters, R. S. *The concept of motivation.* London: Routledge & Kegan Paul, 1958.

Ryle, G. *The concept of mind*. London: Hutchinson, 1949.
Ryle, G. *Dilemmas*. Cambridge, England: Cambridge University Press, 1954.

SUPPLEMENTARY READINGS

GENERAL OVERVIEW OF ANALYTICAL PHILOSOPHY

J. O. Urmson, *Philosophical analysis, its development between the two world wars* (Oxford, 1956) is a perceptive account of its period. R. Rorty, Ed., *The linguistic turn* (Chicago, 1967) is a good anthology of important articles setting forth "linguistic" analysis; it contains an extensive bibliography. H. Feigl & W. Sellars, Ed., *Readings in philosophical analysis* (New York, 1949) is a classic anthology; it is updated in H. Feigl, W. Sellars, & K. Lehrer, Eds., *New readings in philosophical analysis* (New York, 1972). The selections and introductions in W. P. Alston & G. Nakhnikian, Eds., *Readings in twentieth century philosophy* (New York, 1963) give a good picture of the major figures in the development of analytic philosophy.

EARLY BRITISH ANALYTIC PHILOSOPHY

The major figures in the development of analytic philosophy in the first two decades of this century were G. E. Moore and B. Russell. For Moore, see his essays in *Philosophical studies* (London, 1922) and *Philosophical papers* (London, 1959). For Russell, see *Our knowledge of the external world* (Chicago, 1914) and *The philosophy of logical atomism* (in Alston & Nakhnikian). At the end of this period we have L. Wittgenstein's epoch-making work, *Tractatus logico-philosophicus* (London, 1922).

LOGICAL POSITIVISM

The classic papers in this movement are collected in A. J. Ayer, Ed., *Logical positivism* (New York, 1959).

ORDINARY-LANGUAGE PHILOSOPHY

The Wittgensteinian source is *Philosophical investigation* (Oxford, 1953). In addition to the works by Ryle cited earlier, other major contributions include J. L. Austin, *Philosophical papers* (London, 1961) and *Sense and sensibilia* (Oxford, 1962), and J. Wisdom, *Philosophy and psychoanalysis* (Oxford, 1953). Three volumes edited by A. N. Flew contain many of the classic papers of this movement: *Logic and language: First series* (Oxford, 1951) and *Second series* (Oxford, 1953), and *Essays in conceptual analysis* (London, 1960). A. J. Ayer et al., *The revolution in philosophy* (London, 1956) is a series of BBC talks taking a general look at the movement.

ANALYTICAL PHILOSOPHY OF MIND
AND PHILOSOPHY OF PSYCHOLOGY

Armstrong, D. M. *A materialist theory of the mind*. London: Routledge & Kegan Paul, 1968.
Broad, C. D. *The mind and its place in nature*. London: Routledge & Kegan Paul, 1925.

651

Gustafson, C. F. (Ed.). *Essays in philosophical psychology*. New York: Doubleday, 1964.

Hampshire, S. *Thought and action*. London: Chatto & Windus, 1959.

Hampshire, S. (Ed.). *Philosophy of mind*. New York: Harper & Row, 1966.

Kenny, A. *Action, emotion and will*. London: Routledge & Kegan Paul, 1963.

Fodor, J. A. *Psychological explanation*. New York: Random House, 1968.

Rosenthal, D. M. (Ed.). *Materialism and the mind-body problem*. Englewood Cliffs, N.J.: Prentice-Hall, 1971.

Russell, B. *The analysis of mind*. London: George Allen & Unwin, 1921.

Shaffer, J. A. *The philosophy of mind*. Englewood Cliffs, N.J.: Prentice-Hall, 1968.

Taylor, C. *The explanation of behaviour*. London: Routledge & Kegan Paul, 1964.

PSYCHOLOGY AND MATHEMATICS

28

*Mathematical Modeling of Perceptual, Learning, and Cognitive Processes**

R. DUNCAN LUCE

Introductory Outline

Since experimental psychology mostly involves discrete responses at discrete times, it had no great compatibility with the largely continuous mathematics of the nineteenth century. But this has changed radically with the growth of mixed discrete and continuous ideas: set theory, probability and stochastic processes, and ordered algebraic structures. In this paper, a variety of specific examples of modeling are drawn from sensation and perception, learning and memory, measurement and scaling, and cognition and decision-making. Four conclusions are drawn. (1) Not everything that looks both mathematical and psychological is actually very satisfactory modeling. (2) We have not been as successful as we would like in separating theories of the organism from the boundary conditions of specific experiments. And when we fail to do so, it is difficult for knowledge to accumulate. (3) Theories are either stated at just one level (behavioral) or at two levels (cognitive as well as behavioral), and behavior is explained in terms of mental or physiological concepts. The latter, although highly appealing, suffer from severe problems of

*This work was supported in part by a grant from the National Science Foundation to Harvard University. I thank D. M. Green for his comments on an earlier draft.

nonidentifiability of explanatory concepts unless physiological data can be brought to bear. This has only really been done successfully in sensory work. (4) The apparently happy match of stochastic processes with experimental procedures has suffered from the need to cope with the control or strategy flexibility exhibited by subjects. This has led many to believe computer simulation is the easy way out. Some doubts are expressed.

Were one to take seriously the idea that scientific psychology began when Wundt founded a formal laboratory in 1879, one would have considerable trouble in understanding the initial interplay between mathematics and psychology. Among others, Fechner and Helmholtz would be banished, and that makes quite a dent in the early history of psychophysics. Of course, most of our graduate students, close adherents that they be of William James, would applaud the banishment of early psychophysics and would, no doubt, urge it for all of psychophysics.

The Growth of Mathematics Compatible with Experimental Psychology

The Nineteenth-Century Incompatibility: Continuous Mathematics and Discrete Psychology

In a way, it is somewhat surprising that mathematics and psychology were partners early on at all. Consider the mathematics available at the time, say, in the third quarter of the last century. Basically one had Euclidean geometry, which only a few mathematicians were aware was in the process of being dethroned as *the* geometry; various bits and pieces of algebra, especially linear algebra; analytic geometry, which is a lovely exploitation of structural parallels between algebra and geometry; a miscellany of results about the integers (number theory); and most important of all for applications, analysis—the calculus, ordinary and partial differential equations, theory of functions of a complex variable, Laplace and Fourier transforms, and the like—the basis on which physics had become mathematized, general, and predictive over the preceding two centuries. To a good first approximation, the mathematician or physicist who was likely to think about psychology was one who was familiar primarily with the mathematics suited to continuous or mildly discontinuous phenomena.

By contrast, the methods being evolved by experimental psychologists were highly discontinuous. Laboratory responses, then as now, usually were discrete events in time—a key pressed, a word spoken, a peck observed—and more often than not they were forced to be doubly discrete by making the times at which they could occur—trials—discrete as well. Even the moderately popular reaction times, which we now think of as continuous random variables, were not readily captured using the methods of analysis.

655

The widespread use of limited response alternatives occurring at prescribed times is a fact of laboratory psychology that has greatly influenced our history. From the point of view of this symposium, it prescribed rather closely what mathematics is compatible with our data. More generally, however, it has forced a radical idealization of what is involved in the interaction between organism and environment.

One Twentieth-Century Compatibility: Probability and Statistics

At the end of the last century and the beginning of the present one, the development of set theory, which very neatly put in the same framework finite, countable, and continuous sets, was an almost ideal match to the methods of the experimentalist. This became especially apparent with the creation during much the same period of probability theory, with its identification of chance events as sets, with the incorporation of the crucial concept of independence of events into the measure-theoretic ideas underlying the concept of an integral, with the careful isolation of the empirically essential concept of a random variable and its distribution function, and with the resulting evolution of ideas about estimation, inference, and correlation that constitute statistics. As long as one was willing to ignore response times as a measure of behavior, which it was easy to do since their accurate recording was rather awkward until recently, the observed data fit well the developing mathematics. With minor effort, relative frequencies could be extracted from data, and they looked like estimates of probabilities. True, there was the issue of whether the observations are actually independent and the strong possibility that the underlying probabilities sometimes are not fixed, as in learning, but a basic compatibility appeared to exist.

The earlier growth of analysis was symbiotic with both the field theories of physical force—gravity and electromagnetism—and the continuous theories of matter, in solid, liquid, and gaseous states; whereas, the later growth of probability and random variables was highly compatible with the largely discrete methods of psychology. It is, of course, true that statistics and probability have found widespread use throughout the social sciences and to a degree in the biological and physical ones, but I daresay that nowhere has this sort of modeling been more compatible than with experimental psychology.

Some Developing Incompatibilities

This clear compatibility of the probability models and the major methodological constraints of much of experimental psychology—discrete responses at discrete points of time—coupled powerful and developing mathematical methods together with vast aggregates of data and well-explored paradigms for getting additional data when needed. Such coupling was especially conspicuous in two areas: sensation and learning, topics which I discuss more fully later. During the time from 1925 to

1965, when much of the attempt to exploit the possibilities was under way, it was apparent that some limitations marred the picture. Like many obvious things, little was said about them in print, but much informal conversation together with subsequent events makes clear that the limitations were widely recognized. I shall cite three.

First, the great body of operant data was mostly ignored by model-builders. The reason was not so much Skinner's firm opposition, largely accepted by his disciples, to modelers (Skinner, 1950), although that was surely a factor, as it was the fact that the data were from free-response situations and so did not exhibit the familiar discrete trial structure.

Second, most of the models dealt with response probabilities but not response times. Yet a growing body of evidence suggested that these times exhibit an interesting, if complicated, structure. Moreover, the view began to be expressed quite explicitly that perhaps these continuous measures provide an important key to studying hypothesized internal decision processes.

Third, increasing evidence from cognitive experiments showed that subjects have varied strategies of coping with more-or-less complex perceptual, verbal, and memory tasks. And it has been less and less clear how to adapt stochastic processes to deal with them. Among other things, the paradigm of fixed, usually small, sets of response alternatives pretty well excluded any adequate study of verbal behavior and, more generally, of any responses that exhibit a degree of creativeness.

The past fifteen years have seen major attempts to break out of these limitations. The first two are a part of my story and I talk about them below. The third has more to do with the growth of modern linguistics and psycholinguistics, artificial intelligence, and parts of cognitive psychology about which I am not very expert, so I shall leave that to others.

A Second Twentieth-Century Compatibility: Abstract Algebra and Measurement

Before turning to more detailed matters, let me mention another part of my story, a second type of application of set theoretic methods to our problems. This century has seen a flowering of what is called "modern" or "abstract" algebra. It involves the isolation of structures that can be thought of as a collection of objects which are related to one another by means of operations—something like addition or multiplication—and/or by means of an ordering—something like greater than of numbers—and/or by means of other more complex relations. Such structures, whole classes of them, are studied by working out the mathematical consequences of axioms that describe how the operations and other relations behave. The axiomatic method is ancient—it was, after all, Euclid's method for organizing geometric results into a systematic statement of axioms and the development of their consequences as formal theorems—but it played almost no role in the flowering of

657

analysis following the invention of the calculus by Newton and Leibnitz. By contrast, modern mathematics has seen a number of deep and beautiful axiomatic developments, among them group theory and topology.

It had been clear for much of the last century—at least since Helmholtz (1887/ 1930)—that certain classes of ordered algebraic structures have some bearing on the widespread use of numbers in science. True, numbers can enter just by counting instances, which is how we estimate probabilities. But that is not how classical physics got the numerical measures with which we are all familiar, the ones to which units such as meters, ergs, ohms, and so on are attached. Rather, the structure of the system of numbers somehow systematically mimics certain data structures: greater than of numbers more-or-less accurately reflects an empirical ordering such as the tipping of an equal-arm pan balance, and the operation of addition reflects what happens when two objects are combined by placing them together on the same pan. Indeed, one can argue the view that any science must take its start from crude, qualitative changes that can be unambiguously perceived with the unaided senses, and the first theoretical task is to formulate laws about such observations, from which it may then be possible to provide a convenient numerical representation. At least, this is what appears to have been done, almost unconsciously, in developing the number system and using it to represent basic physical phenomena. Thus, for physics, the only purpose in actually developing axiomatic theories of measurement is to understand exactly what had so successfully evolved over centuries of commerce, barter, and finally scientific systematizing.

Matters have not been so simple for the social and behavioral sciences, in particular, psychology. Measurement has not come easily, and it is frustrating. We all speak of endless attributes that seem to exhibit the most essential feature of a measure, namely, order. There is more or less of utility, of intelligence, loudness, hunger, aggressiveness, fear, and so forth.

Such are our variables, our subject matter; yet it is doubtful if we know how to measure any of them in a fully satisfactory manner. That fact, perhaps more than any other, has pervaded our science in its first century. To be sure, we have a multi-million dollar industry based on the "measurement" of intelligence, but I doubt if there are many scientific psychologists who have much confidence that we know a great deal about the concept of intelligence or how to measure it well. Loudness and brightness remain to this today problematic in psychophysics, with no real consensus on how best to measure them in the service of developing psychophysical theory. Hunger we continue to index by hours of deprivation, knowing full well that that is not true for ourselves.

Our measurement problems lie at two levels. First, there is the question of how to order the attributes empirically. How do we decide whether a particular white, middle-class, well-educated male is more or less intelligent than, say, a black, ghetto-educated school-drop-out female? How do we decide whether a rat is equally hungry on two different experimental occasions? For the most part—psychophysics may be the major exception—we have been unable to solve this empirical problem in an intellectually satisfying, principled way. And without a solution, measurement is blocked.

The second problem, the mathematical one, assumes an ordering is given, and it concerns itself with the properties exhibited by the ordering and with the classes of numerical representations that are compatible with those properties. A great deal of work has been carried out on this topic, and we understand quite fully the structures that have been important in physics and the generalizations that may prove important in psychology, once we get adequate empirical orderings of attributes of interest.

Psychophysics and Perception

Representation of Signals as Random Variables

Since mathematics was first applied in psychology to psychophysics, let me begin there. Aside from some curve-fitting techniques, little happened after Fechner until Thurstone (1927a,b,c), who I would say was the first mathematical psychologist in this century. Why the wait? I suspect it was primarily for the arrival of the formal concept of a quantity whose value varies somewhat from observation to observation but which, nonetheless, can be thought of as unitary—what we now call a "random variable." Thurstone did not use that term, but he exploited the concept. He (and almost everyone after him who has modeled psychophysical phenomena) assumed that when signals which vary in one dimension are presented, each may be treated as if it is represented in the mind by a single number which fluctuates a bit from presentation to presentation. By slicing up the scale of the representation into intervals corresponding to possible responses, the exact location of the representation on each trial determines the response on that trial. Although Thurstone was much interested in conceptual matters, his followers tended to be swept up with the complexities of estimation, fitting, and computation, which at the time were grave. He and they failed to note, or to make anything of, the fact that the model strongly suggests that the subject can, by varying the response criterion, effect a trade-off of response errors. It was another twenty-five years before the importance of that was first recognized.

Psychologists connected with the Second World War were brought into contact with two major ideas from engineering and one from statistics: the theory of signal detectability, information theory, and decision theory. All three are a part of our story.

Theory of Signal Detectability

The theory of signal detectability (Green & Swets, 1974; Swets, Tanner, & Birdsall, 1961; Tanner & Swets, 1954) gave a plausible account of how a vector representation of a signal, which probably exists since a number of peripheral neurons are excited by any signal, can lead to a normally distributed random variable much as Thurstone had assumed. But it also placed great emphasis on the error trade-off —called the ROC curve—resulting from criterion changes. And it applied decision theory to explain those changes. When psychologists looked, subjects did indeed exhibit error trade-offs somewhat, but not exactly, like those predicted by decision theory (Green, 1960; Swets et al., 1961). As a result of those discrepancies, attempts have been made to use learning models to account for criterion change (Atkinson & Kinchla, 1965; Dorfman & Biderman, 1971; Dorfman, Saslow, & Simpson, 1975; Luce, 1963). In part because the theory of signal detectability does not generalize in a very satisfactory way beyond two signals, numerous later models have provided alternative accounts of the Thurstonian random variables. One group of these assumes they arise from some sort of aggregation of neural pulses where pattern and/ or rate are affected by the signal (Grice et al., 1979; Green & Luce, 1973; Luce, 1977a; Luce & Green, 1972, 1974; McGill, 1967; Siebert, 1968, 1970). Work along these lines was heavily influenced by the developing understanding of how information is encoded in the peripheral nervous system (Galambos & Davis, 1943; Kiang, 1965; Kiang et al., 1962; Rose et al., 1967, 1971).

Information Theory

Until the late 1950s, information theory (Shannon, 1948; Shannon & Weaver, 1949) was a major psychological fad: many papers resulted, but they had, I fear, little of lasting import for psychology. Since we all agree that much of our concern is information processing, why was this so? There are at least two reasons. First, the theory is concerned entirely with the statistics of messages—with, for example, how to encode a message to combat chance errors in the transmission—but it is not at all concerned with conveying or extracting meaning. Our concern is largely the latter and how that manifests itself in the behavior of organisms. Second, the theory makes much of a measure, the expected value of $-\log P$, called "entropy" or "uncertainty." Whenever a probability vector or distribution is collapsed into a single statistic—be it a mean, a variance, an entropy, or what have you—care must be taken to ensure that nothing much is lost. This was ultimately shown wrong for entropy in psychology. For example, much was initially made of the fact that mean-choice reaction time is linear with the entropy of the stimulus display—Hick's law—until Hyman (1953) carefully studied the component parts and showed their times were not simply related to $-\log P$.

As one would expect, there are some important residues (an early summary is Luce, 1960). One, I believe, is a result made famous by Miller (1956) as one of the three empirical bases for his concept of a magical number 7 ± 2 limiting our information-processing capabilities. One can state the result easily without reference to information theory. Two 1000-Hz tones 5-dB apart can be absolutely identified by anyone with normal hearing. But seven tones spread at 5-dB steps cannot be; the intervals have to be roughly tripled. Why is this important? Because it means that the Thurstonian random variable depends not only on the signal that is presented, but also on those that might have been presented. If a particular tone is presented, the variance of its representation is roughly an order of magnitude larger if it is in the context of identifying one of seven than if it is one of two tones (Braida & Durlach, 1972; Durlach & Braida, 1969; Gravetter & Lockhead, 1973). This strongly violates most peoples' intuitions about signal transduction, and therefore it poses a conceptual problem. Luce, Green, and Weber (1976) have attempted to resolve it in terms of selective attention affecting the neural sample sizes on which the representations are based, and Shaw (1980) has cited some supporting evidence in another area. But not everyone is convinced this explanation is correct.

Sensory Scaling

Another theme dating from Fechner and interlaced with the problems just discussed is sensory scaling. Fechner (1860/1966) thought he had solved it by postulating that a just-noticed sensory change is the same everywhere, no matter the size of the physical change required to produce it (see Falmagne, 1974, for a modern summary of the mathematics). Thurstone (1927b) simply had it as the expected value of his random variable representing the signal, but for computational reasons he wound up being forced essentially into Fechner's mold. Stevens (1957, 1961, 1975) said both were wrong in assuming any necessary interlock between the mean and the variance, citing physical mechanisms of various sorts as cases in point. He invented methods of so-called direct scaling to get at it, but showed little interest in how these measures related to the rest of psychophysics, where variability and error were the data. The debate still swirls actively today. Increasingly, however, scales play a role in theorizing about psychophysical phenomena of all sorts, and the so-called direct methods are more a problem to be explained than a direct insight into the mind.

Criteria for Psychophysical Modeling

For me, there are four criteria that must be met by any proposal to understand psychophysical data. First, the internal representation of a signal should be consistent with peripheral neurophysiological data, and in particular, while it must depend upon the stimulating conditions just before, during, and just after the signal presentation, it should not depend upon the experimental context within which the signal is embedded. Second, a model for any psychophysical experiment, from detection through cross-modality matching, should simply be an account of a plausible decision process carried out on the signal representation. Third, any experimental method, "direct" or not, does not, by fiat, provide a direct avenue to some truth. It requires a theoretical account just as much as any other experimental

661

procedure. If it is shown that some statistic of some method is proportional to the expected value of the signal representation, then that is, indeed, a nice way to estimate a sensory scale. But that needs to be shown, not assumed. Finally, my fourth criterion, which is perhaps more controversial but I think equally valid, is that the theory should give a natural account of response times. In particular, it should explain speed/accuracy trade-off results. Any theory that starts by assuming a random variable representation does not easily meet this criterion. Rather, one must explicitly postulate how information accumulates with time, and this means that the representation must be a sequence of random variables—a stochastic process—in order to account for the times taken to respond. Examples of such models are Green and Luce (1974), Link and Heath (1975), Ratcliff (1978). Although I think these criteria are clear, and possibly philosophically sound, carrying out work along these lines has proved trickier than one might have contemplated, and we are far from a fully articulated comprehensive psychophysical theory that encompasses the best known procedures.

Miscellaneous Visual Models

Once one turns from general matters to specific sensory modalities, there is such an overwhelming amount of research that one hardly knows what to say. Let me, therefore, pick several examples with strong mathematical themes. The first theme is Fourier methods. The concern here is with alternative representations of a wave form, one as a function of time and the other as a function of frequency; or, in statistical terms, a distribution and its characteristic function. This duality has long played a role in audition, and in recent years has come to be highly dominant in vision where it is thought that one aspect of perception may be a spatial Fourier analysis (Graham & Ratliff, 1974; Robson, 1975). Such theories are inherently perceptual since the calculation of the transform is over a large region; it is, by its nature, not a local concept. This has led to a program of experiments involving sine wave gratings. It is premature to say where this is going to end, but it clearly has had several effects, among them that physical scientists have been attracted to work on visual perception, and there is a deepening grip of mathematical methods in these areas. Let no one approach these gratings who is unwilling to study advanced calculus.

The second theme is geometry, in particular, the geometric nature of visual perception. We view an outside world that physics tells us is three-dimensional and, at the speeds with which we can deal, locally Euclidean. It is projected on two two-dimensional surfaces which can be moved in certain ways, and out of that is somehow constructed an internal model of that physical world. What are the geometric properties of such a representation? This is no place to try to detail any results: suffice it to say that the question is less easy to answer than it might seem

(Blank, 1959, 1961; Indow, 1974; Luneberg, 1947; Suppes, 1977), and it continues to be under active investigation.

Continuing for a moment with vision, let me cite a final area, color vision, in which mathematical modeling has and continues to play a role. Empirical evidence has accumulated over the years that makes clear that there is an initial physiological three-color code which is rather radically altered for some behavioral purposes into a coding of opponent colors (DeValois & DeValois, 1975; Hering, 1878; Hurvich & Jameson, 1955; Jameson & Hurvich, 1955). Active work goes on in an attempt to understand mathematically what is involved here and how it relates to other aspects of vision; one lovely axiomatic study of this is Krantz (1975).

Learning and Memory

The attempts mathematically to model learning do not trace back nearly so far as do those for psychophysics. Hull (1943), and to a lesser degree Spence (1956), undertook early mathematical formulations, but today that elaborate program is largely dismissed as not very satisfactory modeling. More mathematically satisfactory work was carried out by Thurstone (1930) and Gulliksen (1934), but it suffered from the fact that it only tried to deal with average performances. As we now know, many quite different theories lead to the same or very similar mean learning curves, and one must provide a much more detailed understanding of the entire process. Just as the entropy measure often results in a combining of dissimilar things, so, too, the mean may cause interesting information to vanish from sight. For example, the mean may be the same whether the distribution of behavior is tightly centered about the mean or is U-shaped, with a fraction of the animals doing one thing and the rest doing something totally different.

The Rise of Markov Models

Serious modeling of learning awaited the development and infusion into psychology of knowledge about stochastic processes. Such processes are simply collections of random variables indexed by time. If the time variable is discrete—conventionally the integers—then it is said to be a "discrete-time stochastic process"; if time is continuous—conventionally the real numbers—then it is called a "continuous-time process." Although the case of independent random variables is of great interest in statistics, in learning, each random variable, which describes the propensity to select among the alternatives at an instant in time, is a function of the past events of the process, and so is by its very nature not independent of the past. The task is to describe the dependence.

In the 1950s two major ideas arose, both involving discrete time processes corresponding to learning experiments with trials. The one was the linear operators of Bush and Mosteller (1955). Basically, on each trial the organism is assumed to be described by a vector of response probabilities over the possible responses. A response is made according to the distribution, a reinforcement occurs, and together they determine a new vector for the next trial, with the changes all being linear. (Later, I suggested a class of nonlinear models in which the order of application of the operators was immaterial [Luce, 1959, 1964].) Note that such models have a very important, simplifying feature known as the "Markovian property": the current vector of probabilities depends on the preceding one, but not on any before that; it does not matter whatsoever how one gets to that vector; there is no memory other than that embodied in the previous vector.

At much the same time, Estes (see Atkinson & Estes, 1963, for a summary) was developing his theory of stimulus sampling for learning. Here the key idea was a mechanism of associative memory, involving what he called stimulus elements that are individually associated with responses. On each trial a sample of the elements is selected, the relative balance of associations thereby determining the response made. Following the response, the conditioning of the sample is or is not changed, depending on the reinforcement of that trial. This, like the Bush-Mosteller model, has the Markovian property, but unlike theirs, the possible probabilities are restricted to a finite set, and this led to what is technically called a "Markov chain." In a certain limiting case, it approached the linear operator model.

The Demise of Markov Models

Under the influence of Atkinson and Bower (for surveys see Atkinson, Bower, & Crothers, 1965; Atkinson & Juola, 1974; Greeno, 1974), it was not long before a family of Markov chain models for learning and memory processes were developed that were entirely independent of the stimulus-sampling interpretation. A characteristic difference between the operator models and the chain ones was that the former suggested the learning occurred in small steps, the latter, in rather discontinuous jumps in memory states. In a classic experiment, Bower (see Atkinson et al., 1965, Chap. 3) showed that of the two types of models, the discontinuous one was clearly the better. This led to a massive program at Stanford University of Markov chain modeling and to the group of people, sometimes more or less affectionately referred to as the Stanford Mafia, who have been major actors in developing the memory part of cognitive psychology. Curiously, as that developed, fewer and fewer mathematical models were involved, and there was more and more computer simulating. Let us examine what happened.

The routing of the operator model was relatively complete. True, Norman (1972) developed a beautiful general theory of them; they continued to play a minor role in psychophysics; and they have come to play a role outside psychology in engineering and elsewhere. Nonetheless, Markov chains won the day; and yet a decade later they were passé. As I see it, there were two related major reasons. The first was the Markov property itself. This made for easy analysis, at least for Markov chains, since their theory is very complete, but these were memory models that denied much real memory or else forced incredibly complex memory states. They could not account in a reasonable way for the fact that an animal resists extinction far longer after partial reinforcement than after 100 percent reinforcement. The models admitted hardly any cognitive power, no notion of analysis of patterns from the past, none but the most primitive memory.

The second problem is far more subtle, but, in my opinion, crucial. Let me state it this way. These models failed to meet the following criterion, which I consider to be essential for successful modeling of behavior: that there should be a theory of the impact of stimuli and reinforcement on the organism separate from a description of the environment within which the organism is placed, and together these two generate a model of the organism in that environment. For those familiar with physics, it is analogous to having a theory of the relevant physical variables embodied in a system of equations and a set of boundary conditions describing the particular context within which the process is unfolding. In particular, parameters about the organism that are estimated from two distinct experiments should agree to within the error resulting from the data. Whenever one has only models of experiments, with no separable theory of the organism, then one has a hopeless feeling that no information is accumulating. The Markov chains were models of the combined subject and experiment, and no separation was suggested. This, by the way, was not really true of Estes's original stimulus-sampling model.

Another fact about these models, although I think it did not especially bother those at Stanford, was that they were limited to discrete trial experiments and did not encompass free responding. There was a little work (Donio, 1969; Norman, 1966) to generalize them to operant situations, but it did not attract much attention. During the past five years or so, however, operant psychologists, largely under the leadership of Herrnstein, have begun to develop mathematical models for various operant procedures (de Villiers, 1977; Herrnstein, 1974). Two major lines are being pursued. One is to try to view the behavior as resulting from some sort of continuous-time stochastic process that is being affected by the experimental reinforcement schedule which is itself a continuous-time stochastic process that may or may not depend on the behavior (Heyman & Luce, 1979; Staddon & Motheral, 1978). The other thrust is to try to involve ideas from economics, treating the rats and pigeons as if they are "economic men." The preliminary evidence is that animals fit that model rather well, better than human beings do (Rachlin, 1979; Rachlin & Burkhard, 1978; Shimp, 1975), providing that one does not insist on maximization of overall reinforcements.

665

Memory and Response Time

As the emphasis shifted from learning and Markov chains to a concentration on memory, another important change occurred. The focus came to be less on accuracy of performance—the studies were mostly designed so that performance was nearly perfect—while the emphasis was on the time to carry out the information processing (Audley, 1974). Perhaps the earliest and clearest example of that was the technique evolved by Sternberg (1969a, b). The basic idea is that by manipulating various stages of the internal processing, one affects the response times. The problem is to infer from the times the nature of the processing involved. This continues to be a very appealing idea, one that should continue to receive a great deal of attention, in particular drawing on the forms of the time distributions rather than just their means. But as Grossberg (1978), Townsend (1976), Theois and Walter (1974), and others have been at pains to point out, it is not without problems. Without information other than the time, it is probably impossible to infer any unique structure generating those times. Added constraints are needed. We run into the same problem in certain psychophysical modeling, but there at least we can draw upon peripheral neurophysiology to limit our choices; it appears to be less easy to do something comparable in cognition.

Measurement and Scaling

I have already made some general remarks about the, to me, important problems of axiomatic measurement, and I shall not pursue that much more except to mention what I consider the two or three most important developments.

Decision Theory

The earliest measurement theory totally distinct from those of physics, the one which convinced many of us that psychological measurement might ultimately prove tractable, was expected-utility theory and its subjective variants resting on the ideas of qualitative probability (Fine, 1973; Fishburn, 1970; Krantz et al., 1971, Chaps. 5, 8; Luce & Raiffa, 1957; Ramsey, 1931/1964; Savage, 1954; von Neumann & Morgenstern, 1944). The main idea was to study choices among alternatives where the outcome is partially under the control of chance. These concepts, together with both the multivariate ideas mentioned below and the use of Bayes's theorem to incorporate information in probability assessments, has spawned an area of some applied value called decision analysis (Bell, Keeney, & Raiffa, 1977; Pratt, Raiffa, & Schlaifer, 1965; Raiffa, 1968; Schlaifer, 1969).

In a sense, this can be viewed as one of the first attempts to provide a cognitive analysis of human responses—it is cognitive because the situation itself is subjected to analysis rather than being dealt with in some relatively reflexive or associative way. The resulting theory appears to provide a fine analysis of what is a rational approach to such problems, one that is partially descriptive of what people do. However, after a good deal of probing experimentation, it is now clear that people are doing something different. The evidence is overwhelming that context affects the decisions in a way we do not yet understand (Coombs, 1969; Coombs & Huang, 1970, 1976; Grether & Plott, 1979; MacCrimmon, 1968; MacCrimmon, Stanbury, & Wehrung, 1980). The area is so important, the data are so tantalizingly regular, and the modeling so elegant, I have no doubt that we will persist in trying to crack this nut.

Conjoint Measurement

Another major measurement development, dating back nearly twenty years (Debreu, 1960; Luce & Tukey, 1964), is conjoint measurement and its close relation, multiattribute utility (Keeney & Raiffa, 1976). This exploits the fact that an ordering of multifactor stimuli is really rather more structured than one first realizes, provided the factors can be manipulated independently. There is a trade-off between factors that can be studied and exploited. Physics has long done so—e.g., saying that kinetic energy is proportional to mass and to the square of velocity describes those trade-offs that leave the energy unchanged—but physicists and mathematicians failed to work out the corresponding qualitative theory. This has now been done not only for the cases of interest to physics, but also for a number of other cases that may be pertinent to psychology, especially ones for which the representation involves distributive mixtures of addition and multiplication (Krantz, 1972, 1974; Krantz & Tversky, 1971; Krantz et al., 1971; Narens, 1976; Narens & Luce, 1976). Elaborate computer programs now exist which make the applications of these methods quite practical, provided that the data are not too plagued by error (Young, 1972). The task of generalizing the models to handle error, important as it is, has only just begun with the work of Falmagne (1976) and Falmagne et al. (1979).

Before turning to other matters, I cannot refrain from mentioning that the development of theories relating additive conjoint and extensive measurement has provided an adequate qualitative account of the entire structure of classical physical quantities (Krantz et al., 1971, Chap. 10). Moreover, by bringing to bear the attempts to clarify the idea of meaningful measurement statements (Stevens, 1946, 1951), there has developed a satisfying explanation why natural laws are dimensionally invariant (Adams, Fagot, & Robinson, 1965; Krantz et al., 1971; Luce, 1978; Pfanzagl, 1971; Suppes & Zinnes, 1963). The upshot is a better understanding of why the useful method of dimensional analysis works.

667

Three Types of Scaling: Probabilistic, Functional-Measurement, and Multidimensional

From the point of view of the working psychologist, much of this work in measurement has seemed esoteric, and three other scaling methods enjoy far wider use.

The oldest are probabilistic—sometimes inappropriately called "stochastic"—models of choice which assume an underlying scale from which the probabilities arise. Thurstone's model, viewed in a wider context than psychophysics, is of this character, as is my 1959 choice-axiom model (Luce, 1959, 1977b) whose relations to Thurstone have been so neatly developed by McFadden (1974) and Yellott (1977). The data have made clear its limitations, which first Restle (1961) and later Tversky (1972a, b) have attempted to overcome by working out explicit notions of the similarity of stimuli which appears to play a crucial role in people's choices.

Next is the work of Anderson (1974) and his students on what they call "functional measurement." The context is similar to that of conjoint measurement, but instead of working with orderings and axioms, they begin with numerical data and an assumed representation and they fit the representation to the data using analyses of variance methods. The range of application has been impressive and influential, especially in the so-called "soft areas" of psychology.

The last and probably the single most successful area of scaling is that of multidimensional scaling, especially the nonmetric version (Carroll & Wish, 1974; Shepard, 1962, 1974; Torgerson, 1952, 1958, 1965). The input data concern the similarity of stimuli, and even numerical data are treated as providing only ordered information about similarity. The model is usually assumed to be n-dimensional, Euclidean space, with the ordinary distance metric reflecting the ordering of the data, although other spaces have been looked at. The procedure is to find that monotonic transformation of the ordering that yields the smallest number of dimensions providing an adequate account of the data. The mathematics of what is involved has never been fully worked out although there has been some partial work (Beals, Krantz, & Tversky, 1968; Tversky & Krantz, 1970); but computer software for doing what I have described is well developed. In a number of applications, the results have been most impressive, almost always giving a much more comprehensible representation of the data than does its major competitor, factor analysis.

Similarity and Categorization

As I said earlier, the major problem in all of these measurement and scaling applications is getting the empirical ordering of the attribute of interest. In the three scaling methods just discussed, this is resolved largely by getting subjects to establish the order. The subject tells the experimenter about the similarity of stimuli. This is fine as far as it goes, but one suspects that in the long run there needs to be developed a theory of similarity or, what I believe to be the same thing, categorization. Tversky (1977) has offered one interesting analysis, discussed by Krumhansl (1978), but perhaps the most striking developments along these lines right now are not theoretical but empirical. Especially important is the work on natural categories of Cerella (1979), Herrnstein (1979), Herrnstein and de Villiers (1980), and Rosch et al. (1976, 1978). It is not unusually difficult, by showing a pigeon slides of trees and branches which are reinforced and nontrees which are not, to draw forth the concept of tree so that the pigeon henceforth responds appropriately to new tree and new nontree slides. More striking, one can do the same thing using underwater shots of fish in natural habitats and fish-free water habitats, an environment not much a part of the recent experience of pigeons. Moreover, pigeons agree with us about what is a typical fish, making errors just when we do. We know little about this area, but it is clear that the instances of natural categories are complexly related to one another, and it invites much, much more work. This is something that seems basic, important for a behaving organism, and approachable in the laboratory. It will be an enormously important conceptual challenge to mathematical psychologists.

Concluding Remarks

In closing, I am supposed to assess where we are. That is complex, and anything I say is bound to be incomplete, unsatisfactory, and, probably, misleading. Nevertheless, I shall try.

1. Not everything published in psychology with equations or mathematical terms in it is, necessarily, a serious or satisfactory attempt to involve mathematics in theory development. Some cases are now easy to recognize—e.g., Lewin's (1935) hand waving of topology or Hull's (1943) ponderous learning theory. Other more recent cases strike me as more subtle, and I approach them with some concern that I am wrong. All the cases I have in mind exhibit a pattern. First, they note that some branch of mathematics, often a highly respected one, exhibits qualities not unlike the empirical ones of some branch of psychology. Second, to suggest that there is something to the analogy, attempts are made to identify certain of the mathematical concepts with usually informal psychological concepts. However, this step is notable for the lack of any detailed identification between the principal terms of the mathematical theory and specific empirical objects or relations. Third, the level of abstraction is usually very high, comparable to that of advanced physical theories such as quantum mechanics or the general theory of relativity, but this is in areas which, unlike physics, have not yet seen detailed, low level, empirically testable theories from which to generalize and abstract. Fourth, the sponsors are usually well-trained and often respected mathematicians whose knowledge of psychology and whose empirical experience, even in the physical sciences, is very sketchy.

669

III. PSYCHOLOGY AND ITS INTERSECTING DISCIPLINES

At the risk of making enemies across the board, let me cite several specific examples of what I have in mind: catastrophe theory for any phenomenon that exhibits discontinuous jumps and hysteresis (Kolata, 1977; Poston & Stewart, 1978; Saari, 1977; Smale, 1978; Sussmann & Zahler, 1978; Zeeman, 1977); tolerance spaces as models of the mind (Zeeman, 1962); fuzzy set theory for anything involving an apparently imprecise boundary; and lie groups as a way to account for visual illusions (Paillard et al., 1977).

2. My second general observation is that we have failed more often than we have succeeded to construct theories of the organism rather than models of an organism in a particular experiment. Only to the extent that we begin to do that will our work achieve a cumulative character. To a degree, this has happened in sensory psychology, and I think that is one of the reasons that mathematics is such an integral part of that area.

3. Our theories are of two types, as in physics. One involves concepts and constructs at only one intellectual level—in our case, observed macro behavior. The operator models for learning and much of measurement and scaling is of this type. The other involves concepts and usually mechanisms at one level, often a postulated, unobserved mental process, to account for observations at a different level. The sensory random variables, the stimulus elements sampled in Estes's early learning theory, and the stages of memory encoding and processing of Sternberg's theory of memory are all of this character. These reductionistic theories seem far richer and intuitive than the wholly behavioral ones, which is both their appeal and their weakness. Only to the degree that one can bring to bear data appropriate to the explanatory level is it possible to avoid endless arguments about the identifiability of concepts. So far, this has been done successfully, and there only to a very limited degree, in sensory psychology. Other concepts that one hopes have a solid physiological basis, such as memory stores of various sorts, have so far eluded physiological isolation. Nonetheless, extremely interesting and deep investigations along these lines are beginning to appear, e.g., the current work of Grossberg (1980).

4. Although there is at least a superficial happy match between stochastic processes—i.e., time-indexed random variables—and our experimental procedures, whether with trials or free response, not all is well. The development of cognitive psychology has departed from that mode. Part of it, that having to do with grammar, draws on ideas of recursive functions and logic, and that having to do with memory has drifted more and more toward computer simulations, where complex options are easy to build in. Subjects seem to have available many alternative ways of behaving and it seems less stressful to most theorists to try to embody this in computer programs (Simon & Newell, 1974). I am yet to be convinced that this use of computer programs is really solving any problem. The difficulties we are having in cognitive psychology may be conceptual or experimental or both. We may be asking the wrong questions, given our current understanding, and we may not be getting under experimental control enough of what goes on in the typical cognitive

experiment. For example, understanding natural categories may be a necessary, though hardly sufficient, precursor to understanding semantic memory, yet many more scientists have been working on memory than on categorization. In any event, I think some cognitive psychologists may have thrown over mathematics for computer programs a bit too fast. Some—those whose knowledge of mathematics is largely restricted to Markov chains—may have found this the easy route, but others—most notably Simon—have made a conscious and well-informed choice. My own hope—and it is little more than that—is that cognitive psychology will be the source of a new interplay of mathematics and psychology, and perhaps in the long run the source of some new mathematics.

My conclusion that mathematics in psychology is here to stay will come as no surprise. To the degree that a scientist thinks there is some redundancy in what he of she observes and reports, that not everything is independent of everything else, then he or she is dealing with structure. And that is exactly what mathematics is the study of. The only problem is to isolate those structures appropriate to psychological phenomena. Our success in doing so, while considerable, is rather less than I should like to be able to claim. Still, mathematics and computer simulation are really the only games in town if you want to understand and to predict data.

REFERENCES[1]

Adams, E., Fagot, R., & Robinson, R. A theory of appropriate statistics. *Psychometrika*, 1965, *30*, 99–127.

Anderson, N. H. Information integration theory: A brief survey. In D. H. Krantz, R. C. Atkinson, R. D. Luce, & P. Suppes (Eds.), *Contemporary developments in mathematical psychology* (Vol. II). San Francisco: Freeman, 1974.

Atkinson, R. C., Bower, G. H., & Crothers, E. J. *An introduction to mathematical learning theory.* New York: Wiley, 1965.

Atkinson, R. C., & Estes, W. K. Stimulus sampling theory. In R. D. Luce, R. R. Bush, & E. Galanter (Eds.), *Handbook of mathematical psychology* (Vol. II). New York: Wiley, 1963.

Atkinson, R. C., & Juola, J. F. Search and decision processes in recognition memory. In D. H. Krantz, R. C. Atkinson, R. D. Luce, & P. Suppes (Eds.), *Contemporary developments in mathematical psychology* (Vol. I). San Francisco: Freeman, 1974.

Atkinson, R. C., & Kinchla, R. A. A learning model for forced-choice detection experiments. *British Journal of Mathematical and Statistical Psychology*, 1965, *18*, 184–206.

Audley, R. J. Some observations on theories of choice reaction times: Tutorial review. In S. Kornblum (Ed.), *Attention and performance* (Vol. IV). New York: Academic Press, 1974.

Beals, R., Krantz, D. H., & Tversky, A. Foundations of multidimensional scaling. *Psychological Review*, 1968, *75*, 127–142.

---

[1] It is quite impractical to give comprehensive references; the compromise I have followed, albeit imperfectly, is to cite both seminal papers and review articles and books, which will permit the reader to recover as much of the earlier history as desired.

Bell, D. E., Keeney, R. L., & Raiffa, H. *Conflicting objectives in decisions.* New York: Wiley, 1977.

Blank, A. A. The Luneburg theory of binocular space perception. In S. Koch (Ed.), *Psychology: A study of a science* (Vol. I). New York: McGraw-Hill, 1959.

Blank, A. A. Axiomatics of binocular vision: The foundations of metric geometry in relation to space perception. *Journal of the Optical Society of America,* 1961, *51,* 335–339.

Braida, L. D., & Durlach, N. I. Intensity perception, II. Resolution in one interval paradigms. *Journal of the Acoustical Society of America,* 1972, *51,* 483–502.

Bush, R. R., & Mosteller, F. *Stochastic models for learning.* New York: Wiley, 1955.

Carroll, J. D., & Wish, M. Models and methods for three-way multi-dimensional scaling. In D. H. Krantz, R. C. Atkinson, R. D. Luce, & P. Suppes (Eds.), *Contemporary developments in mathematical psychology* (Vol. II). San Francisco: Freeman, 1974.

Cerella, J. Visual classes and natural categories in the pigeon. *Journal of Experimental Psychology: Human Perception and Performance,* 1979, *5,* 68–77.

Coombs, C. H. Portfolio theory: A theory of risky decision making. *La decision.* Paris: Centre National de la Research Scientifique, 1969.

Coombs, C. H., & Huang, L. C. Tests of a portfolio theory of risk preference. *Journal of Experimental Psychology,* 1970, *85,* 23–29.

Coombs, C. H., & Huang, L. C. Tests of the betweenness property of expected utility. *Journal of Mathematical Psychology,* 1976, *13,* 323–337.

Debreu, G. Topological methods in cardinal utility theory. In K. J. Arrow, S. Karlin, & P. Suppes (Eds.), *Mathematical methods in the social sciences, 1959.* Stanford, Calif.: Stanford University Press, 1960.

DeValois, R. L., & DeValois, K. K. Neural coding of color. In E. C. Carterette & M. P. Friedman (Eds.), *Handbook of perception* (Vol. V). New York: Academic Press, 1975.

de Villiers, P. A. Choice in concurrent schedules and a quantitative formulation of the law of effect. In W. K. Honig & J. E. R. Staddon (Eds.), *Handbook of operant behavior.* Englewood Cliffs, N.J.: Prentice-Hall, 1977.

Donio, J. Stimulus sampling learning models described as continuous-time stochastic processes. *Journal of Mathematical Psychology,* 1969, *6,* 240–257.

Dorfman, D. D., & Biderman, M. A learning model for a continuum of sensory states. *Journal of Mathematical Psychology,* 1971, *8,* 264–268.

Dorfman, D. D., Saslow, C. F., & Simpson, J. C. Learning models for a continuum of sensory states reexamined. *Journal of Mathematical Psychology,* 1975, *12,* 178–211.

Durlach, N. I., & Braida, L. D. Intensity perception, I. Preliminary theory of intensity perception. *Journal of the Acoustical Society of America,* 1969, *46,* 372–383.

Falmagne, J.-C. Foundations of Fechnerian psychophysics. In D. H. Krantz, R. C. Atkinson, R. D. Luce, & P. Suppes (Eds.), *Contemporary developments in mathematical psychology* (Vol. II). San Francisco: Freeman, 1974.

Falmagne, J.-C. Random conjoint measurement and loudness summation. *Psychological Review,* 1976, *83,* 65–79.

Falmagne, J.-C., Iverson, G., & Marcouici, S. Binaural "loudness" summation: Probabilistic theory and data. *Psychological Review,* 1979, *86,* 25–43.

Fechner, G. T. *Elemente der psychyphysik* (2 vols.). Leipzig: Breitkopf und Härtel, 1860. (English translation, *Elements of psychophysics.* New York: Holt, 1966.)

Fine, T. *Theories of probability.* New York: Academic Press, 1973.

Fishburn, P. C. *Utility theory for decision making.* New York: Wiley, 1970.

Galambos, R., & Davis, H. The response of single auditory nerve fibers to acoustic stimulation. *Journal of Neurophysiology,* 1943, *6,* 39–57.

Graham, N., & Ratliff, F. Quantitative theories of the integrative action of the retina. In D. H. Krantz,

R. C. Atkinson, R. D. Luce, & P. Suppes (Eds.), *Contemporary developments in mathematical psychology* (Vol II). San Francisco: Freeman, 1974.

Gravetter, F., & Lockhead, G. R. Criterial range as a frame of reference for stimulus judgment. *Psychological Review*, 1973, *80*, 203–216.

Green, D. M. Psychoacoustics and detection theory. *Journal of the Acoustical Society of America*, 1960, *32*, 1189–1203.

Green, D. M., & Luce, R. D. Speed-accuracy tradeoff in auditory detection. In S. Kornblum (Ed.), *Attention and Performance* (Vol. IV). New York: Academic Press, 1973.

Green, D. M., & Luce, R. D. Counting and timing mechanisms in auditory discrimination and reaction time. In D. H. Krantz, R. C. Atkinson, R. D. Luce, & P. Suppes (Eds.), *Contemporary developments in mathematical psychology* (Vol II). San Francisco: Freeman, 1974.

Green, D. M., & Swets, J. A. *Signal detection theory and psychophysics.* Huntington, N.Y.: Krieger, 1974. (Corrected reprint, New York: Wiley, 1966.)

Greeno, J. G. Representation of learning as discrete transition in a finite state space. In D. H. Krantz, R. C. Atkinson, R. D. Luce, & P. Suppes (Eds.), *Contemporary developments in mathematical psychology* (Vol. I). San Francisco: Freeman, 1974.

Grether, D., & Plott, C. Economic theory of choice and the preference reversal phenomenon. *American Economic Review*, 1979, *69*, 623–638.

Grice, G. R., Spiker, V. A., & Nullmeyer, R. Variable criterion analysis of individual differences and stimulus similarity in choice reaction time. *Perception & Psychophysics*, 1979, *25*, 353–370.

Grossberg, S. Behavioral contrast in short term memory: Serial binary memory models or parallel continuous memory models? *Journal of Mathematical Psychology*, 1978, *17*, 199–219.

Grossberg, S. How does a brain build a cognition code? *Psychological Review*, 1980, *87*, 1–51.

Gulliksen, H. A rational equation of the learning curve based on Thorndike's law of effect. *Journal of General Psychology*, 1934, *11*, 395–434.

Helmholtz, H. von Zählen und Messen erkenntnis-theoretisch betrachet. *Philosophische Aufsätz Edvard Zeller gewidmet.* Leipzig, 1887. Reprinted in *Gesammelte Abhandl.*, *3*, 1895, 356–391. (English translation by C. L. Bryan, *Counting and measuring.* Princeton, N.J.: van Nostrand, 1930.)

Hering, E. *Zur Lehre vom Lichtsinne.* Vienna: C. Gerold's Sohn, 1878.

Herrnstein, R. J. Formal properties of the matching law. *Journal of the Experimental Analysis of Behavior*, 1974, *21*, 159–164.

Herrnstein, R. J. Acquisition, generalization, and discrimination reversal of a natural concept. *Journal of Experimental Psychology: Animal Behavior Processes*, 1979, *5*, 116–126.

Herrnstein, R. J., & de Villiers, P. A. Fish as a natural category for people and pigeons. In G. Bower (Ed.), *The psychology of learning and motivation* (Vol. 14). New York: Academic Press, 1980. Pp. 59–95.

Heyman, G. M., & Luce, R. D. Operant matching is not a logical consequence of maximizing reinforcement rate. *Animal Learning & Behavior*, 1979, *7*, 133–140.

Hull, C. L. *Principles of behavior: An introduction to behavior theory.* New York: Appleton-Century-Crofts, 1943.

Hurvich, L. M., & Jameson, D. Some quantitative aspects of an opponent-colors theory. II. Brightness, saturation, and hue in normal and dichromatic vision. *Journal of the Optical Society of America*, 1955, *45*, 602–616.

Hyman, R. Stimulus information as a determinant of reaction times. *Journal of Experimental Psychology*, 1953, *45*, 188–196.

Indow, T. Applications of multidimensional scaling in perception. In E. C. Carterette & M. P. Friedman (Eds.), *Handbook of perception* (Vol. II). New York: Academic Press, 1974.

Jameson, D., & Hurvich, L. M. Some quantitative aspects of opponent-colors theory. I. Chromatic responses and spectral saturation. *Journal of the Optical Society of America*, 1955, *45*, 546–552.

673

III. PSYCHOLOGY AND ITS INTERSECTING DISCIPLINES

Keeney, R. L., & Raiffa, H. *Decisions with multiple objectives: Preferences and value tradeoffs.* New York: Wiley, 1976.

Kiang, N. Y-S. *Discharge patterns of single fibers in the cat's auditory nerve.* Cambridge, Mass.: M.I.T. Press, 1965.

Kiang, N. Y-S., Goldstein, M. H., Jr., & Peaks, W. T. Temporal coding of neural responses to acoustic stimuli. *Institute of Radio Engineers, Transactors on Information Theory,* 1962, IT-8, 113–119.

Kolata, G. B. Catastrophe theory: The emperor has no clothes. *Science,* 1977, *196,* 287, 350–351.

Krantz, D. H. Measurement structures and psychological laws. *Science,* 1972, *175,* 1427–1435.

Krantz, D. H. Measurement theory and qualitative laws in psychophysics. In D. H. Krantz, R. C. Atkinson, R. D. Luce, & P. Suppes (Eds.), *Contemporary developments in mathematical psychology* (Vol. II). San Francisco: Freeman, 1974.

Krantz, D. H. Color measurement and color theory: I. Representation theorem for Grassman structures. II. Opponent-colors theory. *Journal of Mathematical Psychology,* 1975, *12,* 283–303, 304–327.

Krantz, D. H., Luce, R. D., Suppes, P., & Tversky, A. *Foundations of measurement* (Vol. I). New York: Academic Press, 1971.

Krantz, D. H., & Tversky, A. Conjoint-measurement analysis of composition rules in psychology. *Psychological Review,* 1971, *78,* 151–169.

Krumhansl, C. L. Concerning the applicability of geometric models to similarity data: The interrelationship between similarity and spatial density. *Psychological Review,* 1978, *85,* 445–463.

Lewin, K. *A dynamic theory of personality.* New York: McGraw-Hill, 1935.

Link, S. W., & Heath, R. A. A sequential theory of psychological discrimination. *Psychometrika,* 1975, *40,* 77–105.

Luce, R. D. *Individual choice behavior.* New York: Wiley, 1959.

Luce, R. D. The theory of selective information and some of its behavioral applications. In R. D. Luce (Ed.), *Developments in mathematical psychology.* Glencoe, Ill.: Free Press, 1960.

Luce, R. D. A threshold theory for simple detection experiments. *Psychological Review,* 1963, *70,* 61–79.

Luce, R. D. Some one-parameter families of commutative learning operators. In R. C. Atkinson (Ed.), *Studies in mathematical psychology.* Stanford, Calif.: Stanford University Press, 1964.

Luce, R. D. Thurstone's discriminal processes fifty years later. *Psychometrika,* 1977, *42,* 461–489. (a)

Luce, R. D. The choice axiom after twenty years. *Journal of Mathematical Psychology,* 1977, *15,* 215–233. (b)

Luce, R. D. Dimensionally invariant numerical laws correspond to meaningful qualitative relations. *Philosophy of Science,* 1978, *45,* 1–16.

Luce, R. D., & Green, D. M. A neural timing theory for response times and the psychophysics of intensity. *Psychological Review,* 1972, *79,* 14–57.

Luce, R. D., & Green, D. M. Neural coding and psychophysical discrimination data. *Journal of the Acoustical Society of America,* 1974, *56,* 1554–1564.

Luce, R. D., Green, D. M., & Weber, D. L. Attention bands in absolute identification. *Perception & Psychophysics,* 1976, *20,* 49–54.

Luce, R. D., & Raiffa, H. *Games and decisions.* New York: Wiley, 1957.

Luce, R. D., & Tukey, J. W. Simultaneous conjoint measurement: A new type of fundamental measurement. *Journal of Mathematical Psychology,* 1964, *1,* 1–27.

Luneburg, R. K. *Mathematical analysis of binocular vision.* Princeton, N.J.: Princeton University Press, 1947.

MacCrimmon, K. R. Descriptive and normative implications of the decision-theory postulates. In K. Borch & J. Mossin (Eds.), *Risk and uncertainty.* New York: Macmillan, 1968.

MacCrimmon, K. P., Stanbury, W. T., & Wehrung, D. A. Real money lotteries: A study of ideal risk, context effects, and simple processes. In T. S. Wallsten (Ed.), *Cognition processes in choice and decision behavior.* Hillsdale, N.J.: Erlbaum, 1980. Pp. 155–177.

674

McFadden, D. Conditional logit analysis of quantitative choice behavior. In P. Zarembka (Ed.), *Frontiers in econometrics*. New York: Academic Press, 1974.

McGill, W. J. Neural counting mechanisms and energy detection in audition. *Journal of Mathematical Psychology*, 1967, *4*, 351.

Miller, G. A. The magical number seven, plus or minus two: Some limits on our capacity for processing information. *Psychological Review*, 1956, *63*, 81–97.

Narens, L. Utility-uncertainty trade-off structures. *Journal of Mathematical Psychology*, 1976, *13*, 296–322.

Narens, L., & Luce, R. D. The algebra of measurement. *Journal of Pure and Applied Algebra*, 1976, *8*, 197–233.

Norman, M. F. An approach to free-responding on schedules that prescribe reinforcement probability as a function of interresponse time. *Journal of Mathematical Psychology*, 1966, *3*, 235–268.

Norman, M. F. *Markov processes and learning models*. New York: Academic Press, 1972.

Paillard, J., et al. The lie transformation group model for perceptual and cognitive psychology. (A report of a conference.) *Cahiers de Psychology*, 1977, *20*, 71–231.

Pfanzagl, J. *Theory of measurement* (2nd ed.). Würzburg: Physica-Verlag, 1971.

Poston, T., & Stewart, I. Nonlinear modeling of multistable perception. *Behavioral Science*, 1978, *23*, 318–334.

Pratt, J. W., Raiffa, H., & Schlaifer, R. O. *Introduction to statistical decision theory*. New York: McGraw-Hill, 1965.

Rachlin, H. Economics of the matching law. In J. E. R. Staddon (Ed.), *Adaptation to constraint: The biology, economics, and psychology of individual behavior*. New York: Academic Press, 1979.

Rachlin, H., & Burkhard, B. The temporal triangle: Response substitution in instrumental conditioning. *Psychological Review*, 1978, *85*, 22–47.

Raiffa, H. *Decision analysis*. Reading, Mass.: Addison-Wesley, 1968.

Ramsey, F. P. Truth and probability. In F. P. Ramsey, *The foundations of mathematics and other logical essays*. New York: Harcourt, Brace, 1931. Reprinted in H. E. Kyburg, Jr., & H. G. Smokler (Eds.), *Studies in subjective probability*. New York: Wiley, 1964.

Ratcliff, R. A theory of memory retrieval. *Psychological Review*, 1978, *85*, 59–108.

Restle, F. *Psychology of judgment and choice*. New York: Wiley, 1961.

Robson, J. G. Receptive fields: Neural representation of the spatial and intensive attributes of the visual image. In E. C. Carterette & M. P. Friedman (Eds.), *Handbook of perception* (Vol. V). New York: Academic Press, 1975.

Rosch, E., & Lloyd, B. B. (Eds.). *Cognition and categorization*. Hillsdale, N.J.: Erlbaum, 1978.

Rosch, E., Mervis, C. B., Gray, W., Johnson, D., & Bayes-Braem, P. Basic objects in natural categories. *Cognitive Psychology*, 1976, *8*, 382–439.

Rose, J. E., Brugge, J. F., Anderson, D. L., & Hind, J. E. Phase-locked response to low-frequency tones in single auditory nerve fibers of the squirrel monkey. *Journal of Neurophysiology*, 1967, *30*, 769–793.

Rose, J. E., Hind, J. E., Anderson, D. J., & Brugge, J. F. Some effects of stimulus intensity on response of auditory nerve fibers in the squirrel monkey. *Journal of Neurophysiology*, 1971, *34*, 685–699.

Saari, D. G. A qualitative model for the dynamics of cognitive processes. *Journal of Mathematical Psychology*, 1977, *15*, 145–168.

Savage, L. J. *The foundations of statistics*. New York: Wiley, 1954.

Schlaifer, R. O. *Analysis of decisions under uncertainty*. New York: McGraw-Hill, 1969.

Shannon, C. E. A mathematical theory of communication. *Bell System Technical Journal*, 1948, *27*, 379–422, 623–656.

Shannon, C. E., & Weaver, W. *The mathematical theory of communication*. Urbana, Ill.: University of Illinois Press, 1949.

Shaw, M. L. Identifying attentional and decision-making components in information processing. In R. S. Nickerson (Ed.), *Attention and performance* VIII. Hillsdale, N.J.: Erlbaum, 1980. Pp. 277–296.

III. PSYCHOLOGY AND ITS INTERSECTING DISCIPLINES

Shepard, R. N. Analysis of proximities: Multidimensional scaling with an unknown distance function. I, II. *Psychometrika*, 1962, 27, 125–140, 219–246.

Shepard, R. N. Representation of structure in similarity data: Problems and prospects. *Psychometrika*, 1974, 39, 373–421.

Shimp, C. P. Perspectives on the behavioral unit: Choice behavior in animals. In W. K. Estes (Ed.), *Handbook of learning and cognitive processes* (Vol. 2). Hillsdale, N.J.: Erlbaum, 1975.

Siebert, W. M. Stimulus transformations in the peripheral auditory system. In P. A. Kolers and M. Eden (Eds.), *Recognizing patterns*. Cambridge, Mass.: M.I.T. Press, 1968.

Siebert, W. M. Frequency discrimination in the auditory system: Place or periodicity mechanisms? *Proceedings of the IEEE*, 1970, 58, 723.

Simon, H. A., & Newell, A. Thinking processes. In D. H. Krantz, R. C. Atkinson, R. D. Luce, & P. Suppes (Eds.), *Contemporary developments in mathematical psychology* (Vol. I). San Francisco: Freeman, 1974.

Skinner, B. F. Are theories of learning necessary? *Psychological Review*, 1950, 97, 193–216.

Smale, S. Review of catastrophe theory: Selected papers by E. C. Zeeman. *Bulletin of the American Mathematical Society*, 1978, 84, 1360–1368.

Spence, K. W. *Behavior theory and conditioning*. New Haven: Yale University Press, 1956.

Staddon, J. E. R., & Motheral, S. On matching and maximizing in operant choice experiments. *Psychological Review*, 1978, 85, 436–444.

Sternberg, S. The discovery of processing stages: Extensions of Donder's method. In W. G. Koster (Ed.), *Attention and performance* II. *Acta Psychologica*, 1969, 70, 276–315. (a)

Sternberg, S. Memory-scanning: Mental processes revealed by reaction time experiments. *American Scientist*, 1969, 57, 421–457. (b)

Stevens, S. S. On the theory of scales of measurement. *Science*, 1946, 103, 677–680.

Stevens, S. S. Mathematics, measurement, and psychophysics. In S. S. Stevens (Ed.), *Handbook of experimental psychology*. New York: Wiley, 1951.

Stevens, S. S. On the psychophysical law. *Psychological Review*, 1957, 64, 153–181.

Stevens, S. S. To honor Fechner and repeal his law. *Science*, 1961, 133, 80–86.

Stevens, S. S. *Psychophysics*. New York: Wiley, 1975.

Suppes, P. Is visual space euclidean? *Synthese*, 1977, 35, 397–421.

Suppes, P., & Zinnes, J. L. Basic measurement theory. In R. D. Luce, R. R. Bush, & E. Galanter (Eds.), *Handbook of mathematical psychology* (Vol. I). New York: Wiley, 1963.

Sussmann, H. J., & Zahler, R. S. Catastrophe theory as applied to the social and biological sciences: A critique. *Synthese*, 1978, 37, 117–216.

Swets, J. A., Tanner, W. P., Jr., & Birdsall, T. G. Decision processes in perception. *Psychological Review*, 1961, 68, 301–340.

Tanner, W. P., Jr., & Swets, J. A. A decision-making theory of visual detection. *Psychological Review*, 1954, 61, 401–409.

Theois, J., & Walter, D. G. Stimulus and response frequency and sequential effects in memory scanning reaction times. *Journal of Experimental Psychology*, 1974, 106, 1092–1099.

Thurstone, L. L. Psychophysical analysis. *American Journal of Psychology*, 1927, 38, 368–389. (a)

Thurstone, L. L. A law of comparative judgment. *Psychological Review*, 1927, 34, 273–286. (b)

Thurstone, L. L. Three psychophysical laws. *Psychological Review*, 1927, 34, 424–432. (c)

Thurstone, L. L. The learning function. *Journal of General Psychology*, 1930, 3, 469–491.

Torgerson, W. S. Multidimensional scaling: I. Theory and method. *Psychometrika*, 1952, 17, 401–419.

Torgerson, W. S. *Theory and methods of scaling*. New York: Wiley, 1958.

Torgerson, W. S. Multidimensional scaling of similarity. *Psychometrika*, 1965, 30, 379–393.

Townsend, J. T. Serial and within-stage independent parallel model equivalence on the minimum completion time. *Journal of Mathematical Psychology*, 1976, 14, 219–238.

Tversky, A. Elimination by aspects: A theory of choice. *Psychological Review*, 1972, 79, 281–299. (a)

676

Tversky, A. Choice by elimination. *Journal of Mathematical Psychology*, 1972, 9, 341–367. (b)

Tversky, A. Features of similarity. *Psychological Review*, 1977, 84, 327–352.

Tversky, A., & Krantz, D. H. The dimensional representation and the metric structure of similarity data. *Journal of Mathematical Psychology*, 1970, 7, 572–596.

von Neumann, J., & Morgenstern, O. *Theory of games and economic behavior*. Princeton, N.J.: Princeton University Press, 1944, 1947, 1953.

Yellott, J. I., Jr. The relationship between Luce's choice axiom, Thurstone's theory of comparative judgment, and the double exponential distribution. *Journal of Mathematical Psychology*, 1977, 15, 109–144.

Young, F. W. A model for polynomial conjoint analysis algorithms. In R. N. Shepard, A. K. Romney, & S. B. Nerlove (Eds.), *Multidimensional scaling: Theory and applications in the behavioral sciences* (Vol. I). New York: Sumner Press, 1972.

Zeeman, E. C. The topology of the brain and visual perception. In N. K. Fort (Ed.), *Topology of 3-manifolds*. Englewood Cliffs, N.J.: Prentice-Hall, 1962.

Zeeman, E. C. *Catastrophe theory: Selected papers*. London: Addison-Wesley, 1977.

29

Multivariate Statistics
WHEN WILL EXPERIMENTAL PSYCHOLOGY CATCH UP?

RICHARD J. HARRIS

My purpose in this paper is threefold: first, briefly to trace the history of the development of multivariate statistics; second, to suggest how one aspect of this history (identification of multivariate statistics with soft-nosed, correlational research) has led to gross underuse of multivariate statistics by experimental psychologists; and, third, to warn against yet another "hangover" from multivariate statistics' history: a tendency to be too dependent on mathematical statisticians and thus to allow mathematical considerations to override sound research practice.

A Brief History

The first task is made easy by a comprehensive, annotated bibliography (Anderson, Das Gupta, & Styan, 1972) of methodological papers relevant to multivariate statistics from 1811 through 1966 and a history (Bose, 1977) of the crucial period from 1908 to 1939.

1811 as a beginning date for multivariate statistics? 1939 as an end point for a crucial period in the development of multivariate statistics? By the most common measure of the age of a field—publication of the first textbook devoted to that area—multivariate statistics was born in 1957 with the publication of Kendall's, Roy's, and DuBois's texts, followed shortly by that of T. W. Anderson (1958).

The answer to this historical puzzle is that the development of the mathematical tools for multivariate analyses preceded by many years the availability of the computational tools necessary to make their use feasible in all but the most trivial problems. Work important to the development of multivariate statistics extends back at least to Gauss's (1823, 1828) work on least-squares methods for the univariate case. (The 1811 date refers to a paper by Laplace on certain definite integrals which subsequently proved useful in statistics.) Even if we restrict our attention to papers dealing with truly multivariate issues, we find several precocious studies published before the turn of the century: Kummell's (1879) "Reduction of observation equations which contain more than one observed quantity," DeForest's (1881) extension of the "law of error" to "the position of a point in space," and Edgeworth's (1884, 1888) papers on ways of handling "observations relating to several quantities." Bose (1977), however, dates the modern development of multivariate statistics from Student's (1908) solution of the small-sample problem for the correlation coefficient. The development of multiple regression followed soon thereafter (Yule, 1907; Pearson, 1914; Fisher, 1922; Hall, 1927; Fisher, 1928). Pearson's (1914) comments "On certain errors with regard to multiple correlation occasionally made by those who have not adequately studied the subject" make it clear that neither misuse of multivariate statistics nor biting criticism thereof are recent inventions. This same period saw the development of path analysis (Wright, 1921; Niles, 1922; Wright, 1923), T^2 and discriminant analysis (Hotelling, 1931; Malahobnis, 1930; Fisher, 1938), and multivariate analysis of variance and canonical correlation (Hotelling, 1936; Hsu, 1939; Roy, 1939).

The three 1939 papers, which took canonical correlation beyond the $p = q = 2$ case, solved the general eigenvalue problem (required when ratios of sums of squares are to be maximized). This, in turn, "led to an explosive development of multivariate analysis" (Bose, 1977). The principal reason for the lag between completion of the essential mathematical work on which multivariate statistics is based and the "birth" of the field eighteen years later was probably the computational infeasibility, with only desk calculators on hand, of the elegant mathematical solutions to the eigenvalue problem—or even just matrix inversion. Anyone who has had the experience of trying to illustrate inversion of even a 3×3 matrix, or calculation of the eigenvalues thereof, in class without having worked the problem in advance can appreciate why practitioners were slow to adopt multivariate techniques. Considerable attention was paid during these "prenatal" years to finding ways of simplifying and increasing the reliability of "hand" analyses (e.g., Hull, 1925; Toops, 1927; Salisbury, 1929; Hall, Welker & Crawford, 1945; Castore & Dye, 1949), but the work remained prodigious until the development of the digital computer.

Multivariate users were quick to make use of the computer, beginning with ORDVAC (Wrigley & Neuhaus, 1952) and the early IBM machines (Walsh, 1964), through the establishment of nationally distributed packages of programs, beginning with BMD (Dixon, 1961). Nevertheless, the long period of solely mathematical feasibility left its mark on the early multivariate textbooks in the form of the assumption that a strong background in calculus and in matrix algebra is a prerequisite to an understanding of multivariate statistics. This assumption led to writing for an audience with the presumed background, thereby excluding all but the most quantitatively inclined psychologists. When I first began to search (in 1968) for a textbook to use in teaching multivariate to graduate and advanced undergraduate psychology students, I was struck by how simple the underlying concepts of multivariate statistics are—and how difficult it was to find a textbook which made that underlying simplicity clear to mathematically unsophisticated students.

It may be perfectly obvious to someone with three years of calculus and one of linear algebra behind him or her that a particular set of equations is simply a mathematical shortcut to maximizing the Pearson correlation between two linear combinations of measures and is conceptually no different than setting a legion of calculator-armed graduate students to work on finding this canonical R—but a psychology student who is perfectly capable of seeing the value of knowing these optimal linear combinations and the maximum correlation they yield, but who has carefully avoided math courses ever since she or he had a choice, cannot be expected to realize that that is what the equations are offering if this is not put into words. Recently a number of texts have appeared (e.g., Tatsuoka, 1971, and Harris, 1975) which fill the spaces between equations with verbal descriptions of what the math is designed to accomplish and what the properties of the resulting statistical tools must therefore be. I should like to believe that the availability of such texts has contributed to the rapidly growing awareness of the need for multivariate statistics and the concomitant growth in the number of multivariate courses and the number of psychological research papers employing multivariate statistics.

Underuse of Multivariate Statistics in Experimental Research

This spread of multivariate techniques has not been uniform throughout all fields of psychology. In particular, the "hardnosed" experimental areas have shown very little awareness of or interest in multivariate approaches. While preparing a plea for students to take a recent offering of UNM's multivariate course, I did a survey of the first six months of the 1974 *Journal of Experimental Psychology* (*JEP*) (118 papers) and the first three months of the 1975 *Journal of Personality and Social Psychology* (*JPSP*) (73 articles). I found that roughly 13 percent of the *JPSP* research papers, but only 3 percent of the *JEP* research papers, employed a multivariate technique—and in each of the *JEP* "multivariate" papers, the technique employed had been least-squares fitting of the relationship between cell means and levels of an independent variable. Scanning of 1978 issues of these two journals suggests that this discrepancy has, if anything, widened, with multivariate statistics having become more common in *JPSP* (perhaps in response to Tony Greenwald's 1976 declaration of editorial policy requiring explicit recognition of and use of statistics appropriate to, multiple dependent measures) while remaining virtually nonexistent in *JEP*.

One explanation we might advance for the rarity of multivariate applications in experimental psychology is that they are not *needed* in experimental research. After all, multivariate statistics is just for those soft-nosed, correlational researchers, isn't it? Historically, this has been the case. Before we can decide whether this is anything more than a historical accident, we need to discuss just what it is that multivariate statistics can do for psychologists, be they soft-nosed or hard-nosed.

What Multivariate Statistics Can Do, Even for Experimentalists

Basically, multivariate statistics provide two things: control of Type I error rate, and identification of linear combinations of correlated measures which may be much more strongly related than any individual measure. This second function of multivariate statistics is basically an exploratory one, so that failure to check for such emergent variables (e.g., to examine the discriminant function which maximally differentiates among levels of one's independent variable) is a matter of missed opportunity—serious enough for scientists, but at least not misleading as to the reliability of the findings one *does* report.

More serious—at least for psychologists who prefer devoting their interpretative efforts to reliable findings, rather than wasting it on chance phenomena—is the inflation of Type I error rate which results when a separate univariate analysis is conducted on each of several dependent variables, using univariate significance levels for each test. It is ironic that the same experimental psychologists who would be scornful of a paper whose analysis of a five-way, single-factor design consisted solely of ten pairwise *t*-tests employing a critical value appropriate for a single test, are apparently unconcerned about the similar compounding of Type I error rate that comes from carrying out several (I've seen up to fifteen in a single paper) Anovas, one on each of the dependent variables. Thus, one thing which multivariate statistics can contribute is control over experimentwise or familywise alpha.

Control of Type I Error Rate   On the other hand, if control of Type I error rate for sets of univariate tests is all multivariate statistics had to offer, we could condense multivariate texts into the paragraph or two needed to explain the Bonferroni inequality. If we carry out k-tests, each at the α_i level, then the overall probability of one or more Type I errors is $\leq \Sigma \alpha_i$. Thus we need only adjust our alpha levels for the individual tests, α_i, downward so that their sum doesn't exceed the desired familywise error rate, α_t. This principle holds true, no matter whether the individual tests' results are correlated or not—though Bonferroni-adjusted critical values become progressively more conservative as the individual tests become more highly intercorrelated.

681

The Bonferroni-adjusted critical value for carrying out p univariate Anovas, or multiple regression analyses (MRAs) or t-tests on each of p dependent variables will always be less stringent (and the tests therefore more powerful) than the critical value for the overall multivariate test since the latter has to provide protection for the infinite number of comparisons on all possible linear combinations of measures. It is the possibility that one or more of these linear combinations will be much more important (show a much higher among-groups F or multiple correlation with the predictors or pairwise t) than any single dependent variable, which makes this loss of power worthwhile. If the researcher is incapable of thinking in terms of new, emergent variables—just as many researchers still can't think of between-group comparisons following a significant overall effect in terms of anything but simple pairwise differences—then use of overall multivariate tests like multivariate analysis of variance (Manova), canonical correlation analysis (Canona), and Hotelling's T^2 simply waste power—just as use of the overall F test in Manova wastes power if you're simply going to follow it up with pairwise tests like the HSD or Newman-Keuls tests, rather than exploring the more general Scheffé contrasts which the overall F maximizes.

Identification of Emergent Variables However, if one *is* willing to consider linear combinations of dependent variables as new variables in their own right, and to devote some effort to providing substantive interpretations of these emergent variables, the gains can be substantial. There are certainly sound theoretical reasons for expecting linear combinations of independent or dependent variables to be especially important—from the greater reliability of simple averages of related but imperfect measures of the same conceptual variable, to the very different norms of social interaction apt to be responsive to the *average* age of two participants versus the *difference* in their ages, or the differential effects of reinforcement on the asymptote (average of last several trials) versus the quadratic curvature of a learning curve.

(Relatively) Assumption-Free Analysis of Repeated Measures This last example brings up one particular area in which univariate and multivariate approaches directly compete—namely, repeated measures designs. By far the most common approach to analyzing such designs is via univariate Anova, testing each within-subject effect and its interactions with other effects against the pooled interaction between subjects and that within-subject factor.

However, as Huynh and Feldt (1970) have made especially clear, this error term is an average of potentially very different variances (across subjects) of various contrasts among the levels of the within-subject factor. Unless all of these contrasts (when normalized such that the sum of the squares of the contrast coefficients is unity) have identical variances across (interactions with) subjects, the overall F-test employing the pooled-error term is positively biased, and the statistical significance of particular contrasts may be either grossly exaggerated or grossly underestimated.

This same design can be handled without the need of any assumptions about homogeneity of the treatment variances and covariances via an application of Manova known as profile analysis (Harris, 1975, Chap. 4 or Morrison, 1976, Chap. 5). Computationally, any Manova program (e.g., Cramer's 1974 MANOVA program) can be used to carry out profile analysis by submitting to it as dependent variables the simple sum of all the original scores on the within-subject factor, together with a set of single-df contrasts among the levels of the within-subject factor or factors. It is still very rare, however, to find a repeated-measures paper which reports even having tested the assumptions necessary for the validity of the univariate Anova approach, let alone applying profile analysis to obviate these assumptions. Among those which do recognize the assumptions required, the most common approach is to apply the Greenhouse and Geisser (1959) adjustment to degrees of freedom so as to provide a conservative test of the overall F for a given effect, followed by specific comparisons using the pooled term. The resulting overall test is perfectly valid, though ambiguous when the effect is significant by the conventional test but not by the Greenhouse-Geisser conservative criterion. The tests of specific comparisons are, however, of unknown validity, since the true variance of any given contrast may be so discrepant from the average variance that it is still highly positively biased, even after downward adjustment of the degrees of freedom for the pooled error term. (See Harris & Ronis, Note 1, for an example.) Instead, each contrast must be tested against its own variance across subjects, using either a Bonferroni-adjusted critical value or the critical value for the Manova test (expressed as a maximized F contrast).

Summarizing Multivariate statistics can provide control of familywise Type I error rates where multiple measures are involved, including repeated-measures designs, and can identify new, "emergent" variables which may be much more important than any single one of the variables with which the analysis was begun. These contributions are just as important for experimental designs as they are for correlational research; experimentalists' low awareness of them is simply an historical accident.

Two Examples of Positive Contributions

I have thus far focused on the properties of multivariate statistics which make them logically suitable for experimental applications. I have avoided pointing out specific examples of such applications, lest I reveal the very low frequency of my reading in traditional experimental areas. However, two examples bear pointing out.

First is Kimble's (1961, pp. 400–402) discussion of studies dating back to 1938 which demonstrate that even such a deceptively simple concept as hunger yields far from perfectly correlated operational definitions, so that multiple measures are necessary whether hunger is employed as an independent or as a dependent variable. Second is Cattell and Dielman's (1974) application of factor analytic techniques to thirty-six different measures of rats' maze-running behavior "under differing conditions of reward and deprivation for fear, gregariousness, and thirst in three separate mazes" and their resulting demonstration of a close correspondence between the basic dimensions of this maze-running behavior and components "which have consistently emerged in human research."

Do Not Leave Multivariate Statistics to the Statisticians

Having just identified one unfortunate consequence of multivariate statistics' history (their underuse among experimental researchers), we now turn to a second historical accident which has direct relevance to the general theme of the relationships between mathematics and psychology: namely, the tendency to adopt techniques developed for us by mathematicians (in this case, mathematical statisticians) uncritically, without subjecting them to constant "reasonableness" tests.

Dangers of Avoiding Mathematics and the Other Side of the Coin

I have complained elsewhere (Harris, 1976a,c) that social psychologists' reliance on verbally stated theories (in preference to mathematical or computer-simulation models) has severed a crucial link in the hypothetico-deductive chain by making it impossible to know what research hypotheses do or do not follow from a given set of assumptions. Thus we have the spectacle of a dissonance theorist testing a "prediction" about the effects of absolute attractiveness of the alternatives involved in a decision which does *not* follow from the postulates of dissonance theory; of three different conformity theorists reporting data which soundly disconfirm a deterministic model of conformity as strong support for the model; of equity theorists claiming to employ definitions of equity which, when actually manipulated algebraically, turn out to yield nonsensical stipulations as to "what's fair"; and so on. I'm confident that much of the continuing effort to "test" verbally stated learning theories or theories in other areas of psychology would prove to be equally misleading if subjected to some simple algebraic checks. It simply isn't possible to know, for any but the simplest, single-process theories, what research hypotheses do or do not follow from a set of verbally stated postulates.

Multivariate statistics, on the other hand, provide examples of the dangers which await us if we let ourselves be awed by mathematical complexity to the point of abdicating our responsibility for deciding where and how mathematical tools are to be applied to psychological problems. This overdependence on mathematical statisticians developed, I believe, as a consequence of the long period (1939–1956) during which the mathematical development of the principal multivariate techniques was essentially complete (though, as Bose, 1977, points out and Anderson, Das Gupta, & Styan's 1972 tables of number of mathematical papers per year make clear, there was feverish activity to extend and refine these mathematical underpinnings), but the actual computations involved in carrying out most of these techniques in all but the simplest problems were prohibitively time-consuming. As a consequence, only mathematical statisticians and those few psychologists who had an extensive mathematical background learned about multivariate statistics, and the first textbooks which presented these techniques naturally assumed such sophistication among their audience, thus keeping knowledge of multivariate statistics relatively exclusive for another thirteen years (1957–1970).

The antidote to such overdependence is, I believe, to acquaint all potential users of multivariate statistics with the amazing simplicity of the goals of multivariate techniques and of the basic strategy (application of well-known univariate techniques to linear combinations of measures) used to accomplish these goals. Arming oneself with such a *heuristic* understanding of multivariate statistics has at least three potential benefits, to which we now turn.

Avoiding Silly Mistakes via Heuristics

One continues to find authors who use the fact that adding, say, locus-of-control scores to a regression equation for predicting some aspect of social behavior increases the resulting multiple R each of the ten times (once for each of ten behaviors) this is done as strong support for the importance of this variable. If we assume that adding LOC as a predictor would, if LOC in fact had an exactly zero population regression coefficient, lead to an increased R in 50 percent of the samples from the population, but to a decreased R in the other 50 percent, this "10 out of 10" statistic provides a very convincing sign test. However, a moment's reflection on the basic properties of multiple regression analysis (MRA) reveals that this is incorrect; adding a predictor to a regression equation *cannot* decrease R under any circumstances and must almost inevitably increase it in *all* samples. This would be very difficult to prove via algebraic manipulation of the scalar or matrix equations used to compute multiple R. It follows immediately, however, from the fact that what these equations accomplish is the selection of combining weights for all of the predictors which has the highest possible Pearson product-moment correlation with the dependent variable. If we add a predictor, the MRA algorithm, whatever its details, always has available the same coefficients it used to obtain R_m based on the original m predictors, and it can therefore achieve an R_{m+1} exactly equal to R_m by simply retaining the old coefficients and assigning the new predictor a weight of zero. Inevitably, then, random variability in the sample will permit finding an R_{m+1}

higher than R_m by assigning a nonzero weight to the new predictor, X_{m+1}, and adjusting the values of the weights for X_1 through X_m. Thus, simply knowing the goals of MRA and having faith that the mathematical algorithm does its job correctly (a faith subject to repeated verification) is sufficient to tell us that the "10 out of 10" statistic is totally uninformative and that we must therefore look at the magnitude of the increment in R (actually, R^2) relative to the increment to be expected in the null case.

Similarly, we continue to find published papers (which I shall refrain from citing) in which authors use the weights various predictors receive in a multiple regression equation as a criterion for selecting the best predictor of the dependent variable. However, MRA is not designed for this application, but instead answers the question of how best to combine *all* the predictors. If we intend to use only one of the predictors, we should simply pick that predictor having the highest Pearson r with the dependent variable, regardless of its relationships with other predictors and whether or not it makes more than a trivial contribution to the regression equation which employs *all* the variables.

Somewhat more subtly, hundreds of pages and a great deal of fretting have been devoted to the fact that regression weights can differ greatly in magnitude and even in sign from the zero-order correlations of these same variables with the dependent variable. Thus we are provided with pejorative-sounding "suppressor variable" terminology and given sets of rules for avoiding such situations or "correcting" them when they arise, when they are simply a reflection of the fact that regression coefficients and zero-order correlations answer conceptually distinct questions: how much does this variable contribute when used in combination with these other predictors versus how useful a predictor is it if it must be used by itself. Within the MRA setting, we should be focusing on interpreting the optimal linear combination as a substantively interesting variable in its own right rather than getting upset about the fact that performance as one of many predictors is not always perfectly predictable from performance as a "loner." It is ironic that many of the researchers who are upset by suppressor variables are thoroughly familiar with and eager to point out context effects in personality, perception, clinical prediction, and so forth.

Keeping the properties of multivariate analysis of variance (Manova) and of canonical correlation analysis (Canona) in mind would be sufficient (as focusing on computational details or computer program setup procedures would not) to set off "alarm bells" whenever a canonical correlation (R_c) comes out lower than one of the pairwise rs between a variable in the X-set and one in the Y-set (after all, the Canona algorithm could have used weights of zero for all but the two variables involved in the highest r) or a Manova results in a maximized F-ratio (computed on the discriminant function) which is less than one of the univariate F-ratios. At a bare minimum, this would save editors' time and authors' embarrassment.

As a final example, I recently reviewed a paper in which a rather involved multidimensional scaling (MDS) procedure had been used as a means of generating two- or three-dimensional sociograms, and the coordinates of each member's position within the resulting sociogram had been used as predictors in a series of regression equations for which the dependent variables were that member's scores on various personality measures. The resulting R^2s were supposed to reflect the extent to which each personality variable was an important criterion in friendship formation. However, had the authors thought a minute about the basic properties of a sociogram, rather than being mesmerized by symmetrizing transformations, eigenvalue solutions, and so on, they would have realized that friendship between two group members is reflected in the distance between their locations within the sociogram, not in either's absolute spatial location, and that it is similarity of two members' scores on a given variable which one would expect to predict friendship.

Avoiding Statistically Elegant Answers to Irrelevant Questions

A second consequence of overdependence on mathematical results is a tendency for choice among alternative multivariate measures (significance criteria, measures of individual variables' contributions, etc.) to be governed by mathematical convenience, so that we wind up with more powerful or more stable answers to irrelevant questions. I shall give two examples: the issues of loading versus computational coefficients and of greatest-characteristic root versus multiple-root tests.

Loadings versus Weights   At issue here is what to use as a basis for interpreting (and naming) the new, emergent or latent variable produced by a multivariate analysis. One obvious approach is to examine the weights by which scores on the original variables are multiplied in actually computing scores on the new variable. Thus we would use the regression coefficients to interpret the regression variable in MRA; the discriminant function coefficients to interpret the discriminant function(s) in Hotelling's T^2 and Manova; the canonical coefficients to interpret the canonical variates in Canona; and the factor score coefficients to interpret the factors in principal components analysis or factor analysis.

The interpretation process consists primarily of interpreting the smallest coefficients (usually the coefficients for combining z-scores, so as to avoid confounding relative magnitudes with the usually meaningless differences in standard deviation) as essentially zero and the remaining coefficients as plus or minus unity, and then identifying what conceptual dimension would distinguish people who obtain high scores on such a function from those who obtain low scores. That your interpretation of the emergent variable does indeed capture its "essence" is then established by showing that scores on the simplified (zeroes and unities) version show very little drop in the test statistic (Pearson r, t-ratio, F-ratio, percentage of variance accounted for) which was maximized by the optimal linear combination. Where more than one emergent variable is identified (as in Manova and Canona), one also wishes to show that their intercorrelations are still very close to zero.

687

Much more traditional, however, is the use of the *loading* of each original variable on the emergent variable, i.e., the Pearson r between that original variable and the optimal linear combination. The major support for this traditional approach comes from the fact that these loadings tend to be much more stable for small sample sizes than are the computational coefficients. However, a moment's reflection should make it clear (but see Section 7.6, pp. 218–220, of Harris, 1975, if you wish a lengthier argument) that the loadings provide a sound answer to the wrong question.

The loading of a given original variable on a given emergent variable only tells us how good a job of estimating scores on the emergent (latent) variable we could do if we had to "make do" with subjects' scores on that single variable. It seems rather silly to name, say, a canonical variate "generosity" on the basis of a positive correlation between generosity and scores on that canonical variate if it turns out that we have to *subtract* a person's generosity score from scores on other variables in computing his or her overall score on the canonical variate. The coefficients used in computing scores on the emergent variable provide a much sounder operational definition of that new variable than do the zero-order correlations between original and emergent variables (the loadings). Thus, we should take the unfortunate instability of computational coefficients for small Ns as a warning that we need larger Ns to answer a multivariate question (what's the optimal linear combination of these variables?) than to answer a univariate question (how well does this variable perform on its own?), *not* as justification for using univariate criteria to answer the multivariate question.

Selection of a Test Statistic for Individual Roots. A second issue where statistical desiderata (in this case, power and robustness) seem to have overcome relevance is that of selecting a statistic on which to base tests of the statistical significance of individual discriminant functions or individual pairs of canonical variates in cases where more than one such canonical variate pair or discriminant function (inevitably of decreasing importance) is produced.

We can summarize the results of such an analysis in terms of the squared correlation between each pair of (mutually uncorrelated) canonical variates or between each discriminant function and the corresponding optimal contrast among our groups. Call these values $r_1^2, r_2^2, \ldots, r_s^2$. The major choice is between tests based on all the roots—most commonly Wilks's lambda, or U-statistic, which equals $(1 - r_1^2)(1 - r_2^2) \ldots (1 - r_s^2)$, or the Lawley-Pillai trace, which is equal to Σr_i^2—and a test criterion based solely on the largest of the r_i^2s, r_1^2, which is Roy's greatest-characteristic root (or g.c.r.) test. A number of authors (e.g., Schatzoff, 1966) have found, via Monte Carlo runs, that multiple-root criteria (like U and the trace) tend to be more powerful than the g.c.r. test under certain circumstances (namely, when the population values, ρ_i^2, are nearly equal) and also tend to be more robust (Olson,

1974) against violations of multivariate normality than the g.c.r. statistic across a wide variety of situations.

These results clearly suggest that U or the trace is to be preferred to the g.c.r. statistic if the researcher's sole interest is in a test of the overall null hypothesis of no relationship between the set of independent and the set of dependent variables in the population. However, simply to reject the overall null hypothesis is *not* an adequate stopping point in any research endeavor. We need to go on to ask whether at least one dimension along which the groups differ or along which the two sets of measures are related can be reliably identified. This obviously requires that we examine the maximum discrimination or intercorrelation provided by any linear combination(s) of the original measures, i.e., r_1^2. As Harris (1976b—but see Mendoza, Markos, & Gonter, 1978, and Harris, Note 2) points out, a test of the statistical significance of r_1^2 must be based on *its* value, not the values of r_2^2, r_3^2, and so on. Thus, rejection of the overall null hypothesis on the basis of U or the trace is useless unless r_1^2 is itself statistically significant, so that the probability of coming to a useful conclusion (versus the rather unsatisfactory conclusion that "we know something is going on, but we can't identify any aspect of what that something is") is higher if we use the g.c.r. statistic for both the test of the overall H_0 and the test of r_1^2. (This is an illustration of Roy's more general union-intersection principle and Gabriel's simultaneous comparison procedures, which imply that one should tailor one's overall test to the family of specific comparisons with which you anticipate following up a significant overall test.)

The lack of robustness of the g.c.r., relative to tests based on all the r_i^2s, is a very useful warning and should be taken as a strong suggestion that we need to develop more robust versions of the g.c.r. test. It *cannot*, however, be taken as justification for treating U or the trace as a test of the significance of r_1^2.

Especially revealing with respect to our current concern with overdependence on mathematical results is the persistence of arguments in favor of the partitioned-U procedure for determining the statistical significance of individual roots. We have already concluded (and Mendoza et al., 1978, agree) that we cannot take rejection of the overall null hypothesis on the basis of the value of $U = (1 - r_1^2)(1 - r_2^2) \ldots (1 - r_s^2)$ as establishing the statistical significance of any individual discriminant function or pair of canonical variates—despite the fact that almost all current multivariate texts and computer programs make this mistake. Nevertheless, the residuals from U, e.g., $U_1 = U/(1 - r_1^2) = (1 - r_2^2)(1 - r_3^2) \ldots (1 - r_s^2)$, might form the basis of a useful test of whether it is worthwhile proceeding to tests of r_2^2, r_3^2, and so forth, or if, instead, *no* dimension of relationship between the two sets of measures other than that identified by r_1^2 exists in the population.

The existing tests of such residuals are equivalent (in the case where all population ρ_i are zero) to assuming that the individual components of $\ln U = \ln(1 - r_1^2) + \ln(1 - r_2^2) + \cdots + \ln(1 - r_s^2)$ are independently chi-square distributed with decreasing degrees of freedom. Harris (1976b) pointed out that using the claimed component distribution of $\ln(1 - r_1^2)$ as a basis for testing the statistical significance of r_1^2 leads to a true alpha of .60 for a test at a nominal alpha of .05 and of .24 for a nominal alpha of .01 for the not unusual situation where $s = 10$ and $m = 0$ (10 variables in one set and 11 in the other), even with a sample size of over 1000. Thus subtraction of this grossly inflated χ_1^2 from the sum of all the component χ^2s (which sum does have the claimed distribution) can't possibly lead to a valid test of U_1.

Nevertheless, when this was brought to the attention of the staff who maintain the SOUPAC package at the University of Illinois, with the recommendation that partitioned-U tests be dropped from the Canona Program (Tatsuoka, Note 3), the statistical consultants pointed out that U_1 is tested only after the null hypothesis has been rejected, and there is a long-standing math-stat theorem which asserts that U_1 has the claimed distribution if and only if $\rho_1^2 \neq 0$ but ρ_2^2, ρ_3^2, and so on are all zero. This statistical argument "carried the day," and was incorporated into Tatsuoka's open letter and into Mendoza et al. (1978).

Application of reasonableness tests (the last refuge of the mathematically un-sophisticated!) suggests, however, that the distribution of U_1 when ρ_1^2 equals, say, 10^{-12} (.000000001) can't be very different from its distribution when the overall null hypothesis is true, i.e., when ρ_1^2 equals zero, under which conditions we know the claimed distribution of U_1 is invalid. The task thus becomes one of specifying how large the first population root must be before the claimed and true distributions are sufficiently close (ρ_1^2 must be unity for the claimed distribution to be strictly true) rather than simply accepting a statistical claim at face value. The results of some Monte Carlo runs suggest that ρ_1 may have to be quite large ($>.4$) before the conservatism of the residual-U test becomes negligible. Six simulation runs were conducted, each based on 600 independent random samples of size 117 from a 15-variable multivariate normal population. The six populations employed all had $\rho_2 = \rho_3 = \cdots = \rho_7 = 0$ for the relationship between the first 7 and the last 8 variables. They differed in that $\rho_1 = .001, .100, .200, .400, .600,$ or $.990$. None of the 600 samples yielded a statistically significant value of U_1 at the .05 level for $\rho_1 = .001, .1,$ or $.2$, and only 9 samples yielded significance when $\rho_1 = .4$ ($p < .001$ for the difference between the observed number of significant results and the expected number of 30 in each case). The $\rho_1 = .6$ and .99 runs yielded 27 and 33 nominally significant U_1 values, respectively. It might be objected that since the test of U_1 is carried out only if the overall U test yields significance, we needn't be concerned about the consequences of such low values of ρ_1. This would be incorrect. Since U is based on all 7 roots, it is possible for the overall test to yield significance at the .05 level when r_1^2 is as low as .0740—a value lower than the minimum value (.0879) observed in the 1200 samples from the $\rho_1 = .001$ and .100 cases of the present runs. Clearly, continued faith in the validity of the partitioned-U procedure for testing residuals is badly misplaced.

The problem, as the original developer of this theorem (Bartlett, 1941) made clear, is that it is an *asymptotic* result, strictly holding only if our sample size is infinite, in which case *any* nonzero first-population root is indeed sufficient to guarantee that the shared variance extracted when $(1 - r_1^2)$ is deleted from U is an unbiased estimate of that attributable to ρ_1^2.

The main point for present purposes is that application of a simple reasonableness test would have been sufficient to avoid the misapplication (or, at least, over-generalized application) of an elegant mathematical result.

Identifying Gaps in Multivariate Statistics

A final consequence of overreliance on mathematical statisticians—who are not, after all, trained to be sensitive to the needs of researchers—is the danger that the need for various techniques not yet available to researchers will go unnoticed. There are indeed some surprising gaps in our armamentarium of multivariate statistical techniques, some of which I surveyed at a workshop sponsored by the Southwestern Division, Society for Multivariate Experimental Psychology in 1978 (Harris, Note 4). That survey included both gaps in theoretical developments and lags in incorporating mathematical results into nationally distributed computer programs. Given the emphasis of the present symposium on relations between mathematics and psychology, I shall focus on needed mathematical developments.

Of course, some of these gaps may be more apparent than real, a product of lack of thoroughness in perusing relevant journals and/or failure to properly translate and/or to see the implications of papers I *have* encountered. I've already committed such self-delusions on at least two occasions: once when I informed an audience which included the senior author of Huynh and Feldt (1970) that no test of the h.o.t.d.v. assumption of repeated-measures Anova was available (Harris, Note 5), and again when I "rediscovered" (Harris, Note 6) a method for finding an optimal explanation of an interaction as a "contrast of contrasts" which is implicit in Gollob's earlier (1968) FANOVA model. However, even if some of the gaps outlined below prove to be equally illusory, their inclusion in the present paper should serve to alert the authors of the solutions to these problems to the need to make these results available to a wider audience. Now for the gaps.

Extending Multiple Regression Tests to Canonical Analysis   There are a number of tools available in MRA for which no analogs are available in Canona. For instance, formulae for the expected value of sample multiple R^2 when the null hypothesis is true and corresponding formulae for estimating population R^2 are well known. However, there appear to be no corresponding formulae for R_c^2, the squared canonical correlation. We know that R_c^2 has an expected value larger than $\max(p, q)/(N - 1)$, since it is the squared multiple R between the canonical variate of the smaller set and the variables in the larger set. We also have some limited Monte Carlo evidence, from the same runs which were the basis for Harris (1976b),

691

that even $(p + q)/(N - 1)$ is an underestimate of $E(R_c^2)$. Formulae of the sort requested here would be of considerable value in giving users a "feel" for the degree of inflation in R_c^2 relative to ρ_c^2.

Similarly, tests for the statistical significance of individual regression coefficients and of contrasts among the various regression coefficients are readily available, but no such tests for the canonical coefficients used to compute the canonical variates exist.

Finally, the statistical significance of the increment in R^2 obtained by adding one or more predictors can be readily tested, but the same is not true of the increment in R_c^2 following addition of a variable or variables to one or the other set. This increment must be greater than the corresponding R^2 increment, since both the coefficients for the incremented set and the coefficients defining the dependent variable the incremented set predicts are changed following an addition to either set.

Current least-squares Manova programs such as Cramer's (1974) MANOVA involve tests of analogous increments as later main effects or interactions are brought into the Anova part of the model, but this is accomplished by treating all preceding corrections to the initial sum of squares matrices as if they were fixed, a priori corrections, and almost certainly yields positively biased tests. The problem is minimal in most applications, however, since the independent variables are usually very nearly orthogonal in experimental designs.

In short, almost none of the statistical apparatus developed for stepwise multiple regression is available for those who might wish to conduct stepwise canonical correlation.

The Repeated-Battery Problem Often we are in a position in which we wish to observe a battery of p measures on several (say, k) occasions. We might be interested in the consistency of these measures across occasions, in which case canonical correlation or a generalization thereof to more than two occasions is involved. Or we might be interested in testing occasion-to-occasion differences in mean vectors, in which case we are essentially interested in a Manova approach to a within-subjects design. We can, of course, use canonical correlation in the first case, and Hotelling's T^2 for flatness (i.e., single-sample T^2 on a $pk - 1$ element vector of differences between adjacent measures or of contrasts among measures) in the second case. However, it seems very natural in many of these cases to restrict our search for optimal linear combinations of the pk measures to those in which the relative magnitudes of the coefficients for the p dependent measures are held constant across occasions, i.e., in which we are examining the same "emergent variable" (linear combination of the p measures) on each occasion. Unfortunately, I've been unable to find (or construct) a mathematical technique for accomplishing such constrained optimization, except in the very special case where we can assume homogeneity across occasions of the $p \times p$ matrix of variances and covariances among the p measures.

Improving the Robustness of the G.C.R. Test   As I pointed out in an earlier version of this paper, greatest-characteristic-root (g.c.r.) tests are not outstandingly robust against violations of multivariate normality, but the relative robustness of multiple-root tests is of no help since we have to get down to the level of a single root (optimal dimension of relationship) before a useful result is obtained. Any technique which can be developed to increase the robustness of g.c.r. tests— perhaps through transformations similar to the variance-stabilizing transformations applied in Anova, or through preliminary factor analysis as in some of the recent root-regression approaches to stabilizing regression coefficients, or through development of a nonparametric analog to the g.c.r. test—would be a significant addition to the body of multivariate techniques.

Using All Roots for Improved Discrimination   The existence of multiple roots (discriminant functions) in Manova is perfectly reasonable in that each root identifies a separate source of relationship between the independent- and dependent-variable sets, each uncorrelated with the others. It is also, however, extremely frustrating in that it seems as though it ought to be possible to use the roots beyond the largest one to achieve even better discrimination among the groups than that provided by use only of the discriminant function associated with the largest root. What *is* clear is that we cannot simply take a linear combination of the various discriminant functions, since such a linear combination is itself a linear combination of the original variables, and the first discriminant function is by definition the optimal linear combination of the original variables.

Morrison (1976, Section 6.5) describes one procedure which *may* improve on the discrimination provided by the first discriminant function, namely selecting $k(k - 1)/2$ pairwise discriminant functions and assigning each S to the group implied by the series of pairwise comparisons. Another obvious choice would be to assign each subject to a group on the basis of his or her Euclidean distance from each centroid in the s-dimensional space of the discriminant functions. However, neither procedure has, to my knowledge, been translated into a test statistic (e.g., the percent correct classification) with a known sampling distribution—nor, for that matter, do we know for sure that they do indeed yield better discrimination than use of the first discriminant function by itself.

Ideally we would like to find some family of comparison procedures whose maximum discriminative ability is indexed, in accordance with the union-intersection principle, by some single statistic—maybe even Wilks's lambda or the trace criterion.

693

Limiting Formulae for G.C.R. Critical Values   The most extensive tables of critical values of the g.c.r. statistic are, to date, those printed in Harris (1975, Appendix A). These tables incorporate Venables's (1974, 1975) algorithm for exact values when $n \leq 5$, and Pillai's (1965) approximation for values of $n > 5$. They cover values of s from 2 through 20; values of $m = -.5, 0, 1, \ldots, 10$, and 15; and values of n through 1000. However, multivariate researchers do not always restrict themselves to problems which fall within the confines of these tables, and the jumps in parameter values (e.g., from $n = 100$ to $n = 500$ and from $m = 10$ to $m = 15$) may make researchers nervous about interpolating within the table.

We can go to computer subroutines for computing g.c.r. critical values, such as the one printed in Appendix B of Harris (1975) incorporating Pillai's approximation and the one provided by Venables (1975). These programs have problems of their own, however, for values of s, m, or n beyond the range of the tables and for desired αs much less than .0001 (as might arise, for instance, if we were carrying out a series of Manovas or Canonas with Bonferroni-adjusted critical values). It is unclear whether the problems encountered by these programs are due to computer difficulties such as round-off error or to violation of hidden assumptions in the Pillai approximation. It would seem reasonable to hope, however, that the limiting forms of the g.c.r. distribution for extreme values of s, m, or n (and possibly of α) would be sufficiently simple to permit circumventing these problems and might even be some member of the family of incomplete beta distributions. If so, it would seem a lot more rational to provide these limiting forms to users, rather than expanding g.c.r. tables ad infinitum.

I suspect that this falls into the heavily populated category of results which are so obvious to any competent mathematical statistician as to seem (to such a person) hardly worth mentioning. Evidence to this effect is provided by Hanumara and Thompson's (1968) casual mention of having made a variable change in the g.c.r. distribution and then having taken the limit as m approached infinity en route to solving a related problem which was the focus of their paper. Let me assure any mathematical statisticians that mentioning the obvious would, in this case, be a considerable service to us users of multivariate statistics, even if it doesn't bring fame in math stat circles.

Summary

Thus there are a number of gaps in the tools presently available to users of multivariate statistics. Please note that neither these gaps nor any of the other consequences we have attributed to overdependence on mathematical statisticians are intended as complaints about the performance of mathematical statisticians. Mathematical statistics is not an empirical science, and mathematical statisticians are not trained to and should not be expected to make judgments on the soundness of the research practices implied by a given mathematical tool. It is we psychologists who have allowed our awe at the complexity of the mathematical statistician's task to lead us into shirking our own responsibility of judging the proper use of these tools within the research context. I take as an encouraging sign the stated goal of the new *Journal of Educational Statistics* to provide a forum for the exchange of ideas, needs, and new developments between researchers and statisticians.

REFERENCE NOTES

1. Harris, R. J., & Ronis, D. T. Specific comparisons in repeated-measures designs: Insufficiency of the Greenhouse-Geisser correction. Unpublished manuscript, 1978.
2. Harris, R. J. The continued invalidity and/or uselessness of partitioned-U tests. In C. Burdsal (Chair), *Applications of multivariate techniques*, Seventh Annual Users' Workshop of the Southwest Division, Society of Multivariate Experimental Psychology. Presented at meeting of the Southwest Psychological Association, San Antonio, April 26, 1979. (Summary appeared in the January 30, 1979 issue of the *Tie-Line*, SW-SMEP's newsletter.)
3. Tatsuoka, M. M. Open letter to Prof. R. J. Harris. February 25, 1976.
4. Harris, R. J. An agenda for multivariate statistics. In C. Burdsal (Chair), *Computer applications*, Sixth Annual Users' Workshop of SW-SMEP. Presented at meeting of the Southwest Psychological Association, New Orleans, April 20, 1978.
5. Harris, R. J. Multivariate analysis of variance. In R. M. Pruzek (Chair), *Four classes of multivariate research methods: Their characteristics and inter-relationships*. Symposium presented at meeting of the American Educational Research Association, Chicago, April 19, 1974.
6. Harris, R. J. Optimal decomposition of interactions into contrasts of contrasts. Paper presented at meeting of the American Psychological Association, Washington, D.C., September 3, 1976.

REFERENCES

Anderson, T. W. *An introduction to multivariate statistical analysis*. New York: Wiley, 1958.

Anderson, T. W., Das Gupta, S. D., & Styan, G. P. H. *A bibliography of multivariate statistical analysis*. New York: Wiley, 1972.

Bartlett, M. S. The statistical significance of canonical correlations. *Biometrika*, 1941, 32, 29–37.

Bose, R. C. Early history of multivariate statistical analysis. In P. R. Krishnaiah (Ed.), *Multivariate analysis -IV*. Amsterdam: North-Holland, 1977.

Castore, G. F., & Dye, W. S., III. A simplified punch card method of determining sums of squares and sums of products. *Psychometrika*, 1949, 14, 243–250.

Cattell, R. B., & Dielman, T. E. The structure of motivational manifestations as measured in the laboratory rat: An examination of motivational component theory. *Social Behavior and Personality*, 1974, 2, 10–24.

Cramer, E. M. *Revised MANOVA program*. Chapel Hill, N.C.: Thurstone Psychometric Laboratory, University of North Carolina, 1974.

DeForest, E. L. Law of error in the position of a point in space. *The Analyst*, 1881, 9, 3–9, 41–48, 73–82.

Dixon, W. J. (Ed.). *BMD: Biomedical computer programs*. Berkeley, Calif.: University of California Press, 1961.

DuBois, P. H. *Multivariate correlational analysis*. New York: Harper & Row, 1957.

Edgeworth, F. Y. On the reduction of observations. *The London, Edinburgh, and Dublin Philosophical Magazine and Journal of Science, Fifth Series*, 1884, *17*, 135–141.

Edgeworth, F. Y. On a new method of reducing observations relating to several quantities. *Dublin Philosophical Magazine and Journal of Science, Fifth Series*, 1888, *25*, 184–191.

Fisher, R. A. The goodness of fit of regression formulae, and the distribution of regression coefficients. *Journal of the Royal Statistical Society*, 1922, *85*, 597–612.

Fisher, R. A. The general sampling distribution of the multiple correlation coefficient. *Proceedings of the Royal Society of London, Series A: Mathematical and Physical Sciences*, 1928, *121*, 654–673.

Fisher, R. A. The statistical utilization of multiple measurements. *Annals of Eugenics*, 1938, *8*, 376–386.

Gauss, K. F. Theoria combinationis observationum erroribus minimis obnoxiae. Pars prior and pars posterior. (Societati Regiae Exhibita, Feb. 15, 1821, and Feb. 2, 1823.) *Commentationes Societatis Regiae Scientiarum Gottingensis. Recentiores. Classis Mathematicae*, 1823, *5*, 33–62, 63–90.

Gauss, K. F. Supplementum theoriae combinationis observationum erroribus minimis obnoxiae. (Societatie Regiae Exhibitum, Sept. 16, 1826.) *Commentationes Societatis Regiae Scientiarum Gottingensis. Recentiores. Classis Mathematicae*, 1828, *6*, 57–98.

Gollob, H. F. A statistical model which combines features of factor analysis and analysis of variance techniques. *Psychometrika*, 1968, *33*, 73–115.

Greenhouse, S. W., & Geisser, S. On methods in the analysis of profile data. *Psychometrika*, 1959, *24*, 95–112.

Hall, D. M., Welker, E. L., & Crawford, I. Factor analysis calculations by tabulating machines. *Psychometrika*, 1945, *10*, 93–125.

Hall, P. Multiple and partial correlation coefficients in the case of an *m*-fold variate system. *Biometrika*, 1927, *19*, 100–109.

Hanumara, R. C., & Thompson, W. A., Jr. Percentage points of the extreme roots of a Wishart matrix. *Biometrika*, 1968, *55*, 505–512.

Harris, R. J. *Primer of multivariate statistics*. New York: Academic Press, 1975.

Harris, R. J. Handling negative inputs in equity theory: On the plausible equity formulae. *Journal of Experimental Social Psychology*, 1976, *12*, 194–209. (a)

Harris, R. J. The invalidity of partitioned-U tests in canonical correlation and multivariate analysis of variance. *Multivariate Behavioral Research*, 1976, *11*, 353–366. (b)

Harris, R. J. The uncertain connection between verbal theories and research hypotheses in social psychology. *Journal of Experimental Social Psychology*, 1976, *12*, 210–219. (c)

Hotelling, H. The generalization of Student's ratio. *Annals of Mathematical Statistics*, 1931, *2*, 360–378.

Hotelling, H. Relations between two sets of variates. *Biometrika*, 1936, *28*, 321–377.

Hsu, P. L. On the distribution of roots of certain determinantal equations. *Annals of Eugenics*, 1939, *9*, 250–258.

Hull, C. L. An automatic correlation calculating machine. *Journal of the American Statistical Association*, 1925, *20*, 522–531.

Huynh, H., & Feldt, L. S. Conditions under which mean square ratios in repeated measurements designs have exact F-distributions. *Journal of the American Statistical Association*, 1970, *65*, 1582–1589.

Kendall, M. G. *A course in multivariate analysis*. London: Charles Griffin, 1957.

Kimbel, G. A. *Hilgard and Marquis' Conditioning and learning* (2nd ed.). New York: Appleton, 1961.

Kummell, D. H. Reduction of observation equations which contain more than one observed quantity. *The Analyst*, 1879, *6*, 97–105.

Malahobnis, P. C. On tests and measures of group divergence. Part I. Theoretical formulae. *Journal and Proceedings of the Asiatic Society of Bengal, New Series*, 1930, *26*, 541–588.

Mendoza, J. L., Markos, V. H., & Gonter, R. A new perspective on sequential testing procedures in canonical analysis: A Monte Carlo evaluation. *Multivariate Behavioral Research*, 1978, *13*, 371–382.

Morrison, D. F. *Multivariate statistical methods* (2nd ed.). New York: McGraw-Hill, 1976.

Niles, H. E. Correlation, causation and Wright's theory of path coefficients. *Genetics*, 1922, *7*, 258–273.

Niles, H. E. The method of path coefficients: An answer to Wright. *Genetics*, 1923, *8*, 256–260.

Olson, C. L. Comparative robustness of six tests in multivariate analysis of variance. *Journal of the American Statistical Association*, 1974, *69*, 894–908.

Pearson, K. On certain errors with regard to multiple correlation occasionally made by those who have not adequately studied the subject. *Biometrika*, 1914, *10*, 181–187.

Pillai, K. C. S. On the distribution of the largest characteristic root of a matrix in multivariate analysis. *Biometrika*, 1965, *52*, 405–414.

Roy, S. N. P-statistics or some generalizations in analysis of variance appropriate to multivariate problems. *Sankhya*, 1939, *4*, 381–396.

Roy, S. N. *Some aspects of multivariate analysis*. New York: Wiley, 1957.

Salisbury, F. S. A simplified method of computing multiple correlation constants. *Journal of Educational Psychology*, 1929, *20*, 44–52.

Schatzoff, M. Sensitivity comparisons among tests of the general linear hypothesis. *Journal of the American Statistical Association*, 1966, *61*, 415–435.

"Student." Probable error of a correlation coefficient. *Biometrika*, 1908, *6*, 302–310.

Tatsuoka, M. M. *Multivariate analysis: Techniques for educational and psychological research*. New York: Wiley, 1971.

Toops, H. A. Statistical checks on the accuracy of intercorrelation computations. *Research Bulletin, Educational Testing Service*, 1927, *6*, 385–391.

Venables, W. N. Null distribution of the largest root statistic. Algorithm AS77. *Journal of the Royal Statistical Society, Series C: Applied Statistics*, 1974, *23*, 458–465.

Venables, W. N. Computation of the null distribution of the largest or smallest latent root of a beta matrix. *Journal of Multivariate Analysis*, 1975, *3*, 123–131.

Walsh, J. A. An IBM 709 program for factor analyzing three mode matrices. *Educational and Psychological Measurement*, 1964, *24*, 669–673.

Wright, S. Correlation and causation. *Journal of Agricultural Research*, 1921, *20*, 557–585.

Wright, S. The theory of path coefficients—a reply to Niles's criticism. *Genetics*, 1923, *8*, 239–255.

Wrigley, C. F., & Neuhaus, J. O. A re-factorization of the Burt-Pearson matrix with the ORDVAC electronic computer. *British Journal of Psychology, Statistical Section*, 1952, *5*, 105–108.

Yule, G. U. On the theory of correlation for any number of variables, treated by a new system of notation. *Proceedings of the Royal Society of London, Series A*, 1907, *79*, 182–193.

PSYCHOLOGY AND THE NEUROSCIENCES

30

Mind and Brain, Psychology and Neuroscience, the Eternal Verities

KARL H. PRIBRAM

We commonly attribute our awareness of the mind-brain issue to Descartes who pointed out that "brain" might well be understood in machinelike terms but that our views on "mind" depend on introspection. "Cogito ergo sum," I think, thus I am. Mind, self, self-consciousness are "subjective," private, and therefore inaccessible to what later came to be called "objective" study.

The advent of behaviorism should have immediately altered our views on the privacy of self-experience, the privacy of perception, thought, and feeling. Though not directly accessible to others, self-experiences can be verbally reported, consensually validated and in this fashion made "objective." Much of science is based on such indirection—we study the light emitted from stars, we do not palpate the stars themselves; we study the tracks made on an oscilloscope by subatomic particles, we do not come into direct contact with those "particles" themselves.

But radical behaviorists eschewed this readily available solution and instead chose to become materialist, physicalist, and "thoroughly scientific." Skinner (1971), for example, has repeatedly warned against the use of subjective terminology because its connotative meanings may corrupt stricter operational definitions based on verbal and instrumental behaviors. As I have indicated elsewhere (Pribram, 1979a), this amounts to throwing out the baby with the bath water, leaving one with a clean behavioral science which overlaps with but does not cover the range of a psychological science. Specifically, what is left out is subjective experience, that fascinating topic which brings most students into this field of inquiry.

The question arises as to why the radical behaviorists took the course they did. Here I want to explore the suggestion that mistaken though that course might be from the standpoint of psychological science, the mistake reflects the physicalistic and mechanistic views developed during the nineteenth century, views which the new science had to live through—to experience, if you will—before it could cope wholly with its own subject matter.

This exploration takes the form of this essay's title. First, the mind-brain issue is shown to have much deeper roots than those expressed by Descartes. Second, the impact of a scientific approach to the issue is illustrated by work on the specific problem of neural-perceptual isomorphism. Finally, the impact of this scientific work is reflected back onto the roots of the mind-brain issue, bringing the very latest understanding to bear on the earliest recorded expressions of men's and women's minds and thus their brains.

Verbalization, Nominalization, and Proposition

"In the beginning was the Verb," i.e., words originally referred to a flow of experience; early communication was "verbal"! The word *word* appears closely related to the word *verb*. At a recent conference on philosophy, during a presentation of the work of Spinoza we were apprised of the fact that initially Hebrew words were verbs denoting being, action, and process. Similar forms are said to exist in preclassical Sanskrit. Be that as it may, there is every evidence that human thought, including scientific thought, begins by nominalizing, reifying what at first are sensed as processes. Piaget has documented this development in children; biochemists routinely operate in this fashion when they isolate first a function of, for example, the pituitary gland, reify that function by giving it a name, for example, ACTH, and then search for "it" until the name is substantiated, that is, found to be a chemical substance.

The power of nominalization can be gleaned not only from its use in science but from such observations as those of Helen Keller whose world came to life once she could name, objectify, items previously experienced only as processes:

> I knew then that w-a-t-e-r meant that wonderful cool something that was flowing over my hand. That living word awakened my soul, gave it light, hope, joy, set it free! There were barriers still it is true, but barriers that could in time, be swept away. I left the well-house eager to learn. Everything had a name, and each name gave birth to a new thought. As we returned to the house, every object which I touched seemed to quiver with life. That was because I saw everything with a

strange new sight that had come to me. On entering the door, I remembered the doll I had broken. I felt my way to the hearth and picked up the pieces. I tried vainly to put them together. Then my eyes filled with tears for I realized what I had done [she had earlier destroyed the doll in a fit of temper], and for the first time I felt repentance and sorrow (Helen Keller, 1903/1954).

As Walker Percy so clearly perceives (Coles, 1978), "Here . . . in a small space and a short time something extremely important and mysterious had happened. Seven year old Helen made her breakthrough from the good responding animal which behaviorists study so successfully to the strange name giving and sentence uttering creature which is Homo Sapiens."

Note that Helen Keller became aware of her thoughts at the same moment that she was able to name objects. She did not make the mistake of the radical behaviorists—subject as well as object were attended. Note also that in doing so, propositions were formed, remembrances, repentances, and sorrows could be entertained. Subject could be responsible for object, cause could lead to effect.

Irrespective of whether process descriptions in terms of verbs preceded or arose coterminally with nominalization and whether nominalization preceded or arose coterminally with propositional utterances, the entire set of linguistic operations described above did occur in human prehistory and do occur in the development of every human being. Thus the mind-brain issue is joined at the very inception of what makes us human—our ability to make propositions, i.e., to conceptualize processes as subjects acting on objects. In order to nominalize a process into a proposition made up of a subject, verb, and object, we must first categorize and then hierarchically arrange categories into logical relationships. We thus become *logical* animals—the word *logical* being derived from the word *logos*, Greek for "word."

Invariance, Rationality, and Harmony

But human beings are not just logical. They are also rational. *Rational* derives from *ratio*, a different sort of relationship than the logical. Ratios are expressed as invariances arranged harmoniously rather than as labels arranged hierarchically. The realm of the rational is music and musical mathematics, not the natural languages and logic.

Greek philosophers and their precursors clearly distinguished between logic and rationality. Pythagoras and Plato recognized music, not logic, as the model of rationality. An excellent account of this early emphasis on rationality can be found in Ernest McClain's *The Myth of Invariance* (1976). In this volume, McClain presents the counterpoint to "In the beginning was the Word (Verb)." He traces the history of rationality from the *Rg Veda*, the Egyptian Book of the Dead, the Bible, to Pythagoras and Plato. And this view of the rational equates it with the spiritual tradition in both Eastern and Western thought.

If the suggestion that indeed words were initially verbs designating process were validated, one might fruitfully inquire whether that process was the establishing of invariances through rationalizing (deriving ratios). In this sense, verbs were expressions of invariances and thus "In the beginning was the verb and the verb was with God." But God also must be understood as a verb, making the phrase read "and the verb was spiritual," i.e., rational. Only when nominalized do hierarchy and logical causality emerge: "And the Word was made flesh, and dwelt among us, and we beheld Her glory, the glory of the only begotten of the Father, was full of grace and truth." Note that the instantiation of the Word was female (notably better at natural languages than males—see, for example, the review by Pribram and McGuinness, 1979) and that "She" is hierarchically and causally related to God the Father, now completely nominalized as subject whose actions give rise to object. Note also that this proposition maintained its rationality, i.e., "was full of grace" but added logic ("and truth").

The point of reviewing this ancient prehistory and early history of thought is to note that the germ of the mind-brain issue is contained in any logical system, i.e., any system that derives from the use of *logos*, words in propositions in which subject(ive) and object(ive) are separated and causally related to one another. In addition, however, the point is also to emphasize that in another system, the rational, which is based on ratios, as in music, the Cartesian dilemma does not exist. In such a system the methods by which invariances are constructed are more patently clear as when a tempered scale is developed (Bernstein, 1976, speaks of tempered as "tampered"). The obvious and inexorable intertwining of the functions of biological brain with physical energies to constitute the psychological process is the hallmark of a rationality which was lost sight of in the Cartesian logic. Let us therefore now turn to current neuroscience and psychology to see where the results of experimental research have led with regard to the mind-brain issue.

The conception that the brain serves as a set of organs of mind inaugurates nineteenth-century psychology. The success of this conception is due largely to the work of anatomist Franz Joseph Gall, who proposed that:

> If . . . man has faculties which essentially distinguish him from the animal, and which give to him the peculiar character of humanity, he also offers in his brain . . . parts which animals have not; and the difference of effects is thus found to be explained by the difference of causes (1835, Vol. 1, p. 1003).

Gall's conceptions were supported by a large volume of clinical pathological observations. Some of these have been summarized in readily accessible form in the first Penguin volume on *Brain and Behavior* (Pribram, 1969a). Of course, Gall's thesis did not go unchallenged, especially when in the hands of a popular following;

it became degraded into the doctrine of phrenology. Nonetheless, these early observations did set the stage for a nineteenth-century physiologically based psychology, a psychology rooted in observation and experiment. By the end of the century the relation between brain and experience and brain and behavior was couched in terms not much different from those currently in use. The psychophysics of Fechner, Weber, Helmholtz, and Mach remains unmatched in wealth of experimental detail and conceptual sophistication. The role of brain function in psychology was modeled in clearly recognizable form by William James (1890) and Sigmund Freud (1895/1950). The work of Francois Magendie and Claude Bernard laid the foundations for the laboratories of physiological psychology of Wilhelm Wundt, Ivan P. Pavlov, and Walter B. Cannon. In this field of inquiry, the leap from the philosophically tortuous pronouncements of the eighteenth century to the scientific, data-based arguments of the twentieth century is indeed great.

However, this forward leap was brought to a sudden halt with World War I. The psychology of the first half of the twentieth century (to about 1960) marched to a different drummer, was infused with a different spirit. That spirit was behaviorism, and, strange as it may seem, the tune and rhythm of behaviorism hark back to another biological nineteenth-century tradition, that of Darwinian evolution. In a most interesting fashion, the conception of brain as man's crowning glory which is responsible for his unique psychology came into unconscious competition with the conception of the descent of man from his animal forebears.

Some of the reasons for this conflict have been reviewed extensively in another manuscript (which also reviews the nineteenth-century contributions alluded to above—Pribram & Robinson, in press). It is worthwhile, nonetheless, to abstract here some of the highlights of this issue and to note where things stand in this year of the centenary celebration of psychology as an experimental discipline.

Evolutionary Psychology

Behaviorism

Psychology, seen solely as "the science of behavior," became a broadly regnant dictum roughly from the mid-1920s to the mid-1950s of this century. The various forms of behaviorism heralded the triumphs of a (roguish) adolescent independence from mother philosophy, aunt education, and whatever other family ties might still bind. The stated aim was to mathematize, to develop laws in the image of the mechanistic physics of Newton. In the words of the founder:

> The behaviorist asks: Why don't we make what we can *observe* the real field of psychology? Let us limit ourselves to things that can be observed, and formulate laws concerning only those things. Now what can we observe? We can observe

behavior—what the organism does or says. And let us point out at once: that *saying* is doing—that is, *behaving.* Speaking overtly or to ourselves (thinking) is just as objective a type of behavior as baseball.

The rule, or measuring rod, which the behaviorist puts in front of him always is: Can I describe this bit of behavior I see in terms of "stimulus and response"? By stimulus we mean any object in the general environment or any change in the tissues themselves due to the physiological condition of the animal, such as the change we get when we keep an animal from sex activity, when we keep it from feeding, when we keep it from building a nest. By response we mean anything the animal does—such as turning toward or away from a light, jumping at a sound, and more highly organized activities such as building a skyscraper, drawing plans, having babies, writing books, and the like.

You will find, then, the behaviorist working like any other scientist. His sole object is to gather facts about behavior—verify his data—subject them both to logic and to mathematics (the tools of every scientist). He brings the new-born individual *into his experimental nursery* and begins to set problems: What is the baby doing now? What is the stimulus that makes him behave this way? He finds that the stimulus of tickling the cheek brings the response of turning the mouth to the side stimulated. The stimulus of the nipple brings out the sucking response. The stimulus of a rod placed on the palm of the hand brings closure of the hand and the suspension of the whole body by that hand and arm if the rod is raised. Stimulating the infant with a rapidly moving shadow across the eye will not produce blinking until the individual is sixty-five days of age. Stimulating the infant with an apple or stick of candy or any other object will not call out attempts at reaching until the baby is around 120 days of age (J. B. Watson, 1924/1959, pp. 6–7).

The behaviorist approach initiated by Watson was elaborated and modified by many successors, among whom the only figure of appreciable current influence is Burrhus Frederic Skinner. Watson was still interested in physiological measurement—behavior for Watson meant movement. For Skinner, behavior became the environmental consequence of the movement, the act of producing a paper record which "could be taken home at night and studied." Environmental consequences, not the physiology of human beings, became the substance and the tool of the behaviorist.

The important advance from this level of explanation [mental] that is made by turning to the nervous system as a controlling entity has unfortunately had a similar effect in discouraging a direct descriptive attack upon behavior. The change is an advance because the new entity beyond behavior to which appeal is made has a definite physical status of its own and is susceptible to scientific investigation. Its chief function with regard to a science of behavior, however, is again to divert attention away from behavior as a subject matter. The use of the nervous system as a fictional explanation of behavior was a common practice even before Descartes, and it is now much more widely current than is generally realized. At a popular level a man is said to be capable (a fact about his behavior) because he has brains (a

705

fact about his nervous system). Whether or not such a statement has any meaning for the person who makes it is scarcely important; in either case it exemplifies the practice of explaining an obvious (if unorganized) fact by appeal to something about which little is known. . . . (I am not attempting to discount the importance of a science of neurology but am referring simply to the primitive use of the nervous system as an explanatory principle in avoiding a direct description of behavior) (B. F. Skinner, 1938, p. 4).

What led to this turn? Why, in this centenary year of Wundt's achievement of a well-rounded, experimentally based biological and social psychology has our inquiry so systematically espoused only the environmental and the social branches and denied its neurobiological roots?

There are, of course, many reasons. Perhaps the major of these was the discovery of methodological behaviorism, i.e., that behavior is indeed a potent measure of mental phenomena. In testing this potency, it is not altogether surprising that the measure became, for a while, its own end. While Watson's psychology (1924/1959) was still physiologically rooted, his message was that behavior should take its own measure, fly free, and leave mind behind in the bosom of philosophy. And in the hands of Tolman (1932), Hull (1943, 1951), and Skinner (1938) behavioral science did just that—successfully. So successfully in fact that the question now can be raised as to just what might be the relationship of a science of behavior to psychology, conceived as the study of the "psyche," i.e., mental processes (see, for example, Pribram, 1979a).

This success of behaviorism was in part due to the technical developments that characterize so much of twentieth-century science. Soon it was recognized that more than the behavior of muscle groups could be measured, the occupation of Sechenov (1863/1965), Pavlov (1927), Bechterev (1911), and Watson (1924/1959). In addition, the behavior of the entire organism could be controlled by mazes (the data base for Tolman, 1932, for instance); by problem and choice boxes (upon which Thorndike, 1898, 1913–1914, and Yerkes, 1904, depended); by check lists (as in "intelligence" tests and "opinion" polls); and by panels and levers (as developed by Skinner, 1938). A wealth of data accumulated, and with the advent of computerized testing mechanisms (e.g., Pribram, 1969b) continued to increase.

Toward the latter part of the twentieth century, a reasonable question was what this wealth had gained for psychology. One certain gain is the wealth itself. There was no question but that reliable data were obtained in controlled situations where before there were only records of subjective experience. Methodological behaviorism, in its accumulation, had constructed a science of behavior in which the variables that control behavior in limited situations had been adumbrated. Tools had been developed to simplify and abstract the problems of psychology much as the inclined plane had been developed to simplify and abstract the problems of mechanics in physics. The behaviorists' tools were applied to pharmacology, neurophysiology, education, and therapeutics, with varying success.

706

But what relevance did these data have to the persistent problems of psychology, problems such as the acquisition and storage of memory; its organization into representations of experience; the access to such representations via thought and attention; the use of these same representations in behaving skillfully and/or intentionally, to name but a few? It remained for the latter part of the century to address the problems of *psychology* with these tools.

Meantime, while a functionalist behaviorism came to hold sway in the second quarter of this century, a new structuralism developed in anthropology and linguistics. This structuralism searched not so much for the anatomical organs of mental faculties as for the structures of process. "Structure" in this new sense meant stable organizations, identifiable orders in ongoing functional relationship—a turning away from an unreconstructed functional behaviorism. In 1942 Merleau-Ponty framed an essentially functional existentialism (being-in-the-world) into *The Structure of Behavior*. Later, George Miller, Eugene Galanter, and Karl Pribram produced *Plans and the Structure of Behavior* (1960).

> As our debate progressed and our conceptions of Plans became clearer, a conviction grew on us that we were developing a point of view toward large parts of psychology. We then began to wonder how we might best characterize our position so as to contrast it with others more traditional and more familiar. The question puzzled us. We did not feel that we were behaviorists, at least not in the sense J. B. Watson defined the term, yet we were much more concerned—in that debate and in these pages, at least—with what people did than with what they knew. Our emphasis was upon processes lying immediately behind action, but not with action itself. On the other hand, we did not consider ourselves introspective psychologists, at least not in the sense Wilhelm Wundt defined the term, yet we were willing to pay attention to what people told us about their ideas and their Plans. How does one characterize a position that seems to be such a mixture of elements usually considered incompatible? Deep in the middle of this dilemma it suddenly occurred to us that we were subjective behaviorists. When we stopped laughing we began to wonder seriously if that was not exactly the position we had argued ourselves into. At least the name suggested the shocking inconsistency of our position (Miller, Galanter, & Pribram, 1960, p. 211).

Skinner, the arch enemy of subjectivism, was ultimately moved to modify his stance, perhaps in part by such developments as have just been noted. He suggested that a distinction could be drawn between behaviorism as method and behaviorism as theory. The result was expressed in terms of a new "radical behaviorism" (patterned perhaps after William James's radical empiricism).

> The statement that behaviorists deny the existence of feelings, sensations, ideas, and other features of mental life needs a good deal of clarification. Methodological behaviorism and some versions of logical positivism ruled private events out of

707

bounds because there could be no public agreement about their validity. Introspection could not be accepted as a scientific practice, and the psychology of people like Wilhelm Wundt and Edward B. Titchener was attacked accordingly. Radical behaviorism, however, takes a different line. It does not deny the possibility of self-observation or self-knowledge or its possible usefulness, but it questions the nature of what is felt or observed and hence known. It restores introspection but not what philosophers and introspective psychologists had believed they were "specting," and it raises the question of how much of one's body one can actually observe.

The position can be stated as follows: what is felt or introspectively observed is not some nonphysical world of consciousness, mind, or mental life but the observer's own body. This does not mean, as I shall show later, that introspection is a kind of physiological research, nor does it mean (and this is the heart of the argument) that what are felt or introspectively observed are the causes of behavior. An organism behaves as it does because of its current structure, but most of this is out of reach of introspection. At the moment we must content ourselves, as the methodological behaviorist insists, with a person's genetic and environmental histories. What are introspectively observed are certain collateral products of those histories.

The environment made its first great contribution during the evolution of the species, but it exerts a different kind of effect during the lifetime of the individual, and the combination of the two effects is the behavior we observe at any given time. Any available information about either contribution helps in the prediction and control of human behavior and in its interpretation in daily life. To the extent that either can be changed, behavior can be changed (Skinner, 1976, pp. 18–20).

Plans and the Structure of Behavior led a sizable portion of the community of experimental psychologists away from a radical behaviorism that eschewed cognitions, thought, ideas, consciousness, and will, into a subjective behaviorism in which these concepts were conceived as based on orderly (structured) interactions between environmental and brain processes and thus amenable to scientific inquiry. Merleau-Ponty had argued for a similar change from the opposite direction. Subjectivity as an existential, unsharable experience was held to be sharable (i.e., observable) as behavior and thus more amenable to inquiry than had been suspected.

At the same time that these developments were taking place in the body of experimental and philosophical psychology, something of a growing conservatism characterized physiological psychology. The trend in this subdiscipline was toward a reductionism which, if continued, would have had physiological psychology absorbed by neurophysiology, an absorption at the expense of physiological psychology as a psychological discipline. (An example may be found in the author's presidential address to the Division of Physiological Psychology of the APA, 1970.) Simultaneously, however, there transpired a courtship of a branch of physiological psychology—neuropsychology—by cognitively oriented psychologists, and this courtship produced a number of results that led in the opposite direction. Not the least of these results was the re-animation of neuropsychology by such issues and phenomena as attention, problem-solving, complex perceptions, contextual determinants of information processing, artificial intelligence, and the like.

Neuropsychology

On a certain construction, Lashley, Hebb, Sperry, and Pribram are all "behavioral scientists," and on an even looser construction they might even be called "technical behaviorists" in their choices of dependent variables. But the classical behaviorism of Watson, the neobehaviorism of Hull, and the radical behaviorism of Skinner involved more than a choice of dependent variables. As an *ism* such positions presupposed something of a philosophy of science, something of an ontology, even something of a system of social ethics. Understood in these terms, the formal tradition of behaviorism is an *ism* that found much to reprove in both the distant and the recent history of neurophysiological psychology, for in the latter discipline there has been a willingness, even a necessity, to accept the verbal reports of subjectively experienced cognitive, ideational, conscious, affective, volitional, and motivational aspects of human psychology (see Pribram, 1962, 1971b). Radical behaviorism took an ontological stand against a causal role for any subjectively labeled central states and representations in the organization of behavior. It insisted that they exist, if at all, only as physically specifiable neural or endocrine states or as epiphenomena of observable behavior.

The issue is important and can perhaps be brought into focus by the following analogy. Physicists studying atoms observe the properties of hydrogen and oxygen. They find lawful relations among their interactions as when two hydrogen atoms combine with one oxygen atom in a certain way to make up a molecule of H_2O. Now, however, the scientists find that H_2O has peculiar properties not shared by H and O while separate. Thus, H_2O liquefies at ordinary earth temperatures and solidifies when the temperature drops just a bit. And when it solidifies it floats on its liquid base, something most other things do not do. The following issues are now raised by the scientists who made these observations. Some want to label the H_2O combination "water" because common language calls it that. Others state that such labeling is unscientific. Next the question is raised whether water as such is in any way causally related to hydrogen and oxygen. Certainly the combination H_2O places constraints on the distribution of H and O, and the uses to which H and O can be put. But also water makes life as we know it possible. These chemical and biological consequences of combining H and O are far-reaching. Are they therefore any less scientific? Is the downward "causation" of the effects of combining H and O on their distribution to be ignored? Are chemists and biologists "soft" in their approach to science when they discuss the properties of water?

Take these statements and substitute *brain*, or more accurately, *body—organ-*

709

ism—for hydrogen and *environment* for oxygen. Behaviorally effective interactions, i.e., combinations, produce a new level of organization. Is it all right to label some of the combinations *vision*, others *attention*, others *love*, and *dignity*, and *freedom*, just as we labeled H_2O *water*? And are there "causal" relationships between freedom and the distributions of brains and organisms in the world? What is wrong with a psychology that holds that, for example, freedom makes spiritual life possible just as the wetness of water makes biological life possible? These were questions addressed by brain scientists such as Sherrington (1955), Sperry (1976), Penfield (1975), Eccles (1976) and Pribram (1979b), and philosophers such as Popper (1977), in response to earlier behavioristic stances such as Gilbert Ryle's logico-linguistic critique of the "ghost in the machine" (1949).

Isomorphism: The Percept, the Cortex, and the World

There are many experimental findings that relate brain, behavior, and experience. Psychophysics, psychophysiology, and neuropsychology abound with illustrations of the relationship between brain and mind, provided one is willing to infer mental constructs from instrumental behavior and the verbal reports of experience. Several of these examples have been detailed elsewhere (see Pribram, 1970, 1971a). For this essay, however, it seems more effective to pursue one line of research and to show how it bears on the mind-brain issue.

The example deals with the problem of isomorphism. Mary Henle (1977) has called attention to the fact that the problem has not been dealt with adequately either at the conceptual or the experimental level. What then is the problem, and how does it relate to the mind-brain issue? Simply stated, the theory of isomorphism suggests that some recognizable correspondence exists between the organization of our perceptions and the organization of our brain states. With regard to the mind-body problems, therefore, isomorphism is of central concern. No form of identity between mind and brain can be entertained if isomorphism does not hold—if it does, identity is still not mandatory, of course. To the extent that isomorphy exists, our existential understanding of the intimate relationship between mind and brain is correspondingly enhanced.

Isomorphism literally means "of the same form." What needs to be shown is that a brain state measured electrically or chemically has the same form, the same configuration as the mental percept. Recently, Roger Shepard (1979) has extended the concept to include what he calls a close functional relationship between brain representation and percept. Henle rightly criticizes this extension by pointing out that a naming response could be interpreted as "functionally related" yet be far from exhibiting the property of sharing the same form.

What are the facts? First, Wolfgang Köhler demonstrated that steady-state current shifts occur in the appropriate receiving areas of the brain cortex when a visual or auditory stimulus is presented. This shift coterminates with the presentation, and in the same and subsequent experiments it was shown that the shift accompanies the desynchronization of the electroencephalogram (see Pribram, 1971b, for review). At the same time a series of experiments undertaken by Lashley (1951) and his students placed gold foil over the cortex in order to short out direct currents, and another series performed by Sperry (1955) placed insulated mica strips into grooves cross-hatched into the cortical surface. Neither of these experimental procedures nor another in which electrical epilepsy was produced (Pribram, 1971b) resulted in *any* deficiency in discrimination performance of cats and monkeys. This led Köhler to remark that not only his theory but every other brain theory of perception had been jeopardized. In personal discussions and letters it was suggested that perhaps microfields centering on synaptic events might substitute for or underlie the macrofields (see, for example, Beurle, 1956; Pribram, 1960). Köhler died before any precise conceptual or experimental implementation of these ideas could be accomplished.

Meanwhile, unit recordings of the responses of single cells in the brain cortex had shown that in the visual cortex the response was especially brisk to lines presented in a specific orientation (Hubel & Wiesel, 1959). In view of the finding that below cortex the responsive field of neurons was circular, a Euclidean interpretation of the neural mechanism of perception became popular: below cortex spots, align the spots (by convergence) to make up lines, and from lines any other figure can be constructed by simply extrapolating the process hierarchically. The appeal of the formulation was the appeal of isomorphism—at last the evidence seemed to indicate that brain geometry and mind geometry were the same.

The basis of this cellular isomorphism is, of course, superficially different from that proposed by Köhler. He had suggested that steady-state currents were the measure of isomorphism while the unit recordings relied on nerve impulse responses. But closer inspection shows that this difference is not critical: the responsive fields of neurons are made up of their dendrites and are therefore ordinarily referred to as receptive *fields*. Receptive fields receive inputs via synapses. Thus the geometry of the receptive field in fact is the geometry of the steady-state microfields (hyper- and depolarizations) engendered in the synapto-dendritic network of the neuron from which the unit recording is obtained. And, as noted, toward the end of his life Köhler had come to entertain the possibility that it was in fact these synapto-dendritic locations which determined his cortical "fields."

Although the relationship between the data obtained with unit recordings and the proposal of brain-percept isomorphism has not been enunciated heretofore, the overwhelming intuitive appeal of this Euclidean solution to the problem, even for Gestalt oriented perception psychologists such as Teuber, has almost certainly stemmed from a tacit acknowledgment of the relationship.

It would be nice if this were where the discussion of isomorphism could end. But nature and especially biological nature is wayward in dealing with those who wish to broach her secrets. In the late 1960s and 1970s it became apparent in several

711

laboratories around the world, e.g., Stanford (Spinelli & Barrett, 1969; Spinelli, Pribram, & Bridgeman, 1970), Harvard (Pollen, Lee, & Taylor, 1971; Pollen & Ronner, 1975), Cambridge (Campbell & Robson, 1968; Movshon, Thompson, & Tolhurst, 1978), Leningrad (Glezer, Ivanoff, & Tscherbach, 1973), and Massachusetts Institute of Technology (Schiller, Finlay, & Volman, 1976), that the line-selective neurons in the visual cortex displayed inhibitory and excitatory sidebands in their receptive fields. Their responsivity varied more as a function of the width and spacings of several parallel lines (gratings) presented in a preferred orientation than as a function of any single line. This was conceptualized by the Cambridge group as indicating that the cells were responding to what Fergus Campbell called the spatial frequency of repetition of such parallel lines in a grating rather than to any single line. This view was based on the fact that repeated presentations of a grating of a particular spatial frequency would influence not only the subsequent response to that grating but to gratings with "harmonic" relationships to the initial grating. Campbell therefore proposed that the visual system operates on spatial patterns of light much as the auditory system operates on temporal patterns of sound. Recently the geometric versus spatial frequency hypotheses have been put to critical test by Russell DeValois at the University of California at Berkeley with a clear quantitative result against the geometric and in favor of the frequency mode of operation (DeValois, Albrecht, & Thorell, 1978a,b).

Evidence has been accumulating for almost a century that such wave form descriptions of sensory processing are valid. Georg Simon Ohm (of Ohm's Law of the relationship between electrical current, voltage, and resistance) suggested in 1843 that the auditory system operates as a frequency analyzer, perhaps according to Fourier principles. The Fourier theorem states that *any* pattern, no matter how complex, can be analyzed into a set of component sine waves, i.e., a set of completely regular wave forms each at a different frequency. Hermann von Helmholtz developed Ohm's suggestion by a series of experiments which provided evidence that such decomposition takes place in the cochlea. Helmholtz proposed that the cochlea operates much like a piano keyboard, a proposal which was subsequently modified by Georg von Bekesy (1960) on the basis of further experimentation which showed the cochlea to resemble more a stringed instrument brought to vibrate at specific frequencies. Nodes of excitation which develop in the vibrating surface (the "strings") account for the piano-keyboard-like qualities described by Helmholtz.

Bekesy further developed his model by actually constructing a multiply vibrating surface which he placed on the forearm of a subject. When the phase relationship between the vibrators (there were five in the original model) are appropriately adjusted, a single point of excitation is tactually perceived (Bekesy, 1967). It was then shown that the cortical response evoked by such vibrations is also single: the percept rather than the physical stimulus (Dewson, 1964) is reflected in the cortical response. Somewhere between skin and cortex, inhibitory interactions among neural elements had produced a transformation. Bekesy went on to show that by

712

applying two such "artificial cochleas," one to each forearm, and once again making the appropriate adjustments of phase, the subject was made to experience the point source alternately on one arm, then on the other, until after some continued exposure, the source of stimulation was projected outward into space between the two arms. Bekesy noted that we ordinarily "project" our somato-sensory experience to the end of writing and surgical instruments; the novelty in his experiments was the lack of solid physical continuity between the experienced source and the actual physical source. In the auditory mode this is, of course, the principle upon which stereophonic high fidelity music systems are based: by appropriate phase adjustment the sound is projected to a location between and forward of the acoustical speakers, away from the physical source of origin.

Another line of support favoring some sort of wave-form operation of the brain cortex comes from the observation that specific engrams or memory traces are not lost when brain tissue is injured. Whatever the nature of memory traces, they must become distributed over some considerable part of the brain to resist disruption. An effective method of distributing information was invented by Dennis Gabor, a mathematician, who suggested that storing the wave forms generated by energies reaching a recording surface rather than their intensities would provide better resolution in image reproduction (1948). Each electron or photon reaching a film creates ripples much as pebbles thrown into a pond. The ripples form wave fronts which intersect, producing nodes of reinforcement and interference. Mathematically, the point energies composing an image are transformed into a frequency, i.e., a wave-form representation, and by performing the inverse transform, the image can be readily reconstructed. Gabor christened the method "holography" because the entire image becomes distributed, i.e., represented, in each part of the hologram record.

In a hologram each quantum of light acts much as a pebble thrown into a pond. The ripples from such a pebble spread over the entire surface of the pond (the mathematical expression for this is in fact called a spread function of which the Fourier transform is a prime example). If there are several pebbles, the ripples produced by one pebble originate in a different location from those produced by another pebble, thus the ripples intersect and form interference patterns with nodes where the ripples add, and sinks where they cancel. The nodes can be captured on film as oxidations of silver grains if the ripples are produced by light falling on film instead of pebbles falling into water. Note that the information from the impact of each and every pebble or light ray is spread over the "recording" surface, thus the property that each portion of that surface is encoding the whole. And as noted earlier, performing the inverse transform reconstructs the image of the origin of that information. Thus the whole becomes enfolded in each portion of the hologram because each portion "contains" the spread of information of the entire image.

The holistic principle of the hologram is totally different from earlier views that wholes develop properties different from their parts. The emergence of properties

713

from appropriate combinations was expressed in the Gestalt principle that "the whole is greater and different from than the sum of its parts." The holistic properties of holograms are expressed in the principle that "the whole is contained or enfolded in its parts" and the very notion of "parts" is altered because parts of a hologram have no specifiable boundaries.

The properties of holograms that are important for brain functioning are (1) the distribution of information which can account for the failure of brain lesions to eradicate any specific memory trace (engram); (2) the tremendous readily retrievable storage capacity of the holographic domain—the entire contents of the Library of Congress can currently be stored on holofiche (microfilm recorded in holographic form) taking up no more space than an attaché case; (3) the capacity for associative recall which is inherent in holograms because of the coupling of inputs when they become distributed; and (4) the powerful technique for correlating provided by this coupling—cross correlations and auto correlations are accomplished almost instantaneously. This is why the Fast Fourier Transform (FFT) is so useful in computer operations when statistical correlations are needed or when image construction, as in X-ray tomography, is required.

The step from showing that cortical cells encode frequencies to viewing the cortical surface as a holographic distributing device for encoding memory is not a completely simple one. The receptive field of each cell may encode holographically, i.e., in the waveform domain, but such receptive fields are small—for example, in the visual system they subtend at most some 5° of visual angle. But, as has been shown by engineers using holographic techniques, such patch holograms—also called "strip" or "multiplex" holograms—have all the image-reconstructing properties of global holograms. Further, when the patches encode overlapping but not identical patterns, movement can be recorded. Global holograms show the property of translational invariance which allows object constancy to result; but this is at the sacrifice of an explicit encoding of space and time which are enfolded into the *wave number*, as physicists term the two-dimensional *spatial frequency* of neurophysiologists.

There are other problems such as the amount of information that can be encoded in wave lengths recorded from neural tissue. But if the wave form is spatially related to dendritic hyper- and depolarizations these can occur angstrom units apart. Furthermore, the wave mechanical treatment of neural holography may not be the most propitious; suggestions have been made to use modified cable theory (Poggio & Torre, 1980); to treat the dendritic net as a manifold in which each polarization point is considered a cell in a lattice of a Lie group (Hoffman, 1970); or to use other mathematical approaches developed in quantum mechanics. Whatever the best quantitative description turns out to be, the current facts are that the dendritic receptive field does encode in such a way that a Fourier-like Gabor transform is appropriate at one level of description (see DeValois et al., 1978a,b), and the

714

Fourier transform has the advantage of being readily invertible so that encoding and subsequent image reconstruction are easily achieved.

The reason for looking at quantum mechanics for mathematical treatments of neural holographic processes is that the issues faced at the microphysical level are in many respects similar to those encountered in current neurophysiology. Thus David Bohm (1971, 1973) has suggested that a holographic-like order which enfolds space and time underlies the observations of quantum physics. Bohm calls this an implicate order to distinguish it from such explicate, explicit orders as those represented by Euclidean geometry and Newtonian physics.

On the basis of these results and formulations, the problem of brain-percept isomorphism takes on added complexity. The brain cortex resembles a spatial filter (Movshon et al., 1979), resonator or interferometer (Barrett, 1969), a musical instrument, or hologram constructing percepts. Such an instrument is not a geometric isomorph of the percepts it constructs. Rather, the isomorphism is seen to be between the brain as an instrument and the arrangement of physical energies elsewhere in the universe. The isomorphism is between two "physical" entities, "brain" and "world," rather than between either of them and our percepts!

Were the Gestalt psychologists wrong therefore in their proposal of psychophysical isomorphism? I do not believe so—only the locus of the isomorphism was misplaced. A possible resolution of the complexities introduced by the recent findings of how the brain cortex operates comes from an observation made by David Bohm with regard to current physics: he suggests that all of our conceptualizations in physics (as opposed to experimental manipulations and their formal mathematical treatment) are based on the use of *lenses*. We have telescopes and microscopes which contain lenses which objectify. Objects are particulate, separated from one another and can thus move with respect to one another to create the appearance of space, time, and causality, i.e., the explicate domain. Take away lenses and one is immersed in the implicate order.

Apply this reasoning to the perceptual isomorphism problem. Our percepts provide us with a Euclidean and Newtonian mechanistic order in which there are objects separated from one another, in which there is space, movement, time, causality. This is the explicate order. Take away our lenses—in this case the lenses and retinal structure of our eyes, the cochlea of the ear, and the tactile senses which, as we have seen, Bekesy showed in a carefully conducted series of experiments to be lens-like due to sensory, i.e., lateral inhibition—and we might well be left with an implicate order much as was Helen Keller before she learned to objectify.

Isomorphy, according to this analysis, is between percept and *sensory* mechanism. Contrary to James Gibson's pronouncements (1979), the lens of the eye does focus an image on the retina which is viewed by most students of comparative neurology when they are given an ox eye to dissect. The eye is, of course, not stationary. Thus the "image" of perception must be composed from a retinal figure

715

which is in continual motion. This is accomplished in two ways. First, the retinal mosaic is anatomically re-presented isomorphically in the gross structure of the cortex. There is a more-or-less point-to-point connectivity between groups of cells in the retina and groups in the cortex. Thus the sensory order is maintained in the macrostructure—the between-receptive-field organization—of the sensory projections to the cortex.

Second, *within*-receptive-field organization of these projections is, as detailed above, holographically organized. The focused retinal image is analyzed into wave forms by the motion of the retina as shown by the "Mexican hat" configuration of the receptive field recorded from the fibers of the optic nerve (Rodieck, 1965). This results in the microstructure of the sensory projections (Pribram, Lassonde, & Ptito, 1981).

Now under intense study in our laboratory (Spinelli & Pribram, 1967; Lassonde, Ptito, & Pribram, 1981) are the relationships between the macro- and microstructures of the cortical sensory receiving areas, and of both to the mechanisms (located in the intrinsic "association" systems of the brain) which are responsible for linguistic logicality and objectivity (Pribram, 1981a,b, 1983). Objectivity apparently results not only from the lens-like structures of the senses but also from the constancies, the invariances, culled from the variegated interactions between the senses and the sensed which result from *movement*. Correlations, facilitated by the holographic microstructure of the sensory systems, play a critical role in establishing invariances. Objective invariance (e.g., experienced event, numerosity) must then be operated upon to produce logos and ratio, and there is evidence that in man these operations are performed to some extent by different hemispheres. Thus the left hemisphere appears to specialize in logical linguistic operations; the right hemisphere (at least in musically untrained subjects) in the rational tonal operations basic to music and perhaps some aspects of mathematics.

The issue of brain-percept isomorphism is thus complex. Basically, however, one can make the statement that phenomenal experience is the result of the operations of the sensory-motor apparatus. *Brain* function is involved only inasmuch as the sensory-motor apparatus is represented in the macrostructure of the sensory and motor systems of the brain. But there is much more to brain function than this sensory-motor re-presentation. The operations of the holographic microstructure and the mechanisms that lead to linguistic logic and musical and mathematical rationality were considered here, but there is also the entire neurochemical apparatus which is involved in the organization of mood-states, the apparatus that organizes emotional and motivational feelings and expressions, to name the most important. Again, these mechanisms show isomorphy with experience only to the extent that they represent the organization of bodily functions (Pribram & McGuinness, 1979; Pribram, 1977, 1981c).

These observations do not mean that the brain remains uninvolved in the organization of experience and behavior. The phenomenon of phantom limbs is but one

716

outstanding example which demonstrates the intimate relationship of brain to psychological processes. This same example shows that the body per se becomes unnecessary to experiencing it once its representation has become imprinted in brain. The converse has also been demonstrated: certain brain lesions result in "neglect" of the part of the body on the side opposite to the lesion. Such body parts are simply not experienced as existing even when they are pointed out to the patient.

In summary then, it is the body and its senses and receptor functions, its glands, and the muscles that beget movement that are *ontologically* responsible for perceptual-brain isomorphism. To the extent that these body functions become represented in the brain, to that extent isomorphism occurs. But the brain has other alternative processing systems which are anisomorphic with experience, though they may correspond to nonsensory aspects of physical reality. It is these alternatives that provide a current frontier for exploration, both in physics and in psychobiology.

The Eternal Verities

Subjectivity, holograms, musical ratios, and harmonies as rational operations; all have become counterintuitive to our contemporary scientific culture. For a century we have been steeped in the virtues of "logical" positivism and "logical" mathematics to the exclusion of "rational" forms of thought. Thus, right or wrong, a Euclidean logic of isomorphy between brain processes and perception comes all too easily while a Gaborian and Bohmian rationality is appreciated with only the greatest of difficulty. The difficulty is compounded for scientists because they have been trained to be "objective" and thus they objectify before all else; because proximate causality is a necessity in performing and interpreting experiments; and because the implicate and rational orders are so closely aligned with subjective, religious, and mystical, i.e., nonlogical, experience.

If, however, the analysis presented in this essay is correct, the evidence gathered in the physical, brain, and psychological sciences will right the current cultural imbalance between *logos* and *ratio*. As noted, physicists have already come to grips with the limitations of objectifying. As the data from the neuro- and behavioral sciences indicate, these physicists are about to be joined by their biological and psychological colleagues. A paradigm shift, to use Kuhn's well-worked phrase, is in the making. But, of course, the shift will be, as revolutions so often are, a return to knowledge and wisdom established long, long ago in the prehistory of mankind. But the scientific mode should add its own luster to these eternal verities. Psychologists especially should benefit from this turn of the scientific weal. A precise, observationally based approach to such problems as aesthetics, ethics, spiritual values, freedom, dignity, religious beliefs, and mystical and other "paranormal" phenomena ought to result. At the moment these problems can be tackled from a social-psychological standpoint, but understanding which might come from an analysis of process and mechanism—especially neural mechanism—appears beyond reach. If, however, the twenty-first century continues the incredibly fruitful course charted by the nineteenth and twentieth, there is every promise that we will look at "psychology's first hundred years as an experimental discipline" with a quiet humor encompassed in phrases such as "and they thought they were psychologists"!

REFERENCES

Barrett, T. W. The cortex as interferometer: The transmission of amplitude, frequency and phase in the cerebral cortex. *Neuropsychologia*, 1969, 7, 135–148.

Bechterev von, V. *Die Funktionen der Nervencentra*. Berlin: Fischer, 1911.

Bekesy, G. von. *Experiments in hearing*. New York: McGraw-Hill, 1960.

Bekesy, G. von. *Sensory inhibition*. Princeton, N.J.: Princeton University Press, 1967.

Bernstein, L. *The unanswered question*. Cambridge, Mass.: Harvard University Press, 1976.

Beurle, R. L. Properties of a mass of cells capable of regenerating pulses. *Philosophical Transactions of the Royal Society of London*, 1956, 240, 55–94.

Bohm, D. Quantum theory as an indication of a new order in physics. Part A. The development of new orders as shown through the history of physics. *Foundations of Physics*, 1971, 1(4), 359–381.

Bohm, D. Quantum theory as an indication of a new order in physics. Part B. Implicate and explicate order in physical law. *Foundations of Physics*, 1973, 3(2), 139–168.

Campbell, F. W., & Robson, J. G. Application of Fourier analysis to the visibility of gratings. *Journal of Physiology*, 1968, 197, 551–566.

Coles, R. *Walker Percy: An American search*. Boston: Little, Brown, 1978.

DeValois, R. L., Albrecht, D. G., & Thorell, L. G. Spatial tuning of LGN and cortical cells in monkey visual system. In H. Spekreijse (Ed.), *Spatial contrast*. Amsterdam: Monograph Series, Royal Netherlands Academy of Sciences, 1978. (a)

DeValois, R. L., Albrecht, D. G., & Thorell, L. G. Cortical cells: Bar and edge detectors, or spatial frequency filters? In S. Cool & E. L. Smith (Eds.), *Frontiers in visual science*. New York: Springer-Verlag, 1978. (b)

Dewson, J. H., III. Cortical responses to patterns of two-point cutaneous stimulation. *Journal of Comparative & Physiological Psychology*, 1964, 58, 387–389.

Eccles, J. C. Brain and free will. In G. G. Globus, G. Maxwell, & I. Savodnik (Eds.), *Consciousness and the brain: A scientific and philosophical inquiry*. New York: Plenum, 1976.

Freud, S. Project for a scientific psychology. In J. Strachey (Ed. and trans.), *Standard edition of the complete psychological works of Sigmund Freud*. New York: Norton, 1950. (Originally written, 1895.)

Gabor, D. A new microscopic principle. *Nature*, 1948, 161, 777–778.

Gall, F. J. *On the origins of the moral qualities and intellectual faculties of man*. Carlsruhe: C. L. Müller, 1835.

Gibson, J. J. *The ecological approach to visual perception*. Boston: Houghton Mifflin, 1979.

Glezer, V. D., Ivanoff, V. A., & Tscherbach, T. A. Investigation of complex and hypercomplex receptive fields of visual cortex of the cat as spatial frequency filters. *Vision Research*, 1973, 13, 1875–1904.

Henle, M. The influence of Gestalt psychology in America. *Annals of the New York Academy of Sciences*, 1977, 291, pp. 3–12.

Hoffman, W. C. Higher visual perception as prolongation of the basic Lie transformation group. *Mathematical Biosciences*, 1970, *6*, 437–471.

Hubel, D. H., & Wiesel, T. N. Receptive fields of single neurones in the cat's striate cortex. *Journal of Physiology*, 1959, *148*, 574–591.

Hull, C. L. *Principles of behavior: An introduction to behavior theory.* New York: Appleton-Century-Crofts, 1943.

Hull, C. L. *Essentials of behavior.* New Haven: Yale University Press, 1951.

James, W. *The principles of psychology.* (2 vols.) New York: Holt, 1890.

Keller, H. *The story of my life.* New York: Doubleday, 1954. (Originally published, 1903.)

Lashley, K., Chow, K. L., & Semmes, J. An examination of the electrical field theory of cerebral integration. *Psychological Review*, 1951, *58*, 123–136.

Lassonde, M. C., Ptito, M., & Pribram, K. H. Intracerebral influences on the microstructure of visual cortex. *Experimental Brain Research*, 1981, *43*, 131–144.

McClain, E. G. *The myth of invariance.* Boulder, Colo.: Shambhala, 1976.

Merleau-Ponty, M. *The structure of behavior.* Boston: Beacon Press, 1963. (Originally published, 1942.)

Miller, G. A. *Psychology: The science of mental life.* New York: Harper & Row, 1962.

Miller, G. A., Galanter, E., & Pribram, K. H. *Plans and the structure of behavior.* New York: Holt, 1960.

Movshon, J. A., & Lennie, P. Pattern-selective adaptation in visual cortical neurones. *Nature*, 1979, *278*, 850–852.

Ohm, G. S. Über die definition des tones, nebst daran geknupfter theorie der sirene und ahnlicher tonvildener vorrichtungen. *Ann. Physik. Chem.*, 1843, *59*, 513–565.

Pavlov, I. P. *Conditioned reflexes. An investigation of the physiological activity of the cerebral cortex* (G. V. Anrep, trans.). London: Oxford University Press, 1927.

Penfield, W. *Mystery of the mind.* Princeton, N.J.: Princeton University Press, 1975.

Poggio, T., & Torre, V. A new approach to synaptic interactions. In H. Palm (Ed.), *Approaches to complex systems.* Berlin: Springer-Verlag, 1980.

Pollen, D. A., Lee, J. R., & Taylor, J. H. How does the striate cortex begin the reconstruction of the visual world? *Science*, 1971, *173*, 74–77.

Pollen, D. A., & Ronner, S. F. Periodic excitability changes across the receptive fields of complex cells in the striate and parastriate cortex of the cat. *Journal of Physiology*, 1975, *245*, 667–697.

Popper, K. R., & Eccles, J. C. *The self and its brain.* New York: Springer International, 1977.

Pribram, K. H. The intrinsic systems of the forebrain. In J. Field, H. W. Magoun, & V. E. Hall (Eds.), *Handbook of physiology, neurophysiology II.* Washington, D.C.: American Physiological Society, 1960.

Pribram, K. H. Interrelations of psychology and the neurological disciplines. In S. Koch (Ed.), *Psychology: A study of science* (Vol. 4). New York: McGraw-Hill, 1962.

Pribram, K. H. (Ed.). *Brain and behavior* (4 vols.). London: Penguin, 1969. (a)

Pribram, K. H. DADTA III: Computer control of the experimental analysis of behavior. *Perceptual and Motor Skills*, 1969, *29*, 599–608. (b)

Pribram, K. H. The biology of mind: Neurobehavioral foundations. In A. R. Gilgen (Ed.), *Scientific psychology: Some perspectives.* New York: Academic Press, 1970.

Pribram, K. H. The realization of mind. *Synthese*, 1971, *22*, 313–322. (a)

Pribram, K. H. Languages of the brain: Experimental paradoxes and principles in neuropsychology. Englewood Cliffs, N.J.: Prentice-Hall, 1971. (2nd ed., Monterey, Calif.: Brooks/Cole, 1977.) (b)

Pribram, K. H. Peptides and protocritic processes. In L. H. Miller, C. A. Sandman, & A. J. Kastin (Eds.), *Neuropeptide influences on the brain and behavior.* New York: Raven Press, 1977.

Pribram, K. H. Behaviorism, phenomenology and holism in psychology: A scientific analysis. *Journal of Social and Biological Structures*, 1979, *2*, 65–72. (a)

Pribram, K. H. Transcending the mind/brain problem. *Zygon*, 1979, *14*, 19–30. (b)

719

III. PSYCHOLOGY AND ITS INTERSECTING DISCIPLINES

Pribram, K. H. The distributed nature of the memory store and the localization of linguistic competencies. *Toronto Semiotic Circle—Proceedings of a Symposium on the Neurological Basis of Signs in Communication Processes*, pp. 127–147. Toronto: Victoria University, 1981. (a)

Pribram, K. H. Context sensitive coding in speech. In T. Myers, J. Laver, & J. Anderson (Eds.), *Proceedings of the International Symposium on the Cognitive Representative of Speech, Edinburgh, Scotland*, pp. 255–262. Amsterdam: North Holland, 1981. (b)

Pribram, K. H. Emotion. In S. B. Filskov & T. J. Boll (Eds.), *Handbook of clinical neuropsychology*. New York: Wiley, 1981. (c)

Pribram, K. H. Brain and the perception of objective reality. In *Absolute values and the creation of the new world*, pp. 1373–1401. New York: ICF Press, 1983.

Pribram, K. H., Lassonde, M. C., & Ptito, M. Classification of receptive field properties. *Experimental Brain Research*, 1981, 43, 119–130.

Pribram, K. H., & McGuinness, D. The origins of sensory bias in the development of gender differences in perception and cognition. In M. Bortner (Ed.), *Cognitive growth and development: Essays in memory of Herbert G. Birch*. New York: Bruner/Mazel, 1979.

Pribram, K. H., & Robinson, D. Biological contributions to the development of psychology. In C. Buxton (Ed.), *A history of modern psychology: Concepts, methods, viewpoints*. New York: Academic Press, in press.

Rodieck, R. W. Quantitative analysis of cat retinal ganglion cell response to visual stimuli. *Vision Research*, 1965, 5, 583–601.

Ryle, G. *The concept of mind*. New York: Barnes & Noble, 1949.

Schiller, P. H., Finlay, B. L., & Volman, S. F. Quantitative studies of single-cell properties in monkey striate cortex. *Journal of Neurophysiology*, 1976, 39, 1288–1374.

Sechenov, I. M. *Reflexes of the brain*. Cambridge, Mass.: M.I.T. Press, 1965. (Originally published, 1863.)

Shepard, R. N. Psychophysical complementarity. In M. Kubovy & J. R. Pomerantz (Eds.), *Perceptual organization*. Hillsdale, N.J.: Erlbaum, 1979.

Sherrington, C. *Man on his nature*. Garden City, N.Y.: Doubleday, 1955.

Skinner, B. F. *The behavior of organisms*. New York: Appleton-Century-Crofts, 1938.

Skinner, B. F. *Beyond freedom and dignity*. New York: Knopf, 1971.

Skinner, B. F. *About behaviorism*. New York: Vintage, 1976.

Sperry, R. W. Mental phenomena as causal determinants in brain function. In G. G. Globus, G. Maxwell, & I. Savodnik (Eds.), *Consciousness and the brain*. New York: Plenum, 1976.

Sperry, R. W., Miner, N., & Meyers, R. E. Visual pattern perception following subpial slicing and tantalum wire implantations in the visual cortex. *Journal of Comparative & Physiological Psychology*, 1955, 48, 50–58.

Spinelli, D. N., & Barrett, T. W. Visual receptive field organization of single units in the cat's visual cortex. *Experimental Neurology*, 1969, 24, 76–98.

Spinelli, D. N., & Pribram, K. H. Changes in visual recovery functions and unit activity produced by frontal and temporal cortex stimulation. *Electroencephalography & Clinical Neurophysiology*, 1967, 22, 143–149.

Spinelli, D. N., Pribram, K. H., & Bridgeman, B. Visual receptive field organizing of single units in the visual cortex of monkeys. *International Journal of Neuroscience*, 1970, 1, 67–74.

Thorndike, E. L. Animal intelligence: An experimental study of the associative processes in animals. *Psychological Review Monograph*, 1898, 2 (No. 8).

Thorndike, E. L. *Educational psychology* (3 vols.). New York: Columbia University Press, 1913–1914.

Tolman, E. C. *Purposive behavior in animals and men*. New York: Appleton-Century-Crofts, 1932.

Watson, J. B. *Behaviorism*. Chicago: University of Chicago Press, 1959. (Originally published, 1924.)

Yerkes, R. M. Inhibition and reinforcement of reactions in the frog: *Rana clamitans*. *Journal of Comparative Neurological Psychology*, 1904, 14, 124–137.

31

The Visceral Systems in Psychology

JOHN I. LACEY

Given limitations of space, time, and competence, I am able to give only a very restricted account of just a few of the many areas that constitute the study of interrelationships among the central and autonomic nervous systems and behavior.

To conform to the historical intent of this volume, it is appropriate to start with the seminal contributions of Wilhelm Wundt. His *Principles of Physiological Psychology* was published in 1874, a date that may be taken as the beginning of a new, formally named, hybrid discipline.

Wundt did *not* think that the study of bodily mechanisms could explain the nature of, the essential subjective qualities of, conscious processes. These were the peculiar province of psychology. He did think that the task of physiological psychology was the study of the "bodily substrate of the mental life." Wundt's thoughts were prophetic. Relatively few physiological psychologists—Karl Pribram, Roger Sperry, and John Eccles being prominent and desirable exceptions—postulate that the subjective qualities of consciousness are suitable topics for neuroscientists. But all physiological psychologists believe that detailed and intimate knowledge of the structure and function of the nervous system is necessary for the understanding of *behavior*, if not of consciousness. Moreover, some believe that the relationship is a reciprocal one: that a theory of behavior in nonphysiological terms may lead to a fuller understanding of neural function.

A major theme of this chapter derives directly from Wundt. I am indebted to a recent letter by Sabat (1979) in the *American Psychologist* for the following quotation from Wundt's *Lectures on Human and Animal Psychology*, as translated in 1894. At issue is the question of the existence of spatial and temporal localization of the physical mechanisms serving as substrates of behavior. This problem is still with us, Sabat points out, as exemplified by the search for reward and punishment centers in the brain. Wundt stated:

> To speak of a number of psychical centres, one must have made assumptions that are equally impossible whether from the standpoint of physiology or of psychology. There is, in reality, but one psychical centre; and that is the brain as a whole, *with all its organs* [my italics]. For in any at all complicated process, these organs are brought into action, if not all together, at any rate over so wide a range and in such various quarters as to forbid the delineation of special psychical centres within the functional whole.

Sophisticated neuropsychologists today do not often use the word *center*, for the notion of specific nuclei and tracts being responsible for single discretely defined behavioral processes, independent of the action of other interacting nuclei and tracts, simply is untenable. Interdependence and interaction among neural structures and processes is the rule, not the exception. That this is so accounts in large part, I think, for the still-present difficulties in "neurologizing" behavior. The difficulties are greater in studies relating behavior to autonomic functions than in studies of behavior and central functions. Primarily this is because autonomic functions are *not* isolated from central functions; and because autonomic structures and functions—for a variety of technical and anatomical reasons—have not been as amenable to detailed and minute scrutiny as the central nervous system.

Interactions among central and autonomic functions must be understood, in my opinion, before the field now known as "the psychophysiology of the autonomic nervous system" (hereafter referred to as ANS psychophysiology) can yield important and wide-ranging understanding of behavior. They are not yet well understood. Only recently have systematic attempts been made to render an orderly, although preliminary and incomplete, account of this vital area. Uchizono in his introduction to a historically important symposium on the central organization of the autonomic nervous system (Sato, 1975, p. iii) puts the matter accurately when he characterizes the physiology of the autonomic nervous system as "comparatively retarded," and states:

> The complexity and vagueness, both structurally and functionally, of this system has caused people to hesitate rather than study it. On the other hand . . . researchers have been fascinated by the simplicity of the somatic nervous system which, since the days of Sherrington, has produced dramatically fruitful results.

722

Hence, in my opinion, ANS psychophysiology is in a relatively primitive state because it lacks extensive development of the underlying basic neurophysiology, and, it may be fairly said, many times ignores what little is known.

In this chapter, I raise two major questions to serve as probes into the current status of ANS psychophysiology. The questions are (1) whether neuropsychology typically goes far enough in the study of the "brain as a whole, with all its organs"; and (2) what conceptual problems are raised, and still need to be solved, if the operation of the "brain as a whole, with all its organs" is to be understood. These questions could be explored in the context of almost any subspeciality of neuroscience. I will restrict myself to two topics that are closely identified with ANS psychophysiology: affective behavior and stress; and I will utilize concepts of systems-control theory, both to order past contributions and to suggest future directions.

Emotion and Affective Behavior

Emotions, however defined, are particularly suitable processes for the study of the "brain as a whole, with all its organs," if only because the major affective states (nonchronic) are accompanied by the appearance of widespread, *centrally regulated*, visceral, motor, and endocrinological perturbations. Consideration of this topic is particularly appropriate, for the still-ongoing development of our understanding of the physical substrate of emotion is highly instructive, both for what is typically included in the major discussions of the neurophysiology of affective behavior and typically excluded. Brief but incisive reviews of the material covered in the next few paragraphs can be found in Zanchetti (1967) and Scheibel and Scheibel (1967).

For James and Lange, as is well-known, the important structure was the neocortex, which first initiated motor and visceral activities, and then, upon receiving interoceptively and proprioceptively derived signals, translated these signals into the "felt" emotion. But for Cannon, the important structure was the thalamus. Diencephalic processes resulted simultaneously in peripherally and centrally directed efferent discharges. In Cannon's view, there was no return from the periphery itself to the neocortical mantle. The peripheral discharges served only to prepare the organism for fight or flight. The controversy between James-Lange and Cannon dominated the first three decades of this century and produced the famous "sham rage" experiments of Bard (Cannon's student).

Bard's experiments on the decorticate cat located the major controlling structures involved in the visceral and motor expressions of sham rage in the caudal half of the hypothalamus—often called the "head ganglion" of the autonomic nervous system—and in the ventral-caudal thalamus.

723

The visceral-motor accompaniments of sham rage are explosive and extensive. They occur both spontaneously and in response to otherwise innocuous stimuli, such as light stroking of the forepaw. Obviously, the inhibitory effects of suprahypothalamic structures had been surgically removed. Cannon and Bard thought the source of the inhibition to be solely cortical. In 1937, Papez proposed his famous figure-of-eight circuit as *the* "mechanism of emotion," which involved coordinated and integrated activities of diencephalic and rhinencephalic structures. Thus what is now known as the limbic lobe was implicated as involved in affective behavior. Limbic lobe structures are now known to exert a variety of autonomic effects, some inhibitory and some facilitatory. The history of the development of our knowledge of the complex interactions among hypothalamic, amygdalar, septal, and hippocampal structures, and their role as substrates of a variety of behaviors, is beyond the scope of this chapter. Each of these structures, with the possible exception of hippocampus, is intimately, but complexly, involved with autonomic functions, and with a variety of important nonemotional behaviors. Given the current emphasis on the role of "cognitive appraisal" and "coping strategies" in the control and modulation of affective behaviors and affective experiences, we must also assume complex neocortical participation in ways that cannot yet be specified in strictly physiological terms.

A fair summary, I think, of our current concept of the locus of the physical substrate of affective behavior is: almost everywhere. Participation of multiple structures is the rule, not the exception, both for affective and nonaffective behaviors. With respect to a general understanding of brain and behavior, Isaacson (1974, p. 239) states—and I think a very large number of neuroscientists would agree—that "it is presumptuous to suggest that the functions of any brain region are understood at all well." This is not for lack of an impressive amount of empirical data, not due to a dearth of ingenious theories or a lack of sophisticated experimental tools and concepts. Nor is it due to the lack of dramatic and major advances in our understanding of the relation of some brain structures to behavior in the past few decades. It is due to the enormous difficulties of attaining meaningful generalizations, of wide scope and applicability, from necessarily limited observations of the operations of multiple interactive structures and processes.

I have a parallel to Isaacson's statement, albeit one that perhaps would not elicit such widespread agreement: it is presumptuous to suggest that the role of any single autonomic response, or even any mixture of autonomic responses, in behavior is understood at all well. This, too, I think, is not due to the lack of an impressive amount of empirical data or of sophisticated experiments. It is due, I think, primarily to three factors. First, there has occurred an unfortunate segregation—both intellectual and institutional—of those who study *only* the relationship of *central* nervous system structures and processes to behavior from those who study the relationship *only* of peripherally accessible autonomic functions to behavior. Second, a similar separation of both groups has occurred from those who study classical problems within physiology proper, such as cardiovascular regulation, respiratory regulation, glucose regulation, and other such specific areas of physiological concern. Third, very complex processes revealed within the central nervous system—such as the so-called "arousal" processes mediated by the ascending reticular system—have been reified and oversimplified, as they are applied to the design of experiments and to the interpretation of experimental data. The result of these three developments has been to impoverish theoretical development and to limit intellectual horizons. For me, the hallmark of this impoverishment and limitation is that the members of each group very rarely refer to the concepts and findings of the other groups. Moreover—in my probably idiosyncratic opinion—when they do make such references, the citations are marked more by narrowness and restriction than by inclusiveness and integration.

The fact is, I think, that we have not made even a respectable start in producing general neuropsychological theories that yield an understanding of how autonomic processes are integrated with central processes in diverse behaviors. Textbooks in neuropsychology commonly segregate peripheral autonomic functions in a chapter on "emotion and arousal," with no hint in the attendant discussion of the fact that autonomic responses occur in a large number of nonaffective behaviors, and, indeed, as I attempt to show later, serve as regulators of behavior. This despite the fact that, for example, students of thermoregulation have long known that quite complex behaviors of the chilled or heated animal are governed by the visceral responses to changes in environmental temperature. The cold rat not only shivers to produce more heat and exhibits peripheral vasoconstriction to reduce heat loss; it also, given the opportunity, will gather material to make a warm nest. These same students of thermoregulation are intensely involved at the same time in the study of how central activities guide and modulate the complex of thermoregulatory responses, both physiological and behavioral. (See, for example, a recent review article by Satinoff, 1978.) An opposite picture is presented by the majority of those who call themselves ANS psychophysiologists. They commonly are concerned only with the details of the peripheral responses and the behavioral conditions that cause their occurrence.

Hence, the answer to my first question is that only in a few highly specific areas of investigation, such as feeding, drinking, and thermoregulation, do students of visceral processes make an attempt to study the "brain as a whole, with all its organs."

Stress, Feedback, and Engineering Control Theory

I return to the decorticate cat, a simplified preparation whose study offers many rewards. The widespread somato-autonomic storm of "sham rage" includes hyperpnoea, hypertension, tachycardia, mydriasis, and violent somatic activity. These same responses, and additional ones, have been recorded and quantitatively evaluated in literally many thousands of experiments, particularly in experiments involving "stress" and "arousal." One would think that by now a satisfactory taxonomy of stress and affect, and a satisfactory theoretical understanding of the role such responses play in behavior, would have been achieved; that the reigning concepts of sympathetic and parasympathetic mediation and the structural allocation of such mediation to anterior and posterior hypothalamus, of homeostatic regulation of the internal milieu, and of viscero-autonomic integration are all that would be needed to enable the physiological psychologist to make an informed and penetrating approach to the study of critical behaviors.

Yet only a little over a decade ago—and the situation would not be different today—the psychologist Teichner (1968) was faced with the problem of evaluating, understanding, and predicting the behavioral and physiological stress reactions of military personnel in unusual physiological environments. He found the studies by psychologists of physiological responses so seriously deficient as to warrant a trenchant and compelling reevaluation. Psychologists, he states,

> have tended to be concerned with autonomic measures, and the search for sensitivity and consistency among them, whereas physiologists concerned with environments have been concerned with *centrally controlled* [my italics] regulatory mechanisms of the body. To a large degree, both interests lead to taking the same physiological measures. But the interpretation given to the measures has been remarkably different (pp. 271–272).

Let me quote at length from Teichner, first from a passage that issues some clear challenges to psychophysiological theory.

> Stressor-stress reaction associations are difficult to demonstrate, . . . without specific consideration of the compensatory action of the regulating systems. For example, the rectal temperature of men exposed to air temperatures of 100°F may show little or no increase. A naive investigator observing only rectal temperature might be tempted to conclude that 100°F is not a stressor. In fact, at this temperature, he could find an increased sweat rate, a raised skin temperature, an increased peripheral blood flow, and a decreased metabolic rate, all of which represent compensatory activities of the thermoregulatory system. Rectal temperature is a *controlled* event; compensatory responses are *controlling* events. It is the controlling event which first exceeds normal limits of variation given a stressor. When the controlled variable exceeds its normal range of fluctuation, the compensation processes are failing in control, but this may not happen short of severe exposure to the stressor. In other words, one level of stress reaction is present when the *compensatory* events exceed their normal limits; a more intense level is present when the *controlled* events exceed their normal limits. For this reason, it cannot be emphasized too strongly that the investigation of stress phenomena must put emphasis on measurement of the activities of controlling or compensatory processes for, except under relatively severe conditions, the variables which they control change very little (p. 272).

Elsewhere, Teichner summarizes his main thesis as follows:

> Emphasis has been put on the measurement of controlling or compensatory reactions as opposed to controlled phenomena. This implies that investigators concerned with physiological measurements should select and interpret their variables in terms of regulatory actions. Measures such as HR, RR, GSR, vasomotor activity, etc. whether considered singly or in combination, cannot be interpreted consistently unless they are interpreted as phenomena which are dependent on regulatory activities on the one hand, and which, in turn, alter the state of other regulatory variables. This is equally true of behavioral phenomena. That is, in the presence of a stressor, behavioral and physiological measures may increase, decrease, or not change at all according to the nature of the on-going regulatory activity and according to whether what is being observed is a controlling or controlled variable. It is not, therefore, a question of which physiological or behavioral event provides a more sensitive measure of stress or what pattern of increases or decreases occurs reliably, or whether a particular measure increases in the presence of a stressor while another one decreases. Instead the organism must be viewed as a system and the on-going state of the system must be known before the experimental conditions are applied. Furthermore, this approach asks that the system state be known for the individual since individuals may vary widely in regard to chronic capacities, activation levels, and bandwidths. Unless the individual is known in these ways, all that can be expected under stress are unpredictable individual differences in performance and in "patterns" of physiological response (p. 282).

These are penetrating observations. I agree wholeheartedly with the general notion that we are dealing with a self-regulating system, organized to produce homeostatically desirable end-results. I also agree that autonomic psychophysiology and neurophysiological behavioral studies are deficient insofar as they ignore such basic physiological concepts. I think, however, that the situation is more complex than Teichner suggests, and that a consideration of these complexities leads to useful insights into the nature of the physical substrate of behavior.

Self-regulating systems are studied in detail in engineering control systems theory. This elegant theory involves quantitatively definable, and strictly defined, processes and attributes, such as set-point, gain, and negative feedback, to name a few key concepts. Many of the *engineering* concepts can be employed to describe the operation of *physiological* systems. Indeed, considerable effort has been expended, and continues to be expended, in the application of control theory to physiological systems, such as temperature regulation, acid-base equilibrium, water exchange, gastric secretion, cardiovascular regulation, regulation of motor activities, glucose regulation, and many others. The results have been enormously useful in promoting understanding of physiological systems. (See, for example, Grodins, 1963, and Milhorn, 1966.) Control theory can handle even quite complex interactions of multiple structures and functions. It is being applied, sparsely now but with increasing frequency, to behavioral and psychophysiological processes. It may offer

727

a solution to the conceptual problems raised in the study of the "brain as a whole, with all its organs." But there are radical differences between man-made engineering control systems and physiological control systems. A consideration of these differences yields some interesting insights into the nature of the neural substrate of behavior.

Visceral Responses as Regulators of Behavior

One of the important differences is that physiological control systems are not sharply separated from each other. One consequence is that what is a *controlled event* in one system becomes a *controlling event* for another system.

The most thoroughly documented example of this phenomena concerns blood pressure, usually considered a *controlled event* in cardiovascular studies because it is a resultant of changes in cardiac output and peripheral resistance. Changes in blood pressure are *sensed* (sensors are indispensable elements in control theory) by strain-sensitive interoceptors—the so-called "baroreceptors"—and are fed back (another key concept in control theory) to the central nervous system as a changed temporal pattern and frequency of nerve impulses via the vagal and glossopharyngeal afferent fibers. Within the central nervous system, corrective actions are then initiated such that blood pressure is regulated downwards if blood pressure has increased, and regulated upwards if blood pressure has decreased. The end-result of this *negative feedback loop* is the constraint of blood pressure within relatively narrow limits—a beautifully organized and well-documented example of homeostatic regulation, in which, to repeat, blood pressure is the *controlled event*.

One of the mechanisms involved is that blood pressure increase results in heart rate decrease (under many but not all conditions) because heart rate partially determines cardiac output, a major factor in blood pressure.

But the inhibitory effects of increases in blood pressure are not limited to heart rate. Baroreceptor feedback invokes a surprisingly large number of inhibitory pathways. Some fourteen years ago, my wife and I began to speculate about the significance of an ever-growing neurophysiological literature, dating back to 1929, which demonstrated such noncardiovascular inhibitory effects (J. I. Lacey, 1967; J. I. Lacey & B. C. Lacey, 1970; Heymans & Neil, 1958). Among such effects caused by increased blood pressure, are: (1) cortical synchronization, a commonly used index of a nonaroused, nonalerted brain; (2) decrease in muscle tone; and (3) abrupt termination of episodes of sham rage, including all its aspects: hyperpnoea, hypertension, mydriasis, violent skeletal movements. More recent experiments even more convincingly demonstrate the translation of blood pressure from a controlled event to a behaviorally important controlling event. Coleridge, Coleridge, and Rosenthal (1976) showed that inflation of the carotid sinus (a major sensor of pulsatile blood pressure changes) resulted in prolonged inhibition of pyramidal cell activity in motor cortex. They conclude:

728

> Evidence has been accumulating for more than 40 years to support the notion that stimulation of carotid sinus baroreceptors exerts widespread and prolonged inhibitory effects on the central nervous system. . . . It is now clear that these effects involve single neurons of the motor cortex (p. 645).

Since each heart beat results in a transitory increase and decrease of arterial pressure, more such episodes of motor inhibition will occur per unit time as heart rate increases. My wife and I think that some such mechanism accounts for our finding, replicated in two very different experiments, that "voluntary" motor responses do not occur randomly within the cardiac cycle but instead are modally displaced to later and later times after the contraction of the left ventricle as momentary heart rate increases (J. I. Lacey & B. C. Lacey, 1979; B. C. Lacey & J. I. Lacey, 1978). This is a result clearly not explicable by current popular interpretations of the significance of heart rate for behavior. Unfortunately, this result itself cannot be clearly explained by reference to known details of baroreceptor feedback. Much remains to be discovered! Indeed, we are only at the very beginning of a detailed understanding of how baroreceptor feedback is involved in behavior. Two very recent animal experiments, showing behaviorally significant inhibition resulting from blood pressure increase, are noteworthy for their wide implications.

Responses of immobility can be induced in animals all along the phylogenetic scale, and have been studied ever since 1646, when "Father Kircher's remarkable experiment of bewitching a fowl" was described (see Braud & Ginsburg, 1973). The protective role of such responses in predator-prey relations has been implicated. In modern studies, attempts are made to understand the phenomenon in terms of neurotransmitters, on the one hand (Thompson et al., 1974; Hatton et al., 1978), or in terms of "fear" or of "learned helplessness" on the other (Braud & Ginsburg, 1973; Leftwich & May, 1974). In 1978, Hatton, Lanthorn, Webster, and Meyer studied the immobility response in rabbits, produced by suddenly inverting the animal from an upright position, and forcibly restraining it for 10 seconds by pressing the thorax with one hand. In experimental animals, either the glossopharyngeal nerve was sectioned (thus eliminating carotid sinus feedback) or the carotid sinus area itself was completely denervated. In comparison with control, nondenervated rabbits, the denervated animals exhibited a significantly reduced incidence of the immobility reflex. When the response was obtained, however, it did not differ in duration from that obtained in controls. Thus, the elimination or marked reduction of blood pressure feedback to the central nervous system modified skeletal motor activity, although in a complex manner.

A second noteworthy experiment has been contributed recently by Dworkin, Filewich, Miller, Craigmyle, and Pickering (1979). In this experiment, blood pressure in rats was raised by phenylephrine infusions, and the effects on escape-avoidance behavior in the response to highly aversive stimulation of the sensory nucleus of the trigeminal nerve were measured. On days when blood pressure was

729

elevated, the rats ran less to escape or avoid the stimulus. On control days, with control saline infusions, they ran more. That baroreceptor feedback is involved is shown by the fact that these results were *not* seen in rats with denervated baroreceptors. "Hypertension-induced baroreceptor activity," these authors conclude, "thus reduced escape-avoidance running either by attenuating the aversiveness of noxious trigeminal stimulation, or by an unknown action on some other link in the response system" (p. 205). Once again, then, visceral afferent feedback is shown to influence motor activity, perhaps because of inhibition, either of pain reception, or, more directly, of motor activity itself.

In human subjects, we repeatedly have found bradycardia and (when measured) either hypotension or irregular effects on blood pressure whenever the task set the subject involved primarily noting and detecting external environments, or making simple responses, in reaction time experiments, to punctate visual or auditory stimuli. (See the references already given to Lacey and Lacey.) But hypertension and tachycardia were regularly found when "mental work" or aversive stimulation was used. Other measures, such as electrodermal activity and respiration did not differentiate among these stimulus situations. Hence, mixed response patterns were the rule in simple sensorimotor tasks, with parasympathetic-like cardiovascular responses, but sympathetic-like electrodermal responses. These phenomena seem to me to be more easily interpreted by reference to baroreceptor feedback mechanisms than by reference to traditional concepts such as ergotropic (sympathetic) or trophotropic (parasympathetic) mechanisms. They also are more easily accommodated within more complex neurobehavioral theories of arousal and attention, such as that by Pribram and McGuinness (1975, which does make a serious attempt at studying the brain as a whole, with all its organs), than by simplified notions of arousal as a quantitatively defined unidimensional continuum that can be indifferently indexed by any one of a number of measures of electrocortical, autonomic, or somatic activity. They also imply that autonomic responses are not just related to intensive or energizing aspects of behavior; autonomic response patterns also reflect the nature of the intended transaction between the organism and its environment, to employ a phrase we have used elsewhere. This is the basis of my second major disagreement with Teichner: important clues to the functions of extended physiological control systems *are* found when attention is paid to which measures reliably increase and which simultaneously decrease in different behavioral contexts. The underlying question is: how is the system preferentially biased?

System Bias in Physiological Systems

This topic has not received formal theoretical development although the concept is implicit in varying physiological contexts. For example, in studies of sham rage, the shifting dominance between baroreceptors (which are inhibitory to all the visceral-motor phenomena) and chemoreceptors (which are excitatory) has been studied by

Baccelli, Guazzi, Libretti, and Zanchetti (1965). In decerebrate animals, they found that the effect of the large afferent (feedback) fibers in decreasing blood pressure could never be reversed by the pressor activity of the chemoreceptive fibers; they could only be partially obliterated. In decerebrate animals, then, the *system* is biased toward inhibition. But in decorticate animals, it was found that the *system* is biased toward excitation. The difference between the preparations shows the importance of suprahypothalamic modulation of somatic and visceral outflow.

System bias is also revealed by preferential association of specific stimuli with complex organized response patterns. Perhaps the clearest and most dramatic example of this kind of behaviorally relevant system bias has been produced by Garcia and his colleagues. Their extended studies—behavioral, physiological, anatomical, and neurophysiological—of conditioned taste aversions and bait-shyness are a landmark in this area. Much of this seminal work is conveniently summarized in Garcia, McGowan, and Green (1972) and Garcia, Kimeldorf, and Hunt (1961). Taste, but not olfaction, can be the basis for one-trial conditioning, with a CS-UCS interval measured in hours rather than seconds. The reasons for this functional preferential association can be found in the anatomy and physiology of the connections among visceral afferent systems (Coil et al., 1978a; Coil et al., 1978b; Hankins, Rusiniak, & Garcia, 1976; Hankins, Garcia, & Rusiniak, 1973; McGowan, Hankins, & Garcia, 1972; McGowan et al., 1969).

We do not have such clear and compelling demonstrations of system bias in, say, the cardiovascular system. This is the source of much confusion because, in the intact human, it is very difficult to make solid, incontrovertible inferences from such mixed autonomic-response patterns as we find in sensorimotor activities. For example, we (my wife and I) have been involved in a continuing controversy: is the anticipatory cardiac deceleration seen, for example, in a reaction-time experiment an instrumental response of the organism which facilitates speedy response, or only a consequence or accompaniment of diminished skeletal-motor activity in task-irrelevant musculature? I doubt that this question can be decisively settled by observations of the responses of intact humans. Only converging bits of evidence will help. One such converging bit of evidence is provided in a simplified model experiment in which such questions become clearly irrelevant. Briefly, it has been known for decades that vagal stimulation, or carotid sinus stimulation, results in a prolongation of the same cardiac cycle in which the stimulus occurs. The degree of slowing depends precisely on the time of stimulation within the cardiac cycle. Early stimuli produce more cardiac slowing than late stimuli; very late stimuli produce no effect on the concurrent cardiac period. The mechanism involved is thought to be a change in the slope of diastolic depolarization of the sino-atrial node, caused by acetylcholine release upon vagal stimulation. In human subjects, we have been able to show precisely this time-dependency phenomenon—and several related ones—not by varying time of vagal stimulation, but by varying the time of occurrence within a single heart beat of auditory or visual stimulation in signal-detection

731

and reaction-time tasks. There would seem to be no question that this effect is not mediated by skeletal-motor activity. The *system* seems *biased* to produce an instantaneously occurring response of cardiac slowing upon the registration of significant external stimulation (B. C. Lacey & J. I. Lacey, 1977, 1978, 1980).

Why? Why should a decrease in heart rate show such a preferential association with external signals? Why should blood pressure exert regulatory control on electrocortical "arousal" responses and on goal-directed, organized motoric sequences and on pain sensitivity? These, given traditional concepts, seem to be inconceivably remote relationships, and they seem to be ridiculously complicated and inefficient ways to design a brain!

One Structure for Many Systems

One clue appears on some reflection: these relations do not constitute a unique set; there are several commonplace examples in which the same bodily structures and processes can be seen to operate in the service of very different organismic activities. This too is not a characteristic of engineering control systems.

My airways and accessory structures are used to satisfy the absolutely vital need for adequate external respiration. They also are used for the exquisitely complex, and absolutely biologically separate, requirements of articulate speech. Another example: Shifts in vasomotor tone and regional shifts in blood flow are essential parts of cardiovascular regulation during exercise; they apparently occur in response to the exercise-induced need for increased metabolism. But the same shifts are prominent processes in thermoregulation. Indeed, as Satinoff (1978) points out (p. 21), a good argument can be made that ". . . most, if not all, thermoregulatory reflexes evolved out of systems that were originally used for other purposes." She draws one example from the work of Cowles. "Cowles has argued that the peripheral vasomotor system . . . first served as a supplemental respiratory organ in amphibia. It then became a heat collector and disperser in reptiles . . . and finally an essential temperature regulatory mechanism for endotherms." The principle involved is that of "evolutionary co-adaptation: a mechanism evolved for one purpose has as a side benefit an adaptive value in an entirely different system." Satinoff insightfully concludes: "The same principle of new controls over an already existing mechanism for a new function can be used to understand the nervous organization of many forms of motivated behavior (p. 21)."

Multiple Structures, Multiple Set Points

A simple engineering control system has a single "set point." Consider the homely negative feedback loop of a thermostatically controlled furnace. If we make the "set point" 70°F, an increase in temperature above that point will cause the furnace to shut off; a decrease below that point will cause it to turn on. A single sensor, a single feedback loop, and a single output mechanism underlie the entire sequence of corrective actions. But now consider the thermoregulatory control system of, say, a rat in a cold environment. He shivers (a reflex motor response); he shows peripheral vasoconstriction (a visceral response); and he creates a warm nest (a complex bit of goal-directed behavior). Multiple peripheral structures and demonstrably physically separated neuronal circuits in the hypothalamus mediate these corrective actions. Each of these structures, integrated into a common regulatory system by evolution-ary co-adaptation, retains its own set point (Satinoff, 1978)! It is theoretically ap-pealing to consider that this (or an analog) is one of the basic mechanisms that allows for the often-demonstrated dissociation of one visceral response from an-other, of electrocortical responses from visceral responses, of motor responses from visceral responses. In a word, it allows for the emergence of different patterns of response in different behavioral conditions. Whether this speculation has any merit or not, the facts again demonstrate the differences between technological and physi-ological systems, and they suggest another conceptual tool for the study of the brain as a whole, with all its organs.

Control of the Control System

Co-adaptation, whether evolutionary or not, does seem to be a fact: the same final output mechanism serves different functions. There is an implied cost. There must be some additional mechanisms to mediate conflicts and competitions among dif-ferent systems vying for the same output apparatus. A singer cannot sustain a high note indefinitely without stopping to draw a breath. Here we encounter a gaping hole in psychophysiological theory. We have no notion of the principles that govern the resolution of competition among contrary demands on the same body structure. What is the order of priority? I am aware of only one study that has even raised the question. The results of that study (Bergman, Campbell, & Wildenthal, 1972) are extraordinarily interesting. They studied heart rate changes, using *simultaneous but contradictory* demands: exercise, which reliably increases heart rate, and apnea plus stimulation of facial cold receptors, simulating the "dive reflex" which reliably decreases heart rate. The oxygen-conserving response of bradycardia in the dive reflex completely won over the oxygen-consuming response of tachycardia in dy-namic exercise. When isometric exercise was combined with the dive reflex, the resultant heart rate level was a compromise, falling between the levels attainable by the two contrary demands taken singly. It is clear that we need many more such studies, and attempts to formulate general principles concerning the resolution of contrary demands by the central and autonomic nervous systems working together.

Quantifiability

Engineering control theory is precise, and it is expressed mathematically and ele-gantly. What I have done so far in this discussion is to use, rather selectively and qualitatively, some of the concepts of control theory to expose gaps in our knowledge and to derive a diverse set of concepts that may serve as guides in the study of the physical mechanisms of behavior. Can biological and psychophysiological systems be treated in such mathematical terms? An exceptionally clear statement of the problem is given by Cronin (1979), who undertook the challenging task of developing a mathematical model of periodic catatonia, starting with mathematical models of the thyroid control system.

> . . . the models we will consider are all systems of ordinary differential equations. The choice of a system of ordinary differential equations . . . is motivated partly by the fact that negative feedback systems in engineering have been described by ordinary differential equations. But there is another somewhat less rational motivation. [They] have been studied for centuries, and extensive theory concerning their solutions exists. It is less intimidating to try to apply a well-established mathematical theory than to use a newer approach. . . . When differential equations are used in physics, they are often mathematical statements of basic assumptions or laws concerning the physical world. . . . In biology there are no such basic laws, and when a biological system is studied quantitatively, the mathematical description is usually of an ad hoc nature and is derived more or less by data fitting . . . in general it says nothing about how the biological system works. For example, the famous Hodgkin-Huxley equations, which were published in 1952, give a fairly accurate quantitative description of how certain ionic currents across the axon membrane are related to the membrane potential. But even today very little is understood of the mechanism by which ionic currents are conducted across the membrane (pp. 88–89).

This is a sobering statement, but also a hopeful one, as her own studies demonstrate. Perhaps, in the next century of development of the science of psychology, we will have more adequate principles and less restrictive mathematics than now.

Coda

This chapter has omitted discussion of most of the work in the past century that has studied visceral systems in the context of behavioral science. This is not because the work is unimportant or undistinguished. It is because I feel that the theories and principles that have so far emerged are inadequate to the study of the "brain as a whole, with all its organs," and that a reformulation of the nature of the approach to this massive task is desirable. For it is clear that visceral systems do not exist as a distinct and separate entity merely tacked onto the central nervous system. They are integrated with the central nervous system at all levels from the spinal cord to the cortex, and they are not merely effector systems. Only in specialized areas of investigation, such as thermoregulation, feeding, and drinking, is there explicit acknowledgment of this fact. As a result, concepts such as arousal, and ergotrophic and tropotrophic functions have persisted too long, even in the face of much evidence that should have led to their modification and perhaps even rejection. I have emphasized, following Isaacson, that we do not yet understand clearly the functions of any single brain region, or any single visceral response. Indeed, I feel that perhaps we should not attempt to. Perhaps we should focus instead on the dynamically changing interactions among diverse brain regions and diverse visceral processes. We do not yet have the tools or the concepts to enable the study of such dynamic interactions in any general way. But it is worth the effort to keep the goal in mind. The concepts of systems-control theory may be useful, particularly as they are modified and enlarged to encompass the facts that, in physiological systems, controlled events can become controlling events; that visceral responses may directly regulate brain activity and behavior; and that single output mechanisms are used in the service of diverse needs.

REFERENCES

Baccelli, G., Guazzi, M., Libretti, A., & Zanchetti, A. Pressoceptive and chemoceptive aortic reflexes in decorticate and in decerebrate cats. *American Journal of Physiology*, 1965, *208*, 708–714.

Bergman, Jr., S. A., Campbell, J. K., & Wildenthal, K. "Diving reflex" in man: Its relation to isometric and dynamic exercise. *Journal of Applied Physiology*, 1972, *33*, 27–31.

Braud, W. G., & Ginsburg, H. J. Effect of administration of adrenalin on immobility reaction in domestic fowl. *Journal of Comparative and Physiological Psychology*, 1973, *83*, 124–127.

Coil, J. D., Hankins, W. G., Jenden, D. J., & Garcia, J. The attenuation of a specific cue-to-consequence association by antiemetic agents. *Psychopharmacology*, 1978, *56*, 21–25. (a)

Coil, J. D., Rogers, R. C., Garcia, J., & Novin, D. Conditioned taste aversions: Vagal and circulatory mediation of the toxic unconditioned stimulus. *Behavioral Biology*, 1978, *24*, 509–519. (b)

Coleridge, H. M., Coleridge, J. C. G., & Rosenthal, F. Prolonged inactivation of cortical pyramidal tract neurones in cats by distension of the carotid sinus. *Journal of Physiology* (London), 1976, *256*, 635–649.

Cronin, J. Biomathematical models of schizophrenia. *Neurological Research*, 1979, *1*, 87–99.

Dworkin, B. R., Filewich, R. J., Miller, N. E., Craigmyle, N., & Pickering, T. G. Baroreceptor activation reduces reactivity to noxious stimulation: Implications for hypertension. *Science*, 1979, *205*, 1299–1301.

Garcia, J., Kimeldorf, D. J., & Hunt, E. L. The use of ionizing radiation as a motivating stimulus. *Psychological Review*, 1961, *68*, 383–395.

Garcia, J., McGowan, B. K., & Green, K. F. Biological constraints on conditioning. In A. H. Black and W. F. Prokasy (Eds.), *Classical conditioning II: Current theory and research.* New York: Appleton-Century-Crofts, 1972.

Grodins, F. S. *Control theory and biological systems.* New York: Columbia University Press, 1963.

Hankins, W. G., Garcia, J., & Rusiniak, K. W. Dissociation of odor and taste in baitshyness. *Behavioral Biology*, 1973, *8*, 407–419.

Hankins, W. G., Rusiniak, K. W., & Garcia, J. Dissociation of odor and taste in shock-avoidance learning. *Behavioral Biology*, 1976, *18*, 345–358.

Hatton, D. C., Lanthorn, T., Webster, D., & Meyer, M. E. Baroreceptor involvement in the immobility reflex. *Behavioral Biology*, 1978, 22, 122–127.

Hatton, D. C., Tankle, R., Lanthorn, T., & Meyer, M. E. Serotonin and tonic immobility in the rabbit. *Behavioral Biology*, 1978, 24, 97–100.

Heymans, C., & Neil, F. *Reflexogenic areas of the cardiovascular system*. Boston: Little, Brown, 1958.

Isaacson, R. L. *The limbic system*. New York: Plenum, 1974.

Lacey, B. C., & Lacey, J. I. Change in heart period. A function of sensorimotor event timing within the cardiac cycle. *Physiological Psychology*, 1977, 5, 383–393.

Lacey, B. C., & Lacey, J. I. Two-way communication between the heart and the brain. *American Psychologist*, 1978, 33, 99–113.

Lacey, B. C., & Lacey, J. I. Cognitive modulation of time-dependent primary bradycardia. *Psychophysiology*, 1980, 17, 209–221.

Lacey, J. I. Somatic response patterning and stress: Some revisions of activation theory. In M. H. Appley and R. Trumbull (Eds.), *Psychological stress: Issues in research*. New York: Appleton-Century-Crofts, 1967.

Lacey, J. I., & Lacey, B. C. Some autonomic-central nervous system interrelationships. In P. Black (Ed.), *Physiological correlates of emotion*. New York: Academic Press, 1970.

Lacey, J. I., & Lacey, B. C. Somatopsychic effects of interoception. In E. Meyer III & J. V. Brady (Eds.), *Research in the psychobiology of human behavior*. Baltimore: Johns Hopkins University Press, 1979.

Leftwich, D., & May, J. G. Effects of conditioned aversive stimuli presented during tonic immobility in guinea pigs. *Journal of Comparative and Physiological Psychology*, 1974, 87, 513–516.

McGowan, B. K., Garcia, J., Ervin, F. R., & Schwartz, J. Effects of septal lesions on bait-shyness in the rat. *Physiology and Behavior*, 1969, 4, 907–909.

McGowan, B. K., Hankins, W. G., & Garcia, J. Limbic lesions and control of the internal and external environment. *Behavioral Biology*, 1972, 7, 841–852.

Milhorn, H. T. *The application of control theory to physiological systems*. Philadelphia: Saunders, 1966.

Pribram, K., & McGuinness, D. Arousal, activation, and effort in the control of attention. *Psychological Review*, 1975, 82, 116–149.

Sato, A. (Ed.). Central organization of the autonomic nervous system. Satellite Symposium of the 26th Congress of the International Union of Physiological Sciences, New Delhi, 1974. *Brain Research*, 1975, 87, 139–437.

Sabat, S. R. Wundt's physiological psychology in retrospect. *American Psychologist*, 1979, 34, 635–638.

Satinoff, E. Neural organization and evolution of thermal regulation in mammals. *Science*, 1978, 201, 16–22.

Scheibel, M. E., & Scheibel, A. B. Anatomical basis of attention mechanisms in vertebrate brains. In G. C. Quarton, T. Melnechuk, & F. O. Schmitt (Eds.), *The neurosciences: A study program*. New York: Rockefeller University Press, 1967.

Teichner, W. H. Interaction of behavioral and physiological stress reactions. *Psychological Review*, 1968, 75, 271–291.

Thompson, R. W., Piroch, J., Fallen, D., & Hatton, D. A central cholinergic inhibitory system as a basis for tonic immobility (animal hypnosis) in chickens. *Journal of Comparative and Physiological Psychology*, 1974, 87, 507–512.

Zanchetti, A. Subcortical and cortical mechanisms in arousal and emotional behavior. In G. C. Quarton, T. Melnechuk, & F. O. Schmitt (Eds.), *The neurosciences: A study program*. New York: Rockefeller University Press, 1967.

PSYCHOLOGY AND
EVOLUTIONARY BIOLOGY

32

Some Thoughts on the
Evolution of
Comparative Psychology*

STEPHEN E. GLICKMAN

Introduction

For it is notorious that from the hour when Mr. Darwin and Mr. Wallace simultaneously propounded the theory which has exerted so enormous an influence on the
thought of the present century, the difference between the views of these two joint
originators of the theory has since been shared by the ever increasing host of their
disciples. We all know what that difference is. We all know that while Mr. Darwin
believed the facts of human psychology to admit of being explained by the general
laws of Evolution, Mr. Wallace does not believe these facts to admit of being thus
explained. Therefore, while the followers of Mr. Darwin maintain that all organisms whatsoever are alike products of a natural genesis, the followers of Mr. Wallace maintain that a distinct exception must be made to this general statement in
the case of the human organism; or at all events in the case of the human mind.
Thus it is that the great school of evolutionists is divided into two sects; according to
one the mind of man has been slowly evolved from lower types of psychical

* I am indebted to my colleagues in the Animal Behavior Proseminar at Berkeley, Frank Beach and
Irving Zucker, for their sustained interest and support. Thanks are also due to Dr. Frank Sulloway for his
advice and encouragement.

738

existence, and according to the other the mind of man, not having been thus evolved, stands apart, *sui generis*, from all other types of existence (Romanes, 1883, pp. 8–9).

The publication in 1859 of Darwin's theory of natural selection provided both a framework and the primary impetus for the modern study of animal behavior. However, the split between Darwin and his "codiscoverer" of the theory of natural selection, A. R. Wallace, over the evolution of humanity, provided a special challenge to the community of evolutionists. The zest of intellectual battle was added to the ongoing search for scientific truth, with particular attention directed to the phyletic junction between animals and people.

In Darwin's words:

> If no organic being excepting man had possessed any mental powers, or if his powers had been of a wholly different nature from those of lower animals, then we should never have been able to convince ourselves that our high faculties had been gradually developed. But it can be clearly shown that there is no fundamental difference of this kind (1871/1873, p. 34).

The heritage of this concern surrounds those of us involved in the contemporary study of animal behavior.

The Darwinian program (1871/1873) involved analyses of both instinctive behaviors and higher intellectual processes. Foresight, reason, and imagination were contrasted with instinct as alternative routes to adaptive behavior. Two research traditions emerged from this kind of thinking. One tradition focused upon instinctive, i.e., species-characteristic, behaviors. In Darwin's own writing, *The Expression of the Emotions in Man and Animals* (1872/1965) provides the most extensive elaboration of this approach. With its emphasis on inherited motor patterns and, to a lesser extent, phyletic relationships, this was the direct precursor of classical ethology as developed by Lorenz and Tinbergen in the period between 1930 and 1950. The second tradition concerned itself with the development of the higher mental faculties as adaptive characteristics. This began as a search for the emergence of human-like mental qualities in animals, a development that, it was hoped, would parallel increasing complexity of presumptive neurological organization. In the hands of Darwin's disciple George Romanes, this meant ranging from the simple "protoplasmic movements" of ovum and spermatozoa upward through many phyletic levels until one reached a sense of "indefinite morality" in apes, dogs, and fifteen-month-old human babies (Romanes, 1883). Although Romanes's conclusions frequently seem arbitrary, particularly as they have been caricatured in one-line historical epigrams, it is this line of inquiry that led directly through Lloyd Morgan to Edward L. Thorndike.

Thorndike's (1898, 1911) studies of learning in cats, chicks, dogs, and monkeys marked a crucial fork in the road to studying the animal mind. Thereafter animal learning would be quantified and inferences regarding mental capacities would be scrutinized with ever sterner criteria. This was to be true for all researchers in these areas. However, there were several messages in Thorndike's writing. One could take the message of objectivity and Thorndike's example of direct species comparison. Thus fortified, one could pursue the classic questions of intellectual continuity and emergence with new vigor. That is indeed what characterized the work of Hunter (1913), Hamilton (1911, 1916), and Yerkes (1916). In updated form, this is the line which includes the studies of learning sets by Harlow and his students (Harlow, 1959; Warren, 1965), and the systematic, methodologically sophisticated efforts of Bitterman and his colleagues to locate continuities and phyletic junctions as they relate to laws of learning or performance (Bitterman, 1960, 1965, 1975). It is also the historic thread that unites Darwin's attempts to understand the roots of human language (pp. 51–60 in *The Descent of Man*, 1873) with the modern studies of the Gardners (1969), Premack (1971), and Rumbaugh (1977) on tutored language in apes, and observations of Seyfarth et al. (1980) on the natural calls of monkeys.

But there was an alternative message in Thorndike's studies, and particularly in his *discussion* of those studies (Thorndike, 1898, 1911). In the right test situations, Thorndike believed the principles of learning were remarkably similar in each species he studied. Although Thorndike obtained and presented records of performance from three Cebus monkeys which could just as easily have been interpreted as indicative of insightful "human performance" (Thorndike, 1911, pp. 199, 204), he chose to emphasize the records coincident with a simpler associative interpretation. The insightful records were explained away and what might have appeared as an emergent property of primates was also discarded. Thorndike carried the line of speculation further. Although human reasoning was seen as unique, perhaps it emerged from the simple accumulation of vast numbers of associations (Thorndike, 1911, p. 239). These were the ideas that came to dominate the American study of the animal mind. These were the ideas that justified the use of animals to understand the human mind. They led to the dominance of the white rat and the pigeon as subjects-of-choice as psychologists grappled with the formulation of general laws from Watson through Skinner (Beach, 1950; Lockard, 1968). Having "settled" the question of species generality, arguments regarding the optimal formal structure for behavioristic theory, or such particular issues as the place of drive reduction in learning, emerged as the primary concerns of psychologists working with animals during the 1930-1940-1950 era. The "peculiar" phenomena of imprinting, bait-shyness, and birdsong learning were ignored until the last possible moment. The more naturalistic field of species-characteristic learning processes, which pulled animal psychology back to its evolutionary roots, did not really gain hold on the scene with appropriate recognition until the 1970s (Hinde & Stevenson-Hinde, 1973; Seligman & Hager, 1972).

To be sure, through the early and mid-twentieth century there was a steady output of comparative psychological research in the United States. Although lacking force of numbers, the work was substantial and recognized as such. Robert Yerkes examined learning in a broad range of vertebrate and invertebrate species (e.g., Yerkes, 1902, 1912; Yerkes & Huggins, 1903; Yerkes & Coburn, 1915) and dealt with central questions of genetics, instinct, and animal behavior broadly defined (Yerkes, 1907, 1913; Yerkes & Bloomfield, 1910). He also pioneered the use of primates as subjects for behavioral research (Yerkes & Yerkes, 1929). Carpenter (1934, 1940) and Schneirla (1933, 1938, 1940) left the laboratory for highly innovative field studies of primates and ants. Stone (1922, 1925, 1926) and Beach (1940, 1947) developed the study of mammalian parental and copulatory behavior within the psychological laboratory, and Beach (1948, 1958) was instrumental in fostering the growth of behavioral endocrinology. Finally, major textbooks were produced which summarized existent knowledge of comparative psychology, sometimes with exceptional phyletic range (e.g., Maier & Schneirla, 1935; Warden, Jenkins, & Warner, 1934).

However, to the extent that there has been a uniquely "American" thrust in comparative psychological research apart from the learning traditions already noted, it has involved the study of the development of behavior. More than that. There has been a succession of psychologists working in the United States (or trained there) who, by theoretical article and by example, have argued that understanding behavior must ultimately involve detailed analysis of its ontogeny. Kuo (1921, 1922, 1976), Schneirla (e.g., Maier & Schneirla, 1935; Schneirla, 1957, 1965), and their intellectual descendants were at the heart of this movement. This was the core group of comparative psychologists that engaged the classical ethologists in debate during the 1950s.

Robert Hinde's book on *Animal Behaviour* (1966) signaled a new synthetic era of interchange between ethology and comparative psychology. But in the ever-accelerating world of modern science, new challenges were in the works even as Hinde's book was being written and reviewed. Novel and influential work on ecological correlates of social behavior was combined with some powerful insights on individual competition and the significance of genetic kinship to produce the field of sociobiology (Wilson, 1975). The results of this latest dialectic between psychologists, animal behaviorists, and sociobiologists are yet to emerge. But it is certainly as heated as any prior debate (Caplan, 1978). The attitudes of psychologists toward evolutionary thought have generally ranged from indifference through ambivalence to antagonism, and the current debate over sociobiology has raised all of the intellectual and political concerns that have forever hovered around Darwinism and social Darwinism.

741

Politics, Personal Style, and the Social Context

Since the 19th century, there have been three influential doctrines which need to be thoroughly criticized in order to diminish or even eliminate their influence. They are: (1) Darwin's theory of "survival of the fittest," (2) Marx's theory of "class struggle" and (3) Freud's theory of "psychoanalysis." These three doctrines have one common ground: namely, they assume that men and animals have hereditary instincts for violence, hatred, and cruelty. If men have such instincts, human beings will never be able to enjoy peace (Zing Yang Kuo, 1970; as cited by Gottlieb, 1976, p. ix).

It is part of the common mythology of science that all can be understood by reference to the logical emergence of theory and data, with, perhaps, a bit of aesthetics thrown in. In practice, however, the history of ideas in general—and of experiments in the study of animal behavior in particular—is also a history of *people*, their personal characteristics, and the environment in which they worked. For example, it is impossible to comprehend more than one hundred years of scientific dispute regarding nature, nurture, and natural selection, without recognizing the de facto link between scientific Darwinism and social Darwinism. To allege that some behavior had been "selected," or was "instinctive," was commonly taken to imply that it was natural, good, and immutable. The very line of evolutionary argument concerning selection and adaptation, which is at the core of much that has occurred in the historic development of research on animal behavior, can be perceived as an obstacle to social change. Arguments over the epigenesis of pecking in chicks or the inevitability of aggression in fish were frequently carried out at several levels. There was a genuine scientific issue regarding ontogenies and mechanisms. There was also, very often, serious political content beneath the surface. It was very likely there for Kuo (1930, 1938) as he demonstrated variability and modifiability in the responses of cats to rats. It appears again, even more openly, in his studies of kittens and dogs reared together, or of predatory birds reared with natural avian prey (Kuo, 1976). Again there is a dual message. For the scientist, there is a lesson of environmentally manipulable plasticity during development; for society, the message is do not prematurely terminate the search for a human environment that can bring out our best. As we shall see, personal experience and social concerns were active in Wallace's critique of Darwin. There was clear political content in Lehrman's (1953) first critique of Konrad Lorenz.[1] All of these issues have surfaced again in the responses of the Sociobiology Study Group to the "biological determinism" of the sociobiologists (e.g., Allen et al., 1975, 1976; Alper et al., 1976). There may be one difference. In keeping with our times, political issues are no longer submerged. Although I find the personal nature of

---

[1] The reader interested in the details of Lorenz's more ideological writings may refer to the interchange between Kalikow and Nisbett (Kalikow, 1979).

some of these critiques distressing, it is often difficult to feel appropriate sympathy for the attacked. There is a persistent suspicion that, in their efforts to reach beyond the normally restricted circle of scientists, some sociobiologists have resorted to "buzz" words and scientific shortcuts, bringing the storm upon themselves and then looking innocently about. Which brings us to the question of personal style and the scientific processes. As Edwin G. Boring noted in his presidential address to the American Psychological Association in 1928:

> Founders are generally promoters, in science as elsewhere, and we therefore have "to consider the mechanisms of public attention" (Boring, 1929, pp. 114–115).

In the group under consideration in this paper, John Watson may be the proto-typical founder, but surely Lorenz, Skinner, and Wilson have their substantial promotional skills, as well as rare scientific talents. We might guess that the ability to write with clarity and vigor is important. So is a sense of what is significant and where the public interest is likely to be captured. Individual goals and the tolerance for ambiguity frequently determine the areas in which people work, as their taste for controversy influences the manner in which they publish. Darwin was a very ambitious scientist who wanted his due as a "founder," but not at the expense of his personal dignity, and his distaste for controversy prevented publication of the theory of natural selection for several decades. What was it that prevented Edward Thorn-dike from founding "behaviorism"? Very early on, he had the data and the basic ideas (Joncich, 1968) as well as a fine writer's hand, a definite taste for controversy, and a sense of what was important. Perhaps there was an emergent conservatism of age, a growing scientific caution, an inability to relinquish the mentalism of his nineteenth-century mentors. Or, perhaps it was simply that, as Thorndike (1936, p. 268) observes in an autobiographical sketch, his tendency was ultimately to say no to ideas and yes to people.

I am not sure of the particular answers to these sorts of questions, but I am confident that they form a basic substrate of the history of comparative psychology. In the remainder of this essay, I review a highly selected set of themes and incidents drawn from the preceding sketch. The continuous interplay between psychological ideas and evolutionary thought in the present treatment is more a commentary on themes and people than on the data that has been generated—and it is a limited commentary at that.

Darwin, Wallace, and Mental Evolution

> As the instincts of a species are fully as important to its preservation and multiplica-
> tion as its corporeal structure, it is evident that if there be the slightest congenital
> differences in their instincts or habits, or if certain individuals during their lives are

743

> induced or compelled to vary their habits, and if such differences are in the smallest degree more favourable, under slightly modified external conditions, to their preservation, such individuals must in the long run have a better *chance* of being preserved and of multiplying. If this be admitted, a series of small changes may, as in the case of corporeal structure, work great changes in the mental powers, habits and instincts of any species (Darwin, 1844; reprinted in de Beer, 1958, p. 143).

As early as 1837, Darwin recognized that the theory on which he was working would have implications for the comparative study of the animal mind: "My theory would give zest to recent and fossil comparative anatomy; it would lead to the study of instincts, heredity and mind heredity. . . ." Before he had articulated the principle of natural selection, Darwin had already perceived that studies of transmutation of species and geographical grouping would lead to attempts "to discover *causes* of change—the manner of adaptation . . . to comprehend true affinities" (Darwin, 1837; as cited by de Beer, 1958, p. 6). The theme is indeed followed up in 1842, when Darwin writes his first sketch of evolution through natural selection. In a section on variation in instincts and other mental attributes, Darwin observes that such qualities of the mind as "courage, pertinicity, suspicion, restlessness, ill-temper, sagacity and the reverse unquestionably vary in animals and are inherited . . . ." Various specific habits and instincts are considered and the concept of selection working upon these features of behavior is discussed with a combination of caution and optimism:

> Although we can never hope to see the course revealed by which different instincts have been acquired, for we have only present animals . . . to judge of the course of gradation, yet once grant the principle of habits, whether congenital or acquired by experience, being inherited and I can see no limit to the . . . extraordinariness of the habits thus acquired" (Darwin, 1842; as cited by de Beer, 1958, pp. 56–57).

The basic ideas of variation, inheritance, and selection, as applied to behavior, are expanded upon in Darwin's essay of 1844 (de Beer, 1958, pp. 136–149). Illustrated with many examples, the 1844 essay contained a discussion of how selection could produce complex instincts such as laying eggs in other birds' nests, slavemaking in ants, and construction of honeycombs from simpler sorts of behavior. These considerations of behavioral evolution were a significant part of Darwin's thought from the earliest points in his evolutionary writing. His reliance on the Lamarckian conception of the inheritance of practiced habits was also characteristic of these early writings. It would remain so for all of Darwin's life, blurring the modern concept of selection and giving a rare antique quality to those aspects of his books.

The section on habit and instinct was modified and expanded for presentation in *The Origin of Species by Means of Natural Selection* when it appeared in 1859. Although the inference was there to be drawn, discussion of human evolution had

744

been essentially omitted from *The Origin*. This problem was attacked by Alfred Russel Wallace in 1864. In a paper read to the British Anthropological Society, Wallace proposed a radically new theory of human origins. At the heart of Wallace's proposal was the belief that, at a critical point in human evolution, we were freed from the pressures of natural selection that affect all other species. The key was human intellect:

> At length, however, there came into existence a being in whom that subtle force we term *mind*, became of greater importance than his mere bodily structure. Though with a naked and unprotected body, *this* gave him clothing against the varying inclemencies of the seasons. Though unable to compete with the deer in swiftness, or with the wild bull in strength, *this* gave him weapons with which to capture or overcome both. . . . From the moment when the first skin was used as covering, when the first rude spear was formed to assist in the chase, the first seed sown or shoot planted, a grand revolution was in effect in nature . . . for a being had arisen who was no longer necessarily subject to change with the changing universe. . . (Wallace, 1864, clxvii–clxviii).

Wallace's paper was received enthusiastically by Darwin, if not by the assembled members of the Anthropological Society. Darwin acknowledged that "the great leading idea is quite new to me, . . . yet I had got as far as to see with you that the struggle between the races of man depended entirely upon intellectual and *moral* qualities." Darwin proceeds to offer some additional complimentary comments, disagrees on some minor (but revealing) issues, and finally offers Wallace "a few notes on Man" which he never expects to use (cited in Marchant, 1916, p. 127).[2] However, between 1864 and 1869–1870 Wallace moved still further in separating the evolution of human beings from the traditional routes of natural selection. He was ultimately to conclude that natural selection could not account for such universal human characteristics as our relative hairlessness, the structure of the feet and hands, the perfection of the larynx, and most significantly, the size of the human brain. Wallace's argument in the latter regard was basically rather simple. The brains of such peoples as those he lived with in the Malay archipelago were much larger than required by their life-style. "They possess a mental organ beyond their needs. Natural selection could only have endowed savage man with a brain a few degrees superior to that of an ape, where he actually possesses one very little inferior to that of a philosopher" (Wallace, 1870/1895).

On first hearing of Wallace's defection, Darwin wrote: "I hope you have not murdered too completely your own and my child." The situation was not improved by reading the actual material. On April 14, 1869, Darwin again writes to Wallace:

---

[2] All of the excerpts from the Darwin-Wallace correspondence cited in this paper can be found neatly clustered in Marchant, 1916.

> As you expected, I differ grievously from you, and I am very sorry for it. I can see
> no necessity for calling in an additional and proximate cause in regard to Man. I
> have been particularly glad to read your discussion because I am now writing and
> thinking much about Man. . . .

The challenge to deal with human evolution in general, and mental evolution in particular, had to be met in any case. But Wallace's joining the ranks of the opposition must have provided a special spur to Darwin, as it was ultimately to provoke other nineteenth-century behaviorists. On November 22, 1870, Darwin wrote to Wallace: "I have finished 1st vol. and am halfway through proofs of 2nd vol. of my confounded book, which half kills me by fatigue, and which I fear will quite kill me in your good estimation." In 1871 Darwin published *The Descent of Man and Selection in Relation to Sex*. Here, for the first time, Darwin dealt with the evolution of the higher mental faculties (e.g., curiosity, reason, imagination, and language), as well as the natural selection of human sociality. He also confronted Wallace directly. Addressing the subject of man, "even in the rudest state in which he now exists," Darwin (1871/1873) writes:

> He has invented and is able to use various weapons, tools, traps, etc. with which he
> defends himself, kills or catches prey, and otherwise obtains food. He has made
> rafts or canoes for fishing or crossing over to neighbouring fertile islands. He has
> discovered the art of making fire, by which hard and stringy roots can be rendered
> digestible, and poisonous roots or herbs innocuous. . . . These several inventions
> . . . are the direct results of the development of his powers of observation, memory,
> curiosity, imagination and reason. I cannot, therefore, understand how it is that
> Mr. Wallace maintains, that "natural selection could only have endowed the
> savage with a brain a little superior to that of an ape" (pp. 131–132).

In *The Descent*, Darwin grapples with the problem of finding the antecedents of human intellect in the world of existent animal species. "My object in this chapter is solely to show that there is no fundamental difference between man and the higher mammals in their mental faculties" (Darwin, 1871/1873, p. 34). Darwin's methods for demonstrating these characters varied. His best evidence came from personal observation, or simple experimentation. For example, to investigate curiosity, along with the instinctive dread of snakes exhibited by monkeys, Darwin placed a series of live and stuffed snakes, as well as other objects and animals, in monkey cages at the Zoological Gardens. After first testing the monkeys' response to a stuffed snake, Darwin tried "a dead fish, a mouse, a living turtle, and other new objects . . . at first frightened, they soon approached, handled and examined them." However, their response to a live snake in a paper bag was quite different as ". . . monkey after monkey, with head raised high and turned on one side, could not resist taking momentary peeps into the upright bag, at the dreadful object lying quiet at the bottom" (Darwin, 1871/1873, p. 42). However, when straining to find evidence of the precursors of human behavior in lower animals, even Darwin was capable of citing anecdotes that strain modern credulity. In that spirit, he enthused that "Even insects play together, as has been described by that excellent observer, P. Huber, who saw ants chasing and pretending to bite each other like so many puppies" (Darwin, 1871/1873, p. 38).

If a primary focus in *The Descent* was upon the search for human-like mental qualities in animals, there is a concern in *The Expression of the Emotions in Man and Animals* with the existence of stereotypic, instinctive motor patterns in people; patterns that would be heritable and have selective advantage. It is an exquisite book. Species differences and adaptive significance were discussed in some, but certainly not all cases of stereotypic emotional expression. In one instance, Darwin observes that "a savage frame of mind" is indicated by "ears drawn closely backwards and pressed to the head," "but only in the case of those animals that fight with their teeth; and the care which they take to prevent their ears being seized by their antagonists, accounts for this position" (Darwin, 1872/1965, pp. 110–111). In this manner, Darwin can account for the widespread appearance of this pattern in the carnivores, as well as its relative absence in "man, the higher apes, and many ruminants."

The instinctive (and hence inherited) nature of emotional expression was evaluated by examining evidence for: (1) appearance of the pattern in young infants without opportunity for experience, (2) appearance of a given pattern in a human being born without sight, and (3) cross-cultural universality of a pattern. These have remained the fundamental research strategies for students of human nature from the psychoanalysts through the classical ethologists and the modern sociobiologists.

Darwin had passed along his remaining notes on animal behavior to George Romanes. Romanes, in turn, carried forward the program initiated by Darwin, examining the emergence and elaboration of emotional and intellectual capacities in the broadest phyletic perspective. His methods, much as Darwin's, were a blend of personal observation, simple experimentation, and anecdote. Once again, where personal observation predominated, Romanes could prove astute and thoughtful. For example, at one point Romanes rears some ferrets under a hen. He notes "that when half-grown and put to a rabbit for the first time, they clearly knew that their attack should be directed against one end of the rabbit, but were not quite certain which. . . ." Several weeks later, Romanes examined the reactions of these same ferrets toward another hen. Now,

> their hereditary instincts prompted attack, while their individual associations inhibited the prompting. There was a manifest conflict of feelings, which had its expression in a prolonged period of indecision. And although eventually the hereditary instincts prevailed over the associations formed by individual experience, the prolonged hesitation proved that the latter exerted a strong modifying force (Romanes, 1883, p. 228).

747

The idea of experimental rearing, followed by systematic behavioral testing, had already been brilliantly demonstrated by Spalding (1873/1954). However, Romanes's observations are interesting in their own right and specifically anticipate the study of Eibl-Eibesfeldt (1963) on prey-killing in isolation-reared ferrets and of Kuo (1938) on the behavior of cats reared with rats.

Romanes also examined the ability of hermit crabs to form what we would today designate as passive avoidance responses. His procedures would not pass my personal animal subjects committee:

> When he had protruded his head from the shell of the whelk in which he was residing, I gently moved toward him a pair of open scissors, and gave him plenty of time to see the glistening object. Then, slowly including the tip of one of his tentacles between the open blades, I suddenly cut off the tip.

The animal withdrew into its shell time and time again following such insult, but "never learnt to associate the appearance of the scissors with the effect which always followed it" (Romanes, 1883, pp. 122–123). These observations are not meant to deny the charges of anecdotalism which have always been associated with Romanes's name, or his insistence of finding those "needed" precursors of the human mind at very suspect places in the animal kingdom.

It is important to recall that Romanes was not an impartial observer. He was seeking to buttress a theory, Darwin's theory, and the opposition had a potent recruit in Wallace. I have previously argued that personal experience and the social context are important determinants of scientific opinion. At this point we may profitably return to consider Darwin and Wallace, the (sometimes) hidden assumptions in their arguments, and the ways in which nonscientific factors influence scientific disputes.

> I hope it is a satisfaction to you to reflect—and very few things in my life have been more satisfying—that we have never felt any jealousy towards each other, though in one sense rivals. I believe that I can say this of myself with truth, and I am absolutely sure that it is true of you (Darwin to Wallace, April 20, 1870).

The story of the independent discovery of the theory of natural selection by Darwin and Wallace has been described sufficiently elsewhere (e.g., Eiseley, 1961; Merton, 1957). In Merton's account of priority disputes in science, which frequently range from the comic to the sleazy, the behavior of Darwin and Wallace is unique and inspiring. Credit was given where credit was due, and both men remained on cordial terms until Darwin's death in 1882. Insofar as their correspondence is preserved, we have a remarkable record of scientific interaction; sometimes supportive, at other times appreciative, questioning, and arguing, but always with honesty and passion. However, they came from very different backgrounds and led very different lives. In the course of their scientific careers, Darwin and Wallace had four general areas of disagreement (Wallace, 1905, pp. 16–22): (1) whether the human species had been naturally selected or specially created; (2) the extent to which sexual selection, operating through female choice of "beautiful" mates, was the preferred explanation of sexual dimorphisms involving, for example, the elaborate display of male plumage or ornaments; (3) if certain peculiarities of the distribution of plant species were the result of climatic changes or the result of aerial dispersal of seeds by birds, gales, or storms; and (4) were acquired characteristics inherited and, if so, could such inheritance be explained by Darwin's theory of pangenesis?

Three of these disagreements have at least some relevance to behavior and, in several instances, scientific positions may be linked to the personal experiences of the men involved. We have already seen the impetus given to the study of the gap between the human mind and the animal mind by Wallace's assumption of the necessity of special creation in regard to people. The Darwin-Wallace divergence on the evolution of the human brain is, as Eiseley (1961, p. 303) has implied, the likely result of their different contacts with native peoples in remote areas. Darwin traveled as a member of a British expedition. Wallace traveled South America and Malaysia "alone," supporting his work by collecting for museums. He lived with the native peoples of different areas rather than observing them. In commenting on the range of human variation in morality and intelligence in *The Descent of Man*, Darwin writes:

> Nor is the difference slight in moral disposition between a barbarian, such as the man described by the old navigator Byron, who dashed his child on the rocks for dropping a basket of sea-urchins, and a Howard or Clarkson, and in intellect, between a savage who uses hardly any abstract terms, and a Newton or Shakespeare (1873, p. 34).[3]

Contrast Darwin's views with those of Wallace (1869/1962, p. 456):

> I have lived with communities of savages in South America and in the East, who have no laws or law courts but the public opinion of the village freely expressed. Each man scrupulously respects the rights of his fellow, and any infraction of these rights rarely or never takes place. . . partly by the influence of public opinion, but chiefly by that natural sense of justice and of his neighbor's right which seems to be, in some degree, inherent in every race of man.

---

[3] John Howard was a leader of the English prison reform movement during the eighteenth century. Thomas Clarkson was an English abolitionist who played an instrumental role in the elimination of the British slave trade.

749

The direction in which Wallace was headed culminates in an essay published in 1912. Here he observes:

> Even the so-long-despised Australians—almost the lowest in terms of material progress—yet show by their complex language, their elaborate social regulations, and often by an innate nobility of character, indications of a very similar nature to our own. If they possess fewer philosophers and moralists, they are also free from so large a proportion of imbalanced minds—idiots and lunatics—as we possess.

Wallace further noted that there existed in the Pacific people who were certainly "our equals, if not our superiors. These we are rapidly exterminating through the effect of *our* boasted civilization" (p. 44).

This is not meant to demean Darwin. In addition to his genius, Darwin was a warm, liberal man for his times: opposed to slavery, in favor of electoral reform, and concerned for the oppressed. But he was, in some areas, *of* his times and not very far ahead of them. For many scientists of the day, the existent native peoples were virtual "missing links." It was only through work in Wallace's tradition that "the Negro's skull is no longer placed on the lecturer's table between that of the gorilla and the Caucasian" (Eiseley, 1961, p. 314). At the time, Wallace's belief in the ultimate intellectual potential of native peoples must have seemed bizarre beyond reason. Consider Romanes writing in the late 1880s:

> One of the most generally applicable statements we can make with reference to the psychology of uncivilized man is that it shows, in a remarkable degree, what we may term a *vis inertiae* as regards upward movement. Even so highly developed a type of mind as that of the Negro—submitted, too, as it has been in millions of individual cases to close contact with minds of the most progressive type, and enjoying as it has in many thousands of individual cases all the advantages of a liberal education—has never, so far as I can ascertain, executed one single stroke of original work in any single department of intellectual activity (Romanes, 1889/1898, p. 13).

This is not the place for a prolonged account of Darwin's and Wallace's remaining points of disagreement. However, their argument over sexual selection is of particular interest. Darwin had created an alternative to natural selection. Wallace insisted on searching for differences in life-style between the sexes in order to account for differences in physical characteristics. For example, he had formulated a law in 1868: "When both sexes of birds are conspicuously coloured, the nest conceals the sitting bird; but when the male is conspicuously coloured and the nest is open to view, the female is plainly coloured and inconspicuous" (Wallace, 1905, pp. 384–385). In the latter case, the female, locked to the nest by duties of incubation, was presumed to require inconspicuous coloration. This line of argument was buttressed by cross-species comparisons in a manner that has a very modern flavor.

It is a convergent evolutionary argument in which the behavioral characteristics of different species, as well as their morphology, are related to a common feature of their life-style rather than common ancestry. Although this sort of disagreement between Darwin and Wallace is not easily linked to differences in personal experience, it is interesting to consider their interchange on sexual selection in humans. Darwin writes:

> I suspect that a sort of sexual selection has been the most powerful means of changing the races of men. I can show that the different races have a widely divergent standard of beauty. Among savages the most powerful men will have the pick of women and they will generally leave the most descendants. . . . Our aristocracy is handsomer? . . . than middle classes, from pick of women (Darwin, May 28, 1864).

Wallace replies expressing his doubts:

> In the very lowest tribes there is rarely much polygamy. . . . I think it rarely happens that any healthy and undeformed man remains without wife and children. I very much doubt the oft-repeated assertion that our aristocracy are more beautiful than the middle classes. . . . Mere physical beauty . . . is quite as frequent in one class of society as the other (Wallace, May 29, 1864).

In addition to their different personal experiences with native peoples, one cannot help but reflect on the fact that Darwin was Cambridge-educated, from an "excellent" family, and relatively affluent. Wallace was the son of a modest-poor family, forced to terminate his schooling at fourteen, and in a financial scramble for much of his life.

Even in the context of his divergence from Darwin's treatment of the mechanisms of plant distribution, Wallace discerned the role of differential personal experience. He believed that the lowering of temperatures required by Darwin's theory of distribution would have destroyed much of the plant and animal life that characterizes tropical regions under consideration. "The only reason why Darwin did not feel this appears to be that he knew nothing personally of the tropics beyond a few days at Bahia and Rio, and could have had no conception of its wonderfully rich and highly specialized fauna and flora" (Wallace, 1905, p. 20).

Finally, there is a parting of opinion about the inheritance of acquired characteristics. Both Darwin and Wallace had accepted such ideas in their early writings. From our vantage point, Darwin's frequent, vivid discussions of the inheritance of habits markedly affected, for example, his views of human social evolution. Casting about for an explanation, Darwin postulated the existence of "gemmules," particles dispersed into the blood from the somatic cells of the body that gathered in the sexual cells of the organism. Inheritance could thus be modified by environmental conditions that affected the "gemmules." Wallace, at first, accepted Darwin's hy-

751

pothesis, but later rejected the scheme. His initial rejection was influenced by the results of transfusion experiments carried out by Galton, which failed to support the Darwinian hypothesis. Later he would be convinced by the studies of August Weismann, although this was after Darwin's death. The story surrounding pangenesis would appear to be more a demonstration of Darwin's relentless search for order and coherence in nature than a comment on diverse lives. Also, it was surely easier for Wallace to give up Darwin's hypothesis than for Darwin to relinquish his own ideas.

Classical Ethology and the Comparative Psychologists

> Darwin was fully aware of a fact which . . . is rightly considered the starting point of ethology. This fact, which is still ignored by many psychologists, is quite simply that behavior patterns are just as conservatively and reliably characters of species as are the forms of bones, teeth, or any other bodily structures (Lorenz, 1965, p. xii).

In the period between 1930 and 1950, Konrad Lorenz, in collaboration with N. Tinbergen, constructed a "field" of ethology with a clearly articulated set of research strategies and methods and a complex matrix of critical concepts and explanatory devices (Beer, 1963, 1964; Lorenz, 1950; Tinbergen, 1951). A complete-as-possible inventory of species-characteristic behavior patterns was to be constructed for species under consideration. Lorenz advocated building this inventory, in part, by naturalistic observation. However, contrary to popular belief, Lorenz was very wary of the limitations of such animal watching. Instead, he advocated the keeping of captive animals where, through environmental distortion, behavior patterns might be seen to miscarry (Lorenz, 1950, p. 236). In this regard, he was surprisingly close to the position taken by his critic Z. Y. Kuo. Kuo's "behavioral neophenotypes" (1976, p. 26) are essentially identical to Lorenz's miscarried behaviors. At any rate, species-characteristic behavior patterns could, in turn, be divided into appetitive and consummatory phases, as had been suggested by Craig (1918). The "invariant" component acts, known as fixed-action patterns, were to provide the heart of a phyletic comparative strategy. Following the writings of Whitman (1899, 1919) and Lorenz's teacher, Heinroth, these fixed-action patterns could be used as taxonomic characters from which phylogenies could be reconstructed and adaptive significance inferred. The next task in line for the classical ethologist involved the determination of the critical characteristics of those environmental stimuli which triggered the various fixed-action patterns. Elaborately constructed models, and occasionally arrays-of-models, were employed to delineate the crucial stimulus elements. Variation in the ease of evoking a particular fixed-action pattern at a particular time was explained by postulating the accumulation and dissipation of "action-specific-energy," which was discharged during the performance of an art. Observations relating to habituation, spontaneous recovery, and even the appearance of fixed-action patterns in the absence of the appropriate sign stimulus (i.e., vacuum activities), were explained by fluctuations in action-specific energy. Lorenz (1950) provided a hydraulic model to aid in visualizing these events. Accumulation and dissipation of energy were represented by fluid accumulating in a vat, with the resulting pressure at a spigot, near the bottom of the vat, held in check by a valve-like device (the innate releasing mechanism) on which the sign stimulus was presumed to act.

Some mention should also be made of various processes introduced to account for the discrepancies between the motivational systems, which were presumed to be activated in any given situation, and the actual behavior that emerged. As Tinbergen (1951) observed, a bird caught in conflict between flight-from and attack-toward a rival might instead increase preening behavior (a displacement activity), or peck at the ground (redirection). Although I am not clear about the true ancestry of these complex motivational postulates, the similarities with the ideas of William McDougall (1923) are quite striking. McDougall also cites Craig's 1918 paper. In describing the mating of birds, McDougall views the male's display as a "key" which can open a "lock" possessed by the female. The "lock" is sensitive only to a specific pattern. Moreover, in 1913 he had proposed a hydraulic model almost identical to that offered by Lorenz. As McDougall (1923, p. 107) summarized the hypothetical system:

> . . . each instinct is in part a sluice-gate in the system of barriers which dams back the energy liberated in the afferent side of the nervous system; that on stimulation of the instinct, on turning of the key in the lock, the sluice-gate swings open and makes the efferent channels of the instinct the principal outlet, "the final common path," for all available free energy.

Perhaps a still earlier anticipation of both McDougall and Lorenz may be found in some passages of Herbert Spencer as cited by Darwin (1872/1965):

> it may be received as an "unquestionable truth that, at any moment, the existing quantity of liberated nerve-force . . . must expend itself in some direction" . . . an "overflow of nerve-force, undirected by any motive, will manifestly take the most habitual routes; and, if these do not suffice, will next overflow into the less habitual ones" (p. 71).

Not quite McDougall and Lorenz, but similar enough to be rather tantalizing.

At its best, classical ethology provided a rich framework for examining behavior. Attention was focused on the orderly accumulation of significant descriptive data in many species. By pulling together concepts and strategies from previous workers, and adding crucial items of their own, Lorenz and Tinbergen had developed a comprehensive theoretical perspective about animal behavior. They bridged a longstanding gap between independent observations of naturalists and systematic science. Unfortunately, the system tended to discourage detailed ontogenetic analysis and made assumptions (e.g., regarding the accumulation and discharge of action-specific energy) that were very vulnerable. Moreover, the introduction of concepts like displacement and redirection, like the defense mechanisms of the psychoanalysts, tended to make direct tests of the theory very difficult. Behavior was no longer directly predictable from its presumptive motivational antecedents. When the ideas of the classical ethologists were finally made commonly available to comparative psychologists in the years following World War II, both interest and confrontation were inevitable.

Comparative Psychology and Developmental Analysis

> Suppose we try an experiment on the walking response of a babe under such conditions as to prevent the influence of habit formation. If it turns out that the babe can walk effectively . . . the instinct psychologist will conclude that walking is an instinct pure and simple. . . . for the non-instinct psychologists the mere statement that walking is innate or acquired is altogether unsatisfactory: if walking could be performed without previous training they would proceed to find out what has made this unlearned activity possible . . . most important of all (*they would analyze*) . . . the nature and intensity of the stimuli and the total situation, which acting together or serially, call out the walking response. In other words, the instinct psychologist ends his investigation where the non-instinct psychologist begins (Z. Y. Kuo, 1922, pp. 349–350).

In the above quote, from the second of several extraordinary articles written by Zing Yang Kuo (1921, 1922) as an undergraduate and graduate student at Berkeley, we find a central theme of comparative psychology for the past half-century. It is a call for developmental analysis: the core of T. C. Schneirla's theoretical writing (Schneirla, 1949, 1959, 1965) and of Daniel Lehrman's powerful critique of Lorenzian views.

> The problem for the investigator who wishes to make a causal analysis of behavior is: How did this behavior come about? The use of "explanatory" categories such as "innate" and "genically fixed" obscures the necessity of investigating developmental *processes* in order to gain insight into the actual mechanisms of behavior and their inter-relations (Lehrman, 1953, p. 345).

In the same spirit as Kuo decried the "vitalistic" motivational concepts of McDougall and Freud, so Lehrman questions Lorenz's concept of action-specific energy: "referring motivation to the action of specific centers in the central nervous system is often like the concept of 'innate behavior' itself, simply a substitute for actual analysis of the biology of the specific case" (Lehrman, 1953, p. 354). From

754

the psychologist's perspective, the use of terms like *innate* or *instinctive* has always carried the dual dangers of giving the illusion of explanation, while prematurely terminating the search for potentially complex, but very important sources of environmental interaction with the developing organism (Beach, 1955; Hebb, 1953).

Not all critiques of Lorenz's concepts came from psychologists. Robert Hinde wrote a very influential series of papers indicating the deficiencies of motivational models of the Lorenz variety (Hinde, 1956, 1959a, 1960), while George Barlow (1968) observed that the apparent stereotypy of the fixed-action pattern was often more the result of too-casual analysis, than true invariance of any given fixed-action pattern on different occasions. Approaching the perceptual side of the organism, Hailman (1967) demonstrated that the classic assumptions of the innate releasing mechanism concept, as applied to the pecking response of gulls, needed to take experiential factors into account.

In contrasting findings of Kuo and Coghill, Maier and Schneirla (1935, p. 278) state that: "The plan of an experiment determines which facts will be brought to light. . . no one experiment brings out all of the processes at work, and it is therefore fruitful for scientific progress that opposing points of view exist among research workers." It would certainly seem a reasonable conclusion in the present case. The pioneering embryonic studies of Kuo, which continue in the hands of Gottlieb, were sparked, at least in part, by rejection of existing doctrine. Similarly, the studies of sequential interaction between organism and environment represented in the work of Schneirla's students (e.g., Lehrman, 1962; Rosenblatt, 1965) were carried out in a framework created, in part, by disagreement. The classical ethological side also had its experimental moments. The early critiques of Lorenz (Beach, 1955; Lehrman, 1953; Schneirla, 1956) cited studies by Birch (1956) on the role of genital self-licking and Riess (1950) on the role of prior experience with object manipulation as essential precursors of maternal behavior and nest construction in the laboratory rat. Eibl-Eibesfeldt (1961) effectively criticized Riess's design and demonstrated that, when properly investigated, object manipulation experience did not appear to have the influence inferred by Riess. Moreover, Eibl-Eibesfeldt's result was confirmed by Wehmer (1965). While genital self-licking may well be important for the emergence of normal maternal function in rats, the maternal cannibalism reported by Birch did not hold up to replication by Christophersen and Wagman (1965). Although references to the Birch and Riess studies were subsequently dropped from the developmentalist bibliographies, the change in data had no impact on the theoretical argument. In a brilliant review of twenty years of disagreement with Lorenz, Lehrman (1970) accurately targets the crux of the matter: Lorenz, as an evolutionist, is primarily focused upon outcome in the normal environment. Lehrman, as a developmental psychologist, has to be concerned with the process of sequential interaction that produces the phenotype. Lehrman's paper is one of those too-rare occasions where one of the participants in a scientific argument steps back for a creative view of the debate in which they are engaged.

Textbooks of the 1930s

In 1934–1935, four textbooks of comparative psychology were published and reviewed in the *Psychological Bulletin*. The books by Munn (1933), Moss et al. (1934), and Warden, Jenkins, and Warner (1934) were assessed by McAllister (1935). Maier and Schneirla (1935) was reviewed by Leeper (1936). Munn's book was restricted to the rat, but it was very comprehensive within that boundary. The Moss et al. text was an edited book, with substantial phyletic range but lacking the unity of perspective that comes from a single-authored or truly co-authored work.

There are some perhaps surprising formal similarities between the Warden, Jenkins, and Warner (WJ & W) and Maier and Schneirla texts. Chapters were arranged by taxonomic groups from plants, through various invertebrates, to vertebrates (and within the vertebrates, from fish to mammals). There were also some striking differences between the texts. WJ & W was more encyclopedic, less theoretical, more oriented toward history and methods per se, and openly referred to natural selection. McAllister (1935, p. 617) noted that: "The systematic treatment of the same topics for the main divisions of plant and animal life makes this book outstanding as an introduction to the general field of comparative psychology both as a textbook and as a book for general reference use." The Maier and Schneirla book was described by Leeper as "one of the finest psychological textbooks that this reviewer has met." He complimented its writing, mechanics, and success at "bringing out the theoretical significance of the research covered."

However, natural selection and the evolution of behavior are never addressed directly. Although evolutionary concepts would ultimately be incorporated in Schneirla's writing, he was at heart a psychologist. Perhaps more than any other psychologist in our times, he grappled with the construction of a comprehensive theoretical framework for analyzing behavior in comparative perspective. Fortunately for the contemporary student of animal behavior, Schneirla's key papers have been collected in convenient fashion by Aronson et al. (1972), with appropriate clusterings and introductory remarks. Unfortunately, Schneirla is not easy reading. It is impossible to do justice to the range of Schneirla's thought in the present article. However, we may note three concepts or themes that are essential aspects of his writing: (1) approach-withdrawal theory; (2) levels of organization in behavioral analysis; and (3) emphasis on the necessity of understanding the ontogeny of behavior in all its complexity. One finds the antecedents of all these themes in the original Maier and Schneirla book. For example, in discussing amoeboid behavior, Maier and Schneirla (1935, p. 16) observe that: "Other things being equal, the energy value of the stimulus determines whether the *Amoeba* moves toward or away from the source. Stimuli of *weak intensity* characteristically elicit movement toward the stimulated locality." On page 12, they had previously described the "principle of the optimum" as "that environmental condition . . . which best promotes the representative physiological processes of the organism." It does not take too much extrapolation to reach the "inverted-U" curves of adaptive behavior as a function of stimulus intensity that characterize approach-withdrawal theory.

Schneirla's emphasis on levels of organization reflected his belief that where there were divergent underlying structures there would be corresponding divergence in psychological processes. There was also a commitment to the idea that with increasing neural complexity there was a parallel development of flexibility in adaptive capacity. Levels of organization, as articulated by Schneirla, is a classical statement of conceptions of emergent processes. The addition of elements or components to an existent system will have novel properties not just because of the individual contributions of the added elements but also because of the emergent matrix of new interrelationships among the parts. Working within this framework, Schneirla discussed such diverse comparisons as the maze learning of rats and ants, and communication in human and insect societies. The superficially similar learning curves of rats and ants were shown to obscure fundamental species differences in what is learned and how things are learned (Schneirla, 1946). Contrasts between human and insect communication emphasizes the vastly greater plasticity of the human situation and warn against the too-glib use of analogies (Schneirla, 1951). Always there is the concern with process rather than mere outcome. This may account for one of the discomforting aspects of Schneirla's writing for the contemporary evolutionary oriented animal behaviorist. Although one can find in Schneirla's writing sophisticated discussions of field methodology (Schneirla, 1950) or the taxonomic and ecological correlates of insect social organization (Schneirla, 1953), the *focus* of his writing is not directed at such questions. In addition, perhaps because of the persistent battles with the instinct theorists that marked his lifetime, Schneirla frequently slights the adaptive questions in the course of arguing against some overly genetic view. This is the feeling that is generated by, for example, Schneirla's (1965) discussion of the fear of hawk shapes exhibited by some birds and described by Tinbergen (1951). The thrust of Schneirla's discussion is toward fitting the behavior into some nonconfigurational, approach-withdrawal framework rather than recognizing the unique adaptive significance of the behavior and then proceeding to an open analysis of mechanism. Given the complexities of visual processing and the existence of cells that respond either to the onset or offset of stimuli, his argument in terms of intensity differences is strained at best. Moreover, Schneirla sounds like any other theorist-clinging-to-his-theory as he attempts to explain away data from studies indicating that animals approach sweet substances and avoid bitter ones by stretching approach-withdrawal theory beyond its credible limits—one *would* see avoidance of sweet, for instance, if only we could get the solutions sufficiently concentrated (Schneirla, 1965, pp. 8–9). Perhaps, but that leaves us with the question of what would constitute evidence of qualitative variation in attractiveness of stimuli. Presumably all natural selection could reasonably have produced would be a system responsive to concentrations found in the natural food sources of the species in question.

757

Although I may find some fault with certain aspects of Schneirla's theorizing and writing style, there is no question that he had a vision of comparative psychology which is still viable and which, in principle, is fully compatible with the research strategies dictated by modern evolutionary perspectives. Unfortunately, Schneirla's views have never had the impact that was warranted within psychology. Possibly a failure of communication. Maybe the army ant just seemed too remote for the bulk of American psychology. The fact remains that the textbooks of the 1930s promised a vigorous field, complete with the healthiest sort of interchange with biology. In the ensuing years it was never achieved. Perhaps some hint of the reasons for this failure may be found through consideration of what did happen to the American psychological study of animals before and after the 1930s.

American Behaviorism and the Study of Animal Learning

Edward L. Thorndike and C. Lloyd Morgan

> The main purpose of the study of the animal mind is to learn the development of mental life down through the phylum, to trace in particular the origin of the human faculty (Thorndike, 1898, p. 2).

> There are really in this field special objections to the acceptance of the testimony about animals' intelligent acts which one gets from anecdotes. . . . Dogs get lost hundreds of times and no one ever notices it or sends an account of it to a scientific magazine. But let one find his way from Brooklyn to Yonkers and the fact immediately becomes a circulating anecdote . . . biologists and psychologists before the pet terrier or hunted fox often become like Samson shorn. . . . All this refers to means of getting knowledge of what animals *do*. The next question is, "What do they *feel?*" (Thorndike, 1898, pp. 4–5).

In his early work, Edward L. Thorndike was concerned with mental evolution, emphasizing the gap between animals and people. This focus, and his persistent attention to what animals "feel," establishes Thorndike's link with his nineteenth-century colleagues from Darwin through Lloyd Morgan. His insistence on systematic, quantitative approaches to gathering data on animal learning, including replication of observations on a number of subjects within a species, and on working under controlled laboratory conditions mark Thorndike as the first twentieth-century animal psychologist.

The detailed history of Thorndike's discoveries is still obscure. He began his studies of maze learning in chicks at Harvard in 1896 and extended his observations to puzzle-box solutions by cats and dogs at Columbia University in 1897–1898 (Joncich, 1968). This was his dissertation research and the substance of his 1898

758

monograph. Studies of three Cebus monkeys engaged in very different latch-box tasks came later and were published as a separate monograph (Thorndike, 1901). Finally, all was collected, with some additional material, in the 1911 book on *Animal Intelligence*. Thorndike's legacy of experimental methodology, trial-and-error learning, the law of effect, and much more, has been lasting and significant. But when he announces early in his monograph that "no work done in this field is enough like the present investigation to require an account of its results" (Thorndike, 1898, p. 3), an interesting problem is raised. As Dewsbury (1979) has recently noted, Lloyd Morgan had used the term *trial and error* to describe the method of associative learning and had further stated that "the successful response is repeated because of the satisfaction that it gives. . . ." Moreover, Morgan had published a description of trial-and-error learning in his fox terrier (!) "Tony" that sounds very much like Thorndike's own systematic work. For Tony, "when he wants to go out into the road, puts his head under the latch of the gate, lifts it, and waits for the gate to swing open" (Morgan, 1894/1896, p. 288). Morgan then goes on to note that an observer coming upon the finished performance might be inclined to give Tony too much credit. Watching the development of the behavior from an early phase, and "sometimes putting him back and making him open it again," Morgan (1894/1896, p. 289) observed that "gradually he went, after fewer pokings of his head out in the wrong place, to the one opening at which the latch was lifted." The process of learning lasted nearly three weeks "before he went at once and with precision to the right place and put his head without an ineffectual fumbling beneath the latch. Even now he always lifts it with the back of his head and not with his muzzle which would be easier for him." Morgan (1894/1896, p. 291) concluded that:

> If those who take a scientific interest in zoological psychology will endeavor to utilize to the full these opportunities, and will record the results of experimental investigation, we shall acquire a better acquaintance with the psychological processes in animals than we could gain with a thousand anecdotes.

Morgan's writings had been studied in William James's seminar at Harvard in which Thorndike was enrolled (Joncich, 1968). Morgan had also lectured at Harvard in 1896 at approximately the time when Thorndike was beginning his work with chicks. Morgan is extensively cited in Thorndike's 1911 book, but no mention is made of the fox terrier opening a gate by lifting a latch, or of Morgan's anticipation of trial and error and the law of effect. Finally, Morgan is omitted from Thorndike's autobiographical sketch, although Romanes and others are cited. History will repeat itself, however, as Thorndike disappears from Watson's (1930) bibliography (except for a minor uncomplimentary reference), and also from Skinner's *Behavior of Organisms* (1938).

I have previously indicated two lines of work that can be traced to Thorndike.

The numerically "weaker" (comparative) line emphasized the evolution of mental capacity. Thorndike himself presented different views on this from one time to the next. His early hopes, expressed in the 1898 monograph, seem to place special emphasis on the gap between monkeys and the other animals that he tested. Perhaps they would show imitation, a presumptive antecedent of human reason. But attempts to demonstrate imitation fail. Thorndike can get them to imitate neither him nor one another, although the latter failure is somewhat mitigated by the overt antagonism between two of the monkeys. Thorndike was to conclude that there was no evidence of reasoning in monkeys, despite observing "a rapid, often apparently instantaneous, abandonment of the unsuccessful movements and a selection of the appropriate one which rivals in suddenness the selections made by human beings" (Thorndike, 1911, p. 189). He pointed to the poor performance of monkeys on some problems, and considered the possibility that their success was more a function of acute vision, manipulatory tendencies, motor skills, and the ability to form rapid associations. Anything but reason. In retrospect, Thorndike could just as easily have inferred insight or thought from his data, as he did infer mere associative skills. A very important question for understanding science is why decisions of this sort are made. Why Thorndike made the conservative choice is not clear to me. He seemed to escalate his criteria, arguing that rate is an inadequate measure, while calling for some variety of considered, interproblem transfer. Indeed, the shape of a learning curve per se was inadequate to the task of inferring reason, but it was also an inadequate basis for rejecting the possible existence of such a process.

The manner in which Thorndike summarized his results, rather than the results themselves, would change the face of American psychology.

> Experiments have been made on fishes, reptiles, birds and various mammals, notably dogs, cats, mice and monkeys, to see how they learned to do simple things to get food. All these animals manifest fundamentally the same sort of intellectual life. Their learning is of the same general type (Thorndike, 1911, pp. 282–283).

As to the gap between people and animals, Thorndike takes an emergent stance. At one point he states that "In man the type of intellect common to the animal kingdom finds its fullest development, and with it is combined the hitherto non-existent power of thinking about things and rationally directing action in accord with thought" (Thorndike, 1911, p. 285). But he had previously noted that "it seems highly probable that the so-called higher intellectual processes of human beings are but . . . [a function of] a very great number of associations" (Thorndike, 1911, p. 239).

Thorndike set the direction for both groups: those who would attempt to scale emergent processes, and those who would opt to study animals in order to learn about people, with the species of animal interchangeable.

Comparative Studies of the Animal Mind: Continuity and Emergence

Hunter's delayed response test, devised with Carr in a search for evidence of ideation in animals, provides the prototypical tale for such comparative investigations. Early results (Hunter, 1913) were promising. As one moved from raccoons, through rats and dogs, the ability to respond to a visual signal after a delay interval increased in systematic fashion, but only in raccoons and a child (Hunter, 1917) were the animals able to bridge the delay interval without maintaining postural orientation. Of some surprise to the modern reader is Hunter's failure to discuss motivational problems in species comparison, but that is really just a lesson in the extent to which we are all bound by the scientific context in which we are embedded. Unfortunately, it soon became clear that the absolute ability to bridge delay intervals was largely determined by the test situation. In their 1934 text, Maier and Schneirla present a rather discouraging tabulation of accumulated studies, concluding that "the value of the delayed response technique is questionable . . . the results may be satisfactorily explained by regarding the situation as one favorable to recall. After the delay period, the animal must merely reproduce the missing part of the stimulus situation and react to it" (p. 452). The latter part of the Maier and Schneirla criticism is debatable. Hunter had his set of assumptions as to what would constitute adequate evidence for ideation in animals and Maier and Schneirla had theirs. Determining whether animals have imagery could be as controversial a process today as it was in the 1930s.

There are several interesting sidelights that relate to the delayed response test. First, it was selected by Tinbergen for special "ethologically oriented" criticism. Tinbergen (1951, pp. 9–10) cites a study by Baerends, who noted that the digger wasp can bridge delays of fifteen hours, first visiting a larval nest to assess the food situation, and then returning after a prolonged interval with an appropriate amount of food. So much for the vaunted higher mental processes of mammals. But, as Tinbergen notes, seeing this capacity means adjusting the test to the specific lifestyle of the digger wasp. A raccoon able to bridge delays of thirty seconds in a wide variety of situations achieves a kind of flexibility that is denied to the wasp and very implicative for questions of adaptation. Second, the most systematic studies of delayed response in various primate species were carried out in the 1930s by Harlow and his colleagues (Harlow, 1932; Harlow, Uehling, & Maslow, 1932). In the hands of Harlow and others, this test was to provide a primary tool for the assessment of brain lesions in the early 1950s. In addition, these early comparative studies may be seen as the logical precursor of the more sophisticated studies on learning-to-learn carried out in truly comparative fashion by Harlow and others in the 1950s and early 1960s (Harlow, 1959; Warren, 1965).

Students interested in the history of direct species comparison should also reexamine the fascinating studies of G. V. Hamilton (1911, 1916) that are in danger of disappearing from view. Hamilton tested the mouse, rat, gopher, horse, dog, monkey, baboon, human child, and normal and deficient human adults in various versions of the same basic apparatus. Hamilton was concerned with strategies of problem-solving. Subjects were confronted with four doors. There was no way of knowing which door would be open on any trial, but it would not be the door open on the previous trial. Five problem-solving strategies were delineated. Hamilton's procedure, although vulnerable to the usual critiques as a scaling device, was unique in examining the qualitative nature of approaches used by different animals and species, rather than merely relying on absolute error scores.

Much more recently, by far the most intellectually comprehensive approach to direct species comparison has been elaborated by Bitterman and his colleagues (Bitterman, 1960, 1965, 1975). It has been an approach characterized by a clearly articulated research strategy: searching for qualitatively different laws of learning or performance in widely divergent species. It has also employed ingenious instrumentation, involved serious sustained effort, and contained a conviction that there are likely to be discontinuities in these laws if one searches in species with sufficiently different nervous systems. This part of Bitterman's view is in accord with the levels of organization conceptualization of Schneirla to which we have previously alluded. In addition, Bitterman at least addressed the usual issues of equating motivation, task demand, and the like, by suggesting the substitution of systematic variation of experimental parameters. It is an approach that might have been expected to attract more researchers than has proved to be the case. Inertia and the technical difficulties involved may be a partial explanation, as well as Bitterman's own record of complex results. However, it may also be the case that Bitterman's rejection of the contributions of his predecessors (e.g., Bitterman, 1960) and his challenge (Bitterman, 1976) to the newer ecological-evolutionary procedures have probably not helped in the "game" of gaining converts.

Finally, there is the eternal problem of language in apes. The early, and largely unsuccessful, attempt to train chimpanzees to "talk" (Kellogg & Kellogg, 1933; Hayes & Hayes, 1951) has been supplanted recently by the gestural sign-language studies of Gardner and Gardner (1969, 1975, 1978) and the more automated investigations of Premack (1971) and Rumbaugh (1977). It is, unfortunately, a field marked by internal conflict and under some external attack (Terrace, 1979). My personal sympathies are with the Gardners as having provided the optimal situation for examining the emergence of a human-like flow of communication, albeit at the sacrifice of certain aspects of control and quantification. There is probably no issue in the field which comes closer to dealing with the Darwin-Wallace argument that split the evolutionists of the nineteenth century. There is also in the modern ape language research a clue to the solution of the dilemma that led Wallace to conclude for the divine creation of the human brain in 1870. A brain evolving in a situation that demands rapid, complex social responses and very varied feeding behaviors is capable of enabling an astonishing set of new and still more complex behaviors in a novel habitat, with basic needs supplied and long-term daily tutelage. Following Wallace's earlier reasoning, and watching Washoe sign, he would have had to declare that the chimpanzee brain was also created by a supreme force for a divine purpose.[4]

Behaviorism and the Age of General Process Learning Theory

As Beach (1950) so beautifully documented, the rich comparative psychology existent in this country in the founding year of the *Journal of Animal Behavior* (1911) was to decline dramatically during the next thirty-seven years. By the 1940s, a typical year found 60–70 percent of articles in the major archival journal of the field devoted to studies of the Norway rat. Investigators employing nonmammalian vertebrates and invertebrates, a thriving field in the early years of the journal, had declined to perhaps 10 percent of the total number of published papers. Coincident with this shift in focal species was a parallel shift in the subject matter of primary concern. Studies of sensory capacities, reflexes, and simple reaction patterns also declined, while research on conditioning and learning came to dominate the field. Thorndike's conclusions had been assimilated. The relative interchangeability of species was also a reasonable inference from the Pavlovian model of conditioned reflexes, as long as one ignored the uniquely human characteristics represented by the second signal system. The scene was thereby set for that uniquely American phenomenon, Watsonian behaviorism: an optimistic, no-nonsense pragmatism that promised not just a technique for studying behavior but for changing it. Listen to the concluding paragraphs of *Behaviorism*:

> Behaviorism ought to be a science that prepares men and women for understanding the principles of their own behavior. It ought to make men and women eager to rearrange their own lives, and especially eager to prepare themselves to bring up their children in a healthy way. . . . I am trying to dangle a stimulus in front of you, a verbal stimulus which, if acted upon will gradually change this universe. For the universe will change if you bring up your children, not in the freedom of the libertine, but in behavioristic freedom—a freedom which we cannot even picture in words, so little do we know of it (Watson, 1930, pp. 303–304).

The book has made clear that this is to be accomplished by applying the principles of conditioning and learning originally derived from studies of dogs, cats, rats and an occasional monkey. Only in the land of Horatio Alger could such a simple

---

[4]The general issue of the natural selection of the human brain is still not settled. G. C. Williams (1966), one of the intellectual leaders of modern Darwinism, has also puzzled over the extraordinary "cerebral hypertrophy" of human beings. He finds little evidence of direction selective advantage but speculates that the ability to understand linguistic instructions early in life could be a partial answer.

763

route to glory become so dominant an intellectual force. It was just eighteen turbulent years since Watson had first announced behaviorism. By referring to Watson's *Behavior: An Introduction to Comparative Psychology* (1914) and comparing it with his *Behaviorism* of 1930, we can examine a case study that is relevant to this essay. It is a study of the detachment of behaviorism from its early broad biological base. Virtually all the books have in common is their uncompromising commitment to elimination of "mentalism." In 1914 Watson was citing pertinent comparative psychological data. Yerkes is the most cited psychologist in his index, with Thorndike and Hunter reasonably close behind. Pavlov (or "Powlow") is mentioned, but only for the utility of his method in studying sensory capacities. Field and laboratory studies were encouraged. Watson (1914, p. 30) noted that "the daily routing adjustments of animals and an accurate knowledge of the environmental conditions under which animals live can come only through field observation." Involved with Lashley in a field study of the nesting behavior of terns, Watson advocates studies that originate in the field, are brought to the laboratory for analysis, and then are submitted to test once again in the field.

Evolution and questions of adaptive significance are dealt with extensively, albeit in sometimes idiosyncratic ways. Watson was already displaying the psychologist's impatience with the all-is-for-the-best inferences drawn by the evolutionists. In discussing certain doubts that he has regarding the preeminent role assigned to the human frontal lobes, Watson observes: "Of course to those who are wedded to the Darwinian theory and who believe that simply because we have the tissue it must have a life and death significance, this argument will not appeal" (1914, p. 320). Watson takes a strong stand on the neutral nature of many mutations incorporated by different species (anticipating a recent serious reconsideration of this problem; see, for example, Dobzhansky, et al., 1977, pp. 130, 303–308). However, in typical Watsonian fashion, he cannot resist pushing his case to its limits. Not only does he grasp at slender evidence to promote consideration of the inheritance of acquired characteristics, he rejects the inheritance of "continuous" natural variation of morphological characters. His ultimate direction is clear—maximize environmental influence, permitting adaptation through flexibility of the individual organism.

Watson is also drawn to the question of continuity and the issue of the critical junction between animals and people. In general, Watson is clearly for continuity. However, he does perceive one gap between people and primates. It has to do with language and thought, but it is a function of our larynx (!), not our brain. Watson allows that introducing linguistic capacity could change our view of the distinction between man and ape, at least within limits. Watson writes that he does not "believe that the putting on of simple language habits in the gibbon, e.g., would make him a fit subject to compete with a cultured European." However, he has less problem when the standard is another racial group:

We do mean that if we could *establish* in the anthropoid even a primitive language and were then to compare him with the primitive Australian bushman, we should at once lose the feeling that there is some qualitative difference between his behavior and our own, i.e., we should lose the feeling at once that he is a brute (Watson, 1914, p. 322).

Even in the twentieth-century roots of American behaviorism, the questions addressed by Darwin and Wallace are present, and we find Watson locating his missing link in Australia.

If the Watson of 1914 is eclectic in approach and oriented toward a broad range of intellectual issues, the Watson of 1930 is much more focused on the conditioned reflex model, people and application. However, Watson's use of conditioned reflex terminology is really much more striking than his use of the conditioned reflex paradigm. For example, in accounting for a fictional case of latch-box problem-solving by a hypothetical white rat, Watson (p. 27) recreates Thorndikean problem-solving without ever referring to its creator. The "instinctive activities" of Thorndike—soon to become the operant behaviors of Skinner—are simply classed by Watson as "unconditioned responses." The lack of identifiable unconditioned stimuli is dismissed. A kind of loose chaining theory is presented to account for the acquisition of a complex sequence of acts that make up the ultimate new "conditioned response." (I sit here in the luxurious position of working from Edward Tolman's copy of the Watson book. In the margin, in Tolman's hand, is written: "The latest Watsonian doctrine of trial and error learning.")

Skinner (1959) has identified Loeb, Pavlov, and Watson as significant early influences on his thinking. Thorndike must have had his impact as well. On pages 13–14 of the 1898 monograph, Thorndike had described "the starting point for the formation of any association" in the puzzle-boxes as the "squeezing, clawing, bitings, etc.," that constitute the instinctive repertoire of the confined cat. Ultimately, experience in other boxes could result in some modification in the cat's approach: "A very pleasant form of this decrease in instinctive impulses was noticed in the cessation of howling and mewing." But here we have Thorndike's account of the origins of "operant" activity. The effects of reward were also being discussed. Even "shaping," of a sort, is anticipated by Thorndike (1911, p. 35) as when, with several cats who were either old or sluggish, "it was necessary to let them out of the box a few times feeding them each time," in order to encourage the emergence of the instinctive repertoire necessary for problem solution. It was a simple, if ingenious, step to liberate the operant from trial-by-trial strictures, permitting the use of rate of response as the critical dependent variable. The law of effect could now be manipulated in terms of reinforcement schedules and emphases shifted to performance rather than acquisition. The Watsonian vision of the behavioristic state was in sight (e.g., Skinner, 1948).

Species differences were not explicitly denied, but what inference was left when Skinner chose the rat and the pigeon as "representative" organisms and published his now famous cluster of cumulative records (Skinner, 1959, Fig. 14, p. 374)? "Pigeon, rat, monkey, which is which? It doesn't matter." Although Skinner proceeds to note that species variation will affect "the ways in which they act upon the environment," he quickly adds that "mice, dogs and human children could have added their curves to this figure." This is not to deny the remarkable creativity and power of Skinner's insights. It was, however, an approach that directed attention away from species variation rather than toward a comparative perspective. As a historical sidelight: Joncich reprints a fascinating letter written by Skinner to Thorndike in 1939. Skinner has read Hilgard's (1939) review of the *Behavior of Organisms* in which Hilgard has noted the debt to Thorndike. Skinner puzzles over the question of the lack of acknowledgment and comes up with two supplementary hypotheses:

> (1) I have never seen an advertised and promoted "system" under your name and (2) I seem to have identified your point of view with the modern psychological view taken as a whole. It has always been obvious that I was merely carrying on your puzzle-box experiments but it never occurred to me to remind my readers of that fact (Joncich, 1968, p. 506).

A brief consideration of Hull can also aid in understanding the decline of comparative psychology. The commitment here was neither to the rapid modification of society or to the exploration of effects of a few simple variables on a single class of behavioral response. Rather, we have a new optimism: if psychology will only follow the formal plan laid out in the physical sciences, and certified by contemporary philosophers of science, all will fall into place. The problem of species differences was not the focus of Hullian theory. However, it was addressed in an interesting and little-cited paper by Hull that appeared in the *Psychological Review* in 1945. It is entitled "The Place of Innate Individual and Species Differences in a Natural-Science Theory of Behavior." A brief article, its basic theme is reflected in this statement: "Innate individual and species differences find expression in the empirical constants which are the essential constituents of the equations expressing the primary and secondary laws of Behavior" (pp. 56–57). However, several revealing paragraphs are contained on the final page of the article: "It is to be regretted that no factual evidence in support of the central hypothesis of the present paper as to the nature of individual or species differences . . . can be given at this time." Further, "Despite the fact that a program of empirical research directed to this latter end has been in progress in the author's laboratory for more than a year, it must be confessed that not a single empirical constant of the twenty or so contained in his systematic approach to behavior . . . has been satisfactorily determined. However, a very promising technique is being developed and we now have renewed hope" (p. 60).

That Hull could not find the empirical constants that he needed in one year's work is not surprising. But, the total commitment to the *form* of the approach rather than to a realistic consideration of evolution and species-characteristic life-styles is retrospectively painful and, from a comparative psychological perspective, unfortunate.

Species-Characteristic Learning Processes

> I think it extremely probable that there are inherited facilities for association, if I may so phrase it. I mean that there very likely exist in the cerebral hemispheres nerve-tracks which facilitate the establishment of such associations as those between sight and taste. What is inherited, however, is the mechanism by which *an* association may be established; what is a matter of individual acquisition is *the* association that is established (Morgan, 1894/1896, p. 89).

Papers concerned with such species-characteristic learning processes as imprinting (Lorenz, 1937; Spalding, 1873/1954), birdsong learning (Thorpe, 1958, 1961; Marler & Tamura, 1964), and bait-shyness (Barnett, 1963) emerged while American learning theory was a thriving enterprise. However, the data were generally ignored. As long as the experiments were zoological, European, or carried out with unfamiliar species, their impact was very slight. The impetus to recognize and deal with learning in a naturalistic context apparently awaited the presentation of such ideas from *within* American psychology. The opening wedge was probably Breland and Breland's (1961) demonstration of species-characteristic intrusions that interfered with the orderly control of operant behaviors. Raccoons that had "learned" to pick up coins for food reinforcement found it difficult to release the coin into a metal container when that additional requirement was introduced and began to rub the coins between their forepaws. Pigs, after learning to carry a wooden coin to a piggy bank, would begin to root about with their objects and delay reinforcement. There had been some anticipation of this sort of result in Thorndike (1911, pp. 47–48). He had rewarded cats with release from a puzzle-box for licking or scratching themselves and had released a chick from a puzzle-box for dressing its feathers. He observed: "There is in all these cases a noticeable tendency, of the cause of which I am ignorant, to diminish the act until it becomes a mere vestige of a lick or scratch." In the Brelands' experiments and in Thorndike's results, there was a progressive failure of the reinforcer to control the emission of the operant in the expected manner.

The papers on bait-shyness by Garcia and his collaborators (Garcia, Ervin, & Koelling, 1966; Garcia & Koelling, 1966; Garcia, Hankins, & Rusiniak, 1976), with the apparent specificity of associations between taste and illness and the ability of subjects to bridge extraordinary intervals between eating and the onset of illness, immediately challenged the implicit assumptions of general process learning

767

theory. Finally, by the end of the decade, Brown and Jenkins (1968) had published an account of autoshaping, while Williams and Williams (1969) had reported the still more counterintuitive finding of negative automaintenance. In the former case, pigeons spontaneously emitted unnecessary operants directed at an illuminated disc that predicted the arrival of food. In the latter instance, it was noted that the pigeons would continue to peck at this disc even when such pecking delayed access to the food hopper. Again, we had the apparent intrusion of species-characteristic response tendencies overriding the traditional dogma of operant reinforcement theory.

The early 1970s found the entire area of species-characteristic learning processes flourishing, and several major collections of papers were published (Hinde & Stevenson-Hinde, 1973; Seligman & Hager, 1972). Although the rate of research in this area has not been all one might wish, the legitimacy of the field is generally established.

Several aspects of the sociology of science should be noted, as they are raised by the literature on species-characteristic learning processes. How were the early announcements of these exciting phenomena greeted? I recall discussing the Breland and Breland article with a creative, prominent Skinnerian at the time. His comment: "Keller has forgotten everything that Fred ever taught him. The animals weren't hungry enough." More recently, Herrnstein (1977a) has reviewed the problems created for general process operant theory by Breland and Breland, for example, or the autoshaping demonstrations. Skinner (1977) has replied. The heart of his answer is: (1) most of the information is familiar; (2) no great revisions of the "theory" are necessary; and (3) phylogeny has always been a recognized part of the Skinnerian program. "*The Behavior of Organisms* has long been out of date, thanks to the efforts of many researchers, of whom Herrnstein is one. But I am continually surprised at how little of the book is actually wrong or no longer relevant" (Skinner, 1977, p. 1012). Like most of us, Skinner can articulate the general principle that the world has changed. Admitting to the significance of specific changes is more difficult. Incidentally, Skinner (1977) also claimed that the Brelands' work had been misinterpreted and was not really intended as a challenge to operant conditioning. But we now have Marion Breland Bailey's word that the challenge truly to integrate phylogeny and learning was exactly what they had in mind (Bailey & Bailey, 1980).

John Garcia was recently awarded the Distinguished Scientific Contribution award of the American Psychological Association. However, his early papers were rejected by the Association's journals. As detailed in Garcia's (1981) recent address (on receipt of his award, Montreal, 1980), his initial reports were greeted with skepticism, not enthusiasm. Entrenched assumptions regarding the necessary and sufficient conditions for learning led to more than the usual editorial scrutiny.

On the Failure of Darwinism and Comparative Approaches in Psychology

> From its inception, American psychology has been strongly anthropocentric. Human behavior has been accepted as the primary object of study and the reactions of other animals have been of interest only insofar as they seemed to throw light upon the psychology of our own species. There has been no concerted effort to establish a genuine comparative psychology in this country for the simple reason that with few exceptions American psychologists have no interest in animal behavior *per se* (Beach, 1950, p. 119).

Beach's argument seems as plausible today as when it was advanced in 1950. Given our preoccupation with people and our classic assumption that plasticity and reason are the hallmarks of the human mind, it is not surprising that the primary use of animals was in fundamental studies of learning and conditioning. The assumptions of general processes that were species independent and/or the supposed existence of "representative" species made the use of animals-as-substitute-people a logical step. There was also the peculiar faith in formal structure and method over content.

But there was probably more to it than that. In our effort to establish psychology as an experimental science, naturalistic observation was suspect as uncontrolled and very limited. Even so comparatively oriented a psychologist as Kuo could write: ". . . naturalistic observations are valuable only insofar as they help the student of behavior broaden his outlook so that in devising experimental programs he will look beyond the narrow confines of the laboratory" (Kuo, 1976, p. 22). Naturalistic observation was the source of ideas. Serious science was a matter for the scientific laboratory. Since the adoption of a truly evolutionary approach *requires* significant attention to the behavior of animals in their natural surround, the poor repute of field research was an inevitable barrier.

In addition, evolutionary theory itself was suspect on three grounds. There was (and is) a common belief that all evolutionary theory is circular—a situation that is not helped by the all-is-for-the-best stories of many popular evolutionists. Second, given the focus on people and the common behavioristic assumption of ultimate human plasticity, there was no relevance to discussions of biological constraints on behavior. Finally, there was (and is) the reasonable concern with the political implications of social Darwinism.

Sociobiology

Sociobiology is defined as the biological basis of all social behavior. For the present it focuses on animal societies, their population structure, castes, and communication, together with all of the physiology underlying the social adaptations. But the discipline is also concerned with the social behavior of early man and the adaptive features of organization in the more primitive contemporary human societies (Wilson, 1975a, p. 4).

The conventional wisdom also speaks of ethology, which is the naturalistic study of whole patterns of animal behavior, and its companion enterprise, comparative psychology, as the central, unifying fields of behavioral biology. They are not; both are destined to be cannibalized by neurophysiology and sensory physiology from one end and sociobiology and behavioral ecology from the other . . . (Wilson, 1975a, p. 6).

The formal advent of sociobiology, as marked by the publication of E. O. Wilson's massive and impressive book (1975a), is so recent an enterprise that placing it in historical perspective is probably a premature enterprise. However, as might be expected from a book with such lofty aspirations on the one side and unrestrained critiques on the other, great controversies have erupted in the brief time since its appearance. Fortunately, there does seem to be some general agreement regarding the immediate scientific spurs to the creation of this latest biological view of social behavior and organization (Alexander, 1975; Barash, 1977; Barlow, 1980).

Individual Competition and Kin Selection

With the higher social animals, I am not aware that any structure has been modified solely for the good of the community, though some are of secondary service to it. For instance, the horns of ruminants and the great canine teeth of baboons appear to have been acquired by the males as weapons for sexual strife, but they are used in defence of the herd or troop. In regard to certain mental faculties the case, as we shall see in the following chapter, is wholly different; for these faculties have been chiefly, or even exclusively, gained for the benefit of the community; the individuals composing the community being at the same time indirectly benefited (Darwin, 1871/1873, p. 149).

As may be gleaned from the above quote, Darwin was concerned about the special role that membership in social groups might play during the operation of natural selection. Both Darwin and Wallace ultimately committed themselves to the view that, within human communities, there existed social motives that had been selected for the good of the group. Darwin extended this view to the higher social mammals as well. The rejection of such group-selectionist arguments has formed one of the cornerstones of modern sociobiology. In 1962, Wynne-Edwards suggested that individual members of animal groups would "voluntarily" restrain their reproductive activities for the good of the group. The "group" thus became the unit of natural selection, and those groups containing appropriately altruistic individuals were seen as more likely to survive in competition with groups where such restraint was not exercised.

G. C. Williams (1966) reanalyzed the situations described by Wynne-Edwards and clearly demonstrated that what might at first appear to be group selection could be more parsimoniously and plausibly explained by reference to individual selection. For example, it could be shown that reduction in clutch size by birds and "investing" a great deal in fewer offspring in times of scarcity might actually produce more *surviving* offspring for individual parents than churning out a large number of smaller birds less able to compete for available resources (Lack, 1968).

Williams's line of argument was greatly expanded in scope by access to several theoretical publications by Hamilton (1964a,b) on the concept of "inclusive fitness." Prior to Hamilton's papers, the tendency had been to limit attention to parents and offspring in analyses of the genetic implications of natural selection. Hamilton noted that although parents and offspring of typical biparental species shared one-half their genes, all members of family groups shared some proportion of genes. Siblings, on the average, shared one-half their genes; grandparents and grandchildren, one-quarter of their genes, and so forth. Thus a "new" theory of seemingly altruistic behavior was born:

> . . . in the world of our model organisms, whose behavior is determined strictly by genotype, we expect to find that no one is prepared to sacrifice his life for any single person but that everyone will sacrifice it when he can thereby save more than two brothers, or four half-brothers, or eight first cousins . . . (Hamilton, 1964a, p. 16).

One can also find in Darwin's writing an anticipation of the basic kin selection argument, first as he grappled with the question of the sterile social insects (Darwin, 1859/1869, pp. 209–215), and then in regard to uniquely human abilities. After positing the development of a novel weapon or means of defense by a single man in a tribe, Darwin discusses the advantages that might accrue to the members of the group, including a potential increment in numbers:

> If such men left children to inherit their mental superiority, the chance of the birth of still more ingenious members would be somewhat better, and in a very small tribe decidedly better. Even if they left no children, the tribe would still include their blood-relations; and it has been ascertained by agriculturists that by preserving and breeding from the family of an animal, which when slaughtered was found to be valuable, the desired character has been obtained (Darwin, 1871/1873, p. 155).

Without Mendelian genetics, Darwin was working at an enormous disadvantage, but his approach to the concept of inclusive fitness, given the paucity of facts available, is truly remarkable. Hamilton and Williams had paved the route to a new examination of social behavior emphasizing competition between individuals to increase the relative proportion of their genes in succeeding generations. There have been both practical and theoretical implications of this line of thought. From a purely empirical standpoint, the investigation of animal social behavior has been permanently changed. Field studies can no longer involve "quick" studies of groups of animals classed only by age, sex, and role. A "complete" understanding of social organization will necessarily involve studies of known *individuals*, preferably with sufficient time to study effects across generations and to allow determination of kinship relations. This seems clear and valuable. Moreover, a burgeoning literature testifies to the heuristic power of kin selection ideas, despite the time requirements and complexity of such studies (Daly & Wilson, 1978; Krebs & Davies, 1978). Long-term investigations of individual animals clearly demonstrate the testability of hypotheses derived from kin selection theory (e.g., Sherman, 1977, 1980). Unfortunately, the theory has still sometimes run far in advance of the data.

This trend was enhanced by the publication of three provocative papers by Robert Trivers (1971, 1972, 1974). One article, concerned with the sometimes competing interests of parents and offspring (Trivers, 1974), fits directly within the framework of inclusive fitness. In this article Trivers argues that parent-offspring conflict is, in general, inevitable because natural selection would have favored different selfish behaviors in parents and offspring. This is the other side of the altruistic coin. All things being equal, parents should favor the success of their offspring over nonrelatives, but not if it is at the expense of greater future personal reproductive potential. A second article by Trivers (1972) pointed toward the differential "investment" of fitness-determining personal resources of males and females in their offspring, usually low for males, high for females. An "explanation" for the generality of male promiscuity and female selectivity in choice of mates is one clear implication, as well as more subtle predictions regarding changes and reversals of behavior in species where the parental burden is shared or reversed.

Reciprocity and the Testing of Sociobiological Propositions

Simply stated, an individual who maximizes his friendships and minimizes his antagonisms will have an evolutionary advantage, and selection should favor those characters that promote the optimization of personal relationships. I imagine that this evolutionary factor has increased man's capacity for altruism and compassion and has tempered his ethically less acceptable heritage of sexual and predatory aggressiveness. There is theoretically no limit to the extent and complexity of group-related behavior that this factor could produce, and the immediate goal of such behavior would always be the well-being of some other individual, often genetically unrelated. Ultimately, however, this would not be an adaptation for group benefit. It would be developed by the differential survival of individuals and would be designed for the perpetuation of the genes of the individual providing the benefit to another (Williams, 1966, p. 94).

772

In 1971 Trivers published an extremely provocative article in which the concept of reciprocal altruism was expanded and developed. The argument was now made that individuals could/would engage in altruistic behavior with nonrelatives through the existence of social contracts that ensured reciprocity. There were requirements for the emergence of such altruistic behavior: the risk to the altruist had to be lower than the net potential benefits to the altruist and the relatives who shared the altruist's genes. It was also suggested that such reciprocity could only function in stable communities of intelligent individuals. It would only be in such social groups that individuals could rely on detection and prevention of "cheating," as well as insuring a high probability of reciprocity. Human societies were the obvious target group for such theorizing.

The ideas contained in Trivers's papers have had major impact in sociobiology and animal behavior. Overt conflict between parents and offspring had been described well before Trivers's paper (e.g., Schneirla & Rosenblatt, 1961, in kittens; Hinde, 1969, in rhesus monkeys). However, reciprocity agreements are relevant to much of human social interaction. The real question is what novel insights have been gained from viewing this behavior in evolutionary terms, and can the theoretical implications be tested, i.e., disproved? I do not feel qualified to answer the first question because it involves anthropological expertise well beyond my domain. Certainly Alexander (1979) has worked very creatively at interpreting human cross-cultural data in terms of both kin-selection and reciprocity arguments. However, the scientific price that has been paid for the free use of reciprocity strikes this reviewer as not worth the benefit. Freed from the kin-related limitations of nepotistic theory, all of human social interactions are now fair game. But one looks in vain for behaviors that necessitate theoretical revision, despite Wilson's statements regarding bad evolutionary speculation (1975b, p. 28) or Alexander's elegant discussion of theory testing in a Darwinian framework (1979, pp. 7–15 and 19–22). In fact, Alexander makes a crucial point that is too frequently overlooked by psychologists. In practice, one does not test the theory of evolution through natural selection:

> . . . there is no single, overall test that is both simply applicable and able to falsify the entire theory of evolution in all its aspects; nor should one necessarily be expected or required. For a process that has led to the diversity and complexity of the life existing throughout geological time, the only reasonable expectation is that we must repeatedly match our predictions with evidence and judge the theoretical significance of those predictions on the basis of their likelihood, individually and collectively, of being met by accident or chance (Alexander, 1979, pp. 21–22).

I would phrase this even more strongly. All a scientist ever does is test a personal hypothesis regarding a particular route to survival. But even the appearance of the theory has led recent workers to focus on a host of new reproduction-related variables, in addition to examining overt conflicts more carefully. It seems fair to

773

conclude that important studies of differential parental behavior of males and females, changes in behavior across successive broods, and the like have indeed been sparked by Trivers's line of speculation. Previous discussions had tended to focus on benefits of maternal rejection for the offspring in terms of fostering independence. Now, for the first time, attention was shifted to parental gains. This heuristic function is very significant and should not be obscured by some of the less pleasing aspects of work carved out in this framework. Both in the parent-offspring paper and the reciprocity article there is an illusion of mathematical precision and testability that is disconcerting. "Testing" the parent-offspring conflict theory requires a cost-benefit analysis that is much more complex than may appear at first glance. Costs are not simply caloric costs or risks of predation and, under the rules of inclusive fitness, the assessment of benefits could require almost staggering quantities of data. These issues are left to the ingenuity of the individual experimenter. Perhaps it will all work out, but my worst fears are that so long as results coincide with Trivers's predictions, no one will be particularly upset with the experimental assumptions. However, negative reports (if they should appear) may receive a different reception. Calculations of costs and benefits could, in such cases, receive the most thorough scrutiny and challenge. This is not unique in the history of science, but that does not mean it is ideal.

The situation in regard to reciprocity theory is probably worse. It seems patently "true" that this is frequently lacking in the sociobiological commentary on human nature. As heroism, homosexuality, suicide, and the like are successively explained, one generally waits in vain for the failure of prediction that would require revision. An exception to this practice is provided by Alexander. At one point in his book, Alexander notes six areas where cross-cultural data obtained by Murdock do not obviously fit with sociobiological prediction (pp. 165–168). We need more such tough-minded reviews, and they must be followed by appropriate tests. Otherwise, this sort of theorizing will forever be vulnerable to the articulate critiques advanced, for example, by Lewontin (1979).

Concluding Thoughts

It is possible to believe that amidst the resulting rubble there is emerging for the first time a synthesis and an accuracy of focus that may yet yield a truly comprehensive and useful theory of behavior: an evolutionary theory yet a predictive theory; a philosophically significant theory, yet a practical and effective one; a theory valuable, acceptable, indeed indispensable, to biological and social scientists alike (Alexander, 1975, p. 79).

If sociobiological theory is to make a lasting contribution to our understanding of evolution, it must abandon the naive adaptationist program that now characterizes human sociobiology and become very much more explicit about the epistemological and methodological difficulties that face it. To do so will require that sociobiologists abandon their claim to universal explanation of all human social phenomena and accept a much more modest goal of providing well-founded explanation of, say, caste formation in social insects, a difficult enough task and one requiring much serious experimental, natural historical, and theoretical work. By being less grandiose in its project, sociobiology may become more fruitful in its outcome (Lewontin, 1979, p. 14).

If the preceding quotations were from a multiple-choice examination, I would have to check both-of-the-above, although I am personally inclined to acknowledge considerably greater contributions by the modern Darwinian behaviorists than is Lewontin's choice. Paradoxically, from the vantage point of a friendly comparative psychologist whose own research has been changed by recent Darwinian ideas, what sociobiology needs most is some failures: overt demonstrations that sociobiologists live by the same rules as the rest of us in a world where hypotheses are formulated to be tested and, at least occasionally, rejected. There are additional problems that many psychologists have had regarding sociobiology: the rush from gene to behavior that bypasses questions of ontogeny, and the distressing sociopolitical implications of genetic determinism (Tobach, 1978; Wyers et al., 1980). The sociopolitical issues have been previously addressed.

However, it may be important to note that in ". . . answer to the question, 'What does evolution have to say about normative ethics, or defining what people *ought* to be doing?' Alexander (1979, p. 276) replies, 'Nothing whatsoever.'" Given the plasticity of human behavior, our cognitive and reflective abilities, and the like, Alexander concludes that humans can ". . . accomplish almost whatever they wish." It is actually an argument very similar in tone and content to the concluding paragraphs of A. R. Wallace's first article on human evolution in 1864. Natural selection does not have to be viewed as providing our species with a genetic straitjacket.

As to the neglect of ontogeny, the scenario bears a striking resemblance to past wars between Kuo and the instinctivists, or Lehrman and the classical ethologists. Ontogenetic analysis is at the heart of psychology. Any system that deals with ends and relegates questions of means to a subsidiary position is likely to receive a skeptical greeting from psychologists in general and comparative psychologists in particular. However, the comparative study of animal behavior by psychologists has been disconnected from its evolutionary roots too long and too frequently. The phyletic, ecological, and genetic messages of natural selection form the essential background from which psychological analysis must proceed. I hope that we will soon be past this latest stage of public-relations-oriented claims and sociopolitical countercharges. There is clearly work to be done. With the careful infusion of evolutionary concepts, continuous critical scrutiny, and a healthy modesty regarding its accomplishments, comparative psychology will indeed make significant and unique contributions to "the psychological studies" (Koch, 1981).

REFERENCES

Alexander, R. D. The search for a general theory of behavior. *Behavioral Science,* 1975, *20,* 77–100.

Alexander, R. D. *Darwinism and human affairs.* Seattle: University of Washington Press, 1979.

Alexander, R. D., & Tinkle, D. W. (Eds.). Natural selection and social behavior: Recent research and new theory. New York: Chiron Press, 1981.

Allen, E., et al. Letter to the editor. *New York Review of Books,* November 13, 1975, pp. 182, 184–186.

Allen, E., et al. Sociobiology—another biological determinism. *BioScience,* 1976, *26,* 183–186.

Alper, J., et al. Letter to the editor. *Science,* 1976, *192,* 424–427.

Aronson, L. R., Tobach, E., Rosenblatt, J. S., & Lehrman, D. S. (Eds.). *Selected writings of T. C. Schneirla.* San Francisco: Freeman, 1972.

Bailey, R. E., & Bailey, M. B. A view from outside the Skinner box. *American Psychologist,* 1980, *35,* 942–946.

Barash, D. P. *Sociobiology and behavior.* New York: Elsevier, 1977.

Barlow, G. W. Ethological units of behavior. In D. Ingle (Ed.), *Central nervous system and fish behavior.* Chicago: The University of Chicago Press, 1968.

Barlow, G. W. The development of sociobiology: A biologist's perspective. In G. W. Barlow and J. Silverberg (Eds.), *Sociobiology: Beyond nature/nurture?* Boulder, Colo.: Westview Press, 1980.

Barnett, S. A. *A study in behaviour.* London: Methuen, 1963.

Beach, F. A. Effects of cortical lesions upon the copulatory behavior of male rats. *Journal of Comparative Psychology,* 1940, *29,* 193–246.

Beach, F. A. A review of physiological and psychological studies of sexual behavior in mammals. *Physiological Reviews,* 1947, *27,* 240–307.

Beach, F. A. *Hormones and behavior.* New York: Hoeber, 1948.

Beach, F. A. The snark was a boojum. *American Psychologist,* 1950, *5,* 115–124.

Beach, F. A. The descent of instinct. *Psychological Review,* 1955, *62,* 401–410.

Beach, F. A. Neural and chemical regulation of behavior. In H. F. Harlow & C. N. Woolsey (Eds.), *Biological and biochemical bases of behavior.* Madison: University of Wisconsin, 1958.

Beer, C. G. Ethology: The zoologist's approach to behaviour, Part 1. *Tuatara,* 1963, *11,* 170–177.

Beer, C. G. Ethology: The zoologist's approach to behaviour, Part 2. *Tuatara,* 1964, *12,* 16–39.

Birch, H. G. Sources of order in the maternal behavior of animals. *American Journal of Orthopsychiatry,* 1956, *26,* 279–284.

Bitterman, M. E. Toward a comparative psychology of learning. *American Psychologist,* 1960, *15,* 704–712.

Bitterman, M. E. Phyletic differences in learning. *American Psychologist,* 1965, *20,* 396–410.

Bitterman, M. E. The comparative analysis of learning. *Science,* 1975, *188,* 699–709.

Bitterman, M. E. Flavor aversion studies. *Science,* 1976, *192,* 266–267.

Boring, E. G. The psychology of controversy. *Psychological Review,* 1929, *36,* 97–121.

Breland, K., & Breland, M. The misbehavior of organisms. *American Psychologist,* 1961, *16,* 681–684.

Brown, P. L., & Jenkins, H. M. Autoshaping of the pigeon's key-peck. *Journal of the Experimental Analysis of Behavior,* 1968, *2,* 1–8.

Caplan, A. L. (Ed.). *The sociobiology debate.* New York: Harper & Row, 1978.

Carpenter, C. R. A field study of the behavior and social relations of howling monkeys. *Comparative Psychology Monographs,* 1934, *10,* 1–168.

Carpenter, C. R. A field study of the behavior and social relations of the gibbon. *Comparative Psychology Monographs,* 1940, *16,* 1–212.

Christophersen, E. R., & Wagman, W. Maternal behavior in the albino rat as a function of self-licking deprivation. *Journal of Comparative and Physiological Psychology,* 1965, *60,* 142–144.

Craig, W. Appetites and aversions as constituents of instincts. *Biological Bulletin*, 1918, *34*, 91–107.

Daly, M., & Wilson, M. *Sex, evolution and behavior*. North Scituate, Mass.: Duxbury, 1978.

Darwin, C. *On the origin of species by means of natural selection*. New York: Appleton, 1869. (Originally published, 1859).

Darwin, C. *The descent of man, and selection in relation to sex* (Vol. I). New York: Appleton, 1873. (Originally published, 1871).

Darwin, C. *The expression of the emotions in man and animals*. Chicago: The University of Chicago Press, 1965. (Originally published, 1872).

de Beer, G. Forward. In C. Darwin & A. R. Wallace, *Evolution by natural selection*. Cambridge: The University Press, 1958.

Dewsbury, D. C. Lloyd Morgan: Something old that's often new. *Contemporary Psychology*, 1979, *24*, 677–680.

Dobzhansky, T., Ayala, F. J., Stebbins, G. L., & Valentine, J. W. *Evolution*. San Francisco: Freeman, 1977.

Eibl-Eibesfeldt, I. The interactions of unlearned behavior patterns and learning in mammals. In W. F. Delfresnaye (Ed.), *Brain mechanisms and learning*. Oxford: Blackwell, 1961.

Eibl-Eibesfeldt, I. Angeborenes und Erworbenes im Verhalten einiger Sauger. *Zeitschrift für Tierpsychologie*, 1963, *20*, 705–754.

Eiseley, L. *Darwin's century*. Garden City, N.Y.: Anchor, 1961.

Garcia, J. Tilting at the paper mills of academe. *American Psychologist*, 1981, *36*, 149–158.

Garcia, J., Ervin, F. R., & Koelling, R. A. Learning with prolonged delay of reinforcement. *Psychonomic Science*, 1966, *5*, 121–122.

Garcia, J., Hankins, W. G., & Rusiniak, K. W. Flavor aversion studies (with reply by M. E. Bitterman). *Science*, 1976, *192*, 265–267.

Garcia, J., & Koelling, R. A. Relation of cue to consequence in avoidance learning. *Psychonomic Science*, 1966, *4*, 123–124.

Gardner, R. A., & Gardner, B. T. Teaching sign language to a chimpanzee. *Science*, 1969, *165*, 664–672.

Gardner, R. A., & Gardner, B. T. Evidence for sentence constituents in the early utterances of child and chimpanzee. *Journal of Experimental Psychology, General*, 1975, *104*, 244–267.

Gardner, R. A., & Gardner, B. T. Comparative psychology and language acquisition. *Annals of the New York Academy of Sciences*, 1978, *309*, 37–76.

Gottlieb, G. Preface and Biography of Ling-Yang Kuo. In Z. Y. Kuo, *The dynamics of behavior development: An epigenetic view*. New York: Plenum, 1976.

Hailman, J. P. The ontogeny of an instinct. *Behaviour*, 1967, Supplement 15, 1–142.

Hamilton, G. V. A study of trial and error reactions in mammals. *Journal of Animal Behavior*, 1911, *1*, 33–66.

Hamilton, G. V. A study of perseverence reaction in primates and rodents. *Behavior Monographs*, 1916, *3* (No. 13).

Hamilton, W. D. The genetical evolution of social behaviour. I. *Journal of Theoretical Biology*, 1964, *7*, 1–16. (a)

Hamilton, W. D. The genetical evolution of social behaviour. II. *Journal of Theoretical Biology*, 1964, *7*, 17–52. (b)

Harlow, H. F. Comparative behavior of primates. III. Complicated delayed reaction tests on primates. *Journal of Comparative Psychology*, 1932, *14*, 241–252.

Harlow, H. F. Learning set and error factor theory. In S. Koch (Ed.), *Psychology: A study of a science* (Vol. 2). New York: McGraw-Hill, 1959.

Harlow, H. F., Uehling, H., & Maslow, A. H. Comparative behavior of primates. I. Delayed reaction tests on primates from the lemur to the orang-outan. *Journal of Comparative Psychology*, 1932, *13*, 313–343.

777

Hayes, K. J., & Hayes, C. The intellectual development of a homeraised chimpanzee. *Proceedings of the American Philosophical Society*, 1951, 95, 105–109.

Hebb, D. O. Heredity and environment in mammalian behavior. *British Journal of Animal Behaviour* 1953, *1*, 43–47.

Herrnstein, R. J. The evolution of behaviorism. *American Psychologist*, 1977, 32, 593–603. (a)

Herrnstein, R. J. Doing what comes naturally: A reply to Professor Skinner. *American Psychologist*, 1977, 32, 1013–1016. (b)

Hilgard, E. R. Review of B. F. Skinner's *The behavior of organisms. Psychological Bulletin*, 1939, 36, 121–125.

Hinde, R. A. Ethological models and the concept of drive. *British Journal of Science*, 1956, 6, 321.

Hinde, R. A. Unitary drives. *Animal Behaviour*, 1959, 7, 130–141. (a)

Hinde, R. A. Some recent trends in ethology. In S. Koch (Ed.), *Psychology: A study of a science* (Vol. 2). New York: McGraw-Hill, 1959. (b)

Hinde, R. A. Energy models of motivation. *Symposia of the Society for Experimental Biology*, 1960, 14, 199–213.

Hinde, R. A. *Animal behaviour: A synthesis of ethology and comparative psychology.* New York: McGraw-Hill, 1966.

Hinde, R. A. Analysing the roles of the partners in a behavioral interaction—mother-infant relations in rhesus macaques. *Annals of the New York Academy of Science*, 1969, 159, 651–667.

Hinde, R. A., & Stevenson-Hinde, J. (Eds.). *Constraints on learning: Limitations and predispositions.* New York: Academic Press, 1973.

Hodos, W., & Campbell, C. B. G. Scala naturae: Why there is no theory in comparative psychology. *Psychological Review*, 1969, 76, 337–350.

Hull, C. L. The place of innate individual and species differences in a natural-science theory of behavior. *Psychological Review*, 1945, 52, 55–60.

Hunter, W. S. The delayed reaction in animals and children. *Behavior Monographs*, 1913, 2 (No. 6).

Hunter, W. S. The delayed reaction in a child. *Psychological Review*, 1917, 24, 74–87.

Joncich, G. Complex forces and neglected acknowledgments in the making of a young psychologist: Edward L. Thorndike and his teachers. *Journal of the History of the Behavioral Sciences*, 1966, 2, 43–50.

Joncich, G. *The sane positivist: A biography of Edward L. Thorndike.* Middletown, Conn.: Wesleyan University Press, 1968.

Kalikow, T. J. Konrad Lorenz's "brown past": A reply to Alec Nisbett. *Journal of the History of Behavioral Science*, 1979, 15, 173–180.

Kellogg, W. N., & Kellogg, L. A. *The ape and the child: A study of environmental influence upon early behavior.* New York: McGraw-Hill, 1933.

Koch, S. The nature and limits of psychological knowledge. *American Psychologist*, 1981, 36, 257–269.

Krebs, J. R., & Davies, N. B. (Eds.). *Behavioural ecology. An evolutionary approach.* Sunderland, Mass.: Sinauer Associates, 1978.

Kuo, Z. Y. Giving up instincts in psychology. *Journal of Philosophy*, 1921, 18, 645–664.

Kuo, Z. Y. How are instincts acquired? *Psychological Review*, 1922, 29, 344–365.

Kuo, Z. Y. The genesis of the cat's responses to the rat. *Journal of Comparative Psychology*, 1930, 11, 1–35.

Kuo, Z. Y. Further study of the behavior of the cat toward the rat. *Journal of Comparative Psychology*, 1938, 25, 1–8.

Kuo, Z. Y. *The dynamics of behavior development: An epigenetic view.* New York: Plenum, 1976.

Lack, D. *Population studies of birds.* London: Oxford University Press, 1966.

Lack, D. *Ecological adaptations for breeding in birds,* London: Methuen, 1968.

Leeper, R. Review of Maier and Schneirla's *Principles of animal psychology. Psychological Bulletin*, 1936, 33, 467–471.

Lehrman, D. S. A critique of Konrad Lorenz's theory of instinctive behavior. *Quarterly Review of Biology*, 1953, 28, 337–363.

Lehrman, D. S. Interaction between internal and external environments in the regulation of the reproductive cycle of the ring dove. In F. A. Beach (Ed.), *Sex and behavior*. New York: Wiley, 1965.

Lehrman, D. S. Interaction of hormonal and experimental influences on development of behavior. In E. L. Bliss (Ed.), *Roots of behavior*. New York: Hoeber, 1962.

Lehrman, D. S. Semantic and conceptual issues in the nature-nurture problem. In L. R. Aronson, E. Tobach, D. S. Lehrman, & J. S. Rosenblatt (Eds.), *Development and evolution of behavior*. San Francisco: Freeman, 1970.

Lewontin, R. C. Sociobiology as an adaptationist program. *Behavioral Science*, 1979, 24, 5–14.

Lockard, R. B. The albino rat: A defensible choice or a bad habit. *American Psychologist*, 1968, 23, 734–742.

Lorenz, K. Z. The companion in the bird's world. *Auk*, 1937, 54, 245–273.

Lorenz, K. The comparative method in studying innate behaviour patterns. *Symposium of the Society for Experimental Biology*, 1950, 4, 221–268.

Lorenz, K. *Evolution and modification of behavior*. Chicago: The University of Chicago Press, 1965.

Maier, N. R. F., & Schneirla, T. C. *Principles of animal psychology*. New York: McGraw-Hill, 1935.

Marchant, J. *Alfred Russel Wallace: Letters and reminiscences*. New York: Harper, 1916.

Marler, P., & Tamura, M. Culturally transmitted patterns of vocal behavior in sparrows. *Science*, 1964, 146, 1483–1486.

McAllister, W. G. Review of three comparative psychology texts. *Psychological Bulletin*, 1935, 32, 614–619.

McDougall, W. The sources and direction of psychophysical energy. *American Journal of Insanity*, 1913.

McDougall, W. *Outline of psychology*. New York: Scribner's, 1923.

Merton, R. K. Priorities in scientific discovery: A chapter in the sociology of science. *American Sociological Review*, 1957, 22, 635–659.

Morgan, C. L. *An introduction to comparative psychology*. New York: Scribner's, 1896. (Originally published, 1894.)

Moss, F. A., et al. *Comparative psychology*. New York: Prentice-Hall, 1934.

Munn, N. L. *An introduction to animal psychology*. Boston: Houghton Mifflin, 1933.

Premack, D. Language in chimpanzee? *Science*, 1971, 172, 808–822.

Riess, B. F. The isolation of factors of learning and native behavior in field and laboratory studies. *Annals of the New York Academy of Science*, 1950, 51, 1093–1102.

Romanes, G. J. *Mental evolution in animals*. London: Kegan Paul, Trench, 1883.

Romanes, G. J. *Mental evolution in man*. New York: Appleton, 1898. (Originally published, 1889.)

Rosenblatt, J. S. The basis of synchrony in the behavioral interaction between the mother and her offspring in the laboratory rat. In B. Foss (Ed.), *Determinants of infant behaviour* (Vol. 3). London: Methuen, 1965.

Rumbaugh, D. M. *Language learning by a chimpanzee*. New York: Academic Press, 1977.

Schneirla, T. C. Studies on army ants in Panama. *Journal of Comparative Psychology*, 1933, 15, 267–299.

Schneirla, T. C. A theory of army-ant behavior based upon the analysis of activities in a representative species. *Journal of Comparative Psychology*, 1938, 25, 51–90.

Schneirla, T. C. Further studies on the army-ant behavior pattern. *Journal of Comparative Psychology*, 1940, 29, 401–460.

Schneirla, T. C. Ant learning as a problem of comparative psychology. In P. L. Haniman (Ed.), *Twentieth century psychology*. New York: Philosophical Library, 1946.

Schneirla, T. C. Levels in the psychological capacities of animals. In R. W. Sellers, V. J. McGill, and M. Farber (Eds.), *Philosophy for the future*. New York: Macmillan, 1949.

779

Schneirla, T. C. The relationship between observation and experimentation in the field study of behavior. *Annals of the New York Academy of Sciences,* 1950, *51,* 1022–1044.

Schneirla, T. C. The "levels" concept in the study of social organization in animals. In M. Sherif & E. Rohrer (Eds.), *Social psychology at the crossroads.* New York: Harper, 1951.

Schneirla, T. C. Insect behavior in relation to its setting. In K. Roeder (Ed.), *Insect physiology.* New York: Wiley, 1953.

Schneirla, T. C. Interrelationships of the "innate" and the "acquired" in instinctive behavior. In *L'instinct dans le comportement des animaux et de l'homme.* Paris: Masson, 1956.

Schneirla, T. C. The concept of development in comparative psychology. In D. B. Harris (Ed.), *The concept of development.* Minneapolis: University of Minnesota Press, 1957.

Schneirla, T. C. An evolutionary and developmental theory of biphasic process underlying approach and withdrawal. In M. R. Jones (Ed.), *Nebraska Symposium on Motivation,* 1959. Lincoln: University of Nebraska Press, 1959.

Schneirla, T. C. Aspects of stimulation and organization in approach/withdrawal processes underlying vertebrate behavioral development. In D. S. Lehrman, R. Hinde, & E. Shaw (Eds.), *Advances in the study of behavior* (Vol. 1). New York: Academic Press, 1965.

Schneirla, T. C., & Rosenblatt, J. S. Behavioral organization and genesis of the social bond in insects and mammals. *American Journal of Orthopsychiatry,* 1961, *31,* 223–253.

Seligman, M. E. P., & Hager, J. L. *Biological boundaries of learning.* New York: Appleton-Century-Crofts, 1972.

Seyfarth, R. M., Cheney, D. L., & Marler, P. Vervet monkey alarm calls: Semantic communication in a free-ranging primate. *Animal Behaviour,* 1980, *28,* 1070–1094.

Sherman, P. W. Nepotism and the evolution of alarm calls. *Science,* 1977, *197,* 1246–1253.

Sherman, P. W. The limits of ground squirrel nepotism. In G. W. Barlow & J. Silverberg (Eds.), *Sociobiology: Beyond nature-nurture.* Boulder, Colo.: Westview Press, 1980.

Skinner, B. F. *The behavior of organisms.* New York: Appleton-Century-Crofts, 1938.

Skinner, B. F. *Walden two.* New York: Macmillan, 1948.

Skinner, B. F. A case history in scientific method. In S. Koch (Ed.), *Psychology: A study of a science* (Vol. 2). New York: McGraw-Hill, 1959.

Skinner, B. F. Herrnstein and the evolution of behaviorism. *American Psychologist,* 1977, *32,* 1006–1012.

Spalding, D. A. Instinct. With original observations on young animals. *MacMillan's Magazine,* 1873, *27,* 282–293. (Reprinted in the *British Journal of Animal Behaviour,* 1954, *2,* 2–11.)

Stone, C. P. The congenital sexual behavior of the young male albino rat. *Journal of Comparative Psychology,* 1922, *2,* 95–152.

Stone, C. P. Preliminary note on the maternal behavior of rats living in parabiosis. *Endocrinology,* 1925, *9,* 505–512.

Stone, C. P. The initial copulatory response of female rats reared in isolation from the age of twenty-days to the age of puberty. *Journal of Comparative Psychology,* 1926, *6,* 73–84.

Terrace, H. S. *Nim.* New York: Knopf, 1979.

Thorndike, E. L. Animal intelligence: An experimental study of the associative processes in animals. *Psychological Review Monograph,* 1898, *2* (No. 8).

Thorndike, E. L. Mental life of the monkeys. *Psychological Review Monograph,* 1901, *3* (No. 15).

Thorndike, E. L. *Animal intelligence: Experimental studies.* New York: Macmillan, 1911.

Thorndike, E. L. Autobiographical sketch. In C. Murchison (Ed.), *A history of psychology in autobiography* (Vol. III). Worcester, Mass.: Clark University Press, 1936.

Thorpe, W. H. The learning of song patterns by birds, with special reference to the song of the chaffinch. *Ibis,* 1958, *100,* 535–570.

Thorpe, W. H. Bird song: The biology of vocal communication and expression in birds. *Cambridge Monographs in Experimental Biology,* 1961, *12,* 129–136.

Tinbergen, N. *The study of instinct.* London: Oxford University Press, 1951.

Tobach, E. The methodology of sociobiology from the viewpoint of a comparative psychologist. In A. L. Caplan (Ed.), *The sociobiology debate.* New York: Harper & Row, 1978.

Tobach, E., & Schneirla, T. C. The biopsychology of social behavior of animals. In R. E. Cooke & S. Levin (Eds.), *Biologic basis of pediatric practice.* New York: McGraw-Hill, 1968.

Trivers, R. L. The evolution of reciprocal altruism. *Quarterly Review of Biology,* 1971, 46, 35–57.

Trivers, R. L. Parental investment and sexual selection. In B. Campbell (Ed.), *Sexual selection and the descent of man.* Chicago: Aldine, 1972.

Trivers, R. L. Parent-offspring conflict. *American Zoologist,* 1974, 14, 249–264.

Wallace, A. R. The origin of human races and the antiquity of man deduced from the theory of "natural selection." *The Anthropological Review,* 1864, 2, clviii–clxx.

Wallace, A. R. The limits of natural selection as applied to man. Chapter IX in *Natural selection and tropical nature: Essays on descriptive and theoretical biology.* London: Macmillan, 1895. (This paper originally appeared in Wallace's contributions to the theory of natural selection, published in 1870.)

Wallace, A. R. *My life* (2 vols.). London: Chapman & Hall, 1905.

Wallace, A. R. Evolution and character. In P. L. Parker (Ed.), *Character and life.* London: Williams & Northgate, 1912.

Wallace, A. R. *The Malay archipelago.* New York: Dover, 1962. (An unabridged republication of the last revised edition of the work first published in 1869 by Macmillan and Company, London.)

Warden, C. J., Jenkins, T. N., & Warner, L. H. *Introduction to comparative psychology.* New York: Ronald, 1934.

Warren, J. M. Primate learning in comparative perspective. In A. M. Schrier, H. F. Harlow, & F. Stollnitz (Eds.), *Behavior of nonhuman primates: Modern research trends* (Vol. 1). New York: Academic Press, 1965.

Watson, J. B. *Behavior: An introduction to comparative psychology.* New York: Henry Holt, 1914.

Watson, J. B. *Behaviorism* (rev. ed.). New York: Norton, 1930.

Wehmer, F. Effects of prior experience with objects on maternal behaviors in the rat. *Journal of Comparative and Physiological Psychology,* 1965, 60, 294–296.

Whitman, C. O. Animal behavior. In E. B. Wilson et al., *Biological Lectures from the Marine Biological Laboratory, Wood's Hole, Massachusetts 1898,* Boston: Ginn, 1899.

Whitman, C. O. The behavior of pigeons. *Publications of the Carnegie Institution,* 1919, 257, 1–161.

Williams, G. C. *Adaptation and natural selection.* Princeton, N.J.: Princeton University Press, 1966.

Williams, D. R., & Williams, H. Auto-maintenance in the pigeon: Sustained pecking despite contingent nonreinforcement. *Journal of the Experimental Analysis of Behavior,* 1969, 12, 511–520.

Wilson, E. O. *Sociobiology: The new synthesis.* Cambridge, Mass.: Harvard University Press, 1975. (a)

Wilson, E. O. Letter to the editor. *New York Review of Books,* December 11, 1975. (b)

Wilson, E. O. Academic vigilantism and the political significance of sociobiology. *BioScience,* 1976, 26, 183, 187–190.

Wilson, E. O. *On human nature.* Cambridge, Mass.: Harvard University Press, 1978.

Wyers, E. J., et al. The sociobiological challenge to psychology: On the proposal to "cannibalize" comparative psychology. *American Psychologist,* 1980, 35, 955–979.

Wynne-Edwards, V. C. *Animal dispersion in relation to social behaviour.* Edinburgh: Oliver and Boyd, 1962.

Yerkes, R. M. Habit formation in the green crab, *Carcinus granulatus. Biological Bulletin,* 1902, 3, 241–244.

Yerkes, R. M. The instincts, habits and reactions of the frog. *Psychological Review Monograph,* 1903, 4, 579–638.

Yerkes, R. M. Space perception in tortoises. *Journal of Comparative Neurology,* 1904, 14, 17–27.

Yerkes, R. M. *The dancing mouse: A study in animal behavior.* New York: Macmillan, 1907.

III. PSYCHOLOGY AND ITS INTERSECTING DISCIPLINES

Yerkes, R. M. The intelligence of earthworms. *Journal of Animal Behavior,* 1912, 2, 332–352.

Yerkes, R. M. The heredity of savageness and wildness in rats. *Journal of Animal Behavior,* 1913, 3, 286–296.

Yerkes, R. M. *The mental life of monkeys and apes.* Boston: Holt, 1916.

Yerkes, R. M., & Bloomfield, D. Do kittens instinctively kill mice? *Psychological Bulletin,* 1910, 7, 253–263.

Yerkes, R. M., & Coburn, C. A. A study of the behavior of the pig, *Sus scrofu,* by the multiple choice method. *Journal of Animal Behavior,* 1915, 5, 185–225.

Yerkes, R. M., & Huggins, G. E. Habit formation in the crawfish, *Cambarus affinis. Psychological Review Monograph,* 1903, 4, 565–577.

Yerkes, R. M., & Yerkes, A. W. *The great apes. A study of anthropoid life.* New Haven: Yale University Press, 1929.

33

*Genes, Consciousness, and Behavior Theory**

RICHARD D. ALEXANDER

During the past two decades, a theoretical revolution has occurred in evolutionary biology. It is a revolution that concerns the generation-to-generation operation of microevolution, and therefore the interpretation of long-term cumulative changes in macroevolution. It has focused our attention on what I believe to be the most profound paradox of human existence, and on phenomena important to everyone concerned with understanding the complexity of human behavior and of the human psyche.

I will approach this topic by considering, first, some of my own personal reflections on disagreements between biologists and psychologists which have fascinated and bothered me since I took my last formal course as a doctoral student over twenty-five years ago. That was a seminar in physiological and comparative psychology taught by Donald R. Meyer at The Ohio State University. I happened to take it shortly after the appearance of Lehrman's (1953) critique of Lorenz (1950), and in a year when the mission of the seminar was to tear to shreds the arguments advanced by Niko Tinbergen (1951) in his then fairly new book *The Study of*

* I appreciate the efforts of those who involved me in the symposium associated with this volume and of Professor Koch in urging me to submit the manuscript. I note that several passages in this paper have been taken with minor changes from my 1979 and 1981 papers and my 1979 book, all published since the APA symposium.

Instinct. In the middle of that same term I had the privilege of hosting T. C. Schneirla while he talked to the entomologists about the behavior of army ants and to the psychologists about the ontogeny of emotions in higher mammals. So I received a sudden and powerful dose of the controversy and excitement in the hybrid arena between biology and psychology during the heyday of what is sometimes called "European ethology." I was made aware that the central questions in this controversy have always involved the ontogeny of behavior. My presentation here is developed with this fact in mind. Let me now describe some thoughts I have had since then about the history of disagreements between our two disciplines.

Differences between Psychology and Biology

First, it seems to me that only the most general discoveries in biology, especially in regard to theory, are likely to attract much attention within psychology. But general biological theory is always evolutionary, and evolutionary theory is about genetic changes. For this reason, it is always easy for social scientists to believe that any new theory about behavior from biology is just another effort to reintroduce genes, probably in an unsupportable way or for ideological reasons rather than scientific ones, or to revive the tired old dichotomies of inherited and acquired, innate (or instinctive) and learned, genetic and environmental. These practices usually have a negative effect on psychologists who, unlike biologists, concentrate on the effects of the environment on ontogenies, not on the effects of genes. Moreover, most psychological theory is about the effects of changes or variations in the environment, while evolutionists most often generalize the environment rather than particularize it and therefore talk about its stable components. Evolutionists may talk about whether environments are certain or uncertain, predictable or unpredictable— things that general—and they often are satisfied to discuss the environments of whole species. Psychologists are interested in environmental variations, not merely in the lives of different individuals within a species but variations occurring within an individual's lifetime as well. These are just differences between the two sciences. They are not good or bad, but they sometimes reduce our ability to communicate.

Precisely unlike psychologists, evolutionists also tend to put ontogenies aside, and they do so for two reasons. First, evolutionists generalize most about the adaptive (reproductive) significance of phenotypes, while the ontogenies underlying adaptive phenotypes (traits) tend to be particular, not general, and may even be unique to the individual. Second, evolutionists presumably always know that there is an ontogeny behind any behavior, and they assume that all ontogenies have been appropriately shaped by natural selection. In studying adaptations, therefore, they feel justified in delaying attention to ontogenies. Psychologists, on the other hand, who focus on ontogenies and on their variations because the question of human individuality lies at the heart of their science must feel that this is putting aside all that is interesting, and their suspicions that we biologists are all genetic determinists are further reinforced.

Evolutionists may make a prediction about sex ratios in broods of offspring or about altruism to relatives. Then they check to see if sex ratios or altruism come out that way. They don't worry—at first—about what developmental experiences or physiological events underlie the attribute that interests them. And they only use ontogenies to put limits on their arguments when it seems that no proximate mechanism could reasonably exist that would explain a postulated trait or function. For example, while serving on a doctoral committee recently, I learned that silver maple trees often behave as females for a few years when very young and then later turn entirely to being males. When I first heard this I suggested that perhaps they reverse their sex if males are scarce, and therefore reproductively valuable, in their particular vicinity. Immediately a botanist responded: how could a tree possibly measure the sex ratio in its vicinity? Somehow I had the gumption to suggest that it might do so by being a female for a while and reacting to the proportion of its ova that are fertilized year after year. The important point, however, is not that I happened to come up with an hypothesis that satisfied the botanist temporarily, but that I was acting like an evolutionary biologist while the botanist was acting more like a social scientist. I wanted to hypothesize a particular evolutionary or adaptive function; he was demanding that I describe a reasonable proximate mechanism before continuing.[1]

A final note on sources of disagreements between us: I think that biologists often use terms like "innate" intending only to emphasize that they are temporarily bypassing the question of ontogeny, or they use it for behaviors with cryptic ontogenies. But it sounds as though they mean the behavior has no ontogeny. When such biologists are challenged by psychologists either to defend concepts like innate or to explain what their theories mean for particular ontogenetic questions, a curious thing happens: many biologists actually seem to become genetic determinists in the course of defending themselves against social scientists' criticisms of their ignoring of ontogenies. To say that maybe a certain percentage of human behavior is genetic, that incest avoidance is an instinct based on genes, or that a birdsong may

[1] It is important that I have used the word *hypothesis* here. Those who criticize the approach of evolutionary biologists or all those who look for the adaptive significance of traits sometimes refer to such predictive statements as "stories," "just-so stories," or "conclusions." To view them as conclusions on the basis of the anecdotal, nonsystematically gathered, or even unconsciously acquired knowledge that led to their formulation is obviously circular, unscientific, and inadmissible. On the other hand, it would be surprising if some proponents of the evolutionary approach did not make this mistake. What is more surprising, however, is that reputable scientists attempt to discredit an entire discipline by parading such mistakes as typical and using them to play upon the sympathies of those for whom the evolutionary approach, especially to human behavior, is still alien and difficult, rather than by using the best examples from evolutionary biology to show how that discipline can help advance our knowledge of ourselves.

be completely inherited with no learning involved are all examples from the recent literature (see discussion by Alexander, 1979b).

Survival of the Fittest What?

With these remarks I will turn to another area of communicative failure between biologists and social scientists. Hamilton (1970) noted that we had still not discovered what it is that organic evolution by natural selection maximizes. Darwin never explicitly addressed this question. If we could resurrect him long enough to ask about it, we might put the question to him as simply: survival of the fittest *what?* For anyone who accepts organic evolution as the underlying process responsible for life and its traits, this is a central question. I think, however, that unless Darwin had somehow acquired knowledge since he died he could not answer it, and for a reason that is completely understandable. Let me explain by considering briefly the possible answers.

First, we talk and think a great deal about our own personal survival as individuals. We like to think it is (or we wish it were) our own survival that is at stake in the great race of life, and our view of the medical profession and our support of it implies that this is indeed our view of life. If that is what evolution is all about, however, it has been a colossal failure, for of all the units in the hierarchy of organization of life, the individual is just about the shortest lived; moreover, individuals in most species are very short-lived compared to the longest-lived in a few species. Scarcely anyone is challenging redwoods and bristlecone pines for life length. The skew is in the wrong direction. Whatever individuals may have evolved to do—and I happen to believe that there are few questions more worth asking— they have not evolved to survive.

Families, social groups, populations, and species all last longer than individuals do. But neither can they be described as having evolved to survive, even though biologists were fooled for a long time on this point. For one thing, all of these units change continually: they don't reproduce themselves accurately or precisely, and that's one way of failing to survive. More importantly, there is a continually growing body of evidence backed by solid theory indicating that at least in general the attributes of living things simply are not there because they perpetuate the species or the group, or even because they perpetuate the family per se, even if they do so incidentally. In other words, the mechanisms of evolution clearly do not favor the survival of species or populations as such. I realize that not all readers will be familiar with the evidence behind this conclusion against what has been called group selection, but it has been around for more than a decade now, beginning with Williams (1966), and it has been widely discussed. I have reviewed the evidence elsewhere (Alexander, 1979a; Alexander & Borgia, 1978). Recent works arguing that group selection does occur (e.g., Wilson, 1980; Wade, 1976) only support its lack of generality by revealing the narrow conditions under which it can be effective. Here I wish to discuss the meaning for psychologists of the conclusion in biology that group selection is not a general explanation for the existence and nature of traits. What effect of selection is such a general explanation?

Because individuals do not survive, and groups do not now appear as appropriate targets for "survival of the fittest," Darwin only had one other unit in the hierarchical organization of life to which he could turn to answer the question we would put to him, and that is traits. In some sense he knew this. For example, consider how he explained the trait of sterility in social insects. First he noted that traits may be carried by individuals that never express them, and if the expression of those traits, when it does occur, contributes to the reproduction of family members who are not expressing the traits but nevertheless carrying them, then the traits themselves, he said, can spread, or as he put it, be "advanced by natural selection." In 1859 Darwin explained it this way: "A breed of cattle always yielding oxen [castrates] with extraordinarily long horns, could be slowly formed by carefully watching which individual bulls and cows, when matched, produced oxen with the longest horns; and yet no one ox could ever have propagated its kind." Similarly, he noted that tasty vegetables could be produced by saving seeds from relatives of the vegetables tasted or eaten, therefore unable themselves to produce seeds, and that cattle with "the flesh and fat . . . well marbled together" could be bred although "the animal has been slaughtered" if "the breeder goes . . . to the same family."

This analysis was almost unbelievably prescient, clearly anticipating the refinements of evolutionary theory that we modern biologists are only belatedly beginning to understand and use.

But we still haven't answered the original question. It cannot be traits as such that have evolved to survive either, and we can use Darwin's own argument to prove it. In his argument, sterility in the social insects would have been facultative from the start, and it remains so today; so it was the potential to be sterile or not that spread and survived. Perhaps it is always, in some sense, the ability or potential to have one or another of two or more alternative traits that tends to survive longer and longer. Such abilities or potentials necessarily derive from the possession of genes. Indeed, that is almost a definition of gene: a heritable potential to produce certain traits in certain environments. So the answer to our rude question to Darwin is that what selection maximizes is the survival of the fittest genes, and the reason he could never know the answer is that for reasons we cannot reconstruct he didn't get around to understanding Gregor Mendel's contemporary studies of sweet peas. Apparently Darwin never knew a thing about genes, although he came very close to describing them in his argument about the evolution of sterility in the social insects.

Genes that survive for long periods—and there are probably many that have been around for billions of years—do so by reproducing or copying themselves exactly, and they yield not traits but potentials for different traits. They reproduce themselves exactly inside localized buffering environments that continually adjust to the rest of the environment (that remains) outside them. Some of these local environ-

787

ments of genes have developed the ability to generalize about all such local environments, and, communicating among themselves, they have agreed on the label "phenotype" to describe such local environments, including themselves. These intelligent, reflective, analytical, local gene environments are called by themselves "humans."

The genes that survive the longest must be the ones whose potential as expressed in traits can match the environment for the longest periods—in other words, those that can best generalize the environment. One way of "generalizing" the environment is to use predictive contingencies or signs within it to modify yourself to meet its variations. Of course we call that "learning." And the potential for traits—even for the trait of learning—resides in the genes of the evolutionist.

Like a good evolutionary biologist, I have reintroduced genes. But, I have introduced them to account for learning. And I mean it just that way—that at one level the existence of certain genes is the only way to explain the existence of learning. It is unfortunate that the kinds of genes I am talking about—those postulated to account for learning—are simultaneously the kind most likely to underlie behavior, as opposed to morphology or physiology (because they are concerned with plasticity), and those most concealed from our analytical efforts. They are the genes least likely to be exposed to our view, again because the variations in the phenotypes they produce are triggered by environmental differences. Sometimes it is not easy to realize that genes are saved because they yield particular phenotypes in two or more particular and recurring environments; but I will venture that this is the rule and that the other kinds of cases, more obvious and better known to us, will turn out to be the exceptions that require special explanations. It is from these circumstances that the unbelievably complex and protracted arguments over heritability derive (e.g., Feldman & Lewontin, 1975); we ought not to allow them to obscure the real issues.

Before this decade no philosopher, no social or biological scientist—not Darwin or Freud or Marx or any of the rest—could have known that we people are, in terms of history, just complicated local gene environments—or genetic replicator vehicles, as Dawkins (1977) has put it. In my view it is the most profound paradox of human existence that throughout the entire evolutionary elaboration of the traits that now enable us to talk or think about genes (consciousness and self-awareness), the tiny objects that underlie it all remained totally outside the range of our senses. This has to mean that, without formal biological training, we could not know what we are really doing in our day-to-day activities and endeavors or what they represent. Whatever we have thought we were doing is either some substitute, as close as possible to being an accurate reflection of "maximizing the likelihood of survival of our genes," or else a matter of self-deception.

For the first time—because we do now know about genes and know their mission (a missing link, so to speak, in our self-understanding)—we are in a position to ask intelligently whether or not it is possible to generalize about what people are doing minute by minute, hour by hour, lifetime by lifetime in their everyday existences. For the first time we have a way to proceed in analyzing conflicts of interest at every level of human social organization, and we know that to be accurate and useful these analyses must be driven right down to the level of the gene. For the first time we can understand that human beings seem to be group-altruists partly because throughout history their associates have carried some of their genes (and partly because the group was otherwise useful to their own reproductive success) and individually selfish because throughout history individuals have carried individualized, unique sets of genes. For the first time we may be able to do more than guess or flounder about with respect to things like the significance of free will, self-awareness, self-deception, introspection, dreams, conscience, the subconscious, and morality.

Inclusive-Fitness-Maximizing

Now let me turn more explicitly to the question: what are human beings really doing? There is just one way to replicate genes that are invariably carried in phenotypes and that is to produce and help other replicators (phenotypes) who carry the same genes. We knew that all the time. There is a twist to it, however, that we never understood from the arguments of Darwin (1859/1967, 1871), Fisher (1930/1958), and Haldane (1932/1966) until William D. Hamilton (1964) explained and applied it: we can help both descendant and nondescendant relatives. For a species in which individuals never interact with anyone but mates and offspring, this frill is irrelevant. For an organism like a human being, in which throughout history individuals tend to interact consistently with a horde of different relatives, scarcely any fact could be a more important clue to understanding its sociality and the development of each individual's social tendencies.

Hamilton called helping all genetic relatives in the way that maximizes survival of one's genes "inclusive-fitness-maximizing." I will use that term from now on.

The theoretical and philosophical significance of the facts that I have just reviewed seems to me as profound as that of Darwin's original development of the theory of evolution, and the most important advance in human knowledge of the twentieth century. Anyone who cannot accept that must somehow deny or trivialize the proposition that what people are doing from hour to hour, day to day, lifetime to lifetime is carrying out activities that, not necessarily in current environments but in terms of our long-term history, represent inclusive-fitness-maximizing. We are doing those things that, if we had not rapidly and radically modified our environment, would actually be enabling and promoting the survival of our genes. To me that notion represents a monumental shortcut—one of unparalleled potential—for all students of human behavior.

Our history of ignorance about genes must be one of the reasons for feeling that

789

we must deny that we have evolved to be vehicles of genic reproduction. But I think there is another fascinating reason for such denials. To introduce a person to genes as the objects that underlie his or her whole behavior is to make genes into the very phenomena that I suspect we are most powerfully evolved to resist in our social behavior: foreign entities who, precisely for the reason that we think of them as foreign, will not be expected to even know about, let alone share, our interests. Entities of that sort usually represent hostile forces. We are in effect xenophobic toward our own genes because and to the extent that they are anthropomorphized (one is tempted to speak of genophobia!). We can be sure that the whole phenomenon of evolutionary self-analysis is a trait wholly unanticipated during the evolutionary organization of genomes. Self-analysis is, in effect, an environment of development created accidentally by the genes, and not necessarily conducive to their long-term survival, but with enormous potential for determining what humans may become.

In some sense this aspect of self-awareness may be the biggest change in an environment of a living thing since life began, for that is what knowledge of the mission of our genes really is: a change in our environment of behavioral development and expression. In part it represents a giant step toward closing the feedback loop between need (or desire) and novelty in evolutionary change, a causal connection which organic evolution has never otherwise managed. Unlike cultural innovations, genetic novelties do not appear because the organism needs them, or in the form needed. But humans are now well on the road to accomplishing this connection for genetic as well as cultural change.

Biologists view the lifetimes of organisms as "effort" (expenditure of energy and taking of risks), and they divide this effort into two general categories: somatic effort and reproductive effort. Somatic effort is that used to build the soma toward later or better possibilities of reproduction. Reproductive effort can be divided into two categories: mating effort and nepotistic effort. Mating effort amounts to beneficence toward one's gametes. Nepotistic effort can in turn be divided into parental effort, or beneficence toward one's offspring, and extraparental nepotistic effort or beneficence toward one's nondescendant relatives (Low, 1978; Alexander & Borgia, 1978).

In terms of sociality the part of effort that concerns us is parental and extraparental nepotistic effort. Elsewhere I have divided nepotism (beneficence toward relatives) into two general kinds: discriminative and nondiscriminative (Alexander, 1977, 1979a). Nondiscriminative nepotism refers to beneficence offered indiscriminately to one's associates or contacts. In my view it is an unlikely kind of behavior in an organism capable of distinguishing relatives of differing degrees and differing needs except when powerful external threats tend to synonymize individual interests. Therefore I assume that discriminative nepotism, including parental behavior—or its surrogates in changed environments—represents the basic or essential element in human sociality. (One can also speak of direct and indirect nepotism—

the latter being sometimes termed reciprocity [Trivers, 1971]—and of discriminative and nondiscriminative reciprocity.)

I assume that identifying the immediate or proximate mechanisms by which discriminative nepotism develops in the individual constitutes a major or central problem of psychology. To say it another way, I assume that it will be useful to psychologists to view the world of human sociality as an enormously complex system of discriminative nepotism and to view the ontogeny of social behavior as patterned toward achievement of maximal reproduction via nepotism, at least in terms of the environments of history. In other words, I am predicting that theories of social learning will someday be explicit efforts to understand discriminative altruism of both nepotistic and reciprocal sorts.

To maximize the effectiveness of discriminative nepotism, the individual requires three kinds of information about potential recipients of its nepotism: the degree of relatedness, the need of the individual (more properly its ability to turn beneficence into reproductive success), and the available alternative uses of any resources that it might invest.

Figure 33.1 is a diagram of the set of genetic relatives potentially associated with a given human individual. Mates are not included, nor are in-laws and other relatives by marriage, although it is possible to quantify one's expected relationship or reactions to them.

Mechanisms of Kin Regulation

Given an ability to evaluate the relative needs of different individuals, this diagram amounts to a blueprint for inclusive-fitness-maximizing. If one does know all of these relatives and is keenly aware of their needs, then he or she is in a position to maximize the effectiveness of reproductive effort via nepotism (in its general sense of beneficence to relatives). It is indisputable that we know who our relatives are: anthropology has proved that for every society it has studied. With regard to ontogenies, we may ask how it is, in fact, that we do know who our actual relatives are. Anyone can fill in actual names of relatives on a diagram of the sort in Figure 33.1, usually out to first cousins or beyond (e.g., Schneider & Cottrell, 1975) unless one's family is extremely large or unusual, or unless, in this modern mobile technological society, one has been geographically divorced from them—a situation quite unlike that in which humans have lived throughout history. I am particularly interested in the problem of modeling the ontogeny of nepotism because it seems to me that this is the only way to bring our two disciplines into accord on the important topics of how to understand the life activities and motivations of humans and how to interpret social learning.

I think it is obvious to all of us that we know who the different relatives are in our various families as a consequence of learning experiences that are often entirely conscious. We know that our parents told us who some of these relatives are. We

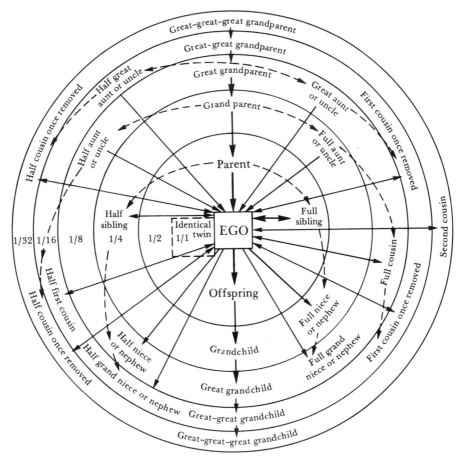

Figure 33.1 Genetic relatives potentially available to an individual, Ego, for reproductively self-serving nepotism. Arrows indicate likely net flows of benefits. Half the genes of parent and offspring are identical by immediate descent. Other relationships are averages. Dotted lines indicate closer relatives other than Ego, of Ego's relatives, thus the most likely alternative sources of nepotistic benefits. Widths of lines indicate likely relative flows of benefits to or from Ego based on the combination of genetic relatedness and ability of recipients to use the benefits in reproduction. Extreme lateral relatives are less likely to be encountered or identified because of social or geographic distance, extreme vertical relatives because of temporal nonoverlap. Double-headed arrows indicate relatives whose statuses in regard to need of benefits or ability to use them to reproduce and ability to give benefits are doubtful owing to the uncertainty of age relationships of the individuals involved. (Thus one's second cousin may be much younger, much older, or about the same age; one's sibling, on the other hand, is much more likely to be of comparable age.) Relatives on the right side of the diagram are those resulting from monogamous marriages; polygyny results in relatives indicated on the left. I argue here that natural selection would save genetic materials leading to behavioral

792

know that our understanding of the identity of siblings and parents and some close relatives has built up through extensive and intimate association across years and decades. On the other hand, some of the learning experiences involved are not conscious—or do not remain so—even if the individuals responsible for causing them do indeed remember them: a parent may recall introducing his child to particular relatives even if the child itself has forgotten.

To use an aside briefly, it has been shown—conclusively, I think—that not only in human but in nonhuman mammals as well, avoidance of sexual relations with close relatives is also a consequence of learning, of intimate social interactions or associations that occur when one or both individuals are prereproductive. In humans this aspect of the association is not necessarily conscious. How many individuals know why they are not interested sexually in their siblings? How many know the laws in detail with regard to incest? How many have even a faint notion of the actual disadvantages of sexual interactions with very close relatives? Yet we avoid those relationships rather consistently, and we know now that we do it as a result of learning experiences—learning experiences that are not for the most part conscious, or not remembered (or even well enough understood to be reliably reconstructed).

I think that much of the informational background of nepotism is much more conscious than is that of incest avoidance. It seems to me that genealogical connections—their length and directness—constitute the principal means by which individuals are apprised of and remember their obligations to relatives. These genealogical relationships are learned. Their significance is learned. Humans do not have a history of knowing what their actual genetic relatedness is, but they do have a keen understanding of closer versus more distant relatives, and in the end that amounts to the same thing. In this connection it is interesting that to count genealogical links and halve the relationship with each additional link—which is precisely what courts of law and churches do in assessing matters like inheritance—is an accurate method of determining fractional relationships in order to put numbers in Hamilton's original formula for maximizing inclusive fitness.

I believe that when social learning is approached as essentially a problem in

---

tendencies (such as learning biases) that in usual social situations promote the assisting of closer relatives over more distant ones, and of more needy relatives among those able to convert assistance into reproduction. Recognition of relatives (except a mother's recognition of her offspring born while she is conscious and observing) most often (at least) occurs as a result of social learning and circumstantial evidence. Numbers and kinds of social interactions (and not some kind of innate kin-recognition mechanism) are likely to be the sources of the cues for behaving socially in reproductively appropriate fashions. How such cues are used in households of different structures in different societies and how social learning is structured as an evolved mechanism of adaptive nepotism are problems that remain to be elucidated. (From Alexander, 1977.)

understanding inclusive-fitness-maximizing through nepotism, evolved in certain kinds of environments that have been variously modified, sometimes with extreme rapidity, many clarifications will occur, with respect to not only patterns of human social behavior but learning itself as a general phenomenon.

Social learning may seem like an adequate mechanism for much of nepotism— much of human sociality—but the question remains whether or not other mechanisms also exist. The biologists who have become excited about the central significance of nepotism in recent years have all been through periods of wondering whether or not mechanisms other than social learning might be involved. I do not believe so, and I would like to present the reasons very briefly (see also Alexander, 1977, 1979a).

First, one might suppose that individual genes would be able to cause their phenotypes to search the phenotypes of other individuals for evidence of their presence or absence in the other genome and then cause the phenotype to act appropriately (Hamilton, 1964). This is a lot of activity for one gene to cause. Leaving that aside, I regard such a mechanism as extremely unlikely on other grounds. Any such gene would continually be serving its own presence in potential recipients of nepotism, and any mutant that suppressed its effect would help itself and everyone else in the genome by that action and would spread on that account. I am saying that "outlaw" genes that help only themselves in nepotism cannot persist (Alexander & Borgia, 1978; Alexander, 1979a). Instead, one expects that the genes in a group as cooperative as a modern genome has to be to produce a successful phenotype will surely be served approximately equally by the actions of the individual genes comprising them, and the only way this can be accomplished is for the genome to act as a whole, through the phenotype, on the basis of each gene's probability of being in a genome that is available for assistance. The way this can be accomplished is through considering whether the relative falls into one or another class of relatives—each class having a certain amount of genetic overlap with the potential altruist—a certain probability of carrying any individual gene. Even if we do use individual traits that are themselves closely tied to the presence of certain alleles—eye color, hair color, ear shape, or the presence of distinctive "family-wide" birthmarks or other features—to place individuals into or out of certain categories of relationship, we do so as a result of learning what the mark, feature, or trait means by seeing it in relatives already known by other means. That is merely a variant of the social-learning model I mentioned first.

Since I originally predicted (Alexander, 1977) that organisms must somehow learn who their relatives are, a number of studies have been conducted which deserve review here. Greenberg (1979) demonstrated that sweat bees learn who their sisters are during their association as young adults in the natal burrow. For several reasons, Greenberg's results have been widely misinterpreted (e.g., May & Robertson, 1980). First, Greenberg used the phrase "innate recognition mechanism" in his title, although he was actually referring to genetically determined differences (presumably in chemicals) used by the bees to recognize one another. Second, Greenberg's note that he reared the bees in individual isolation has been mistaken by some biologists to mean that there was no learning opportunity; but sweat bees always develop isolated in their own earthen cells and learn as young adults whom to accept while guarding the burrow entrance. Third, Greenberg showed that sisters can be recognized as such even though they have never previously been encountered, apparently by comparisons of their chemicals with those of sisters encountered. Finally, it is my feeling that for some biologists the whole notion of "kin selection" loses its flavor if there are no "innate mechanisms" of kin recognition and they see such mechanisms wherever they look.

May and Robertson (1980) reported, apparently with inadvertent correctness, that a mechanism "exactly analogous" to that shown by Greenberg in sweat bees "was reported by K. E. Linsenmaier . . . in a desert-dwelling social isopod." They did not give the reference, but probably referred to a 1972 study in which juvenile woodlice also learn to recognize their parents, and parents their offspring, by association, perhaps using specific chemicals which vary with genetic variation. May and Robertson then asserted that in a third study "Waldman's and Adler's [1979] evidence for kin recognition in frogs [it actually involved toads in the genus *Bufo*] . . . does not distinguish between innate and environmental mechanisms. . . ." This is correct, but they fail to remark that the tadpoles associated in sibling groups before they were mixed and shown to re-aggregate as siblings. It is clear, then, that appropriate learning situations were available. Waldman (1981) has now shown that isolated tadpoles also recognize maternal half-siblings but not paternal half-siblings, indicating that some stimulus provided by the mother, perhaps in the jelly-like milieu of the egg mass, is the critical learning vehicle. Buckle and Greenberg (1981) have shown that sweat bees use other individuals with whom they associate, but not themselves, to learn the attributes of relatives.

The only recent publication with data implying that appropriate situations for learning to recognize relatives are not available seems to be that of Wu et al. (1980) dealing with recognition of paternal half-siblings by infant macaques. These babies were removed from their anesthetized mothers within five minutes after birth, kept in individual wire cages in a room (7.6 m × 11.0 m) housing fifty other macaques, "such that they had no opportunity for visual, physical or olfactory interactions with relatives or any other animals used in the experiments," and allowed play time each day only with four to six nonrelatives. Auditory cues and learning from their own personal attributes were not excluded as possibilities, and no proximate mechanism for the apparent recognition was postulated. Such studies are vulnerable, on the question of innate (versus learned) recognition of relatives, because, like all isolation studies, they depend upon the exclusion of all relevant aspects of the environment rather than the positive demonstration of a particular mechanism, as is possible with studies showing that learning occurs. Merely to identify a possible relevant variable not explicitly eliminated requires that the study be repeated to be useful.

795

Such studies are also problematical because no likely innate mechanism for differentially recognizing relatives, or relatives of different degree, seems ever to have been proposed. The mechanisms suggested so far can be criticized because they involve either unprecedentedly complex activities by single genes or the likelihood of conflict within the genome that could thwart their evolution (see Alexander, 1979a, pp. 103ff).

May and Robertson were probably misled by the demonstration by Greenberg that genetic differences among sweat bees cause the differences (probably in chemicals) that are learned by other bees, enabling differential treatment. But the mechanism Greenberg demonstrated is by no means new: human beings use it all the time. They learn what individuals of their own or other families look like, and then they use those features to remember old individuals and place new ones into the right groups. Every time humans use a heritable physical difference to guess at relationships between humans, they are doing precisely what the sweat bees do (e.g., "Judging by the shape of your nose, I would say you are a Durante"; "That family is from Japan"; "The baby looks just like his father"). That May and Robertson were indeed confused is shown by their remark, "It is not yet known whether vertebrates have similar innate abilities."

It is possible to argue about the definition of innateness. Wilson (1975) defined it so as to include learning (for a comment, see Alexander, 1979b), and another biologist with whom I discussed this problem remarked that he would regard a learning event as "more innate" if it occurred earlier in life. Perhaps, in some sense, this would make it more "inborn." But the more common usage is to oppose innateness and learning, as May and Robertson clearly did. If such opposition of the two concepts eliminates the possibility of proximate mechanisms of particular forms of social behavior alternative to learning, then so be it. It is unfortunate that so many biologists and nonbiologists alike continue to suppose that there must be such alternatives to learning without carefully exploring what would be involved. Until a reasonable model is proposed, or, even better, a mechanism actually demonstrated, it is appropriate to be skeptical about the entire concept of innate recognition of kin. If animals like bees, sowbugs, and tadpoles learn who their kin are, it seems likely that those who argue that various kinds of social learning will prove to be the only vehicle of kin recognition are correct. I predict that the results of Greenberg and Buckle will prove to be general, and that other studies will be planned to test for the same possibilities. Particularly interesting are the questions (1) whether one's own attributes are used in assessing classes to which putative relatives may belong, (2) whether individual relatives not previously encountered are accepted, (3) what kinds of stimuli used in kin recognition, (4) what sex differences in kin recognition correlate with social difference, and (5) how many classes of different relatives are regularly distinguished by the different possible means. In this connection, a particularly interesting—and surprising—finding is that of Sherman (personal communication) that females (but not males) of Belding's ground squirrels seem able to distinguish maternal full- and half-siblings within their own litter.[2]

Learning studies demonstrate mechanisms; studies of innateness typically seek to demonstrate absence of mechanisms (learning). In view of the apparent difficulties in postulating mechanisms not involving learning, and the results with arthropods and lower vertebrates, it seems appropriate to be skeptical about the entire concept of innate recognition of kin. Indeed, Greenberg (personal communication) has pointed out that the word *innate* is inappropriately used to modify *recognition* unless recognition is used not in the usual sense of "previously known" but according to secondary meanings like "to acknowledge, or take notice of."[3]

I conclude that terms like *instinctive* and *innate* and *genetic* might as well be abandoned in considering why and how patterns of discriminative nepotistic assistance arise in social groups of humans. The only thing that is inherited or innate or instinctive is the genes themselves, not the behavior or any other aspect of the phenotype that develops in one or another environment. Moreover, the ontogenetic mechanisms of nepotism are, at least in some large part, ordinary learning phenomena. I believe that a thorough exploration of all this will represent an investigative aid to psychologists of immeasurable importance. I do not deny that one can get along without it, but I would hate to try to ignore all of these things and have to compete with other investigators who understand them well and are continually taking into account how they could assist in their investigations. I would not suppose that any other point need be stressed in this regard.

Past and Future

It should be obvious that several differences exist between the approach of modern evolutionary biologists and that of the ethologists of two or three decades ago: (1) recognition of the importance of understanding the levels at which selection is generally effective, causing an avoidance of the concept of altruism in the context of group selection (as with, for example, Lorenz's notion of forbearance in contests between conspecifics in the interest of preserving the species); (2) an avoidance of

---

[2] For an excellent update of known mechanisms of kin recognition, see Holmes and Sherman, 1983.

[3] Unless one uses a peculiar and rationalizing definition of *innate*, progress toward a demonstration of innateness amounts to a demonstration of the absence of ontogenetic influences, or of an ontogeny. To demonstrate learning, on the other hand, is to show that particular stimuli influence ontogeny. Because of this difference, the usual dichotomy with respect to observed behaviors is not between learned and innate but between behaviors for which some ontogenetic stimuli are known and others for which none is known. To some extent this always means that the ontogeny of the behavior that is termed *innate* is to some extent (or may be) cryptic or hidden. Since it is premature to call all such behaviors innate, I suggest that a new term is needed for behaviors with cryptic ontogenies, and I suggest *cryptonate*, meaning that the origin, its birth, or development of the behavior is difficult to trace.

the dichotomy of innate and acquired (except for some writing of a few sociobiologists; see discussion by Alexander, 1979b); and (3) a keener analytical capability in respect to altruism, egoism, behavioral development, and the functions of learning.

What is likely to happen in the near future in respect to the hybrid discipline lying between the social sciences and evolutionary biology? I have already suggested that efforts will continue in the analysis of the ontogenetic mechanisms of nepotism and of culture in terms of a history of inclusive-fitness-maximizing. I think that increasing attention will be paid to the problem of understanding why social life sometimes, but not always, evolves toward ever greater complexity, and specifically to elucidating the forces that guided the evolution of human traits and human sociality. I believe that great strides will be made in developing the study of communication, and that the entire branch of philosophy concerned with social issues like morality and ethics will be literally transformed—much of it into a science—by incorporation of the principles now evident from evolutionary biology.

Free Will and Individual Interests

Finally, I shall comment briefly on one of the topics I mentioned earlier: free will— a concept that many feel is antithetical to any biological theory of human behavior. Because of my impression that this kind of feeling underlies much of the resistance to biological-evolutionary interpretations of human tendencies, and because I regard it as an unwarranted pessimism, I think it is useful to show that reasonable and testable hypotheses can be generated about the biological nature and function of what we call "free will." There is not much new in what I am about to say, and it is in no way a comprehensive treatment of the subject; but I do not think we have to rely any more on our intuitions alone to decide whether we like our arguments, as I believe has been necessary for such arguments in the past.

An integral aspect of consciousness is the phenomenon of self-awareness, and self-awareness, in turn, at least partly involves what Robert Burns called seeing ourselves as others see us. To a biologist—probably to almost anyone at all—this aspect of self-awareness is easily seen as crucial to success in social matters; in turn, biological reproductive success—the focus of the evolutionary biologists' interest— depends upon social success.

In some large part our conscious awareness of ourselves and our social circumstances is taken up with what might be called social "scenario-building." Almost continually we play out in our minds the possible and probable moves in the game of social living, which of course is not a game at all but the real thing. How can I write this paper (deliver this lecture, study for this examination, approach this policeman or judge or merchant or bully or friend) so as to achieve this or that personal goal? What will he or she do if I do this or that? What action by me will most likely cause my desired ends to be achieved? If I do this, and he does that, and then I do something else, then what? And so on and so forth.

In such scenario-building we seem to see before us alternatives. We actually perceive beforehand—through a marshaling of all the information available to us from the past and present—possible choices that we can make. We assume that we can make any one of those choices that we wish to. We evaluate them, and we apparently make whichever one we decide is best (or preferred or whatever). We cherish the right to make the decision ourselves, on our own bases, and the additional right to keep the reasons private, and not even to review them consciously if we do not wish to.

This projecting and weighing of possibilities, it seems to me, has the obvious correlate that the most unpredictable aspect of our environment is the sets of other social individuals and collectives with which we must interact. They too are building scenarios.

I suggest that free will amounts to the right to build our own scenarios and act on them for our own reasons without having to justify them—in other words, that free will involves nothing in particular about the causes of our behavior except our right to determine them, to weigh costs and benefits in our own terms.

To the extent that this is correct, the problem of understanding free will resolves to that of understanding the bases on which we make our judgments of possible alternatives and why we cherish the right to be personal, private, and individual about such judgments.

The only background I can imagine for a compulsive adherence to such a privilege by every different individual—and at the same time a compelling one in biological terms—is that, throughout evolutionary history, reproductive individuals have been genetically unique.

This means that, in biological terms, the right to make our own personal decisions about our own futures is the ultimately precious possession of individual humans. Even if societal rules and obligations actually place enormous restrictions on this privilege, we strive for the right to apply and interpret these restrictions, as they affect us, by and for ourselves.

I offer the hypothesis that decisions of free will—judged in terms of the environments of history—will tend to be those which maximize our inclusive fitnesses, that we have evolved to be exceptionally good at such decisions, and that this is the precise reason for the existence and nature of consciousness and self-awareness.

I would like to finish by drawing my wild speculation about social scenario-building, or individual social planning, out to its limits—or perhaps well beyond its limits—by suggesting a possible connection between science and the humanities. A sort of no-man's land has always existed between these two arenas of human endeavor, with each proudly disdaining the other in selected regards. As a columnist in the *Ann Arbor News* put it recently, harking back to her college days with respect to her fellow students who went into science, "It just seemed as though they went their way and we went ours."

Scientific studies seek generalizations—kinds of understanding that immediately have the same kind of applicability to large numbers of people. A scientist's discoveries, and therefore fame and fortune, are predicted on the generality of his or her conclusions. In some sense the same is true of a novel or a play or a poem: Shakespeare, after all, lasts because we know deep down in our souls that he understood us—which means that he understood general human nature in a very special way. But there is a difference, and I have wondered if the difference is not in part that we tend to a much greater extent to use those experiences and discoveries that come from the humanities as theater—or, if you will, as condensed scenarios—in terms of our own personal social existences. We use them as experiences that we as individuals can turn to our own advantage by applying their lessons to our own unique existences in our own unique fashions. To some extent this is true of science, but not nearly so much so. Perhaps we are talking here about the romanticism that is widely acknowledged in some realms, and absent—for most— in some others. Science may be romantic for the scientist whose existence—and success or failure—is wrapped up in it, but it is much less so for the ordinary person than is a poem or a deeply moving drama.

Perhaps I can complete this thought appropriately by quoting the social anthropologist Anthony F. C. Wallace (1961) in a statement that seems to me to be entirely consistent with the new evolutionary view of human nature and human activities. It is appropriate that I should be quoting an anthropologist, since anthropology is a discipline that now and then undergoes some formal strife in its annual meeting over whether it wishes to call itself a science or an aspect of the humanities. Wallace wrote as follows:

> The humanist—the poet, the novelist, the dramatist, the historian—has tended to approach . . . with a sense of tragedy (or humor) . . . the paradox, so apparent to him, that despite the continuing existence of culture and the group, the individual is always alone in his motivation, moving in a charmed circle of feelings and perceptions which he cannot completely share with any other human being. This awareness of the limits of human communication, of the impossibility, despite all the labor of God, Freud, and the Devil, of one man fully understanding another, of the loneliness of existence, is not confined to any cult of writers; it is a pan-human theme.

As an evolutionary biologist, all I feel like saying in response to that statement is *yes*. With our individualized sets of genes, and our history of individualized interests, we humans write poetry, philosophize, pursue truth, seek adoption by surrogate kin groups, sometimes commit suicide, and travel on through history trying to decide where we should go from here, given what we seem to have found out about where we have been. A part of that finding out is the new knowledge of the extent and nature of our conflicts of interest during history, measurable only by carrying our analyses of these conflicts right down to the level of the gene.

REFERENCES

Alexander, R. D. Evolution, human behavior, and determinism. *Proceedings of the Biennial Meeting of the Philosophy of Science Association*, 1977, 2, 3–21.

Alexander, R. D. *Darwinism and human affairs*. Seattle: University of Washington Press, 1979. (a)

Alexander, R. D. Evolution, social behavior, and ethics. In T. E. Engelhardt & D. Callahan (Eds.), *The foundations of ethics and its relationship to science* (Vol. 4). Hastings-on-Hudson, N.Y.: Hastings Institute, 1979. (b)

Alexander, R. D. Evolution, culture, and human behavior: Some general considerations. In R. D. Alexander & D. W. Tinkle (Eds.), *Natural selection and social behavior: Recent research and new theory*. New York: Chiron, 1981.

Alexander, R. D., & Borgia, G. Group selection, altruism, and the levels of organization of life. *Annual Review of Ecology and Systematics*, 1978, 9, 449–474.

Buckle, G. R., & Greenberg, L. Nest-mate recognition in sweat bees: (*Lasioglossum zephyrum*): Does an individual recognize its own odor or only odors of its nestmates? *Animal Behaviour*, 1981, 29, 802–809.

Darwin, C. *On the origin of species*. A fascimile of the first edition with an introduction by Ernst Mayr. Cambridge, Mass.: Harvard University Press, 1967. (Originally published, 1859.)

Darwin, C. *The descent of man and selection in relation to sex* (2 vols.). New York: Appleton, 1871.

Dawkins, R. Replicator selection and the extended phenotype. *Zeitschrift für Tierpsychologie*, 1977, 47, 61–76.

Feldman, M. W., & Lewontin, R. C. The heritability hangup. *Science*, 1975, 190, 1163–1168.

Fisher, R. A. *The genetical theory of natural selection* (2nd ed.). New York: Dover, 1958. (Originally published, 1930.)

Greenberg, L. Genetic component of bee odor in kin recognition. *Science*, 1979, 206, 1095.

Haldane, J. B. S. *The causes of evolution*. London: Longmans, Green, 1932. (Reprinted, Ithaca, N.Y.: Cornell University Press, 1966.)

Hamilton, W. D. The genetical evolution of social behaviour, I, II. *Journal of Theoretical Biology*, 1964, 7, 1–52.

Hamilton, W. D. Ordering the phenomena of ecology. *Science* 1970, 167, 1478–1480.

Holmes, W. G., & Sherman, P. W. Kin recognition in animals. *American Scientist*, 1983, 71, 46–55.

Lehrman, D. S. A critique of Konrad Lorenz's theory of instinctive behaviour. *Quarterly Review of Biology*, 1953, 28, 337–363.

Linsenmaier, K. Die Bedeutung familienspezifischer "Abzeichen" für den Familien-Zusammenhalt bei der sozialen Wustenassel *Hemiepistus reamuri* Audovin u. Savigny (Crustacea, Isopoda, Oniscoidea). *Zeitschrift für Tierpsychologie*, 1972, 31, 131.

Lorenz, K. The comparative method in studying innate behaviour patterns. *Symposia on Social and Experimental Biology*, 1950, 4, 221–268.

Low, B. S. Environmental uncertainty and the parental strategies of marsupials and placentals. *American Naturalist*, 1978, 112, 197–213.

May, R., & Robertson, M. Just-so stories and cautionary tales. *Nature*, 1980, 286, 327.

Schneider, D. M., & Cottrell, C. B. The American kin universe: A genealogical study. University of

Chicago Department of Anthropology, *Studies in Anthropology*. Series in *Social, Cultural, and Linguistic Anthropology* (Vol. 3). Chicago: University of Chicago Press, 1975.

Tinbergen, N. *The study of instinct*. Oxford: Clarendon Press, 1951.

Trivers, R. L. The evolution of reciprocal altruism. *Quarterly Review of Biology*, 1971, 46, 35–57.

Wade, M. S. Group selection among laboratory populations of *Tribolium*. *Proceedings of the National Academy of Science*, 1976, 73, 4604–4607.

Waldman, B. Sibling recognition in toad tadpoles: The role of experience. *Zeitschrift für Tierpsychologie*, 1981, 56, 341–358.

Waldman, B., & Adler, K. Toad tadpoles associate preferentially with siblings. *Nature*, 1979, 282, 611–615.

Wallace, A. F. C. The psychic unity of human groups. In B. Kaplan (Ed.), *Studying personality cross-culturally*. New York: Harper & Row, 1961.

Williams, G. C. *Adaptation and natural selection*. Princeton, N.J.: Princeton University Press, 1966.

Wilson, D. S. *The natural selection of populations and communities*. Reading, Mass.: Benjamin/Cummings, 1980.

Wilson, E. O. *Sociobiology: The new synthesis*. Cambridge, Mass.: Harvard University Press, 1975.

Wu, K. M. H., Holmes, W. G., Medina, S. R., & Sackett, G. P. Kin preference in infant *Macaca nemestrina*. *Nature*, 1980, 285, 225.

PSYCHOLOGY AND LINGUISTICS

34

Psychology and Linguistics
THE FIRST HALF-CENTURY

ARTHUR L. BLUMENTHAL

In the last decades of the nineteenth century and early in the twentieth century, psychologists and linguists interacted through a fruitful though often combative exchange of ideas. The result of that interchange was a hybrid discipline known in the dominant German literature as *Sprachpsychologie*. The interests summarized by that term match what we now call "psycholinguistics." What remains today of that earlier psycholinguistics, or *Sprachpsychologie*, is a large body of dust-covered literature, both theoretical writings and experimental or observational reports. Most of this early work is little known today, and yet some parts of it may be relevant and even useful for present-day psycholinguistics. (See Table 34.1—"Chronological Display of References in Linquistics and Psychology of Language.")

It may be asking too much of students of the psychology of language to require that they take time to study the historical intricacies of their subject matter. After all, psycholinguists today even pause at the thought of absorbing the labyrinth of technical development in the present-day linguistic theory.

But having read some of the earlier literature myself, I am still led to the suggestion that we give it more attention.[1] And that suggestion derives from one worrisome thought: It is that one hundred years from today psycholinguists (or whatever

[1] The range of my own acquaintance with this early literature is indicated in my review, *Language and Psychology: Historical Aspects of Psycholinguistics* (New York: Wiley, 1970).

they call themselves in 2079) might have little, or only the vaguest familiarity with the names, the theories, and the accomplishments that concern us today. History offers just too many examples of that sort of lapse.

And those future scholars, as I can imagine, might well be engaged in many of the same issues that concern us today, even though it is likely that their technical jargon, perhaps even their whole working language, will be different from ours. And like some of us today, their accounts of the past may be merely a process of self-definition serving to gratify their own work or their own felt significance.

We could now set examples, for the sake of posterity, of historiographically better efforts to understand and profit from what has gone before—from earlier movements of thought that are not identified as our own (parochial) affiliations. If such examples are well set today, then perhaps our intellectual descendants will be better disposed to remember us and our time, and may not repeat our errors. And more important for our sakes, they then may not be tempted to take credit for discoveries that belong to us.

A brief consideration of the times and efforts of an earlier generation of interaction between psychology and linguistics is the goal of this paper. It is my assignment here to give a general overview of those relations for the period 1879–1929—the first half of that century of psychology with which this volume is concerned. John Carroll will examine psychology-linguistics relations in the second half of that century in the following chapter.

Anyone with access to the resources and who is able to take a serious look at the intellectual accomplishments of the nineteenth century cannot help but observe a landscape littered with linguistic theories. Linguistics then, as now, came in many forms. One that is especially identified with that century is philology—an approach to the study of languages that emphasizes cultural and historical interests. That particular form of language study went out of style, in most places, in the twentieth century; but there are signs of its impending resurrection. Other approaches to language study in the nineteenth century included the physiological study of speech, the investigation of syntax by logicians, and the study of speech sound patterns by phoneticians. And then there was the general area of *Sprachwissenschaft*, as the Germans called it, which may be taken as roughly synonymous with our newer term *linguistics*. The language specialties of a century ago were further subdivided by the cultural and philosophical traditions or theoretical biases which separated their practitioners—divisions that were about the same as those which prevail today. (Again, see Chronological Display of References.)

As for modern psychology, no matter how artificial may be the marking of the year of 1879 as its beginning, one cannot avoid noticing how its institutionalization in the late nineteenth century caught the popular fancy and received the widest notice. For example, the World Fairs that took place around the turn of the century (London, Chicago, St. Louis) presented pavilions filled with artfully displayed marvels of this new science—the dazzling brass instruments that could ostensibly

TABLE 34.1 Chronological Display of References in Linguistics and Psychology of Language (1879–1929)[a]

YEAR	LINGUISTICS		PSYCHOLOGY OF LANGUAGE		YEAR
	Structuralist tradition	Generative tradition	Mechanistic tradition	Cognitive psycholinguistics	
1879	Whitney (1875), Leskien (1876), Sievers (1876)		Geiger (1869)		1879
1880	Paul	Wundt, Miklosich	Stricker	Wundt	1880
1881			Steinthal	Preyer	1881
1882					1882
1883					1883
1884					1884
1885	Brugmann, Schuchardt	Curtius	Wegener		1885
1886				Paulhan	1886
1887		Böthlingk	Wheeler	Fournié	1887
1888					1888
1889					1889
1890	Sweet, Meyer-Lübke, Strong et al.	von der Gabelentz		Sommer, De La Grasserie	1890
1891	Byrne, Bechtel		Bourdon		1891
1892				Goldscheider & Müller	1892
1893				Binet & Henri	1893
1894	Ries	Darmesteter	Dewey	Meringer & Mayer	1894
1895	Baudouin de Courtenay, Grammont				1895
1896			Sully, Lukens	Moore, Erdmann, Jerusalem	1896
1897	Kaeding, Bréal	Svedelius	Quantz, Rousselot	Reichel	1897
1898	Stöhr		Erdmann & Dodge		1898
1899		Reckendorf	Zeitler	Ament, Franke, Gehmlich	1899
1900		Wundt	Zwaardemaker	Wundt, Bagley, Bawden	1900
1901	Delbrück, Martinak	Oertal, Morris	Thumb & Marbe, Mauthner	Croce, Ganzmann	1901

Year				
1902	Barth	Scripture	Sütterlin	
1903	Owen	Meumann, Dittrich		
1904	Mead			
1905	Lalande, Vossler	Leroy	Ravizza, Finck	
1906	Wells	Dearborn, Taylor		
1907	Stern & Stern, Rowland	Doran, Van Ginneken		
1908	Huey	Menzerath		Marty, Séchehaye
1909				Jones
1910	Wartensleben	Kent & Rosanoff		
1911		Meyer		Boas
1912			Sheffield	
1913	Stählin		Broens	Markov
1914		Watson	Bloomfield	
1915		Nice	Kramp	
1916		Woodrow & Lowell		de Saussure
1917		Schmidt		Sturtevant
1918				
1919	Bühler	Magni	Pavlovich	
1920		Buswell		Sapir, Meillet
1921				Curme, Jesperson
1922	Piaget	Gray	Brunot	Ogden & Richards
1923	Delacroix	F. Allport		Palmer
1924	Cohen	Esper, Fröschels, Jousse, Yerkes & Learned		Bartoli, Weiss
1925				
1926	Guillaume, Gvozdev, Richter	Horn, Head		
1927		De Laguna		
1928	Bühler (1934)	Markey, Pillsbury & Meader, Kantor		Hjemslev, Condon
1929		Fletcher		

aFull references appear in the Reference section.

expose one's mental capacities. Several of the young heroes of this new adventure were also exhibited on these occasions—James McKeen Cattell, Francis Galton, G. Stanley Hall, E. B. Titchener, and Hugo Münsterberg.

For a while in those earlier days this "new" psychology was, by virtue of its apparent newness, something of an inspiration in the academic community; or if not that, it at least put some neighboring disciplines on the defensive. Philology, in stark contrast, was at that time already a senior, conservative, and somewhat senile member of the academic community, having been granted its disciplinary independence generations earlier. Many old philology departments were soon to be legislated out of existence or reorganized in various universities, with the spoils of that dissolution to be divided among other newer departments (anthropology, literature, language studies). It was some time later that the newer departments of linguistics began to appear, especially in American universities, and to some observers this may have given the illusion of linguistics as a very new discipline. The appearance of these newer linguistics departments in twentieth-century universities was, as I shall show, in some ways related to events in the interaction of psychology and linguistics around the turn of the century, and it is those events to which I now turn.

A considerable number of language scholars (philologists, phoneticians, speech pathologists, *Sprachwissenschaftlicher*) found inspiration in the nascent scientific psychology of the late nineteenth century. In fact, from approximately the 1870s until about the time of World War I there was a widespread, if not universal attempt to construct the discipline of linguistics by the methods and upon the theories of the new psychology. Most of that attempt was centered in the German universities which then held the dominant position in the world of higher education and research.

In the 1860s and 1870s the program of a group of linguists known as the "neogrammarians" (a mistranslation of *Junggrammatiker*) was that language should be completely describable in terms of the physical shape of utterances. This was an extreme expression of nineteenth-century positivism, but nevertheless one that has continued in some quarters even to the present day. For the so-called "neogrammarian" linguists (who were centered in Leipzig University) positivistic experimental psychology, especially the rigorous methods of psychophysics, seemed to offer an ideal and a guide for the study of language. Other linguists with similar sentiments had become followers of the mathematical and mechanistic psychology of Johann Friedrich Herbart, the most notable examples being Chaim Steinthal and Hermann Paul.

Herbart's psychology remained a significant influence until the end of the century. His psychology constituted a sophisticated brand of associationism modified by German rationalism. As such it offered quantitative descriptions of the associations between and the structure of atomic mental states. Central to these descriptions were notions of assimilation, accommodation, and fusion of mental states (or men-

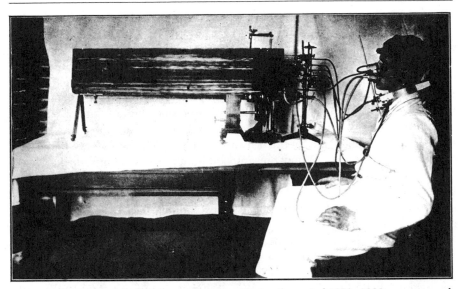

Figure 34.1 Figuring out how language works. During the period 1879–1929, one approach to language study was strongly mechanistic. This approach often implied that language would be explained through the mechanical analysis of the physical shape of utterances. The picture is from Pillsbury and Meader (1928).

tal representations—*Vorstellungen*). Some of Herbart's mathematical formulations have, as I understand, been shown to be identical to some recent formulations in mathematical psychology.

In any case, Herbart's work was taken quite seriously by a good number of linguists in the late nineteenth century. His best spokesman among linguists was certainly Hermann Paul who was also, by all accounts, the leading figure in linguistics at that time. Paul's influential text, the *Principles* . . . , first appeared in 1880 and then went through five editions until the last one in 1920. In this work the notions of mental associations, assimilations, accommodations, fusions, interference, generalization, and other derivative principles formed the basis of his account of language.

No sooner, however, had this celebrated discovery of psychology by linguists begun, than a deep schism opened up among viewpoints within theoretical psychology. It developed from the work of Wilhelm Wundt who came to be a prominent critic of Herbartian psychology and who also came to be the leading psycholinguist.

It is often said in textbook accounts today that the disagreement between Wundt and Herbart concerned only the question of whether psychology could be an experimental science, Herbart denying that possibility, Wundt promoting it. But that is an incomplete account. The difference between Herbart and Wundt was as much

809

theoretical and philosophical as it was methodological, and it was to disturb relations between linguists and psychologists who studied language for at least a generation.

Wundt's argument, in opposition to Herbart (and Paul), was that the human mind is in essence creative—that thoughts, perceptions, and memories do not derive from an inventory of isolated mental impressions strung together in associative chains. Rather, mental states and their expressions are, he argued, internal constructions that are developed from germinal mental impressions. This activity was seen as being under the control of a creative, central control process. In the case of linguistic phenomena, Wundt drew support from the writings of Wilhelm Humboldt who had lived nearly a century earlier. Wundt's citations from Humboldt are, by the way, the same as those of the present-day linguists who trace their ideas back to this same root. Wundt first spelled out his psycholinguistics in detail in his *Logik* of 1880.

Paul and his followers faced the question of creativity (the pervasive novelty of expression in language, in the case of psycholinguistics) with the explanatory devices of "analogy formations" and "generalization." This gave much less prominence to creativity than is found in Wundt's psycholinguistics. And Paul's treatment did not require a central control process.

Wundt's contributions to linguistics began (Wundt, 1880) with his invention of the tree diagram to describe the organization of mental states that underlie sentences. For Wundt the fundamental unit of language was the sentence, and this was because the sentence corresponds to, or is the expressive result of, an underlying germinal mental impression (*Gesamtvorstellung*), a fundamental concept in Wundtian psychology.

Sentences which exhibit the same meanings but whose words are arranged in different syntactic patterns were seen by Wundt as representing different transformations of one underlying mental structure that was common to them all. In Wundt's view, *words* should then be considered as the arbitrary resultants of the act of analysis of mental impressions, and these resultants were seen as attaining greater or lesser stability through the social conventions of particular languages. Wundt's approach to linguistic study may be called the "generative" or the "psychological" approach.

In opposition to Wundt, Paul took the word as his linguistic element. And rather than describing sentences as Wundt did, Paul remained with the older Herbartian system of associative processes which were conceived as the mechanisms that link words together into sentences; this linking process, as he argued, reflects the linking of underlying elemental ideas.

I will not belabor this discussion with attempts to gauge the sheer size of the literature that this controversy generated so many years ago. But it seems to be the most pervasive theme in early psycholinguistics. It certainly was not the only theme, but I mention it alone because it defines that early literature fairly well.

What it all eventually came to was a divorce of the cozy relation between psychology and linguistics and a collapse of *Sprachpsychologie.* The beginning of those divorce proceedings is clearly marked by one influential book: It is Bernard Delbrück's review of the schism between the Wundtian and the Herbartian viewpoints in the study of language (Delbrück, 1901). The book was never translated into English because in that time most all language scholars were fluent in German. (In 1904, however, George Herbert Mead—a student of Wundt's—published a shorter review of the relations between psychologists and linguists, a review that seems to be based in part on Delbrück's book.)

Not only were the views of Wundt and Herbart in active opposition at the turn of the century; there were by then, of course, several other emergent schools of psychology that were beginning to share in the competition. And so the situation for the linguist who attempted to build his linguistics on a basis of psychological theory was growing ever more precarious. Delbrück made the well reasoned argument that it should matter little to the linguist which theory of psychology is correct; for, as he argued, linguists are engaged in a fundamentally different discipline. It is not their purpose, nor within the reach of their conceptual tools, to explain human performance. Instead, linguists are concerned with the structure and interrelations of abstract code systems—German, English, Russian, Chinese, and so on. The description of the formal aspects of these code systems is a logically different task from that of describing how people perceive, remember, or think.

Delbrück's declaration of independence was to have a liberating effect upon linguists. There soon followed a highly productive era in twentieth-century structuralist linguistics, and this was coordinated with pressures within academia to create the new departments of linguistics.

At about the same time, changes were appearing in psychology as the first generation of experimental psychologists, trained primarily in Germany, approached retirement and a restless new generation, with Austrian, French, Russian, and especially American roots, became ascendant. These changes were one aspect of the new wave of positivist viewpoints which swept over much of the academic and scientific community early in this century. Animals were now used increasingly as subjects in psychological research. And the more that this took place, the less did language appear as any sort of problem for psychologists. With the development of conditioning theories, the description of language as sequences of reflexes or of environmentally controlled operants simply did not address much of the subject matter that was of traditional concern to linguists or to early psycholinguists.

The major works of the most influential American linguist in the early twentieth century reflects this historical evolution fairly well. That person was Leonard Bloomfield who, when writing his first book on language (1914), had journeyed to Leipzig to hear Wundt lecture on that topic. The book contains a fair, though incomplete synopsis of the Wundtian approach to language. But before the second edition appeared in 1933, Bloomfield had been converted by his newer behaviorist

811

colleagues, and so there is little trace of Wundtian psychology in the later book. And what is more significant about the second edition of Bloomfield is that psychology—even of the behavioristic school—is no longer a model at all for linguistics. That fact reflects what had happened to the relations between linguists and psychologists in the early decades of this century, events that had been heralded by Delbrück in 1901.

By the 1920s almost no one was interested in the status of the relations between linguists and psychologists. One notable exception, however, was Erwin Esper who described his alarm over that earlier divorce (e.g., Esper, 1935). As he tirelessly argued, there was nothing in the structuralist and functionalist linguistics of his day that rendered it incompatible with early behaviorism. The difficulty in the alienation of linguists from psychology may partly have been an overreaction to the earlier Wundtian era when the distinctions between the two disciplines had been blurred. One may observe how often the linguists of this period (the 1920s and 1930s) refer back to Delbrück's declaration of independence in 1901.

There were certainly other prominent expressions of interest in language made by psychologists during the 1930s (such as those from J. R. Kantor and B. F. Skinner). But they were more concerned with importing their particular behaviorist viewpoints into the study of language than with direct participation in linguistics or with cross-disciplinary contacts with linguists.

I would like to present some review of the early empirical work, but the limits on the present chapter permit mention of only a few examples. I will describe three examples of early psycholinguistic research, each of which was prominent in its day, each focusing on a different type of problem or phenomenon. First is the work of Binet and Henri on memory for sentences. Second is Clara and William Stern's study of language acquisition. And third is Meringer's investigation of speech errors.

Binet and Henri (1894)

One piece of nineteenth-century experimental psychology known today to every psychology undergraduate is Ebbinghaus's study of memory (1885), which employed nonsense syllables as memory items and which gave evidence relevant to the nature of forgetting. Ebbinghaus had deliberately avoided the effects of meaningful natural language on memory. But other nineteenth-century psychologists, particularly cognitive theorists, were interested in just those effects. A notable example, in the sense that it inspired later research, was the joint research of Alfred Binet and Wundt's student Victor Henri (1894).

To study memory for sentences, Binet and Henri read prose passages to subjects who were subsequently asked to recall those passages after the lapse of various time intervals. Recall accuracy was analyzed in terms of linguistic structure. For scoring purposes the passages were divided into short phrases, each of which was seen as representing an underlying kernel idea. Figure 34.2 shows one of the more consistent patterns in their data—the pattern of omissions, substitutions, and synonyms.

For the distribution of errors within sentences, Binet and Henri found that they could explain mistakes only on the basis of sentence meaning and not on word position:

> The meaning of the sentence is quite distinct from the meanings of the words: it does not result from simply adding together word meanings. There are important parts in a sentence that are so essential that if they were omitted, the sentence would have no meaning (Binet & Henri, 1894, p. 35).

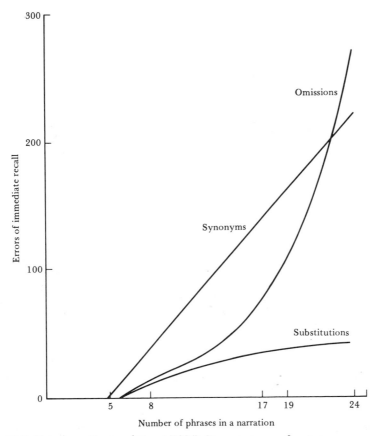

Figure 34.2 Data from Binet and Henri (1894). Errors in terms of omissions, synonyms, and substitutions for the recall of prose passages (narrations) of varying length. Length is measured as the number of kernel phrases.

They continued by describing changes in syntactic form—changes from the passive sentence structure to the active, from the negative to the positive, and so on. This investigation was frequently cited in the immediately following years by those investigators interested in the effects of syntax and verbal meaning upon recall.

Stern and Stern (1907)

For another and more elaborate example of early psycholinguistic research, let us turn to the study of language acquisition. The nineteenth-century literature is filled with "baby biographies"—the results of zealous parents' daily logging of the appearance of language in their own children. "Scientific pedagogy" had appeared in Germany early in the 1800s, and for a while it was almost universally based on Herbart's psychology, Herbart being something of a nineteenth-century Piaget.

In the French-speaking world a strong tradition of child study dating back to Rousseau had led to the establishment of the Jean Jacques Rousseau Institute for Child Study in Geneva (now Piaget's Institute for Genetic Epistemology). Similar movements and institutes were established in other countries. There were those founded by G. Stanley Hall in the United States, James Sully in England, Ladislaus Nagy in Hungary, Ivan Gheorgov in Bulgaria, Lombroso in Italy, and there was the St. Petersburg Society of Experimental Pedagogy in Russia, the National Child Study Museum in Madrid, and I have been told that some similar early child-study centers were founded in the Orient.

Naturally enough, language acquisition was a key concern in such places, and an enormous literature resulted. By the turn of the century the divisions between the linguistic viewpoints of Wundt and of Paul were evident in much of that work. There was also the age-old nature-nurture controversy which loomed large in those days and which was probably sparked by nineteenth-century theories of evolution. Much of this early work culminated in Clara and William Stern's book *Die Kindersprache* (1907), which is still reprinted in Germany.

Many early studies of language acquisition may be ignored because of their superficiality; data often consisted of anecdotes and second-hand reports. But there were other valuable studies. The Sterns's book was one of the best, the most influential work in this area in its time. As many others had done, these investigators made systematic observations of language acquisition in their own children, and then they made systematic comparisons of their observations with those of numerous other investigators, comparisons which involved several languages.

Most early writers can be categorized as arguing for either an *imitation* theory or a *spontaneity* theory of language acquisition. The Sterns effectively showed that either position alone is inadequate. Much of their book elaborates the following position:

814

The fact that children imitate does not permit us to deny the spontaneity of children. Spontaneity by no means need be opposed to imitation, but can occur through and with the material acquired by imitation. The real problem therefore is not one of imitation vs. spontaneity but rather to what extent internal tendencies and forces are at work during assimilation, selection, and internal processing of externally presented forms.

Spokesmen for spontaneity have also gone too far, but in the opposite direction. Some who have hunted down "word inventions," that is, the child's neologisms for which there are no precedents in sound gestures and sound imitations or in words of conventional speech, got far off the track. Others have construed spontaneity too intellectually as a logical formation of concepts, thus contradicting the primitive makeup of children's speech.

We believe that the proper position is a synthesis of these two opinions. In his form of speech the child learning to speak is neither a phonograph reproducing external sounds nor a sovereign creator of language. In terms of the contents of his speech he is neither a pure associative machine nor a sovereign constructor of concepts. Rather, his speech is based on the continuing interaction of external impressions with internal systems, which usually function unconsciously; it is thus the result of a constant "convergence." The detailed investigations pertaining to the development of speech and thought will have to be directed at determining the relative participation of both forces and how they accommodate each other (Stern & Stern, 1907, pp. 122–123).

The first part of the Sterns' work concerns the language development of their own three children. Then they discuss the general psychology of language acquisition with extensive comparisons of other researchers' findings, including discussions of the form-content distinction, expressive gestures, one-word sentences, syntactic structures (negation, clauses, interrogatives, and so forth), the development of word-forms and categories, and then such special problems of child language as phonemic distortions, sound changes, elliptical constructions, and original creations. The following excerpt, taken from Chapter 13, Development of the Sentence, shows the character of their analyses:

On the average the child begins around the middle of the second year of life to speak multiple-word sentences. Table 1 [34.2] shows samples of such early sentences. The orthographic representation, however, does not adequately portray a peculiarity usually to be observed, which is the jerky manner of punctuating the spoken words with pauses. It occurs in various kinds of sentences, usually vocative sentences. When the child says *ata-puppe* (have doll), each word actually has sentence value. To be absolutely accurate, one would have to speak of a primitive chain of sentences. But at the same time real sentences occur, like Hilde's *da ist brbr* (there's an animal) or Ament's *babedd dschidschi* (Babett rode on the train).

In their grammatical structures these sentences are very different. In the earliest

TABLE 34.2 Initial Multiple-Word Sentences[a]

Child	Sentence	Year	Months	Explanation
Hilde Stern	da is brrbrr	1	5½	When pointing at animal pictures
	da sich wauwau	1		When pointing at animal pictures
	alle alle milch	1	7	The milk's been drunk.
	tag, mama!	1	7	Hello (good day) Mama!
Gunther Stern	da is puppe	1	7	There's the doll.
	lda is papa, süs!	1	2	There's Papa. Look!
	mū—herste?	1	2	Do you hear the cow mooing?
	Wo is'n der papa?	1	2½	Where is Papa?
	butte alle	1	4	I've had enough of the roll.
Eva Stern	hilda—kakao!	1	4½	Hilde, come for cocoa!
	ātă—puppe	1	4⅔	Father, I have a doll.
	mama komma	1	4⅔	Mama, come here.
	mama—hilda	1	6	Mama, carry me to Hilde.
Axel Preyer	haim mimi	1	6	I want to go home and drink milk.
	danna kuha	2	11	Auntie gave me cake.
	kaffe nein	2	½	There's no coffee there.
	mama ĕtse	2	½	Mama should sit down
Ament's niece	babedd dschidschi	1	½	Babett rode on the train.
	lulu dai	1	7	Lulu's here.
	lili alden	1	8	Willi should hold (it).
Lindner's son	a, bennt	1	9	Oh, it's burning.
	guckuk papa, guckuk	1	9½	Said while playing hide-and-seek to father, mother, Olga.
	mama geben	1	9½	Mama should give.
Idelberger's son	mama obba obba	1	3	Mama, get up.
	mama ada	1	4	I was walking with Mama.
Tögel's son	papa nö	1	7	Papa's going out in the snow.
	opapa bibip	1	7	Grandpa brought a bird.
	baba bisch bisch	1	7	Papa is sleeping.
Major's child R	gash faw	1	11½	The glass falls.
	aga baw	1	11½	Ball is gone.
	wead moom	2	0	Read the story about the moon.
	betie dat	2	0	I want food for Jack (toy horse).
Tracy's Boy C	papa cacker	1	6½	Papa has firecrackers.
Sully's child M	mama tie	1	6½	Mama, button it.
Taine's girl	a bûle coucou	1	6	The burning (ça brule) is hiding: the sun sets.
Gheorgov's first son	daj chieb	1	7	Give bread.
	daj lep	1	8	Give bread.
Gheorgov's second son	ela nana	1	8	Come brother.
Deville's daughter	i pa	1	1½	Eugène's gone.
	pépé, toutou	1	3	Poupée, coucou (playing hiding game with doll).

[a]From Clara and Wilhelm Stern, 1907.

period, the prevailing type is one in which one part is formed by a vocative or an interjection and the other part represents the actual central matter to be communicated. But sentences with related parts soon take over. For example:

Subject + Object: *danna Kuha* (auntie, give me some cake), Verb + Adverbial Designation: *mama ada* (I was walking with Mama), Subject with Predicate Nominative: *kind kalt* (child is cold).

The combination of Verb and Object appears to be very frequent, as the numerous examples in Table 1 [34.2] show.

The first multiple-word sentences consist of only two parts. But as soon as the child acquires the ability to synthesize, he has no basic difficulty in forming more complex combinations, and they appear quickly. With the first synthesis of three or more words, something similar to what happened during the transition from the one-word sentence to two-part sentences occurs. The new element is not integrated into the grammatical structure of the sentence but is appended as an independent word instead. Through a sentence chain the child thus acquires a sentence structuring that becomes increasingly complex. At one year and ten months, Hilde could already express the main components of such thoughts as "Mama should get me the pictures from the back room" but only by making a chain of six primitive short sentences: *Mama. Bilda hamele. Zimma. Hamele bilda. Hinten. Dada mama eholn.*

The contents of the first multiple-word sentences have one thing in common—they are all positive in nature. Our list shows only one negation, out of forty examples, in Axel Preyer's *Kaffee nein*, and it occurs at a fairly late age. When negating sentences do appear after some time, they almost always have the nature of a primitive sentence chain. Negation is not part of the sentence but an independent expression of attitude that usually does not occur until after the positive part of the sentence has been spoken. The first negating word thus is not *not*, but is *no*, a phenomenon that has analogies in the development of language in general. [The Sterns then give many examples.] (Stern & Stern, 1907, pp. 182–186.)

A rather large portion of the early language acquisition research, particularly in the United States, England, and France, took the form of vocabulary counts, word categorizations, and relative-frequency tabulations of parts of speech sometimes with comparisons of frequencies across age levels. Such attempts to force the taxonomy of the adult language upon descriptions of child language had already been widely criticized by the Wundtian psycholinguists, e.g., Meumann (1903). As the argument ran, the child's first words may correspond to almost any word category in the adult language, or, more accurately, they are much broader and undifferentiated categories than those of adult language.

Meringer (1895)

For the third example of early psycholinguistic research, the work of Meringer provides an impressive example. Rudolf Meringer of Vienna was a philologist by training. Yet his work on language performance had an influence that went well beyond the boundaries of philology, and it was widely cited by early psychologists. Meringer pioneered the study of speech lapses, slips of the tongue, and other errors of language performance. He showed that such observations are useful for gaining insight into the nature of language function. This work was published in two large collections of observations which also contain theoretical analyses: *Versprechen und Verlesen* (1895) written in collaboration with the neurologist Carl Mayer, and *Aus dem Leben der Sprache* (1908). The former volume was actually written entirely by Meringer with Mayer serving as a consultant on matters of psychology and neurology. The 1895 work contains the largest collection of observations. These two works form a body of observations that are still unsurpassed for this area of investigation. They are the most sustained effort to collect and catalogue a large corpus of speech errors observed as they occur in spontaneous conversation.

Meringer's work was a strong influence on thinkers as different as Wundt and Freud, and it was widely cited in the turn-of-the-century psychology literature. Freud, for example, borrowed Meringer's findings in a way that, according to Meringer, twisted them to fit Freud's interpretation that all errors of speech are caused by repressed thoughts. (A series of vitriolic exchanges between Meringer and Freud ensued.) The intent of Meringer's work was to contribute to the understanding of natural language performance and to work toward a theory of that process. Wundt (1900) considered Meringer's observations to be a model of psycholinguistic research, and he claimed that the careful and systematic naturalistic observations made by Meringer were more fruitful than the more common experimental approaches taken by the psychologists of that day who often studied language by means of word-association tasks in controlled laboratory settings. (These episodes and disagreements have been reviewed in more detail by Cutler, 1979.)

Like Wundt, Meringer reacted against the *Junggrammatiker* movement, opposing their aim to limit the description of language to the external forms of utterances. Like Wundt, he argues that this limitation makes language study a sterile pursuit which is out of touch with the nature of living language.

The five major types of speech error, according to Meringer, are: (1) exchanges, (2) anticipations, (3) perseverations, (4) contaminations, and (5) substitutions. The first three types involve either whole words, syllables, single speech sounds, or even component features of single sounds. Contaminations occur between words, phrases, or sentences and involve either the blending or interchanging of alternative means of expressing a thought or displacements, in which the ordering of the output becomes confused or garbled. The fifth type, substitutions, occurs when a word is replaced by some other semantically-related, or sound-related, or other associatively-related word. Meringer noted a number of other—but rare—types of error: omissions of sounds or syllables and grammatical confusions, such as mistaken verb agreement.

On the basis of these observations, Meringer came to significant and broad conclusions. In particular, he found that speech errors are rule-governed (they are not random), and further that all people make speech errors according to the same rules. These conclusions thus lent strength to psycholinguistic notions of language as rule-governed behavior that is in some ways independent of immediate environmental contingencies.

For particular examples of these rules, in the case of the first three types of error (exchange, anticipation, and perseveration) Meringer found that "like replaces like"—a speech component is erroneously replaced only by another component that has a parallel function in another word. Word-terminal sounds exchange, word-initial sounds exchange, and syllabic nuclei exchange. But a word-terminal, for example, does not exchange with the initial sound or with other different parts. Also, stressed syllables exchange only with other stressed syllables; unstressed exchange only with unstressed.

Another interesting part of Meringer's observations include "tip-of-the-tongue" situations—partial recall of words—for which Meringer developed a theory of the relative memory strengths of word parts. The initial sounds and the stressed syllable in polysyllabic words are, as he observed, the easiest to recall.

In other more theoretical generalizations Meringer argued that when we produce utterances we do not simply retrieve words from memory; rather, we have highly automatic rules or procedures for constructing different grammatical forms. And these frequently fail—often under predictable circumstances such as fatigue. He attempted to relate frequency and type of error to the speaker's age and to the momentary rate of speech, but found no significant relations.

Finally, Meringer attempted to make some statement about comprehension errors—hearing errors and reading errors—although these are much more difficult to collect because they are not overt and thus are not easily recorded. Because of his very sketchy observations here, he was unable to draw any firm conclusions relating these errors to speech-production errors.

With the decline of turn-of-the-century *Sprachpsychologie*, Meringer's work was lost sight of. It was not until the 1970s that speech-error research was revived and considered again as being relevant to psycholinguistics (see Fromkin, 1973).

Here I must end this review and call attention again to the question of the relations between psychologists and linguists in earlier years—the question with which I began. I would especially like to direct the reader's attention to one point. In those earlier relations, psychology was very much in the dominant position, and linguists were often in attendance at the lectures of a Wundt, or a Stern, or a Bühler to keep abreast of the latest developments in psychological theory. But then eventually, out of frustration, many linguists gave up on psychology—or perhaps more rationally, the separation was the result of a clearer view of fundamental differences in goals that distinguish the two disciplines.

Years later, in the period that includes our time (which John Carroll reviews in the following chapter), the same ritual is being played out. But the relation between psychologists and linguists as recently developed is the reverse of what it had been at the turn of the century. In an action reversing the patterns of an earlier time, psychologists have more often been the ones to make trips across the disciplinary boundary to attend the lectures of prominent linguists. This is characteristic of the recent effort to build a psychology of language on the basis of, or by analogy to, formal linguistics—rather than the other way around as in the earlier period we have just reviewed.

Perhaps, with the present proliferation of linguistic theories and the new discussions about the respective goals of linguists and psychologists, a reverse replay of the scenario of psychologist-linguist relations earlier in this century should not be surprising. We might then expect a turning away, to some degree, of psycholinguists from the current enterprise of writing "grammars" of language performance, or analyzing subjective "lexicons," or from discussions of the "language of thought."

I have not mentioned one further finding in my historical readings. I suspect it is a phenomenon that is much broader than the special sphere of psychology-linguistics relations. Call it the "Pollyanna Principle." In nearly every decade of the historical period I have reviewed, one finds leading authorities of this field commenting that the controversies that have racked the discipline in the past are just about worked out. The authority then looks forward to a future in which mostly technical details remain to be worked upon, implying that this will not necessarily be easy but that the way at last seems clear. And those comments usually reflect the feeling that earlier ill-guided differences between theorists have just about been cleared away. Such a pattern in intellectual history is one of the more stunning findings one gains from the study of the past as we compare it with the present where we often find the same message.

Whatever the future course of relations between psychology and linguistics, it should be a more intelligent one if we pay attention to what has happened in the past.

REFERENCES

Allport, F. H. *Social psychology*. Boston: Houghton Mifflin, 1924.
Ament, W. *Die Entwicklung von Sprechen und Denken beim Kinde*. Leipzig: Wunderlich, 1899.
Bagley, W. C. The apperception of the spoken sentence: A study in the psychology of language. *American Journal of Psychology*, 1900, 12, 80–134.
Barth, P. Zur Psychologie der gebundenen und der freien Worstellung. *Philosophische Studien*, 1902, 19.
Bartoli, M. *Introduzione alla neolinguistica*. Geneva, 1925.
Baudouin de Courtenay, J., *Versuch einer Theorie der phonetischen Alternationen*. Strassburg, 1895.

Bawden, A. H. A study of lapses. *Psychological Monographs*, 1900, 3 (Whole No. 4).

Bechtel, F. *Die Hauptprobleme der indogermanische Lautlehre siet Schleicher*. Göttingen, 1892.

Binet, A., & Henri, V. La mémoire des phrases. *L'Année Psychologique*, 1894, *1*, 24–59.

Bloomfield, L. *An introduction to the study of language*. New York: Holt, 1914.

Boas, F. *Handbook of American Indian languages*. Washington, D.C.: Smithsonian Institution, 1911.

Böthlingk, O. *Panini's Grammatik*. Leipzig, 1887.

Bourdon, B. *L'expression des émotions et des tendances dans le langage*. Paris: Alcan, 1892.

Bréal, M. *Essai de sémantique*. Paris: Hachette, 1897.

Broens, O. *Darstellung und Würdigung des sprachphilosophischen Gegensatzes zwischen Paul, Wundt und Marty*. Betzdorf: Ebner, 1913.

Brugmann, K. *Zum heutigen Stand der Sprachwissenschaft*. Strassburg, 1885.

Brunot, F. *La pensée et la langue*. Paris: Alcan, 1922.

Bühler, K. Ueber die Prozesse der Satzbildung. *Zeitschrift für Psychologie*, 1919, *81*, 181–206.

Bühler, K. *Sprachtheorie: Die Darstellungsfunktionen der Sprache*. Jena: Fischer, 1934.

Buswell, G. T. *An experimental study of the eye-voice span in reading*. Supplementary Educational Monographs, No. 17. Chicago: The University of Chicago Press, 1920.

Byrne, J. *General principles of the structure of language*. London, 1892.

Cohen, M. Sur les langages successifs de l'enfant. *Mélanges linguistique offerts à M. J. Vendreyes par ses amis et ses élèves*. Paris: Champion, 1925.

Condon, E. V. Statistics of vocabulary. *Science*, 1928, *67*, 300.

Croce, B. *Estetica come scienza dell'espressione e linguistica generale*. Bari, 1901.

Curme, G. O. *A grammar of the German language*. New York: Holt, 1922.

Curtius, G. *Zur Kritik der neuesten Sprachforschung*. Leipzig: Barth, 1885.

Cutler, A. Contemporary reactions to Rudolf Meringer's speech error research. *Historiographica Linguistics*, 1979, *6*, 57–76.

Darmesteter, A. *La vie des mots*. Paris, 1894.

Dearborn, W. F. *The psychology of reading: An experimental study of the reading pauses and movements of the eye*. New York: Science Press, 1906.

Delacroix, H. *Le langage et la pensée*. Paris: Alcan, 1924.

De La Grasserie, R. *Essai de phonétique dynamic ou historique comparée*. Paris, 1891.

De Laguna, G. A. *Speech: Its function and development*. New Haven: Yale University Press, 1927.

Delbrück, B. *Grundfragen der Sprachforschung mit Rücksicht auf W. Wundt's Sprachpsychologie erörtert*. Strassburg, 1901.

Dewey, J. The psychology of infant language. *Psychological Review*, 1894, *2*, 63–66.

Dittrich, O. *Grundzüge der Sprachpsychologie*. Leipzig: Engelmann, 1903.

Doran, E. W. A study of vocabularies. *Pedagogical Seminary*, 1907, *14*, 401–438.

Ebbinghaus, H. *Ueber das Gedächtnis*. Leipzig: Dunker & Humboldt, 1885.

Erdmann, B. Die psychologischen Grundlagen der Beziehungen zwischen Sprechen und Denken. *Archiv für systematische Philosophie*, 1896, *2*, 355–417.

Erdmann, B., & Dodge, R. *Psychologische Untersuchungen über das Lesen*. Halle: Niemeyer, 1898.

Esper, E. A. A technique for the experimental investigation of associative interference in artificial linguistic material. *Language Monographs*, 1925, *1*, 1–47.

Esper, E. A. Language. In C. Murchison (Ed.), *A handbook of social psychology*. Worcester, Mass.: Clark University Press, 1935.

Finck, F. N. *Die Aufgabe und Gliederung der Sprachwissenschaft*. Halle: Niemeyer, 1905.

Fletcher, H. *Speech and hearing*. New York: Holt, 1929.

Fournié, E. *Essai de psychologie*. Paris: Didier, 1887.

Franke, C. Sprachentwicklung der Kinder und der Menschheit. *Encyclopädisches Handbuch der Pädagogik*. Bern, 1899.

Fromkin, V. A. (Ed.). *Speech errors as linguistic evidence*. The Hague: Mouton, 1973.

821

III. PSYCHOLOGY AND ITS INTERSECTING DISCIPLINES

Fröschels, E. *Psychologie der Sprache*. Leipzig: Deuticke, 1925.

Gabelentz, G., von der. *Die Sprachwissenschaft*. Leipzig: Engelmann, 1890.

Ganzmann, O. *Ueber Sprach- und Sprachvorstellungen*. Berlin, 1901.

Gehmlich, E. *Der Gefühlsinhalt der Sprache*. Langensalza, 1899.

Geiger, L. *Der Ursprung der Sprache*. Stuttgart: Cotta, 1869.

Goldscheider, A., & Müller, R. Zur Physiologie und Pathologie des Lesens. *Zeitschrift für klinische Medicin*, 1893, 23, 131–167.

Grammont, M. *La dissimulation consonantique dans les langues indo-européennes et dans les langues romanes*. Dijon, 1895.

Gray, C. T. The anticipation of meaning as a factor in reading ability. *Elementary School Journal*, 1923, 23, 614–626.

Guillaume, P. Les débuts de la phrase dans le langage de l'enfant. *Journal de Psychologie*, 1927, 24, 1–25.

Gvozdev, A. Usvoenie rebenkom rodnogo jazyka. In N. Rybnikov (Ed.), *Detskaja Reč*. Moscow: Biblioteka Pedagoga, 1927.

Head, H. *Aphasia and kindred disorders of speech*. New York: Holt, 1926.

Hjelmslev, L. *Principes de grammaire générale*. Copenhagen, 1928.

Horn, M. D. The thousand and three words most used by kindergarten children. *Childhood Education*, 1926, 3, 118.

Huey, E. B. *The psychology and pedagogy of reading*. New York: Macmillan, 1908.

Jerusalem, W. *Die Psychologie im Dienste der Grammatik*. Vienna, 1896.

Jespersen, O. *Language: Its nature, development, and origin*. London: Allen & Unwin, 1922.

Jones, D. *Intonation curves*. Leipzig, 1909.

Jousse, M. *Etudes de psychologie linguistique*. Paris: Beauchesne, 1925.

Kaeding, F. *Haufigkeitsworterbuch der deutschen Sprache*. Steglitz, 1897–1898.

Kantor, J. R. Can psychology contribute to the study of linguistics? *The Monist*, 1928, 38, 630–648.

Kent, G. H., & Rosanoff, A. J. A study of association in insanity. *American Journal of Insanity*, 1910, 67, 37–96, 317–390.

Kramp, L. *Das Verhältnis von Urteil und Satz*. Bonn, 1915.

Lalande, A. La conscience des mots dans le langage. *Journal de Psychologie*, January, 1905.

Leroy, E. *Le Langage*. Paris: Alcan, 1905.

Leskien, A. *Die Declination im Slawisch-Litauischen und Germanischen*. Leipzig, 1876.

Lukens, H. T. Preliminary report on the learning of language. *Pedagogical Seminary*, 1896, 3, 424–460.

Magni, J. A. Vocabularies. *Pedagogical Seminary*, 1919, 26, 209–233.

Markey, J. F. *The symbolic process*. London: Routledge, 1928.

Markov, A. A. Essai d'une recherche statistique sur le text du roman "Eugène Onêgin," illustrant la liason des épreuves en chain. *Bulletin de l'Academie Imperiale des Sciences de St. Petersbourg*, Sixth Series, 7, 1913, 153–162.

Martinak, E. *Psychologische Untersuchungen zur Bedeutungslehre*. Leipzig, 1901.

Marty, A. *Untersuchungen zur Grundlegung der allgemeinen Grammatik und Sprachphilosophie*. Halle: Niemeyer, 1908.

Mauthner, F. *Sprache und Psychologie*. Stuttgart: Gotta, 1901.

Mead, G. H. The relations of psychology and philology. *Psychological Bulletin*, 1904, 1, 375–391.

Meillet, A., *Linguistique historique et linguistique générale*. Paris: 1921.

Menzerath, P. Die Bedeutung der sprachlichen Geläufigkeit oder der formalen sprachlichen Beziehung für die Reproduktion. *Zeitschrift für Psychologie*, 1908, 48, 1–95.

Meringer, R. *Aus dem Leben der Sprache*. Berlin: Behr, 1908.

Meringer, R., & Mayer, C. *Versprechen und Verlesen: Eine psychologisch-linguistische Studie*. Stuttgart: Göschen, 1895.

Meumann, E. *Die Sprache des Kindes.* Zürich: Zürcher & Furrer, 1903.

Meyer, M. *The fundamental laws of human behavior.* Boston: Gorham Press, 1911.

Meyer-Lübke, W. *Grammatik der romanischen Sprachen.* Leipzig, 1890–1902.

Miklosich, F. Über die Wanderungen der Rumunen in den dalmatinischen Alpen und den Karpaten. Vienna, 1880.

Morris, E. P. *On principles and methods in Latin syntax.* New York, 1901.

Moore, K. C. The mental development of a child. *Psychological Review, Monograph Supplements,* 1896, *1* (Whole No. 3).

Nice, M. M. The development of a child's vocabulary in relation to environment. *Pedagogical Seminary,* 1915, *22,* 35–64.

Oertal, H. *Lectures on the study of language.* New York, 1901.

Ogden, C. K., & Richards, I. A. *The meaning of meaning.* New York: Harcourt, 1923.

Owen, E. T. Interrogative thought and the means of its expression. *Transactions of the Wisconsin Academy,* 1903, *14,* 393–471.

Palmer, H. E. *A grammar of spoken English.* Cambridge, 1924.

Paul, H. *Prinzipien der Sprachgeschichte.* Halle: Niemeyer, 1880.

Paulhan, F. Le langage intérieur et la pensée. *Revue Philosophique,* 1886, *21,* 26–58.

Pavlovitch, M. *Le langage enfantin.* Paris: Alcan, 1920.

Piaget, J. *Le langage et la pensée chez l'enfant.* Neuchâtel: Delacheux & Nestlé, 1923. (Translated by M. Gabain as *The language and thought of the child.* New York: Meridian, 1955.)

Pillsbury, W. B., & Meader, C. L. *The psychology of language.* New York: Appleton, 1928.

Preyer, W. *Die Seele des Kindes.* Stuttgart: Union, 1881. (Translated by H. Brown as *The mind of the child.* New York: Appleton, 1888–1889.)

Quantz, J. O. Problems in the psychology of reading. *Psychological Review, Monograph Supplements,* 1897, 2 (Whole No. 5).

Ravizza, F. *Psychologia della lingua.* Milan: Torino, 1905.

Reckendorf, H. Zur allgemeinen Syntax. *Indogermanische Forschung,* 1899, *10,* 188.

Reichel, W. *Sprachpsychologische Studien.* Halle: Niemeyer, 1897.

Richter, F. *Die Entwicklung der psychologischen Kindersprach-forschung.* Münster, 1927.

Ries, J. *Was ist Syntax? Ein kritischer Versuch.* Marburg, 1894.

Rousselot, J. *Principes de phonétique expérimentale.* Paris, 1897–1908.

Rowland, E. H. The psychological experiences connected with different parts of speech. *Psychological Review, Monograph Supplements,* 1907, 8 (Whole No. 1).

Sapir, E. *Language: An introduction to the study of speech.* New York: Harcourt, 1921.

Saussure, F. de. *Cours de linguistique générale.* Paris: Payot, 1916.

Schmidt, W. A. *An experimental study in the psychology of reading.* Supplementary Educational Monographs, 1 (Whole No. 2). Chicago: The University of Chicago Press, 1917.

Schuchardt, H. *Ueber die Lautgesetze.* Berlin, 1885.

Scripture, E. W. *The elements of experimental phonetics.* New York, 1902.

Séchehaye, C. A. *Programmes et méthodes de la linguistique théorique.* Paris, 1908.

Sheffield, A. D. *Grammar and thinking.* New York: Putnam, 1912.

Sievers, E. *Grundzüge der Lautphysiologie.* Leipzig: 1876.

Sommer, R. Zur Psychologie der Sprache. *Zeitschrift für Psychologie,* 1891, *2,* 151.

Stählin, W. Experimentale Untersuchungen über Sprachpsychologie und Religionspsychologie. *Archiv für Religionspsychologie,* 1914, *1,* 117–194.

Steinthal, H. *Einleitung in die Psychologie und Sprachwissenschaft.* Berlin: Dümmler, 1881.

Stern, C., & Stern, W. *Die Kindersprache.* Leipzig: Barth, 1907.

Stöhr, A. *Algebra der Grammatik.* Leipzig, 1898.

Strong, H., Logeman, W., and Wheeler, B. *Introduction to the study of the history of language.* London, 1891.

823

Stricker, S. *Studien über die Sprachvorstellung.* Vienna: Braumüller, 1880.

Sturtevant, E. *Linguistic change.* Chicago, 1917.

Sütterlin, L. *Das Wesen der sprachlichen Gebilde.* Heidelberg: Winter, 1902.

Sully, J. *Studies of childhood.* New York: Appleton, 1896.

Svedelius, C. *L'analyse du langage.* Upsala, 1897.

Sweet, H. *Primer of phonetics.* Oxford, 1890.

Taylor, C. O. Ueber das Verstehen von Wörter und Sätzen. *Zeitschrift für Psychologie,* 1906, *40,* 225–251.

Thumb, A., & Marbe, K. *Experimentelle Untersuchungen über die psychologischen Grundlagen der sprachlichen Analogiebildung.* Leipzig: Englemann, 1901.

Van Ginneken, J. *Principes de linguistique psychologique.* Paris: Rivière, 1907.

Vossler, K. *Sprache als Schöpfung und Entwicklung.* Vienna, 1905.

Wartensleben, G. Beiträge zur des Uebersetzens. *Zeitschrift für Psychologie,* 1910, *57,* 89–115.

Watson, J. B. *Behavior: An introduction to comparative psychology.* New York: Holt, 1914.

Wegener, P. *Untersuchungen über die Grundfragen des Sprachlebens.* Halle: Niemeyer, 1885.

Weiss, A. P. Linguistics and psychology. *Language,* 1925, *1,* 52–57.

Wells, F. L. *Linguistic lapses.* New York: Science Press, 1906.

Wheeler, B. I. *Analogy and the scope of its application to language.* Ithaca, N.Y.: 1887.

Whitney, W. D. *The life and growth of language.* New York: Appleton, 1875.

Woodrow, H., & Lowell, F. Children's association frequency tables. *Psychological Monographs,* 1916, *22* (Whole No. 97).

Wundt, W. *Logik* (Vol. I). Stuttgart: Enke, 1880.

Wundt, W. *Die Sprache. Völkerpsychologie* (Vol. I). Leipzig, Engelmann, 1900.

Yerkes, R., & Learned, W. *Chimpanzee intelligence and its vocal expression.* Baltimore: Williams & Wilkins, 1925.

Zeitler, J. Tachistoskopische Untersuchungen über das Lesen. *Philosophische Studien,* 1899, *16,* 380–463.

Zwaardemaker, H. Ueber den Accent nach graphischer Darstellung. *Medizinisch-pädagogische Monatschrift für die Sprachheilkunde,* 1900, *10,* Nos. 9–10.

35

Psychology and Linguistics
DETACHMENT AND AFFILIATION IN THE SECOND HALF-CENTURY*

JOHN B. CARROLL

The second half of the century since Wundt's founding of a psychological laboratory began in 1929, and if you will permit me a personal note, that was the year I graduated from what we used to call—more appropriately than we knew—grammar school. It was also the year that I met and became a student of Benjamin Lee Whorf, himself a student of the linguist Edward Sapir. Whorf was later to become known as the chief modern exponent of a very old theory—already considered by von Humboldt, Max Müller, and others in the nineteenth century—that the structure of one's language works some kind of influence on the way one thinks, the theory that is now often cited as the Sapir-Whorf hypothesis and that autogenously requires interdisciplinary study. I will not relate here the circumstances under which I had the good fortune to become associated with Whorf (see Carroll, 1980); suffice it to say that as a consequence of that association I can now look back on a half-century of personal contact with linguistics. In a sense, it also initiated my contact with psychology, for although Whorf was not a psychologist, and not even a

*This is a version, edited and updated for publication here, of an address presented at the Wundt Centennial Symposium: Psychology and Linguistics, at the convention of the American Psychological Association, New York City, September 5, 1979. For partial support of the work involved in its preparation, I am indebted to the Kenan Leave Fund of the University of North Carolina at Chapel Hill and to the James McKeen Cattell Fund which enabled me to take a full sabbatical during the academic year 1979–1980.

professional linguist, he could be said to have been interested in the psychology of language. Certainly his writings, which I edited and published posthumously (Whorf, 1956), give evidence of this.

Although Whorf, through Sapir, was in contact with the "mainstream" linguistics of that day, neither Whorf nor I had any connection with the mainstream of psychology in 1929; I did not enter the mainstream of psychology until 1937, when I went to the University of Minnesota as B. F. Skinner's first graduate student. My task here is not to recount the recent history of the psychology of language, although that is inevitably involved, but to trace the connections between mainstream psychology and mainstream linguistics over the period from 1929 to the present. I do this with the aid of Table 35.1—"Chronological Display of Selected References in Linguistics and the Psychology of Language"—in effect a collection of references, classified and chronologically ordered in separate columns according to principal trends and streams of activity in linguistics and in the psychology of language. The actual bibliographical citations are given in the References at the end of this chapter. The references are of various types, ranging from major theoretical treatises, "landmark" conference proceedings, and seminal journal articles and monographs, through literature reviews, textbooks, and books of readings. A few (Cofer, 1978; Ervin-Tripp, 1974; Hymes & Fought, 1975; Osgood, 1975; Salzinger, 1970) are pertinent historical accounts, personal histories, and the like. I cannot take space to describe or discuss all these references and the bases for my classifications, which were often difficult or essentially arbitrary. (Some authors will find strange bedfellows in their columns.) I make no claim that the collection is complete or exhaustive, but it is representative of developments in the respective fields. [1]

While assembling these references, it occurred to me to examine the relations between psychology and linguistics as evidenced in the way in which each discipline treated the publications of the other, as well as its own, in the book review sections of its principal journals. The reference list thus contains many citations of book reviews, whenever I was able to find them—in part through systematic searches of the journals *Language*, the *Psychological Bulletin*, and *Contemporary Psychology*. [2] The book reviews make highly interesting reading. Despite all the

[1] The collection was assembled from the extensive bibliographical materials that I have maintained in linguistics and the psychology of language more or less continuously since my graduate study years (1937–1940), generally through constant tracking of the principal journals that are pertinent in each field, abstract journals, published bibliographies, and the like. Although the collection represents only a small fraction of the published output, I believe it contains listings of a major proportion of the more important books and monographs that appeared in the respective fields and that could be considered candidates for treatment in book reviews and other critical notices in both fields.

[2] The first volume of *Language*, the official journal of the Linguistic Society of America, appeared in 1925; the journal has been published continuously since then. The issues nearly always contain reviews, sometimes quite lengthy, of books and monographs in linguistics and related fields. Volume 50, Number 4 (Part 2), December 1974, is a complete index to articles and reviews published up to that time. The

vagaries of the book reviewing process—including editors' problems in selecting items for review and finding competent reviewers, and the occasional waywardness of the reviewers—they reveal striking trends. One can appreciate these trends fully only by perusing the reviews themselves, but some indications can be given here.

As one may see from Table 35.2, even in the early years of the period under consideration linguistic journals reviewed publications in the psychology of language more frequently than psychological journals reviewed publications in linguistics, and this contrast in the reviewing practices of the two disciplines persisted throughout the period. Eighty-one percent of the seventy-nine linguistic references had at least one review in a linguistic journal, but only 38 percent of these were reviewed in a psychological or psycholinguistic journal. In some contrast, the rate of review of psychology of language references in journals in this discipline was 91 percent, but 55 percent of these references were also given reviews in linguistic journals. Not being based on any scientific sampling, these figures give only a rough impression, but they are not out of line with what one might expect from a knowledge of the history of contacts between the disciplines. The numbers are not the whole story, of course. From the tenor of the reviews themselves, it appears that until around 1965, linguists were, so to speak, watchfully attentive to any sign that psychological theory and research would give some help in developing a science of linguistics and language behavior, but their feeling was that most of the signs were negative or at least dubious. From the other side, the relatively few reviews of linguistic works by psychologists published in psychological journals tended to express dissatisfaction with the possible contributions of linguistics. Beginning around 1965, reviews on both sides were generally more appreciative of materials in the other discipline, though still very cautious in accepting them at face value.

In tracing relations between two disciplines, a background consideration is the degree to which each might be expected to benefit from the other in the light of its goals. Broadly defined, the goals of linguistic science are to describe and compare natural language systems and to induce general principles governing such systems. The goals of psychology, one may say, are to induce, from observations and experiments, general principles governing the behavior and performance of organisms. In particular, a psychology of language would be expected to yield principles and regularities governing the acquisition and use of natural language systems in human cognition and communication. Insofar as linguistics provides information about particular language systems or language systems in general, we could expect psychology to benefit from such information in the effort to understand the acquisition and use of languages. Conversely, we might expect linguistics to benefit from

---

Psychological Bulletin, an official publication of the American Psychological Association, was the principal medium for the Association's publication of book reviews from 1904 until about 1956, when *Contemporary Psychology, A Journal of Reviews* became the exclusive vehicle for such publication. No cumulative index to reviews in these psychological journals has been published.

TABLE 35.1 Chronological Display of Selected References in Linguistics and the Psychology of Language (1929–1979)[a]

YEAR	LINGUISTICS		PSYCHOLOGY OF LANGUAGE		
	Structuralist tradition	Current tradition	Behaviorist tradition	Transitional positions	Cognitive psycholinguistics
1929			Adams & Powers, Weiss[P]	De Laguna[P,L] (1927)	
1930					
1931	Stern[P]				
1932	Bloomfield[L]				
1933					
1934					
1935	Twaddell[L]		Esper		
1936			Zipf[P,L], Kantor[P,L], McGranahan, Skinner		
1937					
1938					
1939	Gray[L,P]	Trubetzkoy[L]			
1940	Bryant & Aiken[L,P], Fries[L], Whorf[L]				
1941		Jakobson[L,P]			
1942	Bloch & Trager[L], Bloomfield[L]				
1943			Carroll		
1944					
1945					
1946			Pronko		
1947	Sturtevant[L], Wells				

Year					
1948	Joos	Leopold		Shannon & Weaver[L]	
1949					
1950					
1951	Trager & Smith[L]	Harris[L]	Miller(a)[P,L] Miller(b)[P]	Carroll et al.	Lashley
1952	Fries[L]	Harris Jakobson[L]		Olmsted & Moore Osgood	
1953	Carroll[L,P]		Miller(a)		
1954	Hoijer[L,P]		Miller(b) Mowrer	Osgood & Sebeok[L]	
1955	Gleason[L]	Harris			Brown Bruner et al.[P,L]
1956	Whorf[L,P] (posthumous)	Chomsky Jakobson & Halle[L,P] Chomsky[L]	Skinner[P,L]	Osgood et al.[P,L]	
1957	Hockett[L]				Brown[P,L]
1958		Chomsky[P]	Alkon		
1959	Yngve	Lees[L] Halliday			Miller et al.[P,L]
1960	Gleason (see 1955)			Mowrer[P] Saporta[P,L]	
1961					
1962	Hill				Miller
1963	Lounsbury[L]	Greenberg[L,P] Katz & Fodor Bach[L]	Gough & Jenkins	Osgood(a) Osgood(b)[P,L] Carroll[P,L]	Chomsky & Miller
1964		Fodor & Katz[L,P] Gumperz & Hymes[L] Katz Katz & Postal[L,P] Chomsky[L]			Brown & Bellugi[P,L] Lenneberg[P]
1965				Osgood & Sebeok[P] (see 1954)	Miller
1966	Lamb[L]	Quirk & Svartvik[L,P] Sebeok[L]	Esper	Ervin-Tripp & Slobin	Lyons & Wales[P,L] McNeill Smith & Miller[P,L]

TABLE 35.1 Continued

	LINGUISTICS		PSYCHOLOGY OF LANGUAGE		
YEAR	Structuralist tradition	Current tradition	Behaviorist tradition	Transitional positions	Cognitive psycholinguistics
1967		Lieberman[L,P]	Salzinger & Salzinger[P]	Jakobovits & Miron[P]	Lenneberg[P,L] Miller[P] Chomsky[L] Oldfield & Marshall[P]
1968	Bolinger[L] Hockett[L]	Bach & Harms[L] Chomsky & Halle[L] Fillmore Langacker[L] Lyons[L] McCawley	Esper[P,L] Goldman-Eisler Staats[P]	Dixon & Horton[P] Rommetveit Zale	
1969	Cook[L]	Crystal[L] Langendoen[L] Searle[L] Seuren[L]	Suppes	Gardner & Gardner	Miller & McNeill
1970		Chafe[L]	Premack Salzinger	Cowan[P] Deese[P]	Bloom[P] Blumenthal[P,L] Flores d'Arcais & Levelt[P,L] Gleitman & Gleitman[P,L] Hayes[L] McNeill[P]
1971	Olmsted[P]	Dingwall Householder[L,P] Jackendoff[L]	Premack	Fillenbaum Steinberg & Jakobovits[P,L]	Slobin(a)[P,L] Slobin(b)[P]
1972	Trager			Fredle & Carroll[P]	Greene[P,L] Schank
1973	Derwing[L,P]	Halliday[P] Labov[L,P] Stockwell et al.[L]	Esper[P,L] Salzinger & Feldman[P]		Brown[P,L] Weimer

1974		*Cohen*[L,P] *Harman*[P] *Levelt*[L,P] *Sadock*[L]		Carroll *Ervin-Tripp* *Pollio*[P] *Rommetveit*[P]	*Fodor et al.*[P,L] Miller *Weimer & Palermo*[P,L]
1975	*Hymes & Fought*[L]	*Chomsky*[P] *Sampson*[L]		*Aaronson & Rieber*[P] *Kavanagh & Cutting*[P,L] *Massaro*[P]	*Glucksberg & Danks*[P]
1976		*Hudson*[L] *Li*[L] *Parisi & Antinucci*[L]	*Winokur*[P]	Osgood *Carterette & Friedman*[P]	*Bever et al.*[P] *Cairns & Cairns*[P,L] *Greenfield & Smith*[P,L] *Leonard*[L] *Miller & Johnson-Laird*[P,L] *Taylor*[P,L]
1977	*Pike & Pike*[L]	*Fodor*[L,P] *Lyons*[L,P]	*Kantor*[P]	*Curtiss*[P,L] *Lewis & Rosenblum*[P,L] *Rosenberg*[P] *Rumbaugh*[P] *Schlesinger*[P,L] *Sebeok*[P,L]	*Clark & Clark*[P,L] *Ervin-Tripp & Mitchell-Kernan*[P,L] *Morton & Marshall*[P]
1978		*Cole*[L] *Dingwall*[P] (see 1971) *Kac*[L] *Sankoff*[L,P]		*Snow & Ferguson*[P,L] *Bloom & Lahey*[P,L] Cofer *de Villiers & de Villiers*[P,L] *Levelt & Flores d'Arcais*[P] *Palermo*[P]	*Foss & Hakes*[P,L] *Halle et al.*[P]
1979	*Givón*[P,L]	*Fillmore et al.*	Terrace et al.		*Morton & Marshall*[P] *Slobin*[P] (see 1971)

[a] Items in *italics* are considered "reviewable"; the remaining items are articles and similar works not normally treated in reviews.

[L] At least one review is noted in a linguistic journal (see References).

[P] At least one review is noted in a psychological or psycholinguistic journal (see References).

831

TABLE 35.2 Percentages of Works in Linguistics and in the Psychology of Language Reviewed by Journals in Each Discipline, for Three Periods over 1929–1979

PERIOD	WORKS IN LINGUISTICS			WORKS IN THE PSYCHOLOGY OF LANGUAGE		
	Number of items	Percentage reviewed in linguistic journals	Percentage reviewed in psychological journals	Number of items	Percentage reviewed in psychological journals	Percentage reviewed in linguistic journals
1929–1964	35	86	37	19	90	79
1965–1974	29	79	38	27	85	45
1975–1979	15	73	40	33	97	49
1929–1979	79	81	38	79	91	55

whatever psychology might have to offer about how human beings learn and use language systems.

We may characterize the first twenty-five years of the period covered in Table 35.1 as ones of relative detachment: relations between the two disciplines were negligible. There are several reasons for this. First, linguistics was far from being a large, well-organized discipline. In 1929 there were few independent departments of linguistics, even in major universities. Most of the scholars who thought of themselves as linguistic scientists had been trained in departments of English or foreign languages, or of anthropology, and were on the faculties of such departments. The Linguistic Society of America had been founded only as recently as 1925. Few general treatises and textbooks on general linguistics were available; the methodology of linguistic analysis was in effect an art passed down through successive generations of graduate students—and these were few in number. Second, linguistics was only beginning to recognize the importance of "synchronic" rather than "diachronic" studies—that is, the importance of making scientific descriptions of language systems as they existed at a particular point of time in a particular language community as opposed to the study of the development of language systems over long periods of time. For this reason a general theory of language structure was slow to develop. It was not until 1933 that the second edition of Bloomfield's 1914 treatise *Language* offered a formalization of what has since been called, perhaps rather inaccurately, the "structuralist" or "taxonomic" tradition. Under the influence of the behaviorist psychologist A. P. Weiss (1929), Bloomfield (1933) had attempted to develop a rigorous and objective methodology of linguistic analysis that may be characterized as "bottom-up" in nature. That is, through the examination of spoken or written language performances obtained through certain fairly well-defined elicitation procedures with informants or as texts, a language system was to be analyzed first in terms of its elementary phonetic units (phonemes), then in terms of elementary lexical units (free or bound morphemes), and only later in terms of morphological and syntactical composition rules. The problems of identifying elementary phonetic and morphemic units appeared generally so large and difficult that the higher levels of analysis (morphology and syntax) got short shrift in this early period. Semantic considerations came into play only in finding aspects of structure that made for *differences* of meaning; exactly what the meanings were was a matter to be left to lexicographers. Much of the linguistic research of the period was devoted to the description of a wide variety of languages, for example, American Indian languages (then rapidly disappearing), native American English dialects (while they still remained fairly distinct), and languages of military importance in World War II. Linguistic scientists had little time to attend to psychological aspects of language. Language teaching methods developed for the Army during the war featured large amounts of imitation and rote learning and made no explicit appeal to principles of learning derived from psychological research, if indeed any such principles were available (Bloomfield, 1942).

833

Bloomfield and others established an important tradition that has been influential up to the present day. It has in fact had an influence, to an extent that is seldom acknowledged, even on linguists who are working within newer traditions. The references listed in the entire first column of Table 35.2 represent linguistic work carried out generally within the framework of the Bloomfieldian tradition or its variants.

Fundamentally, the detachment of linguistics from psychology during the Bloomfieldian era may be attributed to the theoretical position that it adopted, to the effect that the study of language systems should be conducted independently of considerations of mind or behavior. Although linguists felt that psychology might make contributions to problems like the teaching of native and foreign languages or the influence of language on thought, they preferred to maintain relative autonomy in pursuing what they believed to be the basic goals of their discipline. (To a degree, this position is maintained even by theorists in current traditions, except that a language system is considered to be in some way a property of the mind.)

There are also reasons on the side of psychology for the detachment that existed between the disciplines in the first half of the period we are considering. It is hardly necessary to remind the reader of the preoccupations of psychology during that period. Except for islands of interest in *Gestalttheorie*, psychoanalysis, and other special schools of thought, the generally behavioristic theories expounded by Watson, Hull, Tolman, and Skinner dominated the scene. There was little interest in what we now call "cognitive processes," and what interest there was seldom extended to speech and language. Thus one finds much blank space in the first twenty or twenty-five years of the third column of Table 35.1, headed "behaviorist tradition," and even more white space in the fourth and fifth columns. To be sure, reviews of literature in the psychology of language were dutifully published periodically in the *Psychological Bulletin* and other media (see references for Adams & Powers, 1929; Esper, 1935; McGranahan, 1936; and Pronko, 1946), but these reviews reflected little awareness of, or even interest in, developments in linguistics. Furthermore, with one or two exceptions, important publications in linguistics were not noticed in the book review sections of psychological journals (whereas on the contrary there were a number of instances of psychological works being reviewed in linguistic journals). And like linguistics, psychology was subject to the effects of the economic depression in the 1930s and World War II in the 1940s.

Aside from certain European developments that are deliberately being ignored here (and that were largely ignored by American psychologists—for example, the writings of Karl Bühler), what little work in the psychology of language there was during the period 1929 to, say, 1951, centered around three figures: Esper, Kantor, and Skinner—all of a behaviorist persuasion. Of these, Esper was most closely associated with linguistics; as a graduate student in psychology he had studied under several early linguists and became acquainted with Bloomfield. Some of his research in the learning of miniature language systems had been published, in 1925,

834

in a monograph supplement to the first volume of *Language*. Esper continued publishing in the field up to very late in his life—still advocating a generally associationistic orientation (Esper, 1966, 1968, 1973). In the preface that Esper wrote, at the age of seventy-six, to his last publication, *Analogy and Association in Linguistics and Psychology* (1973), one finds these touchingly plaintive words:

> . . . I have, of course, during the past century, seen many . . . theories, fads, and fancies come and go, and while all the controversial literature which they produced may have supplied motive power [as Boring had suggested], I am depressed by the thought of the enormous waste of energy, goodwill, and paper which they also produced, and I share Bloomfield's wistful vision of a more rational—and courteous—world of science in which workers could respect and mutually stimulate one another, and hostility would be expressed only for really careless and unscholarly publications and not for the work of those with whose point of view one happened to disagree (Esper, 1973, p. xxxi).

Skinner had a curiously peripheral interest in language in the form of what he defined as "verbal behavior," that is, behavior of an individual that arises mainly through the reinforcements supplied by other individuals. Already by the late 1930s he had developed important concepts of verbal responses as varieties of operants. (I was privileged to be introduced to these concepts in Skinner's courses in the psychology of language at the University of Minnesota at that time.) His major work in the field was not published until 1957 (Skinner, 1957), although "underground" mimeographed drafts kept interest in his work alive. It was under Skinner's influence that I published (Carroll, 1944) a paper attempting to relate linguistics to Skinner's system—a paper that received discouragingly little attention from either psychologists or linguists. The war years were apparently not propitious for devotion to theory in the psychology of language.

Kantor's major work, *An Objective Psychology of Grammar* (1936, reprinted 1952), deserves comment. This was a starkly behavioristic treatment that urged psychologists to purge themselves of all traces of "mentalism" in dealing with language, and to address themselves instead to the functions of language in the mutual "adjustments" of speakers and hearers to each other and to stimuli in their environment. Kantor attempted to give an "interbehaviorist," "adjustmental" account of a variety of grammatical phenomena, berating linguists, along the way, for what he regarded as their tendency to treat language symbols as "things" divorced from their function in social interaction. Pronko (1946), one of Kantor's students, carried this theme forward in a literature survey, reviewing a number of experimental studies by himself and other students of Kantor. From today's perspective, these experiments may be said to represent mainly demonstrations of rather obvious referential functions of language symbols.

The great gulf that existed between psychology and linguistics in those early years

835

is best illustrated by the savage (but in my opinion well-justified) review in *Language* of Kantor's treatise. The review was authored by H. V. Velten, one of Kantor's colleagues on the Indiana University faculty, in the department of German. Here are a few extracts from that review:

> Once again a non-linguist rushes to the rescue of the sadly misguided science of linguistics. For according to Kantor, "the fair-minded observer must agree that hardly a beginning has been made in bringing scientific order to the linguistic chaos."
>
> The salvation is to be found in the holistic doctrine that every act of speech, i.e. of "adjustmental behavior," is an indivisible whole which may on no account be dissected into sounds, words, and sentences. . . .
>
> When Marty tried to foist upon linguistics Brentano's system of psychology, he at least offered a completely new terminology of grammar. Kantor offers nothing beyond the suggestion, endlessly repeated on over 300 pages, that acts of speech should be classified according to the situations to which they are adjusted. . . .
>
> . . . Suffice it to say that linguistics will have to do without the aid of the particular brand of psychology expounded in this book (Velten, *Language*, 1938, *14*, 66–68).

It is noteworthy that one of the latest entries in column three of Table 35.1 is for a late work by Kantor (1977) entitled *Psychological Linguistics*. A review by Rieber in *Contemporary Psychology* is gentle and genteel to a fault, but a scanning of the book itself reveals that it contains little more than the same kinds of polemics to be found in the 1936 publication. "Interbehavioristic," "adjustmental" psychology of the Kantorian variety dies hard!

In the last quarter of the centennial century, relations between psychology and linguistics warmed up to a state of what may be characterized as cautious affiliation. The term *affiliation* does not, however, do justice to the relationship, which was asymmetric if not one-sided. One gains insight into the relationship only by becoming acquainted with the several partially overlapping streams of activity that produced it.

First consider events in linguistics, in which by 1951 there were signs of much ferment. Still working essentially within the structuralist tradition, Zellig Harris (1951, 1952) focused on syntactical problems, mainly in English, extending his analyses even to suprasentential relationships in discourse. To many, Harris's work tended to demonstrate that conventional methods of distributional analysis were incapable of dealing adequately with the complexities of syntactic structure. Fries's (1952) attempts along these lines were generally criticized even by linguists. Noam Chomsky (1956), a student of Harris's and in the early 1950s a Junior Fellow at Harvard, felt that it was necessary to reformulate linguistic methodology with what may be called "top-down" procedures, beginning at least at the level of the sentence and working down to something like the phoneme. His 1956 paper described three models of language description; one may say that at least the first two of these were "straw man" models. He showed persuasively that a Markovian "finite state" model was clearly unacceptable, that the "phrase structure" model implicit in some of the work of the structuralists would be only partially successful, and that a "transformational generative" model held much promise. His monograph *Syntactic Structures* (1957) presented an early version of a transformational model for English grammar and captured the attention of a new generation of linguists. In this work or in other writings, he proposed a striking change in linguistic methodology, namely, that linguists be permitted to use intuition about their own language in describing that language, as opposed to the examination of texts and corpuses to which structuralists limited themselves. By the time of the publication of Chomsky's *Aspects of the Theory of Syntax* (1965), Chomsky's theories dominated linguistics, much to the distress of many older members of the profession. But even some of the newer generation of linguists had doubts about some features of Chomskyan theory, and they spawned a variety of further grammatical theories. The complex details cannot be gone into here; some of the names associated with these newer grammatical theories, with dates of principal publications, are the following: Halliday (1961, 1973), Fillmore (1968), McCawley (1968), Lyons (1968), Seuren (1969), Chafe (1970), Hudson (1976), and Parisi and Antinucci (1976).

There is an important point to be made about all these developments in linguistics, referenced in the second column of Table 35.1. To one degree or another, each of these newer grammatical formulations (including Chomsky's, of course) made claims about the psychology of language use and acquisition. In contrast to the structuralist school, which eschewed psychological considerations, Chomsky insisted that the formal analysis of a language somehow specifies what the "ideal speaker" of that language "knows" about the language in order to generate and understand "novel sentences." (There has been much debate over exactly what Chomsky meant by this claim, or what it implies.) Chomsky further speculated that only the postulation of some sort of innate, species-specific endowment could permit explaining how a child could acquire this knowledge. He introduced a distinction between what he called "competence" and "performance" and claimed that associationist psychology would be totally incapable of explaining linguistic knowledge and behavior. In his famous review (Chomsky, 1959) of Skinner's *Verbal Behavior* (1957), he urged the rejection of behaviorism and of the principle of reinforcement as bases for a psychology of language.

The claims made by other grammatical theorists were not as explicit or extreme as those of Chomsky, but they unfailingly impinged upon psychology and seemed to require a frankly cognitive, or perhaps "mentalistic," orientation (Katz, 1964). For example, the "case grammar" approach advocated by those who called themselves "generative semanticists" implies that language behavior involves complex manipulations of conceptual categories; a radical behaviorist might have trouble dealing with such categories, if they were not rejected out of hand.

837

Note that all these developments occurred purely within linguistics; they would probably have taken place even if there had not been parallel developments in psychology, now to be described.

By 1951 it was obvious to a number of psychologists that there was a need for the development of a satisfactory psychological account of language and language behavior. Psychology was expanding after World War II, and language learning and use was seen as a new world to conquer. There was hope and even confidence, among many, that a behavioristic or at least functionalist orientation would be adequate to this task. Skinner had given encouragement to this view in his William James lectures at Harvard in 1948 (later worked into his book, 1957). Two events that occurred in 1951 helped prepare for the assault on language: first, the publication of the first modern textbook of linguistic psychology, George Miller's *Language and Communication* (1951a); and second, the convening of an interdisciplinary summer workshop in linguistics and psychology at Cornell University under my leadership and under the sponsorship of the Social Science Research Council (SSRC).

Miller had acquired his interest in language phenomena partly through his applied work in speech perception and intelligibility during the war years, and indeed much progress in speech analysis had been made through the efforts of communication engineers. Miller was able to make good use of the concepts of information theory that had been introduced by Shannon and Weaver (1949). His theoretical orientation in psychology was at that time frankly behavioristic—"not fanatically behavioristic, but certainly tainted by a preference," Miller stated in his preface. The book relied on the work of Skinner, Hull, Hilgard, and other learning theorists, and therefore it is listed in the column of Table 35.1 identified as representing the behavioristic tradition in psychology. The linguistic theory and methodology recognized by Miller was essentially that of Bloomfield; Bloomfield's *Language* (1933) was cited as "a classic text in linguistics which favors the behavioristic description of verbal behavior" (p. 173).

The 1951 Cornell seminar brought together four psychologists and four linguists who spent a summer introducing each other to the essentials of their respective disciplines and exploring potential relations between them. The mimeographed, unpublished report (Carroll, et al., 1951) that resulted from that seminar is listed under "transitional positions" in Table 35.1 because, from the perspective of the participants, dissatisfaction with the constraints of behaviorist theory was already beginning. Osgood was exploring the possibility of explaining referential behavior through his "mediation hypothesis," and I myself was at pains to point out to my fellow psychologists the problems of trying to use simple associationist theory to explain language acquisition and use. The seminar members were much occupied with problems of specifying units of behavior, concluding that units identified by linguists (phonemes, morphemes, and the like) were not necessarily those employed in actual speech production and understanding, even though they might often coincide. They were also much impressed with the suggestion, arising in linguistics, that units in a language system are hierarchically organized, yet they were puzzled about how to handle such an organization in behavior theory, or even in information theory. Nevertheless, it seemed to them that some kind of complex learning and behavior theory could eventually be developed to account for the facts of language organization, acquisition, and use.

As a result of the Cornell seminar, regular contacts between linguists and psychologists were established through meetings of the Committee on Linguistics and Psychology that the SSRC sponsored over the years from 1952 to 1961. One of the first projects of the committee was the organization of a further and more broadly based summer seminar that occurred in 1953 and resulted in the publication of the monograph *Psycholinguistics* edited by Osgood and the linguist Sebeok (1954). This widely read monograph set the tone and content of much of the work in psycholinguistics for the next few years, perhaps up to a little beyond 1965, when it was reissued with an extensive review, by the social anthropologist A. R. Diebold, Jr., of psycholinguistic research over the period 1954 to 1964 and a reprint of an article by George Miller describing the new wave of psycholinguistic research conducted by those psychologists who had been caught up in what they saw as some kind of revolution in linguistic theory.

By this time, Miller himself, along with a number of other psychologists, had made a complete switch from his former behavioristic position to an advocacy of a psycholinguistic theory that would rely heavily on transformational generative grammar (Miller, 1962, 1965). A large number of references are listed in the last column of Table 35.1 headed "cognitive psycholinguistics," in order to suggest that this brand of psycholinguistics was (and still is) much in harmony with the general trends in psychological theory that set in toward the middle 1950s with the publications of Lashley, Bruner, and many others that might be mentioned. Cognitive psycholinguists often cite Lashley's (1951) paper on the serial order of behavior as sounding the death knell of associationism and posing the basic problems to be addressed by a satisfactory psychology of language. But psychologists must probably give Chomsky—a linguist—credit for providing impetus for the great expansion of cognitive psychology along psycholinguistic lines. It was Miller's work on the psychology of grammar, inspired by Chomskyan theory and reported in his 1962 paper in the *American Psychologist*, that established the new subspecialty, called *experimental psycholinguistics* (Glucksberg & Danks, 1975), which is concerned with the "psychological reality of grammar" and the processes by which mature language users perceive and understand "novel" sentences. Unfortunately, psycholinguistic experimentation was not able to keep up with the rapid developments in linguistic theory; the "kernel and transformation" grammar that was the basis for one of Miller's more elegant experiments, and for much other research of that period, was almost completely overturned by the version of transformational theory proposed by Chomsky in his 1965 *Aspects*. At the same time, psycholinguistic experimentation

839

was outrunning linguistic theory, so much so that by 1966, an Edinburgh conference on psycholinguistics, papers from which were edited by Lyons and Wales (1966), concluded that transformational theory, or in particular the hypothesis of derivational complexity derived therefrom, was not an adequate basis for interpreting sentence comprehension. This conclusion was further addressed in Fodor, Bever, and Garrett's (1974) treatise on the psychology of language, and the arguments surrounding this and related issues are still raging today, taking into consideration also some of the newer grammatical theories mentioned earlier.

Developmental psycholinguistics, the study of child language acquisition, also owes much to Chomsky, if only because Chomsky challenged psychologists to test his claim that child language acquisition involves innate learning mechanisms. Among the psychologists who have been most supportive of this claim were David McNeill (1966, 1970) and the late Eric Lenneberg (1967). However, the founder of developmental psycholinguistics in its modern form was the psychologist Roger Brown (1973; see also Brown & Bellugi, 1964), who has taken a more impartial stance concerning the relevance of transformational as opposed to other candidate theories. Most of the references having to do with child language studies have been placed in the "cognitive psycholinguistics" column of Table 35.1 because those studies have depended heavily on the newer linguistic theories and have tended to eschew behavioristic explanations. Nevertheless, current views (e.g., Snow & Ferguson, 1977) give much more credit to environmental influences, such as the type of "motherese" to which the child is exposed, than did those that proposed the dominant function of a "language acquisition device."

Chomsky's linguistic theories are also partly responsible for psychologists' recent interest in the possibility of arranging conditions whereby primates, such as chimpanzees and gorillas, could communicate with human beings or with each other by means of some form of language system. Chomsky's claim that language is species-specific to human organisms and is acquired through innate mechanisms unique to humans challenged psychologists to attempt to disconfirm this claim. Several psychologists, notably Gardner and Gardner (1969), Premack (1971), and Rumbaugh (1977), have produced language-like behavior in primates, but currently it is moot whether this behavior depends on a system having the properties of human natural language. According to a group of psychologists (Terrace et al., 1979) and the linguist Sebeok (1977), the artificially produced "language" of chimpanzees and gorillas is mainly learned, imitative behavior that shows little evidence of true language structure. The virtue of a joint effort of linguists and psychologists in this work lies in the power of linguistics to define criteria for a true language system and the capability of psychologists to provide tests of whether those criteria are met.

In the meantime, various other branches of language study with obvious roots in both psychology and linguistics have sprung up. Sociolinguistics, insofar as it studies social dialects, was foreshadowed by earlier work on American English dialects and by the work of the linguist Fries (1940) on varieties of grammars found in different social classes. Neurolinguistic studies were inspired in considerable measure by Jakobson's (1941) publication concerning aphasia as a sort of mirror image of early child language acquisition, but they also have origins in psychological work going back to the nineteenth century.

The current situation in both linguistics and psychology is one of healthy diversity of opinion and theory. Toward the bottoms of the two columns of references devoted to linguistics, the one allotted to the "current tradition" and its forerunners is quite dense, but a fair number of references are also found in the column assigned to the "structuralist tradition"; many of these represent reactions to the newer trends. For example, Derwing (1973) has attempted to show the weaknesses of transformational theory in dealing with the grammars of child languages, and Hymes and Fought (1975) have provided an extensive critique of transformational theory and of what they regard as the somewhat irresponsible and erroneous criticisms of the structuralists made by the transformationalists. Likewise, one finds almost as many references in the "transitional positions" column under the psychology of language as one finds under "cognitive psycholinguistics," and there are still those who staunchly support and defend a radical behaviorist position, for example, Winokur (1976). Charles Catania's review of Winokur's text in *Contemporary Psychology* (1977) is entitled "Verbal behavior is alive and well." Actually, the heading "transitional positions" does not aptly characterize all those listed in that column; some of the writers listed there would be better described as attempting to resolve the opposition between behavioristic and more purely "cognitive" theories of language.

The characterization of the whole modern period as one of "cautious affiliation" should also be qualified by pointing out that there are increasingly closer ties between psychology and linguistics with respect to the training of new generations of research workers and specialists. Nowadays, one could find very few psycholinguists who have not had a considerable dose of linguistics in their graduate training. Young linguists are encouraged to take courses in various branches of psycholinguistics, not only to round out their professional education but also to put themselves, if need be, in a position to seek jobs in which they can apply linguistics in various types of practical work in second-language teaching, bilingual education, and clinical studies of language-retarded children, aphasics, and other defectives.

It is also now quite customary for each of the disciplines to include book reviews of publications of the other discipline in its principal journals and to publish reviews and articles by members of the other discipline. Psycholinguists are frequently found attending meetings and conventions in linguistics and vice versa.

Where is psycholinguistics going? To what extent will psychology continue to interact with linguistics? I can give optimistic answers to these questions. I foresee that the next few years will bring much mellowing and reconciliation of the oppositions between different camps and schools of thought. In linguistics, I predict that some fair compromise between "bottom-up" and "top-down" methodologies of linguistic analysis will be arrived at, and in psychology I envision some reasonable

841

resolution of the alleged conflicts between behavioristic and cognitive theories. Further, I foresee continually closer cooperation between linguistics and psychology—not only cognitive psychology, but also social psychology, neuropsychology, and even psychometrics! (Fillmore, Kempler, & Wang, 1979; Diller, 1980; Sankoff, 1978). I believe that together psychology and linguistics are ready to begin the real job of accounting, in a principled way, for language acquisition and use, both in its productive and receptive phases.

With the dust from past frays slowly settling, we may see the realization of one of Chomsky's (1968) most startling claims, namely, that linguistics is really a branch of psychology. But this is no more than what Father Wundt himself envisaged.

REFERENCES

Aaronson, D., & Rieber, R. W. Developmental psycholinguistics and communication disorders. *Annals of the New York Academy of Sciences*, 1975, 263, 5–287.

Adams, S., & Powers, F. F. The psychology of language. *Psychological Bulletin*, 1929, 26, 241–260.

Alkon, P. K. Behaviorism and linguistics. *Language and Speech*, 1959, 2, 37–51.

Bach, E. *An introduction to transformational grammars.* New York: Holt, 1964.

Bach, E., & Harms, R. T. (Eds.) *Universals in linguistic theory.* New York: Holt, 1968.

Bever, T. G., Hurtig, R. R., & Handel, A. D. Analytic processing elicits right ear superiority in monaurally presented speech. *Neuropsychologia*, 1976, 14, 175–181.

Bloch, B., & Trager, G. L. *Outline of linguistic analysis.* Baltimore: Linguistic Society of America, 1942.
> Reviewed: *Language*, 1943, 19, 42–44.

Bloom, L. *Language development: Form and function in emerging grammars.* Cambridge, Mass.: M.I.T. Press, 1970.
> Reviewed: *Contemporary Psychology*, 1971, 16, 519–520 (J. Weil).

Bloom, L., & Lahey, M. *Language development and language disorders.* New York: Wiley, 1978.
> Reviewed: *Contemporary Psychology*, 1979, 24, 367–369 (N. S. Rees).
> *Language*, 1979, 55, 945–947 (C. Garvey).

Bloomfield, L. *Language.* New York: Holt, 1933.
> Reviewed: *Language*, 1934, 10, 40–48 (R. G. Kent), 48–52 (G. M. Bolling).
> *Language*, 1935, 11, 251–252 (G. M. Bolling).

Bloomfield, L. *Outline guide for the practical study of foreign languages.* Baltimore: Linguistic Society of America, 1942.
> Reviewed: *Language*, 1943, 19, 42–44 (E. Sturtevant).

Blumenthal, A. L. *Language and psychology: Historical aspects of psycholinguistics.* New York: Wiley, 1970.
> Reviewed: *Contemporary Psychology*, 1971, 16, 497–498 (J. Macnamara).
> *Language*, 1971, 47, 979–981 (E. A. Esper).

Bolinger, D. *Aspects of language.* New York: Harcourt, Brace, 1968.
> Reviewed: *International Review of Applied Linguistics*, 1970, 8, 78–81 (F. Braun).
> *Journal of Linguistics*, 1970, 6, 125–129 (D. J. Allerton).
> *Language*, 1970, 46, 667–671 (J. H. Hill).

Brown, R. W. Language and categories. In J. S. Bruner, J. J. Goodnow, & G. A. Austin (Eds.), *A Study of Thinking.* New York: Wiley, 1956.

842

Brown, R. *Words and things*. Glencoe, Ill.: Free Press, 1958.
    Reviewed: *Contemporary Psychology*, 1959, 4, 193–195 (J. J. Jenkins).
    Language, 1959, 35, 496–503 (H. Hoijer).
Brown, R. *A first language: The early stages*. Cambridge, Mass.: Harvard University Press, 1973.
    Reviewed: *Contemporary Psychology*, 1975, 20, 97–100 (C. S. Smith).
    Journal of Linguistics, 1975, 11, 322–343 (P. H. Matthews).
    Language, 1975, 51, 764–770 (K. Atkinson-King).
Brown, R., & Bellugi, U. Three processes in the child's acquisition of syntax. *Harvard Educational Review*, 1964, 34, 133–151.
Bruner, J. S., Goodnow, J. J., & Austin, G. A. *A study of thinking*. New York: Wiley, 1956.
    Reviewed: *Contemporary Psychology*, 1957, 2, 249–252 (D. Rapaport).
    Language, 1957, 33, 415–421 (F. W. Householder).
Bryant, M. M., & Aiken, J. R. *Psychology of English*. New York: Columbia University Press, 1940.
    Reviewed: *Psychological Bulletin*, 1941, 38, 761–762 (B. F. Skinner).
    Language, 1941, 17, 158–160 (S. S. Newman).
Cairns, H. S., & Cairns, C. E. *Psycholinguistics: A cognitive view of language*. New York: Holt, 1976.
    Reviewed: *Journal of Psycholinguistic Research*, 1978, 7, 477–492 (A. F. Healy).
    Language, 1977, 53, 480–483 (T. Scovel).
Carroll, J. B. The analysis of verbal behavior. *Psychological Review*, 1944, 51, 102–119.
Carroll, J. B. *The study of language: A survey of linguistics and related disciplines in America*. Cambridge, Mass.: Harvard University Press, 1953.
    Reviewed: *International Journal of American Linguistics*, 1954, 20, 345–346 (T. A. Sebeok).
    Language, 1955, 31, 59–72 (H. L. Smith, Jr.).
    Psychological Bulletin, 1955, 52, 87–88 (I. J. Hirsh).
Carroll, J. B. *Language and thought*. Englewood Cliffs, N.J.: Prentice-Hall, 1964.
    Reviewed: *Contemporary Psychology*, 1968, 13, 296–299 (E. Deaux & K. S. Deaux).
    International Journal of American Linguistics, 1966, 32, 285–288 (M. Anisfeld).
    American Journal of Psychology, 1966, 79, 169 (M. S. Miron).
    Modern Language Journal, 1965, 49, 384–386 (J. A. Fodor).
Carroll, J. B. Towards a performance grammar for core sentences in spoken and written English. *International Review of Applied Linguistics*, 1974, 12, 29–49.
Carroll, J. B. The tale of a theoretical and applied linguistic psychologist. In B. H. Davis & R. O'Cain (Eds.), *First person singular: Papers from the Conference on an Oral Archive for the History of American Linguistics*. Amsterdam: John Benjamins, 1980.
Carroll, J. B., Agard, F. B., Dulany, D. E., Newman, S. S., Newmark, L. D., Osgood, C. E., Sebeok, T. A., & Solomon, R. L. *Report and recommendations of the interdisciplinary seminar in psychology and linguistics, Cornell University*, June 18–August 10, 1951, Ithaca, N.Y., 1951.
Carterette, E. C., & Friedman, M. P. (Eds.). *Handbook of perception. Language and speech* (Vol. 9). New York: Academic Press, 1976.
    Reviewed: *Contemporary Psychology*, 1977, 22, 652–653 (S. Glucksberg).
    Journal of Psycholinguistic Research, 1979, 8, 407–424 (K. Stenning).
Chafe, W. L. *Meaning and the structure of language*. Chicago: The University of Chicago Press, 1970.
    Reviewed: *Language*, 1972, 48, 134–161 (R. W. Langacker).
Chomsky, N. Three models for the description of language. *IRE Transactions*, 1956, IT-2, No. 3, 113–124.
Chomsky, N. *Syntactic structures*. The Hague: Mouton, 1957.
    Reviewed: *Language*, 1957, 33, 375–408 (R. B. Lees).
Chomsky, N. (Review of B. F. Skinner's *Verbal behavior*.) *Language*, 1959, 35, 26–58.
    Reviewed: *Journal of the Experimental Analysis of Behavior*, 1970, 13, 83–99 (K. MacCorquodale).

Chomsky, N. *Aspects of the theory of syntax*. Cambridge, Mass.: M.I.T. Press, 1965.
   Reviewed: *Journal of Linguistics*, 1967, 3, 119–152 (P. H. Matthews).
Chomsky, N. The formal nature of language. In E. H. Lenneberg (Ed.), *Biological foundations of language*. New York: Wiley, 1967.
Chomsky, N. *Language and mind*. New York: Harcourt, Brace, 1968. ("Enlarged edition," 1972).
   Reviewed (1972 edition): *Language*, 1973, 49, 453–464 (G. Harman).
Chomsky, N. *The logical structure of linguistic theory*. New York: Plenum, 1975.
Chomsky, N., & Halle, M. *The sound pattern of English*. New York: Harper & Row, 1968.
   Reviewed: *Language Sciences*, 1969, No. 7, 7–13 (S. Golopentia-Eretescu).
Chomsky, N., & Miller, G. A. Introduction to the formal analysis of natural languages. In R. D. Luce, R. R. Bush, & E. Galanter (Eds.), *Handbook of mathematical psychology* (Vol. 2). New York: Wiley, 1963.
   Reviewed (whole book): *Contemporary Psychology*, 1965, 10, 56–57 (B. F. Green, Jr.).
Clark, H. H., & Clark, E. V. *Psychology and language: An introduction to psycholinguistics*. New York: Harcourt, Brace, 1977.
   Reviewed: *Contemporary Psychology*, 1978, 23, 825–826 (R. R. Hurtig).
         Language, 1979, 55, 436–439 (L. H. Waterhouse).
Cofer, C. N. Origins of the *Journal of Verbal Learning and Verbal Behavior*. *Journal of Verbal Learning and Verbal Behavior*, 1978, 17, 113–126.
Cohen, D. (Ed.). *Explaining linguistic phenomena*. New York: Wiley, 1974.
   Reviewed: *Contemporary Psychology*, 1975, 20, 875–876 (H. S. Cairns).
         Journal of Linguistics, 1976, 12, 177–182 (G. Sampson).
Cole, P. (Ed.). *Pragmatics*. New York: Academic Press, 1978.
   Reviewed: *Language*, 1980, 56, 209–211 (Z. Vendler).
Cook, W. A. *Introduction to tagmemic analysis*. New York: Holt, 1969.
   Reviewed: *Journal of Linguistics*, 1971, 7, 291–293 (R. Huddleston).
Cowan, J. L. (Ed.). *Studies in thought and language*. Tucson, Ariz.: University of Arizona Press, 1970.
   Reviewed: *Contemporary Psychology*, 1971, 16, 558–559 (J. R. Hayes).
Crystal, D. *Prosodic systems and intonation in English*. Cambridge, England: Cambridge University Press, 1969.
   Reviewed: *Contemporary Psychology*, 1970, 15, 547–548 (N. N. Markel).
Curtiss, S. *Genie: A psycholinguistic study of a modern-day "wild-child."* New York: Academic Press, 1977.
   Reviewed: *Contemporary Psychology*, 1979, 24, 456–457 (M. Maratsos).
         Language, 1979, 55, 725–726 (M. W. Salus).
Deese, J. *Psycholinguistics*. Boston: Allyn & Bacon, 1970.
   Reviewed: *Contemporary Psychology*, 1970, 15, 651 (G. A. Miller, brief notice).
De Laguna, G. A. *Speech: Its function and development*. New Haven: Yale University Press, 1927.
   Reviewed: *Language*, 1928, 4, 33–38 (A. P. Weiss).
         Psychological Bulletin, 1930, 27, 65–70 (E. A. Esper).
Derwing, B. L. *Transformational grammar as a theory of language acquisition: A study in the empirical, conceptual and methodological foundations of contemporary linguistics*. New York: Cambridge University Press, 1973.
   Reviewed: *Contemporary Psychology*, 1975, 20, 47–48 (K. Nelson).
         Journal of Linguistics, 1975, 2, 261–270 (N. V. Smith).
         Language in Society, 1975, 4, 375–377 (J. Fought).
de Villiers, J. G., & de Villiers, P. A. *Language acquisition*. Cambridge, Mass.: Harvard University Press, 1978.
   Reviewed: *Contemporary Psychology*, 1979, 24, 230–231 (E. H. Matthei & T. Roeper).
         Journal of Linguistics, 1980, 16, 131–139 (A. Cruttenden).

Diller, K. C. (Ed.). *Individual differences and universals in language learning aptitude.* Rowley, Mass.: Newbury House, 1980.

Dingwall, W. O. (Ed.). *A survey of linguistic science.* College Park, Md.: Linguistic Program, Univ. of Maryland, 1971. (2nd. ed., Stamford, Conn.: Greylock, 1978.)
    Reviewed: 2nd ed.: *Contemporary Psychology,* 1980, *25,* 317–319 (S. Glucksberg).

Dixon, T. R., & Horton, D. L. (Eds.). *Verbal behavior and general behavior theory.* Englewood Cliffs, N.J.: Prentice-Hall, 1968.
    Reviewed: *Contemporary Psychology,* 1969, *14,* 142–144 (C. Clifton, Jr.).

Ervin-Tripp, S. Two decades of Council activity in the rapprochement of linguistics and social science. *Social Science Research Council Items,* 1974, *28,* 1–4.

Ervin-Tripp, S., & Mitchell-Kernan, C. (Eds.). *Child discourse.* New York: Academic Press, 1977.
    Reviewed: *Contemporary Psychology,* 1978, *23,* 718–720 (M. Shatz).

Ervin-Tripp, S. M., & Slobin, D. I. Psycholinguistics. *Annual Review of Psychology,* 1966, *17,* 435–474.

Esper, E. A. Language. In C. Murchison (Ed.), *A handbook of social psychology.* Worcester, Mass.: Clark Univ. Press, 1935.

Esper, E. A. Social transmission of an artificial language. *Language,* 1966, *42,* 575–580.

Esper, E. A. *Mentalism and objectivism in linguistics: The sources of Leonard Bloomfield's psychology of language.* New York: American Elsevier, 1968.
    Reviewed: *Contemporary Psychology,* 1969, *14,* 465–467 (A. L. Blumenthal); rejoinders and replies, 1970, *15,* 253, 255, 319, 381.
        Language, 1970, *46,* 131–140 (D. L. Olmsted).
        Semiotica, 1970, *2,* 277–293 (J. C. Marshall).
        British Journal of Psychology, 1970, *61,* 576–577 (J. P. Thorne).

Esper, E. A. *Analogy and association in linguistics and psychology.* Athens, Ga.: University of Georgia Press, 1973.
    Reviewed: *Contemporary Psychology,* 1975, *20,* 776–777 (J. Torrey).
        Language, 1975, *51,* 514–516 (R. A. Hall, Jr.).

Fillenbaum, S. Psycholinguistics. *Annual Review of Psychology,* 1971, *22,* 251–306.

Fillmore, C. J. The case for case. In E. Bach & R. Harms (Eds.), *Universals in linguistic theory.* New York: Holt, 1968.

Fillmore, C. J., Kempler, D., & Wang, W. S-Y (Eds.). *Individual differences in language ability and language behavior.* New York: Academic Press, 1979.
    Reviewed: *Contemporary Psychology,* 1980, *25,* 548–549 (M. Singer).

Flores d'Arcais, G. B., & Levelt, W. J. M. (Eds.). *Advances in psycholinguistics.* New York: American Elsevier, 1970.
    Reviewed: *Contemporary Psychology,* 1972, *17,* 260–261 (S. Glucksberg).
        Language Sciences, 1975, No. 36, 33–35 (G. Quintling).

Fodor, J. D. *Semantics: Theories of meaning in generative grammar.* New York: Crowell, 1977.
    Reviewed: *Contemporary Psychology,* 1977, *22,* 532 (H. H. Clark).
        Journal of Linguistics, 1978, *14,* 115–118 (D. Wilson).
        Language, 1979, *55,* 425–431 (G. L. Ioup).

Fodor, J. A., Bever, T. G., & Garrett, M. F. *The psychology of language: An introduction to psycholinguistics and generative grammar.* New York: McGraw-Hill, 1974.
    Reviewed: *Contemporary Psychology,* 1975, *20,* 170 (H. H. Clark; brief notice).
        Journal of Psycholinguistic Research, 1977, *6,* 261–270 (E. Wanner).
        Language, 1976, *52,* 682–690 (D. B. Pisoni).
        Canadian Journal of Linguistics, 1976, *21,* 126–131 (J. F. Kess).

Fodor, J. A., & Katz, J. J. *The structure of language: Readings in the philosophy of language.* Englewood Cliffs, N.J.: Prentice-Hall, 1964.

845

Reviewed: *Contemporary Psychology*, 1965, *10*, 350–352 (A. Rapoport).
Journal of Linguistics, 1966, *2*, 243–245 (V. Hope).
Language, 1967, *43*, 526–550 (Y. Bar–Hillel).

Foss, D. J., & Hakes, D. T. *Psycholinguistics: An introduction to the psychology of language.* Englewood Cliffs, N.J.: Prentice-Hall, 1978.

Reviewed: *Contemporary Psychology*, 1978, *23*, 698 (H. S. Cairns); 1979, *24*, 453–454 (K. I. Forster).
Language, 1979, *55*, 491–492 (D. MacKay).

Freedle, R. O., & Carroll, J. B. (Eds.). *Language comprehension and the acquisition of knowledge.* Washington, D.C.: V. H. Winston & Sons, 1972.

Reviewed: *Contemporary Psychology*, 1974, *19*, 485 (D. Fay; brief notice).

Fries, C. C. *American English grammar: The grammatical structure of present-day English with especial reference to social differences or class dialects.* New York: Appleton-Century, 1940.

Reviewed: *Language*, 1941, *17*, 274–275 (M. Joos).

Fries, C. C. *The structure of English: An introduction to the construction of English sentences.* New York: Harcourt, Brace, 1952.

Reviewed: *Language*, 1955, *31*, 312–345 (J. Sledd).

Gardner, R. A., & Gardner, B. T. Teaching sign language to a chimpanzee. *Science*, 1969, *165*, 664–672.

Givòn, T. *On understanding grammar.* New York: Academic Press, 1979.

Reviewed: *Contemporary Psychology*, 1980, *25*, 365–366 (D. T. Langendoen).
Language, 1981, *57*, 436–445 (R. W. Langacker).

Gleason, H. A., Jr. *An introduction to descriptive linguistics.* New York: Holt, 1955. (Rev. ed., 1965.)

Reviewed 1955 ed.: *Language*, 1956, *32*, 469–477 (F. B. Agard & W. G. Moulton).

Gleitman, L. R., & Gleitman, H. *Phrase and paraphrase: Some innovative uses of language.* New York: Norton, 1970.

Reviewed: *Contemporary Psychology*, 1971, *16*, 693–694 (E. Wanner).
Language, 1973, *49*, 519–523 (E. H. Lenneberg).

Glucksberg, S., & Danks, J. H. *Experimental psycholinguistics: An introduction.* Hillsdale, N.J.: Erlbaum, 1975.

Reviewed: *Contemporary Psychology*, 1976, *21*, 404–406 (L. Rips).
Journal of Child Language, 1976, *3*, 291–298 (G. Balfour).
Journal of Psycholinguistic Research, 1978, *7*, 477–492 (A. F. Healy).

Goldman-Eisler, F. *Psycholinguistics: Experiments in spontaneous speech.* London: Academic Press, 1968.

Gough, P. B., & Jenkins, J. J. Verbal learning and psycholinguistics. In M. H. Marx (Ed.), *Theories in contemporary psychology.* New York: Macmillan, 1963.

Gray, L. H. *Foundations of language.* New York: Macmillan, 1939.

Reviewed: *Language*, 1940, *16*, 216–235 (Z. Harris & D. C. Swanson).
Psychological Bulletin, 1940, *37*, 634–637 (J. R. Kantor).

Greenberg, J. H. (Ed.). *Universals of language.* Cambridge, Mass.: M.I.T. Press, 1963. (Rev. ed., 1966.)

Reviewed: *Contemporary Psychology*, 1963, *8*, 417–418 (G. A. Miller).
Rev. ed.: *Contemporary Psychology*, 1968, *13*, 612 (W. S. Stolz, brief notice).
Journal of Linguistics, 1965, *1*, 94–95 (C. E. Bazell).
Language, 1964, *40*, 260–269 (E. Haugen).

Greene, J. *Psycholinguistics: Chomsky and psychology.* Harmondsworth: Penguin, 1972.

Reviewed: *Contemporary Psychology*, 1974, *19*, 277–279 (H. H. Clark).
Language, 1975, *51*, 1003–1005 (E. Clark).

Greenfield, P. M., & Smith, J. H. *The structure of communication in early language development.* New York: Academic Press, 1976.

Reviewed: *Contemporary Psychology*, 1977, 22, 362–364 (M. M. Rodgon).

Language, 1979, 55, 444–449 (D. Keller-Cohen).

Gumperz, J. J., & Hymes, D. (Eds.). The ethnography of communication. *American Anthropologist*, 1964, 66 (6, Part 2, special publication).

Reviewed: *Language*, 1966, 42, 704–712 (H. Landar).

Halle, M., Bresnan, J., & Miller, G. A. (Eds.). *Linguistic theory and psychological reality.* Cambridge, Mass.: M.I.T. Press, 1978.

Reviewed: *Contemporary Psychology*, 1980, 25, 15–17 (J. D. Fodor).

Halliday, M. A. K. Categories of the theory of grammar. *Word*, 1961, 17, 241–292.

Halliday, M. A. K. (Ed.). *Explorations in the functions of language.* New York: American Elsevier, 1973.

Reviewed: *Contemporary Psychology*, 1978, 23, 200 (E. V. Clark).

Harman, G. (Ed.). *On Noam Chomsky: Critical essays.* New York: Anchor Press, 1974.

Reviewed: *Contemporary Psychology*, 1975, 20, 433 (H. H. Clark).

Psychological Reports, 1974, 35, 1347 (brief notice).

Harris, Z. S. *Methods in structural linguistics.* Chicago: The University of Chicago Press, 1951.

Reviewed: *International Journal of American Linguistics*, 1952, 18, 257–260 (M. Mead).

International Journal of American Linguistics, 1952, 18, 260–268 (F. W. Householder, Jr.).

Language, 1952, 28, 495–504 (N. McQuown).

Harris, Z. S. Discourse analysis. *Language*, 1952, 28, 18–23.

Harris, Z. S. From phoneme to morpheme. *Language*, 1955, 31, 190–222.

Hayes, J. R. (Ed.). *Cognition and the development of language.* New York: Wiley, 1970.

Reviewed: *Language*, 1974, 50, 394–412 (L. Bloom).

Hill, A. A. (Ed.). *First [Second, Third] Texas Conference on Problems of Linguistic Analysis in English.* Austin, Texas: University of Texas Press, 1962.

Hockett, C. F. *A course in modern linguistics.* New York: Macmillan, 1958.

Reviewed: *Language*, 1959, 35, 503–527 (F. W. Householder, Jr.).

Hockett, C. F. *The state of the art.* The Hague: Mouton, 1968.

Reviewed: *Journal of Linguistics*, 1970, 6, 129–134 (F. W. Householder, Jr.).

Language, 1969, 45, 616–621 (F. R. Palmer).

Hoijer, H. (Ed.). *Language in culture: Conference on the interrelations of language and other aspects of culture.* Chicago: The University of Chicago Press, 1954.

Reviewed: *Language*, 1955, 31, 241–245 (W. Goodenough).

Psychological Bulletin, 1955, 52, 359–360 (R. Brown).

Householder, F. W., Jr. *Linguistic speculations.* New York: Cambridge University Press, 1971.

Reviewed: *Contemporary Psychology*, 1972, 17, 81 (G. A. Miller; brief notice).

Language, 1975, 51, 977–980 (D. T. Langendoen).

Hudson, R. A. *Arguments for a nontransformational grammar.* Chicago: The University of Chicago Press, 1976.

Reviewed: *Language*, 1978, 54, 348–376 (P. Schachter).

Journal of Linguistics, 1980, 16, 103–109 (N. Ostler).

Hymes, D., & Fought, J. American structuralism. In T. A. Sebeok (Ed.), *Current trends in linguistics, 13: Historiography of linguistics.* The Hague: Mouton, 1975.

Reviewed: Whole vol.: *Language*, 1979, 55, 207–211 (N. E. Collinge).

Jackendoff, R. S. *Semantic interpretation in generative grammar.* Cambridge, Mass.: M.I.T. Press, 1972.

Reviewed: *International Journal of American Linguistics*, 1974, 40, 336–337 (E. Hamp).

Journal of Linguistics, 1975, 11, 140–147 (D. W. Lightfoot).

Language Sciences, 1975, No. 36, 23–31 (M. B. Kac).

Jakobovits, L. A., & Miron, M. S. (Eds.). *Readings in the psychology of language.* Englewood Cliffs, N.J.: Prentice-Hall, 1967.
Reviewed: *Contemporary Psychology,* 1968, *13,* 175 (R. Brown; brief notice).

Jakobson, R. *Kindersprache, Aphasie und allgemeine Lautgesetze.* Uppsala: Almqvist & Wiksell, 1941 (Trans.: *Child language, aphasia, and phonological universals.* The Hague: Mouton, 1968.)
Reviewed: *Language,* 1942, *18,* 253–254 (W. Leopold).
1968 translation: *Contemporary Psychology,* 1969, *14,* 580–581 (A. R. Luria & A. A. Leontiev, Jr.).

Jakobson, R., Fant, C. G. M., & Halle, M. *Preliminaries to speech analysis: The distinctive features and their correlates.* Cambridge, Mass.: Acoustics Laboratory, M.I.T., Technical Report No. 13, 1952.
Reviewed: *Language,* 1953, *29,* 472–482 (P. L. Garvin).

Jakobson, R., & Halle, M. *Fundamentals of language.* The Hague: Mouton, 1956.
Reviewed: *Contemporary Psychology,* 1957, *2,* 133–134 (E. Lenneberg).
Language, 1957, *33,* 408–415 (M. Joos).

Joos, M. Acoustic phonetics. *Language Monographs,* 1948 (No. 23).

Kac, M. B. *Corepresentation of grammatical structure.* Minneapolis: University of Minnesota Press, 1978.
Reviewed: *Language,* 1979, *55,* 670–674 (R. Hudson).

Kantor, J. R. *An objective psychology of grammar.* Bloomington, Ind.: Principia Press, 1936. (1952 reprint.)
Reviewed: *Language,* 1938, *14,* 66–68 (H. V. Velten).
Psychological Bulletin, 1937, *34,* 398–402 (D. Wolfle).
1952 reprint: *International Journal of American Linguistics,* 1953, *19,* 312–313 (S. Newman).

Kantor, J. R. *Psychological linguistics.* Chicago: The Principia Press, 1977.
Reviewed: *Contemporary Psychology,* 1979, *24,* 844–845 (R. W. Rieber).

Katz, J. J. Mentalism in linguistics. *Language,* 1964, *40,* 124–137.

Katz, J. J., & Fodor, J. A. The structure of a semantic theory. *Language,* 1963, *39,* 170–210.

Katz, J. J., & Postal, P. M. *An integrated theory of linguistic descriptions.* Cambridge, Mass.: M.I.T. Press, 1964.
Reviewed: *Contemporary Psychology,* 1965, *10,* 453–454 (S. Rosenberg).
Journal of Linguistics, 1966, *2,* 119–127 (J. Lyons).

Kavanagh, J. F., & Cutting, J. E. (Eds.). *The role of speech in language.* Cambridge, Mass.: M.I.T. Press, 1975.
Reviewed: *Contemporary Psychology,* 1976, *21,* 790–791 (O. K. Garnica).
Language, 1979, *55,* 941–945 (W. S-Y. Wang).

Kess, J. F. *Psycholinguistics: Introductory perspectives.* New York: Academic Press, 1976. (a)
Reviewed: *Contemporary Psychology,* 1977, *22,* 203–204 (M. Maratsos).
Journal of Psycholinguistic Research, 1978, *7,* 477–492 (A. F. Healy).
Language, 1980, *56,* 679–685 (T. Scovel).

Kess, J. F. Reversing directions in psycholinguistics. *Language Sciences,* 1976, No. 42, 1–5. (b)

Labov, W. *Sociolinguistic patterns.* Philadelphia: University of Pennsylvania Press, 1973.
Reviewed: *Contemporary Psychology,* 1975, *20,* 9–10 (C. B. Cazden).
Language, 1975, *51,* 1008–1016 (R. Darnell).

Lamb, S. M. *Outline of stratificational grammar.* With an appendix by L. E. Newell. Washington, D.C.: Georgetown University Press, 1966.
Reviewed: *Journal of Linguistics,* 1968, *4,* 287–295 (F. H. Palmer).
Language, 1968, *44,* 593–603 (W. L. Chafe).

Langacker, R. W. *Language and its structure.* New York: Harcourt, Brace, 1968. (2nd ed., 1973.)
Reviewed: *Journal of Linguistics,* 1970, *6,* 154–156 (J. J. Christie).
Language, 1969, *45,* 886–897 (F. W. Householder, Jr.).

Langendoen, D. T. *The study of syntax: The generative-transformationl approach to the structure of American English.* New York: Holt, 1969.
  Reviewed: *Journal of Linguistics,* 1970, *6,* 267–276 (G. Sampson).
  Language, 1971, *47,* 453–465 (F. W. Householder, Jr.).
Lashley, K. S. The problem of serial order in behavior. In L. A. Jeffress (Ed.), *Cerebral mechanisms in behavior.* New York: Wiley, 1951.
Lees, R. B. *The grammar of English nominalizations.* Bloomington, Ind.: Indiana University Research Center, 1960.
  Reviewed: *International Journal of American Linguistics,* 1962, *28,* 134–146 (P. Schachter).
  Language, 1962, *38,* 434–444 (A. A. Hill).
Lenneberg, E. H. (Ed.). *New directions in the study of language.* Cambridge, Mass.: M.I.T. Press, 1964.
  Reviewed: *Contemporary Psychology,* 1965, *10,* 547–549 (D. Hymes).
Lenneberg, E. H. *Biological foundations of language.* With appendices by N. Chomsky and O. Marx. New York: Wiley, 1967.
  Reviewed: *Behaviorism,* 1974, *2,* 146–161 (S. I. Sulzbacher & D. K. Oller).
  Contemporary Psychology, 1968, *13,* 117–119 (J. B. Carroll).
  International Review of Applied Linguistics, 1971, *9,* 181–183 (H. Steger).
  Journal of the Experimental Analysis of Behavior, 1968, *11,* 497–501 (D. J. Bem & S. L. Bem).
Leonard, L. B. *Meaning in child language: Issues in the study of early semantic development.* New York: Grune & Stratton, 1976.
  Reviewed: *Language,* 1979, *55,* 245–248 (K. T. Kernan).
Leopold, W. F. The study of child language and infant bilingualism. *Word,* 1948, *4,* 1–17.
Levelt, W. J. M. *Formal grammars in linguistics* (3 vols.). The Hague: Mouton, 1974.
  Reviewed: *Contemporary Psychology,* 1977, *22,* 167–169 (R. M. Kaplan).
  Journal of Linguistics, 1976, *12,* 182–188 (G. Sampson).
Levelt, W. J. M., & Flores d'Arcais, G. B. (Eds.). *Studies in the perception of language.* Chichester, England: Wiley, 1978.
  Reviewed: *Contemporary Psychology,* 1979, *24,* 972–974 (H. S. Cairns).
Lewis, M., & Rosenblum, L. A. (Eds.). *Interaction, conversation, and the development of language.* New York: Wiley, 1977.
  Reviewed: *Contemporary Psychology,* 1978, *23,* 838–840 (D. Keller-Cohen).
  Language, 1979, *55,* 717–721 (B. G. Blount).
Li, C. N. *Subject and topic.* New York: Academic Press, 1976.
  Reviewed: *Language,* 1979, *55,* 372–380 (P. Munro).
Lieberman, P. *Intonation, perception and language.* Cambridge, Mass.: M.I.T. Press, 1967.
  Reviewed: *Contemporary Psychology,* 1968, *13,* 314 (I. J. Hirsh; brief notice).
  Journal of Linguistics, 1970, *6,* 138–144 (R. Vanderslice).
  Language, 1968, *44,* 830–842 (C-W. Kim).
Lounsbury, F. G. Linguistics and psychology. In S. Koch (Ed.), *Psychology: A study of a science* (Vol. 6). New York: McGraw-Hill, 1963.
  Reviewed: *Language,* 1965, *41,* 95–100 (S. Saporta).
Lyons, J. *Introduction to theoretical linguistics.* Cambridge, England: Cambridge University Press, 1968.
  Reviewed: *Journal of Linguistics,* 1973, *9,* 71–113 (W. Haas).
  Language, 1971, *47,* 70–71 (S. Starosta).
Lyons, J. *Semantics* (2 vols.). Cambridge, England: Cambridge University Press, 1977.
  Reviewed: *Contemporary Psychology,* 1979, *24,* 176–177 (T. Langendoen).
  Language, 1979, *55,* 199–206 (Ö. Dahl).

849

Lyons, J., & Wales, R. J. (Eds.). *Psycholinguistics papers: The proceedings of the 1966 Edinburgh conference.* Edinburgh: Edinburgh University Press, 1966.
    Reviewed: *Contemporary Psychology*, 1968, *13*, 352–353 (M. Anisfeld); 1969, *14*, 122 (ltr., J. Marshall), 123 (reply, M. Anisfeld).
    Journal of Linguistics, 1968, *4*, 139–140 (H. H. Clark).
Massaro, D. W. (Ed.). *Understanding language: An information-processing analysis of speech perception, reading and psycholinguistics.* New York: Academic Press, 1975.
    Reviewed: *Contemporary Psychology*, 1976, *21*, 562–563 (P. A. Kolers).
McCawley, J. D. The role of semantics in grammar. In E. Bach & R. T. Harms (Eds.), *Universals in linguistic theory.* New York: Holt, 1968.
McGranahan, D. V. The psychology of language. *Psychological Bulletin*, 1936, *33*, 178–216.
McNeill, D. Developmental psycholinguistics. In F. Smith & G. A. Miller (Eds.), *The genesis of language: A psycholinguistic approach.* Cambridge, Mass.: M.I.T. Press, 1966.
McNeill, D. *The acquisition of language: The study of developmental psycholinguistics.* New York: Harper & Row, 1970.
    Reviewed: *Contemporary Psychology*, 1972, *17*, 66–68 (E. V. Clark).
Miller, G. A. *Language and communication.* New York: McGraw-Hill, 1951. (a)
    Reviewed: *American Journal of Psychology*, 1952, *65*, 648–651 (J. B. Carroll).
        Language, 1952, *28*, 113–119 (H. Rubenstein).
        Psychological Bulletin, 1952, *49*, 361–363 (C. E. Osgood).
Miller, G. A. Speech and language. In S. S. Stevens (Ed.), *Handbook of experimental psychology.* New York: Wiley, 1951. (b)
    Critiqued: *Psychological Review*, 1952, *59*, 414–420 (D. Olmsted & O. K. Moore).
Miller, G. A. Communication. *Annual Review of Psychology*, 1954, *5*, 401–420. (a)
Miller, G. A. Psycholinguistics. In G. Lindzey (Ed.), *Handbook of social psychology* (Vol. 2). Cambridge, Mass.: Addison-Wesley, 1954. (b)
Miller, G. A. Some psychological studies of grammar. *American Psychologist*, 1962, *17*, 748–762.
Miller, G. A. Some preliminaries to psycholinguistics. *American Psychologist*, 1965, *20*, 15–20.
Miller, G. A. *The psychology of communication: Seven essays.* New York: Basic Books, 1967.
    Reviewed: *Contemporary Psychology*, 1969, *14*, 156–157 (L. A. Jakobovits).
Miller, G. A. Toward a third metaphor for psycholinguistics. In W. B. Weimer & D. S. Palermo (Eds.), *Cognition and the symbolic processes.* Hillsdale, N.J.: Erlbaum, 1974.
Miller, G. A., Galanter, E., & Pribram, K. H. *Plans and the structure of behavior.* New York: Holt, 1960.
    Reviewed: *Contemporary Psychology*, 1960, *5*, 209–211 (D. O. Hebb).
        Language, 1960, *36*, 527–532 (R. Brown).
Miller, G. A., & Johnson-Laird, P. N. *Language and perception.* Cambridge, Mass.: Harvard University Press, 1976.
    Reviewed: *Contemporary Psychology*, 1977, *22*, 545–547 (D. A. Norman).
        Journal of Linguistics, 1978, *14*, 342–347 (R. Harris).
Miller, G. A., & McNeill, D. Psycholinguistics. In G. Lindzey & E. Aronson (Eds.), *The handbook of social psychology. The individual in a social context* (Vol. 3) (2nd ed.). Reading, Mass.: Addison-Wesley, 1969.
Morton, J., & Marshall, J. C. (Eds.). *Psycholinguistics 1: Developmental and pathological.* Ithaca, N.Y.: Cornell University Press, 1977.
    Reviewed: *Contemporary Psychology*, 1979, *24*, 855–857 (J. M. Anglin).
Morton, J., & Marshall, J. C. (Eds.). *Psycholinguistics 2: Structures and processes.* Cambridge, Mass.: M.I.T. Press, 1979.
    Reviewed: *Contemporary Psychology*, 1980, *25*, 413–414 (M. Maratsos).
Mowrer, O. H. The psychologist looks at language. *American Psychologist*, 1954, *9*, 660–694.

Mowrer, O. H. *Learning theory and the symbolic processes.* New York: Wiley, 1960.
Reviewed: *Contemporary Psychology,* 1961, *6,* 358–361 (W. E. Jeffrey).

Oldfield, R. C., & Marshall, J. C. (Eds.). *Language: Selected readings.* Baltimore: Penguin Books, 1968.
Reviewed: *Contemporary Psychology,* 1969, *14,* 194 (D. J. Foss; brief notice).

Olmsted, D. L. *Out of the mouths of babes: Earliest stages in language learning.* The Hague: Mouton, 1971.
Reviewed: *Contemporary Psychology,* 1974, *19,* 45–46 (C. Stoel).

Olmsted, D. L., & Moore, O. K. Language, psychology and linguistics. *Psychological Review,* 1952, *59,* 414–420.

Osgood, C. E. The nature and measurement of meaning. *Psychological Bulletin,* 1952, *49,* 197–237.

Osgood, C. E. On understanding and creating sentences. *American Psychologist,* 1963, *18,* 735–751. (a)

Osgood, C. E. Psycholinguistics. In S. Koch (Ed.), *Psychology: Study of a science* (Vol. 6). New York: McGraw-Hill, 1963. (b)
Reviewed: (Koch vol.): *Contemporary Psychology,* 1965, *10,* 199–201 (R. A. Bauer).
Language, 1965, *41,* 95–100 (S. Saporta).

Osgood, C. E. A dinosaur caper: Psycholinguistics past, present, and future. *Annals of the New York Academy of Sciences,* 1975, *263,* 16–26.

Osgood, C. E. *Focus on meaning. Explorations in semantic space* (Vol. 1). The Hague: Mouton, 1976.
Reviewed: *Contemporary Psychology,* 1978, *23,* 993–995 (J. Limber).

Osgood, C. E., & Sebeok, T. A. (Eds.). Psycholinguistics: A survey of theory and research problems. *International Journal of American Linguistics,* 1954, *20,* Supplement; and *Journal of Abnormal and Social Psychology,* 1954, *49* (4, Part 2). (Reissued with "A survey of psycholinguistic research, 1954–1964," by A. R. Diebold, Jr., and "The psycholinguists," by G. A. Miller. Bloomington, Ind.: Indiana University Press, 1965.)
Reviewed: *Language,* 1955, *31,* 46–59 (D. L. Olmsted).
1965 reissue: *Contemporary Psychology,* 1966, *11,* 594 (R. M. Krauss).

Osgood, C. E., Suci, G. J., & Tannenbaum, P. H. *The measurement of meaning.* Urbana, Ill.: University of Illinois Press, 1957.
Reviewed: *Contemporary Psychology,* 1958, *3,* 113–119 (R. Brown; H. Gulliksen).
Language, 1959, *35,* 58–77 (J. B. Carroll).

Palermo, D. S. *Psychology of language.* Glenview, Ill.: Scott, Foresman, 1978.
Reviewed: *Contemporary Psychology,* 1978, *23,* 699 (H. S. Cairns); 1979, *24,* 453–454 (K. I. Forster).

Parisi, D., & Antinucci, F. *Essentials of grammar* (E. Bates, trans.). New York: Academic Press, 1976.
Reviewed: *Language,* 1978, *54,* 404–407 (S. F. Schmerling).

Pike, K. L. *Language in relation to a unified theory of the structure of human behavior.* Glendale, Calif.: Summer Institute of Linguistics, 1954 (Part 1), 1955 (Part 2).
Reviewed: *Contemporary Psychology,* 1956, *1,* 19–20 (G. A. Miller).
Language, 1955, *31,* 485–488; 1956, *32,* 477–479 (H. Hoijer).

Pike, K. L., & Pike, E. G. *Grammatical analysis.* Dallas, Texas: Summer Institute of Linguistics, SIL Publications in Linguistics, 1977, *53.*
Reviewed: *Language,* 1979, *55,* 907–911 (P. H. Fries).

Pollio, H. R. *The psychology of symbolic activity.* Reading, Mass.: Addison-Wesley, 1974.
Reviewed: *Contemporary Psychology,* 1975, *20,* 6–8 (G. M. Olson).

Premack, D. A functional analysis of language. *Journal of the Experimental Analysis of Behavior,* 1970, *14,* 107–125.

Premack, D. Language in chimpanzee? *Science,* 1971, *172,* 808–822.

Pronko, N. H. Language and psycholinguistics. *Psychological Bulletin,* 1946, *43,* 189–239.

851

III. PSYCHOLOGY AND ITS INTERSECTING DISCIPLINES

Quirk, R., & Svartvik, J. *Investigating linguistic acceptability*. The Hague: Mouton, 1966.
  Reviewed: *Contemporary Psychology*, 1968, *13*, 244 (W. S. Stolz).
    Language, 1969, *45*, 622–624 (A. A. Hill).
Rommetveit, R. *Words, meanings, and messages: Theory and experiments in psycholinguistics*. New York: Academic Press, 1968.
Rommetveit, R. *On message structure: A framework for the study of language and communication*. New York: Wiley, 1974.
  Reviewed: *Contemporary Psychology*, 1976, *21*, 49–51 (P. A. Hornby).
Rosenberg, S. (Ed.). *Sentence production: Developments in research and theory*. Hillsdale, N.J.: Erlbaum, 1977.
  Reviewed: *Contemporary Psychology*, 1979, *24*, 126–128 (M. Garrett).
Rumbaugh, D. M. (Ed.). *Language learning by a chimpanzee: The LANA project*. New York: Academic Press, 1977.
  Reviewed: *Contemporary Psychology*, 1977, *22*, 808–810 (A. Hodun & C. T. Snowden).
    Journal of Psycholinguistic Research, 1979, *8*, 267–300 (C. A. Ristau & D. Robbins).
Sadock, J. M. *Toward a linguistic theory of speech acts*. New York: Academic Press, 1974.
  Reviewed: *Language*, 1976, *52*, 966–971 (J. R. Searle).
    Journal of Linguistics, 1977, *13*, 133–146 (G. N. Leech).
Salzinger, K. Pleasing linguists: A parable. *Journal of Verbal Learning and Verbal Behavior*, 1970, *9*, 725–727.
Salzinger, K., & Feldman, R. S. (Eds.). *Studies in verbal behavior: An empirical approach*. New York: Pergamon, 1973.
  Reviewed: *American Journal of Psychology*, 1974, *87*, 311–312 (S. Fillenbaum).
    Contemporary Psychology, 1974, *19*, 334 (R. W. Schulz).
Salzinger, K., & Salzinger, S. *Research in verbal behavior and some neurophysiological implications*. New York: Academic Press, 1967.
  Reviewed: *Contemporary Psychology*, 1968, *13*, 676–677 (D. S. Palermo).
Sampson, G. *The form of language*. London: Weidenfeld & Nicolson, 1975.
  Reviewed: *Journal of Linguistics*, 1976, *12*, 206–208 (G. Gazdar).
Sankoff, D. (Ed.). *Linguistic variation: Models and methods*. New York: Academic Press, 1978.
  Reviewed: *Contemporary Psychology*, 1980, *25*, 323 (W. Wolfram).
    Language, 1980, *56*, 158–170 (A. J. Naro).
Saporta, S. (Ed.), with the assistance of J. R. Bastian. *Psycholinguistics: A book of readings*. New York: Holt, 1961.
  Reviewed: *Contemporary Psychology*, 1963, *8*, 6–7 (C. K. Staats & A. W. Staats).
    Language, 1964, *40*, 197–260 (A. R. Diebold, Jr.).
Schank, R. C. Conceptual dependency: A theory of natural language understanding. *Cognitive Psychology*, 1972, *3*, 552–631.
Schlesinger, I. M. A note on the relationship between psychological and linguistic theories. *Foundations of Language*, 1967, *3*, 397–402.
Schlesinger, I. M. *Production and comprehension of utterances*. Hillsdale, N.J.: Erlbaum, 1977.
  Reviewed: *Contemporary Psychology*, 1978, *23*, 313–314 (J. H. Danks).
    Language, 1979, *55*, 440–444 (P. A. Hornby).
Searle, J. R. *Speech acts: An essay in the philosophy of language*. Cambridge, England: Cambridge University Press, 1969.
  Reviewed: *Language*, 1970, *46*, 217–227 (A. Koller).
Sebeok, T. A. (Ed.). *Current trends in linguistics, III: Theoretical foundations*. The Hague: Mouton, 1966.
  Reviewed: *Language*, 1968, *44*, 556–593 (J. McCawley).
Sebeok, T. A. (Ed.). *How animals communicate*. Bloomington, Ind.: Indiana University Press, 1977.

852

Reviewed: *Contemporary Psychology*, 1979, *24*, 965–967 (D. K. Candland).

        Language, 1979, *55*, 736–738 (P. H. Salus).

Seuren, P. A. M. *Operators and nucleus*. Cambridge, England: Cambridge Univ. Press, 1969.

    Reviewed: *International Review of Applied Linguistics*, 1973, *11*, 263–278 (G. Kress).

        Journal of Linguistics, 1971, *7*, 277–287 (R. Hudson).

Shannon, C. E., & Weaver, W. *The mathematical theory of communication*. Urbana, Ill.: University of Illinois Press, 1949.

    Reviewed: *Language*, 1953, *29*, 69–93 (C. F. Hockett).

Skinner, B. F. The verbal summator and a method for the study of latent speech. *Journal of Psychology*, 1936, *2*, 71–107.

Skinner, B. F. *Verbal behavior*. New York: Appleton-Century-Crofts, 1957.

    Reviewed: *Contemporary Psychology*, 1958, *3*, 209–214 (C. E. Osgood; C. Morris).

        Harvard Education Review, 1959, *29*, 264–268 (G. H. Matthews).

        Journal of the Experimental Analysis of Behavior, 1969, *12*, 831–841 (K. MacCorquodale; "a retrospective appreciation").

        Language, 1959, *35*, 26–58 (N. Chomsky).

        Science, 1959, *129*, 143–144 (D. E. Dulany).

        Word, 1959, *15*, 362–367 (O. K. Tikhomirov).

Slobin, D. I. *Psycholinguistics*. Glenview, Ill.: Scott, Foresman, 1971. (2nd ed., 1979.) (a)

    Reviewed: *Contemporary Psychology*, 1973, *18*, 672–673 (R. J. Jarvella).

        Language Learning, 1971, *21*, 249–252 (H. D. Brown).

        2nd ed.: *Contemporary Psychology*, 1980, *25*, 264–265 (J. M. Carroll).

Slobin, D. I. (Ed.). *The ontogenesis of grammar: A theoretical symposium*. New York: Academic Press, 1971. (b)

    Reviewed: *Contemporary Psychology*, 1972, *17*, 647–648 (M. Maratsos).

Smith, F., & Miller, G. A. (Eds.). *The genesis of language: A psycholinguistic approach*. Cambridge, Mass.: M.I.T. Press, 1966.

    Reviewed: *Contemporary Psychology*, 1968, *13*, 49–51 (R. Brown).

        Journal of Linguistics, 1968, *4*, 143–146 (R. Wales).

Snow, C. E., & Ferguson, C. A. (Eds.). *Talking to children: Language input and acquisition*. Cambridge, England: Cambridge University Press, 1977.

    Reviewed: *Contemporary Psychology*, 1979, *24*, 102–104 (C. B. Cazden).

        Language, 1979, *55*, 449–454 (C. B. Farwell).

Staats, A. *Learning, language and cognition*. New York: Holt, 1968.

    Reviewed: *Contemporary Psychology*, 1968, *13*, 624–625 (S. Glucksberg).

Steinberg, D. D., & Jakobovits, L. A. (Eds.). *Semantics: An interdisciplinary reader in philosophy, linguistics, and psychology*. Cambridge, England: Cambridge Univ. Press, 1971.

    Reviewed: *Contemporary Psychology*, 1972, *17*, 428–429 (J. Macnamara).

        Journal of Linguistics, 1973, *9*, 361–364 (F. H. Palmer).

Stern, G. *Meaning and change of meaning, with special reference to the English language*. Göteborg, 1931. (Reprinted, Indiana Univ. Press, 1964.)

    Reviewed: *Psychological Bulletin*, 1935, *32*, 104–105 (S. Newman).

Stockwell, R. P., Schachter, P., & Partee, B. H. *The major syntactic structures of English*. New York: Holt, 1973.

    Reviewed: Preliminary version: *Language*, 1972, *48*, 645–667 (P. Chapin).

Sturtevant, E. H.: *An introduction to linguistic science*. New Haven: Yale University Press, 1947.

    Reviewed: *Language*, 1947, *23*, 437–442 (H. M. Hoenigswald).

Suppes, P. Stimulus-response theory of finite automata. *Journal of Mathematical Psychology*, 1969, *6*, 327–355.

Taylor, I. *Introduction to psycholinguistics*. New York: Holt, 1976.

III. PSYCHOLOGY AND ITS INTERSECTING DISCIPLINES

Reviewed: *Contemporary Psychology*, 1978, 23, 310–311 (C. A. Perfetti).
Journal of Psycholinguistic Research, 1978, 7, 477–492 (A. F. Healy).
Language, 1977, 53, 480–483 (T. Scovel).

Terrace, H. S., Petitto, L. A., Sanders, R. J., & Bever, T. G. Can an ape create a sentence? *Science*, 1979, 206, 891–902.

Trager, G. L. *Language and languages.* San Francisco: Chandler, 1972.

Trager, G. L., & Smith, H. L., Jr. *An outline of English structure.* Norman, Oklahoma: Battenburg Press, 1951. (Studies in Linguistics, Occasional Papers No. 3.)
Reviewed: *Language*, 1955, 31, 312–345 (J. Sledd).

Trubetskoy, N. S. *Grundzüge der Phonologie.* (Travaux du Cercle Linguistique de Prague, No. 7.) Prague, 1939.
Reviewed: *Language*, 1941, 17, 345–349 (Z. S. Harris).

Twaddell, W. F. On defining the phoneme. *Language Monographs*, 1935 (No. 16).
Reviewed: *Language*, 1935, 11, 244–250 (M. Swadesh).

Weimer, W. B. Psycholinguistics and Plato's paradoxes of the *Meno. American Psychologist*, 1973, 28, 15–33.

Weimer, W. B., & Palermo, D. S. (Eds.). *Cognition and the symbolic processes.* Hillsdale, N.J.: Erlbaum, 1974.
Reviewed: *Contemporary Psychology*, 1976, 21, 330–331 (H. S. Cairns).
Language, 1979, 55, 714–717 (A. Munro).

Weiss, A. P. *A theoretical basis of human behavior* (rev. ed.) Columbus, Ohio: R. G. Adams & Co., 1929.
Reviewed: *Psychological Bulletin*, 1931, 28, 172–173 (E. R. Hilgard); (see A. P. Weiss, Linguistics and psychology. *Language*, 1925, 1, 52–57).

Wells, R. S. Immediate constituents. *Language*, 1947, 23, 81–117.

Whorf, B. L. Science and linguistics. *Technology Review* (M.I.T.), 1940, 42, 229–231, 247–248.
Reviewed: As republished in *Four articles in metalinguistics: Language*, 1956, 32, 298–308 (R. E. Longacre).

Whorf, B. L. *Language, thought, and reality: Selected writings of Benjamin Lee Whorf.* With an introduction by John B. Carroll, Ed.; foreword by Stuart Chase. Cambridge, Mass.: M.I.T. Press, 1956.
Reviewed: *Contemporary Psychology*, 1957, 2, 57–59 (O. H. Mowrer).
Language, 1957, 33, 421–423 (G. L. Trager).

Winokur, S. *A primer of verbal behavior: An operant view.* Englewood Cliffs, N.J.: Prentice-Hall, 1976.
Reviewed: *Contemporary Psychology*, 1977, 22, 9–10 (A. C. Catania).

Yngve, V. H. A model and an hypothesis for language structure. *Proceedings of the American Philosophical Society*, 1960, 104, 444–466.
Discussed: J. Greene, *Psycholinguistics: Chomsky and psychology.* Harmondsworth: Penguin, 1972.

Zale, E. M. (Ed.). *Proceedings of the Conference on Language and Language Behavior.* New York: Appleton-Century-Crofts, 1968.

Zipf, G. K. *The psycho-biology of language.* Boston: Houghton Mifflin, 1935.
Reviewed: *Language*, 1936, 12, 196–210 (M. Joos).
Psychological Bulletin, 1936, 33, 218–221 (G. Allport).

PSYCHOLOGY AND AESTHETICS

Editorial Note

In seeking to represent "Psychology and Aesthetics" in the APA program from which this book derives, the editors decided to forego the symposium format followed in the treatment of other topics and invite this century's preeminent psychologist of art, Rudolf Arnheim, to deliver a special address on a theme of his choice. His choice—as the reader will soon discern—was a fascinating one; instead of attempting the history of a field, he essayed the incarnation of a man: Gustav Theodor Fechner, who initiated the field. All psychologists remember Fechner as "father" of experimental psychophysics, and most will recall, though perhaps hazily, that Fechner was also the father of experimental aesthetics. What has dropped out of ken among psychologists is Fechner, whose unique blend of philosophical and mystical views formed the generative context of the two lines of empirical effort for which he is celebrated. In reanimating the "other" Fechner, Arnheim gives all of us an implicit lesson in the difference between history and its conventionalized record. He gives us also a still more important lesson in irony in his subtle elaboration of the suggestion that perhaps Fechner's principal contribution to aesthetics is to be found in the "other" Fechner's "way of looking at the world in the manner of an artist," rather than in the narrow and inhibiting methodic paradigm (essentially that of a "hedonistic psychophysics") governing Fechner's experimental work in aesthetics. It is the latter, of course, which forms the basis for most of the work in experimental aesthetics over the past century.

36

The Other Gustav Theodor Fechner

RUDOLF ARNHEIM

Gustav Theodor Fechner is one of those great figures of the past whose names are attached, in the mind of the average student, to a few items of idea or fact. These items float in empty space, labeled but not interpreted by those authoritative names. The context in which the ideas were conceived and the facts discovered has vanished, and therefore their true meaning has gone. Gone is also the powerful figure to whom we owe them, the richness and originality of a true thinker, whose example we can ill afford to do without.

Fechner is known from the textbooks as the man who founded the science of psychophysics by generalizing Weber's law to state that the arithmetical increase of a perceptual response requires a geometrical increase in the physical stimulus. In addition, the student may be told that Fechner investigated people's preference for certain proportions of rectangles and thereby not only initiated experimental aesthetics but also explored, as a trained mathematician, various ways of measuring statistical distributions quite in general.

As long as one has nothing else to go by, it remains unclear whether Fechner's two noteworthy accomplishments have anything to do with each other or why they should come from the same person. My attempt to describe the matrix from which they sprang will have to be somewhat slanted because I wish to deal with Fechner mainly in his relation to the psychology of art. But Fechner's concern with aesthetics derived so directly from the core of his basic conceptions that my particular perspective might not distort the view unduly. It will be necessary, however, to take a look at those conceptions before their application to aesthetics can be traced.

Fechner's experimental investigations have been selected by the textbook writers for survival because they fit the standards of what is considered relevant and respectable in much psychology. And in fact, Fechner was very much of an empiricist. He proposed to supplement the philosophical aesthetics that proceeded "from above" with an aesthetics "from below" and thereby to furnish its missing factual base. In his paper *Zur experimentellen Aesthetik* of 1871 he praised his precursor Ernst Heinrich Weber for having been the first since Galileo to extend the range of exact research beyond its supposed limits, and this in a direction that he, Fechner, was pursuing himself (Fechner, 1871, p. 555). Throughout his work he insisted that large numbers of observers were needed to make experimental results reliable, and while aesthetics would never be as exact a science as physics, it shared this imperfection with physiology. "Man tut, was man kann," he said. You do what you can.

It is all the more remarkable that the same man was a mystic visionary of compelling power and a playful satirist as well. As a young man he published, under a pseudonym, a humorous essay on the comparative anatomy of the angels. A treatise of 1851, called by the Zoroastrian name *Zend-Avesta*, asserted that everything organic and inorganic in the universe possesses a soul, including the earth itself and the other planets. The spirit of these and other similar works is inseparable from that of the *Elements of Psychophysics*. The same deeply religious pantheist to whom we owe the most poetical ecology ever written collected the measurements of some 20,000 paintings from twenty-two art museums to study their proportions statistically.

Two principal ideas guided Fechner in his thinking. (1) The things and experiences that constitute our world are not merely coordinated and subordinated in separate categories but fit into sliding evolutionary scales, leading from the lowest to the highest levels of existence. (2) The companionship of body and mind pervades the entire universe so that nothing mental is without its physical substratum and, conversely, everything physical is reflected in a corresponding mental experience to the extent to which it reaches beyond the threshold of consciousness.

The first of these principles places Fechner with the evolutionists of the nineteenth century. Although he strongly objected to the notion of blind selection in Darwinism, he preferred evolution to the premise of the traditional taxonomists, who held since the days of Plato and Aristotle that "each higher species was created anew, as it were, from the primordial ooze" (Fechner, 1873, p. III). What distinguishes Fechner from his contemporaries is the sweeping grandeur of his cosmological conception which "basically is only the completion and upper conclusion of what starts from below as psychophysics." His faith in these cosmological visions constitutes "the flower and fruit above the root, for which psychophysics searches in the immediacy of knowledge" (Fechner, 1879/1918, p. 101). In fact, it was those visions that gave the impulse to the empirical research about the scales of thresholds. The modest scale of perceptual responses explorable in experimentation is seen as a tiny token of the giant scale reaching from the infusoria to the solar system within the all-embracing consciousness of God. We are as close to the idealism of the Bishop Berkeley as to the laboratories of Leipzig.

Fechner's second principle derives directly from Spinoza, who stated that body and mind are two aspects of the same unknowable infinite substance. That hypothetical substance appears as mind under the finite attribute of thought and as body under the finite attribute of spatial extension. Fechner gave this view a more psychological turn by insisting that the double aspect was due to different standpoints of the observer. He used the perceptual example of a person looking at a cylinder—actually he said: a circle—from the inside and then again from the outside. The concavity and the convexity of the two views are incompatible and cannot be held at the same time. He also referred to the solar system as seen from the earth and seen from the sun. In fact, Fechner's insistence on standpoints places him in the relativistic tradition that reaches from Copernicus to Einstein and the complementarity principle of Niels Bohr. He proceeded to reason that since the standpoint that offers direct experience of mind is available only to a person's own self and since therefore our assumption that other human beings, and perhaps animals, possess minds like our own must remain conjectural, there was no valid objection to extending the hypothesis and assuming that everything in the material world was endowed with mind. He went so far as to speculate on the soul of plants and to explain in meticulous detail how the earth and the other planets could manage to function as conscious beings without the benefit of nervous systems.

In this connection it is of psychological interest that Fechner's concern with the psychophysics of thresholds was not primary but rather an expedient, to which he resorted because, certainly in his day, the physiological counterpart to conscious experience was inaccessible to research. Only the outer physical stimuli were accessible. He therefore assumed that a direct correlation existed between physical stimulus and physiological response, and this assumption permitted him to substitute the one for the other. What he called his external psychophysics, namely the relationship between physical stimulus and perceptual response, had to serve as a stand-in for the inner psychophysics he was really after, namely the relationship between the mind and its direct bodily equivalent, the physiology of the nervous system.

Although the inner psychophysics eluded the experimenter, Fechner could not refrain from speculating about its nature, and he did so inevitably in terms of what we know today from Gestalt psychology as isomorphism. He said in the *Zend-Avesta* that a person's thoughts cannot differ from what the "motions of the brain" permit and that conversely the motions of the brain cannot deviate from the thoughts to which they are tied (Fechner, 1851/1919, p. 259). And in the

Psychophysics we are told more specifically that although we cannot infer, from what we know by direct exploration, anything about the processes and nature of the physiological substratum, we can make statements about certain structural properties common to both levels of functioning. If such properties as context, sequence, similarity or dissimilarity, intensity or weakness are experienced in the mind, they must have their counterparts in the nervous system (Fechner, 1860/1889, Vol. II, p. 380). He called this isomorphic correspondence his *Funktionsprinzip.*

The conviction that matter is universally endowed with mind served Fechner to avoid the nightview, as he called it, namely the scientific assertion that the beauties of light and color exist only for the conscious mind whereas the physical world in and by itself lies in ghastly darkness. Although as an astute observer he knew the difference between the positive perception of darkness and the absence of sight (Fechner, 1860/1889, Vol. I, p. 167) he needed his mystical biology, which described the stars as superhumanly powerful spherical eyes, to assure him that the splendor of the visual world endures objectively. God's retina, he said in his late work on the dayview as against the nightview *(Die Tagesansicht gegenüber der Nachtansicht)*, consists in the surfaces of all existing things, including the retinae in the eyes of human beings and animals (Fechner, 1879/1918, p. 53). Fechner fought the nightview of science with the same deep-seated passion that impelled Goethe in his theory of color to defend the indivisible purity of white light against Newton's contention that light is composed of the darkness and partiality of the spectral hues. For both men, the ultimate truth resided in direct sensory experience.

This conviction, of course, is the credo and axiom of all art, and in my opinion Fechner's way of looking at the world in the manner of the artist constitutes his principal contribution to aesthetics. It explains his decision to devote his last major work to aesthetics more convincingly than his own reference, in the foreword to his *Vorschule der Aesthetik,* to the few minor studies dealing explicitly with art in his earlier work (Fechner, 1876/1978, Vol. I, p. V). In fact, we must face the vexing paradox that this last extensive effort, almost six hundred pages in length, this final consummation so compellingly requested by the trend of Fechner's entire thinking, fails to embody his guiding ideas in the congenial medium of the arts. (It is only necessary to remember the young Schopenhauer's dealing with a similar task in the third book of his *Die Welt als Wille und Vorstellung* to become aware of the difference.) There are indications that Fechner, once he had decided to embark upon a substantial work on aesthetics, felt obliged to deal with the topics that dominated the major treatises in that field. Thus he holds forth on content and form, unity and complexity, idealism versus realism, art versus nature; he asks whether there is more beauty in the small or in the large, and he thinks that sculpture should be in color to look more real. He does all this and much more quite sensibly and with an occasional Fechnerian flash, and he offers some useful principles and methods, but there is little of his bold originality which would distinguish his book from what professors of philosophy published then and are still publishing now on those same subjects.

There is little in the *Vorschule* to compare, for example, with the inspiration Fechner drew from seeing a waterlily spread its leaves on a pond and offer its open flower to the light. He cites this experience in his book on the soul of the plants to suggest that the lily is enabled by its shape to enjoy the pleasures of the bath and the warmth of the light to the fullest (Fechner, 1848, p. 39). The example can be generalized to imply that by the very appearance of its form and behavior a visual object conveys those basic sensations and strivings which the artist purifies in his work. Note here that Fechner's outlook was mostly visual, although references to sounds and music are not lacking in his writings. His entire life and work is pervaded by a worship bordering on obsession with light and vision. When at the age of thirty-nine he was shaken by a profound spiritual crisis, during which his religious and poetical nature rebelled against the materialism and atheism of his early years as a student of medicine and professor of physics at the University of Leipzig, he became unable to tolerate light, lived for three years in almost total darkness, and came to the brink of death by a concomitant inability to tolerate food. The revenge of the world he felt he had betrayed was meted out by the power of light. He had defied that power by optical experiments carried out in an irreverent spirit; and he was punished by the darkness he feared more than anything else. It was after the sudden recovery from this affliction that he developed his visionary cosmology, which eventually gave the impulse to the works on psychophysics and aesthetics.

Equally characteristic is Fechner's habit of identifying the geometrical symbol of perfection, the sphere, with the eye. The planets are animate beings that demonstrate their superiority by their spherical shape. Their roundness is more beautiful than the lumps and asymmetries of the human body. Since their activities have been sublimated into pure contemplation, they have become eyes. In a playful persiflage of what we now know in Gestalt psychology as the tendency to simplest structure, Fechner describes in his essay on the anatomy of the angels the transformation of the animal head into the body of an angel. In the course of evolution, forehead and chin move forward and the skull bulges around a center located between the eyes. As the eyes move inward and occupy the center of the spherical structure and finally fuse into a single organ, they become the core and symmetry focus of an increasingly transparent sphere. The organism becomes a creature of pure vision. Fechner adds that the angels communicate among themselves through the highest sense known to human beings. They speak in colors rather than sounds by generating beautiful paintings on their surfaces (Fechner, 1825/1875).

This apotheosis of vision, however, is by no means the basic theme of the *Vorschule*. Rather, in a major concession to traditional aesthetics Fechner based his presentation on a motivational approach, the creed of hedonism, according to which human behavior is controlled by a striving for pleasure and the avoidance of unpleasantness. We remember here that in classical philosophy hedonism was conceived as the rationale for every human activity but that in modern times it continued to retain its role as a sufficient explanatory principle only in the philosophy of art. There was a good reason for this. With the increasing secularization of the arts during the Renaissance, their only tangible purpose obvious to the critical observer was that they provided entertainment. This led to the insipid and unfruitful aesthetic conception of art as a source of pleasure. Nevertheless in our century this approach was gratefully adopted by psychologists who attempted to subject people's aesthetic responses to exact measurement in experimentation. It permitted them to reduce the complicated processes that take place when people perceive, organize, and comprehend works of art to a single scalable variable—the condition most favored by scientific method. Just as in perceptual psychophysics the varying intensity of, say, a sensation of light provided the means for measuring thresholds, so the pleasure or unpleasantness of responses yielded the condition for a psychophysics of aesthetics. Fechner's investigation of people's preference for certain proportions of rectangles became the historical prototype of his work.

Thus it came to pass that practically the entire body of experimental aesthetics up to the present time was cast in the convenient format of a hedonistic psychophysics, with the consequence that the more strictly the investigators adhered to the criterion of preference, the more completely their results neglected everything that distinguishes the pleasure generated by a work of art from the pleasure generated by a dish of ice cream. Just as Fechner's study does not tell us why people prefer the ratio of the golden section to others, so most of the innumerable preference studies carried out since his time tell us deplorably little about what people see when they look at an aesthetic object, what they mean by saying that they like or dislike it, and why they prefer the objects they prefer.

Add to this that every respectable experimental setup requires that the stimulus target also should be reducible to a single variable. Accordingly such studies in aesthetics have either followed Fechner's example by limiting their stimuli to very simple patterns or dimensions or by working with actual art objects, whose active ingredients, however, remained unexplored. Therefore the results tended to deal with objects that had little bearing on art or to report on responses to unexamined stimuli.

A less obvious consequence of the derivation from Fechner's psychophysics is the dominant interest in what I would call the "objective percept," rather than in the persons who act as perceivers. Fechner explained with great clarity that since he possessed no means of measuring the intensity of a pleasure response directly, he had to substitute counting for measuring, or, as he himself put it, extensive measure for intensive measure (Fechner, 1876/1978, Vol. II, p. 600). By testing a great many observers, he could use the number of votes given to a particular stimulus as an indicator of the intensity of the pleasure it aroused in the human species as such and in general. Since art criticism is strongly influenced nowadays by a doctrine of relativism, according to which there is no way of assuming that a work of art possesses an objective appearance, let alone an objective value, it is of interest that Fechner considered individual differences as "irregular chance fluctuations" (Fechner, 1860/1889, Vol. I, p. 77). As far as the target of the investigations was concerned, Fechner aimed principally at what he called the "lawful measurement relations of collective objects (i.e., objects consisting of an indefinitely large number of specimens that vary according to laws of chance and can be found in the most different areas)" (Fechner, 1876/1978, Vol. II, p. 273). In recent practice, experimenters have compared the reactions of subject groups distinguished by sex, education, or attitude to complex and meaningful stimuli such as works of art. But aesthetics has yet to discover a cutoff point at which aesthetic stimuli cease to be objective percepts and become, supposedly, the elusive victims of individual or social idiosyncrasies.

Inevitably, the use of fairly simple and neutral stimuli and the reliance on statistical averages lead to results that differ from responses to actual works of art. For example, Fechner attributes much importance to a typical finding which continues to haunt the laboratories of scientific aesthetics. He calls it the "principle of the aesthetic middle" and explains that people "tolerate most often and for the longest time a certain medium degree of arousal, which makes them feel neither overstimulated nor dissatisfied by a lack of sufficient occupation" (Fechner, 1876/1978, Vol. II, pp. 217 and 260). This rule is certainly valid for run-of-the-mill behavior in everyday life. In the arts it would reflect at most a classicistic taste for moderation.

I would like to devote the rest of this paper to the aesthetic relevance of a few other of Fechner's more general ideas. I pointed out earlier that he made aesthetic experience dependent on the pleasure it arouses. He refused to believe, however, that the intensity of such a pleasure corresponded simply to the quantitative strength of the physical stimulus. Instead, in a decisive passage of the *Vorschule* he insisted that the aesthetic effect is brought about by the formal relations within the stimulus configuration, a condition he described as harmony (Fechner, 1876/1978, Vol. II, p. 266). What did he mean by harmony? At times he spoke of it in the conventional sense of the resolution of tension as it is found in the sequences of chords in music. In the above-mentioned passage, however, he related harmony more boldly to one of the key concepts of his work, namely to the principle of the tendency to stability. Let me refer here once more to Fechner's early phantasy about the nature and behavior of angels. There he compares the dignity of the various sense modalities and suggests that higher even than the sense of sight is the sensory awareness of gravity (Fechner, 1825/1875, p. 234). This highest form of perception is "the feeling of the general force of gravity, which relates all bodies to one another and is sensed by their living centers." Now the physical situation of which a perception of gravity would be aware is brought about, according to Fechner, by the tendency to stability. It is a state of equilibrium and tension reduction, envisaged in a similar manner by the Second Law of Thermodynamics and in our own century by the Gestalt tendency to simplest structure (Arnheim, 1971). To be sure, a direct perceptual awareness of the forces held in equilibrium in a physical system such as the universe would indeed be a privilege of the angels. But a physiological system of a similar kind can have its equivalent in perceptual experience. The prime example is the perception of a composition in the arts. The multiplicity of shapes and colors in a work of the visual arts or of sounds in a piece of music is held together by a configuration of forces generated in the nervous system and reflected in the awareness of the artist and every recipient of his work. It is this crucial aesthetic experience to which Fechner referred when he used the term *harmony*.

For a final example I would like to point to a conception developed by Fechner in his book *Some Ideas on the History of the Creation and Evolution of the Organisms* (1873). With his usual idealistic fervor he rejected the biological doctrine that life has derived from inorganic matter. The opposite had to be the case. He asserted that the original state of all being was that of a comprehensive primordial creature, anticipating all existing things in intricate relations and movements and held together in its chaotic fertility only by the force of gravity. From this primordial matrix, articulate organic and inorganic structures derived through a process distinguished from ordinary cell division by what Fechner called the "principle of relational differentiation." It produced at each level opposite entities complementing each other, for example, male and female. Through a Lamarckian kind of mutual adaptation as well as through the gradual slowing down of variability, a state of stability was approached. If that final state were to be fully attained, "each part through the effect of its forces would contribute to bringing the other parts and thereby the whole into a durable, and that means stable, state and maintain them in that state" (Fechner, 1873, p. 89; see also Arnheim, 1971).

Fechner's fantastic biology was as unlikely to find favor with the exact sciences as his other mystical visions. But while it contradicts the facts of nature as we know them, it reminds us forcefully of psychological genesis and especially of the creative process in the arts, where indeed quite typically a global primary conception leads to increasingly articulate shape by a process of differentiation. Components of such a conception develop a shape of their own and search for their place in the whole, whose final composition is strongly influenced by the interrelation of the parts.

A particularly clear example is offered by the growth of form conception in the art work of young children and other early art forms. Here the store of potential shapes in the developing mind concretizes itself first in simple, global figures, such as circles. I have shown elsewhere (Arnheim, 1974, Chap. IV) that the increasing complexity of such art work comes about through a process of differentiation by which each conception becomes the special case of a whole range of variations. Each of these variations, in turn, can subdivide further into an ever richer arsenal of visual expression.

863

The ability of a good work of art to forge a multiplicity of different and often divergent parts into a productive whole has implications for moral conduct which were not lost on Fechner. He viewed the work of art as a symbol of the successful handling of social and personal conflict. As he weighed in his mind the ratio of pleasure and pain in human existence, he was not inclined to underestimate the impact of evil and discord, but he also believed that the life of the individual and the world as a whole progresses from conditions of pain to those of increasing pleasure. He saw the desirable condition of human intercourse symbolized in the work of art, for example, in a piece of music. In his late work on the *Dayview as Against the Nightview* he says: "And so I picture the whole proceeding of the world in the familiar image of a symphony, which, to be sure, produces more, and more severe, dissonances than the symphonies in our concert halls but moves also and nevertheless toward a resolution, for the whole as well as for each individual" (Fechner, 1879/1918, p. 181). In Fechner's view, the human aspiration could attain no higher fulfillment than that of matching the perfection of the work of art.

REFERENCES[1]

Arnheim, R. *Entropy and art.* Berkeley: University of California Press, 1971.

Arnheim, R. *Art and visual perception.* Berkeley: University of California Press, 1974.

Fechner, G. T. *Nanna oder Ueber das Seelenleben der Pflanzen.* Leipzig: Voss, 1848.

Fechner, G. T. *Zur experimentalen Aesthetik.* Abhandlungen der Königl. Sächsischen Gesellschaft der Wissenschaften, XIV. Leipzig: Hirzel, 1871.

Fechner, G. T. *Einige Ideen zur Schöpfungs- und Entwicklungsgeschichte der Organismen.* Leipzig: Breitkopf & Härtel, 1873.

Fechner, G. T. *Vergleichende Anatomic der Engel.* In *Kleine Schriften von Dr. Mises.* Leipzig: Breitkopf & Härtel, 1875. (Originally published, 1825.)

Fechner, G. T. *Elemente der Psychophysik* (2 vols.). Leipzig: Breitkopf & Härtel, 1889. (Originally published, 1860.)

Fechner, G. T. *Die Tagesansicht gegenüber der Nachtansicht.* Berlin: Deutsche Bibliothek, 1918. (Originally published, 1879.)

Fechner, G. T. *Zend-Avesta.* Leipzig: Insel Verlag, 1919. (Originally published, 1851.)

Fechner, G. T. *Vorschule der Aesthetik* (2 vols.). Hildesheim: Georg Holms, 1978. (Originally published, 1876.)

Hermann, I. Gustav Theodor Fechner. Eine psychoanalytische Studie. *Imago, 11.* Leipzig: Intern. Psychoanal. Verlag, 1926.

[1]The German editions of Fechner's writings, on which this paper is based, are listed in these References. Among the translations available in English are the following: *Elements of Psychophysics* (Helmut E. Adler, trans.), New York: Holt, 1966; Walter Lowrie (Ed.), *The Religion of a Scientist*, New York: Pantheon, 1946; *On Life after Death* (Hugo Wernekke, trans.), La Salle, Ill.: Open Court, 1906.

SUPPLEMENTARY READINGS

Any attempt to review even briefly the development of the psychology of art during the decades after Fechner and up to our own time would have been incompatible with the design of the preceding essay. A list of a few relevant titles may be of help to readers who wish to pursue this development on their own.

Closest to Fechner in time but already at the threshold of our own century there appeared another seminal figure, the psychologist Theodor Lipps. His principal work has not been translated: *Aesthetik* (Hamburg, 1903–1906). Among early surveys of the field as a whole see Herbert S. Langfeld, *The Aesthetic Attitude* (New York, 1920); C. K. Ogden, I. A. Richards, and J. Wood, *The Foundation of Aesthetics* (London, 1922); and A. R. Chandler, *Beauty and Human Nature* (New York, 1934). The most recent survey is by H. S. and S. Kreitler, *Psychology of the Arts* (Durham, N.C., 1972). Psychoanalytically oriented are S. Freud, *Leonardo da Vinci*, (London, 1948); E. Kris, *Psychoanalytic Explorations in Art* (New York, 1952); A. Ehrenzweig, *The Psychoanalysis of Artistic Vision and Hearing* (New York, 1953); and E. Neumann, *The Great Mother* (New York, 1955). Two fundamental works on the art work of psychotics are: H. Prinzhorn, *Artistry of the Mentally Ill* (New York, 1972) and A. Bader and L. Navratil, *Zwischen Wahn und Wirklichkeit* (Lucerne, 1976). Finally a few titles of characteristic more recent work: R. Arnheim, *Art and Visual Perception* (Berkeley, 1974); D. E. Berlyne, *Aesthetics and Psychobiology* (New York, 1971); J. W. Getzels and M. Csikzentmihaly, *The Creative Vision* (New York, 1976); James Hogg (Ed.), *Psychology and the Visual Arts* (Harmondsworth, 1969), John M. Kennedy, A *Psychology of Pictorial Perception* (San Francisco, 1974), Pavel Machotka, *The Nude, Perception and Personality* (New York, 1979), and L. B. Meyer, *Emotion and Meaning in Music* (Chicago, 1956).

·

865

IV

PSYCHOLOGY IN RELATION TO SOCIETY, CULTURE, AND SENSIBILITY

PSYCHOLOGY AND THE
PUBLIC GOOD

37

Psychology in Cultural Context
THE DIVISION OF LABOR AND THE
FRAGMENTATION OF EXPERIENCE

STEPHAN L. CHOROVER

We are living in a very singular moment of history. It is a moment of crisis, in the literal sense of that word. In every branch of our spiritual and material civilization we seem to have arrived at a critical turning point. This spirit shows itself not only in the actual state of public affairs but also in the general attitude toward fundamental values in personal and social life (Max Planck, "Where Is Science Going?" 1932).

In ancient times, the Latin word *scientia* meant simply "knowledge." Today, the term "science" refers not only to a body of knowledge and a systematic way of trying to comprehend the world and its contents, but also to a vastly diversified and tremendously complicated human social enterprise. Thus, the direction in which science goes is everywhere and always related to the more general course of human events within the cultural context of which it is a part.

What Is the Problem?

For the most part, my own previous effort to comprehend the mutual and essentially reciprocal interplay that always goes on between scientific psychology and social policy focused upon some past and present controversies over "the meaning of human nature and the power of behavior control" (Chorover, 1979a). My contention here is that psychology as a whole is moving rapidly in the direction of extreme material and conceptual "fragmentation" and that this movement is of more than academic interest. In particular, the widespread propagation and uncritical public acceptance of a partial and fragmentary worldview has something to do with the fact that our culture as a whole is presently unable to cope reasonably, humanely, and effectively with a vast and recursively interpenetrating array of global and local human problems—including the spectres of economic collapse, ecological catastrophe, and nuclear Armageddon.

Today, as when Planck's essay was written, the spirit that is showing itself on all sides is one of growing bewilderment, pessimism, and paralysis. "To prophesy is extremely difficult," says an old Chinese proverb, "especially with respect to the future." I do not suppose that Planck clearly foresaw in 1932 that his "spiritual and material civilization" was about to undergo a horrendously destructive world war, but omniscience is not required in order to see that we are in a comparable predicament today, and that a continuation of present approaches cannot possibly be expected to lead anywhere except toward increasingly violent and humanly destructive conflict among contending social forces. While there are certainly no simple ways to resolve this extremely complicated situation, it may be possible to understand it and hence begin to do something toward its amelioration.

What do I mean by "fragmentation?" Let me give an illustration from my vantage point as a participant-observer within a particular field of scientific and professional specialization. Better yet, let me put it in the form of a personal confession: I cannot seem to keep up with the bewildering variety of things that are going on in my immediate academic neighborhood. The more I try to keep abreast of current developments in the neurobehavioral sciences, the more confused I get. The more I learn about the details of things in my own special area of interest, the more disconnected they seem to be from the issues that drew me into the field of psychology in the first place. What is the explanation?

I really do not think it is just a matter of my personal limitations. From innumerable conversations with colleagues, it is clear that I am not the only one to experience such disconnection, and the bewilderment, pessimism, and paralysis that accompanies it. Though I frequently have real trouble understanding just what my colleagues are doing, saying, and writing these days, I am not trying to project the responsibility for this state of affairs onto them or anyone else.

To "explain" something means to describe its origins, its organization, and its relationship to other things and events. My explanation of the conceptual disconnection phenomenon is based on the already-mentioned idea that there are systematic and structural interrelationships between what is going on in psychology and in the larger world. Could it be that similar factors are responsible for generating the same atmosphere of bewilderment, pessimism, and paralysis in both places?

871

In what way is conceptual disconnection comprehensible as a specific social product of the interplay between science and society? One way is via the development, within psychology (and society), of a mode of intellectual and material production in which things and events are defined and dealt with by dividing them up or breaking them down into supposedly more and more "fundamental" pieces. This is the essence of both analytical atomism and the social division of labor within psychology and many other fields of contemporary human activity. This modus operandi, with its attendant fragmentation of experience, is also a social product of concrete historical conditions. It reflects the interplay of discernible ideas, values, and practices, and it is not a natural or necessary (i.e., sui generis) byproduct of some insensate or autonomous force. In short, the paradigms of contemporary psychology are neither more nor less than the conceptual and material products of the individual and collective experience of psychologists living in contemporary society. Accordingly, they tend to reflect and reinforce the ideas, values, and practices of the culture within which they exist (Chorover, 1979a).

There is nothing particularly original in the idea that a connection exists between the division of labor and the fragmentation of experience. Indeed, many other observers have commented on the growing fragmentation that is now so obvious and widespread in all aspects of human existence. Three authors whose complementary perspectives appear to be particularly pertinent in this connection are the physicist David Bohm, the political economist Harry Braverman, and the metallurgist Cyril Stanley Smith.

In his essay "Fragmentation and Wholeness" (1976), Bohm elaborates on a thesis of "unbroken wholeness" that he has developed in opposition to the Copenhagen interpretation of quantum theory. His goal is to develop a relativistic view of physical reality as "an infinitely complex process of a structure in movement and development." He begins by decrying the widespread and uncritical acceptance of reductionism (or analytic atomism) as the only reasonable way of approaching the problem of comprehending the world and its contents. He characterizes as "an illusion" the idea that the world is constructed of basic objects, particles, or "building blocks" that are ultimately analyzable into separately and independently existing parts. Indeed, he argues that this illusion has been responsible for a

> general confusion of the mind, which creates an endless series of problems and interferes with our clarity of perception so seriously as to prevent us from being able to solve most of them. Thus . . . art, science, technology, and human work in general, are divided up into specialties, each considered to be separate in essence from the others . . . society as a whole . . . is broken up into separate nations and different religious, political, economic, racial groups, etc. [The] natural environment has . . . been seen as an aggregate of separately existent parts . . . each individual human being has been fragmented into a large number of separate and conflicting compartments . . ." (p. 1).

Bohm acknowledges that analytic atomism and the social division of labor in science (and elsewhere) have always been "necessary and proper" to some extent. The central illusion, in his view, is to believe that all the fragments thus produced are actually separately existent.

In his search for the causes of fragmentation, Harry Braverman (1974) looks beyond the limits of the psychological realm. For him, the phenomenon is comprehensible not in terms of disordered individual perceptions or thoughts but in terms of distorted social arrangements and relations. The focus of his analysis is the workplace. He traces the emergence of the "scientific management movement" and the "rational division of labor" during the early twentieth century. In his view, the only reasonable way to understand the contributions of psychologists and other "scientific experts" to the development of modern industrial practices is to consider them in terms of the prevailing social and economic context.

Braverman argues persuasively that the so-called "scientific management movement" and its allegedly rational division of labor was neither scientific nor rational. Its innovations were managerial ploys. They simply reflected the perspective of a managerial class faced with the problem of controlling the behavior of a refractory work force at the point of production within "a setting of antagonistic social relations." As implied by the subtitle of his important book, it is Braverman's central thesis that "the degradation of work in the twentieth century" is a social product of the ideas, values, and practices inherent in a mode of production predicted upon the separation of mental from manual labor and the subdivision of tasks in an assembly-line fashion.

Braverman's thesis is not merely that the rise of the factory system and the social division of labor under corporate capitalism have had an extremely alienating and degrading impact upon the lives of industrial workers in many trades. His further and more pertinent point is that the fragmentation process is actually much more widespread than it once was and that its deleterious effects are no longer limited to workers engaged in traditional industrial occupations. In particular, he contends that the degradation of work is now occurring in many previously exempt occupations—often in connection with various modes of automation. As a consequence, the experience of fragmentation is becoming increasingly familiar to people employed in almost every field of endeavor, including the sciences and allied professions. In short, his interpretation helps to explain what is going on in psychology today.

From a reading of Smith's (1978) essay it becomes apparent that a comparable kind and degree of fragmentation presently prevails within other scientific and professional disciplines as well. "Having spent many years," he writes, "seeking quantitative formulations of the structure of metals . . . I have slowly come to realize that the analytical quantitative approach that I had been taught to regard as the only respectable one for a scientist is insufficient." Smith does not discuss the genesis of analytical atomism and its relationship to the social division of labor in

873

science, but he does point clearly to the availability of an alternative and more holistic perspective from which it is possible to comprehend "aspects of any large and complicated system . . . that cannot be measured easily, if at all." Neither analytic atomism nor the fragmentation of experience it engenders are inexorable "gives." Rather they are parts and products of the prevailing paradigm and of the material and historical conditions that presently exist within the society of which that paradigm is itself a part and product.

In what respects is the shape and texture of contemporary scholarship influenced by the mode of its production? Does it really matter that the effort to comprehend human existence from a scientific perspective is the product of historical processes that include the social division of intellectual work into separate and distinct disciplines? The obvious fact is that knowledge of human nature has generally been pursued in a fragmented way along several somewhat separate and distinct lines. Thus, there now exists a "family" of disciplines—the humanities and human sciences. Included are such diverse "fields" as biology, psychology, sociology, history, and anthropology. In any attempt to evaluate the scholarship that has resulted from this division of labor, it is necessary, first of all, to take into account the conditions under which it has been produced.

Those of us who are psychologists need only refer to our own experience in order to realize that the theories and practices we have learned to regard as significant are the specific products of a particular socially established and consensually maintained system of scientific thought and professional action. As psychologists, we are trained and train others within this historically established and ongoing system. At any given moment, the system is manifested within a given discipline as a "paradigm" (i.e., a particular set of conceptual frameworks entailing certain scientific or professional beliefs, values, and practices).

Within the human sciences there are evidently some differences in prevailing paradigms. However, current developments in all fields tend to reflect and reinforce the general perspective that I have previously described as "analytic atomism." In its more extreme and uncompromising forms, this perspective is consistent with various doctrines of biological determinism, including those which attempt to define such phenomena as social violence as if they were reducible to defects within individual persons or parties. I have discussed this mode of "explanation" elsewhere (Chorover, 1979a; 1980). My present point is that psychologists have traditionally been taught that analytic atomism is the best, indeed the only reasonable and scientific way to approach the problem of understanding the nature of a complex entity or process—be it a brain, a human being, or a social group. "Nothing," as Spinoza noted, "can be understood in isolation," yet as neuropsychologists we were taught to *isolate* the system we aim to comprehend—to separate it from the material or conceptual context within which it originates and of which it is a part; then to *analyze* it—to divide it up or break it down into its identifiable constituent elements.

All of us have been well socialized into the beliefs, values, and practices of our chosen fields. While some of us learned (and taught) that the mental and behavioral activities of organisms—including human beings—were comprehensible as "nothing but" the epiphenomenal correlates of biological (and especially of brain) events, others were learning (and teaching) that human thoughts and feelings and actions were comprehensible as "nothing but" the superficial results of deeper psychodynamic—especially unconscious—causes.

The tendency to pursue the analytic atomistic or reductionistic approach has no doubt been reinforced by the fact that human beings have all sorts of conceptual limitations. The world, accordingly, appears to be altogether too big and its contents too numerous and complex to be comprehended as a whole in any moment or series of moments by any person or persons. This view has, in turn, been reinforced by the general acceptance within the scientific community of the proposition that in order to comprehend the world and its contents, it is both necessary and desirable to divide things up or break them down into units of manageable proportions. By now it should be clear that this circular causal trend has produced a proliferation of "findings," and these have often been interpreted as a token of "progress." But it has also led toward progressive fragmentation within the scientific community. Thus, the differentiation of scientific and professional activity within academic circles— usually referred to, euphemistically, as "specialization"—has already spawned a multitude of narrowly defined and largely self-isolated subdisciplines ranging across a wide spectrum, and including both molecular biology and cultural anthropology. One obvious organizational concomitant of this process has been the proliferation of new and progressively more fragmented institutional entities, often under the rubric of some "interdisciplinary" goal. A more subtle concomitant has been the narrowing of conceptual horizons within each discipline.

What I have suggested, so far, is consistent with the fact that psychology entered the past quarter-century during a period when American society was undergoing a period of substantial economic expansion. During this "post-sputnik" era, the development and deployment of novel tools and techniques for the psychological enterprise was lavishly supported. Nevertheless, the accelerated branching of specialties and its attendant division of labor have caused psychologists to suffer experiences that heretofore were familiar only to workers in putatively less prestigious and rewarding occupations.

Today the growing demand for "specialists" exists in an economic atmosphere of scarcity and extreme competition for limited financial resources, grants, jobs, and so on. Under these conditions, the ever-present feedback loop between science and society engenders even more severe restrictions upon the intellectual perspectives of both students and teachers.

As in many corporate and industrial fields, so in science and technology— including psychology and psychotechnology—the growing division of labor has been and continues to be experienced differently by persons occupying different positions. This does not mean that we have nothing in common, but that the effects of fragmentation are experienced in many different forms. In my opinion, the deleterious effects are numerous and most strongly felt today among students in the relatively early stages of graduate training. That the complaints about fragmentation often tend to wane with time and training only serves to show the power of the scientific and professional socialization process of which we are all products and parts.

Despite determinist claims to the contrary (e.g., Wilson, 1975; Sociobiology Study Group, 1976), personal thoughts, feelings, and actions—and the scientific paradigms, that are among their social counterparts—are subject to change. Thus, we can choose—within limits—the direction in which our science goes. If it is the case that the material and conceptual fragmentation of contemporary psychology is the product of particular historical conditions; and if it is true that the paradigms of contemporary psychology are subject to modification, then it becomes possible to imagine that the trend toward fragmentation is not beyond our power to control, or even to reverse.

What Is to Be Done?

The events recounted did not happen overnight or in a vacuum. Insofar as fragmentation is a social product, it may be reversible. But it will not be easily or instantly reversed. What we commonly call "Western" science has long been almost exclusively predicated upon a fragmentary reductionist epistemology. And Western culture as a whole has long entertained as part of its dualistic tradition the idea that the biological, psychological, and social aspects of existence are essentially separate and distinct.

In attempting to understand the kind of conceptual fragmentation that must be overcome, it may be useful to take note of what is perhaps the oldest and deepest plane of division within the realm of psychological theory: the age-old split that exists in respect to the question of "human nature." The question that has always stood at the very heart of psychological discourse is this: what, precisely, does it mean to be a specifically *human* being? This ancient and still unanswered question arises today, as it always has, in the context of a misleading debate between proponents of ostensibly contradictory doctrines of biological/genetic and social/environmental determinism (see, e.g., Wilson, 1975; Skinner, 1971).

It is obvious to almost everyone who is aware of recent developments in population genetics that the nature-nurture dichotomy is a false one. Phenotypes are products of genotype-environment *interaction*. Thus, there is not the slightest reason to believe in the primacy of *either* the biological *or* the environmental (or social) aspects of human existence. It therefore becomes pertinent to ask why the debate continues to recur in these falsely dichotomous and fragmented terms. More important, since there is every reason to believe that the biological, psychological, and social aspects of human existence continuously interact, it is necessary to ask why they are so consistently regarded as separate and distinct.

One key to answering both questions lies in a consideration of the broader historical context of which the nature-nurture debate is a part. The debate continues to recur, with minor variations in form and content, because it is consonant with traditional categorical ("either/or") logic and because it lends a semblance of meaning to prevailing patterns of social conflict among contending human groups. In short, the effort to invent competing ("either/or") determinist ideas about human nature continues because such ideas continue to be useful as social weapons in the partisan conflicts that inevitably arise whenever some people are trying to regulate the conduct of other people in a context of antagonistic social relations (Chorover, 1979a).

The ideas that we choose to entertain about what it means to be a specifically human being have a powerful effect on our collective ability to resolve the crises that threaten our personal and social existence (Eisenberg, 1972). Can we learn to comprehend ourselves as more than *either* genetically *or* environmentally programmed automatons? Unless we do so, we will forever remain the credulous prey of those whose partisan interests and objectives are well served by the simplistic idea that *either* biology *or* society is destiny.

It it difficult to change. It is not easy to overcome the effects of having been socialized into a scientific and professional system that is organized around a one-dimensional reductionist tradition. It has taken me a long time to realize that I was taught and was teaching too narrow a view of human existence. I now find, however, that I must somehow learn how to overcome the effects of an educational and professional experience that, overall, has encouraged me to believe that there is always to be found a single or main "building block" that can be properly considered as a prime or principal determinant of the development and present organization of any human system.

I am currently trying to establish a perspective broad enough to encompass the narrow disciplinary perspectives of at least a few different psychological subfields. I think that it may thus prove possible to grasp and hold onto a conception of human nature broad enough to include the essentially interdependent biological, psychological, and social facts of human existence. Recently, my own search for some way of transcending the limiting polarities of the nature-nurture debate has led me away from reductionism and toward a composite biological, psychological, and social conception of "human systems" (Chorover & Chorover, 1978).

In "Physician vs. Researcher, Values in Conflict?" (Chorover, 1979b) I asserted that the specialization and fragmentation of the mental health system in our culture enhances the possibility of circumstances arising in which physicians might be inclined to work against the interests of their patients. I concluded that any serious effort to resolve this issue must begin by attempting to deal with those structural features of human society from which the conflicts arise.

In "Violence: A Localizable Problem?" (Chorover, 1980) I began to glimpse a more unified conceptual framework of brain-behavior relationships and the nature of human problems, one that seems to me to be capable of accounting harmoniously for the multiple and reciprocal patterns among the organization of the brain, the behavior of the individual, and the dynamics of the larger social context.

What begins to emerge from my current work is a view of the brain, of human behavior, and of human problems that is consonant with a scientifically sophisticated worldview. Such a view reveals not a set of phenomena comprehensible in either reductionistic or holistic terms, but rather a complex, interpenetrating, and ultimately irreducible web of relationships among events taking place at many levels simultaneously. As one famous physicist put it, "the world thus appears as a complicated tissue of events, in which connections of different kinds alternate or overlap or combine and thereby determine the texture of the whole" (Heisenberg, 1958).

Although still in a preliminary stage, the conceptual frame within which this effort is proceeding may serve as a concluding example of what is entailed in attempting to make a human system—be it a brain, a person, or a social group—humanly comprehensible. Briefly, it is necessary to focus analytically on its mode of internal organization—including a description of the multifarious and recurrent mutual causal connections among its constituent elements or parts. It is also necessary to study its other synchronic aspects, including its organization as a whole: that is, its structure and activity as a coherent unity existing in a particular spatio-temporal context and the nature of the boundaries or interfaces that serve to separate it from (and connect it with) the surrounding systems of which it is a part. Moreover, it is necessary to consider its diachronic aspects and to study its evolution—including its phylogenetic and ontogenetic development as well as its contextual or situational history—and its present position in terms of its life cycle(s).

This approach may or may not turn out to be effective in overcoming the fragmentation of psychology. But if it is the case that the fragmented state of psychology today simultaneously serves to reflect and reinforce the fragmentation of human experience as a whole, and if it is the case that the fragmentation of experience tends to exacerbate the present bewilderment, pessimism, and paralysis that attends all current attempts to deal with urgent human problems, then something must be done to overcome the fragmentation of experience.

Though scientific psychology over its brief history has in the main augmented the fragmentation of experience, it is, by its very conception, the central field of scholarship which could assume leadership in ameliorating the problem. There *may* be a chance that we—who a century ago elected the awesome mission of scientifically illuminating human nature—can begin to contribute, in a meaningful, humane, and effective way, to a resolution of the present crisis. Were that to happen, I should like to think that our successors will still be here to celebrate psychology in its bicentennial year. Perhaps they will be able, with justice, to claim that psychology has begun to make a positive contribution to the public good in relation to the society, culture, and sensibility of which it is a part.

REFERENCES

Bohm, D. *Fragmentation and wholeness.* Jerusalem: Van Leer Jerusalem Foundation, 1976.

Braverman, H. *Labor and monopoly capital: The degradation of work in the twentieth century.* New York: Monthly Review Press, 1974.

Chorover, S. *From genesis to genocide.* Cambridge: M.I.T. Press, 1979. (a)

Chorover, S. Physician vs. researcher, values in conflict? *Wellesley Alumni Magazine,* 1979, 63(4), 21–27. (b)

Chorover, S. Violence: A localizable problem? In E. Valenstein (Ed.), *The psychosurgery debate.* San Francisco: Freeman, 1980.

Chorover, S., & Chorover, B. Towards a theory of human systems. In S. P. R. Rose (Ed.), *Proceedings of the Bressanone Conference on the dialectics of biology and society in the production of mind* (Vol. 2). London: Allison & Busby, 1978.

Eisenberg, L. The human nature of human nature. *Science,* 1972, *176,* 125–128.

Heisenberg, W. *Physics and philosophy.* New York: Harper, 1958.

Planck, M. *Where is science going?* New York: Norton, 1932.

Skinner, B. F. *Beyond freedom and dignity.* New York: Knopf, 1971.

Smith, C. S. Structural hierarchy in science, art, and history. In J. Wechsler (Ed.), *On aesthetics and science.* Cambridge: M.I.T. Press, 1978.

Sociobiology Study Group. Sociobiology: Another biological determinism. *Bioscience,* 1976, 26, 3.

Wilson, E. O. *Sociobiology: The new synthesis.* Cambridge, Mass.: Harvard University Press, 1975.

38

Psychology: Handmaiden to Society

DOROTHEA D. BRAGINSKY

The mainstream of American psychology is far from the objective science that it purports to be. As a scientific enterprise, it is woven from the political, economic, and moral threads of mainstream society. Rather than pursuing the value-free search for truth and understanding in order to help solve human problems, much of psychology is merely the handmaiden of the status quo and of society's prevailing values.

The most immediate example that comes to mind is, of course, psychotherapy and its ancillary technologies. From its very inception, psychotherapy has been the scapegoat of psychology. Suffering attacks from nearly every quarter, the critics range from the person who knows someone who has been in therapy for years and remains "as crazy as ever" to the scientist with his sophisticated, theoretical barrages. Among the most vociferous complainants are psychologists themselves, particularly those from research and university settings.

They have long scorned the clinical "practitioner" for creating and perpetuating a mythology based on social values and morals while eschewing the objective findings of the researchers' laboratories. The rarefied atmosphere of academe makes it all too easy for psychologists in these settings to overlook their own myths and failures as well as the impact social values and morals have upon their scientific endeavors. Furthermore, it is nearly impossible for anyone else to perceive this since few people are aware of what goes on in the psychological laboratory and of what passes for "scientific" research findings.

Clinical psychologists are obvious and vulnerable targets for anyone wanting to find fault with psychology because they deal directly with the public and its welfare. That they, for the most part, fail is not the issue for the moment. The point here is that clinical practitioners are alone among their colleagues in their efforts to grapple with human problems and to ameliorate the pain associated with them. Although other specialties in psychology pay lip service to the ultimate goal of the "public good," particularly when they are applying for federal funding, even a cursory examination of the psychological journals indicates that the human condition is irrelevant to their research.

The literature in the field of psychology is testimony to our failure to explore and investigate meaningful problems in meaningful ways (see Bakan, 1967, 1971; Braginsky & Braginsky, 1974; Jordan, 1968; Koch, 1964, 1969). Indeed, if all that remained of our society for anthropologists of the future were the psychology journals, they would have to conclude that we enjoyed a near paradise. Although we have witnessed during this century some of the most enormous and violent social, political, economic, and personal upheavals, the volumes of psychological research do not reflect upon or record these events.

This apparent apathy toward the human situation is the result of either the psychologists' willful avoidance (e.g., the purists who play "scientist" in their laboratory of glittering gadgets) or their inability to translate concern into meaningful, intelligent, professional behavior. Because mainstream psychology is embedded in the dominant political, economic, and religious ideologies, professional psychologists have upheld these ideologies rather than examining their impact upon the lives of others. Thus, many researchers simply have not looked at the meaningful problems while many others who have looked were unable to see beyond their own social ideologies.

Although negligent of the public welfare, when psychologists remain in their laboratories they do little harm. Working with animals or college sophomores, they create their own realities and impose them upon their "subjects." If their constructions are wrong and the "subjects" do not comply with the hypotheses, no one is wiser since such studies are not published. Even when hypotheses are confirmed in the laboratory, most researchers are well aware that they may not withstand the acid test of the "real world." Nonetheless, they insist that clinical practitioners pay heed to and base their therapies and technologies on the research findings of the laboratory.

This call for greater scientific objectivity in the clinical setting becomes ludicrous when we examine how it functions in a well-controlled research setting. The study to be scrutinized here is singled out because it represents an excellent example of the best in research methodology.

881

Many researchers noted that animals respond more vigorously during early extinction trials than during the end of a reinforced series. In other words, if over a number of trials an animal receives a food pellet for depressing a lever, and if the food pellet suddenly does not appear when the lever is depressed, the animal will press the lever with greater force. The various authors proposed three possible hypotheses to explain this observation: (1) nonreinforcement following the reinforcement series leads to frustration, increasing the general drive level of the animal and thereby heightening the animal's performance; (2) because of associative rather than motivational factors, the animal may have learned during the reinforcement series that it had to press hard on the lever to activate the food pellet apparatus; or (3) vigorous bar-pressing is an earlier habit to which the animal regresses when it is frustrated by nonreinforcement.

Blixt and Ley (1968) attempted to resolve this conflict by designing an experiment that would pit each of the three hypotheses against each other. In it, fifth- and sixth-grade boys were required to push a monitored strain-gauge lever in order to receive reinforcement (M & M candies). When the boys pushed within the predetermined range of force, they received an M & M candy. One group of boys were trained to lever push under light force conditions. After this was established, reinforcement conditions were changed so that a heavy force was needed to get the M & M candy.

Once this new response was established, the subjects were placed on an extinction schedule. A second group was trained to first push with great force and then with light force. With the experiment in place, the authors went on to spell out their predictions:

> . . . The frustration-drive hypothesis would predict that both groups should show an increase in force of responding on the first extinction trial following nonreinforcement, whereas the regression hypothesis would predict that the heavy-to-light group should show an increase in force, but the light-to-heavy group should show a decrease in force (i.e., a return to a previously established mode of responding). The associative hypothesis, however, would predict that the light-to-heavy group should show an increase in force, but the heavy-to-light group should show a decrease (i.e., if a heavy press does not pay off, a lighter press should) (p. 127).

The findings of this study were clear. All experimental groups pushed the lever with great vigor during the first few trials of the extinction (nonreinforcement) series. Specifically, when the boys did not receive an M & M candy after depressing the lever, they pressed harder than when they received the candy. The authors concluded that "the present data are completely consistent with predictions derived from the frustration-drive hypothesis."

As noted before, this study is a fine example of scientific research. The experimenters created the kind of environment necessary to address the problem. The environmental manipulations were explicit and quantifiable, and the dependent variable—the subjects' behavior—was observable and easily measured. Most of all, the logic they followed and the methods they chose were in keeping with the scientific goals of simplicity, directness, and objectivity. Yet their conclusion misrepresents and distorts the empirical observations.

What they omitted from their formulation is the experience we all have had at one time or another. Namely, we have all deposited coins in vending machines expecting to buy gum, soda, or some other item and the machine does not produce the desired item. What typically happens is that we push or pull the lever with more force. If this repeated vigor does not lead to success, we sometimes hit or kick the machine. Why? The most obvious explanation is that we assume that the machine is not operating properly, that it is jammed or that the coins are stuck. We exert this additional force to overcome the malfunction and to receive the desired (and paid for) product. The extra vigor is an entirely appropriate response to a situation that leaves little else to do.

Ten-year-old boys might press the lever harder when the M & M candies did not come out in order to fix a malfunctioning dispensing machine. This very plausible explanation, however, was never mentioned in the discussion of the experiment. Had the authors given any recognition to it, the experiment would probably not have been conducted at all. Indeed, there would be no problem in explaining why boys "respond more vigorously during early extinction trials than during trials at the end of a reinforced series."

Other aspects of this study are noteworthy, informing us further about what one may or may not expect from rigorous experimental methods. For instance, the original hypotheses were based on data compiled from rodents, yet without a word of explanation Blixt and Ley use young boys as subjects to test these same hypotheses. We know that the behavior of ten-year-old boys is not always exemplary, but surely some acknowledgement about the change of species is in order. Moreover, it is possible that rats also try to "unjam" the dispensing machine by hitting it harder. We can never, of course, know because we cannot ask the rats if they have acquired the same knowledge about vending machines as children have. But we can talk to fifth- and sixth-grade boys and ask them why they pushed harder on the machine's lever. Since the experimenters used the same methodological principles they apply to rats (i.e., only observable behavior is recorded), they left a valuable source of information untapped. In short, even the best designed experiments, the most refined quantification and well-grounded hypotheses cannot protect the researcher from the production and perpetuation of myths.

The psychological literature is filled with examples of similar (and often worse) misconstructions of reality. Since experiments are little more than the researchers' constructions, a well-designed study is simply an experiment that fits the ideological stance of a like-minded group of researchers. If this stance is erroneous, misleading, or absurd, the results of the studies will reflect these intellectual shortcomings. Thus, the academic psychologists' plea for clinical psychologists to emulate them by becoming more objective and scientific is hardly the safeguard that researchers imagine. In fact, an analysis of the entire psychological enterprise makes it clear that the clinical myths and failures are, to a great extent, a function of the degree to which practitioners borrow from and emulate mainstream academic psychology (see Braginsky & Braginsky, 1974).

Indeed, the theories upon which the laboratory studies are based can be seen in all their ideological and, often, foolish splendor when transplanted in the therapeutic, clinical setting. After years of emulating the medical profession by using insight and psychoanalytic techniques, clinical psychologists can now turn to therapeutic methods that have directly evolved from psychological research and theory. Although some psychologists have developed their own insight therapies, London (1964) notes that their commonalities with psychoanalysis outweigh their superficial differences.

Let us focus now on psychology's unique contribution to the psychotherapeutic situation, namely, the techniques based upon the theories of Pavlov, Hull, and Skinner. Brought into the clinic by Wolpe, Stampfl, and Skinner, they have evolved what London (1964) calls the "action therapies," the goal of which is for the therapist to "manipulate stimulus-response connections in order to deliberately change specific behavior from one pattern of activity to another." Or as Leifer (1969) phrases it: "It is indoctrination or training for culturally specific traits, attitudes, and actions."

These techniques of behavior modification have been enthusiastically embraced by many clinical psychologists tired of playing stepchild to psychiatrists with regard to the traditional insight therapies (and probably tired of their failures). The behavior-therapy model is rapidly replacing the medical model in many clinical settings. Although the insight therapies were not particularly successful, there was at least some human contact and warmth expressed during the therapeutic encounter. The use of the action therapies, on the other hand, precludes any such humanizing interaction. They, in fact, seem to assure the opposite.

According to Braginsky and Braginsky (1974), compared to the insight therapies, psychology's behavioral therapies: (1) are not transactional—there is no exchange of information between the therapist and the patient; (2) are explicitly manipulative and controlling; (3) are based upon goals set by mainstream norms rather than the person in therapy; (4) are rarely voluntarily engaged in by patients; and (5) are generally undignified, humiliating encounters. In short, these therapies are tailored to the poor, the powerless, and the "misfits" of society.

It is with behavioral therapy that psychology's handmaiden function comes full circle and reaches its most obvious conclusion. First, psychologists help to keep society's house in order by identifying and labeling its deviant citizens (see Becker, 1963; Braginsky, Braginsky & Ring, 1969; Braginsky & Braginsky, 1971; Foucault, 1965; Laing, 1967; Szasz, 1970). This often sets into motion a process of social sanitation (Braginsky & Braginsky, 1974), which removes the deviants from the

884

mainstream of society, placing them in one or another catchment area (e.g., the mental hospital, the training school for the retarded, and so on). Psychologists attempt to somehow correct or "treat" the deviants while residing in these institutions in order to return them to the mainstream of life. In current behaviorist jargon, therapists try to "change unacceptable behaviors into acceptable ones"—socially acceptable ones, of course.

The techniques used to accomplish this goal are as peculiar as the theories and discoveries upon which they are based. For instance, one major contribution of learning theory is the "discovery" of a relationship between deprivation and behavior. In study after study, researchers have been able to demonstrate that hungry or thirsty rats will learn behaviors instrumental to satisfying their hunger or thirst faster than sated rodents. As translated by two behavioral therapists (Schaefer & Martin, 1969) so that it might be understood in human terms and applied to the therapeutic encounter, this discovery now reads: ". . . a man who has starved for three days is likely to do anything for a morsel of bread. On the other hand, someone who has just finished a rich meal would hardly consider a morsel of bread a reinforcer."

Kassorla (1969) with, no doubt, just this kind of "discovery" in mind, conducted the following therapeutic experiment. Taking one of the most deranged patients in a British mental hospital (a mute, catatonic schizophrenic man hospitalized for thirty-two years), Kassorla and her colleagues embarked upon an operant conditioning program. Since Mr. B (the patient) had not spoken to the hospital staff for nearly thirty years, the behavior to be reinforced was speech, "based on the principle that behavior which is reinforced is likely to occur again. . . ."

On the first day of the experiment Mr. B was asked 120 simple questions (e.g., "What is your name?" "How old are you?") to which he responded only 11 percent of the time. He answered with a soft "ugh" sound and twice managed the complex vocalization, "crack 'em." It was this sound that was selected as the behavior to be reinforced. Kassorla had some difficulties regarding the reinforcers and the hospital staff:

> . . . the reinforcement we relied on was food. In spite of considerable resistance from the hospital staff, which felt that Mr. B was too sick to talk and should not be treated "unkindly," we took full control of the patient's feeding (p. 40).

During the initial training sessions Mr. B was given food if, after the experimenter said "crack 'em," he repeated the sound or even moved his lips. After two weeks he vocalized 92 percent of the time and was ready for new words to be introduced. Words such as "dog," "cat," "bird" were repeated after the experimenter. Later still, pictures of objects were shown and Mr. B was required to identify them. A problem arose when for seven days he continued to respond, "I don't know" to a picture of a dog. The experimenters decided to extinguish this "negativistic behavior" since it was interfering with the patient's progress. Whenever

885

Mr. B said "I don't know" when asked to identify the picture of the dog, he was immediately removed from the experimental room where, incidentally, he received his food. Thus, removal from the room assured the patient that he would not receive any reinforcers. After four days, Mr. B responded appropriately when shown the picture of the dog.

The training was completed in about four-and-a-half months (138 days). At that time, the patient responded to 75 percent of those same 120 questions with which the experiment began—no small achievement. Following thirty years of being mute, Mr. B's speech did, indeed, return. The behavioral therapists' explanation of why it returned and of the procedures they used are, however, serious misconstructions of reality. For example, Kassorla maintains that a major difficulty in working with psychotics is to discover what they will find reinforcing and then to figure out a "reliable schedule of positive reinforcements." The most serious distortion here is the therapist's seeing her or himself as the provider of positive reinforcements when, in fact, they are the withholders of reinforcers necessary for survival. To withhold food from a patient until he submits to the therapist might in another context be seen as torture—which is a more accurate representation of reality than Kassorla's.

An extension of the discoveries of the "experts at operant conditioning," if the hospital staff would be willing to stand for it, might include the use of succinyl-choline (a drug that induces respiratory arrest for about two minutes). Surely Mr. B would have relinquished his mute behavior sooner had oxygen been used as a positive reinforcement. In behaviorists' terms one might say that oxygen reinforcers are more reinforcing than food reinforcers.

These linguistic tricks distort what has transpired in two important ways. First, by focusing on what the therapist gives the patient rather than on what he withholds, the therapist can perceive himself as benevolent, not punitive. Second, and more important from a scientific perspective, the behaviorists take what is common knowledge, knowledge used by mankind's oppressors for centuries, and have made it their own "scientific discovery." History is replete with examples of coercive and torturous methods of behavior control. The behaviorists' contribution to the public welfare has been to discover that these methods can be therapeutic and to lend them scientific respectability.

One variation on the reinforcement theme has led to another therapeutic strategy: namely, token economy. In these systems mental patients or schoolchildren or prisoners are given tokens for eliciting the prescribed behavior. These tokens can then be traded for primary reinforcers (food, candy, cigarettes, etc.). Ayllon and Azrin (1968) conducted extensive research using tokens as conditioned reinforcers with hospitalized mental patients. Among some of their major findings are the following discoveries: patients desire the jobs that yield the most tokens; payment of tokens before the performance led to decreased output; discontinuation of payment led to a discontinuation of work.

If the behaviorists had known the rudiments of economic systems, we might have been spared their discovery of capitalism. Surely we all know that people prefer jobs that pay better, be the payment in tokens or dollars; that if you pay someone before a job is completed, his output will be decreased; that if you stop paying someone for his work, he will stop working. Although professional psychologists may enjoy their work to such a degree that these considerations would be irrelevant to their own performance, they should at least appreciate that few working people (particularly those from the social class from which most mental patients come) so enjoy their labors. Moreover, had they seen their work in this context, Ayllon and Azrin might have better understood what they really were doing in the mental hospital: specifically, they replaced the traditional socialist, welfare system of the institution with a system of capitalism.

Although these examples of behavioral therapy ring of antiquity, Schaefer and Martin (1969) report a unique and provocative use of reinforcers in the treatment of "odd behaviors." They suggest, for instance, that foul language or screaming might be dealt with by giving positive reinforcement "for a behavior which in the past was maintained by altogether different reinforcers. . . ." This is so shocking to some patients that researchers have noted a "cure" after a single reinforcement. The schedule they recommend is:

1. One minute of cursing or screaming in the isolation room; 1 cigarette, token, etc.
2. Two additional minutes of continuous louder cursing; 2 cigarettes, tokens, etc. The patient will often cease cursing or screaming after this event. Quiet weeping typically follows (pp. 121–132).

Clearly, this method could be described as treating odd behavior with still odder behavior. The patient is no doubt astonished when he is rewarded by the therapist for a vulgar tirade. The patient is left with two equally strange possible explanations: either he is crazier than he thought (because he must have hallucinated this—it could not have really happened) or that the therapist is, perhaps, sicker than he. Regardless of the patient's conclusions, it is difficult to see just how this technique fits into the behavior modification scheme, since one would predict (based on their theory and research) that the cursing and screaming would increase.

These rather foolish manifestations of behaviorism pale when we explore those techniques that openly subscribe to the use of punishment. Here we find that the behavior modification experts' ignorance of economic systems is matched by their failure to either know or understand or acknowledge the United States Constitution. Because of this, their very pragmatic approach to therapy—"if it works, then it's good"—becomes a threat to our civil and human rights.

Despite a great deal of controversy regarding their use, techniques employing punishment can be found in a variety of settings and enjoy the support of numerous influential psychologists. Under the guise of the principles of negative reinforcement, avoidance learning, and faradic aversive conditioning, these methods all involve the therapist as an agent of punishment—a dispenser of negative reinforcers. Instead of the dialogue between patient and psychologist transacted in the insight therapies, the behavioral therapist administers punishing stimuli to a passive recipient.

An example of the successful use of faradic aversive controls (electric shocks—not to be confused with psychiatry's electroconvulsive shock therapy) is documented by Kushner (1970). He describes the case of a thirty-three-year-old man who at the age of twelve developed a life-long interest in women's undergarments after seeing and being aroused by girls' panties. He would buy panties or sometimes take them from clotheslines, put them on, and masturbate. These symptoms were accompanied by impotence in normal heterosexual relations. The treatment consisted of presenting the fetishistic object followed by a brief, yet uncomfortable electrical shock. The patient could terminate the shock by saying "stop" and putting aside the fetishistic object, picture, or idea. After forty-one sessions and a total of 492 shocks (over a fourteen-week period), the patient stated that panties no longer aroused him. Except for two brief relapses, the man's unwholesome interest in women's undergarments seemed to have vanished. With this out of the way, the therapist was now free to join forces with the patient's considerate girlfriend and attack his impotence (without the use of shocks).

Another more dramatic illustration provided by Kushner (1970) concerns the treatment of a severely retarded boy's self-destructive behavior, specifically, hand-biting. The behavior was so extreme that it caused bleeding and infection. Elbow splints and boxing gloves were used but to no avail. This behavior, although present when he was at home, was intensified during hospitalization when he was placed in a room with a child having a rare congenital disorder that resulted in severe biting of the body. The therapy for this seven-year-old retarded boy was to attach electrodes to the inner part of his thigh and to deliver a shock "contingent with hand-biting." Kushner reports that:

> During the first session there was considerable crying, frantic looking around for nursing personnel who were excluded, and constant moving about on the chair upon which he was seated. He made only one brief effort to remove the electrodes . . . (p. 44).

This session lasted nearly an hour during which time the child put his hands to his mouth or hid his hands about sixty-five times. Each time, he was given a shock. When the second session was conducted two days later, the boy sat quietly and only ten shocks had to be administered. It appeared that in two sessions the child had been encouraged not to bite his hands. Kushner was unable to continue this case, but he cites it nonetheless as an instructive one. Indeed it is.

Of all the postures we have seen assumed by behavioral therapists, this punitive role deserves the most serious criticism. Because it involves the therapist in some form of cruelty, either explicitly or implicitly, the psychotherapeutic function of these methods are clouded. In an effort to elucidate their rationale and to reeducate psychologists who oppose the use of punishment, several position papers have appeared. One of the most articulate advocates, Baer (1970, 1971), reminds us that punishment is a natural part of growing up and that pain is a "good teacher." He exhorts psychotherapists not to be so fainthearted, explaining that ". . . a small number of brief, painful experiences is a reasonable exchange for the interminable pain of a lifelong maladjustment."

Just as insight therapists believe that they are acting in the best interest of their patients, so too do the behavior therapists. Unlike other therapists, however, they further believe that there is a one-to-one relationship between what is good for the patient and what is good for society. As Baer reminds us, the "good" psychotherapist is not necessarily the one who uses benevolent methods while he allows his patient to undergo daily social punishment. The one who uses whatever means are available and who corrects his patient's deviant ways is the commendable therapist. It is implicit in this point of view that the social order, its mores and taboos, are to be preserved at any cost to the individual patient and, for that matter, to the therapist.

Nowhere is the handmaiden function of psychology stated so clearly as in McConnell's (1970) remarks:

> No one owns his own personality. Your ego, or individuality, was forced on you by your genetic constitution and by the society into which you were born. You had no say about what kind of personality you acquired, and there's no reason to believe you should have the right to refuse to acquire a new personality if your old one is antisocial (p. 74).

It is obvious by now that behavioral therapists conduct their activities in an historical and moral vacuum. The values underlying the psychological enterprise, from their perspective, is more befitting a totalitarian regimen than a democratic, free society. For the first time in the history of American psychology, professionals are, in effect, "*instructed*" to offer their services to the authorities in power, those who would determine what is and what is not socially acceptable. Behaviorists have provided a scientifically respectable rationale for employing social controls which are explicitly denied by the Constitution.

Fortunately, the techniques of behavior modification are as ineffectual as those of the other psychotherapies. Their impact upon personality can be presumed often to be limited to eliciting "therapist-desired" behaviors in "therapist-created" settings. Nonetheless, the intention and the implicit message to the human race of these therapists should not go unnoticed. Their ineffectuality aside, there is great potential for harm to the public as well as to the profession of psychology in statements that disguise gross violations of human rights as scientifically sound therapeutic practices. By remaining unaware and uncritical of the possible ramifications of their professional conduct, psychologists can become a destructive force on several fronts.

First, psychologists violate the public good and the trust placed in them by the public at large. Second, they do a disservice to their presumptive beneficiaries by providing inappropriate solutions to misconstrued problems. If psychologists continue to encourage society to avoid confronting its real problems, then meaningful solutions and necessary reforms cannot occur. Finally, by serving as handmaidens to the social order, psychologists degrade their profession and destroy all that it has the potential to become.

REFERENCES[1]

Ayllon, T., & Azrin, N. *The token economy: A motivational system for therapy and rehabilitation.* New York: Appleton-Century-Crofts, 1968.

Baer, D. M. A case for selective reinforcement of punishment. In C. Neurunger & J. Michael (Eds.), *Behavior modification in clinical psychology.* New York: Appleton-Century-Crofts, 1970.

Baer, D. M. Let's take another look at punishment. *Psychology Today,* 1971, 5, 32.

*Bakan, D. The mystery-mastery complex in contemporary psychology. *American Psychologist,* 1965, 20, 186–191.

Bakan, D. *On method: Toward a reconstruction of psychological investigation.* San Francisco: Jossey-Bass, 1967.

Bakan, D. *Slaughter of the innocents.* San Francisco: Jossey-Bass, 1971.

Becker, H. *Outsiders.* New York: Free Press, 1963.

Blixt, S., & Ley, R. Effects of differential force-contingent reinforcement schedules on the frustration effect: A test of alternative hypotheses. *Proceedings of 76th Annual Convention of the American Psychological Association,* 1968.

*Braginsky, B. M., & Braginsky, D. D. *Mainstream psychology: A critique.* New York: Holt, 1974.

*Braginsky, B. M., Braginsky, D. D., & Ring, K. *Methods of madness: The mental hospital as a last resort.* New York: Holt, 1969.

*Braginsky, D. D., & Braginsky, B. M. *Hansels and Gretels: Studies of children in institutions for the mentally retarded.* New York: Holt, 1971.

*Foucault, M. *Madness and civilization: A history of insanity in the age of reason.* New York: Pantheon, 1965.

*Jordan, N. *Themes in speculative psychology.* London: Tavistock, 1968.

Kassorla, I. For catatonia: Smiles, praise and a food basket. *Psychology Today,* 1969, 3, 39–41.

*Koch, S. Psychology and emerging conceptions of knowledge as unitary. In T. W. Wann (Ed.), *Behaviorism and phenomenology.* Chicago: The University of Chicago Press, 1964.

*Koch, S. Psychology cannot be a coherent science. *Psychology Today,* 1969, 3, 14.

[1] References marked with an asterisk are supplementary readings.

890

Kushner, M. Faradic aversive controls in clinical practice. In C. Neuringer & J. L. Michael (Eds.), *Behavior modification in clinical psychology*. New York: Appleton-Century-Crofts, 1970.

*Laing, R. *The politics of experience*. New York: Pantheon, 1967.

*Leifer, R. *In the name of mental health: The social functions of psychiatry*. New York: Science House, 1969.

*London, P. *The modes and morals of psychotherapy*. New York: Holt, 1964.

McConnell, J. W. Criminals can be brainwashed—now. *Psychology Today*, 1970, 3, 14.

Schaefer, H. H., & Martin, P. L. *Behavioral therapy*. New York: McGraw-Hill, 1969.

*Szasz, T. *The manufacture of madness*. New York: Harper & Row, 1970.

891

PSYCHOLOGY AS VIEWED AND PRACTICED BY THE HUMANIST: FOUR PERSPECTIVES

Editorial Note

From the editors' point of view, the four chapters that follow have a unique impor-
tance in this book. For psychology—on any conception of its scope—seeks to address
ranges of human and social phenomena which have been under ardent, disciplined,
and creative scrutiny in the humanities *over millennial stretches of time. Too often*
the psychologist has presumed that the humanist is a muddled obscurantist who
studies complex phenomena and artifacts in "soft" and impressionistic ways—and
who therefore requires replacement or reeducation by adepts in scientific method.
Often the humanist presumes that the psychologist is a philistine usurper who will
trivialize or "explain away," via a feeble and inappropriate armamentarium of
method, problems that have been illuminated by ancient traditions of analysis with
which the psychologist has little or no acquaintance.

It is thus of great importance that any assessment of psychology at the end of its
"first" century include the views of humanists—or better still, samples of what they
do when they pursue specifically psychological themes. To some extent, such objec-
tives have been served by earlier chapters contributed by philosophers. But the histor-
ical and explicative humanities, as well as the arts—fields that both deal with and
generate phenomena which (by definition, if not in practice) are of vital interest to
psychology—have not thus far been represented in this book. Though it is impossible

893

adequately to repair this deficiency within the confines even of a barely portable volume like the present one, we are fortunate to be able to include chapters by four humanists of extraordinary intellectual range and penetration. Jacques Barzun is one of the world's greatest historians of ideas. Elizabeth Sewell comprehends in one distinguished intelligence the multiple competences of poet, literary historian, critic, philosopher, and innovative liberal-arts educator. Alasdair MacIntyre and the late Walter Kaufmann, to be sure, swell the ranks of our philosopher contributors, but they are both philosophers of notably broad humanistic purview—Kulturphilosophs *in the best sense of that honorable but dwindling tradition. MacIntyre's interests comprehend social philosophy, ethics, comparative religion, and ancient philosophy; Kaufmann was as much literary historian as philosopher (with a special interest in the German romantic tradition), and a poet as well.*

There has been a wide disciplinary gulf between psychologists and humanists during the past hundred years. Though this gulf has been crossed in one direction or the other by an occasional adventurer, it is a fair generalization that humanists have set forth on such cross-disciplinary journeys more often than have psychologists. Their destination is usually that part of the psychological shoreline bounding the domains of Freud and Jung—but not always so, as Barzun's chapter on William James and Kaufmann's on Nietzsche reveal. Though a handful of psychologists interested in such matters as empirical aesthetics, "creativity," and psychohistory have crossed the gulf in the other direction, most remain unapprised that the other shore exists by virtue of the narrowly specialized character of the typical psychological education.

Against this background, it is especially regrettable that the four ensuing chapters are among the shortest. The symposium from which they derive had five participants (including the chairman, Sigmund Koch), and a third of the time was set aside for the many questions that we (correctly) anticipated would be asked of our distinguished visitors. The papers thus had to be short ones by design. Though most of the psychologist contributors to this book were asked to expand their original papers to ensure at least minimally adequate coverage of the vast field that psychology has become, at a certain point in the editorial process the need to conserve space could no longer be resisted. We therefore decided to publish the group of "humanist perspectives" in a form very close to the initial proceedings.

The symposium was held on the morning of September 5, 1979—during the final hours of the APA convention. Despite the unpropitious time, an audience of about a thousand persons appeared. If their response to the four brief presentations is any index, the reader will surely conclude that humanists (at least some of them) have a few trade secrets which work toward exceptional idea-to-word ratios.

Each of the chapters speaks for itself with an eloquence that renders editorial comment presumptuous. We should like merely to invite current psychologists—and those of 2079—to ponder the significance of the following circumstances:

1. MacIntyre poses the root paradox of modern psychology, namely, that perhaps it "makes itself true" by virtue of being the one "science" that has a necessarily reflexive impact on its subject matter (i.e., human beings, who, unlike viruses, have direct access to the "scientific" principles that presumably govern their workings), and he does this, we think, more incisively than others who have addressed this issue. In tracing out consequences of the fact "that psychology provides a series of new dramatic texts embodying new histrionic possibilities," MacIntyre, the humanist, trenchantly isolates a set of dangerous effects upon the quality of human life and culture which psychologists should have begun to think about a hundred years ago, if not before! It is also worth noting that during the elaboration of his argument, this humanist shows an easy familiarity with the history of scientific psychology—a degree of familiarity with an "alien" field that few psychologists would be able to command in relation to any issue concerning the humanities!

2. It is significant that Barzun, the humanist, provides the only extended treatment of William James in the pages of this volume. Among psychologists there has been a half-century tradition of celebrating James and claiming to love him—but not of reading him. It takes the humanist, Barzun, to give evidence of deep and sensitive thinking about detailed aspects of James's psychological approach and to come up with an instructive apposition between James's analysis of cognition and Dewey's (another towering figure scarcely read by psychologists in recent decades)—one which develops as a revealing governing metaphor for James's special emphasis, that of "mind as artist."

3. Kaufmann's chapter reminds us that there are great humanist contributors to psychology whose psychological efforts have been largely bypassed by psychologists. If, as Kaufmann makes clear in his interesting study of "Nietzsche as the First Great (Depth) Psychologist," Freud himself has acknowledged Nietzsche's priority and his influence, then it may be well for psychologists to contemplate the more general possibility that there are other humanists in the history of thought who have made seminal contributions to psychology, not only in its "prescientific" phase but in the modern era.

4. It is the poet, Elizabeth Sewell, who as poets should, develops the most dazzling ratio of ideas to words in this symposium. Within a tiny compass of pages she explores the universe of askable questions about the relations (and nonrelations) of psychology to poetry, and of both to sensibility and culture ("high" and "folk"). And her seamless universe of relevant—and witty—observations manifest a fluent mastery of poetry, intellectual history, philosophy, and psychology (not to mention "rock" and country lyrics). The précis of her essay is the essay, but her culminating message— delivered both in prose of eloquent concision and in a poem written for the occasion—is an uncannily fitting one for the final page of the last chapter of this book. It is, quite simply, that there is an essential identity of the creative processes that mediate both *poetry and psychology, art and science*—despite the nonrelatedness,

895

the "uneven" (and "severed") "dance" that currently prevails. There is also the conjoined prophecy that "during the next hundred years there is going to be . . . a move from the unevenness into more unified patterns, a new metaphysic, renewed method, a way out of our current isolation and impoverishment." It is possible to believe that the poet has caught the mood—in some instances inchoate and in others fully formed—of most contributors to this book.

39

How Psychology Makes Itself True—or False

ALASDAIR MacINTYRE

Psychology is not only the study of human thinking, feeling, acting, and interacting: it has itself—like the other human sciences—brought into being new ways of thinking, feeling, acting, and interacting. We ordinary people whom the psychologist studies have turned out to be not quite the same ordinary people that we were before such extraordinary people as William James and Freud and Köhler and Piaget: Psychologists have had varying (sometimes striking) success in interpreting the human world; but they have been systematically successful in changing it. Nor perhaps could it have been otherwise, and for at least two reasons.

The first is that psychology is inevitably a new mode—or rather a set of assorted, even rival new modes—of human *self*-knowledge. And as such it cannot avoid conflict with other older modes of self-knowledge. If St. Augustine is right in thinking that behind the urgings of sexuality lies a suppressed longing for and acknowledgment of God, Freud cannot be right in thinking that behind the urgings of religion lie repressed sexual motivations. If Skinner is right in his judgment of the radical inadequacy of the language of motives, reflection, and deliberation for the purpose of identifying the springs of action, then, as Skinner himself was the first to realize, Henry James was a victim of both his and our linguistic and literary illusions—and so was Conrad and so was Dostoievsky. Think for that matter of how different Luther's reflections on Erikson's life would have been—I suspect are— from Erikson's on Luther. Thus a question initially arises: what happens when it is psychology and not the religious confession or the novel which provides us with our ideals of self-knowledge?

A necessary preliminary to answering this question is to pose another. There is one crucial way in which all the human sciences, and perhaps most of all psychology, differ from the natural sciences. Molecules do not read chemistry textbooks, and articles about viruses in biological journals are never rewritten for magazines in language that viruses themselves will understand. By contrast, actual and aspiring managers systematically read works of social psychology about the behavior of managers, psychiatric patients from time to time delve into manuals of clinical psychology, and there is a whole industry of both high and low vulgarization which communicates the findings of psychology, sometimes, of course, even before they have been found.

The result is that psychology provides a series of new prescriptive models for those whom it is engaged in studying, a set of new dramatic texts embodying new histrionic possibilities. Hence when we find in some psychological text what is clearly a true account of how some particular set of individual people think or feel or act or interact, the question may always arise of whether the account is true because of the accuracy of the methods of observation used by the psychologist who formulated it or whether it is true because the people in question embodied that psychologist's account in their own intentions and thereby in their behavior. Patients may find in Freud, or Sullivan, or whomever the resources to become what Freud, or Sullivan, or whoever says that they are; managers may find in Argyris or Likert both roles to assume and devices to enable them to master the tasks of that kind of role-playing.

So the cultural impact of psychology is two-fold: it provides new models for self-knowledge *and* a partially new self for us to have knowledge of. Partially new, of course, because even in those geographical and social areas where psychology has had the most cultural impact, the new psychological models of self-knowledge and selfhood have to coexist—even in one and the same person—with a variety of older models. But how do the new models achieve cultural power over the old? Sometimes in surprisingly simple ways.

Self-knowledge, as we learned long ago from Hegel and Mead, is only very partially a matter of introspection. We know the self in the mirror of other selves; we see ourselves reflected in the responses and reactions of others to us, and the nature of our self-knowledge depends on which other or others we take as the ideal mirror for the self. That other may be real or imagined; but in either case we not only try to learn about ourselves from what the other says and does in response to our overture, we also mold ourselves in terms of our expectations of how the other will respond. Hence the self's knowledge of itself and its making of itself are indeed two aspects of one and the same process. So it is not at all surprising that the self, confronted by the new forms of self-knowledge made available by psychology, should respond in new ways too. Let me begin with a simple but clear example of how in eliciting such responses psychology may make itself true by helping to provide a new mode of action.

Erwin Stengel argued as early as 1952 that an uncommitted observer would have to recognize two distinct motives in suicide attempts: "the urge to self-damage and possibly self-destruction" *and* "the urge to make other human beings show concern and love and act accordingly" (Stengel, 1964, p. 69). He further argued that within the group who actually commit suicide successfully the first type of motive predominates, but, in the case of a substantial proportion of those who apparently attempt suicide but who do not succeed in killing themselves, it is the second type of motive which matters. "Those who attempt suicide tend, in the suicidal act, to remain near or move towards other people. Suicidal attempts act as alarm signals and have the effect of an appeal for help, even though no such appeal may have been consciously intended" (1964, p. 97).

Thus Stengel distinguishes two kinds of apparently suicidal acts, those which genuinely aim at suicide (and usually achieve it) and those which aim to stage an attempted suicide as an appeal for help, although those who do this may not be consciously aware of what they are doing. When Stengel—and one or two others even before him—first drew this distinction, his reasons do *not* seem to have been adequate to justify his conclusions. There are just too many plausible alternative interpretations of the evidence which he cites. But Stengel's work understandably attracted widespread attention, and the result of that attention was that it was made clear to many genuinely distressed people that if they were to appear to have attempted suicide in a particular way, their action would almost certainly be interpreted as just the type of cry for help which they had already been trying unsuccessfully to utter in different ways. That is to say, the distinction which Stengel alleged to hold without adequate warrant came to hold in fact precisely because of Stengel's advocacy of it plus the publicity accorded to that advocacy. Life imitated psychology. But in this case in one highly specific way—and I use this simple example of the effect of Stengel's work only because of the clarity with which it illustrates the kind of phenomenon with which I am going to be concerned. But the importance of this example lies only in providing an introduction to my other examples.

Let me therefore go on to consider three more general, more important, and certainly more influential ways in which psychology has provided descriptions that have turned into prescriptions, theories which have been reworked as dramatic scripts. Observers before Freud were sometimes keenly aware of motives unacknowledged by the agent him- or herself; but Freud made available the thought of the unacknowledged motive as an all-pervasive presence, so that each of us is encouraged to try and look behind the overt simplicities of the behavior of others to what is actually moving them and equally encouraged to respond to that hidden reality rather than to the surface appearance of the other. The question, "What would his or her therapist take to be going on here?" becomes one of the covert and

899

itself often unacknowledged instruments of everyday deliberation. Behavior is thus not to be taken at its face value: it requires interpretation and often that dialogue of interpretation in which I try to interpret your interpretation of my interpretation of your . . . . What changes when utterances come to be treated as signs or symptoms of something else, when the search for their latent meaning distracts our attention from their manifest meaning?

A first consequence is that it becomes much more difficult to take the notion of an *authoritative utterance* seriously. If we treat such utterances as to-be-psychologically-decoded expressions of the utterer's personality, then we become unable to listen to what fathers say to children, headmasters or headmistresses to pupils, priests and ministers to congregations, presidents to the nation, with the kind of deference to the utterance itself which was once socially prescribed and desired. We interpret, we place, we reduce: or rather we have this done for us by public commentators who interestingly enough expect their own interpretive utterances to be treated with just the kind of seriousness which their own mode of analysis denies to others. But this has been remarked on often enough, and I notice the phenomenon only as a necessary preliminary to identifying a second consequence of the overinterpretative social mode.

It is that when those who inhabit those geographical and social areas which have been most affected by psychological modes—Manhattan or urban California, say, rather than South Carolina or South Boston—do have to become the inhabitants of authoritative roles and thereby the makers of authoritative utterances, they are apt to experience an embarrassing ambiguity and uncertainty in their relationship to their own utterances. How can they straightforwardly mean what they say when the overinterpretative mode has divorced manifest saying from latent meaning? And so we get the characteristic recent and new social performances of the systematically embarrassed father, the embarrassed priest, the embarrassed professor, and the variety of devices for fending off that embarrassment. One brief but not too cryptic way of putting what I am saying is: the publicizing and the vulgarization of the theory of neurotic symptoms has itself created new styles of and perhaps new types of neurosis. And insofar as the classical theory of neurosis fails to capture the roots of these new styles in neurotic belief about the theory of neurosis, it itself needs revision or at least extension. But this is not all that the influence of the overinterpretative mode has achieved.

It is a further consequence of the overinterpretative mode that the notion of understanding other people has taken on a new dimension. It is not just that we are all now urged to understand other people to an extent that is quite new in human culture: parents are urged to understand their children, teachers their students, husbands their wives, and wives their husbands—and one assumption seems to be that the better we understand each other, the better we shall behave toward each other. Yet at the very same time the concept of understanding which accompanies the overinterpretative mode is one in which to understand the other is to perceive in him or her more and other than he or she perceives and acknowledges. The project of understanding comes to involve discrediting the surface appearances. But our surface appearances—what we ourselves take ourselves to be and present ourselves as—are necessarily very clear to us all, and thus understanding is now often enough experienced by its objects as an act of aggression. If I tell you that I am going to understand you, I now threaten you in a way that is culturally new. Hence it has become important in a new way to *not* be understood. Opacity has become a more valuable quality than ever before. And this is just one more consequence of the cultural power of the overinterpretative mode. But now let us turn to a quite different area in which a quite different type of psychology has been at work changing the human mind.

A second area in which psychological description has become social prescription is in the evaluation of human rationality. Where the consequences which produced the overinterpretative mode derived from psychoanalytic theory, those which produced what I shall call *the invisibility of rational agency in other people* derive from social psychology. In a recently published paper, Professor R. P. Abelson (1976), after producing an illuminating and comprehensive survey of the relevant experimental findings on congruity, the balance principle, dissonance theory, and attribution theory, concludes:

> We have pictured the typical individual as overloaded with information which he does not quite know how to process. . . . the individual's mental processes are subject to illusion and oversimplification because of biased or misleading experience, motivated self-enhancement and insufficient awareness of social pressures . . . (p. 83).

Professor Abelson hastens to add that he believes that "increased rationality can be learned and nurtured," but his chief insistence is on "how far away from full rationality the human condition lies." About what he himself calls his gloomy verdict, let me make two points at once. The first is that social psychology's picture of irrational man is indeed culturally influential whenever one person plans to manipulate another; and that advertisers, political campaign managers, and others succeed, not only in acting on the hypothesis that the rest of us are by and large nonrational sheep, but also in communicating to us that that is how they think about us. Notice that this is not how they—or anyone else—think about themselves. What social psychology has provided and apparently warranted is a possible way of thinking about other people which is quite at odds with the way in which each of us inescapably thinks about him- or herself. At the very beginning of his paper, indeed, Abelson pictures the social scientist as endeavoring "to pursue his enquiries according to well-elaborated standards of rationality," and it is quite clear that he does not suppose that the social psychologists whose findings he reports were themselves governed in their judgments by the principle of balance or any of the

901

distorting effects identified by dissonance theory or attribution theory. "Rational us/ irrational them" is the antithesis which clearly emerges. One cannot but recall Freud's view of the French revolution.

Second, it is clear that if the verdict on human rationality is to be rendered by the type of study which Abelson describes, then the gloomy verdict is indeed inescapable. There is, of course, nothing wrong either with the logic of Abelson's argument or with the experimental findings which he reports: what is questionable is one of his additional premises. It is that it is in the kind of situation that can be experimentally isolated and controlled—within a relatively brief period of time, abstracted from normal and ongoing social relations—that rationality or its failure or absence can be studied. My guess is that if the social psychologists whose findings Abelson repeats were themselves studied in this way, they too would appear in poor rational shape. What made the social psychologists rational in their experimental work is that they, precisely unlike those whom they studied while those others were cast as experimental subjects, were operating within and were guided by the norms of a well-developed form of human practice. What I am suggesting is that rationality is a virtue that is only at home within the context of a certain kind of social practice, one within which procedures are available not only for the systematic criticism and improvement of both ends and means, but also for the reevaluation of beliefs and procedures, at appropriate times, including the procedures of rationality itself. Abstract individuals from this kind of temporal and social context—as the subjects of experiments are generally abstracted—and you will have necessarily at least the appearance of anomic, cross-pressured, easily swayed people who seem to warrant the gloomy verdict. Of course the paradigmatic isolated and controlled experimental situation is indeed itself a social situation which is very like many of those characteristic of modern anomic social life, and it is perhaps this resemblance as much as the methodological purity of the experiments which warrants extrapolation from one to the other.

Note that when I discussed the overinterpretative mode of interaction, nothing I said put in question in any way the psychoanalytic theory of the neurotic symptom. Equally, nothing I have said now puts in question the actual experimental findings of social psychology. What I have tried to identify is the effect of a social and cultural tradition of interpreting these findings in a particular way, a tradition which is once more at work in the formulation of Abelson's gloomy verdict and which results more generally in a sharp disjunction between the way in which each of us views ourself and the way in which we view other people taken in the mass. What social psychology thus interpreted has done is to confer upon this egoistic elitism the appearance of the only possible attitude warranted by a scientific approach to the social world. Thus once again psychology has changed the human world in the course of interpreting it and created new phenomena in the course of trying to understand old ones.

Let me finally sketch in the briefest possible way a third crucial area in which psychology has at least contributed to the creation of a new psychological mode. Biography and that part of history which is biography have not remained entirely what they were, and I am not thinking particularly of self-conscious psychohistory. It is now a commonplace among historians that childhood had in some sense to be culturally invented some centuries ago; but even once childhood had been so invented, it was understood for a long time only as a phase to be left behind on entering adult life. We owe it to psychology that many of us now understand adults not only as grown-up children but even as imperfectly grown-up children; in our most heavenly moments we are but echoes of our infancy. And the effect has been, at one level of our culture, a sanctioned commingling of what were once the manners of the nursery with what were once the manners of the adult parts of the house and, at another, yet one more device to reduce the would-be heroic figure to adolescent or preadolescent size. Psychology, that is to say, has contributed to the undecorous and the antiheroic temper of the times.

To this some will reply: what you have argued is nothing other than that psychology has contributed to the creation of a less structured, less authoritarian, more realistic, less hero-worshipping atmosphere. And we like this: we are democrats, we are liberals, and we praise psychology for helping to change the culture in our direction. And this reply does indeed bring into the light my own anti-liberal, pro-authority, and pro-hero-figure presuppositions. But I offer one plea in extenuation. Among the heroes whom I most want to praise are Freud and William James. What I have been saying is that the effect of psychology upon the culture—the effect indeed of psychology publicized and vulgarized, but that is how all sciences have their effects—has been increasingly to foster types of character and modes of action which make it even more difficult than it was already to emulate Freud and James. The final irony of the history of the cultural effects of psychology might well be the dominance of a type of culture in which its founders could never have existed.

REFERENCES

Abelson, R. P. Social psychology's rational man. In S. I. Benn & G. W. Mortimore (Eds.), *Rationality and the social sciences*. London: Routledge & Kegan Paul, 1976.

Stengel, E. *Suicide and attempted suicide*. Baltimore, Md.: Penguin, 1964.

903

40

William James
THE MIND AS ARTIST

JACQUES BARZUN

The part that conventional knowledge plays in the history of culture has never been properly assessed. Nor is this paper the place to attempt a study of it, but one observation on such knowledge may properly introduce the main subject. Conventional knowledge is usually based on some evident truth, above which is reared a superstructure of misunderstanding and fallacy. Conventional knowledge about William James starts with the truth that he expounded the doctrine known as pragmatism. Next, by verbal and historical association, James is linked with John Dewey, also a pragmatist. General opinion then assumes that James's view of the human mind is identical with Dewey's. Now Dewey's being the better known, thanks to his extensive writings on education, the linkage leads directly to the conclusion that James's pragmatic psychology finds the pattern of thought in the mental operations of science: the mind of man is a scientist *in posse*.

In *How We Think* (1910), Dewey gives the outline of this act of mind, which he calls the reflective. It consists of five steps: (1) the occurrence of a difficulty; (2) the definition of it; (3) the occurrence of suggestions to explain or resolve it; (4) the rational elaboration of each suggestion—its bearing and implications; and (5) the corroboration of one of them by experiment or other kinds of testing. Dewey concludes: "thinking comes between observations at the beginning and at the end of a problem" (pp. 72–77).

This "model" is perfectly good as far as it goes, but the first thing to say about it is

904

that it does not begin at the beginning. It takes for granted a mind already full of objects, ideas, abstractions, generalities, concepts, and rules. If we concede that this is "how we think," there appears to be a play on words hidden in the thought-cliché that unites James and Dewey and their pragmatisms.

For what Dewey describes is either deliberate cogitation or well-established habits for meeting difficulty; he is concerned with reasoning, formal and informal. James begins much earlier, biographically speaking. He begins with consciousness and examines how it behaves in its rawest possible state, before it has acquired enough experience to define problems and canvass clear-cut suggestions. What does James find? The complex answer is in Chapter 9 of *The Principles of Psychology* (1890), under the title "The Stream of Thought," a title which in the *Briefer Course* published the following year became the influential phrase, "the stream of consciousness." But although these evocative words have affected literature and philosophy, as well as common speech and the common idea of life, the mental facts that it covers have not become a part of general understanding.

In the first place, according to James, consciousness is not an entity, but a function. The usual notions of a receptacle for ideas, a mirror of external objects, a sensitive plate recording impressions, a subject-spectator watching the "real world" must be given up if we are to understand what goes on not *in* but *as* consciousness. Consciousness is clearly involuntary: not *I think* but *it thinks*, whether I want it to or not. Languages record an awareness of the fact in expressions like *methinks, il m'en souvient, es dünkt mich*, and again in "it occurs to me," "the idea crossed my mind," and so on. *I think* is not parallel to *I walk*. That we have the sensation of owning this self-propelling stream is also true, but making it do our bidding is difficult—and rare. And that is why it is important for education to follow Dewey's analysis and make out of the five steps a conscious method of organized and sequential thought.[1]

But it is equally important (and for much more than education) to understand the working of the mind in its native, original course. It can be shown, for instance, that a great deal of criticism in the arts is vitiated by ignorance of the way the mind perceives and *pre*perceives objects. Thus all theories of "pure" art assume impossibilities in both the making and the witnessing of art. And even in science and mathematics, as more than one great discoverer has testified, the deliberate march of mind in five steps is not so much actual as ideal; it helps to verify rather than to create; the reason being that the mind is natively not a scientist but an artist.

James does not use that figurative way of telling how consciousness works, but the metaphor is not far-fetched, nor is it meant here to bestow an honorific quality, let alone take sides in the foolish, profitless rivalry between art and science. The term is

---

[1]Dewey is not, of course, unaware of thinking in the primitive sense, but he dismisses it quickly as disconnected impressions, fancies, daydreaming, so as to reach his chosen subject, which is marked by "dignity, consecutiveness, and truth" (1910).

used only as a catchword that may help to remove the conventional error caused by Dewey's pedagogic intention.

The mind according to James is a stream composed of waves flowing endlessly without gaps. Each wave (or pulse) presents a crest or focus of intensity surrounded by a fringe. The focus is clear, the fringe dimmer, and what is in the fringe surges forward to become the next clear focus as the previous one fades out. We record this phenomenon in many of our ways of speech. We refer to what is "uppermost" in our minds; we know and speak of what "interests" us and can name what "holds our attention": all these words imply the focus. Compared with it, the fringe, aura, or margin is vague and thus not readily namable. It takes the power of a poet to evoke the fringe by offering a series of images to focus on. In life, we have intimations or presentiments of what may come next to mind, but these escape the net of words because the stream has a way of pressing forward as if driven by a purpose, looking toward an end not yet known—quite as in a story full of suspense. The "interest" at the focus wants each following pulse to be equally interesting or attention wanders off to something more promising.

This rough summary of James's description of the stream shows to begin with that there is a form to thought as it is given to us natively. Thought is not the scattered bits of a kaleidoscope that Dewey dismissed as of no use to him. On the contrary, there is no disconnection at any point, and the sense of making toward a goal on the crest of interest, with troughs of lesser intensity but true connection, is a fundamental form. We find it embodied in every kind of human discourse, from the sentence to the symphony.

To be sure, the products of art or communication are trimmed and compressed by other operations of the mind. Even the so-called "stream-of-consciousness novel" is a simplified artifact and not a transcript of the luxuriant shoots of ideas and feelings in the author's consciousness. The fact remains that the works of the artistic intelligence are not made by imposing on absolute chaos an order from outside, but rather by effecting a distillation of the stream and ultimately respecting its inherent form.

In art, I have said, that form is embodied. The word implies the physical things of whose existence we are aware through consciousness. James shows how they are made, built out of the infant's original welter of sensations and held forever after in fixed forms. Here too, the shaping power of art is visible. For "what are things?" asks James. "Nothing, as we shall abundantly see, but special groups of sensible qualities, which happen practically or aesthetically to interest us. . . . In itself, apart from my interest, a particular dust wreath on a windy day is just as much of an individual thing, and just as much or as little deserves an individual name, as my own body does" (1890, Vol. I, p. 285). Purpose, then, utility, and aesthetic interest dominate consciousness in its fashioning of our world, that is to say, in its role of maker or artist.

The clusters of sensations that the growing mind seizes on may be called perceptions and these become so familiar that thereafter no pure sensation strikes it again. What is more, the recurrence of perceptions leads to preperception at the slightest hint: the mind does not let its creations fade or fall apart. It is in possession not of *the* world, but of *a* world, the one it has individually shaped and which differs in many respects from every other, although—thanks to words and education—we all share a good many objects and relations in common. The different sets of perceptions held by different minds find a parallel in the differences seen in the works of, say, different painters—or philosophers. The differences are due not solely to variations in the sensory organs; they also come from diverse shapings by the mind; they are, so to speak, differences of workmanship.

These objects, moreover, which exist independently of our perceptions and possess relatively permanent features, come to us in many guises according to circumstance, various degrees of light or distance, for example. The developed consciousness deals with these givens quite cavalierly, for its own convenience. At any one moment, what the mind perceives through the open eye is but a shorthand indication of the things outside. An obtuse angle, an expanse of bright color, and to one side an indistinct dark mass are enough to tell us that a desk stands there, under the window. At the same time, we "know" that its angles are no greater than right angles and that the light surface and the dark pedestal are of one uniform shade of brown. We see flat planes and infer solids; we see the same thing large or small and infer distance; most often, unless we are, as we say, *examining*, we see only scraps of perceptions and are guided by them through the maze of our interests or the dangers of physical existence.

In other words, we habitually think and act with the aid of signs and symbols like any conscious artist. On this point the relation of the painter's eye to that of the ordinary man is instructive. The painter, everybody is told, has a better eye and his work makes us see the world as it really is. And it is true that he brings out on his canvas unfamiliar truths of line, color, and relation, whether he is "representative" or not. But he can only do this by assembling for us another set of signs and symbols. He takes our black marble lamp and shows us that, far from being black all over, its rounded shape is a patchwork of black, gray, and golden yellow in irregular gradations. We are humbly grateful and say that our verbal abstraction "black lamp" has blinded us to what was there to see. Yet his artifact is not a view that it would be wise to use in description for an auctioneer's catalogue.

Indeed, when the painter wants to get across the street safely, he must use the ordinary man's perceptual shorthand and not linger on the subtler symbols appropriate to the studio. This obvious truth underscores the Jamesian principle that purpose or interest determines at any time the work of the mind. Since interest at large includes aesthetic interest, the principle further explains why artistic expression can take so many forms and can use so many means. The various schools of painting and sculpture from the dawn of history show widely different techniques, but they speak to us of our same world because they all exemplify the same operations of consciousness. They refine upon its shaping power and stylize its results. In other words, all schools of art are equally "realistic"; their purpose is to show how what is may come to look, and each renders something that the others cannot reach —just like our own various modes of perception.

As for the means, every device from gesture and word to piled-up stones and inarticulate sound can be made to convey meaning because the human consciousness starts life by having to make a world of meanings out of the sensations given off by these same materials. What has once been shaped by the mind in its pursuit of interest can be made interesting once again by rearrangement. The best proof of this is the amazing amount of precise significance that modern critics and connoisseurs have found in the minimal hints of certain abstract, denuded "works" in painting, literature, or music.

One great reason why this can be done is that in the mind as James exhibits it, every focus of thought and every margin around it comes with an affective quality attached. Contrary to all the ancient moral philosophies that depict man as split between intellect and emotion, the two are one. Every thought is suffused with feeling, every feeling goes with a thought. James is careful to add that by thought he does not mean only single and namable ideas, clear and complete. Thoughts are the pulses of consciousness and these may contain any number of objects, ideas, and feelings in one fused mass, as when shock, anger, and indignation make us speechless because our attention is for the moment overcrowded with ideas, memories, visions, and passions. In less confused moments we also note that it is not exclusively the *subjects* of thought that carry feelings, but their relations also. There is, says James, a feeling of *and*, a feeling of *but*, a feeling for every particle indicative of relation.

Finally, the thought and feeling of vagueness are perfectly definite. Vagueness is a mental fact in itself and not the debris of something clear and distinct. James was particularly proud of having restored vagueness to its rightful place in reality, and this achievement may be taken as a good example of his conquest over the rigid intellectualism of preceding psychologies. However much those differed among themselves, they saw the constituent elements of the mind as separate pellets of sensation which had to be brought into order by some mechanical combining device. Nor were the relations perceived among things "given" like other thoughts, as they are in James: they had to be imposed by categories or acquired by inductive observation. In a word, the mind was assembled; it was not an original going concern, a dynamic function, that had the power to carve out its mature contents from the stream. Obviously, thinking by means of an assembly of bits and pieces, and under the waffle-iron of the categories, left no room for the whole range of nuances which we call vagueness and which forms so large a part—all unnamed— of our sentient existence. Nor was it easy to explain by the old scheme how minds could differ so much as they do, even when exposed to very similar blocks of experience.

Once again in this aspect, the Jamesian mind shows how native to it is the response that the artist plays upon and expects of us. If it were not so constituted, how could it be that a work of architecture, by a certain dispositon of its parts, arouses emotion? Or a patch of color in a painting? Or a sequence of notes or chords in a sonata? The answer "association of ideas" will apply in some instances, but in others what is touched and moved lies deeper, in the regions of the unspoken and indefinite. And in any case we must ask how the associated ideas themselves could trigger the feeling if feeling did not inhere in the primary source of all ideas. As Pascal observed, even a proposition in Euclid becomes a sentiment.

The value of establishing consciousness as a flow, of insisting on the distinctness of the vague, of showing all thoughts (including "mere" relations) as charged with feeling—in short, the value of James's account of the mind—appears in its fullness when one knows the importance James ascribed to the subliminal mind, later to be known as the "unconscious." In *The Principles of Psychology*, his concern is with the conscious and the references to the subliminal are few, though indicative. It was later, in the unpublished Lowell Lectures on "Exceptional Mental States" (1896) that James set forth the results of his research into the subliminal[2] and these results influenced his still later studies for the famous *Varieties of Religious Experience* (1902).

There is no pressing reason here to detail how James conceived the subliminal. It is enough to know that he saw it as continuous with the conscious, as it could not be if the conscious were made from discrete elements as in the earlier psychologies. It is also important to know that James ascribed to the subliminal the primary feeling of transcendence which is the germ of religious intimations and convictions. These insights, in turn, are in keeping with the formula here suggested that the Jamesian mind is artist first and last. Out of subliminal apprehendings come superstition and myth; and out of myth come both religion and art, which in nearly all civilizations but ours have been conjoined.

Other suggestive connections exist between James's psychology and the fundamental activity of art.[3] Some are biographical, some cultural. The 1890s, when the *Principles* appeared, was a period of intense aestheticism, inspired in part by a revulsion against the narrowness of dogmatic science. It was the time of Frazer's *Golden Bough* (1890) and Freud's first essays. James, moreover, had much to say about the nature of genius. He interpreted it as a mind no different from the universal type but one more powerfully driven, richer in crests and margins and connections within the stream. And in all these contemporary manifestations of genius and art—think of the doctrines of Impressionism and Symbolism—the

---

[2] The notes for these lectures have survived and have been studied, organized, and reconstructed by Mr. Eugene Taylor (1983) in a form that enables the reader to judge the full scope of James's conception of mind.

[3] A number of them, with supporting quotations from James, may be found in my chapter "William James and the Clue to Art" in *The Energies of Art* (1956).

worth of the indefinite, the value of vagueness, the merit of the evanescent and unrecorded was a cardinal point.

In surveying these interesting relationships and noting the historical antagonism between art and science, one should not suppose that James's description of consciousness ignores—much less combats—Dewey's account of how we think. Inquiry, which we found to be Dewey's limited subject, is taken up in the chapter on reasoning in James's *Principles,* and as a scientist he attaches all due importance to the purposeful conduct of thought. The Jamesian mind goes on to perform a number of tasks beyond the primary "poetic" ones I have mentioned; it takes in all of Dewey's indispensable operations. Abstracting, generalizing, conceptualizing are among them, and they too are universal. Philosophers and psychologists hold no monopoly of these transactions, though theirs may differ from other minds in the amount of time and care they give to the enterprise.

What remains to be said is that in the mode of inquiry Dewey propounds, "purpose" bears the workaday meaning of setting out for results. In the portion of James's work I have discussed, purpose is an intrinsic quality: the stream moves forward from crest to crest and toward an end without effort and without a defined goal. I like to mark the difference by contrasting the purpose*ful* (deliberate) and the purpos*ive* (inherent). The mind's interests, says James, are practical and aesthetic, and these root tendencies must also, I think, be distinguished from deliberate worldly practicality and aesthetic aims. If one does so, it becomes clear that James's pragmatism differs from Dewey's in being, as it were, innate; not exclusively a logic and a method, but simply, long before reflection, the way consciousness pursues and makes the most of its interests: art for life's sake.

REFERENCES

Barzun, J. *The energies of art.* New York: Harper, 1956.

Dewey, J. *How we think.* New York: D. C. Heath, 1910.

Frazer, J. G. *The golden bough: A study in comparative religion* (2 vols.). London: Macmillan, 1890.

James, W. *The principles of psychology* (2 vols.). New York: Holt, 1890.

James, W. *Psychology: Briefer course.* New York: Holt, 1892.

James, W. *The varieties of religious experience: A study in human nature.* New York: Longmans, Green, 1902.

Taylor, E. *William James on exceptional mental states: The 1896 Lowell Lectures.* New York: Scribner's, 1983.

41

Nietzsche as the First Great (Depth) Psychologist*

WALTER KAUFMANN

Nietzsche said in *Ecce Homo*, "That a psychologist without equal speaks from my writings, is perhaps the first insight reached by a good reader—a reader as I deserve him, who reads me the way good old philologists read their Horace" (1908, III. 5).[1] If Nietzsche really was a psychologist without equal, at least up to the time when he wrote this in 1888, then he has certainly had very few good readers by his own standards. Freud was one of the few. Perhaps it takes a psychologist without equal to know one.

Amateur psychologists have often spoken very patronizingly of Nietzsche, offering shallow psychological explanations for his philosophical ideas and discounting *Ecce Homo* in particular as the work of a madman. No sooner had the book been published posthumously, in 1908, than the Vienna Psychoanalytic Society devoted one of its weekly meetings to it. Eleven of the regular members and two guests met at Freud's house on October 28, and after the initial report and some discussion, Freud spoke at some length and said, according to the *Minutes*, that "the degree of introspection achieved by Nietzsche had never been achieved by anyone, nor is it

---

*Readers may also want to consult W. Kaufmann, *Discovering the mind: Nietzsche, Heidegger, and Buber* (Vol. 2) (New York: McGraw-Hill, 1980).

[1] The numerals following the original publication dates of Nietzsche's books denote his Section numbers, which are the same in all editions.

likely ever to be reached again" (Freud, 1967, p. 31ff.). In his great biography of Freud, Jones recorded that "Freud several times said of Nietzsche that he had a more penetrating knowledge of himself than any other man who ever lived or was ever likely to live" (1955, p. 344).[2] And Jones added: "From the first explorer of the unconscious this is a handsome compliment." This comment is surely a paradigm case of British understatement. One would have thought that Freud believed that psychoanalysis made possible deeper self-knowledge than had been possible without it; perhaps also that with its aid he himself had reached a more penetrating self-knowledge than any man before him. Jones, who had no particular liking for Nietzsche, did not follow up Freud's compliment to ask why Freud should have said such a thing. As far as Nietzsche is concerned, it does not matter whether Freud went too far, particularly in his reference to the future. What does matter is that Nietzsche should be taken very seriously as a psychologist.

Nietzsche's claim to having been a psychologist without equal does not rest on a few insights, nor even on a few theories. What we owe to him is an altogether new dimension, a new sensitivity, what one of Freud's pupils, Theodor Reik, called in the title of one of his books (1948) "listening with the third ear." Nietzsche himself had used a similar image in the preface to *Twilight of the Idols* (1889) when he called himself "one who has ears even behind his ears . . . an old psychologist." In *Ecce Homo* he said: "My genius is in my nostrils" (IV.1). He really did have a sense that is not to be found among philosophers before him; and if one looks for predecessors, one must find them among poets and writers. In *Twilight* Nietzsche himself called Dostoevsky, "the only psychologist, by the way, from whom I could learn something."

Nietzsche's psychology, like Freud's, has its roots primarily in imaginative literature, notably including not only Dostoevsky but also Shakespeare and Goethe. But *their* sixth sense had been employed for the most part in the context of entertainment. Who before Nietzsche read his own drafts as well as the books of others with a third ear?

The initial reaction to Freud's remark that Nietzsche knew himself better "than any other man who ever lived or was ever likely to live" will probably be that this is a vast exaggeration. But of what other philosopher could Freud possibly have said this? And do any nonphilosophers come to mind? On reflection it appears that nobody else has done nearly so much to alert us to the psychological background of philosophers and religious figures. It was Nietzsche who first showed how the study of philosophy, religion, and literature can be enriched by listening with the third ear and how every human being, from ourselves to the most famous men and

---

[2] When I asked Jones about this, he referred me to H. Nunberg, the editor of the *Minutes*, and Nunberg wrote me that I had to wait till they got published—as it happened, more than ten years later, in an inadequate translation. The original German text finally appeared in 1977. Jones's recollection of what Freud had said "several times" may well be more accurate than the formulation in the *Minutes*.

women, has dimensions not dreamed of before him. This is surely his greatest psychological achievement.

What is badly needed, however, is a more detailed account. I have distinguished five major contributions (see my *Discovering the Mind*, 1980), though that list could be expanded. In this presentation, I shall have to limit myself to three of these and suggest to the interested reader that my views concerning the remaining two (Nietzsche's pioneering work in psychohistory, and the psychological implications of his "philosophy of masks") can be found in the book just cited.

Nietzsche's *first major contribution* to the discovery of the mind is so complex and has such far-flung implications that one might despair of putting the point briefly if he himself had not stated it once parenthetically in a mere four words: "consciousness is a surface" (*Ecce Homo*, 1908, II.9). In many different contexts he showed how the role of consciousness in our psychic life had been widely and vastly overestimated.

Nietzsche's very concise formulation of the theory of repression is a case in point. Freud, in a footnote added to later editions of one of his major works, *The Psychopathology of Everyday Life* (1904), after mentioning that a recent monograph had listed authors "who appreciate the influence of affective factors on memory," cited it as follows:

> But not one among all of us has succeeded in describing this phenomenon and its psychological reasons as exhaustively and at the same time as impressively as *Nietzsche* did in one of his aphorisms (*Beyond Good and Evil*, chapter II, 68): "*I have done that," says my memory. "I could not have done that," says my pride and remains inexorable. Finally, my memory yields.*

The appeal to "resistance" has often been attacked as a strategy of immunization, and when considering Freud, one must ask whether his claim that Adler and Jung resisted his threatening discoveries was indeed part of an attempt to immunize his views against criticism. In Nietzsche's case, however—and by no means only in his—the concept of resistance is needed to explain the massive neglect of ideas that are felt to threaten the pride of readers and nonreaders. The point is not to discount arguments but rather to explain the lack of arguments and of any serious consideration. There is no dearth of monographs about Nietzsche that deal with all kinds of relatively minor aspects of his thought, and he has been seen in many different perspectives; but despite his own repeated and emphatic claims that he was a psychologist, his psychology has been ignored by almost all writers on Nietzsche, except for passing references here and there.

Nietzsche's *second major contribution* to the discovery of the mind—and the principal one on which I shall dwell—was his theory of the will to power. Resistance to this theory has taken three main forms. First, it is astonishing how many writers on Nietzsche have paid very little attention to his conception of the will to power, although he himself gave it a central place in his books, beginning with *Thus Spoke Zarathustra* (1892). The other forms of resistance also involved a studious neglect of Nietzsche's theory.

The most popular strategy was simple enough: one gave "the will to power" the esoteric, brutal meaning that Nietzsche repeatedly repudiated, and one assumed that there is no power except military or political power. Of course, Nietzsche's choice of the word *power*, and some of his striking formulations, facilitated, if they did not actually invite, misunderstandings.

The third form of resistance to Nietzsche's theory of the will to power is much less widespread than the other two and due almost entirely to a single interpreter. Martin Heidegger, in his bulky two-volume *Nietzsche* (1961) and in some shorter essays, has insisted that Nietzsche was, above all, the last great metaphysician of the West and that the will to power is a metaphysical concept. Such conclusions throw more light on the interpreter than on the man he claims to interpret. In the wake of Heidegger, a new form of resistance to Nietzsche's psychology has developed, chiefly but not only in France. In brief, one discounts what mattered most to Nietzsche himself and plays games with him. Snippets, more often than not from Nietzsche's notebooks, are used as counters, and a premium is placed on clever and surprising moves. Rather oddly, those who play this game seem to think of themselves as avant-garde.

There is no denying that in a few passages, mainly in notes that he himself did not publish, Nietzsche pitted the will to power against the blind irrational will that is the ultimate reality in Schopenhauer's metaphysics. But in his works Nietzsche spoke of psychology as "the queen of the sciences for whose service and preparation the other sciences exist. For psychology is now again the path to the fundamental problems." That is the conclusion of Part I of *Beyond Good and Evil* (1886). In his later works Nietzsche saw himself as a psychologist and not as a metaphysician.

For good measure, the subtitle of *Twilight of the Idols* (1889) is *A Psychologist's Leisure*, and the book contains an incisive attack on Western metaphysics. The chapter on "the four great errors" also contains a section entitled "the psychological explanation of this."

To understand Nietzsche's theory of the will to power, we must contrast it with two alternatives: the will to life and what Freud called, when he moved beyond it, "the pleasure principle." The crucial point is formulated succinctly in *Thus Spoke Zarathustra* (1892): "There is much that life esteems more highly than life itself; but out of the esteeming itself still speaks the will to power."

There is indeed abundant evidence that human beings frequently risk their lives for power or a sense of power. Examples (mine, not Nietzsche's) include mountain climbing, skiing, deep-sea diving, and many other sports. Nor do all who risk their

914

lives in war do so to protect the lives of others; risking one's life and living danger-ously have a fatal attraction that can be understood in terms of the will to power. Skiers who risk life and limb as they speed down a dangerous slope feel vibrantly alive, but it is clear that they are not motivated by any desire for life or survival. What they do experience and seek is a superlative sense of power. We can general-ize that the enormous attraction of great speed—in driving, for example, no less than in skiing—is evidence for Nietzsche's thesis that men and women readily risk life for the sake of power.

Many people claim that "power" has for them predominantly negative associa-tions, but the evidence suggests that they are probably a minority. In any case, what matters is not the term *power* but what motivates people. Clearly, the will to life does not go far in explaining human behavior. The desire to "conquer" Everest or Annapurna is not prompted by the will to life but, rather, by what Nietzsche called the will to power. The widespread admiration for those who scale such high and difficult peaks is quite revealing.

The notion that men seek pleasure is much more widespread in the twentieth century than is the belief that all of human behavior can be explained in terms of a will to life. And Nietzsche pitted his own will to power just as much against the striving for pleasure as against the will to life. It is noteworthy that when Freud developed psychoanalysis he believed that all men seek pleasure. The first major secession in the history of the psychoanalytic movement occurred in 1911 when Alfred Adler left and founded his own school; and Adler (1914) in effect champi-oned the will to power against the pleasure principle. He repudiated the "one magic formula, namely, that of pleasure," and opposed to it "a striving toward power, toward dominance, toward being above."

In the end, Adler's doctrine proved less influential than Freud's revision of his own earlier theories. The central change he made is neatly summed up in the deliberately Nietzschean title of the first major work he published after, and under the influence of, World War I: *Beyond the Pleasure Principle* (1920). Freud came to the conclusion that some important forms of human behavior could not be ex-plained in terms of the pleasure principle, and he introduced a second basic drive known as the death instinct, associated with aggression and destruction. The inter-esting question as to whether Nietzsche's will to power might be able to do the job that the pleasure principle alone could not do has never been explored sufficiently.

The central point of Nietzsche's theory of the will to power is that there is a common denominator for what men really desire and for what they settle for when they give up hope: power. What is wanted, according to Nietzsche, is always power, but not all forms of power are equal.

Unlike many of his detractors, he did not associate "power" exclusively or even primarily with military or political power. John Stuart Mill (1863) once said of some critics of the hedonism of the utilitarians that they "represent human nature in a degrading light; since the accusation supposes human beings to be capable of no pleasure except those of which swine are capable." And many of Nietzsche's detractors have talked and written as if human beings had no powers not shared with beasts of prey.

Once again I shall give my own examples. Why does one become a doctor? It may be because as a child one was impressed by a physician who had the power to help when no one else could, and now one covets such power. Or one may be impressed by the fact that many doctors have a high income and a great deal of prestige—another kind of power. Those who choose to become lawyers or politicians may be similarly motivated. The picture is slightly different when we consider ministers, professors, or artists, but one may still ask whether it is not some kind of power that is desired.

To Nietzsche's mind, one-upmanship, aggressiveness, jingoism, militarism, racism, conformity, resignation to a drab life, and the desire for Nirvana were all expressions of weakness. He did not consider the will to power a trait of the strong only; he explored the manifestations of the will to power in the weak as well.

When he was writing *The Gay Science* (1882), shortly before he hit upon the phrase "the will to power," Nietzsche said in a note: "The Germans think that *strength* must reveal itself in hardness and cruelty; then they submit with fervor and admiration: they are suddenly rid of their pitiful weakness . . . and they devoutly enjoy *terror*. That there is *strength* in mildness and stillness, they do not believe easily. They miss strength in Goethe . . . !" Nietzsche's admiration for Goethe was unwavering, and he always thought of Goethe as a supremely powerful individual.

In a late note that was published posthumously in *The Will to Power* (1910–1911, p. 382) we find this formulation, which I shall call the classical formulation: "I assess the *power* of a *will* by how much resistance, pain, torture it endures and knows how to turn to its advantage." Here Nietzsche was obviously thinking of himself, but not only of himself.

Perhaps the best brief commentary on this note is to be found in a letter Nietzsche wrote to his friend, Frank Overbeck, on Christmas day, 1882, just before he began to write *Zarathustra*: "This last *bite of life* was the hardest I have chewed yet, and it is still possible that I may *suffocate* on it. . . . If I do not discover the alchemists' trick of turning even this—filth into *gold*, I am lost.—Thus I have the *most beautiful* opportunity to prove that for me 'all experiences are useful. . . .'!!!!" The quotation is from Emerson and had appeared on the title page of the first edition of *The Gay Science* a few months before this letter was written. The events alluded to are discussed at length in my *Nietzsche* (1974) but are irrelevant here. What matters is that Nietzsche had reached the ultimate depths of despair, resentment, and dissatisfaction with himself, and then wrote *Zarathustra*. As he realized how much the book owed to the painful experiences that preceded it, resentment gave way to gratitude, and negative emotions to an affirmation of his life and the world in general. This example helps to explain the classical formulation and its intimate connection with one of the central motifs of *Zarathustra*: the celebration of the creative life.[3] Great writers and artists know how to turn suffering to their advantage.

Those who think that they would prefer a life without any obstacles, tensions, failures, and pains give evidence of weakness and lack of imagination. They as much as say that they consider themselves too weak to cope with difficulties, and they fail to realize how soon the kind of life that they think they desire would bore them. All of us derive satisfaction from overcoming obstacles and from turning defeats into victories. At the end of his career, just before his final collapse, Nietzsche put this point beautifully:

> I have often asked myself whether I am not more heavily obligated to the hardest years of my life than to any others. . . . And as for my long sickness, do I not owe it indescribably more than I owe to my health? I owe it a *higher* health—one which is made stronger by whatever does not kill it. *I also owe my philosophy to it.* Only great pain is the ultimate liberator of the spirit. . . . Only great pain, that long, slow pain in which we are burned with green wood, as it were—pain which takes its time—only this forces us philosophers to descend into our ultimate depths and to put away all trust. . . . I doubt that such pain makes us "better," but I know that it makes us more *profound* (*Nietzsche contra Wagner*, Epilogue 1, 1895).

Those who mistrust Nietzsche's witness would do well to reflect on the case of Alexander Solzhenitsyn, who fashioned his great novels out of his experience of the camps, the first circle of hell, and a cancer ward. There is no denying that he is a singularly strong person, and insofar as power is not an external accessory (that goes with a position and is lost when that position is lost) but a quality of a human being, Solzhenitsyn has it to an extraordinary degree—for the reasons Nietzsche spelled out.

A brief evaluation of Nietzsche's theory may help to clarify it. Most readers with some critical acumen are likely to feel that something is wrong with what I have called Nietzsche's second major contribution. But it is not easy to support this intuition.

A familiar attempt to discredit Nietzsche's theory is the claim that if "power" is so elastic that all human behavior can be explained in terms of the desire for it, then actually no behavior is explained by it. But this objection dissolves if one disowns— as I do—*reductionism*: the view that complex phenomena are "merely" or "nothing but" something simple. When we hear a performance of one of Beethoven's late quartets, we hear horsehair drawn over catguts; but the reductionist claim that the quartet is nothing but horsehair drawn over catguts is absurd. Similarly, it is, I think, true and illuminating that Beethoven's compositions were prompted by his

---

[3] The joyous acceptance of the eternal recurrence of the same events represents the ultimate triumph over resentment. Another formula that Nietzsche uses for this total affirmation is *"amor fati:* that one wants nothing to be different, not forward, not backward, not in all eternity" (*Ecce Homo*, 1908, II.10).

will to power; but the reductionist claim that his compositions are nothing but an expression of his will to power is absurd.

Another attempt to discredit the theory that people really want to feel powerful and superior is to claim that one could say just as well that they really want to be submissive. Those who make this point are obviously not motivated by any desire to submit; on the contrary, they want to prove somebody else wrong and show that they are superior. The suggestion that what *all* men really want is to submit cannot be sustained as counterexamples abound. But it could still be true that there are two kinds of people: those who desire power and those who would rather submit.

One kind of evidence that is occasionally adduced for the allegedly widespread desire to submit is the success of Hitler, Lenin, or Stalin. In fact, neither the German nor the Russian people had a choice between power and submission.

Another kind of evidence that is sometimes adduced for the desire to submit is the claim that women differ from men and that while men like to dominate, women prefer to submit. To begin with, however, a mother is hardly a paradigm of submission. She is more nearly a paradigm of power. Moreover, being a wife may confer a social status and the power to do things that in many societies a single woman would find it difficult if not impossible to do. Even to the extent, then, to which a woman does submit, it is arguable that she submits as little as possible in order to attain as much power as possible. The widespread feeling among modern women that the kind of marriage or male-female relationship that involves even a semblance of submission on the woman's part is unacceptable can hardly be said to be motivated by the desire to submit.

A third consideration that is sometimes brought up to illustrate the alleged desire to submit is religion. It is claimed that Muslims and Christians, for example, are motivated by a deep desire to submit to God. Yet here is what Paul wrote to the Corinthians (I.6.2f.):

> Do you not know that the saints will judge the world?
> And if the world is to be judged by you, are you incompetent to try trivial cases?
> Do you not know that we are to judge angels?

That is how Paul converted the Gentiles to Christianity. He appealed to their will to power. And Muhammad appealed to the will to power of those *he* converted, and they went forth and conquered a great empire, fired not only by the desire for power here and now but also by the promise of still greater power after death.

Nietzsche's *third major contribution* to the discovery of the mind was that he virtually founded what Karl Jaspers later called in the title of one of his own books "the psychology of world views." Above all, Nietzsche dealt repeatedly at some length with Christianity, and he also dealt more briefly with Judaism and Buddhism and with some nonreligious worldviews, including anti-Semitism and national-

918

ism—bringing psychology to bear on them. His attempts in this vein should be recognized as pioneering efforts.

It is not only his critique of Christianity that is often profound; Sections 50 through 55 of *The Antichrist* (1895)—about eleven pages in all—furnish the most penetrating "psychology of 'faith' of 'believers'" ever written. Sartre's "Portrait of the Anti-Semite" and Eric Hoffer's *The True Believer* have popularized some of the insights first found here. Incidentally, Sections 54 and 55 also show how wrong most discussions of Nietzsche's theory of knowledge and of his critique of Christianity have been and how thoroughly many writers on Nietzsche have failed to understand his mind. Section 54 begins:

> One should not be deceived: great spirits are skeptics. Zarathustra is a skeptic. Strength, *freedom* that is born of the strength and overstrength of the spirit, proves itself by skepticism. Men of conviction are not worthy of the least consideration in fundamental questions of value and disvalue. Convictions are prisons. . . . Freedom from all kinds of convictions, to be able to see freely, is part of strength. . . . Conversely, the need for faith, for some kind of unconditional Yes and No, this Carlylism, if you will pardon this expression, is a need born of *weakness* (*The Antichrist*, 1895, 54).

Nietzsche sided with Goethe against Kant, espoused hypotheses, and derided certainty. Even the will to power, as we have seen, he presented as a hypothesis, and that is also true of the eternal recurrence of the same events. But the best way to sum up Nietzsche's essentially critical spirit is to recall his note: "a very popular error: having the courage of one's convictions; rather it is a matter of having the courage for an *attack* on one's convictions!!!" (*Gesammelte Werke*, XVI, p. 318).

Kant was afraid of change, while "metamorphosis" was one of Goethe's leitmotifs, also in his life; and Nietzsche said in the poem that concludes *Beyond Good and Evil* (1886): "One has to change to stay akin to me" (*Nur wer sich wandelt, bleibt mit mir verwandt*). Nietzsche's attitude toward convictions and hypotheses was rooted in his openness to change. And Kant's insistence on certainty and necessity was rooted in his dread of change and his need for security. Nietzsche saw that worldviews and strong convictions have a psychological background. Belief systems and convictions are protective shields that impede honesty and openness to experience and change. They bring to mind Goethe's term "ossification," if not calcification. Conversely, those who live with open horizons and hypotheses bring to mind Nietzsche's saying in *The Gay Science*: "The secret for harvesting from existence the greatest fruitfulness and the greatest enjoyment is—to *live dangerously!*" (1882, p. 283).

Nietzsche was a philosopher and should be read as a philosopher. But he was not *only* a philosopher and should not be read only as a philosopher. He also needs to be read as a psychologist and a poet, and his books are works of art. He was as aware as anyone of the tension between the philosophic and the artistic tendency. But even in his first book, *The Birth of Tragedy* (1872), he questioned "whether the birth of an 'artistic Socrates' is altogether a contradiction in terms." *He* was an artistic Socrates. His creative life long, Nietzsche looked at the striving for knowledge, including philosophy and science, in the perspective of art and at art in the perspective of science, as he himself suggested in the magnificent "Attempt at a Self-Criticism" that he used as a preface for the second edition of *The Birth* in 1886. But we could also say that he looked at both art and science, including psychology as well as philosophy, as a psychologist—but as a psychologist who was also a great artist.

REFERENCES

Adler, A. "Verdrängung" und "männlicher Protest." In A. Adler & C. Furtmüller (Eds.), *Heilen und Bilden*. Munich: Reinhardt, 1914. (*See* Ansbacher & Ansbacher, 1956/1964.)

Ansbacher, H. L., & Ansbacher, R. (Eds.). *The individual psychology of Alfred Adler: A systematic presentation in selections from his writings*. New York: Basic Books, 1956. Harper Torchbook, 1964.

Freud, S. *Gesammelte Werke* (18 vols.). London: Imago, 1941–1968.

Freud, S. *Protokolle der Wiener Psychoanalytischen Vereinigung* (Vol. I, 1906–1908; Vol. II, 1908–1910; Vol. III, 1910–1911; Vol. IV, 1912–1918). Frankfurt: S. Fischer, 1976, 1977, 1979, 1981. The volumes first appeared in English as *Minutes of the Vienna Psychoanalytic Society* (M. Nunberg, trans.). New York: International Universities Press, 1962, 1967, 1974, 1975.

Heidegger, M. *Nietzsche* (2 vols.). Pfullingen-Neske, 1961.

Jones, E. *The life and work of Sigmund Freud* (3 vols.). New York: Basic Books, 1953, 1955, 1957.

Kaufmann, W. *Nietzsche: Philosopher, psychologist, antichrist*. Princeton, N.J.: Princeton University Press, 1950. (4th ed., revised and expanded, 1974.)

Kaufmann, W. *Discovering the mind: Nietzsche, Heidegger, and Buber* (Vol. 2). New York: McGraw-Hill, 1980.

Mill, J. S. *Utilitarianism*. London: Parker, Son, & Bourn, 1863.

Nietzsche, F. *Gesammelte Werke, Musarionausgabe* (23 vols.). Munich: Musarion Verlag, 1920–1929. (Citations of Nietzsche's *books* include *original* publication dates in addition to the section numbers, which are the same in all editions.)

Reik, T. *Listening with the third ear*. New York: Farrar, Straus, 1948.

42

Psychology and Poetry
THE UNEVEN DANCE

ELIZABETH SEWELL

We shall start with an image and a poem. Poetry is my business, and with it comes a method other than that habitually practiced in accepted academic work, so it will be as well to plunge into that other method straight away. Our general subject is "psychology and sensibility and culture," but when I was asked to take this on I knew I did not want to attempt any kind of "survey course" about the Arts in general or even literature, despite this country's mysterious passion for survey courses everywhere in education today; so I am attending only to poetry, that and psychology being quite enough to manage. Also when I was first asked, I asked my Muse for a title, and s/he produced, almost at once, "the uneven dance."

The Muse—does that seem to us to be outworn whimsy, I wonder? I name the Muse because once again it is a question of method. We need to shift over into another mythology than the accepted one in psychological usage to which we are all so accustomed that we probably do not recognize it as myth at all. I use the word *myth*, needless to say, in its profound and positive sense, not in the modern and highly current distortion (one hears it in common parlance, in public pronouncements, and on the media all the time) where the word is used as if it meant "delusion" or "lie." May I beg you, while I am at it, to watch your own speech in this regard, and if you mean "delusion" or "lie" to say so?

The myth, familiar to us all in psychology, is that of the "unconscious," or, in one of its variants, the "subconscious." *Sub*conscious, *super*ego—already we are looking at levels within that mansion of the mind. It is part of the great myth or image system constructed by Sigmund Freud, whom George Steiner calls, properly as I believe, "that great Jewish poet." Rebecca West adds another dimension (for poets build on poets, myths on myths) in *The Strange Necessity*. There, having set a context of discussion about the cortex and Pavlov—the "strange necessity" is Art, by the way—she talks about "the people downstairs" and how, if your project is a good one, they will send you up presents from time to time, whereas if you have chosen some unwise course, not merely will they give you no presents but they will hinder you in every way they can, deeming you a fool for having made that choice. Owen Barfield would have things to say about this as well. I am naming names whom I trust, and that certainly includes Freud whom one can love and trust and differ from energetically, which is a good kind of relationship.

Now for the poem, or rather half of it; the other half, the whole poem, waits for us at the end.

> *Clearing on wooded hillside, fitful the moon*
> *Glimpses the several two, dancers, alone,*
> *Pursue their intricate steps, as each to other unknown.*
>
> *The ground slopes steeply, grass unkempt and lush.*

As you will understand, one does not allegorize or encode a poem's images, so I have in my turn to divine by those it produces. If the dance is uneven, it is so in a number of ways, everything in this method tending to be more than one thing. Uneven, then, first in the sense of separated—writing these lines it suddenly struck me that this is what "several" must mean: severed each from each. The dancing-floor is uneven—it is a sharply raked hillside, like Helicon itself in the real Greek landscape. The footing is uneven, tussocks and clumps of herbage where you could easily turn an ankle. And there are two of these dancers. We would be inclined to think of two as an even number, but I am reminded of the dyad in Pythagorean thought where, after the unity of the monad, the division into two is almost a fall, bringing with it matter, change, and corruption. Under these guises we are to think about psychology and poetry, and the relationship between them, in the general picture of contemporary culture.

In terms of general culture there is no question but that psychology has increasingly affected many of the ways in which we think and speak about the world and ourselves. Take dreams, for instance—I find people are often reluctant now to tell their dreams for fear that some hidden sexual symbolism will reveal itself to the listener. Yet interestingly, and here is the uneven dance again, poets continue to make use of their dreams as they have always done, and on their own terms which are not those of psychological technique. This was brought home to me some years ago when at Hunter College in New York I was put in charge of a graduate class whose semester's work was to listen to a series of contemporary poets reading their works, published and unpublished. They were a very varied group, ranging from Robert Lowell and Stanley Kunitz to Adrienne Rich and Jean Valentine, and it was fascinating to me to hear one after the other speak of the centrality of dreams in their poetic work, as poets have always felt and as if no profound changes had taken place in ways of approaching these creations of the sleeping mind.

Clearly those new approaches, insofar as we understand them, do affect us all. The currency of such verbal expressions as the Freudian slip, the Oedipus complex, the collective unconscious, schizophrenia, even an archetype or two, can vouch for our surface familiarity with psychology's domain. In another vein it may be also that our two disciplines, poetry and psychology, share responsibility for the present generation's cult of love and sex, respectively, as the one myth by which supposedly to live. Yet when I turned to that vast popular repository of just such matters, rock and country music, and what it expresses in its lyrics, I could come up with almost nothing about either of our pursuits. For poetry all I recalled, from my own really considerable repertoire, was a mortifying couplet, part of a song used as a kind of booster anthem in my present home state of North Carolina. It says, in its final two lines,

> Lord, it's just like living in a pome—
> I like calling North Carolina home!

If that is not particularly edifying, try to think what you could produce for psychology in its turn. Here all that presented itself was a song, obviously and appropriately enough from California. It is a lament, and in it the following passage occurs:

> My stocks are going down
> And my shrink is out of town
> And my house is on the San Andreas Fault . . .

but who does the singer cry out to in his distress? Freud? Jung? Skinner or even Abe Maslow? Not at all. What he exclaims is:

> I need you, Barry Manilow!

We neither of us seem, Bob Newhart and a few radio commercials notwithstanding, to have gone either far or deep into these sensibilities.

To turn now to connections between the two disciplines themselves, I feel I am in duty bound to spread out a little from poetry, and to encourage us to glance at least at one or two other literary and artistic connections, for they certainly exist. I am thinking mainly of how psychology has influenced letters, but I took the opportunity the other day of looking up the tabulated references to literature of all sorts in

923

the big *Index to Freud's Collected Works,* and I found it instructive both in the quantity and variety of literature which he knew and quoted from. It is also helpful to look at such manifestations of this interest as his Address on Goethe in 1930, read for him because he was already too sick to read it himself. I find him open and generous toward poets, with a judicious sense of limits or boundaries. Somewhere he says (I do not have the exact reference) that it is not the business of psychoanalysis to inquire where the artist's inspiration comes from.[1] I like that. (I should perhaps confess quickly here and get it over that as a poet I do not trust Jung at all.)

When we look now at the other side, it is apparent that there have been mutual relations between psychology and literature of various genres. A Freudian or psychoanalytic approach has been employed in the criticism of a fair number of literary works; we all know about Jones and *Hamlet,* and I think of Lewis Carroll as another example. I can call to mind two really good professional novels which have a psychoanalysis as what the eighteenth century would have called their "machinery," *Arrival and Departure* by Arthur Koestler, so much less well-known and to me so much more interesting than his *Darkness at Noon,* and *The Manticore,* the second work in a remarkable trilogy by the Canadian novelist Robertson Davies. (The second of these portrays a Jungian analysis, by the way.) And in drama there are plays like *Equus,* and I seem to remember a cryptoanalyst years back in T. S. Eliot's play, *The Cocktail Party.*

One could obviously search out a lot more of this kind of thing, but that is "survey" again, and I want to get on to poetry. When I first began to try to make the connection, poetry–psychology, for this piece of work, I found myself thinking, "I shall be 'gravelled for lack of matter.'" The uneven dance—it seemed as if the two dancers were not meeting at all. Hence the start of the poem, and the realization that this very absence of relations *was* my subject matter itself. And it has to do essentially with method, which is why I have been insinuating something at least of poetic method since the beginning.

It seems to me, first, that one reason for the nonmeeting of these disciplines or of their methods is what I might call a difference in phasing, a difference in regard to time. The poetic mode is prophetic. I mean by that nothing bombastic, simply that it has as part of its operations an impulse to speak forward. The poet's voice, therefore, speaking in this strain, is not likely to be heard by that particular generation for some time to come, say, a hundred or a hundred and fifty years. William

---

[1] In elucidating the literary or mythopoeic dream, Freud also comes up consciously against limitations in psychology. When Maxime Leroy sent him an account (not a wholly adequate one, the evidence suggests) of Descartes's three great *Olympica* dreams of 1619, the third of which is all about poetry, Freud does what he can with them but then says, "We have no path open to us which will take us further." It is noteworthy that philosophy, tackling the same dreams in the person of Jacques Maritain, *Le Songe de Descartes,* does not fare much better. The great account of them is given by Muriel Rukeyser in *The Traces of Thomas Hariot,* and since I am writing for those in another discipline may I remind us all that she was a poet, and an eminent one, of our own day.

Blake is a case in point (and since, with the title of Professor Kaufmann's address we seem to be entering horses for the First Depth Psychologist Stakes, I would want to put Blake forward as a possible contestant). He and many of his contemporaries back at the turn of the eighteenth into the nineteenth century, whose wavelength we are perhaps just now getting attuned to, speak to us with a kind of passionate intensity about imagination, the imaginative or poetic method, seen as in no way irrational but rather as "Reason in her most exalted mood," as Wordsworth says of it in Book XIV of his long poem *The Prelude* which bears as subtitle "The Growth of a Poet's Mind," a name which Coleridge glosses somewhere as "The Growth and Revolutions of a Poet's Mind." In either case, psychology, under another mode of working.

As I mention these poets among so many, I wonder how far they seem relevant to the psychologist today, or whether the assumption would be made that the hundred years this Conference is celebrating, a hundred years of psychology as science, have superseded all that. It might be of interest to recall that the relative worth of our two dancing or nondancing disciplines was considered imaginatively in the late and wonderful poem by John Keats, his second "Hyperion," bearing the name *The Fall of Hyperion: A Dream.* It is perhaps unexpected that the question which the poem raises—which is more valuable to humankind, the active loving healer (of body and/or mind) or the poet?—is answered unhesitatingly: the former. One might have thought that this young genius, dying of a tuberculosis no doctor at that period could cure, might in compensation have claimed his own dear vocation, but he hears from the towering priestess in the ruined temple only what we all hear, "Thou art less than they," and accepts it and goes on painfully into the ensuing poem-dream which is his next and almost his last work.

I want at this point to strike briefly a personal note. As I looked at our program here and the speakers who would precede me, I wondered if any of them would be disposed to speak of what psychology had done for them in their lives. Holding to Keats's company, I feel bound to say that I was analyzed in my mid-twenties by an Englishman with the wonderful name of Theodore Faithfull, and that I in some sense date my life from that point. He was a lay analyst as one could be in England, i.e., not a medical practitioner; in fact he had been, he told me, a veterinarian, but "found people more interesting than horses." There was something immensely reassuring, to this nervous patient, in the knowledge that one's analyst had been, so to speak, a horse-doctor. It removed immediately the nightmarish image of the dogmatic, white-coated expert advancing upon one's vitals with a scalpel. Clearly if he could deal with such skittish animals successfully he would know how to deal with an unhappy and unproductive poet. Actually, as I discovered, he treated all his patients as if they were poets, though I do not think he thought of it that way in his Freudian-Jungian-individualistic practice. It is quite simply the rescue from a gray desert of melancholy and powerlessness that I bear witness to here. In doing so, I want also to remind us all of a contrary rescue: if you read the autobiography of that

925

man of the mind, John Stuart Mill, you will recall that at about the same stage of his life, after his intensely intellectual education was completed, he asked himself whether, if all that he had been trained to consider as social betterment came true, would he be any happier? His answer was no, and his depression so great that he thought of suicide. Who rescued him? William Wordsworth, the reading of his poetry, the breaking of the ice. I am insinuating, as you see, that we need each other.

The separation nevertheless is real and continues to be so because obstinately the poets dance their own dance, pursue their own method, as against—what? What is the method which has come to be called, so ironically as I believe, the "scientific method"? That, of course, is a question for you, not for me to answer. This is your method, this Conference marks a hundred years of it, you know full well what it is. Now and then something comes out of this frequently rather rigid and dogmatic framework which really interests a poet: the writings of the neurosurgeon Dr. Joseph Bogen, for instance, or the admirable audacity of the speculations of Dr. Julian Jaynes. I want to point out in passing that this separation is not the only result of the prevailing "scientific method" among yourselves who are, and I mean the phrase solely as a description and not as an adverse comment, the Establishment. When those highly "establishment" institutions, Oxford and Cambridge, have the misfortune to have to make reference to one another, the phrase employed used to be (I do not know if it still is) "the other place." I want to remind you of your "other place" which chooses to call itself "humanistic," splitting off and then splitting again and again, infinitely fissile as left-wing and revolutionary movements so often are. They, too, are interesting to visit, but the dance continues solitary, the poet intent upon another method of choreography.

Of the poetic or imaginative method I want to give only a few indications here: first, an ability to read things and symbols, this depending also upon an ever-alert power of detailed and loving observation (Goethe's *Beobachtung*); next, a fostering and cultivation of memory and prophecy, knowing each connected with the other and both with imagination, and taking prophecy to mean here the ability to think and feel oneself forward in the making of one's life, one's research, the ability to ask and follow up Bacon's *prudens quaestio* which Coleridge transposes into "the forethoughtful question . . . the self-unravelling clue"; next again, the readiness to work by synthesis and so to balance the reliance upon analysis which alone is taught in modern education, learning to operate in terms of multiplicity, complexity irreducible to simple discrete elements, fusion, where everything is always more than one thing and the operative models come in forms such as metaphor, myth, and metamorphosis; to work indirectly, apprehending one thing (or oneself) by looking at another or through another, as is done in all dreams and fictions; to attune oneself to a universe of overlapping networks of correspondences, best grasped perhaps under the form of music or of Needham's "associative logic." You can see that we have run parallel, or merged, with much in the great Neo-Platonic,

Hermetic, and possibly alchemical, tradition, and could certainly add to this method its other notes which hold for poetry as for philosophy, a passion for numbers and mathematical forms, a constant search for precision, order, and due boundaries.

I hope something might have been happening as that list emerged: that you might have been saying to yourself, "But that is what I do." Exactly. The science/art separation which we have taken for granted for so long is senseless. The dance, where dance it is, where the method is living and self-generating and not just manipulation and technique, is one dance, though the dancers remain severed and do not know it yet.

So now I, in my status as poet, am going to prophesy—was not a hundred years the wavelength forward suggested for poets earlier?—that during the next hundred years there is going to be a restitution, or in Bacon's word an instauration of the dance, a move from the unevenness into more unified patterns, a new metaphysic, renewed method, a way out of our current isolation and impoverishment. The poem speaks to this. Here now is all of it:

> *Clearing on wooded hillside, fitful the moon*
> *Glimpses the several two, dancers, alone,*
> *Pursue their intricate steps, as each to other unknown.*
>
> *The ground slopes steeply, grass unkempt and lush.*
>
> *Late or soon wakes what god in underbrush,*
> *Pipes keening and sharp enough*
> *To turn recalcitrant thighs and shins,*
> *Though cold, in half-light, and the footing rough,*
> *As far away the terrible lyre begins,*
> *Thrum becomes thunder, to twine and realign,*
> *First by impulsion, last in full freewill,*
> *All scattered dancers over Helicon's hill.*

The poem says that more than one god is involved, and the effect includes others than just psychology and poetry. I hope we would be agreeable to that.

927

Afterword

SIGMUND KOCH

As senior editor of this book, I had planned to write a detailed epilogue that would specify in some depth the main trends of the contributions: a kind of time capsule preserving the overall "message" of our forty-three distinguished fin-de-siècle commentators for future centuries. It soon became evident that *such* a message could itself assume the proportions of a book, and that this secondary "book" could become a screen occluding the primary one. The message of this book is *the* book; any significant rendering of its essence must be the pattern discerned by each reader willing to dwell thoughtfully within the rich but untidy dispersion of viewpoint, scholarly judgment, and historic detail compressed between these covers.

My own "theory" of the message can in large degree be inferred from the "Foreword," taken together with my contribution on "The Nature and Limits of Psychological Knowledge" (Chapter 4). To compensate for idiosyncratic aspects of my position, I shall here try to trace in the briefest possible way but a few of the most conspicuous tendencies of psychology that are reflected (and often sharpened and intensified) within this book. Though the reporter can in no way excise the personal coefficient of his judgments, my *intention* is to report responsibly. May I apologize to the contributors for the shameless generality in which their views will be represented.

Of greatest current import are, of course, those trends which are discontinuous with psychology's past, especially its recent past. Though the time frame of this book is a century, the particular attitude changes of most compelling interest are best seen against a baseline of circa 1960, when a forty-year behaviorist hegemony and a corollary logical positivist epistemology that had held almost official sway for the preceding thirty years were beginning to break up.

It may be well to recall at this point that the interval (circa) 1930–1960—which was marked by the almost universal observance of an epistemology deriving from logical positivism (and such cognate positions as operationism and neopragmatism) and by the ascendancy of "neobehaviorist" ideas and programs—represented the one period in the history of scientific psychology in which something like a consensus of mission and method had been achieved. The atmosphere of this "Age of Theory" (as I have called it) hardly requires reconstruction for psychologists of appreciable seniority; nor would it seem especially alien to the young who are still residually, though often unwittingly, in its thrall. Its character may be suggested by such of its marks as: the regulation of systematic work by the directives and imagery of hypothetico-deductive method; the subculture surrounding operational definition; the lore concerning the intervening variable; the belief in the imminence (if not achievement) of precisely quantitative behavioral theory of comprehensive scope; the broadly shared judgments with respect to foundation data (usually of a sort generated by one or a few species of infra-human mammals); the belief in automatic refinement and convergence of theories by the device of "differential test"; the belief that the entire pattern of procedural imperatives suggested in shorthand by the preceding rubrics would *guarantee* "objectivism" at the level of theory as well as that of experiment, and thus the emergence of a rigorous, cumulative, predictively powerful science.

This Age of Theory attitude complex was subjected to detailed and rigorous scrutiny in the Study, jointly sponsored by the American Psychological Association and the National Science Foundation, which resulted in the six volumes of *Psychology: A Study of a Science* (Koch, 1959–1963). The Study—which was planned during 1952 and launched in 1953—had as a major aim the comparison of recent systematic practice with the Age of Theory premises. Especially was Study I (Vols. 1–3) designed with such a purpose in view, the central editorial device being a uniform discussion plan which urged contributors to consider their own formulations against a set of topics which synthesized in the most explicit possible way that conception of a scientific "systematic formulation" rendered official by Age of Theory prescriptions. And Study II (Vols. 4–6), though it emphasized empirical problem areas and their relations, also sought to encourage confrontations of *practice*, both research and systematic, with Age of Theory injunctions. The overall project included in its roster of ninety contributors many of the most distinguished psychologists then alive.

The resulting four thousand pages of particulate, probing, and sometimes inspired analysis can be seen as a gigantic critical gloss upon virtually every plank in the Age of Theory platform. To convey the *primary* message in barest essence, one

929

may quote the following two sentences from the editor's "Epilogue" to Study I (Koch, 1959, p. 783):

> *It can in summary be said that the results of Study I set up a vast attrition against virtually all elements of Age of Theory code.* If all contributors are not eager to express their doubts in neon script, neither do they conceal their . . . questioning.

Nevertheless, though the *stability* of the Age of Theory attitude complex was clearly under stress, the message was not without ambiguity. A few paragraphs later, the editor found it necessary to add (pp. 784–785):

> This Epilogue has barely suggested the scope of the attrition . . . against the "reigning" image of systematic practice; yet there is a tendency *still* to funnel activity through its contours . . . . The images which govern *positive* systematic action are still, in the main, Age of Theory images. Often when they do not govern action, they serve as its rationalization. Despite the fact that action can only be fully free when at peace with its presuppositions, there has been very little direct effort towards the creative emendation of Age of Theory doctrine.

The present "Afterword" cannot be the place to document the post-1960 fate of the Age of Theory attitude complex. It is a most intricate story—one which has been enormously complicated not only by the steady diversification and realignment of substantive interests and ideas, but by that fogging of the Age of Theory metaphor system created from the early 1960s onward by the large impact upon psychologists of Thomas Kuhn's analysis of science in terms of the "paradigm" and related notions. Indeed, one could say that an "Age of the Paradigm" soon came to coexist with residues of the Age of Theory imperatives, and to form a mixed (not to say "mixed-up") ideology badly in need of disentanglement (cf. Koch, 1976, pp. 496–511). The notion of "paradigm," together with Kuhn's analysis of the conditions of paradigm change and acceptance, seems to have been broadly perceived as an authoritative body of doctrine that could render the implementation of the Age of Theory objectives "a piece of cake." After all, if the adoption of a paradigm is a matter of "persuasion," and the possession of one makes possible a "puzzle-solving" period of "normal science," then why not agree on a paradigm by some such process as voting? Misreadings of Kuhn almost that primitive were at one time widespread, and their effects are still with us. We cannot here come to serious terms with so large an issue; the intent is merely to note an intervening complication which must be taken into account if we are to take the 1960 status of psychology, as revealed by *Psychology: A Study of a Science*, as a baseline against which to report trends of the present study.

Before proceeding to those trends, it is necessary to mention one further aspect of the 1960 status of psychology that was lushly evident both within the pages of

Psychology: A *Study of a Science* and in the literature of the field at large. During the heyday of the Age of Theory (say, the interval 1930–1945), fundamental psychology had achieved a remarkable constriction of substantive interests. The vast majority of theoretico-experimental psychologists concentrated research attention on elementary "laws" of learning and, to some extent, motivation, in the belief that all significant phenomena associated with other traditionally distinguished problems and processes could ultimately be treated as "secondary derivations" from S-R learning principles. Indeed, the peripheralistic necessities of behaviorism (from Watson onward) led to the virtual extradition of "centralist" areas of psychology (e.g., perception, cognition, affective processes) from direct concern. Direct address of these matters was considered beyond the scientific pale in that the fields at issue were seen to be traditional strongholds of "mentalism" and "subjectivism." To be sure, a trickle of research (much of it highly significant!) on such matters continued throughout the Age of Theory in the efforts of such minority groups as the Gestalt psychologists and of idiosyncratic thinkers like Lewin and Tolman. But such rivulets—with the possible exception of the work of those two men, which could be aligned with orthodoxy in that they drew upon aspects of the Age of Theory epistemology—were barely visible by virtue of the massive concentration on S-R "learning theory."[1]

---

[1] It is to be stressed that so terse a set of generalizations concerning an era as I am forced to make in the above paragraph must fall far short of conveying the "complete" picture. A substantial amount of activity was taking place during even the "classic" Age of Theory in such fields as personality and social psychology. Indeed, Sanford (Chapter 21) notes that the great days of psychodynamically oriented personality research, and of the "culture and personality" movement, were in the 1930s and 1940s. And, of course, not only Freud, Jung, and Adler but, in lesser degree, Murray, Allport, Kluckhohn, and others were visible names. But such fields—which had only recently penetrated into the academy—were viewed as marginal and extrascientific by the vast majority of *fundamental* psychologists. They were granted but second class citizenship by the predominating Age of Theory ideology. Nevertheless, Clark Hull and others of the ruling learning theorists were willing to acknowledge that there were probably some useful ideas lurking under the messy "literary" camouflage of psychoanalytic formulations. This motivated a subtradition of efforts to translate psychoanalytic "hypotheses" into the "system languages" of various S-R learning theories, and also a congeries of experimental attempts toward the "objective" validation of the thus translated principles (cf. Sears's admirable account of these matters in Chapter 8).

Sensory and physiological psychology were also reasonably active at the time but—incredibly—these fields, too, were accorded only second-class citizenship in that they were not projecting comprehensive hypothetico-deductive theories that fulfilled the Age of Theory dictates. (Clifford Morgan once agreed with me on this point by indicating that he in fact felt himself thus stigmatized during that period!) The irony is compounded when we note that so great a physiological psychologist as Karl Lashley was barely heard during the long course of his effort—both experimental and conceptual—to show that the dominating theories of learning were saturated with physiologically impossible presumptions. Though the learning theorists of the day claimed to be operating within a "purely behavioral" universe of discourse (whatever that might be), one can wonder, as Lashley did, about the fruitfulness of making assumptions demonstrably inconsonant with neurophysiological knowledge. It may give one pause to note that a similar issue is *currently* raised by those cognitive theorists who do not think their information-processing theories need be constrained by considerations of neurophysiological plausibility.

931

Circa the early 1950s, however, an appreciable diversification and realignment of substantive interests became apparent—as the result of many factors (far too intricate to unravel here) largely associated with the World War II-induced preoccupations of psychologists, and the challenges and opportunities stemming from the war's aftermath. By our baseline year of 1960, this process of change had gone a considerable distance; it might almost be argued that most of the research interests that are definitive of the current scene had been animated by the early 1960s. There was, for instance, a massive return of the repressed! Long-exiled "centralist" areas like perception and cognition had become active foci of concern. Physiological (or, more generally, "biological") psychology which earlier in the Age of Theory had been sparsely pursued—and denigrated as irrelevant by the "empty-organism" S-R theorists then dominant—had commenced its meteoric post-war trajectory. The study of instinctive behavior had been relegitimated in the United States by the discovery of the work of the European ethologists, and a long-abrogated interest in a "genuine" comparative psychology (rather than the study of rats qua Galilean test objects for "theory") had been rekindled. Developmental psychology—which during the Age of Theory had not been considered as requiring direct address in that the details of developmental process would surely be forthcoming as derivations from the "principles" and "conditions" of learning!—once more became a thriving field.

By 1960, the standard Age of Theory preoccupation with elementary learning and biological deficit motivation had begun to diversify into concerns of more complex character: for example, "learning-sets"; exploration, curiosity and other "exteroceptively" (sic) determined "drives." Sophisticated forms of mathematical modeling (e.g., of learning, of decision and cognitive processes, of neurophysiological process) had begun to form distinct clusters of interest. Entire "new" fields were coming into prominence: information-processing analyses of cognition (along with associated but even more general interests in computer simulation of psychological processes and artificial intelligence), psycholinguistics, and "general system theory," to take one set of examples.

Interest in social psychology and in personality had been diversified and expanded. "Creativity research" had become a focus of interest. A burgeoning interest in applied matters had spawned such new, and massively pursued, specialties as behavior therapy, programmed instruction, sensitivity training and its variants, and a congeries of concerns with critical social dislocations and stresses upon the quality of life.

Against the pressures of such changes, even the "behaviorisms" could no longer sustain their long-enforced repressions. A massive attempt to accommodate, even celebrate, the return of the repressed commenced in (roughly) the mid-1950s. In this effort, the behaviorisms so watered down their conceptual language (especially in re the definition and application ranges of S and R) as to begin to lose distinctiveness. By our reference year of 1960, one was well into the era of the "S-R mediation theories"—which sought to do justice to the "facts" (discriminated by other groupings of psychologists) of perception, cognition, and even of linguistic behavior by assorted efforts to apply S-R concepts and laws to "central events." These liberalized versions of behaviorism are well represented in *Psychology: A Study of a Science* (cf. Neal Miller, 1959, Vol. 2, pp. 196–292; and much of Vol. 5, 1963, which includes a virtual anthology of such positions).

So much for our 1960 "baseline." The present volume can in part be seen as a registration of the status of psychology after a quarter-century more of flux. The story is very much one of an extrapolation of the tendencies already evident in 1960 as multiplied by a steadily expanding work force, and a continuing differentiation of research options.

There has been a marked realignment in the relative "glamor" of major areas of fundamental psychology—mainly in directions presaged by the early 1960s. Without a doubt, cognition, psycholinguistics, perception, developmental psychology, and biological psychology (in the sense comprehending sensory and physiological psychology) have become the most influential and actively pursued fields. Though "radical behaviorism" and a number of "mediation" theories seeking to integrate S-R and cognitive concepts (e.g., "cognitive learning theory," "social learning theory") are still on the scene, interest in learning in most of the senses pursued by the learning theorists of the Age of Theory is approaching the vestigial. And it is of interest to note that the strongholds of influence of both "radical" and "liberalized" behaviorism are *now* to be found in applied (especially clinical) rather than fundamental psychology: the work in "behavior modification" and activities in the milieu of Bandura's and Lazarus's thinking may be taken as examples.

If any one discipline is now perceived as the "basic" field of fundamental psychology, it is certainly *cognitive psychology*—and especially that form of it marked off by the phrase "cognitive science." Developmental psychology—which, of course, crosscuts the concerns of cognitive psychology in the area of "cognitive development"—is as active a field as cognition and is perhaps more heavily populated. Perception thrives, but in that reach of it that leans heavily on information-processing analyses, becomes increasingly difficult to disentangle from cognitive psychology. It need hardly be added that biological psychology—now in closer association with the neurosciences than ever before—has made tremendous strides: not only is it one of the most dynamic of the "fundamental" fields, but it has regained the influence and prestige it commanded in the second half of the nineteenth century.

But there is an outstanding quality of the present situation which was *not* predictable in 1960 or before: *no* field or family of concepts within fundamental psychology commands anything like the breadth of allegiance that did S-R learning theory during the Age of Theory. If "cognitive science" is now, in some sense, the "basic" field, this is so mainly in the eyes of cognitive scientists. It is not necessarily the view

933

of perception theorists, developmentalists, biological psychologists, and so on. Moreover, *within* each of the broad fields of fundamental psychology, diversity of viewpoint is at least as great as the differences *across* them. Psychology is now characterized by a pluralism of conceptual and methodic posit, and of research interest, so great as to suggest a new humility before the actual complexities of the psychological universe: *problems* are being addressed, rather than—as in the past— evaded or liquidated by premanufactured explanations.

It should be added that certain influences originating outside of psychology have had a powerful bearing on the texture of the recent scene. The rapid acceleration of computer technology and theory is perhaps the most conspicuous example. But such developments as Chomskian linguistic theory; advances in mathematics and statistics; sociobiology and, more generally, the "new" evolutionary biology (cf. Alexander, Chapter 33); the reemergence of "philosophy of mind" as an active specialty within philosophy; and the steady emergence of a motley variety of post-positivistic emphases in the philosophy of science have all had important effects on the character of recent psychology.

Note that the generalizations of the preceding paragraphs have borne mainly on what have traditionally been deemed the "process areas" of fundamental psychology. But there has been immensely increased activity in the fields that address the person and the social context, and a growing disposition of their investigators to claim "fundamental" status for those concerns. It has, for instance, become increasingly argued that many of the problems of the process areas cannot be significantly pursued unless the research is conducted within an ambience of knowledge and sensitivity stemming from social and "personological" psychology. "Fundamental psychology" is very much an "open-horizon" concept but, as we shall see later in this "Afterword," never before have its horizons been scanned so differently by so many.

As for the "meta-methodological" imperatives of the Age of Theory, it can be said that its *explicit* superstructure of ideology is almost extinct, and that psychologists working in diverse areas have begun to appeal to a healthy (if confusing) plurality of philosophical rationales, but that certain Age of Theory residues— especially aspects of the mythos surrounding "operational definition"—are still broadly tenacious.

Such changes as have been summarized can hardly have eluded the notice of psychologists whose careers have comprehended the past few decades. These changes are certainly reflected—and their implications creatively explored—within the chapters of this book. The few trends that I wish to emphasize involve attitudinal changes so deep as to challenge the very foundations and scholarly style of our discipline as it has been practiced over its "first" century. It is possible to believe that they portend that the psychology of the "second" century will be played in a different key.

The trends that seem to me most revealing are the following:

1. Resurgence of historical sensibility
2. Ferment concerning the disciplinary status of psychology
3. Doubts concerning the putative "independence" of psychology from philosophy
4. Reanalysis of the role and range of application of experimental method
5. Increased modesty of objective and of claimed accomplishment
6. Serious—rather than merely defensive—concern with the human and social impact of psychology

The first two trends seem sufficiently revealing to merit more than passing attention. The four additional ones are either so clearly related to the initial two, or so patent, as to require only glancing notice.

1. Resurgence of Historical Sensibility

From the moment that psychology was stipulated into life qua formal "science," it was inevitable that the sensibilities of its agents would soon manifest a degree of "instantism" more severe than could be found among other groupings of scholars, even in a largely ahistorical era. The redefinition of an ancient context of inquiry as "science" has much the force of a declaration of war against the past. Even though (as was surmised in the "Foreword") such warfare was no central part of the intention of the generation of the founders, the new image of "independent, experimental science," and the mission suggested by that image, invited of the succeeding generations a pusillanimous attitude toward the past: an initial invidious distinction between the "old psychology" of the schoolman and the metaphysician and the "new" soon led to the virtual disappearance of the "old" from the group memory. And this was but the beginning of a strange dialectic between "old" and "new" such that the psychology of each generation was seen as bearing the counter-scientific stigmata of the "old" by the next generation—whose depraved deviations from scientific purity were dismissed as the "old" psychology by the still next. Indeed, *within* any given generation, the views of one's opponents could be peremptorily dismissed as bearing the metaphysical hallmark of some nameless "old" psychology.

The need for the odd dialectic just described subsided (though not completely) not long after John Watson announced his disposition to "bury subjective subject matter." Watson's "fresh, clean start in psychology, breaking both with current theories and with traditional concepts and teminology" resulted, at least in the United States, in a doctrinal and methodological orthodoxy so complete as to effectuate a virtual blackout of historical interests for fifty years. Indeed, "instantism" became so pronounced during this long interregnum that the successive phases of the behaviorist movement tended to liquidate its own earlier history. There was a time during the *neo*behavioristic hegemony when many of its younger votaries—though they might have been apprised of Watson's name—would not have heard of such prominent "classical" behaviorists as E.B. Holt, A.P. Weiss, or W.S. Hunter. Even currently, it is possible to meet ardent young Skinnerians who draw a blank at the mention of Clark L. Hull—whose "neobehavioristic" thinking, of course, initially sparked, and then dominated the Age of Theory.

Against a background suggested by these remarks, the renaissance of historical perspective implicit in the forty-two essays in this book must be seen as one of the most significant changes in the climate of psychology over the course of this century. It may be thought that this renaissance of sensitivity to history is but an artifact of the charge given to contributors—which, after all, was to assess the areas of their special interest at the end of psychology's "first" century. But the charge was general and open-ended: if anything, oriented more toward the isolation of what the contributor's field could bring into the second century than toward narrative accounts of its first. And indeed, few of the chapters are, in any large part, exercises in historical narrative. What is far more impressive about these essays than their literal historical content is their pervasive quality of *respect* for history, and the frequent evidences of historical considerations playing an organic role in an author's specialized thinking.

Some of the authors report lines of theoretical and research effort which they have self-consciously built upon foundations provided by thinkers who long have been little more than names in the literature. De Rivera (Chapter 15) reanimates neglected aspects of the work of Kurt Lewin and his students (especially Tamara Dembo's 1931 experiments on anger) as a basis for his own interesting phenomenological analysis of "emotional transformation." Loevinger's account (Chapter 19)—at once a history and a resurrection—of the field of "character development" sees long unacknowledged "lines of thought" stemming from James Mark Baldwin (and other late-nineteenth and early-twentieth-century figures) as "still reverberating" in recent work germane to character, including her own.

At least one of the essays (Chapter 34 by Blumenthal on "Psychology and Linguistics") reanimates rather large traditions of nineteenth century effort which have never entered the ken of the psychologists working on related problems, and raises sobering questions as to whether many of the *current* issues had not been anticipated, and perhaps taken in more fruitful directions, by these neglected lines of work. Henle (Chapter 5) repairs a shorter-term but grave lapse of group memory in regard to the contributions of Gestalt psychology by her convincing demonstration that distorted fragments of Gestalt theory and research are being reinvented in important sectors of cognitive psychology, and her exhibition of distinct gains that might ensue if cognitive psychologists established direct scholarly contact with the Gestalt work. Newell (Chapter 16) could be interpreted as fueling Henle's argument in acknowledging the work of Karl Duncker as presaging by thirty years the "cognitive revolution" of the early 1960s. (Those who have remained in sympathetic touch with the Gestalt tradition may be tempted to ask whether the study of cognition needed its information-processing "revolution"—but such an issue is not meet for discussion in this reportorial "Afterword.")

Others of the contributors (e.g., Robinson, Giorgi, Gibson, Sears, Sanford, Gergen, Toulmin and Leary) adduce somewhat similar considerations to the ones just mentioned in pointing to historical circularities and ideational recurrences (some of the latter showing a downward trajectory of quality). Again, *many* of the essays readjust, in revealing ways, misleading historical stereotypes long in the public domain, and fill in gaps in the thin and rather superficial backlog of historical writing that has been deposited by the century (e.g., chapters by Kendler, Rosenzweig, Sears, Hagen, Haber, Kimble, Catania, Bindra, Mischel, McGuire, Zaner, Gleitman, Luce, Harris, Pribram, Lacey, Glickman, Alexander, Carroll, Arnheim, Barzun, Kaufmann).

Several of the essays are of unusual historical interest in that they open up vistas on important figures or issues of a sort for which there is little or no precedent. Rosenzweig's long essay (Chapter 7) documents Freud's attitudes toward experimental psychology, and discusses the more general relations of psychoanalysis to academic psychology, in a degree of specificity and depth that has not been rivalled. Arnheim's evocation of little known aspects of Gustav Fechner's thinking (Chapter 36) contains a revealing moral about the extent to which conventional historiography can distort the essence of persons it may seek to represent. Glickman's masterful delineation of the history of comparative psychology (Chapter 32) lends fresh insight into the vicissitudes of that field by its perceptive tracing of the still active consequences of the dispute between Darwin and Wallace over whether the human mind has *sui generis* characteristics not wholly explicable in terms of the general laws of evolution.

Other chapters of unique historical interest are contributed by our nonpsychologist participants. Though William James's towering early presence is acknowledged in many of the chapters, it is Barzun, the humanist, who actually dwells (Chapter 40) on the texture of James's thought. And another humanist, Walter Kaufmann, reminds psychologists that they tend to overlook much significant psychology within the humanist tradition by his exploration of Nietzsche as psychologist (Chapter 41).

There are of course evidences—most quite explicit—that some of our authors came away from their writing with an enhanced interest in historical matters, and a heightened sense that most problems of current psychological concern have a time dimension which can be disregarded only at great risk to their meaningful treatment. But, from the character of the essays even of these authors, it is hard to believe that the writer was entirely bereft of historical interests and sensitivities until stimulated to wear the historian's mantle by participation in this project. There is, of course, much external evidence to suggest that ahistoricism is broadly, if incipiently, on the wane in our field—as it is, somewhat more conspicuously, in other areas of scholarship. What is hopeful about the testimony of this book is the indication that so many who rank among the leaders of important fields of psychology are so far along in their reassertion of historical sensibility. That may be a happy augury of an increased rate of change for the field as a whole.

2. Ferment Concerning the Disciplinary Status of Psychology

The disciplinary status of psychology—after its century-long march under the banner of "independent, experimental science"—is, in a word, in *doubt*. A strange march in that, though the proudly fluttering banner was reverentially followed by most, the marchers could never quite agree on their map of the terrain they were traversing or exactly whither they were headed. At the end of this century of turmoiled marching, it is possible to say that the deployment of the marchers has rather more the quality of the Napoleonic retreat from Moscow than the initial hopeful advance.

It can be news to no one that recent years have seen an increasing pluralism in conceptions of the disciplinary status of psychology. What is added by the testimony of this book is that such restiveness is now more extensive than at any preceding interval of the last hundred years, including even that unsettled period in the first quarter of this century marked by the constant polemical conflict of the "schools." But the pluralism *now* obtaining has a less embattled, thus less querulous and rhetorical quality. It is a pluralism of *search* rather than assertiveness, marked by humility, not hubris. Were one to contrast this mood with the sordid disciplinary orthodoxy which prevailed in the second third of this century during psychology's Age of Theory, it might *almost* seem that psychology has at last succeeded in transcending its preoccupation with scientistic role playing, and is actually rejoining the tradition of serious Western scholarship. The "almost" in the preceding sentence is merely a reminder that any historic generalization must be shaded in gray. Obviously the geography of sentiment delineated in this book is not the geography of the field at large. But the diversity of our contributors—and their maturity and stature—is such as to ensure that the "field at large" cannot remain far behind.

The rabid and monolithic scientism which dominated so much of the century is, then, giving way to a new pluralism. I can make no attempt to represent the positions of all forty-two of the essays, or convey any position in its differentiated texture, but the more conspicuous changes and realignments of the very conception of our discipline are easy to identify.

Perhaps the outstanding general trend that should at once be noted relates to "pluralism" in something like its ultimate sense: that of the actual conception of our discipline *as plural*. *Many* of our contributors issue a challenge to the conception that psychology is *one* field. Among these, some think it at least two; some think it many. The reference here is not to the obvious fact that psychology has become fractionated into a multitude of specialized research areas (as, e.g., the still pro-

938

liferating substantive Divisions of the American Psychological Association), or to the bifurcation between "fundamental" and "professional" or applied psychology. What is at issue is the conception of *fundamental* psychology per se, and whether there is any sense in which it can be ordered to *one* characteristic set of phenomena, one method, one "theory," one "paradigm," one emulation model as defined by some other field—however generally any of these matters be conceived. It is the eternal question of the one and the many, viewed against a background of the miniature eternity during which the "one" has been ascendant in the conception of fundamental psychology.

Among the contributors to this volume, the most popular version of the "many" is the "two." Whether the centennial occasion has induced an epidemic susceptibility to the views of the founding father, or perhaps because history is inexorably cyclical, a massive neo-Wundtianism is in the making. *Völkerpsychologie* is being reanimated by contributors in other respects as diverse as Miller, Robinson, Gleitman, Gergen, Toulmin (and his collaborator, Leary), and Blumenthal. But "neo-Wundtianism" is a very general metaphor, and there is much variance in the *details* of the conception of disciplinary status offered by these and other authors. A sense of the *range* of positions regarding the "constitutive problem" may be conveyed by brief reference to the viewpoints offered by the contributors whose primary mission was to address the "Disciplinary Status of Psychology" (Chapters 1 through 4).[2]

Among those authors, George Miller's views are perhaps most representative of so-called "mainstream" psychology. If that be true, the mainstream has undergone an acute deflection of course (at least by the standards of but a few years ago). Miller's admirably terse statement is worthy of the kind of *close* analysis that it cannot receive here. He confesses that psychology is increasingly an "intellectual zoo," and emphasizes that it has increasingly "been pulled in two directions," which "Boring once characterized . . . as its biotropic and sociotropic poles," and which have created "a tension that has persistently frustrated scholars who try to define psychology as a unified discipline." Does this not mean that, as E. O. Wilson (in effect) predicts, "all that is valid in contemporary psychology will eventually be cannibalized either into neurophysiology or into sociobiology"? At this point, Miller is quick to remind us: "Did not Wundt, the founding father, limit experimentation to simple sensory processes and warn us that the higher mental processes can be studied only by historical and naturalistic observation? Is this not the same distinction that now threatens to cannibalize Wundt's science?" Miller's answer to his own rhetorical question is important:

---

[2] Though the summaries of these chapters will be brief, it is distressing that the need to keep the "Afterword" within tight space limits makes it impossible to give comparable attention to the other chapters in this book. Chapters 1 through 4 were selected for special attention here because their authors were given the "keynote" charge of examining the *general* "disciplinary status" of psychology. Many of the chapters dedicated to special fields or intersection areas address this theme in comparable depth—and certainly in no less instructive or stimulating ways.

Well, yes. And then again, no. Yes, because Wundt clearly distinguished between physiological and social psychology. No, because he took the explanation of immediate experience as the subject matter of psychology, and immediate experience is of little concern to either a physiologist or a sociologist. . . .

What happened to the unitary substance of Wundt's psychology? An adequate answer would have to recapitulate the history of the field, but it is not too misleading to say that immediate experience took a back seat to other concerns—to behavior, conditioning, the unconscious, mental testing, and a broad range of professional applications in education, industry, and medicine—leading eventually to the intellectual zoo that we inhabit today.

With all the centrifugal forces presently at work, the real question is not whether psychology is a unified discipline, but why so many psychologists believe it should be. Every large psychology department is today a small college unto itself, with a faculty able to teach a little bit of everything: optics, acoustics, physiology, pharmacology, histology, neuroanatomy, psychiatry, pediatrics, education, statistics, probability theory, computer science, communication theory, linguistics, anthropology, sociology, history, philosophy, logic, and, when time permits, psychology. Does something more than historical accident and administrative convenience hold such an array of talent together?

Obviously, no standard method or technique integrates the field. Nor does there seem to be any fundamental scientific principle comparable to Newton's laws of motion or Darwin's theory of evolution. There is not even any universally accepted criterion of explanation. What is the binding force? (Chapter 1, pp. 41–42)

Having in this way isolated the central quandary of our curious discipline, Miller gratefully falls back upon "faith." "I believe the common denominator is a faith that somehow, some day, someone will create a science of immediate experience." He proceeds in the remainder of his essay to develop the view that "psychologists who adopt consciousness as the constitutive problem of their field need reject little of what passes for psychology today." But Miller's faith, as is indicated by the penultimate sentence of his essay, is not boundless: "Perhaps in the next century we will be able to push the constitutive problem of psychology far enough forward to discover principled limits on our ability to understand ourselves."

Miller's essay sounds an almost perfect keynote relative to the objectives of this book. It defines in archetypal vividness and concision most of the issues around which the infinitely shaded turmoils of the current phase of psychology's identity quest are polarized. And it projects—again in an archetypal way—one of the happiest commonalities of this study: a quality of undogmatic civility, responsible tentativeness, that has rarely been conspicuous in the history of our field.

Among our discussants of "disciplinary status," the person whose views are in sharpest opposition to those of Miller is Daniel Robinson (Chapter 3). Robinson returns to Aristotle in an endeavor to show the principled impossibility of a scientific psychology. The distinction between reason and cause implicit in Aristotle's analysis of causality—and developed in a long philosophical and humanistic

940

tradition culminating in the recent work of philosophers of mind—leads him to the conclusion that we are confronted with the alternatives of a nonscientific but *significant* psychology (e.g., "folk-psychology," idiographic analysis using contextually appropriate methods, disciplined armchair psychology, etc.), *or* a scientific *nonpsychology* (as, e.g., physiological psychology), the value of which last he does not derogate.

He uses a version of Hempel's "covering-law" analysis of scientific explanation—which requires the derivability of natural phenomena from universal laws that are both true and symmetric (i.e., time independent in respect to the predictions that they mediate)—as a demarcation criterion for "natural science." But human actions can be defined only in terms of reasons (or other intentional categories) and "the actual and the logical connections between reasons and actions are not the same as those obtaining between causes and effects." Nor can objectivistic behavioral indices of mental events permit their inference—for such indices, as physically specified, are inherently equivocal. What is called "physiological psychology," on the other hand, conforms to the logic of causality, is subsumable under a covering law model of explanation, but is *not* psychology. There is an implication, however, that this acceptably scientific form of "nonpsychology" is of relevance to psychology in the sense that there is a determinable *contingent* relationship between physiological and psychological processes, though the latter can in no intelligible sense be reduced to the former. It is clear that Robinson would perceive most of the mainstream experimental psychology that has been pursued over the last hundred years to have been a form of imitation science: a method-dominated evasion of significant psychological problems in the interests of implementing a succession of misconstrued versions of natural science.

Amedeo Giorgi, perhaps the senior phenomenological psychologist in this country, points (Chapter 2)—more agonizingly than anyone in the group—to the circumstance that "psychology's disciplinary status is ambiguous at best and chaotic at worst." He instructively apposes three quotations, the first from the British psychologist-philosopher, G.H. Lewes in 1879, and the remaining two from J.R. Kantor and an anonymous contributor to the *Psychological Record* in 1979. Both Lewes and his two successors decry with some passion the inability of psychology to establish itself as a natural science. Giorgi notes that "one could easily reverse the dates of these. . . descriptions and find" them "equally applicable." He readily acknowledges the conceptual, philosophic, research, and professional fractionation of the "discipline." But he cannot accept it that coherence of subject matter, method, and objective is precluded *in principle*.

Giorgi's attempt to provide a basis of coherence is especially resistent to summary, for adequate appreciation even of the full text requires some knowledge of the phenomenological tradition. (Zaner's discussion of that tradition in Chapter 26 could provide some of the relevant background.) Giorgi bases his proposals on the view that psychological "phenomena are not comprehensible by means of concepts

941

derived from things, where the natural sciences are at home, nor by means of categories derived from pure ideas, where philosophy reigns supreme." In this view, psychology "introduces us to a range of phenomena that are different from and prior to natural science and philosophy"; thus, "original description of and reflection on our own phenomena" of a sort involving "a minimum number of preconceptions" (i.e., via phenomenological bracketing) is necessary for the correct grasping of "the essence of behavior and experience and their variations."

Such reflection reveals that the "psychological" is bounded: it falls into a zone "between the biological and the logical." The "logical" and related conceptualizations characterized by universality and transparency constitute, in phenomenological thought, "pure idealizations" which "escape the psychological as such, although psychological infrastructures would be presupposed." Within this zone, the "proper object of psychology," which could provide the basis of a coherent discipline, is identified by Giorgi as *expressivity* or "how organisms or persons express themselves in situations." For him, this term is "comprehensive enough to include" both the "commonality" and the "differences" of the three chief competitors for the definition of psychology's object: consciousness, experience, and behavior. In the course of Giorgi's further discussion, "expressivity" becomes tantamount to "the coherent subjective patterning of an objective situation by an individual person or organism."

My own contribution to the theme of "disciplinary status" (Chapter 4) bears mainly on an *explanation* of why psychology has so long embraced its consoling myth of natural science rigor and systematicity—under which aegis it has often proceeded to liquidate its subject matter. But the essay does briefly summarize a conception of the "psychological studies" that I have developed extensively in other sources. Psychology, in this view, "is not a single or coherent discipline but, rather, a collectivity of studies of varied cast, some few of which may qualify as science, while most *do not*."

My *positive* proposal has the merit of what I take to be the clear verdict of 100 years of ardent effort to explore the hypothesis that psychology can be a coherent discipline conformable to any apt construal of the objectives and stratagems of natural science. I suggest that the *noncohesiveness* of psychology finally be acknowledged by replacing it with some such locution as "the psychological studies." These, "if they are really to address the historically constituted objectives of psychological thought, must range over an immense and disorderly spectrum of human activity and experience." Moreover, "problems must be approached with humility, methods must be contextual and flexible, and anticipations of synoptic breakthrough held in check."

The intricate fractionation of theoretical perspectives, foundational philosophies, methods, research interests that has taken place in the century-long pursuit of coherent scientific status is *not* corrigible. There are principled limits upon coherence in *any* sense of that term—nor is such a circumstance regrettable. Psychology has long paid lip service to the complexity and tenuousness of the events in its domain, but in practice has failed to respect the circumstances that (more often than not) they are "multiply determined, ambiguous in their human meaning, polymorphous, contextually environed or embedded in complex and vaguely bounded ways, evanescent and labile in the extreme. This entails obvious constraints upon the task of the inquirer and limits upon the knowledge that can be unearthed." Different theorists will—relative to their different objectives and perspectives—"make asystematically different perceptual cuts upon the 'same' domain. They will identify 'variables' of markedly different grain and meaning contour, selected and linked on different principles of grouping." As a result, different universes of discourse will be established, even if loose ones. Universes of discourse are not (by definition) intertranslatable, nor do they form layers in a logical layer cake: they are just different. I have buttressed this position by developing in other sources (e.g., Koch, 1976) an analysis of the lexical aspect of language which shows that the very processes of definition and word use, whether in natural or technical languages, renders perspective-dependent incommensurabilities and mismatches inevitable in efforts to order psychological (and indeed, other) phenomena by linguistic means.

It is patent that psychology would follow a different course depending on which one of the four analysts of disciplinary status were granted papal authority. But it is not clear *how* different. There are radical differences in the detail of each of the proposals, but there are also some obvious overarching agreements. Though these four essays define no clear-cut coordinate system within which the positions of *all* contributors may be located, it is possible to discern subgroupings of appreciable numbers of the contributors whose positions bear family resemblances to the four points of view just summarized. But even taken by themselves, these four perspectives bear ample testimony to a degree of ferment concerning the disciplinary status of psychology which has been unrivaled throughout most of the twentieth century.

Other chapters which have an especially salient bearing on the *general* "constitutive problem" are those by Henle, Kendler, Rosenzweig, Gibson, McGuire, Gergen, Toulmin and Leary, Zaner, Alston, Pribram, and Chorover.

3. Doubts Concerning the Putative "Independence" of Psychology from Philosophy

We have already stressed that the significance of Wundt's founding of the Leipzig laboratory was soon absorbed into the stereotype that Wundt had launched a "new" psychology—a conception of psychology as "an independent, experimental science." That phrase has echoed throughout the twentieth century as a kind of taken-for-granted constitution edict for the large institutional apparatus that psychology soon acquired, and as *definitive* of both the intent and the reality of the activities environed by that apparatus.

The adjective *independent* has, through most of the twentieth century, been taken to mean "independent from philosophy." That condition has never, in fact, obtained. The late-nineteenth-century psychologists were certainly explicit about their philosophic presuppositions—sometimes too generously so. The psychologists of the early-twentieth-century "schools" (circa 1900–1925) conducted their incessant debates as much in metaphysical and epistemological terms as in psychological ones. But no statement in the history of psychology proved more prophetic than Watson's, when, in 1913, he said in reference to "time honored relics of philosophical speculation," that "I should like to bring my students up in the same ignorance of such hypotheses as one finds among the students of other branches of science" (Watson, 1913, p. 166). Within a few years students were quite generally being brought up in that way. One of the weird sequelae of the antiphilosophical ideology thereby consolidated has been noted in the "Foreword": during the 1930–1960 Age of Theory, when psychologists were accepting their marching orders from a highly tendentious philosophy (logical positivism) with more uniformity and gusto than during any period of its "first" century, the battle cry of "independence from philosophy" was proclaimed with comparable vigor!

Against such a background, it is worth noting that it would be hard to find a contributor to this volume unapprised that the study of mind, experience, action, behavior (or any other "dependent variable" category associated with psychology) is *necessarily* the most philosophy-sensitive enterprise in the gamut of scholarship. Our problems, concepts, terminology, questions have grown out of the history of philosophy; and any position, theory, model, procedural decision, research strategy, or lawlike statement that we assert presupposes philosophical commitments. For special awareness—and stimulating consideration—of such issues, see the chapters by Miller, Giorgi, Robinson, Gibson, de Rivera, Gleitman, Crosson, Loevinger, Elkind, Sanford, McGuire, Gergen, Toulmin and Leary, Zaner, Alston, Pribram, Glickman, Blumenthal, Arnheim, Chorover, Braginsky, MacIntyre, Barzun, Kaufmann, and Sewell.

4. Reanalysis of the Role and Range of Application of Experimental Method

This trend is a clear corollary of matters addressed in "trend 2" concerning "disciplinary status." The stereotype of psychology as homogeneously experimental in its methods in respect to all problems throughout its range has borne no relation to the facts at any point in this century. Literally construed, this would rule out *most* of what psychologists actually do (e.g., all fields, or parts of fields, which depend on naturalistic or historical description, on phenomenal analysis, conceptual analysis, case study, statistically "controlled" observation, "rational" mathematical modeling, test and factorial theory, and so on). What the stereotype actually implies is a *disdain* for nonexperimental method—a sense that such methods are "soft" and inimical to the development of rigorous theories or models.

But it is also possible to argue something like the reverse position: that experimentation, in anything like its strict natural science sense, may be significantly applicable only in delimited areas—the unarguable ones being sensory and physiological psychology, and the more problematic if feasible ones being such "process areas" (whether in whole or in part) as perception, cognition, learning, motivation, etc. Because of the "openness" of the systems dealt with and on other grounds, it may be argued that many laboratory studies—even in the process areas (and more certainly in "complex" fields like social psychology, personology, aesthetics)—are but simulacra of strict natural science experiment, and lead, whether in practice or principle, to distorted, trivial, nongeneralizable, or artifactual findings. Moreover, philosophical and moral objections may be raised against the "use" of human subjects even in experiments involving stresses upon mind or body that may seem innocuous relative to the independent variable "manipulations" deemed permissible in respect to animals.

Debate—occasionally passionate but often desultory—on such issues has taken place throughout the century, but has become almost epidemic in recent years. The essays in this volume certainly suggest that epidemic to be intensifying! This would be evident if only from the emergence of the large number of *Völkerpsychologie*-like positions to which allusion has already been made. Though our neo-Wundtian subgroup of authors certainly conceive the contours of their individual "*Völkerpsychologien*" in different ways, they are at one in resurrecting the distinction between experimental psychology and a psychology of complex intrapersonal, social, and cultural phenomena which can only be pursued by historico-descriptive, phenomenological, and analytic methods of the sort more characteristic of the traditional humanities than the sciences.

But other—and perhaps more fundamental—challenges have been made in this book to mainstream conceptions of the function, feasibility, or appropriateness of experimental method. Robinson, Crosson, Gergen, Zaner, Alston, and MacIntyre imply in their respective chapters that much of psychology must be a matter of *conceptual analysis* of the (often subtle) mental terms and relations which are already in place in the natural language, or of theory-like reanalyses which, while preserving such discriminations, could sharpen and refine them. Giorgi (Chapter 2) and also Zaner (Chapter 26) would see much of the sphere of experimentation displaced by the methods of systematic phenomenology. De Rivera, Loevinger, Elkind, Sanford, and others see a broad role for humble qualitative description and for idiographic methods in general. Toulmin and Leary (Chapter 25)—in the course of their powerful critique of psychology's "cult of empiricism"—encourage

945

informal quasi-experimental study under field conditions (preferably cross-cultural studies such as those of Rosch), and see much work of this character as a precondition to asking significant questions in the laboratory.

In ways consonant with the growing literature on "experimenter effects" and the "social psychology of the psychological experiment," Rosenzweig, Sanford, and others stress the importance of a cooperative, fluently interactive relationship between the investigator and the so-called "subject." Rosenzweig (Chapter 7) would prefer to substitute "experimentee" for "subject," while Sanford (Chapter 21) endorses a form of "action research" or "research encounter" such that a mutually beneficial mode of emotional involvement obtains between "researcher and researched." In similar vein, Zaner (Chapter 26) points out that "*these behaving creatures*, which we seek to take into account, ineluctably *take us into account*," and traces the consequences for psychological research of the "*distinctive mutuality of human life*." It is fair to note that implicit in such positions as the preceding ones is a reconception of the psychological "experiment" or "study" as an *hermeneutic* enterprise, rather than an "objectivistic" one of the sort thought to be definitive of natural science experiment.

Our two social psychologists also advance reconceptions of the function of experiment which are at odds with conventional "logic of science." McGuire (Chapter 24), in advocating a "constructivist" epistemology, sees experiment (and empirical work generally) *not* as a test of a theory but rather as an aid to its construction via the clarification of its latent meanings and its limits. He presumes that typically (at least in social psychology) there will be a plurality of equally "right" theories addressing a given set of phenomena, and that the function of "empirical work" is "to reveal the conditions under which each of the complementary theories obtain." Rather more radically, Gergen (Chapter 23), in developing his "endogenic" assault upon empiricism, sees "research" as bearing neither a corroborative nor an inductive relation to a theory, but as a mode of "vivification": "a means of enhancing the efficacy of theoretical communication." And, for Gergen, a social psychological "theory" is a rational pattern which is not "a 'reflection' of what there is," but " . . a 'transformation' of experience into a linguistic ontology." As such, theory has an "agentive" role which can criticize, guide, or motivate possible modes of social action or organization. Despite differences between McGuire's and Gergen's general positions, they seem to be at one in implying that an experiment can properly be seen as a perspicuous and determinate *illustration* of the import of a theory.

5. Increased Modesty of Objective and of Claimed Accomplishment

This rubric appeared in identical form in the "Epilogue" to Study I of *Psychology: A Study of a Science*. That was in 1959. Why the recurrence?

Commencing in the mid-1950s, it was possible to note a marked decrease in the grandiosity of objective and claimed attainment that had characterized the classic phase of the Age of Theory. Theoretical grandiosity began to contract (regarding intended scope, anticipated predictive richness and specificity, etc.), and both conceptual and methodic options began to diversify. Though some psychologists continued to promote their favored conceptual templates in the messianic spirit of converting the entire psychological community (and, indeed, the world), it was possible, for a decade or so, to discern a new problem-centered modesty on the part of many. These circumstances were clearly registered by the contributors to *Psychology: A Study of a Science,* and were celebratively acknowledged in the editor's "Epilogue."

But, at some point preceding the mid-1960s a strange thing happened. The imagery of the Kuhnian "paradigm" (as noted earlier in this "Afterword") had begun to modulate the still strongly residual Age of Theory epistemology in such a way as to suggest to many that the implementation of the earlier large theoretical objectives was a relatively easy—and largely extraintellectual—matter. If the psychological community could be made to *agree* on a paradigm, then a unitary and progressive science would become inevitable. It was easy to interpret Kuhn's identification of "persuasion," which he intended in a predominantly *rational* sense, as the condition of paradigm acceptance to mean "salesmanship," or perhaps "propaganda." Paradigm promotion became the new form of psychological commerce. Thus commenced a period in which every day saw the propulsion of a brand new paradigm, and every month marked a convention or seminar symposium designed to select a victorious paradigm that would render psychology one and progressive for a tidy stretch of time, if not forever.

Happily, that period is now subsiding. In the past few years it has been possible to derive such an impression from the field at large, but it is rendered conspicuously evident in the pages of this book. A quality of nondefensive professional modesty is manifested by virtually all contributors in a degree rarely, if at all, anticipated in psychology's "first" century. This modesty, tentativeness, openness can be seen in respect to such matters as assessments (explicit or implicit) of the scope and preemptiveness of one's concepts or methods; the generality range and, indeed, the viability of one's research; the feasible objectives of one's field or of psychology generally. What seems to be emerging is an increased ability to live with intellectual tension and doubt—an increased recognition of complexity and limits. All this may be a corollary of the "new" sense of history. But it may point to nothing less than a growing disposition within psychology as a whole to become realigned with the best values of the Western scholarly tradition!

Obviously there are differences among our contributors in the degree to which such saintly attitudes as have just been characterized are manifest. But the variance is much less than might be predicted from one's knowledge of prevailing values within the particular fields that they represent. Areas which are still the bastions of

947

the residual scientism in psychology (e.g., cognitive science, mathematical psychology, biological psychology) are represented by the contributors to this book in modest or liberalized terms—and with a respect for historical antecedents.

Cognitive psychology has certainly in recent years generated a rhetoric of having penetrated the final barricades standing before attainment of some finalist and comprehensive theory of mind, but such optimism is certainly not prominent in Gleitman's (Chapter 17) thoughtful and tentative consideration of problems of "metacognition." Newell (Chapter 16), in chronicling the history of the "cognitive revolution," is confidently perceiving that upheaval to have great promise, but it is significant that he chooses for his major theme the relation between Karl Duncker's brilliant Gestalt-oriented work (of a half-century ago, and little celebrated even in its time) on *thinking*, and major presuppositions of modern information-processing analyses of problem-solving. The philosopher Crosson (Chapter 18) is unhesitantly sympathetic to the value of exploring analogies between cognitive processes and computational transformations as realized by the computer, but is aware of such sharp (if not principled) limits as are posed by the impossibility of any full representation of the "tacit" dimension of knowing (in Polanyi's sense) within a computer program.

Luce's (Chapter 28) masterly and penetrating survey of the principal mathematical strategies pursued in the modeling of perceptual, learning, and cognitive processes over the century is certainly no exercise in specialty-centered chauvinism. He is unrelenting throughout in pointing up limits and failures, and sustains this measured attitude to the very end by concluding on a note of modest, yet undespairing, tentativeness in respect to the future.

Again, there is no trace of specialty-centered grandeur in Glickman's (Chapter 32) admirable isolation of issues (both rational and extrarational) that have beset the history of comparative psychology. And Lacey's lucid discussion (Chapter 31) of the psychophysiology of the autonomic nervous system conceals no skeletons: he sees the field as in a "primitive state," not only because it lacks "development of the underlying basic neurophysiology," but because of the tendency of investigators to neglect the study of "interactions among central and autonomic functions."

Hagen's (Chapter 10) expert and vivid presentation of one of the most important developments in the perception psychology of this century—J.J. Gibson's "ecological" theory—is assuredly partisan; yet it acknowledges areas of mootness in the theory, and generates no rhetoric of "finalism" or completeness. Haber's scholarly discussion (Chapter 11) of recent work on the "six big questions" that he identifies as definitive of perception psychology from its scientific beginnings in the nineteenth century onward is modest and open-ended in attitude throughout.

The traditions stemming from certain of the fields which in the Age of Theory were conspicuously associated with high orders of imperialism and finalism are represented in this book in measured terms.

Kendler (Chapter 6), in his searching analysis of the behaviorist tradition, achieves something like a world record in modesty of allegiance to it by suggesting that of *all* the definitive traits of the historical behaviorisms—to wit: "(1) objectivism, (2) stimulus-response orientation, (3) peripheralism, (4) emphasis on associationistic learning, (5) environmentalism"—only *one* remains viable: "objectivism." Kimble's architectonic article on "Conditioning and Learning" (Chapter 12) is written very much in a "past tense" mood. Catania's (Chapter 13) delineation of the historical circumstances which enforced the isolation of studies of animal from human learning is instructive, and his imaginative suggestions toward an integration of these traditions are put forward in reflective, nonpretentious vein. Mischel's (Chapter 22) sympathy for a "cognitive, social-learning approach" (which can be ordered to the class of current behavior theories that are the descendants of the liberalized "mediation theories" of the late 1950s) is argued with so great a hospitality to the importance of self-regulating intrapersonal factors (e.g., "cognitive-symbolic processes," "self-concept," etc.) that he himself suggests a convergence "with phenomenological viewpoints." Such an attitude is indeed a far cry from the tendentiousness of the Age of Theory.

Bindra (Chapter 14) develops a brilliant rereading of a wide swath of the mainstream research on motivation in terms of his concepts of the "incentive stimulus," and the "central motive state." In so doing, he gives us a hopeful lesson suggesting the possibility that some of the past research which may seem of questionable value when taken in its own terms can acquire substantial significance when reinterpreted by a fertile (yet unpretentious) theoretical mind.

From the evidence of this volume, autistic anticipations of rapid progress in any major field of psychology—or in psychology as a whole—are at lower ebb than at any point in this century. Whether our contributors are more controlled in this respect than are certain of their peers in the fields that they represent is, of course, an open question. But our contributors are non-negligible voices!

6. Serious—Rather than Merely Defensive—Concern with the Human and Social Impact of Psychology

This large issue was raised—in my own terms—at the close of the "Foreword." It bears brief reacknowledgment here as a major trend of this book. The twentieth century has indeed been "the psychological century," and any discipline presuming to give a *scientific* account of the human condition assumes a terrifying responsibility. For, as Alasdair MacIntyre (Chapter 39) points out, psychology has the inherent power of *making itself true*. In addressing its theories of the human condition to its lay beneficiaries, it is necessarily changing that condition. In addressing "technologies" of mitigation, cure or salvation to humanity, it faces the monstrous risks that necessarily supervene when human beings are treated as "objects." Perhaps

Western science has addressed the inanimate universe with similar callousness, but atoms do not perceive their theoretical description, nor do they suffer.

For most of the "first" century, psychologists and psychotechnologists have either sidestepped such issues, or smugly assumed that their armamentarium of "scientific method" *guaranteed* that they could do nothing other than help humankind. In recent decades, there has been growing concern over the consequences of such smugness, both within and outside of psychology. Virtually every prior trend that I have reported suggests that, among our contributors, such concerns are running very high. The two psychologists whose charge it was specifically to address these issues (Chorover, Chapter 37; Braginsky, Chapter 38) mount critiques of psychology's impact on its human clientele which, though brief, have not often been rivalled in severity of judgment and depth of concern.

Coda

The most general import of this book would seem to be that, in large ways, psychology has come full circle in its "first" century. Much of the simplistic scientism which has controlled so large an interval of that century is under question. Indeed, the very conception of the enterprise seems to be undergoing profound alteration. And the dominant quality of the change is a kind of *creative retrogression*. The *intentions* of the pioneers—which had been so largely subverted by the positivistic and other simplifying construals that soon supervened—have been rediscovered. Since action is not fully constrained by rationale, the unbridled expectations spawned by psychology's redefinition as "science" have not precluded solid achievements during its "first" century. But it is especially our failures that have proven instructive. Psychology now seems on the threshold of a period of increased intellectual dignity. It will not conquer the world, but significant fruits are promised because it has largely conquered itself.

REFERENCES

Koch, S. (Ed.) *Psychology: A study of a science* (6 vols.). New York: McGraw-Hill, 1959, 1962, 1963.

Koch, S. Epilogue. In *Psychology: A study of a science* (Vol. 3). New York: McGraw-Hill, 1959.

Koch, S. Language communities, search cells, and the psychological studies. In W. J. Arnold (Ed.), *Nebraska Symposium on Motivation, 1975* (Vol. 23). Lincoln: University of Nebraska Press, 1976.

Miller, N. E. Liberalization of basic S-R concepts. In S. Koch (Ed.), *Psychology: A study of a science* (Vol. 2). New York: McGraw-Hill, 1959.

Watson, J. B. Psychology as the behaviorist views it. *Psychological Review*, 1913, 20, 158–177.

Postscript

THE SECOND CENTURY OF PSYCHOLOGY AT AGE 12 AND THE AMERICAN PSYCHOLOGICAL ASSOCIATION AT AGE 100

SIGMUND KOCH

This Postscript is in recognition of the republication of A *Century of Psychology as Science* by the American Psychological Association (APA) as part of the centennial celebration of its founding. The new release of this book is an appropriate project for the purpose.

The initial basis of the book had been a series of lectures and symposia at the 1979 Annual Convention, sponsored by Divisions 1 (General Psychology) and 24 (Philosophical Psychology) in celebration of the centennial of scientific psychology. The senior editor was president of both Divisions during that year, and David E. Leary served as joint program chairman. At this juncture, it is hardly necessary to note that we had the good fortune of attracting extraordinarily able representatives of a carefully deployed group of fields within psychology and related disciplines. The papers—already brilliant in their initial form—were refined and expanded by their authors into the chapters of this book over several subsequent years. The book was published in 1985, but (to be precise about the historical coverage) the span of most chapters falls a year or two short of that date. (A detailed description of the plan and genesis of the entire project is given in the Introduction, pp. 1–6.)

The present Postscript will be exactly that: a few impressionistic comments about how the trends of the volume have stood up to the tests of the past 10 to 12 years—or, for that matter, vice versa. Even superficial examination of that tiny interval shows that the rate and density of flux have been enormous. It is hard to comprehend that several estimates of the number of "qualified" psychologists in the United States suggest something close to a doubling, while the world population of psychologists has, on the best current estimate, actually doubled. The only way here to address the significance of the mere numbers just cited is to adopt a policy of minimalism—and, with it, a dependence on bold (and therefore rash, therefore idiosyncratic) judgment. Accordingly, I embrace a "first person singular" stance rather more fervently than in the Foreword or Afterword.

In the Foreword, I sought to sketch the institutional development of psychology over the century since its "founding" by Wundt, paying particular attention to its *fin de siècle* institutional status. In the Afterword, I concentrated on substantive and metatheoretical trends of the many contributions to the book. Several of the trends that I emphasized involved attitudinal changes so deep as to challenge the very foundations and scholarly style of our discipline as it had been practiced over its first century. It was possible to believe from these changes that the psychology of the second century would be played in a different key (cf. Afterword, pp. 934–950).

In this Postscript, I shall dwell on (a) the most fundamental of the attitudinal changes just alluded to, those bearing on the Disciplinary Status of Psychology, and consider (b) Institutional Trends Over the Second Century. Finally, I shall offer some glancing comments on (c) Substantive Trends in Fundamental Psychology During the Second Century. Naturally, the fuzzy penumbra of issues surrounding (a) ramifies into (b) and (c).

The Disciplinary Status of Psychology: Circa 1979 and After

In the decade or so preceding A *Century of Psychology as Science*, there had been evidence of an increasing pluralism in conceptions of the disciplinary status of psychology. The testimony added by the book suggested that by 1979, such restiveness was more extensive than during any interval of the preceding 100 years, including even that unsettled period in the first quarter of this century marked by the polemical conflicts of the "Schools." But the pluralism evident in the book was one of search rather than assertiveness, marked by humility, not hubris. The rabid and monolithic scientism that dominated so much of the century seemed almost to have vanished.

Perhaps the outstanding general trend relates to "pluralism" in its ultimate sense: that of the actual conception of our discipline as "plural." Many contributors issued a challenge to the conception that *fundamental* psychology is one field. Among these, some thought it at least two; some thought it many. A massive neo-

Wundtianism seemed in the making in that something akin to a *Völkerpsychologie* was broadly seen as a necessary supplement to whatever kind of fundamental psychology the contributor espoused.

There is no adequate way to convey the range of positions concerning the "constitutive problem" in brief compass. In the Afterword, discussion was largely confined to the initial section of the book (pp. 40–97), which was explicitly given to the Disciplinary Status of Psychology. The contributors to that section were George Miller, Amedeo Giorgi, Daniel Robinson, and Sigmund Koch. At this phase, some overlap with the Afterword becomes unavoidable in that it provides a necessary baseline for many of the second-century trends that will be considered in this Postscript.

Daniel Robinson, in his chapter (pp. 60–74), returned to Aristotle in an endeavor to show the principled impossibility of a scientific psychology. The distinction between reason and cause implicit in Aristotle's analysis of causality led him to conclude that we are confronted with the alternatives of a nonscientific but significant psychology (e.g., "folk psychology," ideographic analysis, disciplined armchair psychology) or a scientific nonpsychology (e.g., physiological psychology, the value of which he did not derogate).

Amedeo Giorgi (pp. 46–59) recognized—perhaps more agonizingly than anyone in the group—the circumstance that "psychology's disciplinary status is ambiguous at best and chaotic at worst." Nevertheless, he could not accept that coherence of subject matter, method, and objective is precluded in principle. By leading the reader over a technical phenomenological route that, though plausible, resists any rapid summary, he arrived at the notion of "expressivity" as the basis of a coherent approach to psychology. This he defined as "the coherent subjective patterning of an objective situation by an individual person or organism."

If George Miller (pp. 40–45) be thought more representative of "mainstream" psychology than the other contributors to this section, one must conclude that the mainstream had undergone an acute deflection of course. Miller's vivid characterization of the "centrifugal forces" within psychology is worthy of requotation:

> With all the centrifugal forces presently at work, the real question is not whether psychology is a unified discipline, but why so many psychologists believe it should be. Every psychology department is today a small college unto itself, with the faculty able to teach a little bit of everything: optics, acoustics, physiology, pharmacology, histology, neuroanatomy, psychiatry, pediatrics, education, statistics, probability theory, computer science, communication theory, linguistics, anthropology, sociology, history, philosophy, logic, and, when time permits, psychology. Does something more than historical accident and administrative convenience hold such an array of talent together?
>
> Obviously, no standard method or technique integrates the field. Nor does there seem to be any fundamental, scientific principle comparable to Newton's laws of

motion or Darwin's theory of evolution. There is not even any universally accepted criterion of explanation. What is the binding force? (pp. 41–42)

Miller prefers to believe that "the common denominator is a faith that somehow, someday, someone will create the science of immediate experience"—that "psychologists who adopt consciousness as the constitutive problem of their field need reject little of what passes for psychology today" (p. 42). Nevertheless this faith is not boundless: "Perhaps in the next century we will be able to push the constitutive problem of psychology far enough forward to discover principled limits on our ability to understand ourselves" (p. 45).

Rather than attempting to convey the intricacies of my own contribution (pp. 75–97) to the "disciplinary status" segment of the book, I will state in bold outline the gist of an analysis that I have been pursuing in print for 23 years, and more privately—though I think it was reflected in a 1961 *American Psychologist* article (Koch, 1961)—for many previous years. I might as well say now that initially I was either ignored or treated as a combined micro-moron and psychopath for entertaining such an analysis. And I might as well anticipate the fact that *now* my position is seen as conservative and simplemindedly tolerant by a substantial number of persons who wish to "deconstruct" traditional (i.e., "pre-postmodern") psychology or trash it via some other pre- or post-structuralist formula.

Since 1969, I have argued that psychology is misconceived when seen as a coherent science or as any kind of coherent discipline devoted to the empirical study of human beings. Psychology, in my view, is not a single discipline but a collectivity of studies of varied cast, some few of which may qualify as science, while most do not. I imply nothing invidious in the distinction between the former and latter classes of studies. I have recommended the desirability of supplanting the term *psychology* by *the psychological studies*, but did not expect to prevail!

The 19th-century belief that psychology can be an integral discipline (which led to its institutionalization as an independent science) has been disconfirmed on every day of the 112 years since its presumptive "founding." When the details of that history are attended to, the patent tendency has been toward theoretical and substantive fractionation (and increasing insularity among the "specialities"), not integration. Moreover, there are many *principled* considerations that underline the futility of seeking theoretical, conceptual, or even paradigmatic unification.

The conceptual ordering devices, technical languages, open to the various psychological studies are—like all human modes of cognitive organization—perspectival, sensibility-dependent relative to the inquirer, and often noncommensurable. Such incommensurabilities will frequently obtain not only between "contentually" different psychological studies, but between perspectivally different orderings of the "same" domain. Characteristically, psychological events are multiply determined, ambiguous in their human meaning, polymorphous, contextually environed or embedded in complex and vaguely bounded ways, evanescent, and labile in the extreme. This entails some obvious constraints upon the task of the inquirer and limits upon the knowledge that he or she can hope to unearth. Different theorists will—relative to their different analytical purposes, predictive or practical aims, perceptual sensitivities, metaphor-forming capacities, preexisting discrimination repertoires—make asystematically different cuts upon the same domain. They will identify variables of markedly different grain and meaning contour, selected and linked on different principles of grouping. The cuts, variables, concepts, that is, will in all likelihood establish different universes of discourse, even if they are loose ones.

Because of the immense range of the psychological studies, different areas of study will bear affinities to different members of the broad groupings of inquiry as historically conceived: fields like sensory, physiological (or broadly, neuroscience-oriented) psychology may certainly be regarded as solidly within the family of the biological and, in some reaches, natural sciences. But psychologists must finally accept the circumstance that extensive and important regions of psychological study require modes of inquiry (and correlative researcher sensibilities and training backgrounds) rather more like those of the humanities than the sciences. And among these latter, I would include important sectors of areas traditionally considered fundamental (e.g., perception, cognition, motivation and learning), as well as such obviously more rarified fields as social psychology, psychopathology, personology, aesthetics, and the analysis of "creativity."

I have buttressed this position by developing in other sources (e.g., Koch, 1976) an analysis of the lexical aspect of language which shows that the very processes of definition and word use, whether in natural or technical languages, render perspective-dependent incommensurabilities and mismatches inevitable in efforts to order psychological (and indeed, other) phenomena by linguistic means.

It is fair to say that views similar to those just sampled have become something like a majority stance over the dozen years of our second century. The integration, integrability, coherence, or unity of psychology—whether as a scientific or some kind if *sui generis* discipline—has been questioned in so many ways that one might raise second-order questions concerning the integrability of the critiques!

The coherence of the increasingly differentiating subfields of fundamental psychology has been broadly questioned. Coherence of the almost nondenumerable congeries of *applied* interest-areas would be maintained by no one. Few could any longer argue for some systematic or clear-cut distinction between all fundamental and applied areas. And the questioning has been at levels ranging from theoretical through paradigmatic to methodic integrability. Furthermore, many would raise questions as to whether any of the traditionally discriminated fields of psychology are in fact "one field." Even the newest and most fashionable of the fields with integrating intentions—"cognitive science"—increasingly shows signs of fuzzy boundaries and fuzzy internal relations that cannot be wholly rationalized via the resources of "fuzzy logic."

At the 1991 Annual Convention of the American Psychological Association, such pluralistic attitudes as have just been summarized were broadly manifested. Indeed, in reporting the convention, the *Chronicle of Higher Education* of September 10, 1991 (Staff, *Chronicle of Higher Education*, 1991) observed that "several scholars here said that they had come to agree with Mr. Koch that psychology should be replaced by the term 'psychological studies' to indicate the diverse and sometimes divisive nature of the field." Even *that* degree of coherence is something I had never anticipated!

In the sequel, there will be many occasions for more particularized reference to trends bearing on disciplinary status.

Institutional Trends Over the Second Century Through Age 12

In the Foreword (pp. 7–35), I sought to discuss the background and meaning of the "founding legend," to trace a little of the developmental line of Wundt's foundling, and, most of all, to portray the startling contrast between "Wundt's creature" at age zero and age 100. The essay intertwines substantive observations with numerical estimates of the size, professional interest distribution, and other characteristics of the psychological work force both in the United States and internationally. Such estimates (however soft: Population statistics is more like abstract expressionism than a science) can be revealing in their bearing on such analyses of disciplinary status as I have reported and can also be ampliative in interesting ways.

In this slender Postscript, I will supplement the rather detailed 1979 analyses (cf. pp. 20–22 and 26–32) with but a few vivid figures and impressionistic generalities concerning the status as of circa 1991. May I here acknowledge the assistance of Pat Miyamoto and others at the American Psychological Association who provided me with masses of facts and figures. John Hogan, who was then (1991) collaborating with Virginia Sexton on *International Psychology: Views From Around the World*, and Mark Rosenzweig, who in 1991 had commenced his presidency of the International Union of Psychological Science (IUPsyS), also provided indispensable help. The Sexton and Hogan book and the results of the survey of member societies of IUPsyS directed in 1991 by Mark Rosenzweig are now generally available (cf. Sexton & Hogan, 1992; Rosenzweig, 1992).

The Size of the Community

By the early 1980s, it was clear that psychology comprised one of the largest groupings within contemporary scholarly-cum-professional areas. Mark Rosenzweig's 1982 estimate of the total number of psychologists in the world (based on 1980 IUPsyS data) was 260,000 (Rosenzweig, 1982). Exactly a month before I gave a paper at the August 1991 American Psychological Association Convention that anticipated the present Postscript, he telephoned to notify me, in an awestruck voice, that the estimate which had just emerged from the then current IUPsyS survey was 500,000. Both of these figures include knowledgeable but uncertain estimates of the ratios of psychologists in each of the component-countries who meet the criteria for membership in their national societies, but who are not members.

These figures are soft, but even if "off" by a substantial factor, are both poignant and challenging in their implications. A world that has been undergoing perhaps the most dramatic political reorientations in modern history, and one beset by social dislocations, economic uncertainties, and environmental challenges of almost unprecedented magnitude is apparently turning to psychologists (and other presumed experts on aberrations of the human condition) for help. We seem to be thriving on *their* despair. What an awesome obligation!

But we are celebrating the centennial of the APA. The total membership in 1892 was 42. In 1979, it was approaching 50,000, and in 1990, the total was 70,266. The rate of growth of the APA was phenomenal from its inception until quite recently. Between 1972 and 1982 there was a seemingly sizeable increase (61%), but this was the smallest rate of growth, by decade, until that period. Between 1982 and 1990 the increase has been 29%—which pretty well ensures that the current decade will show the smallest rate of increase in history. Nevertheless, it is all too obvious that, relative to the membership levels of recent years, a 29%-plus increase is, in absolute terms, still formidable. And it should be noted that the figures just considered are for membership defined in a fairly strict sense: members and Fellows plus associates. In recent years, the APA has often advertised membership totals which include affiliates, of which there are three categories: students, high school teachers, and affiliated foreign psychologists. The total membership, on this basis, has been stated as 114,000 for 1992!

It is more difficult, however, to gauge the current total number of psychologists in the United States. Rosenzweig had estimated that in 1980, the total number of psychologists in the combined United States and Canadian work force was 106,000 (cf. Foreword, pp. 26–29). Available figures for the total as of the last 2 to 3 years vary widely. Pat Miyamoto suggests (personal communication, July 25, 1991) that, as of June 1990, there were some 22,000 doctoral-level and/or licensed psychologists who did *not* belong to the APA. This last figure, when added to the concurrent membership of the APA, yields 92,000 psychologists with PhD or comparable-level professional degrees. But these figures omit the many categories of MA psychologists who have been finding employment in an accelerating variety of contexts.

Jessica Kohout of the APA estimated (personal communication, August 1991), on the basis of data that seemed quite plausible, that the number of all MA and

PhD/PsyD psychologists was 183,000. It is hard to resist the conclusion that the number of "qualified" (or at least employable) psychologists in the United States has almost doubled at this early phase of our second century! Despite this, there is a general sense, shared by Dr. Kohout, that the *rate* of growth in the number of qualified psychologists in the United States has slowed and that this trend will continue.

Trends Regarding Fractionation–Integration

In 1979, there were 36 specialty-centered Divisions in the APA. As of 1991 there are 47. It would be overly literal to spell out the names of all 47 in this Postscript, but one can wonder whether any large number of its readers have actually read the full list of APA Divisions. I had not—at least for a long time. Let me tempt the reader by merely listing the 1978 to 1991 Divisions:

37. Child and Youth Services (1978; changed to Child, Youth and Family Services in 1982)
38. Health Psychology (1978)
39. Psychoanalysis (1980)
40. Clinical Neuropsychology (1980)
41. Psychology and the Law (1981; changed to the American Psychology-Law Society in 1984)
42. Psychologists in Independent Practice (1982)
43. Family Psychology (1985)
44. The Society for the Psychological Study of Lesbian and Gay Issues—a Division of the APA (1985)
45. The Society for the Psychological Study of Ethnic Minority Issues (1986)
46. Media Psychology (1986)
47. Exercise and Sport Psychology (1986)
48. Peace Psychology (1990)
49. Group Psychology and Group Psychotherapy (1991)

NOTE: All Divisional numbers after 11 are inflated by two in that two divisional titles designate "vacant" membership. The "slots" remain, but the original members re-formed in Divisions bearing other names.

Should the gallant reader now look up the names of the preceding 34 (actual) Divisions and experience the inevitable onset-aura of existential hypervertigo, there is an easy remedy! Telephone for a representative of one of the many new *non*-APA specialist organizations: The Society for the Unification of Psychology (formerly entitled, I believe, Society for a Single Paradigm in Psychology). It actually exists.

I have not even tried to make an accounting of the new non-APA societies serving specialized interests and ranging in size from a few dozen to the already mammoth American Psychological Society, which, though it commenced only in 1989, numbered 13,000 members by 1992. For a few examples of smaller organizations, be it known that during the initial 2 days of the 1991 APA Convention in San Francisco (August 16–20, 1991), there concurrently took place the first meeting of the Society for Chaos Theory in Psychology, while in Rome, August 4–8 saw the 13th International Congress of Onto-Psychology—which group may (or may not) have little sympathy for the Society for Quantitative Research in Psychoanalysis.

In parallel with these divisional and societal differentiations, there has been, during the 12 years of the second century, an impressive expansion of the mental health, governmental, business and industrial, public interest, legal, and other contexts in which psychological interests have found new homes. An example is the aforementioned practitioner field of *clinical neuropsychology*, which became a Division in 1980, and which by 1989 had over 2,200 members!

Finally, I will note only in passing the immense increase during our second century of the periodical literature bearing on specialized (and in some few cases, generalist) interests within psychology. This reflection of the increasing fractionation of psychology is evident in new American publications and also internationally. Once again, an example symbolic of the trend may be more suggestive than comprehensive numbers. But a few weeks ago, I received a tabloid-sized flyer from the Haworth Press, Inc. of Binghamton, New York. It announced the addition to its 1992 list of "Seven New Journals for CLINICAL PRACTITIONERS." Three of these (the *Journal of Couples Therapy*, the *Journal of Family Psychotherapy*, and the *Journal of Gay and Lesbian Psychotherapy*) were sufficiently far along to permit the inclusion of representative "rave reviews." These seven additions complement the "established" Haworth list, which had already comprised 30 journals! It is no doubt a mark of overspecialism on my part, but I had never heard of the Haworth Press or any of its 37 journals. For a large part of my professional career, "the literature" consisted of less than a dozen APA journals, the Murchison-initiated journals, and a handful of independents such as the *American Journal of Psychology* and *Character and Personality*, plus a few foreign periodicals that virtually no one read. Currently, the APA publishes 28 journals—nine less than Haworth addresses to a single sector of the far-ranging psychological studies.

Fundamental Versus Implemental Psychology

I prefer the term *fundamental* versus *implemental* to *pure* versus *applied*, which distinction does not reflect the asystematically varied character of "the" theoretical versus "the" applicational components of specific formulations within any large area of inquiry. And the "academic research versus practitioner" distinction is even more misleading: It has too often segregated rather different combinations of fields.

In the Foreword to this book, I told the story of the sweeping realignment, over the century, of the proportion of psychologists pursuing fundamental as against implemental objectives. It is suggestive to note that through 1940, approximately 70% of the PhDs granted in U.S. psychology were in the traditional fundamental areas. Stapp, Fulcher, Nelson, Pallak, and Wicherski (1981) estimated from employment trends among the circa 45,000 members of the APA in 1978 that the ratio of pure to applied psychologists was 1:4. But if one uses a criterion of fundamental psychology prevalent for most of the century among those who think themselves basic scientists (which translates into specialty categories of Stapp et al. as experimental psychology, physiological psychology, comparative psychology, cognitive psychology, and psycholinguistics), the ratio becomes 1:8.

Some recent data made available to me by the APA contrast many characteristics of practitioner-psychologists versus the academic research grouping on the basis of the 54,500 registrants in the 1989 Annual Directory. Of these, the academic research grouping constituted 13,500—which yields an academic research–practitioner ratio of 1:3. But the breakdown by fields for the academic research group suggests that substantially less than half the group pursue areas traditionally considered fundamental. It is possible to derive a fundamental–implemental ratio vaguely in the area of 1:10. Much other evidence suggests a lower ratio.

Perhaps more significant are trends that may be derived from data concerning the annual number, and the subfield distribution of new PhDs. The totals of PhDs granted had become roughly constant at circa 3,000 during 1978 to 1980. From Stapp's (1981) analysis of National Science Foundation (NSF) figures for the average annual percentage of change for 13 subfields for the interval 1970–1980, it can be inferred that in the half-decade 1975–1980, the average annual growth rate was 6.8% in the implemental areas, but had become *negative* at −5.7% in the fundamental areas. Similar analyses bearing on the last decade suggest that this decline has gone further, even though there has been a slight annual increase in the total number of degrees granted.

To this summary of PhD patterns, it must be added that the growth in "health service provider" personnel has been augmented significantly by the PsyD programs of the constantly increasing number of professional schools of psychology. In recent years, the number of PsyD degrees granted per annum has hovered around 1,000.

Psychology in International Perspective

This could be (indeed has been) the theme of several books. Here, but a few sentences!

From an early point in the century until the end of World War II, psychology had been but thinly institutionalized in most countries other than the United States. Though American psychology fed, throughout this period, largely on European ideas, the U.S. dominance in psychological *activity* was overwhelming. It was, however, possible to conclude by the end of our first century that American dominance had begun to wane. In 1982, Mark Rosenzweig was able to report that IUPsyS, which had been founded in 1951, had achieved by 1970 a total of 56,000 members representing 36 component societies, and by 1980 had grown to over 100,000 members and 44 societies. I have already noted that, by making guesses concerning the number of psychologists in each country who are not members of their national organizations, he estimated the 1980 world population at 260,000— and that he believes the current world population to be some 500,000.

As one might expect, his figures for 1980 show an extraordinarily uneven deployment of psychologists around the world. Nevertheless, the breakdown by region showed Western Europe with 78,000 psychologists to be not far behind the aggregate for the United States and Canada. Latin America, with 45,000 psychologists, had the third-largest regional work force. The data from the 1991 survey of IUPsyS (Rosenzweig, 1992) suggest that the number of psychologists in Western Europe has again doubled. This would put that region on something like a par with the presumptive U.S. population of psychologists. The rate of growth in Western Europe over the past 20 years has been greater than in our country. It does, however, show signs of slowing down in the highly industrialized countries.

Of course, the training and occupational patterns vary greatly from country to country, but it is fair to say that virtually everywhere, clinical, school, counseling, and other forms of practitioner psychology occupy the majority of the work force.

Estimates of "densities" or rates of psychologists per million of population (cf. Rosenzweig, 1982) show that already in 1980 there were at least five (primarily small, progressive, welfare-oriented) countries with densities greater than our own. And Sexton and Hogan's recently estimated densities (1992) from some societies (e.g., Spain, Belgium, Finland, Switzerland, and Israel) show even greater disparities with the United States than were evident in 1980.

More important than the numerical trends is that extra-U.S. world psychology no longer can be thought by anyone to be a province of American psychology. European and British conceptual and theoretical predilections have increasingly diverged from our own. Though we were always dependent on the older world for many of our ideas, we now acknowledge this, and indeed have become witting importers of European trends.

Concerns Regarding Institutional Trends

There are many fears in the air concerning some of the matters I have addressed and some that I have not. There is fear that significant numbers of fundamental psychologists have been resigning from the APA, that opportunities for academic positions are slowing down, that there are decreasing numbers of undergraduate majors in psychology, that the field enlists an insufficient proportion of undergraduate men, that overall university employment will continue to drop over the coming decade, and many other concerns. The evidence on which some of these fears are founded seems to me to be ambiguous. Other fears may be just.

What should be emphasized is that the fears generally expressed during the past few years have rarely been related to the extraordinarily problematic changes that have been sweeping the world during much of the past decade. I happen to be writing these lines on January 1, 1992. With half the world facing the instability occasioned by its effort to reinvent democracy, and the other half striving to recapture democracy from those who confuse it with selective governmental concern for the welfare of citizens, the near-range future seems both hazardous and unpredictable. The forces leading to this situation have, thus far, sparked needs in many countries for an expansion and diversification of remedial human services, whether at individual, group, or organizational levels. Psychology, especially implemental psychology, has been perceived as responsive to these needs—and much of the growth that I have reported has been both invited and subsidized by agencies that have become increasingly embattled in recent years and that soon may be even more sorely tested. At some early point, the cost of the "remedial" services required by the pressures I have tried to define may prove too great.

The fact remains that psychology has grown far more rapidly than any field in this century. Perhaps it is well that it is slowing down, and, in some ways, changing course. And it seems also to be the case that, even in these hard times, there has thus far been minimal unemployment in our field.

Some Substantive Trends in Fundamental Psychology During the Second Century

In the Afterword, I noted that since circa 1960, when psychology had begun to drift away from the neobehavioristic cum neopositivistic premises of what I had called "The Age of Theory" (cf. Koch, 1959a, pp. 729–788), there had been a marked realignment in the relative glamour of major areas of fundamental psychology. Cognition, perception, psycholinguistics, developmental psychology, and biological psychology (in the sense comprehending sensory and physiological psychology) had become "the most influential" fields. And I added that if any one discipline was perceived as the basic field, it was certainly cognitive psychology— and especially that form of it marked off by "cognitive science." Nevertheless, I noted that no field, or family of concepts, commanded anything like the breadth of allegiance that did S-R learning theory during the Age of Theory. And, indeed, workers in each of these "glamour" fields tended to diagnose their own field as the principal repository of wisdom. Moreover, *within* each of the fields of fundamental psychology, diversity of viewpoint was about as great as the differences *across* them.

962

The situation at the present time is approximately the same. There has been substantial progress in all these fields, and changing conceptual fashions in some, but the typical worker in all fields of fundamental psychology is perhaps even more problem-oriented and less imperialistic than ever before. Naturally, every field retains a few prophets who will go rather far on public occasions. A recent instance may be found in the address by Herbert Simon to the 1991 national convention of the American Psychological Society (cf. Staff, *APS Observer*, 1991), in which the achieved explanatory range of cognitive science theories was represented as "tremendous,"while their explanatory power was seen to be virtually as rigorous as that of any area of physical science theory. Obviously, Dr. Simon "has a right"—but most members of his own discipline are not likely to go that far.

It requires a fool's courage to address the recent history of cognitive science in a few paragraphs. Within the dozen or so years at issue, the most conspicuous development has been the increasing interest in models of the "parallel distributed processing" or "connectionist" variety, which seek to formalize neural networks, sometimes in ways that try to be responsive to actual neurophysiological knowledge.

Estes, in his informative and characteristically noninflated 1991 *Annual Review* article on "Cognitive Architectures," points out that "in the connectionist approach learning is not viewed as a subsidiary problem to be left for consideration after the big problems are taken care of, but, rather, is a major aspect of the cognitive system from the start. For an investigator who grew up scientifically in the Golden Age of Learning Theory this renewed emphasis on learning is a welcome development" (Estes, 1991a, p. 16). Nevertheless, he notes (p. 23) that "all is not smooth going for connectionistic models." For instance, "they may prove unable to maintain several clusters of successively acquired memories simultaneously and therefore exhibit massive interference effects on recognition or recall tests." And, in concluding, he remarks: "Architecture or architectures? I think pluralism gets the nod, certainly for the present and quite possibly for a long way into the future" (p. 25).

From my view, Estes just about says it all. His remarks are generally (perhaps flagrantly) confirmed in two recent compendia—a three-volume *An Invitation to Cognitive Science*" (Osherson, Lasnik, Kosslyn, Hollerbach, & Smith, 1990) and Posner's (1989) *Foundations of Cognitive Science*—in which the recurrent concern is the actual and/or potential unity versus fractionation of cognitive science taken as a whole. These works, along with Newell's presentation of his SOAR Architecture in the book *Unified Theories of Cognition* (1990), are intelligently reviewed in the September 1991 issue of *Psychological Science*. The editor of that journal is, of course, the redoubtable William K. Estes, who, in a prologue to these reviews states: "Rarely has a label so lacking in any clear referent as cognitive science risen so meteorically to the top level of visibility in psychology" (Estes, 1991b, p. 282). The reviewers (and contributors to the multiauthored volumes) confirm this statement hyperabundantly. Not only is the coherence of the field questioned from extravagantly varied incidences, but its large contour is seen as increasingly indeterminate. The relations of the field to artificial intelligence (AI), however ambiguous they may have seemed in the past, can now be seen as virtually unspecifiable.

The important area of psychology associated with **neuroscience** has continued on its revolutionary redefinition of neural and neuropsychological processes at an impressive pace. Dominant recent concerns have been with "neuronal gating," and real-world studies of "neural nets" (some of which latter, however, seek interfacing with the conceptual neural nets of cognitive science). The long-range interest in neurotransmitters has continued to grow.

If anything deserves the right to be called a revolution, it is the revolution in our conception of the central nervous system in the post–World War II era! Yet the field is facing constraints by the anti–animal research movement, which could severely inhibit further progress, or even—as apparently has almost happened in the United Kingdom—shut it down (cf. Hubel, 1991). I find it difficult myself to take a smug position on this issue, having done, many years ago, rat-behavior research of which I am not proud. And yet . . . !

Much of the work in "classical" areas of experimental psychology has been taking place in the ambience of cognitive science models. This is especially so in perception (and sensory psychology), in the study of memory and of a variety of problem domains relatable to learning (e.g., conditioning, knowledge acquisition, and problem solving). Much of **psycholinguistics** also proceeds in the ambience of cognitive science. Nevertheless, some of the most interesting developments within certain of these areas (as, for instance, the study of everyday memory and implicit memory) have arisen quite independently of cognitive science and often involve designs which, though "empirical," are but loosely subsumable under *experiment*.

Empirical studies of **language development**—and **developmental psychology** in general—require little dependence on the resources of cognitive science. Indeed, some of the most visible current trends in psychology are pitted in principle against so-called quantitative (or, more generally, algorithmic) research and proceed under the banner of **qualitative methods.**

Perhaps the most conspicuous trend, though still incipient, has continued to evolve in the **social psychology** of the past decade. In the Afterword, I did not include social psychology within the fundamental grouping in that I preferred to concentrate on the traditional "process areas." But I noted that there had been a growing disposition within social psychology and related areas to claim fundamental status. It had, for instance, become increasingly argued that many of the problems of the process areas cannot be significantly pursued unless the research is conducted within an ambience of knowledge and sensitivity stemming from social and personological psychology. And we have seen that many of the contributors to the book had tentatively resolved their restiveness regarding disciplinary status by suggesting that nomothetic psychology requires supplementation by a psychology analogous

964

to Wundt's *Völkerpsychologie*—indeed, that laboratory psychology has no meaning unless it is contextualized and qualified by cross-cultural and historical concerns.

A subgroup within social psychology that had already by 1979 been making more radical suggestions concerning the historicity, context-dependence, and socially constituted character of *all* matters bearing on human activity, has grown appreciably in influence. This subgroup forms a cluster with many European psychologists, and many who implement cognate views in the social sciences and humanities.

There are few overarching agreements, other than a largely shared critique of conventional psychology, and indeed "post-enlightenment" science in general. Their dominant ideas, both substantive and methodic, derive largely from structuralist and post-structuralist theories in the humanities, from "hermeneutics" as developed by Gadamer and successors, from modern incarnations of rhetoric, and from the traditions of "narratology" and "discourse analysis" (especially as developed in recent years). They are likely to call themselves "social constructionists"— which can mean many things, but at the extreme entails a view that envisages the "self" as a semitranslucent, historically and interactionally plaited discursive knot within an immense but time-bound matrix of social "discourse." Most have been influenced by Derrida and like to perform "deconstructions" on all positions within the history of thought other than their own. They are, of course, hospitable to the use of qualitative methods, and indeed have influenced the growing interest in such matters. Most like to characterize their positions as "postmodern," and like to deconstruct the ahuman consequences of the "Enlightenment Project."

In this brief Postscript, I can only identify—not assess—the trend at issue. Because their most prized concepts are derivative from the literary humanities, and because they would align psychology (and related social sciences) primarily with the humanities, I suppose I should be pleased. I am. But in my now ancient invitation that psychology, in many humanly relevant areas, pattern itself more on the humanities than on the sciences, I was thinking of different strands within the humanities. I was also suggesting that psychologists be selected and trained relative to humanistic sensibility rather more than has been the case. I think it more important to be deeply conversant with a few great texts than to proclaim that human beings can be read as texts. Or that they *are* texts!

A word about the trend in **history of psychology**: In the Afterword, I noted and saluted the "resurgence of historical sensibility" manifested by the contributors to *A Century of Psychology as Science* (cf. pp. 935–938). This was consonant with a growing interest in history that (though still a mere ripple) had been evident for perhaps the preceding 15 years.

The tendency of fundamental psychologists to see their efforts in a historical frame has grown somewhat during the second century. The amount of writing on historic themes has increased. There is lively discussion of historiographic issues.

965

Cheiron (the International Society for History of the Behavioral and Social Sciences) has, I am told, increased by 100 members or thereabouts. Yet the overall trajectory has, to me, been disappointing. In 1979 there was one doctoral program on this continent (University of New Hampshire) in which a student could specialize in history of psychology; now there is one more, at York University in Canada. It is still the case that no U.S. psychology department would employ a historian per se; the candidate must be prepared to contribute to some other (preferably "empirical") area as well.

A distinguished historian recently agreed with me that our second century has not as yet seen a work comparable in scholarship and scope to the two major historical works that were published during our long ahistorical interregnum. These works have been criticized in telling ways in recent years, but no commensurate efforts have eventuated. Some may feel that psychology departments on average offer more courses in history than do departments of "hard" science. But there is a sense in which we are nothing if not our history. Our history is our binding force. Our problems are not dispatchable ones. All we can do is offer glosses upon permanent problems. How can we gloss that which we do not know!

Because I have long argued that psychology cannot, in principle, be dissociated from philosophy, some observations are in order about the trends in **philosophy** during the interval of our concern. In general, positivism has continued to be exorcised so unrelentingly that one is almost tempted to take pity! Glosses upon Wittgenstein continue to occupy the main efforts of a large (but currently decreasing) fraction of the philosophical work force. Would Wittgenstein really have wanted every one of his jottings, however vagrant, to be taken that seriously?

Philosophers of science have been fervently embracing the context of discovery (in atonement for the earlier emphasis on justification), and indeed every other context that might reflect what I emphasized more than 30 years ago in exploring the "fact that science is by, of, and for human beings, that it is an activity of human agents continuous with other functionings of those agents" (cf. Koch, 1959b, pp. 1–18). The recent emphases overlap with those of the social psychologists already discussed: There is much work on the sociology of science, on the rhetoric of science, the narratological aspect of science, and so on.

Philosophers of mind have continued to pursue "intentionalist" analyses of agents and action. Some philosophers of mind serve as enthusiastic camp-followers of cognitive science who provide intricate epistemological rationales for the efforts of their heroes; others have built careers as critics of cognitive science and cognate "reductionist" endeavors.

In plausible dissonance with some of the other tendencies, a number of philosophers have attempted to reinvigorate various forms of **realism**. Phenomenological

966

philosophies are attracting a resurgence of interest. And forms of neo-neo-pragmatism are integrating pragmatism and phenomenological emphases.

Coda

Is it possible to think that the massive delusion concerning the power and range of neobehaviorist learning theory that dominated psychology from roughly 1930 to 1960 is being rivaled by an even more massive delusion in the form of cognitive science? Yes. But I argued the case contra the neobehavioristically dominated Age of Theory virtually alone before being joined in that critique by many of the very persons who molded that interval. This matter was developed *in extenso* in the NSF/APA-sponsored study of the status of psychology at mid-century, which mobilized the efforts of some 87 of the most distinguished theoretically oriented psychologists then alive. The study was published as *Psychology: A Study of a Science* (cf. Koch, 1959c, 1962, 1963). What seems currently to be taking place is a widespread critique of the imperialism and, indeed, finalism of earlier cognitive science theorizing on the part of many both within cognitive science and without. There is something hopeful in that circumstance.

In this Postscript, I have necessarily focused on the ubiquitous evidences of increasing differentiation and fractionation within psychology. I do not think that recognition of this leads to some ultimate relativism. Differing frameworks, perspectives, hypotheses, theories bearing on the same domain are in no necessary way equally plausible, illuminating, insightful, salient, or true. The "logic of confirmation" as dictated to the world by philosophers of science during much of this century is not well suited to the discrimination of such characters of a formulation as are suggested by the preceding adjectives. I have tried to explore in several publications (1971, 1973, 1985) but especially in "Language Communities" (1976) more fruitful modes of assessment. It is not meet that this Postscript serve as a time capsule in which to deposit my humble thinking on such issues.

More purely in the spirit of Coda, may I say that it is *not* the decreasing ratio of fundamental to implemental psychologists that places psychology in jeopardy. The ratio of fundamental to implemental physicists (e.g., theorists to engineers) is infinitesimal. If we can educate sufficiently sensitive and disciplined connoisseurs of particular areas of human need, human anguish, human growth, human cooperation, we should be all the more gratified as that ratio decreases. What places fundamental psychology in jeopardy is what has placed all fields of scholarship in jeopardy: the increasing commercialization of scholarly and intellectual life. When we allow ourselves to become as uninhibitedly instrumental in our goals and actions as the society around us, we invite a world already in twilight to go dark.

That twilight world has been issuing us an immense invitation for help. To meet

967

that invitation would be a sufficient *raison d'être*. To learn, along the way, some deep yet precisely delineable truths about the human condition would add a touch of glory to our still undefinable mission.

REFERENCES

Estes, W. K. (1991a). Cognitive architectures from the standpoint of an experimental psychologist. *Annual Review of Psychology, 42,* 1–28.

Estes, W. K. (1991b). What is cognitive science? *Psychological Science, 5,* 282.

Hubel, D. H. (1991). Are we willing to fight for our research? *Annual Review of Neuroscience, 14,* 1–8.

Koch, S. (1959a). Epilogue to Study 1. In S. Koch (Ed.), *Psychology: A study of a science: Vol. 3.* New York: McGraw-Hill.

Koch, S. (1959b). General introduction to the series. In S. Koch (Ed.), *Psychology: A study of a science: Vol. 1.* New York: McGraw-Hill.

Koch, S. (Ed.). (1959c). *Psychology: A study of a science: Vols. 1, 2, & 3.* New York: McGraw-Hill.

Koch, S. (1961). Psychological science versus the science–humanism antinomy: Intimations of a significant science of man. *American Psychologist, 16,* 629–639.

Koch, S. (Ed.). (1962). *Psychology: A study of a science: Vol. 4.* New York: McGraw-Hill.

Koch, S. (Ed.). (1963). *Psychology: A study of a science: Vols. 5 & 6.* New York: McGraw-Hill.

Koch, S. (1971). Reflections on the state of psychology. *Social Research, 38*(4), 669–709.

Koch, S. (1973). Theory and experiment in psychology. *Social Research, 40*(4), 691–707.

Koch, S. (1976). Language communities, search cells, and the psychological studies. In W. J. Arnold (Ed.), *Nebraska Symposium on Motivation, 1975* (pp. 447–559). Lincoln: University of Nebraska Press.

Koch, S. (1985). Psychology versus the psychological studies. In J. L. McGaugh (Ed.), *Contemporary psychology: Biological processes and theoretical issues—Proceedings of the XXIII International Congress of Psychology of the International Union of Psychological Science.* Amsterdam: North Holland.

Newell, A. (1990). *Unified theories of cognition.* Cambridge, MA: Harvard University Press.

Osherson, D. N., Lasnik, H., Kosslyn, S. M., Hollerbach, J. M., & Smith, E. E. (Eds.). (1990). *An invitation to cognitive science: Vols. 1, 2, & 3.* Cambridge, MA: The MIT Press.

Posner, M. I. (Ed.). (1989). *Foundations of cognitive science.* Cambridge, MA: The MIT Press.

Rosenzweig, M. (1982). Trends in development and status of psychology: An international perspective. *International Journal of Psychology, 17,* 117–140.

Rosenzweig, M. (1992). *International psychological science: Progress, problems, and prospects.* Washington, DC: American Psychological Association.

Sexton, V. S., & Hogan, J. D. (1992). *International psychology: Views from around the world.* Lincoln: University of Nebraska Press.

Staff. (1991). Psychologists ponder changes in field as discipline enters second century. *Chronicle of Higher Education, 38,* 10–11.

Staff. (1991). Simon delivers inspired perspective on psychology as a successful science. *APS Observer, 4,* 19–20.

Stapp, J., Fulcher, R., Nelson, S. D., Pallak, M. S., & Wicherski, M. (1981). The employment of recent doctorate recipients in psychology: 1975 through 1978. *American Psychologist, 36,* 1211–1254.

Stapp, J. (1981, August). An overview of the production of doctorates in psychology. In J. H. Harvey (Chair), *The "pipeline" in psychology: Training, production, and employment of psychologists.* Symposium conducted at the Annual Convention of the American Psychological Association, Los Angeles.

Author Index

To avoid redundancy, this index includes citations given in the *text* of the chapters but not in the bibliographies. Many of the bibliographies include supplementary readings which identify historically important publications in the field at issue. The reader can locate these only by direct reference to the bibliographies. Authors of chapters in this book are identified by initial citations that list in sequence for their chapters the chapter number (in Roman numerals), the limiting page numbers, and (in parentheses) the page numbers of the bibliography. Thus, "V, 100–120 (118–120)" means that the author has contributed Chapter 5, pages 100–120, and the bibliography runs from page 118 to page 120. An author's citations of his or her own work may, of course, be located in the chapter's bibliography.

969

979

985

Subject Index

The architecture of "fields" and issues in psychology is too amorphous and intertwined to permit a sharply discriminating breakdown of topics. Thus, many of the topics in this index are so widely treated in this book (whether under identical or related rubrics) that it is often not feasible to give more than a focal range of page references. Authors listed in this index are those who have been significantly discussed or quoted in the text, or (occasionally) whose historic stature invites special acknowledgment. For some of these authors, citations additional to those listed here may be found in the Author Index.

989

997

About the Editors

SIGMUND KOCH is currently University Professor of Psychology and Philosophy at Boston University. He has concentrated on theoretical, methodological, philosophical, and historical problems of psychology for more than 40 years. Early in his career he also made experimental contributions to the psychology of learning and motivation. He directed and edited the study of the status of psychology at mid-century, sponsored by the APA and subsidized by the National Science Foundation, which resulted in the six-volume series, *Psychology: A Study of a Science* (McGraw-Hill, 1959, 1962, 1963). Now regarded as a classic, this work was received by reviewers in such terms as "a monument to psychology's first 100 years" and "probably the most important publishing event in psychology." He has lectured at most of the major universities in North America and the United Kingdom and has held four Divisional presidencies within the APA. During the past decade, he has (as director of the Boston University Aesthetics Research Archive) conducted intensive studies of the work processes of outstanding artists in a variety of fields.

DAVID E. LEARY is currently dean of arts and sciences and professor of psychology at the University of Richmond. Previously, he was professor of psychology, history, and the humanities and codirector of the graduate program in the history and theory of psychology at the University of New Hampshire. A former president of the History of Psychology Division of the APA, he is an APA Fellow and has been a Fellow at the Center for Advanced Study in the Behavioral Sciences in Stanford, California. He has published broadly in the history and philosophy of psychology and is the editor of *Metaphors in the History of Psychology* (Cambridge University Press, 1990).